Costa Rica

Matthew D Firestone

Carolina A Miranda, César G Soriano

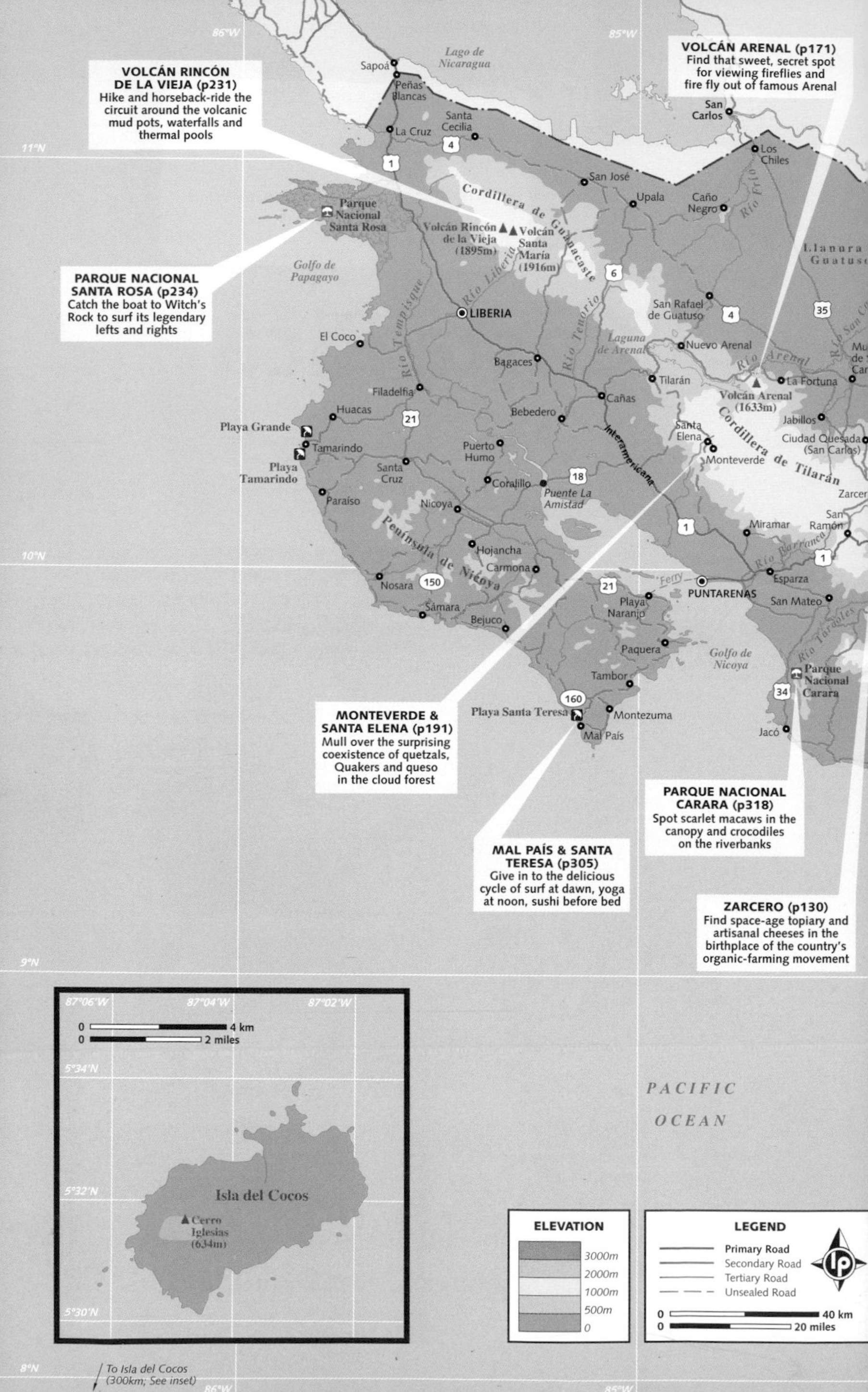
VOLCÁN RINCÓN DE LA VIEJA (p231)
Hike and horseback-ride the circuit around the volcanic mud pots, waterfalls and thermal pools
PARQUE NACIONAL SANTA ROSA (p234)
Catch the boat to Witch's Rock to surf its legendary lefts and rights
VOLCÁN ARENAL (p171)
Find that sweet, secret spot for viewing fireflies and fire fly out of famous Arenal
MONTEVERDE & SANTA ELENA (p191)
Mull over the surprising coexistence of quetzals, Quakers and queso in the cloud forest
MAL PAÍS & SANTA TERESA (p305)
Give in to the delicious cycle of surf at dawn, yoga at noon, sushi before bed
PARQUE NACIONAL CARARA (p318)
Spot scarlet macaws in the canopy and crocodiles on the riverbanks
ZARCERO (p130)
Find space-age topiary and artisanal cheeses in the birthplace of the country's organic-farming movement
Lago de Nicaragua
Sapoá
Peñas Blancas
La Cruz
Santa Cecilia
San Carlos
Los Chiles
San José
Upala
Caño Negro
Cordillera de Guanacaste
Parque Nacional Santa Rosa
Volcán Rincón de la Vieja (1895m)
Volcán Santa María (1916m)
Llanura Guatuso
Golfo de Papagayo
LIBERIA
San Rafael de Guatuso
Laguna de Arenal
Nuevo Arenal
El Coco
Bagaces
Tilarán
La Fortuna
Volcán Arenal (1633m)
Filadelfia
Cañas
Jabillos
Huacas
Bebedero
Playa Grande
Tamarindo
Playa Tamarindo
Puerto Humo
Santa Elena
Monteverde
Ciudad Quesada (San Carlos)
Cordillera de Tilarán
Interamericana
Santa Cruz
Corralillo
Puente La Amistad
Paraíso
Nicoya
Península de Nicoya
Miramar
San Ramón
Zarcero
Hojancha
Carmona
Nosara
Sámara
Bejuco
Ferry
PUNTARENAS
Esparza
Playa Naranjo
San Mateo
Paquera
Golfo de Nicoya
Tambor
Parque Nacional Carara
Playa Santa Teresa
Montezuma
Mal País
Jacó
Río Tempisque
Río Liberia
Río Tenorio
Río Frío
Río Arenal
Río Barranca
Río Tárcoles
PACIFIC OCEAN
Isla del Cocos
Cerro Iglesias (634m)
0 4 km
0 2 miles
ELEVATION
3000m
2000m
1000m
500m
0
LEGEND
Primary Road
Secondary Road
Tertiary Road
Unsealed Road
0 40 km
0 20 miles
To Isla del Cocos (300km; See inset)

SAN JOSÉ (p66)
The cosmopolitan capital has world-class eateries, vintage taverns and the country's main cultural scene

PARQUE NACIONAL TORTUGUERO (p458)
Stay up late to spy endangered sea turtles nesting on wild black-sand beaches

VOLCÁN IRAZÚ (p140)
Allow your jaw to hit volcanic earth after taking in the view from the summit

TURRIALBA (p146)
Ride your adrenaline high after rafting some of the world's fiercest rapids

PUERTO VIEJO DE TALAMANCA (p479)
Surf one of the country's most challenging waves by day and groove to reggaetón at night in this happening Caribbean beach town

PARQUE NACIONAL CHIRRIPÓ (p374)
Climb to the lofty heights of Costa Rica's tallest peak

PARQUE NACIONAL MANUEL ANTONIO (p349)
Get up close and personal with rare squirrel monkeys

DOMINICAL (p354)
Surf until sunset at this terminally laid-back Pacific beach town

PARQUE NACIONAL CORCOVADO (p421)
Endure the multiday trek across the country's last great wilderness

84°W
83°W
11°N
10°N
9°N
8°N
NICARAGUA
CARIBBEAN SEA
PANAMA
Río San Juan
Barra del Colorado
Boca Tapada
Llanura de San Carlos
Llanura de Tortuguero
Río Chirripó
Río Toro
Tortuguero
Parque Nacional Tortuguero
Río Tortuguero
Pital
Puerto Viejo de Sarapiquí
Cariari
San Miguel
Llanura de Santa Clara
Río Reventazón
Parismina
Parque Nacional Volcán Poás
Volcán Poás (2704m)
Cordillera Central
Guápiles
Guácimo
Siquirres
Volcán Irazú (3432m)
ALAJUELA
HEREDIA
Ciudad Colón
SAN JOSÉ
CARTAGO
Pacayas
Lajas
Turrialba
Río Pacuare
PUERTO LIMÓN
Santiago de Puriscal
Paraíso
Tapantí
Moravia
Río Chirripó Atlántico
San Ignacio de Acosta
San Marcos de Tarrazú
Santa María de Dota
Parque Nacional Los Quetzales
Valle de Parrita
Parrita
Quepos
Parque Nacional Manuel Antonio
Savegre
San Isidro de El General
Rivas
Parque Nacional Chirripó
Cerro Chirripó (3820m)
Reserva Biológica Dúrika
Cordillera de Talamanca
Pandora
Cahuita
Río Estrella
Puerto Viejo de Talamanca
Bribrí
Shiroles
Río Telire
Amubri
Río Lari
Río Sixaola
Sixaola
Guabito
Changuinola
Bocas del Toro
Almirante
Dominical
Río General
Ujarrás
Buenos Aires
Uvita
Bahía de Coronado
Valle del General
Potrero Grande
Paso Real
Palmar Norte
Ciudad Cortés
Río Cotón
Valle de Coto Brus
Santa Elena
Sierpe
Interamericana
Fila Costeña
San Vito
Sabalito
Río Sereno
Agua Buena
Boquete
Isla del Caño
Rincón
Parque Nacional Corcovado
Península de Osa
Golfo Dulce
Golfito
Río Claro
Neily
Ferry
Laguna Corcovado
Puerto Jiménez
Playa Zancudo
Paso Canoas
Valle de Coto Colorado
Concepción
David
Carate
Puerto Armuelles
4
32
10
36
2
34

On the Road

MATTHEW D FIRESTONE
Coordinating Author
Península de Osa (p390) is truly a stunning landform, but there is a whole different world lying offshore beneath the surface of the shallow seas. Down here, maritime life of every shape, color and size dashes and darts across your field of vision. Suddenly you hopelessly wish that the remaining oxygen in your tank didn't limit your time in the underwater world.

CEŚAR G SORIANO After weeks of sweltering under the infamous Guanacaste heat, it was time to cool off. So I took the day off for a bit of diving in Sámara (p286), a beautiful beach town whose flora and fauna are equally impressive on land as they are beneath the waves. *¡Pura vida!*

CAROLINA A MIRANDA On this trip I got to explore the absolutely idyllic (and often overlooked) Central Valley. At El Silencio (p131) in Bajos del Toro I planted a tree – with name tag! – in memory of my father and father-in-law. My plan is to go back in a year to see how it's doing.

For full author biographies see p568.

Costa Rica Highlights

Few travel destinations have the vast spectrum of stunning landscapes and exotic wildlife offered by Costa Rica, a tiny Central American country lodged between two great oceans. Of course, what Costa Rica lacks in size, it more than makes up for in biodiversity. In one day you can watch the sunrise over the Caribbean, and the sunset over the Pacific. Or spend the morning trekking through the highland cloud forests, and wind down in the afternoon with a cup of shade-grown brew on an organic coffee plantation. This incredible complement of landscapes is also inhabited by some of the planet's most charismatic species, including the scarlet macaw and squirrel monkey in the canopy above, and the jaguar and tapir on the forest floor.

LUKE HUNTER

1 MONTEVERDE CLOUD FOREST

This iconic cloud forest was first settled by a community of Quakers who sought to protect their invaluable watershed. Home to such rare fauna as the resplendent quetzal, which is the Maya bird of paradise, Monteverde (p191) is partly responsible for Costa Rica's international fame as an ecotourism hot spot.

Matthew D Firestone, Lonely Planet Author, USA

CHRISTOPHER

2 MANUEL ANTONIO

One of the country's original ecotourism destinations, Manuel Antonio (p349) practically put Costa Rica on the map for international jet-setters. While the secret has long been let out, capuchin monkeys bounding across a tropical beach remain an arresting sight.

Matthew D Firestone, Lonely Planet Author, USA

COREY

3 LA FORTUNA AREA

In the shadow of Arenal (p171), one of the most active volcanoes in the world, there's something for everybody including luxurious hotels, romantic restaurants and Tabacón Hot Springs (p159), man's recreation of the Garden of Eden.

César G Soriano, Lonely Planet Author, USA

COREY WISE

4 MONTEZUMA

A laid-back, budget beach town (p298) with a hippie vibe (locals call it 'Montefuma'), beautiful beaches, a chill atmosphere and great restaurants. It's the perfect base for exploring the southern part of the Península de Nicoya.

César G Soriano, Lonely Planet Author, USA

5 PARQUE NACIONAL CORCOVADO

Costa Rica's ultimate outdoor experience is anything but a walk in the park. With the proper gear, ample supplies and a healthy appetite for adventure, Corcovado (p421) is where you can leave behind the tourist crowds and lose yourself in the wilds.

Matthew D Firestone, Lonely Planet Author, USA

JOHNNY HAGLUND

R H PRODUCTIONS / PHOTOLIBRARY

6 JACÓ

I know it's not the 'real' Costa Rica, but I can't deny that Jacó (p322) isn't a blast every time I pass through. Sure, there are better surf spots and cleaner beaches, but its bar, restaurant and club scene is the best you'll find along the entire Pacific coast.

Alex, Traveler, USA

SOUTHERN CARIBBEAN

By day, lounge in a hammock, snorkel uncrowded beaches and visit the remote indigenous territories of the Bribrí and KéköLdi. By night, dip into zesty Caribbean cooking and sway to reggaetón at open-air bars cooled by ocean breezes. The villages of Cahuita (p469) and Puerto Viejo de Talamanca (p479) seem to have it all.

Carolina A Miranda, Lonely Planet Author, USA

7

PAUL K

TORTUGUERO

Watch endangered sea turtles practice the millennia-old ritual of building a nest and laying their eggs on wild black-sand shores in this charming Caribbean jungle town (p458).

Carolina A Miranda, Lonely Planet Author, USA

8

LUKE HU

CARVER MOSTARDI / ALAMY

9 DOMINICAL

A permanently chilled-out beach town where time slows down to a crawl, Dominical (p354) has a way of forestalling your future plans. But when the surf is crashing and the sun is blazing, few travelers seem to really care.

Matthew D Firestone, Lonely Planet Author, USA

CÉSAR G SORIANO

10 LLANOS DE CORTÉS

One of the most dramatic waterfalls (p223) in Costa Rica cascades into a tranquil pond with a white sandy beach. Scramble behind the falls with your sweetie to reach romantic nooks veiled by curtains of water.

César G Soriano, Lonely Planet Author, USA

DAVE AND SIGRUN TOLLERTON /

11 PAVONES

Pavones (p435) is one of my favorite surf spots in the world, even though it doesn't attract as much attention as other, more famous beaches. I like that it's difficult to get to and a bit of an unknown, though the waves here never seem to disappoint.

Daniel, Traveler, Germany

LUKE HU

12 CERRO CHIRRIPÓ

From the lofty heights of Costa Rica's highest summit (p374), you can get a true sense of the country's diminutive size – on a clear day, both the Caribbean and the Pacific are in full and glorious panoramic view.

Matthew D Firestone, Lonely Planet Author, USA

SAN JOSÉ

Museums bursting with pre-Columbian artifacts. World-class eateries serving everything from Costa Rican fusion cuisine to Japanese sushi rolls. And a pumping nightlife that gets roaring after dark. Central America's most cosmopolitan capital (p66) has a little bit of everything.

Carolina A Miranda, Lonely Planet Author, USA

13

RICHARD CUMMINS

COFFEE PLANTATIONS OF THE CENTRAL VALLEY

Soak up plenty of rural idyll and learn all about how Costa Rica's golden bean goes from plant to cup at the valley's picturesque coffee plantations. Among the best spots for a tour: Orosi (p142) and Barva (p137).

Carolina A Miranda, Lonely Planet Author, USA

14

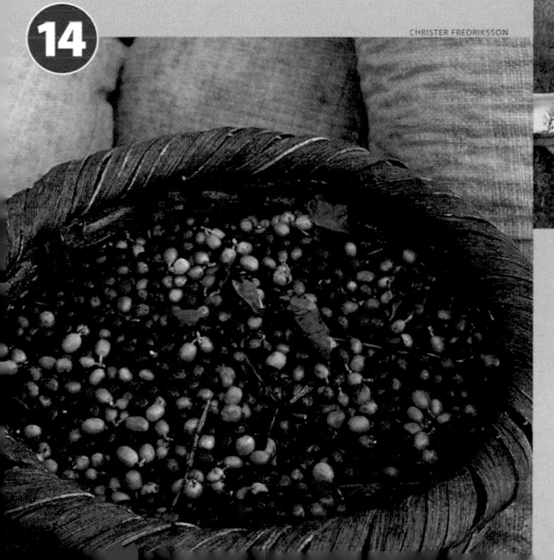

CHRISTER FREDRIKSSON

CÉSAR G SORIANO

15

CAÑO NEGRO

This far-flung, little-visited national park (p516) untouched by modern development has amazing bird-watching and kayaking opportunities. It's a great place to get away from it all.

César G Soriano, Lonely Planet Author, USA

GUAYABO

Nestled into a forested hillside that overlooks the bustling agricultural center of Turrialba, lies Guayabo (p149), the country's most impressive archaeological site, an abandoned mountain city inhabited as early as 1000 BC.

Carolina A Miranda, Lonely Planet Author, USA

THE FORESTS OF PARQUE NACIONAL BRAULIO CARRILLO

This little-visited park (p444) offers a dreamy wonderland of misty forests crisscrossed by cascading rivers and studded by untrammeled volcanic craters – all just 30 minutes from San José.

Carolina A Miranda, Lonely Planet Author, USA

THE SARAPIQUÍ VALLEY

This underrated, ecotourist-friendly area of northern Costa Rica is a mecca for white-water rafters and home to fantastic sustainable lodge resorts, rainforests and gardens (see p499).

César G Soriano, Lonely Planet Author, USA

Contents

Regional Map Contents

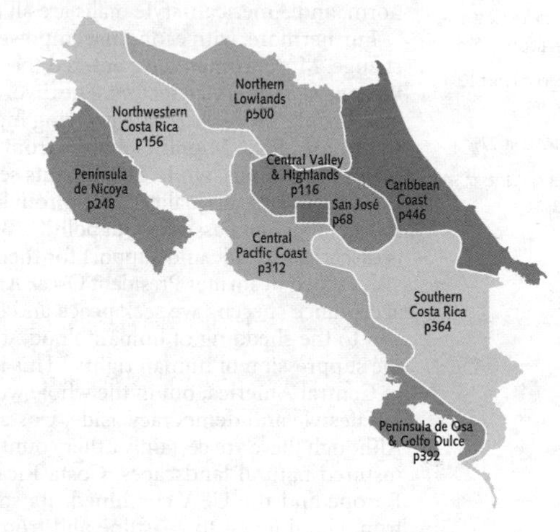

Destination Costa Rica

Costa Rica is sometimes referred to as the Switzerland of Central America because of its comfortable lifestyle, peaceful democracy and overwhelming natural beauty. But is this merely the depiction on a postcard, or does it have relevance for today's Tico (Costa Rican)?

Early in the 20th century, this view could rightly be called an optimistic caricature. At best, Costa Rica was an occasional democracy with widespread poverty and no discernible environmental protection policy. In the second half of the century, however, sustained economic growth created a viable middle class, a generous social welfare state and one of the world's most progressive environmental movements.

To put things in perspective, consider the fact that prior to 1950, half of the country struggled with grinding poverty, and living beyond the age of 50 was an achievement in itself. Today, less than one in five Ticos lives below the poverty line, and life expectancy is on a par with the USA.

FAST FACTS

Population: 4.25 million

Life expectancy at birth: 77.6

Adult literacy: 94.9%

Population living below the poverty line: 16%

Population using the internet: 34%

Annual carbon dioxide emissions per person: 1.85 tons

Annual coffee consumption per person: 3.8kg

Passenger cars per 1000 people: 103

Protected land: 27%

Number of species of birds: 850+

The 'green revolution' kicked off in the 1970s when world coffee prices dropped due to oversupply, and Costa Rica plunged into economic crisis. However, the unpredictable nature of the global commodity markets created a rather unusual alliance between economic developers and environmental conservationists. If wealth could not be sustained through exports, then what about imports – of tourists? By 1985, tourism was annually contributing US$100 million to the Costa Rican economy, and today almost one-third of the entire country is under some form of environmental protection.

Costa Rica annually attracts more than one million tourists each year, and continues to serve as testament to the fact that conservation and development need not be competing interests. Need more proof? As recently as 1980, Ticos lived on family farms, listened to state radio and shopped at the neighborhood *pulpería* (corner grocery store). Today, shopping at supermarkets is a matter of course, satellite TV and wireless internet are the norm, and American-style malls are all the rage.

Furthermore, with economic empowerment has come tremendous social change. More women have entered the workforce though opportunities in the tourist and service sectors. The divorce rate has increased and family size has shrunk. More Ticos are entering higher education, and they are doing so in Costa Rica. Migrant laborers from Nicaragua and Colombia work the coffee plantations, while Tico tenants seek better jobs in the city.

Given the rise in quality of life throughout the country, Ticos are generally self-content and passive about politics. But underneath the easygoing veneer is discernible pride and support for their unarmed democracy.

As stated by former President Oscar Arias Sánchez in his Nobel Peace Prize acceptance speech, 'we seek peace and democracy together, indivisible, an end to the shedding of human blood, which is inseparable from an end to the suppression of human rights.' This is a unique point of view – not only in Central America, but in the whole world.

Lifestyle and democracy aside, Costa Rica is mind-bendingly beautiful. Although there are certainly other countries in the world that enjoy divinely inspired natural landscapes, Costa Rica boasts a higher biodiversity than Europe and the USA combined. Its small size also means that traveling from cloud forest to coastline and from summit to savanna is quick, easy and enjoyable.

Getting Started

Costa Rica is the most user-friendly country in Central America. Most of the tourist hot spots are well connected by cheap buses, accommodations are plentiful and decent eateries are thick on the ground in nearly every corner of the country. Unlike in some other parts of the region, dining without fear for your stomach, meeting and engaging locals, and accessing the internet are all things that can be taken for granted.

Predeparture planning will usually make your trip a bit smoother, but on the whole it's unnecessary unless you're on a tight timetable, and it's usually more enjoyable to give in to the idea of adventure travel. Indeed, Costa Rica has something for everyone, especially if you are an impulsive traveler seeking an adrenaline rush. Of course, if you prefer to spend some quality time with a good book on a sun-drenched beach, Costa Rica has quite a few of those, too.

See the Directory for more information on climate (p529) and festivals (p531).

For shoestringers, transport around the country is plentiful – local buses can carry you to just about every nook and cranny, and boats will pick up where buses leave off. For the more discriminating or time-pressed travelers, minivans with air-con, domestic flights and charters can reach even the most remote corners. Accommodations also range from bargain-basement cabins, campsites and hammock hotels, all the way up to 1st-class resorts loaded with every conceivable luxury.

Lodging is abundant throughout Costa Rica, and it's usually easy to find someplace to stay when you arrive in town. The exceptions to this rule are the weeks between Christmas and New Year's Day, and before and during Semana Santa (the week preceding Easter Sunday). It is also a good idea to book accommodations ahead of time during the school vacation in January and February.

Note that because Costa Rica has a high standard of living, prices here tend to be a good deal higher than those of other Central and South American nations. However, although your dollar may not stretch as far here as in neighboring countries, you can expect an extremely high quality of goods and services throughout Costa Rica.

WHEN TO GO

Generally, the best time to visit Costa Rica is the dry season from December through April, which locals refer to as *verano* (summer). Dry season does not mean it does not rain – it just rains less (so perhaps should be called the 'drier season'). Costa Rican schools are closed from December to February; beach towns are busy during this period, especially on weekends. Lodgings during Semana Santa are usually booked months ahead.

In May begins the rainy season, or *invierno* (winter) as it's known locally. The tourism ministry has come up with the more attractive denomination of 'green season.' The early months of the rainy season are actually a wonderful time to travel to Costa Rica: you can avoid the tourist bustle and lodging is slightly cheaper. During this time, however, rivers start to swell and dirt roads get muddy, making travel more challenging. Some more remote roads may not be accessible to public transportation, so always ask locally before setting out. Bring your umbrella and a little patience.

Because of the number of North American and European tourists, some Costa Rican towns experience a mini high season in June and July, during the northern summer holidays. Expect to pay high-season prices in some towns at this time.

For surfers, the travel seasons vary slightly. For the most part, the Pacific coast sees increased swells and bigger, faster waves during the rainy season, starting in late June and peaking in the worst rainy months of September and October. The Caribbean side has better waves from November through May. Some breaks are consistent year-round.

Wildlife enthusiasts may wish to plan their trip around the seasons of the critters. Turtle season on the Caribbean coast is from late February to October, with the peak season for leatherbacks in April and May, and for green turtles in August and September. On the Pacific coast, the season for leatherbacks is from October to March.

Bird-watchers will be overwhelmed by feathered friends any time of year, but the best season to spot the resplendent quetzal is between November and April. Spring (March through May) and autumn (September through November) are good times to watch the migratory flocks.

Fishing is also good year-round, but you might choose your season if you have your heart set on a specific fish. Anglers head to the Caribbean coast between January and May in search of tarpon, while the autumn (September through November) is the season for snook. On the Pacific coast and in the Golfo Dulce, the best time to snag that sailfish is between November and May.

COSTS & MONEY

Travel costs are significantly higher here than in most Central American countries, but cheaper than in the USA or Europe. And if you're arriving from inexpensive Central American nations, such as Nicaragua, get ready to bust that wallet wide open.

Prices in Costa Rica are frequently listed in US dollars, especially at upmarket hotels and restaurants, where you can expect to pay international prices. Most types of tours are charged in US dollars. In fact, US dollars are

DON'T LEAVE HOME WITHOUT...

- checking the latest visa situation (p537) and government travel advisories (p530)
- insect repellent containing DEET; and, if you're planning large-scale jungle adventures (or staying in budget lodging), a mosquito net
- learning at least a few basic phrases in Spanish
- Pepto-Bismol or an antidiarrheal, in case you get a bad dose of the runs
- sunblock and a hat, so you don't get cooked by the tropical sun
- clothes that you don't mind getting absolutely filthy or wet
- a swimsuit and a beach towel
- a poncho for rainy days and wet boat trips
- a pair of river sandals or reef-walkers and sturdy jungle boots
- an alarm clock for catching early morning buses
- a waterproof, windproof jacket and warm layers for highland hiking and camping
- a flashlight (torch)
- binoculars and a field guide
- miscellaneous necessities: umbrella, padlock, matches, pocketknife
- an appetite for fresh fruit
- a thirst for cold lager
- your sense of adventure

IT MUST BE THE MONEY

Starting in 2010, Costa Rica will roll out some seriously big bills, namely in denominations of 20,000 and 50,000 colones. Since almost two-thirds of the cash currently circulating is in 10,000 colones bills, the Central Bank is hoping that the larger denomination bills will result in a more equal distribution of money.

According to the treasury director of the Central Bank, one side of the six new bills will feature important figures from Costa Rican history, while the other will highlight the country's natural heritage.

Of course, if you're going to roll out some new currency, then why not add a bit of flash to the cash? The new bills will have variable lengths, and there's even talk of switching from cotton fiber to plastic. After all, there's nothing worse than trying to dry out your wallet after a serious surf session!

widely accepted, but the standard unit of currency is still the colón. See also boxed text, p535.

Shoestring travelers can survive on US$25 to US$35 a day, covering just the basics of food, lodging and public transportation. The cheapest hotels start at about US$7 to US$15 per person for a bed, four walls and shared bathroom. Better rooms with private bathroom start at roughly US$15 to US$20 per person, depending on the area. It is possible to eat cheaply at the many *sodas* (lunch counters), where you can fill up on tasty *casados* (set meals) for about US$2 to US$3.

Midrange budgeters can travel comfortably for anywhere from US$50 to US$100 per day. Hotels in this category offer very good value, and double rooms come with comfortable beds, private bathroom, hot water (most of the time) and even breakfast, for US$20 to US$80 per night. Many hotels in this price range also have shared or private kitchenettes, which gives travelers the opportunity to cook – this is a great option for families. A variety of restaurants cater to midrange travelers, offering meals that cost from US$5 to US$10.

Top end visitors can find a good selection of restaurants and hotels in the touristy towns and within some of the major resorts. Luxurious beachside lodges and boutique hotels can cost upwards of US$80, and offer truly world-class meals that begin at around US$15.

Lodging prices are generally higher in the dry season (December to April), and highest during holiday periods (between Christmas and New Year and during Semana Santa). During slower seasons, most hotels are eager for your business, so you can try to negotiate a lower rate. Some of the more popular tourist areas (Monteverde, Jacó, Manuel Antonio and many of the beaches on the Península de Nicoya) are also more expensive than the rest of the country.

HOW MUCH?

Car rental for one week US$200-500

Zip-line adventure through the canopy US$35-60

National park admission fees US$5-15

Taxi from the international airport into central San José US$12

Secondhand longboard from a surf shop US$100-250

TRAVELING RESPONSIBLY

As one of the world's most iconic ecotourism destinations, Costa Rica spoils travelers with a never-ending assortment of environmentally friendly activities. Animal lovers can help baby sea turtles scamper out to sea, while tree huggers can help plant new life in the forest floor. Green thumbs can try their hand at organic agriculture, while nature lovers can explore some of the planet's most pristine landscapes. Indeed, few tourist spots so easily combine wildlife-watching, adventure travel, volunteering and environmental conservation in one earth-friendly package.

However, the greatest challenge to travelers in Costa Rica is preserving the purity of this destination for future generations. The secret is out, the tourism

TOP FIVE ECOLODGES

It's easy to lie down for the night in a hotel when you know that your stay isn't negatively impacting the environment. Although there is certainly no shortage of ecolodges in Costa Rica, the following lists some of our favorites:

- **Esquinas Rainforest Lodge** (p433) A private reserve that is managed by 'Rainforest for the Austrians,' a group that helped establish Parque Nacional Piedras Blancas.
- **Punta Mona** (p496) This remote retreat on the edge of the Caribbean is a working experiment in organic permaculture farming.
- **Hotel Sí Como No** (p344) This ecotourism pioneer is testament to the fact that luxury and sustainability are not incompatible.
- **Celeste Mountain Lodge** (p220) An innovative lodge constructed out of recycled wood, plastic, truck tires, coconut fiber and scrap metal.
- **Tiskita Jungle Lodge** (p438) Set on 100 hectares of orchards, this jungle lodge has more than 100 varieties of tropical fruit from around the world.

industry is booming, and travelers are leaving behind a larger footprint on the country than ever before. As a result, travelers are increasingly looking at ways to minimize the impact of their stay in Costa Rica and to travel in the most sustainable way possible. Fortunately, it's not too hard to think green while in Costa Rica.

Protect the Environment

One of the simplest things you can do before going to Costa Rica is learning about the country's major conservation and environmental issues (see the Environment chapter, p55, for more information). While traveling in Costa Rica, don't be afraid to ask questions, especially since the best source of information about an area is usually a local.

Here is a useful list of author-tested tips:

- Fill up your bottle from a rainwater-collection system, and purify natural water sources while hiking. Reuse plastic bottles.
- When you arrive in a new town, ask around to see if there are any recycling programs. If a system is in place, spread awareness among your fellow travelers.
- While walking along a beach or a trail, pick up any garbage you see. Your actions might inspire another person to do the same.
- Stick to the trails as this reduces the erosion caused by human transit. Likewise, don't damage plants, and always observe wildlife from a distance.
- Always follow the basic snorkel and scuba guidelines, keep garbage out of the water, and remember not to eat or purchase endangered or undersized seafood.
- Feeding the animals interferes with their natural diets and makes them susceptible to bacteria transferred by humans or pesticides contained within fruit.
- When in doubt, remember that common sense and awareness are always your best guides, regardless of where you are in the world.

Stimulate Local Economies

One of the most immediate benefits of tourism is a strong financial boost to the local economy. Keep this in mind if the opportunity arises to spend money at a locally run business or vendor.

Enjoy the creativity of a local artisan. If you spot a piece on display that catches your eye, buy it instead of saying you'll come back later. In all cases, you'll be surprised how far your colones can stretch.

If purchased directly from the source, arts and crafts generate income from the ground up and encourage communities to maintain their traditional practices. Spend your money where it counts and help ensure a culture's future.

In Costa Rica, there are also a number of cooperatives that purchase indigenous crafts from villages around the country, sell them at a premium, and return the profits to the artisan. An excellent example of this commendable practice is Galería Namu (p95) in San José, which is regarded as the premier indigenous art boutique in the country.

A great way of stimulating local economies in a sustainable manner is to frequent businesses that are dedicated to these aims. See boxed text on p539 for more information on various aspects of ecofriendly businesses. For a list of ecofriendly businesses in Costa Rica, see the GreenDex on p586.

Give Back a Little

Costa Rica is justifiably famous as a leading 'voluntourism' destination, particularly because there is a wide range of programs on offer. Depending on your particular needs and interests, you can choose a program in a variety of fields ranging from environmental conservation to community action. For a list of volunteer programs in Costa Rica, see p538.

TRAVELING WITH CHILDREN

Wild animals, active volcanoes, rainforests, beaches – what kid wouldn't love Costa Rica? Parents are guaranteed a good time as well, and will definitely appreciate the country's myriad adventure possibilities as well as a culture that dotes on children. We have authored segments of this guidebook with the needs of little ones in mind, so look for special kid-focused headings.

Families could go just about anywhere in Costa Rica and be perfectly happy. Even San José has a few sights for children, but it's best to get out of town and into the countryside. For an overview of outdoor activities and

TOP FIVE WAYS TO SAVE THE RAINFOREST

- **Plant a tree** At Selva Bananito Lodge (p470) on the Caribbean coast, you can help reforest a former banana plantation while learning about the conservation philosophy from the lodge's conscientious owners, the Stein family.
- **Drink organic, shade-grown coffee** Organic coffee-growing avoids the use of chemical pesticides and fertilizers, minimizing their impact on flora and fauna. Shade-grown coffee ensures the survival of old-growth forests and is planted under shade plants that produce nitrogen and improve the quality of both the soil and the coffee crop.
- **Educate the masses** Work on a community education program with the Fundación Corcovado (p427), a grassroots organization dedicated to preserving one of Costa Rica's last true frontiers – Parque Nacional Corcovado.
- **Say no to beef** One of the main reasons for forest clearing in Central America is to make way for cattle pasture – mostly to feed the export market. If you can't bypass that burger, make sure you know where your cow came from. Consider indulging in grass-fed beef, which is better for your health and better for the environment.
- **Recycle and reuse** Proper waste disposal relieves pressure on crowded landfills and reduces the chance of illegal dumping. Whenever possible, avoid bottled water and purify your own.

TOP 10

COSTA RICA
• San José

For a small country, Costa Rica is jam-packed with sights and attractions. Hopefully, the following lists will inspire you to seek out all that this beautiful country can offer.

IDYLLIC SUNSET SITES

Grab a magic moment in Costa Rica while you enjoy the last rays of the day.

1. Taking in the view from **Crestones Base Lodge** (p377) on Cerro Chirripó.
2. Looking out from **Cabinas El Mirador Lodge** (p399) in Bahía Drake.
3. Viewing the fiery Volcán Arenal from **El Castillo** (p174).
4. Sailing on the deep blue Pacific from **Tamarindo** (p263).
5. Sipping an ice-cold *cerveza* (beer) at **La Taberna** (p465) in Tortuguero.
6. Munching at **Ronny's Place** (p346), high up on the cliffs in Manuel Antonio.
7. Hiking at twilight in **Bosque Eterno de los Niños** (p197) in Monteverde.
8. Reggae-listening at **Johnny's Place** (p487) in Puerto Viejo de Talamanca.
9. Sitting on the dock in the bay at the **Banana Bay Marina** (p431) in Golfito.
10. Relaxing on colonial steps at **Plaza de la Democracia** (p75) in San José.

WORST ROADS

Get ready to shift your transmission into overdrive.

1. Oldie, but goodie – the road from **Tilarán to Monteverde**.
2. The punisher – **Puerto Jiménez to Carate**.
3. Dude, where's the transmission? – bumping and grinding to the waves at **Playa Naranjo**.
4. A river runs through it – crossing the Río Ora between **Playa Carrillo and Islita**.
5. You call this a road? – **Golfito to Pavones**.
6. Bone-cruncher – **Buenos Aires to Reserva Biológica Dúrika**.
7. Car-nivore – the stretch between **Tamarindo and Avellanas** gobbles up vehicles like candy.
8. Road less traveled – the steep climb up to **Altamira and La Amistad**.
9. Keep on truckin' – swerving with the big rigs on the Interamericana between **Cañas and Liberia**.
10. Lake defect – dodging huge potholes on the road around **Laguna de Arenal**.

BEST BEACHES

With two coastlines fringed with sun-kissed beaches, Costa Rica is a beach-lover's paradise.

1. **Manzanillo** (p494) The Caribbean coast's most scenic stretch of sand.
2. **Playas San Miguel and Coyote** (p292) Abandoned beaches, backed by rugged wilderness.
3. **Playa Conchal** (p260) Crushed shells and turquoise water.
4. **Playa Grande** (p260) Sweeping blond sand backed by mangroves, great surf.
5. **Playa Matapalo** (p352) Surfing the waves, hiking to waterfalls.
6. **Playa Montezuma** (p298) Empty white sands, rocky coves and killer sunrises.
7. **Playa Mal País** (p305) Kilometers of huge, crashing surf.
8. **Playa Negra** (p271) Dark sands and crystal-clear waters.
9. **Playa San Josecito** (p433) Scarlet macaws roosting in the almond trees overhead.
10. **Playa Sámara** (p286) A destination for sophisticated beach-goers and fun-loving families.

their required skill levels, see the Costa Rica Outdoors chapter on p405. We've also put together a special 'Fun for Kids' tailored-trip itinerary on p31.

From plush jungle ecolodges to beachside jungle tents, you can find the type of accommodations your family needs pretty much anywhere tourists go. Most midrange and top-end hotels have reduced rates for children under 12, provided the child shares a room with parents. Top-end hotels will provide cribs and usually have activities for children. Throughout this book, we have marked particularly kid-friendly accommodations with this symbol: . If you spot this in a destination listing, you should feel more than free to arrive at check-in with the little ones in tow.

Costa Rican cuisine is simple and hearty and somewhat bland (beans and rice and grilled chicken or steak are omnipresent), making it acceptable for even the most finicky eaters. Special kids' meals are not normally offered in restaurants, though some fancy lodges do them. However, most local eateries will accommodate two children splitting a meal or can produce child-size portions on request. If you're traveling with an infant, stock up on milk formula and baby food before heading to remote areas, and always carry snacks for long drives in remote areas – sometimes there are no places to stop for a bite.

Tired of juice and water? Here are some local drinks that your kids are sure to love: *batidos* (fresh fruit shakes), either *al agua* (made with water) or *con leche* (with milk); coconut milk (sipped through a straw straight from the cracked-open coconut); *horchata* (cinnamon-spiked rice milk). And don't worry too much – generally speaking, tap water and ice cubes in Costa Rica are safe for foreigners to consume.

Some additional tips and resources:

- Children under the age of 12 get a 25% discount on internal air travel, while children under two fly free (provided they sit on an adult's lap).
- If you're traveling with an infant, bring disposable diapers, baby creams, baby aspirin and thermometer from home, or else stock up while in San José.
- For a complete resource on traveling with kids, get Lonely Planet's *Travel with Children* guide.

TRAVEL LITERATURE

While you're in the midst of predeparture planning, check out the following recommended titles to start developing your sense of Costa Rica.

- *Naturalist in Costa Rica* (Dr Skutch) – an icon among bird-watchers, Skutch weaves his philosophies into his beautiful descriptions of flora and fauna in this enchanting memoir and natural history guide.
- *Around the Edge* (Peter Ford) – a story of the author's travels along the Caribbean coast from Belize to Panama, on foot and by boat.
- *Green Dreams: Travels in Central America* (Stephen Benz) – an astute analysis that questions the impact visitors are having on the region and its people.
- *Green Phoenix* (William Allen) – an absorbing and inspiring account of the author's efforts, alongside American and Costa Rican scientists and activists, to conserve and restore the rainforest in Guanacaste.
- *Ninety-Nine Days to Panama* (John and Harriet Halkyard) – a retired couple's detailed and entertaining account of driving an RV (complete with pet dog Brindle) from Texas to Panama.
- *So Far from God: A Journey to Central America* (Patrick Marnham) – the winner of the 1985 Thomas Cook Travel Book Award gives an insightful and amusing account of a leisurely meander from Texas to Panama.

- *Traveler's Tales Central America* (eds Larry Habegger and Natanya Pearlman) – a collection of striking travel essays on the region from renowned writers such as Paul Theroux and Tim Cahill.
- *Walk These Stones* (Leslie Hawthorne Klingler) – this Mennonite service worker writes about her experiences living, working, praying and sharing in the small village of Cuatro Cruces.

INTERNET RESOURCES

CIA Factbook (www.cia.gov/library/publications/the-world-factbook) An excellent overview of Costa Rica's political, economic and environmental standing.

Costa Rica Guide (www.costa-rica-guide.com) Nicely organized website with detailed maps and travel information on each region.

Costa Rica Tourism Board (www.visitcostarica.com) The official website of the Costa Rica Tourism Board (known as the ICT) is a great introduction to the country. You can research your trip and organize accommodations, tours and car rental from this site.

Guías Costa Rica (www.guiascostarica.com) Links that connect you with everything you'd ever need to know – from entertainment to health to government websites.

Lanic (http://lanic.utexas.edu/la/ca/cr) An exceptional collection of links to the websites (mostly in Spanish) of many Costa Rican organizations, from the University of Texas.

Lonely Planet (www.lonelyplanet.com) Provides information on travel in Costa Rica, links to accommodations and traveling tips from the all-important Thorn Tree community forum.

Tico Times (www.ticotimes.net) The online edition of Costa Rica's excellent English-language weekly newspaper.

Itineraries
CLASSIC ROUTES

THE BEST OF COSTA RICA

Two Weeks to One Month / Northwestern Costa Rica & Península de Nicoya

This route takes travelers by bubbling volcanoes, hot springs and tranquil cloud forests before hitting the sun-kissed beaches of the Nicoya.

From **San José** (p66), head north to **La Fortuna** (p158), where you can hike through forest on the flanks of **Volcán Arenal** (p171), then soak in hot springs. Come down from the mountain, take a boat across Laguna de Arenal, then a bus to **Monteverde** (p191), where you can search for the elusive quetzal at **Reserva Biológica Bosque Nuboso Monteverde** (p211).

For a change of scene, head west to the biggest party town in the Nicoya, **Playa Tamarindo** (p263), and enjoy the excellent surf in this brash town. Nature buffs will not want to miss the nesting leatherback turtles at **Playa Grande** (p260), while hard-core surfers should head straight south to **Playas Avellanas** and **Negra** (p271).

Continuing south, don't miss the stunning beaches and cosmopolitan cuisine at **Playa Sámara** (p286) and legendary swells at **Mal País** and **Playa Santa Teresa** (p305). Wind down your trip at laidback **Montezuma** (p298) and head back to San José via **Jacó** (p322) by jet boat and bus.

For a taste of all that Costa Rica has to offer, this classic route will take you into the mountains and cloud forests of the interior before sweeping you down into the Península de Nicoya.

PACIFIC COASTAL EXPLORER

One to Two Weeks / Central Pacific Coast

For days on end of sun, surf and sand, head south along the central Pacific coast for back-to-back beach towns dedicated to the pursuit of hedonism.

Kick things off in the resort town of **Jacó** (p322), a cosmopolitan enclave of fine dining and raging nightlife. In case you need a reminder that you're still in Costa Rica, backtrack a bit north up the coast to **Parque Nacional Carara** (p318), home to large populations of enchanting scarlet macaws.

Heading south along the coast, your next stop is the port town of **Quepos** (p336), which serves as a convenient base for the country's most popular national park, **Parque Nacional Manuel Antonio** (p349). Here, the rainforest sweeps down to meet the sea, providing refuge for rare animals, including the endangered Central American squirrel monkey.

Continue on south to **Hacienda Barú National Wildlife Refuge** (p354), where you can clamber on a canopy platform and sloth-spot in the trees. If you haven't had enough of the postcard-perfect Pacific coast, keep heading south to **Dominical** (p354) to catch some more waves, or to tiny and tranquil **Uvita** (p358) to escape the tourist crowds.

From Uvita, you can either continue south to the far-flung **Península de Osa** (p390), or head back to **San José** (p66) en route to the **Caribbean coast** (p442).

This excursion continues where the Best of Costa Rica route ends, and winds through the beaches and rainforests of the central Pacific region.

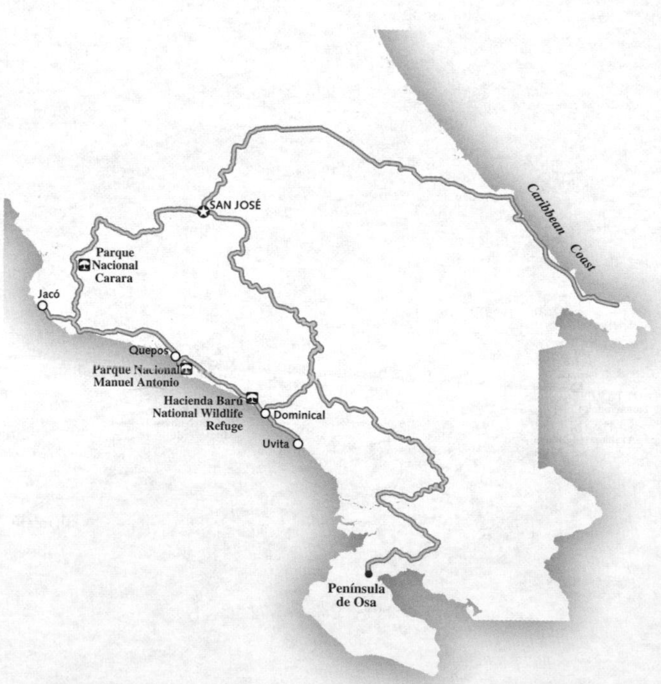

CARIBBEAN COASTAL EXPLORER

One to Two Weeks / Caribbean Coast

Spanish gives way to English, and Latin beats change to Caribbean rhythms as you begin to explore the 'other Costa Rica.'

Hop on the first eastbound bus out of **San José** (p66) and get off at **Cahuita** (p469), capital of Afro-Caribbean culture and gateway to **Parque Nacional Cahuita** (p477). Stick around and get your fill of this mellow little village before moving on to **Puerto Viejo de Talamanca** (p479), the Caribbean's center for nightlife, cuisine and all-round positive vibes.

From Puerto Viejo, rent a good old-fashioned pushbike and ride to **Manzanillo** (p492), from where you can snorkel, kayak and hike in the **Refugio Nacional de Vida Silvestre Gandoca-Manzanillo** (p494).

For the adventurous at heart, head north to grab a boat from **Moín** (p456) and travel the canal-lined coast to the village of **Tortuguero** (p461), where you can watch nesting green and leatherback turtles. Of course, the real reason you're here is to arrange a canoe trip through the mangrove-lined canals of **Parque Nacional Tortuguero** (p458), Costa Rica's mini-Amazon.

After spotting your fill of wildlife amid seemingly endless watery passages, head back to San José via water taxi and bus through **Cariari** (p449) and **Guápiles** (p447).

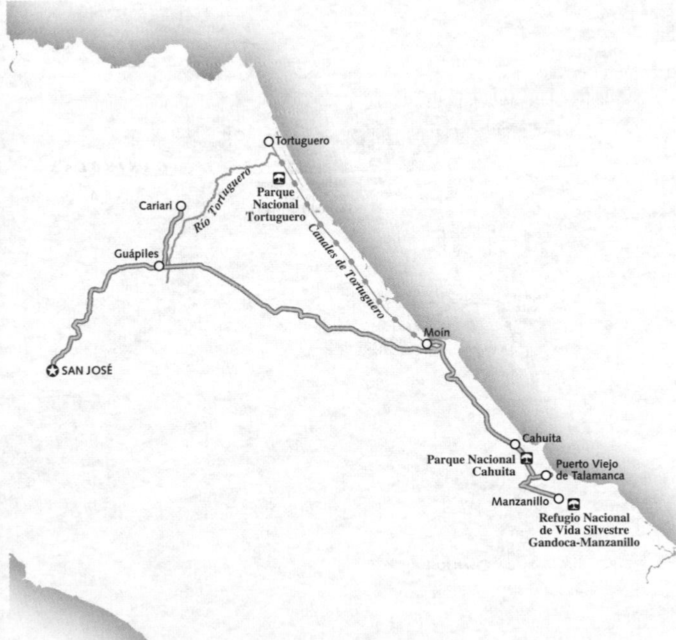

The Caribbean coast is a world unto itself, and provides a striking and memorable contrast to time spent elsewhere in the country.

ROADS LESS TRAVELED

RIDING RÍO SAN JUAN & SARAPIQUÍ

One to Two Weeks / Northern Lowlands & Caribbean Coast

Travel the river route through some of Costa Rica's most remote regions in the sparsely populated northern lowlands and Caribbean coast.

From **San José** (p66), bus to the tiny town of **La Virgen** (p499), a rafting and kayaking mecca where you can take a ride on the Río Sarapiquí and spend the night at the luxurious **Centro Neotrópico Sarapiquís** (p503).

As soon as you've gotten your bearings, follow the Río Sarapiquí on the bus to **Puerto Viejo de Sarapiquí** (p505), where you can wander through banana plantations, spot wildlife and mingle with busy scientists at the **Estación Biológica La Selva** (p508).

Of course, don't wait too long to leave terra firma and grab the morning boat up the Río Sarapiquí to **Trinidad Lodge** (p506), on the south bank of the Río San Juan. Stay on a working ranch, ride horses and go bird-watching before setting out, again by boat, along the Río San Juan, with your eye to the Caribbean coast.

This river (Nicaraguan territory) offers an incredible ride, which will take you through wildlife hot spots, ranches, forest, old war zones (from when Contras inhabited the area) and the remote **Refugio Nacional de Vida Silvestre Barra del Colorado** (p467) to the village of **Barra del Colorado** (p467) and its loose assortment of lodges. There you can go sportfishing, bird-watching and croc hunting (with binoculars, not guns).

You'll have to depend upon tides, weather and independent boatworkers, but if you work it out, you'll see more wildlife and incredible scenery than you have ever imagined.

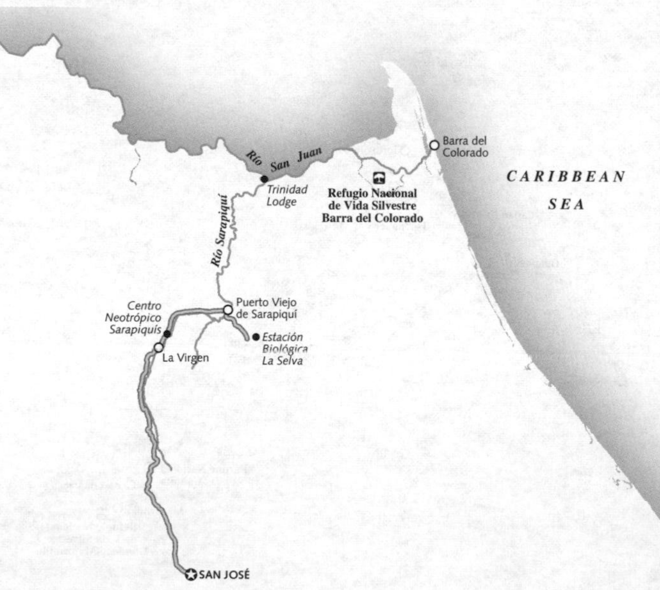

HIKING IN THE TALAMANCAS **Two to Three Weeks / Southern Costa Rica**

Costa Rica's most unexplored mountainous area is home to two spectacular hikes, which can be done separately or bundled together if you've got the time.

Gear up in **San Isidro de El General** (p369) before heading southeast through pineapple plantations to the small agricultural town of **Buenos Aires** (p378). Arrangements can be made here for transport via dirt road to the wonderfully remote **Reserva Biológica Dúrika** (p378), a self-sustaining community nestled in the Cordillera de Talamanca.

From this point, hire a local guide and trek through **Parque Internacional La Amistad** (p385), one of Costa Rica's last true wilderness areas. You can also pay a visit to the neighboring indigenous community of **Ujarrás** (p378).

If you haven't had your fill of nature yet, head from Buenos Aires to **Altamira** (p386), where you'll also find the headquarters for Parque Internacional La Amistad. From here you can take the 20km guided trek through **Valle del Silencio** (p387), one of the most isolated and remote areas in all of Costa Rica, ending up at a small refuge at the base of the **Cerro Kamuk** (p387).

From here, make the return trip through Altamira and back to the rowdy roads near the Interamericana.

The Cordillera de Talamanca is one of the most remote areas in the country and home to indigenous communities and incredible vistas.

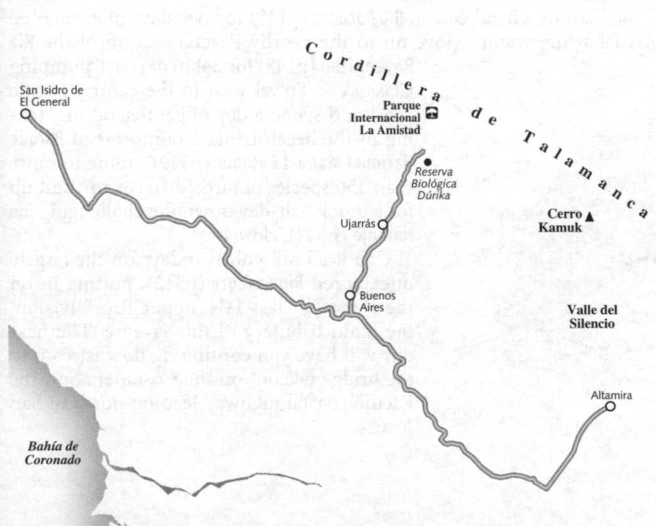

TAILORED TRIPS

SURFING SAFARI

Costa Rican shores have been attracting surfers since *Endless Summer II* profiled some of the country's most appealing breaks.

Playa Tamarindo (p263) serves as a good base for several tasty surfing sites. You can start with a boat trip to the granddaddies of all surf breaks, Witch's Rock and Ollie's Point in the **Parque Nacional Santa Rosa** (p234).

Next, hit the isolated beaches at **Playas Avellanas** and **Negra** (p271), whose famous waves were featured in the movie. Down the coast, **Playa Guiones** (p282) is cooking all year long, and from there it's just a hop, skip and long jump to the legendary **Mal País** (p305).

The next big stop is **Jacó** (p322) and **Playa Hermosa** (p332) on the central Pacific coast, offering consistent waves, but keep moving south for good breaks at **Matapalo** (p352) and **Dominical** (p354).

Afterwards, hightail it way south to **Cabo Matapalo** (p418) on the Península de Osa, before skipping back to the mainland for one of the continent's longest left-hand breaks at **Pavones** (p435).

And don't forget the Caribbean. Catch a boat to the uninhabited **Isla Uvita** (p454) off the coast of Puerto Limón or frolic in the waves east of town at **Playa Cocles** (p489). Further south the famous Salsa Brava at **Puerto Viejo de Talamanca** (p479) is for experts only.

RAFTING SAFARI

Experience the country's world-class rivers while soaking in the sight of pristine rainforests and wildlife on a 10-day safari.

From San José head east to **Río Pacuare** (p148) for two days of enchanted Class IV white water. Move on to the nearby Pascua section of the **Río Reventazón** (p148) for 24km of heart-pumping Class IV+. Travel west to the central Pacific coast and spend a day of gentler rafting, taking in the beach-fringed rainforest of **Parque Nacional Manuel Antonio** (p349), home to more than 350 species of birds. Afterwards, suit up for a quick half-day down the challenging **Río Naranjo** (p342), close by.

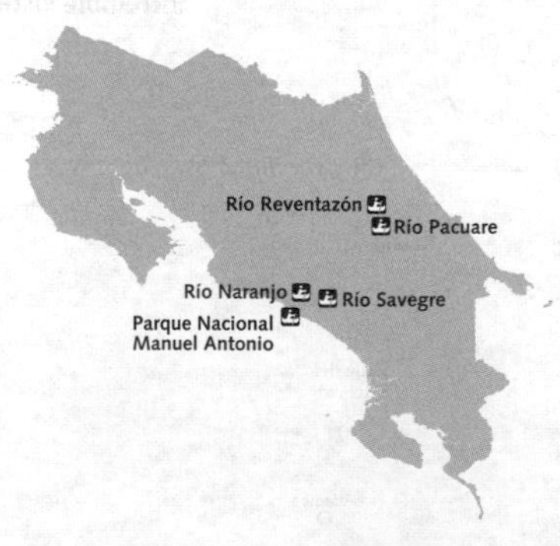

Cap it all off with two days on the largely unexplored **Río Savegre** (p342), putting in on the remote, Class IV+ upper Río División, the main tributary of the Savegre. The next day will have you continuing downstream to the bridge takeout on the Costanera Sur, the Pacific coastal highway leading north to San José.

EXPLORING OSA

Home to Costa Rica's most pristine nature, the Península de Osa is an undeniable draw for anyone wanting some rugged wilderness exploration.

Either head down the Pacific coast or fly into **Puerto Jiménez** (p413), which serves as the gateway to Osa. Here, you can spend a day or so kayaking around the mangroves or otherwise soaking up the charm of this tiny town.

Next, head north to **La Palma** (p403), from where you can visit the **Reserva Indígena Guaymí** (see boxed text, p413) and observe firsthand the traditional lifestyle of one of Costa Rica's indigenous groups.

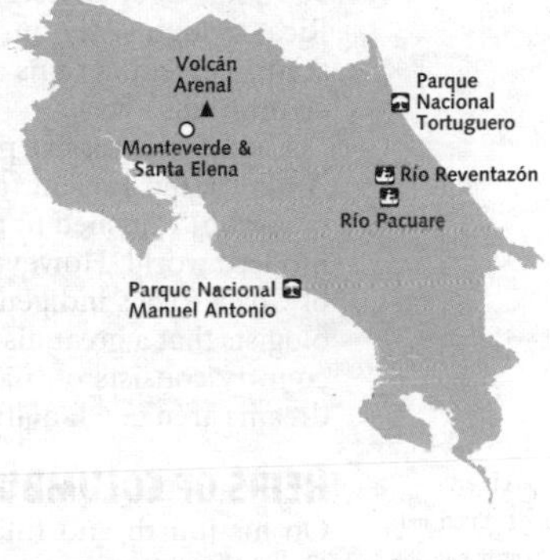

The undisputed highlight of Osa is **Parque Nacional Corcovado** (p421), one of the country's best wildlife-watching spots. It's worth spending a few days exploring the trails with backpack in hand, and particularly well-equipped travelers can even trek across the entirety of the park.

Finally, unwind at **Cabo Matapalo** (p418), where you can chill out for as long as you like, enjoying some of the country's most beautiful beaches.

FUN FOR KIDS

Whether you've got little angels or devilish troublemakers, Costa Rica is 100% kid-friendly and fun for everyone.

Costa Rica's top-billed family destinations are the remote mountain villages of **Monteverde** and **Santa Elena** (p191), where a grocery list of sights and activities awaits. Depending on the ages and the interests of your children, you can take them hiking through rainforest, zip lining through the canopy or even on a tour through a working dairy farm.

Another kid-friendly destination is **Parque Nacional Manuel Antonio** (p349), which woos little hearts and minds with its offering of charismatic creatures. Teach the little ones about the wonders of nature as you spot monkeys bounding through the trees, or simply spend your time sprawling out on gentle ocean-lapped sands.

Continuing with the safari theme, **Parque Nacional Tortuguero** (p458) is traversed by jungle rivers that are chock-full of crocodiles, iguanas and snakes. While little hands and legs should stay inside the boat at all times, the adventure factor runs high here.

White-water rafting on the **Ríos Reventazón** and **Pacuare** (p148) is also a possibility as both rivers have sections with smoother runs that are family-approved. Note, however, that children must be at least nine years old, and even older for tougher runs.

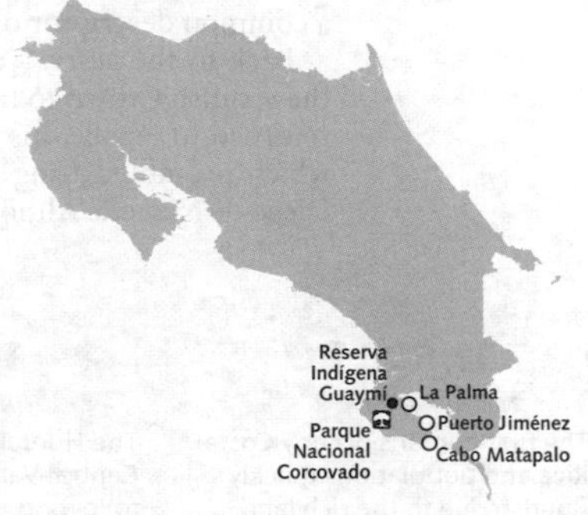

For a taste of the exotic, you can't go wrong with a visit to **Volcán Arenal** (p171). Watching lava spew forth and light up the evening sky is sure to captivate even those with the shortest of attention spans.

History

LOST COSTA RICA

The coastlines and rainforests of Central America have been inhabited by humans for at least 10,000 years. On the eve of European discovery some 500 years ago, an estimated 400,000 people were living in today's Costa Rica, though sadly our knowledge about these pre-Columbian cultures is scant. Torrential rains and Spanish colonization washed the remains of lost civilizations away.

Unlike the massive pyramid complexes found throughout much of Latin America, the ancient towns and cities of Costa Rica (with the exception of Guayabo) vanished in the jungles, never to be seen again by the eyes of the modern world. However, tales of lost cities still survive in the oral histories of Costa Rica's indigenous communities and there is hope among archaeologists that a great discovery lies in waiting. Considering that much of the country consists of inaccessible mountains and rainforests, perhaps these dreams aren't so fanciful.

The origin of Earth – according to Bribrí and Cabécar creation myth – is the subject of the beautifully illustrated story *When Woman Became Sea* by Susan Strauss.

HEIRS OF COLUMBUS

On his fourth and final voyage to the New World in 1502, Christopher Columbus was forced to drop anchor near present-day Puerto Limón after a hurricane damaged his ship. While waiting for repairs, Columbus ventured into the verdant terrain, and exchanged gifts with hospitable and welcoming chieftains. He returned from this encounter, claiming to have seen 'more gold in two days than in four years in Española.' Columbus dubbed the stretch of shoreline from Honduras to Panama as Veraguas, but it was his excited descriptions of *costarrica,* 'the rich coast,' that gave the region its lasting name. At least, that is how the popular story goes.

The reality is a bit more uncertain as the ship's logs from the fourth voyage didn't survive, and the only known record of the journey is a handwritten letter from Columbus to the Spanish Crown, which doesn't actually refer to the 'rich coast' by name. A more likely origin for the *costarrica* moniker is Diego Gutiérrez, the first colonial governor of the territory, who used the phrase in a much later 1543 letter to the Spanish Crown. However, there is no indication whether he himself invented the term, or was simply relaying a common descriptor or even corrupting a local indigenous word.

Back to the story – anxious to claim its bounty, Columbus petitioned the Spanish Crown to have himself appointed governor. But by the time he returned to Seville, his royal patron Queen Isabella was on her deathbed, which prompted King Ferdinand to award the prize to Columbus' rival, Diego de Nicuesa. Although Columbus became a very wealthy man, he never

TIMELINE

11,000 BC

The first humans occupy Costa Rica and populations quickly flourish due to the rich land and marine resources found along both coastlines.

1000 BC

The Huetar power base in the Central Valley is solidified following the construction and habitation of the ancient city of Guayabo, which is continuously inhabited until its mysterious abandonment in AD 1400.

100 BC

Costa Rica becomes part of an extensive trade network that moves gold and other goods and extends from present-day Mexico down though to the Andean empires.

returned to the New World, and died in 1506 after being worn down by ill health and court politics.

To the disappointment of his *conquistador* (conqueror) heirs, the region was not abundant with gold, and the locals were considerably less than affable. Nicuesa's first colony in present-day Panama was abruptly abandoned when tropical disease and warring tribes decimated its ranks. Successive expeditions launched from the Caribbean coast also failed as pestilent swamps, oppressive jungles and volcanoes made Columbus' paradise seem more like a tropical hell.

A bright moment in Spanish exploration came in 1513 when Vasco Núñez de Balboa heard rumors about a large sea and a wealthy, gold-producing civilization across the mountains of the isthmus – almost certainly referring to the Inca empire of present-day Peru. Driven by equal parts ambition and greed, Balboa scaled the continental divide, and on September 26, 1513, he became the first European to set eyes upon the Pacific Ocean. Keeping up

PRE-COLUMBIAN COSTA RICA

The early inhabitants of Costa Rica were part of an extensive trading zone that extended as far south as Peru and as far north as Mexico. The region hosted roughly 20 small tribes, organized into chiefdoms, indicating a permanent leader, a *cacique*, who sat atop a hierarchical society that included shamans, warriors, toilers and slaves.

Adept at seafaring, the Carib dominated the Atlantic coastal lowlands, and served as a conduit of trade with the South American mainland. In the northwest, several tribes were connected to the great Mesoamerican cultures. Aztec religious practices and Maya jade and craftsmanship are in evidence in the Península de Nicoya, while Costa Rican quetzal feathers and golden trinkets have turned up in Mexico. In the southwest, three chiefdoms showed the influence of Andean indigenous cultures, including coca leaves, yucca and sweet potatoes.

There is also evidence that the language of the Central Valley, Huetar, was known by all of Costa Rica's indigenous groups, which may be an indication of their power and influence. The Central Valley is home to the only major archaeological site uncovered in Costa Rica, namely Guayabo (p149).

Thought to be an ancient ceremonial center, Guayabo once featured paved streets, an aqueduct and decorative gold. Here, archaeologists uncovered exquisite gold ornaments and unusual life-size stone statues of human figures, as well as distinctive types of pottery and *metates,* stone platforms that were used for grinding corn. Today, the site consists of little more than ancient hewed rock and stone, though Guayabo continues to stand as testament to a once-great civilization of the New World.

Still a puzzle, however, are the hundreds of hand-sculpted, monolithic stone spheres that dot the landscape of the Diquis Valley in Palmar (p380) and the Isla del Caño (p402). Weighing up to 16 tons and ranging in size from a baseball to a Volkswagen, the spheres have inspired many theories: an ancient calendar, extraterrestrial meddling, or a game of bocce gone terribly awry.

1522

Spanish settlement develops in Costa Rica, though it will be several decades before the colonists can get a sturdy foothold on the land.

1540

The Kingdom of Guatemala is established by the Spanish, and includes much of Central America – Costa Rica, Nicaragua, Honduras, El Salvador, Guatemala and the Mexican state of Chiapas.

1

Spanish
Vásque
in Co
of g
m

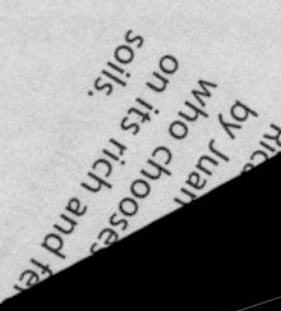

with the European fashion of the day, Balboa immediately proceeded to claim the ocean and all the lands it touched for the king of Spain.

The thrill of discovery aside, the conquistadors now controlled a strategic western beachhead from which to launch their conquest of Costa Rica. In the name of God and king, aristocratic adventurers plundered indigenous villages, executed resisters and enslaved survivors throughout the Nicoya peninsula. However, none of these bloodstained campaigns led to a permanent presence as intercontinental germ warfare caused outbreaks of feverish death on both sides. Since the area was scarce in mineral wealth and indigenous laborers, the Spanish eventually came to regard it as the 'poorest and most miserable in all the Americas.'

Visit World Mysteries at www.world-mysteries.com/sar_12.htm for an investigation of Costa Rica's mysterious stone spheres.

NEW WORLD ORDER

It was not until the 1560s that a Spanish colony was firmly established in Costa Rica. Hoping to cultivate the rich volcanic soil of the Central Valley, the Spanish founded the village of Cartago (p138) on the banks of the Río Reventazón. Although the fledgling colony was extremely isolated, it miraculously survived under the leadership of its first governor, Juan Vásquez de Coronado. Preferring diplomacy over firearms to counter the indigenous threat, Coronado used Cartago as a base to survey the lands south to Panama and west to the Pacific, and secured deed and title over the colony.

Though Coronado was later tragically lost at sea in a shipwreck, his legacy endured: Costa Rica was an officially recognized province of the Viceroyalty of New Spain (Virreinato de Nueva España), which was the name given to the viceroy-ruled territories of the Spanish empire in North America, Central America, the Caribbean and Asia.

For roughly three centuries, the Captaincy General of Guatemala (also known as the Kingdom of Guatemala), which extended from modern-day Texas to Panama, with the exception of Belize, was a loosely administered colony in the vast Spanish empire. Since the political-military headquarters of the kingdom were in Guatemala, Costa Rica became a minor provincial outpost that had little if any strategic significance or exploitable riches.

As a result of its backwater status, Costa Rica's colonial path diverged from the typical pattern in that a powerful landholding elite and slave-based economy never gained prominence. Instead of large estates, mining operations and coastal cities, modest-sized villages of smallholders developed in the interior Central Valley. According to national lore, the stoic, self-sufficient farmer provided the backbone for 'rural democracy' as Costa Rica emerged as one of the only egalitarian corners of the Spanish empire.

Equal rights and opportunities were not extended to the indigenous groups and as the Spanish settlement expanded, the local population decreased dramatically. From 400,000 at the time Columbus first sailed, the number was reduced to 20,000 a century later, and to 8000 a century after that. While

1563

The first permanent Spanish colonial settlement in Costa ... is established in Cartago ... Vásquez de Coronado, ... the site based ... ile volcanic

1737

The future capital of San José is established, sparking a rivalry with neighboring Cartago that will eventually culminate in a civil war between the two dominant cities.

1821

Following a unanimous declaration by Mexico on behalf of all of Central America, Costa Rica finally gains its independence from Spain after centuries of colonial occupation.

disease was the main source of death, the Spanish were relentless in their effort to exploit the natives as an economic resource. Central Valley groups were the first to fall, though outside the valley several tribes managed to survive a bit longer under forest cover, staging occasional raids. However, as in the rest of Latin America, repeated military campaigns eventually forced them into submission and slavery.

THE FALL OF AN EMPIRE

On October 27, 1807, the Treaty of Fontainebleau, which defined the occupation of Portugal, was signed between Spain and France. Under the guise of reinforcing the Franco-Spanish army occupying Portugal, Napoleon moved tens of thousands of troops into Spain. In an act of military genius, Napoleon ordered his troops to abandon the ruse and seize key Spanish fortifications. Without firing a single shot, Napoleon's troops seized Barcelona after convincing the city to open its gates for a convoy of wounded soldiers.

The Last Country the Gods Made, by Adrian Colesberry, is a collection of essays and photographs, providing an overview of Costa Rican history, geography and society.

Although Napoleon's invasion by stealth was successful, the resulting Peninsular War was a horrific campaign of guerrilla combat that crippled both countries. As a result of the conflict as well as the subsequent power vacuum and internal turmoil, Spain lost nearly all of its colonial possessions in the first third of the 19th century.

In 1821, the Americas wriggled free of Spain's imperial grip following Mexico's declaration of independence for itself as well as the whole of Central America. Of course, the Central American provinces weren't too keen on having another foreign power reign over them, and subsequently declared independence from Mexico. However, all of these events hardly disturbed Costa Rica, which learned of its liberation a month after the fact.

The newly liberated colonies pondered their fate: stay together in a United States of Central America, or go their separate national ways. At first, they came up with something in between, namely the Central American Federation (CAF), though it could neither field an army nor collect taxes. Accustomed to being at the center of things, Guatemala also attempted to dominate the CAF, alienating smaller colonies and hastening its demise. Future attempts to unite the region would likewise fail.

Meanwhile, an independent Costa Rica was taking shape under Juan Mora Fernández, first head of state (1824–33). He tended toward nation-building, and organized new towns, built roads, published a newspaper and coined a currency. His wife even partook in the effort by designing the country's flag.

Life returned to normal, unlike in the rest of the region where post-independence civil wars raged on. In 1824, the Nicoya-Guanacaste region seceded from Nicaragua and joined its more easygoing southern neighbor, defining the territorial borders. In 1852, Costa Rica received its first diplomatic emissaries from the USA and Great Britain.

April 1823

The Costa Rican capital officially moves to San José after intense skirmishes with the conservative residents of Cartago, who take issue with the more liberal longings of the power-hungry *josefinos*.

December 1823

The Monroe Doctrine formerly declares the intentions of the USA to be the dominant imperial power in the Western Hemisphere despite protests from European powers.

1824

The Nicoya- votes to s Nicarag of Cos regi in

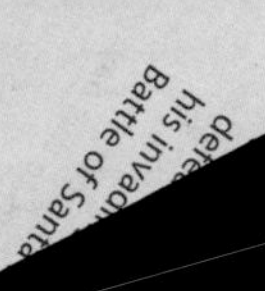

COFFEE RICA

In the 19th century, the riches that Costa Rica had long promised were uncovered when it was realized that the soil and climate of the Central Valley highlands were ideal for coffee cultivation. Costa Rica led Central America in introducing the caffeinated bean, which transformed the impoverished country into the wealthiest in the region.

WILLIAM WALKER

As the Spanish empire receded, another arose. In the 19th century the USA was in an expansive mood and Spanish America looked increasingly vulnerable.

In 1853, a soldier of fortune named William Walker landed in the Mexican territory of Baja California with 45 men intending to privately conquer Mexico and Central America, establish slavery and mandate white control of the region. Walker succeeded in capturing La Paz, the capital of the territory, and declared himself the president of the new 'Republic of Lower California.'

However, less than three months after occupying the region, he was forced to retreat back to the other California due to lack of supplies and an unexpectedly strong Mexican resistance. Although he was later put on trial for conducting an illegal war, his legendary campaign won him popularity among expansionists in the conservative west and south of the USA, which prompted the jury to acquit him in only eight minutes.

In 1856 Walker was back to his old tricks again, this time capitalizing on the civil war that was raging in Nicaragua. After raising a small army, he managed to sack the city of La Virgen and cripple the Nicaraguan national army. One month later, he conquered the capital of Granada and took control of the country through puppet president Patricio Rivas. Soon after, US President Franklin Pierce fully recognized Walker's regime as the legitimate government of Nicaragua.

Before long, Walker was marching on Costa Rica, though Costa Rican President Juan Rafael Mora Porras guessed Walker's intentions and managed to recruit a volunteer army of 9000 civilians. In a brilliant display of military prowess, a ragtag group of fighters surrounded Walker's army as they lay waiting in an old hacienda (estate) in present-day Parque Nacional Santa Rosa (see p234). The battle was over in just 14 minutes and Walker was forever expelled from Costa Rican soil.

During the fighting, a drummer boy from Alajuela, Juan Santamaría, was killed while daringly setting fire to Walker's defenses. The battle became national legend and Santamaría was exalted as a Costa Rican patriot and immortalized in statues (and in an airport) throughout the country.

After returning to Nicaragua, Walker declared himself president of the country. However, Walker's popularity was waning on all sides and soon he found himself being repatriated to the USA. Of course, Walker's messianic ambitions were far from realized, and after a brief hiatus he set out once again for Central America.

On his final (and ultimately fatal) expedition, Walker tried to invade Honduras, which quickly perturbed the British, who saw him as a threat to their affairs in British Honduras (present-day Belize) and the Mosquito Coast (present-day Nicaragua). After being captured by the British Royal Navy, Walker was quickly handed over to the Honduran authorities, who chose death by firing squad as a fitting punishment for trying to take over their country.

1856

Costa Rica puts a damper on the expansionist aims of the war hawks in the USA by [illegible]ating William Walker and [illegible]ing army at the epic [illegible] Rosa.

1889

Costa Rica's first democratic elections are held, a monumental event given the long history of colonial occupation, though unfortunately blacks and women were prohibited by law to vote.

1890

The construction of the railroad between San José and Puerto Limón is finally completed despite years of hardships and countless deaths due to accidents, and diseases such as malaria and yellow fever.

When an export market was discovered, the government actively promoted coffee to farmers by providing free saplings. At first, Costa Rican producers exported their crop to nearby South Americans, who processed the beans and re-exported the product to Europe. By the 1840s, however, local merchants had already built up domestic capacity and learned to scope out their own overseas markets. Their big break came when they persuaded the captain of the HMS *Monarch* to transport several hundred sacks of Costa Rican coffee to London, percolating the beginning of a beautiful friendship.

The Costa Rican coffee boom was on. The drink's quick fix made it popular among working-class consumers in the industrializing north. The aroma of riches lured a wave of enterprising German immigrants to Costa Rica, enhancing the technical and financial skills in the business sector. By century's end, more than one-third of the Central Valley was dedicated to coffee cultivation, and coffee accounted for more than 90% of all exports and 80% of foreign-currency earnings.

The coffee industry in Costa Rica developed differently from the rest of Central America. As elsewhere, there arose a group of coffee barons, elites that reaped the rewards for the export bonanza. But Costa Rican coffee barons lacked the land and labor to cultivate the crop. Coffee production is labor-intensive, with a long and painstaking harvest season. The small farmers became the principal planters. The coffee barons, instead, monopolized processing, marketing and financing. The coffee economy in Costa Rica created a wide network of high-end traders and small-scale growers, whereas in the rest of Central America, a narrow elite controlled large estates, worked by tenant laborers.

In the 1940s children in Costa Rica learned to read with a text that stated 'Coffee is good for me. I drink coffee every morning.'

Coffee wealth became a power resource in politics. Costa Rica's traditional aristocratic families were at the forefront of the enterprise. At midcentury, three-quarters of the coffee barons were descended from just two colonial families. The country's leading coffee exporter at this time was President Juan Rafael Mora Porras (1849–59), whose lineage went back to the colony's founder Juan Vásquez de Coronado. Mora was overthrown by his brother-in-law, after the president proposed to form a national bank independent from the coffee barons. The economic interests of the coffee elite would thereafter become a priority in Costa Rican politics.

BANANA EMPIRE

The coffee trade unintentionally gave rise to Costa Rica's next export boom – bananas. Getting coffee out to world markets necessitated a rail link from the central highlands to the coast, and Limón's deep harbor made an ideal port. Inland was dense jungle and insect-infested swamps, which prompted the government to contract the task to Minor Keith, nephew of an American railroad tycoon.

1900

The population of Costa Rica reaches 50,000 as the country begins to develop and prosper due to the increasingly lucrative international coffee and banana trades.

1914

Costa Rica is given an economic boost following the opening of the Panama Canal. The canal was forged by 75,000 laborers, many thousands of whom died during construction.

1919

Federico Tinoco Granados is ousted as the dictator of Costa Rica in one of the few episodes of brief violence in an otherwise peaceful political history.

The project was a disaster. Malaria and accidents churned through workers as Tico recruits gave way to US convicts and Chinese indentured servants, who were in turn replaced by freed Jamaican slaves. To entice Keith to continue, the government turned over 3200 sq km of land along the route and provided a 99-year lease to run the railroad. In 1890, the line was finally completed and running at a loss.

Keith had begun to grow banana plants along the tracks as a cheap food source for the workers. Desperate to recoup his investment, he shipped some bananas to New Orleans in the hope of starting a side venture. He struck gold, or rather yellow. Consumers went crazy for the elongated finger fruit. By the early 20th century, bananas surpassed coffee as Costa Rica's most lucrative export and the country became the world's leading banana exporter. Unlike in the coffee industry, the profits were exported along with the bananas.

Costa Rica was transformed by the rise of Keith's banana empire. He joined with another American importer to found the infamous United Fruit Company, soon the largest employer in Central America. To the locals, it was known as *el pulpo*, 'the octopus' – its tentacles stretched across the region, becoming entangled with the local economy and politics. United Fruit owned huge swathes of lush lowlands, much of the transportation and communication infrastructure and bunches of bureaucrats. The company drew a wave of migrant laborers from Jamaica, changing the country's ethnic complexion and provoking racial tensions.

For details on the role of Minor Keith and the United Fruit Company in lobbying for a CIA-led coup in Guatemala, pick up a copy of the highly readable *Bitter Fruit* by Stephen Schlesinger and Stephen Kinzer.

BIRTH OF A NATION

The inequality of the early 20th century led to the rise of José Figueres Ferrer, a self-described farmer-philosopher and the father of Costa Rica's unarmed democracy. The son of Catalan immigrant coffee planters, Figueres excelled in school and went to MIT, in Boston, to study engineering. Upon returning to Costa Rica to set up his own coffee plantation, he organized the hundreds of laborers on his farm into a utopian socialist community, and appropriately named the property La Luz Sin Fin, 'The Struggle Without End.'

In the 1940s, Figueres became involved in national politics as an outspoken critic of President Calderón. In the midst of a radio interview in which he badmouthed the president, police broke into the studio and arrested Figueres. He was accused of having fascist sympathies and was banished to Mexico. While in exile, he formed the Caribbean League, a collection of students and democratic agitators from all over Central America, who pledged to bring down the region's military dictators. When he returned to Costa Rica, the Caribbean League, now 700-men strong, went with him and helped protest against the powers that be.

When government troops descended on the farm with the intention of arresting Figueres and disarming the Caribbean League, it touched off a

1940

Rafael Ángel Calderón Guardia is elected president and proceeds to improve working conditions in Costa Rica by enacting minimum-wage laws as well as an eight-hour day.

1940s

José Figueres Ferrer becomes involved in national politics and opposes the ruling conservatives. Figueres' social-democratic policies and criticism of the government angers the Costa Rican elite and President Calderón.

1948

Conservative and liberal forces clash, resulting in a six-week civil war that leaves 2000 Costa Ricans dead, many more wounded and destroys much of the country's fledgling infrastructure.

civil war. The moment had arrived: the diminutive farmer-philosopher now played the man on horseback. Figueres emerged victorious from the brief conflict and seized the opportunity to put into place his vision of Costa Rican social democracy. After dissolving the country's military, Figueres quoted HG Wells: 'The future of mankind cannot include the armed forces.'

As head of a temporary junta government, Figueres enacted nearly 1000 decrees. He taxed the wealthy, nationalized the banks and built a modern welfare state. His 1949 constitution granted full citizenship and voting rights to women, African-Americans, indigenous groups and Chinese minorities. Today, Figueres' revolutionary regime is regarded as the foundation of Costa Rica's unarmed democracy.

THE AMERICAN EMPIRE

Throughout the 1970s and '80s, the sovereignty of the small nations of Central America was limited by their northern neighbor, the USA. Big sticks, gunboats and dollar diplomacy were instruments of a Yankee policy to curtail socialist politics, especially the military oligarchies of Guatemala, El Salvador and Nicaragua.

Thirty-three out of 44 Costa Rican presidents prior to 1970 were descended from just three original colonizing families.

In 1979 the rebellious Sandinistas toppled the American-backed Somoza dictatorship in Nicaragua. Alarmed by the Sandinistas' Soviet and Cuban ties, fervently anticommunist President Ronald Reagan decided it was time to intervene. The Cold War arrived in the hot tropics.

The organizational details of the counterrevolution were delegated to Oliver North, an eager-to-please junior officer working out of the White House basement. North's can-do creativity helped to prop up the famed Contra rebels to incite civil war in Nicaragua. While both sides invoked the rhetoric of freedom and democracy, the war was really a turf battle between left-wing and right-wing forces.

Under intense US pressure, Costa Rica was reluctantly dragged in. The Contras set up camp in northern Costa Rica, from where they staged guerrilla raids. Not-so-clandestine CIA operatives and US military advisors were dispatched to assist the effort. A secret jungle airstrip was built near the border to fly in weapons and supplies. To raise cash for the rebels, North allegedly used his covert supply network to traffic illegal narcotics through the region.

The war polarized Costa Rica. From conservative quarters came a loud call to re-establish the military and join the anticommunist crusade, which was largely underwritten by the US Pentagon. In May of 1984, more than 20,000 demonstrators marched through San José to give peace a chance, though the debate didn't climax until the 1986 presidential election. The victor was 44-year-old Oscar Arias Sánchez, who, despite being born into coffee wealth, was an intellectual reformer in the mold of Figueres, his political patron.

1949

Hoping to heal its wounds while charting a bold new course for the future, the temporary government enacts a new constitution abolishing the army, desegregating the country, and granting women and blacks the right to vote.

1963

Reserva Natural Absoluta Cabo Blanco at the tip of the Nicoya peninsula becomes Costa Rica's first federally protected conservation area through the efforts of Swedish and Danish conservationists.

1987

President Oscar Arias Sánchez wins the Nobel Peace Prize for his work on the Central American peace accords, which brought about greater political freedom throughout the region.

Once in office, Arias affirmed his commitment to a negotiated resolution and reasserted Costa Rican national independence. He vowed to uphold his country's pledge of neutrality and to vanquish the Contras from the territory, which prompted the US ambassador to suddenly quit his post. In a public ceremony, Costa Rican school children planted trees on top of the CIA's secret airfield. Most notably, Arias became the driving force in uniting Central America around a peace plan, which ended the Nicaraguan war and earned him the Nobel Peace Prize in 1987.

In 2006 Arias once again returned to the presidential office, winning the popular election by a 1.2% margin, and subsequently ratifying the controversial Central American Free Trade Agreement (Cafta).

Prior to his re-election, President Oscar Arias Sánchez founded the Arias Foundation for Peace and Human Progress; on the web at www.arias.or.cr.

COSTA RICA TOMORROW

Costa Rica held free and fair presidential elections in February 2010, which were supervised by the Organization of American States. The victor was Oscar Arias Sánchez' former Vice President Laura Chinchilla, who won just under 47% of the vote, thus retaining the political power of her center-right National Liberation Party. Chinchilla campaigned on similar economic platforms as her political mentor, namely the promotion of free trade and further increased access to US markets. However, critics argue that these aims do not protect small farmers and domestic industries, which have struggled to compete with the recent flood of cheap US products.

Unlike Arias, Chinchilla is a staunch social conservative who is diametrically opposed to legalized abortion, same-sex marriage and emergency contraception. In a striking departure from her political mentor, she has pledged to fight against proposed legislation that would strip Costa Rica of its official Roman Catholic designation and establish a secular state.

Costa Rica will most likely continue its reign as the global pioneer in sustainable development, providing a model in which economic and environmental interests are complementary. But it is not without some contention. Conservation and ecotourism are administered by two powerful bureaucracies – the Ministry of Environment & Energy (Minae) and the Costa Rica Tourism Board (ICT) – who frequently clash. There is also a widening gap between the motives of the San José–based eco-elite and the concerns of the rural residents, who still use the land to survive.

The success of the 'green revolution' has created a new concern, namely the need for sustainable tourism. The increasing number of visitors to Costa Rica has led to more hotels, more transportation and more infrastructure upgrades. This tourist-driven encroachment on the rainforest inevitably places stress on the fragile ecosystem that people are flocking to see. However, although Costa Rica is certainly not without its problems, it is one of the few countries in the region where environmental issues are given a proper forum for discussion as opposed to mere lip service.

2000

At the start of the new millennium, the population of Costa Rica tops four million, though many believe the number is far greater due to burgeoning illegal settlements on the fringes of the capital.

2006

Nobel laureate Oscar Arias Sánchez is elected president for the second time in his political career on a pro-Cafta (Central American Free Trade Agreement) platform despite winning by an extremely narrow margin.

2007

A national referendum narrowly passes Cafta. Opinion remains divided as to whether opening up trade with the USA will be beneficial in the long run for Costa Rica.

The Culture

TICO PRIDE

Costa Ricans, or Ticos as they affectionately call themselves, take great pride in defining themselves by what they are not. In comparison with their Central American neighbors like Nicaragua and Honduras, there's little poverty and illiteracy and they aren't beleaguered by political tumult. It's a curious line-up of negatives that somehow adds up to one big positive.

Ticos are also extremely proud of their country, from its ecological jewels, high standard of living and education levels to, above all else, the fact that it has flourished without an army for the past 60 years. They view their country as an oasis of calm in a land that has been continuously degraded by warfare. The Nobel Peace Prize that Oscar Arias Sánchez received for his work on the Central American peace accords is a point of pride and confirms the general feeling that they are somehow different from a grosser, more violent world. Peace is priceless.

Ticos are always well mannered and will do all they can to *quedar bien* (leave a good impression). Conversations start with a cordial greeting such as *buenos días* (good morning) or *buenas tardes* (good afternoon), as well as friendly inquiries about your well-being before delving into business. Bullying and yelling will get you nowhere, but a smile and a friendly greeting goes a long way.

LIFESTYLE

A lack of war and the presence of strong exports and stronger tourism have meant that Costa Rica enjoys the highest standard of living in Central America. For the most part, Costa Ricans live fairly rich and comfortable lives, even by Western standards.

The most comprehensive and complete book on Costa Rican history and culture is *The Ticos: Culture and Social Change in Costa Rica* by Mavis, Richard and Karen Biesanz.

One of the main reasons for the social cohesiveness of Costa Rican society is the strength and influence of family ties. Indeed, the family unit remains the nucleus of life in Costa Rica and serves as a support network for everyone involved. Families socialize together and groups of the same clan will often live near each other in clusters. Furthermore, celebrations, weddings and family gatherings are a social outlet for rich and poor alike, and those with relatives in positions of power – nominal or otherwise – don't hesitate to turn to them for support.

Given this mutually cooperative environment, it shouldn't come as a surprise that life expectancy in Costa Rica is almost the same as that of the USA. In fact, most Costa Ricans are more likely to die of heart disease or cancer, as opposed to the childhood diseases that tend to claim lives in many developing nations. A nationwide healthcare system and proper sanitation systems account for these positive statistics, as does a generally stress-free lifestyle, tropical weather and a healthy and varied diet.

Similar to the industrialized world, families have an average of 2.2 children. For the most part, Costa Rican youths spend ample time on middle-class worries, such as dating, music, belly-baring fashions and *fútbol* (soccer). Primary education is free and compulsory, contributing to the 95% literacy rate. Costa Rica also has a comprehensive socialized medical system and pension scheme that looks after the needs of the country's sick and elderly.

The middle and upper class largely reside in San José, as well as the major cities of the Central Valley highlands (Heredia, Alajuela and Cartago), and enjoy a level of comfort similar to their economic brethren in Europe and the USA. They live in large homes or apartments, have a maid, a car or two and, for the lucky few, a second home on the beach or in the mountains. On the outskirts of these urban areas, the urban poor have hastily constructed shanty towns, but certainly not on the scale of some other Latin American countries.

The home of an average Tico is a one-story construction made of concrete blocks, wood or a combination of both. In the poorer lowland areas, people often live in windowless houses made of *caña brava*, a local cane.

For the vast majority of *campesinos* (farmers) and *indígenas* (indigenous people), life is hard, and poverty levels are higher and standards of living are lower than in the rest of the country. This is especially true along the Caribbean coast where the descendants of Jamaican immigrants have long suffered from a lack of attention by the federal government. However, although poor families have few possessions and little financial security, every member assists with working the land or contributing to the household, which creates a strong safety net.

As in the rest of the developing world, globalization is having a dramatic effect on family ways. These days, society is increasingly geographically mobile – the Tico that was born in Puntarenas might end up managing a lodge on the Península de Osa. And, with the advent of better-paved roads, cell phones, electrification and the increasing presence of North American and European expats, change will continue to come at a steady pace for the Tico family unit.

The expression *matando la culebra* (meaning 'to be idle,' literally 'killing the snake') originates with *peones* (laborers) from banana plantations. When foremen would ask what they were doing, the response was '*¡Matando la culebra!*'.

ECONOMY

For about 20 years, Costa Rica's economy has remained remarkably stable thanks to strong returns on tourism, agriculture and industry. Commerce, tourism and services (hotels, restaurants, tourist services, banks and insurance) account for 67.6% of the total gross domestic product (GDP), while agriculture and industry make up 6.5% and 25.9% respectively.

Principle agriculture exports include pineapples, coffee, beef, sugar, rice, dairy products, vegetables, fruits and ornamental plants, while industrial exports include electronic components (microchips), food processing, textiles, construction materials, fertilizer and medical equipment.

Poverty levels have also been kept in check for more than 20 years by strong welfare programs. Although approximately 16% of the populace lives below the poverty line, beggars are few and far between, and you won't see the packs of ragged street kids that seem to roam around other Latin American capitals.

A subsistence farmer might earn as little as US$100 a year, far below the national average of US$11,500 per capita. However, even in the most deprived region, such as the Caribbean coast, most people have adequate facilities and clean drinking water. In fact, Unicef estimates that more than 90% of households have adequate sanitation systems, while virtually all have access to potable water.

Increased legal and illegal immigration from Nicaragua has started to put a strain on the economic system. There are an estimated 300,000 to 500,000 Nicaraguans in Costa Rica, who serve as an important source of mostly unskilled labor, but some believe they also threaten to overwhelm the welfare state.

In conjunction with two indigenous women, Paula Palmer wrote *Taking Care of Sibö's Gifts*, an inspiring account of the intersection between the spiritual and environmental values of the Bribrí.

Foreign investors continue to be attracted by the country's political stability, high education levels and well-developed tourism infrastructure. At the same time, the government is struggling to curb inflation, tackle its rising debts, reform its antiquated tax system and deal with the fallout of the global recession.

POPULATION

Costa Ricans call themselves Ticos (men or groups of men and women) or Ticas (women). Two-thirds of the nation's more than four million people live in the Meseta Central (Central Valley) and almost one-third is under the age of 15.

In the 1940s, Costa Rica was an overwhelmingly agricultural society, with the vast majority of the population employed by coffee and banana plantations. By the end of the century, the economy had shifted quite dramatically, and only one-fifth of the labor force was employed by agriculture. These days, industry (especially agro-industry) employs another one-fifth, while the service sector employs more than half of the labor force. Banking and commerce are prominent, but tourism alone employs more than 10% of the labor force.

Costa Rica hosts an annual tennis tournament known as La Copa del Café (The Coffee Cup).

Most inhabitants are *mestizos,* having a mix of Spanish and indigenous and/or African roots, though the vast majority of Ticos consider themselves to be white. Although it's difficult to offer a precise explanation for this cultural phenomenon, it is partly due to the fact that Costa Rica's indigenous populations were virtually wiped out by the Spanish *conquistadores* (conquerors). As a result, most Costa Ricans prefer to trace their ancestry back to the European continent and take considerable pride in the purity and clarity of their Spanish.

Indigenous Costa Ricans today make up only 1% of the total population. These groups include the Bribri and Cabécar (p489), the Brunka (p378), the Guaymí (p413) and the Maleku (p521). For more information on their histories, see boxed text, p45.

Less than 3% of the population is black, and the vast majority is concentrated on the Caribbean coast. Tracing its ancestry to Jamaican immigrants who were brought to build railroads in the 19th century, this population speaks Mecatelyu: a creole of English, Spanish and Jamaican English. It identifies strongly with its counterparts in other Caribbean countries; coconut-spiced cuisine and calypso music are only a couple of elements that travelers can enjoy. In Limón, still common are the rituals of *obeah,* or sorcery, passed down from African ancestors.

Chinese immigrants (1%) also arrived in Costa Rica to build railroads in the 19th century, though there have been regular, more voluntary waves of immigration since then. In recent years North American and European immigration has greatly increased, and it is estimated that roughly 50,000 expats from these two regions presently live in the country.

Get player statistics, game schedules and find out everything you ever needed to know about La Sele, the Costa Rican national soccer team, at www.fedefutbol.com (in Spanish).

SPORTS

The national sport is, you guessed it, *fútbol.* Every town has a soccer field (which usually serves as the most conspicuous landmark) where neighborhood aficionados play in heated matches.

The *selección nacional* (national selection) team is known affectionately as La Sele. Legions of rabid Tico fans still recall La Sele's most memorable moments, including an unlikely showing in the quarterfinals at the 1990 World Cup in Italy and a solid (if not long-lasting) performance in the 2002 World Cup. La Sele qualified to participate in the 2006 World Cup in Germany, although the team failed to progress beyond the first round; it didn't manage to qualify in 2010. Costa Rica has also played several times in the Copa América, twice making it to the quarterfinals. Women's soccer is not followed with as much devotion, but there is a female national team. The regular season is from August to May.

Surfing is growing in popularity among Ticos. Costa Rica annually hosts numerous national and international competitions that are widely covered by local media.

Bullfighting is also popular, particularly in the Guanacaste region, though the bull isn't killed in the Costa Rican version of the sport. More aptly described, bullfighting is really a ceremonial opportunity to watch an often tipsy cowboy run around with a bull. The popular Latin American sport of cockfighting is illegal.

MULTICULTURALISM

The mix of mainstream *mestizo* society with indigenous people, African-Americans, Asians and North Americans provides the country with an interesting fusion of culture and cuisine. And while the image of the welcoming Tico is largely true, tensions always exist.

For the black population, racism has been a reality for more than a century. About 75% of the country's black population reside on the Caribbean coast, and this area has been historically marginalized and deprived of services by a succession of governments (black Costa Ricans were not allowed in the Central Valley until after 1948). Nonetheless, times have changed and black visitors as well as other minority groups can feel comfortable traveling around the entire country.

It is Nicaraguans who are currently the butt of some of society's worst prejudice. During the 1980s, the civil war provoked a wave of immigration from Nicaragua. While the violence in this neighboring country has ended, most immigrants prefer to stay in Costa Rica for its economic opportunities. Many nationals like to blame Nicas for an increase in violent crime, though no proof of this claim exists (see boxed text, p230).

Indigenous populations remain largely invisible to many in Costa Rican society. Many indigenous people lead Westernized, inherently Tico lives, and others inhabit the country's reserves and maintain a more traditional lifestyle. Note that *indio* (Indian) is an insulting term; *indígena* is the preferred term, meaning 'indigenous.'

MEDIA

For Costa Rican news in English, check out the weekly *Tico Times* at www.ticotimes.net or the tabloid *Inside Costa Rica* at www.insidecostarica.com.

Satellite TV is fairly ubiquitous in Costa Rica, which means that you can choose anything from Venezuelan *telenovelas* (soap operas) and Hollywood movies to Premier League football and CNN. Likewise, there is a full spectrum of radio programming, though the mix tends to skew toward reggaetón music. If you read Spanish and you want to catch the latest news and politics, look no further than the daily *La Nación*.

The law guaranteeing freedom of the press in Costa Rica is the oldest such law in Central America, dating from 1835. While Costa Rica certainly enjoys more press freedom than most Latin American countries, do not expect a great deal of probity from its media. The outlets are limited and coverage tends to be cautious, largely due to conservative media laws.

Surprisingly, Costa Rica has a *desacato,* an insult law, on its books. This is common in most Latin American countries and allows public figures to sue journalists if their honor has been 'damaged' by the media. A 'right of response' law allows individuals who have been criticized in the media equal attention (time or space) to reply to the charges. Critics of the law claim it limits the freedom of the press and provides officials with a shield from public scrutiny.

The 2001 assassination of radio journalist Parmenio Medina gave reporters another reason not to dig deep. Medina was the host of a popular investigative program called *La Patada* (The Kick). Shortly before broadcasting a series on financial irregularities at a now-defunct Catholic radio station, Parmenio Medina was shot to death outside his home in Heredia. In 2007 the gunmen, in addition to a prominent businessman who ordered the hit, were sentenced to 35 years in prison after the country's longest-ever trial. Six other men were acquitted, while the other alleged mastermind, a Catholic priest, was acquitted of murder but found guilty of fraud.

ENDANGERED CULTURES

The Europeans that made the long journey across the Atlantic did not come to admire the native culture. Spanish conquistadors valued the indigenous populations as an economic resource: they ruthlessly leveled the tribal society, plundered its meager wealth and hunted down and enslaved the survivors. Catholic missionaries followed closely behind, charged with eradicating heathen beliefs and instilling a more civilized lifestyle. As a result, native culture in Costa Rica came close to extinction.

The remnants of a traditional native lifestyle survived at the outer margins, kept alive by isolated families beyond the reach of law and popular culture. The indigenous groups were not even encouraged to assimilate, but instead were actively excluded from Spanish-dominated society. Well into the 20th century, they were forbidden from entering populated regions and were denied fundamental political and legal rights. Indigenous peoples were not granted citizenship until the 1949 constitution, though in practice their status did not change much as a result.

In 1977 the government created the reservation system, which allowed indigenous groups to organize themselves into self-governing communities. The government, however, retained title to the land. With this change, it was now permitted to engage in traditional languages and customs. Ironically, this more tolerant government policy also meant access to public education and job opportunities, which accelerated native language loss and Tico acculturation.

Presently, there are 22 reservations in Costa Rica but indigenous cultures remain highly endangered. The language of the once robust Central Valley Huetar is already extinct. In Guanacaste, the cultural inheritance of the Chorotega tribe, descendants of the rich Mesoamerican tradition, is now all but depleted. Many of the Bribrí and Cabécar who remained in the Caribbean lowlands tended to shed their native ways after finding employment on the banana plantations. The only exception is in remote pockets of the south, where some Guaymí still speak the native tongue, wear traditional garments, and hunt and gather to subsist (see boxed text, p413).

The Brunka, also called Boruca, are what remains of three great chiefdoms that once inhabited the Península de Osa and much of the south; now they are restricted to a reservation in the valley of the Río Grande de Térraba. While their annual Fiesta de los Diablitos attracts much outside attention, their language is nearly extinct and their land is threatened by a proposal for a huge hydroelectric project (see p379).

Libel and slander laws put the burden of proof on reporters and they are frequently required to reveal their sources in court. In July 2004, the Inter-American Court of Human Rights struck down a defamation decision against Mauricio Herrera Ulloa of *La Nación*. The Costa Rican government has promised to abide by the ruling, which called for a revision of the criminal libel laws, though progress has been slow.

RELIGION

More than 75% of Ticos are Catholic (at least in principle). And while many show a healthy reverence for the Virgin Mary, they rarely profess blind faith to the dictates coming from Rome – apparently 'pure life' doesn't require being excessively penitent. Most people tend to go to church for the sacraments (baptism, first communion, confirmation, marriage and death) and the holidays.

Religious processions on holy days are generally less fervent and colorful than those in Latin American countries such as Guatemala or Peru, though the procession for the patron virgin, La Virgen de los Ángeles, held annually on August 2, does draw penitents who walk from all over Central America to Cartago to show devotion. Semana Santa (the week before Easter) is a national holiday: everything (even buses) stops operating at lunchtime on Maundy Thursday and doesn't start up again until the afternoon of Holy Saturday.

Roughly 14% of Costa Ricans are evangelical Christians; increased interest in evangelical religions is attributed to a greater sense of community spirit within the churches. The black community on the Caribbean is largely Protestant, and there are small Jewish populations in San José and Jacó. There are sprinklings of Middle Easterners and Asians who practice Islam and Buddhism, respectively.

WOMEN IN COSTA RICA

Women are traditionally respected in Costa Rica (Mother's Day is a national holiday), and since 1974, the Costa Rican family code has stipulated that husband and wife have equal duties and rights. In addition, women can draw up contracts, assume loans and inherit property; sexual harassment and sex discrimination are against the law. In 1996, Costa Rica passed a landmark law against domestic violence, one of the most progressive in Latin America.

But only recently have women made gains in the workplace, with growing roles in political, legal, scientific and medical fields. In 1993, Margarita Penon (Oscar Arias Sánchez' wife) ran as a presidential candidate. In 1998, both vice presidents (Costa Rica has two) were women: Astrid Fischel and Elizabeth Odio. In February 2010 Arias Sánchez' former Vice President Laura Chinchilla won the elections and became the first female president in Costa Rica's history.

Despite some advances, machismo is not a thing of the past in Costa Rica. Antidiscrimination laws are rarely enforced and women are generally lower-paid and are less likely to be considered for high-level jobs. They also have more difficulty getting loans, even though their repayment record is better than that of men. In the countryside, many women maintain traditional roles: raising children, cooking and running the home.

ARTS

Literature

Costa Rica: A Traveler's Literary Companion, edited by Barbara Ras, is a fine collection of 26 short stories by modern Costa Rican writers, offering a valuable glimpse of society from Ticos themselves.

Few works of Costa Rican writers or novelists are available in translation and, unfortunately, much of what is written about Costa Rica and available in English (fiction or otherwise) is written by foreigners.

Carlos Luis Fallas (1909–66) is widely known for the *Mamita Yunai* (1940), an influential novel that took the banana companies to task for their labor practices, and he remains very popular among the Latin American left.

Carmen Naranjo (1928–) is one of the few contemporary Costa Rican writers who has risen to international acclaim. She is a novelist, poet and short-story writer who also served as ambassador to India in the 1970s, and a few years later as Minister of Culture. In 1996, she was awarded the prestigious Gabriela Mistral medal from the Chilean government. Her collection of short stories, *There Never Was a Once Upon a Time,* is widely available in English. Two of her stories can also be found in *Costa Rica: A Traveler's Literary Companion*.

Tatiana Lobo (1939–) was actually born in Chile, but since 1967 she has lived in Costa Rica, where her many books are set. She received the noteworthy Premio Sor Juana Inés de la Cruz for Latin American women novelists for her novel *Asalto al paraíso* (Assault on Paradise).

José León Sánchez (1930–) is an internationally renowned memoirist. Of Huetar descent and from the border of Costa Rica and Nicaragua, he was convicted for stealing from the famous Basílica de Nuestra Señora de los Ángeles (p138) in Cartago, and sentenced to serve his term at Isla San Lucas, one of Latin America's most notorious jails. Illiterate when he was incarcerated, Sánchez taught himself how to read and write, and clandestinely authored one of the continent's most poignant books: *La isla de los hombres solos* (called *God Was Looking the Other Way* in the translated version). This fictionalized account is based on the 20 years he served out of his original 45-year sentence. He later went on to produce 14 other novels and serve in several high-level public appointments.

Theater

The most famous theater in the country is the Teatro Nacional (p73) in San José. The story goes that a noted European opera company was on a Latin American tour but declined to perform in Costa Rica for lack of a suitable hall. Immediately, the coffee elite put a special cultural tax on coffee exports for the construction of a world-class theater. The Teatro Nacional is now the premier venue for plays, opera, performances by the national symphony orchestra, ballet, poetry readings and various other cultural events. It is also an architectural feature and a landmark in any city tour of San José.

Visual Arts

The visual arts in Costa Rica first took on a national character in the 1920s, when Teodórico Quirós, Fausto Pacheco and their contemporaries began painting landscapes that differed from traditional European styles, depicting the rolling hills and lush forest of Costa Rican countryside, often sprinkled with characteristic adobe houses.

The contemporary scene is more varied and it is difficult to define a unique Tico style. Several individual artists have garnered acclaim for their work, including the magical realism of Isidro Con Wong, the surreal paintings and primitive engravings of Francisco Amighetti, and the mystical female figures painted by Rafa Fernández. Other artists incorporate a variety of themes in a range of media, from painting and sculpture to video and site-specific installations. The Museo de Arte y Diseño Contemporáneo (p76) in San José is the top place to see this type of work and its permanent collection is a great primer.

See a stunning and comprehensive visual database on Central American contemporary art at the Museo de Arte y Diseño Contemporáneo website (www.madc.ac.cr).

Many art galleries are geared toward tourists and specialize in 'tropical art' (for lack of an official description): brightly colored, whimsical folk paintings depicting flora and fauna that evoke the work of French artist Henri Rousseau.

Folk art and handicrafts are not as widely produced or readily available as in other Central American countries. However, the dedicated souvenir hunter will have no problem finding the colorful Sarchí oxcarts (p129) that have become a symbol of Costa Rica. Indigenous crafts, which include intricately carved and painted masks as well as handwoven bags and linens, are also widely available.

Film

Although Costa Rica does not have a prominent film industry, in 2010 director Paz Fabrega won the coveted VPRO Tiger award at the Rotterdam Film Festival for *Agua fría de mar* (Cold Water of the Sea), a story of a young couple and a seven-year-old girl from contrasting social backgrounds who spend Christmas together along the Pacific coast.

Music & Dance

The mix of cultures in Costa Rica has resulted in a lively music scene, incorporating elements from North and South America and the Caribbean islands. Popular dance music includes Latin dances, such as salsa, merengue, bolero and *cumbia*.

One Tico salsa group that has made a significant name for itself at a regional level is Los Brillanticos, who once shared the stage with Cuban legend Celia Cruz during a tour stop she made in San José. Timbaleo is a salsa orchestra founded by Ramsés Araya, who became famous as the drummer for Panamanian salsa superstar Rubén Blades. Taboga Band is another long-standing Costa Rican group that plays jazz-influenced salsa and merengue music.

Follow current events in Costa Rica at the website of the top daily, *La Nación,* at www.nacion.com.

San José features a regular lineup of domestic and international rock, folk and hip-hop artists, but you'll find that the regional sounds are equally vibrant, featuring their own special rhythms, instruments and styles. For instance, the Península de Nicoya has a rich musical history, most of it made with guitars, maracas and marimbas. The traditional sound on the Caribbean coast is calypso, which has roots in the Afro-Carib slave culture. Also check out Costa Rican–born Chavela Vargas (1919–), a folkloric singer with a hauntingly beautiful voice that has influenced generations of Latin American performers.

Guanacaste is also the birthplace of many traditional dances, most of which depict courtship rituals between country folk. The most famous dance – sometimes considered the national dance – is the *punto guanacasteco* (see boxed text, p219). What keeps it lively is the *bomba,* a funny (and usually racy) rhymed verse, shouted out by the male dancers during the musical interlude.

Food & Drink

All it takes is a quick glance at the menu to realize that Costa Rica is firmly rooted in the tropics. With everything from exotic fruits such as mangoes, guavas and lychees and the obligatory cup of shade-grown coffee, to fillets of locally raised fish and a zesty *ceviche* (uncooked but well-marinated seafood) featuring the catch of the day, Costa Rica is just as much a feast for the palate as it is for the eyes.

Of course, Costa Rica remains fiercely true to its Latin roots by featuring rice and beans prominently at most meals. Thatched country kitchens can be found all over Costa Rica, with local women ladling out basic but hearty home-cooked specials known as *comida típica* (literally 'typical food'). And of course, Costa Ricans go wild for a good steak, which partially explains the abundance of cattle ranches throughout the country.

Entradas: Journeys in Latin American Cuisine, by Joan Chatfield-Taylor, has some of Costa Rica's most popular recipes – and many others.

If you prefer your Tico (Costa Rican) fare a bit more upscale with a nouveau twist, try the country's trendier tourist areas. These have seen a high level of immigration from Europe and the US, which assures a wide selection of just about anything you might want to munch on. Whether you're partial to sushi or souvlaki, this little country can go miles to satiate your appetite.

STAPLES & SPECIALTIES

If you're looking for rich and fiery *mole* (rich chocolate sauce), or a perfectly crafted avocado soup, you've come to the wrong country. Sadly, the complex and varied dishes concocted in Mexico and Guatemala never made it south of the border. Traditional Costa Rican staples, for the most part, are very basic, somewhat bland and frequently described as comfort food. The diet consists largely of rice and beans – and beans and rice – though it's fresh, hearty and honest fare.

Breakfast for Ticos is usually *gallo pinto* (literally 'spotted rooster'), a stir fry of rice and beans. When combined, the rice gets colored by the beans, and the mix obtains a specked appearance. Served with eggs, cheese or *natilla* (sour cream), *gallo pinto* is generally cheap, filling and sometimes can be downright tasty. If you plan to spend the whole day surfing or hiking, you'll find that rice and beans is great energy food. If you are not keen on rice and beans, many hotels will provide what they refer to as a 'tropical breakfast,' which is usually bread along with a selection of fresh fruits. American-style breakfasts are also available in many eateries and are, needless to say, heavy on the fried foods and fatty meats.

Costa Rican Typical Foods, by Carmen de Musmani and Lupita de Weiler, is out of print, but it is perhaps the only Tico-specific cookbook ever written.

Most restaurants offer a set meal at lunch and dinner called a *casado*, or a 'married man's' lunch. This meal is always cheap, heavy on the stomach and well balanced with meat, beans, rice and salad. An extremely popular *casado* is the ubiquitous *arroz con pollo*, which is chicken and rice that is usually dressed up with grains, vegetables and a good mix of mild spices. Also look out for *patacones*, fried green plantains cut in thin pieces.

Food is not heavily spiced, unless you're having traditional Caribbean-style cuisine. The vast majority of Ticos have a distinct aversion to hot sauce, though most local restaurants will lay out a spicy *curtido* (a mixture of hot peppers and pickled vegetables) or little bottles of Tabasco-style sauce for the diehards. Another popular condiment is *salsa lizano*, the Tico version of Worcestershire sauce.

Considering the extent of the coastline, it is no surprise that seafood is plentiful, and fish dishes are usually fresh and delicious. Fish is often fried, but may also be grilled or blackened. While it's not traditional Tico fare,

THE GALLO PINTO CONTROVERSY

No other dish in Costa Rica inspires Ticos quite like their national dish of *gallo pinto,* that ethereal medley of rice, beans and spices. Of course, exactly what type and amount of this holy trinity makes up authentic *gallo pinto* is the subject of intense debate, especially since it is also the national dish of neighboring Nicaragua.

Both countries claim that the dish originated on their soil. Costa Rican lore holds that the dish and its iconic name were coined in 1930 in the neighborhood of San Sebastián, which is on the southern outskirts of San José. Nicaraguans claim that it was brought to the Caribbean coast of their country by Afro-Latinos long before it graced the palate of any Costa Rican.

The battle for the rights to *gallo pinto* doesn't stop here, especially since the two countries can't even agree on the standard recipe. Nicaraguans traditionally prepare it with small red beans, while Costa Ricans swear by black beans. And we're not even going to bore you with the subtle complexities of balancing cilantro, salt and pepper.

Much to the dismay of patriotic Costa Ricans, Nicaragua currently holds the world record for making the biggest ever pot of *gallo pinto.* On September 15, 2007, a seething vat of *gallo pinto* fed 22,200 people, which firmly entrenched Nicaragua's name next to *gallo pinto* in the *Guinness Book of World Records.*

ceviche is on most menus, and usually contains octopus, tilapia, dorado and/or dolphin (the fish, not Flipper). Raw fish is marinated in lime juice with chilies, tomatoes and herbs. Served chilled, it is a delectable way to enjoy fresh seafood. Emphasis is on 'fresh' here – this is raw fish (think sushi), so if you have reason to believe it is not fresh, don't risk eating it.

The most popular foreign food in Costa Rica (at least amongst the Ticos) is Chinese. Nearly every town has a Chinese place and even if it doesn't, menus will likely include *arroz cantonés* (fried rice). Italian food is also extremely popular and pizza parlors and Italian restaurants of varying quality abound. The locally produced pizzas are sometimes heavily loaded cheese bombs.

If an establishment doesn't exactly impress you with its cleanliness, then it might be advisable not to eat fruits, vegetables or salads there. If they are improperly washed, you could be sending your stomach a little bacteria surprise, though generally speaking water from the tap in Costa Rica is of sufficient quality to drink.

DRINKS

Coffee is probably the most popular beverage in the country and wherever you go, someone is likely to offer you a *cafecito*. Traditionally, it is served strong and mixed with hot milk to taste, also known as *café con leche*. Most drinkers get *café negro* (black coffee) and for those who want a little milk, you can ask for *leche al lado* (milk on the side). Many trendier places serve cappuccinos and espressos and milk is nearly always pasteurized and safe to drink.

Worried that you'll head back home and dearly miss *salsa lizano* or Tropical drinks? Thankfully www.lapulpe.com sells Costa Rican products and will ship the goods to just about anywhere in the world.

For a refresher, nothing beats *batidos* – fresh fruit drinks (like smoothies) made either *al agua* (with water) or *con leche* (with milk). The array can be mind-boggling and includes mango, papaya, *piña* (pineapple), *sandía* (watermelon), *melón* (cantaloupe), *zarzamora* (blackberry), *zanahoria* (carrot), *cebada* (barley) or *tamarindo* (fruit of the tamarind tree). If you are wary about the condition of the drinking water, ask that your *batido* be made with *agua enbotellada* (bottled water) and *sin hielo* (without ice), though, again, water is generally safe to drink throughout the country.

A bottled, though less tasty alternative, is a local fruit beverage called 'Tropical.' It's sold in many stores and restaurants and the most common flavors are *mora, piña, cas* (a tart local fruit) and *frutas mixtas* (mixed fruit). Just shake vigorously before drinking or the powderlike substance at the bottom will remain intact.

Pipas are green coconuts that have a hole macheted into the top of them and a straw for drinking the 'milk' – a very refreshing and filling drink. *Agua dulce* is sugarcane water, or in many cases boiled water mixed with brown sugar. *Horchata,* found mostly in the countryside, is a sweet drink made from rice milk and flavored with cinnamon.

The usual brands of soft drinks are available, including some favorites you thought were long gone, like Crush and Squirt. In rural areas, and especially on buses, don't be surprised if your soda (or your juice) is served in a plastic bag. Plastic bags are cheaper than plastic bottles or other containers, so locals fill plastic bags with a variety of beverages and sell them from coolers at the side of the road. If you are lucky, it will also have a straw, which makes it a lot easier to enjoy your drink. If it's a long bus ride, don't be surprised if a few people fill up the bags again and toss them from the window!

Order gourmet Costa Rican coffee and other treats at www.cafebritt.com.

The most popular alcoholic drink is beer, and there are several local brands. Imperial is perhaps the most popular – either for its smooth flavor or for the ubiquitous T-shirts emblazoned with their eagle-crest logo. Pilsen, which has a higher alcohol content, is also known for its saucy calendars featuring *las chicas Pilsen* (the Pilsen girls). Both are tasty pilsners. Bavaria produces a lager and Bavaria Negro, a delicious, full-bodied dark beer. This brand is popular among the young and well educated, but it's not so easy to find outside the trendiest spots.

After beer, the poison of choice is *guaro,* which is a colorless alcohol distilled from sugarcane and usually consumed by the shot, though you can order it as a sour. It goes down mighty easily, but leaves one hell of a hangover.

As in most of Central America, the local rums are inexpensive and worthwhile, especially the Ron Centenario, which recently shot to international fame. The most popular rum-based tipple is a *cuba libre* (rum and cola), which hits the spot on a hot, sticky day, especially when served with a fresh splash of lime. Premixed cans of *cuba libre* are also available in stores, but it'd be a lie to say the contents don't taste weirdly like aluminum.

Most Costa Rican wines are cheap, taste cheap, and will be unkindly remembered the next morning. Imported wines are available but expensive and difficult to store at proper temperatures. Chilean brands are your best bet for a palatable wine at an affordable price.

No alcohol is served on Election Day or in the three days prior to Easter Sunday.

WHERE TO EAT & DRINK

The most popular eating establishment in Costa Rica is the *soda.* These are small, informal lunch counters dishing up a few daily *casados.* Other popular cheapies include the omnipresent fried- and rotisserie-chicken stands.

A regular *restaurante* is usually higher on the price scale and has slightly more atmosphere. Many *restaurantes* serve *casados,* while the fancier places refer to the set lunch as the *almuerzo ejecutivo* (literally 'executive lunch').

For something smaller, *pastelerías* and *panaderías* are shops that sell pastries and bread, while many bars serve snacks called *bocas,* which are snack-sized portions of main meals.

Lunch is usually the day's main meal and is typically served around noon. Dinner tends to be a lighter version of lunch and is eaten around 7pm.

Quick Eats

Street vendors sell fresh fruit (sometimes prechopped and ready to go), cookies, chips (crisps) and fried plantains. Many *sodas* have little windows that face the street and from there dispense *empanadas* (corn turnovers stuffed with ground meat, chicken, cheese or sweet fruit), tacos (usually tortillas with meat) or *enchiladas* (pastries with spicy meat).

VEGETARIANS & VEGANS

If you don't mind rice and beans, Costa Rica is a relatively comfortable place for vegetarians to travel.

Cocinando con Tía Florita is a popular Tico cooking show. Check out the recipes and meet Tía Florita herself at www.cocinandocontiaflorita.tv.

Most restaurants will make veggie *casados* on request and many are now including them on the menu. They usually include rice and beans, cabbage salad and one or two selections of variously prepared vegetables or legumes.

With the high influx of tourism, there are also many specialty vegetarian restaurants or restaurants with a veggie menu in San José and tourist towns. Lodges in remote areas that offer all-inclusive meal plans can accommodate vegetarian diets with advance notice.

Vegans, macrobiotic and raw food–only travelers will have a tougher time as there are fewer outlets accommodating those diets. If you intend to keep to your diet, it's best to choose a lodging where you can prepare food yourself. Many towns have health-food stores *(macrobióticas)*, but selection varies. Fresh vegetables can also be hard to come by in isolated areas, and will often be quite expensive.

EATING WITH KIDS

If you're traveling with the tots, you'll find that 'kids' meals' (small portions at small prices) are not normally offered in restaurants, though some fancy lodges do them. However, most local eateries will accommodate two children splitting a meal or can produce child-size portions on request. You can ask for restaurant staff to bring you simple food, rice with chicken or steak cooked *a la plancha* (on the grill).

If you are traveling with an infant, stock up on milk formula and baby food before heading to remote areas. Avocados are safe, easy to eat, nutritious and they can be served to children as young as six months old. Young children should avoid water and ice in drinks as they are more susceptible to stomach illnesses.

Coffee was thought to energize workers, so in 1840 the government decreed that all laborers building roads should be provided with one cup of coffee every day.

Always carry snacks for long drives in remote areas – sometimes there are no places to stop for a bite.

For other tips on traveling with the kids, see p529.

HABITS & CUSTOMS

Costa Ricans are open and informal, and treat their guests well. If you have the good fortune to be invited into a Tico home, you can expect to be served first, receive the biggest portion and perhaps even receive a parting gift. On your part, flowers or wine are both fine gifts to bring, though the best gift you can offer is extending a future dinner invitation to your hosts.

Remember that when you sit down to eat in a restaurant, it is polite to say *buenos días* (good morning) or *buenas tardes* (good afternoon) to the waitstaff and/or any people you might be sharing a table with. It is also

TOP EATS IN COSTA RICA

- Try Peruvian specialties at **Machu Picchu** in San José (p91).
- Savor spicy, delicious fish tacos from **El Loco Natural** (p487) in Puerto Viejo de Talamanca.
- Pan-Asian meets Latin Fusion at **Kapi Kapi Restaurant** (p347) in Manuel Antonio.
- Experience innovative Mediterranean cuisine at **Seasons by Shlomy** (p270) in Tamarindo.
- Try anything off the menu at **Restaurante Exótica** (p361) in Ojochal.

polite to say *buen provecho,* which is the equivalent of *bon appetit,* at the start of the meal.

EAT YOUR WORDS

Don't know your *pipas* from your *patacones*? A *batido* from a *bolita*? Get beneath the surface of Costa Rica's plentiful cuisine by learning the lingo. For pronunciation guidelines, see p559.

Food Glossary

ON THE MENU

almojabanos	al·mo·kha·*ba*·nos	similar to *tortilla de maíz,* but hand-rolled into small sausage-sized pieces
batido	ba·*tee*·do	milkshake made with fresh fruit, sugar and milk
bocas	*bo*·kas	savory side dishes or bar snacks
bolitas de carne	bo·*lee*·tas de *kar*·ne	snack of mildly spicy meatballs
carimañola	ka·ree·ma·*nyo*·la	a deep-fried roll made from chopped meat and boiled yucca
carne ahumada	*kar*·ne a·oo·*ma*·da	smoked, dried ('jerked') meat
casado	ka·*sa*·do	a cheap set meal usually served at lunchtime
ceviche	se·*vee*·che	raw fish or shellfish marinated in lemon or lime juice, garlic and seasonings
chicha	*chee*·cha	heavily sweetened fresh fruit drink
comida corriente	ko·*mee*·da ko·*ryen*·te	a mixed plate of typical regional foods
corvina	kor·*vee*·na	a flavorful white fish
empanada	em·pa·*na*·da	corn turnover filled with ground meat, chicken, cheese or sweet fruit
gallo pinto	*ga*·yo *peen*·to	literally 'spotted rooster'; a soupy mixture of rice and black beans
hojaldres	o·*khal*·dres	fried dough, similar to a doughnut; popular with breakfast
huevos fritos/ revueltos	*we*·vos *free*·tos/ re·*vwel*·tos	fried/scrambled eggs
licuado	lee·*kwa*·do	shake made with fresh fruit, sugar and water
mondongo	mon·*dong*·go	tripe soup
patacones	pa·ta·*ko*·nes	green plantains cut in thin pieces, salted, pressed, then fried
pipa	*pee*·pa	coconut water, served straight from the husk
plátano maduro	*pla*·ta·no ma·*doo*·ro	ripe plantains baked or broiled with butter, brown sugar and cinnamon; served hot
raspados	ras·*pa*·dos	shaved ice flavored with fruit juice
ropa vieja	*ro*·pa *vye*·kha	literally 'old clothes'; a spicy shredded beef combination served over rice
seco	*se*·ko	alcoholic drink made from sugarcane
tajadas	ta·*kha*·das	ripe plantains sliced lengthwise and fried
tamales	ta·*ma*·les	ground corn with spices and chicken or pork, wrapped in banana leaves and boiled
tasajo	ta·*sa*·kho	dried meat cooked with vegetables
tortilla de maíz	tor·*tee*·ya de ma·*ees*	a thick, fried cornmeal tortilla

BASICS

azúcar	a·*soo*·kar	sugar
cuchara	koo·*cha*·ra	spoon
cuchillo	koo·*chee*·yo	knife

hielo	*ye*·lo	ice
mantequilla	man·te·*kee*·ya	butter
pan	pan	bread
plato	*pla*·to	plate
sal	sal	salt
servilleta	ser·vee·*ye*·ta	napkin
sopa	*so*·pa	soup
taza	*ta*·sa	cup
tenedor	te·ne·*dor*	fork
vaso	*va*·so	glass

MEALTIMES

almuerzo	al·*mwer*·so	lunch
cena	*se*·na	dinner
desayuno	de·sa·*yoo*·no	breakfast

FRUITS & VEGETABLES

aguacate	a·gwa·*ka*·te	avocado
ensalada	en·sa·*la*·da	salad
fresa	*fre*·sa	strawberry
guanábana	gwa·*na*·ba·na	soursop
manzana	man·*sa*·na	apple
maracuyá	ma·ra·koo·*ya*	passion fruit
naranja	na·*ran*·kha	orange
piña	*pee*·nya	pineapple
zanahoria	sa·na·*o*·rya	carrot
zarzamora	sar·sa·*mo*·ra	blackberry

SEAFOOD

camarón	ka·ma·*ron*	shrimp
filete de pescado	fi·*le*·te de pes·*ka*·do	fish fillet
langosta	lan·*gos*·ta	lobster
langostino	lan·gos·*tee*·no	jumbo shrimp
pescado	pes·*ka*·do	fish
pulpo	*pool*·po	octopus

MEATS

bistec	bee·*stek*	grilled or fried beef; steak
carne	*kar*·ne	meat
chuleta	choo·*le*·ta	pork chop
hamburguesa	am·boor·*ge*·sa	hamburger
salchicha	sal·*chee*·cha	sausage

DRINKS

agua	*a*·gwa	water
bebida	be·*bee*·da	drink
café	ka·*fe*	coffee
cerveza	ser·*ve*·sa	beer
leche	*le*·che	milk
ron	ron	rum
vino	*vee*·no	wine

COOKING TERMS

a la plancha	a la *plan*·cha	grilled
frito	*free*·to	fried

Environment

David Lukas

THE LAND

Despite its diminutive size, 51,000-sq-km Costa Rica is a study in contrasts and contradictions. On one coast it fronts scenic Pacific shores while only 119km away lies the muggy Caribbean coast, with a range of active volcanoes and alpine peaks in between. Rich in natural resources, Costa Rica has gone from suffering the highest rates of deforestation in Latin America in the early 1990s to being a global model for tropical conservation. Now in charge of an exemplar system of well-managed and accessible parks, Costa Rica is perhaps the best place in the world to experience rainforest habitats, while its stunning natural landscape is easily the top reason tourists visit this delightful country.

The world-famous Organization for Tropical Studies runs three field stations and offers numerous classes for students seriously interested in tropical ecology. See www.ots.ac.cr.

With a length of 1016km, the Pacific coastline is infinitely varied as it twists and turns around gulfs, peninsulas and many small coves. Rugged, rocky headlands alternate with classic white- and black-sand beaches and palm trees to produce an image of a tropical paradise along some stretches. Strong tidal action creates an excellent habitat for waterbirds as well as a visually dramatic crashing surf (perfect for surfers). Inland, the landscapes of the Pacific lowlands are equally dynamic, ranging from dry deciduous forests and open cattle country in the north, to lush, magnificent tropical rainforests in the south.

Monotonous in comparison, the Caribbean coastline runs a straight 212km along a low, flat plain that is inundated with brackish lagoons and waterlogged forests. A lack of strong tides allows plants to grow right over the water's edge along coastal sloughs, creating walls of green vegetation. Broad, humid plains that scarcely rise above sea level and murky waters characterize much of this region.

The fabulous limestone caves of Parque Nacional Barra Honda were formed in the remains of ancient coral reefs after they were uplifted out of the ocean.

Running down the center of the country, the mountainous spine of Costa Rica is a land of active volcanoes, clear tumbling streams and chilled peaks clad in impenetrable cloud forests. These mountain ranges generally follow a northwest to southeast line, with the highest and most dramatic peaks in the south near the Panamanian border (culminating at the 3820m-high Cerro Chirripó). The difficulties of traveling through and farming on these steep

OUT ON A REEF

Compared to the rest of the Caribbean, the coral reefs of Costa Rica are small fry. Heavy surf and shifting sands along most of the Caribbean coast produce conditions that are unbearable to corals, but on the southern coast two beautiful patches of reef are protected on the rocky headlands of Parque Nacional Cahuita and Refugio Nacional de Vida Silvestre Gandoca-Manzanillo.

These diminutive but vibrant reefs are home to more than 100 species of fish and many types of coral. Countless damselfish, sergeant majors, parrot fish and surgeonfish gather to feed on abundant marine algae, while predatory barracudas come to prey on the fish. Gandoca-Manzanillo is a famous nesting ground for four species of sea turtle. Even better, turtle volunteers have been patrolling these beaches since 1986 to prevent poachers and the turtle populations are doing really well thanks to their efforts.

Unfortunately, the reefs are in danger due to sediments washing downriver from logging operations, and from toxic chemicals that wash out of nearby agricultural fields. In 1991 an earthquake lifted the reefs up as much as 1.5m, stranding and killing large portions of this fragile ecosystem.

So far the coral reefs of Costa Rica have been largely overlooked, but with these threats hanging over them, there's little time to lose.

slopes have, until recently, saved much of this area from development and made it a haven for wildlife.

In the midst of the highlands is the Meseta Central – Central Valley – which is surrounded by mountains (the Cordillera Central to the north and east and the Cordillera de Talamanca to the south). It is this fertile central plain, 1000m and 1500m above sea level with abundant rainfall and consistently mild temperatures, that contains four of Costa Rica's five largest cities and more than half of the country's population.

The seven species of poison-dart frog in Costa Rica are beautiful to look at but have exceedingly toxic skin secretions that cause paralysis and death.

Like most of Central America, Costa Rica's geologic history can be traced to the impact of the Cocos Plate moving northeast and crashing into the Caribbean Plate at a rate of about 10cm every year – quite fast by geological standards. The point of impact is called a 'subduction zone,' and this is where the Cocos Plate forces the edge of the Caribbean Plate to break up and become uplifted. It is not a smooth process, and hence Central America is an area prone to earthquakes and ongoing volcanic activity (see p530). Arenal, in the north, is one of the world's most active volcanoes.

WILDLIFE

Nowhere else in the world are so many types of habitats squeezed into such a tiny area. In terms of number of species per 10,000 sq km, Costa Rica tops the list of countries at 615 species, compared to a wildlife-rich country such as Rwanda that has 596, or to the comparatively impoverished USA with its 104 species. This simple fact alone (not to mention the ease of travel and friendly residents) makes Costa Rica the premier destination for nature-lovers from all over the world.

The large number of species in Costa Rica is also due to the relatively recent appearance of the country. Roughly three million years ago Costa Rica rose from the ocean, and formed a land bridge between North and South America. As species from these two vast biological provinces started to mingle, the number of species essentially 'doubled' in the area where Costa Rica now sits.

Animals

Though tropical in nature – with a substantial number of tropical animals such as poison-dart frogs and spider monkeys – Costa Rica is also the winter home for more than 200 species of migrating birds that arrive from as far away as Alaska and Australia. So don't be surprised to see one of your familiar backyard birds feeding alongside trogons and toucans. Individual animals and insects are given more coverage in the Costa Rica Wildlife Guide chapter, p181.

Two-toed sloths descend from the trees once every two weeks to defecate.

With a total of 850 species recorded in Costa Rica, it's understandable that birds are one of the primary attractions for naturalists, who could stay for months and still barely scratch the surface in terms of seeing all these species. Birds in Costa Rica come in every color, from strawberry-red scarlet macaws to the iridescent jewels called violet sabrewings (a type of hummingbird). Because many birds in Costa Rica have restricted ranges, you are guaranteed to find different species everywhere you travel.

Visitors will almost certainly see one of Costa Rica's four types of monkeys or two types of sloths, but there are an additional 230 types of mammals awaiting the patient observer. More exotic sightings might include the amazing four-eyed opossum or silky anteater, while a lucky few might spot the elusive tapir, or have a jaguarundi cross their path.

The extensive network of national parks, wildlife refuges and other protected areas are prime places to spot wildlife. But remember that these creatures do not know park boundaries, so keep your eyes peeled in the forested areas and buffer zones that often surround these sanctuaries. Early morning is the best time to see animals because many species sleep during the hottest part of the day. Spotting one of the nocturnal species – such as Baird's tapir, the silky anteater and the kinkajou – requires going out at night with a strong flashlight (a great item to pack for your Costa Rica trip).

If you are serious about observing birds and animals, the value of a knowledgeable guide cannot be underestimated. Their keen eyes are trained to notice the slightest movement in the forest, and they recognize the many exotic sounds. Most professional bird guides are proficient in the dialects of local birds, greatly improving your chances of hearing or seeing these species. Furthermore, a good local guide will often have an idea where certain species tend to congregate – whether it's quetzals eating fruit in an avocado tree, or American crocodiles catching fish at the mouth of a river. Through its National Biodiversity Institute, Costa Rica now trains locals to be professional nature guides as an alternative to letting this skilled work go to foreign guides.

No season is a bad season for exploring Costa Rica's natural environment, though most visitors arrive during the peak dry season when trails are less muddy and more accessible. An added bonus of visiting between December and February is that many of the wintering migrant birds are still hanging around. A trip after the peak season means fewer birds, but is a stupendous time to see dried forests transform into vibrant greens and it's also when resident birds begin nesting.

Dr Alexander Skutch is famous for the *Guide to the Birds of Costa Rica*, but he also wrote several other contemplative books about his feathered friends, including *A Naturalist in Costa Rica* and *The Minds of Birds*.

ENDANGERED SPECIES

As expected in a country with unique habitats and widespread logging, there are numerous species whose populations are declining or in danger of extinction. Currently, the number-one threat to most of Costa Rica's endangered species is habitat destruction, followed closely by hunting and trapping.

Costa Rica's four species of sea turtles – olive ridley, leatherback, green and hawksbill – deservedly get a lot of attention. All four species are classified as

LOOK BUT DON'T JUMP IN

In 2006 swimming with dolphins and whales in Costa Rica was made illegal. It is also illegal to attempt to capture or harass them. Dolphin- and whale-watching tours have become increasingly popular in recent years, leading to an explosion in the number of operators. Unfortunately, too many operators are out for a quick buck, often at the expense of the animals.

In a survey conducted by the Cetacean Society International a few years back, 17 of the operators refused to cooperate by answering survey questions, and all of the tour companies investigated made mistakes such as harassing animals, not carrying life jackets and having motor problems. Only one company had knowledgeable guides that could provide 'reasonable natural-history information.' Lacking experience and knowledge, many operators have been conducting their tours without due attention to the integrity of the star players – the animals themselves.

In short, too much attention from tourists has caused some dolphins and whales to stress out. Research indicates that in some heavily touristed areas, dolphins are leaving their natural habitat in search of calmer seas. Some scientists believe that having humans at close proximity in the water disrupts feeding, nursing and other behavior. There is growing concern about the long-term human impact on the health of these marine mammals. The 2006 legislation banning swimming with marine mammals was enacted with their best interests in mind.

When your boat comes across these amazing creatures of the sea, do not jump in the water. From the comfort of the boat you can have an awe-inspiring and longer-lasting experience (the dolphins and whales usually swim away quickly when humans are in the water, but they might stay and swim around a boat indefinitely). And more importantly, you won't disturb the peace of these gentle giants.

endangered or critically endangered, meaning they face an imminent threat of extinction. While populations of some species are increasing, thanks to various protection programs along both coasts, the risk for these *tortugas* is still very real.

Destruction of habitat is a huge problem. With the exception of the leatherbacks, all of these species return to their natal beach to nest. That means that the ecological state of the beach directly impacts that turtle's ability to reproduce. All of the species prefer dark, undisturbed beaches, and any sort of development or artificial lighting (including flashlights) will inhibit nesting.

The tale of the green turtle's rebound in Tortuguero is told in two popular books by Archie Carr: *The Windward Road: Adventures of a Naturalist on Remote Caribbean Shores* and *The Sea Turtle: So Excellent a Fishe*.

Hunting and harvesting eggs are two major causes of declining populations. Green turtles are actually hunted for their meat. Leatherbacks and olive ridleys are not killed for meat, but their eggs are considered a delicacy – an aphrodisiac no less. The hawksbill turtles are hunted for their unusual shells, which are sometimes used to make jewelry and hair ornaments. Of course, any trade in tortoise-shell products and turtle eggs and meat is illegal, but a significant black market exists.

The legendary resplendent quetzal – the bird at the top of every naturalist's must-see list – teeters precariously as its home forests are felled at an alarming rate. Seeing a noisy scarlet macaw could be a bird-watching highlight in Costa Rica, but trapping for the pet trade has extirpated these magnificent birds from much of their former range. Although populations are thriving in the Península de Osa, the scarlet macaw is now extinct over most of Central America, including the entire Caribbean coast.

Central America's largest land mammal, the 300kg Baird's tapir, is a sought-after source of protein, making it a target for hunters. The tapir's habit of commuting between feeding patches and water holes on distinctive 'tapir trails' makes it extremely vulnerable to hunting. Tapirs are now restricted to the least accessible wilderness areas. Similarly, the gigantic 600kg West Indian manatee is an easy victim for hunters, especially since they are placid and have no defenses. Manatees still populate the canals of Parque Nacional Tortuguero, though they are elusive.

Carol Henderson's *Field Guide to the Wildlife of Costa Rica* is a handy all-in-one resource.

Costa Rica's sexiest endangered species is undoubtedly the reclusive jaguar. Jaguars require a large area to support enough prey to survive. Annually, an individual jaguar needs the equivalent of 53 white-tailed deer, 18 peccaries, 40 coatis, 25 armadillos and 55 iguanas. That is for one jaguar! Owing to clearing for cattle ranches and overhunting of jaguar prey, suitable habitat for viable populations of jaguars now exists in only a handful of protected

DREAM OF THE BOUNTIFUL TURTLES

The following list outlines the current endangerment levels for each of Costa Rica's turtles and the places where you can (still) see them.

Green Endangered – the world population of nesting females is estimated to be less than 90,000. Green turtles nest in Parque Nacional Tortuguero (p458) and surrounding beaches from mid-June to mid-September.

Hawksbill Critically endangered – the world population of nesting females is estimated to be less than 23,000. These beauties only make rare appearances on beaches around Tortuguero between February and September, while they are more common at Parque Nacional Marino Ballena (p359) from May to November.

Leatherback Critically endangered – the world population of nesting females is estimated to be 35,000. Leatherbacks nest on the northern Caribbean coast around Parque Nacional Tortuguero (p458) and the beaches of Parismina (p457) from March to June. Pacific leatherbacks lay eggs on Playa Grande in the Parque Nacional Marino Las Baulas de Guanacaste (p262), but the number of nesting turtles has declined dramatically in recent years.

Olive ridley Endangered – the world population of nesting females is estimated to be around 800,000. Olive ridleys are unique in that thousands of turtles descend on one beach to nest en masse. This happens in Parque Nacional Santa Rosa (p234) and Refugio Nacional de Fauna Silvestre Ostional (p285) between July and November.

areas, such as Parque Nacional Corcovado (p421) and Parque Internacional La Amistad (p385).

Plants

Floral biodiversity is also high – close to 12,000 species of vascular plants have been described in Costa Rica, and more are being added to the list every year. Orchids alone account for about 1400 species.

Experiencing a tropical forest for the first time can be a bit of a surprise for visitors from North America or Europe, where temperate forests tend to have little variety. Such regions are either dominated by conifers, or have endless tracts of oaks, beech and birch. Tropical forests, on the other hand, have a staggering number of species – in Costa Rica, for example, almost 2000 tree species have been recorded. If you stand in one spot and look around, you'll see scores of different plants, and if you walk several hundred meters you're likely to find even more.

Costa Rica's national tree is the guanacaste, commonly found on the lowlands of the Pacific Slope.

The diversity of habitats created when this many species mix is a wonder to behold – one day you may find yourself canoeing in a muggy mangrove swamp, and the next day squinting through bone-chilling fog to see orchids in a montane cloud forest. If at all possible, it is worth planning your trip with the goal of seeing some of Costa Rica's most distinctive plant communities, including rainforests, mangrove swamps, cloud forests and dry forests.

Classic rainforest habitats are well represented in parks of the southwest corner of Costa Rica or in mid-elevation portions of the central mountains. Here you will find towering trees that block out the sky, long looping vines and many overlapping layers of vegetation. Large trees often show buttresses, winglike ribs that extend out from their trunks for added structural support.

Few organizations are as involved in building sustainable rainforest-based economies as the Rainforest Alliance. See the website for special initiatives in Costa Rica: www.rainforest-alliance.org.

Along brackish stretches of both coasts, mangrove swamps are a world unto themselves. Growing stiltlike out of muddy tidal flats, five species of trees crowd together so densely that no boats and few animals can penetrate. Striking in their adaptations for dealing with salt, mangrove trees thrive where no other land plant dares tread. Though often thought of as mosquito-filled backwaters, mangrove swamps play extremely important roles. Not only do they buffer coastlines from the erosive power of waves, they also have high levels of productivity because they trap nutrient-rich sediment and serve as spawning and nursery areas for innumerable species of fish and invertebrates.

Most famous of all, and a highlight for many visitors, are the fabulous cloud forests of Monteverde (p211), with fog-drenched trees so thickly coated

COSTA RICA'S EASTER BLOSSOM

Among Costa Rica's 1400 species of orchids, the guaria morada *(Cattleya skinneri)* is celebrated with special reverence. Blooming around the time of Lent and Easter, this gorgeous orchid with dense clusters of lavender-rose flowers is prominently displayed on altars, homes and churches everywhere in Central America. In the old days these flowers grew liberally on the walls and roofs of old houses and courtyards, where they added a special charm. However, this ancient custom fell by the wayside and they are no longer a common sight.

In honor of its links to history and tradition, the orchid was chosen as Costa Rica's national flower in 1937. Unfortunately, the plant's amazing popularity has resulted in wild populations being harvested without restraint, and an alarm was raised in 2004 that it could become extinct in the wild without immediate action. Hopefully, the orchid's numbers will begin to increase again, because although they are easy to grow commercially, no quantity of orchids in a greenhouse can replace the flowers found in the wild forests of Costa Rica.

in mosses, ferns, bromeliads and orchids that you can hardly discern their true shapes. Cloud forests are widespread at high elevations throughout Costa Rica (such as the Parque Nacional Chirripó area, p374) and any of them would be worth visiting. Be forewarned, however, that in these habitats the term 'rainy season' has little meaning because it's always dripping wet from the fog.

While the female scarlet macaw sits on her nest, the male regurgitates food for her to eat, and later does the same for their chicks.

For a complete change of pace try exploring the unique drier forests along the northwest coast. During the dry season many trees drop their foliage, creating carpets of crackling, sun-drenched leaves and a sense of openness that is largely absent in other Costa Rican habitats. The large trees here, such as Costa Rica's national tree, the guanacaste, have broad, umbrella-like canopies, while spiny shrubs and vines or cacti dominate the understory. At times, large numbers of trees erupt into spectacular displays of flowers, and at the beginning of the rainy season everything is transformed with a wonderful flush of new green foliage.

If you can't make it to one of the areas above, check out the fantastic orchid gardens at Jardín de Orquídeas (p196) or Lankester Gardens (p142), which is near Cartago and home to more than 800 types of orchids.

NATIONAL PARKS & PROTECTED AREAS

The national-park system began in the 1960s, and has since been expanded into a National Conservation Areas System with an astounding 186 protected areas, including 32 national parks, eight biological reserves, 13 forest reserves and 51 wildlife refuges. At least 10% of the land is strictly protected and another 17% is included in various multiple-use preserves. Costa Rican authorities enjoy their claim that more than 27% of the country has been set aside for conservation, but multiple-use zones still allow farming, logging and other exploitation, so the environment within them is not totally protected.

For maps and descriptions of the national parks, go to www.costarica-nationalparks.com.

Travelers will be surprised to learn that, in addition to the system of national preserves, there are hundreds of small, privately owned lodges, reserves and haciendas (estates) that have been set up to protect the land, and many of these are well worth visiting.

Although the national-park system appears glamorous on paper, a report a few years ago from the national conservation body (Sinac; Sistema Nacional de Areas de Conservación) amplified the fact that much of the protected area is, in fact, at risk. The government doesn't exactly own all of this land – almost half of the areas are in private ownership – and there isn't a budget to buy it. Technically, the private lands are protected from development, but there have been reports that many landowners are finding loopholes in the restrictions and selling or developing their properties, or taking bribes from poachers and illegal loggers in exchange for access to their lands.

On the plus side is a project by Sinac that links national parks and reserves, private reserves and national forests into 13 conservation areas. This strategy has two major effects. First, these so-called megaparks allow greater numbers of individual plants and animals to exist. Second, the administration of the national parks is delegated to regional offices, allowing a more individualized management approach in each area. Each conservation area has regional and subregional offices delegated to provide effective education, enforcement, research and management, although some regional offices play what appear to be only obscure bureaucratic roles.

Although many of the national parks were expressly created to protect Costa Rica's habitats and wildlife, a few parks preserve other resources such as the country's foremost pre-Columbian ruins at Monumento Nacional Arqueológico Guayabo (p149), an important cave system at Parque Nacional

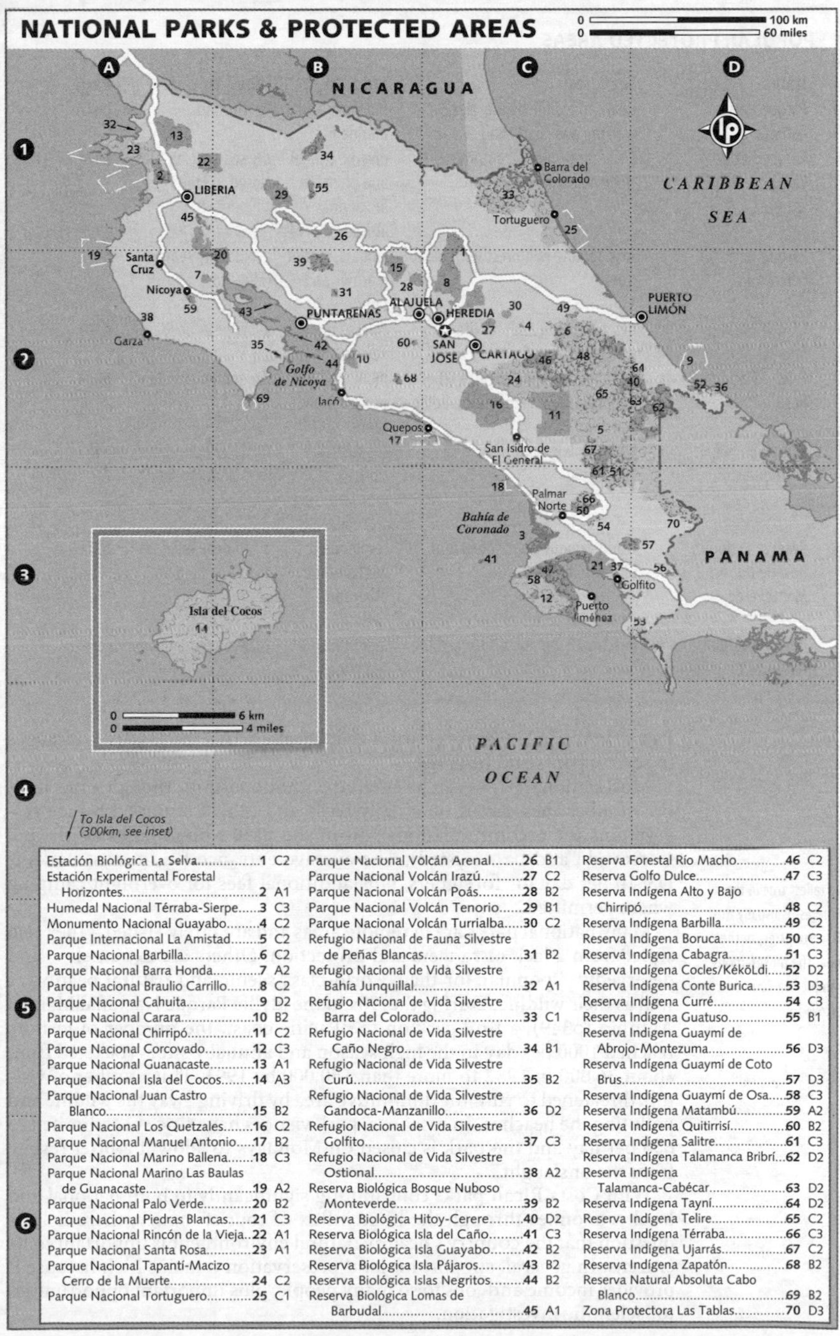
NATIONAL PARKS & PROTECTED AREAS
0 100 km
0 60 miles
NICARAGUA
CARIBBEAN SEA
PACIFIC OCEAN
PANAMA
LIBERIA
Santa Cruz
Nicoya
Garza
PUNTARENAS
ALAJUELA
HEREDIA
SAN JOSE
CARTAGO
PUERTO LIMÓN
Barra del Colorado
Tortuguero
Golfo de Nicoya
Jacó
Quepos
San Isidro de El General
Palmar Norte
Bahía de Coronado
Golfito
Puerto Jiménez
Isla del Cocos
0 6 km
0 4 miles
To Isla del Cocos (300km, see inset)
Estación Biológica La Selva....1 C2
Estación Experimental Forestal Horizontes....2 A1
Humedal Nacional Térraba-Sierpe....3 C3
Monumento Nacional Guayabo....4 C2
Parque Internacional La Amistad....5 C2
Parque Nacional Barbilla....6 C2
Parque Nacional Barra Honda....7 A2
Parque Nacional Braulio Carrillo....8 C2
Parque Nacional Cahuita....9 D2
Parque Nacional Carara....10 B2
Parque Nacional Chirripó....11 C2
Parque Nacional Corcovado....12 C3
Parque Nacional Guanacaste....13 A1
Parque Nacional Isla del Cocos....14 A3
Parque Nacional Juan Castro Blanco....15 B2
Parque Nacional Los Quetzales....16 C2
Parque Nacional Manuel Antonio....17 B2
Parque Nacional Marino Ballena....18 C3
Parque Nacional Marino Las Baulas de Guanacaste....19 A2
Parque Nacional Palo Verde....20 B2
Parque Nacional Piedras Blancas....21 C3
Parque Nacional Rincón de la Vieja....22 A1
Parque Nacional Santa Rosa....23 A1
Parque Nacional Tapantí-Macizo Cerro de la Muerte....24 C2
Parque Nacional Tortuguero....25 C1
Parque Nacional Volcán Arenal....26 B1
Parque Nacional Volcán Irazú....27 C2
Parque Nacional Volcán Poás....28 B2
Parque Nacional Volcán Tenorio....29 B1
Parque Nacional Volcán Turrialba....30 C2
Refugio Nacional de Fauna Silvestre de Peñas Blancas....31 B2
Refugio Nacional de Vida Silvestre Bahía Junquillal....32 A1
Refugio Nacional de Vida Silvestre Barra del Colorado....33 C1
Refugio Nacional de Vida Silvestre Caño Negro....34 B1
Refugio Nacional de Vida Silvestre Curú....35 B2
Refugio Nacional de Vida Silvestre Gandoca-Manzanillo....36 D2
Refugio Nacional de Vida Silvestre Golfito....37 C3
Refugio Nacional de Vida Silvestre Ostional....38 A2
Reserva Biológica Bosque Nuboso Monteverde....39 B2
Reserva Biológica Hitoy-Cerere....40 D2
Reserva Biológica Isla del Caño....41 C3
Reserva Biológica Isla Guayabo....42 B2
Reserva Biológica Isla Pájaros....43 B2
Reserva Biológica Islas Negritos....44 B2
Reserva Biológica Lomas de Barbudal....45 A1
Reserva Forestal Río Macho....46 C2
Reserva Golfo Dulce....47 C3
Reserva Indígena Alto y Bajo Chirripó....48 C2
Reserva Indígena Barbilla....49 C2
Reserva Indígena Boruca....50 C3
Reserva Indígena Cabagra....51 C3
Reserva Indígena Cocles/KékōLdi....52 D2
Reserva Indígena Conte Burica....53 D3
Reserva Indígena Curré....54 C3
Reserva Indígena Guatuso....55 B1
Reserva Indígena Guaymí de Abrojo-Montezuma....56 D3
Reserva Indígena Guaymí de Coto Brus....57 D3
Reserva Indígena Guaymí de Osa....58 C3
Reserva Indígena Matambú....59 A2
Reserva Indígena Quitirrisí....60 B2
Reserva Indígena Salitre....61 C3
Reserva Indígena Talamanca Bribrí....62 D2
Reserva Indígena Talamanca-Cabécar....63 D2
Reserva Indígena Tayní....64 D2
Reserva Indígena Telire....65 C2
Reserva Indígena Térraba....66 C3
Reserva Indígena Ujarrás....67 C2
Reserva Indígena Zapatón....68 B2
Reserva Natural Absoluta Cabo Blanco....69 B2
Zona Protectora Las Tablas....70 D3

POPULAR PROTECTED AREAS

Name	Features	Wildlife	When to Visit	Page
Parque Nacional Cahuita	easily accessible hiking, beach walking and snorkeling	monkeys and marine life	year-round	p477
Parque Nacional Chirripó	Costa Rica's highest summit, cloud-forest trekking	diverse animal and plant life at varying altitudes	dry season (Jan-Mar), closed in May	p374
Parque Nacional Corcovado	vast, remote rainforest with giant trees	jaguars, scarlet macaws and tapirs	avoid rainy season (May-Nov)	p421
Parque Nacional Manuel Antonio	beach walking and wildlife-watching	diverse monkey species	avoid peak holidays	p349
Parque Nacional Santa Rosa	dry forest with guanacaste (the national tree), hiking and wildlife-watching	monkeys, peccaries and coatis	dry season (Jan-Mar)	p234
Parque Nacional Tortuguero	beach walking and sea turtle egg-laying	sea turtles, sloths, manatees and crocodiles	turtle season, check with park for details	p458
Reserva Biológica Bosque Nuboso Monteverde	world-famous cloud forest and bird-watching	resplendent quetzals and other rare birds	avoid peak holidays	p211
Reserva Natural Absoluta Cabo Blanco	beach walking and bird-watching	monkeys and sea birds	year-round	p304

Barra Honda (p279) and a series of geologically active and inactive volcanoes in several parks and reserves.

Most national parks can be entered without permits, though a few limit the number they admit on a daily basis and others require advance reservations for accommodations within the park's boundaries (Chirripó, Corcovado and La Amistad). The average entrance fee to most parks is US$10 per day for foreigners, plus additional fees for overnight camping where permitted.

The tallest tree in the rainforest is usually the silk-cotton tree, or the ceiba. The most famous example is a 70m elder in Corcovado.

Many national parks are in remote areas and are rarely visited – they also suffer from a lack of rangers and protection. Others are extremely – and deservedly – popular for their world-class scenic and natural beauty, as well as their wildlife. During the '90s in the idyllic Parque Nacional Manuel Antonio (p349), a tiny park on the Pacific coast, the number of visitors reached 1000 per day in the high season and annual visitors rocketed from about 36,000 in 1982 to more than 150,000 by 1991. This number of visitors threatened to ruin the diminutive area by driving away the wildlife and polluting the beaches. In response, park visitors have since been limited to 600 per day and the park is closed on Mondays to allow it a brief respite from the onslaught.

With Costa Rican parks contributing significantly to both national and local economies through the huge influx of tourist money, there is little question that the country's healthy natural environment is important to its citizens. In general, support for land preservation remains high because it provides income and jobs to so many people, plus important opportunities for scientific investigation.

ENVIRONMENTAL ISSUES

Costa Rica is a mixed bag in terms of environmental issues. No other tropical country has made such a concerted effort to protect the environment and in 2008 Costa Rica was ranked one of the top five nations in the world for its overall environmental performance. At the same time, as the global leader in the burgeoning ecotourism economy, Costa Rica is proving to be a case study in the pitfalls and benefits of ecological tourism.

Adrian Forsyth has written several colorful children's books about the rainforest, including *Journey Through a Tropical Jungle* and *How Monkeys Make Chocolate*.

Deforestation

Can you believe that this tropical paradise was once entirely carpeted in lush rainforests? Tragically, after more than a century of clearing for plantations, agriculture and logging, Costa Rica lost about 80% of its forest cover before the government stepped in with a plan to protect what was left. Through its many programs of forest protection and reforestation, 52% of the country is forested once again – a stunning accomplishment.

Despite protection for two-thirds of the remaining forests, cutting trees is still a major problem for Costa Rica, especially on private lands being cleared by wealthy landowners and multinational corporations. Even within national parks, some of the more remote areas are being logged illegally because there is not enough money to hire guards to enforce the law.

Green Phoenix, by science journalist William Allen, is an absorbing account of his efforts, alongside scientists and activists, to conserve and restore the rainforest in Guanacaste.

Apart from the direct loss of tropical forests and the plants and animals that depend on them, deforestation leads directly or indirectly to other severe environmental problems. Forests protect the soil beneath them from the ravages of tropical rainstorms; after deforestation much of the topsoil is washed away, lowering the productivity of the land and silting up watersheds and downstream coral reefs.

Cleared lands are frequently planted with a variety of crops, including Costa Rica's main agricultural product, bananas, the production of which entails the use of pesticides as well as blue plastic bags to protect the fruit. Both the pesticides and the plastic bags end up polluting the environment. See boxed text, p448, for information on how this has also impacted humans.

THE ESSENTIAL RAINFOREST

One of the most common media buzzwords these days is 'climate change' or 'global warming,' particularly in regard to humans negatively impacting the health and sustainability of the planet. As developing nations continue to modernize, global carbon emissions rise and evidence of the greenhouse effect can be felt across the planet.

One of the best defenses humans have against rising carbon dioxide (CO_2) levels is the tropical rainforest. Tropical rainforests limit the greenhouse effect of global warming by storing carbon and hence reducing the amount of CO_2 in the atmosphere – they act as a 'carbon sink.' Unfortunately, our best defense against climate change is rapidly being destroyed the world over. In an example of the interconnectedness of environments, scientists have found that the deforestation of Latin American rainforests is impacting global ecosystems, such as the Sahel in Africa, where desertification has increased as deforestation in Latin America increases.

Unfortunately, the total picture is even bleaker. In 2004, scientists made an announcement following a 20-year study in the Amazon, claiming the world's tropical forests may become less able to absorb CO_2. In some areas of the forest scientists discovered that bigger, quicker-growing species were flourishing at the expense of the smaller ones living below the forest canopy. Since plant growth is dependent upon CO_2, the team hypothesized that the bigger plants in tropical rainforests were getting an extra boost from rising levels of global emissions.

As a result of changing rainforest dynamics, specifically the decline of densely wooded subcanopy trees, the ability of tropical rainforests to act as a carbon sink is in jeopardy.

Because deforestation plays a role in global warming, there is a lot of interest in rewarding countries like Costa Rica for taking the lead in protecting their forests. The USA has forgiven millions of dollars of Costa Rica's debt in exchange for increased efforts to preserve rainforests. The Costa Rican government itself sponsors a program that pays landowners for each hectare of forest they set aside, and has petitioned the UN for a global program that would pay tropical countries for their conservation efforts.

The National Biodiversity Institute is a clearing-house of information on both biodiversity and efforts to conserve it; see www.inbio.ac.cr.

Tourism

The other great environmental issue facing Costa Rica comes from the country being loved to death, directly through the passage of more than one million foreign tourists a year, and indirectly through the development of extensive infrastructure to support this influx. Every year, more resort hotels and lodges pop up, most notably on formerly pristine beaches or in the middle of intact rainforest. Many of these projects are poorly planned, and necessitate additional support systems, including roads and countless vehicle trips, with much of this activity unregulated and largely unmonitored.

There is growing concern that many hotels and lodges are simply dumping wastewater into the ocean or nearby creeks rather than following expensive procedures for treating it. With an official estimate that only 4% of the country's wastewater is treated, and with thousands of unregulated hotels in operation, there's a good chance that some hotels and lodges aren't taking care of their waste.

It is worth noting, however, that many private lodges and reserves are also doing some of the best conservation work in the country, and it's really

THE PRICE OF ECOTOURISM

Traditionally, tourism in Costa Rica has been on a small and intimate scale. The great majority of the country's hotels are small (fewer than 50 rooms) and staffed with friendly local people who work closely with tourists, to the benefit of both. This intimacy and friendliness has been a hallmark of a visit to Costa Rica.

But this is changing. The financial bonanza generated by the tourism boom means that new operations are starting up all the time – some are good, many are not. The big word in Costa Rica is 'ecotourism' and everyone wants to jump on the green bandwagon. These days, there is everything from 'ecological' car-rental agencies to 'ecological' menus in restaurants.

Taking advantage of Costa Rica's 'green' image, a growing number of developers are promoting mass tourism by building large hotels with accompanying environmental problems. Apart from the immediate impacts, such as cutting down vegetation, diverting or damming rivers and driving away wildlife, there are secondary impacts such as erosion and lack of adequate waste-treatment facilities for huge hotels in areas far from sewage lines.

The government tourist board (ICT; Instituto Costarricense de Turismo) has launched mass-marketing campaigns all over the world, touting 'Costa Rica: No Artificial Ingredients,' yet hasn't followed up with the kind of infrastructure necessary to preserve those ingredients (nor does it lobby for them). Many people feel a certain degree of frustration with the ICT for selling Costa Rica as a green paradise but doing little to help preserve it.

The big question is whether future tourism developments should continue to focus on the traditional small-hotel, ecotourism approach, or turn to mass tourism, with planeloads of visitors accommodated in 'megaresorts' such as the ones in Cancún, Mexico. From the top levels of government down, the debate has been fierce. Local and international tour operators and travel agents, journalists, developers, airline operators, hotel owners, writers, environmentalists and politicians have all been vocal in their support of either ecotourism or mass tourism. Many believe that the country is too small to handle both forms of tourism properly. It remains to be seen which faction will win – or if both can coexist successfully.

inspiring to run across homespun efforts to protect Costa Rica's environment spearheaded by hardworking families or small organizations tucked away in some forgotten corner of the country. These include projects to boost rural economies by raising butterflies or native flowers, efforts by villagers to document their local biodiversity, or amazingly resourceful campaigns to raise funds to purchase endangered lands.

The Refugio Nacional de Vida Silvestre Curú (p297), Tiskita Jungle Lodge (p437) in Pavones, La Amistad Lodge (p388), and Rara Avis (p509) near Puerto Viejo de Sarapiquí are but a few examples. Costa Rica is full of wonderful tales about folks who are extremely passionate and generous in their efforts to protect the planet's resources.

Michael Crichton's book *Jurassic Park* is set on Isla del Cocos. In it, he refers to Ticos as 'Ticans.'

San José

San José is not a pretty city. It's studded with unremarkable concrete towers, clogged pedestrian arcades and fast-food outlets redolent of everything fried. On some days, it is sensory overload: walk its teeming streets and you'll get jostled by businessmen grunting into cell phones and street vendors hawking fried bananas, all set to a soundtrack of tooting horns and roaring bus engines. But linger long enough and 'Chepe' – as San José is affectionately known – will begin to reveal its charms.

Duck into an anonymous-looking restaurant and you might find yourself in the middle of a garden, sipping wine beside a gushing fountain. A vintage house might conceal a cutting-edge contemporary art space. An unremarkable-looking hotel may have been the place where presidents once slept. It is a place rife with history. San José, after all, is where forward-thinking leaders once gathered to decide that this would be a country without an army.

Over the last century, the transformation from prewar agrarian coffee town to 21st-century urban sprawl has been unkind to the city's physical form. But regardless of what it may look like, San José is the beating heart of Costa Rica – home to its most influential thinkers, its finest museums and its most sophisticated restaurants. In a country that has been culturally transformed by vast amounts of tourism, there's nowhere better to begin to understand what it means to be Tico. For to truly love Costa Rica, you must first learn to love its capital.

HIGHLIGHTS

- Admiring Costa Rica's artistic traditions past and present at the **Museo de Jade** (p76) and **Museo de Arte y Diseño Contemporáneo** (p76)
- Dancing until the break of dawn at one of San José's hopping **nightclubs** (p92)
- Ogling the rich marbled floors and beaux arts interiors of the graceful **Teatro Nacional** (p73)
- Reveling in cold beer and country cooking at **La Casona de Laly** (p110) in the suburb of Escazú
- Grooving to live bands in San Pedro at **Jazz Café** (p105), the city's most storied music venue

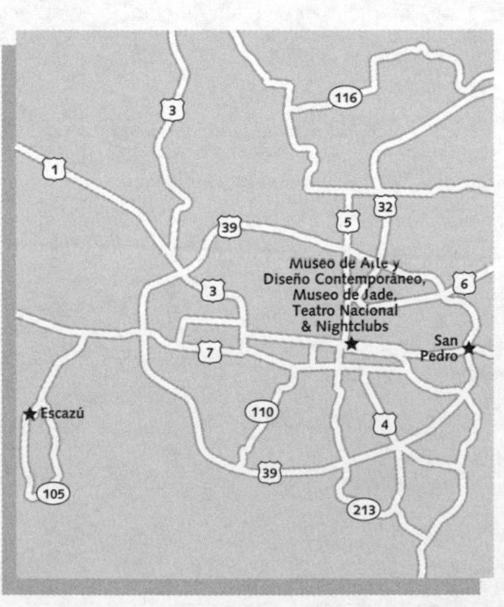

- POPULATION: CITY 350,000, GREATER METRO AREA OVER 1.5 MILLION
- AREA: 2366 SQ KM

HISTORY

For much of the colonial period, San José played second fiddle to the bigger and relatively more established Cartago, a city whose origins date back to 1563 and which, during the colonial era, served as the provincial capital. Villanueva de la Boca del Monte del Valle de Abra – as San José was first known – was not founded until 1737, when the Catholic Church issued an edict that forced the populace to settle near churches (attendance was down).

The city remained a backwater for decades, though it did experience some growth as a stop in the tobacco trading route during the late 18th century. Following independence in 1821, rival factions in Cartago and San José each attempted to assert regional supremacy. The struggle ended in 1823 when the two sides faced off at the Battle of Ochomongo. San José emerged the victor and subsequently declared itself capital.

Despite its new status, the city remained a quiet agricultural center into the 20th century. The calm was shattered in the 1940s, when parts of San José served as a battlefield in the civil war of 1948, one of the bloodiest conflicts in the country's history. Out of that clash, José Figueres Ferrer of the Partido de Liberación Nacional (National Liberation Party) emerged as the country's interim leader – signing a declaration that abolished the army at the armory that now serves as the Museo Nacional (p73).

The rest of the 20th century would see the expansion of the city from diminutive coffee-trading outpost to sprawling urban center. In the 1940s San José had only 70,000 residents. Today, the population stands at more than 1.5 million. Recent years have been marked by massive urban migration as Ticos (Costa Ricans) and, increasingly, Nicaraguans have moved to the capital in search of economic opportunity (see boxed text, p230). As part of this, shantytowns have mushroomed on the outskirts, and crime is increasingly becoming a part of life for the city's poorest inhabitants.

Even so, the city remains a vital economic and arts hub, home to important banks, museums and universities – as well as the everyday outposts of culture: live music spaces, art centers, bookstores and the corner restaurants where *josefinos* (people from San José) gather to chew over ideas.

ORIENTATION

The city is in the heart of a wide and fertile valley called the Meseta Central (Central Valley). San José's center is arranged in a grid with *avenidas* (avenues) running east to west and *calles* (streets) running north to south. Av Central is the nucleus of the downtown area and is a pedestrian mall between Calles 6 and 9. It becomes Paseo Colón to the west of Calle 14. There are no exact street addresses, so these are given by the nearest street intersection. Thus, the address of the tourist office is Calle 5 between Avs Central and 2.

The downtown has several districts, *barrios,* which are all loosely defined. The central area is home to innumerable businesses, bus terminals, hotels and cultural sites. West of downtown is La Sabana, named after the park, and just north of it is the elegant suburb of Rohrmoser. Further west is the affluent outer suburb of Escazú. Immediately east (and within walking distance) of the downtown area are the contiguous neighborhoods of Los Yoses and San Pedro.

Note that the maps used in this book show streets and avenues. However, most locals do not use street addresses. To learn how to decipher Tico directions, see boxed text, p534.

You can pick up a free map of the city at the tourist office (p72).

INFORMATION

Look for free copies of **San José Volando** (www.sanjosevolando.com), a monthly pocket-sized guide that has arts, food and other cultural listings in English. You can find it at art galleries, museums and better restaurants and hotels.

Bookstores

English-language magazines, newspapers, books and maps are widely available in shops throughout the city. The following stores offer the best selection:

7th Street Books (Map p74; ☎ 2256-8251; Calle 7 btwn Avs Central & 1; 🕑 10am-5pm) The headquarters of all things English-language also carries maps.

Librería Lehmann (Map p74; ☎ 2223-1212; www.librerialehmann.com; Av Central btwn Calles 1 & 3; 🕑 8am-6:30pm Mon-Fri, 9am-5pm Sat, 11am-4pm Sun) Good selection of English-language books, guidebooks (including Lonely Planet), as well as topographic and other maps (available upstairs).

Librería Universal (Map p74; ☎ 2222-2222; www.universalcr.com; Av Central btwn Calles Central & 1) On the

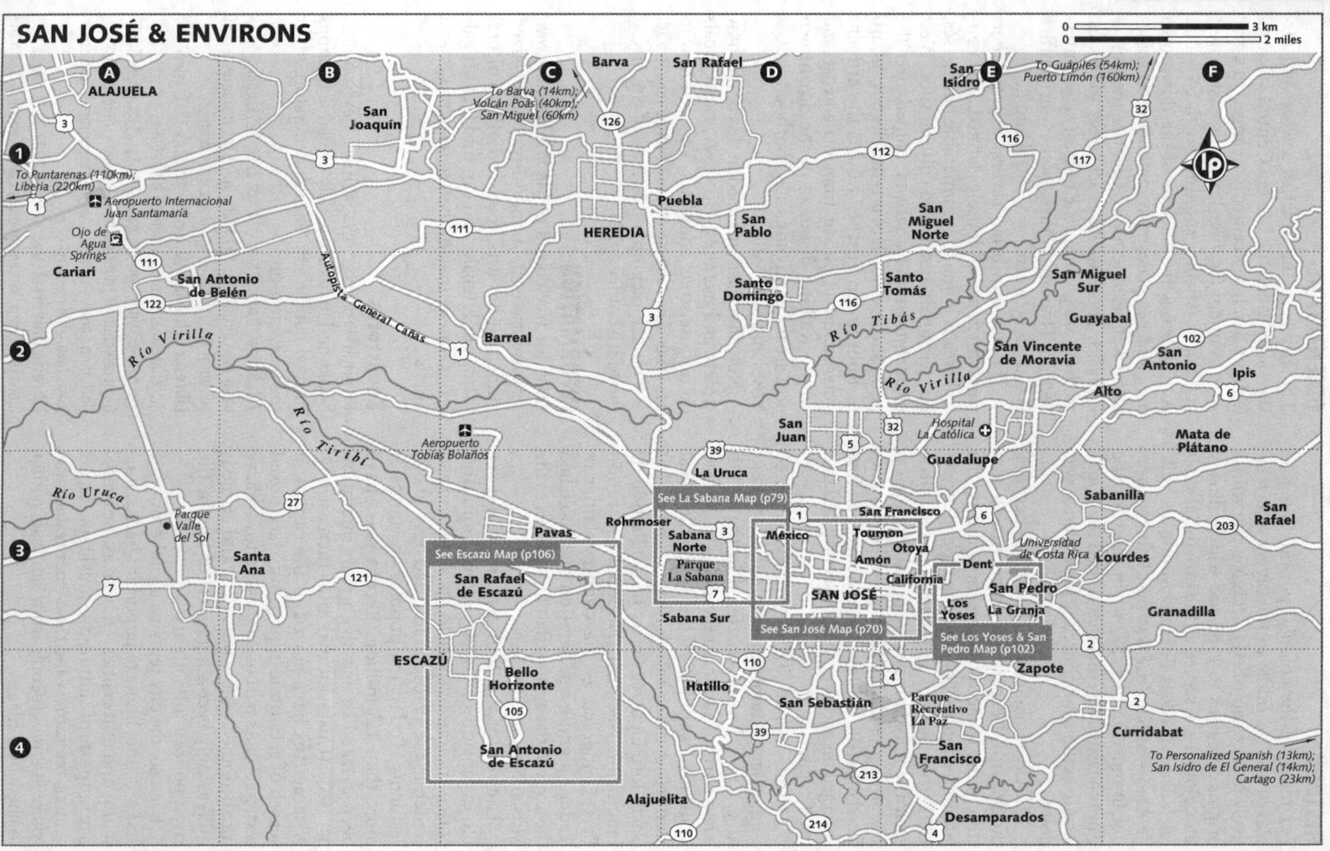
SAN JOSÉ & ENVIRONS
0 3 km
0 2 miles
ALAJUELA
San Joaquín
Barva
San Rafael
To Barva (14km); Volcán Poás (40km); San Miguel (60km)
San Isidro
To Guápiles (54km); Puerto Limón (160km)
To Puntarenas (110km); Liberia (220km)
Aeropuerto Internacional Juan Santamaría
Ojo de Agua Springs
Cariari
San Antonio de Belén
HEREDIA
Puebla
San Pablo
San Miguel Norte
Autopista General Cañas
Barreal
Santo Domingo
Santo Tomás
San Miguel Sur
Guayabal
Río Tibás
Río Virilla
San Vincente de Moravia
San Antonio
Ipis
Alto
Río Tiribí
Aeropuerto Tobías Bolaños
San Juan
Hospital La Católica
Guadalupe
Mata de Plátano
Río Uruca
Parque Valle del Sol
Santa Ana
La Uruca
See La Sabana Map (p79)
Rohrmoser
Pavas
San Francisco
Sabanilla
San Rafael
See Escazú Map (p106)
San Rafael de Escazú
Sabana Norte
Parque La Sabana
México
Toumon
Otoya
Amón
California
SAN JOSÉ
Universidad de Costa Rica
Lourdes
Dent
San Pedro
Los Yoses
La Granja
Granadilla
Sabana Sur
See San José Map (p70)
See Los Yoses & San Pedro Map (p102)
ESCAZÚ
Bello Horizonte
Hatillo
San Sebastián
Zapote
Parque Recreativo La Paz
Curridabat
San Antonio de Escazú
San Francisco
To Personalized Spanish (13km); San Isidro de El General (14km); Cartago (23km)
Alajuelita
Desamparados

GETTING INTO TOWN

International flights arrive at Aeropuerto Internacional Juan Santamaría in nearby Alajuela. There are a number of ways to get from the airport into town: taxi, bus and door-to-door shuttle service (for details, see p99). Many hotels can also arrange for private airport pickup at reasonable rates.

If traveling by bus, you'll arrive at one of several international bus terminals sprinkled around the western and southern parts of downtown. Some of this area is walkable provided you aren't hauling a lot of luggage and are staying nearby. But, if you're arriving at night, take a taxi, since most terminals are in dodgy areas.

Note that many taxi drivers in San José are commissioned by hotels to bring them customers, and the hotel scene is so competitive that drivers will say just about anything to steer you to the places they represent. Among other things, they will 'call' your hotel and a voice on the other end will tell you that they're fully booked. Be skeptical. Tell drivers firmly where it is you would like to go. And if you have concerns about where you have chosen to stay, ask to see a room before settling in for the night.

2nd floor, the shop has a tiny selection of English-language books, as well as a rack devoted to Costa Rican literature.

Libro Azul (Map p74; Av 10 btwn Calles Central & 1; 🕑 8:30am-12:30pm & 1:30-5:30pm Mon-Fri, 9am-noon Sat) A tiny shop with secondhand books, mostly in Spanish.

Cultural Centers

San José's growing cultural scene is supported by various foreign institutions, which host film nights, art exhibits, theater, live music and academic conferences. Call ahead in the summer months of January and February, when these spots tend to have limited hours.

Alianza Francesa (Map p74; ☎ 2222-2283; www.afsj.net; cnr Calle 5 & Av 7) The Alliance has French classes, a small library and rotating art exhibits in a historic Barrio Amón home.

Centro Cultural de España (☎ 2257-2919; www.ccecr.org; Rotonda del Farolito, Barrio Escalante) One of the city's most vibrant cultural institutions, this Spanish-run center offers a full roster of events. There is also an audio-visual center and a lending library.

Centro de Cine (Map p74; ☎ 2223-0610/2127; http://centrodecine.go.cr; cnr Calle 11 & Av 9) Located in a rambling Victorian mansion, the government-run cinematheque hosts festivals, lectures and events dedicated to Latin American film.

Emergency

See the inside front cover for more emergency numbers.

Red Cross (☎ 128)

Traffic police (☎ 2222-9330)

Internet Access

Checking email is easy in San José, where cybercafes are more plentiful than fruit peddlers. Rates are generally ₡300 to ₡500 per hour, though these days most hotels (even budget hostels) provide free internet access, mostly via wi-fi.

Café Internet Omni Crisval (Map p74; Av 1 btwn Calles 3 & 5; 🕑 9am-9pm Mon-Sat; per hr ₡400) A dozen terminals with speedy connections located on the main floor of the Omni shopping center.

Más Móvil Internet (Map p74; Av 5 btwn Calles Central & 1; ☎ 2221-4080; per hr ₡300) Sixteen machines, some of which have Skype for online calling.

Laundry

Do-it-yourself laundry services are hard to find in San José. However, most hotels and hostels offer this service. Expect to pay in the vicinity of ₡4400 to ₡5500 for a load. High-end places may charge by the piece, which is generally more expensive.

Medical Services

For medical services in Escazú, see p105.

Clínica Bíblica (Map p70; ☎ 2522-1000/1030; www.clinicabiblica.com; Av 14 btwn Calles Central & 1) The top private clinic in the downtown area. Doctors speak English, French and German, and an emergency room is open 24 hours.

Hospital La Católica (Map p68; ☎ 2246-3000; www.hospitallacatolica.com; Guadalupe) A pricey private clinic located north of downtown. In 2009 the hospital debuted an adjacent 34-room hotel – geared at patients who arrive for treatments from abroad.

Hospital San Juan de Dios (Map p74; ☎ 2257-6282; cnr Paseo Colón & Calle 14) The free public hospital – incidentally, Costa Rica's oldest (founded 1845) – is open 24 hours. It offers a wide variety of medical services and there is a children's wing. Expect long waits.

Money

ATMs that accept foreign bank cards are widely available all over San José. In addition, banks will exchange most foreign currencies and traveler's checks. It is also worth noting that most businesses in San José (and Costa Rica, for that matter) will accept cash US dollars as payment. Credit cards are widely accepted, though Visa tends to be preferred over MasterCard and American Express.

For general information on money issues, see p535.

Banco de Costa Rica La Sabana (Map p79; ☎ 2233-7055; cnr Paseo Colón & Calle 40; ⏰ 9am-4pm Mon-Fri); San José (BCR; Map p74; ☎ 2284-6600; www.bancobcr

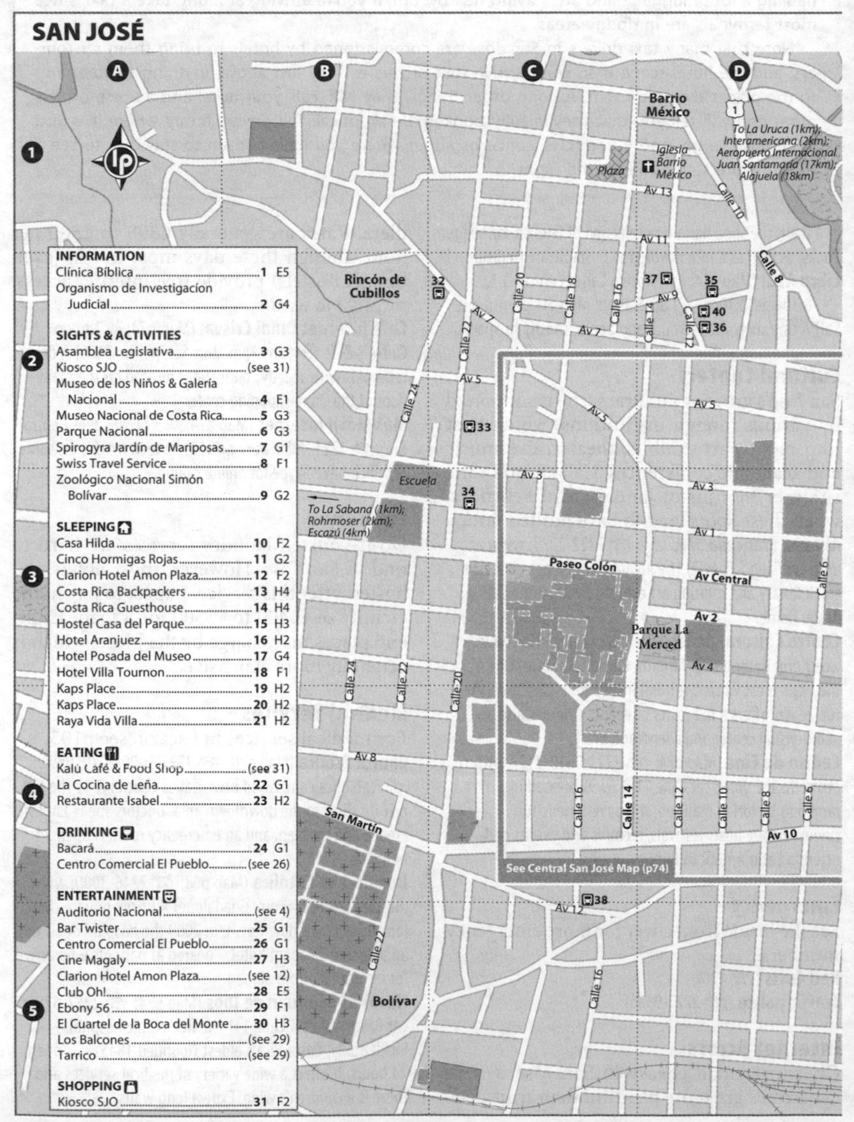

.com; cnr Calle 7 & Av 1; 8:30am-6pm Mon-Fri) A top local bank, with ATMs that dispense colones and US dollars.

Banco de San José (Map p74; 2295-9797; www.bac.net; Av 2 btwn Calles Central & 1; 8am-6pm Mon-Fri, 10am-2pm Sat) A reliable full-service bank with ATMs on the Plus and Cirrus systems.

Banco Nacional de Costa Rica Exchange House (Map p74; cnr Av Central & Calle 4; 10:30am-6pm Mon-Fri, 8am-3:45pm Sat & Sun) A good find in the event of a Sunday cash-exchange emergency since it's open seven days; expect long lines.

Citibank (Map p74; 2239-9091; www.latinamerica.citibank.com/costarica/index.html; Av 1 btwn Calles Central & 1; 8:30am-6pm Mon-Fri, 9am-5pm Sat) Can cash Citibank traveler's checks, plus they have ATMs on the Cirrus, Plus and Visa systems.

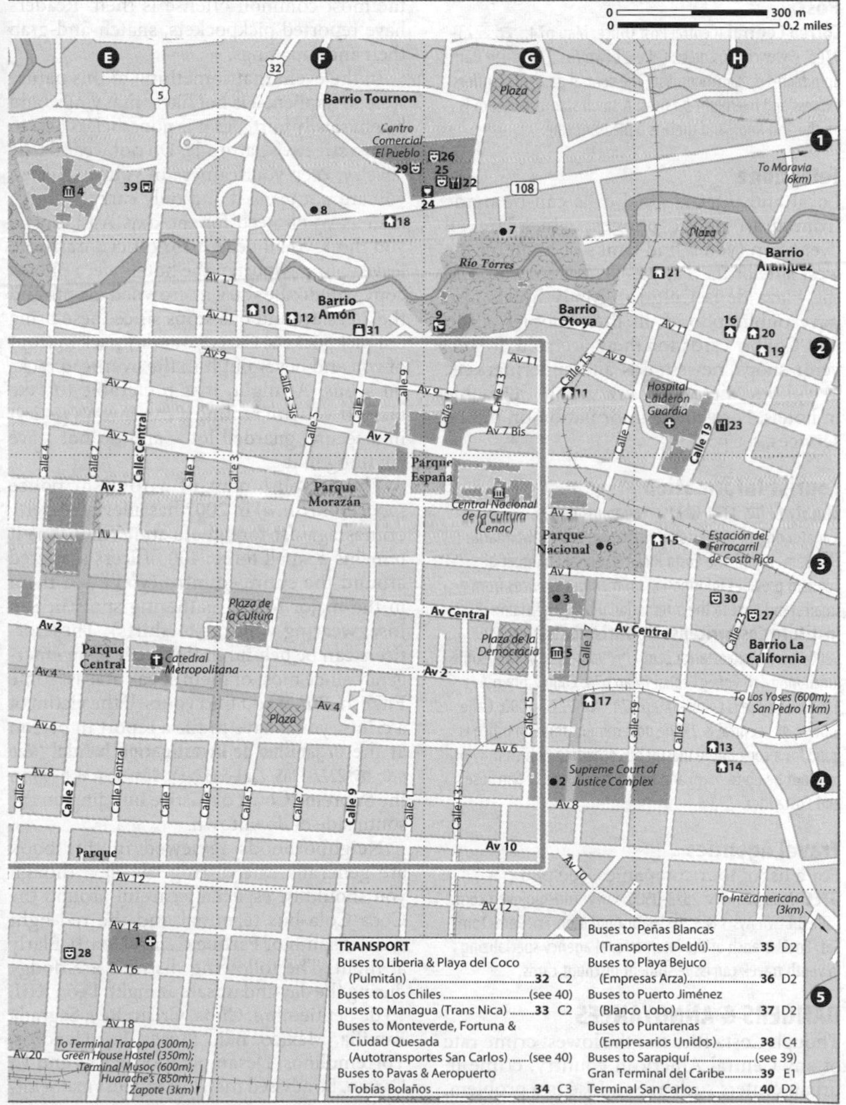

Credomatic (Map p74; ☎ 2295-9898; www.credomatic.com; Calle Central btwn Avs 3 & 5) A subsidiary of the Banco de San José, it gives cash advances on Visa and MasterCard.

Scotiabank (Map p74; ☎ 2521-5680; www.scotiabankcr.com; Calle 5 btwn Avs Central & 2; 9am-5pm Mon-Fri) Good service and 24-hour ATMs on the Cirrus system that dispense US dollars and colones.

Post

Correo Central (Central Post Office; Map p74; ☎ 2223-9766; www.correos.go.cr; Calle 2 btwn Avs 1 & 3; 8am-6pm Mon-Fri, 8am-noon Sat) The central post office offers express and overnight services. A small stamp museum is on the 2nd floor, and there is a pleasant cafe.

Telephone

Local and international calls can be made from most public phones, which are all over town (you'll find banks of them on the west side of the Parque Central and around the Plaza de la Cultura). Many hotels also have public phones in their lobbies. Chip and Colibrí cards for these are sold at souvenir shops, newsstands and supermarkets. Telephone directories are usually available in hotels. For general information on phone services, see p537.

Tourist Information

Canatur (☎ 2234-6222; www.tourism.co.cr, www.canatur.org; Aeropuerto Internacional Juan Santamaría; 8am-10pm) The Costa Rican National Chamber of Tourism provides information on member services from a small stand next to the international baggage claim.

Instituto Costarricense de Turismo (ICT; ☎ 2299-5800; www.visitcostarica.com; 9am-5pm with flexible lunch Mon-Fri) Correo Central (Map p74; Calle 2 btwn Avs 1 & 3); Plaza de la Cultura (Map p74; ☎ 2222-1090; Calle 5 btwn Avs Central & 2) The government tourism office is good for a copy of the master bus schedule (which may or may not be up to date) and handy free maps of San José and Costa Rica.

Travel Agencies

For a list of tour companies, see p80.

OTEC (Map p74; ☎ 2523-0500; www.turismojoven.com; Calle 3 btwn Avs 1 & 3; 8am-6pm Mon-Fri, 9am-1pm Sat) Local branch of the international agency specializing in youth travel; can issue student discount cards.

DANGERS & ANNOYANCES

Though Costa Rica has the lowest crime rate of any Central American country, crime in urban centers such as San José is a problem. Within Costa Rica, reported robberies have skyrocketed by more than 50% since 1998 and the rate of homicides in San José has grown by almost two-thirds, according to a report issued by the UN in 2009. It is worth noting, however, that despite this trend, the country still retains one of the lowest homicide rates in the Americas. Not surprisingly, in a city where one in five people live below the poverty line, the most common offense is theft. Readers have reported pickpockets, snatch-and-grab theft and muggings.

In the event that something of this nature were to happen, it is not likely that you would be physically hurt, but it is nonetheless best to keep a streetwise attitude. Do not wear flashy jewelry, keep your camera in your bag when you are not using it and only carry as much cash as you'll need for the day. And, unless you think you'll need it for official business, leave your passport in the hotel safe; a photocopy will do. Be wary at crowded events and the areas around bus stops since these bring out pickpockets. Carry your day pack in front of you and never put it in the overhead racks on a bus. At night, it is preferable to take taxis. If you are renting a car, always park it in a secure, guarded lot – and do not leave anything in it.

The establishment of a tourism police *(policía turística)* in 2007 has alleviated petty crimes against foreigners somewhat, but it remains a small force: 400 officers scattered around the entire country (you'll see them in the major tourist gathering spots in San José, wearing white polo shirts). These officers can be helpful in the event of an emergency since most of them speak at least some English. But, if you find yourself the victim of a crime, you'll have to file a report in person at the **Organismo de Investigacíon Judicial** (Map p70; ☎ 2222-1365, 2221-5337; 9am-5pm Mon-Fri) in the Supreme Court of Justice building on the south side of downtown.

Neighborhoods reviewed in this book are generally safe during the day, though you should be especially careful around the Coca-Cola bus terminal and the red-light district south of Parque Central, particularly at night. The following districts are dodgy during the day and unsafe at night: León XIII, 15 de Septiembre, Cuba, Cristo Rey, Sagrada Familia, México, Bajo Piuses, Los Cuadros, Torremolinos, Desamparados, Pavas and La Carpio. Be advised that, like in most major cities, adjacent neighborhoods can vary greatly in terms of safety; inquire locally before setting out.

Like anywhere else in the world, women traveling alone should take extra precautions. Do not walk around alone at night and stick to licensed taxis (further information is available on p536). In addition, men should be aware that prostitutes are known for their abilities to take more than their customers bargained for – namely their wallets. Needless to say, if having sex with a prostitute, use condoms: AIDS is on the rise in Central America, and although prostitution is legal in Costa Rica, it is not regulated.

Other factors affecting quality of life include the city's gridlocked traffic and its pit-sized gutters and potholes. Noise and smog are unavoidable components of the San José experience – and most central hotels are victim to a considerable amount of street noise, no matter how nice they are. Most significantly, be skeptical of unaffiliated touts and taxi drivers who try to sell you tours or tell you that the hotel you've booked is a crime-infested bordello. Many of these folks will say anything to steer you to the places that pay them commissions. For general tips on safe travel in Costa Rica, see p530.

SIGHTS

San José is small and best explored on foot, where you can join locals along teeming sidewalks and pedestrian boulevards that lead to vintage theaters, crowded cafes, lush parks and some of the finest museums in Central America.

Central San José East

PLAZA DE LA CULTURA

For many Ticos, Costa Rica begins here. This architecturally unremarkable concrete **plaza** (Map p74; Avs Central & 2 btwn Calles 3 & 5) in the heart of downtown is usually packed with locals slurping ice-cream cones and admiring the wide gamut of San José street life: juggling clowns, punk-rock teenagers and pop-lite Christian bands. It is perhaps one of the safest spots in the city since the entire plaza serves as the ceiling of the Museo de Oro Precolombino y Numismática, which is located one level down, and is therefore considered private property (this gives security guards the right to shoo away 'unsavory' characters).

Museo de Oro Precolombino y Numismática

Beneath the plaza is this three-in-one **museum** (Map p74; ☎ 2243-4221; www.museosdelbancocentral.org; basement, Plaza de la Cultura; admission US$9; 9am-4:45pm Tue-Sun). It is owned by the Banco Central, and the dim, brutalist architecture brings to mind all the warmth and comfort of a bank vault. But the museum is an important repository of Costa Rica's most priceless pieces of pre-Columbian gold, and the collection – which contains hand-tooled ornaments that date back to AD 400 – is beautifully lit and presented. Look for intricate depictions of regional fauna, such as frogs, bats, crabs and jaguars. A smaller exhibit area details the history of Costa Rican currency, while another features a rotating selection of regional art.

Teatro Nacional

On the southern side of the plaza resides the **Teatro Nacional** (Map p74; ☎ 2221-1329; Calles 3 & 5 btwn Avs Central & 2; admission US$7; 9am-4pm Mon-Sat), San José's most revered public building. Constructed in 1897, it features a columned neoclassical facade that is flanked by statues of Beethoven and Calderón de la Barca, a 17th-century Spanish dramatist. The lavish marble lobby and auditorium are lined with paintings depicting various facets of 19th-century life. The most famous is *Alegoría al café y el banano*, an idyllic canvas showing coffee and banana harvests. The painting was produced in Italy and shipped to Costa Rica for installation in the theater, and the image was reproduced on the old ₡5 note (now out of circulation). It is clear that the painter never witnessed a banana harvest because of the way the man in the center is awkwardly grasping a bunch (actual banana workers hoist the stems onto their shoulders).

For information on performances, see p94. If you're looking to rest your feet, try the excellent onsite cafe (p89).

Across the street, also belonging to the national theater is the **Galería García Monge** (Map p74; cnr Av 2 & Calle 5; admission free), which features temporary exhibitions by contemporary Costa Rican and Central American artists.

MUSEO NACIONAL DE COSTA RICA

The **Museo Nacional** (Map p70; ☎ 2257-1433; www.museocostarica.go.cr; Calle 17 btwn Avs Central & 2; adult/child US$6/3; 8:30am-4:30pm Tue-Sun) is located inside the old Bellavista Fortress, which served as the

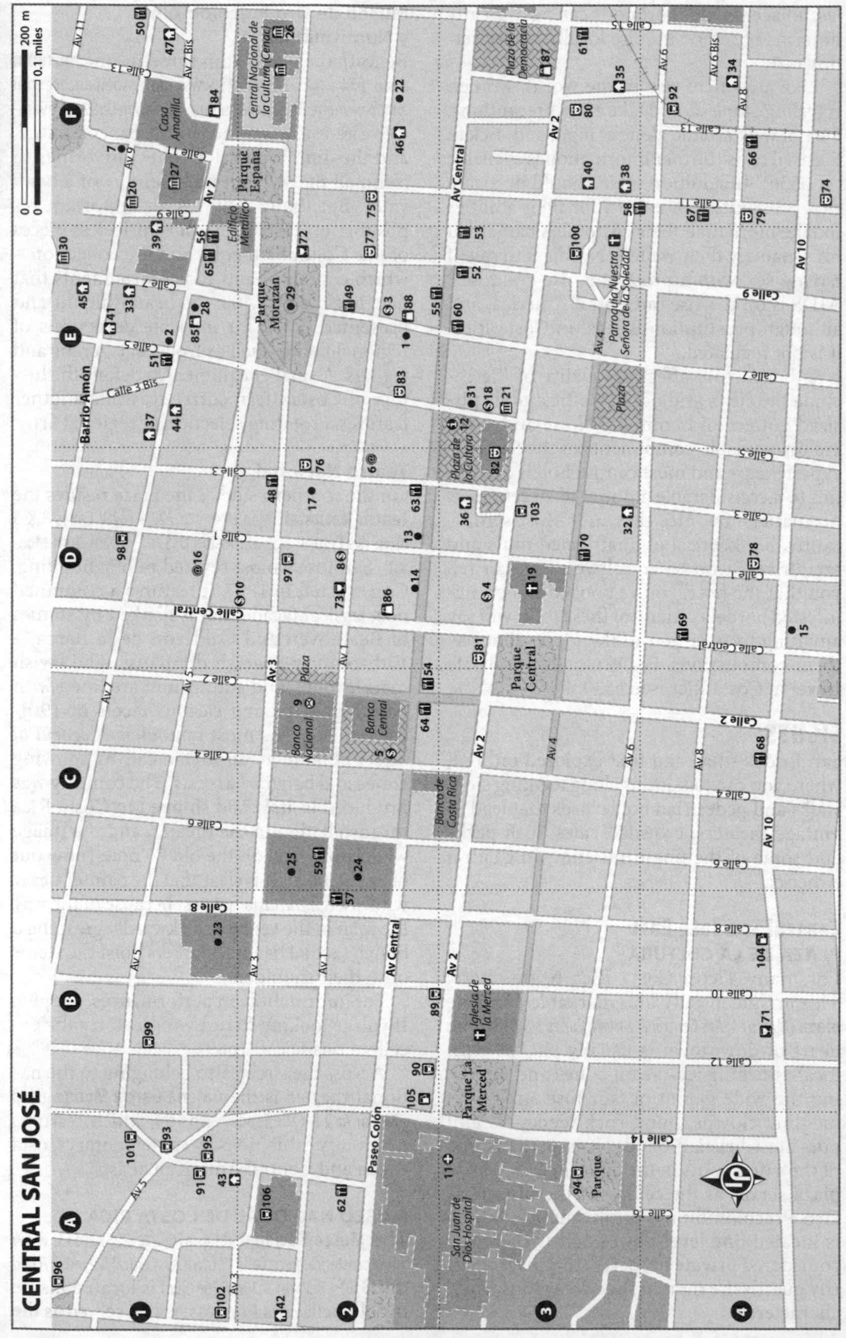
CENTRAL SAN JOSÉ
0 200 m
0 0.1 miles
Barrio Amón
Casa Amarilla
Central Nacional de la Cultura (Cenac)
Parque España
Edificio Metálico
Parque Morazán
Plaza de la Democracia
Plaza de la Cultura
Parque Central
Banco Nacional
Banco Central
Plaza
Banco de Costa Rica
Iglesia de la Merced
Parque La Merced
San Juan de Dios Hospital
Parque
Parroquia Nuestra Señora de la Soledad
Paseo Colón
Av 11
Av 9
Av 7 Bis
Av 7
Av 5
Av 3
Av 1
Av Central
Av 2
Av 4
Av 6
Av 6 Bis
Av 8
Av 10
Calle 15
Calle 13
Calle 11
Calle 9
Calle 7
Calle 5
Calle 3 Bis
Calle 3
Calle 1
Calle Central
Calle 2
Calle 4
Calle 6
Calle 8
Calle 10
Calle 12
Calle 14
Calle 16

old army headquarters and saw fierce fighting (hence the pockmarks) in the 1948 civil war. It was here that President José Figueres Ferrer announced, in 1949, that he was abolishing the country's military.

The museum provides a quick survey of Costa Rican history, with exhibits of pre-Columbian pieces from ongoing digs, as well as artifacts from the colony and the early republic. Among the many notable pieces is the fountain pen that Figueres used to sign the 1949 constitution. Don't miss the newly restored period galleries in the northeast corner, which feature turn-of-the-20th-century furnishings and decor from when these rooms served as the private residences of the fort's various commanders.

Immediately west of the museum is the stark **Plaza de la Democracia** (Map p74; Avs Central & 2 btwn Calles 13 & 15), which was constructed by President Oscar Arias in 1989 to commemorate 100 years of Costa Rican democracy. The

INFORMATION
7th Street Books....1 E2
Alianza Francesa....2 E1
Banco de Costa Rica....3 E2
Banco de San José....4 D3
Banco Nacional de Costa Rica Exchange House....5 C2
Café Internet Omni Crisval....6 D2
Centro de Cine....7 F1
Citibank....8 D2
Correo Central....9 C2
Credomatic....10 D2
Hospital San Juan de Dios....11 A3
ICT (Tourist Office)....(see 9)
ICT (Tourist Office)....12 E3
Librería Lehmann....13 D2
Librería Universal....14 D2
Libro Azul....15 D4
Más Móvil Internet....16 D1
OTEC....17 D2
Scotiabank....18 E3

SIGHTS & ACTIVITIES
Catedral Metropolitana....19 D3
Galería Andrómeda....20 F1
Galería García Monge....21 E3
Jacob Karpio Galería....22 F2
Mercado Borbón....23 B1
Mercado Central....24 C2
Mercado Central Annex....25 C2
Museo de Arte y Diseño Contemporáneo....26 F2
Museo de Jade....27 F1
Museo de Oro Precolombino y Numismática....(see 12)
Museo Postal....(see 9)
Rainforest Aerial Tram Office....28 E1
Teatro Melico Salazar....(see 81)
Teatro Nacional....(see 82)
Templo de Música....29 E2
TEOR/éTica....30 E1
Tico Train....31 E3

SLEEPING
Casa Alfi....32 D3
Casa Morazán....33 E1
Casa Ridgway....34 F4
Fleur de Lys Hotel....35 F3
Gran Hotel Costa Rica....36 D3
Hostel Pangea....37 E1
Hotel Colonial....38 F3
Hotel Don Carlos....39 E1
Hotel Doña Inés....40 F3
Hotel Kekoldi....41 E1
Hotel Mesón del Angel....42 A2
Hotel Musoc....43 A1
Hotel Santo Tomás....44 E1
Kabata Hostel....45 E1
Pensión de la Cuesta....46 F2
Rincón de San José....47 F1

EATING
Auto Mercado....48 D2
Bar Morazán....49 E2
Café del Correo....(see 9)
Café del Teatro Nacional....(see 82)
Café Mundo....50 F1
Café Parisienne....(see 36)
Café Valandra....51 E1
Chelle's....52 E3
Churrería Manolo's....53 E3
Churrería Manolo's....54 C2
Don Wang....(see 67)
El Patio....55 E2
El Torito....56 E1
Helados de Sorbetera....57 B2
La Esquina de Buenos Aires....58 F3
Mariscos Poseidón....59 C2
Mercado Central....(see 24)
News Café....60 E3
Nuestra Tierra....61 F3
Pastelería Merayo....62 A2
Perimercado....63 D2
Q Café....64 C2
Restaurante La Criollita....65 E1
Restaurante Shakti....66 F4
Restaurante Tin-Jo....67 F4
Soda Castro....68 C4
Vishnu....69 D4
Vishnu....70 D3

DRINKING
Bar Chavelona....71 B4
Bar Morazán....(see 49)
Chelle's....(see 52)
El Morazán....72 E2
La Embajada....73 D2

ENTERTAINMENT
Bochinche....74 F4
Casino Club Colonial....75 F2
Complejo Salsa 54 y Zadidas....76 D2
Hotel del Rey....77 E2
La Avispa....78 D4
Pucho's Nightclub....79 F4
Teatro Fanal....(see 26)
Teatro La Máscara....80 F3
Teatro Melico Salazar....81 D3
Teatro Nacional....82 D3
Teatro Variedades....83 E2

SHOPPING
eÑe....84 F1
Galería Namu....85 E1
La Casona....86 D2
Mercado Artesanal....87 F3
Mercado Central....(see 24)
Rincón del Habano....88 E2

TRANSPORT
Buses to Alajuela (Tuasa)....89 B2
Buses to Alajuela, Volcán Poás & Airport (Tuasa)....90 B2
Buses to Cañas and Tilarán (Empresa Cañas)....91 A1
Buses to Cartago & Turrialba....92 F4
Buses to Changuinola/Bocas del Toro (Transportes Bocatoreños)....93 A1
Buses to Dominical & Uvita (Transportes Morales)....(see 106)
Buses to Escazú....94 A3
Buses to Escazú & Santa Ana....95 A1
Buses to Grecia & Sarchi....96 A1
Buses to Guadalupe....97 D2
Buses to Heredia....98 D1
Buses to Jacó (Transportes Jacó)....(see 106)
Buses to Montezuma & Mal País....(see 106)
Buses to Nicaragua, Honduras & El Salvador (King Quality)....99 B1
Buses to Nicaragua, Panama, Guatemala, El Salvador & Honduras (Tica Bus)....100 E3
Buses to Nicoya, Nosara, Sámara, Santa Cruz & Tamarindo (Empresas Alfaro)....101 A1
Buses to Panama City & Managua (Panaline)....(see 93)
Buses to Playas Brasilito, Flamingo, Hermosa & Panamá (Tralapa)....102 A1
Buses to Quepos/Manuel Antonio (Transportes Morales)....(see 106)
Buses to Volcán Irazú....103 D3
Enersol Gas Station....104 B4
Gas Station....105 B2
Terminal Coca-Cola....106 A2

concrete plaza is architecturally dull, but it has recently received a needed cleaning and some of its elevated terraces provide decent views of the mountains surrounding San José (especially at sunset). On its western flank is an open-air crafts market (see p96).

MUSEO DE ARTE Y DISEÑO CONTEMPORÁNEO

Commonly referred to as MADC, the **Contemporary Art and Design Museum** (Map p74; ☎ 2257-7202; www.madc.ac.cr; Av 3 btwn Calles 13 & 15; admission US$3; ⏲ 9am-4:45pm Mon-Sat) is housed in the historic National Liquor Factory building, which dates from 1856. The largest and most important contemporary art museum in the region, MADC is focused on showing the works of contemporary Costa Rican, Central American and South American artists and occasionally features temporary exhibits devoted to interior design, fashion and graphic art.

MUSEO DE JADE

You will find the world's largest collection of American jade (pronounced '*ha*-day' in Spanish) at this small **museum** (Map p74; ☎ 2287-6034; 1st fl, Edificio INS, Av 7 btwn Calles 9 & 11; admission adult/child under 11yr US$7/free; ⏲ 8:30am-3:30pm Mon-Fri, 9am-1pm Sat) on the 1st floor of the Instituto Nacional de Seguros (INS; National Insurance Institute). The pieces are varied: expect to see display cases cluttered with translucent jade carvings that depict fertility goddesses, shamans, frogs and snakes, as well as some incredible pottery (some of which reflects Maya influences), including a highly unusual ceramic head displaying a row of serrated teeth. The craftsmanship is generally excellent and pieces are in a fine state of conservation.

PARQUE ESPAÑA & PARQUE MORAZÁN

Surrounded by heavy traffic and flanked by MADC and the Museo de Jade, the **Parque España** (Map p74; Avs 3 & 7 btwn Calles 9 & 11) may be small, but it becomes a riot of birdsong every day at sunset when the local avian population comes in to roost. In addition to being a good spot for a shady break, the park is home to an ornate statue of Christopher Columbus that was given to the people of Costa Rica in 2002 by his descendants, commemorating the quincentennial of the explorer's landing in Puerto Limón.

To its west stands the recently remodeled **Edificio Metálico** (Map p74; cnr Av 7 & Calle 9), a century-old two-story metal building that was prefabricated in Belgium. The structure was shipped piece by piece to San José and today it functions as a school and local landmark. On the Parque España's northeast corner is the **Casa Amarilla** (Map p74; Av 7 btwn Calles 11 & 13), an elegant colonial-style house that is home to the ministry of foreign affairs (and is closed to the public). The glorious ceiba tree in front was planted by John F Kennedy during his 1963 visit to Costa Rica. If you walk around to the property's northeast corner, you can see a graffiti-covered slab of the Berlin Wall standing in the rear garden.

To the southwest of the Parque España is another park, the **Parque Morazán** (Map p74; Avs 3 & 5 btwn Calles 5 & 9), named for Francisco Morazán, the 19th-century general who attempted to unite the Central American nations under a single flag. Once a notorious center of prostitution, the park is now beautifully illuminated in the evenings. At its center is the **Templo de Música** (Music Temple; Map p74), a concrete bandstand that serves as an unofficial symbol of San José.

BARRIO AMÓN

North and west of the Jade Museum lies this pleasant, historic **neighborhood** (Map p70), home to a cluster of *cafetalero* (coffee grower) mansions constructed during the late 19th and early 20th centuries. In recent years, many of the area's historic buildings have been converted into hotels, restaurants and offices, making this a popular district for an architectural stroll. You'll find everything from art-deco concrete manses to brightly painted tropical Victorian structures in various states of upkeep. It is a key arts center.

On Amón's northern limit lies **TEOR/éTica** (Map p74; ☎ 2221-6971; www.teoretica.org; cnr Calle 7 & Av 11; admission by donation; ⏲ 10am-6pm Tue-Fri, 11am-6pm Sat), a contemporary art museum housed in a vintage mansion, each of its elegant rooms featuring cutting-edge works by established and emerging figures from Latin America (such as Costa Rican artist Priscilla Monge, who is well known for her wry embroideries). This young museum features the private collection of the TEOR/éTica foundation, a nonprofit organization that supports Central American art and culture. It is an important gathering spot for regional artists, who arrive to attend lectures, workshops and other events.

Just across the street is **Kiosco SJO** (Map p70; ☎ 2258-1829; www.kioscosjo.com; cnr Av 11 & Calle 7; 🕑 11am-6pm Mon, 11am-10pm Tue-Sat), a gallery and design boutique run by architect Juan Ignacio Salom that is focused on showcasing sustainable design and the work of Latin American artists and artisans. If all the browsing makes you hungry, head to the lovely onsite cafe, Kalú (p89).

On Amón's southeastern edge, the smaller yet charming **Galería Andrómeda** (Map p74; ☎ 2223-3529; andromeda@amnet.co.cr; cnr Calle 9 & Av 9; 🕑 10am-7pm Mon-Fri, 10:30am-5pm Sat) is a free local art space featuring works by emerging artists, as well as a selection of literary magazines (in Spanish), among other publications.

ZOOLÓGICO NACIONAL SIMÓN BOLÍVAR

It may seem ironic to visit a **zoo** (Map p70, ☎ 2233-6701; www.fundazoo.org; Av 11 btwn Calles 7 & 9; adult/child US$4/3; 🕑 8am-3:30pm Mon-Fri, 9am-4:30pm Sat & Sun;) in one of the most biologically rich countries in the world. But this is a popular spot with local families, who pour in on weekends to peek at the animals. It's rough around the edges – the cages are cramped and a few readers have complained of the animals' filthy living spaces – but it can serve as a basic primer on area wildlife for small children. If you have time for a day trip, a *much* better option is Zoo Ave outside Alajuela (see p127).

PARQUE NACIONAL & ENVIRONS

One of the nicest of San José's green spaces is the **Parque Nacional** (Map p70; Avs 1 & 3 btwn Calles 15 & 19), a shady spot where retirees arrive to read newspapers and young couples smooch coyly on concrete benches. At its center is the **Monumento Nacional**, a dramatic statue (erected in 1953) that depicts the Central American nations – with Costa Rica in the lead – driving out American filibuster William Walker (see boxed text, p36 for more on that episode). The park is studded with myriad monuments devoted to key figures in Latin American history, including Cuban poet, essayist and revolutionary José Martí, Mexican independence figure Miguel Hidalgo and 18th-century Venezuelan poet and thinker Andrés Bello.

Across the street, to the south, stands the **Asamblea Legislativa** (Legislative Assembly), which also bears an important statue: this one a depiction of Juan Santamaría – the young man who helped kick the pesky Walker out of Costa Rica – in full flame-throwing action.

Less than a block to the east is the old train station to the Atlantic, the **Estación del Ferrocarril de Costa Rica** (Map p70; Av 3 btwn Calles 17 & 23), which was built in 1908. Though the building is closed (it most recently housed a children's museum), it's nonetheless a remarkable example of tropical architecture (and a good photo op), with swirling art nouveau–inspired beams and elaborate stonework all along the roofline.

One block to the west of the park, is **Jacob Karpio Galería** (Map p74; ☎ 2257-7963; Av 1 btwn Calles 11 & 15; 🕑 10am-5pm Mon-Fri), the city's preeminent gallery, featuring established contemporary artists from around the region, including Priscilla Monge.

Central San José West

PARQUE CENTRAL AREA

The city's **central park** (Map p74; Avs 2 & 4 btwn Calles Central & 2) is more of a run-down plaza than a park. At its center is a grandiose bandstand that looks as if it was designed by Mussolini:

WORD ON THE STREET

Alfonso Peña is a born-and-bred *josefino* who edits the literary magazine *Matérika* (www.materika.org) and helps manage Galería Andrómeda in Barrio Amón (above).

What makes San José a compelling cultural center? Naturally, the city has incredible museums, such as the Museo de Arte y Diseño Contemporáneo (opposite), the Teatro Nacional (p73), the Galería Nacional (p78), and TEOR/éTica (opposite). But it goes beyond that. I've been a writer for 25 years and I'm constantly observing things. And San José is a city that wherever you go, there's something to see, from the architecture to the people on the street. Every visitor should consider it an absolute necessity to take a stroll through Barrio Amón. It's got these little streets that are full of magic. It's the oldest part of the city – there are houses here from the 19th century – and it's where much of our cultural life has taken place. This is where Costa Rican writers have tangled with issues like eroticism and crime and esoteric themes. There's so much to discover here. You just have to be willing to look for it.

massive concrete arches support a florid roof capped with a ball-shaped decorative knob.

To the east of the park is the Renaissance-style **Catedral Metropolitana** (Map p74; Avs 2 & 4 btwn Calles Central & 1), built in 1871, after the previous cathedral was destroyed in an earthquake. The interiors, in keeping with the period, are graceful neoclassic, with colorful Spanish tile floors, stained-glass windows, and a Christ figure (near the main entrance) that was produced by a Guatemalan workshop in the late 17th century. On the north side of the nave, along the passage to the Capilla del Santisímo (Chapel of the Holy One), a recumbent Christ that dates back to 1878 draws devout Ticos, who arrive here to pray and deposit pleas scribbled on small slips of paper.

On the north side of the park is the **Teatro Melico Salazar** (Map p74; Av 2 btwn Calles Central & 2), which was built in 1928 in a beaux-arts style. It is named after the well-known Costa Rican tenor Melico Salazar (1887–1950), who performed internationally (among other places, he sang at the Metropolitan Opera in New York City). The theater was the site of the 2002 presidential inauguration, and regularly hosts fine arts engagements (see p94).

MUSEO POSTAL, TELEGRÁFICO Y FILATÉLICO DE COSTA RICA

A few blocks north of the Parque Central, the diminutive **postal museum** (Map p74; ☎ 2223-6918; 2nd fl, Correo Central, Calle 2 btwn Avs 1 & 3; admission US$0.50; 8am-5pm Mon-Fri) has a small exhibit of Costa Rican stamps (including one that commemorates John F Kennedy's 1963 visit). It's a good way to kill time if your friends are waiting in line to mail letters home.

MERCADOS (MARKETS)

Though *josefinos* mainly do their shopping at chain supermarkets, San José's crowded indoor markets retain an old-world feel. The main market is the **Mercado Central** (Map p74; Avs Central & 1 btwn Calles 6 & 8; 6am-6pm Mon-Sat), lined with vendors hawking everything from cheese and spices to coffee beans and obligatory *pura vida* souvenir T-shirts. One block to the north is the **Mercado Central Annex** (Map p74; Avs 1 & 3 btwn Calles 6 & 8), which is less touristy, crowded with butchers, fishmongers and informal counters dishing out typical Costa Rican *casados* (a set meal of rice, beans and cabbage slaw served with chicken, fish or meat). To the northwest is the similar **Mercado Borbón** (Map p74; cnr Av 3 & Calle 8), which is more focused on produce – though all three markets sell a bit of everything. (Be aware: the streets get sketchy around the Borbón.)

Central San José North

MUSEO DE LOS NIÑOS & GALERÍA NACIONAL

If you were wondering how to get your young kids interested in art and science, this unusual **museum** (Map p70; ☎ 2258-4929; www.museocr.com; Calle 4, north of Av 9; adult/child US$2/1.50; 8am-4:30pm Tue-Fri, 9am-5pm Sat & Sun;) – actually two museums in one – is an excellent place to start. Housed in an old penitentiary built in 1909, it is part children's museum and part art gallery. Small children will love the hands-on exhibits related to science, geography and natural history, while grown-ups will enjoy the unusual juxtaposition of contemporary art in abandoned prison cells.

SPIROGYRA JARDÍN DE MARIPOSAS

Another great spot for kids is this small **butterfly garden** (Map p70; ☎ 2222-2937; www.infocostarica.com/butterfly; adult/child US$7/3; 8am-4pm;), which houses more than 30 species of butterfly – including the luminescent blue morpho – in plant-filled enclosures. Visit in the morning to see plenty of fluttering. An airy new cafe serves fresh juices, sandwiches and salads. The garden is 150m east and 150m south of Centro Comercial El Pueblo, which can be reached on foot (about a 20- to 30-minute walk from downtown), by taxi, or by bus to El Pueblo, where there is a sign.

La Sabana

West of downtown, the bustle of the city's congested center gives way to private homes, condo towers and shopping areas chock-full of Ticos. At the heart of this district lies the sprawling Parque Metropolitano La Sabana, a popular recreation center – and a welcome patch of green amid the concrete of the capital.

At the time of writing, many of the park's installations were undergoing needed remodeling.

PARQUE METROPOLITANO LA SABANA

Known simply as **Parque La Sabana** (Map p79), this 72-hectare green space at the west end of the Paseo Colón was once the site of the country's main airport. Today it is home to two museums, a lagoon, a fountain and a va-

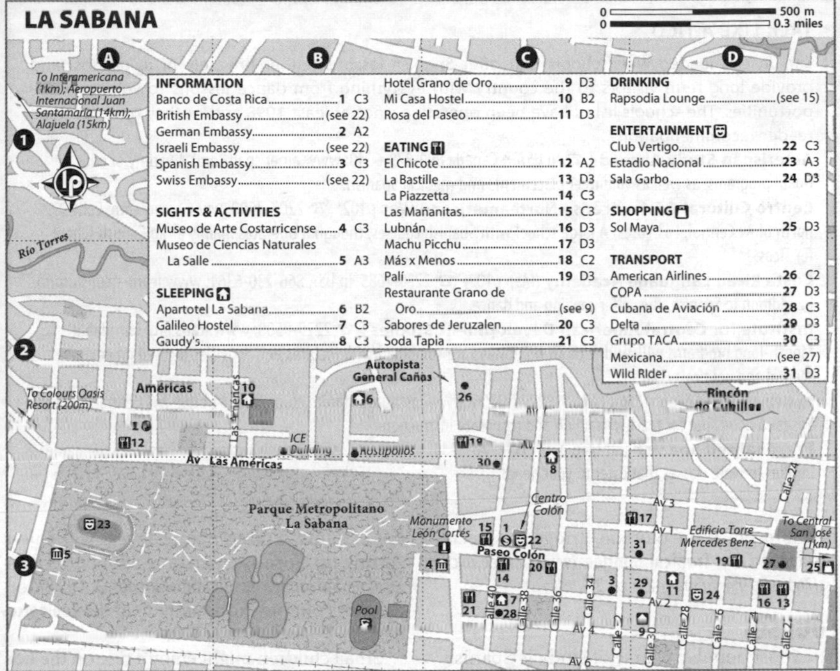

riety of sports facilities. It is also home to the Estadio Nacional (National Stadium), where international and Division 1 soccer matches are played (it will soon be replaced by a bigger stadium that, at the time of writing, was under construction in the northwest corner of the park). During the day, it's a great place for a stroll, a picnic or a relaxed jog. On weekends, it is packed with picnicking families and kids playing ball.

At the eastern entrance to the park is the **Museo de Arte Costarricense** (Map p79; ☎ 2256-1281; www.musarco.go.cr; Parque La Sabana), in a Spanish-style structure that served as San José's main airport terminal until 1955. In the midst of a top-to-bottom remodel (reopening in late 2010), the museum features regional art and other exhibits.

On the other end of the park, near the southwest corner, is the **Museo de Ciencias Naturales La Salle** (Map p79; ☎ 2232-1306; adult/child US$2/1.50; 8am-4pm Mon-Sat, 9am-5pm Sun;), which has an extensive collection of dusty stuffed animals and minerals. The exhibit has definitely seen better days, and although some of the animals look like they're about to disintegrate, you'd be hard pressed to find a more bizarre display of taxidermy. It's in the old Colegio La Salle (high school).

ACTIVITIES

Parque Metropolitano La Sabana (Map p79; ☎ 2284-8700) has a variety of sporting facilities, including tennis courts, volleyball, basketball and baseball areas, jogging paths and soccer pitches. Pickup soccer games can be had on most days, though you'd better be good: Ticos can sink a drop shot by age seven. There is also an Olympic-sized **swimming pool** for serious lap swimmers (again, call ahead – it was under construction in 2010). If you want to swim with the kiddies and your hotel doesn't have a pool, head to the Ojo de Agua springs in San Antonio de Belén, a popular swim spot for Tico families (see p118).

Golfers can hit the greens at the **Parque Valle del Sol** (Map p68; ☎ 2282-9222, ext 218/9; www.vallesol.com; 1.7km west of HSBC Bank, Santa Ana; 18 holes with a cart per person US$94; 6:30am-6pm Tue-Sun, 8am-6pm Mon) in the nearby suburb of Santa Ana, while adrenaline junkies can opt to take the plunge with one of the daily bungee jumps off

TALK LIKE A TICO

San José is loaded with schools that offer Spanish lessons (either privately or in groups) and provide long-term visitors to the country with everything from dance lessons to volunteer opportunities. The schools listed have been operating since at least 1998 and/or they have received reader recommendations.

Amerispan Study Abroad (☎ in USA & Canada 800-879-6640; www.amerispan.com) A variety of educational programs, as well as volunteer placements and medical Spanish.

Centro Cultural Costarricense Norteamericano (Map p102; ☎ 2207-7500; www.cccncr.com; Calle 37, north of Av Central, Los Yoses) A large school with Spanish courses, though it operates mainly as an English school for Ticos.

Costa Rican Language Academy (Map p102; ☎ 2280-1685, in USA 866-230-6361; www.learn-spanish.com) In addition to Spanish, they offer cooking and dance.

Institute for Central American Development Studies (☎ 2225-0508; www.icads.org; Curridabat) Month-long programs with and without homestays are combined with lectures and activities focused on environmental and politicals issues.

Instituto Británico (Map p102; ☎ 2225-0256; www.institutobritanico.co.cr; Calle 41 btwn Avs Central & 8, Los Yoses) A good spot for teacher-training and corporate instruction.

Personalized Spanish (off Map p68; ☎ 2278-3254; www.personalizedspanish.com; Tres Ríos) Like the name implies, private classes that cater to your needs.

the 80m-tall Río Colorado Bridge in Grecia organized by **Tropical Bungee** (www.bungee.co.cr; 1st/2nd jump US$65/30) – see p128.

COURSES

The most popular course of study is Spanish (see boxed text, above). While many of these academies can arrange cooking and dance lessons, you can improve your dance moves on your own at **Merecumbé** (www.merecumbe.net), a chain of studios that will get you grooving to everything from salsa to waltz. Most courses are for locals, but some sessions are geared at foreign travelers. Schedules vary; call ahead.

The company has various studios, though, unfortunately, nothing in downtown. See these nearby locations:

Merecumbé Escazú (Map p106; ☎ 2289-4774, 8884-7553; cnr Av 3 & Calle Cortés, Escazú)

Merecumbé Guadalupe (☎ 2234-7000; Centro Comercial Uniplaza, Guadalupe)

Merecumbé San Pedro (☎ 2224-3531; 100m south & 25m west of the Banco Popular, San Pedro)

SAN JOSÉ FOR CHILDREN

Chances are that if you're in Costa Rica on a short vacation you'll be headed out to the countryside fairly quickly. But if for some reason you're going to be hanging out for a day – or two or three – with your kids, here are a few activities to keep them busy.

The **Museo de los Niños** (p78) is a hit with children who just can't keep their hands off the exhibits. Young nature-lovers will enjoy getting up close and personal with butterflies at the **Spirogyra Jardín de Mariposas** (p78) or checking out the exotic animals at the **Zoológico Nacional Simón Bolívar** (p77).

Small children might enjoy a ride on the **Tico Train** (Map p74; adult/child US$2/1; ⌚ Sunday only), which picks up passengers from the eastern side of the Plaza de la Cultura and takes them on a 45-minute joyride through the city. The train itself looks like it was stolen from an American carnival, though the *cumbia* music emanating from the train's speakers is about as Central American as it gets.

Teens might dig checking each other out at the **Plaza de la Cultura** (p73), which has a number of nearby fast-food outlets and ice-cream shops. In the suburbs, **Mall San Pedro** (p105) and the sprawling **Multiplaza Escazú** (p112) are good for young consumers craving serious mall action.

If you're planning on spending more than a week in the city, note that many Spanish language academies offer special custom-made lessons for teens (see boxed text, above). In addition, both the **Teatro Eugene O'Neill** (p105) and **Teatro Fanal** (p94) have children's theater groups. If your child is learning Spanish, this experience might make a vivid lesson.

TOURS

The city is small and easily navigable, but if you're looking for a walking tour that will guide you to key sites, here are some recommendations:

Costa Rica Art Tour (☎ 2288-0896, 8359-5571; www.costaricaarttour.com; per person US$95) This small outfit run by Molly Keeler organizes a recommended day tour that visits five different artist studios, where you can view (and buy) the work of local painters, sculptors, printmakers, ceramicists and jewelers. Lunch and hotel pickup is included in the price. Reserve at least one week in advance.

Swiss Travel Service (Map p70; ☎ 2221-0944; www.swisstravelcr.com) This long-standing agency offers a three-hour walking tour of San José that hits all the key sites. Their offices are inside the Radisson Europa, 250m west of Centro Comercial El Pueblo.

TAM Travel (Map p102; ☎ 2527-9700; www.tamtravel.com; Los Yoses Travel Center, Calle 39 btwn Avs Central & 8; per person US$35) This reputable agency organizes half-day walking tours of the city, along with travel throughout Costa Rica.

For a directory of specialty tours beyond San José, see p524.

FESTIVALS & EVENTS

Festival de Arte Every even year, San José becomes host to the biennial citywide arts showcase that features theater, music, dance and film. It's held for two weeks in March. Keep an eye out for information in the daily newspapers.

Día de San José (St Joseph's Day; March 19) San José marks the day of its patron saint with mass in some churches.

Festival de las Carretas (Oxcart Festival) Takes place every November, and is a celebration of the country's agricultural heritage. The highlight is a parade of oxcarts down Paseo Colón.

Festival de Luz (Festival of Light) A month after Paseo Colón's oxcart parade is the Christmas parade, marked by an absurd amount of plastic 'snow.'

Las Fiestas de Zapote (December 25 to January 1) If you're in the San José area between Christmas and New

SAN JOSÉ IN…

One Day

Start at the city's most beautiful building, the graceful **Teatro Nacional** (p73), a theater that dates back to the 19th century. Take time to enjoy a sip of espresso and a pastry at the theater's atmospheric **cafe** (p89) before heading around to the east side of the **Plaza de la Cultura** (p73) and ducking in to the **Museo de Oro Precolombino y Numismática** (p73), which catalogues the country's pre-Columbian gold treasures. From here, stroll northeast through the **Parque Morazán** (p76) to the **Museo de Arte y Diseño Contemporáneo** (p76), Central America's most prominent contemporary arts institution.

Snack at one of the area's pleasant terrace eateries, such as **Café Mundo** (p89) or **Kalú** (p89). Afterwards, stroll through historic **Barrio Amón** (p76), browsing shops such as **Kiosco SJO** (p95), **Galería Namu** (p95) and **eÑe** (p95). For the evening happy hour, circle back to the Parque Morazán for a cocktail at **El Morazán** (p92), a historic bar with park views.

Two Days

On your second day in town, get a primer on Costa Rican history at the **Museo Nacional** (p73) and explore the neighboring **Mercado Artesanal** (p96) for crafts. From here, head west on bustling Av Central to the **Catedral Metropolitana** (p78), where Ticos still pack the pews for daily mass. Afterward head northwest to the **Mercado Central** (p78), where you can shop for T-shirts and Costa Rican coffee. If you like to eat cheap, this is an ideal spot for lunch.

In the evening, head east to Los Yoses and San Pedro, where you will find some of San José's best neighborhood eateries (p103) and bars (p104), as well as the city's most esteemed venue for live music, the **Jazz Café** (p105).

Three Days

If you are ready for a day trip out of town, consider a pilgrimage to the historic **Basílica de Nuestra Señora de los Ángeles** in Cartago (p138), where the penitent arrive on their knees or arrange for a tour of the coffee farms that surround the idyllic mountain village of **Orosi** (p142). If you're feeling adventurous, you can try a day-long river-running trip in the vicinity of **Turrialba** (see boxed text, p148) or peek into the craters of the **Poás** (p124) or **Irazú** (p140) volcanoes. Families with small children will enjoy an excursion on the **Rainforest Aerial Tram** (p445), which glides along lush cloud-forest canopy within sight of birds and monkeys.

Year's Eve, you absolutely have to visit this week-long holiday celebration of all things Costa Rican (namely rodeos, cowboys, carnival rides, fried food and a whole lot of drinking). The celebration, which annually draws in tens of thousands of Ticos, takes place at the bullring in the suburb of Zapote, just southeast of the city.

SLEEPING

Accommodations in San José run the gamut from grim little boxes to sumptuous luxury. You'll find the cheapest sleeps in the city center, with nicer midrange and top-end spots clustered in more well-to-do districts such as Barrio Amón and La Sabana. Also worthwhile for their charm, safety and serenity are the adjacent neighborhoods of Los Yoses and San Pedro (p101), which lie within walking distance from downtown.

For tonier options, the upscale suburb of Escazú (p108) – a 20-minute bus ride away – is a good choice. If you're flying into or out of Costa Rica, it may be more convenient to stay in Alajuela (p119), as the town is minutes from the international airport.

Reservations are recommended in the high season (December through April), in particular the two weeks around Christmas and Semana Santa (Holy Week, the week preceding Easter). Before reserving with a credit card, see boxed text, p525. For general information on hotels in Costa Rica, see p523.

Hostels

The city overflows with hostels geared at backpackers. Keep in mind that the arrangements at these spots are basic: you'll have a bunk and access to a shared bathroom, but plan on bringing amenities such as soap, shampoo and towels. Many places, however, are equipped with 21st-century goodies like wi-fi and TV lounges. Many hostels also have affordable private rooms. All hotels listed below have hot-water showers.

For ease of use, all of San José's hostels we've covered are listed here, regardless of the part of town they're in. For some excellent alternatives, see the Los Yoses district (p101).

Galileo Hostel (Map p79; ☎ 2248-2094; www.hostelgalileo.com; cnr Calle 40 & Av 2; dm US$9-10, s without bathroom US$22, d US$30, d without bathroom US$24-26; 💻 📶) In a vintage house east of Parque La Sabana, this snug little hostel has several dormitories and half a dozen private rooms of various sizes. The freshly painted dorms are tight (it's bunk to bunk), but the rooms are clean and the prices the cheapest in town. There is free wi-fi, a communal kitchen, a small garden patio and an onsite bar, where you can sip Pilsens and watch the game. The best part: the laid-back American owners host Sunday BBQs during football season.

Costa Rica Backpackers (Map p70; ☎ 2221-6191; www.costaricabackpackers.com; Av 6 btwn Calles 21 & 23; dm US$12, d without bathroom US$28; 🅿 💻 📶 🏊) About a block east of the Supreme Court complex, this extremely popular hostel has 15 dormitories and 13 private double rooms spread out over several structures that surround a nice garden with hammocks and a free-form pool. Chill-out music completes the laid-back ambience, though you can always take things up a notch in the attached bar-restaurant, which serves breakfast (₡1800 to ₡2500) and other basic meals (*casados* ₡3000). Rooms and shared bathrooms are basic but clean, and decorated with tropical-themed murals. There is a communal kitchen and TV lounge, as well as free luggage storage and internet access.

Gaudy's (Map p79; ☎ 2258-2937, 2248-0086; www.backpacker.co.cr; Av 5 btwn Calles 36 & 38; dm US$12, d with/without bathroom US$30/26; 💻 📶) You'll find this homey hostel inside a sprawling modernist house in a residential area east of Parque La Sabana. Popular among shoestring travelers for years, it has 13 private rooms and two dormitories. The Colombian owners keep the design scheme basic and the vibe mellow, but the service is professional and the rooms well maintained. There's a communal kitchen, TV lounge, pool table and foosball, a courtyard strung with hammocks, as well as free internet. Find it 200m north and 150m east of the Banco de Costa Rica.

Hostel Casa del Parque (Map p70; ☎ 2233-3437; www.hostelcasadelparque.com; cnr Calle 19 & Av 3; dm US$12, d with/without bathroom US$40/30; 📶) A vintage art-deco manse from 1936 houses this quiet spot on the eastern edge of the Parque Nacional. Six large, basic private rooms and one dormitory have parquet floors and simple furnishings, while a private double features a vintage '30s boudoir. A somewhat bare upstairs roof deck has nice city views, and there is a shared kitchen and free wi-fi. The bilingual young owner, Federico Echeverría, is a good source of local dining information.

our pick **Hostel Pangea** (Map p74; ☎ 2221-1992; www.hostelpangea.com; Av 7 btwn Calles 3 & 3bis; dm US$12, d with/without bathroom US$35/30, presidential ste US$60; 🅿 💻 📶 🏊) This industrial-strength,

Tico-owned hostel – 25 dorms and 25 private rooms – has been a popular twenty-something backpacker hangout in San José for years. It's not difficult to see why: it's smack in the middle of the city and comes stocked with a pool, a rooftop restaurant-lounge with stellar views and a combination bar–movie theater furnished with beanbags and a stripper pole. Needless to say, this is a party spot. But the rooms are clean, the mattresses firm and the shared bathrooms freshly remodeled. The hostel's two new 'presidential suites' have dreamy views and flat-screen TVs. Plus, there is free internet, free phone calls to North America and the bilingual staff can help you arrange luggage storage, onward travel within Costa Rica as well as airport pickup and drop-off in their private van (from US$9). Of all the amenities, it is the restaurant, in particular, that is a godsend – open until midnight, it serves lip-smacking quesadillas, veggie burritos and what has to be San José's tastiest burgers (₡2200 to ₡3300).

Kabata Hostel (Map p74; ☎ 2255-0355/3264; www.kabatahostel.com; Calle 7 btwn Avs 9 & 11; dm US$12, d without bathroom US$32, all incl breakfast; P 💻 📶) Run by a a Tico family that lives onsite, this modern, no-frills spot in Barrio Amón has its lobby-lounge painted in bright colors. Small, carpeted rooms are basic but clean and share a couple of roomy bathrooms. There is a small shared kitchen and free wi-fi. The helpful bilingual owners also organize adventure tours all over Costa Rica.

Green House Hostel (off Map p70; ☎ 2258-0102; www.greenhousehostel.altervista.org; Calle 11 btwn Avs 16 & 18; dm with bathroom US$13, s/d/tr US$21/32/43; P 📶) This attractive hostel is adorned with hanging plants, historic photographs and antiques. The rooms themselves are a bit modest, though the perk here is that they all have private bathrooms (even the dorms). There is a TV lounge, a small bar that sells beer and a communal kitchen. It's a bit pricey compared with other hostels, and it's somewhat inconveniently located in Plaza Víquez, which isn't the nicest of neighborhoods, but the charming owners make a stay worthwhile.

Mi Casa Hostel (Map p79; ☎ 2231-4700; www.micasahostel.com; dm US$12, r with/without bathroom US$30/28, all incl breakfast; P 💻 📶 ♿) A converted modernist home in La Sabana has polished wood floors, vintage furnishings and half a dozen eclectic guest rooms to choose from (two of which are dormitories). One room is wheelchair-accessible. Mellow communal areas are comfortably furnished, and the shared kitchen is clean and roomy. There is a pleasant garden, where a tiny bar stocks cold beer for guests, and other perks include a pool table, free internet, and laundry service (₡5500). Find it 50m west and 150m north of the ICE building.

Central San José East

Most of downtown's better sleeping options are located east of Calle Central, many of them in historic Victorian and art-deco mansions.

BUDGET

Pensión de la Cuesta (Map p74; ☎ 2256-7946; www.pensiondelacuesta.com; Av 1 btwn Calles 11 & 15; dm US$10, s/d/tr/q without bathroom incl breakfast US$20/28/30/40, d apt US$40; 📶) Situated on a hill behind the Asamblea Legislativa is this 1920s wooden house, whose exterior looks as if it was painted by Ken and Barbie. It's a ramshackle spot, with 14 dim rooms (with shared bathrooms), most of which are painted an institutional shade of turquoise. However, it is cheap and generally clean, and the sunny lounge is a good spot to read or watch TV. There is also a small, basic two-person apartment equipped with kitchenette.

Casa Ridgway (Map p74; ☎ 2222 1400, 2233-6168, www.amigosparalapaz.org; cnr Calle 15 & Av 6bis; dm US$14, s/d US$22/34, without bathroom US$16/30; P 🚭 📶) A small, welcoming guesthouse, on a quiet side street near the Supreme Court complex is run by the adjacent Friends' Peace Center, a Quaker organization that promotes social justice and human rights. The rooms are immaculate, as are the shared showers and communal kitchen – and the atmosphere is, well,

HOMESTAYS

Bell's Home Hospitality (☎ 2225-4752; www.homestay-thebells.org; s/d/tr incl breakfast US$30/50/75) This recommended agency is run by the bilingual Marcela Bell, who has operated the business for more than 20 years. She can arrange stays in more than a dozen homes around San José, each of which has been personally inspected. All are close to public transportation and readers have sent only positive comments about these places. Note that there is a US$5 surcharge for one-night-only stays; dinner is available at an extra cost.

peaceful. There is a small lounge and a lending library offers an extensive collection of books on Central American politics and society. This isn't the place for party people – no smoking or alcohol is allowed and quiet hours are from 10pm to 6am.

Casa Hilda (Map p70; ☎ 2221-0037; c1hilda@racsa.co.cr; Av 11 btwn Calles 3 & 3bis; s/d/tr US$20/30/45) Run by the charming Quesada family, this simple peach-colored guesthouse has five basic, clean rooms with private bathrooms surrounding a peaceful courtyard. Check out the natural spring in the center of the house that has been bubbling potable water for more than 90 years (even during dry season). Credit cards accepted.

our pick **Hotel Aranjuez** (Map p70; ☎ 2256-1825; www.hotelaranjuez.com; Calle 19 btwn Avs 11 & 13; s/d/tr from US$29/42/49, s/d without bathroom US$22/25, all incl breakfast; P) This rambling hotel in Barrio Aranjuez consists of several nicely maintained vintage homes that have been strung together with connecting gardens. The 35 spotless rooms come in a variety of configurations, and the private ones are equipped with lockboxes and cable TV. The hotel's best attribute, however, is the lush garden patio, where a heaping breakfast buffet is served every morning (don't miss the omelet bar). Though the architecture can be a bit creaky and the walls thin, the service is efficient and the hotel is a solid, family-friendly, budget option. Credit cards accepted.

Cinco Hormigas Rojas (Map p70; ☎ 2255-3412; www.cincohormigasrojas.com; Calle 15 btwn Avs 9 & 11; r incl breakfast US$30-58;) A one-of-a-kind B&B that is a riot of plants – literally, you have to walk through a tunnel of branches just to get to the front door – as well as a riot of everything else. Every nook and cranny of this snug, four-room inn features a piece of art or embellishments crafted out of papier-mâché (not to be missed: the Frida Kahlo altar and the papier-mâché toilet). All of it is the vision of multilingual hippie chick Mayra Güell, who – in addition to being terrifically friendly – treats her guests to daily breakfasts featuring macrobiotic breads, fresh jams and juices and organic coffee. Art is available for purchase, and every traveler leaves with a small handmade gift.

Casa Alfi (Map p74; ☎ 2233-1805, 8866-0572; www.casaalfihotel.com; Calle 3 btwn Avs 4 & 6; s/d/tr incl breakfast US$30/40/50;) Steps from the Teatro Nacional, a simple two-story structure surrounds a bright covered courtyard, around which nine guest rooms are located. The rooms (which vary in size and layout) are simple but come equipped with TV, telephone, private bathroom and lockbox, and feature folk-art touches. It's a sleepy spot, despite being in the middle of the downtown hubbub. Credit cards accepted.

Costa Rica Guesthouse (Map p70; ☎ 2223-7034; www.costa-rica-guesthouse.com; Av 6 btwn Calles 21 & 23; d with/without bathroom US$45/35; P) In a house dating from 1904, this recent addition to the San José budget scene (it opened in 2009) has simple, graceful rooms with spacious bathrooms and hallways lined with Spanish tiles. Furnishings are basic (the beds are creaky), but it's a tranquil, couples-friendly spot – operated by the owners of Costa Rica Backpackers, which lies across the street (guests of the hotel are welcome to use the swimming pool at the hostel). There's a small internet lounge and there are plans to open a small onsite restaurant.

MIDRANGE

our pick **Kaps Place** (Map p70; ☎ 2221-1169; www.kapsplace.com; Calle 19 btwn Avs 11 & 13, Av 11 btwn Calles 19 & 21; s US$25-40, d US$50-60, tr US$70, apt US$80-115, all incl breakfast; P) A colorful little guesthouse on a residential street in Barrio Aranjuez, Kaps has 24 small, homey rooms of various configurations spread over two buildings. Run by Karla Arias, this is decidedly a family place: expect to see kids playing in the yucca plant–filled courtyard or hopping on the trampoline. Also, the guesthouse staff can arrange babysitting upon request. Patios are strung with hammocks and the public areas are wonderfully decorated in bright mosaics. There is free internet and Spanish, English and French are spoken.

Hotel Doña Inés (Map p74; ☎ 2222-7443/553; www.donaines.com; Calle 11 btwn Avs 2 & 6; s/d/tr incl breakfast US$45/55/70;) This friendly, frayed-at-the-edges hotel near the Supreme Court has 20 small, carpeted rooms that surround a small but pleasant courtyard. The atmosphere is all Spanish colonial, with vintage-style furnishings to set the mood. Rooms are set back from the street, so it's reasonably quiet; airier upstairs units are the better bet. The staff speak English, Spanish and Italian. Credit cards accepted.

Hotel Posada del Museo (Map p70; ☎ 2258-1027; www.hotelposadadelmuseo.com; cnr Calle 17 & Av 2; s US$52-

86, d US$63-86;) This *posada* (country-style inn) is at a diagonal from the Museo Nacional, in a 1928 structure with a dramatic entrance that features a Juliet balcony overlooking the foyer. French doors line the entrances to each of the rooms (no two of which are alike), which are all named after Costa Rican birds and flowers. Some rooms accommodate up to four people, making this a good spot for families. Plus, there is no charge for children under 10. The amiable Argentine managers speak English, Spanish, French and Italian. Note to light sleepers: the hotel's proximity to the train tracks can mean you'll hear some early morning hooting when the trains barrel through. Credit cards accepted.

Hotel Colonial (Map p74; 2223-0109; www.hotelcolonialcr.com; Calle 11 btwn Avs 2 & 6; s/d/ste US$52/64/102;) Guests at this 1940s Spanish-style inn near the Supreme Court complex are greeted by an intricately carved baroque-style carriage door and an arched poolside promenade. The 17 rooms are either whitewashed or painted an earthy shade of mustard yellow, with dark wood furnishings and bright bedspreads. Those on higher floors have sweeping views of the city and outlying mountains, while three of the ground-level rooms are wheelchair-accessible. Credit cards accepted.

Rincón de San José (Map p74; 2221-9702; www.hotelrincondesanjose.com; Av 9 btwn Calles 13 & 15; s/d/tr/q incl breakfast US$52/66/84/100;) Centered on three colonial-style houses in Barrio Amón, this tidy spot, popular with couples and families, has 40 guest rooms – some of which are modern with bright linens and ceramic tile, while others are equipped with period-style pieces and polished wood floors. There is an attractive interior garden courtyard where breakfast is served. Laundry service and luggage storage are available, and credit cards are accepted.

Casa Morazán (Map p74; 2257-4187; www.casamorazan.com; cnr Calle 7 & Av 9; s/d incl breakfast US$55/65;) This art-deco house in Barrio Amón was built in the 1930s as the residence of John Keith, the cousin of Minor Keith, the famous banana baron who helped construct the Atlantic railroad. It is fully furnished in period-style pieces and bathrooms are well appointed, with bathtubs and bidets.

Hotel Kekoldi (Map p74; 2248-0804; www.kekoldi.com; Av 9 btwn Calles 5 & 7; s/d/tr from US$57/69/79;) The Kekoldi is set in an airy art-deco building in Barrio Amón that has 10 expansive, light-drenched rooms of various sizes, painted in light shades of pastel and equipped with cable TV. Murals of beach landscapes adorn the common areas and there is a garden for lounging. A relaxed spot, the hotel is gay-friendly and English and German and are spoken. Credit cards accepted.

Hotel Don Carlos (Map p74; 2221-6707; www.doncarloshotel.com; Calle 9 btwn Avs 7 & 9; s/d US$65/75, s/d deluxe US$75/85, all incl breakfast;) Built around an early 20th-century house that once belonged to President Tomás Guardia, this lovely Barrio Amón inn exudes a colonial-era vibe. Thirty-three rooms in various sizes, configurations and decor are nestled around a pre-Columbian–themed sculpture garden with a sundeck, tables and a small swimming pool (ideal for kids). All rooms come equipped with cable TV, lockbox and hair dryer. Don't miss the Spanish-tile mural, just outside the onsite restaurant, which beautifully depicts central San José in the 1930s. Rates include a welcome cocktail; credit cards are accepted.

Hotel Santo Tomás (Map p74; 2255-0448; www.hotelsantotomas.com; Av 7 btwn Calles 3 & 5; d incl breakfast US$80-120;) This stately early 20th-century colonial-style mansion is a Barrio Amón landmark that once belonged to the Salazar family of *cafetaleros*. There are 30 rooms of varying sizes, some of which are located within the mansion itself (expect slightly frayed accommodations, with high ceilings and period furnishings), while others occupy a recent addition in the back. These newer rooms are the best: equipped with brocaded bedspreads, modern bathroom, balcony and flat-screen TV. There is a garden courtyard with a solarium, swimming pool, a Jacuzzi and a small open-air gym. English is spoken; the hotel is also gay-friendly.

Fleur de Lys Hotel (Map p74; 2223-1206; www.hotelfleurdelys.com; Calle 13 btwn Avs 2 & 6; s/d US$82/93, junior ste/master ste US$110/127, all incl breakfast;) A pristinely maintained century-old Victorian mansion painted a bright shade of lavender houses 30 spotless wood-paneled rooms with firm beds, ceiling fans and wicker furnishings. There is a small onsite bar that hosts a daily happy hour – and, on special occasions, there is live music. The staff is attentive and the location central (note the proximity of the train tracks). Credit cards accepted.

Raya Vida Villa (Map p70; 2223-4168; www.rayavida.com; Calle 15, off Av 11; s/d incl breakfast US$85/95, extra person US$20; P) This long-running B&B, housed in a secluded hilltop villa, reflects owner Michael Long's interest in art and antiques. The house, built in the Spanish colonial style, has a patio with a fountain, a fireplace and a small garden, while an upstairs deck is a pleasant spot with city views. Five well-appointed rooms have polished wood floors, bright floral linens and expansive bathrooms, one of which has a whirlpool tub. For the taxi driver: the hotel is 100m north of Hospital Calderón Guardia on Calle 17, then 50m west on Av 11, then another 50m north.

TOP END

All of the following hotels accept credit cards.

Hotel Villa Tournon (Map p70; ☎ 2233-6622; www.costarica-hotelvillatournon.com; 100m west of Centro Comercial El Pueblo; s/d US$95/125, s/d superior US$125/135; P) A pleasant, modern hotel has 80 simple, businesslike rooms with wood floors and cable TV, and amenities such as a swimming pool, Jacuzzi, gym and casino. Rooms facing south have nice views.

Gran Hotel Costa Rica (Map p74; ☎ 2221-4000; www.grandhotelcostarica.com; Calle 3 btwn Avs Central & 2; d standard/superior US$96/121, junior ste/ste/master ste US$168/260/283, all incl breakfast; P) The city's first prominent hotel was constructed in 1930 and is today recognized as a national landmark (John F Kennedy and soccer legend Pelé have both stayed here). Frequent renovations have kept the 104 rooms modern and comfortable, though they retain period touches such as brass bed frames and wood furnishings. Some of the units have wonderful views of the Teatro Nacional, and here and there are subtle architectural reminders of the hotel's history: exposed beams, molded ceilings and the dramatic entrance hall – lined with vintage photographs of San José. The alfresco Café Parisienne (p90) is one of the most popular tourist cafes in the city. There are two restaurants and a bar.

Another worthwhile chain option is **Clarion Hotel Amon Plaza** (Map p70; ☎ 2523-4600; www.hotelamonplaza.com; Av 11; d standard/superior from US$140/170, d ste from US$230, all incl breakfast;), with spacious, well-equipped rooms that have a formal Edwardian feel.

Central San José West

Accommodations on the western side of downtown are limited: the area is commercial and crime is an issue, especially in the streets surrounding the Coca-Cola bus terminal. However, this can be a convenient spot to stay if you're catching an early bus. After sundown, use taxis to get around.

Hotel Musoc (Map p74; ☎ 2222-9437; Calle 16 btwn Avs 1 & 3; s/d US$13/16, without bathroom US$9/11;) This large building next to the Coca-Cola terminal is a nicer option than it would appear on the outside. The linoleum-tiled rooms look institutional, but they are clean and sunny and the showers are hot. The staff speak some English.

VOLUNTEERING IN SAN JOSÉ

For travelers who want an experience beyond vacation, there are dozens of not-for-profit organizations in San José that gladly accept volunteers. The sheer number of groups means that some experiences are less than fabulous. That said, there are plenty of organizations that could use the assistance. Here are some of them:

Amerispan (☎ in USA & Canada 800-879-6640; www.amerispan.com) Manages programs devoted to everything from animal rescue to women's education. In San José, there are opportunities to work in educational settings or with the elderly.

Central American Service Expeditions (☎ 8839-0515; www.serviceexpeditions.net) A Costa Rican nonprofit that creates custom volunteer expeditions for families and teens, focused on sustainability. Around San José the group has helped build roads and day-care centers in unincorporated city slums.

GeoVisions (☎ in USA & Canada 877-949-9998; www.geovisions.org) An international nonprofit with school, hospital and orphanage-related placements.

Sustainable Horizon (☎ in USA & Canada 718-578-0420; www.sustainablehorizon.com) Arranges a wide variety of volunteer trips, including opportunities to help out at children's shelters.

United Planet (☎ in USA & Canada 800-292-2316; www.unitedplanet.org) For volunteers interested in health-, child- and elder-care fields.

Volunteer Abroad (☎ in USA & Canada 888-649-3788; www.volunteerabroad.ca) Among other options, they place volunteers in the children's hospital.

Hotel Mesón del Angel (Map p74; ☎ 2222-1997/3405; www.hotelmesondelangel.com; Calle 20 btwn Avs 1 & 3; s/d/tr/q incl breakfast US$49/59/69/79; P) A nicer, midrange option is this secure, family-owned spot, with 38 small, tidy rooms painted in warm, earthy tones. All are equipped with cable TV, lockbox and private bathroom. There is a garden in the back, making this a surprisingly charming spot for the neighborhood. A few rooms are wheelchair-accessible. Credit cards accepted.

La Sabana & Surrounds

You'll find modern inns and vintage B&Bs in the neighborhoods that surround Parque Metropolitano La Sabana.

Apartotel La Sabana (Map p79; ☎ 2220-2422, www.apartotel-lasabana.com; 150m north of Rostipollos; d/q/apt incl breakfast from US$50/72/96; P) This lovely new brick apartment complex has 32 units in various configurations that draw long-term business travelers as well as families. Rooms (with and without kitchen) are decorated in graceful, neutral tones and accented with wood furnishings and folk art, plus an interior courtyard has a nice pool. Service is attentive. Special rates are available for weekly stays; credit cards are accepted.

Rosa del Paseo (Map p79; ☎ 2257-3258; www.rosadelpaseo.com; Paseo Colón btwn Calles 28 & 30; s/d/ste from US$76/88/93; P) Though it's right on Paseo Colón, don't let the small facade fool you: this sprawling Victorian mansion (built in 1897 by the Montealegre family of coffee exporters) reaches into an interior garden courtyard that provides a respite from city noise. The hotel still maintains the original tile floors and polished wood ceilings, as well as antique oil paintings and sculptures. Rooms are simple, with polished wood floors and period-style furnishings. The garden, where breakfast is served each morning, is filled with heliconias and bougainvilleas. Credit cards accepted.

Colours Oasis Resort (off Map p79; ☎ 2296-1880, in USA 866-517-4390; www.coloursoasis.com; Blvr Rohrmoser, cnr of El Triangulo; d/ste from US$89/149;) This longtime gay and lesbian hotel in the elegant Rohrmoser district (to the northwest of La Sabana) is located in a sprawling Spanish colonial–style complex. Here, rooms and mini-apartments of various sizes and configurations have paddle fans, modern furnishings and impeccable bathrooms. Facilities include a TV lounge, minigym, pool, sundeck and Jacuzzi – as well as an onsite bar-restaurant, an ideal spot for an evening cocktail. The helpful owners speak English, French and Spanish and can offer all kinds of helpful insights on gay travel in the country. Call ahead for directions.

our pick **Hotel Grano de Oro** (Map p79; ☎ 2255-3322; www.hotelgranodeoro.com; Calle 30 btwn Avs 2 & 4; d US$115-165, f/garden/vista-del-oro ste US$175/210/305; P) In the central part of San José, Grano de Oro is a favorite of honeymooners and it's not difficult to see why. Built around a sprawling early 20th-century Victorian mansion, this elegant inn has 40 demure 'Tropical Victorian' rooms furnished with wrought-iron beds and rich brocade linens. Remodeled in 2007, eight units maintain the hotel's historic look while boasting private courtyards with gurgling fountains. The lobby is punctuated by a dramatic mahogany staircase and the public areas sparkle with fresh tropical flowers and polished wood accents. If you want to experience the Costa Rica of a gilded age, this would be the place to do it. The hotel is also home to the recommended Restaurante Grano de Oro (p91).

Cariari Area

The residential district of Cariari is located in the nether region between San José and Alajuela and is convenient if you need to stay close to the airport. The following places are best reached by private vehicle or taxi.

Cariari Bed & Breakfast (☎ 2239-2585, in USA 866-224-8339; www.cariaribb.com; Av de la Marina 12; d incl breakfast US$75-90; P) This charming B&B is run by a friendly North American named Laurie and features three guest rooms of varying sizes and amenities, including one with a private deck. There are plenty of common areas in this stunning Spanish-colonial home, including a tropical garden, a TV lounge and a roof deck.

There are also a number of top-end chain resorts, which are equipped with all manner of amenities, including golf privileges at the nearby country club:

Doubletree Cariari by Hilton (☎ 2239-0022; doubletree1.hilton.com; d/ste/2-bedroom ste from US$119/189/259; P)

Hotel Ramada Plaza Herradura (☎ 2209-9800/9841; www.ramadaherradura.com; d/ste/master ste incl breakfast from US$130/205/535; P)

Marriott San José (☎ 2298-0000, in USA & Canada 888-236-2427; www.mariott.com; d standard/d superior/

master ste from US$170/240/450; P) The best of the chain bunch.

EATING

From humble corner stands dishing out gut-filling *casados* to contemporary bistros serving fusion everything, in cosmopolitan San José you will find the country's best restaurant scene. Dedicated eaters should also check out the dining options in Los Yoses and San Pedro (p103), as well as Escazú (p110).

Top-end restaurants tend to get busy on weekend evenings; make a reservation.

Central San José East

Long-standing neighborhood *sodas* (lunch counters) mix effortlessly with contemporary cafes and Asian-fusion eateries on San José's eclectic east side.

GROCERIES

Auto Mercado (Map p74; ☎ 2233-5511; www.automercado.co.cr; cnr Calle 3 & Av 3; 7am-8pm Mon-Sat, 8am-3pm Sun) One of the better supermarkets, with a good selection of cheeses, produce, liquor, coffee and chocolate.

Perimercado (Map p74; ☎ 2222-2252; Calle 3 btwn Avs Central & 1; 7am-9pm Mon-Sat, 8am-3pm Sun) A more economical chain.

RESTAURANTS

Budget

Café Valandra (Map p74; ☎ 2248-2196; cnr Av 7 & Calle 5; sandwiches ₡400-2700; 10am-7pm Mon-Fri) This new French-run spot in Barrio Amón is a good spot for coffee – as well as a traditional French *croque monsieur* (a grilled, smoked-ham sandwich topped with melted cheese).

El Torito (Map p74; ☎ 2256-0220; Av 7 btwn Calles 7 & 9; breakfast ₡990, casados ₡3000; 7am-8pm) Within sight of the Museo de Jade, El Torito is an informal cafe-bakery stocked with sweet and savory turnovers and freshly baked breads. They also serve a short list of lunch specials (think roasted chicken with rice and beans) at comfortable prices.

Restaurante La Criollita (Map p74; ☎ 2256-6511; Av 7 btwn Calles 7 & 9; breakfast ₡1200, casados ₡3500-3600; 7am-9pm Mon-Fri, 7am-4pm Sat) A couple of doors down from El Torito is this homier local spot popular with office types, which dishes out a changing menu of simple Costa Rican specialties, such as stewed chicken or grilled fish. The setting is pleasant, the service efficient and you can accompany your meal with a glass of Chilean cabernet (₡1600).

Huarache's (off Map p70; ☎ 2239-2828; Av 22 btwn Calles 5 & 7; mains ₡1700-3000; 11am-11pm) This bustling Mexican restaurant on a nondescript block near Plaza Víquez (350m east of the Hospital de la Mujer) makes up for all the bland meals you've had in Costa Rica. Here you'll find fresh honest-to-goodness tacos, quesadillas, guacamole, tortilla soup and hot sauces that'll make you think you've died and gone to Mexico.

Vishnu (Map p74; Calle Central btwn Avs 6 & 8, cnr Av 4 & Calle 1; breakfast ₡1800, casados ₡2400-3000, mains ₡2400-5500; 8am-7pm Mon-Fri, 9am-6pm Sat & Sun; V) You'll find a rainbow of fresh local produce, vegetable stews and well-rendered soy burgers at this informal chain of vegetarian cheapies. Most folks pile in for the inexpensive lunch specials, which generally include salad, fresh juice and dessert. There are vegan specialties as well.

Restaurante Shakti (Map p74; ☎ 2222-4475; cnr Av 8 & Calle 13; mains ₡2200-4500, casados ₡2700; 7:30am-7pm Mon-Fri, 8am-6pm Sat; V) This informal neighborhood health-food outpost has simple, organic-focused cooking as well as freshly baked goods. Favorites include veggie burgers, along with various fish dishes, but most people arrive for the *casado* of the day – which is always vegetarian.

Bar Morazán (Map p74; ☎ 2222-4622; 2nd fl, Calle 7 btwn Avs 1 & 3; lunch casados ₡2300; 11am-2pm) Walk through the dim, smoky lobby casino of the Hotel Costa Rica Morazán up to the 2nd floor and you will be rewarded with one of the cheapest, most filling *almuerzos ejecutivos* (set lunches) in San José. On weekdays, the bar serves a rotating daily special that pulls in local office workers for platters piled with items like fried fish with lentils, rice and green salad. The price includes juice *and* dessert. The best part: you get to enjoy your meal before a sublime wall-sized mural of dogs playing poker.

Restaurante Isabel (Map p70; ☎ 2233-4687; Calle 19 btwn Avs 7 & 9; casados ₡2400; 8am-11pm Mon-Sat) A mix of regulars and medical professionals (the Hospital Calderón Guardia is right across the street) jam into the long Formica tables for generously portioned daily specials – such as grilled chicken with rice, beans and fresh cabbage slaw.

Chelle's (Map p74; cnr Av Central & Calle 9; casados ₡2500; 24hr) This unpretentious spot serves basic sandwiches and *casados* – none of which are very exciting. Regardless, *josefinos* will tell you that you haven't experienced San José until you've had a wee-hours breakfast here after a night of drinking – and there's a bar in case you want to keep going.

Café del Teatro Nacional (Map p74; Plaza de la Cultura; dishes ₡2700-4400; 9am-5pm Mon-Fri, 9am-12:30pm & 1:30-5:30pm Sat) One of the most beautiful cafes in the city, this atmospheric spot evokes early 20th-century Vienna. In other words, a perfect place to sip cappuccino and take in the lovely ceiling frescoes.

Midrange

Kalú Café & Food Shop (Map p70; 2221-2081; www.kalu.co.cr; cnr Calle 7 & Av 11; breakfast ₡2500-3250, sandwiches ₡4100-4600, mains ₡5450-8650; 9:30am-6pm Mon-Fri, 11:30am-9:30pm Sat; V) Sharing a sleek space with the Kiosco SJO design store (p76), this style-conscious cafe is the new restaurant by noted chef Camille Ratton. The menu is a global fusion of salads, sandwiches (try the miniburgers) and pastas, such as homemade gnocchi cooked in Malbec with wild mushrooms (₡6750). Whatever you do, don't miss dessert: their light and airy cheesecake (₡2500), served with stewed fresh strawberries in balsamic is mind-meltingly good.

Café Mundo (Map p74; 2222-6190; cnr Av 9 & Calle 15; mains ₡2800-6500; 11am-10:30pm Mon-Thu, 5pm-12:30am Fri & Sat; V) Location. Location. Location. This longtime Italian cafe and expat favorite has it. Set on a sprawling terrace in a vintage Barrio Otoya mansion, it's a perfect spot to enjoy a glass of wine and good (if not earth-shattering) pizzas and pastas within sight of a splashing outdoor fountain. The wine list is good and even includes a selection of bubbly Spanish cavas.

La Cocina de Leña (Map p70; 2222-1883/8782; Centro Comercial El Pueblo; mains ₡3500-6000; 11am-11pm Sun-Thu, to midnight Fri & Sat) 'The Wood Stove' is a charming spot with terra cotta tiles, a wood-beam ceiling and the endearing tradition of printing its menu on brown paper bags. The fare is all Costa Rican country cooking, strong on dishes like tamales and *olla de carne*, a hearty meat-and-vegetable soup that warms the bones on chilly nights. There is live marimba music on some evenings.

Don Wang (Map p74; 2223-5925/6484; www.donwangrestaurant.com; Calle 11 btwn Avs 6 & 8; mains ₡4000-7800; 11am-3pm & 5:30-10pm Mon-Fri, 11am-11pm Sat, 11am-10pm Sun; V) This hopping Cantonese eatery is an ideal place for dim sum (they serve it all day every day), as well as a long list of Chinese specialties, from stir-fried shrimp with cashews to *mu shu* vegetables (there are more than a dozen veggie dishes to choose from). Parents will love the children's play area in the corner – ideal for restless toddlers.

News Café (Map p74; cnr Av Central & Calle 7; mains ₡4200-11,000; 6am-10pm;) On the ground floor of Hotel Presidente is the most popular cafe in the city among gringo expats. The main draw is the daily selection of foreign newspapers and the free wi-fi, as well as a simple menu strong on American specialties such as sandwiches, salads and steaks.

Restaurante Tin-Jo (Map p74; 2221-7605; www.tinjo.com; Calle 11 btwn Avs 6 & 8; mains ₡5000-8500; 11:30am-3pm & 5:30-10pm Mon-Thu, 11:30am-3pm & 5:30-11pm Fri & Sat, 11:30am-10pm Sun; V) The interiors of this popular Asian standard-bearer are a riot of pan-Asian everything – just like the menu. Expect a wide range of fare from various regions – from kung pao shrimp to spicy tuna maki to pad thai – as well as an extensive vegetarian menu.

Nuestra Tierra (Map p74; cnr Av 2 & Calle 15; mains ₡5200-10,000; 24hr;) A taxidermied bull's

---

BEST EATS IN THE METROPOLITAN AREA

Every restaurant has a specialty that it does better than anyone else. Here's our guide to the best…

- **Bocas** La Casona de Laly, Escazú (p110)
- **Caribbean cooking** Restaurante Whapin, Los Yoses (p104)
- **Casados** Nuestra Tierra, San José (right)
- **Cheesecake** Kalú, San José (above)
- **Cinnamon rolls** Giacomin, Los Yoses (p103)
- **Gallo pinto** El Buen Comer, Los Yoses (p103)
- **Historic atmosphere** Restaurante Grano de Oro, La Sabana (p91)
- **Hummus** Aya Sofya, Los Yoses (p104)
- **Pizza** Pane e Vino, San Pedro (p104)
- **Spanish-style tapas** Olio, Los Yoses (p104)
- **Steak** La Esquina de Buenos Aires, San José (p90)

head greets you at this country restaurant, where the theme is Costa Rican spit and sawdust. Cheery waiters deliver wooden platters piled with heaping *casados* to hordes of hungry tourists and Tico families seated at rustic picnic-style tables. Portions are large, the food is good and the prices reasonable.

Top End

El Patio (Map p74; ☎ 2221-1700; www.elpatiodelbalmoral.com; Av Central btwn Calles 7 & 9; sandwiches ₡1400-2200; mains ₡5200-11,000; 🕑 6am-10:30pm) Filled with chattering gringos and suited Ticos, this all-purpose cafe-restaurant is a good place to chill out while taking in the pedestrian action on Av Central. Bonus: on sunny days, the restaurant opens its retractable roof. On some weekday evenings, the upstairs terrace bar (🕑 4pm to 11pm) hosts live bands.

La Esquina de Buenos Aires (Map p74; ☎ 2223-1909; cnr Calle 11 & Av 4; dishes ₡4900-13,000; 🕑 11:30am-3pm & 6-11pm Mon-Fri, noon-11pm Sat & Sun; Ⓥ) Spanish-tile floors, bright white linens and the sound of old tangos evoke the atmospheric bistros of San Telmo – making this one of the top spots in the city for a steak and a glass of Malbec. Also tasty are the house-made *empanadas* (turnovers stuffed with meat or cheese) and the extensive selection of fresh pastas, including vegetarian options such as tender raviolis stuffed with mozzarella and fresh basil. There's a good wine list (bottles from ₡4500), attentive service and flickering candlelight, making this an ideal place for a date.

Café Parisienne (Map p74; ☎ 2221-4000; Plaza de la Cultura; mains ₡8200-18,000; 🕑 24hr) Part of the Gran Hotel Costa Rica, this European-style cafe is perfect for people-watching, and you can't beat the views of the Teatro Nacional. The meals are overpriced and fairly ordinary, though the waitstaff will leave you alone if you just order a coffee (espresso ₡1000).

Central San José West

The city's hectic commercial heart has some of the cheapest eats in town – with a modern cafe or two to keep things interesting.

Churrería Manolo's (Map p74; Av Central btwn Calles Central & 2, Av Central btwn Calles 9 & 11; churros ₡200-275, mains ₡2400-3500, casados ₡2420; 🕑 7am-10pm) This San José institution is famous for its cream-filled *churros* (doughnut tubes), which draw crowds of *josefinos* in search of a quick sugar rush. Here's a tip – *churros* are the freshest around 5pm when hungry office workers beeline here straight from work. Otherwise, this is a popular spot for breakfast and lunch (though the food and service are uninspired).

Pastelería Merayo (Map p74; Calle 16 btwn Paseo Colón & Av 1; pastries ₡400-1000; 🕑 closed Sun) This informal pastry shop has a wide variety of freshly baked, cavity-inducing goodies. The coffee is strong and it's a sweet way to pass the time if you're waiting for a bus at the Coca-Cola terminal.

Café del Correo (Map p74; ☎ 2257-3670; Correo Central, Calle 2 btwn Avs 1 & 3; coffee ₡850-1600; 🕑 9am-7pm Mon-Fri, 10am-5pm Sat) Adjacent to the central post office is this mellow cafe that draws everyone from businessmen to teenagers on dates – and is a nice, central place to rest your feet. The *cortados* (espresso with a dollop of steamed milk) are good, and there are some sinful drinks, too – such as whiskey-laced Irish coffee (from ₡2250).

Soda Castro (Map p74; Av 10 btwn Calles 2 & 4; dishes ₡1800-3000, sundaes ₡2300; 🕑 11am-9:30pm; 👪) It's not in the best neighborhood, but this casual, six-decade-old Tico spot is a good place to feed the sweet tooth. You'll find sundaes and banana splits, but it's the house-made *paletas* (fresh fruit pops) that make this spot worth the walk. They come in a variety of seasonal flavors, including fantastically dreamy toasted coconut.

Q Café (Map p74; ☎ 2221-0707; www.quecafe.com; 2nd fl, cnr Av Central & Calle 2; mains ₡3900-5900; 🕑 8am-8:30pm Mon-Sat) A sleek, monochromatic cafe with excellent views of the ornate Correo Central in the distance, this modern 2nd-story spot is perfect for coffee drinks (including delicious iced mocha) and pastries. There is also a full menu of savory snacks. Try the *empanadas*, which go well with the cafe's homemade hot sauce.

One of the cheapest places for a good lunch is at the **Mercado Central** (Map p74; Av Central btwn Calles 6 & 8), where you'll find a variety of *sodas* serving *casados*, tamales, seafood and everything in between. A good spot is **Mariscos Poseidon** (Map p74; Mercado Central Annex; mains ₡2000-3800), a narrow, blue-and-yellow seafood joint run by the congenial Doris in the central market's northern annex, just off Av 1. The *ceviche mixto* appetizer (fish, shrimp and octopus marinated in lime juice) is tasty and cheap, as are the generous portions of seafood-studded rice. Afterwards, head across the street to the main market for dessert at **Helados de Sorbetera** (Map p74; Mercado Central; frozen custard ₡400-

700), a century-old local favorite that serves up cinnamon-laced frozen custard. Do as the locals do and order *barquillos* (cylindrical sugar cookies) to accompany your icy treat.

La Sabana & Surrounds

The residential area around the park is dotted with family eateries.

GROCERIES

There are two good neighborhood supermarkets here:

Más x Menos (Map p79; www.masxmenos.co.cr; ☎ 2248-0968; cnr Autopista General Cañas & Av 5; 7am-midnight Mon-Sat, 7am-9pm Sun)

Palí (Map p79; www.pali.co.cr; ☎ 2256-5887; Paseo Colón btwn Calles 24 & 26)

RESTAURANTS

Budget

Soda Tapia (Map p79; ☎ 2222-6734; www.sodatapia.com; cnr Av 2 & Calle 42; sandwiches from ₡1000, breakfast from ₡1600, casados ₡2300-3000; 6am-2am Sun-Thu, 24hr Fri & Sat;) An unpretentious '50s-style diner, this place is perpetually filled with couples and families noshing on grilled sandwiches and generous *casados*. If you have the nerve, try the monstrous 'El Gordo,' a pile of steak, onions, gouda cheese, lettuce and tomato served on Spanish bread. But save room for dessert: Tapia specializes in sundaes (from ₡1800).

Sabores de Jeruzalen (Map p79; ☎ 2221-6715; cnr Paseo Colón & Calle 36; mains ₡2900-3500; 8am-7pm Mon-Thu, 8am-6pm Fri & Sun; V) This small, informal Middle Eastern shop sells plates of hot shawarma and sandwiches stuffed full of fresh hummus and falafel.

Las Mañanitas (Map p79; ☎ 2256-5737; Calle 40 btwn Paseo Colón & Av 3; mains ₡2900-7900; 11am-10pm Mon-Sat, noon-8pm Sun) You can get your Mexican fix at this charming garden restaurant that serves a variety of well-rendered specialties. It's the tacos that are tops: corn tortillas stuffed full of chicken, steak, sea bass or *carne al pastor* (spiced pork) – best when accompanied by one of the restaurant's refreshing margaritas.

Midrange

our pick **Machu Picchu** (Map p79; ☎ 2255-1717; Calle 32 btwn Avs 1 & 3; mains ₡4200-11,000; 10am-10pm Mon-Sat, 11am-6pm Sun;) This locally renowned Peruvian restaurant will do you right if you have a hankering for all things Andean. A popular spot for a leisurely Sunday lunch, it has an encyclopedic menu featuring tasty Peruvian classics such as *pulpo al olivo* (octopus in olive sauce), *ají de gallina* (a nutty chicken stew) and *causa* (chilled potato terrines stuffed with shrimp and avocado), among *many* other things. There is also a children's menu (₡4500).

Lubnán (Map p79; ☎ 2257-6071; Paseo Colón btwn Calles 22 & 24; mains from ₡4800; 11am-3pm & 6-11pm Tue-Sat, 11am-4pm Sun) This cozy Lebanese spot serves a mix of Middle Eastern dishes, including shish kebabs, falafel and *kebbeh* (bulgur wheat and lamb fritters). Want to try a little bit of everything? Order the meze – a platter of small portions, ideal for two.

La Piazzetta (Map p79; ☎ 2222-7896; cnr Paseo Colón & Calle 40; mains ₡5000-16,000; noon-2:30pm & 6:30-11pm Mon-Fri, 6-11pm Sat) This old world Italian spot (expect waiters with bow ties) serves a lengthy list of traditional specialties: antipasto, creamy risottos, homemade pastas and tender veal. There is an extensive list of imported wines, and several luscious desserts – including a celebrated chocolate mousse.

Top End

Restaurante Grano de Oro (Map p79; ☎ 2255-3322; Calle 30 btwn Avs 2 & 4; lunch mains ₡5900-12,000, dinner mains ₡7500-15,600; noon-2pm & 6-10pm Mon-Sat) One of San José's top dining destinations is the stately, flower-filled restaurant at the Hotel Grano de Oro (p87). Known for its Costa Rican–fusion cuisine, the menu is laced with unique specialties such as pork loin roasted in coffee and seared duck crowned with caramelized figs. There is an encyclopedic international wine list (from ₡11,900 per bottle), including half a dozen types of champagne and cava. For dessert, don't miss the coffee cream pie. Reservations are recommended for dinner; credit cards are accepted.

El Chicote (Map p79; ☎ 2232-0936; Av Las Américas; mains ₡6000-14,000; 11am-3pm & 6-11pm Mon-Fri, 11am-11pm Sat & Sun) A pleasant family spot that draws carnivores for long Sunday lunches, El Chicote grills up beefy sirloins in the middle of the restaurant and then serves them with black beans, fried bananas and steamy baked potatoes. If you don't do red meat, there are plenty of chicken and seafood options as well. There is also a six-page wine list, strong on Mediterranean and South American vintages (from ₡3100).

La Bastille (Map p79; ☎ 2255-4994; www.la-bastille-restaurante.com; cnr Paseo Colón & Calle 22; mains ₡6800-11,000; noon-2pm & 6-10pm Mon-Fri, 6-10pm Sat) This five-decade-old bistro serves French classics such as escargot, onion soup, steak tartare and cordon bleu dishes.

DRINKING

Whatever your poison may be (ours is *guaro* sour – local firewater made with sugarcane), San José has plenty of venues to keep you lubricated – from local dives to trendy lounges. For many more drinking options, see the nearby neighborhoods of Los Yoses and San Pedro (p104). The price of a beer will vary depending on the venue, but count on spending ₡1200 and up. Take your ID; some places card everyone upon entering.

Note that some enterprising thieves have taken to lurking around popular spots, waiting to relieve drunken party people of their wallets. When leaving a bar late at night, keep your wits about you and take a taxi.

Bar Chavelona (Map p74; ☎ 2221-6094; Av 10 btwn Calles 10 & 12; 🕑 5pm-5am) Nestled amid a row of auto body shops on the west side of town (in other words: take a taxi), this renowned bar, which dates back to 1927, was the spot where Costa Rican author Carlos Luis Fallas (1909–66) once enjoyed happy hour in the company of the local intelligentsia. The bohemian atmosphere is long gone – replaced by an '80s decor that screams Duran Duran – but it remains a pleasant Tico spot for beer and *bocas* (savory bar snacks).

Bar Morazán (Map p74; ☎ 2222-4622; 2nd fl, Hotel Costa Rica Morazán, Calle 7 btwn Avs 1 & 3; 🕑 11am-2am) Decidedly local, in the heart of the San José tourist belt, this humble little bar has reasonably priced drinks, a sports-betting window, a stack of TVs displaying the games *and* a supersized mural of dogs playing poker. Awesome.

Centro Comercial El Pueblo (Map p70; Ⓟ) This Spanish Mediterranean outdoor mall is a warren of bars, clubs and music venues. The proximity of one place to the next makes it ideal for a pub crawl and there is stringent security, which keeps the atmosphere generally safe (though it can get unruly in the wee hours). Things usually get going at about 9pm and shut down by 3am. One of the best spots to sip is the newly opened Bacará (Map p70; ☎ 2222-1883/8782; open from 11am to 3am), on the southwest corner of the complex, which has a broad, open terrace with excellent city views.

Chelle's (Map p74; ☎ 2221-1369; cnr Av Central & Calle 9; 🕑 24hr) If you're boozing the night away with Ticos, you might find yourself here at 4am, clutching a cold one and telling people you just met that you love them. The greasy menu will help you soak up the booze.

El Morazán (Map p74; ☎ 2256-5110; cnr Calle 9 & Av 3; cocktails ₡2500-3000; 🕑 noon-midnight) Facing the Parque Morazán, this exposed-brick, Spanish tile–clad space dates back to 1904. Throughout its long life it has hosted all manner of historical figures (including Che Guevara, according to one account). Though it recently came under new ownership, it remains a popular hangout among Chepe's young artsy set. In addition to beer, there is a full menu of classic cocktails and snacks. On some nights, there is live music.

La Embajada (Map p74; Av 1 btwn Calles Central & 1; 🕑 10am-1am) This cavernous, smoke-filled spot – occupied largely by men – is an ideal daytime drinking dive. Its main advantage is that if anyone asks where you're headed, you can simply say 'The Embassy.'

Rapsodia Lounge (Map p79; ☎ 2248-1720; www.rapsodialounge.com; cnr Paseo Colón & Calle 40; 🕑 5pm-2am) A hyper-chic see-and-be-seen lounge clad in stark black-and-white furnishings has an extensive list of cocktails and a menu of Mediterranean-inspired dishes and snacks. Guest DJs can often be found setting the mood.

Other good spots for a tipple include the Café Parisienne at the Gran Hotel Costa Rica (p90) or El Patio (p90), overlooking the pedestrian walkway on Av Central.

ENTERTAINMENT

Pick up *La Nación* on Thursday for listings (in Spanish) of the coming week's attractions. The *Tico Times* 'Weekend' section (in English) has a calendar of theater, music and museum events. The free monthly magazine *San José Volando* is also a good guide for nightlife and cultural events.

Nightclubs

From thumping electronica to hip-hop to salsa, merengue and reggaetón, Chepe's clubs offer a wide variety of ways to get your groove on. Most spots open at around 10pm, but don't truly get going until after midnight. Admission charges vary (generally ₡2000 to ₡5000) depending on the location, the DJ and the night. Places come and go with alarming regularity, so ask around before heading out. The website Tico Party (www.ticoparty.com)

keeps an up-to-date rundown of the latest spots (in Spanish).

For the trendiest nightspots, make your way to Escazú (p111). Be safe: travel by taxi at night.

CENTRAL SAN JOSÉ EAST & NORTH

Centro Comercial El Pueblo (Map p70; Ⓟ) The most popular nightspot in San José is dense with human activity on weekends. Clubs here come and go; here are a few standard-bearers:

Bar Twister (Map p70; ☎ 2222-5746; 🕑 5pm-3am Wed-Sat) Catering to the Jaegermeister crowd, this cavernous club has nightly DJs that play contemporary international and Latin music.

Ebony 56 (Map p70; ☎ 2223-2195; 🕑 8pm-4am Tue-Sat) A sprawling disco spins a mix of reggae, dance hall, hip-hop and reggaetón.

Tarrico (Map p70; ☎ 2222-1003) A popular watering hole where hard-drinking *josefinos* pile in to play foosball and hit the dance floor.

Complejo Salsa 54 y Zadidas (Map p74; ☎ 8865-6919; Calle 3 btwn Avs 1 & 3) More low-rent than El Pueblo, this vast 2nd-story club is a good place to shake it if you want to go Latin, playing a mix of merengue, salsa, cumbia and Latin swing. Be prepared to cut some serious rug here – the local dancers are expert *salseros*.

LA SABANA

Club Vertigo (Map p79; ☎ 2257-8424; www.myspace.com/vertigocr; Paseo Colón btwn Calles 38 & 40) Located on the ground floor of a nondescript office tower, the city's premier club packs in Chepe's beautiful people with a mix of house, trance and electronica. Downstairs is an 850-person-capacity sweat-box of a dance floor, while upstairs you'll find a chill-out lounge lined with red sofas. Dress to the nines and note that admission charges can skyrocket on guest-DJ nights (from ₡7000).

Gay & Lesbian Venues

The city is home to Central America's most thriving gay and lesbian scene. As with other spots, admission charges vary depending on the night and location (from ₡2000 to ₡5000). Some clubs close on various nights of the week (usually Sunday to Tuesday) and others host women- or men-only nights; inquire ahead or check individual club websites for listings. For general information on gay travel, see p532.

The clubs listed below are on the south side of town, which can get rough after dark. Take a taxi.

Bochinche (Map p74; ☎ 2221-0500; www.bochinchesanjose.com; Calle 11 btwn Avs 10 & 12) A club that features everything from classic disco to electronica, as well as special themed nights.

Club Oh! (Map p70; ☎ 2221-9341; www.clubohcostarica.com; Calle 2 btwn Avs 14 & 16; 🕑 from 9pm Fri & Sat) This massive dance club with an attached lounge attracts a mixed crowd of gays, lesbians and their allies. There's drinking, dancing and midnight drag shows every Friday.

La Avispa (Map p74; ☎ 2223 5343; www.laavispa.co.cr; Calle 1 btwn Avs 8 & 10) A gay establishment that has been in operation for more than three decades, La Avispa has a bar, pool tables and a boisterous dance floor that's been recommended by readers. There are lesbian nights twice a month.

Pucho's Nightclub (Map p74; ☎ 2256-1147; www.puchosnightclub.com; cnr Calle 11 & Av 8) More low-rent (and significantly raunchier) than some is this gay male outpost that features scantily-clad go-go boys and over-the-top drag shows.

Cinemas

Many cinemas show recent Hollywood films with Spanish subtitles and an English soundtrack. Occasionally, films are dubbed over in Spanish *(hablado en español)* rather than subtitled; ask before buying a ticket. Movie tickets cost about ₡2000 to ₡2500, and generally Wednesdays are cheaper. Check newspaper listings or individual theater websites for schedules.

There are bigger multiplexes in Los Yoses and San Pedro (p105), while the most modern theaters are in Escazú (p111).

Cine Magaly (Map p70; ☎ 2223-0085; www.ccmcinemas.com; Calle 23 btwn Avs Central & 1) The latest releases.

Sala Garbo (Map p79; ☎ 2222-1034; cnr Av 2 & Calle 28) Art-house and classic films.

Teatro Variedades (Map p74; ☎ 2222-6108; Calle 5 btwn Avs Central & 1) An old show palace that dates from 1894 screens independent and Hollywood films.

Live Music

Centro Comercial El Pueblo (Map p70; Ⓟ) has a number of spots that feature live Latin combos and rock bands – and everything in between. As with everything else at El Pueblo, these come and go like the tides. One long-standing space is Los Balcones (Map p70; ☎ 2221-4619; open on Fridays and Saturdays), which specializes in the socially conscious Latin American folk music known as *nueva trova*.

El Cuartel de la Boca del Monte (Map p70; ☎ 2221-0327; Av 1 btwn Calles 21 & 23; ⏲ 4pm-1am) Though not strictly a live-music venue, this atmospheric old bar with exposed brick walls has long drawn in cheek-to-jowl crowds for live bands on most nights of the week (especially Fridays). It's popular with university students, who arrive to flirt and drink and various combinations thereof.

For a more upscale scene, try the 2nd-story bar at El Patio (p90), which hosts live bands on Thursday, Friday and Saturday nights, as well as the artsy El Morazán (p92). Otherwise, serious musical aficionados should head to the neighboring district of San Pedro, where Jazz Café (p105) serves as the city's pre-eminent live-music venue.

Theater

There is a wide variety of theatrical options in San José, including some in English. Local newspapers, including the *Tico Times*, list current shows. Most theaters are not very large so performances tend to sell out; get tickets as early as possible.

Auditorio Nacional (Map p70; ☎ 2256-5876; www.museocr.com; Museo de los Niños, Calle 4, north of Av 9) A grand stage for concerts, dance theater and plays – and the site of the Miss Costa Rica pageant.

Little Theatre Group (☎ 2289-3910; www.littletheatregroup.org) This English-language performance troupe has been around since the 1950s and presents several plays a year; call or go online to find out when and where the works will be shown.

Teatro Fanal (Map p74; ☎ 2257-5524/8304; Cenac Complex, Av 3 btwn Calles 11 & 15) Adjacent to the contemporary art museum, it puts on a variety of works, including children's theater – all in Spanish.

Teatro La Máscara (Map p74; ☎ 2222-4574; Calle 13 btwn Avs 2 & 6) Dance performances as well as repertory theater.

Teatro Melico Salazar (Map p74; ☎ 2233-5424; www.teatromelico.go.cr; Av 2 btwn Calles Central & 2) The restored 1920s theater has regular fine-arts performances, including music, theater, ballet and other dance.

Teatro Nacional (Map p74; ☎ 2221-5341; www.teatronacional.go.cr; Calles 3 & 5 btwn Avs Central & 2) Costa Rica's most important theater stages plays, dance, opera, symphony, Latin American music and other major events. The main season runs from March to November, but there are performances throughout the year.

Casinos

Gamblers will find casinos in several of the larger hotels. Most of these are fairly casual, but in the nicer spots it is advisable to ditch the T-shirts in favor of a button-down shirt as there may be a dress code. Gents: be advised that casinos are frequented by prostitutes (high-class and otherwise), so be wary if suddenly you're the most desirable person in the room.

Casino Club Colonial (Map p74; ☎ 2258-2807; www.casinoclubcolonial.com; Av 1 btwn Calles 9 & 11; ⏲ 24hr) San José's most elegant casino.

Clarion Hotel Amon Plaza (Map p70; ☎ 2523-4600; www.hotelamonplaza.com; cnr Av 11 & Calle 3bis; ⏲ 3-4pm) A quieter, out-of-the-way spot.

Hotel del Rey (Map p74; ☎ 2258-4880; www.delreyhotel.com; cnr Calle 9 & Av 1; ⏲ 24hr) A jam-packed shocking-pink building offers everything from roulette to slot machines and what has to be the highest density of prostitutes in the city.

Sports

International and national *fútbol* (soccer) games are played at the **Estadio Nacional** (Map p79; ☎ 2284-8700), which is currently under construction. Located in Parque Metropolitano La Sabana since 1924 – in a structure that has hosted everyone from Pope John Paul II to soccer legend Pelé – the old stadium was torn down in late 2008 to make way for an US$83 million stadium that is being built with money and labor from China. It will seat 35,000 spectators and feature a retractable roof and a field made of natural grass. At the time of research, it was scheduled to open in March of 2011.

Bullfighting is another popular sport, and fights are held seasonally in the southern suburb of Zapote over the Christmas period. Members of the public (usually drunk) are encouraged to participate in the action (the bull isn't killed in the Costa Rican version of the sport).

For information on sports activities, see p79. For other general information on sports in Costa Rica, turn to p43.

SHOPPING

Whether you're looking for indigenous carvings, high-end furnishings or a plastic howler monkey, San José has no shortage of shops, running the gamut from artsy boutiques to tourist traps stocked full of tropical everything. With the exception of markets, hag-

GRAPPLING WITH THE SEX TRADE

Exit the baggage claim at the international airport in San José and you'll be welcomed by a sign that reads 'In Costa Rica sex with children under 18 is a serious crime. Should you engage in it we will drive you to jail.' For decades, travelers have arrived in Costa Rica in search of sandy beaches and lush mountainscapes. Unfortunately, an unknown percentage of them also come in search of sex – not all of it legal.

Prostitution by men and women over the age of 18 is perfectly legal. But the tourist juggernaut of the last few decades has fueled illicit activities at its fringes – namely child prostitution and, to a lesser degree, human trafficking. To be clear: having sex with a minor in Costa Rica is illegal, carrying a penalty of up to 10 years in jail. But child prostitution has nonetheless flourished. In fact, a number of aid groups, along with the country's national child-welfare agency (Patronato Nacional de la Infancia; PANI), estimate that there may be as many as 3000 child prostitutes in San José alone. In turn, this has led to women and children being trafficked for the purpose of sexual exploitation, as documented in a 2008 report issued by the US State Department.

Alarm over the problem has crescendoed steadily since 1999, when the UN Committee on Human Rights issued a statement saying that it was 'deeply concerned' about child-sex tourism in Costa Rica. Since then, the government has taken a number of measures to crack down. They've established national task forces to combat the problem, trained the police force in how to deal with issues of child exploitation and formed a coalition against human trafficking. But enforcement remains weak – largely due to lack of personnel and funding On its end, the USA – the principal source of sex tourists to Costa Rica – has made it a prosecutable crime for Americans to have sex with minors anywhere in the world.

There are also countless challenges in fighting the problem. Tourism remains one of the country's primary sources of revenue – and, unfortunately, that includes the countless travelers who arrive specifically to seek sex. Along with Thailand and Cambodia, Costa Rica is one of the most popular sex-tourism destinations in the world, according to Ecpat International, a nonprofit dedicated to ending child prostitution. The phenomenon has been magnified by the internet: there are entire sex-tourism websites that chronicle – in grotesque detail – where and how to find sex or, in the words of one, how to find '18-year-old girls for less than the price of a good steak.' In all of these, Costa Rica figures prominently. While these sites are not necessarily illegal, they do promote a permissive image of the country – one that can lead some travelers to think that child sex is acceptable.

Various organizations fight the sexual exploitation of children in Costa Rica, which you can contact to learn more about the problem or to report any incidents you encounter. For details, see boxed text, p540.

gling is not tolerated in stores and shops. In touristy shops, keep an eye peeled for 'authentic' woodworks that have 'Made in Indonesia' stamped on the bottom.

For general information on shopping in Costa Rica, turn to p536.

eÑe (Map p74; ☎ 2222-7681; cnr Avs 7 & 7bis; 🕒 10am-6:30pm Mon-Sat) This hip little design shop across from the Casa Amarilla sells all manner of pieces crafted by Costa Rican designers and artists, including a limited selection of clothing, jewelry, silk-screened T-shirts, handbags, picture frames, zines and works of graphic art.

Galería Namu (Map p74; ☎ 2256-3412; www.galerianamu.com; Av 7 btwn Calles 5 & 7; 🕒 9:30am-6:30pm Mon-Sat, 9am-1:30pm Sun) A fair-trade gallery run by Aisling French does a great job of bringing together artwork and crafts from a diverse population of regional ethnicities. Here, you'll find a lovely array of Boruca masks, finely woven Wounaan baskets, Guaymí dolls, Bribrí canoes, Chorotega ceramics and Huetar carvings, as well as contemporary urban and Afro-Caribbean crafts. They can also help arrange visits to remote indigenous territories in different parts of Costa Rica. See their website for details.

our pick **Kiosco SJO** (Map p70; ☎ 2258-1829; www.kioscosjo.com; cnr Av 11 & Calle 7; 🕒 11am-6pm Mon, 11am-10pm Tue-Sat) With a focus on sustainable design by Latin American artisans, this sleek shop stocks art books, original photography, artisanal chocolates, fashion and contemporary home decor by established regional designers.

It's pricey, but rest assured that everything you find here will be of exceptional quality.

La Casona (Map p74; Calle Central btwn Avs Central & 1; Mon-Sat) Welcome to the number-one tourist trap in Chepe! What you give up in authenticity, however, you'll make up for in convenience. Various stalls spread out over two floors stock T-shirts, banana-leaf paper journals and tree-frog stickers. Shop around as some quality crafts can be found.

Mercado Central (Map p74; Avs Central & 1 btwn Calles 6 & 8; 6am-6pm Mon-Sat) The bustling Central Market is the best place in the city for, well, just about anything you'd want. This is the cheapest place to buy a hammock *(Hecho en Nicaragua)* or a *pura vida* T-shirt (Made in China), or a vast assortment of forgettable knickknacks. For something decidedly more Costa Rican, export-quality coffee beans can be bought at a fraction of the price you'll pay in tourist shops.

Mercado Artesanal (Crafts Market; Map p74; Plaza de la Democracia; Avs Central & 2 btwn Calles 13 & 15; midmorning-sunset) A touristy open-air market that sells everything from handcrafted jewelry and Bob Marley T-shirts to elaborate woodwork and Guatemalan sarongs.

Rincón del Habano (Map p74; Calle 7 btwn Avs Central & 1; 9am-6:30pm Mon-Fri, 9:30am-5:30pm Sat) You'll find a wide selection of cigars in this tiny decade-old shop that sells stogies from all over, including brands from Costa Rica, the Dominican Republic, Nicaragua and Cuba.

Sol Maya (Map p79; ☎ 2221-0864; cnr Paseo Colón & Calle 20; Sun-Fri) A simple corner shop in La Sabana carries fabric from all over the world, including a decent selection of hand-loomed Guatemalan textiles. Prices are reasonable.

For the country's finest woodcrafts, it is absolutely worth the trip to visit the Biesanz Woodworks workshop in Escazú (see boxed text, p112).

GETTING THERE & AWAY

San José is the country's transportation hub, and it's likely that you'll pass through the capital a number of times throughout your travels (whether you want to or not).

Air

There are two airports serving San José (see p99 for information on how to get to them). If you're leaving the country, be advised that there is an international departure tax of US$26.

Aeropuerto Internacional Juan Santamaría (Map p68; ☎ 2437-2400; Alajuela) handles international air traffic in its main terminal, which is stocked with the usual airport facilities: sundry stores, duty-free outlets and a grim selection of fast-food outlets. Immediately to the north of the main terminal, a small blue building houses the operations of **Sansa** (☎ 2290-4100; www.flysansa.com), one of the country's two domestic airlines.

Aeropuerto Tobías Bolaños (Map p68; ☎ 2232-2820; Pavas), which lies in the San José suburb of Pavas, services domestic flights on **NatureAir** (☎ 2220-3054; www.natureair.com), the country's other domestic airline.

INTERNATIONAL AIRLINES

International carriers that have offices in San José are listed here. Airlines serving Costa Rica directly are marked with an asterisk; they also have desks at the airport.

Air France (☎ 2220-4111; www.airfrance.com; Oficentro Ejecutivo La Sabana, 7th fl, Edificio 6, Sabana Sur; 8am-noon & 1-5pm Mon-Fri)

American Airlines* (Map p79; ☎ 2248-9010; www.americanairlines.co.cr; Edificio Centro Cars, across from Crown Plaza Corobicí, Sabana Este; 8am-6pm Mon-Fri, 8am-4pm Sat)

Avianca* (☎ 2441-2827/2776; www.avianca.com; Aeropuerto Internacional Juan Santamaría, Alajuela; 8am-5pm Mon-Fri)

Continental* (☎ 2296-4911; www.continental.com; No 2, Oficentro La Virgen, Zona Industrial, Pavas; 8am-5pm Mon-Fri, 9am-1pm Sat)

COPA* (Map p79; ☎ 2222-6640; www.copaair.com; 1st fl, Torre Mercedes Benz, cnr Calle 24 & Paseo Colón, La Sabana; 8am-6pm Mon-Fri, 8am-4pm Sat)

Cubana de Aviación* (Map p79; ☎ 2221-7625/6918; www.cubana.cu; Calle 40 btwn Avs 2 & 4, La Sabana)

Delta* (Map p79; ☎ 2256-7909; www.delta.com; Edificio Elizabeth, 100m east & 50m south of Toyota on Paseo Colón, La Sabana; 8am-5pm Mon-Fri)

Grupo TACA* (Map p79; ☎ 2299-8222; www.taca.com; cnr Calle 40 & Av Las Américas, across from Nissan dealer, La Sabana; 8am-8pm Mon-Fri, 8am-5pm Sat, 9am-5pm Sun)

Iberia* (☎ 2431-5633; www.iberia.com; Oficentro Tical, 1km east of Aeropuerto Internacional Juan Santamaría, Alajuela; 8am-noon & 1-5pm Mon-Fri)

Mexicana* (Map p79; ☎ 2295-6969; www.mexicana.com; 1st fl, Torre Mercedes Benz, cnr Calle 24 & Paseo Colón, La Sabana; 8am-5pm Mon-Fri)

United Airlines (☎ 2220-4844; www.united.com; Oficentro Ejecutivo La Sabana, 1st fl, Edificio 2, Sabana Sur; 8am-10pm Mon-Fri, 9am-1pm Sat)

CHARTER AIRCRAFT

Sansa and NatureAir both offer charter flights out of San José, as do the companies listed below. Most charters are small (three- to five-passenger) aircraft and can fly to any of the many airstrips around Costa Rica. Each listing below indicates which San José airport the company operates from.

Aero Bell (☎ 2290-0000; aerobell@racsa.co.cr; Tobías Bolaños)

Aviones Taxi Aéreo SA (☎ 2431-0160/0293; www.airchartercentralamerica.com; Juan Santamaría)

Helicópteros Turísticos Tropical (☎ 2220-3940; Tobías Bolaños)

Pitts Aviation (☎ 2296-3600; Tobías Bolanos)

Viajes Especial Aéreos SA (Veasa; ☎ 2232-1010/8043; Tobías Bolaños)

Bus

Bus transportation in San José can be bewildering. There is no public bus system and no central terminal. Instead, dozens of private companies operate out of stops scattered throughout the city. Many bus companies have no more than a stop (in this case pay the driver directly); some have a tiny office with a window on the street, while some operate from a terminal. The bigger stations service entire regions. These include the following:

Gran Terminal del Caribe (Map p70; Calle Central, north of Av 13) A roomy station on the north end of town is the central departure point for all buses to the Caribbean.

Terminal Coca-Cola (Map p74; Av 1 btwn Calles 16 & 18) A well-known landmark. Numerous buses leave from the terminal and the four-block radius around it to points all over Costa Rica; in particular, the Central Valley and the Pacific coast. This is a labyrinthine station with ticket offices scattered all over.

Terminal Musoc (off Map p70; Av 22 btwn Calles Central & 1) On the south end of town, this terminal has buses to San Isidro and points south.

Terminal San Carlos (Map p70; cnr Av 9 & Calle 12) A small, rather decrepit terminal serving destinations in the north and northwest, such as Monteverde, La Fortuna and Sarapiquí.

Bus schedules change regularly. Pick up the useful but not always up-to-date master bus schedule at the ICT office (p72), or you can download a PDF copy from their website (www.visitcostarica.com; click on the link that says 'General Info'). Buses are crowded on Friday evening and Saturday morning and packed to the gills at Christmas and Easter.

For buses that run infrequently, it is advisable to buy tickets in advance. If you want to avoid hassle, book your travel through **A Safe Passage** (☎ 8365-9678; www.costaricabustickets.com), which can purchase bus tickets in advance for a small fee. They also arrange airport transfers.

Be aware that thefts are common in many bus terminals. Stay alert, keep your valuables close to you and don't stow anything important (such as passports and money) in the overhead racks or luggage compartment of a bus.

Schedules and prices change regularly. Inquire locally before setting out.

INTERNATIONAL BUSES FROM SAN JOSÉ

International buses get booked up fast. Buy your tickets in advance – and take your passport. For more on border crossings, see p543.

Changuinola/Bocas del Toro, Panama Transportes Bocatoreños (Map p74; ☎ 2227-5923; cnr Av 5 & Calle 16, in front of Hotel Cocorí) US$28; six hours; departs 9am.

David, Panama Tracopa (off Map p70; Calle 5 btwn Avs 18 & 20) US$25; nine hours; departs 7:30am.

Guatemala City, Guatemala Tica Bus (Map p74; www.ticabus.com; cnr Calle 9 & Av 4) US$74; 60 hours; departs 6am, 7:30am and 12:30pm.

Managua, Nicaragua King Quality (Map p74; ☎ 2258-8834; Calle 12 btwn Avs 3 & 5) US$36; nine hours; departs 3am; Panaline (Map p74; cnr Av 5 & Calle 16, in front of Hotel Cocorí) US$23; nine hours; departs 5am; Tica Bus (Map p74; cnr Calle 9 & Av 4) Normal/executive US$21/32; nine hours; departs 6am, 7:30am and 12:30pm; Trans Nica (Map p70; Calle 22 btwn Avs 3 & 5) US$21 to US$31; nine hours; departs 4am, 5am, 9am and noon.

Panama City, Panama Panaline (Map p74; ☎ 2256-8721; cnr Av 5 & Calle 16, in front of Hotel Cocorí) US$25; 15 hours; departs 1pm; Tica Bus (Map p74; www.ticabus.com; cnr Calle 9 & Av 4) Normal/executive US$26/37; 15 hours; departs noon and 11pm.

San Salvador, El Salvador King Quality (Map p74; ☎ 2258-8834; Calle 12 btwn Avs 3 & 5) US$62; 48 hours; departs 3am; Tica Bus (Map p74; cnr Calle 9 & Av 4) Normal/executive US$53/58; 48 hours; departs 6am, 7:30am, 12:30pm and 11pm.

Tegucigalpa, Honduras King Quality (Map p74; ☎ 2258-8834; Calle 12 btwn Avs 3 & 5) US$60; 48 hours; departs 3am; Tica Bus (Map p74; cnr Calle 9 & Av 4) US$42; 48 hours; departs 6am, 7:30am and 12:30pm.

DOMESTIC BUSES FROM SAN JOSÉ

For destinations within Costa Rica, consult the following listings.

To the Central Valley

Alajuela Tuasa (Map p74; Av 2 btwn Calles 12 & 14) ₡400; 40 minutes; departs every 10 minutes from 4am to 11pm, every 30 minutes after 11pm.
Cartago (Map p74; Calle 13 btwn Avs 6 & 8) ₡500; 40 minutes; departs hourly between 5:15am and 10pm.
Grecia (Map p74; Av 5 btwn Calles 18 & 20) ₡900; one hour; departs every 20 minutes from 6am to 10:20pm.
Heredia (Map p74; Calle 1 btwn Avs 7 & 9) ₡400; 20 minutes; departs every 10 minutes from 5am to 11pm.
Sarchí (Map p74; Av 5 btwn Calles 18 & 20) ₡1000; 1½ hours; departs every 30 minutes from 5am to 10pm.
Turrialba (Map p74; Calle 13 btwn Avs 6 & 8) ₡1100; two hours; departs hourly from 5am to 10pm.
Volcán Irazú (Map p74; Av 2 btwn Calles 1 & 3) Round-trip ₡2500; two hours; departs 8am.
Volcán Poás Tuasa (Map p74; Av 2 btwn Calles 12 & 14) Round-trip ₡3400; five hours; departs 8:30am.

To Northwestern Costa Rica

Cañas Empresa Cañas (Map p74; ☎ 2258-5792; Calle 16 btwn Avs 1 & 3) ₡2300; 3¼ hours; departs 5:30am, 8:30am, 11:40am, 12:20pm, 1:30pm, 3:30pm and 5pm.
Ciudad Quesada (San Carlos) Autotransportes San Carlos (Map p70; ☎ 2255-4300; Terminal San Carlos) ₡2500; 2½ hours; departs every 30 to 45 minutes from 5am to 6:15pm.
La Fortuna (Map p70; Terminal San Carlos) ₡2900; four hours; departs 6:15am, 8:30am and 11:30am.
Liberia Pulmitan (Map p70; ☎ 2666-0458; Calle 24 btwn Avs 5 & 7) ₡2800; four hours; departs hourly from 6am to 8pm.
Monteverde/Santa Elena (Map p70; Calle 12 btwn Avs 7 & 9) ₡3200; 4½ hours; departs 6:30am and 2:30pm. (This bus fills up quickly – book ahead.)
Peñas Blancas, Nicaragua border crossing Transportes Deldú (Map p70; ☎ 2256-9072; www.transportesdeldu.com; Av 9 btwn Calles 10 & 12) ₡4400; six hours; departs 4am, 5am, 5:50am, 7:45am, 9:30am, 10:30am, 1:30am, 4:15pm and 7pm.
Tilarán Empresa Cañas (Map p74, ☎ 2258-5792; Calle 16 btwn Avs 1 & 3) ₡3100; four hours; departs 7:30am, 9:30am, 12:45pm, 3:45pm and 6:30pm. (On Sunday there is no bus at 9:30am.)

To Península de Nicoya

Montezuma and Mal País (Map p74; Terminal Coca-Cola) ₡6800; six hours; departs 6am and 2pm.
Nicoya Empresas Alfaro (Map p74; ☎ 2256-7050; Av 5 btwn Calles 14 &16) ₡3200; five hours; departs 5:30am, 7:30am, 10am, noon, 1pm, 3pm, 5pm and 5:30pm.
Playa Bejuco Empresas Arza (Map p70; ☎ 2258-3883; Calle 12 btwn Avs 7 & 9) ₡4000; 5½ hours; departs 6am and 3:30pm. (These buses stop on the street outside the Terminal San Carlos.)
Playa del Coco Pulmitán (Map p70; Calle 24 btwn Avs 5 & 7) ₡3300; five hours; departs 8am, 2pm and 4pm.
Playa Flamingo, via Brasilito Tralapa (Map p74; Calle 20 btwn Avs 3 & 5) ₡4600; six hours; departs 8am, 10:30am and 2pm.
Playa Nosara Empresas Alfaro (Map p74; ☎ 2256-7050; Av 5 btwn Calles 14 & 16) ₡3900; six hours; departs 5am.
Playa Sámara Empresas Alfaro (Map p74; ☎ 2256-7050; Av 5 btwn Calles 14 & 16) ₡3600; five hours; departs 12pm.
Playas Panamá and Hermosa Tralapa (Map p74; Calle 20 btwn Avs 3 & 5) ₡4600; five hours; departs 3:30pm.
Playa Tamarindo Empresas Alfaro (Map p74; 2256-7050; Av 5 btwn Calles 14 & 16) ₡4400; five hours; departs 11:30am and 3:30pm.
Santa Cruz Empresas Alfaro (Map p74; 2256-7050; Av 5 btwn Calles 14 & 16) ₡4200; five hours; departs 6am, 8am, 9:45am, 11am, noon, 12:30pm, 2pm, 4:30pm, 5:30pm and 7pm.

To the Central Pacific Coast

Dominical and Uvita Transportes Morales (Map p74; Terminal Coca-Cola) ₡2500; seven hours; departs 6am and 3pm.
Jacó Transportes Jacó (Map p74; ☎ 2290-2922; Terminal Coca-Cola) ₡2000; three hours; departs 6am, 7am, 9am, 11am, 1pm, 3pm, 5pm and 7pm.
Puntarenas Empresarios Unidos (Map p70; ☎ 2222-8231; cnr Av 12 & Calle 16) ₡1500; 2½ hours; departs hourly at 6am and 7pm.
Quepos/Manuel Antonio Transportes Morales (Map p74; Terminal Coca-Cola) ₡3500 to ₡3700; four hours; departs roughly every 90 minutes from 6am to 7:30pm.

To Southern Costa Rica & Península de Osa

Ciudad Neily Tracopa (off Map p70; ☎ 2221-4214; Calle 5 btwn Avs 18 & 20) ₡5000; eight hours; departs 5am, 1pm, 4:30pm and 6:30pm.
Golfito Tracopa (off Map p70; ☎ 2221-4214; Calle 5 btwn Avs 18 & 20) ₡4700; eight hours; departs 7am, 3:30pm and 10:15pm.
Palmar Norte Tracopa (off Map p70; ☎ 2221-4214; Calle 5 btwn Avs 18 & 20) ₡2800; five hours; departs 5am, 7am, 8:30am, 10am, 1pm, 2:30pm and 4:30pm.
Paso Canoas, Panama border crossing Tracopa (off Map p70; ☎ 2221-4214; Calle 5 btwn Avs 18 & 20) ₡5000; six hours; departs 5am, 1pm, 4:30pm and 6:30pm.
Puerto Jiménez Blanco Lobo (Map p70; ☎ 2221-4214; Calle 12 btwn Avs 9 & 11) ₡5900; eight hours; departs 6am and 12pm. (This bus fills up quickly in high season; buy tickets in advance.)
San Isidro del General Tracopa (off Map p70; ☎ 2221-4214; Calle 5 btwn Avs 18 & 20) ₡2100; three hours; departs hourly from 5am to 6:30pm; Transportes Musoc

(Calle Central btwn Avs 22 & 24) ₡2100, three hours, departs hourly from 5:30am to 5:30pm.
San Vito Tracopa (off Map p70; ☎ 2221-4214; Calle 5 btwn Avs 18 & 20) ₡4200; seven hours; departs 6am, 8:15am, noon and 4pm.

To the Caribbean Coast

All of the following buses depart from the Gran Terminal del Caribe (Map p70):
Cahuita (Autotransportes Mepe) ₡3700; four hours; departs 6am, 10am, 12pm, 2pm and 4pm.
Cariari, for transfer to Tortuguero (Empresarios Guapileños) ₡1400; 2¼ hours; departs 6:30am, 9am, 10:30am, 1pm, 3pm, 4:30pm, 6pm and 7pm.
Guápiles (Empresarios Guapileños) ₡1100; 1½ hours; departs hourly from 5:30am to 10pm.
Puerto Limón (Autotransportes Caribeños) ₡2500; three hours; departs roughly every 30 minutes from 5am to 7pm.
Puerto Viejo de Talamanca (Autotransportes Mepe) ₡4300; 4½ hours; departs 6am, 10am, 12pm, 2pm and 4pm.
Siquirres (Líneas del Atlántico) ₡1400; 1½ hours; departs 6:30am, 8am, 11am, noon, 1pm, 3pm, 4pm and 5pm.
Sixaola, Panama border crossing (Autotransportes Mepe) ₡5300; six hours; departs 6am, 10am, 12pm, 2pm and 4pm.

To the Northern Lowlands

Ciudad Quesada (San Carlos) See departures to Northwestern Costa Rica, opposite.
Los Chiles, Nicaragua border crossing (Map p70; Terminal San Carlos) ₡2100, five hours, departs 5:30am and 3:30pm.
Puerto Viejo de Sarapiquí Autotransportes Sarapiquí (Map p70; Gran Terminal del Caribe) ₡1400, two hours, departs 6:30am, 7:30am, 10am, 11:30am, 1:30pm, 2:30pm, 3:30pm, 4:30pm, 5:30pm and 6pm.

TOURIST BUSES

Grayline's Fantasy Bus (☎ 2220-2126; www.graylinecostarica.com) and **Interbus** (☎ 2283-5573; www.interbusonline.com) shuttle passengers in air-con minivans from San José to a long list of popular destinations around Costa Rica. They are more expensive than the standard bus service, but they offer door-to-door service and can get you there faster. Turn to p548 for more information.

GETTING AROUND

Central San José frequently resembles a parking lot – narrow streets, heavy traffic and a complicated one-way system mean that it is often quicker to walk than to take the bus. The same applies to driving: if you rent a car, try to avoid downtown. If you're in a real hurry to get somewhere that is more than 1km away, take a taxi.

To/From the Airports

TO AEROPUERTO INTERNACIONAL JUAN SANTAMARÍA

You can reserve a pickup with **Taxi Aeropuerto** (☎ 2221-6865; www.taxiaeropuerto.com), which charges a flat rate of between US$21 and US$30 for trips to and from most parts of San José. (These are a bright orange color.) You can also take a street taxi, but the rates may vary wildly. Plan on spending at least ₡11,000 to ₡14,000 (roughly US$20 to US$25); more in heavy traffic. **Interbus** (☎ 2283-5573; www.interbusonline.com) runs an airport shuttle service that will pick you up at your hotel (US$10 per person), good value if you're traveling alone. The cheapest option is the red **Tuasa bus** (Map p74; cnr Calle 10 & Av 2; ₡400) bound for Alajuela. Be sure to tell the driver that you are getting off at the airport (just say: *Voy al aeropuerto, por favor.*).

From downtown, the drive to the airport can take anywhere from 20 minutes to an hour (more if you take the bus) – and vice versa. Plan accordingly.

TO AEROPUERTO TOBÍAS BOLAÑOS

Buses to Tobías Bolaños depart every 30 minutes from Av 1, 250m west of the Terminal Coca-Cola. A taxi to the airport from downtown starts at about ₡6600 (or about US$12). **Interbus** (☎ 2283-5573; www.interbusonline.com) also has an airport shuttle service for US$10.

Bus

Local buses are useful to get you into the suburbs and surrounding villages, or to the airport. Most buses run between 5am and 10pm and cost in the vicinity of ₡200 to ₡300.

Buses from Parque La Sabana head into town on Paseo Colón, then go over to Av 2 at the San Juan de Dios hospital. They then go three different ways through town before eventually heading back to La Sabana. Buses are marked Sabana–Estadio, Sabana–Cementerio or Cementerio–Estadio. These buses are a good bet for a cheap city tour. Buses going east to Los Yoses and San Pedro go back and forth along Av 2 and then switch over to Av Central at Calle 29. (These are easily identifiable by the big sign that says 'Mall San Pedro' on the front window.) The route starts at the corner of Av 2 and Calle 7, near Restaurante El Pollo Campesino.

Buses to the following outlying suburbs and towns begin from bus stops at the indicated blocks. Some places have more than one stop – only the main ones are listed here.

Escazú Avenida 6 (Map p74; Av 6 btwn Calles 14 & 16); Calle 16 (Map p74; Calle 16 btwn Avs 1 & 3)
Guadalupe (Map p74; Av 3 btwn Calles Central & 1)
Pavas (Map p70; Av 1 btwn Calles 20 & 22)
Santa Ana (Map p74; Calle 16 btwn Avs 1 & 3)

Car

It is not advisable to rent a car just to drive around San José. The traffic is heavy, the streets narrow and the meter-deep curb-side gutters make parking nerve-wracking. In addition, break-ins are frequent and leaving a car – even in a guarded lot – might result in a smashed window and stolen belongings. Hire one of the plentiful taxis instead.

If you are renting a car to travel throughout Costa Rica, you will not be short of choices: there are more than 50 car-rental agencies – including many of the global brands – in and around San José. The travel desks at travel agencies and upmarket hotels can arrange rentals; you can also arrange rentals online and at the airport. Within Costa Rica, you can check the local yellow pages (under 'Alquiler de Automóviles') for a complete listing. Note that there is a surcharge of about US$25 for renting cars at Aeropuerto Internacional Juan Santamaría.

One excellent local option is **Wild Rider** (Map p79; ☎ 2258-4604; www.wild-rider.com; Paseo Colón btwn Calles 30 & 32; 🕑 8am-6pm), run by a charming trio of Germans. While their specialty is motorcycles, they have a fleet of about 40 small sports utility vehicles. Prices are reasonable (from US$300 per week in high season) and some of the newer vehicles even have stereos with iPod hookups. Reserve well in advance.

For general information on rental agencies, see p548.

Motorcycle

Given the apparent homicidal nature of most San José drivers, renting a motorcycle to get around the city is recommended only to those who are truly qualified. Rentals are usually small and rates start at about US$50 per day for a 350cc motorcycle and climb from there. Plan on paying more than US$150 a day or more for a Harley.

Wild Rider (Map p79; ☎ 2258-4604; www.wild-rider.com; Paseo Colón btwn Calles 30 & 32; 🕑 8am-6pm) rents sports bikes like the Honda XR-250 or the Suzuki DRZ-400S. Prices start at US$420 per week in high season (including insurance, taxes and helmets). They organize on- and off-road guided tours as well.

For Harleys, see Harley Davidson Rentals (p112) in Escazú.

Taxi

Red taxis can be hailed on the street day or night, or you can have your hotel call one for you. You can also hire taxis at the stands at the Parque Nacional, Parque Central and near the Teatro Nacional.

Marías (meters) are generally used, though a few drivers will tell you they're broken and try to charge you more – especially if you don't speak Spanish. (Not using a meter is illegal.) Make sure the *maría* is operating when you get in, or negotiate the fare up front. Short rides downtown cost ₡1000 to ₡2000. A taxi to Escazú from downtown will cost roughly ₡4500, while a ride to Los Yoses or San Pedro will generally cost about ₡2000. There's a 20% surcharge after 10pm that may not appear on the *maría*.

You can hire a taxi and a driver for half a day or longer if you want to do some touring around the area, but rates vary greatly depending on the destination and the condition of the roads. For these trips, it is best to negotiate a flat fee in advance.

AROUND SAN JOSÉ

Over the years, as San José's urban sprawl has crawled up the hillsides of the Central Valley, the boundary lines have blurred between the heart of the city and the villages that encircle it. Here you will find a little bit of everything: from crowded slums filled with immigrant workers to stylish residential neighborhoods where modernist houses hide behind 3m-high walls. Within this belt, there are a number of areas that offer an appealing alternative to staying in the city proper.

Just a few hundred meters east of San José's downtown are the contiguous neighborhoods of Los Yoses and San Pedro, home to a number of embassies as well as the most prestigious university in the country, the Universidad de Costa Rica (UCR). To the west, about 7km away, is Escazú, where Americanized housing developments lie alongside old Tico homesteads. Looking for a more relaxing alternative to the urban grind? These areas are a great place to start.

LOS YOSES & SAN PEDRO

These two side-by-side neighborhoods may lie in close proximity, but their characters are each totally unique. Los Yoses is a charming residential district dotted with modernist structures, historic homes, cozy inns and chilled-out neighborhood eateries. San Pedro, on the other hand, which houses the university district, is more boisterous – brimming with bars, clubs and all manner of student activity. Both of these areas provide an enticing (and convenient) alternative to staying in San José.

Orientation & Information

These districts are centered on a roundabout where Av Central meets the road to Zapote. The traffic circle is punctuated by the Fuente de la Hispanidad (a large fountain), which serves as an area landmark. Be careful crossing the streets that surround the circle; vehicles like to careen through at full throttle. To the west lies the district of Los Yoses; to the east, you'll find San Pedro, anchored by a small plaza and the Iglesia de San Pedro. About three blocks to the north of this point is the tree-lined campus of the UCR.

Most streets in Los Yoses and San Pedro are unnamed, and locals rely almost entirely on the landmark method to orient themselves (see boxed text, p534, for details). In Los Yoses, major area landmarks include the Subaru dealership, the old ICE building *(El Antiguo ICE)*, the Spoon restaurant and the Mall San Pedro. In San Pedro, common points of reference include the old Banco Popular building *(El Antiguo Banco Popular)* and the Iglesia de San Pedro.

There are dozens of internet cafes in the streets surrounding Calle La Amargura, so you will have no problem logging on. Rates begin at ₡300 per hour.

Burbujas (Map p102; ☎ 2224-9822; 150m east & 25m south of the Scotiabank, San Pedro; 🕑 9am-5pm Mon-Sat) Laundry service; about ₡3000 for a regular-sized load.

OTEC (Map p102; ☎ 2234-9468; www.turismojoven.com; 2nd fl, Outlet Mall, cnr Av Central & Calle Central, San Pedro; 🕑 10am-7pm Mon-Sat) The San Pedro office of the international youth travel agency.

Post Office (Map p102; ☎ 2253-6895; 1st fl, Outlet Mall, cnr Av Central & Calle Central, San Pedro; 🕑 8am-5:30pm Mon-Fri, 8am-noon Sat)

Scotiabank (Map p102; ☎ 2280-0604; Av Central btwn Calles 5 & 7, San Pedro) Changes cash and has a 24-hour ATM on the Cirrus network.

TAM Travel (Map p102; ☎ 2527-9700; www.tamtravel.com; Calle 39 btwn Avs Central & 8, Los Yoses) Airline ticketing, local travel and more.

Sights & Activities

The **Museo de Insectos** (Insect Museum; Map p102; ☎ 2511-5318; admission US$2; 🕑 1-5pm Mon-Fri; ♿), also known as the Museo de Entomología, has a fine collection of insects assembled by the Facultad de Agronomía at the Universidad de Costa Rica. It is housed (somewhat curiously) in the basement of the music building (Facultad de Artes Musicales), a brutalist structure painted an incongruous shade of Barbie pink. It is claimed that this is the only insect museum of its size in Central America. The collection is certainly extensive and provides a good opportunity to view a vast assortment of exotic creepy crawlies. The museum is signposted from the Iglesia de San Pedro.

For contemporary art, pay a visit to the lobby of the Hotel Milvia (p103), which serves as a noted area gallery, during daytime hours.

If you're interested in knocking down some pins, **Boliche Dent** (Map p102; ☎ 2253 5745; www.bolichedent.com; Calle 37, north of Av Central, Los Yoses; lane per hr US$18; 🕑 11am-midnight) in Los Yoses is an old-school bowling alley that looks straight out of 1969 (when it was built). Just east of the rotunda in San Pedro, the 1970s are alive and well at **Salón Los Patines** (Map p102; ☎ 2224-6821; northeast cnr of traffic circle, San Pedro; 🕑 7-10pm), a throwback roller rink.

Sleeping

Intimate inns, relaxed hostels, atmospheric B&Bs – this area offers some blessedly tranquil spots to hang your hat for the night, much of it just a short stroll from downtown San José.

All of the hotels listed have hot water.

HOSTELS

our pick **Hostel Bekuo** (Map p102; ☎ 2234-1091; www.hostelbekuo.com; 325m west of Spoon, Los Yoses; dm US$12, d with/without bathroom US$35/30, d with bathroom & TV US$40, all incl breakfast; P 💻 Wi-Fi) This restful spot feels more like a home than a hostel. The airy modernist structure has nine rooms (four of

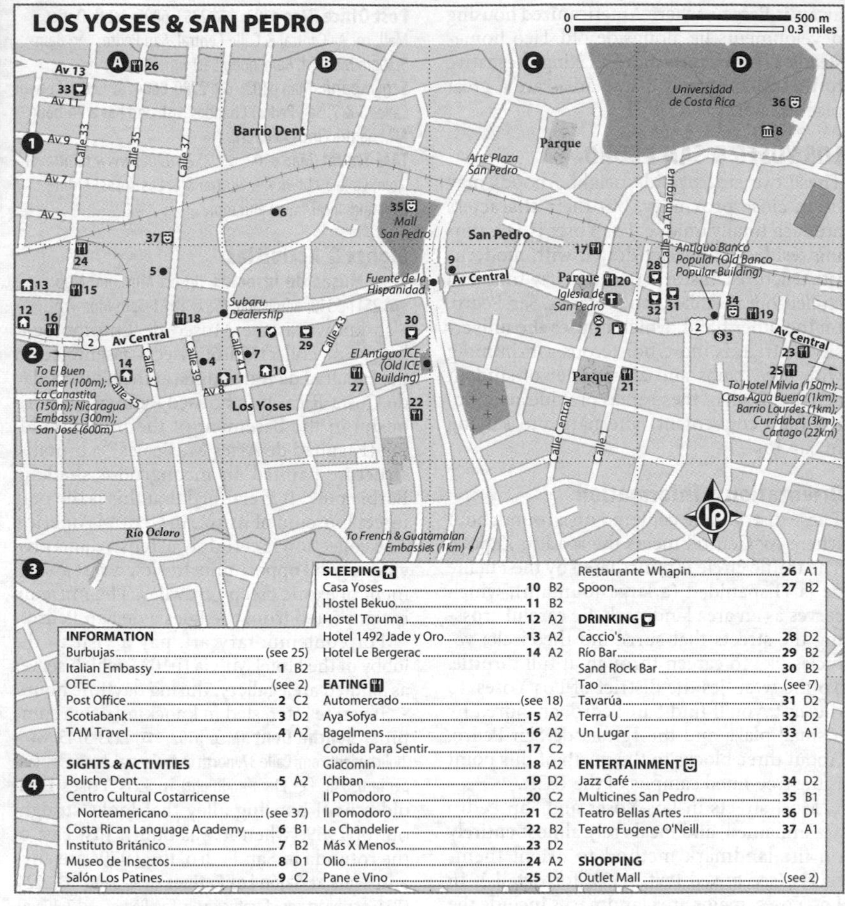

which are dormitories; one of which is reserved especially for women), as well as large tiled bathrooms, an expansive TV lounge dotted with bean bags, and an interior courtyard with a pre-Columbian granite sphere right in the center. The shared kitchen is comfortable and well equipped and there is free internet.

Casa Yoses (Map p102; ☎ 2234-5486; www.casayoses.com; Av 8; dm US$12, r per person with/without bathroom US$18/15, all incl breakfast; P 💻 📶) Another mellow spot, this nine-room Spanish Revival–style house from 1949 is perched on a hill that offers lovely views of the valley from the front garden. Here you'll find 10 rooms (six of them dorms) of varying decor and style, but all of which are spotless, with wood floors and tiled hallways. There is a shared kitchen, a lounge with a pool table and foosball, and even an area for BBQs. The young Tico owners speak Spanish, English and French.

BUDGET

our pick Hostel Toruma (Map p102; ☎ 2234-8186; www.hosteltoruma.com; Av Central btwn Calles 29 & 33; dm/s/d US$12/35/45; P 💻 📶 ♿) Overlooking Av Central from a small hill, this graceful neoclassical home once belonged to José Figueres, the Costa Rican president who abolished the army and granted women the right to vote. In late 2009, the hotel completed a top-to-bottom makeover that preserved the Spanish-tile floors and left the facade's decorative friezes sparkling. While the Toruma contains four dormitories, it feels much more like an inn, with 17 large private rooms, each of which is equipped with a modern bathroom, a sofa, wi-fi and flat-screen TV. Upstairs, an internet lounge is dotted with bean bags; downstairs, a small poolside restaurant serves breakfast, light snacks and beer. It's a mellow spot, popular with chilled-out solo travelers, couples and young families – and one of the best budget deals in San José.

Casa Agua Buena (off Map p102; ☎ 2280-3548; www.aguabuena.org/casabuena/index.html; Barrio Lourdes; r per week US$60-80) East of San Pedro, these ramshackle group houses are popular among international students and long-term travelers on tight budgets. Accommodations consist of two simple peach-colored homes with rooms of various sizes, equipped with shared kitchen, washing machine and a lounge with cable TV. Some rooms share bathrooms, while others have private ones. The Casa is gay-friendly.

MIDRANGE & TOP END

All of the hotels below accept credit cards.

Hotel Milvia (off Map p102; ☎ 2225-4543; www.hotelmilvia.com; s/d/tr incl breakfast US$59/69/75; 💻 📶) This lovely Caribbean-style plantation building once served as the home of Ricardo Fernández Peralta, an artillery colonel who fought in Costa Rica's 1948 civil war. Now owned by Brit expat Steve Longrigg and his Tica wife, Florencia Urbina, it serves as a hotel and art gallery. Nine eclectic rooms – some carpeted, others with shining wood floors, all dotted with bright pieces of art – surround a pleasant courtyard with a trickling fountain. An upstairs terrace provides incredible views of the mountains in the distance. For taxi drivers: from the Más x Menos in San Pedro, it's 250m east, 100m north and 100m east.

Hotel 1492 Jade y Oro (Map p102; ☎ 2256-5913; www.hotel1492.com; Av 1 btwn Calles 29 & 33, Los Yoses; d standard/deluxe incl breakfast US$70/80; P 📶) On a quiet Los Yoses side street, you'll find this intimate B&B, in a Spanish-style house built in the 1950s by the Volio family. The rooms vary in size, but all are nicely accented, with Portuguese tilework and some original furnishings. Breakfast is served in a charming rear garden.

Hotel Le Bergerac (Map p102; ☎ 2234-7850; www.bergerachotel.com; Calle 35 btwn Avs Central & 8, Los Yoses; d standard/superior/deluxe/grande US$90/115/135/145, all incl breakfast; P 💻) A whitewashed building contains a bright lobby accented with fresh flowers and 25 rooms that overlook a tropical garden at this Los Yoses standard-bearer. Though sizes and configurations vary, they are all comfortable and sunny, accented with wood floors and floral bedspreads, and equipped with immaculate bathroom, cable TV, telephone and safe. There is an onsite restaurant with a full bar.

Eating

Succulent Turkish sandwiches, Caribbean-style *rondón* (seafood gumbo), steaming pizzas – you can find just about every type of food in the narrow streets of San Pedro and Los Yoses, including quaint neighborhood spots well off the tourist trail.

BUDGET

our pick **Giacomin** (Map p102; ☎ 2224-3463; Av Central east of Calle 37, Los Yoses; pastries from ₡700; 🕑 8am-noon & 2-7pm Mon-Fri, 8am-noon & 2-6:30pm Sat) Obscured by a parking lot to the east of the Automercado is this small, 1960s pastry shop that *josefinos* swear is the best in town. Here you'll find delicious mushroom minipizzas, flaky croissants and what has to be Central America's best cinnamon roll *(arrollado de canela)*. There's a sweet selection of chocolate-dipped butter cookies, too. The tranquil upstairs lounge is a perfect haven in which to sip cappuccino and read a book.

El Buen Comer (off Map p102; ☎ 2233-3857; Av Central, 200m west of Bagelmens, Los Yoses; breakfast ₡800-1750, lunch casados ₡1900; 🕑 8am-3pm Mon-Fri) Popular with office workers, this homey, two-story *soda* is an excellent bet for budget-minded folks looking for tasty Tico home-style cooking, including *casados* and *gallo pinto* (a common meal of blended rice and beans).

Bagelmens (Map p102; ☎ 800-212-1314; www.bagelmenscr.com; cnr Av Central & Calle 33; breakfast ₡1000-2000; 🕑 7am-9pm; 📶) It's not Brooklyn, but if you've been on the *gallo pinto* diet, you'll be glad to know that Bagelmens offers decent bagels – as well as delicious freshly made waffles, supermoist banana bread and surprisingly good Italian gelatos (pistachio is our favorite). Bonus: there's free wi-fi for customers.

Spoon (Map p102; ☎ 2253-1331; Av 8; dishes ₡1500-6000; 🕑 7am-9pm Mon-Fri, 9am-5pm Sat & Sun) The Los Yoses branch of this local chain also serves as a local landmark. The menu is extensive and the big breakfasts are tops (especially after a long night of drinking). Better yet, the tables are made out of refurbished Regina sewing machines. Sew cool.

Comida Para Sentir (Map p102; 100m north of Iglesia de San Pedro, San Pedro; casados ₡1600-2800; 10am-6pm Mon-Fri; V) This informal, bustling student spot serves an international menu of veggie everything including curried rice with cashews, vegetable *casados,* whole-grain sandwiches and a mean cappuccino.

La Canastita (off Map p102; 2221-3816; cnr Av Central & Calle 25, Los Yoses; mains ₡1800-3000; 11:30am-11pm) This strip-light-and-plastic-table joint serves up delicious *casados* and blares out soccer to animated punters. It is a local favorite.

Aya Sofya (Map p102; 2224-5050; cnr Calle 33 & Av 1, Los Yoses; dishes ₡2600-7900; 7am-7pm Mon-Sat; V) A hidden gem with a diminutive outdoor patio serves a variety of Turkish and Mediterranean specialties, including fresh hummus, green salads laced with feta cheese, chicken sandwiches doused with tangy yogurt sauce and a rotating selection of daily specials. Don't miss their impeccable (and razor-thin) apple tart, perfect with an inky shot of Turkish coffee.

Pane e Vino (Map p102; 2280-2869; 150m east & 25m south of Scotiabank; pizzas ₡3100-8000; 5pm-midnight Mon-Sat, 5-10pm Sun; V) Delicate superthin-crust pizza comes in 90 different variations at this rustic San Pedro family spot, where you can satisfy your cravings for *salame picante* (pepperoni). The heaping bowls of pasta are a deal, including the delicious Pasta Pane e Vino, penne in a light tomato sauce studded with artichokes and mushrooms. There is a decent selection of wine (from ₡4100). Recommended.

For self-caterers, try **Más x Menos** (Map p102; Av Central, San Pedro) and **Automercado** (Map p102; Av Central btwn Calles 39 & 41, Los Yoses) – large, modern supermarkets that stock plenty of everything. The latter has a good selection of healthy items, including veggie burgers.

MIDRANGE

Olio (Map p102; 2281-0541; cnr Calle 33 & Av 3; tapas ₡2300-5500, dishes ₡5700-8900; 11:30am-1am Mon-Fri, 4pm-midnight Sat; V) This cozy, Mediterranean-flavored gastropub serves a long list of tempting tapas, including divine stuffed mushrooms *(hongos madrileños),* goat-cheese croquettes and garlic shrimp. There are also more than 17 house-made pastas to choose from and a decent beer and wine list (bottles from ₡13,500). Don't miss desert, specifically vanilla ice cream doused in coffee liqueur.

Ichiban (Map p102; 2291-5220; Centro Comercial Calle Real, Av Central, 50m east of Antiguo Banco Popular; maki rolls ₡2500-11,000, mains ₡3500-13,000; noon-3pm & 6:30-11pm Mon-Fri, noon-10pm Sat & Sun) You'll find all things Japanese at this modern San Pedro sushi bar, which dishes up well-rendered ramen, teppanyaki and specialty sushi rolls. They even have a Tico Roll (₡6200), which comes loaded with cream cheese, shiitake mushrooms, fried plantains and crab.

Il Pomodoro (San Pedro; pizzas ₡3300-10,000; V) Iglesia (Map p102; 2224-0966; 75m north of Iglesia de San Pedro; closed Tue); Parque (Map p102; 2283-1010; 100m south of Outlet Mall; closed Mon;) This very popular family chain draws office workers, families and packs of expats for fresh-from-the-oven pizzas topped with everything from olives to shellfish. Parents will appreciate the expansive location on the park, and there are even high chairs and changing stations.

Le Chandelier (Map p102; 2225-3980; 100m west & 100m south of El Antiguo ICE, Los Yoses; mains ₡5500-13,500; 11:30am-2pm & 6:30-10pm Mon-Fri, 6:30-10pm Sat) Whether you're sitting next to the fireplace or outside on the patio, it's hard to find a more romantic place than this two-decade-old Los Yoses outpost. Here, chef Claude Dubuis serves traditional French specialties (think duck *à l'orange*) with a few Costa Rican flourishes. Save room for the crêpes suzette for two (₡6000) – and *bon appétit*!

our pick **Restaurante Whapin** (Map p102; 2228-1480; cnr Calle 35 & Av 13, 200m east of El Farolito, Barrio Escalante; mains ₡7600-10,500; 8am-2:30pm & 6-10pm Mon-Sat) If you don't make it to the Caribbean, then absolutely make sure you eat here: an intimate corner spotpainted Rasta red, yellow and green, and serving up spectacularly delicious meals. Enjoy a steamy bowl of *rondón* (seafood gumbo cooked in coconut milk), a plate of rice and red beans, or fish simmered in spicy coconut sauce. Don't forget the fried plantains and, in season, the crisp breadfruit. Wash it all down with *agua de sapo,* a zesty sweet ginger drink.

Drinking

Calle La Amargura (Sorrow Street; Map p102; San Pedro) This is what Calle 3 is known as, to the north of Av Central. However, it should be called Calle de la Cruda (Street of Hangovers) because it has the highest concentration of bars of any single street in town, and many of these are packed with customers (mainly university students) even during daylight hours. Places come and go, but Terra U (50m north of Av Central), Caccio's (150m north of Av Central) and Tavarúa (across the street) are longtime party spots. The area gets rowdy in the wee hours: watch out for drunks and pickpockets.

Río Bar (Map p102; Av Central, west of Calle 43, Los Yoses) Just west of the fountain, this popular bar with an upstairs lounge has live bands on some nights and a pyrotechnic house drink called the *cucaracha* (cockroach). Early in the evening it's a good spot to watch the rush-hour traffic crawl by in the company of an after-work crowd.

Sand Rock Bar (Map p102; Centro Comercial Cocorí, 50m south of Fuente de la Hispanidad, Los Yoses) A raucous beer-swilling spot that gets rolling at 5pm and keeps going until the last customer leaves. Expect the soundtrack to be rock, rock and more rock – with some heavy metal thrown in to spice things up.

Tao (Map p102; ☎ 2225-5696; www.taorestolounge.com; Calle 41 btwn Avs Central & 8; cocktails from ₡3000) A dimly lit lounge decorated with lots of Buddhas, this hip spot has fusion cocktails and decent Vietnamese appetizers, including satay and spring rolls (from ₡2000).

our pick **Un Lugar** (Map p102; Calle 33 btwn Avs 11 & 13) This small wood-lined bar serves as a neighborhood hangout that draws artsy types and young professionals for cold beer and *bocas* (₡1800 to ₡3300). This is a good spot for solo women travelers.

Entertainment

Multicines San Pedro (Map p102; ☎ 2283-5715/6; www.ccmcinemas.com; 2nd fl, Mall San Pedro; admission US$4) This popular multiplex has 10 screens showing the latest Hollywood flicks.

For live theater, there are a couple of choices in the area. **Teatro Eugene O'Neill** (Map p102; ☎ 2207-7554; www.cccncr.com; Calle 37, north of Av Central, Los Yoses) has performances sponsored by the Centro Cultural Costarricense Norteamericano (Costa Rican–North American Cultural Center). On the east side of the UCR campus is the **Teatro Bellas Artes** (☎ 2207-4327; www.teatro.ucr.ac.cr), which has a wide variety of programming, including works produced by the university's fine-arts department.

Jazz Café (Map p102; ☎ 2253-8933; www.jazzcafecostarica.com; ⏲ 6pm-2am) is *the* destination in San José for live music, with a different band every night. Countless performers have taken to the stage here, including legendary Cuban bandleader Chucho Valdés and Colombian pop star Juanes. Admission charges vary, but plan on spending about ₡4000 to see local groups. It's 50m east of the Antiguo Banco Popular.

Shopping

Mall San Pedro (Map p102; ☎ 2283-7516; northwest of Fuente de la Hispanidad, Los Yoses) This busy four-story mall comes chock-full of clothing shops, a food court, a video arcade and even an Apple computer store.

Outlet Mall (Map p102; cnr Av Central & Calle Central, San Pedro) Smaller and more economical is this spot right across from the Iglesia de San Pedro.

Getting There & Away

From the Plaza de la Cultura in San José, take any bus marked 'Mall San Pedro.' A taxi ride from downtown will cost about ₡2000, depending on traffic. To get into San José, take one of the buses that make stops all along Av Central heading west into the city.

ESCAZÚ

You can find an unusual juxtaposition of gringo expats, moneyed aristocrats and old-world Tico village life in this sprawling suburb that climbs a steep hillside overlooking San José and Heredia. The area is really made up of three adjoining neighborhoods: San Rafael de Escazú, Escazú Centro and San Antonio de Escazú, each of which has its own unique character.

At the bottom of the hill is San Rafael, which is one part Costa Rica, two parts USA, dotted with strip malls, top-end car dealerships, tract housing and chain restaurants. Escazú Centro retains an unhurried Tico ambience, where narrow streets are cluttered with shops, *sodas* and old-world country taverns. At the top of the hill, the area around San Antonio remains almost entirely residential, a mix of humble rural homes, sprawling estates and a handful of hotels with spectacular views. The further you get up the hill, the more scarce public transportation becomes, so it's best to have a car.

Escazú's proximity to Pavas and Alajuela makes it a convenient place to stay if you want to be near San José's airports.

Information

Banco de Costa Rica ATM (Map p106; Av Central btwn Calles Central & 1, Escazú Centro) A 24-hour ATM on various international networks, including Cirrus.

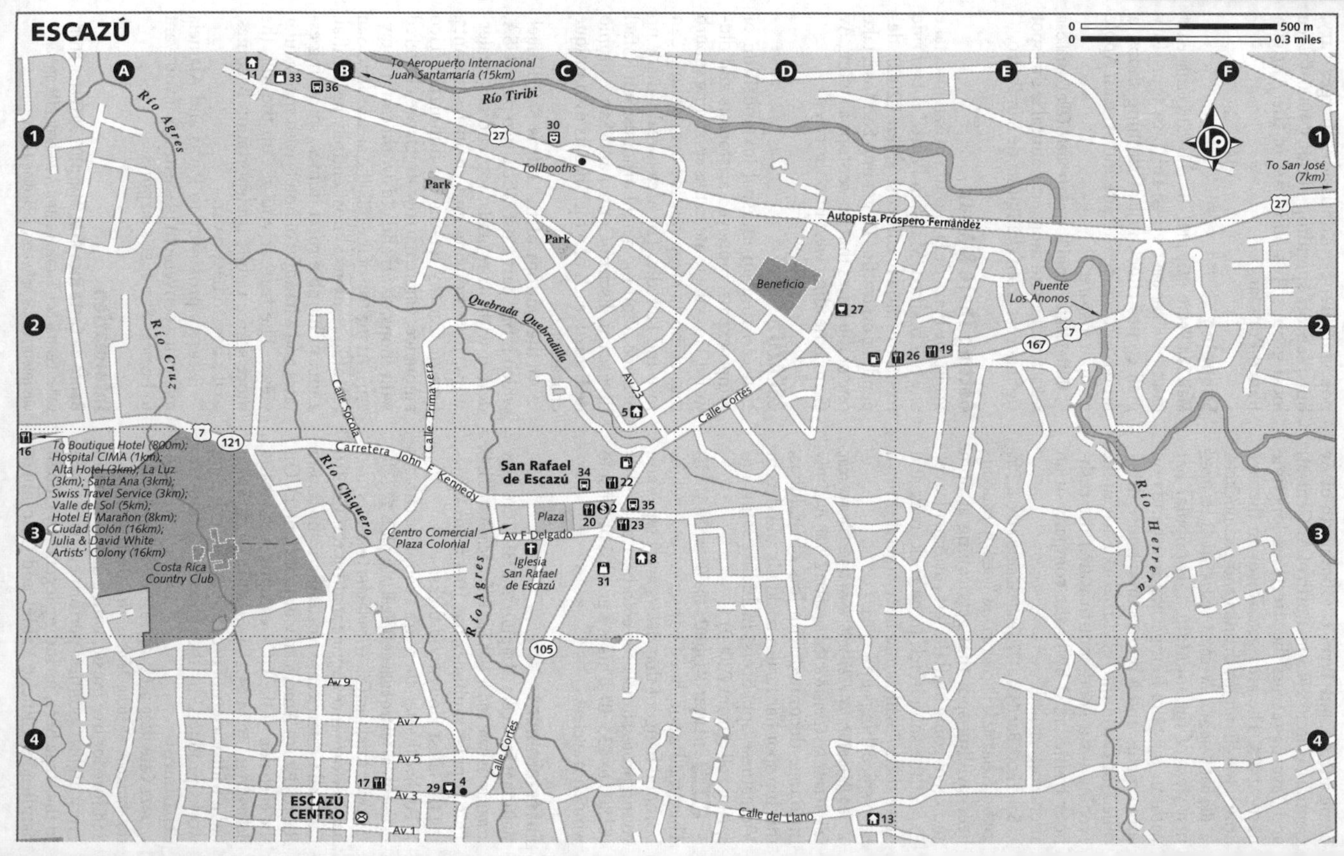
ESCAZÚ
0
0
500 m
0.3 miles
A
B
C
D
E
F
1
2
3
4
To Aeropuerto Internacional Juan Santamaría (15km)
Río Tiribi
Río Agres
27
Tollbooths
Park
Park
Autopista Próspero Fernández
To San José (7km)
Beneficio
Puente Los Anonos
167
7
Quebrada Quebradilla
Av 23
Calle Cortés
Río Cruz
Calle Socola
Calle Primavera
Carretera John F Kennedy
121
To Boutique Hotel (800m); Hospital CIMA (1km); Alta Hotel (3km); La Luz (3km); Santa Ana (3km); Swiss Travel Service (3km); Valle del Sol (5km); Hotel El Marañon (8km); Ciudad Colón (16km); Julia & David White Artists' Colony (16km)
16
Río Chiquero
Costa Rica Country Club
San Rafael de Escazú
Plaza
Centro Comercial Plaza Colonial
Av F Delgado
Iglesia San Rafael de Escazú
Río Agres
105
Río Herrera
Av 9
Av 7
Av 5
Av 3
Av 1
Calle Cortés
ESCAZÚ CENTRO
Calle del Llano
11
33
36
30
27
26
19
5
34
22
2
20
35
23
8
31
17
29
4
13

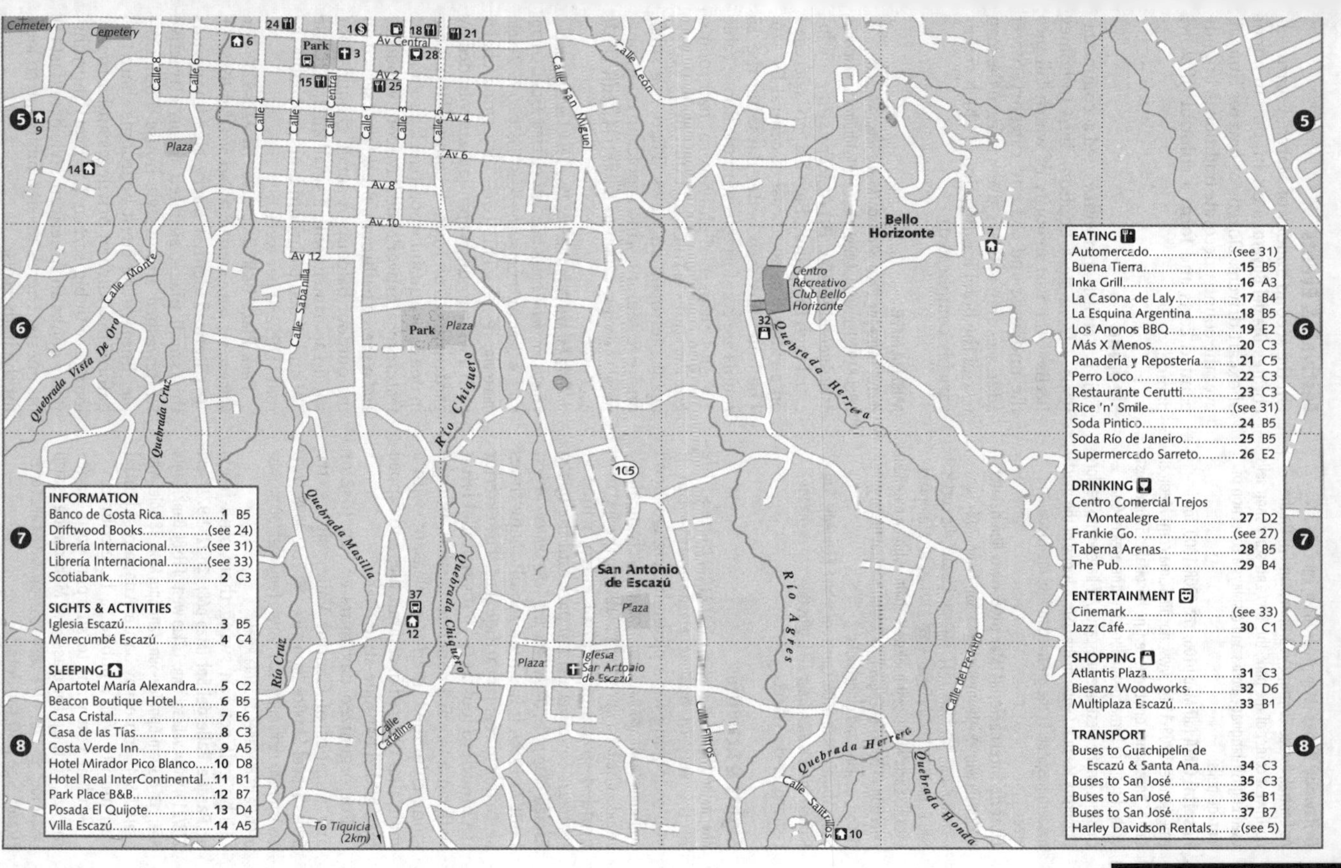
INFORMATION
Banco de Costa Rica....................1 B5
Driftwood Books....................(see 24)
Librería Internacional...........(see 31)
Librería Internacional...........(see 33)
Scotiabank....................2 C3
SIGHTS & ACTIVITIES
Iglesia Escazú....................3 B5
Merecumbé Escazú....................4 C4
SLEEPING
Apartotel María Alexandra.......5 C2
Beacon Boutique Hotel............6 B5
Casa Cristal....................7 E6
Casa de las Tías....................8 C3
Costa Verde Inn....................9 A5
Hotel Mirador Pico Blanco.....10 D8
Hotel Real InterContinental....11 B1
Park Place B&B....................12 B7
Posada El Quijote....................13 D4
Villa Escazú....................14 A5
EATING
Automercado....................(see 31)
Buena Tierra....................15 B5
Inka Grill....................16 A3
La Casona de Laly....................17 B4
La Esquina Argentina.............18 B5
Los Anonos BBQ....................19 E2
Más X Menos....................20 C3
Panadería y Repostería..........21 C5
Perro Loco....................22 C3
Restaurante Cerutti...............23 C3
Rice 'n' Smile....................(see 31)
Soda Pintico....................24 B5
Soda Río de Janeiro...............25 B5
Supermercado Sarreto...........26 E2
DRINKING
Centro Comercial Trejos
Montealegre....................27 D2
Frankie Go....................(see 27)
Taberna Arenas....................28 B5
The Pub....................29 B4
ENTERTAINMENT
Cinemark....................(see 33)
Jazz Café....................30 C1
SHOPPING
Atlantis Plaza....................31 C3
Biesanz Woodworks..............32 D6
Multiplaza Escazú..................33 B1
TRANSPORT
Buses to Guachipelín de
Escazú & Santa Ana..........34 C3
Buses to San José..................35 C3
Buses to San José..................36 B1
Buses to San José..................37 B7
Harley Davidson Rentals........(see 5)
Cemetery
Park
Plaza
Av Central
Av 2
Av 4
Av 6
Av 8
Av 10
Av 12
Calle 8
Calle 6
Calle 4
Calle 2
Calle Central
Calle 1
Calle 3
Calle 5
Calle San Miguel
Calle León
Calle Monte
Calle Sabanilla
Quebrada Vista De Oro
Quebrada Cruz
Río Chiquero
Quebrada Masilla
Quebrada Chiquero
Río Cruz
Calle Catalina
To Tiquicia (2km)
San Antonio de Escazú
Iglesia San Antonio de Escazú
Bello Horizonte
Centro Recreativo Club Bello Horizonte
Quebrada Herrera
Río Agres
Calle Filtros
Calle Salitrillos
Calle del Pedrero
Quebrada Honda
105

Driftwood Books (Map p106; 2nd fl, cnr Calle 2 & Av Central, Escazú Centro; 3-6pm Mon-Fri) On the northwest corner of the park, this tiny 2nd-story shop sells used English-language books and displays a collection of vintage bells.

Hospital CIMA (off Map p106; 2208-1000, for emergencies 2208-1144; www.hospitalcima.com) Medical care – emergency or otherwise. The hospital is 500m west of the Próspero Fernández tollbooth in the area of Guachipelín, on the west side of Escazú. Affiliated with Baylor University Medical Center in the USA, it is one of the most modern hospitals in the greater San José metropolitan area.

Librería Internacional (Map p106; www.libreriainternacional.com; 10am-8pm Mon-Sat, 10am-7pm Sun) Atlantis Plaza (2588-1817; Atlantis Plaza, Calle Cortés, San Rafael); Multiplaza Escazú (2201-8320; Multiplaza Escazú) Costa Rica's best bookstore chain, with an excellent selection of books in English, including natural history, fiction, cooking and guidebooks.

Scotiabank (Map p106; Carretera John F Kennedy, San Rafael) There is a 24-hour ATM, plus they can exchange cash and traveler's checks.

Sights & Activities

Because this is a residential area, there's little in the way of tourist attractions – but if you're looking for a pleasant neighborhood to browse shops and enjoy a leisurely meal, it's ideal. The best spot for a walk are the narrow, gridded streets of Escazú Centro, which at its heart contains a small park and the **Iglesia Escazú** (Map p106; cnr Av Central & Calle Central). First built in 1799, it has been rebuilt many times since due to regular earthquakes. The exterior isn't much to look at (a 1990s remodel left it with an awkward concrete facade), but the stone-columned interior is pleasant, with a main altar covered in ceramic tiles and capped by a gilded baroque-style altar.

For organized day tours of San José or any number of Central Valley sights, try **Swiss Travel Service** (Map p106; 2282-4898; www.swisstravelcr.com; Autopista Próspero Fernández, 300m west of Cruce de Piedades de Santa Ana).

The golf set can swing their nine-irons at **Parque Valle del Sol** (Map p68; 2282-9222, ext 218/219; www.vallesol.com; 1.7km west of HSBC Bank, Santa Ana; 6:30am-6pm Tue-Sun, 8am-6pm Mon; 18 holes with a cart US$94), in nearby Santa Ana, a residential community with a public 18-hole course.

And, if you want to sharpen your dance moves, sign up for classes at **Merecumbé Escazú** (Map p106; 2289-4774, 8884-7553; cnr Av 3 & Calle Cortés, Escazú). See p80 for details.

Festivals & Events

On the second Sunday of March, Escazú celebrates **Día del Boyero**, a celebration in honor of oxcart drivers. Dozens of *boyeros* from all over the country decorate traditional, brightly painted carts and form a colorful (if slow) parade.

Sleeping

This is a stylish area with varied accommodations – from sleek boutique inns to homey B&Bs – the vast majority of which fall into the midrange and top-end category. Street addresses aren't always given; refer to the map or call the hotel for directions (which are invariably complicated).

MIDRANGE

Hotel Mirador Pico Blanco (Map p106; 2228-1908, 2289-6197; hotelpicoblanco.com; Calle Salitrillos, San Antonio; d standard/ste US$40/50; P) A sleepy stone inn located high in the hills, Pico Blanco is perched on a ridge 3km southeast of central Escazú. The hotel has seen better days, but the 15 rooms are comfortable, with tile floors, cable TV and clean, if slightly worn, bathrooms. For the money, you won't find more extravagant metropolitan views. There is a small onsite restaurant, which cooks up traditional meals (dishes ₡2000 to ₡4000). Credit cards accepted.

Villa Escazú (Map p106; 2289-7971; inezchapman29@yahoo.com; www.hotels.co.cr/vescazu.html; Escazú Centro; s/d/tr without bathroom incl breakfast US$50/60/75, 2-night minimum; P) This two-story wood chalet with a wraparound veranda is surrounded by gardens and fruit trees. Accommodations are in one of two quaint wood-paneled rooms that feature local artwork and have comfy couches and a shared bathroom. Breakfast is served on the outdoor balcony. A small, ground-floor studio apartment with a small kitchen, cable TV and a tiled bathroom is also available for rent (US$280 per week).

Park Place B&B (Map p106; 2228-9200; San Antonio; s/d without bathroom incl breakfast US$55/60; P) Retired dentist Barry Needman runs this small place, situated in an attractive whitewashed alpine-style house. Four simple, immaculate guest bedrooms share two bathrooms, kitchen privileges and a roomy lounge with big-screen TV. Every morning, Barry cooks an American-style breakfast for his guests. There's no sign out front, so look for the high eaves.

Costa Verde Inn (Map p106; ☎ 2228-4080; www.costaverdeinn.com; Escazú Centro; s/d/tr US$55/65/75, d apt from US$85, all incl breakfast; P wi-fi) The sister lodge of the famous Manuel Antonio hotel, this homey stone inn is surrounded by lush gardens that contain a hot tub, a mosaic-tile swimming pool, a BBQ area and even a sundeck with wi-fi. Fourteen simple rooms of various sizes have king-sized beds, comfy rocking chairs and folk-art accents. Five apartments come with fully equipped kitchen. A generous Tico breakfast is served on the outdoor terrace. Weekly rates are available; credit cards accepted.

Casa de las Tias (Map p106; ☎ 2289-5517; www.hotels.co.cr/casatias.html; s/d/tr incl breakfast US$72/82/92; P wi-fi) In a quiet area of San Rafael, this yellow-and-turquoise Cape Cod–style house (complete with picket fence) has five immaculate, individually decorated rooms, all with private bathrooms. The house is adorned with crafts that owners Xavier and Pilar have picked up on their travels in Latin America, lending the place a cozy, intimate feel.

Apartotel María Alexandra (Map p106; ☎ 2228-1507; www.mariaalexandra.com; cnr Calle 3 & Av 23, San Rafael, d apt from US$80; P wi-fi) This centrally located apartment-hotel in San Rafael has 15 clean, wood-paneled apartments with private bedroom, kitchen and laundry area – all of which channel a late-'70s *Brady Bunch* vibe. There is a sauna, mosaic-tile swimming pool and a small gym. Housekeeping is included.

Boutique Hotel (off Map p106; ☎ 2288-6762; www.bedandbreakfastcr.com; Carretera John F Kennedy; d standard/junior/deluxe/ste incl breakfast US$85/95/115/125; P wi-fi) One kilometer west of the Costa Rica Country Club, on the road to Santa Ana, this friendly two-story inn has five simple rooms with blond-wood floors, large, comfortable beds, painted sinks with folk-art motifs, minirefrigerators and in-room coffeemakers. Two units come with air-con and two are wheelchair-accessible. A broad outdoor deck with pleasant views is stocked with rocking chairs for lounging.

Posada El Quijote (Map p106; ☎ 2289-8401; www.quijote.cr; Calle del Llano, Bello Horizonte; d standard/superior/deluxe incl breakfast US$95/105/115; P wi-fi) This Spanish-style *posada* on a hillside rates as one of the top B&Bs in the San José area. Standard rooms are simple yet homey, with wooden floors, throw rugs, cable TV and private hot-water bathrooms, while larger superior and deluxe units have either a small patio or a private terrace. All guests are invited to take a nip at the honor bar, and then relax on the outdoor patio while soaking up the sweeping views of the Central Valley.

TOP END

Credit cards are accepted at all of the following establishments.

Beacon Boutique Hotel (Map p106; ☎ 2228-3110; www.mybeaconescazu.com; Av Central btwn Calles 4 & 6, Escazú Centro; d incl breakfast US$129-299; P wi-fi) A stylish 27-room inn situated at the heart of Escazú Centro, this top-end spot comes stocked with all manner of luxury goodies: high thread count linens, down comforters, king-sized beds, plush robes, in-room coffeemakers and even a pillow menu. Room decor is contemporary Spanish Mediterranean (think mahogany furnishings and sedate earthy tones). There is an onsite gym, spa and wine bar (open from 7pm to midnight), as well as a lush courtyard garden with a pool.

our pick Casa Cristal (Map p106; ☎ 2289-2530; www.casacristalcr.com; Bello Horizonte; d incl breakfast US$130-225; P wi-fi) This chic, whitewashed boutique hotel is situated on what has to be the best piece of real estate in Escazú: at the end of a winding mountain road, on a hillside overlooking several dozen hectares of uninhabited parkland, with the twinkling lights of San José in the distance. There are eight individually decorated contemporary guest rooms with king-sized beds, flat-screen TVs and large bathrooms (some with Jacuzzi tubs) – most of which have floor-to-ceiling windows that allow for uninterrupted views of the Central Valley. It's a serene spot, with a pool, a small bar and a cafe. Upon arrival, all guests are treated to a welcome mojito by the inn's hospitable Cuban owners. Excellent value. Note that the hotel does not accept children under the age of 12.

Other top-end options include **Hotel Real InterContinental** (Map p106; ☎ 2289-7000; www.interconti.com; d/ste/presidential ste from US$250/550/1800; P wi-fi), an outpost of this esteemed luxury chain located across the street from the Multiplaza mall.

OUTSIDE ESCAZÚ

Three kilometers west of Escazú is the affluent expat suburb of Santa Ana. On the road between the two is the **Alta Hotel** (off Map p106; ☎ 2282-4160; www.thealtahotel.com; d/ste from US$149/169; P wi-fi), a graceful

A COSTA RICAN ART COLONY

If you work in the arts and want to spend some time in Costa Rica, the **Julia and David White Artists' Colony** (off Map p106; ☎ 2249-1414; www.forjuliaanddavid.org; studio apt for 2 weeks from US$425;) offers the perfect refuge. Located 16km west of Escazú, the 5-hectare compound in the hills surrounding Ciudad Colón comes equipped with a swimming pool, hiking trails and comfortable studios.

Mediterranean-style villa with 23 white-washed rooms decked out in terra-cotta tiles and contemporary wood furnishings. Expansive bathrooms are clad in Spanish tiles and come equipped with hair dryers and robes. Rooms on the 4th and 5th floors have the best views: on a clear day it's possible to see all the way to the Pacific. Service is attentive and there is a pool, concierge services and a restaurant, La Luz (see opposite).

Five kilometers beyond Santa Ana, on the old, picturesque road to Ciudád Colón, you'll find **Hotel El Marañon** (off Map p106; ☎ 2249-1271; www.cultourica.com; s/d/tr/q incl breakfast US$49/69/85/99; P). A bright mustard-yellow building, surrounded by fruit orchards, it has 20 simple cabins with firm beds. Some rooms have staggering views of the Central Valley. This is an environmentally minded place, powered by solar energy and scrubbed with biodegradable cleansers. A small onsite restaurant serves three meals daily; yoga is sometimes available.

Eating

You'll find a little bit of everything in Escazú, from homey Tico spots to global fusion eateries.

BUDGET

Panadería y Repostería (Map p106; ☎ 2289-7750; cnr Av Central & Calle 5, Escazú Centro; items from ₡300; 7am-5pm Mon-Sat; V) This bright-red corner bakery is a great spot to pick up fresh bread, cookies and doughnuts.

Rice 'n' Smile (Map p106; Atlantis Plaza, San Rafael; rice pudding ₡1000; 10am-8pm Sun-Thu, 10am-9pm Fri & Sat; V) This contemporary new spot in the Atlantis Plaza shopping center serves a rotating selection of more than 30 scrumptious flavors of rice pudding. *Dulce de leche* (caramel) is a sticky-sweet favorite.

our pick **La Casona de Laly** (Map p106; cnr Av 3 & Calle Central, Escazú Centro; bocas ₡1000-2200, casados ₡1900, mains ₡2200-7000; 11am-12:30am Tue-Sat, 11am-6pm Sun) At the heart of Escazú Centro, this much-loved restaurant-tavern specializes in country-style Tico fare. Locals and expats alike pack the joint for cheap, lip-smacking *bocas*, ice-cold beers and a soundtrack of merengue accompanied by the cackling of the owner's pet birds, who inhabit the cages that line the entire west wall of the restaurant. Be sure to try the *dados de queso* (fried cheese cubes) – they are the best.

Soda Pintico (Map p106; 2nd fl, cnr Av Central & Calle 2, Escazú Centro; mains ₡1100-2800; casados ₡1700; 7am-6pm Mon-Sat) This cheap and charming *soda* located on the 2nd floor of the Escazú Centro Commercial Plaza is tiny but the *casado* portions are just right. There is no menu to speak of; ask what's cooking.

La Esquina Argentina (Map p106; ☎ 2288-2811; cnr Av Central & Calle Cortés, Escazú Centro; dishes ₡1200-4400; 7am-2pm Mon-Fri) This popular roadside stand sells piping-hot *empanadas*, smoked meats and tasty mashed potatoes. The outdoor patio is a good spot to linger over a cup of coffee.

Perro Loco (Map p106; Centro Comercial El Cruce, cnr Calle Cortés & Carretera John F Kennedy, San Rafael; hot dogs ₡1680-4470; noon-8pm Mon-Tue, noon-4am Wed-Sat, 4-10pm Sun) If you've been boozing it up, this greasy spoon is what you need. 'Crazy Dog' serves eight internationally themed hot dogs. Our favorite: the Chihuahua dog, loaded with fresh guacamole.

Buena Tierra (Map p106; ☎ 2288-0342; cnr Calle Central & Av 2, Escazú Centro; dishes ₡2200-3500; 8am-5pm Mon-Fri, 9am-2pm Sat; V) A cute and friendly organic cafe and cafeteria in Escazú Centro, south of the Iglesia Escazú, has an outdoor balcony with wonderful views of the town center. It's a great spot to sip herbal tea and eat cake.

Soda Río de Janeiro (Map p106; ☎ 8811-5263; cnr Calle 1 & Av 2, Escazú Centro; mains ₡2700; 6am-6pm Mon-Sat) Located southeast of the Iglesia Escazú, this charismatic little *soda* decked out with bright-red tablecloths is frequently full. Typical Tico fare includes pork chops, chicken or fish accompanied by big jars of spicy, pickled vegetables. There's a tiny aquarium of angelfish that you can watch while you wait for a seat.

Self-caterers can hit the **Más x Menos** (Map p106; ☎ 2228-0954; Carretera John F Kennedy, San Rafael; 6:30am-midnight Mon-Sat, 6:30am-10pm Sun) or the **Supermercado Saretto** (Map p106; ☎ 2228-0247; San

Rafael). The best supermarket in the area is the sprawling new **Automercado** at Atlantis Plaza (Map p106; ☎ 2588-1742; San Rafael; ⏲ 7am-10pm Mon-Sat, 8am-9pm Sun).

MIDRANGE

Inka Grill (Map p106; ☎ 2289-5117; www.graninka.com; Centro Comercial Los Pacos, on the road to Santa Ana; dishes ₡4000-13,000; ⏲ noon-4pm & 6-10pm Mon-Thu, noon-11pm Fri & Sat, noon-9:30pm Sun) The San José outpost of this venerable international chain serves all the Peruvian classics, including *ceviche* (marinated seafood), stuffed potatoes and an exceptionally well-made *ají de gallina* (walnut-chicken stew). Don't miss the *pisco sours* (grape-brandy cocktails). There is also a children's menu.

Los Anonos BBQ (Map p106; ☎ 2228-0180; mains ₡5500-16,000; ⏲ noon-3pm & 6-10pm Tue-Sat, 11:30am-9pm Sun) On the road between San José and Escazú is this meat-centric place, which has been in continuous operation since the early '60s. It's a rustic family spot, with wood tables and historic photos of Costa Rica – and if you've got a hankering for a good steak, this would be the place to dip into USDA-approved cuts. Credit cards accepted.

Restaurante Cerutti (Map p106; ☎ 2228-4511/9954; www.ceruttirestaurante.com; Calle Cortés, San Rafael; dishes ₡5585-11,170; ⏲ noon-2:30pm & 6:30-11pm Wed-Mon; Ⓥ) This pricey restaurant, south of Carretera JF Kennedy in San Rafael, delivers predictably top-notch Italian specialties, including fresh seafood and house-made pastas. The ravioli stuffed with ricotta and mushrooms is a local favorite, and you can't go wrong with the long list of delicious risottos. Credit cards accepted.

Tiquicia (off Map p106; ☎ 2289-5839; miradortiquicia.com; mains ₡6500-11,000; ⏲ 5pm-midnight Tue-Thu, noon-2am Sat, noon-6pm Sun) This long-running hilltop Tico restaurant serves up bounteous platters, in addition to live folk music on weekends. Without a doubt, it's a tourist trap – an expensive one – but you're not here to eat, you're here to admire the extravagant views of the Central Valley. The restaurant is 5km south of Escazú Centro on a paved road. It's tricky to find; call for directions or check the website for a map.

La Luz (off Map p106; ☎ 2282-4160; www.thealtahotel.com; mains ₡7700-15,500; ⏲ 6:30am-10pm) Tucked into the bottom floor of the Alta Hotel (p109), this elegant dining spot has lovely valley views and a Costa Rican fusion menu featuring more than half a dozen lobster specials daily. Favorites include dishes such as *camarones flamboyán* (shrimp flambéed in tequila) and grilled beef tenderloins bathed in a sauce made of local strawberries. Credit cards accepted.

Drinking

Centro Comercial Trejos Montealagre (Map p106; Calle Cortés, San Rafael) This nightlife and drinking complex on the northern edge of San Rafael is one of the hottest – and trendiest – drinking and dancing outposts in the capital. The scenesters usually start rolling in at 9pm and keep going until the wee hours. As with other San José party places, bars come and go quickly, so inquire locally before setting out. One of the few enduring spots is Frankie Go (☎ 2289-5937), which regularly screens soccer matches and hosts ladies' nights.

Taberna Arenas (Map p106; cnr of Av Central & Calle 3; Escazú Centro; ⏲ from 4pm) This delightful, old-fashioned Tico bar is an Escazú institution. Arenas has good *bocas* and a wide selection of domestic and imported beers. Owner don Israel is a true charmer, and has his photos with various heads of state on the walls, along with the agricultural implements that are de rigueur in any country bar.

The Pub (Map p106; Av 3 btwn Calles 3 & 5; ⏲ from 11am) The small American-owned pub has a list of more than two dozen international beers, a dozen local brews and a selection of shots with scary-sounding names like 'Test Tube Baby' and 'Anti-Freeze.' A greasy bar menu is available to soak up the damage.

If you're looking to sip fine vintages, visit the stylish ground-floor wine bar at the Beacon Boutique Hotel (p109). For local flavor, nothing beats the always awesome La Casona de Laly (see opposite).

Entertainment

The **Cinemark** (Map p106; ☎ 2201-5050; www.cinemarkca.com; Multiplaza Escazú; admission ₡2200) inside the Multiplaza mall has first-run movies. Wednesday admission is knocked down to ₡1300.

If you're seeking a little live music, the **Jazz Café** (☎ 2288-4740; www.jazzcafecostarica.com; north side of Autopista Próspero Fernández; admission from ₡3000) – the sister club of the San Pedro standard-bearer (p105) – has a roomy new performance outpost featuring local and international bands. If you're coming from San José, take the exit immediately after the tollbooth.

THE FINE WOODCRAFTS OF BARRY BIESANZ

Located in the hills of Bello Horizonte in Escazú, the workshop of **Biesanz Woodworks** (Map p106; ☎ 2289-4337; www.biesanz.com; 8am-5pm Mon-Fri, 10am-4pm Sat & Sun) can be difficult to find, but the effort will be well worth it. This shop is one of the finest woodcrafting studios in the nation, run by celebrated artisan Barry Biesanz. His bowls and other decorative containers are exquisite and take their inspiration from pre-Columbian techniques, in which the natural lines and forms of the wood determine the shape and size of the bowl. The pieces are expensive (from US$85 for a palm-size bowl), but they are unique – and so delicately crafted that they wouldn't be out of place in a museum.

Club Gaira (☎ 2288-2367; www.clubgaira.com; next to Ferretería EPA; 8pm-2:30am Wed-Sat) is Escazú's new trendy, design-conscious club with a geometric-meets-tribal decor (think zebra pelts and striped couches), plus two bars, two dance floors and DJs that spin hip-hop, Latin and electronica. Admission charge varies.

The Centro Comercial Trejo Montealegre (p111) also has a number of dance spots.

Shopping

Atlantis Plaza (Map p106; Calle Cortés, San Rafael) A symphony of brutal-looking steel is home to a small shopping center lined with boutiques, a bookstore (see p108), an Automercado supermarket and various eateries.

Multiplaza Escazú (Map p106; ☎ 2289-8984; www.multiplazamall.com; 10am-8pm Mon-Sat, 10am-7pm Sun) Costa Rica's most stylish – and massive – shopping mall has everything you need (or don't). Of particular interest to campers is the Cemaco (☎ 2289-7474), a budget department store that sells basic fishing and camping supplies, including propane gas for your portable stove. If you're coming from San José, the mall can be reached by taking any bus marked 'Escazú Multiplaza' (see p99 for more information).

Getting There & Around

Frequent buses between San José and Escazú cost about ₡300 and take about 25 minutes. All depart San José from east of the Coca-Cola Terminal or south of the Hospital San Juan de Dios. They take several routes: buses labeled 'San Antonio de Escazú' go up the hill to the south of Escazú and end near the Iglesia San Antonio de Escazú; those labeled 'Escazú Centro' end in Escazú's main plaza; others, labeled 'Guachipelín' go west on the Carretera John F Kennedy and pass the Costa Rica Country Club. All buses go through San Rafael.

For motorcycle rental, see **Harley Davidson Rentals** (Map p106; ☎ 2289-5552; www.mariaalexandra.com; cnr Calle 3 & Av 23, San Rafael), inside the Apartotel María Alexandra. Riders have to be more than 25 years of age and have a valid motorcycle driver's license. Rates start at US$150 per bike per day and include helmet, goggles and unlimited mileage (insurance and tax are not included).

Central Valley & Highlands

It is on the coffee-draped hillsides of the Central Valley that you will find Costa Rica's heart and soul. This is not only the physical center of the country, it is its cultural and spiritual core. It is here that the Spanish first settled. It is here that coffee built a prosperous nation. And it is here that picturesque highland villages still gather for centuries-old fiestas. It is also here that you'll get to fully savor Costa Rica's country cooking: artisanal cheeses, steamy corn cakes, crisp pieces of pork and fresh-caught river trout. It's a simple cuisine, but it is comforting – one that feels like home.

For the traveler, the Central Valley offers a break from the tourist industrial complex on the coasts. In this mountainous region of nooks and crannies, entertainment consists of hanging out in a bustling mountain town, and watching folks gather for market days and church. That doesn't mean, however, that there is nothing to do. You can ride raging rapids, see space-age shrubbery, visit the country's oldest colonial church, attend solemn religious processions, look for trogons in mist-shrouded forests and hike myriad volcanoes – the geological phenomena that have provided the country with its indescribably fertile soil and its long-running agricultural traditions. So take you're your time. When you explore the Central Valley, you'll not only witness great beauty – you'll see the landscape that gave Costa Rica its character.

HIGHLIGHTS

- White-knuckling it down the cascading rapids of the **Ríos Reventazón** or **Pacuare** (p148)
- Seeing the country's most venerated religious relic at the **Basílica de Nuestra Señora de Los Ángeles** (p138) in Cartago
- Peering into the mammoth craters of the area's grumbling volcanoes: **Irazú** (p140), **Poás** (p124) and **Turrialba** (p151)
- Winding along scenic mountain roads to **Zarcero** (p130), home of trippy topiary and organic farming
- Hiking through the serene surroundings at the country's major archaeological site, **Monumento Nacional Arqueológico Guayabo** (p149)

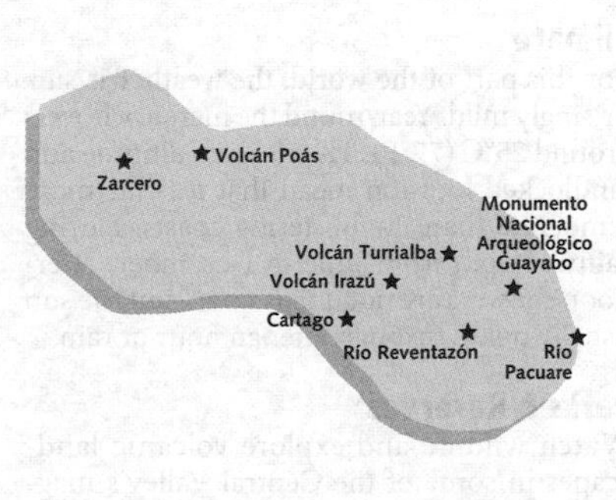

History

As in other parts of the country, there is little in the historical record about the ethnicities that inhabited the Central Valley prior to the arrival of the Spanish. What is known is that the people of the area – largely the Huetar – practiced an animist religion, produced stone sculpture and clay pottery, and communicated in a Chibchan dialect that is now extinct. They also developed and maintained the ancient highland city of Guayabo (p149) – which is today the biggest and most significant pre-Columbian archeological site in the country.

Though Columbus grazed the country's shore in 1502, European settlement in Costa Rica would not begin in earnest until 1563, when Juan Vásquez de Coronado founded the colonial capital of Cartago, what is today Costa Rica's oldest Spanish city. Over the next two centuries, Spanish communities would pop up in Heredia, San José and Orosi. Throughout this period, however, the area remained a colonial backwater, a checkerboard of Spanish farming communities and *indios bravos* ('fierce Indians'), native ethnicities that had not come under colonial dominion – and who practiced a largely itinerant agriculture.

It was only after independence, in the 1830s, that the area began to prosper with the expanded cultivation of coffee. The *grano de oro* (golden bean) transformed the country, providing the revenue to invest in urban infrastructure such as electricity and pavements, not to mention many baronial mansions. Coffee has since been overtaken as a key agricultural export by pineapples and bananas. But its legacy lives on, reflected in the culture, architecture and traditions of many highland towns.

Climate

For this part of the world, the weather is surprisingly mild. Year-round the mercury hovers around 25°C (77°F). The elevated altitude and landlocked location mean that it is far more temperate than the blistering coasts. During rainy season, from June to December, afternoon showers are not uncommon, but the sun usually pokes through after an hour of rain.

Parks & Reserves

Watch wildlife and explore volcanic landscapes in some of the Central Valley's magnificent national parks.

Los Ángeles Cloud Forest Adventure Park (p133) This away-from-the-crowds reserve offers the chance to whiz through the treetops on a canopy tour or trot through hills on horseback.

Monumento Nacional Arqueológico Guayabo (p149) See the outline of an ancient forest village nestled into a lush hillside at the country's biggest and most important pre-Columbian archeological site.

Parque Nacional Tapantí-Macizo Cerro de la Muerte (p144) This little-visited park receives more rainfall than any other part of the country, so it's full of life – a perfect outpost for dedicated bird-watchers.

Parque Nacional Volcán Irazú (p140) One of the few lookouts in the country that affords views of both the Caribbean and the Pacific, Irazú also lays claim to being the country's highest active volcano.

Parque Nacional Volcán Poás (p124) Easily accessible, this park has a shimmering crater lake and plenty of surrounding cloud forest.

Dangers & Annoyances

While the area is generally considered to be very safe, there are regular reports of car break-ins. Try to always secure guarded parking and never leave valuables in your car.

Getting There & Around

While all of the towns in this area are connected by regular buses, renting a car makes sense if you want to explore the many worthwhile hard-to-reach corners. Locals occasionally wave down passing cars. If you do this, beware that there are risks (see p550), and always offer to help with gas costs.

ALAJUELA & THE NORTHERN VALLEY

Volcanoes shrouded in mist, undulating coffee *fincas* (plantations), bustling agricultural centers. The area around the provincial capital of Alajuela, 18km northwest of San José, seems to have it all – including Juan Santamaría international airport, just 3km outside the city. The proximity to the airport is key, for this area makes a highly convenient transit point if you are entering or leaving the country. And for travelers seeking to avoid San José, it offers a good selection of bustling eateries, atmospheric B&Bs and well-equipped city inns.

ALAJUELA

pop 43,000

Costa Rica's second city is also home to one of the country's most famous figures: Juan Santamaría, the humble drummer boy who died putting an end to William Walker's campaign to turn Central America into slaving territory in the Battle of Rivas in 1856 (for more on Walker, see boxed text, p36). A busy agricultural hub, it is here that farmers bring their products to market – which means that on any given day (except Sunday), the place is teeming.

Alajuela is by no means a tourist 'destination.' Much of the architecture is unremarkable, the streets are often jammed and there are only a few offerings in the way of sights. But it's an inherently Costa Rican city. And, in its more relaxed moments, it can unveil a few charms – a place where Tico families have leisurely Sunday lunches and teenagers steal kisses in the park. It's also a good base for exploring the countryside to the north, including the Parque Nacional Volcán Poás (p124).

Orientation & Information

Central Alajuela is a pedestrian-friendly grid that is easy to navigate, but as with all Costa Rican cities, signage is nonexistent (see boxed text, p534).

Citibank (☎ 2443-6011; cnr Calle 2 & Av 6; 🕑 9am-6pm Mon-Fri, 9am-12:30pm Sat) Alajuela is cluttered with banks; this one has a drive-through and two ATMs on the Plus, Cirrus and Maestro networks.

Conexion (☎ 2431-2623; Calle 1 btwn Avs 3 & 5; per hr ₡350; 🕑 7am-7pm Mon-Sat) Next to Jalapeños Central, this place offers internet access, photocopying and international calling.

Hospital San Rafael (☎ 2436-1000) A bells-and-whistles hospital housed in a brand-new three-story complex on the southern edge of town.

Instituto Costarricense de Turismo (ICT; ☎ 2442-1820) There's no tourist office in Alajuela proper, but the ICT has a desk at the international airport.

Libros Chiloé (Av 5 btwn Calles 2 & 4; 🕑 8:30am-6pm Mon-Sat) Dusty little shop packed to the rafters with Spanish-language historic and literary tomes, including a large section devoted to Costa Rican history. There is a small selection of English and French titles, too.

Post office (☎ 2443-2653; Av 5 btwn Calles Central & 1; 🕑 8am-5:30pm Mon-Fri, 8am-12pm Sat)

Scotiabank (☎ 2430-9560; cnr Av Central & Calle 1; 🕑 8:30am-5pm Mon-Fri, 9am-1pm Sat) Has a 24-hour ATM on the Cirrus network.

Sights

ALAJUELA CITY CENTER

The shady **Parque Central** is a pleasant place to relax beneath a cluster of mango trees. It is surrounded by several 19th-century buildings, including the **cathedral**, which suffered severe damage in an earthquake in 1991. The hemispherical cupola is constructed of sheets of red corrugated metal. The interior is spacious and elegant rather than ornate; two presidents are buried here.

Six blocks to the east, a Renaissance-inspired structure, built in 1941, houses the **Iglesia La Agonía**, a popular local spot for mass (the first one is at 6am). The columned interiors are airy and graceful, with ornate wood altars and, interestingly, a main altar encrusted with a fluorescent crucifix (somehow, it works).

Two blocks south of the Parque Central is the rather bare **Parque Juan Santamaría**, where there is a statue of the hero (see below) in action, flanked by cannons – an area frequented by canoodling teenagers. Across the way, the **Parque de los Niños** has slightly more pleasant landscaping, in addition to playground equipment and plenty of chattering toddlers.

Situated in a century-old structure that has served as both a jail and an armory, north of the Parque Central, the **Museo Juan Santamaría** (☎ 2441-4775; www.museojuansantamaria.go.cr; cnr Av 3 & Calle 2; admission free; 🕑 10am-5:30pm Tue-Sun) chronicles the life and history of Juan Santamaría, the legendary drummer boy who helped route American filibuster William Walker in 1856 by torching the building that he and his men were hiding out in. A basic exhibit area contains vintage maps, paintings and historical artifacts related to the conflict. They also host rotating arts and crafts exhibitions and there is a small auditorium where performances are occasionally staged.

AROUND ALAJUELA

Three kilometers to the southeast, in Río Segundo de Alajuela, is the important **Amigos de las Aves** (☎ 2441-2658; www.hatchedtoflyfree.org; suggested per person donation US$20; 🕑 by appointment), a successful green and scarlet macaw breeding program housed on a 3-hectare *finca* also known as Flor de Mayo. Founded in 1992 by Richard and Margot Frisius, the organization is working to revive endangered macaw populations in collaboration with the Minae, the government ministry that oversees the national park system. They also have volunteer opportunities (from US$15 to US$18 per person per day). See the website for details. Two-hour guided tours of the

CENTRAL VALLEY & HIGHLANDS

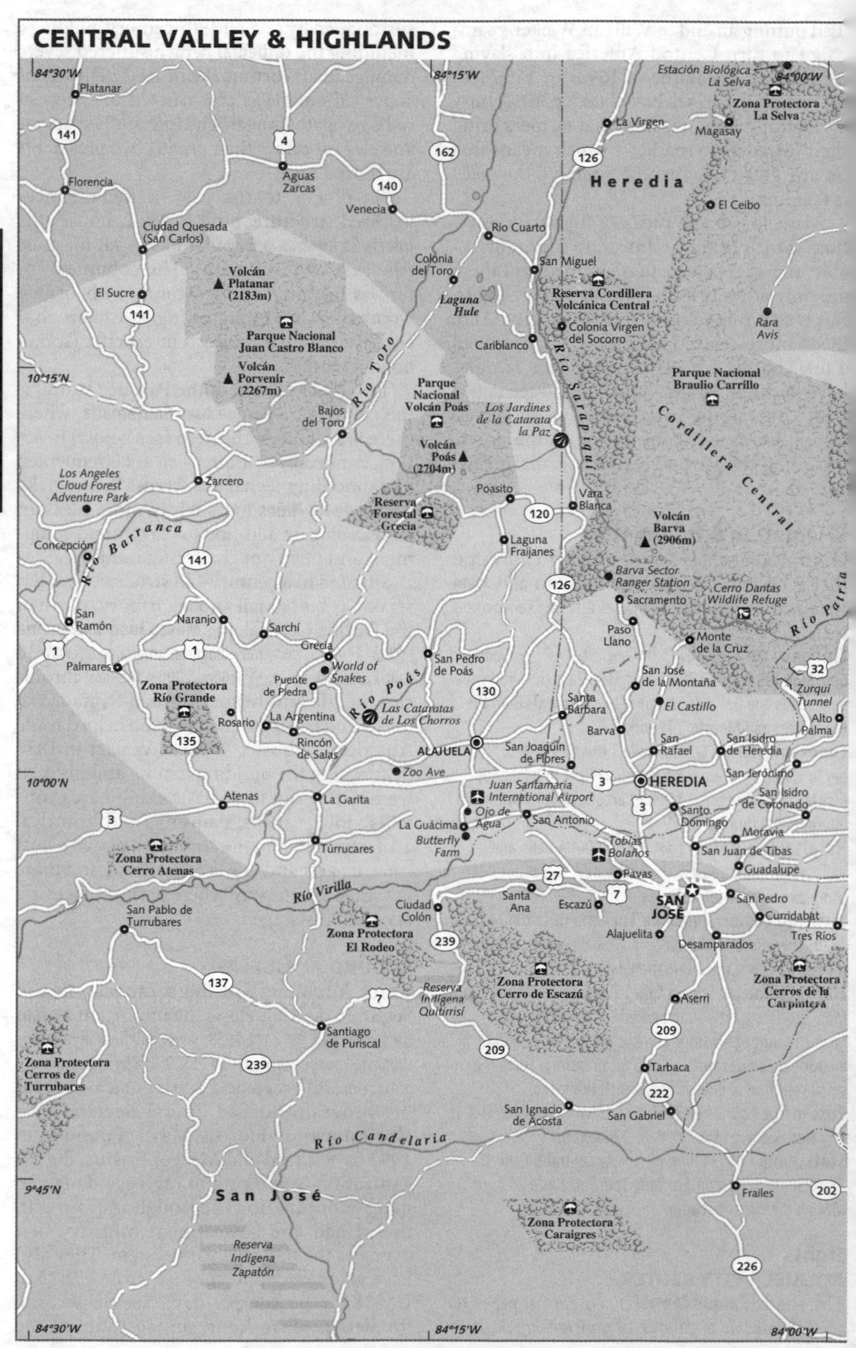

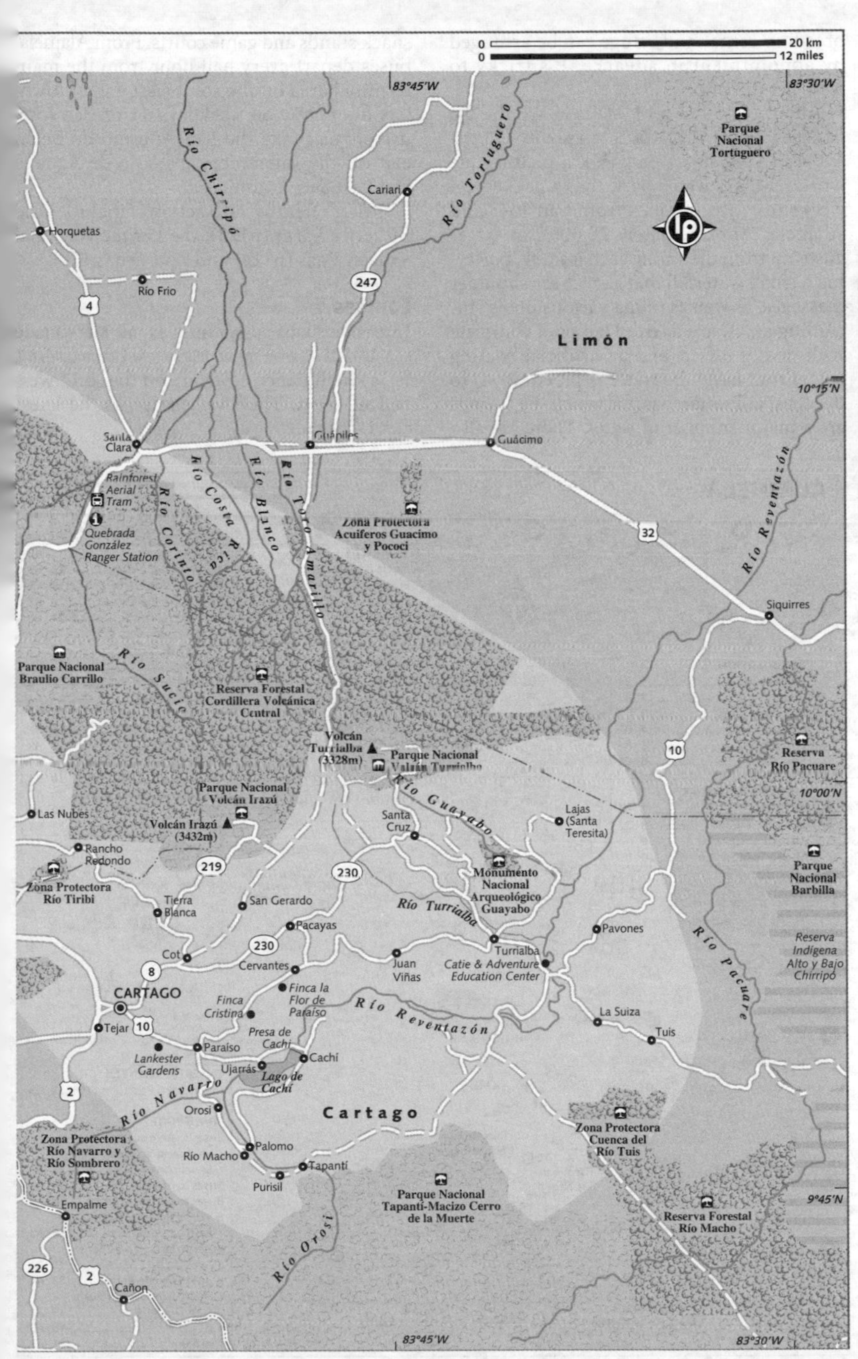

CENTRAL VALLEY & HIGHLANDS

breeding center and refuge can be arranged by appointment in advance. It's tricky to find; get directions.

About 6km south of Alajuela are the **Ojo de Agua springs** (☎ 2441-0655; admission US$1.50, children under-6 free; 8am-5pm;), a picturesque working-class water park that's packed on weekends with families from San José and Alajuela. Approximately 20,000L of water gush out from the spring each minute, powering a small waterfall that's great for shoulder massages, as well as filling various pools (including an Olympic-sized lap pool complete with diving tower) and an artificial boating lake. From here, the water is piped down to the coast at Puntarenas, for which the springs are a major supplier of water. There are also snack stands and game courts. From Alajuela buses depart every half hour from the main terminal area on the southwest end of town, less frequently on weekdays. From San José drivers can take the San Antonio de Belén exit off the Interamericana; Ojo de Agua is just past San Antonio.

Other nearby attractions include the Butterfly Farm (p123), the Parque Nacional Volcán Poás (p124) and Zoo Ave (p127).

Courses

Improve your salsa moves at **Merecumbé** (☎ 2442-3536; www.merecumbe.net; Av 2 btwn Calles 8 & 10), a small dance academy on the southwest end of town. Their website posts the latest class schedule.

A CLEAN, WELL-LIGHTED PLACE

Book-a-holics rejoice! You'll find one of the best English-language bookstores in the country right in Alajuela. **Goodlight Books** (☎ 2430-4083; www.goodlightbooks.com; Av 3 btwn Calles 1 & 3; 9am-6pm), managed by longtime expat Larry Coulter, offers a mind-boggling selection of tomes: 9000 well-organized books (both used and new) that cover everything from literature to history to sci-fi. He also keeps a worthwhile stock of difficult-to-find books on Costa Rica and the region, and there is a small array of volumes in Dutch and German. You will also find maps, guidebooks and a tiny cafe serving very tasty iced coffee.

The best part: the name. It was inspired by the Ernest Hemingway short story, *A Clean, Well-Lighted Place*.

For details about Spanish-language study, see boxed text, p128.

Festivals & Events

In the town that gave birth to Juan Santamaría, it would be expected that the anniversary of the **Battle of Rivas**, on April 11, would be particularly well celebrated. This momentous event is commemorated with all manner of civic events, including a parade and *lots* of firecrackers.

Sleeping

Since Alajuela is so close to the international airport, most hotels and B&Bs can arrange airport transfers for a small fee (or even for free). If you are driving your own car, note that many places in the city center don't have their own parking area, but there are many guarded lots around the city. Also, expect street noise to be a fact of life in the center of town.

As in other spots, taxi drivers will try to steer you to places that pay them a commission. Remember: be skeptical, don't believe everything you hear and if you're unsure about where you've chosen to stay, ask to see a room.

HOSTELS

A few of the hotels listed in the Budget section, right, also offer dorm rooms.

Hotel Trotamundos (☎ 2430-5832; www.hoteltrotamundos.com; Av 5 btwn Calles 2 & 4; dm US$12, d US$25-30, all incl breakfast; internet) This spot is basic, but the rooms are clean and the service is super-friendly. Three dorms and seven private units with cable TV – one of which has an outdoor balcony facing the street – are nestled into a two-story house that surrounds a tiny interior courtyard. There is a shared kitchen, public phones, free internet and a small communal area. Credit cards accepted.

our pick **Hostel Maleku** (☎ 2430-4304; www.malekuhostel.com; 50m west of Hospital San Rafael; dm US$12, s/d without bathroom US$25/35; internet) This sweet little backpackers' abode located on the south edge of town, 50m west of the Hospital San Rafael, has tight spic-and-span rooms tucked into a vintage home on a quiet street. There are also two private rooms, with shared bathrooms, a communal kitchen, a TV lounge and free internet. It's a wonderful, serene spot and the staff is very helpful.

BUDGET

Mango Verde Hostel (☎ 2441-6330; mirafloresbb@hotmail.com; Av 3 btwn Calles 2 & 4; s/d US$15/25, without bathroom US$10/20) This small hotel has nine bare and basic rooms, though there's a decent-sized shared kitchen, a garden patio, plenty of hammocks and a lounge space.

Hotel Cortéz Azul (☎ 2443-6145; Av 5 btwn Calles 2 & 4; dm US$10, d with/without bathroom US$30/25; P) The owner, Eduardo Rodríguez, is a local artist who displays his unique work throughout the property (don't miss the mural of the *Last Supper*). The hotel has 10 homey, clean rooms with polished wood floors, a common area and two kitchens. Original art is available for purchase at reception.

Cala Inn B&B (☎ 2441-3219; www.hotelcalacr.com; Calle 2 btwn Avs 2 & 4; dm US$12, d with/without bathroom US$40/30, all incl breakfast; wi-fi) This small, modern eight-room spot overlooking the Parque Juan Santamaría has tidy parquet-floor rooms that are simple and spotless. The rooms vary in size and furnishings, from a dorm that sleeps four to a private room with king-sized bed. All share a kitchen and a cozy lounge with cable TV and foosball. Credit cards accepted.

our pick **Alajuela Backpackers Boutique Hostel & Hotel** (☎ 2441-7149; www.alajuelabackpackers.com; cnr Av 4 & Calle 4; dm US$15, s/d standard US$30/45, s/d deluxe US$38/58, s/d junior ste US$48/68; internet wi-fi) This

CENTRAL VALLEY & HIGHLANDS

AWAY FROM SAN JOSÉ

For most visitors to Costa Rica, a night in San José is practically obligatory at the beginning or end of every trip. But if you have a car, you can instead arrange to stay at one of the following country inns. All lie within a two-hour range of the international airport – and all have incredible mountain scenery.

- Just outside of Alajuela, **Trapp Family Lodge** (p121) and **Xandari Resort Hotel & Spa** (p122) have pastoral settings – just 10 minutes away from the airport.
- To the north, **Poás Volcano Lodge** (p125) has smashing volcano views, at a drive time of 45 minutes.
- A 30-minute cruise along the Interamericana leads to **Vista del Valle Plantation Inn** (p128), which serves up extravagant views of the Río Grande gorge and amazing *tres leches* (literally 'three milk') cake.
- A sleek new B&B in San Ramón, **Casa Amanecer** (p133) is under an hour's drive – as is the **Villa Blanca Cloud Forest Hotel Spa** (p134) in the nearby Los Ángeles Cloud Forest Adventure Park.
- Outside of Heredia, **Hotel Bougainvillea** (p136) and the dreamy **Finca Rosa Blanca** (p137) will have you at less than 30 minutes from the airport check-in.
- A little more than 90 minutes away, in the Valle de Orosi, **Sanchirí Mirador** (p142) and **Orosi Lodge** (p143) offer picturesque views of wild forest and coffee *fincas*.

brand-new 21-room inn facing the Parque de los Niños is less a hostel than a full-blown hotel equipped with a smattering of dormitory rooms. An interior atrium is draped in plants and a 4th-floor beanbag lounge offers a prime opportunity to sip beers while watching the planes take off at the international airport in the distance. Dormitories are wonderfully uncluttered (only four people to a room) and each come with their own bathroom, while the private rooms are graceful, decorated in serene earth tones and equipped with cable TV and double-pane windows. More expensive 'junior suites' have plasma TV and comfy king-sized bed. Plus, there is wi-fi all over the hotel. Credit cards accepted.

Arilapa (☎ 2443-6941; www.arilapa.com; dm/s/d/tr incl breakfast US$17/30/35/45; P 💻) Just outside of town, this lovely family home with bright rooms clad in terra-cotta tile floors can take you straight from the airport to nature. Set in an orange grove, it is run by Arnold and Ileana, who offer free airport pickups and tortilla-making lessons at the in-house bakery.

Pensión Alajuela (☎ 2443-1717; www.pensionalajuela.com; Av 9 btwn Calles Central & 2; d with shared bathroom US$24, d with/without air-con US$33/28; ❄ 💻 📶) A dozen different rooms (some without windows) are simple, but clean and surround a pleasant garden terrace filled with plants. There's a communal kitchen, wi-fi and laundry service. Credit cards accepted.

Hotel Pacandé (☎ 2443-8481; www.hotelpacande.com; Av 5 btwn Calles 2 & 4; s US$27-50, d US$28-50, tr US$45-60, all incl breakfast; P 💻) This popular, locally run option is very clean throughout, offering 10 large rooms with wood furnishings, frilly toilets, folk-art touches and cable TV. Rooms come in a variety of configurations, with some sleeping up to six people and others sharing bathrooms. The outdoor breakfast nook is a great spot for a morning brew and fresh pineapple.

Hotel Alajuela (☎ 2441-1241; alajuela@racsa.co.cr; Calle 2 btwn Avs Central & 2; s/d/tr/q US$28/32/35/40) Twenty-eight simple rooms make up this centrally located hotel to the south of the Parque Central. It's not going to win any beauty contests, but the rooms are clean and smell like disinfectant and come equipped with industrial-strength fans. Corner rooms are best (though a bit noisy), with nice views of the park. A downstairs lounge has cable TV. Credit cards accepted.

Vida Tropical B&B (☎ 2443-9576; www.vidatropical.com; Calle 3, north of Av 11; s/d incl breakfast US$30/45, additional person US$10, children under 12 free; P 💻 👶) In a quiet residential neighborhood just north of downtown is this Colombian-American-run B&B, operated by the owners of the Jalapeños Central restaurant. The house has five snug, simple guest rooms awash in bright murals and a well-tended backyard that's perfect for getting some sun. There are plenty of hammocks and comfy couches, plus laundry service is available.

MIDRANGE

Hotel Los Volcanes (☎ 2441-0525; www.hotellosvolcanes.com; Av 3 btwn Calles Central & 2; s US$35-60, d US$46-75, all incl breakfast; P ⊠ ✻ ▣ ≋) A refurbished, 1920s home with 15 rooms of differing sizes and amenities – from vintage units with period-style furniture and clean, shared bathrooms, to shining, contemporary rooms with flat-screen TV and safe. There's also an enjoyable courtyard in the back, complete with gurgling fountain. Plus the helpful Tico owners can arrange free airport drop-off at the end of your stay. Credit cards accepted.

Welcome to CR B&B (☎ 2265-6563; www.welcometocr.com; d incl breakfast US$50; P ▣ ≋) The Tico-American owners of this charming little place used to manage the Hostal Toruma in Los Yoses and now have this B&B of their own. Located about 5km east of the airport on the road to San Joaquín, it's a homey spot, with three double rooms with private bathroom and à la carte breakfast. They can book all manner of package tours.

Hotel Villa Bonita (☎ 2441-0239; www.hotelvillabonita.com; cnr Av 8 & Calle 9; s/d US$50/60, children under 10 free; P ▣) A charming B&B with five simple, whitewashed rooms located on the outskirts of the city center. Units are comfy, with plump white pillows and firm mattresses. The main draw is the well-manicured garden where guests can swing away the afternoon in hammocks.

our pick Hotel 1915 (☎ 2441-0495; www.1915hotel.com; Calle 2 btwn Avs 5 & 7; d US$55-85; P ✻ ▣ ≋) The exteriors may not look like much, but step through the front door and you'll find yourself in a quaint 16-room inn built around a century-old home. Rooms have adobe walls, wood-beam ceilings, period-style furnishings and most are equipped with a minifridge. In addition, the graceful living room has a stained-glass window and many of the floors are clad in vintage Spanish tile. The lovely open-air lounge is a great space to chill and there is a tour agency onsite. Credit cards accepted.

Las Orquídeas Inn (☎ 2433-9346; www.orquideasinn.com; s US$69-140, d US$79-150; P ⊠ ✻ ≋ ◙) About 5km west of Alajuela on the road to San Pedro de Poás, this stately colonial-style structure houses 19 well-appointed rooms. Bright standard units with terra-cotta tile floors are decked out in rich textiles and are situated just steps away from a garden with a pool and Jacuzzi. Nicer suites, in various configurations, come with polished wood floors (our favorite is the loft-style geodesic dome), and some have great views of the valley. The popular restaurant-bar is well known for its bounteous Marilyn Monroe paraphernalia. Credit cards accepted.

Trapp Family Lodge (☎ 2431-0776; www.trappfam.com; d US$95, additional person US$15, children 3-11 US$6; P ▣ ◙ ♿) This highly recommended family spot is the comfiest, most attractive option within reach of the airport landing strip. A bright, mustard-yellow Spanish country-inn houses 20 terra-cotta–tiled rooms with comfortable polished-wood beds and a graceful hacienda vibe. The best units have balconies overlooking a lovely garden studded with bougainvillea and fig trees, as well as a bean-shaped swimming pool. It's located 20km from the international airport on the road to La Guácima; free airport transfers are provided. Credit cards accepted.

TOP END

The following top-end hotels are located on the road that leads north from Alajuela, towards Volcán Poás; all accept credit cards.

Hotel Buena Vista (☎ 2442-8595; www.hotelbuenavistacr.com; d standard/deluxe/junior ste incl breakfast US$85/100/120; P ⊠ ▣ ◙) About 5km north of Alajuela, this whitewashed Mediterranean-style hotel is perched on a mountaintop and has panoramic views of the nearby volcanoes. Tidy, carpeted rooms have floral spreads and fresh flowers; the more expensive of which come with private balcony with valley views (worth the price). A small trail leads from the hotel through a coffee plantation and down to the main road. There is also a nice garden for relaxing.

Pura Vida Retreat & Spa (☎ in USA 888-767-7375; www.puravidaspa.com; per person incl 3 meals US$125-185; P ⊠ ≋ ◙) A renowned yoga and alternative-health center that's a destination in and of itself, this plush, hillside retreat 4km from Alajuela offers 'tentalows' in addition to well-appointed indoor suites. Roomy tiled units have comfy beds, private bathrooms, and some have private balcony with views. Most folks come here on package retreats, so inquire ahead to see what will be on offer. Call ahead for directions; it's tricky to find.

Xandari Resort Hotel & Spa (☎ 2443-2020; www.xandari.com; d villa US$230-315; P ⊠ ✿ ≋) Set in a coffee plantation overlooking the Central Valley, about 6km north of Alajuela, this romantic spot (ideal for honeymooners) has postcard-perfect views and modern bungalows painted in tropical colors, each accented with textile spreads and well-designed folk-art motifs. Individually decorated units all have garden-view showers, minifridge and sitting area. The grounds offer more than 3km of trails for exploring and there are three pools (including one shaped like a half moon), a Jacuzzi, a spa, and a restaurant that specializes in organic local foods and vegetarian cooking (see right for details). There is also an excellent gift shop.

Eating

BUDGET & MIDRANGE

For the cheapest meals, head to the enclosed **Mercado Central** (Calles 4 & 6 btwn Avs 1 & Central; 7am-6pm Mon-Sat) for produce stands, inexpensive lunch counters and much, much more.

Soda El Puntalito (cnr Calle 4 & Av 3; snacks ₡1000-2000) Do as the locals do and grab a stool under the old blue awning at this cheap, unassuming corner sidewalk stand.

Dolcelato (☎ 2441-6672; Plaza Real Alajuela; ice cream from ₡1000; noon-9:30pm Mon-Thu, noon-10:30pm Fri-Sun) A fantastical array of Italian ice creams in flavors of both fruit and chocolate can be found at this contemporary *gelateria* at the strip mall on the south edge of town. In a nod to local palates, they even have the mysterious flavor known as 'Churchill' (see boxed text, opposite).

Panadería Santa Clara (Av 1 btwn Calles 6 & 8; items ₡200-600) Follow your nose to this outstanding bakery, which is stocked with all types of homemade breads as well as eye-popping pastries, cookies and cakes. The macaroons *totally* rule!

Coffee Dreams Café (☎ 2430-3970; cnr Calle 1 & Av 3; dishes ₡900-4200; 8am-8pm Mon-Sat) This adorable cafe is a great place to sample the local blend, but it's worth bringing your appetite along, too, as the tamales here are hot and heavenly.

Café Las Delicias (☎ 2440-3681; cnr Av 3 & Calle 1; dishes ₡1300-3100; 8am-8pm Mon-Sat) A cute corner spot for cappuccino, iced coffee, chilled drinks, cheesecake and a highly yummy *pastelito de piña* (pineapple pastry).

Ambrosia (☎ 2201-5057; Av 5 btwn Calles Central & 2; mains ₡1350-2200; 10am-9pm Mon-Sat) This pretty, open-air cafe in a yellow building is good for a pick-me-up espresso. The menu features a mix of Italian-influenced options, including sandwiches, pasta and several types of tasty lasagna (including one made with hearts of palm).

Jalepeños Central (☎ 2430-4027; Calle 1 btwn Avs 3 & 5; dishes ₡1400-3400; 11am-9pm Mon-Sat) Run by an animated Colombian-American from New York City, this popular Tex-Mex spot will introduce some much-needed spice into your diet – as well as some super jumbo burritos. You'll also find Tico specialties, spit-roasted chicken and New York–style cheesecake.

Ceviche del Rey (☎ 2440-0779; www.cevichedelreycr.com; Calle 2, north of Río Alajuela; mains ₡2200-9000; 11am-11pm) It's worth the trek to the northern outskirts of town for Peruvian food at this favorite family outpost. Expect all manner of Andean classics, including fresh *ceviche* (seafood marinated in lime juice), the tender stir-fries known as *saltados* and even harder-to-find regional specialties such as *cabrito a la norteña* (stewed goat in cilantro). They even have Peruvian beer.

La Mansarda (☎ 2441-4390; Calle Central btwn Avs Central & 2, 2nd fl; meals ₡2600-7500; 11am-11pm) An old standby for traditional Costa Rican fare is this casual balcony restaurant overlooking the street. Grilled fish and chicken dishes are the specialty, and can be complemented by a good selection of wines by the glass (from ₡1400). Save room for the *flan de coco* (coconut flan) or, better yet, a belt of Flor de Caña rum. The best!

Los Olivos (cnr Calle 4 & Av 4; breakfast ₡300, mains ₡3000-5900; 7am-10pm) This bright corner spot facing the Parque de los Niños serves tasty *café con leche* (coffee with milk), along with a mix of international specialties, from burritos to steak. The best part: if you pick up fresh strawberries from the roadside vendors near the Poás volcano, the kitchen will clean them and whip them up into a delicious *natural de fresa* (strawberry shake without milk) – with the purchase of a main dish.

Self-caterers can stock up on groceries at the **Palí supermarket** (cnr Av 2 & Calle 10; 8am-8pm) or **Más x Menos** (Av 1 btwn Calles 4 & 6; 7am-9pm Mon-Sat, 7am-8pm Sun).

TOP END

Xandari (☎ 2443-2020; www.xandari.com; mains ₡4500-10,000; V) If you want to impress a date, then you can't go wrong at this elegant restaurant with incredible views, housed at the hotel of the same name (opposite). The menu is a mix of organically focused Costa Rican and international meals (with plenty of vegetarian options), from catch of the day seared in olive oil and wasabi to healthy interpretations of local *casados* (set meals). For dessert, try the chocolate macadamia nut cake.

Como en Casa (☎ 2441-7607; Plaza Real Alajuela; mains ₡5100-14,000; 🕑 11am-10pm Sun-Wed, 11am-11pm Thu-Sat) In a new strip mall on the south edge of town, this Argentinean grill is a popular weekend lunch spot, serving a comprehensive round-up of grilled meats and a strong selection of pastas (including vegetarian options). There is a good wine list (from ₡6600 a bottle), as well as desert crepes stuffed with local strawberries.

Entertainment

The perennial Costa Rican soccer champions, Alajuela's own La Liga, play at the Estadio Morera Soto at the northeast end of town on Sundays during soccer season. If you can't get seats, stop by **Cugini Bar & Restaurant** (☎ 2440-6893; cnr Av Central & Calle 5; 🕑 noon-midnight Mon-Sat) and you can catch the game over a brew or two.

There's no shortage of dive bars, and there's a good chance that karaoke will be on offer after 10pm. If this is your first night in Costa Rica, we recommend the Guaro Cacique. Bottoms up! (And don't call us in the morning.)

Getting There & Away

For details of flights to Aeropuerto Internacional Juan Santamaría, see p96 and p546. You can take a taxi (from ₡1800) to the airport from the Parque Central.

There is no central terminal; instead, a number of small terminals and bus stops dot the southwestern part of the city. Note that there are two Tuasa terminals (east and west) – right across the street from each other.

Atenas (Calle 10 btwn Avs Central & 2) ₡300; 30 minutes; departs every 30 minutes from 6am to 9pm.
Butterfly Farm (cnr Av 2 & Calle 8) ₡300; 30 minutes; departs at 6:20am, 9am, 11am and 1pm.
Heredia (Tuasa Terminal East; Calle 8 btwn Avs Central & 1) ₡300; 30 minutes; departs every 15 minutes from 5am to 11pm.
La Garita/Zoo Ave (Calle 10 btwn Av 2 & Central) ₡300; 30 minutes; departs every 30 minutes from 6am to 9pm.
San José (Tuasa Terminal West; Calle 8 btwn Avs Central & 1) ₡400; 45 minutes; departs from Alajuela bus terminal every 10 minutes from 5am to 11pm, some of these stop at the international airport.
San José via Aeropuerto Internacional Juan Santamaría (Station Wagon; Av 4 btwn Calles 2 & 4) ₡400, 45 minutes; departs every 15 to 20 minutes during the day, less frequently at night; operates 24 hours a day. Locally, these buses are referred to as *los buses amarillos de la liga* (the league's yellow buses).
Sarchí (Calle 8 btwn Avs Central & 1) ₡300; 30 minutes; departs every 30 minutes from 5am to 10pm.
Volcán Poás (Tuasa Terminal West; Calle 8 btwn Avs Central & 1) ₡3000; 4½ hours round-trip, including time to visit the summit; departs at around 9:15am. (This bus originates in San José so departure times are approximate.)

BUTTERFLY FARM

Started in 1983, the **Butterfly Farm** (☎ 2438-0400; www.butterflyfarm.co.cr; adult/children ages 4-11 US$15/7.50, with transportation from San José US$35/20; 🕑 8:30am-5pm) opened as the first commercial butterfly farm in Latin America. In the wild it's estimated that less than 2% of caterpillars survive to adulthood, while breeders at the farm boast an astounding 90% survival rate. This ensures a steady supply of pupae for gardens, schools, museums and private collections around the world.

The butterflies are busiest when it's sunny, particularly in the morning. Your entrance fee includes a guided two-hour tour, where you

¿QUÉ ES UN 'CHURCHILL'?

Enter any Tico ice-cream shop and you're likely to encounter a rather mysterious-looking menu item known as the 'Churchill' – a viscous bright purple drink that looks like it emerged from the *Star Wars* cantina scene. For the uninitiated: the Churchill is a milkshake crafted from *helado de colita,* a tutti-frutti ice-cream that is less frutti and more tutti (especially in the artificial dyes department) and is blended with milk and sugar syrup into an achingly sweet, lavender-hued goo that is topped off by an architectural dollop of dried powdered milk. What does it taste like? We're still trying to figure that out – but rest assured that it's not like anything that exists in nature. And yes, we drank the whole thing.

can learn about the butterfly life cycle, visit the lab and stroll around a netted garden amid the fluttering. Tours in various languages run four times daily. In addition, there is an option to purchase a package tour (adult/child US$75/60) that includes transportation from San José, lunch and a visit to the Café Britt Finca.

Drivers can reach the Butterfly Farm by heading 12km south of Alajuela to the village of La Guácima; it's almost in front of the well-signed El Club Campestre Los Reyes. From Alajuela, you can take a direct bus (see p123).

PARQUE NACIONAL VOLCÁN POÁS

Just 37km north of Alajuela by a winding and scenic road is the most heavily trafficked **national park** (admission US$10; 8am-3:30pm) in Costa Rica. And for those who want to peer into an active volcano – without the hardship of hiking one – it's ideal. The centerpiece is, of course, Volcán Poás (2704m), which had its last blowout in 1953. This event formed the eerie and enormous crater, which is 1.3km across and 300m deep – and offers the wonderful opportunity to watch the bubbling, steaming cauldron belch sulfurous mud and water hundreds of meters into the air. There are two other craters, as well, one of which contains a sapphire-blue lake ringed by high-altitude forest.

The main crater at Poás continues to be active to varying degrees. In fact, the park was briefly closed in May 1989 after a minor eruption sent volcanic ash spouting more than 1km into the air, and lesser activity closed the park intermittently in 1995. In recent years, however, Poás has posed no imminent threat, though scientists still monitor it closely. See boxed text, p173, for more on volcanic eruptions.

In the meantime, the most common issue for visitors is the veil of clouds that gather around the mountain at about 10am (even in dry season). Even if the day looks clear, get to the park as early as possible or you won't see much.

Information

Some 250,000 people visit the park annually, making Poás the most packed national park in the country; weekends get especially jammed. The best time to go is on a weekday in the dry season. In particular, go early in the morning before the clouds obscure the view. If the summit is cloudy, take a hike to the other craters and return to the cauldron later – winds shift and sometimes the cloud cover is blown away.

Near the entrance, there is a visitors center with a souvenir stand, a small museum and informative videos that play hourly between 9am and 3pm. There is also a coffee shop – but the menu is limited. However, the road up to the park is lined with stands selling fruit, cheese and snacks – as well as countless touristy spots serving typical Tico fare – so you won't go hungry. Bring your own bottled water, though, as the tap water is undrinkable.

There is no camping or other accommodations inside the park. For lodging and eating in the vicinity, see opposite.

Be advised that overnight temperatures can drop below freezing, and it may be windy and cold during the day. Also, Poás receives almost 4000mm of rainfall each year. Dress accordingly.

Hiking

From the visitors center, there is a paved wheelchair-accessible path that leads to a crater lookout. Because of the toxic sulfuric-acid fumes that are emitted from the cauldron, visitors are prohibited from descending into the crater.

From the lookout, two trails branch out – to the right is Sendero Botos, to the left Sendero Escalonia. **Sendero Botos** is a short, 30-minute round-trip hike that takes you through dwarf cloud forest, which is the product of acidic air and freezing temperatures. Here you can wander about looking at bromeliads, lichens and mosses clinging to the curiously shaped and twisted trees growing in the volcanic soil. Birds abound, especially the magnificent fiery-throated hummingbird, a high-altitude specialty of Costa Rica. The trail ends at **Laguna Botos**, a peculiar cold-water lake that has filled in one of the extinct craters.

Sendero Escalonia is a slightly longer trail through taller forest, which gets significantly less traffic than the other parts of the park. While hiking on the trail, look for other highland specialties, including the sooty robin, black guans, screech owls and even the odd quetzal (especially from February to April). Although mammals are infrequently sighted in the park, coyotes and the endemic montane squirrel are present.

Tours

Numerous companies offer daily tours to the volcano, but these can be an overpriced affair. Depending on the number of additional activities they include, they can cost US$40 to US$100, and the kicker is that you'll usually arrive at the volcano at around 10am – right when the clouds start rolling in. Also, readers complain that they're often rushed off the crater, though there always seems to be time for stopping at a souvenir shop on the way back. As always, shop around and ask questions.

It's just as easy to visit the volcano using public transportation from San José or Alajuela. And, if you have two or more people in your group, the best deal is to rent a car or hire a private taxi for the day and visit the volcano at your leisure.

Sleeping & Eating

ON THE ROAD TO POÁS

The area around the Parque Nacional Volcán Poás is largely agricultural (expect to see lots of dairy and fruit farming), but there are still a number of places to sleep, eat and visit. This is scenic, rural countryside – and makes for a lovely afternoon drive or overnight stay.

Lo Que Tu Quieres Lodge (☎ 2482-2092; d US$20, additional person US$10; Ⓟ) About 5km before the park entrance, this creaky budget option has five bare-bones *cabinas* in various sizes equipped with heater and electric shower – and the larger ones have private chimney that you can have lit on request. The owners will usually let you camp for a few dollars. There is a small restaurant (*casados* from ₡3000) with staggering views – on a clear day, you can see all the way to the Golfo de Nicoya – that serves simple, typical food.

Lagunillas Lodge (☎ 2448-5837, 8389-5842; d US$30, d cabinas US$40; Ⓟ) This lodge and farm is the closest accommodation to the volcano, and while it's basic, the family that operates it is charming and the rustic log cabins offer stellar views. Rooms and stand-alone cabins, which can accommodate up to six people, have hot-water showers and heaters, and all are surrounded by hiking trails. There's also a fish pond where you can catch your dinner, and a restaurant (mains from ₡2500) that will cook it up for you. They can also arrange horseback rides. To get here, take the signed turnoff about 2km before the park entrance and head west, about 1km down a steep dirt road; 4WD absolutely, positively required. Call ahead.

In season, expect to see vendors along the road to the volcano selling artisanal foods and fresh-picked fruit. Pick up a bag of strawberries take it with you back to Alajuela. The folks at Los Olivos (p122) will whip it into a shake with the purchase of a main dish.

EAST OF POÁS

About 10km before the entrance to the national park, a winding, paved road heads east through Poasito, before arriving in the village of Vara Blanca, where it turns north and leads to the famed La Paz Waterfall Gardens. This is scenic, uncluttered countryside – the ideal place for a pleasant drive or to spend the night. (This area was greatly affected by the 2009 earthquake. See boxed text, p126 for more info.)

Places are listed as you head east from Poasito to La Paz.

Villa Calas (☎ 2482-2222; www.villacalas.com; d US$40-50, q US$90; Ⓟ) Just 4km east of Poasito, you'll find this small, rustic outpost, with 10 A-frame cabins in various configurations. All come with chimney; more expensive ones are equipped with kitchenette, while the largest have full kitchen. A pleasant restaurant (mains ₡3100 to ₡5900) serves typical Costa Rican fare – including river trout prepared myriad ways (in season). Parents will appreciate the toddler play set. Credit cards accepted.

our pick **Poás Volcano Lodge** (☎ 2482-2194; www.poasvolcanolodge.com; d standard/junior ste US$95/110, additional adult/child under 12yr US$25/15, all incl breakfast; Ⓟ) Roughly another 8km east along the road, you'll find this high-altitude dairy farm that offers attractive lodging in an idyllic rural setting. Six comfortable, well-appointed rooms in a converted stone horse-stable (some units are still equipped with the old hitching rings) have a rustic flair. In addition, the grounds have more than 3km of hiking trails that offer views of the volcano – and all the way to Nicaragua – on clear days. A games room, destroyed by the earthquake, should be fully rebuilt by late 2010.

Colbert Restaurant (☎ 2482-2776; www.colbert.co.cr; mains ₡2600-8500; noon-9pm Fri-Wed) Two kilometers east of the Poás Volcano Lodge, you'll find this charming French restaurant with nice views and a chef that looks like he's straight out of Central Casting: Joël Suire is not only French, he is bequeathed with an ample moustache and wears a toque. Expect a menu loaded with traditional French items

THE 2009 VARA BLANCA EARTHQUAKE

In January 2009, the area around Vara Blanca, to the east of the Volcán Poás, was rocked by a massive 6.2 quake that split roads, triggered deadly avalanches and leveled the village of Cinchona. Out of 170 homes in the town, 60 were wrecked outright and another 60 were declared uninhabitable the next day. Almost three dozen people were killed, and several went missing; hundreds were left homeless

The quake also claimed a 3km stretch of road that connected Vara Blanca in the Central Valley to San Miguel on the northern slope. Engineers have concluded that the area remains too unstable for the road to be rebuilt – which means that a new road, along a different route, will be constructed. At the earliest, it will be finished in late 2010. (If you're looking to drive it, inquire locally before setting out.) Furthermore, the families that once inhabited Cinchona will be relocated. At press time, the government had unveiled a plan to create a new development in the vicinity of Cariblanco, to the north.

Travelers, in the meantime, can still visit all the many lovely points from Poás to just beyond the La Paz Waterfall Gardens – a gesture of support that many area businesses would no doubt welcome in the wake of this tragedy.

such as onion soup, house-made paté and beef tenderloin grilled with green peppercorns. There is a good wine list (bottles from ₡7800), strong on vintages from South America and France. Don't miss the fresh bread or to-die-for lace cookies.

La Paz Waterfall Gardens (☎ 2482-2720, 2482-2100; www.waterfallgardens.com; adult/child under 12yr US$35/20; 8am-5pm; P) This garden and hotel complex is host to 3.5km of hiking trails and five scenic waterfalls, the largest one of which – La Catarata de la Paz (Peace Waterfall) – is probably one of the most photographed sights in Costa Rica. (The earthquake, sadly, destroyed 90% of the garden's trails, but these should all be cleared and ready to go at some point in late 2010.) Visitors can also tour a butterfly conservatory, an aviary, an orchid display, a serpentarium and a historic Tico farmhouse that dates back to 1900. It's an ideal spot for active seniors and small children (there are even special children's activities), since many of the trails are smooth and well-maintained.

If you want to stay onsite, book a room at the adjacent **Peace Lodge** (☎ 2482-2100; www.waterfallgardens.com; d standard/deluxe/villa US$275/345/415, additional adult/child US$40/20, all incl breakfast; P), which has 17 over-the-top units, all with gorgeous valley views. These all have private deck, fireplace, canopy bed, staggeringly large bathroom and, in the event that you are suffering from acute Jacuzzi withdrawal, each unit comes stocked with two hot tubs (one inside and one out). An extravagant loft-style villa sleeps up to six. There's also a heated outdoor infinity-edge swimming pool, complete with heated waterfall. Credit cards accepted.

Getting There & Away

You can take a taxi to the park for around ₡50,000 from San José or ₡22,000 from Alajuela. If you're driving, the road from Alajuela to the volcano is well signed. Most visitors using public buses come from San José. Get to the terminal early.

From San José (₡3400, five hours), Tuasa buses depart 8:30am daily from Av 2 between Calles 12 and 14, stopping in Alajuela at about 9:15am and returning at 2:30pm. Most of these buses also make a pit stop at one of the roadside restaurants along the way.

WEST TO ATENAS

From Alajuela, a narrow, paved highway leads 25km west to the lovely mountain town of Atenas. It's a nice day trip, with perfect climate and a charming rural atmosphere.

La Garita

In an area that attracts scientists who do research on maize, it is not surprising that this town – spread out along the road that connects Alajuela to Atenas – is lined with restaurants whose specialty is corn: corn soup, cornbread, tamales and *chorreadas* (savory corn pancakes) to be exact. It is located 11km west of Alajuela and worth the pilgrimage if you are looking for good country eats.

All places are listed as you travel west, from Alajuela to Atenas.

In a quiet spot, surrounded by forest, you'll find **Martino Resort & Spa** (☎ 2433-8382; www.hotelmartino.com; d standard/deluxe incl breakfast US$135/180; P), a Las Vegas-meets-Central America extravaganza of classical mythology and polished hardwood everything. Forty-eight rooms with Greek porticos are spacious and well appointed and there's a large swimming pool guarded by a knockoff of Michelangelo's *David*. There is also a gym, sauna and spa – as well as an Italian restaurant, **La Focaccia** (mains ₡4500-7000), which serves a mix of specialties, including risottos and pastas. The hotel is 2km north of the Alajuela exit from the Interamericana, about 15 minutes from the airport.

About 10km west of Alajuela, you'll find **Zoo Ave** (☎ 2433-8989/9966; adult/child US$15/13; 8:30am-5pm), a well-designed animal park boasting more than 15 species of reptile and 115 species of birds – all on colorful, squawking display in a relaxing 14-hectare park. In addition, you'll find all four species of Costa Rican monkey, as well as many other critters. Though technically a zoo, it is also an important breeding center that aims to reintroduce native species into the wild. There is also a cafe. This is an excellent place for families.

Continue west and the road slides right over the Interamericana. Just north of the intersection, you'll find **La Casona del Maíz** (mains ₡2400-6400; 7am-9pm), a jam-packed family spot that offers unparalleled views of a verdant valley and…a working pit mine (seriously). But the food is spectacular – a lengthy menu of Tico country cooking – heavy on the grilled meats and corn dishes, though there are veggie *casados* as well. The *chorreadas* (savory corn pancakes) are excellent, but don't leave without sampling the tasty corn soup, studded with sweet, fresh kernels, or the falling-off-the-bone pork ribs (*costillas de cerdo*). Divine.

South of the highway, you'll find **La Fiesta del Maíz** (☎ 2487-7057; mains ₡2400-3100; 10am-8pm Wed-Mon), a humble roadside place that sells whole roasted chickens, *chorreadas,* tamales and cornbread by the bag.

A few more kilometers to the west, is **La Casa del Viñedo** (☎ 2487-6086; mains ₡3200-8500; noon-close), a family restaurant on the edge of La Garita that grills up ribs and steaks. It also sells a selection of pastas, *empanadas* and locally crafted wines. Our advice: avoid the wine.

GETTING THERE & AWAY

Buses (₡400, 30 minutes) run between Alajuela and La Garita, via Zoo Ave, every half hour.

Atenas

This small village, on the historic *camino de carretas* (oxcart trail) that once carried coffee beans as far as Puntarenas, is best known as having the most pleasant climate in the world, at least according to a 1994 issue of *National Geographic*. It's not too heavy on sights, though springtime is always in the air here.

About 1km before the center of town, you'll see the **Monumento al Boyero** (Monument to the Oxcart Driver) on the north side of the road – a grey metallic sculpture that looks like an oxcart on a rocket launchpad.

In town, you can dine on the main plaza at **Haedel's** (☎ 2446-0810; mains ₡3800-4900; 8am-2pm & 5-8pm Wed-Sun), a rustic German spot that serves all manner of sausage, pork and sauerkraut dishes. You can also get healthy yogurt and muesli breakfasts for only ₡1900.

On the eastern end of town, you'll find the typical **Restaurant La Trocha del Boyero** (☎ 2446-0533; casados ₡2500, mains ₡3100-5500; 11am-9pm). Tico families pour into the pleasant outdoor deck on weekends for a variety of *casados* on offer, fresh trout (in season) and heaping bowls of *chifrijo* (rice and beans with fried pork, corn chips and fresh tomato salsa). It is located on the main road to Alajuela, 300m east of the gas station, and 100m to the south. Look for a sign at the turnoff.

There is no place to stay in the village, but travel north for 5km, on the road to Grecia, and you'll find **El Cafetal Inn B&B** (☎ 2446-5785; www.cafetal.com; d incl breakfast US$75-120; P), a simple country inn set in the midst of a hillside coffee plantation. Fourteen guest rooms have clay-colored walls and eclectic tropical decor (think floral murals), as well as private balconies with rocking chairs. There is a swimming pool and two easy trails lead to waterfalls. A small restaurant, **Rincón Llanero** (4-9pm), serves basic dishes, as well as the plantation's signature brand of coffee, La Negrita. Credit cards are accepted.

Half-hourly buses connect the village of Atenas to Alajuela and San José from 6am to 9pm. The area is quite spread out, however, and best navigated by car.

NORTHWEST TO SARCHÍ

To the northwest of Alajuela, the carefully cultivated hills are home to the picturesque agricultural towns of Grecia (22km), Sarchí (29km), Naranjo (35km) and Zarcero (52km) – among others – many of which are popular weekend getaways for *josefinos* (inhabitants of San José) in search of fresh mountain air. The region boasts excellent coffee and dairy products and an interesting collection of eccentric attractions, including the country's most curious topiary bushes.

Rosario Area

From the Interamericana, near the road to Grecia, you'll see the well-signed turnoff for the **Vista del Valle Plantation Inn** (☎ 2450-0800; www.vistadelvalle.com; d incl breakfast US$100-175; P ⊠ ≋ ♨), adjoining the Zona Protectora Río Grande. Here you'll find a total of 17 individually designed units overlooking a forested gorge. Newer ones are better, but all come stocked with private deck, books and handcrafted soap. In addition, private trails lead to a 90m-high waterfall in the adjoining reserve and the staff can arrange horseback tours and massages. There is also a pool and Jacuzzi. The open-air restaurant (mains ₡5000 to ₡8800) serves Costa Rican fusion cuisine – including vegetarian specials that feature homegrown produce. Do not miss the moist *tres leches* cake or the homemade jams. Credit cards accepted.

Two kilometers west of the turnoff to Grecia, you'll find the offices of **Tropical Bungee** (☎ 2248-2212, 8398-8134; www.bungee.co.cr; 1st/2nd jump US$65/30), where you can arrange to hurl yourself off the 80m-high bridge over the Río Colorado. It's easiest to make a reservation online.

Grecia

pop 12,000

The village of Grecia – once named the 'Cleanest Little Town in Latin America' – is centered on a pleasant **Parque Central** (central plaza) that is anchored by one of the most charming churches in Costa Rica.

On the south side of the cathedral, you'll find a branch of the **Banco de Costa Rica** (🕑 9am-4pm), which has a 24-hour ATM operating on various international systems. For those who want to refine their moves, there's a branch of the dance academy **Merecumbé** (☎ 2495-1313; www.merecumbe.net), in a gray building on the main road into town.

SIGHTS

At the heart of town you'll find the incredibly quaint **Catedral de la Mercedes**, a red metal structure that was prefabricated in Belgium and shipped to Costa Rica in 1897 – and resembles a gingerbread church. It has an airy nave, bright Spanish tile floors and a Gothic-style altar covered in marble.

The small **Centro de la Cultura** (☎ 2444-6767), north of the church, maintains a small exhibit of Spanish-colonial artifacts and articles about the city's status as the cleanest in America.

Grecia's premiere attraction, **World of Snakes** (☎ 2494-3700; adult/child US$11/6; 🕑 8am-4pm), lies 1.5km south of the bus station. It is a well-

SPANISH SCHOOLS IN THE CENTRAL VALLEY

Unless otherwise noted, prices are given for five four-hour days of instruction, with/without a week's homestay. Prices include two meals a day.

Adventure Education Center (Map p146; ☎ 2556-4609, 2556-4614; www.adventurespanishschool.com; US$575/440) Combine Spanish classes and white-water rafting at this Turrialba school that also offers medical Spanish.

Centro Panamericano de Idiomas (☎ 2265-6306; www.cpi-edu.com; US$480/330) Based in San Joaquín de las Flores, just outside of Heredia, this popular school also has a teen program.

Finca la Flor de Paraíso (☎ 2534-8003; www.la-flor.org; with homestay US$450) This organic farm (see boxed text, p140), outside of Cartago, offers small group classes.

Intensa (☎ 2442-3843, in USA 866-277-1352; www.intensa.com; US$279/404) Schools in Alajuela and Heredia teach everything from medical to business Spanish.

Intercultura (Map p135; ☎ 2260-8480, in USA 800-552-2051; www.interculturacostarica.com; US$285/425) School in Heredia also arranges volunteer opportunities and offers cooking and dance classes.

Montaña Linda (☎ 2533-3640; www.montanalinda.com; with homestay US$230) All classes are one-on-one at this Orosi hostel and inn (p143).

run breeding center focused on supporting endangered snake populations. More than 150 snakes (45 species in all) are displayed in large cages. Informative tours are given in English, German or Spanish and there may be a chance to handle reptiles. Buses between Grecia and Alajuela can drop you at the entrance.

A couple of kilometers to the south, a bend in the road leads to an 18th-century **rock bridge**, which connects the hamlets of Puente de Piedra and Rincón de Salas. Locals say that the only other rock bridge like this is in China, and some tales have it that it was built by the devil. In 1994 it was declared a National Site of Historic Interest. It's small, so don't expect the eighth wonder of the world. Ask for directions, as it's hard to find.

About 5km south of Grecia, toward Santa Gertrudis, are **Las Cataratas de Los Chorros** (admission US$5; 8am-5pm), two gorgeous waterfalls and a swimming hole surrounded by picnic tables. It's a popular spot for weekending couples.

SLEEPING & EATING

B&B Grecia (☎ 2494-2573; www.bandbgrecia.com; s US$35-45, d US$45-55, additional person US$10, all incl breakfast;) This tiny three-room B&B located 150m south of the Parque Central has tidy, clean rooms in various sizes, including one that comes with a Jacuzzi tub. The owner can help arrange area tours.

Healthy Day Country Inn Resort (☎ 2444-5903; s/d without bathroom US$40/48; P V) This ramshackle resort has seen better days, but it's decent (and ideal if you're on a health kick). Rooms share bathrooms – but all have access to the onsite tennis court, gym and Jacuzzi. In addition, you can order massages and macrobiotic meals. It's more than 1km north of the cathedral on the road to Grecia.

Hotel Aeromundo (☎ 2494-0094; www.hotelaeromundo.com; s US$40, d US$60-70, apt US$75-100, all incl breakfast; P) About 100m east of the cathedral, this clean, tidy spot administered by the efficient Doris has 14 snug, carpeted rooms with cable TV surrounding an interior courtyard draped in plants. Three apartments are stocked with full kitchens. Credit cards accepted.

For rich coffee drinks and snacks – as well as free wi-fi – hit **Café Delicias** (☎ 2494-2093; dishes ₡700-1900; 8am-7pm;), an enjoyable spot near the southwest corner of the park.

A good dinner place is the popular **Don Efraín** (☎ 2494-0923; dishes ₡3000-8000; 11am-11pm Tue-Sun), which serves grilled meats and seafood in an open-air patio. It is located just north of the Healthy Day Country Inn.

Self-caterers will find the **Supermercado Palí** (☎ 2444-6696) to the southeast of the church. A farmers' market takes place north of town on Saturday mornings.

GETTING THERE & AWAY

The bus terminal is 300m west of the church.

San José ₡800; one hour; departs every 15 minutes from 5:30am to 8:30pm, every 30 minutes on weekends.

Sarchí, connecting to Naranjo ₡200; 30 minutes; departs every 25 minutes from 5am to 8:30pm.

Sarchí

pop 5500

Welcome to Costa Rica's most famous crafts center, where artisans produce the ornately painted oxcarts and leather-and-wood furnishings for which the Central Valley is known. (You'll know you've arrived because just about everything is covered in the signature geometric designs – even city hall.) Yes, it's a tourist trap – organized excursions from San José bring in travelers by the busload – but it's a pretty one. The town is stretched out along a road that weaves through hilly countryside.

Most people come in for an afternoon of shopping and call it a day. But there are more than 200 artisanal workshops in the area. If you have time on your hands, it is possible to meet different artisans and custom-order a creation.

For the lowdown on the goods, see boxed text, p130.

ORIENTATION & INFORMATION

Sarchí is divided by the Río Trojas into Sarchí Norte and Sarchí Sur, and is rather spread out, straggling for several kilometers along the main road from Grecia to Naranjo. In fact, it's easiest to explore by private car.

In Sarchí Norte, you'll find the heart of the village, including a twin-towered **church**, some restaurants and hotels, as well as a public plaza that contains what is purported to be the **world's largest oxcart** (the photo-ops are priceless).

Also on the north end of town is the **Jardín Botánico Else Kientzler** (☎ 2454-2070; www.elsekientzlergarden.com; adult/child US$15/10; 8am-4pm;). This recommended botanical garden has 2km of trails, ideal for a refreshing stroll among more than 2000 types of clearly labeled plants, including succulents, fruit trees, heliconias and orchids. There is a picnic area and a small playground for children. Find it 800m north of the stadium.

On the soccer field, about 100m south of the church, there is a branch of the **Banco Nacional** (☎ 2454-4262; ⏰ 8:30am-3pm Mon-Fri) for changing money.

SLEEPING & EATING

Cabinas Mandy (☎ 8814-1555; d US$13; P) About 300m north of the fire station, in Sarchí Norte, is this small, basic budget option with simple well-kept rooms that have cable TV and private hot shower.

Hotel Daniel Zamora (☎ 2454-4596; d US$35; P) On a quiet street north of the soccer field, the Zamora is a slightly more upmarket choice. Seven clean tile-floor rooms have cable TV, private hot shower and even a small sitting area. Credit cards accepted.

Villa Sarchí Lodge (☎ 2454-5000; hotelvillasarchi@ice.co.cr; d US$35; P) Run by the same owners as Hotel Daniel Zamora, here you'll find eight rooms set into a nice garden with a swimming pool. It is located 800m west of town, on the road to Naranjo. Credit cards accepted.

Las Carretas (☎ 2454-1636; mains ₡3800-6200; ⏰ 11am-9pm) One of the most popular spots for a lunch break is the restaurant adjacent to the Fábrica de Carretas Joaquín Chavarrí. Expect a mix of Tico classics along with international items such as burgers and burritos.

A great farmers' market is held on Fridays behind Taller Lalo Alfaro, where you can grab homemade snacks, *queso palmito* (a local cheese) and lots of produce.

GETTING THERE & AROUND

If you're driving from San José, from the Interamericana, take the signed exit to Grecia and from there, follow the road north to Sarchí. If you're coming from the west, take the turnoff north to Naranjo, then head east to Sarchí.

Buses arrive and depart from Sarchí Norte.

Alajuela ₡300; 30 minutes; departs every 30 minutes from 6am to 11pm.

Grecia ₡300; 20 minutes; departs every 25 minutes from 5am-8:30pm.

San José ₡1000; 1½ hours; departs every 30 minutes between 5am and 10pm.

ZARCERO

pop 3200

North of Naranjo, the road winds for 20km until it reaches Zarcero's 1736m perch at the western end of the Cordillera Central. This s

A SHOPPERS GUIDE TO SARCHÍ

Most travelers come to Sarchí for one thing and one thing only: *carretas,* the elaborate, colorfully painted oxcarts that are the unofficial souvenir of Costa Rica – and official symbol of the Costa Rican worker. In Sarchí, these come ready for the road (oxen sold separately) or in scaled-down versions (ready to display in gardens or used as minibars). But the area produces plenty of other curios as well: leather-and-wood furniture (including those incredible rocking chairs that collapse, Ikea-style for shipping), wood tableware and an infinite array of trinkets emblazoned with the colorful mandala-design popularized by *carretas*.

Workshops are usually open from 8am to 4pm daily, and they accept credit cards and US dollars. For your shipping ease, find a **UPS office** (☎ 2454-5555) in Sarchí Sur. Below is a list of some of the most respected and popular spots, though with more than 200 places to choose from, it pays to shop around. Prices and quality vary; choose carefully.

Coopearsa (☎ 2454-4196/4050; www.coopearsa.com) In Sarchí Norte, 200m west of the soccer field, is this kitsch-filled paradise of *carretas,* woodwork and painted feathers.

Fábrica de Carretas Joaquín Chaverri (☎ 2454-4411) The oldest and best-known factory in Sarchí Sur. In the back, the small studio is a good place for watching artisans emblazon those incredible patterns on the oxcarts by hand.

Los Rodríguez (☎ 2454-4097); **El Arte Sarchiseño** (☎ 2454-1686); **Muebles El Artesano** (☎ 2454-4422) All are located along the main road and specialize in rocking chairs and other furniture.

Taller Lolo Alfaro (☎ 2454-4131) One block north of the Palí supermarket in Sarchí Norte, this renowned workshop (the country's oldest) produced the massive oxcart in Sarchí's main plaza.

a gorgeous location: the mountains look as if they've been lifted from landscape paintings and the climate is famously fresh. But the real reason you're here is to look at the country's most intense shrubbery.

Parque Francisco Alvarado, in front of the peach-and-blue Iglesia de San Rafael (built 1895), was just a normal plaza until the 1960s, when a gardener named Evangelisto Blanco suddenly became inspired to shave the ordinary, mild-mannered topiary into a bizarre series of drippy, abstract shapes. Over the years, these have morphed into statuesque heads, freaky octopi straight out of *Star Trek* and a double tunnel of surreal, melting arches. In other words, bring your camera.

In addition to the space-age trees, Zarcero is a center for Costa Rica's organic-farming movement. You can find unusual varieties of pesticide-free goodies all over town, and the surrounding mountains are just perfect for an afternoon picnic.

If there was ever a place where the roadside stands are worth it, this is it. Winding country lanes in the area are all lined with stands selling fresh cashews, honey, sweets (the coconut *cajeta* is good) and *queso palmito*, a locally made cheese that has a delicate taste and goes well with fresh tomatoes and basil. Once you've packed your picnic basket, find a grassy spot – or have a feast within view of the bizarre bushes in Zarcero's main plaza.

If you brought your swimsuit, stop at **Piscinas Apamar** (☎ 2463-3674; admission US$2; 7am-4pm Mon-Sat), 500m west of the park on the road to Guadalupe (up the hill, behind the Musmanni), where there's not only a huge swimming pool but also three hot tubs.

Just north of the town church is **Hotel Don Beto** (☎ 2463-3137; d with/without bathroom US$33/28, tr US$39; P), a comfortable spot with eight tidy rooms accented in bright floral linens, and hardwood floors – many of which come with private balcony. The helpful Tico owners can organize trips throughout the area, including excursions to the nearby Los Ángeles Cloud Forest Adventure Park or the Parque Nacional Juan Castro Blanco.

Hourly buses traveling between San José and Ciudad Quesada stop at Zarcero, though some buses may be full by the time they reach Zarcero, particularly on weekends. There are also buses from Alajuela, San Ramón and Grecia.

BAJOS DEL TORO

pop 250

A road snakes east out of Zarcero, through winding hillsides dotted with family farms, up into the lower reaches of the area's cloud-forest ecosystem. If you were looking for a little piece of Costa Rica where everybody knows everybody, then look no further. This 250-person town is rural idyll at its finest. Besides, the mountain air couldn't possibly be any fresher.

There are no banks or internet cafes. Bring all the cash you need. Businesses are all listed in order as you drive into town.

Bosque de Paz Rain/Cloud Forest Lodge & Biological Reserve (☎ 2234-6676; www.bosquedepaz.com; per person incl 3 meals US$114-150; P V) This 1000-hectare reserve has more than 22km of trails in tropical old-growth forest, as well as a 12-room hacienda-style inn with a dozen whitewashed, terra-cotta–tiled rooms with large windows that offer forest views. More significantly, the area is part of an important wilderness corridor between Parque Nacional Volcán Poás and Parque Nacional Juan Castro Blanco, so you might just run into a group of researchers during your stay. Needless to say, bird-watching is a specialty. Vegetarian and vegan diets can be accommodated; rates are based on double occupancy.

our pick El Silencio (☎ 2761-0301; www.elsilenciolodge.com; per person incl 3 meals US$240; P ⊠ V) When it comes to absolute serenity, there are few places in Costa Rica that can beat this superbly designed mountain lodge that doesn't just talk the environmental talk, but walks it as well. No earth was moved to construct the 15 simply designed (but very luxurious) individual cabin suites stocked with minibar, fireplace, rocking chair and private deck with Jacuzzi tub – which are positively amazing when the stars are out. In addition, there is a spa, 8km worth of trails (one of which leads to a stunning waterfall) and a health-conscious menu stocked with organic, local foods and strong on vegetarian dishes. Plus the charming, bilingual Tico staff all hail from the region – and no one leaves without planting a tree. Highly recommended. Credit cards accepted.

Soda Restaurante Nené (☎ 2761-1932; mains ₡3000-3500; 8am-5pm) This small tourist complex has stocked tilapia and trout ponds where you can catch your own and then have it fried or grilled up with garlic at the onsite *soda* (cheap, informal lunch counter).

CENTRAL VALLEY & HIGHLANDS

Hotel y Villas Bajo del Toro (☎ 2761-0284; r US$54; P) Four spacious ceramic-tile rooms with bright bedspreads have private balcony, rocking chair and views of a rushing river. Units sleep up to four and come equipped with hot-water bathroom, coffeemaker and minifridge. A small *soda* (*casados* ₡2500) serves typical meals. This is a weekend spot, so if you're visiting midweek, prices may be flexible.

Down the street, in a circular wood building, you'll find **Rancho Típico Toro Amarillo** (☎ 2761-1918; breakfast ₡1200-1500, casados ₡2300-2500; 6am-6pm), a rustic country eatery – with a changing daily menu – run by a local women's cooperative. They have two tidy *cabinas* (double US$22) in the back, both with private bathrooms and hot water.

Getting There & Away

If driving north from the Interamericana through Zarcero, take a right immediately after the church and head north about 15km. The road is almost entirely paved but the last stretch is steep and rocky; 4WD is recommended. There are daily buses from Zarcero.

PARQUE NACIONAL JUAN CASTRO BLANCO

This 143-sq-km **national park** (admission US$10, camping per person US$3) was created in 1992 to protect the slopes of Volcán Platanar (2183m) and Volcán Porvenir (2267m) from logging. The headwaters for five major rivers originate here as well, making this one of the most important watersheds in the country.

The park is in limbo, federally protected but still privately owned by various plantation families – only those parts that have already been purchased by the government are technically open to travelers. As yet, there is almost no infrastructure for visitors, though there is a **Minae office** (☎ 2460-7600) in El Sucre, north of Zarcero, where you can pay fees for camping or day use. However, the office is frequently closed, and fees are rarely collected.

The park is most popular among anglers as each of the five rivers is brimming with trout. The lack of infrastructure and tourist traffic means that your chances of spotting rare wildlife (such as quetzals, black guans and curassow) are very high – but it also means that maintained trails are almost nonexistent. It is best to go with a guide, which can be arranged through tour agencies and hotels in the area.

PALMARES

pop 8900

Palmares' claim to fame is the annual **Las Fiestas de Palmares**, a 10-day beer-soaked extravaganza that takes place in mid-January and features carnival rides, a *tope* (horse parade), fireworks, big-name bands, small-name bands, exotic dancers, fried food, *guaro* tents and the densest population of merry Ticos you've ever seen. It is one of the biggest events in the country – crowds can reach upwards of 10,000 people – and is covered widely on national TV. For the other 355 days of the year, Palmares is a tumbleweed town, where life is centered on the ornate stained-glass **church** in the central plaza.

There's little in the way of accommodations, so unless you know someone with a house, give up any plans on staying here during the party. At other times, a good spot to lay your head is **Casa Marta** (☎ 2452-1010; www.hotelcasamarta.com; d incl breakfast US$70; P), which has a dozen clean, whitewashed rooms with polished wood ceilings. It's located 800m south of the highway, near the bullring. The area around the plaza is lined with *sodas* and bakeries.

Buses run continuously from San José to Palmares throughout the festival. For information on the musical lineup, visit **Fiestas Palmares** (www.fiestaspalmares.com).

If you're driving, the road from Sarchí continues west to Naranjo, where it divides – head south for 13km to reach Palmares. It is well signed.

SAN RAMÓN

pop 2500

The colonial town of San Ramón is no wallflower in the pageant of Costa Rican history. The 'City of Presidents and Poets' has sent five men to the country's highest office, including ex-president Rodrigo Carazo, who built a tourist lodge a few kilometers to the north at the entrance to the Los Ángeles Cloud Forest.

At the center of this charming agricultural town, you'll see the twin spires of the ash-gray **Iglesia de San Ramón**. The interiors are definitely worth checking out: it has a lovely baroque-style altar, Spanish-tile floors and neat rows of wood pews. In front of the church is the **Parque Central**, which is surrounded by a few low-lying colonial-style buildings and is studded with several *torii*, the traditional Japanese gates found at the entrance to a Shinto shrine. (Go figure.) The best time to visit is on Saturdays during the farmers' market, when all manner of cheeses and chorizo are on display and the local ladies can be found shopping and gossiping.

On the north side of the park, the **Museo de San Ramón** (☎ 2437-9851; admission free; 8am-noon & 1-5pm Mon-Fri) maintains a few simple exhibits devoted to detailing life in Costa Rica during the colony and the early republic. Towards the back, a gallery shows rotating art exhibits.

There is a **Banco de Costa Rica** (9am-4pm), with an ATM, 300m west of the park.

Sleeping & Eating

Hotel San Ramón (☎ 2447-2042; r per person US$18; P) About 300m west and 100m north of the church is this decent budget option with a helpful owner and 31 basic rooms scattered over two buildings. All of these have hot-water bathroom and cable TV. Credit cards accepted.

Hotel La Posada (☎ 2445-7359; www.posadahotel.net; d standard/deluxe incl breakfast US$50/60; P) This nicer midrange inn has 28 well-maintained rooms surrounding a lush, plant-filled courtyard with a fountain. They are somewhat baroque-looking, stocked with massive, handcrafted beds, each of which lie somewhere on the design continuum between Louis XIV and African safari. All have minifridge and cable TV; the more expensive units come with Jacuzzi tubs. A few rooms are wheelchair-accessible. Find it 400m north of the church.

Casa Amanecer (☎ 2445-2100; www.casa-amanecer-cr.com; d incl breakfast US$62; P V) Located a 10-minute drive northeast of San Ramón, on the road to Concepción, is this new, sleekly designed B&B, run by Christopher and Luisa. Here you'll find four graceful contemporary rooms with wonderful valley views. In addition, the hotel stocks bicycles and there is regular yoga. The owners put great effort into being environmentally conscious, from the veggie breakfasts to the biodegradable cleaning products. Additional meals and in-room massages (US$40) can be arranged with advance reservation.

About 100m west and 50m south of the central plaza in San Ramón, **Aroma's Café** (☎ 2447-1414; coffees ₡700-1350, dishes ₡700-2800; 10:30am-7pm Mon-Sat, noon-7pm Sun) is a bright, attractive spot – good for lounging – that serves up a variety of coffee drinks, pastries and light meals.

Inexpensive *sodas* abound.

Shopping

For something truly unique, head to **El Tejano** (☎ 2447-0001; 8:30-noon & 1:30-6pm Mon-Sat), a small shop selling saddles, cowboy hats and highly spectacular cowboy-boot lamps. The shop is located 100m south of the hospital, on the north end of town.

Getting There & Away

There are hourly buses to San José as well as frequent buses to Ciudad Quesada via Zarcero. Buses depart from Calle 16 between Avs 1 and 3.

LOS ÁNGELES CLOUD FOREST ADVENTURE PARK

This **private reserve** (☎ 2461-0643; www.cloudforestcostarica.com; per person US$20; 9am-4pm), 18km north of San Ramón, is centered on a lodge and dairy ranch that was once owned by ex-president Rodrigo Carazo. Some 800 hectares of primary and secondary forest have a short boardwalk and 11km of foot trails that lead to towering waterfalls and misty cloud forest vistas. The appeal of this cloud forest (which is actually adjacent to the reserve at Monteverde, see p211) is that it is comparatively untouristed, which means you will have a good chance of observing wildlife (jaguars and ocelots have been spotted), and the birdwatching is fantastic.

Bilingual naturalist guides are available to lead hikes (per person US$30) and guided horseback-riding trips (per hour US$20). Alternatively, you can zip along the tree tops on the reserve's obligatory canopy tour (per person US$45).

A taxi to the reserve and hotel costs about US$15 from San Ramón, and the turnoff is well signed from the Interamericana.

Sleeping

Tierras Enamoradas (☎ 2447-9331; www.landsinlove.com; d incl breakfast US$105, additional person US$22; P V) Adjacent to another private reserve featuring 20km of cloud-forest trails, this Israeli-run vegetarian B&B has eclectic rooms with bright floral motifs, a lounge, an outdoor swimming pool and good views. The restaurant serves an international mix of Costa Rican, Mediterranean and Middle

Eastern items, though plan on spending for it: *gallo pinto* (stir-fried rice and beans) will set you back US$9. It's about halfway between Villa Blanca Cloud Forest Hotel Spa and the village of La Tigra.

Villa Blanca Cloud Forest Hotel Spa (☎ 2228-4603; www.villablanca-costarica.com; d superior/deluxe/honeymoon US$170/192/215, additional person US$25, child under 6 free, all incl breakfast; P 💻 V 👶) Nestled into a well-manicured garden that sits alongside the reserve, this recommended lodge has 30 blue-and-white adobe *casitas* (little houses) that come with varying levels of amenities. All have fireplaces, minibars and coffeemakers; more expensive units are bigger and come equipped with Jacuzzi tubs. There's a fine restaurant that serves a Central American menu, including veggie dishes. All manner of excursions can be arranged, such as hikes to a nearby peak to see quetzals and kid-friendly trips to a local dairy farm. Credit cards accepted.

HEREDIA AREA

Despite its proximity to the capital, Heredia isn't just another San José suburb. Since the late 1990s the city has served as Costa Rica's center of technology: microchips produced here have become one of the country's most important exports, turning Heredia into a magnet for highly educated tech heads. The town itself has a very young vibe, particularly around the western edge of town, where students lounge around cafes and bars at all hours of the day. In addition to the tech boom, the region remains a vital coffee producer – and a gateway to one of Costa Rica's largest swaths of highland forest, the Parque Nacional Braulio Carrillo.

HEREDIA

pop 33,000

During the 19th century, *La Ciudad de las Flores* (The City of the Flowers) was home to a *cafetalero* (coffee grower) aristocracy that made its fortune exporting Costa Rica's premium blend. Today, the historic center retains some of this well-bred air, with a leafy main square that is overlooked by a stocky cathedral, and low-lying buildings that channel the architecture of the Spanish colony.

Though only 11km from San José, Heredia is – in personality – at a remove from the grit and grime of the capital. Yet, it still maintains a cosmopolitan vibe – largely due to the high-tech corporations (such as Intel) that have settled amid the area's coffee *fincas*. In addition, the Universidad Nacional (National University) keeps things a touch bohemian and on any afternoon, you're bound to find local bars and cafes abuzz with young folk idling away their time.

Information

There's no tourist office but most other services are readily available.

Hospital San Vicente de Paul (☎ 2261-0001; Av 8 btwn Calles 14 & 16)

Internet Café (Av Central btwn Calles 7 & 9; per hr ₡300; 🕒 24hr) For 24-hour access to the web, plus, there are no shortage of internet spots in the immediate area.

Scotiabank (☎ 2262-5303; Av 4 btwn Calles Central & 2; 🕒 8:30am-5pm Mon-Fri, 9am-1pm Sat) They change money and have a 24-hour ATM that dispenses US dollars.

Sights

Heredia was founded in 1706, and in true Spanish-colonial style it has several interesting old landmarks arranged around the **Parque Central**. To the east is **Iglesia de la Inmaculada Concepción**, built in 1797 and still in use. Opposite the church steps you can take a break and watch old men playing checkers at the park tables while weddings and funerals come and go. Built in a neoclassical, Renaissance style, the church's thick walls and squat construction has withstood the earthquakes that have damaged or destroyed most other historic buildings from this period.

To the north of the park is an 1867 guard tower called simply **El Fortín**, the last remaining turret of a Spanish fortress and the official symbol of Heredia – and a national historic site. Because of its fragile state, its passageways are closed to the public.

At the park's northeast corner, in a low-lying Spanish structure that dates back to the 18th century is the **Casa de la Cultura** (☎ 2261-4485; cnr Calle Central & Av Central; admission free; 🕒 hours vary), which at one point served as the residence of President Alfredo González Flores, who governed from 1913 to 1917. It is beautifully maintained and now houses permanent historical displays as well as rotating art exhibits.

The campus of **Universidad Nacional**, six blocks east of Parque Central, is a great place for doing a little guerrilla learning. Keep an eye out for posters advertising cultural offer-

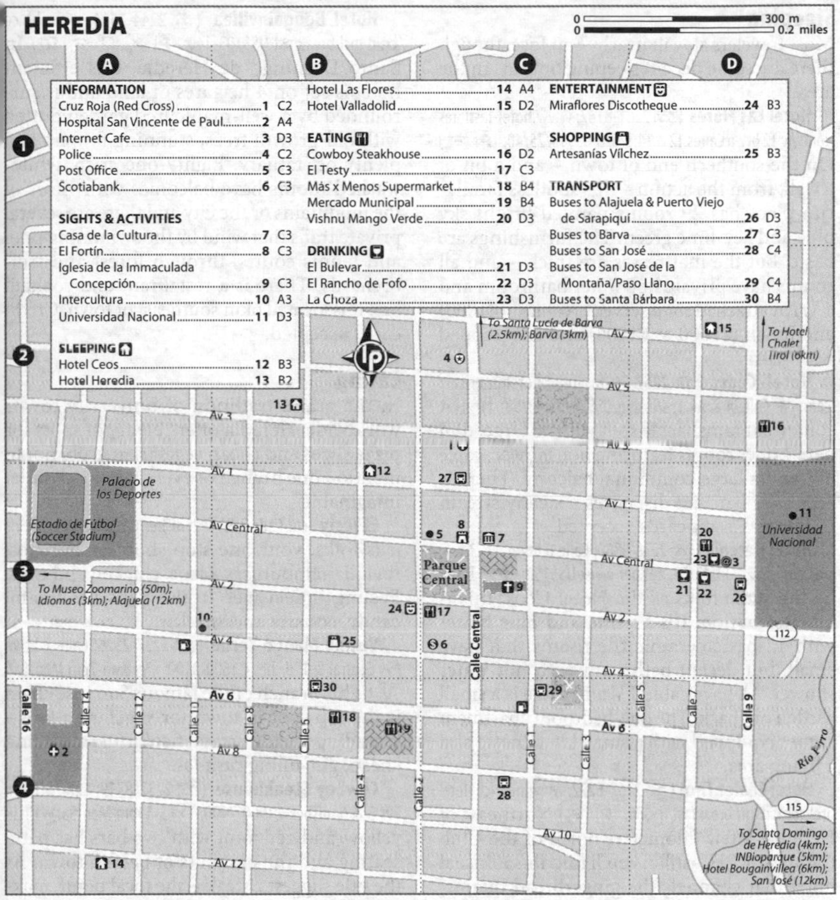

ings and special events happening around the city. Also, check out the marine biology department's **Museo Zoomarino** (☎ 2277-3240; admission free; 🕑 8am-4pm Mon-Fri), where more than 2000 displayed specimens give an overview of Costa Rica's marine diversity. The Museo Zoomarino is not on campus, but located about 1km west of the university.

About 4km to the southeast of town, in the neighborhood of Santo Domingo, is **INBioparque** (☎ 2507-8107; www.inbioparque.com/en/; adult/student/child US$23/17/13; 🕑 8:30am-2pm Tue-Fri, 9:30am-3:30pm Sat & Sun; 🚸 ♿), a wildlife park and botanical garden run by the non-profit INBio (National Biodiversity Institute), which catalogs Costa Rica's biodiversity and promotes its sustainable use. Visitors can admire 531 species of plant, creatures such as sloths, boas and tarantulas, and visit a livestock and a butterfly farm. On weekends there is children's theatre, plus the park is wheelchair-accessible. Closing times listed above are when the last guests are admitted; the park itself doesn't shut until sunset. See the website for a list of specialty naturalist tours and directions.

Heredia is also an excellent base from which to explore the little-visited Volcán Barva, within the Parque Nacional Braulio Carrillo. See p445 for all the details.

Courses

For a list of language schools in the area, see boxed text, p128.

Sleeping

Most travelers stay in nearby San José, though there are some decent sleeping options in the area.

Hotel Las Flores (☎ 2261-8147; www.hotel-lasflores.com; Av 12 btwn Calles 12 & 14; s/d/tr US$13/25/40; P wi-fi) On the southern end of town – and a bit of a walk from the action – this spotless family-run place has 29 rooms painted bright sky blue and key-lime green. The furnishings are basic, but the mattresses are thick – and all rooms have private hot-water bathroom and TV. An attached *soda* serves breakfast (₡1000) and lunch (₡1600 to ₡1900) and is equipped with wi-fi.

Hotel Ceos (☎ 2262-2628; info@hotelamericacr.com; cnr Calle 4 & Av 1; s/d/tr/q US$24/33/43/53; P) A somewhat ramshackle spot with 10 large, dim bare-bones rooms featuring hot shower, cable TV and a large communal balcony. There is an onsite bar that dispenses a steady stream of Pilsen. Credit cards accepted.

Hotel Heredia (☎ 2238-0880; Calle 6 btwn Avs 3 & 5; s/d/tr/q US$24/33/43/53, apt per week US$150; P) Run by the same folks as the Hotel Ceos, this is a better option. It's a white-and-blue house with 12 basic ceramic-tile rooms that have small, but decent bathroom with hot-water shower. All have cable TV and there is a small garden out back. The one-bedroom apartment comes equipped with a small kitchenette and a living area.

Hotel Chalet Tirol (☎ 2267-6222; www.hotelchaletel tirol.com; d incl breakfast US$85; P wi-fi) Northeast of Heredia, a few kilometers north of the Club Campestre El Castillo, you'll find this unusual hotel that channels the gingerbread quaintness of the Alps. (It was once covered in fake snow and used as a backdrop for a German beer advert.) The 23 rooms, all of which come equipped with cable TV, could stand an upgrade, but they are generally charming, and come in a variety of configurations, including rustic stand-alone 'chalets.' In July and August, the hotel hosts a small international music festival.

Hotel Valladolid (☎ 2260-2905; www.hotelvalladolid.net; cnr Calle 7 & Av 7; d US$87; P air-con wi-fi) This business hotel on a quiet street on the northeast end of town has 12 bright, clean, tiled rooms that aren't beautiful, but are very well maintained. They all have microwaves, minifridge, bar, cable TV and private bathroom with hot water. The staff is quite helpful; credit cards accepted.

Hotel Bougainvillea (☎ 2244-1414; www.hb.co.cr; d incl breakfast US$103-140; P nonsmoking internet wi-fi pool) In Santo Domingo de Heredia, this efficient hotel is set on 4 hectares of land and is surrounded by a well-manicured garden dotted with old-growth trees, stunning flowers and plenty of statuary. Eighty-one crisp, white-washed rooms have balconies with views of the mountains or the city and there are several private trails that wind by the swimming pool and tennis courts, through forest and fruit orchards. There is a restaurant and cocktail bar. It is located 6km southeast of town. Credit cards accepted.

Eating

In the grand tradition of university towns worldwide, Heredia offers plenty of spots for pizza slices and cheap vegetarian grub, not to mention one branch of every fast-food outlet imaginable.

El Testy (cnr Calle 2 & Av 2; dishes ₡1200-2800) Here it is folks, your one-stop shop for burritos, ravioli, hamburgers, tacos, chicken and fries. Feeling indecisive? It also sells ice cream, candy, cookies and snacks!

Vishnu Mango Verde (☎ 2237-2526; Calle 7 btwn Avs Central & 1; dishes ₡1600-3100; ⏰ 8am-7pm Mon-Sat; V) This branch of the famous San José chain is the top spot in town for vegetarian fare – including a wide array of colorful salads and cheap, gut-filling *casados*.

Cowboy Steakhouse (☎ 2237-8719; Calle 9 btwn Avs 3 & 5; dishes ₡1900-7400; ⏰ 5-11pm Mon-Sat) This yellow-and-red joint with two bars has patio seating and the best cuts of beef in town. As the title suggests, steak is the focal point, making it a meat-lover's must. But the hearty salads and extensive list of *bocas* (savory bar snacks) are worth a nibble as well.

You can fill up for a couple of thousand colones at the **Mercado Municipal** (Calle 2 btwn Avs 6 & 8; ⏰ 6am-6pm), which has *sodas* to spare and plenty of very fresh groceries. **Más x Menos** (Av 6 btwn Calles 4 & 6; ⏰ 8:30am-9pm) is a supermarket with everything else.

Drinking & Entertainment

With a thriving student body, there's no shortage of live music, cultural events and the odd happening. Stay aware: Heredia can get dodgy at nighttime, though there is an established police presence.

The university district is hopping most nights of the week (Tico students live it up ike you wouldn't believe). **La Choza** (Av Central btwn Calles 7 & 9), **El Bulevar** (cnr Calle 7 & Av Central) and **El Rancho de Fofo** (Av Central btwn Calles 7 & 9) are three long-running watering holes.

After a few rounds of beers, the party really kicks off at the **Miraflores Discotheque** (cnr Av 2 & Calle 2), on the southern edge of the Parque Central, where locals get groovy to a mix of international beats.

Shopping

At **Artesanías Vílchez** (☎ 2237-9641; Mon-Sat) the selection of crafts is crude, but you're here for one reason, and one reason only: to buy an authentic Tico cowboy hat. Saddle up and ride!

Getting There & Away

There is no central bus terminal, and buses leave from bus stops scattered around the southern part of town.

Alajuela (cnr Av Central & Calle 9) ₡400; 20 minutes; departs every 15 minutes from 6am to 10pm.

Barva (Calle Central btwn Avs 1 & 3) ₡300; 20 minutes; departs every 30 minutes from 5:15am to 11:30pm.

Puerto Viejo de Sarapiquí (cnr Av Central & Calle 9) ₡1200; 3½ hours; departs at 11am, 1:30pm and 3pm.

San José (Av 8 btwn Calles Central & 1) ₡300; 20 minutes; departs every 20 to 30 minutes from 4:40am to 11pm.

San José de la Montaña/Paso Llano – for Volcán Barva (Transportes del Norte; Calle 1 btwn Avs 4 & 6) ₡400; one hour; departs 5:25am, 6:25am, noon and 4pm Mon-Fri, 6:40am, 11am and 4pm Sat-Sun.

Santa Bárbara (Calle 6 btwn Avs 4 & 6) ₡300; 20 minutes; departs every 10 to 30 minutes from 5:15am to 11:30pm.

BARVA

pop 4900

Just 2.5km north of Heredia is the historic town of Barva, a settlement that dates back to 1561 and which has been declared a national monument. The town center is dotted with low-lying 19th-century buildings and is centered on the towering **Iglesia San Bartolomé**, which was constructed in 1893. Surrounded by picturesque mountains, it just oozes colonial charm. In addition, the surrounding area was once popular with the Costa Rican elite: Cleto González Víquez (1858–1937), twice president of Costa Rica (he built the original National Library), was born and raised here. It's a perfect spot for a lazy afternoon stroll – and though Barva proper doesn't have any lodgings, there are some attractive inns in the hillsides outside of town.

Sights

The most famous coffee roaster in Costa Rica, **Café Britt Finca** (☎ 2277-1600; www.coffeetour.com; adult with/without lunch US$35/20, student US$30/16; tours 11am;) is headquartered just 1km south of Barva – and offers a 90-minute bilingual tour of its area plantation that includes a video presentation and a hokey stage play about the history of coffee (small kids will likely dig it). Naturally, there's plenty of coffee tasting and gift-shop browsing. For an extra US$10, you can combine the tour with a one-hour trip to a *beneficio* (processing plant). Plus the company operates a daily shuttle that can pick you up from San José for an extra fee; reserve ahead. If you are driving, you can't miss the *many* signs between Heredia and Barva.

Located in Santa Lucía de Barva, about 1.5km southeast of Barva, the small **Museo de Cultura Popular** (☎ 2260-1619; admission US$3; 9am-4pm), run by the Universidad Nacional, is located in a restored 19th-century farmhouse that exhibits period pieces, such as domestic and agricultural tools. It is best to reserve a tour ahead of time, when staff can arrange a hands-on visit – which might include using the beehive-shaped clay oven to make traditional foods (though this may require a minimum number of people).

Barva is also an excellent base from which to hike the little-visited Volcán Barva (see p445).

Festivals & Events

Every March the town is home to the famous **Feria de la Mascarada**, a tradition with roots in the colonial era, in which people don massive colorful masks (some of which weigh up to 20kg), and gather to dance and parade around the town square. Demons and devils are frequent subjects, but celebrities and politicians also figure in the mix (you haven't lived until you've seen a 6m-tall Celia Cruz). The festival is usually held during the last week of the month, but dates vary from one year to the next; inquire locally.

Sleeping

More affordable accommodations can be found in nearby Heredia (opposite).

Finca Rosa Blanca (☎ 2269-9392; www.fincarosablanca.com; d US$295-520; P) Set in the midst of a hillside coffee plantation just outside of Santa Bárbara, this honeymoon-ready confection of suites and villas is cloaked in fruit

CENTRAL VALLEY & HIGHLANDS

trees that shade private trails. Fifteen sparkling white adobe rooms with wood-beam ceilings and private balconies are lavishly appointed; one tops a tower with a 360-degree view, reached by a winding staircase made from a tree trunk. Shower in an artificial waterfall, take a moonlit dip in the pool, have an organic citrus-coffee bath soak at the spa – or, better yet, dip into a *very* romantic dinner at the hotel's recommended restaurant (mains US$18-26; V), which serves locally focused dishes, such as mountain trout with sweet-corn ragout. Credit cards accepted.

Getting There & Around

Half-hourly buses travel between Heredia and Barva (₡400, 20 minutes), picking up and dropping off in front of the church.

CARTAGO AREA

The riverbank setting of the city of Cartago was handpicked by Spanish Governor Juan Vásquez de Coronado, who said that he had 'never seen a more beautiful valley.' Cartago was founded as Costa Rica's first capital in 1563, and Coronado's successors endowed the city with fine colonial architecture. However, as things tend to happen in Costa Rica, the city was destroyed during a 1723 eruption of the Volcán Irazú. Any remaining landmarks were toppled by the earthquakes in 1841 and 1910.

Although the city was relegated to backwater status when the seat of government moved to San José in 1823, the surrounding area, particularly the Orosi Valley, flourished during the days of the coffee trade. Today much of the region continues to be devoted to the production of coffee, among other agricultural products. And though Cartago no longer has the prestige of being a national capital, it nonetheless remains a vital commercial hub – not to mention the site of the most important religious monument in the country.

CARTAGO

pop 24,100

After the rubble was cleared, in the early 20th century, nobody bothered to rebuild Cartago to its former quaint specifications. As in other commercial towns, expect plenty of functional concrete structures. One exception is the bright white Basílica de Nuestra Señora de los Ángeles, which is visible from many parts of the city, standing out like a snowcapped mountain above a plane of one-story edifices. It is considered to be the holiest religious shrine in Costa Rica and has been rebuilt several times, after each of the city's natural disasters.

The city is thrown briefly into the spotlight every August, when pilgrims from every corner of the country descend on the basilica to say their most serious prayers. The remainder of the year, Cartago exists mainly as a commercial and residential center, though the beauty of the surrounding mountains helps take the edge off modern life.

Orientation & Information

The city is based on a grid system with a public square at its heart. As always, street signs are infrequent. There is no tourist office.

Hospital Max Peralta (☎ 2550-1999; www.hmp.sa.cr; Av 5 btwn Calles 1 & 3) Offers emergency health care, among other services.

Internet Alta Velocidad (Calle 1 btwn Avs 1 & 3; per hr ₡300; 🕑 7:30am-7pm Mon-Fri, 8am-7pm Sat, 9am-6pm Sun) You can check email here, 50m south of the Parque Central.

Scotiabank (☎ 2591-9000; cnr Av 2 & Calle 2; 🕑 9am-5pm Mon-Fri) Changes money and has a 24-hour ATM that accepts foreign cards.

Sights

The most important site in Cartago – and the most venerated religious site in the country – the **Basílica de Nuestra Señora de los Ángeles** (cnr Av 2 & Calle 16) channels any airy Byzantine grace, with fine stained-glass windows and ornate side chapels featuring carved wood altars. Though the structure has changed many times since 1635, when it was first built, the relic that it protects remains unharmed inside.

La Negrita, 'the Black Virgin,' is a small (less than a meter tall), probably indigenous, representation of the Virgin Mary, found on this spot on August 2, 1635 by a native woman. As the story goes, when she tried to take the statuette with her, it miraculously reappeared back where she'd found it. Twice. So the townspeople built a shrine around her. In 1824, she was declared Costa Rica's patron Virgin. She now resides on a gold, jewel-studded platform at the main altar. Each August 2, on the anniversary of the statuette's miraculous discovery, pilgrims from every corner of the country (and beyond) walk the 22km from San José to the basilica. Many of the penitent complete the last few hundred meters of the pilgrimage on their knees.

At other times, the best time to visit the basilica is during mass. Noon mass is the best, when the sun is up and the stained-glass shimmers – and the organist bangs away at the massive pipe organ that hovers over the main doorway. (During ceremonies, please be respectful. Take a seat and refrain from taking pictures.) Otherwise, the church – with its hand-painted interiors and clerestory windows – is lovely any time of day.

Las Ruinas de la Parroquia (Iglesia del Convento; cnr Av 2 & Calle 2) was built in 1575 as a shrine to St James the Apostle (Santiago, in Spanish), destroyed by the 1841 earthquake, rebuilt a few years later and was then destroyed again in the 1910 earthquake. Today only the outer walls of the church remain, but 'the Ruins' are a pleasant spot for hanging out and people-watching – though legend has it that the ghost of a headless priest wanders the ground on foggy nights.

For an insight into regional cultures, visit the **Elias Leiva Museum of Ethnography** (☎ 2551-0895; Colegio Luis Gonzaga, Calle 3 btwn Avs 3 & 5; admission adult/student US$7/4; 7am-2pm Mon-Fri), located in the basement of the Colegio Luis Gonzaga. It has a few small displays of pre-Columbian and colonial artifacts.

Sleeping & Eating

Lodging options are limited and your best bet for food is to stroll along Avs 2 and 4 downtown, where *sodas* and bakeries can be found.

Hotel Dinastía (☎ 2551-7057; Calle 3; r with/without bathroom US$19/15) This bare-bones spot near the San José bus station has 27 aging rooms with thin walls. Rooms with private bathroom have hot water; others do not.

Los Ángeles Lodge (☎ 2551-0957, 2591-4169; Av 4 btwn Calles 14 & 16; d with breakfast US$50; P) With its balconies overlooking the Plaza de la Basílica, this decent B&B stands out with spacious and comfortable rooms, hot showers and a big breakfast made to order by the cheerful owners.

Panadería Araya (☎ 2551-0739; Av 4 btwn Calles 8 & 10; pastries from ₡125; 5am-9pm) A tidy little bakery with tasty breads and pastries (try the flaky palm-leaf cookies) and a narrow counter where you can sip fresh-brewed coffee.

La Puerta del Sol (Av 4 btwn Calles 14 & 16; casados ₡2600-3000, mains ₡2400-5000; 8am-midnight) Located downstairs from Los Ángeles Lodge, this pleasant *soda* has been around since 1957 and serves myriad Tico specialties as well as burgers and sandwiches. Don't miss the vintage photos of Cartago displayed on the walls.

Self-caterers can find supermarkets in the vicinity of the Parque Central and fresh veggies and other items at the **Mercado Central** (cnr Av 4 & Calle 1).

Shopping

Vendors set up in front of the basilica to sell all manner of religious articles. **Bazar Mafalda** (☎ 2552-3592; Av 4 btwn Calles 12 & 14; 9am-5pm), to the west of the church, stocks an interesting selection of rosaries, scapulars and ex-votos – and, rather incongruously, soccer paraphernalia and nail polish. One block to the west is **Remembranzos** (☎ 2553-0005, 8981-9749; remembranzoscr@yahoo.com; Av 4 btwn Calles 10 & 12), a tiny cluttered shop selling vintage coins, stamps, photographs and company scrip from coffee plantations. Hours are erratic, so call ahead.

On the main highway, about 8km west of Cartago in Tres Ríos, you'll find the massive new **Terra Mall** (☎ 2278-6970; Autopista Florencio del Castillo), stocked with everything from a high-end multiplex (you can get cocktails served inside some of the movie theaters) to brand-name boutiques – not to mention *lots* of teenagers.

Getting There & Away

Bus stops are scattered around town. The following buses serve destinations in the area:

Paraíso, for Finca la Flor de Paraíso (Calle 6 btwn Avs 1 & 3) ₡600; 40 minutes; for the *finca,* take buses labeled Birrisito/La Flor/El Yas.

Paraíso & Lankester Gardens (Calle 6 btwn Avs 1 & 3) ₡500; 20 minutes; departs hourly from 7am to 10pm. For the gardens, ask the driver to drop you off at the turnoff.

Orosi (Calle 6 btwn Avs 1 & 3) ₡400; 40 minutes; departs hourly from 8am to 10pm Monday to Saturday.

San José (Calle 5, north of Av 6) ₡500; 45 minutes; departs every 15 minutes.

Turrialba (Av 3 btwn Calles 8 & 10) ₡600; 1½ hours; departs every 45 minutes from 6am to 10pm weekdays, 8:30am, 11:30am, 1:30pm, 3pm and 5:45pm weekends.

Volcán Irazú (Calle 6 btwn Avs 1 & 3) ₡2000; one hour; the bus originates in San José at 8am, stops in Cartago at about 8:30am and returns from Irazú at 12:30pm. Get there early.

PARQUE NACIONAL VOLCÁN IRAZÚ

Looming on the horizon, 19km northeast of Cartago, Irazú, which derives its name from the indigenous word *ara-tzu* (thunder-point), is the largest and highest (3432m) active volcano in Costa Rica. In 1723, the Spanish governor of the area, Diego de la Haya Fernández, watched helplessly as the volcano unleashed its destruction on the city of Cartago (one of the craters is named in his honor). Since the 18th century, 15 major eruptions have been recorded.

One of the most memorable occurred in March of 1963, welcoming visiting US President John F Kennedy with a rain of volcanic ash that blanketed most of the Central Valley (it piled up to a depth of more than 0.5m). During two years' worth of subsequent activity, agricultural lands northeast of the volcano were devastated, while clogged waterways flooded the region intermittently. In 1994, Irazú unexpectedly belched a cloud

A NATURAL EDUCATION

If you really want to experience the Central Valley's rural culture, pay a visit to the **Finca La Flor de Paraíso** (☎ 2534-8003; www.la-flor.org) outside of Cartago. This not-for-profit organic farm operated by the Association for the Development of Environmental and Human Consciousness (Asodecah) has a recommended volunteer-work program that will allow you to get your hands dirty on projects related to agriculture, reforestation, animal husbandry and even medicinal-herb cultivation. There is also an onsite Spanish school.

The cost of the volunteer-work programs, including room and board (in simple wood cabins and dormitories), is US$20 daily. Vacationers can arrange day trips (per person US$10) or overnight stays (US$50) – both of which include meals. Family rates are available. Advance reservations are necessary.

The *finca* is 7km northeast of Paraíso on the road to El Yas. From Cartago, take a La Flor/Birrisito/El Yas bus; get off at the pink church in La Flor. The entrance to the *finca* is 100m to the south.

of sulfurous gas, though it quickly quieted down. At the time of writing, the volcano was slumbering peacefully, aside from a few hissing fumaroles (for more information on the mechanics of eruptions, see boxed text, p173).

The national park was established in 1955 to protect 23 sq km around the base of the volcano. The summit is a bare landscape of volcanic-ash craters. The principal crater is 1050m in diameter and 300m deep; the Diego de la Haya Crater is 690m in diameter, 100m deep and contains a small lake; and the smallest, Playa Hermosa Crater, is slowly being colonized by sparse vegetation. There is also a pyroclastic cone, which consists of rocks that were fragmented by volcanic activity.

Information & Orientation

There's a small **information center** (☎ 2551-9398, 2200-5025; park admission US$10, parking ₡600; ⏲ 8am-3:30pm) and basic cafe but no accommodations or camping facilities. Note that cloud cover starts thickening, even under the best conditions, by about 10am, about the same time that the bus rolls in. If you're on one of those buses, do yourself a favor and don't dally – head straight for the crater. If you have a car, make an extra effort to arrive early and you'll be rewarded with the best possible views and an uncrowded observation area. The park is busiest on Sundays and holidays, when a line of cars up to 1km-long queues up at the park entrance.

At the summit it is possible to see both the Pacific and the Caribbean, but it is rarely clear enough. The best chance for a clear view is in the very early morning during the dry season (January to April). It tends to be cold and windy up here and there's an annual rainfall of 2160mm – come prepared with warm, rainproof clothes.

From the parking lot, a 200m trail leads to a viewpoint over the craters; a longer, steeper trail leaves from behind the toilets and gets you closer to the craters (note that this trail is intermittently closed). While hiking, be on the lookout for high-altitude bird species, such as the volcano junco.

Tours

Tours are arranged by a variety of San José operators and cost US$40 to US$60 for a half-day tour, and up to US$100 for a full day combined with lunch and visits to sights such as the Lankester Gardens or the Orosi Valley.

Tours from hotels in Orosi (US$25 to US$40) can also be arranged – these may include lunch and visits to the basilica in Cartago or sights around the Orosi Valley.

Eating

Restaurant 1910 (☎ 2536-6063; casados ₡2900; ⏲ closed Mon) On the road up to the park entrance, 100m north of the Pacayas turnoff, this homey spot is worth a stop for lunch to see its collection of old photographs documenting the 1910 earthquake that completed the destruction of colonial Cartago. Expect a long list of Tico specialties, including fresh grilled river trout.

Getting There & Away

Barring a 20km hike, there are three ways to get here: an organized tour; a ₡27,500 (approximately) taxi from Tierra Blanca, which includes having the driver wait for a few hours; or by car. If you're in a group, renting a car is the best deal: you can get to the park early (it's easy to find) and afterwards, follow it up with a leisurely lunch – with incredible views – at the Mirador Sanchiri (p142) in nearby Orosi – an ideal day trip.

To get to the volcano, drivers can take Hwy 8 from Cartago, which begins at the northeast corner of the plaza and continues 19km to the summit. The road is well signed.

The only public transportation to Irazú departs from San José (₡2500) at 8am, stops in Cartago (₡2000) to pick up passengers at about 8:30am and arrives at the summit a little after 9:30am. The bus departs from Irazú at 12:30pm.

VALLE DE OROSI

This charming river valley is famous for its mountain vistas, a quaint colonial church, hot springs, an orchid garden, a lake formed by a hydroelectric facility, a truly wild national park and coffee – lots and lots of coffee. A 60km scenic loop (freshly paved in 2009) winds through a landscape of rolling hills terraced with shade-grown coffee plantations and expansive valleys dotted with pastoral villages. If you're lucky enough to have a rental car (or a good bicycle), you're in for a treat, though it's still possible to navigate most of the loop via public buses.

The loop road starts 8km southeast of Cartago in Paraíso, and then heads south to Orosi. At this point you can either continue south into Parque Nacional Tapantí-Macizo Cerro de la Muerte or loop back to Paraíso via Ujarrás.

Paraíso Area

This busy town has been engulfed by the urban sprawl of Cartago, only 8km away. The village itself is not terribly picturesque (rows of concrete houses generally aren't), but the wonderful Orosi Valley emerges just outside of it. A few kilometers along the road to Orosi is the **Mirador Orosi**, which is the official scenic overlook, complete with toilets, a parking lot and plenty of great photo opportunities. There are also two noteworthy sights near Paraíso that are definitely worth exploring.

The University of Costa Rica runs the exceptional **Lankester Gardens** (☎ 2552-3247; www.jardinbotanicolankester.org; admission adult/student US$7/5; ⌚ 8:30am-4:30pm; ♿), which was started as a private garden by British orchid enthusiast Charles Lankester in 1917, but was turned over to the university for public administration in 1973. Orchids are the big draw at this tranquil 11-hectare spot, with more than 1100 at their showiest from March to May. There is also a new Japanese garden, as well as areas full of bromeliads, palms, heliconias and other tropical plants. There is a good gift shop (this is one of the few places where foreigners can legally purchase orchids to take home) and a cafe was in the works at the time of research. Guided tours in English and Spanish can be arranged with prior reservation; the garden is wheelchair-accessible. Find it 5km west of Paraíso on the road to Cartago; look for a blue sign with an image of an orchid.

Two kilometers east of Paraíso on the road to Turrialba is **Finca Cristina** (☎ 2574-6426, in USA 800-355-8826; www.cafecristina.com; guided tour per person US$12), an organic coffee farm that is open to visitors by appointment only (call ahead for a reservation). Linda and Ernie have been farming in Costa Rica since 1977, and a 90-minute tour of their *microbeneficio* (miniprocessing plant) is a fantastic introduction to the processes of organic-coffee growing, harvesting and roasting. Finca Cristina also sells its product to guests at wholesale prices.

The most beautiful places to stay are just outside of town. On the road from Paraíso to Orosi stands **Orosi Valley Farm B&B Hostel** (☎ 2533-3001; www.orosivalleyfarm.com; dm US$10, d US$45; Ⓟ), a picturesque old farmhouse with a trickling creek and jaw-dropping views of the lush green valley. It was being remodeled in 2010 – so call ahead to double-check prices and availability.

About 2km south of Paraíso, and 1km off the main road, you'll find **Sanchirí Mirador** (☎ 2574-5454; www.sanchiri.com; d incl breakfast US$75; Ⓟ), a delightful, family-run B&B that offers an excellent reason to break up a road trip. There are 12 superclean, ceramic-tiled rooms with comfortable wood furnishings and staggering vistas of Parque Nacional Tapantí-Macizo Cerro de la Muerte and the Reventazón river in the valley below. Alongside lie five slightly older, but equally spic-and-span wood *cabinas* that are nestled a little more deeply into the forest (though these also have nice views). All have roomy stone bathroom with hot water. If you're not staying overnight, but need a place to break for lunch, the open-air **Sanchiri Restaurante** (casados ₡4000; ⌚ 7am-8pm) is a good choice. The friendly staff serve generous portions of good regional cooking – but you're not here for the food, you're here for the extravagant valley views. Recommended.

Orosi

pop 3900

Named for a Huetar chief who lived here at the time of the conquest, Orosi charmed Spanish colonists in the 18th century with its perfect climate, rich soil and wealth of water – from lazy hot springs to bracing waterfalls. So, in the typical fashion of the day, they decided to take the property off Orosi's hands. Today the area remains picturesque – and is a good spot to revel in beautiful scenery and a small town atmosphere.

Orosi is one of the few colonial-era towns to survive Costa Rica's frequent earthquakes, which have thankfully spared the postcard-perfect village church, the **Iglesia de San José Orosi**. Built in 1743, it is the oldest religious site still in use in Costa Rica. The roof of the church is a combination of thatched cane and ceramic tiling, while the carved wood altar is adorned with religious paintings of Mexican origin. Adjacent to the church is a small **museum** (☎ 2533-3051; admission US$1; ⌚ 9am-5pm Tue-Sun) with interesting examples of Spanish-colonial religious art and artifacts, some of which date back to the 17th century.

Being in a volcanic region also means Orosi has the perks of hot springs. Though not on the scale of the steaming-hot waters found near Fortuna (p159), Orosi does offer a couple of nice modest pools with warm water. You'll find **Los Balnearios** (☎ 2533-2156; admission US$2; 7:30am-4pm Wed-Mon) on the southwest side of town next to the Orosi Lodge, and **Los Patios** (☎ 2533-3009; admission US$2; 8am-4pm Tue-Sun) 1.5km south of town. Los Balnearios is more convenient as it's in town, but Los Patios is a larger complex with a few more springs.

INFORMATION

Find more information on the area on the village website (www.orosivalley.com).

Banco Nacional (300m south of the park) has an ATM and changes money.

Otiac (Orosi Tourist Information & Arts Café; ☎ 2533-3640; 9am-4pm Mon-Sat; wi-fi) is run by the multilingual Toine and Sara, two long-term residents who have collected a wealth of information on all there is to do in the valley. They can help arrange tours and are a good source of information about volunteer and teaching opportunities. In addition, their roomy space – equipped with wi-fi – functions as cultural hall, cafe, resource center and book exchange. Find their office (it's prominently signed) 200m south of the park and one block west of the main road.

Aventuras Orosi (☎ 2533-4000; www.aventurasorosi.com; 9am-4pm) is another good source of information. Operated by the charming Luis, who served as a guide for the venerable Ríos Tropicales rafting company for manlake-sy years, this small outfit can organize short, local rafting expeditions (US$40), tours of neighboring coffee *fincas* (US$30), as well as custom itineraries to the Volcán Irazú or the little-visited Parque Nacional Tapantí-Macizo Cerro de la Muerte. The office is tucked into a U-shaped courtyard 25m north of the park.

ACTIVITIES

The town is a perfect base from which to explore Parque Nacional Tapantí-Macizo Cerro de la Muerte, which offers excellent bird-watching.

If you want to study Spanish, Toine and Sara also run **Montaña Linda** (☎ 2533-3640; www.montanalinda.com), one of the most affordable language schools in the country. For details, see boxed text, p128.

SLEEPING & EATING

Montaña Linda (☎ 2533-3640; www.montanalinda.com; camping per person US$3.50, dm US$7.50, d US$30, s/d without bathroom US$15/20, additional person US$5; P internet) Two blocks south and three blocks west of the bus stop is this great, chilled-out budget option. Eleven tidy dorms and brightly accented private rooms surround a homey terrace with flowers and hammocks. Units all come with access to hot showers, and kitchen privileges are available for a small additional fee (US$1).

Hotel Reventazón (☎ 2533-3838; d incl breakfast US$31-55; P wi-fi) A functional two-story cement structure with seven large, clean tile-floor rooms that come equipped with cable TV, hot water and fridge. There's free wi-fi and a laundry service is available (₡5000). More expensive units are bigger and have better views.

our pick Orosi Lodge (☎ 2533 3578; www.orosilodge.com; d/tr US$55/65, d chalet US$85, additional person US$15; P wi-fi wheelchair) This peaceful hotel, run by a friendly German couple, has eight bright rooms with wood-beam ceilings. Each comes with a minifridge, coffeemaker and plenty of organic coffee – and most face a lovely garden courtyard with a fountain. A new three-bedroom duplex chalet is great for families or traveling couples, with a master suite that offers incredible views of the volcanoes in the distance. One room is wheelchair-accessible; credit cards are accepted. The lodge is south of the park, near the entrance to Los Balnearios.

Tetey Lodge (☎ 2533-1335; www.teteylodge.com; d/tr/q US$62/79/96; P wi-fi) On the outskirts of town, about 800m south of the park, Tetley Lodge is set in a low-lying mustard-yellow building that faces the main road. Rooms are spotless, with ceramic-tile floors, bright wicker and wood furnishings, minifridge and cable TV – all facing a small interior courtyard. Breakfast is available for an additional fee. Credit cards accepted.

Hotel Tapantí Media (☎ 2533-9090/9393; s/d/tr incl breakfast US$40/55/71; P wi-fi) Follow the road for another 500m and you'll find Tapantí Media situated right in the middle of a coffee *finca* on the right-hand side. Rooms are simple, but clean, with tile floors and TV. The views are excellent from the onsite Italian restaurant (mains ₡3950-12,000, pizzas ₡5300-6800; open from 7am to 9pm, bar open until 11pm), which serves respectable pizzas and has a bar with a cozy lounge and fireplace.

Cafetería Orosi (dishes ₡2100-3500; 7am-7pm) Adjacent to the Orosi Lodge is this recommended cafe that serves organic local coffee, as well as a mix of homemade pastries, salads and sandwiches – and even an excellent apple cake.

GETTING THERE & AWAY

All buses stop about three blocks west of the *fútbol* (soccer) field; ask locally about specific destinations. Buses from Cartago (₡400, 40 minutes) depart hourly from the corner of Calle 4 and Av 1.

Cachí Dam & Ruinas ₡300; 20 minutes; departs every 30 minutes from 6am to 9pm.

Cartago ₡400; 40 minutes; departs every 45 minutes from 5am to 9pm.

Parque Nacional Tapantí-Macizo Cerro de la Muerte

This 580-sq-km **national park** (admission US$10; 6am-4pm) protects the lush northern slopes of the Cordillera de Talamanca, and has a rainy claim to fame: it is the wettest park in the country, getting almost 8000mm of precipitation a year. In 2000 it was expanded to include the infamous Cerro de la Muerte (p368) – otherwise known as the 'Mountain of Death.' This precipitous peak is the highest point on the Interamericana and the northernmost extent of *páramo*, a highland shrub and tussock grass habitat that's most commonly found in the Andes and is home to a variety of rare bird species.

Known simply as Tapantí, the park also protects wild and mossy country that's fed by, literally, hundreds of rivers. Waterfalls abound, vegetation is thick and the wildlife is prolific, though not always easy to see because of the rugged terrain. Nevertheless, this is a popular destination for dedicated bird-watchers, opening at 6am to accommodate all bird-nerd needs.

INFORMATION

There is an **information center** (☎ 2200-0090; 6am-4pm) near the park entrance and a couple of trails leading to various attractions, including a picnic area, a swimming hole and a lookout with great views of a waterfall. Rainfall is about 2700mm in the lower sections but reaches almost 8000mm in some of the highest parts of the park, so make sure you pack rain gear. Fishing is allowed in season (from April to October; permit required), but the 'dry' season (from January to April) is generally considered the best time to visit.

WILDLIFE-WATCHING

Quetzals are said to nest on the western slope of the valley, where the park information center is located. More than 300 other bird species have also been recorded in the park including hummingbirds, parrots, toucans trogons and eagles. Though rarely sighted due to the thick vegetation, monkeys, coatis pacas, tayras and even pumas, ocelots and oncillas are present.

HIKING

There are three signed trails leading from the information center, the longest of which is a steep 4km round-trip, while a well-graded dirt road that is popular with mountain bikers runs through the northern section of the national park. Unfortunately, Tapantí is not open to backcountry hiking. However, the bird-watching opportunities here are legendary, and most people are satisfied simply being able to spot a large variety of birds in such a small area.

SLEEPING & EATING

About 1km before the park entrance is **Kiri Mountain Lodge** (☎ 2591-7601; www.kirilodge.net; s/d incl breakfast US$24/45; P), which has six rustic cabins with private hot shower resting on 50 mossy hectares of land. Trails wind into the nearby Río Macho Forest Preserve, which is adjacent to Tapantí and inhabited by much of the same wildlife. A restaurant specializes in trout, which can be caught in the well-stocked pond and then served up any way you like.

Five kilometers north out of town, on the road to Tapantí, **Monte Sky** (☎ 2231-3536; www.intnet.co.cr/montesky/; per person incl meals US$45; P) is a 536-hectare private reserve that is teeming with bird species (290 at last count). There is a basic lodge and plenty of hiking trails. The folks at Otiac (p143) in Orosi can help arrange overnight stays.

GETTING THERE & AWAY

If you have your own car, you can take a bumpy gravel road (4WD recommended) from Purisil to the park entrance.

Buses are trickier. From Cartago, take an Orosi–Purisil bus (make sure it's going to Purisil; not all of them do). The bus can drop you 5km from the entrance. Inquire at Otiac or Aventuras Orosi about guides and other transport options (p143).

rosi to Paraíso

rom Orosi, a loop road heads north and parllels the Río Orosi before swinging around he artificial **Lago de Cachi**. The lake was created ollowing the construction of the **Cachí Dam** the largest in the country), which supplies an José and the majority of the Central Valley vith electricity. Buses run from Orosi to the lam and nearby ruins, though this stretch is est explored by car or bicycle – and it's worth xploring as this is beautiful countryside.

Sights here are all listed traveling north long the eastern shore of the lake, from Orosi round to Ujarras.

La Casona del Cafetal Restaurant (☎ 2577-414/1515; www.lacasonadelcafetal.com; mains ₡4800 0,000; 🕑 11am-6pm;) About 3km southeast of the dam, on the left-hand side of the road, ou'll find this charming lakeside restaurant n the middle of a coffee plantation. It is popular with local families who arrive to dip into resh river trout or grilled pork loins glazed with tamarind sauce. Don't miss the coffeeaced deserts, such as flan and ice cream. There is a small playground for the kiddies, as well as short trails and a lagoon with paddle boats for rent (in high season). This is a popular spot on Sundays.

Cabañas de Montaña Piedras Albas (☎ 2577-1462; www.cabinas.co.cr/costa_rica1.htm; s/d/q US$40/46/79; P) Across the main road from La Casona is the turnoff to these well-equipped *cabinas* in the hills beyond Cachi – an ideal place if you're here to slow down and enjoy the scenery. Bright wood cabins come with fully stocked kitchen, cable TV, private deck with lake and mountain views, and there are private trails for hiking. Ideal for families.

Another 2km along the main road, and 1km south of the dam, on the right-hand side, is **Casa del Soñador** (Dreamer's House; ☎ 2577-1186, 2577-1021; admission free; 🕑 8am-6pm), an artisanal woodworking studio run by Hermes Quesada. The son of renowned Tico carver Macedonio Quesada, Hermes maintains the *campesino* (peasant farmer) tradition of whittling gnarled coffee-wood branches into ornate religious figures and whimsical characters. His workshop displays sculptures of all sizes, with pieces available for purchase.

Past the dam, you'll find the small village of **Ujarrás** at the bottom of a long, steep hill – a couple of store signs with the word 'Ujarrás' tell you that you've arrived. Turn left at a sign for Restaurant La Pipiola to head toward the old village (about 1km), which was damaged by a flood in 1833 and abandoned. The sign may not be visible so ask around.

The waters have since receded, revealing the ruins of the 1693 **Iglesia de Nuestra Señora de la Limpia Concepción**, a colonial stone church that was once home to a miraculous painting of the Virgin discovered by a local fisherman. According to the lore, the relic refused to be moved, forcing clerics to build the church around it. In return, the Virgin helped locals defeat a group of marauding British pirates in 1666. After the floods and a few earthquakes, however, the painting conceded to move to Paraíso, leaving the ruins to deteriorate photogenically in a remarkable overgrown park. Every year, usually on the Sunday closest to April 14, there is a procession from Paraíso to the ruins, where mass, food and music help celebrate the day of **La Virgen de Ujarrás**. The church's grassy grounds are a popular picnicking spot on Sunday afternoons – but go in the middle of the week and chances are that you will have them all to yourself.

After Ujarrás, the road continues for a few more kilometers before looping back to Paraíso.

TURRIALBA AREA

In the vicinity of Turrialba, at an elevation of 650m above sea level, the Río Reventazón gouges a mountain pass through the Cordillera Central. In the 1880s this geological quirk allowed the 'Jungle Train' between San José and Puerto Limón to roll through, and the mountain village of Turrialba grew prosperous from the coffee trade. Later, the first highway linking the capital to the coast exploited this same quirk. Turrialba thrived.

However, things changed by the early 1990s when the straighter, smoother Hwy 32 through Guápiles was completed and an earthquake succeeded in shutting down the railway for good. Suddenly, Turrialba found itself off the beaten path. Even so, the area remains a key agricultural center, renowned for its mountain air, strong coffee and Central America's best white-water rafting. To the north, the area is home to two important sites: the majestic Volcán Turrialba and the archeological site of Guayabo (p149).

TURRIALBA

pop 27,000

When the railway shut down in 1991, Turrialba ceased to be an important commercial pit-stop in the San José–Limón trade route. Commerce slowed down, but the town nonetheless remained a regional agricultural center, where local coffee planters could bring their crops to market. Things didn't remain quiet for long, however. With tourism on the rise in the 1990s, it wasn't long before this modest mountain town became known for having access to some of the best white-water rafting on the planet. By the early 2000s, Turrialba was a simmering hot-bed of international rafters looking for Class-V thrills.

But this new economy faced a troubled future. In the early part of the new millennium, the national power company (ICE) began to make good on a long-running plan to dam the lower Río Pacuare – the most popular stretch of white water in the country – to increase hydroelectric production. The dam, however, would destroy the rapids and, with them, part of Turrialba's economy. Townspeople united with conservation groups to successfully oppose the dam. The project was shelved, bu other plans are afoot, perhaps to dam th upper part of the river. It's a long way of however. For more details on dam project see boxed text, p150.

Information

There's no official tourist office, but bette hotels and most white-water rafting outfit can organize tours, accommodations an transportation throughout the region.

Banco de Costa Rica (cnr Av Central & Calle 3; 9am 4pm Mon-Fri) Has a 24-hour ATM on the Cirrus and Visa Plus systems.

ECA Internet (2nd fl, Calle 1 btwn Avs 4 & 6; per hr ₡30C 9am-9pm) Check your email here, on the northeast corner of Parque Central.

Sights

About 4km east of Turrialba, **Catie** (Centr Agronómico Tropical de Investigación; Center for Tropica Agronomy Research & Education; ☎ 2556-6431; www .catie.ac.cr; admission US$1, guided tours US$15-20; 7am 4pm) consists of 1000 hectares dedicated t tropical agricultural research and education Agronomists from all over the world recog-

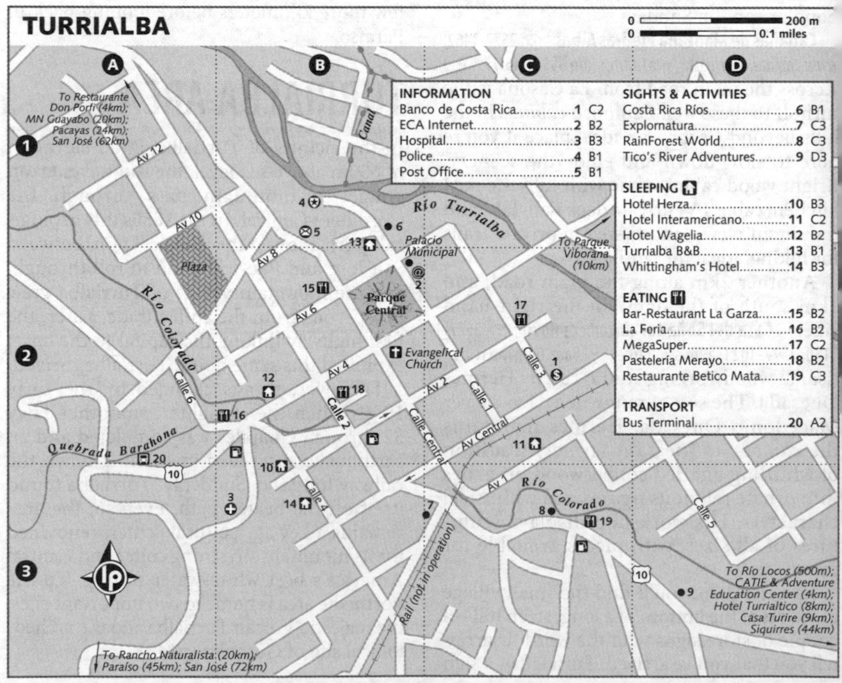

nize this as one of the most important centers in the tropics. You need to make reservations for one of several available guided tours through laboratories, greenhouses, a seed bank, experimental plots and one of the most extensive libraries of tropical-agriculture literature in the world. You can also easily pick up a map (or print one off their website) and take a self-guided walk through the gardens to a pond, where waterbirds such as the purple gallinule are a specialty. You can walk to Catie or get a taxi (₡1500) from Turrialba.

About 10km east of Turrialba, in the village of Pavones (500m east of the cemetery), **Parque Viborana** (☎ 2538-1510; admission US$7; 9am-4pm Mon-Fri) is a small serpentarium run by a local family. Here you can see (and even handle) a variety of Costa Rican snakes, including some very large boas. A rustic visitors area has a small exhibit.

Tours

The following operators all offer either kayaking or rafting in the area. For the particulars on river runs, see boxed text, p148.

Costa Rica Ríos (☎ in USA 888-434-0776; www.costaricarios.com; Calle 1, north of Av 6) Offers week-long rafting trips that must be booked in advance. It's 25m north of Parque Central.

Explornatura (☎ 2556-4932; www.explornatura.com) This longtime outfitter also runs reader-recommended canyoning expeditions, among other tours.

Río Locos (☎ 2556-6035; www.whiteh2o.com) A popular local company does rafting as well as other area tours.

RainForest World (☎ 2556-0014; www.rforestw.com) Offering rafting trips since 1981, this company organizes multiday camping and rafting excursions, one of which goes into the Reserva Indígena Cabécar.

Tico's River Adventures (☎ 2556-1231; www.ticoriver.com) Another good local outfit offers all manner of rafting trips and runs a kayaking school.

Sleeping

TURRIALBA

Whittingham's Hotel (☎ 2556-8822; Calle 4 btwn Avs 2 & Central; d with/without bathroom US$10/8) Seasoned budget travelers won't mind the seven basic (but reasonably clean) concrete rooms at this hotel operated by the friendly Gerald Whittingham. All come with TV and have access to warm showers. Reception closes at 5pm, so get there early.

Hotel Interamericano (☎ 2556-0142; www.hotelinteramericano.com; Av 1; s/d/tr/q US$25/35/45/55, without bathroom US$11/20/30/40; P wi-fi) On the south side of the old train tracks is this simple 22-room hotel, regarded by rafters as *the* meeting place in Turrialba. The showers are immaculate, the tiled rooms are bright, the 2nd-story lounge is an ideal spot to sip beer, and Luis, the bilingual manager, is a good source of local information. Breakfast is available on request (US$4).

Hotel Herza (☎ 2556-1097; hotelherza@gmail.com; 2nd fl, cnr Av 2 & Calle 4; d US$25; wi-fi) This welcome new budget place has eight simple, very clean and airy ceramic-tile rooms with firm beds and is run by the helpful Franklin and his wife. A common terrace overlooks the street, with views of the hills in the background.

Turrialba B&B (☎ 2556-6651; www.turrialbahotel.com; Calle 1, north of Av 6; s/d/tr incl breakfast US$40/60/80; P nonsmoking wi-fi) This charming and tranquil, five-year-old spot has clean, bright, well-appointed rooms, a cozy living-room area, a lovely garden patio equipped with a Jacuzzi and a library chock-full of travel guides on Latin America. There is also a shared kitchen and a small bar. Excellent value.

Hotel Wagelia (☎ 2556-1566; www.hotelwagelia.com; Av 4 btwn Calles 2 & 4; d/tr incl breakfast US$83/94; P nonsmoking wi-fi) Simple, modern and clean no-frills rooms come with cable TV and face a quiet, interior courtyard. A restaurant serves many Tico specialties (₡3100 to ₡7500) and a pleasant terrace bar is a good place for a drink and wi-fi. Nonguests can use the wi-fi with the purchase of a drink.

AROUND TURRIALBA

There are some stellar hotels around the Turrialba area. All have private hot-water bathrooms, and can arrange tours and rafting trips.

Off the highway to Siquirres, 8km east of town, **Hotel Turrialtico** (☎ 2538-1111; www.turrialtico.com; d US$64-75) is a Tico-run lodge that's been owned and managed by the García family since 1968. There are 14 polished-wood-panel rooms in an old farmhouse that have bright, floral spreads and paintings by local artists. A pleasant open-air restaurant (mains ₡2200 to ₡7000) serves up country cooking (including excellent fresh fish) – and it's hard to beat the dramatic views.

From the highway, take the turnoff to La Suiza/Tuis, head south for 2km and you'll see signs leading to **Casa Turire** (☎ 2531-1111; www.hotelcasaturire.com; d standard/ste/master ste incl breakfast US$135/210/350, additional person US$25-55, child under

WHITE-WATER RAFTING IN THE CENTRAL VALLEY

There are two major rivers in the Turrialba area that are popular for rafting – the Río Reventazón and the Río Pacuare. The following is a quick guide to the ins and outs (and ups and downs) of each.

Río Reventazón

This storied rock-lined river has its beginnings at the Lago de Cachí, an artificial lake created by a dam of the same name. It begins here, at 1000m above sea level, and splashes down the eastern slopes of the cordilleras to the Caribbean lowlands. It is one of the most difficult, adrenaline-pumping runs in the country – and with more than 65km of rapids, you can get as hardcore as you like.

Tour operators divide the river into four sections between the dam and the take-out point in Siquirres. **Las Máquinas** (Power House) is a Class II–III float that's perfect for families, while **Florida**, the final and most popular segment, is a scenic Class III with a little more white water to keep things interesting. The **Pascua** section has 15 Class-IV rapids – featuring names like 'the Abyss' – and is considered to be the classic run. The Class-V **Peralta** segment is the most challenging; tours do not always run it due to safety concerns.

Water levels stay fairly constant year-round because of releases from the dam. There are no water releases on Sunday, however, and although the river is navigable, it's generally considered the worst day.

Río Pacuare

The Río Pacuare is the next major river valley east of the Reventazón, and has arguably the most scenic rafting in Costa Rica, if not Central America. The river plunges down the Caribbean slope through a series of spectacular canyons clothed in virgin rainforest, through runs named for their fury and separated by calm stretches that enable you to stare at near-vertical green walls towering hundreds of meters above.

The Class III–IV **Lower Pacuare** is the more accessible run: 28km through rocky gorges and isolated canyons, past an indigenous village, untamed jungle and lots of wildlife curious as to what the screaming is all about.

The **Upper Pacuare** is also classified as Class III–IV, but there are a few sections that can also go to Class V, depending on conditions. It's about a two-hour drive to the put-in, though it's worth it – you'll have the prettiest jungle cruise on earth all to yourself.

The Pacuare can be run year-round, though June to October are considered the best months. The highest water is from October to December, when the river runs fast with huge waves. March and April is when the river is at its lowest, though it is still challenging.

Trips & Prices

A number of reputable national companies organize trips (see p527), as can agencies in Turrialba (see p147).

Day trips usually raft the Class III–IV Lower Pacuare or Class-III segments of Río Reventazón, which both have easy-access put-ins. There are other runs – such as the Upper Pacuare and Pascua segment of Reventazón – but these will require more time spent in a van (though, for the dedicated adrenaline junkie, it will be worth it). Multiday excursions with camping or lodge accommodations are offered by numerous companies.

For day trips (many of which originate in San José), you can expect to pay anywhere from US$85 to US$120 depending on transportation, accessibility and amenities. It is generally less expensive to leave from Turrialba, and put-in on the Lower Pacuare or Class-III segments of the Reventazón (from US$75). For two-day trips, prices vary widely depending on accommodations, but expect to pay between US$195 to US$300 per person. Children must be at least nine years old for most trips, and older for tougher runs.

free;). An elegant three-story plantation inn, it has 16 graceful well-appointed rooms with high ceilings, wood floors and wrought-iron beds; a massive master suite comes with a Jacuzzi and excellent views of the coffee and macadamia-nut plantations in the distance. Spa services are available, there is a restaurant (dishes US$7 to US$33) and the helpful staff can arrange area activities. Parents will appreciate the small climbing gym. Credit cards accepted.

About 1.3km south of Tuis, a signed dirt road (4WD needed) leads to **Rancho Naturalista** (2554-8101/8100; www.ranchunaturalista.net; per person incl 3 meals US$100;), a small lodge set on 50-hectares of land that lies 900m above sea level – and attracts dedicated bird-watchers in search of the snowcap hummingbird, among other species. (There have been 433 species recorded in the area; more than 200 of them from the lodge balcony alone.) Fifteen simple rooms are scattered around the main lodge or separate *casitas* (which are nicer), with wood furniture, tile floors and a comfortable deck stocked with hammocks and rockers. Meals include organic produce grown on the grounds.

Eating

Sodas and bakeries abound.

Pastelería Merayo (Calle 2 btwn Avs 2 & 4; pastries ₡350-600) Founded in 1928, this informal bakery produces made-to-order coffee that is strong and delicious, as well as some excellent pastries. Tip: anything with custard – *crema pastelera* – is guaranteed to be good.

our pick **Restaurant Betico Mata** (Hwy 10; gallos ₡600-800; 11am-midnight, until later on weekends) This carnivore's paradise on the south end of town specializes in *gallos* (open-faced tacos on corn tortillas) piled with succulent, fresh-grilled meats including beef, chicken, sausage or pork, all soaked in the special house marinade. All go smashingly well with an ice-cold beer. The restaurant has a counter that faces the street – making it easy to park and pick-up a snack if you're driving through town.

La Feria (Calle 6, north of Av 4; casados ₡1700, mains ₡2100-5550; 11am-10pm Wed-Mon, 11am-2pm Tue;) This unremarkable-looking eatery has friendly service and excellent, inexpensive home cooking. Try the *pollo a la milanesa*, a crisp chicken cutlet served with cucumber-yogurt dipping sauce. Tasty!

Restaurant Don Porfi (2556-9797; ₡2700-5400; 11am-11pm) Four kilometers north of town (and a ₡2000 taxi ride), on the road to the volcano, this longtime local favorite whips up a mix of international and Tico cuisine, from grilled steaks to stacked seafood platters to chicken bathed in garlic. A wine list features a selection of South American vintages.

Bar-Restaurant La Garza (2556-1073; cnr Av 6 & Calle Central; mains ₡4000-5300; 10am-11pm) A Turrialba institution, this corner place has been serving traditional Tico dishes to locals and tourists alike as long as anyone can remember. It's an excellent place for an evening beer.

Self-caterers can find supplies at the well-stocked **MegaSuper** (cnr Calle 3 & Av 2).

Getting There & Away

A modern bus terminal is located on the western edge of town off Hwy 10.

Monumento Nacional Arqueológico Guayabo ₡400, one hour, departs at 11:15am, 3:10pm and 5:30pm Monday through Saturday, 9am, 3pm and 6:30pm on Sunday.

San José via Paraíso & Cartago ₡1200; two hours; departs every 45 minutes 5am to 6:30pm.

Siquirres, for transfer to Puerto Limón ₡1000; 1¾ hours; departs every 60 to 90 minutes from 6am to 6pm.

La Suiza & Tuis ₡300; departs every 60 to 90 minutes from 7am to 10pm Monday through Saturday; every two hours on Sunday 7am to 8:30am.

MONUMENTO NACIONAL ARQUEOLÓGICO GUAYABO

Nestled into a patch of stunning hillside forest 19km northeast of Turrialba is the largest and most important archaeological site in the country. Guayabo is composed of the remains of a pre-Columbian city that was thought to have peaked at some point in AD 800, when it was inhabited by as many as 20,000 people. Today, visitors can examine the remains of old petroglyphs, residential mounds, an old roadway and an impressive aqueduct system – built with rocks that were hauled in from the Río Reventazón along a cobbled, 8km road. Amazingly, the cisterns still work, and (theoretically) potable water remains available onsite.

The settlement, which may have been occupied as early as 1000 BC, was mysteriously abandoned by AD 1400 and Spanish explorers left no record of ever having found the ruins. For centuries, the city lay largely untouched under the cover of the area's thick highland forest. But in 1968, archaeologist Carlos Aguilar Piedra of the University of Costa Rica, began systematic excavations of Guayabo, finding polychromatic pottery and gold artifacts that are now exhibited at San José's Museo Nacional (see p73).

In 1973, as the site's importance became evident, Guayabo was declared a National Monument, with further protections set forth in 1980. The site occupies 232 hectares, most of which remains unexcavated. It's a small place – so don't go expecting Mayan pyramids.

Information

There's a small information and **exhibit center** (☎ 2559-1220; admission US$7; ⏲ 8am-3:30pm) that provides an overview of what the city may have once looked like. (The best archaeological pieces can be found at the Museo Nacional in San José.) Guided tours are not available but the very well-maintained trails are well signed.

Camping (per person US$5) is permitted and services include latrines and running water. Keep in mind that the average annual rainfall is about 3500mm; the best time to go is during the dry season (January to April), though it might still rain. And make sure you pack the insect repellent; it gets mighty buggy.

Wildlife-Watching

The site currently protects the last remaining premontane forest in the province of Cartago, and although mammals are limited to squirrels, armadillos and coatis, there are good bird-watching opportunities here. Particularly noteworthy among the avifauna are the oropendolas, which colonize the

DAMNING THE RIVERS?

Considered one of the most beautiful white-water rafting rivers in the world, the wild Río Pacuare became the first federally protected river in Central America in 1985. Within two years, however, Costa Rica's national power company, the Instituto Costarricense de Electricidad (ICE), unveiled plans to build a 200m gravity dam at the conveniently narrow and screamingly scenic ravine of Dos Montañas.

The dam would be the cornerstone of the massive Siquirres Hydroelectric Project, which would include four dams in total, linked by a 10km-long tunnel. If built, rising waters on the lower Pacuare would not only flood 12km of rapids up to the Tres Equis put-in, but also parts of the Reserva Indígena Awari and a huge swath of primary rainforest where some 800 animal species have been recorded.

The project was intended to help ICE keep up with the country's rapidly increasing power demands (per capita consumption of energy in Costa Rica has grown more than 73% since 1975, according to the World Bank). But as the proposal moved from speculation to construction, a coalition of local landowners, indigenous leaders, conservation groups and, yep, white-water rafting outfits organized against it. (Rafael Gallo, of the Fundación Ríos Tropicales, the charitable arm of the venerable rafting company, was a key figure in this fight.)

The group filed for the first Environmental Impact Assessment (EIA) in the region's history – and won. The move required ICE to seek an independent study of the dam's environmental impact and economic feasibility, effectively stalling its construction. In the meantime, organizers were able to draw international attention to the situation. In 2005, residents of the Turrialba area held a plebiscite on the issue of the dam. Of the 10,000 residents polled, 97% gave the project a thumbs down – a resounding 'No.'

As a result of these efforts, the project was shelved – and the lower part of the river is now protected as a forest reserve. But there is talk of, at some point down the line, installing a dam further up the river. For now, it's nothing more than conjecture. But it's worth noting that the neighboring Río Reventazón has already lost a third of its Class-V rapids due to the first phase of the Siquirres Project. If you were thinking of going rafting in Costa Rica, the time to do it is now.

monument by building sacklike nests in the trees. Other birds include toucans and brown jays – the latter are unique among jays in that they have a small, inflatable sac in their chest, which causes the popping sound that is heard at the beginning of their loud and raucous calls.

Getting There & Away

It's easy to get here by car. Head north out of Turrialba and make a right after the metal bridge. The road is well signed from there. It's mostly paved, but the last 3km of the drive is not; 4WD is recommended.

Buses from Turrialba (₡400, one hour) depart at 11:15am, 3:10pm and 5:30pm Monday through Saturday and at 9am, 3pm and 6:30pm on Sunday. Buses travel from Guayabo to Turrialba at 5:15am, 6:30am, 12:30pm and 4pm Monday through Saturday; 6:30am, 12:30pm and 4pm on Sunday. You can also take a taxi from Turrialba (from ₡8000).

PARQUE NACIONAL VOLCÁN TURRIALBA

This rarely visited active volcano (3328m) was named Torre Alba (White Tower) by early Spanish settlers, who observed plumes of smoke pouring from its summit. Since its last eruption in 1866, Turrialba has generally slumbered quietly. However, in January of 2010, a small eruption rained a fine sprinkle of ash on its slopes. It was nothing major as far as eruptions go – but something that has vulcanologists closely monitoring the situation. At press time, the volcano had been regularly releasing small clouds of gas (largely helium) and areas within 2km of the summit were put on alert.

Turrialba was declared a national park in 1955, and protects a 2km radius around the volcano. Below the summit, the park consists of mountain rainforest and cloud forest, dripping with moisture and mosses, full of ferns, bromeliads and even stands of bamboo. Although small, these protected habitats shelter 84 species of birds and 11 species of mammals.

If the summit is open, you can peer into the **Central Crater**, which has minor fumarole activity bubbling sulfurous mud. The **Main Crater**, which had its last major eruption in 1866, is spewing jets of sulfur and steam, and is therefore closed to the public. The smaller **Eastern Crater** lacks fumarole activity, though moisture is present in the crater during the rainy season.

Although the craters are not nearly as dramatic as Poás or Irazú, the lack of infrastructure (and tourists) gives the summit a wild and natural feeling. Because of the recent eruption, inquire locally about conditions before setting out – and be sure to let someone know of your whereabouts.

Information

At the time of writing, there was neither a ranger station nor admission fee, though there are frequently rangers at the top of the summit. The average temperature is only about 15°C (59°F), so dress accordingly.

Volcán Turrialba Lodge (see below) arranges a variety of guided hikes and horseback and mountain-biking expeditions through the park.

If it's closed, you can always admire the summit on the volcano's very own webcam at www.ovsicori.una.ac.cr/videoturri.html.

Hiking

From the end of the road, trails through montane forest lead to the Eastern Crater and the Central Crater. They are unmarked, so ask a ranger if you can't find the way. Be advised that the summit is not developed for tourism, so keep your distance from the craters and be especially careful along the edges – they are brittle and break easily.

From the rim there are views of Irazú, Poás and Barva volcanoes – weather permitting, of course.

Sleeping

Volcán Turrialba Lodge (☎ 2273-4335; www.volcanturrialbalodge.com; r per person with 1/2/3 meals US$45/55/65; Ⓟ) About 14km northwest of Santa Cruz (accessible by 4WD only), this working cattle ranch is perched between the Turrialba and Irazú volcanoes, and recommended for adventurous travelers. Tidy, lemon-yellow *cabinas* are heated by wood stoves and the area offers fantastic views of the volcano. The staff can also organize hikes and horseback rides (minimum two people). Meals are all typical country-cooking, served in front of a blazing stove at the restaurant-lounge, where there is a TV, board games and a small bar. It gets chilly up here, so bring warm clothes and pajamas. Rates are based on double occupancy.

Getting There & Away

The volcano is only about 15km northwest of Turrialba as the crow flies, but more than twice as far by car than foot. From the village of Santa Cruz (which is 13km from Turrialba and connected via public buses), an 18km road climbs to the summit. The road is paved fo the first 10km, and then becomes increasingl rough; 4WD is necessary. You can also get 4WD taxi from Santa Cruz for about ₡14,00 each way. There are signs along the way, anc this is the official route into the national park

Northwestern Costa Rica

Iconic Costa Rica lives in the northwest. Whether it's for a glimpse of Volcán Arenal spitting fiery lava, the flash of green from a quetzal's wing or the perfect barrel ride at Witch's Rock, this region is heavily traveled for these and a wealth of other reasons. The landscape ranges from the blazing, dry beaches of the Guanacaste coast to the mist-shrouded heights of Volcán Miravalles (2028m) along the region's chain of volcanoes. The number and diversity of national parks and reserves alone sums up northwestern Costa Rica's classic ecodestination status.

Many visitors make Arenal and Monteverde their first and last stops in the region, but if you have more time, it's worth seeking out the smaller, less-visited spots for a taste of something more authentic. Fumaroles and bubbling mud pots, impossibly aquamarine waterfalls and jewel-toned frogs and toucans add unexpected wonder to swaths of tropical wet forest and the humid slopes of the Cordillera de Guanacaste. At lower elevations, the open stretch of big-sky country along the Interamericana is lined with *fincas* (farms) and the odd guanacaste tree, for which the province is named. Just short of the Nicaraguan border, a detour west off the Interamericana leads to out-of-the-way bays – some kick up consistent wind for kiteboarding addicts while others shelter tranquil sands for unruffled sunbathers.

While the hot spots in the northwest are undoubtedly well traveled, the infinitude of natural attractions and remote destinations means that the experience can be as small, or as sprawling, as you want to make it. Back roads abound, offering independent travelers endless opportunities to explore the lesser-known, tucked-away treasures of the region.

HIGHLIGHTS

- Watching lava light the night above the peak of **Volcán Arenal** (p171) from viewpoints in La Fortuna or El Castillo
- Waking early to hike in the magical mists of **Reserva Biológica Bosque Nuboso Monteverde** (p211) and **Reserva Santa Elena** (p214) before the busloads arrive
- Satisfying your need for speed on windy **Bahía Salinas** (p240) with a kitesurfing course, or taking the chance to bronze on a deserted bay
- Trekking the circuit of waterfalls, thermal pools and volcanic vents of **Volcán Rincón de la Vieja** (p231) by foot and horseback
- Hiking out to the otherworldly cerulean-blue waters of the Río Celeste at **Parque Nacional Volcán Tenorio** (p219)
- Watching wildlife at Costa Rica's largest wetland sanctuary, **Parque Nacional Palo Verde** (p223)

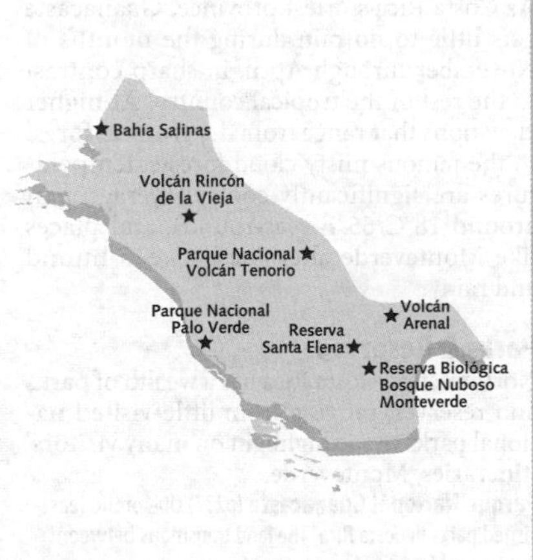

History

The first occupants of Guanacaste are believed to have been the Chorotega, who inhabited large tracts of land throughout Costa Rica, Honduras and Nicaragua in the 8th century BC. Unfortunately, our knowledge about the group is incomplete due to the lack of extensive ruins typical of populations in other parts of Central America. For more information on the Chorotega, see boxed text, p279.

Although their civilization prospered for over 2000 years, the Chorotega were wiped out by warfare and disease during the Spanish colonial period. During this era, the Spanish systematically clear-cut large tracts of dry tropical rainforest as the table-flat landscape was perfect for growing crops and raising cattle.

Following the independence of Central America from Spain, the newly independent provinces formed the Central American Federation. At the time, Guanacaste was part of Nicaragua, although border disputes resulted in skirmishes with Costa Rica. But on July 25, 1824, *guanacastecos* voted to separate and join Costa Rica. Contemporary Guanacastecos take pride in their unique origin and culture, and it's not uncommon to see flags proclaiming an independent Guanacaste.

Climate

The climate in northwestern Costa Rica varies widely from the heat of Guanacaste to the peaks of the chain of volcanoes in the region. As Costa Rica's driest province, Guanacaste gets little to no rain during the months of November through April, in sharp contrast to the rest of the tropical country. At higher elevations that range from dry tropical forest to the famous misty cloud forests, temperatures are significantly cooler (averaging at around 18°C/65°F year-round), and places like Monteverde alternate between humid and rainy.

Parks & Reserves

Northwestern Costa Rica has a wealth of parks and reserves, ranging from little-visited national parks to the highlight on many visitors' itineraries, Monteverde.

Parque Nacional Guanacaste (p237) One of the least-visited parks in Costa Rica. The land transitions between dry tropical forest to humid cloud forest.

Parque Nacional Palo Verde (p223) Stay at the research station here and take a guided tour to see some of the 300-plus bird species that have been recorded in this rich wetland.

Parque Nacional Rincón de la Vieja (p231) Peaceful, muddy isolation can be found just outside of Liberia, where bubbling thermal activity abounds.

Parque Nacional Santa Rosa (p234) Access legendary surf, hike through the largest stand of tropical dry forest in Central America and visit a historical battle site.

Parque Nacional Volcán Arenal (p171) Centered on the perfect cone of Volcán Arenal, the clouds will sometimes disperse to reveal red-hot lava or a plume of smoke.

Refugio Nacional de Fauna Silvestre Peñas Blanca (p189) If you're self-sufficient, it's possible to visit this wild refuge in the southern Cordillera de Tilarán.

Refugio Nacional de Vida Silvestre Bahía Junquillal (p237) Another small, peaceful protected site, this refuge has a beach backed by mangrove swamp and tropical dry forest.

Reserva Biológica Bosque Nuboso Monteverde (p211) Costa Rica's most famous cloud forest, Monteverde receives a steady stream of visitors without having lost its magic.

Reserva Biológica Lomas de Barbudal (p224) If you're here in March, you might be lucky enough to catch the yellow blooms of the *corteza amarilla* tree in this tropical dry forest reserve.

Reserva Santa Elena (p214) Slightly less crowded and at a higher elevation than Monteverde, this is also a good spot to seek a quetzal sighting.

Dangers & Annoyances

While foreign women generally have no problems traveling in Costa Rica, they may sense a whiff of machismo in Guanacaste, most often if traveling alone, and usually in the form of harmless hissing or catcalls. This constant annoyance may become exasperating (especially when combined with heat and humidity), and the best way to combat it is simply to ignore it.

Getting There & Around

More and more visitors are flying directly into Liberia, a convenient international airport that makes for quick escapes to both northwestern Costa Rica and the beaches of the Península de Nicoya. Liberia is also a major transportation center for buses traveling the Interamericana, from the border with Nicaragua to San José. Regular buses also serve the Península de Nicoya to hubs such as Santa Cruz and Nicoya and coastal points beyond. The most unusual mode of transport in the area is the jeep-boat-jeep transfer between Monteverde and La Fortuna, but it's also possible to do the trip on horseback.

ARENAL ROUTE

If you've got your own wheels and you've got a little time, take the road from Ciudad Quesada to the Arenal area – you are in for one beautiful ride. With the backdrop of Volcán Platanar, the road winding through this green, river-rich agrarian region passes through prosperous, quaint towns bright with bougainvillea. In front of you, if the weather cooperates, the smoking peak of Arenal will loom in the distance.

Past La Fortuna, the paved road (beware of potholes) hugs the north bank of Laguna de Arenal. On either side of the road, up the green slope and down on the lakeside, turnouts and driveways for lovely inns, kooky ersatz Austrian mini-villages, hip coffeehouses and eccentric galleries appear invitingly like pictures in a pop-up book. Scattered in between, you can't help but notice the scads of real-estate signs offering lots for sale, but the area is bucolic and not overdeveloped, and each stop feels far enough away from the next to give a sense of isolation.

Heading back around the western edge of the lake, you'll pass through the lakeside Nuevo Arenal and down to the pleasant mountain town of Tilarán before descending back toward the Interamericana. Note that the route is also well served by public transportation.

CIUDAD QUESADA (SAN CARLOS)

pop 27,300

The official name of this small city is Ciudad Quesada (sometimes abbreviated to 'Quesada'), but all the locals know it as San Carlos, and local buses often list San Carlos as the destination. It's long been a bustling ranching and agricultural center, known for its *talabaterías* (saddle shops), where some of the most intricately crafted leather saddles in Costa Rica are made and sold; a top-quality saddle can cost US$1000. The city is also home to the **Feria del Ganado** (cattle fair and auction), which is held every April and accompanied by carnival rides and a *tope* (horse parade).

Although San Carlos is surrounded by pastoral countryside, the city has developed into the commercial center of the region – it's also gritty and congested, and driving here can be harrowing for the uninitiated driver. Fortunately, there's no real reason to enter the city, except to either change buses or visit one of the area's fine hot springs.

As the regional market town, you'll find plenty of ATMs, internet cafes and groceries and shops around Parque Central.

If you're not staying at one of the two private hot-springs resorts, you can visit the budget-friendly **Aguas Termales de la Marina** (☎ 2460-1692; admission US$2). The springs, on the outskirts of town, are referred to locally as 'El Tucanito' (El Tucano is the name of the most expensive resort in town).

Sleeping & Eating

There is no shortage of budget hotels and eateries around town. Apart from the plethora of chain restaurants, you'll find a few decent local spots on or near the park.

Hotel Don Goyo (☎ 2460-1780; s/d US$20/30; P) This is the most established hotel in San Carlos proper, and has small, pleasant, salmon-colored rooms with private hot shower. The attached restaurant (mains ₡2300 to ₡5800) is well respected for its high-quality food, including traditional Tico favorites and a good variety of Western dishes. It's 100m south of Parque Central.

Loma Verde Hotel (☎ 2460-1976; s/d incl breakfast US$40/62; P) Located about 2km north of town on the road to Florencia, this hotel is on a hilltop garden with great vistas. It's popular with Christian retreat groups and features a games room, internet cafe and pretty landscaping. It's a good, quiet budget option if you just need a place to crash for the evening. All rooms have private bathroom with hot water, air-con and TV. The hotel is well signed from the highway.

Termales del Bosque (☎ 2460-4740; www.termalesdelbosque.com; s/d incl breakfast US$62/78; P) Several airy cottages are arranged around the jungle-like grounds at this recommended resort designed with Tico tourism in mind, though it's popular with foreigners who don't want to fork out the cash at nearby El Tucano. Luxury here is low-key with therapeutic soaking taking place in seven natural hot- and warm-water springs (adult/child US$22/6), which are arranged on the riverbank in a forested valley populated by morpho butterflies. To reach the resort, turn right behind the cathedral and continue for 7km to the east; you will see a sign on the left.

Hotel Occidental El Tucano & Spa (☎ 2460-0600; http://en.occidentalhotels.com/hotels/ElTucano.asp; d

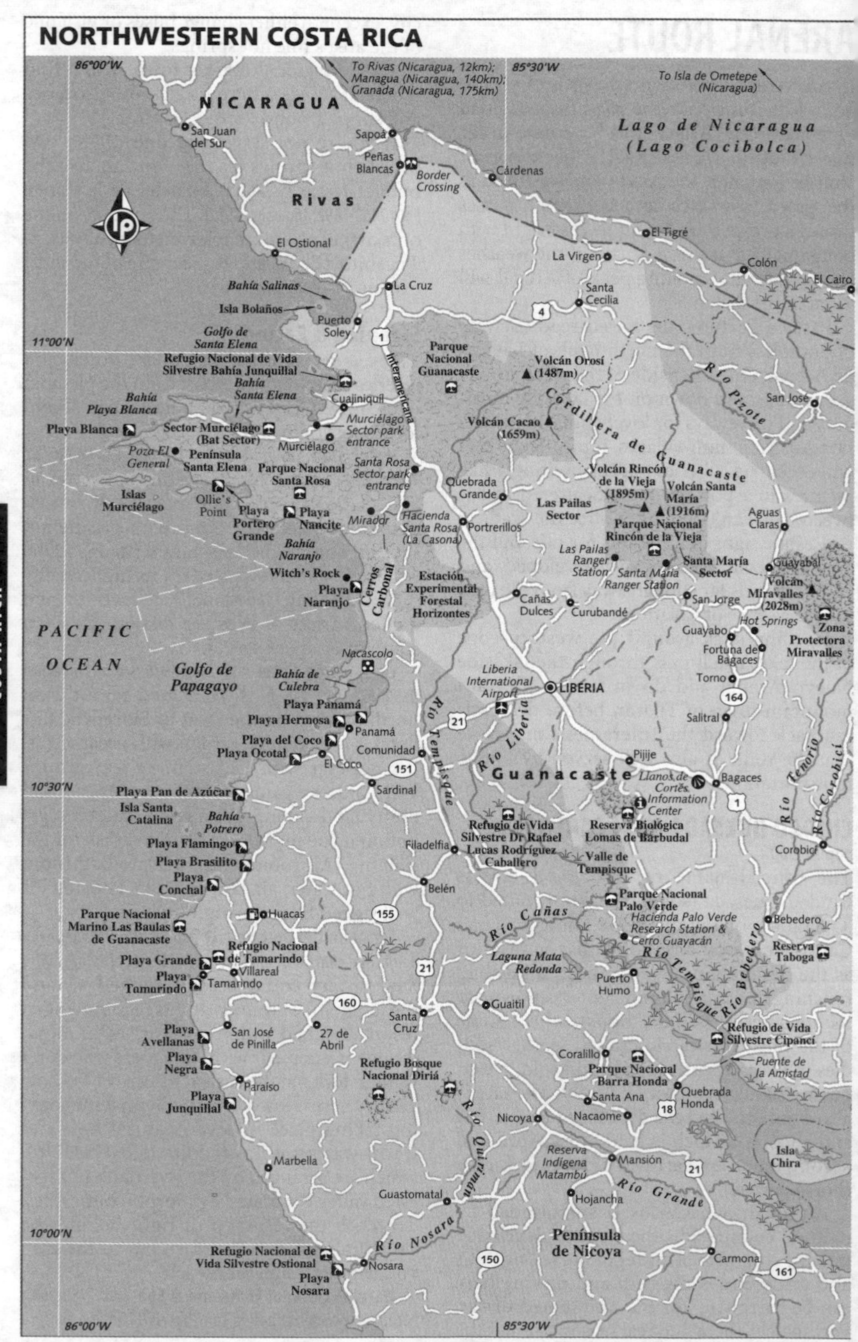
NORTHWESTERN COSTA RICA
NICARAGUA
To Rivas (Nicaragua, 12km); Managua (Nicaragua, 140km); Granada (Nicaragua, 175km)
To Isla de Ometepe (Nicaragua)
Lago de Nicaragua (Lago Cocibolca)
San Juan del Sur
Sapoá
Peñas Blancas
Border Crossing
Cárdenas
Rivas
El Tigré
La Virgen
Colón
El Cairo
El Ostional
La Cruz
Santa Cecilia
Bahía Salinas
Isla Bolaños
Puerto Soley
Golfo de Santa Elena
Refugio Nacional de Vida Silvestre Bahía Junquillal
Bahía Santa Elena
Parque Nacional Guanacaste
Volcán Orosí (1487m)
Río Pizote
San José
Bahía Playa Blanca
Playa Blanca
Cuajiniquil
Sector Murciélago (Bat Sector)
Murciélago Sector park entrance
Murciélago
Volcán Cacao (1659m)
Cordillera de Guanacaste
Poza El General
Península Santa Elena
Parque Nacional Santa Rosa
Santa Rosa Sector park entrance
Quebrada Grande
Volcán Rincón de la Vieja (1895m)
Volcán Santa María (1916m)
Islas Murciélago
Ollie's Point
Playa Portero Grande
Playa Nancite
Mirador
Hacienda Santa Rosa (La Casona)
Portrerillos
Las Pailas Sector
Parque Nacional Rincón de la Vieja
Aguas Claras
Bahía Naranjo
Las Pailas Ranger Station
Santa María Ranger Station
Santa María Sector
Guayabal
Witch's Rock
Playa Naranjo
Cerros Carbonal
Estación Experimental Forestal Horizontes
Cañas Dulces
Curubandé
San Jorge
Volcán Miravalles (2028m)
Hot Springs
Zona Protectora Miravalles
Guayabo
Fortuna de Bagaces
PACIFIC OCEAN
Golfo de Papagayo
Nacascolo
Bahía de Culebra
Liberia International Airport
LIBERIA
Torno
Playa Panamá
Playa Hermosa
Panamá
Río Tempisque
Río Liberia
Salitral
Playa del Coco
Playa Ocotal
Comunidad
El Coco
Pijije
Guanacaste
Llanos de Cortés
Bagaces
Río Tenorio
Río Corobicí
Sardinal
Information Center
Playa Pan de Azúcar
Isla Santa Catalina
Bahía Potrero
Refugio de Vida Silvestre Dr Rafael Lucas Rodríguez Caballero
Reserva Biológica Lomas de Barbudal
Playa Flamingo
Filadelfia
Corobicí
Playa Brasilito
Valle de Tempisque
Playa Conchal
Belén
Parque Nacional Palo Verde
Hacienda Palo Verde Research Station & Cerro Guayacán
Parque Nacional Marino Las Baulas de Guanacaste
Huacas
Río Cañas
Bebedero
Refugio Nacional de Tamarindo
Reserva Taboga
Playa Grande
Villareal
Laguna Mata Redonda
Río Tempisque
Río Bebedero
Playa Tamarindo
Tamarindo
Puerto Humo
Guaitil
Santa Cruz
Playa Avellanas
San José de Pinilla
27 de Abril
Refugio de Vida Silvestre Cipancí
Playa Negra
Refugio Bosque Nacional Diriá
Coralillo
Parque Nacional Barra Honda
Puente de la Amistad
Paraíso
Playa Junquillal
Santa Ana
Quebrada Honda
Río Quiriman
Nicoya
Nacaome
Reserva Indígena Matambú
Mansión
Isla Chira
Marbella
Río Grande
Guastomatal
Hojancha
Río Nosara
Península de Nicoya
Refugio Nacional de Vida Silvestre Ostional
Nosara
Carmona
Playa Nosara
86°00'W
85°30'W
11°00'N
10°30'N
10°00'N
1
4
21
151
155
160
150
164
18
161
NORTHWESTERN COSTA RICA

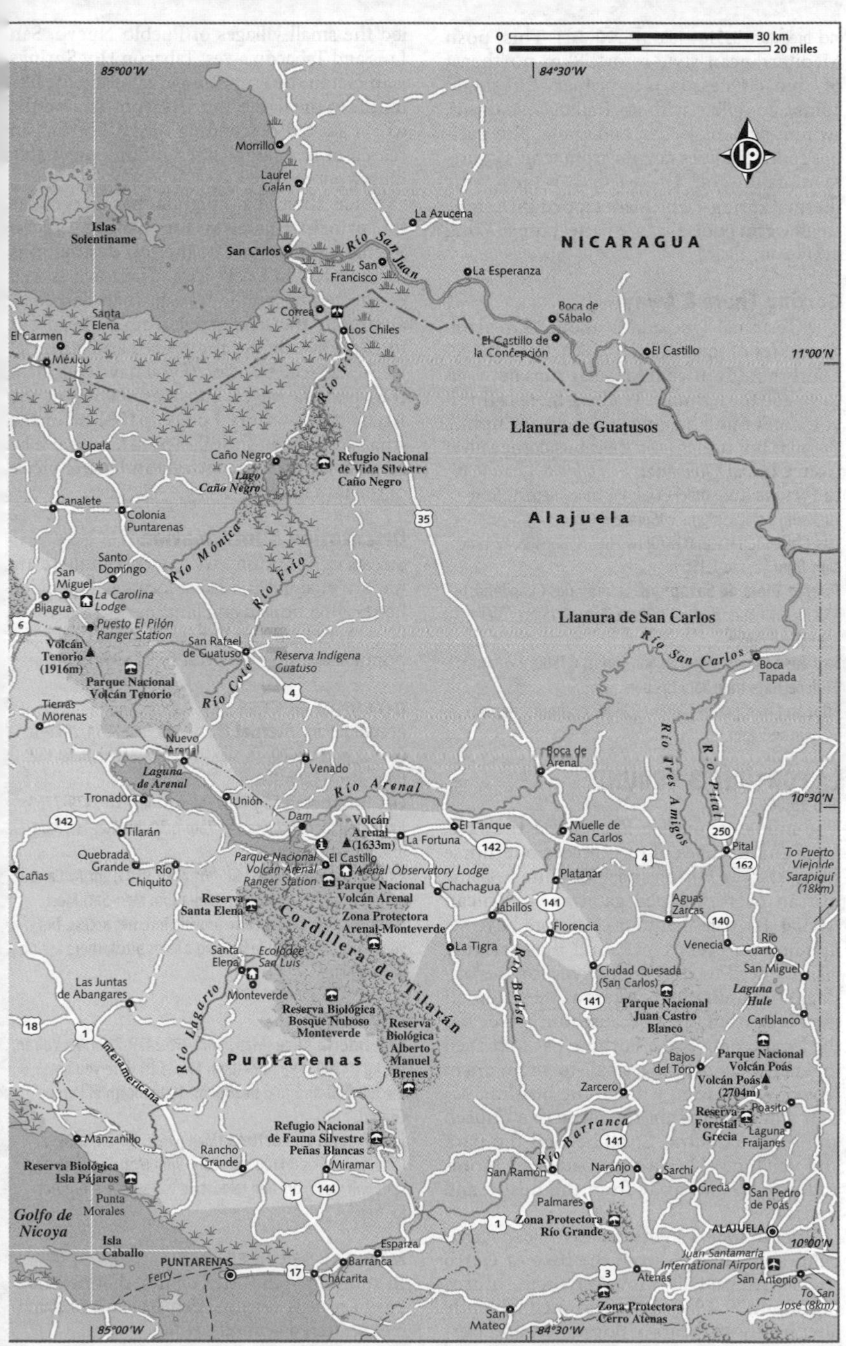
0 30 km
0 20 miles
85°00'W
84°30'W
11°00'N
10°30'N
10°00'N
NICARAGUA
Alajuela
Puntarenas
Llanura de Guatusos
Llanura de San Carlos
Cordillera de Tilarán
Islas Solentiname
Morrillo
Laurel Galán
La Azucena
San Carlos
Río San Juan
San Francisco
La Esperanza
Boca de Sábalo
El Castillo de la Concepción
El Castillo
Correa
Los Chiles
Santa Elena
El Carmen
México
Río Frío
Upala
Caño Negro
Lago Caño Negro
Refugio Nacional de Vida Silvestre Caño Negro
Canalete
Colonia Puntarenas
Río Mónica
Santo Domingo
San Miguel
La Carolina Lodge
Bijagua
Puesto El Pilón Ranger Station
Volcán Tenorio (1916m)
Parque Nacional Volcán Tenorio
San Rafael de Guatuso
Reserva Indígena Guatuso
Río Cote
Río San Carlos
Boca Tapada
Tierras Morenas
Nuevo Arenal
Venado
Laguna de Arenal
Boca de Arenal
Río Tres Amigos
Río Pital
Tronadora
Unión
Río Arenal
Dam
Volcán Arenal (1633m)
La Fortuna
El Tanque
Muelle de San Carlos
Tilarán
Quebrada Grande
Río Chiquito
Cañas
Parque Nacional Volcán Arenal Ranger Station
El Castillo
Arenal Observatory Lodge
Parque Nacional Volcán Arenal
Chachagua
Platanar
Pital
To Puerto Viejo de Sarapiquí (18km)
Reserva Santa Elena
Zona Protectora Arenal-Monteverde
Jabillos
Florencia
Aguas Zarcas
Venecia
Río Cuarto
La Tigra
Santa Elena
Ecolodge San Luis
Monteverde
Río Balsa
Ciudad Quesada (San Carlos)
San Miguel
Laguna Hule
Parque Nacional Juan Castro Blanco
Cariblanco
Las Juntas de Abangares
Reserva Biológica Bosque Nuboso Monteverde
Reserva Biológica Alberto Manuel Brenes
Río Lagarto
Interamericana
Parque Nacional Volcán Poás
Bajos del Toro
Volcán Poás (2704m)
Zarcero
Reserva Forestal Grecia
Poasito
Laguna Fraijanes
Río Barranca
Manzanillo
Refugio Nacional de Fauna Silvestre Peñas Blancas
Rancho Grande
Miramar
Reserva Biológica Isla Pájaros
San Ramón
Naranjo
Sarchí
Grecia
San Pedro de Poás
Punta Morales
Palmares
Golfo de Nicoya
Zona Protectora Río Grande
ALAJUELA
Isla Caballo
Esparza
Juan Santamaría International Airport
PUNTARENAS
Ferry
Barranca
Chacarita
Atenas
San Antonio
To San José (8km)
Zona Protectora Cerro Atenas
San Mateo
35
4
6
142
250
162
141
140
18
1
144
17
3

incl breakfast US$104-180; P ✖ ☒) This posh Mediterranean-style resort, 8km northeast of Ciudad Quesada, is in primary forest and comes complete with an Italian restaurant, swimming pool, Jacuzzi and sauna, plus various sports facilities ranging from tennis courts to miniature golf. The real draw is the nearby thermal springs, which are tapped into three small warm pools that are perfect for soaking away your ills.

Getting There & Away

The Terminal Quesada is about 2km from the center of town. Taxis (₡580) and a twice-hourly bus (₡150) make regular runs between town and the terminal. Walking there is fine if you don't mind hauling your luggage uphill. Popular bus routes (and their bus companies) from Ciudad Quesada:

La Fortuna (Coopatrac) ₡600; 1½ hours; departs 6am, 10:30am, 1pm, 3:30pm, 5:15pm and 6pm.
Los Chiles (Chilsaca) ₡1870; two hours; departs 12 times daily from 5am to 7:15pm.
Puerto Viejo de Sarapiquí (Empresarios Guapileños) ₡1250; 2½ hours; departs 4:40am, 6am, 9:15am, 10am, 3pm and 5:30pm.
San José (Autotransportes San Carlos) ₡1800; 2½ hours; 11 departures from 5am to 6pm.
Tilarán (Transportes Tilarán) ₡2600; 4½ hours; departs 6:30am and 4pm.

LA FORTUNA & AROUND

pop 10,000

The influx of tourism has altered the face, fame and fortunes of this former one-horse town; still, La Fortuna has not quite become just an overdeveloped gateway to Volcán Arenal. It's true that tour operators have set up shop on every block, and that arriving visitors need to steel themselves for the onslaught of touts and hawkers as they step off their buses, but that's because tourism drives the local economy. La Fortuna has managed to retain an underlying, small-town *sabanero* (cowboy) feel to it, with all the bustling action still centered on the attractive church and Parque Central. Stroll beyond the park and you'll quickly hit dirt roads and mom-and-pop *cabinas* away from the hustle and traffic flow.

Prior to 1968, La Fortuna was a sleepy agricultural town, 6km from the base of Cerro Arenal (Arenal Hill). However, on the morning of July 29, 1968, Arenal erupted violently after nearly 400 years of dormancy, and buried the small villages of Pueblo Nuevo, San Luís and Tabacón – yes, Tabacón Hot Springs is in fact in the eruption path. Suddenly, like moths to the flame, tourists from around the world started descending on La Fortuna in search of fiery night skies and the inevitable blurry photo.

Since then, La Fortuna has served as the principal gateway for visiting Volcán Arenal, and it's one of the top destinations for travelers in Costa Rica. The town is well connected by public transport to San José, and many travelers arrive from or head out to Monteverde via the scenic and unusual jeep-boat-jeep transfer. If you have your own transport, however, consider staying at the Arenal Observatory Lodge (p173) or in the small town of El Castillo (p174), as you'll be rewarded with fewer crowds and better views of the lava flows.

Orientation & Information

Streets in La Fortuna are named, but there are few street signs and most locals will provide better directions using landmarks. The town is centered on the Parque Central plaza, a popular evening hangout for Tico teens.

INTERNET ACCESS

Arenal Rocks Internet (Map p160; ☎ 8854-2898; Av Central; per hr ₡600; ⏰ 8am-11pm) Located under the Hotel Arenal Carmella.
Ciro Internet Café y Mas (Map p160; ☎ 2479-7769; Av Central; per hr ₡500; ⏰ 7am-6:30pm Mon-Fri, 8am-6:30pm Sat).
Expediciones (Map p160; ☎ 2479-9101; cnr Av Central & Calle 1; per hr ₡450; ⏰ 7am-10pm Mon-Sat) Most tour operators in town also provide internet access, but if you're not interested in hearing a sales pitch, there are no hassles here.

LAUNDRY

Lavandería Alice (Map p160; ☎ 2479-7111; Av Volcán; per kg ₡1800; ⏰ 7am-10pm Mon-Sat) Here you get the full fluff-and-fold treatment, 100m north of Parque Central.
Lavandería La Fortuna (Map p160; ☎ 2479-9547; Calle 4; per 4kg ₡4100; ⏰ 8am-9pm Mon-Sat) Friendly staff will wash, dry and fold while you surf the internet for free.

MEDICAL SERVICES

In addition to the listed clinics, there are dozens of private doctors, dentists and pharmacies scattered around town.

Centro Médico Arenal Vital (Map p160; ☎ 2479-7027; Calle 1; 🕑 24hr) Located in the Hotel Las Colinas building, this private clinic is open 24/7 and has English-speaking staff.

Clínica Fortuna (Map p160; ☎ 2479-9461; Calle 3 btwn Avs Volcán & Fort; 🕑 7am-10pm Mon-Thu, 7am-8pm Fri-Sun) Look for the hidden bust of US President John F Kennedy, unceremoniously propped next to a generator.

MONEY

Note that banks listed below have 24-hour ATMs.

BAC San José (Map p160; ☎ 2295-9797; cnr Av Fort & Calle 3) Can change traveler's checks.

Banco de Costa Rica (Map p160; ☎ 2479-9113; Av Central)

Banco Nacional (Map p160; ☎ 2479-9355; cnr Calle 1 & Av Fort)

Banco Popular (Map p160; cnr Av Central & Calle 5)

POST

Correos de Costa Rica (Map p160; Av Fort; 🕑 8am-5:30pm Mon-Fri, 7:30am-noon Sat) Mail your volcano postcards and packages from here.

TOURIST INFORMATION

There is no independent tourist information center in La Fortuna, though any tour operator or hotel front desk will be happy to give you information out of enlightened self-interest. However, we highly recommend Diego and the staff at Arenal Backpackers, and Pete of Gringo Pete's for honest, candid information on local sights and attractions. They also offer some of the best rates for activities and attractions. If you find cheaper prices, it's probably too good to be true (see boxed text, below).

Sights

HOT SPRINGS

What's the consolation prize if you can't actually see the volcano? Why, hot springs, of course, and you'll be glad to know La Fortuna has some doozies.

If a movie director ever needed a setting for the Garden of Eden sequence in Genesis, **Tabacón Hot Springs** (Map p169; ☎ 2519-1900; www.tabacon.com; day pass adult/child incl lunch or dinner US$85/40, evening pass incl dinner US$70/35; 🕑 10am-10pm) would be it. Enter through the gratuitously opulent ticket counter, flanked by an outrageous buffet on one side and glittering gift shop on the other. Then, with a thundering announcement, rare orchids and more florid tropical blooms part to reveal, oh yes, a 40°C (104°F) waterfall pouring over a cliff, concealing natural-looking caves complete with camouflaged cup holders. Lounged across each well-placed stone, in various stages of sweat-induced

NORTHWESTERN COSTA RICA

SCAMS

If you're taking the bus to La Fortuna, scammers start before you even get there, boarding a few kilometers out of town, then working the crowd: 'That hotel is overpriced, but I have a friend...' You know this scam, right? But it gets worse.

In addition to steering travelers to poor hotels, we've heard of some people in La Fortuna who'll also book you on 'half-price tours.' Usually you'll just show up for your tour and learn that your receipt is invalid, though we've also heard about people taken to pricey hot springs, then abandoned without transportation or their entry fees paid as promised. Or to save admission fees on lava-viewing tours, these scammers will just take you to the public roadside bridge rather than to the better observation points in the private reserves. We've even heard of touts selling vouchers for phony tours in such far-flung locales as Monteverde and Caño Negro. In a disturbing recent development, these scam artists have set up several professional-looking 'information booths' around town.

After milking a batch of tourists, the scammers trade off between La Fortuna, Monteverde and other hot spots for a couple of weeks; it's worked hassle-free for years. Why hasn't anything been done about this? That's a good question, but basically it comes down to the fact that no one wants to wait around for months to bring these people to trial.

It's worth going through a reputable agency or hotel to book your tours around here. You may pay twice as much, but at least you'll get to go. On the bright side, the recent upswing in tourism in the La Fortuna area has brought promises from the Instituto Costarricense de Turismo (ICT) that there will be a crackdown on touts, though it remains to be seen if this situation will improve soon.

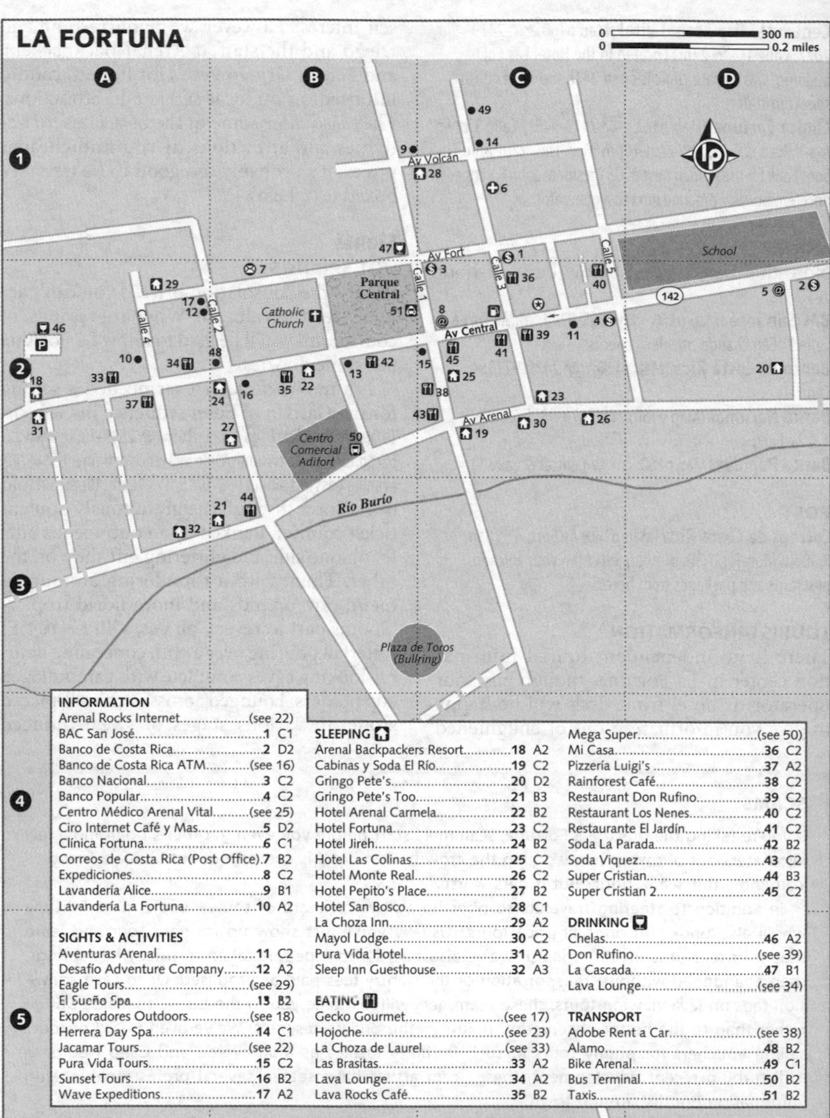

exhaustion, relax reddening tourists all enjoying what could be called a hot date.

This hedonism comes at a price – on top of the exorbitant admission fee, that is. The spa, 14km west of La Fortuna, is actually on the site where a volcanic eruption ripped through in pretouristed 1975, killing one local. The former village of Tabacón was destroyed in the 1968 eruption, killing 78. Chances are you'll be fine, but remember that as an active volcano, Arenal always poses the risk of unpredictably acting up. That said, if you have time and money to visit only one hot spring in Costa Rica, make it Tabacón.

The newest entry into the spring scene is the **Springs Resort & Spa** (Map p169; ☎ 2401-3313, in USA 954-727-8333; www.thespringscostarica.com; admission US$40). This over-the-top, luxury resort, partially opened in 2008, is giving Tabacón a run for its money. The Springs features 18 free-form pools with various temperatures, volcano views, landscaped gardens, waterfalls and swim-up bars, including a jungle bar with a water slide. During our recent visit, the resort was still partially under construction. But the parts that have opened, including the hot springs and the main lodge, are quite impressive.

Baldi Hot Springs Hotel Resort & Spa (Map p169; ☎ 2479-9651; www.baldihotsprings.cr; with/without buffet US$34/25; ⏰ 10am-10pm) sports concrete Roman pillars and a Maya pyramid sprouting waterslides; the ambience of these springs 5km west of La Fortuna falls somewhere between Caesar's Palace and Epcot Center. The 25 thermal pools here range in temperature from 32°C (90°F) to a scalding 67°C (153°F). At night, Baldi is especially popular with the younger backpacker crowd, attracted by the three swim-up bars, loud music, and decent buffet – but be aware that drink prices are ridiculously expensive.

Across the street, a large forbidding gate that leads to the recommended **Eco Thermales Hot Springs** (Map p169; ☎ 2479-8484; adult/child US$30/20, with dinner US$55/45; ⏰ 10am-9pm) complex, which is by reservation only. The theme here is minimalist elegance, and everything from the natural circulation systems in the pools to the soft, mushroom lighting is understated yet luxurious. Just 100 visitors per four-hour slot are welcomed at 10am, 1pm and 5pm, and you can phone ahead or book online at www.anywherecostarica.com. During the evening session, guests have the option to choose from one of three set menus, which feature home-style food served in earthenware pots.

We're certainly not going to let out the secret, but there are several free **hot springs** in the area that any local can take you to.

DAY SPAS

Many top-end hotels have spas that are open to nonguests including Tabacón Grand Spa Thermal Resort Lodge, the Springs Resort & Spa, Hotel Nayala and Casa Luna Lodge, among others. **El Sueño Spa** (Map p160; ☎ 2479-8261; Av Central; massages US$35-60; ⏰ 9am-9pm) offers massages, facials and reflexology treatments in its peaceful little salon just across from the south side of Parque Central. It also sells volcanic mud so you can relive the spa experience at home.

Herrera Day Spa (Map p160; ☎ 2479-9016; cnr Av Volcán & Calle 3; massages US$20-85; ⏰ 9am-10pm), 200m northeast of Parque Central, has an intimate, European atmosphere and sells its own line of homemade beauty products.

WATERFALLS

Even if you can't see Arenal, La Fortuna has another natural wonder that pales only in comparison with an erupting volcano: **La Catarata de la Fortuna** (Map p169; admission US$10; ⏰ 8am-5pm), a sparkling 70m ribbon of clear water pouring through a sheer canyon of dark volcanic rock arrayed in bromeliads and ferns. It's photogenic, and you don't have to descend the canyon – a short, well-maintained and almost vertical hike paralleling the river's precipitous plunge – to get the shot, though you do have to pay the steep entry fee.

It's worth the climb out (think Stairmaster with a view) to see the rare world at the jungle floor. Though it's dangerous to dive beneath the thundering falls, a series of perfect swimming holes with spectacular views tiles the canyon in aquamarine – cool and inviting after the hike or ride here. Keep an eye on your backpack.

From the turnoff on the road to San Ramón, it's about 4km uphill to the falls. If you decide to walk up, you'll enjoy spectacular views of Cerro Chato as you hike through pastures and past the small hotels lining the road. You might appreciate a stop at **Neptune's House of Hammocks** (Map p169; ☎ 2479-8269; hammocks ₡25,000-85,000), which sells soft drinks and hammocks (cat-sized models also available) that you can try out while you take a breather.

You can also get to the waterfall on horseback (US$25 to US$35 per person) or by car or taxi (₡3000 one way); several outfits offer overpriced tours that include a shuttle. A handful of snack and souvenir stands are at the entrance to the falls, but it's worth packing your own lunch and making a day of it.

The falls are also the trailhead for the steep, five- to six-hour **Cerro Chato** climb, a seriously strenuous but rewarding trek to a beautiful lake-filled volcanic crater, where you can have a swim once you summit Cerro Chato. Starting from here, you'll have to pay a US$10 fee for crossing the *finca* leading to Cerro Chato; a slightly cheaper (though you'll still pay a fee) and less physically taxing alternative would be to hike up the other side from Arenal Observatory Lodge (p172).

Can't handle the hike? Just past the turnoff to the *catarata* (waterfall), at the third bridge (Río Fortuna) as you leave La Fortuna for San Ramón, there's a short trail on the left leading to a pretty **swimming hole** just under the road, with a rope swing and a little waterfall of its own – thank you very much.

ECOCENTRO DANAUS

The reader-recommended **Ecocentro Danaus** (ecological center; Map p169; ☎ 2479-7019; www.ecocentrodanaus.com; admission with/without guide US$12/7; 🕑 8am-4pm Mon-Sat, 9am-3:30pm Sun), 3km east of town then 600m down a dirt road, has a well-developed trail system that's good for bird-watching, and there are frequent sightings of sloth, coati and howler monkey. The price of admission also includes a visit to a butterfly garden, a ranarium featuring poison-dart frogs and a small lake containing caiman and turtles. Various tour operators in town run guided night tours (US$25) to the ecological center.

Activities

There's no shortage of things to do around La Fortuna, but it's going to cost you.

BUNGEE JUMPING

It was bound to spring up here sometime – **Arenal Bungee** (Map p169; ☎ 2479-7440; www.arenalbungee.com; jump US$50; 🕑 9:30am-9:30pm) lets you fling yourself through the air from its 'Extreme Machine' structure in several ways, including launching upwards from the ground. Confused? Try it for yourself at this outfit, safety-certified by the Costa Rica Tourism Board. During our visit, Arenal Bungee was in the process of moving to a new location by Ecoglide (right).

CANOEING

Highly recommended, **Canoa Aventura** (Map p169; ☎ 2479-8200; www.canoa-aventura.com; 🕑 6:30am-9:30pm) is about 1.5km west of town on the road to Arenal and specializes in canoe and float trips led by bilingual naturalist guides. Most are geared toward wildlife-watching, with birds (green macaw, roseate spoonbill, honeycreeper etc) being the focus of various tours. Popular paddles include the full-day trip to Caño Negro (US$150, including breakfast and lunch) and an overnight (US$311) to the northern rainforest for an opportunity to spot the great green macaw.

CANOPY TOURS

Opened in 2008, **Ecoglide** (Map p169; ☎ 2479-7120; www.arenalecoglide.com; adult/student/child 5-12yr $45/35/22.50; 🕑 8am-4pm; ♿) is the newest and biggest game in town, featuring 15 cables, 18 platforms and a 'Tarzan' swing. Ecoglide is highly recommended for families with young children; the dual-cable safety system provides extra security and peace of mind.

Try **Arenal Paraíso Canopy Tours** (Map p169; ☎ 2479-1100; www.arenalparaiso.com; adult/student & child US$45/35) for two-hour tours along 12 zip lines. A bit further west, **Canopy Los Cañones** (Map p169; ☎ 2479-1000; www.caopyloscanones.com; US$45) is based at the Hotel Los Lagos, with 15 cables over the rainforest. You can also do canopy tours inside the park itself with SkyTrek, see p174. Then there's **Arenal Mundo Aventura** (Map p169; ☎ 2479-9762; www.arenalmundoaventura.com; canopy tour adult/child US$65/33), an ecological park where you can take a canopy tour over La Fortuna Waterfall, go rappelling, horseback riding and catch Maleku performances all in one go.

CANYONING

The reputable **PureTrek Canyoning** (Map p169; ☎ 2479-1313, 2479-1315; www.puretrek.com; 🕑 7am-10pm) leads guided rappels down four waterfalls, one of which is 50m in height. The four-hour tour costs US$85 and includes transportation and lunch. It's located several kilometers west of town, on the road to Arenal Nayara Hotel & Gardens.

HIKING

There are many great hiking trails in and around Parque Nacional Volcán Arenal, some with excellent views of the lava flows. Most of the trails are located on private nature reserves, none of which are free. For more information, see p172.

HORSEBACK RIDING

Desafío Adventure Company (Map p160; ☎ 2479-9464; www.desafiocostarica.com; Calle 2; 🕑 6:30am-9pm) treats its horses well and has been recommended for the trek to Monteverde (US$75). Along with horseback-riding trips, the company organizes adventure tours rappelling down waterfalls, and community-based tours visiting a local women's recycling collective and animal rescue shelter. Look for the building shaped like a castle turret.

KITESURFING & WINDSURFING

You're only a short drive from the premier spot in Costa Rica for wind sports – Laguna de Arenal (p175).

WHITE-WATER RAFTING & KAYAKING

Desafío Adventure Company (Map p160; ☎ 2479-9464; www.desafiocostarica.com; Calle 2; 6:30am-9pm) is recommended for its expertise in river rafting. White-water rafting and kayaking on the Ríos Toro, Peñas Blancas and Sarapiquí are convenient day trips from La Fortuna, and rapids ranging from Class I to Class IV cater to all skill levels. Depending on access and the difficulty of the rapids, trips cost between US$45 and US$100.

Wave Expeditions (Map p160; ☎ 2479-5250; www.waveexpeditions.com; cnr Calle 2 & Av Fort; 7am-9pm), run fun, professional river trips for all experience levels. Prices are competitive, and readers have raved about the excellent staff running these trips.

Aguas Bravas (Map p169; ☎ 2479-7645; www.aguas-bravas.co.cr; 7am-7pm), 2km east of Fortuna, offers a gentle safari float trip (US$50) on Peñas Blancas that's a good choice for families, plus Class-III and Class-IV trips for US$65 and US85 per person, respectively.

Festivals & Events

The big annual bash is **Fiestas de la Fortuna**, held in mid-February and featuring two weeks of Tico-rules bullfights, colorful carnival rides, greasy festival food, craft stands and unusual gambling devices. It's free, except for the beer (which is cheap) and you'll have a blast trying to decide between the temporary disco with go-go dancers getting down to reggaetón or the rough and wild tents next door with live ranchero and salsa.

Tours

You could have someone blindfold you and spin you around on Av Central and chances are you'd manage to stumble right into a tour-operator's desk – unless a tout got a hold of you first. While exploding development in La Fortuna means there's a lot of healthy

THE RAIN OF FIRE

William Bogarin-Solano was just seven years old when Volcán Arenal erupted on July 29, 1968. He was born and raised in a small village just west of La Fortuna. He is one of the few people who has hiked to the summit of Arenal (a major no-no). Today he works as a guide, leading international visitors on nightly lava-viewing hikes on the slopes of Arenal.

What do you remember about the day Arenal erupted? For about 24 hours before the eruption, the ground was shaking violently. Our cows stopped drinking, because the cool spring waters had turned quite hot. On July 29, we awoke to a beautiful clear morning. Suddenly at about 7:30am we heard a huge explosion like a bomb had gone off. In a matter of minutes, the sky grew dark and filled with ash. Rocks the sizes of cars were spit from the volcano and hurled 5km away, exploding on impact. We ran for our lives. Luckily we lived on a hilltop; that saved us from the dangerous volcanic gases that settled on the villages below. About 80 people were killed when they succumbed from the toxic gases.

Why did you hike Arenal? The eruption traumatized me as a child, and I remained scared of Arenal even as an adult. To conquer my fear I started spending more time around the volcano. I began working as a tour guide at Arenal Observatory Lodge. I started hiking up Arenal, getting closer and closer to the top. Finally in 1996 I reached the summit and placed a banner in honor of those who died in 1968. I've since climbed to the top of Arenal eight times. It's very difficult, very dangerous and now very illegal. I won't do it again, and neither should you.

How dangerous is Arenal? Over the years, several hikers have been killed when they were consumed by the toxic fumes. In August 2000 a small sightseeing airplane that got too close crashed into the side of Arenal, killing 10 people; I was part of the team sent to recover the bodies. You must always have respect for volcanoes because you can never predict what they will do.

What do you enjoy most about working on Arenal? I love meeting people from all over the world. I love nature. And yes, I love Arenal volcano. It's part of my life. The volcano is like my friend…a very dangerous friend.

competition, you'll need to shop around, compare prices and not buy your tour from some friendly dude on the street. This is one place where the freedom of having your own wheels can save you money and hassles.

There's usually a two-person minimum for any trip, and groups can work out discounts in advance with most outfitters. If you don't want to deal with the tour operators, most hotels can arrange trips for you, though you will probably be charged a US$5 per person commission. It's also becoming standard practice in La Fortuna to sell tourists pricey tours to distant destinations, such as Caño Negro. If you're turned off by the idea of public transportation, this is a fine option, though you'll save yourself a ton of money (and probably have a much better experience) if you actually go to these places on the local bus and then organize a tour upon arrival.

Most tourists are interested in taking the obligatory trip to Volcán Arenal, which is generally an afternoon excursion to either the national park or a private overlook to appreciate the mountain by day, combined with a trip to one of the hot springs and usually dinner. Then it's off to another overlook in the evening, where lucky souls will see some lava. Prices vary widely, but generally run US$25 to US$65 per person. Make sure your tour includes entry fees to the park and hot springs, which could easily add another US$25 to the total. Also remember that there's a better-than-even chance that Arenal will remain demurely wrapped in cloud cover for the duration of your trek. There are no refunds if you can't see anything, but nighttime soaks in the hot springs are pretty damn great anyway.

Most agencies in town can also arrange jeep-boat-jeep transportation to Monteverde (see p170), which is the easiest, most scenic way to visit the cloud forests.

The tour operators listed below are a few of the more established agencies, but this list is by no means exhaustive.

Aventuras Arenal (Map p160; ☎ 2479-9133; www.arenaladventures.com; Av Central; 🕑 7am-8pm) Has been around for over 15 years, organizing a variety of local day tours via bike, boat and horseback.

Desafío Adventure Company (Map p160; ☎ 2479-9464; www.desafiocostarica.com; Calle 2; 🕑 6:30am-9pm) This highly recommended company offers a variety of tours including rafting, lava-viewing hikes, horseback riding, mountain biking, spelunking and more. Look for the castle-like building.

Eagle Tours (Map p160; ☎ 2479-9091; www.eagletours.net; 🕑 6:30am-9pm) Budget travelers rave about this professionally run tour agency. It's located on the premises of La Choza Inn, about 150m west of the church.

Jacamar Tours (Map p160; ☎ 2479-9767; www.arenaltours.com; 🕑 7am-9pm) Recommended for its incredible variety of naturalist hikes. It's located on the ground level of Hotel Arenal Carmela.

Pura Vida Tours (Map p160; ☎ 2479-9045; www.puravidatrips.com; cnr Calle 1 & Av Central; 🕑 7am-10pm)

Sunset Tours (Map p160; ☎ 2479-9800; www.sunsettourcr.com; Calle 2; 🕑 6:30am-9pm) This is La Fortuna's most established tour company, recommended for high-quality tours with bilingual guides.

Sleeping

Costa Rican holidays call for merrymaking and explosions, and what better fireworks show is there than the famous lava of La Fortuna? Visitors both foreign and domestic are drawn to La Fortuna for the chance to see the volcano spit some magma, particularly on weekends and holidays, so for those times try to make advance reservations.

There are a bazillion places to stay in town, and we've only listed a handful. The great thing about La Fortuna is the number of small, family-run places, usually a few simple rooms with electric showers and maybe a private bathroom, offering meals by arrangement and good conversation. You may hear about them through word of mouth or just by roaming around for a few minutes. These places will help arrange local tours and are a good way to help locals cash in on the tourism boom. Hotel touts meet the buses and can be more strong-armed than in most of Costa Rica; not all are trustworthy (see boxed text, p159).

If you're driving, consider staying on the pastoral road to Cerro Chato, a few kilometers south of town, where several appealing hotels have cropped up. Note that hotels west and south of town are listed separately.

Rates given are high-season prices, but low-season rates plummet by as much as 40%.

IN TOWN

Hostels

Gringo Pete's (Map p160; ☎ 2479-8521; gringopetes2003@yahoo.com; camping per person US$2, dm US$3, r per person with/without bathroom US$5/4; Ⓟ) With a clean and cozy vibe, it's hard to believe that this purple hostel, 100m south of the school, is so cheap! Whether you're in the comfy dorms sleeping four or your own private room with sink and shower, you'll flock to the breezy covered common areas, which are great spots to chat with other backpackers. Pete, from the USA, can point you toward cut-rate tours and store your bags for you while you're on them. Amenities include a communal kitchen, BBQ and laundry service. If it's full, stroll about 750m along the river toward Arenal and see if there's room at Gringo Pete's Too.

our pick Arenal Backpackers Resort (Map p160; ☎ 2479-7000; www.arenalbackpackersresort.com; Av Central; dm US$14, tents s/d US$14/20; d/tr/q US$45/75/84;) This self-proclaimed 'five-star hostel' with volcano views is among the cushier hostels in Costa Rica. Dorm rooms have private hot-water bathroom, and you'll sleep easy on the thick, orthopedic mattresses. Private rooms definitely cater to midrange travelers, though with cable TV, two superior double beds and tiled bathrooms, they're worth the splurge. The newest budget accommodations option is the covered tent city; each raised tent contains a double air mattress, sheets, pillows and electricity. But the real draw is the landscaped pool with swim-up bar, where backpackers spend lazy days lounging with a cold beer. Other amenities include hammocks, free internet and wi-fi, lockers in every room, 24-hour security and a decent but pricey restaurant and bar with great happy-hour specials. To top it off, manager Diego (a former Costa Rican professional footballer) and his staff are some of the friendliest, most helpful and informed hostel employees we've ever met.

Budget

Prices are quoted here with taxes excluded, since paying in cash usually means no taxes.

Sleep Inn Guesthouse (Map p160; ☎ 8394-7033; misterlavalava@hotmail.com; Av Arenal; r with/without bathroom per person US$7/5) If you're looking for a welcoming Tico family to stay with, you've found them. It's owned by Carlos and Cándida, who also manage Gringo Pete's Too. Carlos, whose nickname is Mr Lava-Lava Man, guarantees you'll see lava (or you get to go again for free), and his tours (US$16) are the cheapest in town.

La Choza Inn (Map p160; ☎ 2479-9361; www.lachozainnhostel.com; Av Fort btwn Calles 2 & 4; dm US$7, s/d with shared bathroom US$13/17, standard s/d US$34/51, deluxe s/d US$51/68, all incl breakfast;) This popular budget inn 100m west of Parque Central has a great variety of rooms, a well-stocked communal kitchen, an extreme[...] staff and is consistently packed [...] nating travelers. The onsite lo[...] recommended Eagle Tours is a huge bonus.

Mayol Lodge (Map p160; ☎ 2479-9110; www.mayollodge.com; Av Arenal; s/d with fan US$20/35, with air-con US$35/50;) Small, bright rooms done up in cheery blue-and-yellow tile are centered on a cool, refreshing pool with volcano views. It's 200m southeast of Parque Central.

Pura Vida Hotel (Map p160; ☎ 2479-9495; www.hotelpuravida.net; Av Central; s/d/tr US$25/35/50;) Although Pura Vida is nothing too out of the ordinary, it's reasonably priced and extremely comfortable with features like good shower pressure and firm mattresses. The Chinese family that owns the hotel also runs a Chinese restaurant (₡2000 to ₡5600) downstairs.

Hotel Pepito's Place (Map p160; ☎ 2479-9238; Calle 2; s/d US$30/40;) A cute family-run choice with flowerpots on the balconies, this is a good deal within this price range. Find it 100m southwest of the church.

Cabinas y Soda El Río (Map p160; ☎ 2479-9341; Av Arenal; r US$40;) Next to the river and run by a friendly family, rooms here are secure, homey and comfortable. Plus there's the *soda* (open from 6am to 9pm) out front.

Midrange

All of the following accommodations have private bathrooms with hot water.

Hotel Las Colinas (Map p160; ☎ 2479-9305; www.lascolinasarenal.com; Calle 1 btwn Avs Central & Arenal; s/d/tr/q incl breakfast from US$45/60/84/88;) The superfriendly owners of Las Colinas have completely remodeled this hotel, creating modern, airy rooms and a 2nd-story terrace with great views of the volcano. All rooms have cable TV and solar-generated hot water, but rates increase with amenities like air-con, minibar and sitting rooms.

Hotel Monte Real (Map p160; ☎ 2479-9357; www.monterealhotel.com; Av Arenal btwn Calles 3 & 5; d US$50-90;) Next to the Río Burío with a pool in the middle of the landscaped grounds, this comfortable hotel is run by an attentive Tico couple named Francisco and Nury. Pricier rooms are larger and have balconies with river or volcano views, and the setting means that you'll sometimes see sloths hanging out in the hotel trees.

Hotel Arenal Carmela (Map p160; ☎ 2479-9010; www.hotelarenalcarmela.com; Av Central; s/d incl breakfast US$50/60;) They've crammed quite a few rooms into this small area – if anyone's on the balcony while you take a dip in the pool, you may feel like a performing seal. But the rooms are modern and clean, if on the small side, and as it's just across from the church it's right in the center of town.

Hotel Jireh (Map p160; ☎ 2479-9004; www.hotelarenaljireh.com; cnr Calle 2 & Av Central; s/d incl breakfast US$50/65; P) This pretty yellow hotel has 12 spacious rooms with balconies, some overlooking a cute courtyard with a small pool. All rooms have air-con, cable TV, fridge, coffeemaker and hot-water bathroom with hairdryer. This is a great budget option during low season when prices plummet.

Hotel San Bosco (Map p160; ☎ 2479-9050; www.arenal-volcano.com; Av Volcán; s/d incl breakfast US$66/80; P) The most established hotel in town is one of the priciest, though the perks include free wi-fi in all the spotless rooms, free coffee and tea all day, a guarded parking lot, lovely pool and superfriendly staff.

Hotel Fortuna (Map p160; ☎ 2479-9197; www.lafortunahotel.com; cnr Av Arenal & Calle 3; s/d incl breakfast US$68/79, with volcano views add US$10; P) The tallest building in town, this five-story, 44-room hotel is the newest and most modern hotel in downtown La Fortuna. The well-appointed rooms have balconies (some with volcano views), cable TV, private bathroom with hot water and hairdryer, and even room service. There's an elevator, and most rooms are wheelchair-accessible. The gorgeous open-air lobby houses one of the best restaurants in town, Hojoche.

our pick **Hotel Cabañitas** (Map p169; ☎ 2479-9343; www.hotelcabanitas.com; standard cabin s/d/tr US$80/95/115; superior cabin s/d/tr US$100/115/135; ste s/d/tr US$110/125/145; P) Located about 1km east of downtown, this quiet complex of 43 private cabins surrounding lush gardens is a great place to get away from it all, but still close enough to walk to town. Each cabin features dark polished wood from floor to ceiling, bathroom with hot water, air-con, coffeemaker, telephone and balcony with rocking chairs. The larger superior rooms have cable TV and minibar. There's also a large swimming pool, a kiddie pool, spa, bar and restaurant onsite. Children under eight stay for free.

WEST OF TOWN

There are a few recommended places to stay along the road to Arenal, some of which have more character than others.

Budget

Hotel Las Flores (Map p169; ☎ 2479-9307; hotellasfloreslodge@ice.co.cr; s/d/tr incl breakfast US$20/30/40; P) This is a great budget option. Attractive, wood-paneled *cabinas* 2.5km west of town (near Lomas del Volcán) have hot-water bathroom, cable TV and fridge. There's a nice *soda* onsite too.

Cerro Chato Lodge (Map p169; ☎ 2479-9522; www.cerrochato.com; r incl breakfast US$35-65; P) Owned by Miguel Zamora, an avid naturalist who delights in leading tourists on nature tours. Rooms here are simple and sweet, with hot-water bathroom and great views of the volcano. About 1.5km west of La Fortuna, turn left at the Super Christian £4 grocery store and continue 800m to the lodge. Miguel can pick you up for free from La Fortuna.

Midrange

Hotel Sueño Dorado (Map p169; ☎ 2479-7222; www.suendodorado.com; standard s/d/tr US$45/71/97, superior s/d/tr US$58/85/111, all incl breakfast; P) It's nothing fancy, but this family-run motel with good volcano views is a good deal in low season. The yellow and green complex has 11 spotless rooms, all with private bathroom, hot water and TV, next to a bird-filled garden, restaurant and small pool. The wheelchair-accessible villa is the best room. It's about 4km west of La Fortuna.

Erupciones Inn B&B (Map p169; ☎ 2479-1400; www.erupcionesinn.com; s/d incl breakfast US$80/90; P) The colorful *cabinas* at this appealing B&B are adorned with ornamental tiles and windows facing the volcano. And each one comes with its own private patio with chairs, looking onto the green scenery or the volcano. There's even a Jacuzzi at this sweet spot, 9km west of La Fortuna.

Lomas del Volcán (Map p169; ☎ 2479-9000; www.lomasdelvolcan.com; s/d/tr/q incl breakfast US$97/105/135/165; P) Although Lomas del Volcán is one of the original resorts lining this stretch of road, it's recommended because of its quiet location (you can hear monkeys in the trees) and stunning volcano views (especially when you're soaking in the outdoor hot tub). Comfy, hardwood cabins have private hot-water bathroom with stained-glass accents, and there are plenty of opportunities for hiking through the surrounding primary forest. Find it about 2km west of La Fortuna and then another signposted 1.5km down a dirt road.

Top End

Arenal Volcano Inn (Map p169; ☎ 2461-1122; www.arenalvolcanoinn.com; s/d/tr incl breakfast from US$103/119/133; P ✻) The beautifully landscaped grounds of this quaint inn surround a pool and bungalow-style rooms, about 6.5km from La Fortuna. The tiled rooms are simple but include kitchenette and cable TV, and the management do all they can to make your stay relaxing and comfortable.

Hotel el Silencio del Campo (Map p169; ☎ 2479-7055; www.hotelsilenciodelcampo.com; d/tr/q incl breakfast US$149/169/189; P ✻) This lovely resort 4km west of town has cabins that are luxurious without being showy, and have attractive tiling, plush bedding and soft lighting. Unfortunately, a hideously ugly and huge hotel has rudely put up its walls right next to the property.

our pick **Arenal Nayara Hotel & Gardens** (Map p169; ☎ 2479-1600; www.arenalnayara.com; r US$232, ste US$309, both incl breakfast; P ✻) Opened in 2008, Nayara has quickly become our favorite hotel in the Arenal region. This intimate hotel has 24 *casitas* with Asian-inspired architecture and minimalist decor. All rooms have exquisite furnishings and bedding, rich woods, flat-screen TV, DVD player, iPod dock and an indoor and separate outdoor shower. But the best feature is outside: your own private balcony with a Jacuzzi where you can soak up surreal views of Arenal volcano. Other amenities include a pool, wine bar and one of the best restaurants in the region. Nayara is one of the most romantic and relaxing hotels in Costa Rica. If you're planning a honeymoon, anniversary or other romantic event, you simply can't do better than beautiful Nayara.

Tabacón Grand Spa Thermal Resort Lodge (Map p169; ☎ 2256-1500; www.tabacon.com; d incl breakfast US$245-450; P ✻) The original and still one of the finest luxury resorts in the area, the classy complex features 114 recently remodeled rooms and suites, spread out over several buildings that tastefully blend into the tropical rainforest background. All rooms have all the upscale amenities you'd expect, while suites add spacious Jacuzzi tubs. Hot water in showers is naturally heated by the thermal springs. Property amenities include a gym, restaurant, bar, pool and onsite transportation. But the best attraction is the thermal resort and spa across the street. Tabacón lodge guests have unlimited access to the hot springs, which is where you'll want to spend most of your time if you stay here. The hot springs also offers the best dining options. Tabacón is 13km west of La Fortuna.

Arenal Kioro (Map p169; ☎ 2479-1700; www.hotelarenalkioro.com; s/d incl breakfast US$378/435; P ✻) With in-your-face volcano views, it's almost scary to think about just how close this hotel is located to Arenal. The 53 all-suite rooms feature floor-to-ceiling windows with panoramic volcano or mountain views, whirlpool tub, balconies and floral decor. There are eight beautiful thermal hot-spring pools surrounded by lush gardens. Onsite amenities include a restaurant, gym, gameroom and full-service spa.

SOUTH OF TOWN

Just a few kilometers south of town, a mostly dirt road trundles up to the base of Cerro Chato, and hotels now dot either side of the path where before there were *fincas*. A few of these hotels are listed in order of distance from the main road.

Even further flung is the village of Chachagua, about 8km south along the road to San Ramón. Crisscrossed by local rivers, this area is a quiet place in the rainforest, away from the touristy brouhaha of La Fortuna.

Cabinas La Catarata (Map p169; ☎ 2479-9753; r US$30; P) About 1km further up the road, you'll see a few places offering *cabinas;* of these, this riverside, family-run spot is by far the best value. Though the wood-walled cabins are simple, they're spotlessly clean and come with fully equipped kitchen, TV and hot water. Some sleep up to eight people, and the setting is peaceful and rustic.

Catarata Eco-Lodge (Map p169; ☎ 2479-9522; www.cataratalodge.com; s/d incl breakfast US$63/69; P) Well, they do recycle and don't automatically throw your linens in the wash every day; apart from that, the 'eco' of this lodge extends to simply caring about the environment. But it has a gorgeous setting at the base of Cerro Chato, and the staff takes beautiful care of the garden, pool and guests.

Villas Josipek (Map p169; ☎ 2430-5252, 2479-9555; www.costaricavillasjosipek.com; s/d/tr US$40/75/93; P) In the village of Chachagua, these immaculate, simple wooden cabins with volcano views are surrounded by private rainforest trails that penetrate the Bosque Eterno de los Niños. All eight of the cabins have full kitchen, and the largest sleeps up to 12. There's a well-kept pool on the quiet, jungle-fringed property, and the family can arrange tours in the region.

Hotel Arenal Green (Map p169; ☎ 2479-8383; www.arenalgreen.com; d/tr/q US$65/75/90, villas US$110-125; P ❄ wi-fi) On the road to Cerro Chato is this reader-recommended, family-friendly hotel comprising six clean and spacious cabins with private hot-water bathroom, coffee-maker and fridge. The villa sleeps six and has a kitchenette and cable TV. A great choice for families.

Chachagua Rainforest Hotel (Map p169; ☎ 2468-1010; www.chachaguarainforesthotel.com; s/d incl breakfast US$87/103; P ⊠) This hotel is a naturalist's dream, situated on a private reserve that abuts the Bosque Eterno de Los Niños. Part of the property is a working orchard, cattle ranch and fish farm, while the rest is humid rainforest that can be accessed either through a series of hiking trails or on horseback. Request the older, Frank Lloyd Wright–esque wooden cabins, which have low windows for watching the birds. There's also a pool within the exquisitely lush grounds, as well as a restaurant that features some produce and meats raised on the premises. The 2km dirt road forking off the main road may require 4WD in the rainy season.

Casa Luna Lodge (Map p169; ☎ 2479-7368; www.casalunalodge.com; r incl breakfast US$116; P ❄ wi-fi ♿) Wooden doors open into elegant rooms tiled in terra-cotta. Some rooms are wheelchair-accessible, and have large orthopedic beds. There's wi-fi access, secure parking, spa treatments (US$40 to US$130) and the pleasant pool area is edged with landscaped garden walkways leading to an open-air restaurant. It's 1.5km from the main road, on the right.

Eating

BUDGET

Rainforest Café (Map p160; ☎ 2479-7239; Calle 1 btwn Avs Central & Arenal; pastries ₡750-2750; 🕑 7am-8:30pm; wi-fi) Superb coffee and espresso is served in what feels like an industrial tent, all glass walls and aluminum bathroom door. There's a dash of urban coffeehouse atmosphere as well, in the burlap coffee bags on the floor and coffee beans under the glass tabletops. The pastry case is a marvel, and the menu has some sandwich-type items along with specialty coffee drinks.

Restaurante El Jardín (Map p160; ☎ 2479-9360; cnr Av Central & Calle 3; mains ₡1400-8000; 🕑 5am-1pm) You can either relax over a shrimp pizza in this bustling eatery 100m east of the Parque Central, or grab a chair beneath the Pollo Pito Pito sign and snack on a few pieces of greasy (but delicious) fried chicken.

our pick **Soda Viquez** (Map p160; ☎ 2479-7132; mains ₡1500-4000; 🕑 7am-10pm) Locals swear this is the best *soda* in town, and we won't dispute their opinion. Located just left of the Rainforest Café, this cute, open-air, family place serves great Tico favorites including awesome *casados* (₡2700). Don't miss the grilled fish with garlic. Wash it down with a fresh juice smoothie. Divine!

Restaurante Linda Vista (Map p169; ☎ 2468-0660; mains ₡1800-3000; 🕑 10am-midnight) Down in Chachagua, this roadside *soda* with fabulous views is about 500m south of Villas Josipek. The nice ladies running this place serve typical Costa Rican dishes.

Soda La Parada (Map p160; ☎ 2479-9547; www.restaurantelaparada.com; Av Central; mains ₡2200-9500; 🕑 24hr) Facing Parque Central and all the street action, this popular *soda* serves great steak *casados*, decent pizza and a couple of bizarre Tico health drinks – *chan* (slimy) and *linaza* (good for indigestion) – to after-hours revelers and folks waiting for their buses.

Gecko Gourmet (Map p160; ☎ 2479-8905; cnr Calle 2 & Av Fort; ₡2500-4000; 🕑 low season 8:30am-5pm, high season 6am-6pm; V) Tired of *casados*? Stop by this little deli for great sandwich and salad offers, including several vegetarian options. Or start the morning with homemade bagels or a breakfast burrito. It's in the same building as Wave Expeditions.

Lava Rocks Café (Map p160; ☎ 2479-9222; Av Central; mains ₡3000-9500; 🕑 7am-10pm) This popular cafe dishes out big breakfasts, hearty *casados* and fresh salads, and has breezy, open-air seating in the shade. It's a magnet for tourists, who can also book tours from the desk here.

For groceries, stop by the well-stocked **Super Cristian 2** (Map p160; cnr Av Central & Calle 1; 🕑 7am-9pm) on the southeast corner of Parque Central; there's another branch (corner Av Arenal and Calle 2) down by the river. The new **Mega Super** (Map p160; Av Arenal; 🕑 7am-9pm Mon-Sat, until 8pm Sun) at the bus terminal is a good place to visit before boarding a long bus ride.

MIDRANGE & TOP END

Lava Lounge (Map p160; ☎ 2479-7365; Av Central btwn Calles 2 & 4; mains ₡2500-6000; 🕑 11am-10:30pm) This hip, open-air restaurant is a breath of fresh air when you just can't abide another *casado*. There's pasta, fish, burgers, wraps and a fair selection of other such well-executed international standbys, brought to you by friendly waiters. Skip the sushi.

Restaurant Los Nenes (Map p160; ☎ 2479-9192; Calle 5; mains ₡3000-11,000; ⏰ 10am-11pm) This classic La Fortuna establishment 200m east of Parque Central is adored by locals and tourists alike. If you're in the mood for fine dining, the seafood platters here can't be beat, and the *ceviche* (₡1500) is as good as it gets.

Las Brasitas (Map p160; ☎ 2479-9819; Av Central; mains ₡3000-10,000; ⏰ 11am-11pm) Sometimes you just need some good Mexican food – nothing against Lizano sauce, but there's just no burn. Check out this breezy but elegant open-air spot 200m west of Parque Central, with good fajitas and something called a *choriqueso* (sort of like a sausage fondue). Hey, if you're going to have a heart attack, go happy.

Vagabondo (Map p169; ☎ 2479-9565; mains ₡3000-8000; ⏰ noon-11pm) Of the many Italian restaurants in the region, Vagabondo has the best wood-fired pizzas around, plus great pasta dishes. There's also a popular sports bar. It's 1.5km west of La Fortuna near a sharp bend in the road.

La Choza de Laurel (Map p160; ☎ 2479-9231; www.lachozadelaurel.com; mains ₡4000-9000; ⏰ 6:30am-10pm) This place serves good, reasonably priced *comida típica* (typical food), and it always seems to be bustling. Live large and order a banana split, served on the half-shell of a pineapple.

Hojoche (Map p160; ☎ 2479-9197; www.lafortunahotel.com; cnr Av Arenal & Calle 3; mains ₡4000-10,000; ⏰ 7am-11pm; 📶) Named for the gorgeous dark wood liberally used throughout the decor (check out the ceiling!), this open-air restaurant at La Fortuna Hotel is one of our favorite new dining spots. The international menu specializes in fresh seafood dishes. There's live music on weekends, sports and movies on TV and even a Wii video game corner. The tropical Jungle bar has daily happy hour specials.

Ginger Sushi (Map p169; ☎ 2401 3310; www.thespringscostarica.com; mains ₡6000-10,000; ⏰ 2pm-11pm) This fabulous, open-air restaurant on the ground level of the Springs Resort & Spa has fantastic sushi rolls. It's a bit out of the way, but you'll find it's worth the drive once you

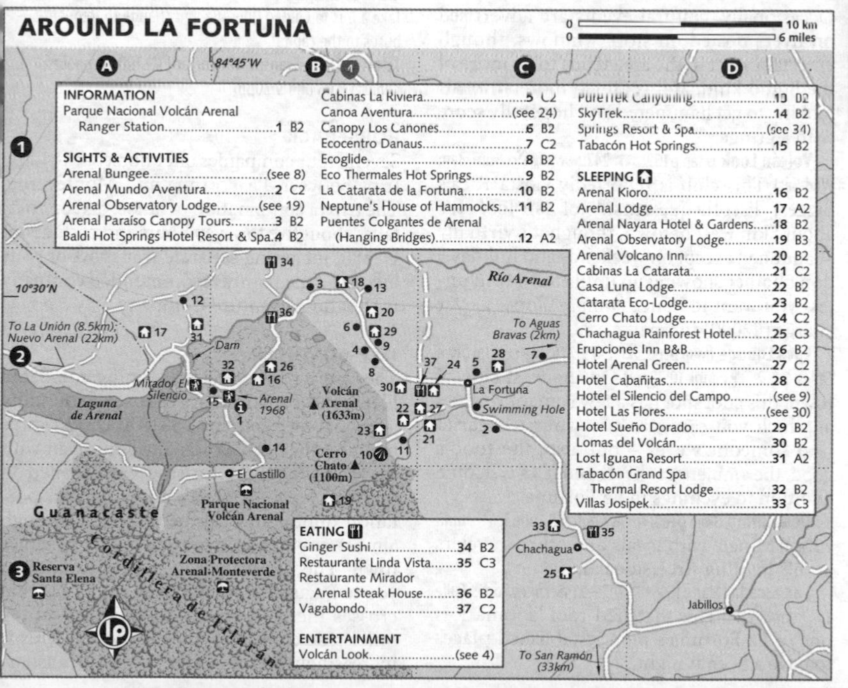

take your first bite of the fabulous creations, such as our favorite, the sunset roll.

Restaurante Mirador Arenal Steak House (Map p169; ☎ 2479-1926; mains ₡7000-15,000; ⌚ 10am-11pm) Go West, young (wo)man! If you're craving a good *churrasco* (steak), that is. This *sabanero*-themed steakhouse has the grilling technique down pat, with great volcano views from the patio. It's located 8km west of La Fortuna.

our pick **Restaurant Don Rufino** (Map p160; ☎ 2479-9997; www.donrufino.com; cnr Av Central & Calle 3; mains ₡5000-23,000; ⌚ 10am-11pm) Fortuna's best restaurant is formal enough to justify buttoning up your shirt and putting on a little lipstick. The contemporary, open-air restaurant is popular with locals and tourists alike. Continental cuisine with judiciously applied Tico flavor makes up the menu here including gigantic shrimp, fish, filet mignon and prime rib. The half-in and half-out bar is also a prime place to chill with a cocktail (as late as 2:30am, if you're in that kind of mood).

Drinking & Entertainment

Despite the tourist influx, La Fortuna unfortunately remains a cultural wasteland. Occasionally, cultural events are advertised on flyers posted on store windows, though entertainment in the area tends to be more of the liquid kind, and is aimed more at locals looking to get hammered and hopefully score with a gringa.

Volcán Look (Map p169; ☎ 2479-9690; ⌚ 8pm-3am Wed-Sat) This club is reportedly Costa Rica's biggest discotheque outside of San José. It's about 5km west of town, though it's virtually abandoned except on weekends and holidays: don't bother showing up until after 11pm unless you want to dance *cumbia* alone. Cover charge (₡2000) for men.

Lava Lounge (Map p160; ☎ 2479-7365; Av Central btwn Calles 4 & 2; ⌚ until 10:30pm) On the west side of town, this cool spot has a few romantic tables at which you can gaze over your margarita into someone's eyes – but also, the food's good, the ambience is lively and it's a welcome addition to evenings in La Fortuna.

Don Rufino (Map p160; cnr Av Central & Calle 3; ⌚ until 2:30am) Mingle with locals and other travelers at this inviting streetside bar.

La Cascada (Map p160; ☎ 2479-9145; cnr Av Fort & Calle 1; ⌚ until 2am) This thatched-roof landmark is one of La Fortuna's more established places to have a beer at night.

Chelas (Map p160; ☎ 2479-9594; bocas ₡1600-2600; ⌚ 5pm-2am Mon-Fri, noon-midnight Sat) This popular open-air local bar behind Arenal Backpackers Resort has great *bocas* (small, savory dishes), including *chicharrones* (stewed pork) and *ceviche de pulpo* (raw octopus marinated in lemon juice). The best nights of the week to visit are Monday (karaoke) and Thursday (disco). Arenal Backpackers guests get a 10% discount just by asking.

Getting There & Away

BUS

All domestic buses stop at the Centro Comercial Adifort bus terminal (Av Arenal). The Tica Bus to Nicaragua (₡12,000) passes by El Tanque between 6:30am and 7am daily; to catch the bus you'll have to take an early taxi to El Tanque (15 minutes, ₡4500).

Keep an eye on your bags, particularly on the weekend San José run.

Ciudad Quesada (Auto-Transportes San José–San Carlos) ₡650; one hour; 15 departures per day from 5am to 7pm.
Monteverde ₡1400; six to eight hours; departs 8am (change at Tilarán at 12:30pm for Monteverde).
San José (Auto-Transportes San José–San Carlos) ₡1955; 4½ hours; departs 12:45pm and 2:45pm. Alternatively, take a bus to Ciudad Quesada and change to frequent buses to the capital.
Tilarán (Auto-Transportes Tilarán) ₡1100; 3½ hours; departs 8am and 5:30pm.

HORSEBACK

Several tour companies offer horseback-riding trips between La Fortuna and Monteverde. The trip (a combination of horse, taxi or boat) takes about five to seven hours and costs about US$85, including separate transport of your luggage. One highly recommended company is Desafío Adventure Company.

JEEP-BOAT-JEEP

The fastest route between Monteverde-Santa Elena and La Fortuna is the sexy-sounding jeep-boat-jeep combo (US$18 to US$25, three hours) – the 'jeep' is actually a minivan with the requisite yellow 'turismo' emblazoned on the side. Jeep or not, it's a terrific transportation option and can be arranged through almost any hotel or tour operator in either town. The minivan from La Fortuna takes you to Laguna de Arenal, meeting a boat that crosses the lake, where a 4WD taxi on the other side continues to Monteverde. This is increasingly becoming the primary transportation between La Fortuna and Monteverde as it's incredibly scenic, reasonably priced and it'll save you half a day of travel over rocky roads.

Getting Around

BICYCLE

Some hotels rent bikes to their guests, though **Bike Arenal** (Map p160; ☎ 8835-2877; www.bikearenal.com; Calle 3; half-/full day US$16/22, guided tours US$67-96; ⏲ 7:30am-6pm) has the best-maintained mountain and road bikes in town. It also offers guided bike tours, including beautiful rides to El Castillo and around Laguna de Arenal. Note that cycling after dark is illegal in La Fortuna.

The classic mountain-bike trip to La Catarata (about 7km from town) climbs to a fairly brutal, if nontechnical, last few kilometers, although we've heard stories of hardy pack-a-day smokers who've made it (just barely).

CAR

La Fortuna is easy to access by public transportation, but nearby attractions such as the hot springs, Parque Nacional Volcán Arenal and Laguna de Arenal require a bit more of an effort without internal combustion. Luckily, you can rent cars at **Alamo** (Map p160; ☎ 2479-9090; www.alamocostarica.com; cnr Av Central & Calle 2; ⏲ 7:30am-6pm) or **Adobe Rent a Car** (Map p160; ☎ 2478-7202; www.adobecar.com; ⏲ 7am-7pm), located behind the Rainforest Café.

PARQUE NACIONAL VOLCÁN ARENAL

Arenal was just another dormant volcano surrounded by fertile farmland from about AD 1500 until July 29, 1968, when something snapped. Huge explosions triggered lava flows that destroyed three villages, killing about 80 people and 45,000 cattle. The surrounding area was evacuated and roads throughout the region were closed. Eventually, the lava subsided to a relatively predictable flow and life got back to normal. Sort of.

Although it occasionally quietens down for a few weeks or even months, Arenal has been producing menacing ash columns, massive explosions and streamers of glowing molten rock almost daily since 1968. Miraculously, the volcano has retained its picture-perfect conical shape despite constant volcanic activity, though its slopes are now ashen instead of green.

The degree of activity varies from year to year and week to week – even from day to day. Sometimes there can be a spectacular display of flowing red-hot lava and incandescent rocks flying through the air; at other times the volcano subsides to a gentle glow. During the day, the lava isn't easy to see, but you might still see a great cloud of ash thrown up by a massive explosion. Between 1998 and 2000, the volcano was particularly active (which is when many of those spectacular photos you see in tourist brochures were taken), and while the lava of late hasn't been quite that photogenic, it's still an awe-inspiring show.

The best nighttime views of the volcano these days are from its southwestern side, which you can appreciate by taking a night tour or by spending the night at either the Arenal Observatory Lodge (p173) or one of several accommodations in El Castillo (see p174). However, be aware that clouds can cover the volcano at any time, and on rainy days a tour can be a miserably cold affair – thank goodness for all those hot springs nearby!

Orientation & Information

The **ranger station** (Map p169; ☎ 2461-8499; admission to the park US$10; ⏲ 8am-4pm) is on the western side of the volcano. Most people arrive as part of a group tour, but you can reach it independently. To get here by car, head west from La Fortuna for 15km, then turn left at the 'Parque Nacional' sign, and take the 2km good dirt road to the entrance on the left side of the road. You can also take an 8am bus toward Tilarán (tell the driver to drop you off at the park) and catch the 2pm bus back to La Fortuna.

The ranger station complex includes an information center and parking lot. From here, trails lead 3.4km toward the volcano. Rangers will tell you how far you are allowed to go. At the time of writing, this area was not in a danger zone.

If you are heading to Arenal Observatory Lodge, continue driving on the dirt road. About 3km past the ranger station you will come to a small one-lane bridge and parking area; this is a popular (and free) night lava-viewing spot. Shortly after you cross the bridge, you'll reach a fork in the road; left goes to Arenal Observatory Lodge and right goes to the village of El Castillo. Turn left and continue 2.6km to reach the lodge. You'll first pay a US$2 entry fee at the front gate. This steep, hard-packed gravel and partially paved road is fine for most vehicles, but a 4WD is recommended.

A taxi from La Fortuna to either the lodge or to El Castillo will cost about US$25.

Sights & Activities

Arenal was made a national park in 1995, and it is part of the Area de Conservación Arenal, which protects most of the Cordillera de Tilarán. This area is rugged and varied, and the biodiversity is high; roughly half the species of land-dwelling vertebrates (birds, mammals, reptiles and amphibians) known in Costa Rica can be found here.

Birdlife is very rich in the park, and includes such specialties as trogons, rufous motmots, fruitcrows and lancebills. Commonly sighted mammals include howler monkeys, white-faced capuchins and surprisingly tame coatis (though it's tempting, don't feed the wild animals).

ARENAL OBSERVATORY LODGE

The **Arenal Observatory Lodge** (Map p169; ☎ reservations 2290-7011, lodge 2479-1070; www.arenalobservatorylodge.com; day pass per person US$4; Ⓟ) was built in 1987 as a private observatory for the Universidad de Costa Rica. Scientists chose to construct the lodge on a macadamia-nut farm on the south side of Volcán Arenal due to its proximity to the volcano (only 2km away) and its relatively safe location on a ridge. Since its creation, volcanologists from all over the world, including researchers from the Smithsonian Institute in Washington, DC, have come to study the active volcano. Today, the majority of visitors are tourists, though scientists regularly visit the lodge, and a seismograph in the hotel continues to operate around the clock. The lodge is also the only place inside the park where you can legally bed down.

The lodge offers massages (from US$60), guided hikes and all the usual tours at good prices. You can swim in the pool, wander around the macadamia-nut farm or investigate the pine forest that makes up about half of the 347-hectare site. You can also rent horses for US$8 per hour.

A tiny **museum** (admission free) on the old observation deck has a seismograph and some cool newspaper clippings.

HIKING

From the ranger station (which has trail maps available), you can hike the 1km circular **Sendero Los Heliconias**, which passes by the site of the 1968 lava flow (vegetation here is slowly sprouting back to life). A 1.5km-long path branches off this trail and leads to an overlook, where you might hear the growling sounds of Arenal volcano.

The **Sendero Las Coladas** also branches off the Heliconias trail, and wraps around the volcano for 2km past the 1993 lava flow before connecting with the **Sendero Los Tucanes** (US$4). This trail extends for another 3km through the tropical rainforest at the base of the volcano. To return to the car-parking area, you will have to turn back. You'll get good views of the summit on the way back since you're now at a better angle to view it.

From the park headquarters (not the ranger station), there is also the 1.2km **Sendero Los Miradores**, which leads you down to the shores of the lake, and provides a good angle for viewing the volcano.

Near the highway turnoff to the park, there are two other trail systems worth checking out. The newest is **Arenal 1968** (Map p169; ☎ 2462-1212; www.arenal1968.com; adult/child under 10yr US$7/free; 🕑 7am-10pm), a system of trails and lookouts along the original 1968 lava flow. It's located 1.2km from the turnoff, just before the ranger station. Just before the turnoff, **Mirador El Silencio** (Map p169; adult/child under 7yr US$6/free; 🕑 7am-9pm) is a private 556-acre nature reserve with four hiking trails.

Every once in a while, perhaps lulled into a sense of false security by a temporary pause in the activity, someone tries to climb to the crater and peer within it. This is very dangerous – climbers have been killed and maimed by explosions. The problem is not so much that the climber gets killed (that's a risk the foolhardy insist is their own decision) but rather that the lives of Costa Rican rescuers are placed at risk.

If you're not staying at Arenal Observatory Lodge, it's worth visiting as there are 6km of **trails** in total. A handful of short hikes include views of a nearby waterfall, while sturdy souls could check out recent lava flows (2½ hours), old lava flows (three hours) or the climb to Arenal's dormant partner, Volcán Chato, whose crater holds an 1100m-high lake only 3km southeast of Volcán Arenal (four hours). For the best nighttime views, a guided hike is

FEELIN' HOT, HOT, HOT!

Volcanoes are formed over millennia as a result of the normal shifting processes of the earth's crust. For example, when oceanic crust slides against continental crust, the higher-density oceanic crust is pushed into a deep region of the earth known as the asthenosphere. This process, along with friction, melts the rocky crust to form magma, which rises through weak areas in the continental crust due to its comparatively light density. Magma tends to collect in a chamber below the earth's crust until increasing pressure forces it upward through a vent and onto the surface as lava. Over time, lava deposits can form large, conical volcanoes with a circular crater at the apex from which magma can escape in the form of gas, lava and ejecta.

Although our understanding of volcanoes has greatly progressed in the past few decades, scientists are still unable to predict a volcanic eruption with certainty. However, it is possible to monitor three phenomena – seismicity, gas emissions and ground deformation – in order to predict the likelihood of a volcanic eruption. Seismicity refers to the ongoing seismic activity that tends to accompany active volcanoes. For example, most active volcanoes have continually recurring low-level seismic activity. Although patterns of activity are difficult to interpret, generally an increase in seismic activity (which often appears as a harmonic tremor) is a sign that an eruption is likely to occur.

Scientists also routinely monitor the composition of gas emissions as erupting magma undergoes a pressure decrease that can produce a large quantity of volcanic gases. For example, sulfur dioxide is one of the main components of volcanic gases, and an increasing airborne amount of this compound is another sign of an impending eruption. Finally, scientists routinely measure the tilt of slope and changes in the rate of swelling of active volcanoes. These measurements are indicators of ground deformation, which is caused by an increase in subterranean pressure due to large volumes of collecting magma.

Since Volcán Arenal is considered by scientists to be one of the 10 most active volcanoes in the entire world, comprehensive monitoring of the volcano occurs daily. Although there is constant activity and frequent eruptions, nothing has thus far rivaled the deadly 1968 eruption. In recent years, the lava flow switched directions to the southwest (much to the chagrin of hotel owners in La Fortuna), though scientists are predicting that the flow might reverse itself in years to come.

suggested. Maps and local English-speaking guides are available for these hikes. The lodge also has a 4.5km bike trail that winds through secondary forest, as well as a 1km sidewalk trail that is completely wheelchair-accessible.

Note that camping is not allowed inside the park, though people do camp (no facilities) off some of the unpaved roads west of the volcano by the shores of the lake.

Sleeping & Eating

Arenal Observatory Lodge (Map p169; ☎ 2479-1070, 2290-7011; www.arenalobservatorylodge.com; La Casona s/d/tr/q US$74/87/103/116, standard r US$104/118/125/147, Smithsonian r US$134/154/163/174, junior ste US$167/175/183/193, White Hawk Villa for 8 people US$511, all incl breakfast; P ⊠ 💻 🏊 ♿) Although most of the lava flows are on the southwest side of Arenal (the lodge is positioned to the west), the views of the eruptions are excellent, and the constant rumbling is enough to make you sleep a bit uneasily at night. The lodge has a variety of rooms spread throughout the property, five of which are wheelchair-accessible (along with the pool and several trails – this lodge hasn't slouched). Rates include a buffet breakfast and guided hike. La Casona is about 500m away in the original farmhouse. It now houses four rustic double rooms sharing two bathrooms; there are volcano views from the house porch. Standard rooms, adjacent to the main lodge, were originally designed for researchers but have been renovated to acceptably plush standards. Smithsonian rooms, accessible via a suspension bridge over a plunging ravine, are the best and have the finest views. The White Hawk Villa, with a kitchen and several rooms, is perfect for groups.

The restaurant (lunch/dinner mains ₡6000 to ₡25,000), though overpriced, has a good variety of international dishes and is decorated with jars of venomous snakes in formaldehyde.

EL CASTILLO

The tiny mountain village of El Castillo is a wonderful alternative to staying in La Fortuna – it's bucolic, untouristed and perfectly situated to watch the southwesterly lava flows. There are also some delightful accommodations options, and a number of worthwhile sights. Unfortunately you'll need your own wheels as no buses serve this lovely little enclave.

On the road to El Castillo, **SkyTrek** (Map p169; ☎ 2645-7070; www.skytrek.com; adult/student/child tram only US$55/44/28, canopy tour US$66/52/42; 7:30am-4pm) runs canopy tours on the south side of Arenal. This canopy tour gives stellar views of Laguna de Arenal, the volcano and the lush rainforest. A silent gondola (the SkyTram) slowly conveys visitors up above the canopy, and at the top you can either tram it back down or fly down the zip lines.

On the only road in town, you'll find two noteworthy ecological attractions. The **El Castillo-Arenal Butterfly Conservatory** (☎ 2479-1149; www.butterflyconservatory.org; with/without guide US$10/8; 8am-4pm) is run by an American expat named Glenn, whose conservation project far exceeds your normal butterfly garden. He is seeking to understand life cycles and hatching times for different species, and routinely works with students and volunteers to rigorously catalog every scrap of data. Here you'll find seven different gardens pertaining to each habitat as well as a ranarium, an insect museum, a medicinal herb garden, botanic garden trails and a river walk. The conservatory has one of the largest butterfly exhibitions in Costa Rica, and is one of the few places that raises all of the butterflies and frogs on exhibit. The center proportionally releases these species for repopulating habitats within the area. Glenn is also actively involved in local reforestation programs, and is always looking for a few good volunteers.

Next door is the **Arenal EcoZoo** (☎ 2479-1059; www.arenalecozoo.com; admission adult/child US$13/10; 8:30am-5:30pm), where local snake-handler Victor Hugo Quesada will introduce you to some of the most dangerous snakes in the world like Eliza, a 3.8m-long Burmese python. Victor will also demonstrate how to handle and milk a venomous snake. The EcoZoo, more commonly known as El Serpentario, is also home to many frogs, lizards, iguanas, turtles, scorpions, tarantulas and butterflies.

Sleeping & Eating

If you've got your tent, you can pitch it for free on the shores of Arenal Lake. Across the street from Templo Cristiano church, just before Pizza John's Jardín Escondido, a dirt road leads down to a beautiful lakeside spot with priceless volcano views.

OUR PICK **Essence Arenal** (☎ 2479-1131; www.essencearenal.com; dm US$16, d with/without bathroom US$43/32; P) Perched on an 100-acre hilltop with incredible volcano and lake views, this 'boutique hostel' is one of the most exciting new projects in the Arenal region. Essence owners Nico and Kelly have created the perfect budget resort. The basic but clean rooms have orthopedic mattresses and hypo-allergenic pillows. Common area amenities include a fireplace and Japanese soaking tub, cable TV, video games, movie nights, laundry service, cafeteria, hiking trails and small pool with killer views of the lava flows. Possibly the best reason to stay is the onsite restaurant, Essence Demo Cuisine. Resident gourmet chef Isaac Weliver of Chicago lovingly prepares all-vegetarian meals (US$10) right before your eyes. Guests are encouraged to take part in the creation of dishes that will delight even the most hardcore carnivore. It's not easy getting here, but it's well worth the trip. After crossing the bridge into El Castillo, turn left towards the Butterfly Conservatory and go 1km uphill; a 4WD is required. The hostel can provide transportation from La Fortuna. English, French, Spanish and German are spoken.

Cabinitas El Castillo Dorado (☎ 2479-1146; cabinitaselcastillo@hotmail.com; s/d US$40/55; P) Here you'll find simple cabins with private warm-water bathrooms and volcano views through enormous picture windows. The onsite restaurant (mains ₡1100 to ₡3500) is recommended for its fresh tilapia and, needless to say, great vistas.

Hummingbird Nest B&B (☎ 8835-8711, 2479-1174; www.hummingbirdnestbb.com; s/d incl breakfast US$50/75, 2-night minimum; P) At the entrance to town, you'll see a small path that leads up the (steep) hill to one of our favorite B&Bs in all of Costa Rica. It's owned by Ellen, a former Pan Am stewardess and all-round world traveler who has finally found a small slice of paradise to call her own. Her quaint little home has two guest bedrooms with private hot showers and enough frilly pillows to make you miss home – but that's not even the best part! In her immaculately landscaped front garden, you can soak the night away in a huge outdoor Jacuzzi while watching the lava flow down Arenal. You can even arrange to have a massage (US$45) while watching the lava. Ellen (who's also charming and full of grace) is active in the local schools, and is a good person to talk to about volunteering in the area.

Hotel Linda Vista del Norte (☎ 2479-1551; www.hotellindavista.com; s/d standard US$66/76, ste US$112-146, all incl breakfast; P) The first accommodations you'll pass on the road into town is a lodge consisting of 25 rooms with smashing views, perched high on a mountaintop. The dated rooms were being remodeled during our recent visit. Even better is the restaurant-bar (mains ₡5500 to ₡8500), lined with picture windows for spectacular views of the Arenal lava flows. There's also a small infinity pool with swim-up bar.

Rancho Margot (☎ 2479-7259; www.ranchomargot.org; P) Like many projects in Costa Rica, Rancho Margot began with such promise. The goal was to create a completely self-sufficient organic farm and resort lodge. Unfortunately, we've received many complaints from readers and locals alike, coupled with our own recent experience, and we can no longer recommend staying here. However, day-trippers might be interested in visiting for the many activities on offer including horseback riding, mountain biking, rappelling, kayaking, yoga and fishing.

our pick **Pizza John's Jardín Escondido** (☎ 2479-1155; mains ₡2500-4250; noon-9pm) On the road to Rancho Margot, look for the small sign leading to this lovely pizzeria hidden at the end of a grassy alley. The intimate, two-story structure is covered in graffiti left by international visitors to this hidden garden. Owner John DiVita of Los Angeles is lively and entertaining, and he'll have you in stitches with stories about his past life as a punk rocker and his escape from corporate America. John – a second-generation pizza-maker – cooks up an awesome pizza pie and also whips up delicious homemade ice cream. He unapologetically proclaims, 'I clog arteries, and I'm proud of it.'

LAGUNA DE ARENAL AREA

About 18km west of La Fortuna, you'll arrive at a 750m-long causeway across the dam that created Laguna de Arenal, an 88-sq-km lake that is the largest in the country. Although a number of small towns were submerged during the lake's creation, the lake currently supplies valuable water to Guanacaste, and produces hydroelectricity for the region. High winds also produce power with the aid of huge, steel windmills, though windsurfers and kitesurfers frequently steal a breeze or two.

If you have your own car (or bicycle), this is one of the premier road trips in Costa Rica. The road is lined with odd and elegant businesses, many run by foreigners who have fallen in love with the place, and the scenic views of lakeside forests and Volcán Arenal are about as romantic as they come. Strong winds and high elevations give the lake a temperate feel, and you'll be forgiven if you suddenly imagine yourself in the English Lakes District or the Swiss countryside.

But, things are changing – quickly. Baby boomers, lured to the area by the cool climate and premier fishing, are snapping up every spot of land with a 'For Sale' sign on it. Costa Rican law does not require would-be-realtors to possess a valid real-estate license, and there's been heavy foreign investment in the region. Costa Ricans are not happy about the impending loss of their lakeside paradise, and it doesn't seem likely that the construction boom is going to slow.

Most of the road is paved and in decent condition, though you'll encounter some big potholes. Buses run about every two hours, and hotel owners can tell you when to catch your ride. If you're heading to Monteverde via the jeep-boat-jeep transfer, you're in for a lovely ride.

Dam to Nuevo Arenal

This beautiful stretch of road is lined on both sides with cloud forest, and there are a number of fantastic accommodations strung along the way.

AROUND THE DAM

Unlike the fly-by view you'll get on a zip-line canopy tour, a walk through **Puentes Colgantes de Arenal** (Arenal Hanging Bridges; Map p169; ☎ 2479-1128; www.hangingbridges.com; adult/student/child under 12yr US$22/12/free; 7:30am-4:30pm) allows you to explore the rainforest and canopy from trails and suspended bridges at a more natural and peaceful pace. Reservations are required for guided bird-watching tours (three hours, from 6am) or informative naturalist tours (8am and 2pm).

The bridges are easily accessible by car and well signed, though most tourists arrive on a package tour from La Fortuna. The Tilarán bus can drop you off at the entrance, but it's a 3km climb from the bus stop.

If you want to stay in the area, **Arenal Lodge** (Map p169; ☎ 2290-4232; www.arenallodge.com; d standard US$88, superior US$124, junior ste US$155, chalet US$161, matrimonial ste US$185, all incl breakfast; P) is 400m west of the dam, at the top of a steep 2.5km ascent, though the entire lodge is awash with views of Arenal and the surrounding cloud forest. Standard rooms are just that, but junior suites are spacious, tiled and have wicker furniture, a big hot-water bathroom and a picture window or balcony with volcano views. Ten chalets sleep four and have kitchenette and good views. The lodge also has a Jacuzzi, a billiards room, a sophisticated restaurant (mains ₡4000 to ₡9000), complimentary mountain bikes and private stables.

Alternatively, **Lost Iguana Resort** (Map p169; ☎ 2267-6148, 2479-1331; www.lostiguanaresort.com; r US$215-300, ste US$300-535, casitas US$460, all incl breakfast; P) is easily the area's most stylish place to lay your head. This resort occupies a serene mountainside that affords phenomenal volcano views, sequestered far from the activity in La Fortuna. Even the standard rooms have private balconies looking out on Arenal, beds boasting Egyptian cotton sheets, satellite TV, and an invaluable sense of peace and privacy. Surrounded by rainforest, the rooms are tastefully decorated with bamboo furniture, open-beamed ceilings and large windows. Reception and restaurant areas are romantic enough to appeal, even if leaving your cozy *casita* seems a tragedy.

UNIÓN AREA

Attractions below are listed in order of their distance from the dam.

You can't miss **Hotel Los Héroes** (☎ 2692-8012/3; www.hotellosheroes.com; d with/without balcony US$65/55, tr US$80, apt US$115, all incl breakfast; P), a slightly incongruous alpine chalet 13.5km west of the dam, complete with carved wooden balconies and Old World window shutters – and that's just on the outside. Large, immaculate rooms with wood paneling and hot-water bathrooms are decorated with thickly hewn wood furniture that may make Swiss-Germans a little homesick, particularly when viewing paintings of tow-headed children in lederhosen smooching innocently. There are also two apartments (each sleeps up to five) with full kitchen, huge bathroom and balcony overlooking the lake. Facilities include a Jacuzzi, swimming pool, a church complete with Swiss chimes, and a restaurant (mains ₡3000 to ₡7000; open from 7:30am to 4pm and 6pm to 8:30pm) that allows Swiss folks who've been on the road too long to indulge in authentic *Zürcher Geschnetzeltes* (Zurich-style veal served over potatoes) and fondues. Former US President Jimmy Carter once dined here. The owners have even built a miniature train (₡5500) that brings you up a hill to an underground station beneath the Rondorama Panoramic Restaurant (mains ₡5000 to ₡10,000), a revolving restaurant (seriously!) that's reportedly one-of-a-kind in Central America. There's also a hiking trail that leads to the restaurant and is great for wildlife-watching. English, German, French, Spanish and Portuguese are spoken.

Rates for the simply gorgeous two-person cottages – works of art, really – at **La Mansion Inn Arenal** (☎ 2692-8018; www.lamansionarenal.com; cottages incl breakfast US$204-640; P) also include a champagne breakfast, fruit basket, welcome cocktail, canoe access and horse rides, all conspiring with the magnificent views to make this the most romantic inn in the region. The cottages feature huge split-level rooms with private terrace, lake view, high ceiling, Italianate painted walls and arched, bathroom doors. There's also an ornamental garden featuring Chorotega pottery, an infinity swimming pool that appears to flow into the lake, a pool table, a formal restaurant (four-course dinner excluding wine US$22 to US$38) and a cozy bar shaped like the bow of a ship. It's 15.5km west of the dam.

Indio Pelado (Bald Indian; ☎ 2692-8036; mains ₡2800-6000; 11am-11pm) If you can get past the politically incorrect name, this roadside restaurant cooks up a great pizza in their wood-fired oven, plus pastas and steaks. It's perched on a steep hill with lake views. There are also 10 basic rooms for rent (doubles US$30) with private bathroom, hot water and patio with views. It's 17.4km west of the dam.

A serene, German-run escape, **La Ceiba Tree Lodge** (☎ 2692-8050, 8814-4004; www.ceibatree-lodge.com; d US$84; P) is 22km west of the dam and centered on a 500-year-old ceiba tree. Its five spacious, cross-ventilated rooms are entered through Maya-inspired carved doors and decorated with original paintings. Views of Laguna de Arenal, the lush, tropical gardens and utterly lovely dining-hangout area make this mountaintop spot a tranquil retreat from whatever ails you. A small apartment (price negotiable) is also available for rent

Another accommodation option is **Villa Decary B&B** (☎ 2694-4330, from US or Canada 1-800-556-0505; www.villadecary.com; r US$99, casitas with kitchen US$129-149, extra person US$15, all incl breakfast; P), an all-round winner with bright, spacious, well-furnished rooms, delicious full breakfasts and fantastic hosts. Five rooms have private hot shower, a queen and a double bed, bright Latin American bedspreads and artwork. They also have balconies with excellent views of the woodland immediately below and the lake just beyond. There are also three separate *casitas* with a kitchenette. Paths into the woods behind the house give good opportunities for bird-watching and wildlife-watching, and there's a good chance that howler monkeys will wake you in the morning. Guests can borrow binoculars and a bird guide to identify what they see. Decaray (named for a French botanist who discovered a new species of palm) also boasts one of the best collections of palm trees in Costa Rica. The American-owned B&B is family-friendly and gay-friendly. It's 24.5km west of the dam, and 2km east of Nuevo Arenal.

If you're a gourmand suffering from a lack of memorable cuisine, make absolutely sure to book dinner reservations at the **Gingerbread Hotel & Restaurant** (☎ 2694-0039, 8351-7815; www.gingerbreadarenal.com; r incl breakfast US$100; 5-9pm Tue-Sat, lunch by reservation only), arguably the best restaurant in northwestern Costa Rica (if not the entire country). Better yet, stay at the charming boutique hotel, where the beds are sumptuous and the rooms adorned with murals by renowned local artists – this way, you'll get homemade preserves and pastries at breakfast. With the freshest local fare providing the foundation of his weekly menus, Chef Eyal turns out transcendent meals (mains US$9 to US$40, wines US$30 to US$200) and is choosy about his wine list, emphasizing top Chilean and Spanish vino. And yet there's no pretension in this very cozy, out-of-the-way, lake-view dining room with walls covered in paintings by artists in the community (including manager Coryn). A word to the wise: do not pass up dessert. And come prepared – credit cards are not accepted.

Nuevo Arenal

The only good-sized town between La Fortuna and Tilarán is the small Tico settlement of Nuevo Arenal, which is 27km west of the dam, or one hour drive from La Fortuna. In case you were wondering what happened to the old Arenal (no, it wasn't wiped out by the volcano), it's about 27m below the surface of Laguna de Arenal. In order to create a large enough reservoir for the dam, the Costa Rican government had to make certain, er, sacrifices, which ultimately resulted in the forced relocation of 3500 people. Today, the humble residents of Nuevo Arenal don't seem to be fazed by history, especially since they now own premium lakeside property.

Nuevo Arenal is something of a rest stop for travelers heading to Tilarán and points beyond, though it's certainly a pleasant (and cheap) place to spend the night. The tiny downtown also has a gas station, a Banco de Costa Rica, SuperCompro and a bus stop near the park.

SLEEPING & EATING

Cabinas Catalina (☎ 8819-6793; d US$18; P) Across from the gas station, find these budget digs which consist of sterile *cabinas* with concrete walls and warmish showers that will do in a pinch. The onsite restaurant, Moya's Place, serves pizza and other local favorites.

Aurora Hotel (☎ 2694-4071; r with/without views US$30/20; P) With spectacular volcano and lake views, this American-run hotel on the east side of the square has simple but clean rooms with hot-water bathroom, cable TV and patio. Amenities include a pool, Jacuzzi and sauna. The hotel also houses the office of Paradise Adventures; owner Jonathan can arrange wakeboarding trips and other water sports.

Bar y Restaurant Bambú (☎ 2694-4048; mains ₡1100-3500; 6am-10pm) In addition to doing good *casados* and *gallos* (not to mention another round of beer on Friday night when there's live music), the owner has tourist information and can arrange fishing trips, guided hikes and horseback rides.

Lava Java (☎ 2694-4753; mains ₡4000-9000; 6am-8:30pm;) Check your email here (₡500 per hour) on the main road as you sip a fresh smoothie or slurp down a quick coffee. Lunch and dinner are also served.

Restaurant La Casa de Doña Celina (☎ 2694-4609; mains ₡2200-5000; 7am-9pm) This is just your basic *soda*, next door to Lava Java, but the views make your lunch taste better, as do the retro diner tables on the patio, and you can work up your appetite with a game of pinball.

Rumours Bar & Grill (☎ 8330-4123; mains ₡2200-3500; 11am-midnight) Next door to Banco de Costa Rica, this loud restaurant is popular with gringos and Ticos alike. The menu features American and Tex-Mex favorites like hamburgers, chile con carne, quesadillas and grilled cheese sandwiches.

Tom's Pan (☎ 2694-4547; mains ₡4500-8000; 7am-4pm Mon-Sat; P) Better known as 'the German Bakery,' this slightly overrated landmark is a famous rest stop for road-trippers heading to Tilarán. Its breads, strudels and cakes are all homemade and delicious, though heartier eaters will rave over the big German breakfasts, goulash with homemade noodles, spätzle, bratwurst, weisswurst and real German beer.

Nuevo Arenal to Tilarán

Continue west and around the lake from Nuevo Arenal, where the scenery becomes even more spectacular just as the road gets progressively worse. Tilarán is the next 'big' city, with a reasonable selection of hotels and restaurants, plus roads and buses that can take you to Liberia, Monteverde or beyond.

SLEEPING & EATING

All attractions below are listed in order of their distance from Nuevo Arenal.

Agua Inn (☎ 2694-4818, 8981-4735; www.aguainn.com; d incl breakfast US$78, apt US$141; P) The sounds of nature will lull you to sleep at this intimate B&B on the banks of the raging Río Cote that overlooks a primary rainforest and beautiful pool. Four rooms in a kaleidoscope of colors all featuring full-sized comfy beds, fan, hot-water bathroom and tiled floors. There's also a one-bedroom apartment with full kitchen (three nights minimum) and a studio with a kitchen. Nearby, a great hiking trail follows the old road to Laguna de Arenal. Ask Californian owner Trent Deushane about his days as a tour bus driver for such acts as the Rolling Stones and Alicia Keys. It's 2.5km west of Nuevo Arenal down a very steep dirt road.

Chalet Nicholas (☎ 2694-4041; www.chaletnicholas.com; d incl breakfast US$79, extra person US$15; P) This attractive mountain chalet 2.7km west of Nuevo Arenal is owned by Catherine and John Nicholas, though their co-owners, five very playful Great Danes (don't be alarmed when they come bounding out to greet you) really know how to steal the show. Two downstairs rooms have private bathroom, while the upstairs loft has two linked bedrooms (for families or groups) and shares a downstairs bathroom. On clear days, all rooms have views of the volcano at the end of the lake. The owners enjoy natural history and have a living collection of dozens of orchids, which attract numerous species of birds. This place has many repeat guests.

Lucky Bug B&B & Caballo Negro Restaurant (☎ 2694-4515; www.luckybugcr.com; r incl breakfast US$69-120; P V) Set on a rainforest lagoon, the bungalows at the Lucky Bug are not only blissfully isolated but feature unique art and decorative details by local artisans. The Caballo Negro (Black Horse; mains US$8 to US$14; open 8am to 8pm) serves excellent organic, vegetarian and European fare handcrafted by owner Monica, who speaks English and German and makes a mean schnitzel. Also here is the fabulously quirky Lucky Bug Gallery, which features high-quality work from local and national artisans, not least of whom are Monica's triplets Kathryn, Alexandra and Sabrina. The artistry really is outstanding, and should you fall in love with a painting of a bug or something bigger, they can ship it for you. It's 3km west of Nuevo Arenal.

Lago Coter Ecolodge (☎ 2440-6768; www.ecolodgecostarica.com; s/d/tr standard US$76/87/99, cabin US$93/105/122, all incl breakfast; P) This environmentally friendly lodge caters mostly to visitors that come on a complete package, including meals, rental equipment and guided naturalist hikes. Built in 1990 with an endowment from the World Bank, the hotel is committed to preserving its 250 hectares of primary-forest private reserve and 50 hectares of secondary-growth forest and pastures. Standard rooms with hot-water shower are in a handsome wood-and-stone lodge that has a large fireplace and a relaxation area with billiards, TV and a small library. There are also 14 larger cabins that have picture windows overlooking the lake. Go 4.5km west of Nuevo Arenal then turn 3km down an unpaved road.

La Rana de Arenal (☎ 2694-4031; www.dorislakearenal.com; s/d incl breakfast US$30/45; P) Watch out for the hairpin turnoff at the driveway to La Rana, a quaint German-run spot with seven comfortable rooms. The restaurant

WORLD-CLASS WIND

Some of the world's most consistent winds blow across northwestern Costa Rica, and this consistency attracts windsurfers from all over the world. Laguna de Arenal is rated one of the three best windsurfing spots in the world, mainly because of the predictability of the winds. From December to April, the winds reliably provide great rides for board sailors who gather on the southwest corner of the lake for long days of fun on the water. Windsurfing is possible in other months, too, but avoid September and October, which are considered the worst.

Although there are plenty of fly-by-night operators, there are really only two places you should consider for all your surfing needs. The best company for windsurfing is **Tico Wind** (☎ 2692-2002, 8813-7274; www.ticowind.com; rentals half-day US$42, full-day incl lunch US$78, lessons per hr US$50), which sets up a camp on the western shores of the lake each year from late November to late April. It has state-of-the-art boards and sails that are replaced every year, with different equipment to suit different wind conditions and client experience. First-timers should consider the 'Get on Board' package (US$120). Lessons are offered in English, Spanish, German, Italian and Portuguese. The launch area is located 15km west of Nuevo Arenal, about 400m after the Equus Bar-Restaurant. The entrance is by the big white chain link fence with 'ICE' painted on it, then follow the dirt road 1km to the lake shore. Staff can also help book accommodations and transportation.

Hotel Tilawa (see p180) has emerged as a popular destination for windsurfers (and increasingly kitesurfers, too), and has an excellent selection of sailboards for rent at comparable rates. Although some folks think that the high winds, waves and world-class conditions are too much for a beginner to handle, the folks at Tilawa disagree. They run the reader-recommended **Tilawa Windsurf Center** (www.windsurfcostarica.com; half-/full day US$100/150), offering windsurfing and kitesurfing lessons. After the first day, lessons become more expensive (US$60 per hour) and cater to all skill levels – once you've learned the basics, self motivated practice with short instructional periods is the best way to learn. If you're staying at the hotel, you can also take advantage of discount rates on rental equipment (half-/full day US$45/55).

Laguna de Arenal is also now attracting wakeboarders. **Paradise Adventures Costa Rica** (☎ 8856-3618; www.paradise-adventures-costa-rica.com; per hr US$150), based at the Aurora Hotel in Nuevo Arenal (p177), has the latest wakeboarding equipment. Rates are for up to seven people including equipment, lessons and boat ride. Owner Jonathan can create a variety of tailored packages, including leisure boat rides.

It gets a little chilly on Laguna de Arenal, and rentals usually include wet suits, as well as harnesses and helmet. For a warm change, head up to Bahía Salinas on Costa Rica's far northwestern coast. Resorts here offer windsurfing year-round, and though the wind may not be quite as world class as at Laguna de Arenal, it comes pretty close. The seasons are the same as for the lake.

(mains US$6 to US$11; open from 11am to 10pm) serves good international food, with an emphasis on German cuisine, in an airy upstairs pub-style dining room. There are tennis courts on the property, which is excellent for bird-watching, and the staff can arrange horseback and boat tours. It's 5.7km from Nuevo Arenal.

our pick **Café y Macadamia de Costa Rica** (☎ 2692-2000; cafeymacadamia@yahoo.com; pastries & coffee ₡1000-2000, mains ₡1200-4500; ⌚ 8:30am-5pm) Pull over for a cup of coffee – and maybe a salad or Thai chicken curry, and leave room for a tasty pastry – all best savored along with the spectacular views of the lake (or clouds and fog, as the weather dictates). The gigantic, wood-floored room and equally large outdoor terrace alone make it worth a stop to stretch your legs. It's 10.5km west of Nuevo Arenal.

Casa Delagua (☎ 2692-2101; mains ₡1000-4000; ⌚ 6am-5:30pm) Two parts art gallery, one part music and bookstore, and one part cafe, this cool roadside shop is worth a detour to check out the amazing works by local artist Juan Carlos Ruiz. The restaurant serves breakfast and lunch specials including salads, fish and fajitas. It's 15km west of Nuevo Arenal.

Equus Bar-Restaurant (⌚ 3-9pm Fri, 11am-10pm Sat, 11am-9pm Sun) This lakeside spot 14.5km west of Nuevo Arenal is perennially popular among windsurfers looking to brag about their exploits over a cold Imperial. There's a good mix of Costa Rican and Western dishes, and on some nights there's live music here.

Mystica Resort (☎ 2692-1001; www.mysticaretreat.com; s/d incl breakfast US$96/116, villas US$226; P) About 15km west of Nuevo Arenal, this Mediterranean-style retreat lies on a hill 1km after the Tierras Morenas turnoff, and is another good midrange option. The resort has several comfortable, colorful rooms with blue tiles, vibrant woven bedspreads, hot showers and volcano views. Even if you're not staying here, it's a great place to stop for a wood-fired pizza lunch (mains ₡2500 to ₡5000, open from noon to 9pm). The Essence, a yoga and meditation center, is on the grounds for all your holistic-healing needs (treatments US$55 to US$60).

Hotel Tilawa (☎ 2695-5050; www.hotel-tilawa.com; d US$68-98; P) It's something of a legend among windsurfers and kitesurfers, and whether you're semiprofessional or just starting out, you'll find a great community of wind warriors here. As for the rooms, well, they're definitely spacious and they cater to different budgets, though the Grecian theme – frescoes and all – is sort of over the top. Tilawa also has the best collection of amenities on the lake, including a huge skateboard park, pool, tennis courts and free bike rental. It's 20km west of Nuevo Arenal.

TILARÁN

pop 7300

Near the southwestern end of Laguna de Arenal, the small town of Tilarán has a prosperous air to it – probably because it has served as a regional ranching center since long before there was a lake to speak of. Every year, this tradition is honored on the last weekend in April with a rodeo that's popular with Tico visitors, and on June 13 with a bullfight-filled fiesta that's dedicated to patron San Antonio.

Because it's situated on the slopes of the Cordillera de Tilarán, this little hub is a much cooler alternative (in climate and atmosphere) to, say, Cañas, and makes a pleasant stop between La Fortuna and Monteverde.

The city also boasts several supermarkets, ATMs, gas stations and internet cafes. Check email while waiting for your bus at **Cybercafé Tilarán** (☎ 2695-9010; per hr ₡600; 9am-10pm Mon-Sat), 25m west of the bus terminal.

If you're passing through here on your way to Monteverde, take a detour to visit **Viento Fresco Waterfalls** (☎ 2695-3434; www.vientofresco.net; adult/student/child 6-12yr US$15/12/10; 7:30am-5pm), a series of five cascades including the amazing Arco Iris (Rainbow Falls), which drops 75m into a refreshing shallow pool that's perfect for swimming. You can also pitch a tent here (US$20 per person, including park admission) or take a horseback-riding tour (US$65 including lunch, three hours). It's located 11km south of Tilarán on the road to Santa Elena/Monteverde.

Sleeping & Eating

All of the hotels listed below have private warm(ish) showers.

Hotel Tilarán (☎ 2695-5043; r with/without bathroom US11/7; P) If you can get one of the rooms toward the back, this is a decent budget choice on the west side of Parque Central. The tiny rooms have cable TV and are clean enough to lay your head for a night.

Hotel Mary (☎ 2695-5479; per person US$21; P) On the south side of Parque Central, Hotel Mary is an excellent option with clean rooms that feature the kind of linens your grandma would love. Plan on street noise in the parkside rooms, or just enjoy it from the balcony. The attached restaurant (mains ₡1500 to ₡3500; open from 6am to midnight) has a mix of some Tico and Chinese favorites.

Hotel El Sueño (☎ 2695-5347; s/d standard US$20/30, with balcony US$25/35) Near the bus terminal, this beautiful hotel (in an ageing, baroque sort of way) has antique decorated rooms, but it's worth splurging for the balcony, where you can bask in the faded glory. Downstairs is Restaurante El Parque (☎ 2695-5425; mains ₡1600 to ₡3000; open from 7am to 11pm) with a selection of *bocas* that discriminating barflies also appreciate.

Hotel La Carreta (☎ 2695-6593; www.lacarretacr.com; s/d incl breakfast US$40/55; P) Owners Rita and Ed have beautifully refurbished these skylit rooms, installing orthopedic beds, reading lights and hand-painted murals by local artists. In addition to the indoor dining area, there's a pleasant garden terrace for sipping coffee and reading something you've picked up from the book exchange in the front room. Breakfasts feature homemade pastries, and nonguests can also stop by for lunch. It's located directly behind the big church.

Five Corners Grill (☎ 8887-7175; mains ₡2800-4000, 8am-2pm) You'll smell the wonderful

(Continued on page 189)

COSTA RICA WILDLIFE GUIDE

The range of habitats in Costa Rica, a consequence of its unique geography, creates an incredible diversity of flora and fauna. Measured in terms of number of species per 10,000 sq km, Costa Rica tops the country list with more than 600. From flamboyant tropical birds and multicolored tree frogs to fleeting glimpses of rare mammals and migrating whales offshore, Costa Rica has some of the most diverse wildlife on the planet.

7

INSECTS & BIRDS

No less than 35,000 species of insects have been recorded in Costa Rica, yet it's estimated by entomologists that thousands more remain undiscovered. The country also hosts more bird species (approximately 850, including six endemics) than Europe, North America or Australia.

10

❶ Blue Morpho

This butterfly flaps and glides along tropical rivers and through openings in the forests. When it lands, the electric-blue upper wings close, and only the mottled brown underwings become visible, an instantaneous change from outrageous display to modest camouflage.

❷ Frigate Bird

This distinctive black bird, with an inflatable red throat pouch, is large, elegant and streamlined. It makes an acrobatic living by aerial piracy, harassing smaller birds into dropping their catch, and then swooping in to steal their meal midair.

❸ Roseate Spoonbill

The descriptively named roseate has a white head and a distinctive spoon-shaped bill, and feeds by touch. It swings its open bill back and forth, submerged underwater, until it feels food and then snaps the bill shut.

❹ Northern Jacana

The northern jacana has extremely long, thin toes that enable it to walk on top of aquatic plants. At first glance it appears nondescript, but when disturbed, the bird stretches its wings to reveal startling yellow flight feathers.

❺ Hummingbirds

More than 50 species of hummingbird have been recorded – their delicate beauty is matched only by their extravagant names. The largest is the violet sabrewing, which has a striking violet head and body with dark green wings.

❻ Toucans

Toucans are classic rainforest birds, and six species are found in Costa Rica. Huge bills and vibrant plumage make species such as the chestnut-mandibled toucan and the keel-billed toucan hard to miss. See the photo on p181.

❼ Scarlet Macaw

Of the 16 species of parrot recorded in Costa Rica, none is as spectacular as the scarlet macaw unmistakable for its large size, bright-red body, blue-and-yellow wings, long red tail and white face.

❽ Blue-Gray Tanager

About half of Costa Rica's birds are passerines, a sprawling category that includes warbler, sparrow, finch, cotinga and tanager. The blue-gray tanager is the ubiquitous songbird of tropical woodlands and gardens.

❾ Resplendent Quetzal

A type of trogon, this is easily the most dazzling and culturally important bird in Central America. The quetzal had great ceremonial significance for the Aztecs and the Maya, and remains the national bird and symbol of Guatemala.

❿ Tarantula

Easily identified by its enormous size and hairy appendages, the tarantula is an intimidating arachnid perfectly capable of killing animals as large as mice, birds and lizards. Surprisingly, however, most species are completely harmless to humans.

REPTILES & AMPHIBIANS

More than half of the 220 species of reptiles in Costa Rica are snakes, though fortunately there are only a couple of deadly ones to watch out for. Of the 160 species of amphibians, the frogs and toads garner the most attention, and are being studied by ecologists as early warning indicators of climate change.

❶ Fer-de-lance

Literally 'iron of the lance,' this much vilified pit viper can be anything from olive to brown or black in color, and has a warning pattern of Xs and triangles on its back – take heed as this snake is not to be trifled with.

❷ Bushmaster

An aptly named lord of its terrain, the bushmaster is the world's longest viper, and the only neotropical specimen known to lay eggs. The snake is usually tan-colored with dark diamond-shaped blotches, and is capable of multiple-bite strikes.

❸ Basilisk

This bright-green lizard is notable for the huge crest running the length of its head, body and tail. Common along watercourses in lowland areas, it has the appearance of a small dinosaur.

❹ Poison-Dart Frog

The Dendrobatidae family of frogs has skin glands exuding toxins that can cause paralysis and death in animals. Indigenous populations traditionally used them as a poison for the tips of their hunting arrows.

❺ Whiptail Lizard

The most frequently seen reptile in Costa Rica is this abundant lizard, which has a white stripe running down its back. Take particular note of the juveniles, who often have distinct metallic-blue tails.

❻ Golden Toad

Now extinct, this golden-colored amphibian was once found throughout the high-altitude cloud forests. It's now believed that its sudden disappearance can be attributed to a fungal epidemic possibly brought on by global warming.

❼ Green Iguana

This stocky beast is regularly encountered draping its 2m-long body across a branch over water. Despite their enormous bulk, iguanas are incessant vegetarians, and prefer to eat young shoots and leaves.

❽ Red-Eyed Tree Frog

The unofficial symbol of Costa Rica, these boldly colored amphibians have red eyes, green bodies, yellow and blue side stripes and orange feet. Despite this vibrant coloration, they're well camouflaged in the rainforest, and rather difficult to spot.

❾ Crocodile

One of nature's most perfect predators, the crocodile is an ancient species with an evolutionary history stretching back more than 200 million years. True apex predators, crocodiles will eat anything they can seize with their massive jaws.

❿ Boa Constrictor

An enormous nonvenomous snake, the boa is nevertheless an efficient predator capable of dispatching prey through constriction. Relying on brute muscle and girth, a boa can strangle cat-sized prey before swallowing it whole.

LAND MAMMALS

Although land mammals inhabit all of Costa Rica's multitudinous biomes, the rainforest in particular captures the imagination of most people. Here, you'll find fierce predators and their crafty prey, as well as a few extended members of our primate family tree.

4

❶ Sloths
Costa Rica is home to the brown-throated three-toed sloth and Hoffman's two-toed sloth. Both are 50cm to 75cm in length with stumpy tails, and tend to hang motionless from branches, or slowly progress upside down along a branch toward leaves, their primary food.

❷ Spider Monkey
This New World primate is named for its long and thin legs, arms and tail, which enable it to pursue an arboreal existence in forests. They swing from arm to arm through the canopy, and can hang supported just by their prehensile tail.

❸ Mantled Howler Monkey
The loud vocalizations of a male mantled howler monkey can carry for more than 1km even in dense rainforest. Variously described as grunting, roaring or howling, this crescendo of noise is one of the most characteristic and memorable of all rainforest sounds.

❹ White-Faced Capuchin
The small and inquisitive monkey has a prehensile tail that is typically carried with the tip coiled. Capuchins occasionally descend to the ground, where food such as corn and even oysters is part of their diet.

❺ Squirrel Monkey
This adorable but diminutive monkey travels in small to medium-sized groups during the day, squealing or chirping noisily and leaping and crashing through vegetation in search of insects and fruit.

❻ White-Nosed Coati
This frequently seen member of the raccoon family is brownish and longer, but slimmer and lighter than your average raccoon. Its most distinctive feature is a long, mobile, upturned whitish snout with which it snuffles around in search of food.

❼ Jaguar
These big cats are extremely rare and well camouflaged, so the chance of seeing one is remote. They do have large territories, however, so you may see their prints or droppings, or even hear their roar – a sound more like a series of deep coughs.

❽ Anteater
Anteaters lack teeth and use a long, sticky tongue to slurp ants and termites. The giant anteater reaches almost 2m in length, and has a tongue that protrudes an astonishing 60cm up to 150 times a minute.

❾ Ocelot
This felid is little more than 1m in length with a short tail and a pattern of many beautiful rosettes. Though it is the most common of the Costa Rican wild cats, it is very shy and rarely seen.

❿ Baird's Tapir
This pudgy, pig-like browsing mammal has a characteristic prehensile snout, and lives deep in the tropical forests. Although humans rarely encounter them, past hunting and slow reproduction rates have pushed the species to the edge of extinction.

4 TIM ROCK / 5 BOB HALS

5

4

MARINE ANIMALS

Costa Rica has one of the most biologically diverse marine ecosystems in the world and an astounding variety of marine animals. Deepwater upwellings are constant year-round, making these waters extremely productive and creating ideal viewing conditions at any season.

❶ West Indian Manatee

In a few of the rivers, estuaries and coastal areas, you may catch a glimpse of this endangered manatee, a large marine mammal (up to 4m long and weighing 600kg) that feeds primarily on aquatic vegetation.

❷ Whales

Migrating whales, which arrive from both the Northern and Southern hemispheres, include orca, blue and sperm whale, and several species of relatively unknown beaked whale. Humpback whales are commonly spotted along the Pacific coast by tour boats.

❸ Dolphins

These charismatic cetaceans are year-round residents in Costa Rica, particularly the common, bottle-nosed and spotted dolphins. They are among the most intelligent animals on the planet, and have been observed exhibiting complex sociocultural behaviors.

❹ Sea Turtles

The massive 360kg leatherback turtle is a stunning creature. The smaller olive ridley is legendary for its remarkable synchronized nesting, when tens of thousands of females emerge from the sea on the same night. The hawksbill (see picture above) is another impressive species.

❺ Hammerhead Shark

Aptly named, this intimidating species of shark has a unique cephalofoil that enables it to maneuver with incredible speed and precision. Scuba divers can see enormous schools of hammerheads around the remote Isla del Cocos.

(Continued from page 180)

barbecue aroma long before you even see this new restaurant, 4km east of Tilarán. The menu specializes in what owner Jim Aoki calls 'gringo comfort food' – eggs Benedict, nachos, bratwurst, peanut butter and jelly milkshakes, french fries and the best flame-grilled burgers on Laguna de Arenal. It's only open for breakfast and lunch, but plans were underway to begin serving dinner. And if you decide to stick around (permanently), note there's an onsite real estate agency.

Cheap meals can be found in the *mercado* (market) beside the bus terminal, or pop into the **SuperCompro** (8am-8pm) for groceries; it's located just across from the park.

Getting There & Away

Tilarán is usually reached by a 24km paved road from the Interamericana at Cañas. The route on to Santa Elena and Monteverde is unpaved and rough, though ordinary cars can get through with care in the dry season.

Buses arrive and depart from the bus terminal, which is half a block west of Parque Central. Be aware that Sunday-afternoon buses to San José may be sold out by Saturday. The route between Tilarán and San José goes via Cañas and the Interamericana, not the Arenal–La Fortuna–Ciudad Quesada route. Regular services go to the following locations:

Cañas ₡350; 30 minutes; departs 5am, 7am, 8am, 9am, 10am, 11:30am and 3:30pm.
Ciudad Quesada, via La Fortuna ₡1550; four hours; departs 7am and 12:30pm.
Nuevo Arenal ₡500; 1¼ hours; departs 5am, 6am, 8am, 9am, 10am, 11am, 1pm, 2:30pm and 3:30pm.
Puntarenas ₡1530; two hours; departs 6am and 1pm.
San José (Auto-Transportes Tilarán) ₡3650; four hours; departs 5am, 7am, 9:30am, 2pm and 5pm.
Santa Elena/Monteverde ₡1200; 2½ hours; departs 7am and 4pm.

INTERAMERICANA NORTE

Even between the Tico speed demons and lumbering big rigs, the Interamericana offers up a wide-angle view of the region. This highway, the main artery connecting San José with Managua, Nicaragua, runs through kilometers of tropical dry forest and neat roadside villages, to the open grasslands and *fincas* of the northern end of Guanacaste Province. Vistas across vast expanses of savanna, which seem more suited to Africa or the American southwest, are broken only by windblown trees, some of which shed their leaves during the hot, dry summer. But complex communications between these seemingly dormant giants will suddenly inspire an entire species to erupt into fountains of pink, yellow or orange blossoms, welling up from the dry grasses in astounding syncopation. This is also where you'll see the signature gait of the *sabanero* (cowboy) as he rounds up a herd of cattle with grace and precision.

For travelers, this is the main route for accessing Monteverde, Liberia, the northern volcanoes, Parque Nacional Santa Rosa and the extreme northwest. The Arenal route connects with the Interamericana Norte in Cañas.

REFUGIO NACIONAL DE FAUNA SILVESTRE PEÑAS BLANCAS & AROUND

This 24-sq-km refuge, not to be confused with the Nicaraguan border crossing of the same name, is along the steep southern arm of the Cordillera de Tilarán. Elevations in the small area range from less than 600m to over 1400m above sea level, variations that result in different types of forest, such as tropical dry forest in the lower southwestern sections, semideciduous dry and moist forests in middle elevations, and premontane forest in the higher northern sections. The terrain is very rugged, and while there are some hiking trails, they are unmaintained and difficult to follow.

The name Peñas Blancas (White Cliffs) refers to the diatomaceous deposits, similar to a good-quality chalk, found in the reserve. The whitish deposits, remnants of unicellular algae once common here when Central America was under water, are found in the steep walls of some of the river canyons in the refuge.

The refuge was created to protect the plant species in the varied habitats as well as an important watershed, and until the Ministerio del Ambiente y Energía (Minae; Ministry of Environment & Energy) develops some tourist infrastructure, the region is inaccessible to all but the most diligent visitors. There are no facilities at the refuge. **Camping** (per person US$2) is allowed, but you must be self-sufficient and in good shape to handle the very demanding terrain. The dry season (January to early April) is the best time to go – it's unlikely that you'll see anyone else there.

The closest town to the refuge is **Miramar**, a historic gold-mining town about 8km northeast of the Interamericana. In town you can visit **Las Minas de Montes de Oro** (guided tour US$79), an old, abandoned gold mine that dates back to 1815. The tour is coupled with horseback riding and a guided hike to a waterfall. The mine is administered by **Finca Daniel Adventure Park** (☎ 2639-9900; www.finca-daniel.com; 2hr horseback-riding tour $45, waterfall canopy tour $89), which has the usual assortment of pricey tours. The onsite lodge, **Hotel Vista Golfo** (s/d/tr standard US$64/67/82, with view US$75/78/94;), is a pleasant hotel with a tranquil, mountain setting that's perfect for getting a little fresh air. Rustic rooms have private hot-water bathroom, and some have sweeping views of the Golfo de Nicoya. There's also a shady pool and a good restaurant. A much more personal option is the German-run **Finca El Mirador B&B** (☎ 2639-8774; www.finca-mirador.com; d US$35-60;), which has three adorable bungalows, each equipped with full kitchen – perfect for self-caterers.

In the small town of Zapotal, 18km northeast of Miramar, is the **Reserva Biológica Alberto Manuel Brenes** (☎ 2437-9906; resbiol@cariari.ucr.ac.cr), a cloud-forest reserve administrated by the University of Costa Rica. The park is famous among bird-watchers for its quetzal population, and travelers usually arrive here on a private tour.

Although there are infrequent buses connecting Miramar to San José and Puntarenas, this is a difficult area to travel in without your own car. Also, be advised that the roads here are frequently washed out during the rainy season, so a 4WD is highly recommended.

COSTA DE PÁJAROS

The 40km stretch of road between Punta Morales in the south and Manzanillo in the north is famous for its mangrove-lined shores, which attract countless varieties of birds (and bird-watchers). The most famous sight in the area is **Isla Pájaros** (Bird Island), which lies less than 1km off the coast at Punta Morales. There are no facilities on the 3.8-hectare islet, which protects a rare colony of brown pelicans. It also acts as a refuge for various seabirds, and the island is a virtual forest of wild guava trees. Aside from becoming an ornithologist, you can visit the island on an organized tour (from US$30), which can be arranged at La Ensenada Lodge.

Popular among the bird-watching population, **La Ensenada Lodge** (☎ 2289-6655; www.laensenada.net; s/d/tr/q US$44/56/72/76;) is a 380-hectare *finca* and working cattle ranch, salt farm and papaya orchard. Comfortable villas, which face out onto the Golfo de Nicoya, have private bathroom heated by solar panels and private patio with hammocks – perfect for watching sunsets (or birds). There's also a pool, restaurant and tennis courts, and you can help out with reforestation projects or on the farm.

JUNTAS

pop 4700

Las Juntas de Abangares (its full name) is a small town on the Río Abangares that was once the center of the gold-mining industry in the late 19th and early 20th centuries. Juntas was once the premier destination in Costa Rica for fortune seekers and entrepreneurs from all over the world, who wanted a part of mine-owner Minor Keith's other golden opportunity. Today, it's simply a pleasant mountain town full of ranchers and farmers.

With the gold boom over, Juntas is trying to reel in travelers by flaunting its ecomuseum and a recently constructed hot-springs resort. Most travelers aren't making special detours here on their way to or from Monteverde, but Juntas makes for a pleasant enough stop if you've got your own wheels. If it's starting to get dark, it's a good place to spend the night rather than misguidedly attempting the muddy slip-and-slide commonly known as the road to Monteverde.

Orientation & Information

The town of Juntas is centered on the Catholic church, which has some very nice stained glass, and the small but bustling downtown is about 300m north of the church, with a Banco Nacional and several *sodas* and small markets. The Ecomuseo is 3km from the main road.

Sights

OK, so the terms 'eco' and 'mining' don't exactly go together like bees and honey to us either, but it's still worth visiting the small

Ecomuseo de las Minas de Abangares (☎ 2662-0310; adult/child $US4/2; 8am-4pm Tue-Sun), which has a few photographs and models depicting the old mining practices of the area. In the grounds outside the museum are a picnic area and children's play area, and there's a good system of trails that pass by old mining artifacts, such as bits of railway. There's also good **bird-watching** (and iguana-ing) along the trails, and monkeys are occasionally sighted.

From the Interamericana, take the paved road 100m past the Parque Central, turn left, cross a bridge, then turn right at the 'Ecomuseo 4km' sign. About 2km past Juntas, the road forks – a sign indicates a road going left to Monteverde (30km) and to the right to the Ecomuseo (2km).

Tours

Mina Tours (☎ 2662-0753; www.minatours.com; 8am-5pm Mon-Fri), behind the church, is a family-run tour outfit that can arrange transportation and accommodations reservations, and offers several gold-themed tours, including the Ecomuseo and abandoned mines, beginning at about US$30 per person for day trips and more for overnight excursions.

Sleeping & Eating

Cabinas Las Juntas (☎ 2662-0153; s/d US$6/10; P) The cheapest bed in town is perfectly acceptable if you're just looking to get a bit of shuteye before heading to Monteverde. There are basic but clean, small, tiled rooms with a cold private shower and cable TV. América, the proprietor, will fix breakfast for US$2 extra. It's 200m south of the gas station.

our pick **Restaurante y Cabinas Mirador el Angel** (☎ 2693-8489, 8994-9452; r incl breakfast per person US$13; mains ₡1200-7000; restaurant 8am-9:30pm Mon-Sun; P) Halfway between Juntas and Monteverde, a well-signed, steep dirt road leads up to this hidden gem with amazing views of the valley and Golfo de Nicoya. The restaurant menu features terrific *casados* like grilled fresh fish, plus burgers and other fast food. The rustic cabins overlook the family's coffee plantation and have private bathroom with hot water, TV and balcony. Owners Angel and Concha are wonderfully hospitable, though little English is spoken. It's located about 4km south of the tiny village of San Rafael.

Centro Turístico Cayuco (☎ 2662-0868; d with/without air-con US$15/10; P) This is a popular option with vacationing Ticos as there's an onsite pool, hot spring, restaurant and bar, all 200m north of the mining statue. Unfortunately, the pool barely looks swimmable, and the hot spring is a concrete dish that's fed by a pipe bearing 'springwater' of dubious origins. The rooms, however, are decent, and have cable TV and private bathroom with cold water.

Pueblo Antiguo Lodge & Spa (☎ 2662-0033; www.puebloantiguo.com; s/d incl breakfast US$50/64; P) This rustic mountain getaway next to the Ecomuseo caters to tourists looking for a rejuvenating escape; and its onsite hot springs, swimming pool, Jacuzzi, sauna, nature trails and restaurant ensure you will be sufficiently entertained (and relaxed). Ten rooms in wooden cabins have private bathroom and scenic mountain views, and there's a good chance wildlife will appear on your front doorstep. The friendly staff members also arrange tours to the nearby Ecomuseo and gold mines.

Restaurante Los Mangos (☎ 2662-0410; mains ₡1500-3000; 11am-2am Tue-Sun) The nicest restaurant in town (we know it's run-down, but there aren't exactly a lot of options here) is on the main road, and does your standard mix of *casados*, *ceviche* and fried chicken, and it'll get you liquored up at night.

Getting There & Away

Buses from Cañas (₡400, 45 minutes) depart at 9:30am and 2:15pm. Buses to San José (₡2500, three hours) depart at 8:30am, 10:30am and 3pm. There are no buses to the Ecomuseo, but a taxi will cost about ₡2300 one way.

Drivers can take the turnoff from the Interamericana, 27km south of Cañas at a gas station called **La Irma** (☎ 2645-5647), where you can also catch buses between Liberia and San José. Monteverde is 30km northeast from Las Juntas on a mostly paved road; the last 12km are a rough dirt road, though it's passable to normal cars in the dry season. From Juntas, take your first left after the plaza, cross the one-lane bridge, turn right and follow the signs to Monteverde.

MONTEVERDE & SANTA ELENA

Strung between two lovingly preserved cloud forests is this slim corridor of civilization, which consists of the Tico village of Santa Elena and the Quaker settlement of Monteverde. A 1983 feature article in

National Geographic described this unique landscape and subsequently billed the area as *the* place to view one of Central America's most famous birds – the resplendent quetzal. Suddenly, hordes of tourists armed with tripods and telephoto lenses started braving Monteverde's notoriously awful access roads, which came as a huge shock to the then-established Quaker community. In an effort to stem the tourist flow, local communities lobbied to stop developers from paving the roads. And it worked. Today, the dirt roads leading to Monteverde and Santa Elena have effectively created a moat around this precious experiment in sustainable ecotourism.

The cloud forests near Monteverde and Santa Elena are Costa Rica's premier destination for everyone from budget backpackers to well-heeled retirees. On a good day, Monteverde is a place where you can be inspired about the possibility of a world where organic farming and alternative energy sources help to salvage the fine mess we've made of the planet. On a bad day, Monteverde can feel like a cross between a natural reserve and Disneyland. But the upside is that the local community continues to maintain the fragile balance of this ecopark and fight against the threat of overdevelopment.

History

The history of these settlements dates back to the 1930s when a few Tico families left the gold-mining settlement of Juntas, and headed up the mountain to try to make a living through logging and farming. In a completely unrelated turn of events, four Quakers (a pacifist religious group also known as the 'Friends') were jailed in Alabama in 1949 for their refusal to be drafted into the Korean War. Since Quakers are obligated by their religion to be pacifists, the four men were eventually released from prison. However, in response to the incarceration, 44 Quakers from 11 families left the USA and headed for greener pastures – namely Monteverde.

The Quakers chose Monteverde (Green Mountain) for two reasons – a few years prior, the Costa Rican government had abolished its military and the cool, mountain climate was ideal for grazing cattle. The Quakers found their isolated refuge from the ills of the world, and adopted a simple, trouble-free life of dairy farming and cheese production amid a new-found world of religious freedom. In an effort to protect the watershed above its 15-sq-km plot in Monteverde, the Quaker community agreed to preserve the mountaintop rainforests.

Climate

When ecologists arrived in the area to investigate the preserve, they discovered that the cloud forests were actually two different ecosystems that straddled both sides of the continental divide. In the Reserva Biológica Bosque Nuboso Monteverde, the warm, moisture-laden trade winds from the Caribbean sweep up the slopes of the divide where they then cool and condense to form clouds. These clouds also pass over the Reserva Santa Elena, though the absence of the trade winds means that the forests here are a few degrees warmer than in Monteverde. As a result, each ecosystem boasts several distinct species (most of which you probably won't be able to see, however).

Orientation

Driving from either of the Interamericana's first two turnoffs to the region, you'll first arrive in Santa Elena, a bustling little community with lots of budget hotels, restaurants and attractions. A road beginning at the northern point of the triangle leads to Juntas and Tilarán, with a turnoff to Reserva Santa Elena. From the westernmost point of the triangle (to the right as you enter town) you can access a scenic and heavily rutted 6km road to the Monteverde reserve.

This road forms the backbone of a spread-out community, and is lined with hotels and restaurants of varying degrees of attractiveness. About 2km from Santa Elena, the neighborhood of Cerro Plano has a neat nucleus of cute businesses centered on Casem and the Monteverde Cheese Factory. Almost 5km from town, a turnoff leads a steep 3km to the Ecolodge San Luis and research station and San Luis Waterfall. Roads are generally paralleled by pedestrian trails.

Information

BOOKSTORES

Librería Chunches (☎ 2645-5147; Santa Elena; 🕑 8am-7pm Mon-Fri, 8am-6pm Sat; 📶) A bookstore and coffee shop with a fine selection of books (many in English), including travel and natural history guides and some US newspapers and magazines. There's laundry service (₡3500 to wash and dry up to 4kg) and its bulletin board is a good source of information. Also see Bromelias Books (p210).

EMERGENCY

Police (☎ 2645-5127; Santa Elena)

INTERNET ACCESS

Internet access is widely available around Santa Elena and at many hotels.

Hotel & Info Center Camino Verde (☎ 2645-6304; www.exploringmonteverde.com/hotel-camino-verde; 6:30am-10pm) Has a busy internet cafe in front, with international Internet calling available; across from the Santa Elena bus terminal.

Internet Pura Vida (☎ 2645-5683; www.internetpuravida.com; per hr ₡800; 10am-8pm;) Located within a converted yellow American school bus, they also offer computer repair and CD burning. There's also a laundry service (₡3800 to wash and dry up to 5kg).

Tree House Restaurant & Café (☎ 2645-5751; www.canopydining.com; 6:30am-10pm) Has a few terminals downstairs that you can use for free (!) for half an hour.

MEDICAL SERVICES

Consultorio Médico (☎ 2645-7778, 8304-2121; 24hr) Across the intersection from Hotel Heliconia.

Red Cross (☎ 2645-6128; 24hr) A hospital located just north of Santa Elena.

Vitosi (☎ 2645-5004; 8am-8pm Mon-Sat, 9am-8pm Sun) German-run pharmacy and department store, across from the Chamber of Tourism.

MONEY

Euros, US dollars and traveler's checks can be exchanged at Hotel & Info Center Camino Verde, although you can expect to pay a fairly hefty commission.

Banco de Costa Rica (☎ 2645-5519; 8am-4pm Mon-Fri, 8am-noon Sat) Has a 24-hour ATM; located next to La Guarida del Sapo.

Banco Nacional (☎ 2645-5027; Santa Elena; 8:30am-3:45pm) 24-hour ATM in the new building behind the parking lot.

Banco Popular A 24-hour ATM.

POST

Correos de Costa Rica (8am-4:30pm Mon-Fri, until noon Sat) Across from the new shopping mall.

TOURIST INFORMATION

Chamber of Tourism (☎ 2645-6565; www.monteverdecr.com; Santa Elena; 8am-8pm) Operated by the local chamber of commerce, this office only promotes hotels and tour companies that pay the membership fee, so come in with the understanding that you'll get biased information.

Hotel & Info Center Camino Verde (☎ 2645-6296; www.exploringmonteverde.com; Camino Verde; 8am-8pm;) Offers maps, hotel and tour bookings, internet access (per hour ₡1600), domestic and international bus reservations and a small hostel (US$8 to US$10 per person).

Pensión Santa Elena (p201) A better option than the tourist office, even if you're not staying at this place. Talk to its friendly staff or check out its comprehensive website.

Sights

Ecotourism is big business in Monteverde and Santa Elena, so it's unsurprising that there are a number of ecoriffic attractions scattered around both towns. And if there's a certain critter you're itching to see, there are plenty of places where your view won't be obscured by all those pesky trees.

As places possessed of such sublime beauty are apt to do, the Monteverde–Santa Elena corridor is attracting an impressive art scene, and there are a growing number of galleries scattered throughout the cloud forest. One specialty here is woodwork, but not at all like that of the Sarchí scene – sculpture, figurative and fluid, is a local art movement worth checking out. Artists from all over the country also display their work in town.

EL JARDÍN DE LAS MARIPOSAS

One of the most interesting activities is visiting the **El Jardín de las Mariposas** (Butterfly Garden; ☎ 2645-5512; www.monteverdebutterflygarden.com; adult/student $10/8; 9:30am-4pm). Admission entitles you to a naturalist-led tour (in Spanish or English) that begins with an enlightening discussion of butterfly life cycles and the butterfly's importance in nature. A variety of eggs, caterpillars, pupae and adults are examined. Visitors are taken into the greenhouses, where the butterflies are raised, and on into the screened garden, where hundreds of butterflies of many species are seen. The tour lasts about an hour, after which you are free to stay as long as you wish. There's also a theater that presents an informational video in English, Spanish, French, Dutch or German. It's best to visit in the morning when the butterflies are most active. There are good volunteer opportunities available here. To save a few bucks, consider purchasing an adult combo

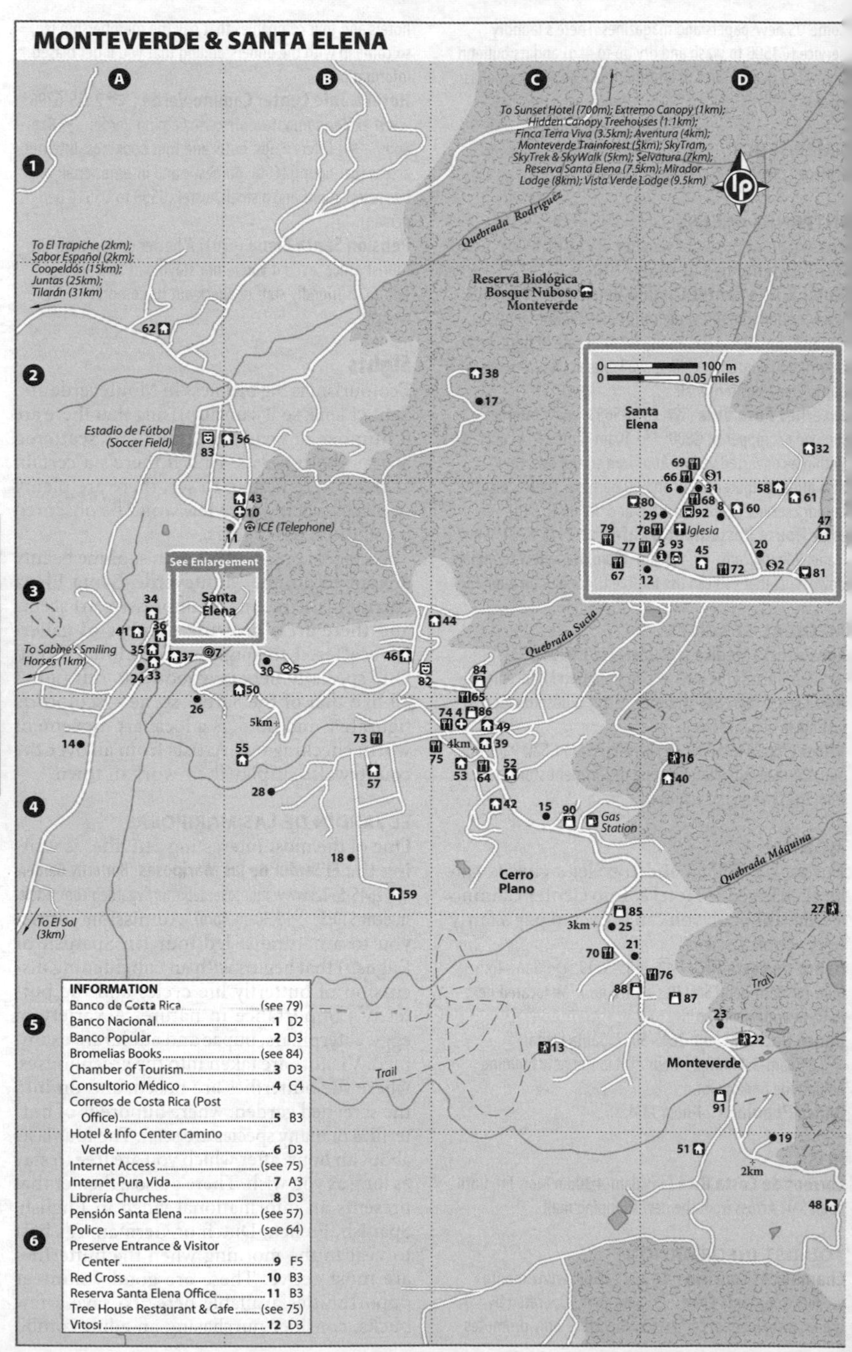
MONTEVERDE & SANTA ELENA
To Sunset Hotel (700m); Extremo Canopy (1km); Hidden Canopy Treehouses (1.1km); Finca Terra Viva (3.5km); Aventura (4km); Monteverde Trainforest (5km); SkyTram, SkyTrek & SkyWalk (5km); Selvatura (7km); Reserva Santa Elena (7.5km); Mirador Lodge (8km); Vista Verde Lodge (9.5km)
Quebrada Rodríguez
To El Trapiche (2km); Sabor Español (2km); Coopeldós (15km); Juntas (25km); Tilarán (31km)
Reserva Biológica Bosque Nuboso Monteverde
Estadio de Fútbol (Soccer Field)
ICE (Telephone)
See Enlargement
Santa Elena
To Sabine's Smiling Horses (1km)
Quebrada Sucia
Santa Elena
Iglesia
100 m
0.05 miles
5km
4km
Gas Station
Cerro Plano
Quebrada Máquina
To El Sol (3km)
3km
Trail
Trail
Monteverde
2km
INFORMATION
Banco de Costa Rica (see 79)
Banco Nacional 1 D2
Banco Popular 2 D3
Bromelias Books (see 84)
Chamber of Tourism 3 D3
Consultorio Médico 4 C4
Correos de Costa Rica (Post Office) 5 B3
Hotel & Info Center Camino Verde 6 D3
Internet Access (see 75)
Internet Pura Vida 7 A3
Librería Churches 8 D3
Pensión Santa Elena (see 57)
Police (see 64)
Preserve Entrance & Visitor Center 9 F5
Red Cross 10 B3
Reserva Santa Elena Office 11 B3
Tree House Restaurant & Cafe (see 75)
Vitosi 12 D3

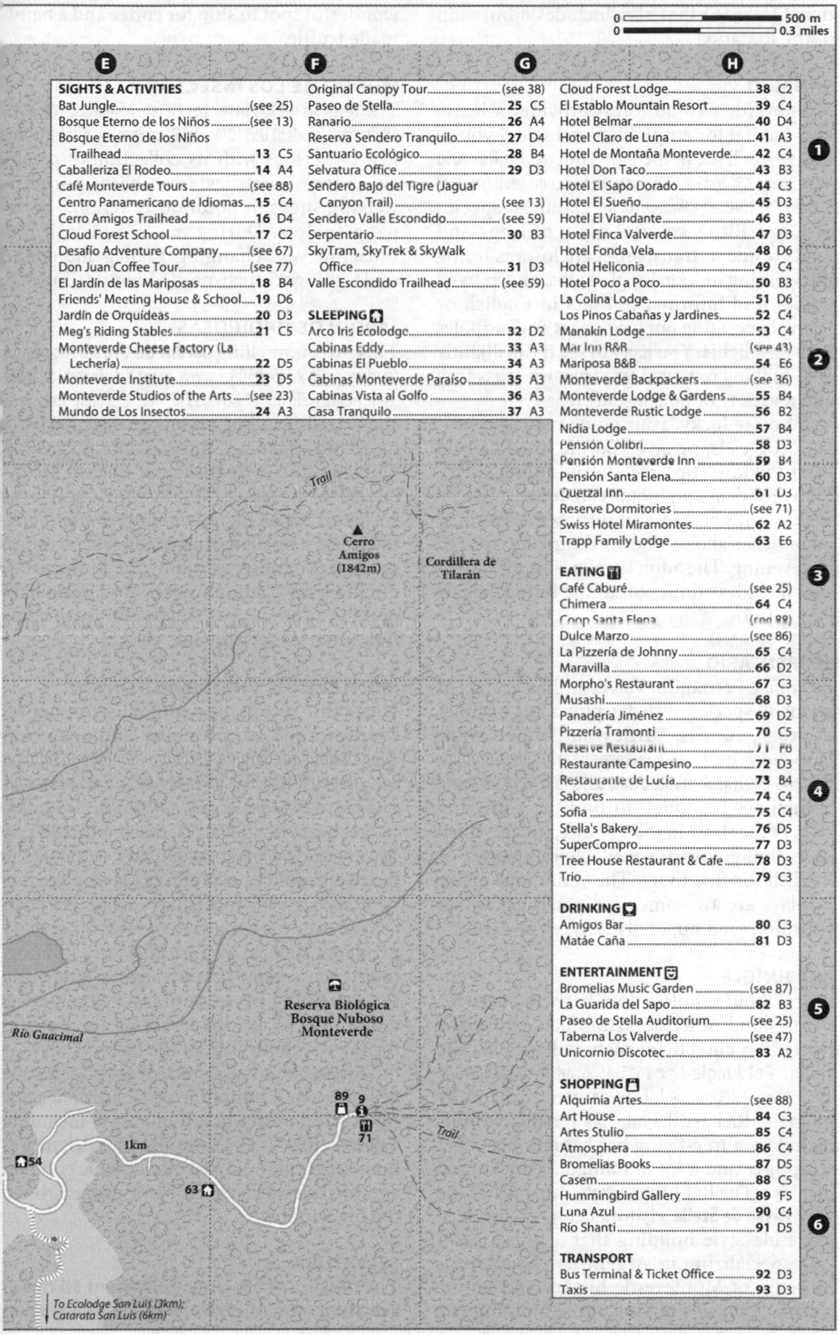

0 500 m
0 0.3 miles

E F G H

SIGHTS & ACTIVITIES

Bat Jungle (see 25)
Bosque Eterno de los Niños (see 13)
Bosque Eterno de los Niños Trailhead 13 C5
Caballeriza El Rodeo 14 A4
Café Monteverde Tours (see 88)
Centro Panamericano de Idiomas 15 C4
Cerro Amigos Trailhead 16 D4
Cloud Forest School 17 C2
Desafío Adventure Company (see 67)
Don Juan Coffee Tour (see 77)
El Jardín de las Mariposas 18 B4
Friends' Meeting House & School 19 D6
Jardín de Orquídeas 20 D3
Meg's Riding Stables 21 C5
Monteverde Cheese Factory (La Lechería) 22 D5
Monteverde Institute 23 D5
Monteverde Studios of the Arts (see 23)
Mundo de Los Insectos 24 A3
Original Canopy Tour (see 38)
Paseo de Stella 25 C5
Ranario 26 A4
Reserva Sendero Tranquilo 27 D4
Santuario Ecológico 28 B4
Selvatura Office 29 D3
Sendero Bajo del Tigre (Jaguar Canyon Trail) (see 13)
Sendero Valle Escondido (see 59)
Serpentario 30 B3
SkyTram, SkyTrek & SkyWalk Office 31 D3
Valle Escondido Trailhead (see 59)

SLEEPING

Arco Iris Ecolodge 32 D2
Cabinas Eddy 33 A3
Cabinas El Pueblo 34 A3
Cabinas Monteverde Paraíso 35 A3
Cabinas Vista al Golfo 36 A3
Casa Tranquilo 37 A3
Cloud Forest Lodge 38 C2
El Establo Mountain Resort 39 C4
Hotel Belmar 40 D4
Hotel Claro de Luna 41 A3
Hotel de Montaña Monteverde 42 C4
Hotel Don Taco 43 B3
Hotel El Sapo Dorado 44 C3
Hotel El Sueño 45 D3
Hotel El Viandante 46 B3
Hotel Finca Valverde 47 D3
Hotel Fonda Vela 48 D6
Hotel Heliconia 49 C4
Hotel Poco a Poco 50 B3
La Colina Lodge 51 D6
Los Pinos Cabañas y Jardines 52 C4
Manakín Lodge 53 C4
Mar Inn B&B (see 43)
Mariposa B&B 54 E6
Monteverde Backpackers (see 36)
Monteverde Lodge & Gardens 55 B4
Monteverde Rustic Lodge 56 B2
Nidia Lodge 57 B4
Pensión Colibrí 58 D3
Pensión Monteverde Inn 59 B4
Pensión Santa Elena 60 D3
Quetzal Inn 61 D3
Reserve Dormitories (see 71)
Swiss Hotel Miramontes 62 A2
Trapp Family Lodge 63 E6

EATING

Café Caburé (see 25)
Chimera 64 C4
Coop Santa Elena (see 88)
Dulce Marzo (see 86)
La Pizzería de Johnny 65 C4
Maravilla 66 D2
Morpho's Restaurant 67 C3
Musashi 68 D3
Panadería Jiménez 69 D2
Pizzería Tramonti 70 C5
Reserve Restaurant 71 F6
Restaurante Campesino 72 D3
Restaurante de Lucía 73 B4
Sabores 74 C4
Sofia 75 C4
Stella's Bakery 76 D5
SuperCompro 77 D3
Tree House Restaurant & Cafe 78 D3
Trio 79 C3

DRINKING

Amigos Bar 80 C3
Matáe Caña 81 D3

ENTERTAINMENT

Bromelias Music Garden (see 87)
La Guarida del Sapo 82 B3
Paseo de Stella Auditorium (see 25)
Taberna Los Valverde (see 47)
Unicornio Discotec 83 A2

SHOPPING

Alquimia Artes (see 88)
Art House 84 C3
Artes Stulio 85 C4
Atmosphera 86 C4
Bromelias Books 87 D5
Casem 88 C5
Hummingbird Gallery 89 F5
Luna Azul 90 C4
Río Shanti 91 D5

TRANSPORT

Bus Terminal & Ticket Office 92 D3
Taxis 93 D3

1 2 3 4 5 6

Trail
Cerro Amigos (1842m)
Cordillera de Tilarán
Reserva Biológica Bosque Nuboso Monteverde
Río Guacimal
89 9 71
Trail
1km
54
63
To Ecolodge San Luis (3km); Catarata San Luis (6km)

NORTHWESTERN COSTA RICA

ticket (US$16) that also includes admission to the Ranario.

RANARIO

Monteverde's cloud forest provides a heavenly habitat for amphibians, which, if you're lucky, you'll see in the park. But at the **Ranario** (Frog Pond; ☎ 2645-6320; www.ranario.com; adult/student & child US$10/8; 9am-8:30pm) about 30 species of Costa Rica's colorful array of frogs and toads reside in transparent enclosures lining the winding indoor-jungle paths. Sharp-eyed guides lead informative tours in English or Spanish, pointing out frogs, eggs and tadpoles with flashlights. You'll get to see the brilliantly fake-looking red-eyed tree frog, the glass frog and a variety of poison-dart frogs.

If you're lucky, your guide may also imitate frog calls, or give you the lowdown on local folklore (tips are always appreciated). Many resident amphibians are more active by night, so it's best to visit during the evening; your ticket allows you to return for free in the evening. The adult combo ticket (US$16) also includes admission to the butterfly garden (p193).

SERPENTARIO

Biologist Fernando Valverde has collected about 40 species of snake, plus a fair number of frogs, lizards, turtles and other cold-blooded critters at his **serpentario** (serpentarium; ☎ 2645-6002; adult/student/child US$8/6/5; 9am-8pm). Sometimes it's tough to find the slithering stars of the show in their comfy, foliage-filled cages, but guides are available in Spanish or English for free tours. The venomous snake displays are awesome, and you'll get to see your first (and hopefully last) fer-de-lance.

BAT JUNGLE

Learn about echolocation, bat-wing aerodynamics and other amazing facts about the (incredibly cute) flying mammal, the bat. The stellar **Bat Jungle** (☎ 2645-6566; adult/child US$10/8; 9:30am-7:30pm), a labor of love realized by biologist Richard Laval, has terrific exhibits including a free-flying bat habitat, beautiful sculptures and a lot of bilingual educational displays. The Bat Jungle makes up part of the new **Paseo de Stella** visitors center, a modern hacienda-style building that also houses a cafe specializing in Argentine chocolate, a museum of Monteverde history and an art gallery. The wide terrace of the building is a wonderful spot to stop for coffee and a handmade truffle.

MUNDO DE LOS INSECTOS

The **Mundo de los Insectos** (World of Insects; ☎ 2645-6859; adult/student US$10/6; 9am-8pm) goes beyond just butterflies with its collection of creepy cloud-forest crawlies, from hermaphroditic walking sticks to notoriously venomous banana spiders. During our recent visit, the museum was changing management and undergoing a much-needed remodeling.

JARDÍN DE ORQUÍDEAS

This sweet-smelling **Jardín de Orquídeas** (Orchid Garden; ☎ 2645-5308; www.monteverdeorchidgarden.com; adult/child under 12yr US$10/free; 8am-5pm) has shady trails winding past more than 400 types of orchid organized into taxonomic groups. Guided tours in Spanish and English are included with admission, on which you'll see such rarities as *Plztystele jungermannioides*, the world's smallest orchid, and several others marked for conservation by the Monteverde Orchid Investigation Project. And if you have orchids at home, you might also learn some tips and tricks for organic care.

MONTEVERDE CHEESE FACTORY

Until the recent upswing in ecotourism, Monteverde's number-one employer was this **cheese factory** (La Lechería; ☎ 2645-5522; tours adult/child US$10/8; tours 9am & 2pm Mon-Sat, store open 7:30am-5pm Mon-Sat, 7:30am-4pm Sun), also called La Lechería (The Dairy). Started in 1953 by Monteverde's original Quaker settlers, the factory produces everything from a creamy Gouda to a very nice sharp, white cheddar, sold all over the country, as well as other dairy products such as yogurt and, most importantly, ice cream. If you've got a hankering for something sweet, our favorite treat is the coffee milk shake. Reservations are required for the two-hour tour of the factory.

Stop by the small, attached shop for a cone of soft-serve scrumptiousness here or at a few other select locations around town, including Sabores (p207). The shop also sells deli meats, homemade granola and other picnic goodies, and you can watch cheese being made through the big window.

SELVATURA

The makers of eco-fun really went all out at **Selvatura** (☎ 2645-5929, 2645-6200; www.selvatura

com; admission hummingbird garden US$5, butterfly garden US$12, reptile museum US$12, hanging bridges adult/student/child under 12yr US$25/20/15, canopy tour adult/student/child under 12yr US$45/35/30; 7:30am-4pm), a huge ecocomplex 150m from Reserva Santa Elena and approximately 12km northeast of Santa Elena, complete with butterfly and hummingbird gardens, a herpetarium (reptiles and amphibian museum), a canopy tour (p199) and a series of hanging bridges. The star attraction is the slightly overwhelming Jewels of the Rainforest Exhibition. This exhibition houses the world's largest private collection of the strangest and most stunning insects you've ever seen. The exhibit is the life's work of entomologist Richard Whitten (with a little help from his wife, Margaret), and is masterfully presented using a combination of art, video and music. If you only have time for one sight in Monteverde, this is the one. Check the website for package deals.

COFFEE PLANTATIONS

Coffee-lovers will be excited to find some of the finest coffee in the world right here. Late April is the best time to see the fields in bloom, while the coffee harvest (done entirely by hand) takes place from December to February. Any time is a good time to see how your favorite beverage makes the transition from ruby-red berry to smooth black brew. Advance reservations are required for all tours, which you can book direct by phone or through many hotels. Most charge about US$30 for adults, including transportation to the *fincas*.

Café Monteverde (☎ 2645-5901; www.monteverde-coffee.com) Run by Cooperative Santa Elena, this highly recommended tour takes visitors to coffee *fincas* that use entirely organic methods to grow the perfect bean. You can help pick some beans, after which you'll be brought to the *beneficio* (coffee mill), where you can watch as the beans are washed and dried, roasted and then packed. Of course, you'll also get to taste the final product with a snack. The cafe (open from 7:30am to 6pm) itself offers free samples of six roasts, or buy some beans to take home.

Coopeldós (☎ 2693-8441; www.coopeldos.com) This cooperative of 450 small and medium-sized, organic coffee growers is Fairtrade-certified. One of their main clients is Starbucks. It's about halfway between Tilarán and Monteverde.

Don Juan Coffee Tour (☎ 2645-7100; www.donjuancoffeetour.com) Book this two-hour tour at their downtown shop near the SuperCompro.

El Trapiche (☎ 2645-5834; www.eltrapichetour.com; tours 10am & 3pm Mon-Sat, 3pm Sun) This reader-recommended, family-run coffee plantation also grows sugar cane. Besides coffee, you can also sample the area's other famous beverage, *saca de guaro,* a liquor made from sugar cane.

FRIENDS MEETING HOUSE

The Quakers (or more correctly, the Society of Friends) who settled in Monteverde played a direct role in preserving the cloud forest, and they remain extremely active in the local community, though they're not recognizable by any traditional costume. Quakerism began as a breakaway movement from the Anglican Church in the 1650s, founded by the young George Fox, who in his early 20s heard the voice of Christ, and claimed that direct experience with God was possible without having to go through the sacraments. Today, this belief is commonly described by Quakers as the 'God in everyone,' and the community continues to lead a peaceful lifestyle in the Monteverde area.

If you're interested in learning more about the Society of Friends, prayer meetings at the Friends Meeting House in Monteverde are held on Sunday at 10:30am and Wednesday at 9am. If you're willing to give at least a six-week commitment, there are numerous volunteer opportunities available. For more information, contact the **Monteverde Friends School** (www.mfschool.org).

Activities

Don't forget your hiking boots, bug spray and a hat – there's plenty to do outdoors around here, including lots of action either on horseback or in the jungle canopy.

HIKING

The best hikes are at the two cloud-forest reserves bookending the main road, Reserva Biológica Bosque Nuboso Monteverde (see p213) and Reserva Santa Elena (see p215).

If you've ever felt cynical about schoolchildren asking for money to save the rainforest, then you really must stop by **Bosque Eterno de los Niños** (Children's Eternal Forest; ☎ 2645-5003; www.acmcr.org; adult/student day use US$8/5, guided night hike US$15/10; 7:30am-5:30pm) and see what they purchased with all that spare change. Keep in mind, however, that this enormous 220-sq-km reserve, which dwarfs both the Monteverde and Santa Elena reserves, is largely inaccessible. The

THE FABLE OF THE GOLDEN TOAD

Once upon a time, in the cloud forests of Monteverde, there lived the golden toad *(Bufo periglenes),* also known as the *sapo dorado*. Because this bright-orange, exotic little toad was often seen scrambling amid the Monteverde leaf litter – the only place in the world where it appeared – it became something of a Monteverde mascot. Sadly, the golden toad has not been seen since 1989 and is now believed to be extinct.

In the late 1980s, unexplained rapid declines in frog and toad populations all over the world spurred an international conference of herpetologists to address these alarming developments. Amphibians once common were becoming rare or had already disappeared, and the scientists were unable to agree upon a reason for the sudden demise of so many amphibian species in so many different habitats.

Several factors may be to blame for these declines, including the fact that amphibians breathe both with primitive lungs and through their perpetually moist skin, which makes them susceptible to airborne toxins. Their skin also provides little protection against UV light, which studies have shown can result in higher mortality rates to amphibian embryos and damaged DNA that in turn causes deformities. Pesticides also have been proven to cause deformities and hermaphroditism. And then there's the global issue of habitat loss. If all that didn't tell a bleak enough story, scientists have since discovered that the worldwide spread of chytridiomycosis disease (caused by the fungus *Batrachochytrium dendrobatidis,* in case you were wondering) has decimated amphibian populations everywhere.

According to the Global Amphibian Assessment, an entire 39% of New World amphibians (that would be 1187 species) are currently threatened with extinction. In response to this dire statistic, an international coalition of zoos and wildlife conservation organizations have jointly established **Amphibian Ark** (www.amphibianark.org), an attempt to 'bank' as many species as possible in the event of further die-offs. We may never know what happened to the golden toad, but as one of the first warning signs that the ecosystem is off balance, its mysterious disappearance might have given a chance for survival – and a happy ending? – to other amphibian species.

international army of children who paid the bills decided that it was more important to provide a home for local wildlife among the primary and secondary forest (and to allow former agricultural land to be slowly reclaimed by the jungle) than to develop a lucrative tourist infrastructure.

The effort has allowed for one fabulous trail that hooks into a system of unimproved trails that are primarily for researchers, the 3.5km **Sendero Bajo del Tigre** (Jaguar Canyon Trail), which offers more open vistas than do those in the cloud forest, so spotting birds tends to be easier. The reason is that a good portion of the surrounding area was clear-cut during the mid-20th century, though there has been significant regrowth since it was granted protected status. The resulting landscape is known as premontane forest, which is unique in Costa Rica as most things that are cut down stay cut down. Visitors also report that wildlife-watching tends to be better here than in the reserves at Monteverde or Santa Elena since the tourist volume is considerably lower.

Make reservations in advance for the popular night hikes, which set off at 5:30pm for a two-hour trek by flashlight (bring your own) through a sea of glowing red eyes. The Estación Biológica San Gerardo at the end of the trail has dorm beds for researchers and students, but you may be able to stay overnight with prior arrangements. If you're looking for a good volunteer program, the administration of the Bosque Eterno de los Niños is always looking for help.

Offering hikes of varying lengths, **Santuario Ecológico** (Ecological Sanctuary; ☎ 2645-5869; admission adult/student/child US$10/8/6, guided night tour US$15/12/10; 🕑 7am-5:30pm) has four loop trails (the longest takes about 2½ hours at a slow pace) through private property comprising premontane and secondary forest, coffee and banana plantations, and past a couple of waterfalls and lookout points. Coati, agouti and sloth are seen on most days, and monkey, porcupine and other animals are also common. Bird-watching is also good. Guided tours are available throughout the day, but you'll see even more animals on the guided night tours (5:30pm to 7:30pm).

An 81-hectare private reserve, **Reserva Sendero Tranquilo** (Tranquil Path Reserve; ☎ 2645-5010; admission US$20; ⏲ tours 7:30am & 1pm) is located between the Reserva Biológica Bosque Nuboso Monteverde and the Río Guacimal. Trails here are narrow to allow for minimal environmental impact, and the group size is capped at six people, which means you won't have to worry about chattering tourists scaring away all the animals. The trails pass through four distinct types of forest, including a previously destroyed area that's starting to bud again.

Sendero Valle Escondido (Hidden Valley Trail; ☎ 2645-6601; day use US$5, night tour adult/child US$20/10; ⏲ 7am-4pm) begins behind the Pensión Monteverde Inn and slowly winds its way through a deep canyon into an 11-hectare reserve. In comparison with the more popular reserves, Valle Escondido is quiet during the day and relatively undertouristed, so it's a good trail for wildlife-watching. However, the reserve's two-hour guided night tour (at 5:30pm) is very popular, so it's best to make reservations for this in advance.

Take a free hike up **Cerro Amigos** (1842m) for good views of the surrounding rainforest and, on a clear day, of Volcán Arenal, 20km away to the northeast. Near the top of the mountain, you'll pass by the TV towers for channels 7 and 13. The trail leaves Monteverde from behind Hotel Belmar and ascends roughly 300m in 3km. From the hotel, take the dirt road going downhill, then the next left. Note that this trail does not connect to the trails in the Monteverde reserve, so you will have to double back.

Another popular (but strenuous) hike is to visit the **Catarata San Luis**, a gorgeous ribbon of water streaming from the cloud forests into a series of swimming holes just screaming for a picnic. The distance from the parking area to the falls is only a few kilometers, but it's steeply graded downhill, and the rocky, mud-filled terrain can get very slick. Readers report that their entire families have been OK on the trail, but it's important to go slow and turn back if it becomes too difficult. However, your efforts will be worth it as the waterfall is simply breathtaking.

Drivers will need a 4WD to ford the little river and climb the muddy road out. You can park (US$6 per car) at a private farm, which is next to the trailhead. Several horseback-riding companies offer excursions to the falls (US$50 per person), but note that much of the road is now paved and this is hard on the horses' knees. A taxi from town to the falls will cost about U$12.

CANOPY TOURS

Wondering where the whole canopy tour craze was born? Santa Elena is the site of Costa Rica's first zip lines, today eclipsed in adrenaline by the nearly 100 imitators who have followed, some of which are right here in town. You won't be spotting any quetzals or coatis as you whoosh your way over the canopy, and questions remain over the ecological value of this type of adventure tourism, but this is the best way to burn your holiday buck.

Before you tighten your harness and clip in for the ride, you're going to have to choose which canopy tour will get your hard-earned cash – this is more challenging than you'd think. Much like the rest of Costa Rica, Monteverde works on a commission-based system, so be skeptical of the advice that you're given, and insist on choosing the canopy tour that you want. We provide basic information on the five major players in town below, though it's good to talk to the friendly, unbiased staff at the Pensión Santa Elena if you want the full scoop.

Aventura (☎ 2645-6388; www.monteverdeadventure.com; adult/student US$40/30; ⏲ 7am-4pm) Aventura has 16 platforms that are spiced up with a Tarzan swing and a 15m rappel. It's about 3km north of Santa Elena on the road to the reserve, and transportation from your hotel is included in the price.

Extremo Canopy (☎ 2645-6058; www.monteverdeextremo.com; adult/child US$40/30; ⏲ 8am-4pm) The newest player on the Monteverde canopy scene, this outfit runs small groups and doesn't bother with extraneous attractions if all you really want to do is fly down the zip lines. There's also a new Superman canopy ride (US$5 extra), allowing you to fly Superman-style through the air.

Original Canopy Tour (☎ 2645-6950; www.canopytour.com; adult/student/child US$45/35/25; ⏲ 7:30am-4pm) On the grounds of Cloud Forest Lodge, this has the fabled zip lines that started an adventure-tourism trend. These lines aren't as elaborate as the others, but with 14 platforms, a rappel through the center of an old fig tree and 5km of private trails worth a wander afterward, you can enjoy a piece of history that's far more entertaining than most museums.

Selvatura (☎ 2645-5929; www.selvatura.com; adult/child US$45/30; ⏲ 7:30am-4pm) One of the bigger games in town, Selvatura has 3km of cables, 18 platforms and one Tarzan swing through primary forest. The office is across the street from the church in Santa Elena.

SkyTrek (☎ 2645-5238; www.skywalk.co.cr; adult/student/child US$75/60/48; 🕑 7:30am-5pm) If you're not buying the whole 'eco' element of canopy tours, then this is definitely for you. This seriously fast canopy tour consists of 11 platforms attached to steel towers that are spread out along a road. We're talking serious speeds of up to 64km/h, which is probably why SkyTrek is the only canopy tour that has a real brake system. The price includes admission to the SkyTram gondola and SkyWalk hanging bridges; cheaper ticket options are available.

HANGING BRIDGES, TRAMS & TRAINS

OK, so you're too scared to zip through the canopy on a steel cable, but fear not: the makers of eco-fun have something special for you – hanging bridges and trams, the safe and slightly less expensive way to explore the tree tops.

Aventura, Selvatura and SkyWalk (owned by SkyTrek) have systems of hanging bridges across which you can traipse and live out your Indiana Jones fantasies. There are subtle differences between all of them (some are fat, some are thin, some are bouncy, some are saggy), though you're going to enjoy the views of the canopy regardless of which one you pick. They're all priced around US$30 for adults and US$20 for students and children.

SkyTram (☎ 2645-5238; www.skywalk.co.cr; ♿), also owned by SkyTrek, is a wheelchair-accessible cable car that leads you on a gentle ride through the cloud forest; tickets can only be purchase in conjunction with SkyWalk or SkyTrek.

Monteverde Trainforest (☎ 2645-5700; www.trainforest.com; adult/student/child under 12yr US$65/33/free; 👪) is a miniature train system that travels four miles through the forest, crossing one tunnel and four bridges. The scenic railroad offers amazing views of Monteverde and Arenal lake and volcano. This is a great option for families with young children, as kids under 12 ride free. It's located 5km north of downtown Santa Elena, on the road to Reserva Santa Elena.

HORSEBACK RIDING

Until recently, this region was most easily traveled on horseback, and considering the roads around here, that's probably still true. Several operators offer you the chance to test this theory, with guided horseback rides ranging from two-hour tours to five-day adventures. Shorter trips generally run about US$15 per hour, while an overnight trek including meals and accommodations runs between US$150 and US$200.

Some outfitters also make the trip to La Fortuna, an intriguing transportation option (US$60 to US$100) with several caveats including only going in the dry season. Though a few operators will charge less, you (or more likely, the horse) get what you pay for.

Caballeriza El Rodeo (☎ 2645-5764, 2645-6306; elrodeo02@gmail.com) Does local tours on private trails, as well as trips to San Luis Waterfall and a sunset tour to a spot overlooking the Golfo de Nicoya. Average price is $30 for two hours.

Desafío Adventure Company (☎ 2645-5874; www.monteverdetours.com) Does local treks for groups and individuals around town, day trips to San Luis Waterfall (US$60 per person including admission, six hours) and several multiday rides. This established outfitter will arrange rides to La Fortuna for US$85, usually on the Lake Trail. The company also arranges white-water rafting trips on the Ríos Toro, Sarapiquí and others, and can help with transport and hotel reservations. Located next door to Morpho's Restaurant.

Meg's Riding Stables (☎ 2645-5560, 2645-5052; 👪) Takes folks on private trails nearby plus treks to San Luis Waterfall. Kid-sized saddles and gentle horses are also available. The horses are well looked after, and this is the longest-established operation in Monteverde.

Mirador Lodge (☎ 2645-5354; Monteverde to Arenal ride US$70) The Quesada family at this isolated cloud-forest lodge takes riders on horseback tours as well as to Arenal, starting from the lodge. If the weather and trail conditions are not perfect, they will arrange a taxi-boat-taxi transfer as an alternative.

Sabine's Smiling Horses (☎ 2645-6894, 8385-2424; www.horseback-riding-tour.com) Run by Sabine, who speaks English, French, Spanish and German, Smiling Horses offers a variety of treks, from US$15 per-hour day trips to specialty tours, including a Full Moon Ride (US$50 per person, three hours). Several multiday treks are also on offer, and Sabine may also take experienced riders on the Castillo Trail, weather permitting. This outfitter has been highly recommended by readers year after year.

Festivals & Events

The **Monteverde Music Festival** is held annually on variable dates from late January to early April. It's gained a well-deserved reputation as one of the top music festivals in Central America. Music is mainly classical, jazz and Latin, with an occasional experimental group to spice things up. Concerts are held on Thursday, Friday and Saturday, at different venues all over town and at Monteverde

Institute, which sponsors it. Some performances are free, but most events ask US$5 to US$15 – proceeds go toward teaching music and the arts in local schools.

The **Sol y Música** festival is sponsored by Bromelias Books, with weekly shows happening from February through April at its amphitheater. In July and August it also hosts the **Gotas y Notas** festival to keep spirits afloat during the wet season; ask around town about shows during your visit.

Courses

Centro Panamericano de Idiomas (CPI; ☎ 2265-6306; www.cpi-edu.com; classes with/without homestay US$480/330; 8am-5pm) Specializes in Spanish-language education, with some courses geared to teenagers, medical professionals or social workers. Also has locations in Heredia and Playa Flamingo, with the opportunity to transfer from campus to campus.

Monteverde Institute (☎ 2645-5053; www.mvinstitute.org) A nonprofit educational institute, founded in 1986, that offers interdisciplinary courses in tropical biology, conservation, sustainable development and Spanish, among other topics. Courses are occasionally open to the public, as are volunteer opportunities in education and reforestation – check the website. Spanish classes start at $290 per week, with homestays with local families available for $18 per night. Long courses (US$4000, 10 weeks) are university-accredited programs for undergraduates and they emphasize tropical community ecology. Internships and volunteer opportunities are also available.

Monteverde Studios of the Arts (☎ 2645-5053) Administered by Monteverde Institute, this offers a variety of classes and workshops, sometimes open to visitors, covering everything from woodworking to papermaking, with a special emphasis on pottery.

Sleeping

During Christmas and Easter, many hotels are booked up weeks in advance. During the January-to-April busy season and also in July, reservations are a good idea, though you can almost always find somewhere to stay. Note that Monteverde can get very cool at night, so don't be surprised if your room doesn't have a fan (but do be if it doesn't have a warm blanket!).

The rates given are high-season rates, but low-season rates could be as much as 30% to 40% lower.

HOSTELS

our pick **Pensión Santa Elena** (☎ 2645-5051, 2645-6240; www.pensionsantaelena.com; camping per person US$4, dm US$7, d US$25-30, d without bathroom US$16-20, cabinas US$35-50; P) This full-service hostel is a perennial favorite, located right in central Santa Elena. Ran and Shannon, the brother-sister duo from Austin, Texas, are committed to offering budget travelers top-notch, four-star service and *pura vida* hospitality. They're also environmentalists at heart, and work with the local community on projects such as the reduction of gray water by installing a water treatment plant. Each room is different, with something to suit every budget and group, including some wheelchair-accessible rooms. The best rooms are in the new annex building, which features great little touches like superior beds, stone showers and iPod docks in every room. Hostel amenities include hot showers, internet cafe, shared well-stocked kitchen and huge lounge, a taco stand and free wi-fi, coffee and tea all day. The charming Costa Rican staff is fully bilingual (Spanish and English), offering the most unbiased tourist information in town.

Cabinas El Pueblo (☎ 2645-6192; www.cabinaselpueblo.com; s/d US$20/30, without bathroom US$15/20, all incl breakfast; P) This pleasant hostel run by an attentive Tico couple is one of the best-value deals in town. The price includes free breakfast, wi-fi and free coffee or tea all day. The well-furnished rooms are big and comfy, with firm mattresses and private hot-water shower. Some rooms also have TV and fridge. You'll also find a fully equipped kitchen, balcony, garden and hammocks.

BUDGET

Competition has kept costs low and budget spots usually offer warm showers, an absolute must in these cold mountain temperatures.

Cabinas Monteverde Paraíso (☎ 2645-5933; monteverdeparaiso@costarricense.cr; r with/without bathroom per person US$10/7; P) Housed in a contemporary, bright yellow-green structure, this little hotel is a great option for those on a tight budget. The 10 clean rooms have comfy beds, TV and frilly, grandmotherly decor. Owner Yesenia is superfriendly and a great cook; don't miss dining at her excellent, onsite *soda*.

Monteverde Backpackers (☎ 2645-5844; www.monteverdebackpackers.com/home.html; dm US$10, s/d/tr/q US$20/30/39/44, all incl breakfast; P) Part of the Costa Rica Hostel Network (along with Arenal Backpackers, Tamarindo Backpackers, Pangaea), Monteverde Backpackers is smaller and more basic than some other cheapies in town. But it's clean and friendly, with wood-paneled rooms, comfy beds and some of the hottest, most powerful showers we've ever felt. Ahhh! You'll also find a communal kitchen, outdoor patio and TV lounge. Note that parking here is extremely limited. Find Monteverde Backpackers on a hill just above Cabinas Vista al Golfo.

Hotel El Sueño (☎ 2645-5021; www.hotelelsuenocr.com; s US$15-25, d US$30-50, all incl breakfast; P) This Tico-run hotel has huge wooden rooms with private hot shower. The pricier, upstairs rooms are airier, though the best ones are toward the back. There's a great balcony with sweeping views of the area.

Cabinas Vista al Golfo (☎ 2645-6321; www.cabinasvistaalgolfo.com; s with/without bathroom US$20/15, d with/without bathroom US$25/20; P wi-fi) This is a very comfortable locale run by a congenial Costa Rican family. Rooms are well kept, the showers are hot and the owners will make you feel right at home. The upstairs balcony rooms ($5 extra) have great views of the rainforest and, on a clear day, the Golfo de Nicoya. There's a small, communal kitchen.

Manakín Lodge (☎ 2645-5080, 2645-5835; www.manakinlodge.com; r per person incl breakfast standard/superior US$18/25; P internet wi-fi) This simple Tico family-run lodge in Cerro Plano has a very friendly, laid-back feel. All of the rooms have homey furnishings, wi-fi and private hot-water shower, though the 2nd-floor superior rooms have better views of the forest and have TV and fridge.

Pensión Monteverde Inn (☎ 2645-5156; r per person incl breakfast US$20; P) In a tranquil corner of Cerro Plano is this small inn, next to the trailhead for the Sendero Valle Escondido. Spartan rooms have private hot shower, and its remote location means lots of peace and quiet. The owners can pick you up at the bus stop if you have a reservation.

Casa Tranquilo (☎ 2645-6782; www.casatranquilohostel.com; r per person incl breakfast with/without bathroom US$25/20; P internet wi-fi) This wonderful little hotel is owned and managed by a delightful Tico couple, David and Elena (and their little one, Josue). Some of the wood-paneled rooms have skylights and views of the gulf. Check out the great upstairs terrace, perfect for a few late-night ballads on the guitar. There's also a communal kitchen, free internet (and wi-fi), free coffee and tea, CD burning and printing, and a buffet breakfast with granola, bread, eggs and fruit.

Pensión Colibrí (☎ 2645-5682; r US$20-30; P) Another popular budget option, this small, family-run *pensión* is on a quiet lane and feels like it's perched among the trees. The larger rooms are worth the money as they have a fridge and balconies overlooking the woods, which are perfect for breathing in the cool, mountain air. There's also a small communal kitchen.

Cabinas Eddy (☎ 2645-6635; www.cabinas-eddy.com; d US$20-35, without bathroom US$20; P internet) This reader-recommended budget spot continues to get raves for its delightful, English-speaking staff and the marimba-playing owner and manager Eddy. Breakfast is an extra US$3, but there's a shared kitchen. The balcony is a great place to relax with a cup of free coffee and take in the view.

Mar Inn B&B (☎ 2645-5279; www.monteverdemarinn.com; s/d incl breakfast US$25/40; P internet wi-fi family) On a hill about 50m north of the high school, this family-run B&B is a great option, as the managers are welcoming and breakfasts filling. Wood-paneled rooms are rustic and airy, and the quiet location means a restful night's sleep. The tastefully decorated rooms have private bathroom with hot water; some rooms have TV. Relax on the shared balcony rocking chairs for lovely sunset views of Santa Elena and the Golfo de Nicoya.

Quetzal Inn (☎ 2645-6076; www.quetzalinn.com; s/d $35/45, without balcony $30/40, all incl breakfast; P internet) Up the same quiet alley as Pensión Colibrí is this lovely little lodge. With wood-plank walls, high sloped ceilings and green surroundings, this family-run inn embodies the perfect combination of central location, thoughtfully designed accommodations and a personable, hospitable ambience.

Sunset Hotel (☎ 2645-5048; s/d/tr incl breakfast US$30/40/55; P) About 1.5km out of Santa Elena toward Reserva Santa Elena, this intimate guesthouse is in a secluded location with great views of the Golfo de Nicoya and ample opportunities for bird-watching on private trails. Clean, standard rooms with porches have two little luxuries: real hot showers (not suicide machines) and toilets with enough pressure to flush paper. German and English are spoken.

our pick **Arco Iris Ecolodge** (☎ 2645-5067; www.arcoirislodge.com; s US$30-64, d US$40-128, cabins US$107-200, honeymoon ste US$193; P internet) This clutch of pretty cabins is on a little hill overlooking Santa Elena and the surrounding forests, and has the privacy and intimacy of a mountain retreat. The lodge features a system of private trails that wind throughout the property, including one that leads to a lookout point where you can see the Pacific on a clear day. There are a variety of different room sizes and styles to choose from, so you can either go rustic or live it up. If you're traveling in a group, the four- to five-person split-level cabin is highly recommended – it's adorned with rich tapestries and features volcanic rock–laden showers. The multilingual German owners are delightful, and they make excellent meals that sometimes feature organic vegetables grown on the grounds. Breakfast is an additional US$7. English, Spanish, German and French spoken.

Hotel Don Taco (☎ 2645-5263; www.cabinasdontaco.com; d standard/cabinas incl breakfast US$34/51, cabañas s/d US$40/62; P) The name sounds a little silly, but with big porches, great murals and an outdoor dining and chill-out area, this spot is fabulous. *Cabañas* come with TV, refrigerator and a balcony overlooking the Golfo de Nicoya. It's just north of Santa Elena proper, so you can rest easy at night.

Mariposa B&B (☎ 2645-5013; vmfamilia@costarricense.cr; s/d incl breakfast US$35/55; P) Just 1.5km from the Monteverde reserve, this friendly family-run place has simple but very nice rooms with private hot showers, all nestled into the forest. In addition to breakfast (a *real* breakfast of fruits, pancakes, eggs and tortillas), there's also a little balcony for observing wildlife, because nothing is cuter than a passel of *pizotes* (coatis).

MIDRANGE

Finca Terra Viva (☎ 2645-5454; www.terravivacr.com; d US$40, extra person US$5, 3 meals extra US$14, casitas US$60; P 💻) This 135-hectare *finca* 3.5km or so out on the road toward Reserva Santa Elena is being gradually returned to the forest; about 60% is already there. In the meantime, cattle, pigs, goats, horses and chickens offer guests a typically Costa Rican rural experience – kids love this place. Each of the six rustic, wooden rooms sleeps up to four and has a private hot shower; a few free-standing *casitas* (cottages), each sleeping four and fitted with kitchenette, are available for those desiring more privacy. Owner Federico is a well-known naturalist and guide who has long envisioned living in a *finca* that combines education, conservation and farming – this is the result. Horseback riding can be arranged, and you can try your hand at milking cows and making cheese at the organic dairy.

La Colina Lodge (☎ 2645-5009; www.lacolinalodge.com; camping per person US$5, d with/without bathroom incl breakfast US$52/44; P) This is the former Flor Mar opened in 1977 by Marvin Rockwell, one of the area's original Quakers, who was jailed for refusing to sign up for the draft in 1949 and then spent three months driving down from Alabama. Nowadays, the gringo owners are as gracious and unpretentiously welcoming as the lodge itself. All of the rambling rooms on this peaceful property are hand-painted in cheery colors with unique furniture and decor, and the kitchen and communal areas provide either shade or sun, and always a relaxed vibe.

Swiss Hotel Miramontes (☎ 2645-5152; www.swisshotelmiramontes.com; s/d US$45/56, d chalets US$85, all incl breakfast; P) Just outside Santa Elena on the road to Juntas is this charming European-inspired retreat, well situated in a grove of pine trees and tropical flowers. Eight rooms of varying size come with fabulous private hot-water bathroom, while the two chalets have a little more breathing space, and a private porch where you can kick off your shoes. Kids love the expansive landscaped grounds, with trails through the well-stocked orchid garden (US$5 for nonguests) and everyone enjoys the huge, pretty chalets. The restaurant (mains ₡2200 to ₡5600, open from 1pm to 10pm) specializes in Swiss treats and, as this is a Swiss-run Costa Rican hotel, staff speak English, German, French and Spanish.

Hotel El Viandante (☎ 2645-6475; www.hotelelviandante.com; d $60 incl breakfast; P 💻 📶 👶) Perched on a small but steep hill with views of the gulf, this small B&B is a great choice for families. It's not superfancy, but the 12 recently remodeled rooms have pinewood interiors with high ceilings, huge private bathroom with hot water and hairdryers, cable TV, orthopedic mattresses and baby cribs on request. Enjoy an American breakfast with a view from the top-floor lounge. Hosts Grace and Renzo are wonderfully hospitable and have a wealth of local knowledge. This is the only place in town that rents bikes.

Monteverde Rustic Lodge (☎ 2645-6256; www.monteverderusticlodge.com; s/d/tr incl breakfast US$42/65/75; P) The tree-branch posts and tree-trunk table tops play along with the theme, but the remodeled rooms are spotless, comfortable and not at all rustic. Rooms have private hot-water shower and tile floors and open on to the garden. It's a short walk from the center of Santa Elena and the Tico owners will happily arrange tours for you.

Nidia Lodge (☎ 2645-5236, 2645-6082; www.nidialodge.com; s/d standard US$58/76, deluxe US$81/99, junior ste US$93/116, all incl breakfast; P 💻 wi-fi) The proprietor of Pensión Flor de Monteverde, Eduardo Venegas Castro, has a beautiful new inn named for his wife. The area is peaceful and just steps away from the Santuario Ecológico, so there's a good chance that wildlife will grace your front doorstep and the motmots will hang out in the trees out back. First-rate accommodations feature hot water and private balconies upstairs, with free wi-fi to boot. There's a nice restaurant where breakfast is served. Nidia provides a superchill presence around the inn, and Eduardo, an expert naturalist, clearly revels in offering guided walks of the area's forests.

Mirador Lodge (☎ 2645-5354; www.miradorlodge.com; s/d/tr incl breakfast US$82/92/102; P 💻 wi-fi) About 9km north of Santa Elena, the Quesada family has established this 55-hectare private reserve in the mists of virgin cloud forest. With views of Arenal, the wooden cabins have gas-heated water, and some have wood-burning stove. There's generator-powered electricity, but candles are provided as a backup, and it's advisable to bring a flashlight. The lodge provides free transfers from town, and transportation in the area for a small fee. The owners also run reputable horseback-riding tours.

Cloud Forest Lodge (☎ 2645-5058; www.cloudforestlodge.com; s/d/tr/q US$90/102/113/125; P 💻 wi-fi) Simple, wood-walled rooms at this hilltop lodge have hot-water shower, but lack extras like satellite TV. Instead, there are trails to walk, birds and sometimes sloths to be seen in the garden and surrounding cloud forest, and views of the Golfo de Nicoya. The helpful staff can arrange tours. It's a pleasant walk into town, but you might want a car to get around.

Los Pinos Cabañas y Jardines (☎ 2645-5252; www.lospinos.net; cabañas standard/junior ste/family US$65/80/125; P) Eleven free-standing *cabañas* are scattered around the peaceful, forested gardens of this nine-hectare property, which once formed a part of the family *finca*. Each *cabaña* affords a sense of privacy, with plenty of space between each one, and has a fully equipped kitchen and small terrace. It's a superb setting for those seeking a little solitude in easy walking distance of restaurants and shops around Cerro Plano. Though all of the *cabañas* are very comfortable and cozy, family rooms are the largest. Junior suites and family cabins are outfitted with hair dryers, cable TV and more upscale furnishings.

Hotel Claro de Luna (☎ 2645-5269; www.clarodelunahotel.com; s standard/deluxe US$59/68, d standard/deluxe US$68/88, all incl breakfast; P) This sweet mountain chalet just southwest of Santa Elena is the perfect getaway for lovers. If you squint your eyes just a bit while staring at the hotel's Swiss-inspired architecture, you could convince yourself you're summering high up in the Alps. All nine rooms have hardwood floors and ceilings, and feature luxurious, hot-water bathroom with regal tiles.

El Sol (☎ 2645-5838; www.elsolnuestro.com; d small/large cabins US$60/80; P 🏊) Located 5km outside of Santa Elena near Guacimal is this 'sunny' spot. This small farm with two guest cabins is at a lower elevation than Santa Elena – the climate is drier and the sun is warmer. The owners of this highly recommended accommodations, Elisabeth and Ignacio, are a German-Spanish couple who will pamper you with strong massages and delicious home cooking. Their teenage son, Javier, is a great guide around the private trails on foot or on horseback.

Hotel de Montaña Monteverde (☎ 2645-5046; www.monteverdemountainhotel.com; r standard/superior US$78/135; P 💻) Opened in 1978 as the first top-end accommodations in Monteverde, this hotel has had a recent renovation to show off its expansive lobby views to better advantage; though the rooms didn't benefit from any added character, they're still perfectly comfortable. Standard rooms have wood accents, thick mattresses and cable TV, and they can sleep up to three people. The superior rooms can accommodate up to four people, and they have a huge bathtub, a private balcony and a minibar. The spacious gardens and forests of the 15-hectare property are pleasant to walk around, and there's also a sauna and Jacuzzi.

Hotel Finca Valverde (☎ 2645-5157; www.monteverde.co.cr; d standard/cabin/superior US$87/93/111, extra person US$17-23; P) Just outside Santa Elena, this working coffee farm is a great choice if you're looking for something a bit different. Cabins each have two bare units with private hot-water shower, an upstairs loft and a balcony, though the real reason you're here is to soak up the rural atmosphere. Junior suites are only slightly more expensive, though they have full bathroom and cable TV. A simple but pleasant restaurant (mains ₡2300 to ₡6200; open from 6am to 9:30pm) serves good fish and meat dishes as well as vegetables from the backyard garden. The attached bar is popular with locals.

Vista Verde Lodge (☎ 8380-1517; www.info-monteverde.com; s/d standard US$87/107, junior ste US$93/116, extra person US$14, all incl breakfast; P) When you really want to get away from it all, take the signed side road just east of Selvatura and head 2.5 rough kilometers (4WD only) to this marvelous lodge, where you'll fall asleep to the sounds of the surrounding rainforest. Wood-paneled rooms with picture windows take in views of Volcán Arenal, and the current direction of the lava flow means that on a clear night you will see plenty of fireworks. There's also a great common area where you can unwind in front of the TV and warm your feet beside the fire. Some 4km of trails through the primary forest surrounding this gorgeous spot can be explored on horseback. Staff can pick you up from the airport with advance notice, and they provide a shuttle service into Santa Elena. If you're expecting luxury at this price, look elsewhere (plus generator power can mean dim lights and quickly cooling showers), but solitude you'll find in spades.

Trapp Family Lodge (☎ 2645-5858; www.trappfam.com; d superior/ste US$96/113, extra person US$17; P ⊠ 💻 ♿) The closest lodge to the reserve entrance (just under 1km away) has 20 spacious rooms with high wooden ceilings, big bathrooms and fabulous views from the picture windows (which overlook either gardens or cloud forest). Suites come complete with TV and refrigerator, and there's no smoking anywhere, so you can breathe easy. There's a homey restaurant (mains ₡5600 to ₡9000), a bar and sitting room with cable TV that's open till 10pm. The emphasis here is on creating a family atmosphere, so bring the kids along and teach them a thing or two about nature.

TOP END

Many of the pricier hotels are experimenting with alternative technologies, from solar-heated showers to elaborate gray-water systems. Owners are usually more than happy to offer impromptu tours with full explanations of how these technologies work, and can offer suggestions to those who'd like to implement similar systems back home.

Hotel Heliconia (☎ 2645-5109; www.hotelheliconia.com; d standard/junior ste/family ste/master ste incl breakfast US$100/112/137/155; P 💻) In Cerro Plano, this attractive, wooden, family-run hotel consists of the main lodge and several bungalows that are spread out across a mountainside. Standard rooms have breezy views while junior suites are ridiculously luxurious with two double beds, full bathroom and stained-glass windows. The two master suites, which can each accommodate up to six people or be connected for a party of 12, are downright palatial with huge sitting areas, whirlpool tubs and outdoor terraces overlooking the Golfo de Nicoya. Owners arrange all the usual tours, and operate a spa and aesthetic center where you can soak your stresses away in the Jacuzzi, or indulge in an endless list of beauty treatments. The onsite Restaurante Mediterráneo (mains US$8 to US$12; open from 6:30am to 9pm) offers innovative Italian and seafood specialties as well as a smattering of typical Costa Rican dishes.

Monteverde Lodge & Gardens (☎ 2257-0766; www.costaricaexpeditions.com; d US$111-190; P ⊠ 💻 🏊) A progressive recycling strategy, a solar-energy system and a huge solar-powered – but nice and hot – Jacuzzi are among this nonsmoking hotel's noteworthy environmentally sound practices. Large rooms with full bathroom and wraparound picture windows have garden or forest views. The large lobby is graced by a huge fireplace, and there's an impeccable bar that looks down on the huge Jacuzzi. The grounds are attractively landscaped with a variety of native plants, emphasizing ferns, bromeliads and mosses, and a short trail leads to a bluff with an observation platform at the height of the forest canopy, with good views of the forest and a river ravine. Most people are here on all-inclusive package deals that include three meals, served à la carte and featuring quality international cuisine, as well as guided tours and transportation from San José.

Hotel Poco a Poco (☎ 2645-6000; www.hotelpocoapoco.com; s/d/tr incl breakfast US$102/113/124; P ⊠ 💻 📶 🏊) A short walk from Santa Elena will bring you to this funky property, which is adorned with ceramic mushrooms, tree frogs and other Costa Rican critters. Yellow-stuccoed rooms sleep three, and they have some great perks – full bathtub, a heated and covered swimming pool, free wi-fi, big cable TV and a DVD library (rental US$3) to dip into during those rainy nights. The best draw, however, is the excellent restaurant (mains ₡3500 to ₡6000; open from 6:30am to 9am and from 11:30am to 9:30pm), which is also open to the public and specializes in barbecues.

Hotel Belmar (☎ 2645-5201; www.hotelbelmar.net; s/d/tr chalet US$90/114/116, standard US$117/130/149, all incl breakfast; P 🖳) Despite being a 'real' eco-resort (the most unusual attraction is the on-site 'Biodigestor' used to create gas for cooking and heating), the Swiss-style Hotel Belmar admirably doesn't flaunt this in its name. Rooms here are definitely upscale, though even their design scheme is commendable as all the artwork is from Casem (see p210). The biggest bonus is right out back: this is the trailhead for Cerro Amigos. Amenities include a Jacuzzi, pool table, pond and great restaurant with tremendous views of cloud forest and the gulf.

Hotel Fonda Vela (☎ 2645-5125; www.fondavela.com; s/d US$109/120, junior ste US$120/141, extra person US$9; P ⊠ 🖳 ♿) With a convenient location near the Monteverde reserve, unique architectural styling, 14 hectares of trail-laden grounds and a private stable, this classy retreat is a sophisticated home base for enjoying the pleasures of the area. Standard rooms are spacious and light, with wood accents and large windows; and the suites are among the nicest rooms in town, featuring bathtub, balcony and sitting room with huge TV. Many rooms are wheelchair-accessible. The restaurant (mains US$8 to US$16; open from 6:15am to 9am, noon to 2pm and 6:30pm to 8:30pm) is open to the public, and recommended for its excellent food that emphasizes fresh, local ingredients. The hotel is owned by the two sons of Paul Smith, who first arrived in Monteverde in the 1950s and is a well-known local artist whose work graces the walls.

Hotel El Sapo Dorado (☎ 2645-5010; www.sapodorado.com; s/d incl breakfast US$116/138, extra person US$30; P ⊠ 🖳 V) This hotel is owned by the Arguedas family, which first settled in the Monteverde area 10 years prior to the Quakers. Today the family is extremely active in the community, and they're regular promoters of the virtues of sustainable tourism. The 'Golden Toad' has 30 spacious rooms mostly in duplex cabins. All have two queen-sized beds, a table and chairs, and private hot shower. Various deluxe suites have minibar, refrigerator and French doors that open to private terraces with views of the Golfo de Nicoya. The private forest behind the hotel has an extensive system of trails, and the restaurant (mains US$10 to US$20; open from 6:30am to 9am, noon to 3pm and 6pm to 9pm) is renowned for its use of locally grown produce and wide range of vegetarian dishes.

our pick **Hidden Canopy Treehouses** (☎ 2645-5447; www.hiddencanopy.com; d garden rooms US$186, tree houses US$242-322, all incl breakfast & afternoon tea; P ⊠) One of the most unique accommodations in Costa Rica, this new boutique hotel lets guests live out their wildest childhood tree-house fantasies, but in a grown-up, blissfully luxurious setting. Hidden within 13 acres of private rainforest are four standalone, wood and glass tree houses, each with a unique floor plan, decor and name. All feature a treetop balcony, luxurious bedding, private bathroom, waterfall shower, custom-made furniture, paintings by local artist Stella, plus high-end amenities such as minibar, coffeemaker, hair dryer, alarm clock and safe. The two-level Eden tree house has a fireplace, glass-enclosed Jacuzzi and canopied bed – perfect for honeymooners. The Neverland tree house sleeps four and overlooks its own Koi pond and has 1½ baths. There are two less-expensive rooms in the main house, where breakfast and sunset teas are held. Simply put, American owner Jennifer and her Tico partner Christhiam have created one of the most romantic hotels we've ever seen.

El Establo Mountain Resort (☎ 2645-5110; www.hotelelestablo.com; d deluxe/ste incl breakfast US$194/267; P ⊠ 🖳) This is a seriously upscale lodge offering a variety of rooms, which are among the most luxurious that the Monteverde-Santa Elena area has to offer. Deluxe rooms have an orthopedic mattress, cable TV, fridge, safe and hair dryer. Junior suites have all of those amenities in addition to split bathroom and sitting area, while the open-plan suites are A-frame lofts with private terraces. Some of the suites have Jacuzzi tubs facing wonderful views, while others have private flagstone terraces. Other amenities include a spa, two indoor pools, two restaurants, hiking trails, and tennis and basketball courts. It's a steep hike to the best rooms, but the resort runs a shuttle on request.

Eating

The top-end hotels in town often have good restaurants, most of which are open to the public. Santa Elena has most of the budget eateries in the area.

The giant **SuperCompro** (☎ 2758-7351; 🕒 7am-9pm) grocery store in Santa Elena has everything you could possibly need including organic produce. **Coop Santa Elena** (🕒 7:30am-6pm) in Cerro Plano has a smaller selection, but profits are reinvested in the community (it's part of the Casem cooperative).

BUDGET

Sabores (☎ 2645-6174; cones ₡560-1700; 🕒 11am-8pm Wed-Mon) With longer hours than La Lechería, this place serves Monteverde's own brand of ice cream, plus coffee and a variety of homemade desserts. It's the perfect place for a civilized scoop after a morning hike through primitive forest.

Panadería Jiménez (☎ 2645-5035; items ₡560-3000; 🕒 5am-6:30pm Mon-Sat, 5am-10am Sun) This bakery has the best goods in town, like whole-wheat breads, pastries and coffee for folks booked on the early bus.

Dulce Marzo (☎ 2645-6568; items ₡650-4500; 🕒 11am-7pm) Yummy home-baked sweets, wraps, sandwiches, good espresso drinks and a favorite-cafe feel make this one of those places to linger over a late-morning coffee as you skim the paper or your guidebook. Foreign magazines scatter the tables and there's also a book exchange if you need reading material for the next leg of your trip. Located next door to Atmosphera gallery.

Stella's Bakery (☎ 2645-5560; mains ₡800-3200; 🕒 6am-10pm) Order your choice of sandwich on delicious homemade breads with a convenient order form (one side is in English), and don't skimp on the veggies, many of which are locally grown (and organic). You can also get soups, salads, quiches and lots of tempting sweet pastries.

Maravilla (☎ 2645-6623; mains ₡1500-3500; 🕒 6am-9pm) Just about the cheapest and most authentic restaurant in Santa Elena, this charming *soda* serves typical Costa Rican specialties including excellent *casados*. The menu also features American favorites such as fajitas, pancakes, French toast and 12 kinds of milk shakes. This place gets very crowded during lunch hour, so plan accordingly.

INSPIRATION IN THE CLOUD FOREST

Born and raised in Monteverde, Marco Tulio Brenes moved to San José, where he worked with established artists, at age 18. He ran the gallery Éxtasis for a decade, lived in the USA, and exhibited his work there in group and solo shows, and found inspiration for recent work in his travels through Europe and Turkey. He's been an artist – or at least wished to be one – since he was very small. Now he is dedicated to working mostly in sculpture and painting in his open studio, Artes Stulio (p210), in the cloud forest.

What are your artistic influences? In my sculptures I always find that nature is my biggest influence, and when I saw the works of Henry Moore, they also influenced me for some time. In painting, my primary influence was the surrealists, especially Dalí; after some time, I discovered that the true influence of my work I found inside myself, through the investigation of the intense colors and organic shapes of the tropics.

How would you describe your style, and in what media do you work? It's difficult for me to describe my own style. It's imaginative, visionary art. In painting, I work in oil and acrylic on canvas. And in sculpture, I work in stone, ceramics and principally in clay. Stone and clay are my favorite media.

Describe the arts scene in Monteverde. I live in Monteverde because it's the place that brings me the most inspiration, with its marvelous forests and its spectacular views of the Pacific. Furthermore, it's a place where I meet good artists working in different media, and who live the artistic life very intensely, and with a dedication to diverse cultural activities. For this reason it's a great place where I can show the public my work in my studio and at the same time demonstrate my process.

What is it like being an artist in Monteverde? Monteverde is a unique place to feel and live art. There's a definite feeling of a dedicated artistic community, whose art manifests itself in diverse media – music, poetry, sculpture, yoga, photography, makers of musical instruments… There are quite a few arts events here, but the artists and the art-appreciating community always wish there were more events and opportunities to share artistic experiences.

our pick Café Caburé (☎ 2645-5020; mains ₡2300-5000; 8am-8pm Mon-Sat;) Looking for something different? Argentine owner Susana Salas has created one of the most eclectic menus around, including Mexican chicken *mole,* chipotle-rubbed steak, sweet-and-sour chicken wraps, curries and mouth-watering, homemade chocolates and other desserts. The balcony has some of the most incredible sunset views in town. Located in Paseo de Stella.

MIDRANGE & TOP END

Chimera (☎ 2645-6081; tapas ₡1700-5000; 11:30am-9:30pm) Latin-infused tapas are complemented by an excellent wine list featuring robust reds like Chilean Syrah-cabernets and crisp whites like pinot grigio. Dine alfresco at the trellis patio or the big-windowed dining room with beautiful jungle views. Charming staff will lay out a spread of cocktails (like kiwi caipirinhas, with lime, sugar and rum) and tapas like sea bass with passion-fruit cream and spicy mayo, or fried yucca with chipotle garlic aioli, all on white tablecloths.

Musashi (☎ 2645-7160; sushi ₡2500-4000, rolls & mains ₡2500-9000; 11am-11pm Tue-Sun) Who ever thought you'd find good sushi in the middle of the rainforest? But look no further than this tiny restaurant in the heart of Santa Elena. Venezuelan owner Jesus is a classically trained sushi chef with an eye for perfection. The sushi boats are a good deal for groups. You'll also find other favorite Japanese dishes including tepanyaki, teriyaki and lunch bento box specials.

La Pizzería de Johnny (☎ 2645-5066; www.pizzeriadejohnny.com; mains ₡2200-8300; 11:30am-10pm) Woodfired, thin-crust pizzas will warm you right up after a long hike through the cloud forests (or up the hill from Santa Elena). The warm atmosphere and lovely dining area makes it feel as though you are having a nicc dinner out without paying the price.

Sabor Español (☎ 2645-5387; saborespanola@hotmail.com; mains ₡3000-7500; noon-9pm) She's from Barcelona. He's from Ibiza. And together, Heri and Montse have created one of the most authentic and lovely Spanish restaurants in Costa Rica. The couple specialize in paella, fresh fish, meats and chicken. We loved the stuffed avocado appetizer, followed by shrimp flambéed in whiskey. Wash it down with some of the best sangria this side of the Atlantic. The ambience is *super tranquillo* and well worth the trip 2km north of downtown.

Restaurante Campesino (☎ 2645-6883; mains ₡3000-10,000; 9am-11pm) Relax beneath about 80 stuffed animals won from machines by the dexterous owner, who also serves up amazing *casados,* salads and a variety of sublime *ceviche* with a smile. The blue shopfront also has our favorite mural in town, and we've never seen toilet cozies quite like these.

Morpho's Restaurant (☎ 2645-5607; mains ₡3800-10,000; 11am-9pm; V) This romantic, downtown restaurant spices up typical Costa Rican food by adding a gourmet flair. *Casados* feature a variety of European-influenced sauces (think sea bass in a fruity demiglaze), and are served with a traditional *batido* (fruit shake) or a more sophisticated glass of wine. The menu also has a good variety of vegetarian dishes.

Restaurante de Lucía (☎ 2645-5337; www.costa-rica-monteverde.com; mains ₡4000-8500; 11am-9pm) On the same road as El Jardín de las Mariposas, this Chilean-owned place is Monteverde's most famous restaurant. Chef José Belmar, who speaks more languages then you and your friend put together, regularly chats to guests and asks for feedback on the cuisine, and dishes (a good mix of Italian and South American specialties) are always flawless, and reasonably priced.

Tree House Restaurant & Café (☎ 2645-5751; www.canopydining.com; mains ₡4000-9000; 6am-10pm;) Built around a half-century-old *higuerón* (fig) tree, this hip cafe serves up your favorite Mexican dishes from burritos to *huevos rancheros* (eggs served with tortillas and a tomato sauce), and has a healthy selection of salads and sandwiches. The burlap-bag ceiling and jungle-themed murals painted on the yellow stucco walls surround the airy atrium. It's a cool, lively space to have a bite, linger over wine and sometimes catch good live music.

our pick Trio (☎ 2645-7254; mains ₡5000-7000; lunch & dinner) From the same people who brought us Chimera and Sofia comes this amazing new fusion restaurant. We were in heaven after savoring the *camarones mojitos* – grilled shrimp drenched in a garlic, cumin, onion, rum and orange-juice sauce, served on a bed of potatoes, veggies and avocados. Follow up the flavor explosions with to-die-for desserts like the mango split sorbet. The contemporary, stilted building is oddly located in a dark corner behind the SuperCompro supermarket. It may not have the ambience of its sister restaurants, but this is hands-down our favorite dining experience in Monteverde.

Pizzería Tramonti (☎ 2645-6120; mains ₡5000-12,500; ⏲ 11am-10pm Mon-Sat) It's worth the trip out here if you hanker for authentic Italian, as the pizzas are baked in a wood-fired oven, and the pastas and seafood are consistently fresh. The atmosphere is also relaxed yet romantic, and the picture windows are perfect for admiring the cloud forest and passers-by.

Sofia (☎ 2645-7017; mains ₡6800-9000; ⏲ 11:30am-9:30pm) Sofia has established itself on the Monteverde restaurant scene as one of the best places in town with its Nuevo Latino cuisine – a modern fusion of traditional Latin American cooking styles. The ambience is flawless – soft lighting, hip music, picture windows, romantic candle settings, sloping wooden ceilings, pastel paintwork and potent cocktails to lighten the mood.

Drinking & Entertainment

Monteverde and Santa Elena nightlife generally involves a guided hike into one of the reserves, but since this misty green mountain draws artists and dreamers, there's a smattering of regular cultural offerings. When and if there's anything going on, you'll see it heavily advertised around town with flyers. Look for events at the **Paseo de Stella Auditorium**, located in the Paseo de Stella shopping center, or **Bromelias Music Garden** (☎ 2645-6272; www.bromelias musicgarden.com), the long-running and constantly metamorphosing haven for the arts in Monteverde.

If you desire aural pleasure, pop into the **Tree House Restaurant & Café** (☎ 2645-5751; www.canopydining.com) for nightly live music.

Unicornio Discotec (⏲ noon-midnight) is an almost exclusively local hangout near the northern end of the soccer field; it's the only place in town that has Imperial on tap (pro), but also has karaoke (con). Two popular bars that usually have a good mix of locals and tourists are **Amigos Bar** (☎ 2645-5071; ⏲ noon-1am), a great place to drink and shoot pool, and the **Taberna Los Valverde** (☎ 2645-5157; www.monteverde.co.cr; ⏲ 11am-1am), at Hotel Finca Valverde, which has a dance floor made for shaking your moneymaker.

Other nightlife venues worth checking out include the following.

La Guarida del Sapo (☎ 2645-7010; ⏲ 6pm-midnight Mon-Thu, 6pm-2am Fri & Sat) This cathedral of music built by the Hotel El Sapo Dorado resembles an old church – right down to the stained-glass windows with Costa Rican nature scenes. But about the only praying you may do here is to the porcelain god. Fridays are the most lively nights when the place is transformed into a discotheque. There's live music on most Mondays and Saturdays. The international restaurant (mains ₡6000 to ₡12,000) serves everything from filet mignon to escargot. A small cover charge applies for special events.

Housed in Santa Elena's original tavern, **Matáe Caña** (☎ 2645-4883; ⏲ noon-late Tue-Sun) is a chic new lounge that fills the void long been present in Monteverde. Opened in late 2009 by the folks behind Pensión Santa Elena, Matáe Caña features the same passion and attention to detail. A waterfall graces one entire wall of the bar. There are numerous padded nooks and crannies where you can sip a drink with your date. During warm weather, guests can lounge on beds in the outdoor patio. The women's bathroom even has its own lounge with couch and huge mirrors. The bar has a good selection of rums and specialty drinks; don't miss the Howler Monkey Shot. The lounge also hosts occasional live salsa bands.

Shopping

During our recent visit, a very large, looming and ugly shopping mall was being constructed on a hill overlooking Santa Elena. Following is a list of some of our favorite local galleries, listed in geographical order from Santa Elena to Monteverde reserve.

Art House (Casa de Arte; ☎ 2645-5275; www.monteverdearthouse.com; ⏲ 9am-6:30pm) Several rooms stuffed with colorful Costa Rican artistry is what you'll find at the Art House. There's jewelry, ceramic work, Boruca textiles and paintings. Though styles here differ quite a bit, it's more along the crafty end of the artsy-craftsy spectrum. It's a great place to find a unique local souvenir.

Atmosphera (☎ 2645-6555; complejoatmosphera@yahoo.com.mx; ⏲ 9am-6pm) An upscale Cerro Plano gallery that specializes in wood sculpture created by artists from all over Costa Rica. Several are from the Monteverde area, and the pieces run the gamut of style and function. They're also priced accordingly, from about US$25 to US$5000. If you fall in conflicted love with some sinuous piece here, may we suggest you think it over with a massage (US$50 to US$60) at the in-house natural spa.

Luna Azul (☎ 2645-6638; lunaazulmonteverde@gmail.com; 9am-6:30pm) This funky boutique is decked out in celestial murals, and it's a relaxing spot to do a little souvenir shopping for your friends…or yourself. There's a great variety of clothing, handmade jewelry and local art up for grabs as well as various aromatherapy products. Check out the fused-glass jewelry – some of our favorite pieces here.

Río Shanti (☎ 2645-6121; www.rioshanti.com; 10am-5pm Mon-Sat, noon-5pm Sun;) The real reason to come here is for a spa treatment, massage or yoga class for adults and children (be sure to call ahead for an appointment or schedule), but this calming space on the road into Monteverde also has a gallery of local art for sale.

Artes Stulio (☎ 2645-5567; artestulio@yahoo.com; 11am-5pm Mon-Sat) A working studio where you can browse the gallery and also roam upstairs to watch the artists at work. The art here is a bit more experimental and an intriguing look into the contemporary scene fostered by the magical Monteverde atmosphere.

Alquimia Artes (☎ 2645-5847; www.alquimiaartes.com; 10am-5pm) The work here is a tad more affordable than at some other places (check out the jewelry by Tarsicio Castillo from the Ecuadorian Andes), but this doesn't mean its collection of wood sculpture, paintings and prints by Costa Rican artists isn't astounding.

Casem (Cooperativa de Artesanía Santa Elena Monteverde; ☎ 2645-5190; www.casemcoop.org; 8am-5pm Mon-Sat, 10am-4pm Sun high season) Begun in 1982 as a women's cooperative representing eight female artists, today Casem has expanded to include almost 150 local artisans, eight of whom are men. Embroidered and hand-painted clothing, polished wooden tableware, handmade cards and other work, some even priced for budget souvenir shoppers, make for an eclectic selection.

Bromelias Books (☎ 2645-6272; www.bromeliasmusicgarden.com; 10am-5:30pm) Don cute felt shoes before entering this bookstore, with its polished-wood Cerro Plano expanse of local arts and crafts, including some intricate batik. There are also books about the region, in particular natural history, in English and Spanish, plus lots of excellent Costa Rican and Central American music. The small amphitheater outside the bookstore has regular theater and musical performances – be on the lookout for posters advertising events.

Hummingbird Gallery (☎ 2645-5030; 8:30am-5pm) This gallery just outside Monteverde reserve has beautiful photos, watercolors, art by the indigenous Chorotega and Boruca people and, best of all, feeders that constantly attract several species of hummingbird. Great photo ops include potential hot shots of the violet sabrewing (Costa Rica's largest hummer) and the coppery-headed emerald, one of only three mainland birds endemic to Costa Rica. An identification board shows the nine species that are seen here. If you'd like a closer look, slides and photographs of the jungle's most precious feathered gems (and other luminous critters) by renowned British wildlife photographers Michael and Patricia Fogden are on display.

Getting There & Away

The government has been planning to build a series of bridges across the several rivers that feed Laguna de Arenal's southwestern shore for about 20 years. If completed, this would provide a road connection between Monteverde and La Fortuna, which would probably be the end of the eco-paradise formerly known as Monteverde. There are always a few scattered spots where some construction work is going on but, for the time being, they're not making too much progress.

BUS

All intercity buses stop at the **bus terminal** (☎ 2645-5159; 5:45-11am & 1:30-5pm Mon-Fri, closes 3pm Sat & Sun) in downtown Santa Elena, and most continue on to the Cheese Factory in Monteverde. On the trip in, keep an eye on your luggage, particularly on the San José–Puntarenas leg of the trip, as well as on the Monteverde–Tilarán run.

Purchase tickets to the Monteverde and Santa Elena reserves at Hotel & Info Center Camino Verde (p193), which can also make reservations for pricier trips with private companies. Destinations, bus companies, fares, journey times and departure times are as follows:

Las Juntas ₡960; 1½ hours; departs from bus station at 4:30am and 3pm. Buses to Puntarenas and San José can drop you off in Las Juntas.

Managua, Nicaragua (Tica Bus) ₡14,000; eight hours; a small shuttle bus (₡1000) departs from the bus station

at 6am and brings you to the Interamericana in Lagartos, where you can pick it up.
Puntarenas ₡1235; three hours; departs from the front of Banco Nacional at 6am.
Reserva Monteverde ₡600; 30 minutes; departs from front of Banco Nacional at 6:15am, 7:20am, 1:20pm and 3pm, returns at 6:45am, 11:30am, 2pm and 4pm.
Reserva Santa Elena ₡1200; 30 minutes; departs from front of Banco Nacional at 6:30am, 8:30am, 10:30am, 12:30pm, 1pm and 3pm, returns 11am, 1pm and 4pm.
San José (TransMonteverde) ₡2500; 4½ hours; departs the Santa Elena bus station at 6:30am and 2:30pm.
Tilarán, with connection to La Fortuna ₡1800; seven hours; departs from the bus station at 6am. This is a long ride as you will need to hang around for two hours in Tilarán. If you have a few extra dollars, it's recommended that you take the jeep-boat-jeep option (see right) to La Fortuna.

There's no direct bus to Cañas. Most people take a bus to Juntas, then transfer from there to frequent Interamericana-route buses for Cañas, Liberia and beyond.

CAR

While most Costa Rican communities regularly request paved roads in their region, preservationists in Monteverde have done the opposite. All roads here are shockingly rough, and 4WD is necessary all year, especially in the rainy season. Many car-rental agencies will refuse to rent you an ordinary car during the rainy season if you admit that you're headed to Monteverde.

There are four roads from the Interamericana: coming from the south, the first turnoff is at Rancho Grande (18km north of the Puntarenas exit); a second turnoff is at the Río Lagarto bridge (just past Km 149, and roughly 15km northwest of Rancho Grande). Both are well signed and join one another about a third of the way to Monteverde. Both routes boast about 35km of steep, winding and scenic dirt roads with plenty of potholes and rocks to ensure that the driver, at least, is kept from admiring the scenery.

A third road goes via Juntas, which starts off paved, but becomes just as rough as the first two roads a few kilometers past town, though it's about 5km shorter than the previous two options. Finally, if coming from the north, drivers could take the paved road from Cañas via Tilarán and then take the rough road from Tilarán to Santa Elena.

During our recent visit, the one and only gas station in Monteverde was indefinitely closed. Fill up in Tilarán or the Interamericana near Juntas. If you're really in a pinch, there's a black-market gas station in Santa Elena; ask any taxi driver for directions.

HORSEBACK

There are a number of outfitters that offer transportation on horseback (per person US$75 to US$100, five to six hours) to La Fortuna, usually in combination with jeep rides. There are three main trails used: the Lake Trail (safe year-round), the Chiquito Trail (safe most of the year) and the gorgeous but infamous Castillo Trail (passable only in dry season by experienced riders). Some unscrupulous tour operators may try to save money by taking shorter, more dangerous routes and overworking horses. Cheaper is *not* better. Stick to established reputable tour companies (p200), ask lots of questions and confirm the route before booking.

JEEP-BOAT-JEEP

The fastest route between Monteverde-Santa Elena and La Fortuna is a jeep-boat-jeep combo (around US$25 to US$30, three hours), which can be arranged through almost any hotel or tour operator in either town. A 4WD taxi takes you to Río Chiquito, meeting a boat that crosses Laguna de Arenal, where a taxi on the other side continues to La Fortuna. This is increasingly becoming the primary transportation between La Fortuna and Monteverde as it's incredibly scenic, reasonably priced and saves half a day of rough travel.

Getting Around

BICYCLE

Hotel El Viandante (p203) is the only place in town that rents mountain bikes (three hours/full day US$10/15). The price includes new Trek 4300 bikes, helmet, tire pump and water bottle. Guided bike tours (US$20 to US$50) to regional attractions are also available. That said, cycling in Monteverde–Santa Elena is not for the lighthearted beginner. The area is extremely hilly, rocky and muddy. Be prepared.

RESERVA BIOLÓGICA BOSQUE NUBOSO MONTEVERDE

When Quaker settlers first arrived in the area, they agreed to preserve about a third of their property in order to protect the watershed above Monteverde. By 1972, however, encroaching squatters began to threaten the region. The community joined forces with environmental organizations such as the Nature Conservancy and the World Wildlife Fund to purchase 328 hectares adjacent to the already preserved area. This was called the Reserva Biológica Bosque Nuboso Monteverde (Monteverde Cloud Forest Biological Reserve), which the Centro Científico Tropical (Tropical Science Center) began administrating in 1975.

In 1986 the Monteverde Conservation League (MCL) was formed to buy land to expand the reserve. Two years later it launched the International Children's Rainforest project, which encouraged children and school groups from all over the world to raise money to buy and save tropical rainforest adjacent to the reserve. Today the reserve totals 105 sq km.

The most striking aspect of this project is that it is the result of private citizens working for change rather than waiting around for a national park administered by the government. The reserve relies partly on donations from the public. Considering that the underfunded Minae struggles to protect the national-park system, enterprises like this are more important than ever for maintaining cohesive wildlife corridors.

Visitors should note that some of the walking trails are very muddy, and even during the dry season (late December to early May) the cloud forest is rainy (hey, it's a rainforest – bring rainwear and suitable boots). Many of the trails have been stabilized with concrete blocks or wooden boards and are easy to walk on, though unpaved trails deeper in the preserve turn into quagmires during the rainy season.

Because of the fragile environment, the reserve allows a maximum of 160 people at any time. During the dry season this limit is almost always reached by 10am, which means you could spend the better part of a day waiting around for someone to leave. The best strategy is to get there before the gates open, or better (and wetter) to come during the off season, usually May through June and September through November.

There are a couple of important points to consider. If you only have time to visit either the Monteverde or Santa Elena reserve, you should know that Monteverde gets nearly 10 times as many visitors, which means that the infrastructure is better and the trails are regularly maintained, though you'll have to deal with much larger crowds. Also, most visitors come to Monteverde (and Santa Elena) expecting to see wildlife. However, both reserves cover large geographic areas, which means that the animals have a lot of space to move around in. Taking a night tour or staying overnight in one of the lodges deep within the reserve will maximize your chances of spotting wildlife; still, it's best to enter the parks without any expectations. The trees themselves are primitive and alone worth the price of admission, though a lot has changed since the quetzal-spotting days of 1983. The animals have adapted to the increased tourist volume by avoiding the main trails, but most people who visit either reserve are more than satisfied with the whole experience.

Information

The **visitors center** (☎ 2645-5122; www.cct.or.cr; park entry adult/student & child/child under 6yr US$17/9/free; ⏲ 7am-4pm) is adjacent to the reserve gift shop, where you can get information and buy trail guides, bird and mammal lists, and maps. The shop also sells T-shirts, beautiful color slides by Richard Laval, postcards, books, posters and a variety of other souvenirs, and rents binoculars (US$10); you'll need to leave your passport. The annual rainfall here is about 3000mm, though parts of the reserve reportedly get twice as much. It's usually cool, high temperatures around 18°C (65°F), so wear appropriate clothing.

It's important to remember that the cloud forest is often cloudy (!) and the vegetation is thick – this combination cuts down on sound as well as vision. Also keep in mind that main trails in this reserve are among the most trafficked in Costa Rica. Some readers have been disappointed with the lack of wildlife sightings. The best bet is, as always, to hire a guide.

The reserve is supported by donations through the **Friends of Monteverde Cloud Forest** (Map p194; www.friendsofmonteverde.org).

If you're looking for a volunteer opportunity, you could try the **Cloud Forest School** (Map p194; ☎ 2645-5161; www.cloudforestschool.org), a kindergarten-through-11th-grade bilingual school locally known as the Centro de Educación Creativa (Center for Creative Education). The school was founded in 1991 to increase educational opportunities for a growing population of school-age children in the area. This independent school offers creative, experiential education to 220 students with an emphasis on integrating environmental education into all aspects of the school. For more information about volunteering as well as a few intern positions, you can contact the Volunteer Coordinator at opportunities@cloudforestschool.org.

Activities

HIKING

There are 13km of marked and maintained trails – a free map is provided with your entrance fee. The most popular of the nine trails, suitable for day hikes, make a rough triangle (El Triángulo) to the east of the reserve entrance. The triangle's sides are made up of the popular **Sendero Bosque Nuboso** (1.9km), an interpretive walk (booklet ₡400 at gate) through the cloud forest that begins at the ranger station, paralleled by the more open, 2km **El Camino**, a favorite of bird-watchers. The **Sendero Pantanoso** (1.6km) forms the far side of El Triángulo, traversing swamps, pine forests and the continental divide. Returning to the entrance, **Sendero Río** (2km) follows the Quebrada Cuecha past a few photogenic waterfalls.

Bisecting the triangle, the gorgeous **Chomogo Trail** (1.8km) lifts hikers 150m to 1680m, the highest point in the triangle, and other little trails crisscross the region, including the worthwhile **Sendero Brillante** (300m), with bird's-eye views of a miniature forest. There's also a 100m suspension bridge about 1km from the ranger station. However, keep in mind that despite valiant efforts to contain crowd sizes, these shorter trails are among the most trafficked in the country, and wildlife learned long ago that the region is worth avoiding unless they want a good look at hominids.

There are also more substantial hikes, including trails to the three backcountry shelters (p214) that begin at the far corners of the triangle. Even longer trails, many of them less developed, stretch out east across the reserve and down the Peñas Blancas river valley to lowlands north of the Cordillera de Tilarán and into the Bosque Eterno de los Niños. If you're strong enough and have the time to spare, these hikes are highly recommended as you'll maximize your chances of spotting wildlife, and few tourists venture beyond the triangle. If you're serious about visiting the backcountry shelters, you should first talk to the park service as you will be entering some fairly rugged terrain, and a guide is highly recommended and at times essential. Camping is normally not allowed.

For advice on deep-jungle trekking and reputable local guides, contact trekking guide **Andres Vargas** (www.euforiaexpeditions.com), a socially responsible, very knowledgeable adventure specialist.

WILDLIFE-WATCHING

Monteverde is a bird-watching paradise, and though the list of recorded species tops out at more than 400, the one most visitors want to see is the resplendent quetzal. The Maya bird of paradise is most often spotted during the March and April nesting season, though you could get lucky any time of year.

For those interested in spotting mammals, the cloud forest's limited visibility and abundance of higher primates (namely human beings) can make wildlife-watching quite difficult, though commonly sighted species (especially in the backcountry) include coatis, howler monkeys, capuchins, sloths, agoutis and squirrels (as in 'real' squirrel, not the squirrel monkey).

Tours

Although you can hike around the reserve on your own, a guide is highly recommended, and not just by us but by dozens of readers who were inspired by their adventures to email Lonely Planet. The park runs a variety of guided tours: make reservations *at least* one day in advance. As size is limited, groups should make reservations several months ahead for dry season and holiday periods. Guides speak English and are trained naturalists, and proceeds from the tours benefit environmental-education programs in local schools.

The reserve offers guided **natural history tours** (☎ reservations 2645-5112; tours excl entry fee US$15) at 7:30am daily, and on busy days at 8:30am as well. Participants meet at the Hummingbird Gallery (p210), where a short 10-minute orientation is given. A half-hour slide show from renowned wildlife photographers Michael and Patricia Fogden is followed by a 2½- to three-hour walk. Once your tour is over, you can return to the reserve on your own, as your ticket is valid for the entire day.

The reserve also offers recommended two-hour **night tours** (incl entry fee with/without transportation US$20/17) at 7:15pm nightly. These are by flashlight (bring your own for the best visibility), and offer the opportunity to observe the 70% of regional wildlife with nocturnal habits.

Guided **bird-watching tours** (5-hr tour incl entry fee per person US$40-50) in English begin at Stella's Bakery (p207) at 6am, and usually sight more than 40 species. There's a two-person minimum and six-person maximum. Longer tours go on by request at a higher fee, and usually more than 60 species are seen.

Several local businesses can arrange a local to guide you within the reserve or in some of the nearby surrounding areas. Staff can also recommend **private guides** (guide@monteverdeinfo.com), or ask at your hotel or tour operator.

The reserve can also recommend excellent guides, many of whom work for it, for a private tour. Costs vary depending on the season, the guide and where you want to go, but average about US$60 to US$100 for a half-day. Entrance costs may be extra, especially for the cheaper tours. Full-day tours are also available. The size of the group is up to you – go alone or split the cost with a group of friends.

Sleeping & Eating

Near the park entrance are **dormitories** (Map p194; ☎ reservations 2645-5122; www.cct.or.cr; dm adult/student without bathroom per person US$20, with bathroom & meals per person $30) with 43 bunks. These are often used by researchers and student groups but are often available to tourists – make reservations. Full board can be arranged in advance.

There are also three **backcountry shelters** (dm US$5), with drinking water, showers, propane stoves and cooking utensils. You need to carry a sleeping bag, candles, food and anything else (like toilet paper) you might need. **El Valle** (6km, two hours) is the closest; **Alemán Hut** (8km, four hours) is near a cable car across Río Peñas Blancas; and **Eladios Hut** (13km, six hours) is the nicest, with separate dorm rooms and a porch. Trails are muddy and challenging, scenery mossy and green, and the tourist hordes that inundate the day hikes a far-off memory. This may be the best way to appreciate the reserve. Reservations are highly recommended, and they can be made at the park office prior to setting out on your hike.

There is a small **restaurant** (plates ₡1000-2500; 🕑 7am-4pm) at the entrance to the reserve, which has a good variety of healthy sandwiches, salads and typical dishes.

Getting There & Away

Public buses (₡600, 30 minutes) depart the Banco Nacional in Santa Elena at 6:15am, 7:20am, 1:20pm and 3pm. Buses return from the reserve at 6:45am, 11:30am, 2pm and 4pm. You can flag down the buses from anywhere on the road between Santa Elena and the reserve – inquire at your hotel about what time they will pass by. Taxis are also available for around ₡2800.

The 6km walk from Santa Elena is uphill but lovely – look for paths that run parallel to the road. There are views all along the way, and many visitors remark that some of the best bird-watching is on the final 2km of the road.

RESERVA SANTA ELENA

Though Monteverde gets all the attention, this exquisitely misty reserve, at 310 hectares just a fraction of the size of that other forest, has plenty to recommend it. You can practically hear the canopy, draped with epiphytes breathing in humid exhales as water drops on to the leaf litter and mud underfoot. The odd call of the three-wattled bellbird or low crescendo of a howler monkey punctuates the higher-pitched bird chatter and chirps.

While Monteverde Crowd…er…Cloud Forest entertains almost 200,000 visitors annually, Santa Elena sees fewer than 20,000 tourists each year, which means its dewy trails through mysteriously veiled forest are usually far quieter. It's also a bit cheaper and much less developed; plus your entry fee is helping support another unique project.

This cloud-forest reserve was created in 1989 and opened to the public in March 1992. It was one of the first community-managed conservation projects in the country, and is now managed by the Santa Elena high school board and bears the quite unwieldy official name of Reserva del Bosque Nuboso del Colegio Técnico Profesional de Santa Elena. You can visit the **reserve office** (☎ 2645-5693; 🕑 8am-4pm Wed-Fri) at the high school.

The reserve is about 6km northeast of the village of Santa Elena. This cloud forest is slightly higher in elevation than Monteverde, and as some of the forest is secondary growth, there are sunnier places for spotting birds and other animals throughout. There's a stable population of monkey and sloth, many of which can be seen on the road to the reserve. Unless you're a trained ecologist, the old-growth forest in Santa Elena will seem fairly similar in appearance to Monteverde, though the lack of cement blocks on the trails means that you'll have a much more authentic (note: muddy) trekking experience.

This place is moist, and almost all the water comes as fine mist, and more than 25% of all the biomass in the forest are epiphytes – mosses and lichens – for which this place is a humid haven. Though about 10% of species here won't be found in Monteverde, which is largely on the other side of the continental divide, you can see quetzal here too, as well as Volcán Arenal exploding in the distance – theoretically. Rule No 407 of cloud forests: it's often cloudy.

Information

You can visit the **reserve** (☎ 2645-5390, 2645-7107; www.reservasantaelena.org; adult/student US$14/7; 🕒 7am-4pm) on your own, but a guide will enhance your experience tenfold.

There's also a simple restaurant, coffee shop and gift store. Note that all proceeds go toward managing the reserve as well as to environmental-education programs in local schools. Donations are graciously accepted.

If you have some extra time, there's a good volunteer program here – possible projects include trail maintenance, surveying, administration and biological research. You're expected to make at least a one-week commitment, and very basic dorm-style accommodations (no electricity and very cold showers) are available free to volunteers, though all but the most rugged will prefer a US$10-per-day homestay, including three meals. Although at times it's possible to simply show up and volunteer, it's best to contact the reserve in advance.

Activities

More than 12km of trails are open for hiking, featuring four circular trails offering walks of varying difficulty and length, from 45 minutes to 3½ hours (1.4km to 4.8km) along a stable (though not 'concrete-blocked') trail system. Rubber boots can be rented (₡600) at the entrance. Unlike Monteverde, Santa Elena is not developed enough to facilitate backcountry hiking, and at the time of writing it was not possible to overnight in the reserve.

Tours

The reserve offers guided **daylight tours** (3-hr tours excl admission per person US$15) at 7:30am and 11:30am daily; try to make the earlier hike. Popular **night tours** (1½-hr tour excl admission per person US$15) leave at 7pm nightly. Tours have a two-person minimum and six-person maximum, so reservations are recommended for both tours during the dry season. The reserve can also arrange three-day private tours through various guides for US$20.

Getting There & Away

A daily shuttle (₡1200, 30 minutes) between the village of Santa Elena and the reserve departs from the Banco Nacional in town at 6:30am, 8:30am, 10:30am, 12:30pm, 1pm and 3pm, and returns at 11am, 1pm and 4pm. A taxi from Santa Elena costs ₡5000.

ECOLODGE SAN LUIS & RESEARCH STATION

Formerly a tropical-biology research station, this facility now integrates research with ecotourism and education, and is administrated by the University of Georgia. The 70-hectare site is on the Río San Luis and adjoins the southern part of the Monteverde reserve. Its average elevation of 1100m makes it a tad lower and warmer than Monteverde, and bird-watchers have recorded some 230 species attracted by the slightly nicer weather. There are also a number of trails into primary and secondary forest, and there's a working farm with tropical fruit orchards and a coffee harvest from November to March.

A variety of comfortable accommodations at the **lodge** (☎ 2645-8049; www.ecolodgesanluis.com; dm US$65, cabins s/d US$85/160; Ⓟ) are available for anyone interested in learning about the cloud-forest environment and experiencing a bit of rural Costa Rican life. Rates include all meals and most activities. There are a host of day and night hikes guided by biologists, as well as slide shows, seminars, horseback rides and even an introduction to research activities. Discounts can be arranged for students, researchers, large groups and long stays.

The ecolodge also runs a resident naturalist volunteer program, though there is a preference for University of Georgia students and graduates, and a six-month commitment is required. The position entails running a number of teaching workshops and guided walks, as well as participating in development projects on the station and in the community. Training, room and board are provided.

From the main road between Santa Elena and Monteverde, it's a steep 3km walk from the signed road where the bus will drop you off. A 4WD taxi from town costs about US$12 each way, and the lodge can also arrange transportation from San José in advance.

PUENTE LA AMISTAD

About 23km south of Cañas on the Interamericana, a turnoff leads 25km on Route 18 to the Puente de la Amistad Costa Rica–Taiwan (Costa Rica–Taiwan Friendship Bridge). The 780m bridge spans the Río Tempisque and was built and financed by the Taiwanese government in 2003. The 'Friendship Bridge' has greatly reduced travel time to and from the beaches in Nicoya.

Long before you get here, you'll notice dozens of signs on the Interamericana advertising the best steakhouse in Guanacaste – **Bar-B-Q Tres Hermanas** (2662-8584; www.treshermanas.co.cr; cnr Interamericana & Rte 18; mains ₡3500-9100; 11am-9pm;). Believe the hype! This local landmark's specialty is barbecue beef and pork ribs, marinated and slow cooked for eight hours. Kids will love the playground and noisy bull and monkey animatronics. Leave your vegetarian friends at home.

CAÑAS

pop 25,000

If you're cruising north on the Interamericana, Cañas is the first town of any size in Costa Rica's driest province, Guanacaste. *Sabanero* culture is evident on the sweltering and quiet streets, where full-custom pickup trucks share the road with wizened cowboys on horseback, fingering their machetes with a swagger you just don't see outside the province. It's a dusty, typically Latin American town, where everyone walks slowly and businesses shut down for lunch, all centered on the Parque Central and Catholic church – which are most definitely not typical.

You're better off basing yourself in livelier Liberia, which has more traveler-oriented services. That said, Cañas is a good place for organizing rafting trips on the nearby Río Corobicí or for exploring Parque Nacional Palo Verde. And if you need to stop here for gas, you'll find there are a couple of interesting sights to check out.

Information

You can find public phones, a post office, library, a Banco Nacional and Banco Popular with ATMs, as well as many simple *sodas* and hotels here.

Emergency clinic (2669-0092; cnr Av Central & Hwy 1; 7am-4pm Mon-Fri) Has 24-hour on-call service.

Internet Ciberc@ñas (2663-5232; Av 3 btwn Calles 1 & 3; per hr ₡700; 8:15am-9pm Mon-Sat, 2-9pm Sun;) Has fast computers, air-con and, if you get here at 8:15am, two hours for the price of one.

Minae/ACT office (2669-0533; Av 9 btwn Calles Central & 1; 8am-4pm Mon-Fri) Has limited information about nearby national parks and reserves.

Sights & Activities

Though most visitors to Cañas simply use the town as a base for visits to nearby Parque Nacional Palo Verde or for rafting on the Río Corobicí, it's worth the trip just to see the Catholic church's **psychedelic mosaics** designed by famed local painter Otto Apuy. Sinewy vines and colorful starbursts that have enveloped the modern church's once clean lines are enhanced by jungle-themed stained glass that's completely different from anything on offer at the Vatican. In **Parque Central** opposite, park benches and the pyramid-shaped bandstand are equally elaborate. The **Plaza de Toros** hosts bullfights in January and February.

LAS PUMAS

Directly behind the office of Safaris Corobicí is **Las Pumas** (2669-6044; www.laspumas.org; adult/child US$7/2; 8am-4pm), a wild-animal shelter started in the 1960s by the late Lilly Hagnauer, a Swiss environmentalist. It's the largest shelter of its kind in Latin America, housing big cats including pumas, jaguars, ocelots, jaguarundis and margays – plus a few deer, fox, monkeys, peccaries, toucans, parakeets and other birds that were either orphaned or injured.

This is a labor of love. The shelter does not receive any government funding and relies on visitor admission and donations to survive. Volunteers are always welcomed, but you must make arrangements beforehand. The shelter is still operated by the Swiss Family Hagnauer, a local Cañas institution; Lilly's husband Werner manages Las Pumas, their daughter Verena runs Rincón Corobicí (p218) and Verena's son Dany runs Ríos Tropicales (see opposite).

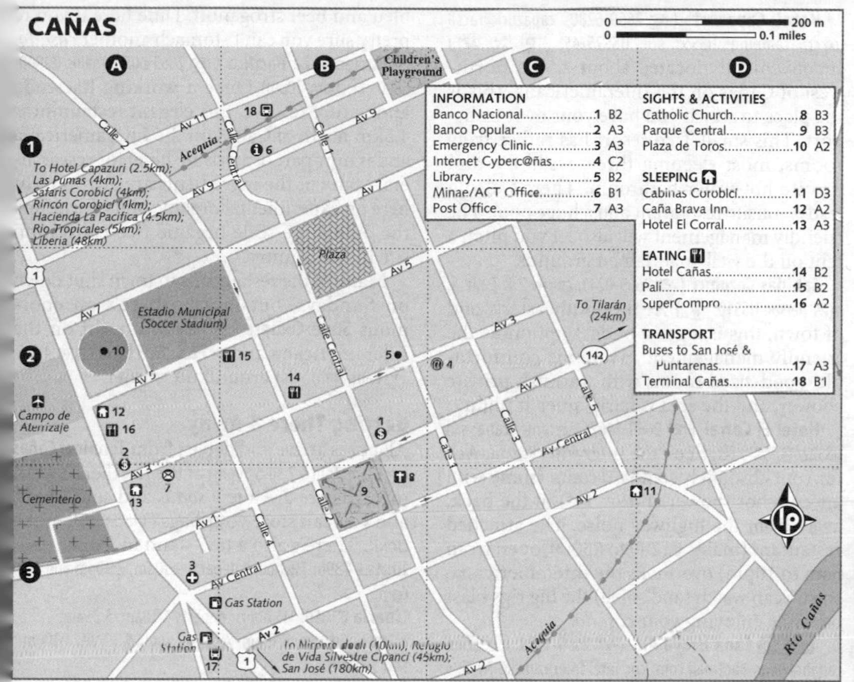

REFUGIO DE VIDA SILVESTRE CIPANCÍ

New in 2001, this small wildlife refuge is at the confluence of the Ríos Tempisque and Bebedero, at the southern end of Parque Nacional Palo Verde. It's a good spot for **bird-watching** and **fishing**, though it's virtually untouristed. Local fishers offer passenger boats for tours on these two rivers. A three-hour guided tour costs around US$20 per person (US$150 minimum), and can usually be arranged at the docks; show up early.

The Minae/ACT office in Cañas has more information on the park. Boats leave from the Níspero dock, just north of the Tempisque ferry.

RAFTING

Gentle rafting trips down the Río Corobicí can be made with **Safaris Corobicí** (☎ 2669-6191; www.safaricorobici.com; Interamericana Km 193; ⏰ departures 7am-3pm; 👪). Bookings can be made at its office on the Interamericana about 4.5km north of Cañas. The emphasis is on wildlife observation rather than exciting white-water rafting. The river is Class I–II (in other words, pretty flat) but families and nature-lovers enjoy these trips. Swimming holes are found along the river. Per person, based on a two-person minimum, a two-hour float costs US$38/19 per adult/child under 14 years, a three-hour bird-watching float covering 12km costs US$46/23, and a half-day 18km float including lunch costs US$60/30. The company also rents out a little guesthouse nearby.

The popular **Ríos Tropicales** (☎ 2233-6455; www.rinconcorobici.com; www.riostropicales.com; ⏰ departures 7am-3pm; 👪) offers similar Class I–II family 'float tours' including its popular two-hour, flora and fauna viewing tour (US$40 per person, including snacks). For the more adventurous, there are Class III–IV white-water rafting trips (US$90 per person) on the Tenorio River that features a death-defying 3.6m (Class V) drop! Ríos Tropicales operates out of the Rincón Corobicí restaurant (p218).

Sleeping

Cañas is a cheaper place to stay than Liberia, though the following places cater more to truckers than travelers. Rooms have cold showers unless otherwise stated.

Hotel Capazuri (☎ 2669-6280; capazuri@racsa.co.cr; camping US$5, s/d US$25/45; P) Inconveniently located about 2.5km northwest of Cañas on the Interamericana, this is the place to stay if you have your own transport. This small Tico resort has rather frilly rooms, most sleeping three, with TV and private hot-water bathroom. There's also a festive, onsite restaurant and a huge pool. The friendly management will also let you pitch a tent on the well-maintained grounds.

Cabinas Corobicí (☎ 2669-0241; cnr Av 2 & Calle 5; r per person US$10; P) At the southeastern end of town, this is a good budget option as the friendly management maintains comfortable, good-sized rooms with warmish private shower, and the area is fairly quiet at night.

Hotel El Corral (☎ 2669-1467; Interamericana; s/d US$22/44;) Right on the Interamericana. Ask for your absolutely standard room (some with air-con, hot shower and/or TV) in the back, away from the highway noise. The attached restaurant (mains ₡1200 to ₡3000, open from 6am to 10pm) overlooks the Interamericana, so you can watch (and smell) the big rigs blast by while enjoying your *casado*.

our pick **Caña Brava Inn** (☎ 2669-1294; recepcioncanabravainn@hotmail.com; cnr Interamericana & Av 5; s US$35-57, d US$71-113; P) The newest and most upscale hotel in town, Caña Brava has all the modern amenities including well-insulated rooms with flat screen TV, wi-fi, huge comfy bedding and contemporary decor. Pricier rooms have Jacuzzi. The hotel also houses an international restaurant (mains from ₡3200 to ₡6000), a small casino and the area's largest disco (open from 6pm to 1am Wednesday to Saturday).

NORTHWESTERN COSTA RICA

Eating

our pick **Rincón Corobicí** (☎ 2669-1234; mains ₡1700-6000; 8am-6pm) This attractive Swiss-run restaurant is 4km north of Cañas on the banks of the Río Corobicí, and is a great lunch spot. A terrace provides river and garden views, and a short trail follows the riverbank where you can take a cool dip. English, French and German are spoken here, and you can book tours with Ríos Tropicales for the Río Corobicí or other destinations in Costa Rica.

Hotel Cañas (☎ 2669-0039; cnr Calle 2 & Av 3; mains ₡1800-5000; 6am-9pm Mon-Sat, 7am-2pm Sun) You can count on the most reliable quality at this hotel restaurant, serving up a number of Western dishes, including chicken cordon bleu and beef stroganoff. Dine here if you're pretty sure you can't stomach another *casado*.

Hacienda La Pacífica (☎ 2669-6050; mains ₡2800-6800; 6am-10pm) Once a working hacienda and nature reserve, this elegant restaurant is 4.5km north of Cañas on the Interamericana and is now part of a private hotel for researchers. Many of the ingredients are grown right here on experimental organic plots, including the only large-scale organic rice cultivation site in the country.

Many of the restaurants in town shut down on Sundays, but luckily there's an enormous **SuperCompro** (8am-8pm) right on the Interamericana and a **Palí** (Av 5 btwn Calles 4 & 2; 8am-8pm) just around the corner.

Getting There & Away

All buses arrive and depart from **Terminal Cañas** (8am-1pm & 2:30-5:30pm) at the northern end of town. There are a few *sodas* and snack bars, and you can store your bags (US$0.50) at the desk. There's also a taxi stand in front.

Juntas ₡390; 1½ hours; departs 9:30am, 2:30pm and 6pm.
Liberia ₡1050; 1½ hours; departs 4:30am, 5:35am, 6:10am, 6:40am, 7:15am, 7:45am, noon, 1:30pm, 4:30pm and 5:30pm.
Puntarenas ₡1400; two hours; departs 6am, 9:20am, 10:30am, 11:30am, 12:30pm, 3:30pm and 4:30pm.
San José ₡2280; 3½ hours; departs 4am, 4:50am, 5:40am, 6:30am, 8:30am, 11:20am, 1:30pm, 2:30pm and 5:30pm.
Tilarán ₡450; 45 minutes; departs 6am, 8am, 9am, 10:30am, noon, 1:45pm, 3:30pm and 5:45pm.
Upala ₡1260; two hours; departs 4:30am, 6am, 8:30am, 11:15am, 1pm, 3:30pm and 5:15pm.

VOLCÁN TENORIO AREA

A paved road 6km northwest of Cañas branches off the Interamericana and heads north to Upala, passing between Volcán Miravalles to the west and Volcán Tenorio (1916m) to the east. Parque Nacional Volcán Tenorio, part of the Area de Conservación Arenal (ACA), is one of the highlights of northwestern Costa Rica.

The park entrance is located just north of Bijagua (pronounced 'bee-*hag*-gwa'), the only sizeable town in the Tenorio area. Bijagua has a few hotels, a Banco Nacional ATM, several small *sodas* and bars, but no gasoline; the nearest gas stations are in Upala or Cañas. If you have your own wheels, the park is an easy day trip from Liberia or Cañas.

LAS FIESTAS DE GUANACASTE

Guanacastecos love their horses, almost as much as they love their fiestas. And what better way to get the best of both worlds than with a *tope* (horse parade), a mix of a Western rodeo and a country fair complete with a cattle auction, food stalls, music, dancing, drinking and, of course, bullriding? In Costa Rica the bulls are never killed, so watching the insane helmetless, bareback, bucking bronco action is exciting and (usually) gore-free. Even better than watching the bullriding is the aftermath of the rider getting tossed, as it's fairly common for the local drunks and young machos to jump into the ring to act as volunteer rodeo clowns, which is simultaneously hilarious and scary.

Though the bullriding usually draws the biggest crowds, the main event is the *tope* itself, where you can see the high-stepping gait of the *sabanero* (cowboy), which demands endurance and skill from both horse and rider.

Topes are also a great place to catch the region's traditional dance, known as the Punto Guanacasteco. Perhaps the showiest aspect of the dance is the long, flowing skirts worn by the women. This skirt is meant to resemble an oxcart wheel, which is a traditional Costa Rican craft most often associated with the town of Sarchí. Punto Guanacasteco traditionally served as a means of courtship, and it's common for the dance to be frequently interrupted by young men who shout rhyming verses in order to try to win over a love interest. The dance and accompanying music are fast paced and full of passion, and they're similar to most other Central American styles.

Topes are a fairly common occurrence in Guanacaste, so ask a local about where one might be happening, or look out for posters. Generally, *topes* occur on Costa Rican civic holidays (p533), though you can bet on finding big parties during Semana Santa (the week before Easter), the week between Christmas and New Year, and on July 25, the anniversary of Guanacaste's annexation.

Parque Nacional Volcán Tenorio

They say when God finished painting the sky blue, he washed his paintbrushes in the **Río Celeste.** The heavenly blue-colored river, waterfalls and ponds of Parque Nacional Volcán Tenorio are one of the most spectacular natural phenomena in Costa Rica.

Established in 1976, this magical 184-sq-km national park remains one of the most secluded and least-visited parks in the country due to the dearth of public transportation and park infrastructure. As a result, it remains a blissfully pristine rainforest abundant with wildlife. Soaring 1916m above the cloud rainforest is the park's namesake, Volcán Tenorio, which actually consists of three peaked craters: Montezuma, Tenorio I (the tallest) and Tenorio II.

Your first stop will be the **Puesto El Pilón ranger station** (☎ 2200-0135; www.sinac.go.cr/acat_volcantenorio.php; admission US$10; 🕑 8am-4pm), which houses a small exhibit of photographs and dead animals. Pick up a free English or Spanish hiking map.

The well-signed trail begins at the ranger station parking lot and winds 1.5km through the rainforest until you reach an intersection. Turn left and climb down a very steep and slippery staircase to the **Catarata de Río Celeste**, a milky-blue waterfall that cascades 30m down the rocks, like heavy cream being poured out of a jug and into a fantastically aquamarine pool.

Climb back up to the main trail and continue 700m further until you reach the technicolored **Pozo Azul** (blue lagoon). The trail loops around the lagoon 400m until you arrive at the confluence of rivers known as **Los Teñidores** (The Stainers). Here, two small rivers – one whitish blue and one brownish yellow – mix together to create the blueberry milk of Río Celeste.

For the final reward, continue 300m to the **Aguas Termales** (hot springs) to soak your weary muscles. This is the only place in the park where you're permitted to enter the water; bring your own towel and swimsuit. Plans for a circuit trail are afoot, but for now the trail ends here. Retrace your steps to return to the ranger station. Hiking to the volcano crater is strictly prohibited.

Allow three to four hours to complete the entire hike. It's only about a 7km round-trip, but parts of the trail are steep and rocky. And because this is a rainforest, the trail can be wet and muddy almost year-round. Good hiking shoes or boots are a must. After your hike, you'll find an area to wash your footwear near the trailhead.

SLEEPING & EATING

There are a few simple *sodas* in Bijagua, but other than that, you'll probably be eating at your lodge.

Around Bijagua

Cabinas Vista Miravalles (☎ 2466-8015; cabinasvistamiravalles@hotmail.com; s/d/tr US$14/22/27; P) Located in the heart of Bijagua behind the Salon 5R bar, these little pink cabins are a good budget option. Each has a double and single bed, private bathroom with hot water, TV and fan.

Tenorio Lodge (☎ 2466-8282; www.tenoriolodge.com; s/q/tr/q incl breakfast US$90/95/120/135; P) Located on a lush hilltop with amazing views of Volcán Tenorio, Tenorio Lodge has some of the most romantic and private accommodations around. There are eight roomy bungalows, each containing two orthopedic beds (one king and one queen), private bathroom with solar-heated water, and panoramic windows and balcony with volcano views. The gorgeous lodge has a lovely restaurant featuring a daily changing dinner menu. On the 17-acre property, you'll find two ponds, a heliconia garden and two hot tubs to enjoy after a long day of hiking. It's located 1km south of downtown.

our pick **Celeste Mountain Lodge** (☎ 2278-6628; www.celestemountainlodge.com; s/d/tr incl all meals US$130/160/190, child US$25; P) One of the most innovative and sustainable hotels we've ever seen, Celeste Mountain Lodge is proof that one can be ecofriendly without giving up comfort or style. The French-owned, Belgian-designed contemporary hotel is absolutely stunning – an open-air hilltop lodge in the shadow of Volcán Tenorio. It was built in 2007 using ecofriendly materials such as recycled wood, plastic, 1000 old truck tires and coconut fiber as seat cushions. Lamps, sculptures and other decorative items are made of scrap metal. Hot water comes from solar power, and cooking gas is partially produced by kitchen waste. There's even an ingenious hot tub heated by burning salvaged wood. Nothing in the building was imported, except for French owner Joel Marchel. The former tour operator and self-proclaimed 'radical' believes we all need to change the way we travel, including 'unplugging' on holiday, so you won't find TV, internet, hairdryer or other gizmos here. The 18 rooms are comfy and stylish, but bathrooms are purposefully small to reduce water consumption. The property features a 2.3km interpretive hiking trail and is located in one of Costa Rica's prime bird-watching areas. The price includes all meals at the amazing, organic restaurant. The lodge is located at the end of a 3.5km-long, very rough (4WD required) access road that begins at the north end of Bijagua.

Around Parque Nacional Volcán Tenorio

Rio Celeste Lodge (☎ 8365-3415; www.riocelestelodge.com; camping US$2, r per person US$20) This simple set of rustic *cabinas* is the cheapest accommodations in the area, and is a good option if your day trip suddenly turns into an overnight stay. Rooms have fan and warm shower, and the lodge is conveniently located on the hill near the trailhead. Staff can also arrange horseback riding and guided hikes.

Posada La Amistad (☎ 8356-0285; posadalaamistad@hotmail.com; camping per person US$7; r incl breakfast/all meals per person US$15/40; P) This very basic but lovely all-wood lodge 1km past the park entrance has four cabins with rustic beds and mosquito netting and tin roofs. The Tico owners are part of China Verde, a tourism association of six local families who own several private reserves, including an area of the Río Celeste where swimming is permitted.

Cabinas Piuri (☎ 2479-8462, 8384-9630; s/d incl breakfast US$15/30; P) Located on the banks of the Río Celeste, this is the nicest and newest hotel near the national park. There are three huge cabins each with a king and queen bed, living room, fridge, tiled floors, hot-water bathroom and shared terrace with chairs rescued from an old movie theatre. A path leads 100m down to the riverbank, where you can swim or lunch at the picnic area. This is a great choice for families. It's about 1km west of the park entrance.

Tenorio's Door (☎ 8306-6878; www.tenoriodoor.es.tl; s/d US$20/40, incl meals US$40/80; P) At the closest hotel to the national park (500m), everything from the walls to the bath towels is Río Celeste blue. Run by the amiable Tica Marielos, it's basic but clean, with hammocks, an onsite restaurant and laundry service.

La Carolina Lodge (☎ 8380-1656; www.lacarolinalodge.com; s/d incl 3 meals & horseback rides from US$75/130;

(P) (icon)) This isolated lodge run by a gracious American named Bill is on a working cattle ranch on the slopes of the volcano, and is highly recommended for anyone looking for a beautiful escape from the rigors of modern life. The remote location means there's limited electricity – but candlelight only adds to the ambience. Amazing meals (organic beans, rice, fruits, cheeses, chicken and pork from the farm), cooked over an outdoor wood-burning stove, are a treat, as is soaking in the wood-fired hot tub. Rooms with hot shower are basic, but you'll be spending most of your time in the nearby hot springs, swimming holes or on the riverside (where you can lounge, swim, fish or go bird-watching). The lodge is about 1.3km west of San Miguel.

GETTING THERE & AWAY

There are no direct buses to the national park. Buses between San Jose and Upala stop in Bijagua (₡3500, four daily). Buses also run between Upala and Canas via Bijagua (₡750, three daily). Most lodges can pick you up in Bijagua, and for a pricey fee will arrange transport to the park.

By car, the turnoff for Parque Nacional Volcán Tenorio is 5km north of Bijagua; turn right just past Bar El Mirador, continue 4.4km on the good gravel road to the village of San Miguel, turn right at the intersection and continue 6km to the park entrance. A 4WD is recommended.

Turning left at the San Miguel intersection would bring you to La Carolina Lodge (1.3km). The rough dirt road (4WD required) continues another 13km until it meets up with Hwy 4, the main Upala–Fortuna thoroughfare.

VOLCÁN MIRAVALLES AREA

Volcán Miravalles (2028m) is the highest volcano in the Cordillera de Guanacaste, and although the main crater is dormant, the geothermal activity beneath the ground has led to the rapid development of the area as a hot-springs destination. As more travelers land in Liberia, they're starting to discover this nearby refuge from the ubiquitous cold shower.

Volcán Miravalles isn't a national park or refuge, but the volcano itself is afforded a modicum of protection by being within the Zona Protectora Miravalles. You can also take guided tours of the government-run Proyecto Geotérmico Miravalles, north of Fortuna, an ambitious project inaugurated in 1994 that uses geothermal energy to produce electricity, primarily for export to Nicaragua and Panama, but also producing about 18% of Costa Rica's electricity. A few bright steel tubes from the plant snake along the flanks of the volcano, adding an eerie touch to the remote landscape. But the geothermal energy most people come here to soak up comes in liquid form. All the listed hot springs are north of the tiny village of Fortuna de Bagaces (not to be confused with La Fortuna de Arenal).

our pick **Thermo Manía** (☎ 2673-0233; www.thermomania.net; adult/child US$10/8; ⏲ 8am-10pm; (wi-fi)) is the biggest complex in the area, with seven thermal pools that are connected by all manner of waterslides, heated rivers, waterfalls and faux-stone bridges. There's also a full spa, playground, museum, zoo, soccer field and picnic tables; the busy restaurant-bar (mains US$4 to US$10) is housed in a 170-year-old colonial cabin furnished with museum-worthy period pieces. Guests who stay in the 26 log-cabin rooms (per person

NORTHWESTERN COSTA RICA

HERE'S MUD IN YOUR EYE

Actually…you'll want to keep thermal mud *out* of your eyes. To get the most out of your mud bath, local hot-springs devotees suggest this general regimen.

If there's a sauna, start with a nice steam for about 15 minutes to open your pores; otherwise, have a few minutes' soak in a warm pool. Then get dirty – squish your hands into the basin of gray volcanic mud (never directly from the pools themselves, which could ruin the experience by burning the flesh off your hands) and apply liberally, avoiding the eye area. Find a spot to relax and let the mud dry on your skin for 10 to 15 minutes before rinsing off under a hot shower and/or having a good soak in the hot pools (the recommended duration depends on the location of the hot springs). Ending with a brave dip in a cold pool, if there is one, not only recharges you in a big way but also sends a healthy jolt of blood to your internal organs.

Before getting into hot water – the thermal kind, at least – remove any silver jewelry to prevent it from oxidizing and turning black.

adult/child US$22/11) have free access to the pools during their stay, with TV and cold-water bathroom (neatly counterbalancing the lack of cold-water pools).

El Guayacán (☎ 2673-0349; www.termaleselguayacan.com; adult/child US$5/3), whose hissing vents and mud pots (absolutely stay on the trail!) are on the family *finca*, lies just behind Thermo Manía. With its five thermal pools and one cold pool in front of its simple, cold-water *cabinas* (adult/child US$22/11), this unpretentious place has a mellow, family vibe to it. There's an onsite restaurant (mains ₡1000 to ₡3000).

Nearby **Yökö Hot Springs** (☎ 2673-0410; www.yokotermales.com; adult/child US$8/6; 7am-11pm;) has four hot springs with a small waterslide and waterfall, set in an attractive meadow at the foot of Miravalles. The 12 elegant *cabinas* (single/double with breakfast US$40/75) have huge bathrooms and gleaming wood floors. Extra amenities include a Jacuzzi, sauna and a relaxed restaurant (mains ₡1000 to ₡5000) serving everything from burgers to filet mignon.

For some local flavor, **Termales Miravalles** (☎ 8357-8820, 8305-4072; adult/child US$4/3) has two pools, a waterslide and lies along a thermal stream. The owners have set up a small restaurant and offer camping (US$6 per person) on the property. They're usually open on weekends year-round, and daily during high season. The access road is directly across from Yökö Hot Springs.

On the southern slopes of Miravalles, **Las Hornillas** (☎ 8839-9769; www.lashornillas.com; admission US$20; 9am-5pm) is the center of volcanic activity in the area. The entrance fee includes an informative tour around the small crater (again, stay on the trail, kids) and allows you to soak in the thermal pools. This wonderfully isolated, family-run spot also offers hiking and tractor tours (US$40) via hanging bridges to a waterfall, including lunch and access to the mud and pools.

Just north of Fortuna de Bagaces is the lovely new **Ailanto Bed & Breakfast** (☎ 8353-7386; www.ailantocostarica.com; d/ste incl breakfast US$75/125;). Judith and David have created this little bit of paradise at the foothill of Miravalles on 33 acres of primary and secondary forest. The Tuscan-style villa has four rooms with comfy furnishings; some have shared bathroom. Property amenities include a shared kitchen, TV lounge, terrace with views, a thermal pool and hiking trails. The hosts can also help book area tours. It's located about 1.5km north of Fortuna de Bagaces; at the Y intersection, go right toward Las Homillas; Ailanto is on the right behind the big rock wall.

Near the base of the volcano is **Centro de Aventuras** (☎ 2673-0469; www.volcanoadventuretour.com; camping US$5, d US$30;), which has a number of offerings including a canopy tour (with/without lunch US$28/20) and horseback riding (US$25 to US$50). The clean, brightly painted *cabinas* have private hot-water bathroom and are centered on a pool that's fed by mountain springwater. This is a good place to inquire about local guides who can take you on independent tours, eg a two-day hike to the summit of Miravalles.

Volcán Miravalles is 27km northeast of Bagaces and can be approached by a paved road that leads north of Bagaces through the communities of Salitral and Torno, where the road splits. From the left-hand fork, you'll reach **Guayabo**, with a few *sodas* and basic *cabinas*; to the right, you'll find **Fortuna de Bagaces** (so named as not to confuse it with La Fortuna), with easier access to the hot springs. Both towns are small population centers, and are not of much interest to travelers. The roads reconnect north of the two towns and toward Upala, and also make a great scenic loop.

Buses (₡500, one hour) from Liberia to Guayabo or Aguas Claras (via Fortuna) depart at 6am, 9am, 11am and 2pm and pass by all the hot-spring entrances. Return buses to Liberia (via Guayabo) pass by the hot springs at about 2:30pm, 3:30pm and 4:30pm.

BAGACES

pop 4100

This small town is about 22km northwest of Cañas on the Interamericana, and is the headquarters of the **Area de Conservación Tempisque** (ACT; ☎ 2200-0125; 8am-4pm Mon-Fri), which, in conjunction with Minae, administers Parque Nacional Palo Verde, Reserva Biológica Lomas de Barbudal, and several smaller and lesser-known protected areas. The office is on the Interamericana opposite the signed main entry road into Parque Nacional Palo Verde. The office is mainly an administrative one, though sometimes rangers are available. Any buses between Cañas and Liberia can drop you off in Bagaces. If you're heading to

Miravalles, there are hourly local buses to both Fortuna and Guayabo.

Llanos de Cortés Waterfall

If you have time to visit only one waterfall in Costa Rica, make it Llanos de Cortés. This beautiful hidden waterfall is located about 3km north of Bagaces; head north on the Interamericana, turn left on the dirt road after the Río Piedras bridge, then follow the bumpy road (4WD required) about 500m until you reach a guard shack on the right. Admission is by donation and proceeds help fund the local primary school. Continue down the dirt road about 300m to the parking area, then scramble down the short, steep trail to reach this spectacular 12m-high, 15m-wide waterfall. The falls drops into a tranquil pond with a white sandy beach that's perfect for swimming and sunbathing. Go 'backstage' and relax on the rocks behind the waterfall curtain, or shower beneath the lukewarm waters. On weekends this is a popular Tico picnic spot, but on weekdays you'll often have the waterfall to yourself.

Apart from a portable toilet, there are no services here except for the occasional vendor selling fruit and cold coconut milk. The parking area is guarded (tips appreciated), but you shouldn't leave anything valuable in your car. If you don't have a car, any bus trawling this part of the Interamericana can drop you at the turnoff, but you'll have to hike from there to the falls.

PARQUE NACIONAL PALO VERDE

The 184-sq-km Parque Nacional Palo Verde is a wetland sanctuary in Costa Rica's driest province that lies on the northeastern banks of the mouth of Río Tempisque at the head of the Golfo de Nicoya. All of the major rivers in the region drain into this ancient intersection of two basins, which creates a mosaic of habitats, including mangrove swamps, marshes, grassy savannas and evergreen forests. A number of low limestone hills provide lookout points over the park, and the park's shallow, permanent lagoons are focal points for wildlife.

The park derives its name from the *palo verde* (green tree), which is a small shrub that's green year-round and abundant within the park. The park is also contiguous in the north with the 73-sq-km Refugio de Vida Silvestre Dr Rafael Lucas Rodríguez Caballero and the Reserva Biológica Lomas de Barbudal, which, along with Parque Nacional Barra Honda, make up part of the **Area de Conservación Tempisque**, a large conservation area containing some of Costa Rica's last remaining strands of dry tropical forest. A recent addition to this project was Refugio do Vida Silvestre Cipancí, which protects the corridors linking the various parks from being clear-cut by local farmers.

Palo Verde has the greatest concentrations of waterfowl and shorebirds in Central America, and over 300 different bird species have been recorded in the park. Bird-watchers come particularly to see the large flocks of heron (including the rare black-crowned night heron), stork (including the endangered jabirú), spoonbill, egret, ibis, grebe and duck; and forest birds, including scarlet macaw, great curassow, keel-billed toucan, and parrots are also common. Frequently sighted mammals include deer, coati, armadillo, monkey and peccary, as well as the largest population of jaguarundi in Costa Rica. There are also numerous reptiles in the wetlands including crocodiles that are reportedly up to 5m in length.

The dry season, from December to March, is the best time to visit as flocks of birds tend to congregate in the remaining lakes and marshes and the trees lose their leaves, thus allowing for clearer viewing. However, the entire basin swelters during the dry season, so bring adequate sun protection. There are also far fewer insects in the dry season, and mammals are occasionally seen around the water holes. Take binoculars or a spotting scope if possible. During the wet months, large portions of the area are flooded, and access may be limited.

Orientation & Information

The **park entrance** (☎ 2200-0125; admission US$10; 🕑 8am-4pm) is 28km along the turnoff from the Interamericana near the town of Bagaces. However, your best source of information on the park is the Hacienda Palo Verde Research Station (p224). There is a fairly extensive system of roads and hiking trails that originate from the park entrance and lead to a series of lookout points and observation towers.

Tours

To fully appreciate the size and topography of the park, it's worth organizing a boat trip.

NORTHWESTERN COSTA RICA

Travelers recommend the **guided tours** (2/3/4 people half-day US$35/60/75) that can be arranged through the Hacienda Palo Verde Research Station. The station also offers **bird-watching tours** (half-/full day per person US$30/38) through the park. Tour operators in San José and La Fortuna run package tours to Palo Verde, but you'll save money by arranging everything yourself.

Sleeping & Eating

Overnight visitors should make reservations and must also pay the US$10 entry fee.

Camping (per person US$4) is permitted near the Palo Verde ranger station, where toilets and hot-water showers are available. Meals and box lunches (₡6000) are available at the Organization of Tropical Studies (OTS) research station by advance arrangement.

Run by the OTS, **Hacienda Palo Verde Research Station** (☎ 524-0607; www.ots.ac.cr; r incl meals adult/child per person $65/34) conducts tropical research and teaches university graduate-level classes. Researchers and those taking OTS courses get preference for dormitories with shared bathrooms. A few two- and four-bed rooms with shared bathrooms are also available. The rates for visitors include a guided hike. The research station is on a well-signed road 8km from the park entrance.

Getting There & Away

The main road to the entrance, usually passable to ordinary cars year-round, begins from a signed turnoff from the Interamericana, opposite Bagaces. The 28km gravel road has tiny brown signs that usually direct you when the road forks, but if in doubt, take the fork that looks more used. Another 8km brings you to the limestone hill, Cerro Guayacán (and the Hacienda Palo Verde Research Station), from where there are great views; 2km further are the Palo Verde park headquarters and ranger station. You can drive through a swampy maze of roads to the Reserva Biológica Lomas de Barbudal without returning to the Interamericana.

Buses connecting Cañas and Liberia can drop you at the ACT office in Bagaces, opposite the turnoff to the park. If you call the ACT office in advance, rangers may be able to pick you up in Bagaces. If you're staying at the Hacienda Palo Verde Research Station, the staff can also arrange to pick you up in Bagaces.

RESERVA BIOLÓGICA LOMAS DE BARBUDAL

The 26-sq-km Lomas de Barbudal reserve forms a cohesive unit with Palo Verde, and protects several species of endangered trees, such as mahogany and rosewood, as well as the common and quite spectacular *corteza amarilla*. This tree is what biologists call a 'big bang reproducer' – all the yellow cortezes in the forest burst into bloom on the same day, and for about four days the forest is an incredible mass of yellow-flowered trees. This usually occurs in March, about four days after an unseasonal rain shower.

Nearly 70% of the trees in the reserve are deciduous, and during the dry season they shed their leaves as if it were autumn in a temperate forest. This particular habitat is known as tropical dry forest, and occurs in climates that are warm year-round, though characterized by a long dry season that lasts several months. Since plants lose moisture through their leaves, the shedding of leaves allows the trees to conserve water during dry periods. The newly bare trees also open up the canopy layer, enabling sunlight to reach ground level and facilitate the growth of thick underbrush. (Dry forests were once common in many parts of the Pacific slopes of Central America, but little remains. They also exist north and south of the equatorial rainforest belt, especially in southern Mexico and the Bolivian lowlands.)

Lomas de Barbudal is also known for its abundant and varied wasps, butterflies, moths and other insects. There are about 250 different species of bee in this fairly small reserve – representing about a quarter of the world's bee species. Bees here include the Africanized 'killer' bees – if you suffer from bee allergies, this is one area where you really don't want to forget your bee-sting kit.

There are more than 200 bird species, including the great curassow, a chickenlike bird that is hunted for food and is endangered, as well as other endangered species including the king vulture, scarlet macaw and jabirú stork. Much like Palo Verde, Lomas de Barbudal is also home to a variety of mammal species as well as some enormous crocodiles – you might want to leave your swimsuit at home.

Orientation & Information

At the reserve entrance, there's a small **information center** (☎ 2671-1029; reserve admission by donation; 7am-4pm), though the actual reserve is on the other side of the Río Cabuyo, behind the museum. The infrastructure of the park is less geared to tourists than at Palo Verde, though there is a small network of hiking trails that radiates from the information center. A small map is provided. It is not possible to overnight in the park and backcountry hiking is not permitted.

Getting There & Away

The turnoff to Lomas de Barbudal from the Interamericana is near the small community of Pijije, 14km southeast of Liberia or 12km northwest of Bagaces. It's 7km to the entrance of the reserve. The road is unpaved, but open all year – some steep sections may require 4WD in rainy season. Buses between Liberia and Cañas can drop you at the turnoff to the reserve.

LIBERIA

pop 45,300

Well, the secret's out. Before the boom in Costa Rican tourism, deciphering the bus timetables and fighting your way through the crowds at the Coca-Cola terminal in San José was a rite of passage for the uninitiated traveler. Even just a few years ago, getting to the beaches on the Península de Nicoya took determination, patience and – depending on the state of Costa Rica's dreadful roads – a little luck. These days, though, travelers are getting their first glimpse of *pura vida* Costa Rica at Liberia's own Aeropuerto Internacional Daniel Oduber Quirós, which is roughly the size of a Wal-Mart parking lot, but more of a breeze to exit.

Previously, the sunny capital of Guanacaste served as a transportation hub connecting Liberia with both borders, as well as the standard-bearer of Costa Rica's *sabanero* culture (see boxed text, p219). Even today, a large part of the greater Liberia area is involved in ranching operations, but tourism is fast becoming a significant contributor to the economy. Liberia has long been a base for visiting the nearby volcanoes, national parks and beaches, and nowadays the sight of gringos heading for their second homes in Tamarindo, or surfers toting their boards, is commonplace.

For now, Liberia is a much safer and surprisingly chill alternative to San José, although the government is looking to expand the airport in several years, with an eye to accommodating as much traffic, or more, as Juan Santamaría airport.

Liberia is still a great base for exploring the attractions in the northwest and the beaches of the Península de Nicoya. And, though most of the historic buildings in the city center are a little rough around the edges and in desperate need of a paint job, the 'white city' is a pleasant one, with a good range of accommodations and services for travelers on all budgets. The streets in downtown Liberia are surprisingly well signed, a rarity in Costa Rica.

Information

INTERNET ACCESS

Cyberm@nia (2666-7240; Av 1 btwn Calles 2 & Central; per hr ₡600; 8am-10pm) With the friendliest staff ever, this spot is also good for cheap long-distance calls, charging ₡150 per minute to most parts of the world.

Planet Internet (2665-3737; Calle Central btwn Avs Central & 2; per hr ₡560; 9am-9pm;) Has speedy machines in a spacious, frigidly air-conditioned room; also offers internet calls.

MEDICAL SERVICES

Hospital Dr Enrique Baltodano Briceño (2666-0011, emergencies 2666-0318) Behind the stadium on the northeastern outskirts of town.

MONEY

Most hotels will accept US dollars, and may be able to change small amounts. Liberia probably has more banks per square meter than any other town in Costa Rica.

BAC San José (2666-2020; Centro Comercial Santa Rosa; 9am-6pm Mon-Fri, 9am-1pm Sat) Changes traveler's checks; try this 24-hour ATM if others won't accept your card.

Banco de Costa Rica (2666-2582; cnr Calle Central & Av 1) Has a 24-hour ATM.

Banco Nacional (2666-0191; Av 25 de Julio btwn Calles 6 & 8; 8am-3:45pm Mon-Fri, 9am-1pm Sat) Has a 24-hour ATM.

Banco Popular (cnr Calle 12 & Av 25 de Julio) Has a 24-hour ATM.

Citibank (cnr Interamericana & Av 25 de Julio; 9am-6pm Mon-Fri, 9am-12:30pm Sat) Has 24-hour ATM and changes money.

HSBC (Av 25 de Julio btwn Calles 6 & 4; 9m-6pm Mon-Fri, 9am-12:30pm Sat) Has a 24-hour ATM.

Sights & Activities

Though there's not much of historical or cultural interest in town, the lack of sights gives you an excuse to relax in one of the local restaurants or bars as you plan your next trip to a beach or volcano.

Near the entrance of town, a **statue** of a steely-eyed *sabanero*, complete with an evocative poem by Rodolfo Salazar Solórzano, stands watch over Av 25 de Julio, the main street into town. The blocks around the intersection of Av Central and Calle Central contain several of the town's oldest houses, many dating back about 150 years.

The pleasant Parque Central frames a modern church, **Iglesia Inmaculada Concepción de María**. The park is also the seasonal hangout of the Nicaraguan grackle, a tone-deaf bird that enjoys eating parrot eggs and annoying passers-by with its grating calls.

A new **museum of archaeology** featuring the collection of ex-president Daniel Oduber is scheduled to open in late 2010. The museum will be located in the old city jail, a castle-like building worth a look.

Walking six blocks northeast of the park along Av Central brings you to the oldest church in town, popularly called **La Agonía** (although maps show it as La Iglesia de la Ermita de la Resurección). Strolling to La Agonía and around the surrounding blocks makes a fine walk.

About 9km south of Liberia, **Africa Mía** (☎ 2666-1111; www.africamia.net; self-guided walking tour adult/child US$16/11, guided van tour adult/child US$27/22; ⏲ 9am-5pm) is a private wildlife reserve with free-roaming elephants, zebras, giraffes,

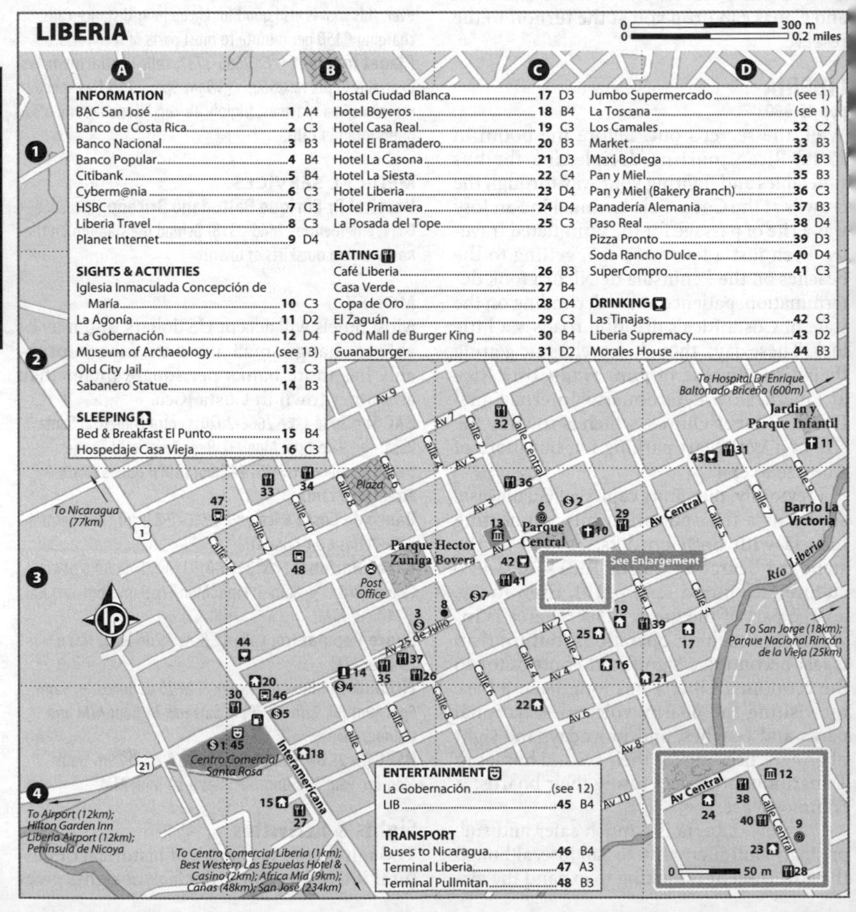

ostriches and other animals. Splurge for the deluxe African Safari Wildlife Tour (adult/child US$65/55) in an open-top Hummer with a stop at a waterfall.

Tours

Hotel Liberia and La Posada del Tope are great budget hotels that can organize trips and tours throughout Costa Rica. La Posada del Tope has the best deals on rental cars and is the exclusive downtown vendor for Tica Bus tickets to Nicaragua.

Sleeping

Liberia is at its busiest during the dry season – reservations are strongly recommended over Christmas, Easter, Día de Guanacaste and on weekends. During the wet season, however, most of the midrange and top-end hotels give discounts.

BUDGET

Hotel Liberia (☎ 2666-0161; www.hotelliberia.com; Calle Central btwn Avs Central & 2; dm US$10, r with/without bathroom US$15/13; P) Rooms in this rambling, century-old building surround an outdoor lounge complete with TV, hammocks and jet-lagged backpackers chatting about their past and present travel plans. Rooms are tidy and bright but pretty basic. The hotel is recommended for its vibrant atmosphere that's in part created by the Peruvian manager Beto.

La Posada del Tope (☎ 2666-3876; hotelposadadeltope@gmail.com; Calle Central btwn Calles Central & 2; r without bathroom per person US$9-18; P) This budget hotel is housed in an attractive mid-19th-century house that's decorated with old photos, antiques and mosquito nets, and has a bit of an old-plantation feel to it. Rooms have shared bathrooms and are fairly basic, though the hotel is recommended as the bilingual Tico owner, Denís, is a wealth of information and can help book tours and transportation. The newer annex across the street (known as Casa Real but actually part of the same hotel) has nicer rooms with TV, set around a lovely little courtyard.

Hotel La Casona (☎ 2666-2971; casona@racsa.co.cr; cnr Calle Central & Av 6; s/d with fan US$16/24, with air-con US$20/30; P) This pink, wooden house has simple rooms with private bathroom and cable TV. There's no hot water (which shouldn't be an issue), and there is also an apartment at the same rates per person as the rooms.

Hospedaje Casa Vieja (☎ 2665-5826; Av 4 btwn Calles Central & 2; s/d with fan US$18/22, s/d with air-con US$36/44;) Just a couple of blocks from Parque Central, this quiet, homelike place has 10 comfortable rooms with private bathroom and TV. Rates do not include breakfast, but there's a small yard out back with a shaded raised patio where you can enjoy the granola that you bring yourself.

Hostal Ciudad Blanca (☎ 2666-3962; Av 4 btwn Calles 1 & 3; s/d with fan US$30/40, with air-con US$35/45; P) One of Liberia's most attractive hotels is in a historic colonial mansion that has been completely refurbished. Tree-shaded rooms have air-con, fan, cable TV, nice furnishings and private hot-water bathroom. The charming little restaurant-bar downstairs is perfect for a nightcap – or a game of pinball.

Hotel Primavera (☎ 2666-0464; Av Central btwn Calles Central & 2; s/d with fan US$37/62, with air-con US$43/66; P) Just off Parque Central but set back from the street a bit, rooms at this small hotel are a little worn, but they have attractive wood accents and come furnished with microwave, cable TV and private cold shower. Not the best value in town, but perfectly OK.

MIDRANGE & TOP END

Hotel La Siesta (☎ 2666-0678; lasiestaliberia@hotmail.com; Calle 4 btwn Avs 4 & 6; s/d incl breakfast US$40/50; P) Spotless, standard rooms with cable TV and private cold-water shower are arranged around a pretty poolside garden. Rooms upstairs are slightly larger, but all are very quiet and the place has a relaxed feel. There's also an attached restaurant (meals ₡2500 to ₡4000, open for breakfast and lunch), which is regarded by locals as having the best *casado* in town.

Hotel El Bramadero (☎ 2666-0371; www.hotelelbramadero.com; cnr Interamericana & Hwy 21; s/d US$40/58; P) El Bramadero is a comfortable, midrange hotel that has well-appointed rooms with air-con, hot shower and cable TV. It has a *sabanero* theme, so it follows that the restaurant (meals ₡3500 to ₡7900, open for lunch and dinner) has some of the thickest and juiciest steaks you've ever feasted on.

Hotel Boyeros (☎ 2666-0722, 2666-0809; www.hotelboyeros.com; cnr Interamericana & Av 2; s/d/tr US$56/65/76; P) The largest hotel in Liberia feels like a cross between a dude ranch and the Holiday Inn. Immaculate rooms all have comfortable furnishings, air-con and cable TV, and the upstairs rooms have private balcony. There's also a 24-hour restaurant, free wi-fi, pool with waterslide, kiddie pool and a shaded sitting area. Look for the sculpture of the *boyero* (oxcart driver) out front.

our pick **Bed & Breakfast El Punto** (☎ 2665-2986; www.elpuntohotel.com; cnr Interamericana & Av 4; s/d US$60/97; P ❄ 💻 📶) This converted elementary school is now a chic hotel, and would definitely feel more at home in trendy Miami than in humble Guanacaste. The saturated tropical colors of the loft apartments manage also to be understated and minimalist. All rooms have beautifully tiled bathroom, kitchenette, hammocks, free wi-fi and colorful modern art. The common area features low outdoor sofas and even crayons for the kids, and the bilingual architect-owner Mariana is charm personified.

Hilton Garden Inn Liberia Airport (☎ 2690-8888; www.hilton.com; d US$80-160; P ⊠ ❄ 💻 📶 🏊) Liberia's newest hotel is also the fanciest, with all the usual four-star amenities including pool, gym and tennis courts. All rooms have fridge, microwave, flat-screen TV, and free internet and wi-fi access. It's directly across from Liberia Airport, perfect if you have an early-morning flight.

For all your overpriced chain-hotel needs, there's a **Best Western Las Espuelas Hotel & Casino** (☎ 2666-0144; www.bestwestern.com; s/d incl breakfast US$75/80, ste US$150; P ⊠ ❄ 💻 🏊) about 2km south of Liberia, with all the standard amenities and rooms you'd expect.

Eating

Panadería Alemania (☎ 2665-2061; Av 25 de Julio btwn Calles 10 & 8; mains ₡500-3000; ⏰ breakfast, lunch & dinner) A German bakery with beautifully flaky croissants, a respectably authentic sushi counter doing what it can with the local rice and an international kitchen turning out Euro-style numbers can all be found at this local hangout. The patio is also a great place for a beer under the canopy of the huge guanacaste tree.

our pick **Café Liberia** (☎ 2665-1660; www.cafeliberia.com; Calle 8 btwn Avs 25 de Julio & 2; items ₡600-3500; ⏰ 8:30am-6pm Mon-Fri, 10am-6pm Sat; ❄ 💻 📶 V) Run by a sweet Tica named Radha, this hip spot is a dream: serving organic juices, Costa Rican coffee, fresh sandwiches, salads and crepes, pastries, wines and lots of vegetarian items. Plus, there's free wi-fi, a gallery and sometimes live music. The lovely Radha also runs a small boutique shop on the premises.

Guanaburger (☎ 2666-7194; cnr Calle 5 & Av 1; ⏰ noon-10pm) This famous homegrown institution packs in the locals with its ₡1800 burger-fries-drink bargain combo.

Los Comales (☎ 2666-0105; Calle Central btwn Avs 7 & 5; plates ₡1000-3000; ⏰ 6:30-9pm) This convivial, popular local spot is run by a women's collective, and serves native Guanacaste dishes as well as typical cuisine. The specialty is chicken and salsa, but the *casados* are just as tasty.

Soda Rancho Dulce (Calle Central btwn Avs Central & 2; mains ₡1100-2200; ⏰ breakfast, lunch & dinner) Sometimes a *casado* is more than a *casado*, and this outstanding open-air *soda*, with groovy wooden tables and good *batidos* (fruit shakes), serves some of the best.

Pan y Miel (☎ 2666-0718; Av 25 de Julio btwn Calles 10 & 8; mains ₡1100-2800; ⏰ 6am-6pm) The best breakfast in town can be had at this branch of the local bakery, which serves its excellent bread as sandwiches and French toast, as well as offering a buffet line with *casado* fixings, pastries and fresh fruit. There's a surlier bakery-only branch a block north of Parque Central.

Pizza Pronto (☎ 2666-2098; cnr Av 4 & Calle 1; mains ₡2800-5000; ⏰ lunch & dinner) Situated in a handsome 19th-century house, this romantic pizzeria is in a class of its own. You can choose from a long list of toppings for your wood-fired pizza, including fresh, local seafood or pineapple; the pastas are also good.

La Toscana (☎ 2665-0653; Plaza Santa Rosa; mains ₡2200-8000; ⏰ noon-11pm; ❄) Satisfy those pangs for gnocchi or spaghetti carbonara at one of the most authentically Italian restaurants in the region. Tuscan wine, tablecloths and tiramisu await.

Copa de Oro (☎ 2666-0532; cnr Calle Central & Ave 2; mains ₡3250-6800; ⏰ 11am-11pm Wed-Mon; 👶) Our favorite family restaurant is popular with locals and gringos alike. There's an extensive food and drink menu. The dish we loved best is the rice and seafood house specialty, *arroz copa de oro.*

El Zaguán (☎ 2666-2456; cnr Ave Central & Calle 1; mains ₡3300-8500; ⏰ 11:30am-10pm; 👶) Located in a beautiful colonial building, this family-friendly restaurant has an extensive international menu specializing in meat including New York Strip, filet mignon and burgers. You'll also find fish, pasta and rice dishes. The outdoor balcony is a great people-watching spot.

our pick **Casa Verde** (☎ 2665-5037; Interamericana; mains ₡4000-10,000; ⏰ 11am-11pm Tue-Sun; 📶)

California-Asian chic comes to Liberia. The sophisticated and stylish Casa Verde is one of the best dining experiences in northwest Costa Rica. Located near the Bed & Breakfast El Punto, the restaurant has contemporary decor, with a slate bar, black leather couches, candlelit tables, an outdoor patio lit by tiki torches, plus chill ambient music, with live music on Fridays. The fusion menu specializes in fish and meat dishes and has an extensive wine list. Sushi-lovers should visit between Thursday and Sunday for awesome rolls and tempura. Don't miss this dining experience.

Paso Real (☎ 2666-3455; Av Central btwn Calles Central & 2; mains ₡4400-7600; 11am-10pm) Liberia's most famous restaurant has a breezy balcony overlooking Parque Central, and is locally known for its inventive cuisine, like mahimahi in a white sauce with apple and chipotle. The huge portions are big enough to share.

Liberia has many inexpensive *sodas* and Chinese take-out restaurants. If you're yearning for gringo-style fast food, head to the **Food Mall de Burger King** (Interamericana). Not to be outdone, there's a new McDonald's at the main entrance to town.

Before you board that long bus ride, pick up cheap eats and fresh fruit and veggies at the traditional covered **market** (Ave 7 btwn Calles 8 & 10, 6am-7pm Mon-Sat, 6am-noon Sun), conveniently located next to Terminal Liberia. Or grab groceries at the **SuperCompro** (Av Central btwn Calles 2 & 4; 8am-8pm Mon-Fri, 8am-6pm Sat & Sun) or the humongous **Maxi Bodega** (Av 7 btwn Calles 8 & 10; 8am-10pm Mon-Sat, 8am-9pm Sun). For a good selection of international groceries, stop by **Jumbo Supermercado** (Plaza Santa Rosa) to load up on supplies before heading to the beach.

Drinking & Entertainment

Live music and dance performances are often held at the Parque Central gazebo and at the nearby **La Gobernación** (cnr Av Central & Calle Central), an old municipal building. Your best chance of seeing Punto Guanacasteco is to be in town for a *tope* (see boxed text, p219).

Las Tinajas (Calle 2 btwn Avs Central & 1; lunch & dinner) Sip a cold beer and nosh on some greasy fries at this parkside pub, an ideal place to watch the happenings in Parque Central. It occasionally has live music.

Liberia Supremacy (Av 1 btwn Calles 5 & 7; 4pm-late Tue-Sun) A bit of Jamaica comes to Liberia at this popular reggae bar decorated with posters of Bob Marley and Che. There's a friendly vibe, cheap beer, an extensive Mexican *bocas* menu and the most uncomfortable bar stools ever made.

Morales House (☎ 2665-2490; cnr Av 1 & Interamericana; bocas ₡1500-3000; 3pm-2am) A real Guanacaste *sabanero* hangout, this barnlike bar with cowboy motif has bulls' heads on the walls, blaring *ranchera* music and American sports on TV.

our pick **LIB** (Plaza Santa Rosa; 5pm-2am Mon-Sat) The best nightspot in town, this open-air disco bathed in neon is on the 2nd floor of Plaza Santa Rosa, blaring salsa and rock music on to the masses below. There's a good *bocas* menu to help soak up the alcohol. A varying cover charge applies for men on weekends.

If you're looking for your Hollywood fix, the American-style shopping mall **cinema** (Centro Comercial Liberia; adult/child ₡1600/1200) has a decent offering of mainstream American films.

Getting There & Away

AIR

Since 1993, Aeropuerto Internacional Daniel Oduber Quirós (LIR), 12km west of Liberia, has served as the country's second international airport, providing easy access to all those beautiful beaches without the hassle of dealing with the lines and bustle of San José. It's a tiny airport, jam-packed with increasing traffic. A new US$35 million airport terminal is currently under construction.

There are no car-rental desks at the airport; make reservations in advance, and your company will meet you at the airport with a car. You'll find a money-exchange, cafe and gift shop. Taxis to Liberia cost ₡6000. Downtown-based **Liberia Travel** (☎ 2666-4383; cnr Av 25 de Julio & Calle 6; 8am-6pm Mon-Fri, 8am-noon Sat) can help book flights worldwide.

The majority of international flights are through the USA, though some airlines fly directly between Liberia and the USA including American Airlines, Continental, Delta, United and US Airways. Charter airlines now fly seasonally from Canada, Belgium and the UK. Domestic airline destinations include:

NatureAir (☎ 2220-3054; www.natureair.com) To/from San José, Quepos, Fortuna, Tambor and Tamarindo.

Sansa (☎ 2668-1047; www.flysansa.com) To/from San José and Tamarindo.

BUS

Buses arrive and depart from **Terminal Liberia** (Av 7 btwn Calles 12 & 14) and **Terminal Pulmitan** (Av 5

NICA VS TICO

Ticos have a well-deserved reputation for friendliness, and it's rare for travelers of any sex, race or creed to experience prejudice in Costa Rica. However, it's unfortunate and at times upsetting that the mere mention of anything related to Nicaragua is enough to turn an average Tico into a stereotype-spewing anti-Nico (note that the term 'Nica' is used by *some* Ticos in a somewhat derogatory manner, so watch your language). Despite commonalities in language, culture, history and tradition, Nica versus Tico relations are at an all-time low, and rhetoric (on both sides) of *la frontera* (the border) isn't likely to improve anytime soon.

Why is there so much hostility between Nicas and Ticos? The answer is as much a product of history as it is of misunderstanding, though economic disparities between both countries are largely to blame.

Though Nicaragua was wealthier than Costa Rica as little as 25 years ago, decades of civil war and a US embargo quickly bankrupted the country, and today Nicaragua is the second-poorest country in the western hemisphere (after Haiti). For example, the 2009 CIA World Factbook lists the GDP per capita purchasing power parity of Costa Rica as US$10,900, while Nicaragua is listed at only US$2800. The main problem facing Nicaragua is its heavy external debt, though debt relief programs implemented by the International Monetary Fund (IMF) and the free-trade zone created by the Central American Free Trade Agreement (Cafta) are both promising signs.

In the meantime, however, Nica families are crossing the border in record numbers, drawn to Costa Rica by its growing economy and impressive education and health systems. However, immigration laws in Costa Rica make it difficult for Nicas to find work, and the majority end up living in shantytowns. Also, crime is on the rise throughout Costa Rica, and though it's difficult to say what percentage is actually attributable to Nica immigrants, some Ticos are quick to point the finger.

It's difficult to predict whether or not relations will improve between both countries, although current signs are fairly negative. Costa Rica, whose civil guard is better funded than many countries' militaries, has a bad habit of being caught on the Río San Juan with a patrol boat of combat troops. Nicaragua, on the other hand, recently passed a law requiring all visiting Ticos to be in possession of a valid visa. Like with all instances of deep-rooted prejudice, the solution is anything but clear.

btwn Calles 10 & 12). Routes, fares, journey times and departures are as follows:

Cañas ₡1050; 1½ hours; departs Terminal Liberia 5:30am, 6:30am, 7:30am, noon, 1:30pm, 4:30pm, 5:30pm, 6:45pm and 7:45pm. It's quicker to jump off the San José–bound bus in Cañas.

Guayabo de Bagaces ₡1000; one hour; departs Terminal Liberia 6am, 9am, 11am and 2pm.

La Cruz/Peñas Blancas ₡750; 1½ to two hours; departs Pulmitan every hour from 5am to 6pm.

Managua, Nicaragua ₡6000; five hours; departs Pulmitan 7am, 8am and noon (buy tickets one day in advance). You can also flag down Nicaragua-bound buses on the Interamericana at McDonald's.

Nicoya, via Filadelfia & Santa Cruz ₡1000; 1½ hours; departs Terminal Liberia every 30 minutes from 4:30am to 9pm.

Potrero Bay, Playa Flamingo, Playa Brasilito ₡1000; 1½ hours; departs Terminal Liberia 4:30am, 6:10am, 11:10am and 6pm.

Playa del Coco ₡580; one hour; departs Pulmitan every hour from 5am to 11am, then 12:30pm, 2:30pm and 6:30pm.

Playa Hermosa, Playa Panamá ₡800; 1¼ hours; departs Terminal Liberia 4:30am, 4:40am, 4:50am, 7:30am, 11:30am, 1pm, 3:30pm and 5:30pm.

Playa Tamarindo ₡1180; 1½ to two hours; departs Terminal Liberia hourly between 3:50am and 6pm. Some buses take a longer route via Playa Flamingo.

Puntarenas ₡1400; three hours; eight buses from 5am to 3:30pm. It's quicker to jump off the San José–bound bus in Puntarenas.

San José ₡2700; four hours; 11 departures from Pulmitan from 4am to 8pm.

CAR

Liberia lies on the Interamericana, 234km north of San José and 77km south of the Nicaraguan border post of Peñas Blancas. Highway 21, the main artery of the Península de Nicoya, begins in Liberia and heads southwest. A dirt road, passable to all cars in dry season (4WD is preferable), leads 25km from Barrio la Victoria to the Santa María entrance of Parque Nacional Rincón de la Vieja; the gravel road to the Las Pailas entrance begins from the Interamericana, 5km north of Liberia (passable to regular cars, but 4WD is recommended).

There are at least 30 rental-car agencies in Liberia (none of which have desks at the airport), all charging about the same rates. Most can arrange pickup in Liberia and drop-off in San José, though they'll try to charge you extra. Rental agencies are on Hwy 21 between Liberia and the airport, but should be able to drop off your car in town. Some recommended car-rental agencies:

Adobe (☎ 2667-0608; www.adobecar.com)
Avis (☎ 2668-1196; www.avis.co.cr)
Budget (☎ 2668-1024; www.budget.com)
Europcar (☎ 2668-1023; www.europcar.co.cr)
Hola (☎ 2667-4040; www.hola.net)
Mapache (☎ 2665-4444; www.mapache.com)
Toyota Rent a Car (☎ 2666-8190; www.carrental-toyota-costarica.com)

PARQUE NACIONAL RINCÓN DE LA VIEJA

Given its proximity to Liberia – really just a hop, skip and a few bumps away – this 141-sq-km national park feels refreshingly uncrowded and remote. Named after the active Volcán Rincón de la Vieja (1895m), the steamy main attraction, the park also covers several other peaks in the same volcanic range, including the highest, Volcán Santa María (1916m). The park breathes geothermal energy, which you can see for yourself in its multihued fumaroles, hot springs, lively *pailas* (mud pots) bubbling and blooping clumps of ashy gray mud, and a young and feisty *volcancito* (small volcano). All these can be visited on foot and horseback on well-maintained but sometimes steep trails.

The park was created in 1973 to protect the 32 rivers and streams that have their sources within the park, an important watershed. Its relatively remote location means that wildlife, rare elsewhere, is out in force here, with the major volcanic crater a rather dramatic backdrop to the scene. Volcanic activity has occurred many times since the late 1960s, with the most recent eruption of steam and ash in 1997. At the moment, however, the volcano is gently active and does not present any danger – ask locally for the latest, as it's in their nature for volcanoes to act up.

Elevations in the park range from less than 600m to 1916m, so visitors pass through a variety of different habitats as they ascend the volcanoes, though the majority of the trees in the park are typical of those found in dry tropical forests throughout Guanacaste. One interesting tree to look out for is the strangler fig, a parasitic tree that covers the host tree with its own trunk and proceeds to strangle it by competing for water, light and nutrients. The host tree eventually dies and rots away, while the strangler fig survives as a hollow, tubular lattice. The park is also home to the country's highest density of Costa Rica's national flower, the increasingly rare purple orchid *(Cattleya skinneri),* locally known as *guaria morada*.

Most visitors to the park are here for the hot springs, where you can soak to the sound of howler monkeys overhead. Many of the springs are reported to have therapeutic properties, which is always a good thing if you've been hitting the Guaro Cacique a little too hard. Several lodges just outside the park provide access and arrange tours. You can also book transportation and tours directly from Liberia.

Orientation & Information

Each of the two main entrances to the park has its own ranger station, where you sign in and get free maps. Most visitors enter through **Las Pailas ranger station** (☎ 2661-8139; www.acguanacaste.ac.cr; admission US$10; 🕑 7am-5pm, no entry after 3pm, closed Mon) on the western flank. Trails to the summit and the most interesting volcanic features begin here. Note that on the way to Las Pailas, you must pay a fee of US$1.50 for the privilege of passing through the private property of Hacienda Guachipelín. The fee is ostensibly for road maintenance but is fairly ludicrous considering its hotel rates.

The **Santa María ranger station** (☎ 2661-8139; admission US$10; 🕑 7am-5pm, no entry past 3pm, closed Mon), to the east, is in the Hacienda Santa María, a 19th-century *rancho* with a small public exhibit that was reputedly once owned by US President Lyndon Johnson. It's closest to the sulfurous hot springs and also has an observation tower and a nearby waterfall.

Activities

WILDLIFE-WATCHING

The wildlife of the park is extremely varied. Almost 300 species of bird have been recorded here, including curassow, quetzal, bellbird, parrot, toucan, hummingbird, owl, woodpecker, tanager, motmot, dove and eagle.

Insects range from beautiful butterflies to annoying ticks. Be especially prepared for ticks in grassy areas – long trousers tucked into boots and long-sleeved shirts offer some protection. A particularly interesting insect is a highland cicada that burrows into the ground and croaks like a frog, to the bewilderment of naturalists.

Mammals are equally varied; deer, armadillo, peccary, skunk, squirrel, coati and three species of monkey make frequent appearances. Tapir tracks are often found around the lagoons near the summit. Several of the wild cat species have been recorded here, including the jaguar, puma, ocelot and margay, but you'll need patience and good fortune to observe one of these.

HIKING

A circular trail east of Las Pailas (about 3km in total) takes you past the boiling mud pools (Las Pailas), sulfurous fumaroles and a *volcancito* (which may subside at any time). About 700m west of the ranger station along the **Sendero Cangreja** is a swimming hole, which is prescribed for lowering your body temperature after too much time in the hot springs. Further away along the same trail are several waterfalls – the largest, **Catarata La Cangreja**, 5km west, is a classic, dropping straight from a cliff into a small lagoon where you can swim. Dissolved copper salts give the falls a deep blue color. This trail winds through forest, then on to open grassland on the volcano's flanks, where you can enjoy views as far as the Golfo de Nicoya. The slightly smaller **Cataratas Escondidas** (Hidden Waterfalls) are 4.3km west on a different trail.

The longest and most adventurous hike in the area is the 16km round-trip trek to the summit of Rincón de la Vieja and to nearby **Laguna de Jilgueros**, which is reportedly where you may see tapirs – or more likely their footprints, if you are observant. The majority of this hike follows a ridge trail, and is known for being extremely windy and cloudy – come prepared for the weather. It's also advised that you hire a guide from the ranger station or a nearby hotel as the trail is dotted with sulfurous hot springs and geysers, and hikers have been severely burned (and occasionally boiled) in the past.

From the Santa María ranger station, a trail leads 2.8km west through the 'enchanted forest' and past a waterfall to sulfurous **hot springs** with supposedly therapeutic properties. Don't soak in them for more than about half an hour (some people suggest much less) without taking a dip in one of the nearby cold springs to cool off. An observation point is 450m east of the station.

SIMBIOSIS SPA

Affiliated with Hacienda Guachipelín, this **spa** (☎ 2666-8075; www.simbiosis-spa.com; admission US$15; 🕑 9am-5:30pm) is also open to the public. With spring-fed hot pools, volcanic mud, a sauna, showers and lounge chairs, all in a natural outdoor setting, this is a lovely place to unwind. You can also arrange massages and spa treatments (US$35 to US$75) on the spot, though it's recommended you reserve ahead.

Tours

All of the tourist lodges can arrange a number of tours, including horseback riding (US$25 to US$35), mountain biking (US$10 to US$30), guided waterfall and hot-springs hikes (US$15 to US$25), rappelling (US$20 to US$50), rafting and tubing on the lesser-known Río Colorado (US$45 to US$60), hanging bridges (US$15 to US$20) and everyone's favorite cash-burner, canopy tours (US$30 to US$50). Rates vary depending on the season, and there are a number of package deals available. If you're staying in Liberia, it's possible to organize these activities in advance either through your hotel, or by contacting the lodges directly.

Sleeping & Eating

CAMPING

Camping is permitted only at the Santa Maria ranger station (US$2 per person). The campground has water, pit toilets, showers, tables and grills but you'll have to be self-sufficient. Be prepared for cold and foggy weather year-round. The wet season is very wet (October is the rainiest month), and very full of mosquitoes. Insect repellent and mosquito nets are needed in the wet season, as is a strategy to keep your food secure from marauding raccoons and coatis. Dry-season camping in December, March and April is recommended. January and February are prone to strong winds.

LAS PAILAS SECTOR

Note that all of the following are a long way from any eateries, so you're stuck with pay-

HOTTEST SPOTS FOR THERMAL POOLS & MUD POTS

Costa Rica's volcano-powered thermal pools and mud pots provide plenty of good, *clean* fun for beauty queens and would-be mud wrestlers alike.

- On the slopes of Volcán Rincón de la Vieja, **Simbiosis Spa** (opposite) has several pools, a wood sauna and quiet vibe, all in a jungle setting.
- While some hot spots around Arenal charge outrageous fees to soak in sparkly surrounds, **Eco Thermales Hot Springs** (p161) maintains its sense of elegance by limiting guest numbers.
- **Las Hornillas** (p222) keeps it real on the southern slope of Volcán Miravalles, with a steaming, bubbling crater you can pick your way around before taking the plunge in its mud pots and hot pools.
- The pinnacle of luxury dirt exists in the remote heights of Rincón de la Vieja at **Borinquen Mountain Resort & Spa** (p234), where, if mineral mud is not your thing, you can opt instead for a wine or chocolate skin treatment.
- Tico-run and family-friendly, **El Guayacán** (p222) has a waterslide, several thermal pools, a trail encircling bubbling mud pots and inexpensive *cabinas* so you can take your time enjoying it all.

ing for (usually pricey) meals at your hotel restaurant.

Rincón de la Vieja Mountain Lodge (☎ 2200-0238; standard s/d incl breakfast US$45/65, bungalows US$60/75; P) Closest to the Las Pailas entrance, this rustic hacienda is on 400 hectares of protected land and has 49 spacious standard rooms, some with wildly painted walls or exposed-beam roofs, and even larger cottages with balconies. The electricity is produced by water falling into a turbine, but the eco-friendly power goes out after 10pm (candles are thoughtfully provided). Staff here are utterly charming.

Hacienda Guachipelín (☎ 2666-8075; www.guachipelin.com; s with/without air-con US$85/70, d with/without air-con US$100/89, all incl breakfast; P) On the road to Las Pailas, this appealing, 19th-century working cattle ranch is on 12 sq km of primary and secondary forest, and has over 100 attractively designed, spacious rooms and suites with private hot-water bathroom and porch. There is a garden-fringed pool and free wi-fi, and guests are received at check-in with a welcome drink. The downside (aside from charging all and sundry to cross the property) is that this place feels like a factory farm, catering largely to package-tour clientele.

Cropping up on the road to the park is an eclectic collection of truly lovely lodges that are worth considering if you've got your own wheels. The following are listed in the order you'll encounter them from the Interamericana.

Rancho Curubandé Lodge (☎ 2665-0375; www.rancho-curubande.com; s/d/tr incl breakfast US$60/65/70, villas s/d/tr US$85/90/95; P) Quiet, peaceful *finca* setting with garden rooms; also has horses for hire.

Canyon de la Vieja Lodge (☎ 2665-5912; www.canyonlodgegte.com; standard s/d/tr/q US$70/90/114/134; P) Riverside rooms surround a *palapa* (shelter with a thatched, palm-leaf roof and open sides) bar and pool, and the attractive accommodations are a comfortable place to crash after a day of adventure tours.

Posada El Encuentro (☎ 8848-8149, 8875-0257; r incl breakfast US$75-85, cottages US$105; P) A few stylish rooms in the cozy house, plus a stand-alone cottage with five beds; has expansive ocean and volcano views from its isolated orchard locale.

El Sol Verde (☎ 2665-5357; www.elsolverde.com; campsites US$5, incl tents & bedding US$18, r US$40-60; P) The lovely Dutch couple here in Curubandé village offer three lovely stone-floored, wood-walled rooms and a camping area with shared outdoor kitchen.

Casa Rural Aroma de Campo (☎ 2665-0008; www.aromadecampo.com; s/d/tr/q incl breakfast US$57/68/94/113; P) This serene, epiphyte-hung, hammock-strung oasis has elegantly designed rooms with polished clay floors, open bathrooms, mosquito nets and classy rural sensibility.

SANTA MARIA SECTOR

Rinconcito Lodge (☎ 2200-0074; www.rinconcitolodge.com; camping per person US$3, standard s/d US$23/35, superior incl breakfast d/tr/q US$55/70/80; P) Just 3km from the Santa María sector of the park, this recommended budget option has attractive, rustic cabins with private hot-water showers, and is surrounded by some of the prettiest pastoral scenery imaginable. Meals are available for around US$5. Breakfast, complimentary with superior rooms, features eggs and milk straight from the lodge's farm. Since it primarily caters to budget travelers, it also offers inexpensive local tours. It also shuttles travelers to and from Liberia (one way US$30).

Buena Vista Lodge (☎ 2690-1414; www.buenavistalodgecr.com; d incl breakfast US$78-92, extra person US$25; P) On the way to Borinquen, this friendly *finca* lodge is home to the new Tizate Wellness Garden hot springs and spa. There are also spring-fed pools, a 400m-high mountain waterslide, canopy trail, hanging bridges, four restaurants, a herpetarium, great views, live entertainment and loads more activities to keep kids (and grown-ups) busy. This is the best option for families.

our pick **Borinquen Mountain Resort & Spa** (☎ 2690-1900; www.borinquenresort.com; s incl breakfast US$188-329, d US$210-365; P) If you want to splurge, wallow here. The most luxurious resort in the area features plush, fully air-conditioned bungalows with private deck, minibar and satellite TV. The onsite hot springs, mud baths and natural saunas are beautifully laid out and surrounded by greenery, but a treatment at the unbelievable Anáhuac Spa (treatments US$35 to US$100; open from 10am to 6pm), suspended over the river and jungle, is the icing on this decadent mud pie.

NORTHWESTERN COSTA RICA

Getting There & Away

The Las Pailas sector is accessible via a good, 20km gravel road that begins at a signed turnoff from the Interamericana 5km north of Liberia; a private road is needed to reach the park and costs ₡700 per person. The Santa María ranger station, to the east, is accessible via a rougher road beginning at Barrio La Victoria in Liberia. Both roads are passable to regular cars throughout the dry season, but a 4WD is required during the rainy season and is highly recommended at all other times (or it will take you twice as long). There's no public transportation, but any of the lodges can arrange transport from Liberia for around US$20 per person each way (two or three people minimum). Alternately, you can hire a 4WD taxi from Liberia for about US$25 to Las Pailas, or US$45 to Santa María, each way.

PARQUE NACIONAL SANTA ROSA

Among the oldest (established in 1971) and largest national parks in Costa Rica, Santa Rosa's sprawling 386 sq km on the Península Santa Elena protects the largest remaining stand of tropical dry forest in Central America, and some of the most important nesting sites of several species of sea turtle. Santa Rosa is also famous among Ticos as a symbol of historical pride – Costa Rica has only been invaded by a foreign army three times, and each time the attackers were defeated in Santa Rosa.

The best known of these events was the Battle of Santa Rosa, which took place on March 20, 1856, when the soon-to-be-self-declared president of Nicaragua, an American named William Walker, invaded Costa Rica. Walker was the head of a group of foreign pirates and adventurers known as the 'Filibusters' that had already seized Baja and southwest Nicaragua, and were attempting to gain control over all of Central America. In a brilliant display of military prowess, Costa Rican President Juan Rafael Mora Porras guessed Walker's intentions, and managed to assemble a ragtag group of fighters that proceeded to surround Walker's army in the main building of the old Hacienda Santa Rosa, known as La Casona. The battle was over in just 14 minutes, and Walker forever driven from Costa Rican soil.

Santa Rosa was again the site of battles between Costa Rican troops and invading forces from Nicaragua in both 1919 and 1955. The first was a somewhat honorable attempt to overthrow the Costa Rican dictator General Federico Tinoco, while the second was a failed coup d'état led by Nicaraguan dictator Anastasio Somoza. Today, you can still see Somoza's abandoned tank, which lies in a ditch beside the road just beyond the entrance to the park. However, the military history surrounding the park didn't end with Somoza, as Santa Rosa was later used as a staging point for the US military during the Sandinistas–Contra war.

Although the park was established mainly due to historical and patriotic reasons, in a surprising coincidence Santa Rosa has also become extremely important to biologists. Upon seeing its acacia thorn trees and tall *jaragua* grass, first impressions of the park are likely to make you believe you've suddenly landed in the African savanna, though closer inspection reveals more American species of plants, including cacti and bromeliads. Santa Rosa is also home to Playa Nancite, which is famous for its *arribadas* (mass nesting) of olive ridley sea turtles that sometimes number up to 8000 at a single time.

However, a good number of travelers are here for one reason – the chance to surf the near-perfect beach break at Playa Naranjo, which is created by the legendary offshore monolith known as Witch's Rock (also known locally as Roca Bruja). The park is also home to another break of arguably equal fame, namely Ollie's Point, which was immortalized in the film *Endless Summer II*, and is named after US Marine Lieutenant Colonel Oliver North. North is most famous for illegally selling weapons to Iran during the Reagan Era, and using the profits to fund the Contras in Nicaragua – Ollie's Point refers to the nearby troop staging area that everyone but the US Congress knew about.

Difficult access means that Santa Rosa is fairly empty, though it can get reasonably busy on weekends in the dry season when Ticos flock to the park in search of their often-hard-to-find history. In the wet months from July through December, particularly September and October, you'll often have the park virtually to yourself.

Orientation & Information

Parque Nacional Santa Rosa's entrance is on the west side of the Interamericana, 35km north of Liberia and 45km south of the Nicaragua border. The **Santa Rosa Sector park entrance** (☎ 2666-5051; admission US$10, camping per person US$2; 8am-4pm) is close to the Interamericana, and it's another 7km to park headquarters, with the administrative offices, scientists' quarters, an information center, three basic campgrounds, museum and nature trail. This office administers the Area de Conservación Guanacaste (ACG).

From this complex, a very rough track leads down to the coast to Playa Naranjo, 12km away. Even during the dry season, this road is only passable to a high-clearance 4WD, and you must sign a waiver at the park entrance stating that you willingly assume all liability for driving this road. The park also requires that you be completely self-sufficient should you choose to undertake the trip, which means bringing *all* your own water and knowing how to do your own car repair. The rangers simply do not have the resources to bail you out or perform vehicle repair if you get into trouble. During the rainy months (May to November), the road is open to hikers and horses but closed to all vehicles; if you want to surf here, it's infinitely easier to gain access to the beach by hiring a boat from Playa del Coco or Tamarindo, further south. Be aware that rangers can and will shut down Playa Nancite to all visitors during the turtle nesting season. From the campsite at Playa Naranjo, it's a 5km hike to the beach. Playa Nancite is generally closed to visitors unless you have permission from the park office.

The park's Sector Murciélago (Bat Sector) encompasses the wild northern coastline of the Península Santa Elena, and is not accessible from the main body of the park. From the Interamericana, continue north past the entrance to the Santa Rosa sector for 10km and then turn left once you pass through the police checkpoint. Continue on this road for a few more kilometers until you reach the village of Cuajiniquíl and then bear left. Continue on this road for another 15km, which will bring you past such historic sights as the former hacienda of the Somoza family (it's currently a training ground for the Costa Rican police) and the old airstrip that was used by Oliver North to 'secretly' smuggle goods to the Nicaraguan Contras in the 1980s. Just after the airstrip is the **Murciélago Sector park entrance** (admission US$10; camping per person US$2; 8am-4pm), which is in the village of Murciélago. From here, it's another 16km to the isolated white-sand beach of Playa Blanca and the trailhead for the Poza el General watering hole, which attracts birds and animals year-round.

Ollie's Point in Playa Portero Grande is in this sector of the park and can only be reached by boat from Playa del Coco or Tamarindo. Or you can do as Patrick and Wingnut did in *Endless Summer II* and crash-land your chartered plane on the beach (not actually recommended).

Sights

The historic **La Casona**, the main building of the old Hacienda Santa Rosa, is near the park headquarters in the Santa Rosa sector. Unfortunately, the original building was burnt to the ground by arsonists in May 2001, but was rebuilt in 2002 using historic photos and local timber. The battle of 1856 was fought around this building, and the military action, as well as the region's natural history, is described with the help of documents, paintings, maps and other displays (mostly in Spanish). If you remember your dictionary, this will be an inspiring (and perhaps humbling) history lesson in how not to invade a country.

The arson was set by a local father-son team of poachers who were disgruntled at being banned from hunting here by park rangers. They were caught and sentenced to 20 years in prison for torching a building of national cultural and historical value. Unfortunately, poaching continues in the park since it's difficult for rangers to effectively patrol such a large area.

Activities

WILDLIFE-WATCHING

The wildlife is certainly both varied and prolific, especially during the dry season when animals congregate around the remaining water sources and the trees lose their leaves. More than 250 bird species have been recorded, including the raucous white-throated magpie jay, unmistakable with its long crest of maniacally curled feathers. The forests contain parrot and parakeet, trogon and tanager, and as you head down to the coast, you will be rewarded by sightings of a variety of coastal birds.

Bats are also very common; about 50 or 60 different species have been identified in Santa Rosa. Other mammals you have a reasonable chance of seeing include deer, coati, peccary, armadillo, coyote, raccoon, three kinds of monkey, and a variety of other species – about 115 in all. There are also many thousands of insect species, including about 4000 moths and butterflies (just bring insect repellent).

Reptile species include lizards, iguanas, snakes, crocodiles and four species of sea turtle. The olive ridley sea turtle is the most numerous, and during the July to December nesting season tens of thousands of turtles make their nests on Santa Rosa's beaches. The most popular beach is Playa Nancite, where, during September and October especially, it is possible to see as many as 8000 of these 40kg turtles on the beach at the same time. The turtles are disturbed by light, so flash photography and flashlights are not permitted. Avoid the nights around a full moon – they're too bright and turtles are less likely to show up. Playa Nancite is strictly protected and entry restricted, but permission may be obtained from park headquarters to observe this spectacle; call ahead.

The variety of wildlife reflects the variety of habitat protected within the boundaries of the park. Apart from the largest remaining stand of tropical dry forest in Central America, habitats include savanna woodland, oak forest, deciduous forest, evergreen forest, riparian forest, mangrove swamp and coastal woodland.

HIKING

Near Hacienda Santa Rosa is **El Sendero Indio Desnudo**, a 1km trail with signs interpreting the ecological relationships among the animals, plants and weather patterns of Santa Rosa. The trail is named after the common tree, also called *gumbo limbo,* whose peeling orange-red bark can photosynthesize during the dry season, when the trees' leaves are lost (resembling a sunburned tourist…or 'naked Indian,' as the literal translation of the trail name implies). Also seen along the trail is the national tree of Costa Rica, the guanacaste. The province is named after this huge tree species, which is found along the Pacific coastal lowlands. You may also see birds, monkeys, snakes, iguanas, as well as petroglyphs (most likely pre-Columbian) etched into some of the rocks on the trail.

Behind La Casona a short trail leads up to the **Monumento a Los Héroes** and a lookout platform. There are also longer trails through the dry forest, including a gentle 4km hike to the Mirador, with spectacular views of Playa Naranjo, which is accessible to hikers willing to go another 9km along the deeply rutted road to the sea. The main road is lined with short trails to small waterfalls and other photogenic natural wonders as well.

From the southern end of Playa Naranjo, there are two hiking trails – **Sendero Carbonal** is a 20km trail that swings inland and then terminates on the beach at Cerros Carbonal, while **Sendero Aceituno** parallels Playa Naranjo for 13km and terminates near the estuary across from Witch's Rock. There's also a 6km hiking trail that starts where the northern branch of the access road terminates – this leads to the biological research station at Nancite; you'll need prior permission to access this beach.

Although it's not officially recommended by the park service, the opportunities for long-distance beach hiking abound, especially if you're an experienced hiker who's prepared to carry large quantities of food and water. Inquire locally about the feasibility of long-distance trekking (especially in regards to permanent water sources). We have heard a rumor that it's possible to hike from Santa Rosa to Playa del Coco (if you make it, let us know!).

SURFING

The surfing at Playa Naranjo is truly world-class, especially near Witch's Rock, a beach break famous for its fast, hollow 3m rights (although there are also fun lefts when it isn't pumping). Beware of rocks near the river mouth, and be careful near the estuary as it's a rich feeding ground for crocodiles during the tide changes. The surfing is equally legendary at Ollie's Point off Playa Portero Grande, which has the best right in all of Costa Rica with a nice, long ride, especially with a south swell. The bottom here is a mix of sand and rocks, and the year-round offshore is perfect for tight turns and slow closes. Shortboarding is preferred by surfers at both spots.

Sleeping & Eating

There's a shady developed **campground** (per person US$2) close to the park headquarters, with picnic benches, grills, flushing toilets and cold-water showers. Playa Naranjo has pit toilets and showers, but no potable water – bring your own. Other camping areas in the park are undeveloped. There's a 25-person, two-night maximum for camping at Playa Naranjo. There's also a small campsite with pit toilets and showers near the ranger station in the Sector Murciélago, though you'll have to carry in your own food and water.

Make reservations in advance to stay at the **research station** (☎ 2666-5051; dm US$15); eight-bed bunkrooms have cold showers and electricity. Researchers get priority, but there's usually some room for travelers. Good meals (₡1700 to ₡4000) are available, but you must make arrangements the day before.

Getting There & Away

The well-signed main park entrance can be reached by public transportation: take any bus between Liberia and the Nicaraguan border and ask the driver to let you off at the park entrance; rangers can help you catch a return bus. You can also arrange private transportation from the hotels in Liberia for about US$20 per person round trip.

To get to the northern Sector Murciélago, go 10km further north along the Interamericana, then turn left to the village of Cuajiniquíl, which has a couple of *sodas* and a *pulpería* (corner grocery stores), 8km away by paved road. Keep your passport handy, as there may be checkpoints. The paved road continues beyond Cuajiniquíl and dead-ends at a marine port, 4km away – this isn't the way to Sector Murciélago but goes toward Refugio Nacional de Vida Silvestre Bahía Junquillal. It's about 8km beyond Cuajiniquíl to the Murciélago ranger station by poor road – 4WD is advised, though the road may be impassable in the wet season. You can camp at the Murciélago ranger station, or continue 10km to 12km on a dirt road beyond the ranger station to the remote bays and beaches of Bahía Santa Elena and Bahía Playa Blanca.

REFUGIO NACIONAL DE VIDA SILVESTRE BAHÍA JUNQUILLAL

This 505-hectare wildlife refuge is part of the ACG, administered from the park headquarters at Santa Rosa. There is a **ranger station** (☎ 2679-9692; admission US$10 incl Parque Nacional Santa Rosa US$10, camping per person US$2; 8am-4pm) in telephone and radio contact with Santa Rosa.

The quiet bay and protected beach provide gentle swimming, boating and snorkeling opportunities, and there is some tropical dry forest and mangrove swamp. Short trails take the visitor to a lookout for marine bird-watching and to the mangroves. Pelicans and frigate birds are seen, and turtles nest here seasonally. Volcán Orosi can be seen in the distance. Campers should note that during the dry season especially, water is at a premium and is turned on for only one hour a day. There are pit latrines.

To get here from Cuajiniquíl, continue for 2km along the paved road and then turn right onto a signed dirt road. Continuing 4km along the dirt road (passable to ordinary cars) brings you to the entrance to Bahía Junquillal. From here, a poorer 700m dirt road leads to the beach, ranger station and camping area.

PARQUE NACIONAL GUANACASTE

Opened on July 25, 1989 (Guanacaste Day), Parque Nacional Guanacaste is the newest part of the Area de Conservación Guanacaste and forms a protected nature corridor

A WHOPPER OF A PROBLEM

Although there is a long history of deforestation in Costa Rica, massive clear-cutting of the rainforests (particularly in Guanacaste) intensified during the 1970s. Currently, there is much debate regarding the causes of this wide-scale deforestation, but research suggests that a shift in governmental philosophy likely sparked the event. Specifically, national policies were implemented at the time that promoted increased land use relating to agriculture, wood production, pasture land creation and improved transit infrastructure. It is argued that these initiatives were aimed at speeding up the country's economic development, especially in response to the decrease in the international demand for Costa Rican coffee.

Clearly, development is a double-edged sword as it's impossible to argue that the philosophies of the 1970s did not in fact improve the quality of life in Costa Rica. Today, Guanacaste is one of the richest provinces in Costa Rica, and the country as a whole is often regarded as the gem of Central America. Quality of life in Costa Rica is among the highest in Latin America, and Ticos have never had to starve like their neighbors to the north and south. However, cattle ranchers in Costa Rica produce an abundance of meat, much of which is destined for the international fast-food market. Thus the devastation of the rainforest is not solely a product of national improvement.

The body of evidence supporting these claims is astounding, and consists of everything from court testimonials to recorded data on imports and exports. Officially, most fast-food companies maintain that they are in favor of rainforest preservation, and that they do not use hamburger meat of foreign origin in their products. However, although imported beef is only a small portion of the total meat consumed in the USA, this accounts for a significant percentage of Central American beef production. One documented problem is that when Central American beef arrives at a US point of entry, it is often marked as 'US inspected and approved,' which disguises the origin of the product. Furthermore, since the meat in a single burger can be derived from multiple cows, it's difficult to verify that a product is in fact free of foreign beef.

As a consumer, it's virtually impossible to ensure that you're not eating beef that's been raised on recently deforested areas, aside from boycotting the major fast-food retailers. In late 2007 Costa Rica approved the Central American Free Trade Agreement (Cafta), which took effect on January 1, 2009. The law reduced tarriffs on beef exports. Several fast-food companies have started adopting healthier menus (though much of this is attributable to recent declines in profits). In the meantime, researchers in Costa Rica are hard at work investigating the natural processes of reforestation.

that now stretches from the Pacific to the Caribbean coast. The park is adjacent to Parque Nacional Santa Rosa, separated from it by the Interamericana, and is only about 5km northwest of Parque Nacional Rincón de la Vieja. It's one of the least-visited and most exclusive parks in the country, because tourist access is highly restricted.

The 345 sq km of Parque Nacional Guanacaste are much more than a continuation of the lowland habitats found in Santa Rosa. In its lower western reaches, the park is indeed composed of the dry tropical rainforest characteristic of much of Guanacaste, but the terrain soon begins to climb toward two volcanoes – Volcán Orosi (1487m) and Volcán Cacao (1659m). Here the landscape slowly transitions to the humid cloud forest that's found throughout much of the highland Cordillera de Guanacaste. This habitat, which is similar in function to Parque Nacional Carara, provides a refuge for altitudinal migrants that move between the coast and the highlands. Thus the national park allows for the ancient migratory and hunting patterns of various animal species to continue as they have for millennia.

However, this ecosystem is more the domain of biologists than tourists (admission is by reservation only), and there are three major research stations within the borders of the park. In addition to observing animal migratory patterns, researchers are also monitoring the pace of reforestation as much of the park is composed of ranch land. Interestingly enough, researchers have found that if the pasture is carefully managed (much of this management involves just letting nature take its course), the natural forest will reinstate itself in its old territory. Thus crucial habitats n the national park are not just preserved, but n some cases they are also expanded.

For information on visiting the park, contact the **ACG headquarters** (☎ 2666-5051; admission US$10, reservations required) in Parque Nacional Santa Rosa.

Sights & Activities

Hiking trails in the national park are among the least developed in the entire country, and are principally used by researchers to move between each of the stations. It's advisable to talk to the staff before setting out on any of the hikes, as infrastructure in the park is almost nonexistent. If you have a relevant background in biology or ecology, volunteer positions are available, though it's best to contact ACG well in advance of your arrival.

MARITZA BIOLOGICAL STATION

This is the newest station and has a modern laboratory. From the station, at 600m above sea level, rough trails run to the summits of Volcán Orosi and Volcán Cacao (about five to six hours). There is also a better trail to a site where several hundred petroglyphs have been found that are chipped into volcanic rock. As with most indigenous sites in Costa Rica, little is known about the origins of the petroglyphs, though the area was believed to be inhabited by the Chorotega (see p154). There is also another trail that leads to the Cacao Biological Station.

To get there, turn east off the Interamericana opposite the turnoff for Cuajiniquíl. The station is about 17km east of the highway along a dirt road that may require a 4WD vehicle, especially in the wet season.

CACAO BIOLOGICAL STATION

High on the slopes of Volcán Cacao (about 1060m), this station offers access to rough trails that lead to the summit of the volcano and to Maritza Biological Station. Cacao Biological Station is reached from the southern side of the park. At Potrerillos, about 9km south of the Santa Rosa park entrance on the Interamericana, head east for 7km on a paved road to the small community of Quebrada Grande (marked 'Garcia Flamenco' on many maps). A daily bus leaves Liberia at 3pm for Quebrada Grande. From the village plaza, a 4WD road that is often impassable during the wet season heads north toward the station, about 10km away.

PITILLA BIOLOGICAL STATION

This station lies on the northeast side of Volcán Orosi, which is on the eastern side of the continental divide. The surrounding forests here are humid, lush and unlike anything you'll find in the rest of Guanacaste.

To get to the station, turn east off the Interamericana about 12km north of the Cuajiniquíl turnoff, or 3km before reaching the small town of La Cruz. Follow the paved eastbound road for about 28km to the community of Santa Cecilia. From there, a poor dirt road heads 11km south to the station – you'll need a 4WD.

Sleeping & Eating

INSIDE THE PARK

You can **camp** (per person US$2.50) near the stations, but there aren't any facilities.

If there's space, you may be able to reserve dorm-style accommodations at **Maritza** or **Pitilla Biological Stations** (☎ 2666-5051; dm US$15). The stations are quite rustic, with room for 30 people, and shared cold-water bathrooms. Meals are also available and should be arranged in advance.

OUTSIDE THE PARK

Hacienda Los Inocentes (☎ 2679-9190; d incl breakfast US$70; P) Part biological research station, part ecolodge, this 1000-hectare former cattle has a spectacular location below the Volcán Orosi and is slowly being reforested. The attractive hacienda building dates to 1890 and has 11 spacious wooden bedrooms with private (but separate) bathroom with solar-heated hot water, plus several larger separate cabins. The upper floor is surrounded by a beautiful, shaded, wooden veranda with hammocks and also volcano views – a good spot for sunset/moonrise. There's also a bar, restaurant, pool and horse rentals. The staff can arrange guided hikes throughout the park as well as to the top of Volcán Cacao. It's located 15km east of the Interamericana on the paved road to Santa Cecilia. Buses between Liberia and Santa Cecilia pass the lodge entrance twice a day. The hotel can arrange transfers.

LA CRUZ

pop 4300

La Cruz is the closest town to the Peñas Blancas border crossing with Nicaragua (see boxed text, p242), and it's the principal gateway to Bahía Salinas (p240), one of Costa

Rica's premier windsurfing and kitesurfing destinations. Although La Cruz itself is a fairly sleepy provincial town, its hilltop location is awash with scenic views of the coastline, and you can easily bus down to several stunning, isolated white-sand beaches on Bahía Salinas. La Cruz is an underrated place to spend the night before heading to Nicaragua.

Information

Changing money at the border post often yields a better exchange rate than in town.

Banco Nacional (☎ 2679-9296) At the junction of the short road into the town center and the Interamericana; has a 24-hour ATM.

Banco Popular (☎ 2679-9352) In the town center, has an ATM.

Cruz Roja (☎ 2679-9004, emergency 2679-9146) A small clinic just north of the town center on the road toward the border.

Internet Cafe (☎ 2679-8190, 8838-8128; per hr ₡560; 8am-7pm Mon-Sat)

Sleeping & Eating

La Cruz may possibly have the most *heladerías* (ice-cream shops) per capita in Costa Rica, for which you'll be glad when the mid-afternoon heat smites you. Pick up groceries at the neighboring Almacén Super Único and SuperCompro La Cruz, on the east side of the plaza. There are a handful of *sodas* scattered around town; otherwise, La Cruz is a gastronomic wasteland.

Hotel Bella Vista (☎ 2679-8060; per person with fan/air-con US$7/10; P) With a lovely mosaic-bottomed pool and breezy restaurant at the top of the hill, this Dutch-run hotel is a great place for a beer in the evenings, although it's a bit run-down. All rooms have private hot-water bathroom, and those upstairs are a bit brighter with partial views of the bay. There's also an attached restaurant (open for breakfast, lunch and dinner).

Cabinas Santa Rita (☎ 2679-9062; s/d US$9/13, with air-con US$15/23; P) The best budget option in town has clean, though dark, rooms with private bathroom and is popular with migrant workers. Across the street, the newer annex has frillier rooms with private bathroom, cable TV, hot shower and air-con.

our pick **Amalia's Inn** (☎ 2679-9618; s/d US$20/35; P) By far the best place in La Cruz to kick back with a cool drink at sunset, the shared terra-cotta terraces at Amalia's look out on to huge, stupendous bay views. The white stucco house on a cliff isn't a bad place to spend the night, either – cozy, homey rooms are decorated with anything from white wicker to modular leather, each with private hot-water bathroom and air-con. Walls in the meandering house are hung with modernist paintings by Amalia's late husband Lester Bounds. Amalia's niece is now the lady of the house, and short of offering meals, she'll make you feel right at home.

Getting There & Away

A **Transportes Deldú counter** (7am-12:30pm & 1:30-5pm) sells tickets and stores bags. To catch a TransNica bus to Peñas Blancas, you'll need to flag a bus down on the Interamericana. Buses to the beaches depart from the bus terminal just up the hill from Hotel Bella Vista; a taxi to the beach costs about ₡7000.

Liberia (Transportes Deldú) ₡1000; 1½ hours; eight departures per day from 5:30am to 6:30pm. Alternatively, catch any San José–bound bus.

Peñas Blancas ₡580; 45 minutes; 10 departures per day from 5am to 6:30pm.

Playa Jobó ₡560; 30 minutes; departs at 8:30am, 11:15am, 2pm and 5pm.

San José via Liberia (Transportes Deldú) ₡3400; five hours; departs 4am, 5:45am, 8am, 10am, 11am, 12:30pm, 2pm, 4pm and 6pm.

BAHÍA SALINAS

Bahía Salinas is the second-best place in all of Costa Rica (after Laguna de Arenal) for windsurfing, and is arguably the best place in the country for kitesurfing because the vegetation around Arenal can be quite dangerous for kiters in the air. The bay otherwise happens to be a bit under the radar, so you'll often find that you have an entire jungle-edged crescent of white-sand beach to yourself. The bay is also home to Isla Bolaños, which protects a large colony of seabirds, including the endangered brown pelican (present from January to May).

Sights & Activities

A dirt road (normally passable to cars) leads down from the lookout point in La Cruz past the small coastal fishing community of **Puerto Soley** and out along the curve of the bay to the consistently windy beaches of **Playa Papaturro** and **Playa Copal**. If wind isn't your thing but sunbathing is, head around the point to **Playa Jobó**, a perfect horseshoe of a bay with calm water, or **Playa Rajada** just beyond. Boats can be rented in the village of El Jobó or at one of the local resorts to visit **Isla Bolaños** (visits are restricted to April through November to avoid disturbing nesting seabirds). Or try contacting **Frank Schultz** (☎ 8827-4109; franksdiving@costaricense.co.cr), who also organizes fishing and diving trips.

WINDSURFING & KITESURFING

The strongest and steadiest winds blow from November through March, but the wind is pretty consistent here year-round. The shape of the hills surrounding the bay funnels the winds into a predictable pattern, and the sandy, protected beaches make this a safe place for beginners and experienced windsurfers and kiteboarders alike. It's important to remember that there are inherent dangers to kiteboarding (namely the risk of losing a limb – yikes!), so it's best to seek professional instruction if you're not an experienced kiteboarder. Responsible instructors recommend at least two days of lessons before you can safely go out on your own. Windsurfing rentals and lessons can be found at **Ecoplaya Beach Resort** (☎ 2676-1010; www.ecoplaya.com).

If windsurfing is too tame for you, then enroll at **Kitesurf School 2000** (☎ 8826-5221; www.bluedreamhotel), a sporty combination of wind and waves (which school instructors insist is much easier to learn than regular surfing) where you are attached to a large kite, then pulled across the bay by the breeze, allowing more advanced students to do flips and other aerial acrobatics above the froth and swells – really cool. If you want to give this a try, make reservations a couple of days in advance for two days of lessons (US$240) or just equipment rental (basic gear per day US$65). Italian and English spoken.

Another reputable kitesurfing school is **Cometa Copal** (☎ 2676-1192; www.islandsurf-sail.com; lguardbl@gmail.com), a seasonal shop run by American Bob Selfridge, who not only offers kitesurfing lessons with PASA (Professional Air Sports Association) certified instructors, but is himself an instructor, lifeguard *and* emergency medical technician. It's open November to June. Lessons are US$40 per hour, or US$45 for a private lesson.

Sleeping & Eating

Most hotels in Bahía Salinas offer transfers from San José or Liberia airports.

Blue Dream Hotel (☎ 2676-1042, 8826-5221; www.bluedreamhotel.com; dm US$15, s/d US$33/42; P) Home base of Kitesurf School 2000, this friendly little hotel looks out over Playa Papaturro from its terraced hillside, with simple, comfortable tiled rooms at the top of the hill. Along with the hammock-strung garden, there's a yoga terrace, Mediterraneo restaurant (open for breakfast, lunch and dinner) serving local and Mediterranean food, and spa services to boot, all run by Italian kiteboarding instructor Nicola and his Tica wife Katya.

Cometa Copal (☎ 2676-1192; www.islandsurf-sail.com; lguardbl@gmail.com; dm US$15, r US$25, cabinas US$40-55; P) A seasonal operation that contracts with different rooms and *cabinas* every year – the ones we saw were clean colorful little *cabinas* at the top of a hill with gorgeous views of the bay. In addition to organizing kitesurfing lessons and rentals, the friendly American couple running Cometa Copal also rents gear and beachfront villas for the short or long term. Bob and Kirsten offer sweet extras like shiatsu massage, overnight kite repairs and home-baked goodies.

our pick **Bolaños Bay Resort** (☎ 2676-1163; www.hotelbolanosbay.com; s/d incl breakfast US$71/83, ste US$109, all-inclusive per person US$54; P) Completely remodeled in 2009, this remote, low-key resort is a great place to get away from it all. Spectacularly set on a high bluff above deserted Playa La Coyotero, the property features a huge thatched-covered lobby and restaurant, a pool with swim-up bar, a disco and tropical gardens. The 72 superclean rooms are scattered around the property, all featuring TV, air-con and private hot water bathroom with bidet; some have kitchenette. All-inclusive packages include lodging, three meals a day and two alcoholic drinks per meal. Four rooms are wheelchair-accessible. Onsite activities include fishing, snorkeling and a seasonal kiteboarding school (late November to May). The beach here is a bit too rough and windy to swim, but a dirt road 2km past the hotel leads to the secluded Playa Jobó, a beautiful cove with a soft beige-sand beach embraced by forest.

Ecoplaya Beach Resort (☎ 2676-1010; www.ecoplaya.com; r & villas US$98-290; P) About 16km from La Cruz, Ecoplaya's luxury rooms and bungalows range from elegant studios, complete with kitchenette and sustainable-teak furniture, to full luxury suites containing minibar, sitting room and

HEADING NORTH OF THE BORDER

Peñas Blancas is a busy border crossing, open 6am to 8pm daily. You won't be charged to exit or enter Costa Rica, but leaving Nicaragua costs US$2. The fee to enter Nicaragua is US$7. Driving a car across the border is another $22, but most car-rental companies in Costa Rica won't allow you to cross borders; check before you sign your contract. Alternatively, leave your car in the 'no man's land' parking area between borders for $5 per day. Banks on either side will change local colones and córdobas for dollars but, inconveniently, not for each other. Independent moneychangers will happily make the exchange for you – at whatever rates they feel like setting.

The border posts are about 1km apart; if you're in the mood you can hire a golf cart (US$2) to make the run. Hordes of totally useless touts will offer to 'guide' you through the simple crossing – let them carry your luggage if you like, but agree on a fee beforehand. You'll also be charged US$1 to enter the state of Rivas. Should you have any hard currency left at this point, there's a fairly fabulous duty-free shop, with fancy makeup and lots of liquor, waiting for you in Sapoá, the Nicaraguan equivalent of Peñas Blancas.

Relax with your purchases on the 37km bus ride (US$1, 45 minutes), departing every 30 minutes, to Rivas. The city is a quiet transport hub, though its well-preserved 17th-century center is worth exploring (think a more run-down version of Granada without all the crowds).

If you're good at bargaining (and you will have to bargain hard), there are a number of taxis waiting on the Nicaraguan side of the border to whisk you to Rivas ($15).

San Juan del Sur

After standing in line in the hot sun and negotiating the chaos of crossing the border, all you might feel up for is collapsing on a beach with a shot of Flor de Caña in hand – if your answer to that is *'sí, por favor,'* then make tracks to San Juan del Sur. This Nicaraguan fishing village has geared itself to tourism, so you can pick up a used novel, go surfing, diving or deep-sea fishing, and then party in the evening with other travelers and local expats. Buses and water taxis also make trips to some of the stunning beaches north and south of San Juan.

There are several places to stay along the market street where the buses pull in. The beachfront is lined with breezy cafes, and you'll find lots of cheap eateries at San Juan's market.

- **Casa Oro** (☎ 505-568-2415; www.casaeloro.com; dm US$7.50-8.50, r with/without bathroom US$19/17; 💻 📶) This well-run hostel is deservedly popular and always heavily booked. Quieter upstairs rooms have more space and private bathroom.
- **Piedras y Olas** (☎ 505-568-2243; www.piedrasyolas.com; r US$207-305; P 🏊) Located on a hilltop with stunning ocean views, this highly recommended luxury beach resort has infinity pools, restaurant, bar and ritzy rooms with kitchens. Note that this property requires lots of stair-climbing.
- **El Timón** (☎ 505-568-2243; dishes US$5-10) This excellent beach restaurant is the place to go for a more upmarket seafood dinner, with professional service and delicious seafood; the *pulpo al vapor* (steamed octopus with a tasty garlicky sauce) is highly recommended.
- **Bambu Beach Club** (☎ 505-568-2101; www.thebambubeachclub.com; mains ₡2500-5500; 🕒 11am-1am; 📶) European-run with Nico charm, this upscale restaurant is located on a quiet stretch of beach and has an international menu including beef, fish, chicken and more. Movie nights are held on Monday and Thursday evenings.

Buses to and from Rivas (US$0.70, 45 minutes), with connections to the border, depart every 30 minutes or so from 3:30am to 7pm. Taxis from Sapoá to San Juan del Sur cost about US$11.Isla de Ometepe

One of Nicaragua's highlights, Isla de Ometepe is like something from a fantasy landscape. The island's twin volcanoes – **Volcán Concepción** (1610m above the lake) and **Volcán Maderas**

(1394m) – rise dramatically from Lago de Nicaragua and are connected by an isthmus formed by lava flow.

Parts of Ometepe are still covered in primary forest, which shelters abundant wildlife, including howler monkey and green parrot. The island is also famous for its ancient Chorotega stone statues and petroglyphs.

It's possible to hike both volcanoes, though these are serious, eight- to 12-hour treks that are best attempted with a local guide. There are also great beaches for sunning and swimming all around the island. The most popular beach, **Playa Santo Domingo**, is on the isthmus and has plenty of places to stay and eat. Many local accommodations have horses, bikes or kayaks to hire at reasonable rates.

The island's two major settlements, Altagracia and Moyogalpa, both offer accommodations and restaurants, but to experience the true charms of Ometepe, travel further out: Charco Verde, Playa Santo Domingo, Balgüe and Mérida all offer lovely settings amid the island's rich biodiversity.

The fastest way of reaching Ometepe is via San Jorge near Rivas, from where boats make the 15km crossing to Moyogalpa on Ometepe. There are two types of boat: significantly more comfortable car/passenger ferries (San Jorge–Moyagalpa 1st/2nd class US$3.50/2.50, departures 7:45am, noon, 2:30pm, 4:30pm and 5:30pm) and fairly basic *lanchas* (small motorboats; US$1.60, departures at 9am, 9:30am, 10:30am, 11:30am, 1:30pm and 3:30pm). Taxis from Sapoá to the San Jorge ferry will cost about US$15 if you bargain hard.

Granada

The lovely colonial city of Granada is a sight for sore eyes after the brutally bland architecture of Costa Rica. The carved colonial portals, elegant churches and fine plaza, as well as its location on Lago de Nicaragua, have enchanted visitors for centuries since the city was founded in 1524. And not only is it a beautiful city to enjoy for a few days, it also makes a convenient launching point for Nicaragua's other attractions. Stop by the **Intur office** (☎ 505-552 6858; granada@intur.gob.ni; Calle Arsenal; 🕑 8am-noon & 2-5pm Mon-Fri, 8am-12:30pm Sat & Sun), across from the San Francisco church, to pick up a good map of the city's historic buildings.

A few blocks northeast of Parque Central is the striking light-blue facade of the **Convento y Iglesia de San Francisco** (Calle Cervantes). It fronts a complex that was initiated in 1585, burned to the ground by William Walker in 1856, and rebuilt in 1867–68. It houses the city's must-see **museum** (admission US$2; 🕑 8:30am-5pm Mon-Fri, 9am-4pm Sat & Sun). Admission includes a bilingual guided tour.

Some recommended places to stay:

- **Hostal Esfinge** (☎ 505-552-4826; Calle Atravesada; dm US$4, d with/without bathroom US$12/7, d with bathroom & air-con US$20; P) A gracious, old-style ambience pervades this gorgeous historic building. Rooms surround a large courtyard, and guests have access to a communal kitchen.
- **Patio del Malinche** (☎ 505-552-2235; www.patiodelmalinche.com; Calle El Caimito; s/d incl breakfast US$66/83;) This lovingly restored colonial home is one of Granada's most appealing places to stay. The personal attention and delicious, massive breakfasts make it feel more like a guesthouse than a hotel.
- **Hotel Colonial** (☎ 505-552-7581; www.hotelcolonialgrande.com; d with/without breakfast US$75/65; P) This relatively new, romantic hotel, built in colonial mansion style, has lovely rooms with canopy bed, private bathroom and cable TV.

Buses from Rivas (US$1, 1½ hours) depart eight times daily until midafternoon. Taxis from Sapoá can take you to Granada for around ₡15,000.

NORTHWESTERN COSTA RICA

air-con in every room. All rooms have satellite TV and private terrace or balcony. Opt for the full American plan (adult/child additional US$84/42, two-night minimum), and all meals are included, as are all drinks from 10am to 10pm (yes, you read that right). The hotel's stretch of white-sand beach is picture-perfect, although the pool with swim-up bar is also perfectly self-indulgent. The hotel has plenty of activities on offer as well.

Restaurant Copal (☎ 2676-1006; mains ₡2000-3500; ⏰ lunch & dinner) This glassed-in *palapa* on a hilltop has little competition here in Playa Copal, but it still turns out excellent Italian food, and the romantic locale can't be topped. Stop by on Thursday nights for wood-fired pizza.

Getting There & Away

Buses (₡580) along this road depart the La Cruz bus terminal to the village of Jabó at 5am, 8:30am, 11:15am, 2pm and 5pm. Buses from Jabó to La Cruz depart at 6am, 9:30am, noon, 3pm and 5:45pm. A taxi to the beaches will cost about ₡6500.

Península de Nicoya

The allure of the Península de Nicoya needs no explanation. Archetypical tropical beaches edge this jungle-trimmed coast, whose shores have been imprinted on the memories of the millions of marine turtles who return to their birthplaces to nest. The travelers, too, descend on these beaches, seeking to witness such magical patterns of nature for themselves. Humans, however, make more of an environmental impact than the leatherbacks do.

Development is the name of the game at the moment, and Nicoya is the high-stakes playing field. That field is in danger of being paved over – in fact, it's in that very process in various parts of the peninsula – but it's difficult to call an outcome. Optimists will point out that Costa Rica is one of the most eco-conscious nations on the planet, and grassroots community activism by both Ticos (Costa Ricans) and foreigners is leading to instances of government enforcement of sustainable development. The next moves will require a sustained effort to maintain the peninsula's intrinsic wildness, but we are betting on the Ticos and local expats to rise to the occasion.

Easy accessibility to all this beauty may be to blame for its exploitation, but who can be blamed for wanting to play, beckoned by waves that never seem to close out, tropical forests teeming with wild things, the slow, sane pace of *la vida costarricense* (Costa Rican life) and what lies beyond that next turn down a potholed dirt road?

HIGHLIGHTS

- Catching the morning swell and perfecting afternoon asanas in **Nosara** (p281)
- Taking the gringo trail and observing the contrasts between **Playa Tamarindo** (p263) and mellow **Montezuma** (p298)
- Hiking to the tip of the peninsula at **Reserva Natural Absoluta Cabo Blanco** (p304), Costa Rica's first wildlife park
- Surfing uncrowded breaks at **Playas Grande** (p260), **Avellanas** and **Negra** (p271)
- Kayaking to Isla Chora for a morning snorkel at **Playa Sámara** (p286)
- Fording rivers on the bumpy route to the 'bad country' and good waters of **Mal País** (p305)

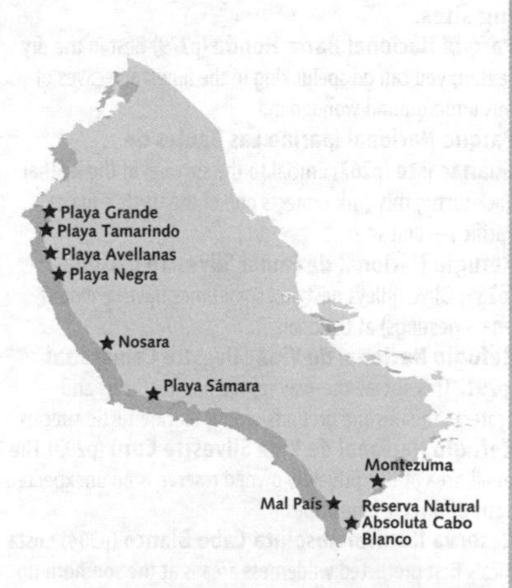

History

Following the independence of Central America from Spain, the peninsula (along with northwestern Costa Rica) comprised the bulk of Guanacaste, a province of the newly formed country of Nicaragua. However, on July 25, 1824, *guanacastecos* voted to secede and join Costa Rica, creating yet another grievance between Nicas and Ticos (see boxed text, p230). Today, some in the region still hold on to the dream of independence, and it's not uncommon to see the Guanacaste flag flying high – sometimes higher than the national one. Tellingly, the Guanacaste coat of arms states 'De la Patria por Nuestra Voluntad': literally, 'Of the Country of our Will.'

Climate

The northern Península de Nicoya has one of the driest climates in Costa Rica, with its coastline mostly characterized by dry tropical forest. Moving further south, as the peninsula transitions from dry tropical forest to tropical rainforest, the amount of moisture increases. Rainfall gradually increases during the green season in the southern Nicoya, typically wettest in September and October and making some regions impassable due to dirt roads being washed out and rivers too swollen to ford.

Parks & Reserves

Most of Nicoya's parks and reserves lie along the shoreline, with several stretching out to sea to protect marine turtles and their nesting sites.

Parque Nacional Barra Honda (p279) Best in the dry season; you can go spelunking in the limestone caves of this underground wonderland.

Parque Nacional Marino Las Baulas de Guanacaste (p262) Crucial to the survival of the leatherback turtle, this park protects one of the turtle's major Pacific nesting sites.

Refugio Nacional de Fauna Silvestre Ostional (p285) Olive ridleys nest and sometimes have *arribadas* (mass nestings) at Ostional.

Refugio Nacional de Vida Silvestre Camaronal (p291) This out-of-the-way refuge has good surf and protects the nesting grounds of four marine turtle species.

Refugio Nacional de Vida Silvestre Curú (p297) The small area of this privately owned reserve is an unexpected oasis of diverse landscapes.

Reserva Natural Absoluta Cabo Blanco (p304) Costa Rica's first protected wilderness area is at the southern tip of the Península de Nicoya.

Getting There & Around

Now that more international air traffic flies directly to Liberia, the Península de Nicoya has become easier to access. Small airstrips serving Tamarindo, Nosara, Sámara, Punta Islita and Tambor are host to daily flights, so you can bypass tough (or impossible) drives on bad roads.

The most popular destinations are served by public buses; Santa Cruz and Nicoya are the region's hubs. Private shuttles run to those destinations not regularly served by public transportation. Sámara and Montezuma are good places to arrange onward travel to more remote places on the southwestern coast.

To drive the roads less traveled, it's mandatory to have a 4WD, but be aware that during the rainy season many roads in the southern peninsula are impassable. Always ask locally about conditions before setting out.

NORTHERN PENINSULA

The northern Nicoya coastline in a snapshot: white-sand beaches, wild green yonder, azure waters. It's no wonder that this is some of the most coveted real estate in the country. What it means when you zoom in is bustling construction of resorts and retirement properties among the trees behind the high-tide line. On the ground it doesn't take supersharp focus to pick out the high gringo-to-Tico ratio around these parts.

Though the dry forests of the northern peninsula have been cut down over the generations to be transformed into farms and pastureland, these days trees are being felled – more selectively, sure – to put up second homes. The Costa Rican lifestyle here has traditionally revolved around the harvest and the herd, but today Ticos live by the tourist season. Each year from December to April, when the snow falls on Europe and North America, Guanacaste experiences its dry season and tourists descend en masse.

While the booming tourism buoys the economy, local Ticos and expats alike are becoming increasingly aware of the tricky balance of development and conservation. But even as construction goes up, the waves keep rolling in and the sun continues to smile on the beaches of the northern peninsula.

The main artery into this region, Hwy 21, runs southwest from Liberia, with coastal access roads branching out from the small towns of Comunidad, Belén and Santa Cruz.

PLAYA DEL COCO

Thirty-seven kilometers west of Liberia and connected by good roads to San José, Playa del Coco is the most easily accessible of the peninsula's beaches. Its name is derived from the cocoa-colored sand that lies between its two rocky headlands, though it can appear, well, dirty. While nearby Tamarindo has become the enclave of moneyed foreigners, Playa del Coco is more the party destination for young Ticos on weekends, the playground of sportfishers and divers during the week and – judging by the many Confederate flags around town – Southern US expats all year round. Though slick development continues its creep, Coco retains a languid, slightly trashy charm.

Although most travelers either pass through quickly or skip Coco in favor of beaches further south, the town is a growing scuba diving center and a preferred jumping-off point for surfers heading to the celebrated Witch's Rock and Ollie's Point (see p237).

Information

The police station and a small post office branch are on the southeast side of the plaza by the beach. Banco Nacional, south of the center on the main road into town, exchanges US dollars and traveler's checks. The few people arriving at Playa del Coco by boat will find the *migración* (immigration) office across from Deep Blue Diving Adventures.

BAC Bank (Pacífico Plaza) Has a 24hr ATM.

BCR Bank (9am-4pm Mon-Fri) Changes US dollars. The ATM is operational from 5am to 10pm.

Café Internet Pillis (per hr ₡800; 7am-9pm) Internet access and international phone calls. On the 2nd floor of a souvenir shop.

Lava Max (☎ 2670-1860; per kg ₡1000; 8am-5pm) Get your laundry washed, dried and folded here.

Main post office (8am-noon & 1-5:30pm) Located near the entrance of town next to Flor de Itabo hotel.

Activities

DIVING & SNORKELING

The following agencies are thoroughly recommended.

Deep Blue Diving Adventures (☎ 2670-1004; www.deepblue-diving.com) Inside the Coco Bay Hotel & Casino, this outfitter runs two-tank boat dives for US$80, including equipment rental and snacks. It also rents bicycles for US$10 per day.

Rich Coast Diving (☎ 2670-0176, in USA & Canada 800-434-8464; www.richcoastdiving.com) On the main street, this Dutch-owned dive shop has a trimaran for overnight diving trips. A two-tank dive costs US$80, plus US$20 for equipment rental.

Summer Salt (☎ 2670-0308; www.summer-salt.com) This friendly little Swiss-run dive shop has professional, bilingual staff who are as interested in showing you a good time as they are in your safety. Two-tank dive trips are US$100 with snacks included.

SWIMMING

Travelers are generally dissatisfied with the quality of the beach at Playa del Coco, but it's just a 4km drive or walk along the paved road to Playa Ocotal (p255), which is clean, quiet and perfect for both swimming and snorkeling.

SURFING

There's no surf in Playa del Coco, but the town is a jumping-off point for Costa Rica's most legendary surf destinations: Witch's Rock and Ollie's Point, which are inside Parque Nacional Santa Rosa (p234). The best way to reach them is by boat, and boat operators *must* be licensed by Minae (Ministerio del Ambiente y Energía; Ministry of Environment and Energy) to enter the park. Several surf shops in Coco and Tamarindo (p266) run trips to Santa Rosa.

OTHER ACTIVITIES

Sportfishing, sailing, horseback riding and sea kayaking are other popular activities. Many places will rent sea kayaks, which are perfect for exploring the rocky headlands to the north and south of the beach as well as the nearby beaches. You will find no shortage of tour companies around town that can book these and many other activities.

Blue Marlin (☎ 2670-0707; bluemarl@racsa.co.cr) Offers sportfishing trips, regional land tours and surf trips to Witch's Rock.

Coco Xtreme (☎ 8886-0712/67; 9am-sunset) This recommended tour operator offers Jet Ski rentals, surfing and fishing trips, and 'party cruises' like the all-you-can-drink, sunset booze cruise aboard an 11m-long yacht (US$65 per person).

Papagayo Marine Supply (☎ 2670-0774; 8am-5pm) has bounteous information and supplies for anglers. It also rents snorkeling gear

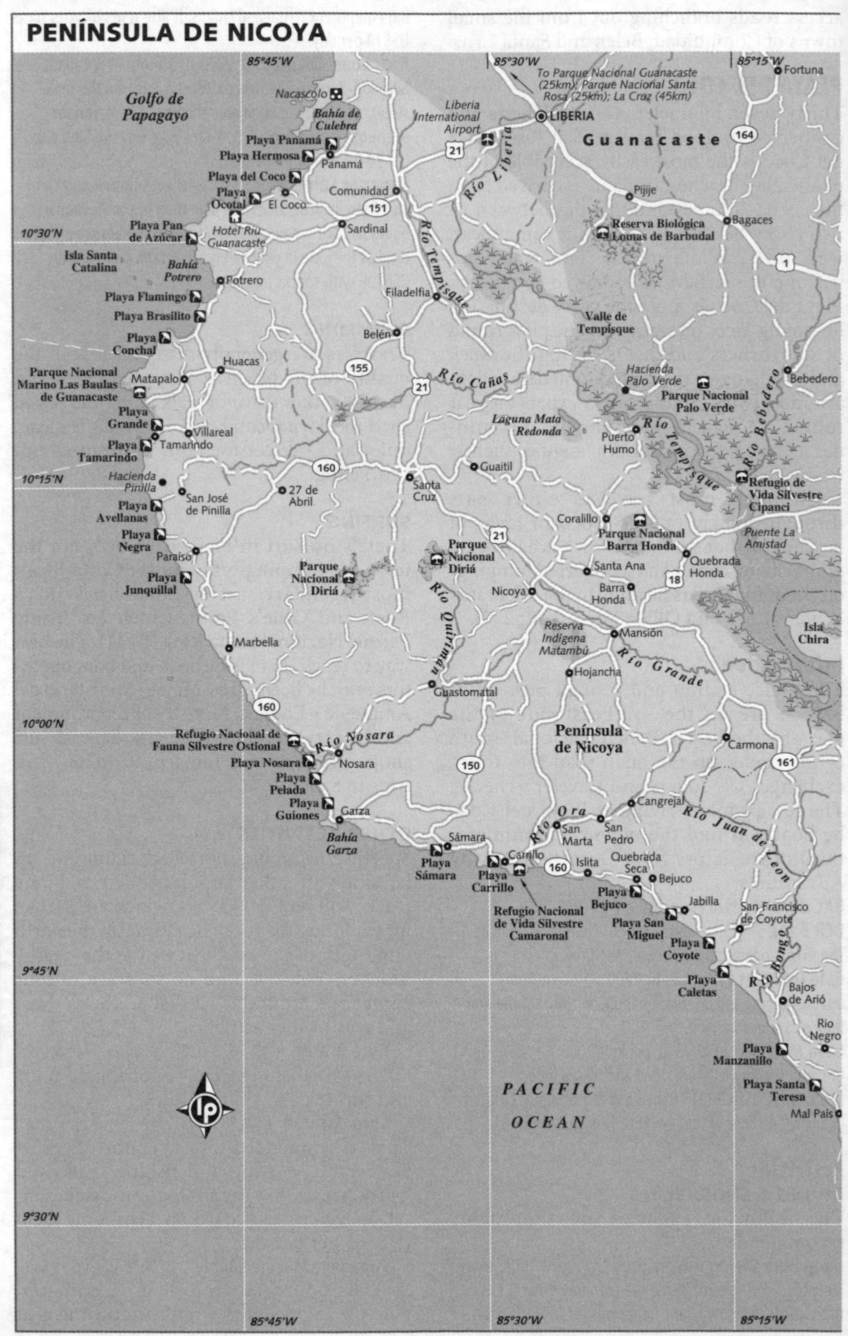
PENÍNSULA DE NICOYA
85°45'W
85°30'W
85°15'W
10°30'N
10°15'N
10°00'N
9°45'N
9°30'N
To Parque Nacional Guanacaste (25km); Parque Nacional Santa Rosa (25km); La Cruz (45km)
Fortuna
Golfo de Papagayo
Nacascolo
Bahía de Culebra
Liberia International Airport
LIBERIA
Guanacaste
Playa Panamá
Playa Hermosa
Panamá
Playa del Coco
Playa Ocotal
El Coco
Comunidad
Río Liberia
Pijije
Hotel Riu Guanacaste
Sardinal
Reserva Biológica Lomas de Barbudal
Bagaces
Playa Pan de Azúcar
Isla Santa Catalina
Bahía Potrero
Potrero
Río Tempisque
Filadelfia
Playa Flamingo
Playa Brasilito
Valle de Tempisque
Belén
Playa Conchal
Huacas
Río Cañas
Hacienda Palo Verde
Parque Nacional Palo Verde
Bebedero
Parque Nacional Marino Las Baulas de Guanacaste
Matapalo
Playa Grande
Villareal
Laguna Mata Redonda
Río Tempisque
Puerto Humo
Río Bebedero
Playa Tamarindo
Tamarindo
Guaitil
Refugio de Vida Silvestre Cipanci
Hacienda Pinilla
San José de Pinilla
27 de Abril
Santa Cruz
Playa Avellanas
Coralillo
Parque Nacional Barra Honda
Puente La Amistad
Playa Negra
Paraíso
Parque Nacional Diriá
Quebrada Honda
Santa Ana
Playa Junquillal
Barra Honda
Nicoya
Río Quiriman
Reserva Indígena Matambú
Mansión
Isla Chira
Marbella
Río Grande
Hojancha
Guastomatal
Refugio Nacional de Fauna Silvestre Ostional
Río Nosara
Península de Nicoya
Carmona
Playa Nosara
Nosara
Playa Pelada
Playa Guiones
Garza
Bahía Garza
Cangrejal
Río Ora
Río Juan de Leon
San Marta
San Pedro
Sámara
Playa Sámara
Carrillo
Playa Carrillo
Islita
Quebrada Seca
Bejuco
Refugio Nacional de Vida Silvestre Camaronal
Playa Bejuco
Jabilla
Playa San Miguel
San Francisco de Coyote
Playa Coyote
Playa Caletas
Río Bongo
Bajos de Arió
Rio Negro
Playa Manzanillo
Playa Santa Teresa
Mal País
PACIFIC OCEAN
1
18
21
150
151
155
160
161
164

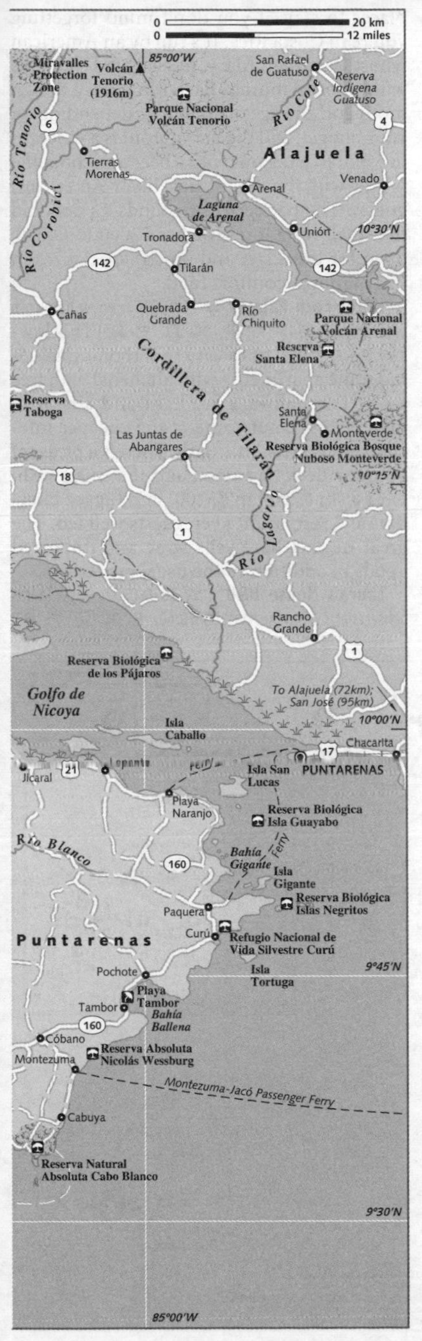

(US$10 per day) and has a small *soda* (informal lunch counter) with Tico cuisine.

Papagayo Golf & Country Club (☎ 2697-0169; 9/18 holes US$55/95, putting green US$6; 🕐 6:30am-5pm Tue-Sun) An 18-hole course located 10km southeast of Playa del Coco.

Festivals & Events

In late January the town hosts a **Fiesta Cívica**, with bullfights, rodeos, dancing and plenty of drinking. But the biggest festival in Coco is the **Fiesta de la Virgen del Mar**, celebrated in mid-July with a vivid religious-themed boat procession in the harbor and a horse pageant.

Sleeping

HOSTELS

El Oasis Backpackers Hostel (☎ 2670-0511; dm per person US$15;) Playa del Coco's first true hostel is a friendly lodge with segregated men's and women's dorms, communal kitchen and lounge area with TV, DVD, laundry service, bike rentals and a lovely garden with hammocks. It's located behind Papagayo Steak House.

BUDGET

The following lodgings have cold-water showers and fans unless otherwise noted, and primarily cater to Tico weekenders. It's popular for Ticos to camp near the beach, though you need to be careful as things can get dodgy when the clubs let out.

Cabinas Don Carlos (☎ 8887-3192; r per person with/without bathroom US$15/10; P) The cheapest place in town has simple, clean and tiny rooms, most with shared bathroom. Pricier rooms have private bathroom, TV and kitchenette. Look for the sign that says 'Rooms for Rent: Backpackers US$8,' advertising the low-season rate.

Cabinas Coco Azul (☎ 2670-0431, 8879-3832; cabinas cocoazul_cr@yahoo.com; s/d US$15/20; P) This two-story, white and brick building is the best of several budget *cabinas* located in a gated complex behind the church. Rooms are sparkling clean and comfy.

Cabinas Marimar (☎ 2670-1212; r per person with/without fridge US$27/18; P) Across the road from the beach are these 16 simple rooms in a two-story brown building with shared balconies. It's no-frills but friendly, and hey, it's beachfront, baby.

Hotel Savannah (☎ 2670-0367; r with/without air-con US$40/30; P) Owned by the same folks behind Hotel Coco Palms, Savannah is a good deal for budget travelers. It's on a quiet side road, with a swimming pool, communal kitchen, barbecue grills and pleasant garden. Rooms, however, are bare-bones; most have bunk beds and cold-water bathroom.

Ruby's Lodging (☎ 8389-6746, 8932-9002; s/d US$30/40; P) Californian-run with Tico charm, this brand-new hotel has eight clean and comfy rooms, all with hot-water bathroom, air-con and TV. Deals or long-term stays are available. There's no sign outside; look for the white building behind the red gate.

Cabinas Donde Claudio y Gloria (☎ 2670-1514; d/tr/q US$35/45/45; P) Located smack-dab on the beach, these clean *cabinas* are a fantastic deal. All rooms have air-con, TV, two double beds, bathroom, and patio with ocean views. The adjoining restaurant (p252) is one of the most established eateries in town.

MIDRANGE

Pato Loco Inn (☎ 2670-0145; www.costa-rica-beach-hotel-patoloco.com; d US$40-60; P) This small inn is one of Coco's most pleasant places to stay, if you don't mind forgetting you're in Costa Rica. It's run by an American whose daughter, Mary, has covered the walls with colorful murals. Each room has a design motif and a range of amenities depending on your budget, and the bar in front is a welcoming spot to hang out with a beer and shoot the breeze with the other (most likely American) guests. The backyard surrounds a pool, and the small restaurant (dishes ₡2000 to ₡4000, open for breakfast and lunch) specializes in international comfort food.

Hotel Coco Palms (☎ 2670-0367; www.hotelcocopalms.com; r US$49-195; P) This low-key resort hotel has a variety of rooms (including some apartments with kitchens) with free wi-fi. The hallways are light and airy with high ceilings, but some of the cheaper interior rooms are a little dark. There's a pleasant outdoor deck and pool, and the small sushi bar (sushi ₡2600 to ₡5200) and bigger international restaurant keep guests well fed. The great market here sells wine and imported goods in addition to the usual groceries.

Laura's House B&B (☎ 2670-0751; www.laurashousecr.net; s/d incl breakfast US$50/60; P)

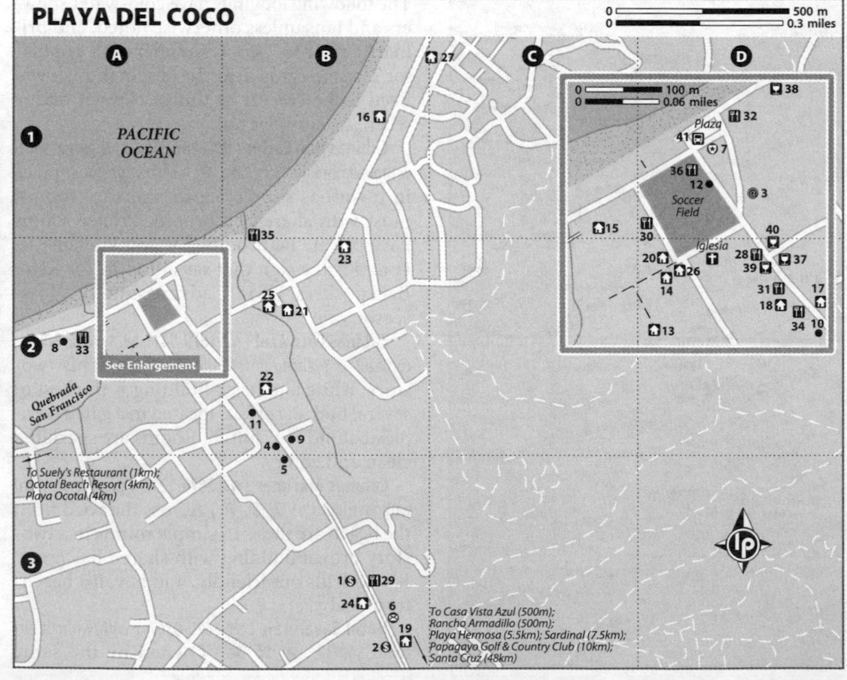

The eight spotless rooms at this homey B&B overlook a small pool and have wi-fi access and cable TV. The place has a friendly, family vibe and it is a short walk to the center of town.

Villa del Sol B&B (☎ 2670-0085, in USA 866-815-8902, in Canada 866-793-9523; www.villadelsol.com; s US$50-65, d US$65-75; t US$90;) This quiet French-Canadian–run place is 1km north of the town center and has a good mix of spotless, well-furnished rooms and studio apartments. There are also six pricey villas that sleep up to 16, though these cater primarily to long-term renters. The hotel is about 100m from the beach, which isn't as crowded at this end.

Flor de Itabo (☎ 2670-0438; www.flordeitabo.com; bungalows US$60, s/d US$70/85, apt US$70-105;) If you're into sportfishing, this is your spot, as the owners have a reputation for catching big game and can organize expeditions throughout Nicoya and the Pacific coast. All rooms have air-con, satellite TV, phone and fridge, while deluxe rooms also have whirlpool tubs. Apartments, with full kitchens, sleep four or six. There's a restaurant serving Italian and international food, a casino and a bar.

our pick Hotel La Puerta del Sol (☎ 2670-0195; lapuertadelsolcostarica@hotmail.com; s/d/tr/ste incl breakfast US$70/90/120/120;) A five-minute walk from town, this unpretentiously luxurious Mediterranean-inspired hotel has two large suites and eight huge pastel-color rooms, each with its own private terrace. The well-manicured grounds have a pool and an open-air, trellis-shaded gym, and the excellent Sol y Luna Restaurant & Bar (see p252) is one of the best eats in town. Dive packages are available through Deep Blue Diving Adventures.

Toro Blanco (☎ 2670-1707; www.toroblancoresort.com; s/d US$90/140;) The newest hotel in town, this bright-yellow, colonial-style building surrounds a courtyard with a lovely swimming pool with swim-up bar. Apartments are rather plain, but all have a full kitchen, flat-screen TV and private balcony overlooking the pool. This is a good choice for families and self-catering groups.

TOP END

In addition to the hotels listed here, see also the listings under Playa Ocotal (p255), 4km to the south, and Playa Hermosa (p253), 5.5km to the north.

Casa Vista Azul (☎ 2670-0678; www.hotelvistaazul.com; r incl breakfast US$101, apt US$124;) This new hotel has seven rooms and two apartments, all of which have air-con and bathroom and are flooded with light and wide-open ocean views. There's also a breezy rooftop dining area, and the owner can help arrange tours. To get here, head west off the main road, just south of Flor de Itabo, and follow the signs.

Coco Beach Hotel & Casino (☎ 2670-0494; www.cocobeachhotelandcasino.com; s/d/tr/q US$108/116/125/130;) It's hard to miss this two-story, salmon-pink hotel, one of the largest buildings in town. Recently remodeled, spacious rooms are generic but comfortable with cable TV and air-con. Amenities include a pool, restaurant, bar and the town's largest casino.

INFORMATION
BAC Bank (see 29)
Banco Nacional 1 B3
BCR Bank 2 B3
Café Internet Pillis 3 D1
Immigration 4 B2
Lava Max 5 B3
Main Post Office 6 B3
Police 7 D1
Post Office (see 7)

SIGHTS & ACTIVITIES
Blue Marlin (see 12)
Coco Xtreme 8 A2
Deep Blue Diving Adventures 9 B2
Papagayo Marine Supply 10 D2
Rich Coast Diving 11 B2
Summer Salt 12 D1

SLEEPING
Cabinas Coco Azul 13 D2
Cabinas Don Carlos 14 D2
Cabinas Donde Claudio y Gloria (see 35)
Cabinas Marimar 15 C1
Café de Playa 16 B1
Coco Beach Hotel & Casino 17 D2
El Oasis Backpackers Hostel 18 D2
Flor de Itabo 19 B3
Hotel Coco Palms 20 D2
Hotel La Puerta del Sol 21 B2
Hotel Savannah 22 B2
Laura's House B&B 23 B2
Pato Loco Inn 24 B3
Ruby's Lodging 25 B2
Toro Blanco 26 D2
Villa del Sol B&B 27 C1

EATING
Andre's Beach Bar 28 D2
Auto Mercado 29 B3
Coco Palms Supermercado 30 D1
Coconutz 31 D2
El Chinamo Caribeño 32 D1
Jardín Tropical (see 36)
La Vida Loca 33 A2
Papagayo Sushi 34 D2
Restaurante Donde Claudio y Gloria 35 B1
Soda Teresita 36 D1
Sol y Luna Restaurant & Bar (see 21)
Zouk Santana (see 40)

DRINKING
La Vida Loca (see 33)
Lizard Lounge 37 D2
Restaurante CocoMar 38 D1
Zi Lounge 39 D2
Zouk Santana 40 D2

TRANSPORT
Bus Stop 41 D1

Rancho Armadillo (2670-0108; www.ranchoarmadillo.com; d incl breakfast US$170, ste US$170-232;) Near the entrance to town, this private estate is on a hillside about 600m off the main road (all paved). The view from the common areas is the best in Playa del Coco, and it's a perfect retreat from the heavily touristed coastline. The seven rooms are light, spacious and nicely decorated with individually crafted furniture. Suites sleep four; some have two bathrooms and two entrances. There's a pool, outdoor gym and plenty of decorative armadillo sculptures, though the location itself makes for a relaxing, meditative stay. The US owners arrange fishing, sailing, diving and surfing trips. Gourmands will enjoy comparing recipes with chef and owner Rick Vogel and using the fully equipped professional kitchen.

Café de Playa (2670-1471/1621; www.cafedeplaya.com; d incl breakfast US$200;) Several elegant rooms at this beach club, adorned with gallery-worthy contemporary art, look on to the pool area and provide easy access to the beach, open-air sushi bar and beachfront restaurant. It's about 15 minutes' walk into the town center, but you may not feel the need to leave.

Eating

El Chinamo Caribeño (mains ₡1000-3500; 7:30am-10pm) East-coast Costa Rican cuisine comes to the Coco at this Caribbean-owned and operated *soda* featuring supercheap and tasty Caribbean-style fish, chicken and rice dishes. Yeah mon!

Soda Teresita (sandwiches ₡1200-2200; lunch & dinner) On the west end of the soccer field, this popular pink *soda* is your best bet for a *torta* (sandwich) and some chitchat with the locals.

La Vida Loca (2670-0181; mains ₡1200-4000; 11am-2pm) Across a creaky wooden footbridge on the south end of the beach is where you'll find the most popular gringo hangout in town. Opened in 1999 by Oregonian 'Jimbo' Jensen, the beachfront bar specializes in US-style comfort food such as burgers, nachos, meat loaf, chili dogs and more.

Jardín Tropical (2670-0428; mains ₡1700-5000; 7am-8:30pm) Also on the soccer field, this well-established, neat and efficient *soda* has a wide selection of menu items, including filling pizzas and freshly caught fish. It's also a great place for a big breakfast by the beach.

Zouk Santana (2670-0191; www.zouksantana.com; mains ₡1700-6000; 11am-late;) Most definitely the hippest place to eat in Coco – you won't be surprised to know it's Italian-owned. The kitchen serves fusion cuisine late into the night to fuel your second wind at the downstairs bar.

Papagayo Sushi (2670-0298; mains ₡2800-5700; lunch & dinner) One of three eateries at this big restaurant complex, this boat-shaped branch features sushi rolls, bento boxes and seafood specialties such as fresh fish sautéed in chipotle orange sauce. The food is good, but don't come if you are in a hurry; service is slow as molasses and some waiters seem more interested in selling time-share tours than taking your order.

Andre's Beach Bar (2670-2052; mains ₡2900-7000; 6:30am-late;) The best pizza place in town also has one of the best breakfast spots, serving omelettes and eggs Benedict. English and French are spoken.

Sol y Luna Restaurant & Bar (Hotel La Puerta del Sol; dishes ₡4000-5500; 6-10pm Wed-Mon) Dine on authentic Italian pasta while soaking up the Mediterranean atmosphere at this restaurant at Hotel La Puerta del Sol (p251). But make sure you save room for a slice of the heavenly homemade tiramisu.

our pick **Suely's Restaurant** (2670-1696; sti-costarica@hotmail.com; mains ₡4000-8000; 6-10:30pm Mon-Sat) A much-welcomed gourmet addition to Coco's dining scene, this extraordinary restaurant is the brainchild of French chef Sebastien and his Brazilian-Belgian wife Thais. The daily changing menu focuses on fresh fish and seafood, such as the truly divine tempura jumbo shrimp in Thai sauce. The simple but tastefully decorated venue is open-air with candlelit tables and ambient chill-out music. And for dessert, don't miss The Volcano – a chocolate cake with melted-chocolate 'lava' sauce in the middle and drizzled with caramel.

Restaurante Donde Claudio y Gloria (2670-1514; www.dondeclaudioygloria.com; mains ₡4200-21,600; 7am-9pm Sun-Thu, to 10pm Fri & Sat) Founded by Playa del Coco pioneers don Claudio and Gloria Rojas, this casual, beachfront seafood restaurant has been a local landmark since 1955. This is a must for seafood-lovers, with such interesting dishes as spicy mahimahi Catalan in an almond, raisin and white-wine sauce.

Coconutz (2670-1982; mains ₡4500-10,000; noon-late;) Across the road from the

Coco Beach Hotel, this is the latest US sports bar–restaurant competing for gringo dollars. The BBQ ribs are terrific, though the house specialty is Tex-Mex. Big screens are constantly airing live (mostly US) sports.

For groceries, you can stock up at **Coco Palms Supermercado** (☎ 2670-0367; 24hr), or the massive **Auto Mercado** (☎ 2670-2232; 8am-8pm, to 9pm Fri & Sat) at the new Pacífico Plaza shopping center near the entrance of town.

Drinking

Playa del Coco has a boisterous mix of Ticos looking to get toasted, and sunburned sportfishers cooling their heels and swapping fish stories. If you're looking for entertainment that doesn't involve drinking, you've come to the wrong town.

The restaurants surrounding the plaza double as bars. The **Lizard Lounge** (3pm-2am) attracts a livelier crowd of dancers. It's a nice place to start out the evening with a game of pool, a cocktail and *bocas* (the Costa Rican equivalent of tapas) on the streetside terrace. **Restaurante CocoMar** (10am-10pm) is a good place for a sunset drink on the beach. Keep the party moving at **La Vida Loca** (☎ 2670-0181; 11am-2am), with live music on weekends.

If you're looking for a more stylish venue, head to **Zouk Santana** (☎ 2670-0191; www.zouksantana.com; 5pm-2am), where there's an open seating area, dance floor and streetside bar. The hot new spot is **Zi Lounge** (☎ 2670-1978; 4pm-2:30am), an outdoor lounge where you can relax on big sofas under large white tents while DJs spin an eclectic mix of electronica, salsa and hip-hop.

Getting There & Away

All buses arrive and depart from the main stop on the plaza, across from the police station.

Filadelfia, for connection to Santa Cruz ₡450; 45 minutes; departs 11:30am and 4:30pm.

Liberia ₡700; one hour; departs eight times from 5:30am to 6pm.

San José (Pulmitan) ₡3200; five hours; departs 4am, 8am and 2pm.

A taxi from Liberia to Playa del Coco costs ₡17,000. Taxis between Playa del Coco and Playas Hermosa or Ocotal will cost about ₡6000.

Note that there's no gas station in town; the nearest one is in Sardinal, about 7.5km inland from Playa del Coco.

PLAYA HERMOSA

If you're looking for the legendary surf beach, see p332. For those of you still with us, Playa Hermosa is a gently curving and tranquil gray-sand beach stretching for about 2km. Although it's only 5.5km (by road) north of Playa del Coco, and development is springing up rapidly along this entire coastline, Hermosa feels less dissipated and more dignified than Coco. The hillsides may be up for sale, but they're still pretty green and the locals are not so jaded.

If you are keen to get in the water, **Bill Beard's Diving Safaris** (☎ 2453-5044, in USA & Canada 877 853-0538; www.billbeardcostarica.com) at the Villas Sol Hotel has been scuba diving and snorkeling since 1970. **Aqua Sport** (☎ 2672-0050) has boats for fishing, water tours and snorkeling.

From the main road, there is a southern and northern access road leading to the beach.

Sleeping

Do it the Tico way and camp for free under a few shady spots near the main beach, but don't expect any facilities.

The second (or northern) entrance to the beach is lined with a variety of hotels and inns, should none of the following options pan out.

Iguana Inn (☎ 2672-0065; s/d US$20/30;) Set 100m back from the beach, this rambling bi-level terra-cotta inn has 10 simple, slightly beat-up rooms with bathroom, though the price is definitely right. The Tico owners are also super laid-back, which makes for a relaxing, worry-free stay.

Cabinas La Casona (☎ 2672-0025; gaviotalouise@hotmail.com; s/d US$30/45; P) The seven cutesy *cabinas* here, with whitewashed rooms, small kitchenette, TV and hot-water bathroom, are ideal for self-caterers, and they're just steps from the beach.

Playa Hermosa B&B (☎ 2672-0063; s/d incl breakfast US$45/70; P) Centered on a gigantic tree right on the beach, this B&B has a certain decaying appeal to it; though it seemed a bit neglected when we stopped by, it does have character and a quiet, beachfront location. You'll find it at the end of the dirt road on the left of the northern access road as you head toward the beach.

Hotel El Velero (☎ 2672-0036/1017; www.costaricahotel.net; d US$90; P) Just steps from the beach, this resort hotel has 22 spacious and fully equipped rooms decorated with

PENÍNSULA DE NICOYA

DIVERS DO IT DEEPER

The northern area of the peninsula is one of the best and most easily accessible sites in the country for diving. As beach diving in this area isn't the greatest, dives are made either around volcanic rock pinnacles near the coast, or from a boat further off at **Isla Santa Catalina** (about 20km to the southwest) or **Isla Murciélago** (40km to the northwest, near the tip of Península Santa Elena).

Diving here is not like diving the Caribbean – do not expect to see colorful hard coral on the scale of Belize. Conditions can be mediocre from a visibility standpoint (9m to 15m visibility, and sometimes up to 20m), but the sites make up for it in other ways: namely, their abundant marine life. The richness, variety and sheer number of marine animals is astonishing. This is the place to see large groupings of pelagics, such as manta rays, spotted eagle rays, sharks, whales, dolphins and turtles, as well as moray eels, starfish, crustaceans and huge schools of native tropical fish. Most of the dive sites are less than 25m deep, allowing three dives a day. Keep in mind, however, that since February 2006 it is now illegal to swim in close proximity to dolphins and whales.

The Papagayo winds blow from early December to late March and make the water choppy and cooler, cutting down on visibility, especially for the four days around the full moon. June and July are usually the best months for visibility.

Isla Santa Catalina and Isla Murciélago both have a rich variety of marine life living and cruising around these rocky outcrops. Manta rays have been reported from December to late April, and at other times you can expect to spot eagle rays, eels, Cortez angelfish, hogfish, parrot fish, starfish, clown shrimp and other bottom dwellers. The far point of Murciélago is known for its regular sightings of groups of bull sharks, which can be a terrifying sight if you're not an experienced diver. Divers also head to **Narizones**, which is a good deep dive (about 27m), while **Punta Gorda** is an easy descent for inexperienced divers.

The good thing about scuba diving here is that the sheer cost of starting and maintaining a dive center discourages fly-by-night operators from setting up shop. As a general rule, though, it's good to feel out a dive shop before paying for a trip – talk to the divemaster, inspect the equipment and make sure you're comfortable with everything before heading out (you should never feel pressured into diving!).

If you haven't been scuba diving before, consider taking a 'Discovery Course,' which costs about US$125 and will teach you all the basics. If you're interested in getting your Open Water Diver certification, which allows you to dive anywhere in the world, a three- to four-day course is about US$400. Compared to what these courses can cost in either North America or Europe, this price is a bargain.

woodwork and colorful bedspreads. The complex has a pool, patio lounge and US-style restaurant and bar, though the real draw is the owner's 11.5m sailboat. Guests are invited on a number of cruises through the crystal-blue waters of the Bahía de Culebra, including daily sunset cruises (US$60 per person, minimum four people).

Hotel Playa Hermosa (☎ 2672-0046; www.hotelplayahermosa.com; r US$198-283; P ⊠ 💻 📶 🏊) *Hermosa* (pretty) would be the simplest way to describe this lovely hotel after the renovation a few years ago. On the southern end of the beach via the first entrance road, the luxurious rooms are screened by branches and greenery of the property's old-growth trees. The well-appointed rooms, with cable TV, comfortable furniture and a simple, tropical aesthetic, ring around a pool and beautifully landscaped garden. There's wi-fi access in the central area.

Villas Sol Hotel (☎ 2672-0001; www.villassol.com; d US$356, villas US$528; P ⊠ 📶 🏊) If an all-inclusive resort deal sounds attractive, this hillside is your place. Standard rooms are equipped with everything you'd want, and the views of the gulf are breathtaking. The villas are definitely pricier, but they have three bedrooms, a kitchen and a private pool option, so gather a few of your friends who have a bit of cash and live it up. There are also tennis courts, a restaurant and a bar, and the owners can arrange all types of activities (Bill Beard's Diving Safaris is also based here).

Eating & Drinking

Whether you're just passing through Playa Hermosa or spending the night, there are some great spots to eat here. Food and other basic supplies are available at Mini Super Cenizaro, on the paved road into town.

Restaurante Pescado Loco (☎ 2672-0017; mains ₡2800-7800; 9am-1am) The 'Crazy Fish' serves up some of the freshest seafood around, including Costa Rican standards such as red snapper and *ceviche* (uncooked, marinated seafood), though we got excited about the *pulpo de gallego* (Galician octopus). The restaurant is between the first and second entrances to Playa Hermosa.

our pick **Ginger** (☎ 2672-0041; mains ₡8300-11,200; 5-10pm Tue-Sun) If you're driving north, look toward the hills on the right and you'll see this stunner of an open-air restaurant (it was designed by the famous Costa Rican architect Victor Cañas). The chic ambience, which feels more like New York than Costa Rica, is complemented by a gourmet list of Asian- and Mediterranean-inspired tapas.

Monkey Bar (☎ 2672-0267; 5pm-midnight) For all your liquid needs visit this huge tree house between the first and second entrances to Playa Hermosa, where you can sip a sundowner to the tune of howlers bleating overhead.

Getting There & Away

There is a daily bus from San José, but you can always take a bus to Liberia and switch there for more frequent buses to Playa Hermosa. A taxi from Liberia costs about ₡8500, and a taxi from Coco about ₡6000. If you're driving from Liberia, take the signed turnoff to Playa del Coco. The entire road is paved.

Buses to Liberia and San José depart from the main road on the northern end of the beach and make a stop in Sardinal.

Liberia ₡450; 1¼ hours; departs seven times from 5:30am to 7:30pm.

San José (Empresa Esquivel) ₡3000; six hours; departs 5am.

PLAYA OCOTAL

This small but attractive gray-sand beach with tidal pools on both ends is 4km southwest of Playa del Coco by paved road. Aside from a few privately owned villas (which are mostly rented as vacation houses), there isn't an actual town here, though it's close enough to Coco that you can either drive or take a leisurely stroll here along the road. Although it's a fairly quiet beach, Ocotal can get mobbed on weekends by Ticos looking to escape the Coco scene.

If you feel like diving, **Ocotal Beach Resort** (☎ 2670-0321; www.ocotalresort.com) offers dive packages, such as an eight-day, seven-night deal including accommodations, breakfast and six days of boat and beach diving (US$1167 per person, based on double occupancy). It also offers fishing charters (it has six boats) and kayak rentals. Complete fishing packages are also available.

Sleeping & Eating

Los Almendros de Ocotal (☎ 2670-1744; www.losalmendrosrentals.com; studios/apt/villas US$82/181/265; P) Perched on the hillside just above Playa Ocotal, these apartments are a great deal for self-caterers or longer-term visitors. They're quiet, have superb views, and are well maintained and comfortable. Apartments sleep four while villas sleep six, and some units have a private pool and terrace.

Villa Casa Blanca (☎ 2670-0518; www.hotelvillacasablanca.com; d/ste incl breakfast US$105/125, additional person US$10; P) Between Playa del Coco and Ocotal, this attractive villa is perched on a pleasant hilltop just a few minutes' walk from the beach. The rooms are beautifully decorated with either Victorian motifs or more modern accents. Three honeymoon suites are larger and feature a step-up bathtub and ocean views. The pool has a swim-up bar, and there's wi-fi access.

Ocotal Beach Resort (off Map p250; ☎ 2670-0321; www.ocotalresort.com; s/d incl breakfast from US$175/200, bungalows US$175, ste US$378; P) This beachside resort on the bay has a relaxed vibe and it is a great choice for divers and sportfishers. There are several swimming pools, tennis courts, and a notable Mediterranean-fusion restaurant whose chef was trained at the Cordon Bleu. Suites are a bit cramped, with gigantic beds, but they have ocean views and Jacuzzi tubs, while duplex-style bungalows share small private pools. All rooms include the creature comforts you'd expect.

Father Rooster Bar & Grill (☎ 2670-1246; www.fatherrooster.com; mains ₡2800-9000; 11am-11pm) This awesome beachside eatery serves up a good variety of grilled dishes, including fish, snacks and burgers, and you cannot beat the location: sit in the coolness of the restaurant, on the shaded wooden terrace or under the palms on the beach. The bartenders make a good margarita as well as a killer frozen Tica Linda, whose knockout punch is naturally Cacique Guaro.

BEACHES SOUTH OF PLAYA OCOTAL

Although they're next to one another, Playas Pan de Azúcar, Potrero, Flamingo, Brasilito and Conchal have relatively little in common. The beaches range from gray sand to white sand to crushed seashells, while the range of development is also a seemingly random pattern.

Although it's tempting to take the 'road' from Sardinal to Potrero, there's a reason why locals call this route the 'Monkey Trail.' The first 8km of gravel road leading to the small town of Nuevo Colón is fine, but the second half is pretty brutal, and should only be tackled in dry season with a 4WD (and after you've talked to a few locals). The Monkey Trail begins 5km west of El Coco; turn right at the Castrol Oil sign and follow the signs for Congo Canopy. At the 'T' intersection in Nuevo Colón, turn left, bear left at the fork and continue for 5km until you reach Congo Canopy. From there, it's a hair-raising 6km drive to Bahía Potrero.

To avoid the rough roads, return to the main peninsular highway from El Coco, then head south through Filadelfia and on to Belén (a distance of 18km), from where a paved road heads 25km west to Huacas (where there's a gas station). Then take the road leading north until you hit the ocean at the village of Brasilito. Turn right and head north: you'll pass Playa Flamingo and Bahía Potrero before reaching Playa Pan de Azúcar. If you make a left instead and head south, you will end up at Playa Conchal.

Buses from San José, Liberia or Santa Cruz can also get you to most of the beaches. If you're into sea kayaking, the proximity of the beaches to one another makes for some great day trips.

About 1km west of Nuevo Colón, you can take the **Congo Trail Canopy Tour** (☎ 2666-4422; US$45) if you're looking for adventure without broken axles.

The mammoth 701-room, all-inclusive **Hotel Riu Guanacaste** (☎ in USA 888-666-8816; www.riu.com; d US$360-598; P ✕ 💻 📶 🏊 👶) is the newest and one of the largest megaresorts in Costa Rica. Opened in 2009, this five-star, oceanfront palace has a huge casino (open from noon to 3am), nine restaurants and bars (open 24/7!), disco, spa, kids' club, conference center and an open-air theater with live Broadway musical productions. From the Nuevo Colón 'T' intersection, continue straight for 4km on the new paved road. It's hard to miss!

Playa Pan de Azúcar

Although the buses stop at Potrero, those with their own ride (it'd better be a 4WD in the rainy season) can head 3km north on a rough dirt road to 'Sugar-Bread Beach,' which derives its name from the crystalline strip of white sand that's protected at both ends by rocky headlands. Difficult access and the lack of cheap accommodations create an atmosphere of total seclusion, and the ocean here is calm, clear and perfect for snorkeling.

Although the beach is fronted by the Hotel Sugar Beach, don't be afraid to walk down to the shore as beaches are public property in Costa Rica.

Luxury at the **Hotel Sugar Beach** (☎ 2654-4242; www.sugar-beach.com; d incl breakfast from US$164; P ✕ 💻 📶 🏊) is simple and understated, which is the right approach considering how difficult it is to compete with the natural beauty of the beach. The 22 lovely rooms are brightly painted and entered via elaborately hand-carved wooden doors. Deluxe rooms are slightly larger and have stunning ocean views. There are also four two-bedroom apartments, two beach houses (with two or three bedrooms sleeping 10 to 12) and a small restaurant. But the real reason you're here is to slow down and linger on one of the most isolated beaches in all of Costa Rica.

Bahía Potrero

This stretch of bay is separated from Playa Flamingo by a rocky headland. Although the overdeveloped eyesore that is Playa Flamingo can be seen across the bay, monkeys can still be heard in the trees here. The hillsides and shoreline are seeing development, and tourists in quad caravans kick up dust along the roads, but the bay has a decidedly lower-key – and shall we say, classier – scene.

Several undeveloped beaches are strung along the bay. The black-sand beach is **Playa Prieta**, the white-sand beach is **Playa Penca**, and **Playa Potrero**, the biggest, is somewhere in between. (These names, it should be noted, are used loosely.) The rocky islet 10km west of Playa Pan de Azúcar is **Isla Santa Catalina**, a popular diving spot (see boxed text, p254). Hotels on the beaches rent water-sports equipment. A recommended surf school is

Point Break Surf (☎ 8866-4133; www.pointbreaksurf.com; per lesson US$45).

There's a small community at **Potrero**, just beyond the northern end of the beach. This is where the bus line ends, and the beaches here don't get the weekend rush found at Brasilito. Further south in the center of the bay, the village of **Surfside** is home to a growing number of US and Canadian expats.

In Potrero, the **Casa del Sol** strip mall has a small gringo-run **Welcome Center** (☎ 2654-5460; 9am-5pm Mon-Sat), where you can pick up free maps and brochures. Nearby on the road toward the Monkey Trail, Banco de Costa Rica has a 24-hour ATM.

SLEEPING

If you're looking for budget accommodations, consider staying 7km south in Brasilito (p259).

Cabinas Christina (☎ 2654-4006; www.cabinascristina.com; s or d US$56, tr or q US$102; P) The cheapest accommodations in town, these simple *cabinas* are scattered under a lovely palm-grove garden. All rooms have air-con, TV and a kitchen.

Bahía Esmeralda (☎ 2654-4480; www.hotelbahiaesmeralda.com; s/d/q incl breakfast from US$70/81/108, apt/villas US$157/215; P) A short walk from the beach, this Italian-owned resort offers supercomfortable accommodations at a bargain price. Standard rooms are a little on the small side, though the relaxed atmosphere, pool and excellent Italian restaurant (open for breakfast and dinner, meals from ₡1550 to ₡6200) more than make up for it. The apartments sleeping up to four have fold-out futons and a kitchen, while larger villas sleep six.

Hotel Isolina (☎ 2654-4333; www.isolinabeach.com; d/tr/q incl breakfast from US$73/75/102, d/tr/q villas incl breakfast US$91/102/124; P) These attractive yellow buildings are set back from the northern end of the beach and completely surrounded by huge bushes of fragrant hibiscus. Rooms have tiled hot showers, cable TV and air-con, while larger villas have two bedrooms and a fully equipped kitchen. There's wi-fi access outside, and the attached restaurant serves up some Tico-Mediterranean specialties.

our pick **Bahía del Sol** (☎ 2654-4671, 2224-7290; www.potrerobay.com; d/ste incl breakfast from US$186/339; P) With a prime beachfront location at Playa Potrero (by the cute baby-turtle sign admonishing quad drivers to stay off the beach), this luxurious resort gets high marks for laid-back elegance. Large, tiled rooms and suites have all the amenities you would want (suites include a fully equipped kitchen and private terrace) and surround a lovely garden with a spa area. Out front, there's a pool with a waterfall and swim-up bar, and a lawn leading out to the beach is peppered with *palapas* (shelter with a thatched, palm-leaf roof and open sides).

Hotel Mediterraneus (☎ 2654-5349; www.hotelmediterraneus.com; d incl breakfast US$192; P) Built in traditional Mediterranean colonial architecture, this posh new hotel is the nicest place in town. The 52 spacious rooms all have balconies or patios overlooking a huge free-form pool with a waterfall. You'll also find an onsite spa and a good but pricey restaurant.

EATING & DRINKING

The Shack (☎ 8336-3497; mains ₡1000-4500; 8am-11pm) Our favorite new watering hole in town, this thatched-roof bar-restaurant is run by a lovely Nashville couple, Susan and Cham, and their business partner Jude. Come here for breakfast, when homemade bagels and sausages are served. Lunch and dinner fare is mainly Tex-Mex, but there are also special evenings such as Sushi Saturdays, Meatloaf Wednesdays and Margarita Madness Fridays. Plus, free coffee and wi-fi anytime.

Maxwell's Café & Bar (☎ 2654-4319; mains ₡1200-4000; 8am-11pm) Sooner or later, every gringo expat and tourist ends up at this popular, open-air restaurant in Surfside. The Californian-American menu features fish tacos, fajitas and burgers. There's also a popular farmer's market every Friday from 1pm to 5pm, when Tico and gringo vendors sell fresh bread, pastries, fruits, sausages and other treats.

Arabica (mains ₡2000-4000; 10am-7pm Mon-Wed, 10am-9pm Fri & Sat, 10am-4pm Sun) Tucked at the Casa del Sol plaza in Potrero is a lovely Middle Eastern–themed coffee lounge with Levantine cuisine including hummus, tabouleh, kebabs, pita and, of course, strong coffee.

Las Brisas Bar & Grill (☎ 2654-4047; mains ₡2500-6000; noon-late) Just off the northwest corner of the soccer field in Potrero, this popular beachfront bar has been a local favorite since 1950. Villagers pack the joint nightly for *bocas*, beers and brilliant sunsets. The pool table here is probably the most exciting entertainment offering in town. Wednesday is ladies' night.

GETTING THERE & AWAY

Many buses begin their route in Potrero on the southeast corner of the soccer field. See Playa Flamingo (below) for schedules. Ask locally before setting out as not every bus goes all the way into Potrero.

Playa Flamingo

The crescent strip of white sand known as Playa Flamingo is postcard-worthy, which is probably why it was billed decades ago as Costa Rica's most sophisticated beach destination. These days the beach has gone completely upscale, though the scene ain't so pretty. The hills above the bay are lined with private villas and expensive condos. Bars are filled with guys bragging about the size of their yachts, and overly friendly ladies willing to go along for the ride. Package tourists and sportfishers still frequent the old resorts that line the bay, but there are definitely better places to spend your time and money. That said, the white-sand shoreline itself is a blue-flag beach, making it a lovely place to while away a free hour or two.

The original name of the beach was Playa Blanca; it changed its name in the 1950s to coincide with the construction of the area's first major hotel, the Flamingo Beach Resort. Funnily enough, flamingo season here runs from never to never.

ACTIVITIES

At the entrance to Playa Flamingo, **Groupo Brandisi** (☎ 2654-4946; www.theedgeadventure.com; 7am-6pm) has a range of rentals and tours. A two-tank dive is US$75, and snorkeling gear, bikes and body boards are available for rent. Fishing charters are also available.

Many boat operators offer cruises and snorkeling trips. The **Lazy Lizard** (☎ 2654-5900; www.lazylizardsailing.com; adult/child US$75/55) catamaran offers a four-hour sunset-snorkeling cruise with equipment, snacks and unlimited booze. Playa Flamingo's marina is indefinitely closed; all boats depart from Bahía Potrero.

SLEEPING & EATING

Budget options are practically nonexistent in Playa Flamingo, though you will find a few local supermarkets. If you want to visit the beach but save a few bucks, consider staying in nearby Brasilito (p259).

Mariner Inn (☎ 2654-4081; marinerinn@hotmail.com; s/d US$34/45; P) Just next to the marina, the Mariner Inn has a sweet terrace bar with beautiful views of the bay where you can have a cocktail before turning in. The small rooms have seen better days, but they are clean and comfortable, with air-con, hot water, cable TV and some with a fridge.

Flamingo Beach Resort (☎ 2654-4444; www.resortflamingobeach.com; r US$120-300; P) The Flamingo is the granddaddy of the area's resorts, with 91 rooms, tennis courts, a pool and a wide restaurant terrace that looks out on the beautiful beach out back. It has a 1950s Vegas look and feel, with no dearth of amenities or gaudy aesthetic.

Marie's (☎ 2654-4136; meals ₡2000-12,000; 6:30am-9:30pm) One of the longest-established eateries in town has a breezy round dining terrace, and such offerings as yogurt, granola and fruit at breakfast, avocados stuffed with shrimp, and spinach-and-ricotta ravioli. The pancakes, burgers and rotisserie chicken are locally famous.

Mar y Sol (☎ 2654-4151; www.marysolflamingo.com; mains ₡3400-14,000; lunch & dinner) For a special night out, you can't go wrong at this hilltop treasure with stunning panoramic sea and sunset views. It's run by the French-American Taulere family, including accomplished chef Jean-Luc. Go for the specialty, filet mignon and lobster brochette with béarnaise and lemon butter.

our pick **Angelina's** (☎ 2654-4839; mains ₡4500-18,000; 5-9:30pm) The stunning interior of this gorgeous restaurant is surpassed only by the masterpiece on your plate. The creative fusion menu features such dishes as Dorado Tico – plantain-encrusted mahimahi with mango-avocado salsa, coconut-jasmine rice and jalapeño-rum glaze. After dinner, pop in for a cocktail at the adjacent Yellowfin Lounge (drinks ₡3900 to ₡7000; open from 5pm to midnight).

GETTING THERE & AWAY

Air

The closest airport is at Tamarindo (p271), which has regular scheduled flights and is about 16km away by paved road.

Bus

Buses depart from the traffic circle near the entrance of town and travel through Brasilito on the way out. Schedules change often, so ask locally about departure times as well as the best place on the road to wait for the bus.

Liberia ₡1200; two hours; departs every hour from 4:30am to 6:30pm.
San José (Tralapa) ₡4800; five hours; departs 2am, 9am and 2pm Monday to Saturday, and 9am, 10:30am and 2pm on Sunday.
Santa Cruz ₡870; one hour; departs nine times per day from 5am to 10pm.

Playa Brasilito

Underrated Brasilito has managed to avoid the overdevelopment that's plagued much of northern Nicoya. It might be that the gray-sand beach here isn't as pretty as the nearby strips of palm-fringed white sand, and the lack of resorts and big hotels gives the town a laid-back atmosphere. This is still very much a working fishing village. Playa Brasilito is popular with weekending Ticos and travelers 'in the know,' who are drawn here for the relaxed beach scene, pleasant swimming, cheap accommodations and spectacular Pacific sunsets.

Brasilito Excursiones (☎ 2654-4237; www.brasilito.com), which operates out of Hotel Brasilito, can book horseback rides, sunset sails and two-tank dives.

Internet is available (₡1200 per hour) at Hotel Nany, but you won't find any bank or gas station. The nearest ATM is in Playa Flamingo.

SLEEPING

The town of Brasilito consists of a few small stores and *sodas*, as well as some great budget and midrange accommodations. In addition to the hotels below, a number of budget *cabinas* have popped up along the dirt road 200m east of the bridge.

Cabinas La Gloria (☎ 2654-4878; d/tr US$40/50; P ❄ 💻 wi-fi) Run by an amiable Tico named Santos, these spruced-up rooms with air-con, fridge, coffee maker, cable TV and free wi-fi are a bit upmarket but a great deal if you're a traveling trio. It's 200m south of the plaza.

Cabinas Ojos Azules (☎ 2654-4346; www.cabinasojosazules.com; s/d US$40/50, tr or q US$60; P ❄) The best budget option in town is a somewhat ramshackle collection of rooms featuring big, comfy beds, some with saucy mirrored headboards. Fancy doubles are upstairs, and simpler downstairs quarters fit up to eight people. All units have bathroom with hot water, and there's a small shared kitchen. It's 200m south of the plaza.

Hotel Brasilito (☎ 2654-4237; www.brasilito.com; r with/without air-con US$46/39; P ❄ wi-fi) On the beach side of the plaza, this recommended hotel is the perfect place to slow down and chill out for a few days. The rooms are simple and clean, though you'll scream with joy when you take a steamy shower with some serious pressure. If it's available, splurge for the sea-view room in the front that has a private hammock-strung patio ideal for soaking up the sunset, after which you can hang out at the popular restaurant. The friendly owners speak German, English and Spanish, and will help arrange tours.

Hotel Nany (☎ 2654 4320; apartotelnany.com; d/q US$65/105; P ❄ 💻 wi-fi 🏊) This is an impressive Tico-run complex complete with its own internet cafe, steakhouse, supermarket, swimming pool and *cabinas*. Large rooms are painted in cheerful tropical colors and come with cable TV, air-con and warm shower. The hotel is managed by the López family, who have been in the area for four decades.

our pick **Conchal Hotel** (☎ 2654-9125; www.conchalcr.com; d incl breakfast US$85; P ❄ 💻 wi-fi 🏊) Rooms at this recommended hotel are simply stunning – whitewashed walls are offset by exposed wooden beams, ceramic tiling and elegant bathroom. London native Simon, the owner, and his staff make every effort to make your holiday comfortable and memorable. And like with any self-respecting British hotelier, you'll also find great curries at the onsite Papaya restaurant (mains ₡2200 to ₡9900).

EATING & DRINKING

Soda Brasilito (☎ 8812-0252; mains ₡1300-10,000; 🕑 7am-8pm) This little green shack on the main plaza attracts locals and tourists alike who swear this is the best place in town for genuine Tico cuisine including beef, chicken and fish dishes.

La Casita de Pescado (☎ 2654-5171; mains ₡1800-9800; 🕑 9am-9pm) Located directly on the beach, this little Tico-owned eatery has cheap yet delicious seafood dishes including octopus, shrimp, fish and squid dishes.

our pick **La Guinguette** (mains ₡2000-9000; 🕑 lunch & dinner) He's Tico. She's French. And when Yohann and Geraldine combined their talents, the result was this fabulously imaginative fusion restaurant that's part Costa Rican *soda*, part French gastropub and 100% pure passion. You'll find a few meat dishes on the daily changing menu, but the house specialty is fresh seafood, caught that morning just meters away. We sampled a wonderful filet of *loro* (parrot fish) in a vanilla sauce, one of many sauces on offer including lobster and curry. 'I'm French, so of course I love sauce,' says Geraldine. Between them and their Romanian waiter Andrei, the staff speak English, Spanish, French, Romanian and Portuguese. The simple open-air restaurant is located on the main plaza, 50m from the beach.

Outback Jack's Roadkill Café (☎ 2654-3465; mains ₡2700-9000; 🕑 6am-11pm) A good spot for a beer, this open-air restaurant-bar attached to Hotel Brasilito looks out on the beach. Though its Ozzie-themed decor would have you believe otherwise, the cuisine is more about international basics with a Tico accent.

Il Forno Restaurant (☎ 2654-4125; mains ₡2800-12,900; 🕑 lunch & dinner; V) This recommended Italian restaurant is in a romantic garden, and has such delightful menu items as thin-crust pizza, homemade pastas and risottos, and enough fresh eggplant dishes to keep vegetarians happy and healthy.

Happy Snapper (☎ 2645-4413; mains ₡3500-10,300; 🕑 8am-noon;) Got kids? Bring the whole family down to this thatched-roofed, friendly seafood restaurant with a swimming pool (free for customers), plus TVs and a huge grassy lounge area.

Indira Bar (☎ 2654-4028; 🕑 noon-late) That crumbling puke-green cement structure on the beach is NOT an abandoned building. This local hole-in-the-wall (literally) has no food, no atmosphere, no decor – just cheap beer and loud music.

GETTING THERE & AWAY

Buses to and from Playa Flamingo travel through Brasilito; see p258 for details. There is a bus ticket office at the north end of Brasilito – look for the blue house with the 'Tralapa Agencia' sign.

Playa Conchal

Just 1km south of Brasilito is Playa Conchal, which is widely regarded as the most beautiful beach in all of Costa Rica. The name comes from the billions of *conchas* (shells) that wash up on the beach, which are gradually crushed into coarse sand. The ocean water is an intense turquoise blue, which is indeed a rarity on the Pacific coast. If you have snorkeling gear, this is the place to bust it out.

On weekends, the beach is often packed with locals and tourists, plus countless vendors hawking everything from cold beer and barbecued snacks to beach chair and snorkel gear rentals, horseback rides and Jet Skis. But on weekdays, especially during low season, Playa Conchal is pure paradise.

The easiest way to reach Conchal is to simply walk 15 minutes down the beach from Playa Brasilito. You can also drive along the sandy beach road, though you may be charged ₡1000 to park.

Why is it that the most expensive resorts always seem to have the most ridiculous names? With 285 hectares of property, including an over-the-top free-form pool and a championship golf course, it's not like **Paradisus Playa Conchal Beach & Resort** (☎ 2654-4123; www.paradisus-playa-conchal.com; d from US$478; P) really needs a fancy name to compensate for any inadequacies. Guests have got it all here, and everything from the marble columns to the gold-trimmed toothbrush holder is a class act. Needless to say, the whole shebang is about as non–Costa Rican as it can get.

PLAYA GRANDE

From Huacas, the southwesterly road leads to Playa Grande, a beach famous among conservationists and surfers alike. By day, the offshore winds create steep and powerful waves, especially at high tide and in front of Hotel Las Tortugas. By night, an ancient cycle continues to unfurl as leatherback sea turtles bearing clutches of eggs follow the ocean currents back to their birthplace.

Since 1991 Playa Grande has been part of the Parque Nacional Marino Las Baulas de Guanacaste (p262), which bars beachfront development to ensure that one of the most important leatherback nesting areas in the world is preserved for future generations. However, this is not to say that Playa Grande is pristine. The park's official boundary ends 50m from the high-tide line, and government agencies have been lax about permitting real-estate development that is technically within the boundaries of the park. In 2007 the Supreme Court of Costa Rica restated a 2005 moratorium on all construction within park boundaries; meanwhile, conservation groups are lobbying to prevent development near the central beach, where turtles can still nest undisturbed by lights and the presence of development. Although Playa Grande does have a few accommodations near the beach, they are set back from the shoreline and carefully managed to ensure that ambient light is kept to a minimum.

Activities

Surfing is most people's motivation for coming to Playa Grande, and if you don't surf, there are people who will happily teach you.

Frijoles Locos (☎ 2652-9235; www.frijoleslocos.com; 9am-5pm) On the road into town, the friendly Ian and Corynne Bean rent and sell surfboards (US$15 to US$20 per day), give lessons (US$45 for one person, US$60 for two people), and offer massage therapy and naturopathic treatments.

Matos Films Surf Store (☎ 2652-9227; www.matosfilms.com; 8am-7pm) This Uruguayan-run surf shop rents surfboards (US$20 per day) and has free internet access for customers. You can even do a weekly rental arrangement for US$100 per week, swapping out boards from their quiver as often as you like.

Playa Grande Surf Camp (☎ 2653-1074; www.playagrandesurfcamp.com) Gerry and his cohorts will rent you short or long boards (US$20 per day), and show you how to ride 'em.

Sleeping & Eating

Hotels are well signposted from the main road into Playa Grande. It's a good idea to bring a flashlight for walking around at night, as the roads are necessarily dark (and uneven).

Playa Grande Surf Camp (☎ 2653-1074; www.playagrandesurfcamp.com; r per person with/without air-con US$25/15; P) Next to El Manglar is this great budget option, run by surfing brothers Gerry and Patrick. The three A-frame *cabinas* with thatch roofs and two stilt *cabinas* (each sleeps four) with private hammock-strung porches, are just steps from the beach. Plus there's surf lessons and board rentals.

El Manglar (☎ 2653-0952; www.hotel-manglar.com; d standard/deluxe/apt US$40/70/120; P) Near the southern end of the beach is this funky, friendly spot with brightly painted stuccoed rooms and lush, tropical grounds. Standard rooms have private cold showers, while deluxe rooms have hot water and slightly more space. The apartment has full kitchen and upstairs loft that's perfect for kids.

Playa Grande Inn (☎ 2653-0719; www.playagrandeinn.com; r/ste US$58/87; P) Around the corner from the Rip Jack Inn, air-conditioned rooms at this laidback place are decked out with polished stained-wood floors, ceilings and walls, and have cable TV and hot water. There's also a cozy bar area and small pool.

Villa Baula (☎ 2653-0644/493; www.hotelvillabaula.com; d/tr US$60/75, bungalows with/without air-con US$110/100; P) Across from the estuary near the southern end of the beach, this rustic beachfront hotel emits virtually no ambient light at night. All rooms come with hot-water bathroom, while more expensive bungalows have air-con and optional kitchen. There's an attractive pool, and this end of the beach is much quieter as it's further from the best surfing.

Rip Jack Inn (☎ 2653-0480; www.ripjackinn.com; d/cabin US$70/90; P) Just south of Hotel Las Tortugas on the inland road, this comfy, convivial inn has a handful of clean, modern rooms with bathroom and air-con. There's also a beautiful open-air bar-restaurant with stunning ocean views, plus regular yoga classes on offer.

our pick **La Marejada Hotel** (☎ 2653-0594, in USA & Canada 800-559-3415; www.lamarejada.com; r incl breakfast US$70) Hidden behind a bamboo fence, this stylish boutique hotel is the friendliest, most relaxing hotel in Playa Grande. The eight elegantly understated rooms have air-con, a queen bed, bathroom with hot water, and a shared balcony overlooking the lush gardens and pool. The lovely owners, Carli and Gail, are friendly and attentive to your every need. A palm-shaded common area is strung with hammocks and leads to Marbar restaurant, famous for its breakfast treats such as eggs Benedict and French toast. And after a hard day of surfing, treat yourself to an in-house massage.

Hotel Las Tortugas (☎ 2653-0423; www.lastortugashotel.com; d/ste US$95/135, apt US$35-100; P) The owner of this hotel, Louis Wilson, is a local hero as he was instrumental in helping to designate Playa Grande as a national park. Although his hotel is near the beach, it was carefully designed to keep ambient light away from the nesting area, and to block light from development to the north. Eleven spacious rooms have air-con and hot-water bathroom, plus thick walls and small windows to enable daytime sleep after a night of turtle-watching. The hotel also has two apartments with kitchens for rent up the hill. Surfboards, body boards, sea kayaks, snorkels and horses can be rented. There's a pool, Jacuzzi and a popular restaurant, and tours can be arranged.

Una Ola (☎ 2653-2682, in USA & Canada 888-958-7873; www.unaola.com; r US$100;) Throw away your 'surf camp' clichés. Una Ola ('one wave' – we love the name) has redefined the scene with boutique chic. The intimate resort has eight whitewashed rooms in minimalist design, some with king-sized bed. Resort amenities include a communal kitchen with honor bar, large pool and a high-tech media entertainment room. For a serious surf vacation, consider the seven-night package (US$945 per person for a double) that includes transportation to and from the Liberia airport, lodging, breakfast, surf lessons, and surfboard and bike rentals.

Hotel Bula Bula (☎ 2653-0975; www.hotelbulabula.com; r incl breakfast US$120;) A few hundred meters inland near the Tamarindo estuary is this recommended hotel, owned by two US expats (one of whom is a professional chef). The rooms are exquisite, with full amenities and original artwork on all the walls, and the landscaped grounds and free-form pool are perfect for relaxing after a hard day of surfing. But one of the biggest draws is The Great Waltini's (dishes US$9 to US$16), the onsite restaurant serving only the freshest local seafood and some truly excellent grilled meats.

Kike's Place (☎ 2653-0834; www.kikesplace.com; breakfast, lunch & dinner) On the road into town, take note of Kike's (pronounced 'kee-kays'), the friendly local bar and restaurant where you can shoot some pool, eat some *ceviche* and let your hair down.

Aside from eating at the hotels, try tasty **Los Malinches** (☎ 2653-0236; mains ₡2600-5000; 8am-9pm Mon-Sat), where you can dine on good, fresh seafood underneath a giant *palapa*. Next door, the **Supermercado** (7:30am-noon & 3-7pm Mon-Sat) sells produce, booze and other staples.

Getting There & Away

There are no buses to Playa Grande. You can drive to Huacas and then take the paved road to Matapalo, followed by a rough dirt road to Playa Grande. If you don't have your own car and are staying in Playa Grande, call ahead and the hotel owners can arrange pickup from the Matapalo turnoff (where the bus from San José can drop you off).

Alternatively, you can cut your travel time in half by catching a boat across the estuary from Tamarindo to the southern end of Playa Grande (around ₡650 per person).

PARQUE NACIONAL MARINO LAS BAULAS DE GUANACASTE

Playa Grande is considered one of the most important nesting sites in the entire world for the *baula* (leatherback turtle). In 1991 the entire beach and adjacent land (379 hectares), along with 220 sq km of ocean, was designated as **Las Baulas** national marine park. This government act followed a 15-year battle between conservationists and various self-motivated parties, including poachers, developers and tour operators.

However, the actual impetus for the creation of the national park came from the owner of the Hotel Las Tortugas (see p261). In fact, the sole stipulation for designating Playa Grande as a protected area was that the beach needed to generate revenue based on tourism. Fortunately, tourists perennially pay the park fees to watch the turtles nest, and local guides ensure that the beach (and their economic livelihood) stays intact.

The ecosystem of the park is primarily composed of mangrove swamp, and it's possible to find here all of the six mangrove species native to Costa Rica. This habitat is ideal for caiman and crocodile, as well as numerous bird species, including the beautiful roseate spoonbill. Other creatures to look for when visiting are howler monkey, raccoon, coati, otter and a variety of crab. But, as is to be expected, the main attraction is the nesting of the world's largest species of turtle, which can weigh in excess of 400kg. Nesting season is from October to March, and it's fairly common for three or four leatherbacks to lay their eggs here on any given night.

The leatherback is critically endangered from overhunting, a lack of protected nesting sights and coastal overdevelopment (beachside lights disorient the turtles when they come up to nest). Despite increased conservation efforts, fewer and fewer leatherbacks are nesting on Playa Grande each year. In 2004 an all-time low of 46 leatherbacks visited the beach, which was a vast departure from the estimated 1000 turtles that nested here in the 1990s. While it's easy to point fingers at developers in Tamarindo, park rangers attribute the decline in nesting turtles to longline commercial fishing, though the construction of high-rise apartments and beachside fast-food joints certainly isn't helping.

In an effort to protect the dwindling leatherback population, park rangers collect the eggs daily and incubate them to increase their chances of survival. Even so, sea turtles must hatch on the beach and enter the water by themselves, otherwise memory imprinting does not occur, and the hatchlings will never return to their birthplace to nest. It's estimated that only 10% of hatchlings will survive to adulthood, though leatherbacks can live more than 50 years, and females can lay multiple clutches of eggs during a single nesting season.

During the day, the beach is free and open to all, which is a good thing as the breaks off Playa Grande are fast, steep and consistent. During the nighttime, however, it is only possible to visit the beach on a guided tour, which is also a good thing as it ensures that the nesting cycles of the leatherback will continue unhindered.

Turtle-Watching

The **park office** (☎ 2653-0470; admission US$10, with guided tour US$25; 🕑 8am-noon & 1-5pm) is by the northern entrance to Playa Grande. Reservations for turtle-watching can be made up to seven days in advance, and they're highly recommended as there is a limited number of places each evening. If you phone ahead, you will be promised a spot within a week, though there is usually a vacancy within a day or two. You can also show up in the evening as there are frequent no-shows, though this is less likely on weekends and during the busy winter holiday season.

Many hotels and tourist agencies in Tamarindo can book tours that include transportation to and from Playa Grande, admission to the park and the guided tour. The whole package costs about US$45. If you don't have your own transportation, this is the best way to go. When making a reservation, passport numbers and full names are required as this prevents big hotels in Tamarindo from reserving blocks for their guests.

The show kicks off anytime from 9pm to as late as 2am, though there is no guarantee that you will see a turtle – this is nature, not the San Diego Zoo. This also means that you might only have to wait for 10 minutes before a turtle shows up, or you could be there for five hours. A small stand at the exhibit sells snacks and sodas, but bring a (thick) book or a deck of cards for entertainment. It could be a very long night – but well worth it.

To minimize the impact of viewing the turtles, guidelines for the tours are very strict; see boxed text, below. Tourists are not allowed on the beach until the turtles have made it to dry sand. Guards with two-way radios are posted on the beach and they will alert your guide when a turtle is ready for its close-up. As a group, you will be accompanied by a guide to a designated viewing area, though photography, filming or lights of any kind are *not* allowed. Over the span of one to two hours, you can watch as the turtle digs its nest, lays about 150 silver shiny eggs and then buries them in the sand (while grunting and groaning the whole time).

If you're looking for a worthwhile volunteer project, the park office usually accepts volunteers to help monitor and catalog each nesting.

PLAYA TAMARINDO

Well, they don't call it Tamagringo for nothing. Call it what you will, but Tamarindo's long status as Costa Rica's top surf and party destination has made it the first and last stop for many tourists and expats. This is

CAMERA-SHY

A picture might be worth a thousand words, but sometimes it's better to say nothing at all. Take, for instance, the miracle of birth – who would want to share that with random gawkers and paparazzi? This is not to poke fun at a serious situation. One of the reasons why turtles no longer nest on Playa Tamarindo is that they're extremely sensitive to ambient light. You can see why a string of beachside bars might deter a turtle from laying her clutch of eggs on that particular beach. So you'll understand why flash photography is strictly forbidden at the beaches where endangered turtles still do return to nest.

When you take a turtle tour, the rangers will politely ask that you refrain from photographing or filming the turtles, but we'd like to underscore the fact that by experiencing it in the moment and not committing it to film, you are helping to maintain a fragile cycle that has renewed itself continually for millions of years.

the most developed beach on the peninsula with no shortage of hotels, bars, restaurants, strip malls and pricey condos. After years of unchecked development, the pace is finally slowing down, partly because of the Great Recession and partly thanks to the work of concerned residents (see boxed text, p266). Tamarindo is slowly recapturing its Tico roots.

Despite having a party-town reputation, Tamarindo is more than just drinking and surfing. It forms a part of the Parque Nacional Marino Las Baulas de Guanacaste (p262). The beach and surf retain their inherent allure for kids and adults alike. Foodies will find some of the best restaurants in the country. Families and students will appreciate that fierce competition has kept prices reasonably low. And Tamarindo's central location makes it a great base for exploring the rest of the peninsula. So drop your pretensions and come on down, because there's plenty to see and do here.

Orientation

Once a sleepy fishing village that turned into a little surf town, Tamarindo now channels the spirit of rush hour in southern California on the weekends, when traffic gridlocks along the two-lane main drag. Just before the main street dead-ends at the southeastern end of the beach, a road branches off to the left and passes the new Plaza Conchal mall. If you turn left again where that road forms a Y, you'll find several hotels along the dirt road. Turn right and you'll be headed for Playa Langosta, where the coast is crowded with condos and villas, a casino resort and a couple of exquisite little inns.

Amazingly, even though Tamarindo is possessed of frozen yogurt, yoga studios and air-conditioned malls, there's no gas station. For that, you'll have to drive 15 paved kilometers to Huacas – from Tamarindo, make a left at the intersection in Villareal, drive to Huacas, hang a right and go up the hill. The gas station is 4km up the road, on the right.

Information

Tourist information is available from any of the tour operators in town, or your hotel. Keep up on the local happenings by picking up a copy of the *Tamarindo News* – it's available all over town or online at www.tamarindo news.com.

BAC San José (☎ 2653-1617; Plaza Conchal; ⏰ 8:30am-3:30pm) Has an ATM and exchanges US dollars and traveler's checks.

Backwash Laundry (per kg ₡1000; ⏰ 8am-8pm Mon-Sat) Get your filthy unmentionables washed, dried and folded. Most hotels also offer laundry service.

Banco de Costa Rica (Plaza Conchal) 24-hour ATM.

Banco Nacional 24-hour ATM.

Coastal Emergency Medical Service (☎ 2653-0611/1974; ⏰ 24hr) It does house calls! Can you say that about your hometown doc?

Cyber Bakanos (⏰ 9am-10pm) On the 2nd floor above a pizza shop, offers high speed internet connections and international phone calls.

HSBC 24-hour ATM.

Internet Café del Mar (☎ 2653-1740; www.cafedel marinternet.com; per hr ₡800; ⏰ 8:30am-9pm)

Jaime Peligro (☎ 8820-9004; ⏰ 9am-6pm Mon-Sat, 10am-3pm Sun) A local spot for new and used foreign-language books and the best Central American CDs and DVDs.

Dangers & Annoyances

The tourist invasion has left Tamarindo with a growing drug and prostitution problem. Vendors openly ply their wares (and women) on the main road by the rotunda, and some bars can get rough at closing time. Theft is a problem. Leave your hotel room locked, use room safes and don't leave valuables on the beach. If you're driving, never leave anything in your car.

In March 2005 an Australian man vanished from a Tamarindo beach and was later found dead. In October 2009 British journalist Michael Dixon walked out of his Tamarindo hotel room and was never seen again. In December 2009 a 67-year-old American was found strangled to death in nearby Playa Potrero. Their cases have not been solved. We're not telling this to alarm you, but as a reminder: although Costa Rica is by far the safest country in Central America, it's important to keep your wits about you. Travel in pairs. If you're alone, tell somebody where you're going. Tamarindo is a party town; have fun, but don't get so wasted that you become vulnerable to crime or accident. Just common-sense precautions that you should practice anywhere in the world.

Activities

CYCLING

The local expert on mountain biking, distance cycling, bike tours and repairs is **Blue Trailz**

(☎ 2653-0221; www.bluetrailz.com; 🕓 7am-7pm Mon-Sat). And if mountain biking ain't your thing, you can also rent a beach cruiser (two hours US$10, all day US$20).

DIVING

There is only one dive shop in Tamarindo, and we don't recommend it due to (from our experience) poor customer service and old equipment. You're better off diving in Playa del Coco (p247) or Playa Sámara (p287).

GOLF

Just outside Tamarindo, near the village of San José de Pinilla, lies a residential development project that boasts one of the finest golf courses in Central America. **Hacienda Pinilla** (☎ 2680-3000; www.haciendapinilla.com) has a 7km par-72 course that was designed by noted architect Mike Young. Greens fees are US$125/165 per person during the low/high season. If you just want to practice your skills, head to Tamarindo Diria's **driving range**, located by the Tamarindo airstrip.

SAILING

For sunset and day-long sailing excursions, book in advance by phone or online with **Blue Dolphin Sailing** (☎ 2653-0867, 8842-3204; www.sailbluedolphin.com). Reader-recommended trips on Captain Jeff's catamaran include a 4½ hour snorkel and sunset sail (US$75/38 per adult/child under 12) with gear, open bar and snacks.

PENÍNSULA DE NICOYA

SKATEBOARDING

If you happen to have your deck with you, there's a fun little one-bowl **skate park** behind the Voodoo Lounge.

SPORTFISHING

There are more than 30 fishing outfitters offering a variety of tour packages. Prices vary wildly depending on boat size and other factors, but expect to pay at least US$400 for a half-day tour. Just about any tour office can help you book a fishing trip, or look for flyers around town. One highly recommended resource is Diego Caicedo of **Tamarindo Bay Tours** (☎ 8821-9978; tamarindobaytours@hotmail.com). With more than 20 years of experience, Diego is a walking wiki of the Tamarindo fishing scene. He knows every boat and captain in town and will help you pick the perfect tour to fit your needs without trying to oversell. He'll even arrange to cook your catch.

SURFING

The most popular wave in Tamarindo is a medium-sized right that breaks directly in front of the Tamarindo Diria hotel. The waters here are full of virgin surfers learning to pop up, most of whom can't help but play aquatic bumper cars. There is also a good left that's fed by the river mouth, though be advised that crocodiles are occasionally sighted here, particularly when the tide is rising (which is, coincidentally, the best time to surf). You'll have to get a local to let you in on some of their favorite spots, as we're not going to ruin it for them.

More advanced surfers will appreciate the bigger, faster and less crowded waves at **Playa Langosta** (on the other side of the point), **Playas Avellanas** and **Negra** (p271) and **Junquillal** (p274) to the south, and **Playa Grande** (p260) to the north. Note that the best months for surfing coincide with the rainy season.

A number of surf schools and tour operators line the main stretch of the road in Tamarindo. Surf lessons hover at around US$40 for 1½ to two hours, and most operators will let you keep the board for a few hours beyond that to practice. All outfits can organize day-long and multiday excursions to popular breaks, rent equipment and give surf lessons.

Banana Surf Club (☎ 2653-0130/2463; www.bananasurfclub.com; 🕑 8am-6pm) This Argentine-run outfit has fair prices on new and used boards.

Blue Trailz (☎ 2653-0114; rasurfshop@yahoo.com; 🕑 7am-7pm) One of the largest and best shops in town, it offers lessons and trips and rents surfboards, bodyboards and skimboards.

Costa Rica Surf Club (☎ 2653-1270; www.costaricasurfclub.com; 🕑 8am-8pm Mon-Sat, 9am-7pm Sun) Two locations in town offering rentals, lessons, repairs and sales. The main location by Sharky's even has a falafel stand.

Witch's Rock Surf Camp (☎ 2653-0239; www.witchsrocksurfcamp.com; 🕑 8am-8pm) Board rentals, surf camps, lessons and regular excursions to Witch's Rock and Ollie's Point are available, though they're pricey. There are beachside accommodations for surfers who sign up for multiday packages.

YOGA

Yoga and pilates **classes** (☎ 8346-8005; per hr US$15) are offered every morning and some

SAVING TAMARINDO

The price of blithely disregarding the pressure on Tamarindo's environment is coming due. At the end of 2007 Playa Tamarindo lost its Bandera Azul Ecológica (Ecological Blue Flag) designation, which marked it as a community with high water quality, safety and environmental responsibility. Frankly, it was about time the flag got pulled, as it was an open secret that the water quality had been deteriorating.

Tamarindo was teetering on the brink of sustainability. The levels of fecal contamination were so high that visitors were warned against swimming or surfing. Losing the Bandera Azul, and watching the alarming spate of high-density construction rising in the middle of tiny Tamarindo sparked concerned residents and businesses into action. The Asociación Pro Mejoras de Playa Tamarindo and the Save Tamarindo campaign appealed for an urban development plan to curb high-density development and require stricter government regulation. The government's National Water Laboratory, Water Supply and Sewerage (AyA) cited more than 80 businesses and forced them to clean up their act.

So far, their efforts seem to be working. In December 2009 AyA gave Tamarindo's beaches a clean bill of health. At the time of writing, Tamarindo was still awaiting the return of its Bandera Azul.

evenings in the Bar 1 building. Call for the latest schedule.

Courses

Use your vacation time wisely by learning to speak Spanish. There are several language schools in Tamarindo. All charge about US$420 for a week-long intensive course (beginner to advanced) including 'homestay' accommodations with a Tico family. Most schools offer multiple-week discounts, and 'Spanish & Surf' packages that include language lessons, surf classes, accommodations and board rentals for about US$610 per week.

Coastal Spanish Institute (☎ 8878-6106; www.coastalspanish.com)

Wayra (☎ 2653-0359; www.spanish-wayra.co.cr)

Tours

Boat tours, snorkeling trips and scooter rentals can be arranged through the various tour agencies in town. Many also rent equipment. The most reputable ones include the following:

Hightide Aventuras (☎ 2653-0108; www.tamarindoaventuras.com; scooters per 4hr US$25, dirt bikes per 4hr US$34) Also rents water-sports equipment, including kayaks, snorkeling gear and surfboards.

Papagayo Excursions (☎ 2653-0254; www.papagayoexcursions.com) The longest running outfitter in town organizes a variety of tours, including visits to turtle-nesting sites.

Sleeping

The rates given are high-season rates; low-season rates can be about 25% to 40% lower.

HOSTELS

The number of hostels in Tamarindo has quadrupled in recent years. Often, these so-called 'hostels' are nothing more than a couple of bunk beds thrown into a scary back room of a private home or business.

Coral Reef Hostel (☎ 2653-0291; dm US$6, r without bathroom per person US$10; P 💻 📶) The 10 rooms here are clean and fairly basic. Though it's on a noisy section of the road, the guys running the place are friendly and offer a variety of services, such as surfboard rental, internet access and a BBQ area.

La Botella de Leche (☎ 2653-0189; labotelladeleche@racsa.co.cr; dm with bathroom US$12, s/d US$26/36; P ❄ 💻 📶) With a relaxed vibe and over-the-top cow theme, this Argentine-run spot is highly recommended for its warm and attentive management, fully air-conditioned rooms and dormitories, and a quiet location at the eastern edge of town. Facilities include a shared kitchen, surfboard racks, hammocks and a TV lounge.

Beach House Tamarindo (☎ 2653-2848; www.beachhousetamarindo.com; dm incl breakfast US$13; P 💻 📶) The only hostel located directly on the beach, this funky new resort opened in late 2009 and shows a lot of potential. The small rooms are simple but clean, all with lockers and fans. There's a big communal kitchen, living room, patio, balcony, private beach access and free breakfast.

our pick **Tamarindo Backpackers** (☎ 2653-4545; www.tamarindobackpackers.com; dm US$15, r per person US$20; P ❄ 💻 📶 🏊) Hidden down a quiet cul-de-sac in a wooded, residential neighborhood, you'll find our favorite hostel in Tamarindo. Part of the Costa Rica Hostel Network, this intimate, all-star backpacker spot in a gorgeous yellow hacienda is big enough to make new friends, but small enough to feel more like a home. The common area has a large full-stocked shared kitchen, TV, computers and free coffee all day. Dorm and private rooms are clean and comfy, with plenty of storage space (the private room upstairs is the nicest for couples). Outside you'll find lovely tropical gardens, a small pool and hammocks, all surrounded by woods where you'll hear howler monkeys every morning.

BUDGET

We constantly receive complaints about Tamarindo hotels, so choose wisely. Unless otherwise noted, the budget hotels listed here have cold water only.

Chocolate Hotel & Hostel (☎ 2653-1311; www.thechocolatehotel.com; dm US$15, s/d US$60/75; ❄ 💻 📶 🏊) Up the same road as the 'Milk Bottle' hostel, this sweet little hotel has several well-appointed rooms done up in dark wood and terra-cotta–tiled floors, with orthopedic mattresses, fully equipped kitchen and hot-water bathroom. Rooms upstairs have higher ceilings and get more light, but all are elegant and comfortable and surround the garden-fringed pool.

Hotel Mono Loco (☎ 2653-0238; elmonoloco@racsa.co.cr; d with fan/air-con US$35/60; ❄ 🏊) This quiet hotel is on the road into Playa Langosta, so you can definitely sleep soundly at night. The hotel itself is a yellow-stucco and thatched-roof building that surrounds a beautifully landscaped pool. Bright and airy rooms have cable TV and optional air-con. The onsite restaurant serves reasonably priced Costa Rican fare all day long.

Villas Macondo (☎ 2653-0812; www.villasmacondo.com; s/d/tr US$35/40/50, with air-con US$60/65/75, 2-/4-person apt US$105/145, extra person US$10; P) Although it's only 200m from the beach, this German-run establishment is an oasis of serenity in an otherwise frenzied town – it's also one of the best deals around. Beautiful modern villas with private hot showers and hammock-strung patios surround a solar-heated pool and tropical garden, while larger apartments are equipped with cable TV, a full kitchen and air-con, which makes it ideal for families.

MIDRANGE

All the following hotels have rooms with hot-water bathroom.

Cabinas Marielos (☎ 2653-0141; www.cabinasmarieloscr.com; r US$40-90; P) One of the best deals in town, this underrated property has a variety of *cabinas* to fit every budget. All rooms have firm beds, a colorful patio and share a communal kitchen. Some rooms face the lush garden, and the place is decorated with Sarchi-style accents. It's one of the few remaining Tico-owned hotels in town. Owner Marielos, a retired university professor known as 'La Tica,' has owned the property since 1978, when she paid a whopping US$100 for the land!

Hotel La Laguna del Cocodrilo (☎ 2653-0255; www.lalagunadelcocodrilo.com; d US$68-79, ste US$130; P) A beachfront location blesses this charming French-owned hotel, with luxurious, well-kept rooms overlooking either the shady grounds or the ocean and estuary. Adjacent to a crocodile-filled lagoon (hence the name), the hotel has a private trail leading to the beach. There's also a restaurant specializing in seafood, but lovers of pastry will be most delighted with the sublime items from the onsite French bakery.

La Palapa (☎ 2653-0362; lapalapatamarindo.com; s/d/tr/q US$75/85/95/105; P) Despite the attached bar-restaurant being one of the most popular places for a sunset cocktail, this little beachfront hotel is surprisingly quiet and secluded. All six stylish rooms have loft beds, ocean views and big-screen TV with DVD player, and the terra-cotta–tiled floors lead to shaded terraces directly on the beach. Though it's only 20m from the roundabout, the hotel's size makes it feel intimate and relaxed.

our pick **Hotel Arco Iris** (☎ 2653-0330; www.hotelarcoiris.com; d standard/deluxe incl breakfast US$99/109; P) A cluster of garden bungalows and deluxe rooms makes up this wonderfully reclusive boutique hotel. Richard, the new US owner, has completely remodeled and transformed the property. The contemporary rooms have wonderful touches such as bamboo ceiling and bathroom with slate walls, plus cable TV, fridge, minibar, hair dryer and safe. Deluxe rooms are larger and sleep up to four. The gorgeous pool and patio garden is home to one of the best restaurants in town, Seasons by Shlomy (p270).

TOP END

All hotels can arrange tours in the area, and all accept credit cards.

Best Western Tamarindo Vista Villas (☎ 2653-0114; www.tamarindovistavillas.com; r US$101-135; ste US$179-229; P) Perched on a hill overlooking the entrance to Tamarindo, this hotel is one of the most popular places in town for well-to-do travelers, and the 33 rooms and suites have all the amenities (and institutionalized blandness) you associate with the Best Western chain. But, it does have an ocean-view pool, the popular Monkey Bar, a dive shop, the Robert August Surf Shop and a tour desk.

Hotel Pasatiempo (☎ 2653-0096; www.hotelpasatiempo.com; d US$115-127, ste US$150, additional person US$15; P) This well-established Tamarindo landmark is known for its popular live-music nights at the bar-restaurant, though it's also a great place to stay. Rooms are awash in tropical-themed murals, and have comfortable beds, modern bathroom, air-con and a private hammock-strung patio. Suites have a living room with fold-out couch, which is perfect if you're traveling with the offspring. Though breakfast isn't included, there's free coffee and pastries offered in the morning.

El Jardín del Edén (☎ 2653-0137; www.jardindeleden.com; d/apt/ste incl breakfast from US$152/186/249; P) On a hill overlooking Tamarindo, this luxurious French-run hotel has 36 exquisite rooms, each with a sitting area and private patio or balcony (and some of Tamarindo's best views). Rooms are gorgeously designed according to one of four themes: Balinese, Japanese, African and Tunisian. There are also two apartments (sleeping five) with a kitchenette, plus a Jacuzzi, pool with a swim-up bar, and a Mediterranean-inspired bar-restaurant.

Villa Alegre B&B (☎ 2653-0270; www.villaalegrecostarica.com; r US$170-185, villas US$230, all incl breakfast; P) This beachside B&B in nearby Playa Langosta has five rooms of various sizes, each decorated with memorabilia from the owners' world travels (you can choose between the Caribbean, USA, California, Guatemala or Mexico rooms). Or stay in the Japan or Russia villas, which are equipped with a full kitchen. There's an honor bar, a comfortable guest living room and plenty of games for children. Bounteous breakfasts are served on the deck, and your hosts Barry and Suzie make their home as sunny and welcoming as they are.

our pick **Hotel Capitán Suizo** (☎ 2653-0075; www.hotelcapitansuizo.com; r with/without air-con US$210/190, bungalows with/without air-con US$290/250, additional person US$40, all incl breakfast; P) On the southern end of the beach is this Swiss-run hotel, which belongs to the group of Small Distinctive Hotels of Costa Rica. The 22 rooms and seven larger, thatched-roof bungalows are decorated with natural stone floors, polished hardwoods and soft, pastel hues. The entire complex is centered on a free-form pool that's shaded by expansive gardens, and all units are just steps from a quiet strip of sand. There's also a six-person beachfront apartment (US$525). Tico charm combined with impeccable Swiss hospitality makes this our favorite boutique accomodations in Tamarindo.

Sueño del Mar B&B (☎ 2653-0284; www.sueno-del-mar.com; d US$195-295, ste US$220-240; P) This stunning Spanish-style *posada* (country-style inn) in nearby Playa Langosta is run by lovely innkeepers Ashton and Tui, and decorated with handcrafted rocking chairs, hammocks and a cozy living room that's perfect for relaxing with the other guests. The six rooms have four-poster beds, artfully placed crafts and open-air garden showers, while the romantic honeymoon suite has a wraparound window with sea views. There's private beach access beyond the pool and tropical garden, and a priceless, pervasive atmosphere of seclusion and beauty…so, no children under 12 allowed.

Eating

You can't have sophisticated modern living without boutique gourmet eateries, so it's unsurprising that Tamarindo has some of the best restaurants in Costa Rica. But be prepared to pay – a cheap meal in this town is about as common as a nesting turtle.

If you're self-catering, the **Super 2001** (7am-9:30pm Mon-Sat, 8am-8:30pm Sun) and **Super Compro** (8am-9pm Mon-Sun) are well stocked with international groceries.

Beach Burger (☎ 2653-2574; burger.beach@gmail.com; items ₡1000-2000; 24 hr) The only 24/7 eatery in Tamarindo, this Colombian-run shack has burgers, subs, hot dogs, *arepas* (corn pancakes) and other hangover-curing treats.

Smilin' Dog Taco Stop (☎ 2653-1370; mains ₡1500-3900; 11:30am-10pm Mon-Sat) Those hankering for Mexican grub will appreciate the quality of offerings at this popular eatery, while shoestringers will revel in the generous portions and low prices.

Bar Nogui (☎ 2653-0029; mains ₡1580-14,000; 11am-11pm) This beachside restaurant offers upscale *casados* (set meals) with grilled fish, mixed meats and unbelievable shrimp and lobster. It's consistently popular with locals and tourists alike, so come early for dinner or be prepared to wait at the bar for a couple of Imperiales with the rowdy regulars.

Sushi Club (☎ 2653 0082; sushi & rolls ₡2200-5000; 5-10pm) We are real sushi snobs, so trust us when we say: this is the best sushi restaurant in Tamarindo. The Argentine-run, intimate (just four tables), open-air restaurant is located poolside at the boutique Hotel Luna Llena. The fresh sushi is divine and reasonably priced, including specials like the 40-piece 'Love Boat' of rolls, nigri and sashimi. With cool, chill-out music and atmosphere and superb service, this is a must for any sushi-lover.

Eat@Joe's (☎ 2653-1262; mains ₡2200-5000; 7am-late) The best snack in town is at this US-run surf camp, where you can order the famous 'nachos as big as your ass' (or sushi rolls) while sucking down cold ones on the outdoor deck until 2am.

Elevation Gallery Café (☎ 8302-3590; mains ₡2500-6100; 8am-3pm Wed-Sun) Readers rave about the breakfast and lunch menu at this stylish coffeehouse. Co-owner Lane Patrick is a former Four Seasons chef. His partner Tara, a fashion photographer, runs the attached Raindolls Boutique and shot the amazing 'babes and bowling' photos gracing the walls of this open-plan, contemporary cafe. On Thursday and Friday nights the cafe is transformed into a tapas and wine bar.

Lazy Wave (☎ 2653-0737; meals ₡2700-13,200; 6-10pm Sat-Thu) Dine at a table if you must, but the best place to enjoy your meal and glass of wine is on the covered pavilion, where you can curl up amid pillows in cushy lounge chairs. If you're out to woo that hot thing you met last night, this hip nightspot, built around a huge tree, is a good place to start the evening. There's a solid wine list, good mix of cocktails and Asian- and Euro-influenced *bocas*, as well as a full menu.

La Baula (☎ 2653-1450; mains ₡4400-6300; 5:30-11pm;) By far the best pizza in Tamarindo – this casual open-air restaurant has real wood-fired pizzas, pastas and other Italian fare. It's also one of the most family-friendly restaurants in town, with a nice playground to keep the kids entertained.

El Coconut (☎ 2653-0086; mains ₡4000-24,000; dinner Tue-Sun) Another recommended choice for seafood and pasta dishes. You can get a special dinner at this Norwegian-owned restaurant without having to get formal about it. The ambience is laid-back but elegant, with a tropical flair and a dessert menu that begs you to save room.

Nibbana (☎ 2653-0447; www.nibbana-tamarindo.com; ₡4400-11,000; lunch & dinner;) One of the nicest beachfront dining areas in town, Nibbana has tables scattered underneath the palms. It serves great pizza at lunch, and Tico-flavored continental cuisine, such as shrimp, lemon and basil risotto, or grilled tuna with a fresh mint-and-tomato compote. It also has free wi-fi access.

Restaurante La Vita Bella & Bruno's Pizzeria (☎ 2653-0147; lavitabellacr@yahoo.com; mains ₡4900-9000; lunch & dinner) The amazing sunset ocean views from the 4th-floor location are surpassed only by the delicious Spanish, Italian, Lebanese and Jamaican cuisine. Somehow it works, because owner Tony Ziade is Lebanese-Spanish and raised in Jamaica. The eclectic menu includes sea bass with chimichurri sauce, chicken kebabs, steak, paellas and authentic pizzas.

Dragonfly Bar & Grill (☎ 2653-1506; mains ₡5000-8500; dinner Mon-Sat) Dragonfly is a local favorite, probably not just for its refined menu, but also for its lovely atmosphere in the festive tent-like structure of the dining room. The menu has a Californian bent, featuring fresh items such as pork chop with chipotle-apple chutney and the Thai-style crispy fish cake with curried corn. Linger a while over your wine and perhaps you can also find room for a divine dessert.

our pick **Seasons by Shlomy** (☎ 8368-6983; www.hotelarcoiris.com; mains ₡6600-8500, fixed-price menu ₡14,000; 6-10pm Mon-Sat) Don't leave town without eating here – it may be the best meal you have in Costa Rica. Israeli chef Shlomy serves innovative dishes with Mediterranean accents that change daily depending on the availability of local ingredients. One of our favorite plates was the Pacific yellow seared tuna in a chili marinade and honey glaze. Located at Hotel Arco Iris, the understated yet elegant open-air restaurant has indoor seating or romantic poolside tables. The food and service here are simply impeccable. Reservations are recommended.

Carolina's Fine Dining (☎ 2369-6834; mains ₡7700-14,300; 6-11pm Thu-Tue) This is one place worth the splurge. Sophisticated continental cuisine highlights skillfully prepared sauces, tender cuts of meat, delectable fish and an impressive selection of imported wines. To truly appreciate the culinary experience, opt for the five-course tasting menu with a full wine tasting (₡38,000).

Drinking & Entertainment

In Tamarindo, all you really have to do is follow the scene wherever it happens to be on that night. On weekends especially, cruising the main drag has the festive feel of a mini Mardi Gras or spring break. And nearly every bar hosts a ladies' night, when women drink free for two hours.

Bars and clubs in this town come and go as often as the waves. Last season's 'it' nightspot may be out the next, so we can't promise this party place recap will be accurate when you visit. But starting on Friday, head to the Monkey Bar inside the Best Western Tamarindo Vista Villas for the ever-popular ladies' night. Sharky's is the place to be on Saturday, when crowds spill out onto the street for the Ladies' 80's Night. Pacífico is the best bet for dancing on Sunday and ladies' night on Wednesday. On Thursday, reggae night at Babylon is a crazy party on the beach.

Aqua Disco is the only real nightclub in Tamarindo. The best nights for clubbing are Monday for ladies' night, Wednesday for live salsa bands and Friday for after-hours dancing. It also has a sushi lounge upstairs.

For those looking for something a bit tamer, fear not. Nibbana and La Palapa are good beachside spots to have a quiet getting-to-know-you cocktail. La Barra is a popular bar for locals and gringos alike. The classy Bar 1 is a great people-watching spot from its open-air, 3rd-floor lounge at Plaza Tamarindo. Our favorite new place to chill is Le Beach Club, with beds and hammocks on the sand and live DJs on Saturday. There's often live music on the weekends at Voodoo Lounge, which has a great outdoor bar and stage in the back; Tuesday is Latin night.

For the best (nonalcoholic) smoothies, juices and iced coffee, you can't beat **Mandarina** (Plaza Esmeralda; 🕑 8am-6pm), with two locations in town – the larger and better one is at Plaza Esmeralda near the entrance to town.

Cine-Mas (Plaza Tamarindo; adult/child ₡3000/2000; 🕑 9pm, plus 6pm matinee weekends) – get it? – is Tamarindo's first movie theater. The intimate 24-seat cinema screens second run films. It's located below Bar 1.

Getting There & Away

AIR

The airstrip is 3km north of town; a hotel bus is usually on hand to pick up arriving passengers, or you can take a taxi. During high season, Sansa has seven daily flights to and from San José (one way/return US$89/178), while NatureAir has three (US$96/192).

Sansa (☎ 2653-0012) has an office on the main road, and the travel desk at the Tamarindo Diria hotel can book trips on NatureAir. The airstrip belongs to the hotel and all passengers must pay a US$3 departure tax.

BUS

Buses for San José depart from the Empresas Alfaro office behind the Babylon bar. Other buses depart across the street from Zullymar Hostel. It's possible to get to Montezuma or Mal País and Santa Teresa by bus for about ₡5500 total, but it will take all day and multiple changes: take the 5:45am bus to Liberia, bus to Puntarenas, ferry to Playa Naranjo, bus to Cobano and bus to Montezuma or Mal País.

Liberia ₡1200; 2½ hours; departs 13 times per day from 4:30am to 6:30pm.

San José ₡4860; six hours; departs 3:30am and 5:30am. Alternatively, take a bus to Liberia and change for frequent buses to the capital.

Santa Cruz ₡300; 1½ hours; departs 6am, 9am, noon, 2pm, 3pm and 4pm.

CAR & TAXI

By car from Liberia, take Hwy 21 to Belén, then Hwy 155 via Huacas to Tamarindo. If you're coming from the southern peninsula, drive just past Santa Cruz, turn left on the paved road to 27 de Abril, then northwest on a decent dirt road for 19km to Tamarindo. These routes are well signed.

A taxi to or from Santa Cruz costs about ₡11,000, and ₡22,000 to or from Liberia. Alternatively, consider a minibus shuttle service. **Tropical Tours** (☎ 2640-1900) offers door-to-door service to Montezuma and Mal País (US$40 per person, 4½ hours). **Tamarindo Shuttle** (☎ 2653-2727; www.tamarindoshuttle.com) services Liberia (US$18 per person, 1½ hours).

Getting Around

Boats on the northern end of the beach can be hired to cross the estuary for daytime visits to the beach at Playa Grande. The ride is roughly ₡690 per person, depending on the number of people.

Many visitors arrive in rental cars. If you get here by air or bus, you can rent bicycles and dirt bikes in town (see p264). There's no gas station, but you can buy expensive gas from drums at the hardware store near the entrance to town. (It's cheaper to fill up in Santa Cruz or at the gas station in Huacas.) Cars can be rented from **Alamo** (☎ 2653-0727) or **Economy Rent-a-Car** (☎ 2653-0752).

PLAYAS AVELLANAS & NEGRA

These popular **surfing beaches** have some of the best, most consistent waves in the area, made famous in the surf classic *Endless Summer II* (one of the breaks off Avellanas is known as 'Pequeño Hawaii'). The beaches begin 15km south of Tamarindo. To get there from Tamarindo, backtrack 5km to the village of Villareal, and turn right onto the dirt road. This road gets progressively worse and requires a 4WD most times of the year (in the wet season there are three rivers to cross). Though the difficult access keeps the area refreshingly uncrowded, development here is inevitable. But concerned locals have taken steps to create a plan for sustainable growth *before* development has a chance to get out of hand, forming the Association of Playa Avellanas to that end.

Playa Avellanas is a long stretch of white sand backed by mangroves, and Playa Negra, a few kilometers further south, is a darker, caramel-color beach broken up by rocky outcrops. At Avellanas, **Little Hawaii** is a powerful and open-faced right at medium tide, while **Beach Break** barrels at low tide (though the surfing is good any time of day). Playa Negra has a world-class right that barrels, especially with a moderate offshore wind. In between is the community of **Playa Lagartillo**, with a few *cabinas* and *sodas* scattered along the road.

If you're not coming from Tamarindo, head west on the paved highway from Santa Cruz, through 27 de Abril to Paraíso, then follow the signs or ask locals. (This is a confusing area to drive through as road signs sometimes face only one direction.)

While you're at the beach, be absolutely certain that nothing is visible in your car as professional thieves operate in this area, and they will remove your window even for a broken flip-flop or moldy sarong.

The recommended **Avellanas Surf School** (☎ 2652-9042; www.avellanassurfschool.com), near the southern entrance of the beach, has surfboard lessons (US$35) and board rentals (US$15 per day). **Café Playa Negra** (☎ 2652-9351; www.playanegracafe.com; 🕑 7am-9pm) has a laundry service (₡3500 per load) and internet access (₡1000 per hour).

Sleeping & Eating

PLAYA AVELLANAS

The following places to stay and eat are very spread out around Playa Avellanas.

Rancho Iguana Verde (☎ 2652-9045; r without bathroom per person US$10; P) About 50m from the beach on the road toward Playa Negra, these six *cabinas* are a bit dark but reasonably clean, with shared cold-water showers. The owner Josué also runs a great *soda* here, serving up excellent, inexpensive *casados* (set meals).

Casa Surf (☎ 2652-9075; www.casa-surf.com; r without bathroom per person US$12; P) Look for the 'Casa Surf' across from Cabinas Las Olas, and pull over – if not for espresso and yummy banana bread, then for a clean, quiet place to stay. Run lovingly by Giovanni and Eve, a Tico-Swiss surfer couple, this place has five simple rooms with shared bathroom and a full kitchen. They also offer surfboard and bike rentals (US$10 per day), surf lessons (US$30), language classes (US$12 per hour) and professional board repair. The bakery is

WHAT TO DO IF YOU'RE CAUGHT IN A RIPTIDE

Riptides account for the majority of ocean drownings, though a simple understanding of how these currents behave can save your life. Rip currents are formed when excess water brought to shore by waves returns to the sea in a rapidly moving depression in the ocean floor. They are comprised of three parts: the feeder current, the neck and the head.

The feeder current consists of rapidly moving water that parallels the shore, though it's not always visible from the beach. When this water reaches a channel, it switches direction and flows out to sea, forming the neck of the rip. This is the fastest-moving part of the riptide, and can carry swimmers out to sea at a speed of up to 10km/h. The head of the riptide occurs past the breakers where the current quickly dissipates.

If you find yourself caught in a riptide, immediately call for help as you only have a few seconds before being swept out to sea. However, it's important to conserve your energy and not to fight the current – this is the principal cause of drownings. It's almost impossible to swim directly back to shore. Instead, try one of two methods for escaping a rip. The first is to tread water and let yourself be swept out past the breakers. Once you're in the head of the rip, you can swim out of the channel and ride the waves back to shore. Or you can swim parallel or diagonally to the shore until you're out of the channel.

Rip currents usually occur on beaches that have strong surf, though temporary rips can occur anywhere, especially when there is an offshore storm or during low tide. Fortunately, there are indicators, such as the brownish color on the surface of the water that is caused by swept-up sand and debris. Also look for surface flattening, which occurs when the water enters a depression in the ocean floor and rushes back out to sea. If you're ever in doubt about the safety of a beach, inquire locally about swimming conditions.

Remember, rips are fairly survivable as long as you relax, don't panic and conserve your energy.

open in high season only, but breakfast and dinner are available for guests year-round. And as Eve is a vegetarian, you'll find plenty of meat-free choices.

Las Avellanas Villas (2652-9212; www.lasavellanasvillas.com; d/tr/q US$65/75/85; P) Stunningly designed by Costa Rican architect Victor Cañas, these four *casitas* (cottages) are covetable as permanent residences. With an aesthetic balancing of the interior environment with the exterior, they have sunken stone floors crossed by wooden bridges, open-air showers, and large windows looking out on front and back terraces. The *casitas* have full kitchens, but dinner is available, and the grounds are just 300m from the beach.

Mauna Loa Surf Resort (2652-9012; www.hotelmaunaloa.com; d US$70; P) This pleasant Italian-run spot is a great place for families, with a secure location that's a straight shot to the beach. Paths lead from the pool area through a well-tended garden, and the cute bungalows have orthopedic beds and hammocks hanging on the terraces.

Cabinas Las Olas (2652-9315; www.cabinaslasolas.co.cr; s/d/tr US$81/93/105; P) On the road from San José de Pinilla into Avellanas, this pleasant hotel is set on spacious grounds only 200m from the beach. Ten airy, individual bungalows have shiny woodwork, stone detailing, hot-water showers and private decks. There's a restaurant, and a specially built boardwalk leads through the mangroves down to the beach (good for wildlife-spotting). Kayaks and surfing gear are available for hire.

Lola's on the Beach (2652-9097; meals ₡5500-11,000; lunch & dinner Tue-Sun) Lola's is the place to hang out, in low-slung plank chairs on a palm-fringed stretch of Avellanas sand, if the water is looking a bit glassy. Try the amazing *poke* (Hawaiian raw-fish salad) or green papaya salad with a beer.

PLAYA NEGRA

In Playa Negra there is a variety of surfer-oriented places.

Kontiki (2652-9117; www.kontikiplayanegra.com; dm US$10;) Along the road from Avellanas, this low-key Peruvian-run place has a rambling collection of tree-house dorms on stilts that are frequented by both surfers and howlers. In the middle of it all is a rickety pavilion where guests hang out in hammocks and benches. There's a small restaurant serving up traditional Peruvian dishes.

Aloha Amigos (2652-9023; r with/without bathroom from US$25/15; P) Friendly, self-described 'haole from Hawaii' Jerry and his son Joey keep basic, screened *cabinas* with shared cold-water bathroom and more expensive doubles with private hot-water bathroom. There's a spacious shared kitchen in the center of the grassy grounds, and the atmosphere is about as chilled as it gets.

our pick Café Playa Negra (2652-9351; www.playanegracafe.com; s/d/tr/q US$25/40/55/70, with air-con US$37/52/67/82, all incl breakfast; 7am-9pm; P) This small hotel has a handful of sparkling-clean rooms upstairs from the cafe at street level. Ranging in size to accommodate pairs or small groups, these stylish, minimalist digs have cool, polished concrete floors, elevated beds neatly covered with colorful bedspreads and open-door bathroom. The shared deck facing the road has lounge sofas and big pillows, and amenities include laundry service, internet access and a free continental breakfast with homemade baguettes – a superb deal for these prices. The cafe serves Tico-Peruvian food (mains ₡4500 to ₡6000).

Mono Congo Surf Lodge (2652-9261; www.monocongolodge.com; r/ste from US$60/95; P) This large, open-air, Polynesian-style tree-house lodge is surrounded by howler-filled trees and is the pinnacle of tropical luxury in Playa Negra. High-ceilinged, polished wood rooms are exquisite, and private bathrooms have hot water and Spanish tiles. A patio has hammocks, and a star-watching deck on the roof provides 360-degree views of the area.

Hotel Playa Negra (2652-9134; www.playanegra.com; s/d/tr/q US$81/93/105/116; P) This charming hotel, right on the beach at Playa Negra's reef break, is a collection of 10 spacious, circular bungalows with thatched roofs, bright tropical colors and traditional indigenous-style tapestries and linens. Each cabin has a queen-sized bed, two single beds, and a bathroom with hot water and roomy showers. There's also a thatched-roof international restaurant (mains ₡2700 to ₡7000) and a surf shop with internet access (₡1600 per hour).

Pablo Picasso (2652-9158; mains ₡1250-4000; 6am-9pm;) 'Burgers as big as your head' is the house specialty at this US-owned restaurant. Other Yank comfort items include whale-sized fish tacos and Philly cheesesteak subs. Too full to move? There are six simple *cabinas* for rent (double with/without air-con US$45/30).

Getting There & Away

The new daily bus to Playa Avellanas departs Santa Cruz's Terminal Diria at 11:30am and 6pm (₡800, 1½ hours), passing by most of the above businesses. Buses to Santa Cruz depart at 5:30am and 1:30pm. Note that there are no afternoon buses on Sundays.

The daily bus to Playa Negra leaves Santa Cruz at 8am; the bus for Santa Cruz departs at 1:30pm from the V on the main road (₡800, 1½ hours).

PLAYA JUNQUILLAL

It's hard to pronounce and almost as difficult to find. Junquillal (say 'hoon-kee-yal') is a 2km-wide gray-sand wilderness beach that's absolutely stunning and mostly deserted – probably because the surf is high and the rips are fierce. It's best to leave your swimming trunks at home, though there are clean lefts and rights when the waves drop a bit in size. Olive ridley turtles nest here from July to November, with a peak from August to October, though in smaller numbers than at the refuges; Junquillal is also an important nesting site for leatherbacks. Though Junquillal is not a protected area, conservation groups have teamed up with local communities to protect the nesting sites and eliminate poaching.

The nearest village is 4km inland at **Paraíso**, which has a few local *sodas* and bars. Accommodations are spread out along the beach.

Sleeping & Eating

El Castillo Divertido (☎ 2658-8428; hotelcastillodivertido@hotmail.com; s/d US$30/40; P) On a hilltop about 500m down the road, you'll find the entrance to this quirky inn owned by an affable German-Tica couple and son. The hotel's rooftop bar has panoramic views – a breezy place to laze in a hammock. Paulo, one of the owners, plays his guitar for guests at sunset. Tiled rooms are clean and have hot showers, and it's worth splurging for the ones with ocean views. The restaurant (dishes ₡2000 to ₡6000) has good breakfasts and dinners with plenty of German favorites.

Hotel Hibiscus (☎ 2658-8437; s/d/tr incl breakfast US$40/50/60; P ❄) This charming German-Nica-run hotel has five spotless rooms with hammock-strung patios overlooking the palm-fringed garden. There's a small restaurant withs a good variety of international cuisine, and the breakfasts are immense and delicious.

Mundo Milo Ecolodge (☎ 2658-7010; www.mundomito.com; d US$55; P wi-fi pool) This new Dutch-owned resort was partially opened during our visit but already showed lots of potential. The thatch-covered, open-air restaurant is open for lunch and dinner; Saturday night Latin dances attract locals and gringos alike. There is currently one African-motif cabin with with a hot-water bathroom and kitchenette, surrounded by trees full of howler monkeys.

Villa Roberta (☎ 2658-8127; dietzcon@racsa.co.cr; d incl breakfast US$58, apt US$87; P ❄ pool) This hospitable two-room B&B is intimate, quaint and full of personality, and its location in the trees makes it feel tranquil in the extreme. The room has a fridge, fan and open-air bathroom facing the jungle, where a monkey might spot you doing your business. The apartment sleeps four and has air-con, bidet, 'his and hers' sinks and a small kitchen. For long stays, Roberta rents Casa Bob (US$85 per night, three nights minimum) across the street, a fully furnished house that sleeps six and has a washer and dryer, full kitchen and a rooftop sundeck with partial sea views.

Hotel Tatanka (☎ 2658-8426, in USA & Canada 800-498-0824; www.hoteltatanka.com; s/d US$58/76; P internet pool) Ten ranch-style rooms with hot-water bathrooms are pretty in pink and have rustic wooden furnishings. There's an inviting pool as well as an open-air pizzeria that serves authentic wood-fired pizza pies (₡2000 to ₡5000) in the evenings.

Guacamaya Lodge (☎ 2658-8431; www.guacamayalodge.com; s/d US$62/67, apt s/d/tr/q US$84/90/95/100, villas US$147; P ❄ internet wi-fi pool) Next door to El Castillo, this quiet Swiss-run place has six quaint bungalows, a two-bedroom villa with a kitchen and four apartments with balcony views. There's also a pool, tennis courts and a restaurant-bar with ocean views and a smattering of Swiss delicacies. The warm and wonderful brother and sister owners speak a remarkable six languages.

Hotel Iguanazul (☎ 2658-8124; www.hoteliguanazul.com; s/d/tr US$68/79/91, with air-con from US$91/102/113, with air-con & ocean view US$113/124/135, all incl breakfast; P ❄ internet wi-fi pool) Don't let the gaudy fountain out front put you off; the aesthetics at this well-established resort hotel are much more relaxed and attractive. The 24 brightly painted and cool, tiled rooms have garden or ocean views. Amenities include a pool, pool table, volleyball and a restaurant-bar with killer views.

our pick **Plumita Pacífica** (☎ 2658-7125, 8335-5142; www.plumitapacifica.com; d US$75; P) When all you need is your sweetie and a secluded palm-fringed beach, these isolated apartments are the answer. There are two modern apartments, each with a fully equipped kitchen, queen bed, iPod dock, beachfront patio and a hot-water shower big enough for two (wink, wink!). And just steps from your front door, the dark-sand, desolate beach has hammocks, picnic tables and an outdoor shower. If you're not in the mood to cook, it's a short drive or pleasant walk to the scattered restaurants.

Aside from the hotel restaurants, your best option for cheap eats is to head to nearby Paraíso, though there a few small spots on the beach, including the locally popular **Bar y Restaurant Junquillal** (dishes ₡1700-3500) and **Rudy's** (☎ 2658-8114; mains ₡1700-4000; breakfast, lunch & dinner), a mellow little bar and restaurant serving Tico standbys and casual fare.

Getting There & Away

Buses depart from Junquillal to Santa Cruz (₡400, 1½ hours) at 6am, 9am, 12:30pm and 4:30pm; you can catch the bus anywhere along the main road. Buses from Santa Cruz's Terminal Diria to Junquillal depart at 4:45am, 6:45am, 10:15am, 12:15pm, 2:15pm and 5:30pm.

If you're driving, it's about 16km by paved road from Santa Cruz to 27 de Abril. From there, it's another 17km on one of the best roads we've seen in all of Costa Rica; it even has separate bike lanes!

From Junquillal, it's possible to drive 35km south to the Nosara area via the legendary surf spot of Marbella. However, this is a very rough dirt road for 4WD only and may be impassable in the rainy season. There are no gas stations on the coastal road and there is little traffic, so ask before setting out. It's easier to reach beaches south of Junquillal from Nicoya.

A taxi from Santa Cruz to Junquillal costs about ₡20,000.

SANTA CRUZ

A stop in Santa Cruz, a *sabanero* (cowboy) town typical of inland Nicoya, provides some of the local flavor missing from foreign-dominated beach towns. Unfortunately, there aren't any attention-worthy sights in town, so most travelers' experience in Santa Cruz consists of changing buses and buying a mango or two. It doesn't help much that Santa Cruz (with Liberia a close second) holds the dubious title of being the hottest city in Costa Rica (we're talking temperature, not sex appeal). However, the town is an important administrative center in the region, and serves as a good base for visiting Guaitil (see boxed text, p276).

About three city blocks in the center of Santa Cruz burned to the ground in a devastating fire in 1993. An important landmark in town is a vacant lot known as **Plaza de Los Mangos**, which was once a large grassy square with three mango trees. However, soon after the fire the attractive and shady **Parque Bernabela Ramos** was opened up 400m south of Plaza de Los Mangos.

Information

Kion, on the southwest plaza corner, is a Wal-Mart style department store selling English-language newspapers and more. There's a gas station off the main intersection with the highway. There is one ATM and at least three internet cafes facing Plaza de Los Mangos. Change money at **Banco de Costa Rica** (☎ 2680-3253), three blocks north of Plaza de Los Mangos.

Festivals & Events

There is a rodeo during the **Fiesta de Santa Cruz** in the second week in January, and on July 25 for **Día de Guanacaste** (see boxed text, p219). At these events, you can check out the *sabaneros*, admire prize bulls and drink plenty of beer while listening to eardrum-busting music.

Santa Cruz is considered the folklore center of the region and is home to a longtime marimba group, Los de la Bajura. The group plays traditional *bombas*, a combination of music with funny (and off-color) verses. Keep an eye out for wall postings announcing performances, or ask hotel staff for information.

Sleeping & Eating

Any directions that mention the 'plaza' are making reference to Plaza de Los Mangos. Note that all of the following places have cold showers, though you'll wish they were even colder.

GUAITIL

An interesting excursion from Santa Cruz is the 12km trip by paved road to the small pottery-making community of Guaitil. Attractive ceramics are made from local clays, using earthy reds, creams and blacks in pre-Columbian Chorotega style. Ceramics are for sale outside the potters' houses in Guaitil and also in San Vicente, 2km beyond Guaitil by unpaved road. If you ask, you can watch part of the potting process, and local residents would be happy to give you a few lessons for a small price.

If you have your car, take the main highway toward Nicoya and then follow the signed Guaitil road to the left, about 1.5km out of Santa Cruz. This road is lined by yellow corteza amarilla trees and is very attractive in April when all of them are in bloom. Unreliable buses (₡225, 45 minutes) serve the village from Santa Cruz every two hours from dawn to dusk on weekdays and until 2pm on Saturday. However, a round-trip taxi should only cost about ₡8000, depending on how long you stay.

If you don't have time to get to Guaitil, visit the small *depósito* (outlet) selling ceramics on the peninsular highway, about 10km north of Nicoya on the eastern side of the road. Be aware that if you take a tour to Guaitil, you may be taken to one particular shop on a commission basis; try to browse other shops in town and share the wealth.

Hotel Diriá (☎ 2680-0080/402; hoteldiria@hotmail.com; s/d US$30/45; P ✲ ☐) Though once in grander shape, this long-standing hotel 500m north of the plaza is looking a little tired. But rooms come with air-con, bathroom and cable TV, and the pleasant shared terraces have lovely rattan rocking chairs.

La Calle de Alcalá (☎ 2680-0000; s/d US$54/73; P ✲ ☐) With its stucco arches and landscaped garden around a pool with a swim-up bar, this inn gets points for design details. Carved wooden doors open into cool, tiled rooms with amenities like hair dryers, wicker furniture and window seats. The pleasant alfresco restaurant-bar (mains ₡3000 to ₡12,000) is the best in town.

Hotel La Pampa (☎ 2680-0586; d with/without air-con US$58/45; P ✲) A good midrange option, 50m west of the plaza, this terra-cotta–color building houses 33 simple and clean modern rooms, all equipped with bathroom and cable TV.

El Milenio (☎ 2680-3237; mains ₡1600-3300; ⏲ 9am-9pm) With a notable Chinese population, Santa Cruz has its share of Chinese food – El Milenio tops them all with its colossal portions of fried rice, decent stir-fries, big-screen TV and blessed air-con. It's 100m west of the plaza.

El Chile Dulce (☎ 8833-1880; mains ₡1760-3000; ⏲ 7am-6pm; V) This ridiculously cheap, contemporary cafe next to Terminal Diria has terrific panini sandwiches, soups, *casados* and even barbeque ribs. Lots of vegetarian options too.

Among the several supermarkets in town, the SuperCompro, just east of the Empresas Alfaro ticket office, is the biggest.

Getting There & Away

Santa Cruz is 57km from Liberia and 25km south of Filadelfia. It's on the main peninsular highway and is often an overnight stop for people visiting the peninsula. A paved road leads 16km west to 27 de Abril, from where dirt roads continue to Playa Tamarindo, Playa Junquillal and other beaches.

Some buses depart from Terminal Tralapa on the north side of Plaza de Los Mangos. For Empresas Alfaro buses, buy tickets at the Alfaro office, 200m south of the plaza, but catch the bus on the main road north of town.

Liberia (La Pampa) ₡770; 1½ hours; departs every 30 minutes from 4:10am to 8:40pm.

Nicoya (La Pampa) ₡310; one hour; departs every 30 minutes from 4:50am to 9:20pm.

San José ₡4690; 4½ hours; seven buses from 4:30am to 5pm (Tralapa); eight buses from 3am to 4:30pm (Empresas Alfaro).

Other local buses leave from Terminal Diria 400m east of the plaza. The schedules fluctuate constantly, so ask around.

Bahía Potrero, via Playa Brasilito & Playa Flamingo ₡600; one hour; departs 19 times per day.

Playa Junquillal ₡400; 1½ hours; departs 4:45am, 6:45am, 10:15am, 12:15pm, 2:15pm and 5:30pm.

Playa Tamarindo ₡400; 1½ hours; departs 4:20am, 5:30am, 9am, 10:30am, 1pm, 3:30pm and 5pm. The last bus does not operate on Sundays.

CENTRAL PENINSULA

Long the political and cultural heart of Guanacaste, the inland region of the central peninsula looks and feels palpably more 'Costa Rican' than the beach resorts of the northern coast. Over the generations, the dry tropical forest has been cut down to make way for the *sabaneros'* (cowboys) cattle, but stands of forest remain, interspersed between *fincas* (plantations) and coastal villages, sometimes backing stretches of wild, empty beaches.

Hwy 21 snakes through the higher el evations of the interior, from the population center of Santa Cruz down through Nicoya, where Hwy 150 branches southward toward Sámara in a winding road through the forest.

There is considerably less development in this region than in the north of the peninsula, though the areas around Sámara and Nosara are developing slowly. Most foreigners who are drawn to the rugged coastal landscapes of the central peninsula are actively committed to its conservation. This part of the coast is rife with secluded beaches, small villages where authenticity reigns, and endless possibilities for getting 'off the map.'

NICOYA

Situated 23km south of Santa Cruz, Nicoya was named after an indigenous Chorotega chief, who welcomed Spanish conquistador Gil González de Ávila in 1523 (a gesture he regretted – see boxed text, p319). In the following centuries, the Chorotega were wiped out by the colonists, though the distinctive facial features of the local residents are a testament to their heritage.

Although Nicoya is in fact a colonial city, very little remains of the original architecture, and what is left is usually in a state of disrepair. However, Nicoya is one of the most pleasant cities in the region, and the bright buildings and bustling streets contribute to the welcoming atmosphere.

For travelers, Nicoya primarily serves as a transportation hub for the region, though the city is a good base for exploring Parque Nacional Barra Honda (p279). It's also a good base for visiting **Puerto Humo**, a small town about 27km northeast on the road past Coralillo that has good opportunities for bird-watching.

Information

Alf@Net (☎ 2685-4182; Calle 1; per hr ₡500; 🕑 8am-10pm) Has air-con and roughly a dozen terminals with very good connections.

Area de Conservación Tempisque (ACT; ☎ 2685-5667; Av Central; 🕑 8am-4pm Mon-Fri) The office of the ACT can help with accommodations and cave exploration at Parque Nacional Barra Honda.

Banco de Costa Rica (Calle Central; 🕑 8:30am-3pm Mon-Fri) Exchanges US dollars.

Banco Popular (Calle 3; 🕑 9am-4:30pm Mon-Fri, 8:15-11:30am Sat) Exchanges US dollars. It also has a 24-hour ATM at Hospital La Anexión.

Cyber Center (Calle 1; per hr ₡400; 🕑 7am-10pm) Internet access.

Hospital La Anexión (☎ 2685-5066) The main hospital on the peninsula is north of town.

Internet Good Times (Av 2; per hr ₡400; 🕑 9am-10pm) Internet access.

Sights

In Parque Central, a major town landmark, is the attractive white colonial **Iglesia de San Blas**, which dates back to the mid-17th century. The appealingly peaceful, wood-beamed church is under continuous restoration, and its mosaic tiles are crumbling, but it can be visited when **mass** (🕑 6pm Mon & Fri, 7am Tue, 7am & 7pm Thu) is not in session. It has a small collection of colonial religious artifacts, or have a look at the wooden Jesus with articulated joints and bleeding stigmata. The park outside is an inviting spot to people-watch from one of the shady stone benches.

On the opposite side of the park is **La Casa de la Cultura**. This small area has cultural exhibits a few times a year and features work by local artists. The exhibit schedule and hours of operation are erratic, but it's worth a peek if the doors are open.

Festivals & Events

The town goes crazy for **Día de Guanacaste**, on July 25, so expect plenty of food, music and beer in the plaza to celebrate the province's annexation from Nicaragua. The Festival de La Virgen de Guadalupe (see boxed text, p279) is one of the most unique festivals in Costa Rica.

Sleeping & Eating

All places have cold showers unless otherwise stated.

Hotel Chorotega (☎ 2685-5245; s/d US$17/22, without bathroom US$6/12; 🅿) Next to the Río

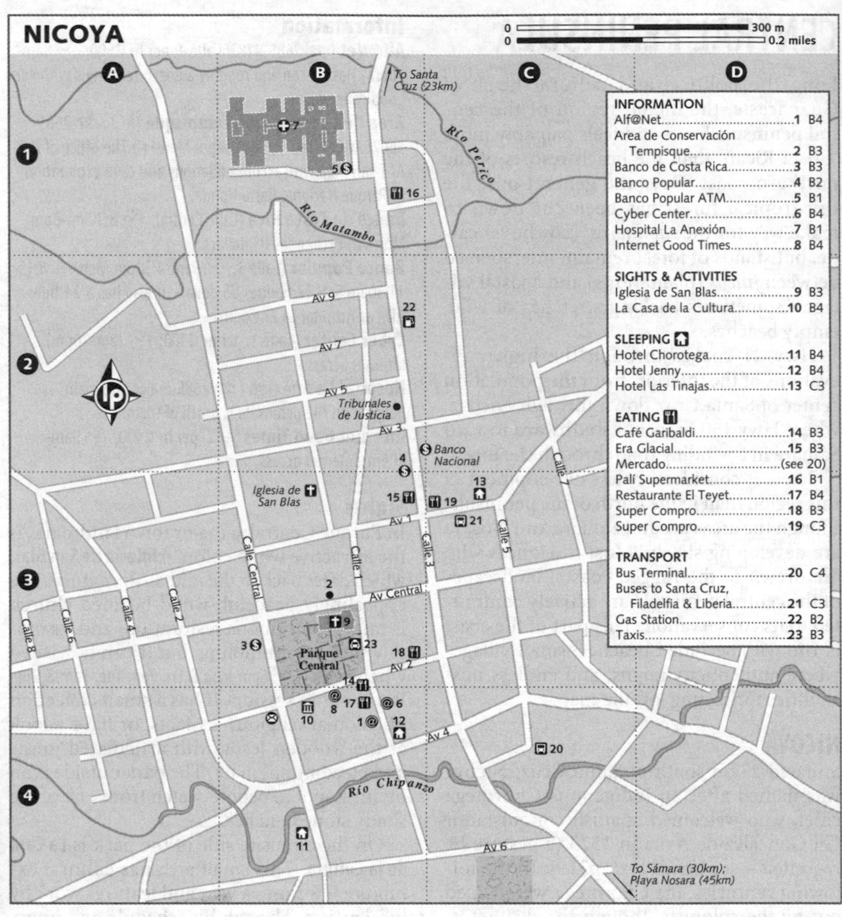

Chipanzo and run by a pleasant family that keeps bare-bones rooms that could use a face-lift but are reasonably clean and neat. You won't find a cheaper bed elsewhere.

Hotel Las Tinajas (☎ 2685-5081; Av 1; s/d US$11/17, d with air-con US$22; P ❄) This hotel is decent and mercifully far from the noise of the plaza, though it's on a relatively busy road. The 28 rooms are clean (although a little rough around the edges), with cable TV and bathroom.

Hotel Jenny (☎ 2685-5050; cnr Calle 1 & Av 4; s/d/tr/q US$18/25/29/37; P ❄) This is one of the best deals in town – all 24 spic-and-span rooms have air-con, cable TV and bathroom. Try to get a room in the cooler, darker halls rather than the noisier ones facing the street.

Café Garibaldi (☎ 2685-5969; cnr Calle 1 & Av 2; items ₡500-2500; 🕒 8am-5pm Mon-Fri, 8am-3pm Sat) At the southwest corner of Parque Central, this outdoor patio-cafe is a pleasant place to people-watch with a coffee, juice or sandwich.

Restaurante El Teyet (Calle 1; mains ₡1500-2800; 🕒 lunch & dinner) Chinese restaurants such as this one are some of the tastiest and cheapest spots to eat in the city. Grab a seat on the patio or in the air-conditioned interior and feast on huge portions of chow mein and other noodle dishes.

Era Glacial (☎ 2675-3227; Calle 3; mains ₡1500-5000; 🕒 noon-9:30pm) At the main intersection downtown, this new pizzeria has 30 types of pies cooked in a real wood-fire oven, plus pastas, meat and fish dishes, and for dessert, ice cream.

Super Compro and Palí supermarkets provide food and supplies for self-caterers. There is also a number of cheap *sodas* in the *mercado* (market) that are good for a quick bite, as well as all your favorite Costa Rican fast-food chains.

Getting There & Away

Most buses arrive at and depart from the bus terminal southeast of Parque Central.

Liberia ₡1000; 2½ hours; departs every 30 minutes from 3:30am to 8pm.

Playa Naranjo, connects with ferry to Puntarenas ₡1300; three hours; departs 5am, 9am, 1pm and 5pm.

Playa Nosara ₡1050; 2½ hours; departs 5am, 10am, noon, 3pm and 5:30pm.

Sámara ₡850; two hours; 13 buses per day from 5am to 9pm.

San José, via Liberia (Empresas Alfaro) ₡3750; five hours; departs five times daily.

San José, via Puente La Amistad ₡3500; four hours; departs eight times daily from 3am to 5pm (Empresas Alfaro), and five times daily from 3:20am to 1:45pm (Tralapa).

Santa Ana, for Barra Honda ₡700; one hour; departs 12:30pm Monday to Saturday.

Other buses for Santa Cruz, Filadelfia and Liberia depart every 30 minutes from 3:50am to 8:30pm from the terminal northeast of the park.

PARQUE NACIONAL DIRIÁ

Since 2004 **Parque Nacional Diriá** (☎ 2680-1820; admission US$10; 🕗 8am-4pm) covers 54 sq km, 1500 of which are primary tropical dry forest and river basins of the Ríos Diriá, Enmedio, Tigre and Verde. At its higher altitudes are stands of tropical humid forest as well. In addition to protecting these vital watersheds, the park is also a refuge for wildlife, such as howler monkeys, deer, anteaters and over 100 bird species.

Two trails, El Venado and El Escabel, lead through the forest and to the lovely Brasil waterfall.

It's possible to stay in a basic bunkhouse here, which has running water and electricity, but otherwise you'll have to be self-sufficient. Call the Santa Cruz Minae office (at the number listed above) to make arrangements.

The park is 14km southwest of Santa Cruz; there is no public transportation.

PARQUE NACIONAL BARRA HONDA

Situated about halfway between Nicoya and the mouth of the Río Tempisque, this 23-sq-km **national park** protects a massive underground system of caves and is one of the most

A BRIEF HISTORY OF THE CHOROTEGA

Although there were several pre-Columbian ethnic groups in the Nicoya peninsula, the most prominent were the Chorotega, which translates as 'Fleeing People.' The Chorotega arrived on the peninsula around the 8th century BC, and are believed to be descendants of the Olmec in Mexico. They were also contemporaries of the Maya, and a part of a cultural link extending from Mexico through Central America to the Andes.

Unlike their contemporaries, however, the Chorotega were not prolific builders. As a result, most of our understanding of the group is based on the representations that appear in their artwork. The Chorotega are best known for their elaborate jade work, though they were also talented potters and sculptors.

Archaeologists believe that the Chorotega were a hierarchical and militaristic society that kept slaves and regularly practiced both cannibalism and human sacrifice. It's also believed that shamanism, fertility rites and ritualistic dance played an important role in their society, though little is actually known about their belief structure.

Although their civilization survived for more than 2000 years, the Chorotega were wiped out by warfare and disease during the Spanish colonial period, though their artisan tradition is still evident among the surviving indigenous populations of Península de Nicoya (see boxed text, p276). The December 12 **Festival de La Virgen de Guadalupe** in the city of Nicoya incorporates the Chorotega legend of *La Yequita,* which relates how a little mare stopped two brothers from killing one another over the love of a princess. The celebration blends Catholic and Chorotega elements by parading a statue of the Virgin to the tune of indigenous music and loud fireworks, while revelers drink copious amounts of *chicha,* a traditional liquor of fermented corn and sugar that's served in hollowed gourds.

unusual (and also highly memorable) national parks in all of the country. The caverns, which are composed of soft limestone, were carved by rainfall and erosion over a period of about 70 million years. Speleologists have discovered more than 40 caverns, with some of them reaching as far as 200m deep, though to date only 19 have been fully explored. There have been discoveries here of pre-Columbian remains dating back to 300 BC.

The caves come with the requisite cave accoutrements: stalagmites, stalactites and a host of beautiful formations with intriguing names such as fried eggs, organ, soda straws, popcorn, curtains, columns, pearls, flowers and shark's teeth. However, unlike caverns in your own country perhaps, Barra Honda is not developed for wide-scale tourism, which means that the caves here feel less like a carnival attraction and more like a scene from *Indiana Jones*. So, don your yellow miner's hat, put on some sturdy boots and be prepared to get down and dirty.

Information

The dry season is the only time that tourists are allowed to enter the caves, though hiking is good any time of year. In the dry season, carry several liters of water and let the rangers know where you are going. Two German hikers died at Barra Honda in 1993 after getting lost on a short hike – they had no water and succumbed to dehydration. Sneakers or, preferably, boots are necessary if you will be caving.

The **ranger station** (☎ 2659-1551; ⌚ 8am-4pm) in the southwest corner of the park takes the US$10 admission fee and provides information. Plan to arrive by noon to tour the caverns, as tours last three to four hours and guides won't start them much later than that.

Sights

You can only explore the **caves** with a guide from the Asociación de Guías Ecologistas de Barra Honda, which can be arranged in the national park offices in **Nicoya** (☎ 2686-6760), **Santa Cruz** (☎ 2680-1920) or **Bagaces** (☎ 2671-1455). A guide charges about US$35 per person, including park admission and equipment. The descent involves using ladders and ropes, so you should be reasonably fit and you must be at least 12 years of age.

A guide service is available for hiking the trails within the park and also for descending into the most popular caves. Guides speak Spanish, though a few of the rangers speak some English.

The only cave with regular access to the public is the 62m-deep **La Terciopelo**, which has the most speleothems – calcite figures that rise and fall in the cave's interior. The best known of these is **El Órgano**, which produces several notes when lightly struck. Scientists and other visitors are required to have permits from the park service to enter other caves. These include **Santa Ana**, the deepest (249m); **Trampa** (Trap), 110m deep with a vertical 52m drop; **Nicoya**, where early human remains were found; and, our favorite, **Pozo Hediondo**, or Fetid Pit, which is famous for its huge piles of bat droppings. Remember that caves cannot be entered after 1pm.

Activities

While **wildlife-watching** underground, you'll have the chance to see such fun-loving creatures as bat, albino salamander, blind fish and a variety of squiggly little invertebrates. On the surface, howler and white-faced monkey, armadillo, coati, kinkajou and white-tailed deer are regularly spotted, as are striped hog-nosed skunk and anteater.

For **hiking**, the Barra Honda hills have a few trails through deciduous, dry tropical rainforest that lead to waterfalls (in the rainy season) adorned with calcium formations. It's also possible to hike to the top of Cerro Barra Honda, which has a lookout with a view that takes in the Río Tempisque and Golfo de Nicoya. Since this national park is comparatively untouristed and undeveloped, it is advised that you either inquire about the state of the trails before setting out, or hire the services of a guide.

Sleeping & Eating

At the entrance to the park, there is a **camping area** (per person US$2) with bathrooms and showers. If you're willing to help clear brush or maintain trails, the park has three dorm-style **cabins** (per person US$12) reserved for volunteers; each has a shower and six beds. Reserve accommodations and meals through the **ACT office** (☎ 2685-5667) in Nicoya or by calling the ranger station. Spanish is necessary.

Getting There & Away

The easiest way to get to the park is from Nicoya. No buses go directly to the park; however, buses to Santa Ana (1km away) will get you close. These leave Nicoya at 12:30pm Monday to Saturday. Return buses leave Santa Ana at noon and 4:30pm. There are no buses on Sunday. The better option is to take a taxi from Nicoya, which will cost about ₡8000. You can arrange for your driver to pick you up later at a specified time.

If you have your own vehicle, take the peninsular highway south out of Nicoya toward Mansión and make a left on the access road leading to Puente La Amistad. From here, continue another 1.5km and make a left on the signed road to Barra Honda. The dirt road will take you to the village of Barra Honda and will then wind to the left for another 6km before ending up at the entrance to the national park. The community of Santa Ana is passed en route. The road is clearly marked, and there are several signs along the way indicating the direction of the park. After the village of Barra Honda, the road is unpaved, but in good condition. However, there is no telling what the next rainy season will do to it, so ask locally before setting out.

If you are coming to the park from Puente La Amistad, you will see the access road to Barra Honda signed about 16km after leaving the bridge. From this point, follow the above directions.

PUENTE LA AMISTAD

Once made exclusively by ferry (car and passenger), the trip over the Río Tempisque has been completely transformed by the recent construction of a 780m bridge, now the largest in Costa Rica. The Puente La Amistad (Friendship Bridge) was built with Taiwanese financial support and opened in July 2003. There is a small parking area and observation platform on the western side of the river so that you can admire it and take photos (as the locals proudly do).

NOSARA AREA

The attractive beaches near the small Tico village of Nosara are backed by a pocket of luxuriant vegetation that attracts birds and wildlife. The area has seen little logging, partly because of the nearby wildlife refuge, and partly because of real-estate development – an unlikely sounding combination.

There are a few hundred foreigners living permanently in the Nosara area (mainly North Americans), the majority of them keen on protecting the rainforest. One resident described the area as 'sophisticated jungle living,' and indeed blending retirement with conservation is an interesting experiment. However, Ticos remain hostile to the development of the area, mainly because land prices have been driven through the roof in just under a decade.

The Nosara area is a magical destination as you can sometimes see parrots, toucans, armadillos and monkeys just a few meters away from the beaches. There are three distinct beaches here. North of the river is **Playa Nosara**, which is difficult to access and primarily used by fishermen. Further south is **Playa Pelada**, a small crescent-shaped beach with an impressive blowhole that sends water shooting through the air at high tide. The southernmost beach is **Playa Guiones**, a 7km stretch of sand that's one of the best surf spots on the central peninsula.

Nosara is not for everyone. If you're not stoked on surf culture, you may find yourself bored silly. The upscale destination caters to monied surfers who live, eat and breathe the waves. And if you're on a budget and looking for a more chilled surf town, head to Mal País and Santa Teresa (p305).

Orientation

The Nosara area is spread out along the coast and a little inland (making a vehicle a bit of a necessity). Nosara village, where you'll find supplies and gas, and the airport are 5km inland from the beach. The main areas with accommodations, restaurants and beaches are Playa Pelada to the north and Playa Guiones to the south. There are many unidentified little roads, which makes it hard to get around if you don't know the place – look for hotel and restaurant signs, and ask for help. Log on to Nosara Travel's website (www.nosaratravel.com/map.html) for a handy map.

Information

There are two gas stations in Nosara village, but only one was open during our visit.

Banco Popular (☎ 2682-0267/011; 🕑 9am-3pm Mon-Fri) Changes US dollars and traveler's checks, and gives cash advances on Visa cards only; the ATM also only accepts Visa cards.

Laundry Mat (🕑 8am-noon & 1-4pm) Coin-operated laundromat located next to Robin's restaurant.

Nosara Travel (☎ 2682-0300; www.nosaratravel.com; 🕑 9am-3pm Mon-Fri) In Playa Guiones, this office books air tickets, arranges car rentals and books hotel reservations or vacation homes.

Nosaranet & Frog Pad (☎ 2682-4039; www.thefrogpad.com; internet per hr ₡2000; 9am-8pm) The going rates for internet use are pretty astronomical in Nosara. The Frog Pad also has used books for sale, and DVDs, bikes and surfboards for rent.

Police (☎ 2682-0317) Next to the Red Cross and post office on the southeast corner of the soccer field in Nosara village center.

Seekret Spot (☎ 2682-0173; per hr ₡2000; 10am-4pm) Internet access and international phone calls. Located on the main road to Playa Pelada.

Super Nosara (8am-7pm Mon-Sat, to 3pm Sun) Southwest of the soccer field, it changes US dollars and traveler's checks. It's also a good place to stock up on supplies – it's cheaper than anything by the beaches.

Activities

CANOPY TOURS

Miss Sky (☎ 2682-0969; www.missskycanopytour.com; adult/child US$60/30; 7am-5pm) has brought a canopy tour to Nosara. It's the longest one in the world – at least for now – with a total length of 11,000m above a pristine, private reserve. The zip lines don't go from platform to platform, but from mountainside to mountainside, and have double cables for added safety. The last of 21 zip lines whisks you directly into the top floor of the onsite disco-bar! Tours leave twice daily, at 8am and 2pm.

HIKING

The **Reserva Biológica Nosara** (☎ 2682-0573; www.lagarta.com) behind the Lagarta Lodge has private trails leading through a mangrove wetland down to the river (five minutes) and beach (10 minutes). This is a great spot for bird-watching, and there's a good chance you'll see some reptiles as well (look up in the trees as there are occasionally boa constrictors here). Nonguests can visit the reserve for US$6.

MASSAGE

After a hard day of surfing, treat yourself to a (totally legit) massage or spa treatment at **Tica Massage** (☎ 2682-0096; www.ticamassage.com; services US$35-80; 9am-6pm), across from Casa Tucan. Next door there's a small gym (US$10 per day) with free weights and machines. Credit cards and traveler's checks are accepted.

SURFING

Check out **Playa Guiones** for the best beach break in the central peninsula, especially when there is an offshore wind. Although the beach is usually full of surfers, there are fortunately plenty of take-off points.

At the main intersection in Guiones, the surf shop **Coconut Harry's** (☎ 2682-0574; www.coconutharrys.com; 7am-5pm) offers private surfing lessons (US$35 per hour), board rental (US$20 per day) and repair, and long-term board storage (US$90 per year).

From here, turn left on the main road into Guiones past Café de Paris and you'll find **Nosara Surf Shop** (☎ 2682-0186; www.nosarasurfshop.com; 7am-6pm). It rents surfboards (US$15 to US$20 per day), does board repairs and arranges surf lessons (US$40 per hour) and tours. Across the street from Kaya Sol, Tico-owned **El Punto** (☎ 2682-1081; www.surfocostarica.com; 8am-6pm) is a highly recommended surf shop that offers lessons (US$40 per hour) and rents surfboards (US$15 per day) and bicycles (US$10 per day).

TURTLE-WATCHING

Most hotels in the area can arrange guided tours to Refugio Nacional de Fauna Silvestre Ostional (p285), where you can watch the mass arrivals of olive ridley turtles.

YOGA

In the hills near Playa Guiones is the famous **Nosara Yoga Institute** (☎ 2682-0071, toll-free 866-439-4704; www.nosarayoga.com). The institute offers regular classes, open to the public, as well as workshops, retreats and instructor training courses. To practice in such a beautiful jungle setting, in airy studios ventilated by ocean breezes, is a wonderful experience for beginners or yogis (and yoginis) alike.

Sleeping & Eating

All prices listed are for high season; low-season prices can be 20% lower or better.

PLAYA GUIONES

Kaya Sol (☎ 2682-1459; www.kayasol.com; dm with/without kitchen US$15/12, d US$30-85, cabin US$47-58;) The heart of this sprawling surfer-and-seeker retreat is the dorm-style accommodations in the 'flop house.' The shared bathrooms are spotless and the pool, with waterfall shower, is perfect for cooling off. There are also a few rooms and private cabins with hot-water bathroom in the back of the property, as well as a beach house (US$110 per night). The restaurant serves US-style food, and the bar

PENÍNSULA DE NICOYA

is *the* place to hang out at night. It's down the road from the Mini Super Delicias.

Rancho Congo (☎ 2682-0078; rcongo@racsa.co.cr; r incl breakfast US$25-50; P) This three-room B&B is a sweet, German-run retreat with big rooms, hammocks and a quiet garden setting just off the main road.

Gilded Iguana Bar & Restaurant (☎ 2682-0259; www.thegildediguana.com; d US$51-62, ste US$85; P) Down the second access road to Guiones, this long-standing hotel for anglers and surfers has well-furnished, tiled rooms of varying sizes with hot-water bathroom and refrigerator. The tasty restaurant will grill your catch for you, and the attached bar is a popular gringo hangout.

Giardino Tropicale (☎ 2682-0258; www.giardinotropicale.com; s/d from US$68/79, ste US$141; P) On the main road, north of Marlin Bill's, this collection of white-walled cabins offers various sizes and views. The pleasant quarters with solar-heated showers all look out to a lawn shaded by a huge tree, and there's a pool for taking a cool dip. Deluxe rooms include a kitchen (without stove). There's also a rambling, rustic restaurant (dishes ₡2800 to ₡5500) that's popular for its thin-crust pizzas.

Café de Paris (☎ 2682-0087/1035; www.cafedeparis.net; d/tr US$80/92; P) This pleasant hotel is located at the corner of the main road and the first access road that leads to Playa Guiones. Shiny, clean rooms have plenty of polished woodwork, a bathroom and air-con, while larger bungalows and villas are great deals if you're traveling in a group. The bakery-restaurant turns out heavenly French breads and pastries and is an excellent place to eat or pick up a lovely brioche.

Casa Romántica (☎ 2682-0272; www.casa-romantica.net; d incl breakfast from US$90; P) Right next to Playa Guiones is this recommended Spanish colonial mansion with several rooms with bathroom. The rooms all have views of the manicured gardens surrounding the pool. There is also private beach access, a small restaurant featuring international cuisine and well-being services (yoga and massage). Tours can be arranged. Credit cards are accepted.

Harbor Reef Lodge (☎ 2682-0059; www.harborreef.com; d US$95-149; ste US$129-239, casas per week from US$1495; P) These cool, tiled rooms with hot-water bathroom, air-con and fridge have wood detailing and attractive Latin American textiles. Suites are located on Playas Pelada and Guiones, and are much more expansive with a full kitchen. There are also two- and three-bedroom *casas*, and suites within *casas*, available for rent. They are pristine, secluded and guests can use the hotel's facilities. To get here, continue beyond Nosara Surf Shop to where the road bends to the left as it hits the shore.

our pick **Harmony Hotel** (☎ 2682-4114; www.harmonynosara.com; d US$214, 2-person bungalows US$305, 4 person ste US$463; P) Designed with clean lines and fostering a tranquil, happy atmosphere, this effortlessly stylish hotel lives up to its name in look and feel. Better, it also strives for harmony with the environment, employing a full-time sustainability coordinator and involving itself with the community and environmental initiatives. Simple but luxurious rooms have a spacious, private deck with outdoor shower and hammock, and bungalows afford even more privacy and space. Using

TOP SPOTS FOR A SPECTACULAR SMOOCH

The Península de Nicoya is blessed with endless romantic beaches, but if you're looking for a dramatic backdrop for that cinematic kiss, here's where to set the scene.

- Head to **Soda Piedra Mar** (p308) in Mal País for breakfast with a view, then scramble on the rocks and find a secluded spot to watch the waves swoon.
- Perched high on a bluff, **Restaurante Mirador Barranquilla** (p292) is stunning at sunset with the Pacific at your feet.
- Wake up early and hike up to the **Montezuma Waterfall** (see boxed text, p300) to have the pools to yourself.
- Book a bungalow at romantic **El Pequeño Gecko Verde** (p289), canoodle over cocktails followed by a sunset stroll on the secret beach, Playa Izquierda.
- Pack picnic provisions, rent kayaks in the morning and paddle away from **Sámara** (p286) to play castaway on uninhabited Isla Chora.

fresh, organic ingredients as much as possible, the restaurant and bar (mains ₡4000 to ₡11,000) are worth a visit if you're not staying here (reservations are recommended).

L'Acqua Viva Hotel & Spa (☎ 2682-1087; www.lacquaviva.com; r US$232, ste US$350-385, villas US$593-831; P) A bit of Bali in Nosara, L'Acqua Viva is one of the most luxurious hotels in the central peninsula. Inside and out, the property is simply stunning, with water, wood and bamboo features throughout. The open-air restaurant and funky lounge bar are the best in town. The 36 contemporary rooms are decorated in minimalist style with all the five-star amenities you'd expect. Yet we do have one major complaint: the location sucks, backing a busy road that's far from the beach. Bring earplugs and a car.

our pick Beach Dog Café (snacks ₡1000-3500; 7am-7:30pm) Just steps from the beach, our favorite new cafe in Nosara has the best breakfast in town. The delicious lunch menu includes organic salads, sandwiches, wraps, pasta and more. Early birds can come for free coffee from 7am to 7:30am. Otherwise, order your favorite espresso drink or smoothie from the warm and friendly staff. There's also free wi-fi.

Marlin Bill's (☎ 2682-0548; meals ₡3400-8000; 11am-2pm & 6pm-late Mon-Sat) Across the main road is this popular bar-restaurant with fantastic ocean views. It's worth grabbing lunch here when the menu is cheaper, though it's worth the price anytime for a hearty filet of blackened tuna and a slab of key lime pie.

Stock up on groceries at the **Mini Super Delicias del Mundo** (☎ 2682-0291; 8:45am-1pm & 2:30-6:15pm Mon-Sat) near Kaya Sol; the bulletin board advertises local events and job openings.

PLAYA PELADA

Refugio del Sol (☎ 2682-0287; www.refugiodelsol.com; d/ste US$45/65; P) Five cozy rooms surround a garden courtyard at this small hotel across from Pancho's. It's a very mellow place to stay, and just a short stroll down to Playa Pelada from here.

Nosara B&B (☎ 2682-0209; www.nosarabandb.net; s/d incl breakfast US$48/64) Further north, on a signed access road, this cute, clean and very quiet option is set back in the trees near a quiet strand of beach. All of the homey rooms have hot-water bathroom and simple decorative motifs.

Lagarta Lodge (☎ 2682-0035; www.lagarta.com; s/d/tr US$75/81/87; P) North of Pancho's Resort, a road dead-ends at this six-room hotel, a recommended choice high on a steep hill above the private 50-hectare Reserva Biológica Nosara. Bird-watching and wildlife-spotting are good here – and you can watch from the comfort of the hotel balcony or see many more species if you go on a hike. Large rooms have high ceilings, hot shower and small private patio or balcony. The balcony restaurant (breakfast and lunch ₡2100 to ₡3800, dinner ₡4700 to ₡7800; closed Tuesday) is worth a visit just for the spectacular view and sunsets, though the rotating menu of international and Tico specialties is equally appealing.

Pancho's Resort (☎ 2682-0591; www.panchosresort.com; bungalows US$76-145; P) On the main road between Playa Pelada and Nosara village, this large property has it all: supermarket, bar, restaurant and *cabinas*. Comfortable bungalows sleeping four to six people have attractive tiled floors, high ceilings, hot-water bathroom, loft and kitchenette. To top it off, Pancho and his bilingual family are all incredibly nice.

Villa Mango B&B (☎ 2682-0130; www.villamangocr.com; s/d incl breakfast US$78/89; P) You can't help but relax at this tiny B&B in the trees, with ocean views and hosts who enjoy chatting with their guests. While there's a pool on the property, you can also take a short stroll down to an isolated stretch of beach.

Olga's Bar & Restaurant (mains ₡1700-3500; breakfast, lunch & dinner) A few hundred meters to the north of La Luna, on a separate side road, lies this perennially popular beachside institution. The Tico-owned joint whips up cheap, yummy *casados* (set meals) and very reasonable fish dinners.

La Luna (☎ 2682-0122; dishes ₡3000-10,000; lunch & dinner) On the beach, to the right of Hotel Playas de Nosara, you'll find this impressive stone building that houses a trendy restaurant-bar and art gallery. The eclectic menu has Asian and Mediterranean flourishes, and the views (and cocktails) are intoxicating. Call ahead for reservations.

Drinking & Entertainment

Aside from the bars and restaurants previously listed, there are a few places in the village of Nosara.

Near the soccer field are two Tico-riffic spots – Tropicana, which is a great place for showing off your salsa moves, and Bar Bambú, another hot spot for Saturday nights. Tropicana runs a nightly shuttle bus (₡1000), which makes the hotel rounds at 10:30pm, returning to Guiones at 2am. The bar at Kaya Sol has a popular ladies' night on Monday, regular live music and comedy shows and always a good vibe. La Banana rocks on Saturday (ladies' night) and Thursday (reggae night). The popular bar at Casa Tucan attracts a slightly older crowd for live music on Wednesday and Sunday and beer-pong tournaments (!) on Friday.

Getting There & Away

AIR

Both Sansa and NatureAir have one daily flight to and from San José for about US$95 each way.

BUS

Local buses depart from the *pulpería* (corner grocery store) by the soccer field. Traroc buses depart for Nicoya (₡800, two hours) at 5am, 7am, noon and 3pm. Empresas Alfaro buses going to San José (₡4500, five to six hours) depart from the pharmacy by the soccer field at 12:30pm.

For ₡150 any of these buses will drop you off at the beach. To get to Sámara, take any bus out of Nosara and ask the driver to drop you off at *la bomba de Sámara* (Sámara gas station). From there, catch one of the buses traveling from Nicoya to Sámara.

CAR

From Nicoya, a paved road leads toward Playa Sámara. About 5km before Sámara (signed), a windy, bumpy (and, in the dry season, dusty) dirt road leads to the village (4WD recommended). It's also possible to continue north (in the dry season), to Ostional, Junquillal and Paraíso, though you'll have to ford a few rivers. Ask around before trying this road in the rainy season, when the Río Nosara becomes all but impassable.

REFUGIO NACIONAL DE FAUNA SILVESTRE OSTIONAL

This 248-hectare coastal **refuge** extends from Punta India in the north to Playa Guiones in the south, and includes the beaches of Playa Nosara and Playa Ostional. It was created in 1992 to protect the *arribadas,* or mass nesting of the olive ridley sea turtles, which occurs from July to November with a peak from August to October. Along with Playa Nancite in Parque Nacional Santa Rosa, Ostional is one of two main nesting grounds for this turtle in Costa Rica.

The olive ridley is one of the smallest species of sea turtle, typically weighing around 45kg. Although they are endangered, there are a few beaches in the world where ridleys nest in large groupings that can number in the thousands. Scientists believe that this behavior is an attempt to overwhelm predators, which contributes to increased species survival.

Prior to the creation of the park, coastal residents used to harvest eggs indiscriminately (drinking raw turtle eggs is thought to increase sexual vigor). However, an imaginative conservation plan has allowed the inhabitants of Ostional to continue to harvest eggs from the first laying, which are often trampled by subsequent waves of nesting turtles. By allowing locals to harvest the first batches, the economic livelihood of the community is maintained, and the villagers in turn act as park rangers to prevent other poachers from infringing on their enterprise.

Rocky **Punta India** at the northwestern end of the refuge has tide pools that abound with marine life, such as sea anemone, urchin

PENÍNSULA DE NICOYA

TRACKING TURTLES

Since 1998 **Programa Restauracíon de Tortugas Marinas** (Pretoma; Marine Turtle Restoration Program) has collaborated with locals to monitor turtle-nesting activity and the operation of hatcheries in order to guarantee the efficient protection of nesting sea turtles and the production of hatchlings. Members of the community are hired as field assistants, and environmental education activities are held with the children in town. The project also involves tagging, measuring and protecting nesting turtles, which has resulted in a drastic reduction in poaching levels.

At the time of writing, Pretoma was operating projects in Playa Ostional, Playa San Miguel, Playa Costa de Oro (on the central Pacific coast) and Punta Banco, near the border with Panama. For more information on volunteering, visit the website at www.tortugamarina.org.

and starfish. Along the beach, thousands of almost transparent ghost crabs go about their business, as do the bright-red Sally Lightfoot crabs. The vegetation behind the beach is sparse and consists mainly of deciduous trees, and is home to iguanas, crabs, howler monkeys, coatis and many birds. Near the southeastern edge of the refuge is a small mangrove swamp where there is good bird-watching.

Activities

Mass arrivals of **nesting turtles** occur during the rainy season every three or four weeks and last about a week (usually on dark nights preceding a new moon), though it's possible to see turtles in lesser numbers almost any night during nesting season. In the dry season, a fitting consolation prize is the small number of leatherback and green turtles that also nest here. Many of the upmarket hotels and tour operators in the region offer tours to Ostional during nesting season, though you can also visit independently.

Aside from turtle-watching, **surfers** can catch some good lefts and rights here just after low tide, though the beach is notorious for its strong currents and huge, crashing surf – it's definitely not suitable for swimming unless you're green and have flippers.

Sleeping & Eating

Camping (per person US$3) is permitted behind the centrally located Soda La Plaza, which has a portable toilet available. The *soda* is open for breakfast, lunch and dinner.

Cabinas Guacamaya (☎ 2682-0430; r without bathroom per person US$10; Ⓟ) In the village of Ostional, this place has several small and dark rooms with shared cold showers, though you'll be thrilled to spend the night here as demand is high during nesting season. The same folks run the attached *pulpería,* which can sell you basic supplies.

Cabinas Ostional (☎ 2682-0428; s/d/q US$12/24/36; Ⓟ) The rooms are slightly better here, with private cold-water shower and a cozy garden. This place, too, fills up quickly.

Rancho Brovilla (☎ 2280-4919, 8821-5910; www.brovill.com; s US$35-45, d US$55-65, apt US$60-80, casas US$125-200, all incl breakfast; Ⓟ ❄ 🏊) In the hills, 2km north of town, Rancho Brovilla is an upscale lodge that's a world away from the more modest accommodations in Ostional. Rooms are adorned with stained-wood accents and come equipped with hot-water bathroom. There's also a restaurant-bar (dishes ₡3100 to ₡11,000) featuring international food.

Getting There & Away

Ostional village is about 8km northwest of Nosara village. During the dry months there are two daily buses from Santa Cruz (times change, so ask around), but at any time of the year the road can get washed out by rain. Hitchhiking from Nosara is reportedly easy.

If you're driving, plan on taking a 4WD as a few rivers need to be crossed. From the main road joining Nosara beach and village, head north and cross the bridge over the Río Nosara. After the bridge, there's a T-junction after about 2km; take the left fork (which is signed) and continue on the main road north to Ostional, about 6km away. There are several river crossings on the way to Ostional, so ask locally about conditions before setting out.

Beyond Ostional, the dirt road continues on to Marbella before arriving in Paraíso, northeast of Junquillal. Be careful and ask before attempting this drive and use a 4WD.

PLAYA SÁMARA

The crescent-shaped strip of pale-gray sand at Sámara is one of the most beloved beaches in Costa Rica – it's safe, tranquil, reasonably developed and easily accessible by public transportation. Not surprisingly, you'll find it's popular with vacationing Tico families, backpackers, wealthy tourists, snorkelers and surfers alike (even Oscar Arias, the ex-president, has a vacation house near here). The calm waters make it an ideal destination for families.

In recent years the village has undergone a bit of a transformation. Sámara is becoming increasingly more sophisticated. Although the village is trying to hang on to the authenticity of its relaxed vibe, Sámara is one of the more sophisticated destinations in the central peninsula.

If you've got some extra time and a 4WD, explore the hidden beaches north of Sámara such as Playa Barrigona, equally famous for its pristine beach as for its celebrity resident, Mel Gibson.

Information

Go to www.samarabeach.com to get the skinny on Sámara.

Banco Nacional (☎ 2656-0086; 🕑 9am-5pm Mon-Fri) Change money at this bank next to the church; there's also an ATM.

Banco Popular A 24-hour ATM located on the north side of the soccer field.

Internet Sámara (☎ 2656-1102; per hr ₡1000; 🕑 9am-9pm) On the main road next to Bar Arriba.

Post Office (🕑 8am-noon & 1:15-5:30pm Mon-Fri) Located in the same building as the police station, on the main road where it meets the beach.

Sámara Computers (☎ 2656-0973; per hr ₡800; 🕑 8am-7pm Mon-Fri, to noon Sat) Internet access, located directly across the street from Banco Nacional.

Sámara Beach Travel Center (☎ 2656-0922; www.samara-tours.com; 🕑 9am-9pm) On the main road, this place has an Internet cafe (per hour ₡1000), and can book flights and Interbus tickets and arrange tours. It also rents bicycles (US$10 per day), scooters (US$25 per day) and kayaks (US$20).

Sámara Laundry (☎ 2656-3000; per kg ₡700; 🕑 8:30am-6:30pm Mon-Sat) Laundry service located on the main road, one block up from the beach.

Activities

CANOPY TOURS

The local zip line operator is **Wing Nuts** (☎ 2656-0153; adult/child US$55/35), located on the eastern outskirts of town off the main paved road.

FISHING

The French-owned **Samara Fishing Trip** (☎ 2656-1033; www.samarafishingtrip.com; US$450-550) offers a variety of inshore and offshore sportfishing trips.

FLIGHTS

Several kilometers west, in Playa Buenavista, the **Flying Crocodile** (☎ 2656-8048; www.flying-crocodile.com) offers ultralight flights (20-minute tour US$75). It also offers flight lessons (US$170 per hour).

SNORKELING & DIVING

The highly recommended **Pura Vida Dive Center** (☎ 2656-0643, 8313-3518; www.puravidadive.com; 2-tank dive incl equipment US$95) arranges diving, snorkeling, fishing and dolphin- and whale-watching tours. Or get your PADI open-water certification (US$400) in three or four days. Ecuadorian dive master Oscar has thousands of dives under his belt, speaks English and has excellent equipment. His shop is located across from Posada Matilori, about 100m east of the main road.

Cabinas Kunterbunt (p288) has an onsite dive school and offers diving and lodging package deals.

SURFING

Experienced surfers will probably be bored with Sámara's inconsistent waves, though beginners can have a blast here.

The experienced and personable Jesse at **Jesse's Sámara Surf School** (☎ 2656-0055; www.samarasurfschool.com) has been teaching wannabe surfers for years, as does his daughter Sunrise. Their friendly, expert instruction is highly recommended by readers (private one-hour lesson US$40). Jesse also arranges custom surfing safaris to secret spots all over the coast and offers yoga and pilates classes.

Another great choice is the **C&C Surf School** (☎ 2656-0590; cncsurfsamara.webs.com; 🕑 8am-8pm), which gives one-hour private lessons for US$30; the fee includes another hour of board rental afterwards, and the school donates 10% from every surf lesson to a local children's school and a turtle conservation project. It also rents kayaks and surfboards and arranges a variety of tours and trips throughout Costa Rica. Its shop at the north end of town also has a basketball court, skate ramp and gym.

Courses

Centro de Idiomas Intercultura (☎ 2656-0127, 2260-8480; www.samaralanguageschool.com) has a campus right on the beach. Language courses begin at US$285 per week, or US$425 with homestay accomodations.

Sleeping

HOSTELS

ourpick **Hostel Casa Brian** (☎ 2656-0315; casabrian@hotmail.com; dm US$16, s/d US$30/40) The only hostel in town, these spartan but comfy and clean rooms are owned by Brian, a superfriendly Canadian and former commercial fisherman. Amenities include a shared kitchen, all-you-can-eat breakfast (Sunday is banana pancake day) and free use of bikes, snorkeling gear, toys, coolers and more. It's only 60m from the beach, about 300m east of the main road.

BUDGET

Showers are all cold unless otherwise noted.

Camping Los Coco (☎ 2656-0496; camping per person US$5) On the eastern edge of the beach, this attractive site has well-maintained facilities but can sometimes be absolutely packed. There are several other campsites along this road if Los Coco has no space.

Cabinas Kunterbunt (☎ 2656-0235; www.cabinas-villa-kunterbunt.com; s/d/tr US$30/40/50, s/d without bathroom US$20/25; P) Tommy and Antje, the German owners, have built a beachfront house and 'multicolored' (in case you were wondering what Kunterbunt meant) *cabinas* right beside a peaceful section of the beach. From the communal outdoor kitchen to the lawn area leading on to the beach, the place has a bare-bones, marooned-on-a-desert-island feel. Antje is a certified dive master and offers dive trips and PADI certification courses. It's 3km from town, so you'll want your own wheels.

Posada Matilori (☎ 2656-0984; posadamatilori@racsa.co.cr; s/d without bathroom US$25/35, with air-con US$35/45; P) With seven new rooms in a cozy and secure home and annex, Stefano and Yorlenny, the extremely friendly Italian-Tica couple running this inn, provide every comfort – orthopedic beds, flowers and soap on your bed, free laundry, free coffee and tea, free use of the boogie boards, a fully equipped kitchen (with a waffle iron!) and lots of comfy hammocks. Shared bathrooms have hot water. The entire property is absolutely spotless (Yorlenny admits she's a bit OCD when it comes to cleaning) and on a quiet side street close to the beach.

La Locanda (☎ 2656-0036; www.locandasamara.com; d with/without bathroom US$35/30, d with air-con US$70, apt US$110-150; P) These clean, bright rooms are right on the beach, and there's a bar and cafe out front. Rooms with air-con also have a fridge and cable TV, and the hotel has secure parking.

Hotel Casa del Mar (☎ 2656-0264; www.casadelmarsamara.net; d with/without bathroom incl breakfast US$85/34; P) Just east of the Super Sámara Market and close to the beach is this agreeable US-run hotel, which has a good mix of rooms for travelers of all budgets. If you don't need your own bathroom, rooms here are a steal (and you can still use the Jacuzzi), though those with bathroom are bright, airy and well worth the money.

Tico Adventure Lodge (☎ 2656-0628; www.ticoadventurelodge.com; s/d/apt US$34/68/130; P) The US owners are proud of the fact that they built this lodge without cutting down a single tree, and they have every reason to be – it's stunning. Nine double rooms with bathroom and wood accents are surrounded by lush vegetation and old-growth trees, while the tree-top apartment for four lets you swing on the patio hammock from three stories high. Or you can stay in the poolside house for five (US$151) with a fully equipped kitchen and dining room and dream about a life in the tropics. Cheaper weekly and monthly rates are available.

Casa Valeria (☎ 2656-0511; casavaleria_af@hotmail.com; d/tr/q from US$35/52/81; P) This intimate little inn is right on the beach about 100m east of the main road. The rooms and bungalows vary in size and are fairly simple, though it's the hammock-strung palm trees and tranquil garden setting that make this place a winner. There's a communal kitchen.

MIDRANGE

All showers are hot unless otherwise stated.

Hotel Belvedere (☎ 2656-0213; www.samara-costarica.com; s/d/tr/q US$45/65/75/85, bungalows US$75, all incl breakfast; P) Set in a breezy garden with nice views at the northern end of town, the Belvedere has 24 whitewashed rooms with exposed wooden beams, solar-heated private shower, cable TV and a small private terrace. Two larger bungalows include a kitchenette – perfect for self-caterers looking for a quiet spot in town. The German owners also speak English. Credit cards are accepted.

our pick **Entre Dos Aguas B&B** (☎ 2656-0998; www.hoteldosaguas.com; s/d/tr/q incl breakfast US$47/52/60/70; P) This fantastic little inn, on the way into town, is what one reader accurately describes as 'Mercedes Benz accommodations on a Toyota budget.' Seven brightly colored rooms have a private stone shower, vibrant woven linens and homey little touches such as incense and candles. A well-manicured garden surrounds the pool, and the common courtyard is invitingly strung with hammocks and set with heavy tables. There's an outdoor wood-fired oven if you're inspired to grill your supper.

Sámara Pacific Lodge (☎ 2656-1033; www.samara-pacific-lodge.com; d/tr/q US$85/96/107; P) Located 1.4km west of downtown, this quiet, colonial-style hotel has been returned to its previous glory by the new French owners. Spacious whitewashed, individually decorated rooms have a high ceiling and bathroom and terrace, some with king-sized beds. Onsite amenities include a huge swimming pool, a baby pool, a lounge with foosball and a European restaurant and bar. Though it's a bit far from the beach, this is an excellent choice for families.

Hotel Mirador de Sámara (☎ 2656-0044; www.miradordesamara.com; tr incl breakfast US$95, apt US$105; P) Perched on a hill on the northern edge of town is this architecturally unusual hotel, complete with looming towers that offer dizzying views of the area. The 'sky rooms' can accommodate up to three, while the large apartments with kitchen can sleep up to six. There's also a small private restaurant with panoramic views of the entire area.

TOP END

Sámara Tree House Inn (☎ 2656-0733; www.samaratreehouse.com; bungalows incl breakfast from US$110; P) These five stilt tree houses for grown-ups are so appealing that you might not want to move out. Fully equipped kitchens have pots and pans hanging from driftwood racks, the cable TVs spin on lazy Susans to face whichever room you're in, and there's wi-fi throughout. Even the bathroom tiling is gorgeous. Huge windows let in light and breezes, and hammocks are hung underneath the raised bungalows.

Villas Pepitas (☎ 2656-0747; www.villaspepitas.com; d/tr/q apt US$110/130/150, d/tr/q villas US$120/140/160; P) On the west side of town, just before crossing the river, these cheery yellow villas are like a sunny slice of Italy in a tropical garden setting. It's quiet on this road, but just a short walk into town and to the beach. The owner is friendly but completely respectful of guests' privacy and comfort.

our pick **El Pequeño Gecko Verde** (☎ 2656-1176; www.gecko-verde.com; s/d/t $141, q $186; P) A hidden slice of heaven on earth, this stunning French-owned hotel is our favorite new B&B in Península de Nicoya. Five contemporary and beautifully decorated bungalows all have a fully equipped kitchen, flat-screen cable TV, a private terrace with hammock and outdoor dining area, plus our favorite feature, outdoor stone shower. A tropical garden of Eden surrounds the bungalows. Onsite amenities include a saltwater swimming pool with waterfall and a fabulous open-air restaurant and bar. Behind the property, a 400m jungle trail and steep cement staircase lead to a secret beach that doesn't appear on any map – Playa Izquierda, a stunning cove beach backed by high cliffs with amazing sunset views.

Eating

'Out with the old and in with the new' is the name of the game in Sámara. There are still some simple *sodas* left in town, but with each passing year the restaurant scene is reinventing itself to cater to a more sophisticated palate. Self-caterers can stock up on supplies at Super Sámara Market, east of the main road, or the smaller Super La Amistad on the main road by the beach.

Soda Sheriff Rustic (mains ₡1500-2800; breakfast, lunch & dinner) One of a few classic *sodas* in town. The beachside location sells itself, though the filling breakfasts, killer *casados* and low, low prices aren't too bad either.

Restaurante Jardín Marino (☎ 2656-0934; mains ₡2000-10,500; lunch & dinner) This large, airy *soda* is always packed, and if you sit yourself down and order something here, you'll see why. The typical food is fresh and of high quality – a *casado de pescado* here means grilled fish, not a deep-fried filet. It's on the main road leading to the beach.

Restaurante Las Brasas (☎ 2656-0546; mains ₡2500-15,000; noon-late) This upscale Spanish restaurant on the main street has all the signature dishes including tortillas, paellas and roast suckling pig. It also has a well-stocked wine cellar, and the upstairs balcony is perfect for people-watching.

Shake Joe's (☎ 2656-0252; mains ₡2800-8500; 11am-late) This hip beachside spot is awash with chilled-out electronica and cool, calm travelers lounging on the huge wooden outdoor couches. You can grab a burger here after your surf session, but the ambience is tops when the sun goes down and the drinks start to flow.

our pick **Al Manglar** (☎ 2656-0096; mains ₡3000-5000; 5pm-10pm) Consistently the best restaurant in town, this thatched-roof, open-air restaurant serves some of the best Italian food in town at reasonable prices. The pasta dishes such as gnocchi and ravioli are real winners. Pizza-lovers, don't miss the Manglar special, with ham, bacon, onions, tomatoes and mushrooms, cooked to perfection. It's tucked on a side street behind El Lagarto.

Casa Esmeralda (☎ 2656-0489; mains ₡3000-10,000; noon-9:30pm Mon-Sat) A favorite with locals, the extensive menu here has a good selection of Tico and international dishes. We loved the fish with avocado sauce, and the friendly staff. There are also a few sunny but overpriced rooms for rent upstairs.

Tabanuco (☎ 2656-1056; mains ₡6500-16,500; ⏰ lunch & dinner) Named for the founder of Sámara, Esteban 'Tabanuco' Castillo Vargas, this posh beachfront bar-restaurant is the most upscale and romantic eatery in town. The open-air deck with driftwood beams is bathed in twinkling lights. The international menu features seafood and grilled meats. Don't miss the *crema de mariscos* (cream of seafood soup).

El Lagarto (☎ 2656-0750; ww.ellagartobbq.com; mains ₡9000-16,000; ⏰ 11am-11pm; 📶) Grilled meats are the big draw at this beachfront alfresco restaurant draped by old trees. Watching the chefs work their magic on the giant wood-fired oven is part of the fun. Our New York strip steak was cooked to perfection. Wash it all down with the biggest margaritas you've ever seen. It's a bit touristy and pricey but worth the splurge.

Drinking & Entertainment

The coolest nightspot in town is the separated beachfront bar at Tabanuco (above), with a big tiled dance floor and surf videos; Friday is reggae night.

La Vela Latina, on the beach, serves sophisticated *bocas* and perfectly blended cocktails and sangría to guests sitting on wooden seats or rocking in comfy leather chairs. To settle in for the evening with some *bocas* and beers with the locals, check out Pablito's Bar way on the west side of town.

On the main road, Shake Joe's (p289) really gets going in the evenings with low lighting and trendy tunes. Tutti Frutti Discotheque (on the beach) keeps the music pumping late most weekends of the year, and is perennially popular with Ticos. Bar Olas is a good place to get started with an Imperial on a beach log.

The poshest new bar in town is Bar Arriba. As the name suggests, it's located upstairs of an office building, offering prime people-watching views of the main drag below, and it serves Spanish tapas and airs US sports on TV.

Shopping

Numerous vendors sell crafts and handmade jewelry at stands along the main road.

Koss Art Gallery (☎ 2656-0284) Visit Jaime at his outdoor studio on the beach, where he frequently displays his richly hued works in the high season. Call ahead for a viewing.

Galería Dragonfly (☎ 2656-0964; www.samaraarte.com) You'll see Leonardo Palacios' mural as you walk the main street; the gallery inside houses uniquely wrought jewelry in all sorts of media such as leather and seashells, along with sculpture, paintings and decorative pieces in a very organic style.

Also worth a stop is Mama Africa, which sells beautiful beaded leather sandals from Kenya. The Italian owners work directly with a Masai collective that crafts the sandals, and purchases support this work.

Getting There & Away

The beach lies about 35km southwest of Nicoya on a well-paved road.

AIR

The airport serving Playa Sámara is nearer to Playa Carrillo (and is often referred to as Carrillo). Sansa flies daily to and from San José (one way/round-trip US$89/178). Book flights at Sámara Beach Travel Center (see p287).

BUS

Empresas Alfaro has a bus to San José (₡3600, five hours) that departs at 4:30am, 8:30am and 1pm Monday to Saturday. On Sunday there is only one bus at 9am. All buses depart from the main intersection just south of Entre Dos Aguas B&B.

Traroc buses to Nicoya (₡900, two hours) depart 11 times daily from the *pulpería* by the soccer field; there's a more limited schedule on Sunday.

PLAYA CARRILLO

About 4km southeast of Sámara, this lazily curving beach with its palm-fringed boulevard is quieter and less developed. With its clean white sand, rocky headlands and backdrop of jungle, Carrillo is a postcard-perfect tropical beach. During weekends and holidays, the boulevard is lined with cars and the beach crowded with Tico families camped out festively beneath the palms.

The little town is on a hillside above the beach and attracts a trickle of surfers working their way down the coast, as well as schools of American sportfishers chasing billfish. About 200m east of the beach, **La Selva** (☎ 2656-2236; adult/child US$8/5; ⏰ 8am-7pm) is a small wildlife refuge and botanical garden with monkeys, iguanas, alligators, coatis and other critters.

Activities

SPORTFISHING

Kingfisher Sportfishing (☎ 2656-0091; www.costaricabillfishing.com) is a well-known local outfit, offering half- and full-day excursions from US$600.

SURF CASTING

You don't have to drop big bucks to catch some nice-sized fish – do as the Ticos do and try your hand at surf casting. Most hotels and tour outfitters can set you up for a few dollars.

SURFING

Surfing here is better than at nearby Playa Sámara, though it's nothing great. Mid- to high tide is when you can catch some decent waves.

Tours

Carrillo Tours (☎ 2656-0543; www.carrillotours.com; 8am-7pm), on the road up the hill, organizes snorkeling, dolphin-watching, kayaking, horseback riding and trips to Palo Verde (p223).

Sleeping & Eating

All of the hotels listed below are at the eastern end of the beach on a hill. The beach is a five- to 10-minute walk down from most of these places.

Camping Mora (☎ 2656-0118; per person US$5; P) At the western end of the beach, this campsite has showers, bathrooms, electricity and potable water.

Casa Buenavista (☎ 2656-0385; www.samarabeach.com/casabuenavista; d incl breakfast US$45-55; P) A sweet Italian couple runs this two-room B&B. Each basic but homey room has its own hot-water bathroom, porch and entrance, and there's a small shaded yoga terrace in the garden.

Cabinas El Colibrí (☎ 2656-0656; www.samarabeach.com/elcolibri; s/d/tr incl breakfast US$50/60/70; P ✻) These Argentine-run *cabinas* are high on the hilltop, and come fully equipped with hot-water bathroom. Mini-apartments with kitchenette are the same price but don't include breakfast. It's a relaxed and comfortable spot, and you'll be well fed at the attached restaurant, which serves traditional Argentine *parrilladas* (grilled meats) and *empanadas* (corn turnovers with minced meat).

Carrillo Club (☎ 2656-0316; www.carrilloclub.com; s/d/tr/q incl breakfast US$60/85/95/105, apt US$85; P ✻) This pretty yellow inn on the hillside has a clutch of comfortable *cabinas* with a private terrace and hot-water bathroom. The two-person apartments are equipped with a kitchen. There's a pool with ocean views, and the beach is a short walk downhill. Taking breakfast on the big front terrace is a treat, with beautiful, expansive views of Playa Carrillo below.

Hotel Arena Blanca (☎ 2656-2025; www.arenablancahotel.com; d incl breakfast US$111; P ✻) Designed like a modern-day hacienda, this hotel employs rustic detail with contemporary polish. Backed by trees, the low-lying building circles a pool area, and the beach is only 150m away. Staff can arrange tours.

Hotel Esperanza (☎ 2656-0564; www.hotelesperanza.com; d incl breakfast US$120; P ✻) Cheerful rooms at this recently remodeled hotel are set back from a columned promenade and open on to the pool area. The rooms are a bit small, but packed with amenities such as cable TV, DVD player, hair dryer and tropical artwork.

There is a number of small *sodas* along the road and soccer field.

Getting There & Away

Regularly scheduled Sansa flights to and from San José (one way/round-trip US$89/178) use the airstrip just northwest of the beach. Some Traroc buses from Nicoya to Sámara continue on the well-paved road to Playa Carrillo – check with the driver first.

ISLITA AREA

The coast southeast of Playa Carrillo remains one of the most isolated and wonderful stretches of coastline in the Nicoya peninsula, mainly because it's largely inaccessible and lacking in accommodations. Regardless, if you're willing to tackle some rugged roads or venture down the coastline in a sea kayak (or possibly on foot), you'll be rewarded with abandoned beaches backed by pristine wilderness and rugged hills.

There are a few smaller breaks in front of the Hotel Punta Islita. Another good beach break lies north of Punta Islita at **Playa Camaronal**. This beach also happens to be a protected nesting site for leatherback, olive ridley, hawksbill and black turtles, and is officially known as **Refugio Nacional de Vida Silvestre Camaronal**.

Playas Corzalito and **Bejuco** to the south of Punta Islita are both backed by mangrove swamps, and offer good opportunities for bird- and wildlife-watching.

Also worth a visit is the small town of **Islita**, which is home to the Museo de Arte Contemporáneo al Aire Libre, an open-air exhibition of contemporary art featuring mosaics, murals, carvings and paintings that adorn everything from houses to tree trunks. This project was organized by Hotel Punta Islita, which sells local art in its gift shop and invests proceeds in the community. If you're interested in helping with the project, inquire at the hotel about volunteer possibilities in the community.

Sleeping & Eating

You can camp on the beaches (without facilities) if you have a vehicle and are self-sufficient.

our pick **Hotel Punta Islita** (☎ 2656-2020; www.hotelpuntaislita.com; d/ste incl breakfast US$349/489, casitas from US$559; P ✖ 💻 📶 🏊) This luxury resort should serve as an example of how to ethically operate a hotel in Costa Rica. In addition to organizing community arts projects, the hotel has sponsored the construction of various public buildings, including a new church, and is consistently working to integrate the rural community of Islita into its development. The hotel is on a hilltop, and has 40 fully equipped rooms with staggering ocean views; spend up for a suite (with a private outdoor Jacuzzi). The infinity pool and surrounding grounds are simply stunning, and the staff can arrange any tour you desire.

Restaurante Mirador Barranquilla (mains ₡2000-7000; 🕑 11am-midnight Wed-Mon) On the crest of a hill about 2km southeast of the hotel, the Mirador Barranquilla has breathtaking 180-degree views of Punta Islita and Playas Bejuco and San Miguel, and is the top place in the area for a sunset beer.

Cambute (mains ₡2800-5000; 🕑 lunch & dinner) For something more low-key, this dressed-up *soda* serves excellent *ceviche* (uncooked, marinated seafood) and *casados* in a relaxed, riverside setting.

1492 Restaurant (☎ 2661-4044; mains ₡7000-14,000; 🕑 breakfast, lunch & dinner) The movie *1492* was shot on location in Punta Islita, and some of the set pieces adorn the restaurant. The cuisine here, which is a fusion of Costa Rican and international food, is top quality – and the view is superlative.

Getting There & Away

AIR

NatureAir and Sansa each fly once daily between San José and Punta Islita (one way/round-trip around US$95/190).

BUS

The closest you can get to Islita by bus is to take one of Empresa Arza's two daily buses from San José that go through San Francisco de Coyote and on to Playas San Miguel and Bejuco. Keep in mind, though, that from Bejuco there is still a long uphill hike to Islita – and hitchhiking is almost impossible due to the lack of traffic.

CAR

Although Punta Islita is less than 10km by road southeast of Playa Carrillo, the coastal 'road' is wicked and requires some river crossings that are impossible in the wet season. See boxed text, p304, for more information. The 'easiest' route is for you to head inland on the paved road from Playa Carrillo to the village of Estrada. When you come to the fork in the road, bear left (turning right would take you down the aforementioned scary road). At the 'T' intersection in Santa Marta, turn right onto the gravel road to Islita. At the next 'T' intersection, you can turn right on the rough but decent dirt road to reach Islita (11km), or left to reach Playas San Miguel and Coyote via San Pedro, Cangrejal and Bejuco.

PLAYAS SAN MIGUEL & COYOTE

Just south of Playa Bejuco are arguably two of the most beautiful and least visited beaches in Costa Rica. Playa San Miguel, to the north, and Playa Coyote, to the south, are wilderness beaches of fine, silver-gray sand that are separated by the mouth of the Río Jabillo. Despite opportunities for great surfing, kayaking and just about anything else you want to do on a sandy strip of paradise, the beaches are nearly always abandoned (the lack of reliable public transportation is probably to blame). As if there weren't enough reasons to visit, San Miguel and Coyote also serve as nesting grounds for olive ridley turtles.

There are no coastal villages to speak of, though a number of in-the-know foreigners have settled in the area and have built some beautiful accommodations near the shoreline. The nearest village is **San Francisco de Coyote**, which is 4km inland and has a few small *sodas*, *cabinas* and an internet cafe. For a good online map of the area, visit www.nicoyapeninsula.com/coyote/map.php.

Activities

You can revel in the crowd-free beach breaks to **surf** off San Miguel, particularly when the tide is rising. At Coyote there is an offshore reef that can be surfed at high tide.

If **swimming**, you are advised to take precautions as the surf can pick up, and there are not many people in the area to help you in an emergency.

If you have your own sea kayak, these beaches (as well as nearby Islita) are perfect for coastal exploration.

Sleeping & Eating

You can camp on both beaches if you're self-sufficient, as there are no services.

Soda Familiar y Cabinas Rey (☎ 2655-1055; s/d US$8/15; P 💻 📶) For those taking the more direct (and treacherous) route to Mal País, this Tico-run *soda* in the village of San Francisco de Coyote is a good place to stock up on provisions and get some local advice. If it's getting late, you might want to stay here as there are simple *cabinas* with private cold-water shower for rent. Believe it or not, this is a wi-fi hot spot.

Hotel Arca de Noé (☎ 2655-8065; dm US$10, d incl breakfast US$70, extra person US$10; P ❄ 🏊) Inland from the beach, this pleasantly landscaped, critter-friendly complex has 10 attractive doubles with a private hot-water shower and air-con. It grows many of its own fruits and herbs, has a dairy that provides the milk and cheese for the restaurant and has begun a community recycling program in the area.

Blue Pelican (☎ 2655-8046; d incl breakfast US$35-45; P 💻) Near the center of Playa San Miguel is this quirky, purple wooden house. There's a variety of rooms suited for singles to groups, including a great upstairs suite with ocean views and a private terrace. Just steps from the beach, the inn has an outdoor shower and board storage racks. The bar-restaurant (mains ₡2500 to ₡6500) has international dishes emphasizing fresh seafood, and the beer is cold.

Flying Scorpion (☎ 2655-8080; escorpionvolador.com; d incl breakfast US$45, apt US$75, houses US$100-250; P) Turn right at the Blue Pelican and continue on the dirt road along the beach for a few hundred meters to find this mellow inn with a handful of clean, very comfortable rooms, with new teak beds and an assortment of eclectic folk art. It has direct beach access for long days of surfing, and you'll be happy to come back to the bar-restaurant's homemade bread, pasta and ice cream. Run by an amiable couple and their pack of Weimaraners, this is a great spot to zone out for a few days or weeks.

Casitas Azul Plata (☎ 2655-8209; www.casitas-azulplata.com; d/tr apt US$70/80; P ❄ 🏊) This homey, German-run spot has a couple of two-bedroom apartments with a full kitchen, cable TV and hot-water shower. It's a great choice for families, located on a quiet hillside.

our pick **Casa Caletas** (☎ 2289-6060; www.casacaletas.com; d/ste/villas incl breakfast US$206/247/746; P ❄ 🏊) Down at the end of the road before turning toward Mal País, this beautiful little boutique hotel sits on the bank of the Río Coyote and feels blissfully isolated. There's an airy *palapa* (shelter with a thatched, palm-leaf roof and open sides) restaurant, cushy rooms and an infinity pool overlooking the river and ocean. The beach is accessible by crossing the river or via trails, and the hotel can arrange horseback rides, kayaking and fishing trips. To get here, take the road from San Francisco de Coyote toward Mal País and follow the signs for the hotel.

Bar.Co Nico (☎ 2655-1205; www.barco-nico.com; bocas ₡900-1600, mains ₡2500-7500; 🕒 10am-late; 💻 📶) A few kilometers past the village on the turnoff for Costa de Oro, this German-run beachfront restaurant (which looks like a giant ship) has reinstated the old Tico tradition of giving away a free *boca* with every beer. The beer is cold and the *bocas* (appetizers) are delicious – what are you waiting for? There's also free wi-fi, and Nico now rents a few simple *cabinas*.

Getting There & Away

BUS

Empresa Arza (☎ 2650-0179) has two daily buses from San José that cross the Golfo de Nicoya on the Puntarenas ferry and continue through Jicaral to San Francisco de Coyote, and on to Playas San Miguel and Bejuco. Buses depart San José at 6am and 3:30pm, pass through San Francisco de Coyote at about 11:30am and 10pm, and arrive at Playa San Miguel at noon and 10:30pm. Return buses leave Bejuco at 2:15am and 12:30pm, pass through Playa San Miguel at around 3am and 1:15pm, and San Francisco de Coyote at 3:30am and

1:45pm. This service is sketchy in the rainy season and the trip may take longer if road conditions are bad.

There aren't any other bus services frequenting this area from Nicoya – or from any other of the peninsula towns, for that matter.

In addition, there is no bus service (because there is barely an actual road) along the coast between Playa Coyote and Mal País.

CAR

See p292 for information about heading north along the coast from here. Also see boxed text, p304, for details on how you could *possibly* travel further south along the coast.

SOUTHEASTERN PENINSULA

At the very southern tip of the Península de Nicoya lies the first and one of the most pristine natural reserves in Costa Rica – and there's a reason it has remained so untouched. An arduous drive down the rugged southeastern coastal route crosses several rivers through the thick rainforest before dropping back down toward the beach at Mal País, just north of the reserve. From the other side, it used to require hours of dusty bus rides and sluggish ferries from the mainland to access this tropical land's end, but these days more roads in the region are slowly being paved and regular shuttles are dropping tourists right into Mal País and Montezuma, making Cabo Blanco a day trip from either burgeoning base.

Word has spread about the miles of surf breaks in Mal País and the chilled vibe of hippie outpost Montezuma – and transportation options have sprung up to meet the demands of surfers and wanderers steadily streaming in to the southeastern peninsula. Growth is somewhat limited by geography in Montezuma and the pulse there beats at the same relaxed pace, but Mal País is pumping. The beauty and wildness on either side of the peninsula can hold you under its thrall, so give yourself the luxury of time here.

As in the rest of the peninsula, Ticos in this region primarily live rural lives centered on agriculture and ranching, though the recent influx of travelers has created a number of jobs in the tourism market.

PLAYA NARANJO

This tiny village next to the ferry terminal is nothing more than a few *sodas* and small hotels that cater to travelers either waiting for the ferry or arriving from Puntarenas. There really isn't any reason to hang around, and thankfully you probably won't have to, as the ferries tend to run reasonably on time.

If you get stuck at the port for a night, the **Hotel El Ancla** (☎ 2661-3887; d with/without air-con US$60/50; P) is just 200m from the pier. Rooms with cold-water bathroom seem a bit pricey, but there's a pool, bar and restaurant to help kill the time.

There's a small *soda* next to the ferry port, as well as a few vendors selling shaved ice and other goodies.

Getting There & Away

All transportation is geared to the arrival and departure of the Puntarenas ferry, so don't worry – if either is running late, the other will wait.

BOAT

The **Coonatramar ferry** (☎ 2661-1069; www.coonatramar.com; adult/child/car ₡860/515/1850) to Puntarenas departs daily at 8am, 12:30pm, 5:30pm and 9pm, and can accommodate both cars and passengers. The trip takes 1½ hours. If traveling by car, get out and buy a ticket at the window, get back in your car and then drive on to the ferry. You cannot buy a ticket on board. Show up at least an hour early on holidays and busy weekends, as you'll be competing with a whole lot of other drivers to make it on.

BUS

Buses meet the ferry and take passengers on to Nicoya (₡1000, three hours). Departure times are (approximately) 7am, 10:50pm, 2:50pm and 7pm.

Regular buses journey from Paquera to Montezuma, though there are none that go southeast from here.

CAR & TAXI

It's possible to get to Paquera via a scenic, bumpy and steep dirt road with some great vistas of Bahía Gigante. For this, a 4WD is recommended, especially in the rainy season when there are rivers to cross. The only public transportation is 4WD taxi, which costs about ₡15,000, depending on the number of passengers and road conditions.

ISLANDS NEAR BAHÍA GIGANTE

The waters in and around the isolated Bahía Gigante, 9km southeast of Playa Naranjo, are studded with rocky islets and deserted islands, 10 large enough to be mapped on a 1:200,000 map. Since there is no public transportation here, and a 4WD is a necessity almost year-round, the area feels very quiet and unhurried (read: completely abandoned).

However, travelers are drawn to this off-the-beaten-path destination for its range of activities, namely sportfishing, snorkeling, diving and kayaking, which can all be arranged through hotels and travel agencies in the area. There are also plenty of opportunities for some serious adventure here: kayak between the islands, camp on a deserted island or explore the crumbling ruins of an island prison – the choice is yours.

Isla San Lucas

The largest island in Bahía Gigante (just more than 600 hectares) is about 5km off the coast from Playa Naranjo, and from a distance seems like a beautiful desert island. However, the 'Island of Unspeakable Horrors' has a 400-year history as one of the most notorious jails in Latin America. The island was first used by Spanish conquistadors as a detention center for local tribes in the 16th century. In 1862 the job of warden was inherited by the Costa Rican government, which used the island to detain political prisoners up until 1992. The prison was also the inspiration for Costa Rica's most internationally famous memoir: *La isla de los hombres solos* (available in English as *God Was Looking the Other Way*) by José León Sánchez, who was imprisoned on the island for stealing *La Negrita* from the cathedral in Cartago.

Visitors to the island can expect to see the 100-year-old overgrown remains of the prison. Although there are still guards living on the island, their primary purpose is to discourage poachers, which means that travelers are usually permitted to wander freely through the prison grounds and even camp on the island.

Isla Gigante

In the middle of Bahía Gigante is the 10-hectare Isla Gigante, which is shown on most maps as Isla Muertos (Island of the Dead) because it is home to a number of Chara burial sites (and believed by locals to be haunted).

The island once served as a rustic resort for yachters, but is now completely abandoned and covered with cacti. Isla Gigante is an interesting place to explore, especially since most Ticos are afraid to set foot on the island (good luck trying to convince anyone to spend the night).

Isla Guayabo, Islas Negritos & Los Pájaros

This cluster of islands was recently established as a biological reserve to protect nesting seabird populations, including the largest breeding colony of brown pelicans in Costa Rica along with frigate birds, boobies, egrets, peregrines and petrels. Although they're not geographically close to one another, the islands are managed as a single unit. For the protection of the birds, no land visitors are allowed except researchers with permission from the park service. However, the reserves can be approached by boat, and the bird populations are large enough to be visible from the ocean.

Isla Tortuga

Isla Tortuga, which consists of two uninhabited islands just offshore from Curú, is widely regarded as the most beautiful island in Costa Rica. The white-sand beaches feel like baby powder, there are gargantuan coconut palms overhead, and the coral reef is perfect for snorkeling. Unfortunately, Tortuga receives heavy boat traffic from tour operators from Montezuma and Jacó, but if you can visit during the week in low season it can be a magical place.

Tours

Most travelers arrange tours either through the hotels listed here or with an operator in Montezuma (p300) or Jacó (p326). However, this is one region where independence (and language skills) can make for a good adventure – inquire locally to find out if someone with a boat is willing to take you where you want to go for a fair price.

The most luxurious excursion is with **Calypso Tours** (☎ 2256-2727; www.calypsocruises.com). The company transports passengers to Isla Tortuga in a luxurious 21m motorized catamaran called the *Manta Raya.* It's all flash with this boat, which has air-con, a couple of outdoor Jacuzzis and an underwater

COSTA RICAN WILDCAT CONSERVATIONISTS

Since 1992 Programa para la Conservación de Felinos (Profelis; Feline Conservation Program) has taken care of confiscated felines that were given to the center by the Ministerio del Ambiente y Energía (Minae; Ministry of Environment and Energy). The project concentrates on smaller felines, including the margay, ocelot and jaguarundi, and aims to rehabilitate and, when possible, reintroduce animals into the wild. In addition, a large component of the program involves the environmental education of the public.

Profelis is headquartered in Hacienda Matambú, a private wildlife reserve in San Rafael de Paquera, about 5km west of Paquera. Volunteers are sought after, especially those that have experience in either keeping animals or veterinary science. For more information on volunteering, visit www.grafischer.com/profelis or contact **Profelis** (☎ 2641-0644/6; profelis@racsa.co.cr).

viewing window. The cost is US$199 – not a bad deal considering that the price includes transportation from San José, Quepos or Manuel Antonio, food and drinks.

Sleeping

Hotels come and go quickly in these parts, but one place that has stood the test of time is **Hotel Maquinay** (☎ 2641-8011; www.maquinaylaperla.com; s/d US$30/50; P). In Playa Naranjo, this quaint hacienda-style hotel is a great deal, with comfortable fan-cooled rooms and shared terraces that look on to a tropical garden and swimming pool. It's located on the road between Naranjo and Paquera.

Getting There & Away

There is no public transportation in the area. The dirt road from Playa Naranjo to Paquera requires a 4WD for most of the year.

PAQUERA

The tiny village of Paquera is about 25km by road from Playa Naranjo and 4km from the ferry terminal. Paquera is more of a population center than Playa Naranjo, though there's little reason to stay here longer than you have to.

Banco Popular (8:15am-4pm), on the side street, can change US dollars and traveler's checks. On the main road, across from the gas station, you'll find **Turismo Curú** (☎ 2641-0004; www.curutourism.com; 7am-9pm), operated by the knowledgeable Luis Schutt of the Curú refuge. Luis offers a tour that combines a visit to Curú and a snorkeling trip to Isla Tortuga for US$30 per person (a great deal!). It also has internet access.

There are a number of *cabinas* in the village, though the best option is **Cabinas & Restaurante Ginana** (☎ 2641-0119; d US$32; P), which has 28 simple and clean rooms with bathroom and optional air-con. There's also a good restaurant (dishes ₡1500 to ₡3000) in case you need a bite to eat before getting on the ferry.

Getting There & Away

All transportation is geared to the arrival and departure of the Puntarenas ferry. If either is running late, the other will wait.

BOAT

Ferry Naviera Tambor (☎ 2641-2084; www.navieratambor.com; adult/child/car ₡810/485/1900) leaves daily at 6am, 9am, 11am, 1pm, 3pm, 5pm, 7pm and 9pm (the last ferry doesn't run in low season). The trip takes about an hour. Buy a ticket at the window, reboard your car and then drive onto the ferry; you can't buy a ticket on board. Show up at least an hour early on holidays and busy weekends. The terminal contains a *soda* where you can grab a bite while waiting for the boat.

BUS

Buses meet passengers at the ferry terminal and take them to Paquera, Tambor and Montezuma. The bus can be crowded, so try to get off the ferry fast to get a seat.

Most travelers take the bus from the terminal directly to Montezuma (₡1400, two hours). Many taxi drivers will tell you the bus won't come, but this isn't true. There are no northbound buses.

TAXI

Getting several travelers together to share a taxi is a good option since the ride will take half as long as the bus. The ride to Montezuma is about ₡5000 per person, and to Mal País it's about ₡7000 – provided you can get enough people together.

A 4WD taxi to Playa Naranjo costs about ₡15,000 for up to four people.

REFUGIO NACIONAL DE VIDA SILVESTRE CURÚ

This small 84-hectare **refuge** (☎ 2641-0100; www.curuwildliferefuge.com; day fee US$10; 🕑 7am-3pm), which is now part of a larger protected area of almost 15 sq km, is a wilderness gem in the largely deforested peninsula. Situated at the eastern end of the peninsula and only 6km south of Paquera, the tiny Curú holds a great variety of landscapes, including dry tropical forest, semideciduous forest and five types of mangrove swamp. The rugged coastline is also home to a series of secluded coves and white-sand beaches that are perfect for snorkeling and swimming.

The refuge is privately owned by the Schutts, a Tico family whose roots in the area go back more than 75 years. They have long been active in environmental efforts, and were instrumental in having the area designated a wildlife refuge. Currently, they are working to reintroduce species to the area, including the scarlet macaw and the rare *mono tití*, or squirrel monkey.

The entrance to the refuge is clearly signed on the paved road between Paquera and Tambor (it's on the right-hand side). Day visitors can show up anytime during operating hours and pay the day fee to hike the trails and visit the reserve. In addition, a variety of tours are available – from horseback riding and kayaking through the estuary to snorkeling and guided hikes. The Schutts can arrange transportation to the reserve from Paquera, and travel agencies in Montezuma (p300) can arrange guided day tours.

Seventeen well-marked, easy to moderate trails take visitors through the different ecosystems; maps are available at the entrance. Readers recommend hiring a guide as it greatly increases your chances of spotting wildlife. The forested areas are the haunts of deer, monkey, agouti and paca, and three species of cat have been recorded. Iguana, crab, lobster, chiton, shellfish, sea turtle and some other marine creatures can be seen on the beaches and in the tide pools. Bird-watchers have recorded more than 232 bird species throughout the reserve, though there are probably more.

Camping is not allowed in the reserve, though there are six rustic **cabinas** (r per person incl 3 meals US$35) with private cold showers. Stays must be arranged in advance either through the Turismo Curú office in Paquera, your tour operator or at the entrance. There is no electricity, so take a flashlight and batteries.

PLAYAS POCHOTE & TAMBOR

These two mangrove-backed gray-sand beaches are protected by Bahía Ballena, the largest bay on the southeastern peninsula, and are surrounded by a few small fishing communities. In the past 15 years, however, the area has slowly developed as a resort destination; the outcome has been less than green. Fortunately, there are a few good choices for accommodations in the area, and for the most part Pochote and Tambor are untouristed, providing plenty of opportunities for hiking, swimming, kayaking and even whale-watching.

The beaches begin 14km south of Paquera, at the community of Pochote, and stretch for about 8km southwest to Tambor – they're divided by the narrow and wadeable estuary of the Río Pánica.

Activities

Both beaches are safe for **swimming**, and there are occasional **whale sightings** in the bay. The gentle waters also make this a good spot for **kayaking**. Although the mangroves are not set up for hiking, Curú is just down the road.

Sleeping

There are a number of all-inclusive, very expensive, environmentally questionable resorts around here – if you want more information, talk to your travel agent.

Cabinas Cristina (☎ 2683-0028; s/d US$22/27; P ⊠) These recommended *cabinas* are run by the always welcoming Eduardo and Cristina, a Tico couple who are eager to show you the *real* beauty of the area. Rooms are simple and spotless, and accommodate travelers of all budgets. There's also a small restaurant, and the owners can give you good advice about booking tours in the area.

Costa Coral Hotel (☎ 2683-0105; www.hotelcostacoral.com; d incl breakfast US$105-120; P ⊠ 🏊) Canadian-owned and Texan-managed, this newly remodeled boutique hotel is better than ever, with 10 colorful Spanish-colonial villas that accommodate up to four people, with hot-water bathroom, cable TV, DVD player and your own terrace overlooking the gardens and pool. The real highlight is the excellent restaurant and bar that's popular with guests and locals alike.

Tambor Tropical (☎ 2365-2872; www.tambortropical.com; ste US$163-222; P) Romantically set on the beach amid a palm-fringed garden, Tambor Tropical is a lovely boutique hotel with stunning architecture. The 12 suites all have dark wood interiors, full kitchen and private veranda. There's no air-con but the ocean breeze will keep you cool on all but the hottest days.

Getting There & Away

The airport is just north of the entrance to Hotel Barceló Playa Tambor. Hotels will arrange pickup at the airport for an extra fee. Between them, Sansa and NatureAir (one way/round-trip US$75/150) have about six daily flights to San José.

Paquera–Montezuma buses pass through here.

CÓBANO

Cóbano has two gas stations, a post office, clinic, pharmacy, Mega Super grocery store and **Banco Nacional** (☎ 2642-0210; 8:30am-3:45pm Mon-Fri, 9am-1pm Sat), making it the only real 'city' (it's hardly even a town) in the southeastern peninsula. Although there are a few hotels and restaurants here, there's no reason to stay since Montezuma is only 5km away.

Paquera–Montezuma buses pass through here, and a 4WD taxi to Montezuma costs about ₡5000.

MONTEZUMA

Up until the late 1990s, a traffic jam in Montezuma was getting off your bike to shoo some cows off the road, a tourist was someone who left after only a month, a night out was rolling a spliff on the beach instead of in your hammock, a good time was – OK, you get the idea. Montezuma was one of the original 'destinations' in Costa Rica, and its remote location and proximity to Costa Rica's first nature reserve, Cabo Blanco, attracted hippies, artists and dreamers alike. You had to work to get here, and no one had plans to leave quickly.

Montezuma is still a charming village, and foreign travelers continue to be drawn here by the laid-back atmosphere, cheap hotels and sprawling beaches. And while nothing ever stays the same, Montezuma has managed to hang on to its tranquil appeal. Typical touristy offerings, such as canopy tours, do a brisk trade here, but you'll see – in the yoga classes, the volunteer opportunities, the arts festivals, the vegan food and the neo-Rastafarians hawking ganja – that the town stays well in touch with its hippie roots. It's no surprise that locals lovingly call this town 'Montefuma.'

Information

The only ATM in town is located across from Chico's Bar, and it's regularly empty of cash on busy weekends. Plan ahead. The nearest full-service bank is in Cóbano (see above). For money exchange, tour operators in town will take US dollars, euros or traveler's checks, though you can expect to pay a heavy commission.

El Parque (per kg ₡900; 7am-8pm) The best place in town to get your laundry done. It also rents bikes (US$10 per day) and scooters (US$35 per day).

Librería Topsy (☎ 2642-0576; 8am-1pm & 3-5pm Mon-Fri, 8am-noon Sat) Has US newspapers and magazines, and a large lending library with books in several languages. It also serves as the unofficial post service, selling stamps and making regular mail drops at Cóbano's post office.

Sun Trails (☎ 2642-0808; per hr ₡1000; 9am-9pm) Internet access.

Sights & Activities

Kerri Bowers and César Benavides of **Proyecto Montezuma** (www.proyectomontezuma.com) run an innovative volunteer program that not only gives to the community, but fosters cultural exchange, pays fair wages to its employees and gifts you something for giving of your time and energy. You choose the project in which you'd like to participate, such as teaching local classes or removing trash from the beach and jungle, and you also sign up for a sustainable adventure tour around Montezuma. Long-term opportunities are also available; hit the website for details.

BEACHES

Picture-perfect white-sand beaches are strung out along the coast, separated by small rocky headlands and offering great beachcombing and tide-pool studying. Unfortunately, there are strong rips along the entire coastline, so inquire locally before going for a swim and take care. For more information on riptides see boxed text, p272.

The beaches in front of the town are nice enough, but the further northeast you walk, the more isolated and pristine they become. During low tide, the best **snorkeling** is in the tide pools, and at Playa Las Manchas, 1km west of downtown. There's great **surf** if you're willing to walk the 7km up the coastline to Playa Grande, or if you head south about 3km to Playa Cedros.

Because of the town's carefree boho feel, topless and (sometimes) nude sunbathing have become de rigueur on some beaches. No one is likely to say anything if you choose to go topless, but keep in mind that Ticos are fairly conservative and many residents find the scene disrespectful of their town.

BUTTERFLY GARDEN

The **Montezuma Gardens** (☎ 8888-4200; www.montezumagardens.com; admission US$8; 🕒 8am-4pm) are about 1km up the hill toward Cóbano, alongside the waterfall trail. You can take a tour through this lush *mariposario* (butterfly garden) and nursery where the mysterious metamorphoses occur. On your walk, you'll learn about the life cycles and benefits of a dozen local species, of which you'll see many colorful varieties. The lovely Oregonian family running the gardens also has a B&B here and offers excellent live-work opportunities.

CANOPY TOURS

After you've flown down nine zip lines, the **Montezuma Waterfall Canopy Tour** (☎ 2642-0808;

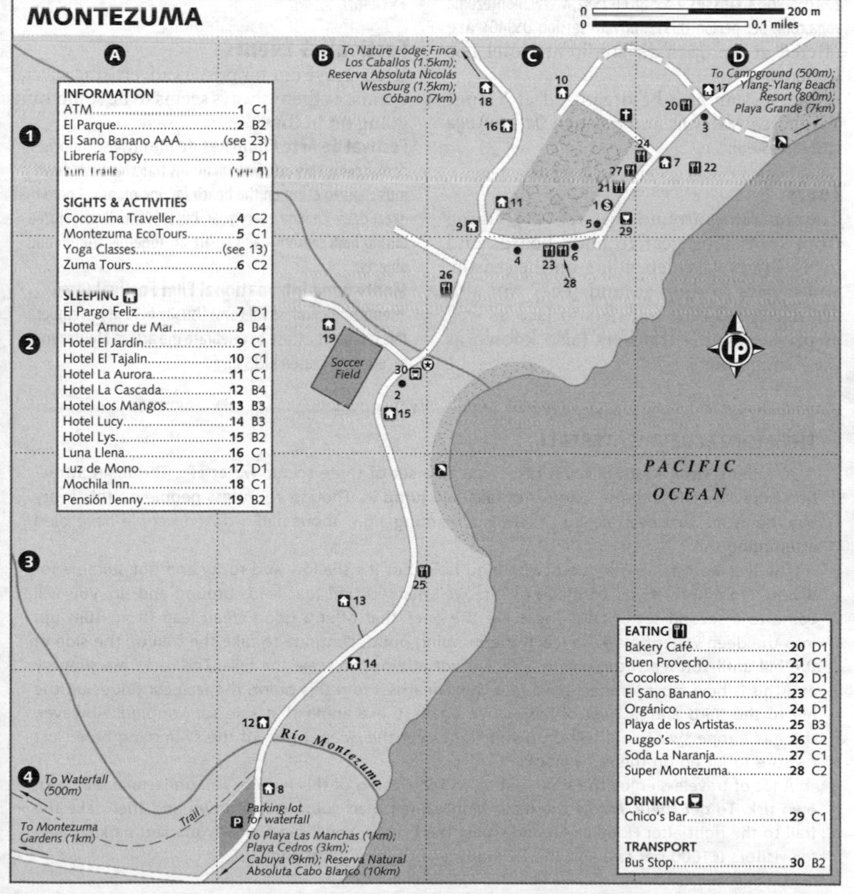

www.montezumatraveladventures.com; US$45) winds up with a hike down – rather than up – to the waterfalls; bring your swimsuit. Book at the Sun Trails office.

HIKING & HORSEBACK RIDING

Inland from Montezuma is the **Reserva Absoluta Nicolás Wessburg**, a private conservation area that was the original site of Nicholas Olof Wessburg and Karen Mogensen's homestead (for more information, see p304). Although the reserve is closed to visitors, you can either hike or go horseback riding along its perimeter – tours can be arranged through operators in town or at the Nature Lodge Finca Los Caballos (p302).

YOGA

Daily **yoga classes** (☎ 8811-7582; www.montezumayoga.com; per person US$12, private session US$40) are offered at the open-air studio at Hotel Los Mangos.

Classes can also be organized at Ylang-Ylang Beach Resort and through **Devaya Yoga** (☎ 8833-5086).

Tours

Tour operators around town rent everything from snorkeling gear to body boards and bikes. Prices vary depending on the season, and it pays to shop around. They can also arrange speed-boat transfers to Jacó as well as private shuttle transfers (also known as the 'Gringo Bus').

The most popular tour is a boat trip to Isla Tortuga, which costs around US$40 a person and should include lunch, fruit, drinks and snorkeling gear. Although the island is certainly beautiful, travelers complain that the whole outing feels like a tourist circus, especially during high season when the entire island is full of boat tours.

Another popular excursion is to take a guided hike (US$55) or a half-day horseback ride (US$50) to nearby Cabo Blanco.

The following three tour operators are recommended:

Cocozuma Traveller (☎ 2642-0911; www.cocozumacr.com; 🕑 24hr)
Montezuma EcoTours (☎ 2642-0467; www.ecotoursmontezuma.com; 🕑 8am-9pm)
Zuma Tours (☎ 2642-0024; www.zumatours.net; 🕑 24hr)

Festivals & Events

Keep an eye out for posters advertising special events, as there always seems to be something going on in town.

Festival de Arte Chunches de Mar (www.chunchesdemar.com) This arts festival brings together artists and musicians to camp on the beach for one month – note that exact dates change every year, but it is usually organized during high season – and create art together from found objects.

Montezuma International Film Festival (www.montezumafilmfestival.com) Usually held in November, this is a great excuse to celebrate the arts in Montezuma before high season kicks in.

THE MONTEZUMA WATERFALL

A 20-minute stroll south of town takes you to a set of three scenic waterfalls. The main attraction here is to climb the second set of falls and jump in. Though countless people do this every day, be aware that even though there is a warning sign, about half a dozen people have died attempting this.

The first waterfall has a good swimming hole, but it's shallow and rocky and not suitable for diving. From here, if you continue on the well-marked trail that leads around and up, you will come to a second set of falls. These are the ones that offer a good clean leap (from 10m up) into the deep water below. To reach the jumping point, continue to take the trail up the side of the hill until you reach the diving area. Do *not* attempt to scale the falls. The rocks are slippery and this is how most jumpers have met their deaths. From this point, the trail continues up the hill to the third and last set of falls. Once again, these aren't that safe for jumping. However, there is a rope swing that will drop you right over the deeper part of the swimming hole (just be sure to let go on the out-swing!).

A lot of travelers enjoy the thrill, but as with anything of this nature, you undertake it at your own risk. To get there, follow the main Montezuma road south out of town and then take the trail to the right after Hotel La Cascada, past the bridge. You'll see a clearly marked parking area for visitors (₡1000 per car) and the beginning of the trail that leads up.

Sleeping

The high season gets crowded, though with so many hotels dotting such a small town you're bound to find something. Note that some hotels have a three-night minimum during Christmas and Easter weeks.

BUDGET

All of the following hotels have shared cold-water showers unless otherwise stated. Be careful with your stuff – travelers frequently complain about theft from hotel rooms in Montezuma.

Camping is illegal on the beaches. There is a small, shaded **campground** (per person US$3) with bathrooms and cold-water showers only a 10-minute walk north of town.

Hotel Lys (☎ 2642-1404; www.hotellysmontezuma.net; camping US$6, r without bathroom per person US$16) This beachside budget hotel with laid-back vibe is run by a group of funky Italians who are bursting with creativity. The owners have also launched a project known as Libre Universidad de Montezuma. This evolving concept is based on communication through artistic expression. Unfortunately, maintenance is slipping and the tiny rooms could use a spring cleaning.

Pensión Jenny (r without bathroom per person US$10) This lovely white-and-blue country house north of the soccer field is a bit removed from the action, which makes it a good option if you want a quiet night's sleep.

Hotel Lucy (☎ 2642-0273; dm US$10, s/d without bathroom US$13/26; P) This beachside *pensión* is popular with shoestring travelers, and was the first budget place to open up in town. It's an excellent deal in this price range, with hammocks, tables and chairs on the shared terraces. There's free coffee and fruit in the mornings, a communal fridge and a new communal kitchen. Ask for a room upstairs – the ocean views and verandas make all the difference.

Mochila Inn (☎ 2642-0030; d without bathroom US$19, d/tr cabinas from US$25/30; P) On a quiet hillside north of town, this secluded inn is brimming with wildlife and is silent (except for the sounds of the rainforest) at night. There are a variety of rooms available that cater to different budgets, though everyone can use the outdoor toilets, which offer only a thin curtain between yourself and nature. (If you bring binoculars, you can watch nature from the throne.)

our pick **El Pargo Feliz** (☎ 2642-0065; d US$25-35; wi-fi) The best budget deal in town – you can't beat the location of these beachfront *cabinas* in the heart of Montezuma. Simple but clean rooms have fan, bathroom and free wi-fi. The communal balcony and garden terrace have relaxing hammocks with sea views, and at night the surf will lull you to sleep.

Luna Llena (☎ 2642-0390; www.lunallenahotel.com; s without bathroom US$25, d without bathroom US$35-50; P) On the northern edge of town on a hilltop overlooking the bay is this delightful German-US–run budget option that's terrific value. There are 12 rooms in a variety of sizes and prices, all with mosquito net, fan and safe large enough to fit a laptop. All rooms have shared bathrooms except the villa with a private bathroom and a covered patio. There are two fully equipped kitchens, a BBQ grill and a communal lounge with stunning ocean views. You can also rent surfboards and bicycles (US$15 per day).

Hotel La Aurora (☎ 2642-0051; www.playamontezuma.net/aurora.htm; s without bathroom US$25-45, d without bathroom US$30-50; extra person US$5; P air-con wi-fi) Reader recommended Hotel La Aurora has a pretty, vine-covered yellow building with an assortment of 15 comfortable rooms with fan, orthopedic bed and mosquito net; others have varying degrees of cold or hot water and air-con. There's a communal kitchen and plenty of hammocks for chilling out.

Hotel Los Mangos (☎ 2642-0076; www.hotellosmangos.com; d with/without bathroom US$75/35, tr bungalows US$95; P pool) This is a charming hotel offering bright, clean orange-and-blue doubles with shared hot-water bathrooms in the main building and bungalows with private bathrooms scattered around the mango-dotted gardens. There is also a small wooden pavilion near the base of the hills where daily yoga classes (see p300) take place.

MIDRANGE & TOP END

Montezuma

All hotels have private hot-water showers.

Hotel La Cascada (☎ 2642-0057; www.hotellacascadamontezuma.com; d incl breakfast US$50, extra person US$15; P) By the river en route to the waterfalls, this classic Montezuma hotel has 15 simple wooden rooms with ocean views and a 2nd-floor deck that's fully strung with cozy hammocks – perfect for swinging or snoozing.

our pick **Hotel El Tajalin** (☎ 2642-0061; www.tajalin.com; d US$50, d superior US$60-70; air-con wi-fi) This delightfully quiet hotel is located on a dead-end road behind the church, but still stumbling distance from the beach and bars. The 14 clean and spacious rooms are nothing fancy, but they all have comfy beds, rich wood floors, air-con and wi-fi. The larger, superior rooms have a safe and a fridge. Upstairs you'll find hammocks and a communal lounge with satellite TV, comfy couches and free coffee all day. Friendly Italian owner Antonio can help book tours and excursions.

Hotel Amor de Mar (☎ 2642-0262; www.amordemar.com; d US$58-124, houses from US$210; P) At the southern end of town, this charming, serene place has a well-manicured lawn strewn with palms and strung with luxurious hammocks, all fronting a beautiful beach with a tide pool big enough to swim in. There are 11 rooms of different shapes and sizes with varying amenities depending on your budget.

Hotel El Jardín (☎ 2642-0548; www.hoteleljardin.com; d US$85-95, 4-person villas US$135; P) This hillside hotel has 15 luxurious stained-wood *cabinas* of various sizes and amenities (some have a stone bathroom and ocean views). The grounds are landscaped with tropical flowers and lush palms, and there's a pool and Jacuzzi for soaking your cares away.

Luz de Mono (☎ 2642-0090; www.luzdemono.com; d/ste/casitas incl breakfast US$85/100/140; P) Once the landmark hotel in town, Luz de Mono is now tired and worn out. The once popular bar and restaurant has shut down and service is slipping. That said, the rooms are clean with a solar-heated shower (some with Jacuzzi), ceramic tiles and wooden accents.

Around Montezuma

Nature Lodge Finca Los Caballos (☎ 2642-0124; www.naturelodge.net; d incl breakfast US$97-165, extra person US$20; P) North of Montezuma on the road to Cóbano, this 16-hectare ranch is adjacent to the Reserva Absoluta Nicolás Wessburg. The lodge has a variety of rooms around the property with either jungle or ocean views. The Canadian owner prides herself on having some of the best looked-after horses in the area, and there are great opportunities here for riding on the trails around the reserve. You can also rent bikes, go hiking, have a meal in the restaurant or splash around the infinity pool.

our pick **Ylang-Ylang Beach Resort** (☎ 2642-0636; www.ylangylangresort.com; luxury tents US$160, d/ste US$195/235, standard/deluxe bungalows US$265/295, all incl breakfast & dinner) About a 15-minute walk north of town along the beach is this resort catering to holistic holiday-seekers. Here you'll find a collection of beautifully appointed rooms, suites and polygonal bungalows with hot showers (some open-air). The newest accommodations option are 'jungalows,' six raised, ecofriendly luxury tents with fan, fridge and shared bathroom. The lush property contains a palm-fringed swimming pool, yoga center, gourmet organic restaurant and spa. The bar is one of the best places in town to enjoy a sunset cocktail. Oh, and you can't actually drive here, though staff will pick you up in their custom beach cruisers from El Sano Banano.

Eating

Self-caterers should head to the Super Montezuma for fresh food.

Buen Provecho (☎ 2642-0717; mains ₡1500-3500; 6am-1pm & 5-10pm Mon-Sat) By day, it's a quaint cafe with homemade bagels, bread and breakfast sandwiches. At night, it becomes a popular hookah bar with tasty tapas.

Bakery Café (☎ 2642-0458; sanforest@hotmail.com; mains ₡2500-5200; 6am-10pm) Grab a chair on the outdoor patio of this homey place with an international menu featuring everything from Indian and Thai to Mexican and Italian. The best time to dine is breakfast, for fantastic omelettes, pancakes, homemade banana bread and French toast. The frolicking bird and monkey show in the garden is free.

Soda La Naranja (☎ 2642-1001; mains ₡2800-5000; 7:30am-10pm Mon-Sat) With typical food on the main strip, this *soda* has a nice shaded patio next to Orgánico and reasonably priced eats.

Puggo's (☎ 2642-0308; mains ₡4000-7000; 8am-10:30pm) A welcomed addition to Montezuma, this promising new Israeli-owned restaurant decorated like a Bedouin tent specializes in Middle Eastern cuisine including falafel, hummus, kebabs, and aromatic fish and seafood dishes cooked in imported spices and herbs. Cap it off with strong cup of Turkish coffee and an amazing dessert.

Cocolores (☎ 2642-0348; mains ₡4000-11,000; 5-10pm Tue-Sun) One of the best restaurants in Montezuma, beachside Cocolores has a pleasant, thatched-roof patio for candlelit dinners. The menu focuses on French-influenced cuisine, as well as some Tico-fusion standards. The curry and coconut shrimp with spicy mango chutney is divine. However, with only

12 tables, long lines and haughty hosts at the front door, it's one of the toughest tables in town.

Orgánico (www.organicomontezuma.com; mains ₡4400-5500; 8am-late; V) When they say 'pure food made with love,' they mean it – this healthy cafe turns out all vegetarian or vegan dishes including spicy Thai burgers, sushi and noodles, nachos, burritos, falafel, smoothies and other meat-free treats you can feel good about.

El Sano Banano (2642-0638; mains ₡4500-12,700; breakfast, lunch & dinner;) This restaurant is way overpriced for simple dishes – 12 bucks for a *casado*? But it's worth showing up in the evening when the restaurant shows nightly films for ₡3000 minimum consumption.

our pick **Playa de los Artistas** (2642-0920; www.playamontezuma.net/playadelosartistas.htm; mains ₡5000-10,000; lunch & dinner Thu-Sat, lunch only Mon-Wed, closed Sun) This artfully decorated beachside spot is the most adored and romantic restaurant in town. The international menu with heavy Mediterranean influences changes daily depending on locally available ingredients, though you can always count on fresh seafood and impeccable culinary sophistication.

Drinking & Entertainment

There are a few bars in town, and you can stop by El Sano Banano to check out which movie it's screening that night.

Chico's Bar is a sprawling complex of bars, tables, beach chairs and dance space with the music turned up loud – making it party-central most nights, especially reggae-night Thursdays. If you can score a table outside, it can be sort of romantic. The bar area seems to be a magnet for local cougars, which, depending on your viewpoint, may not be such a bad thing.

Getting There & Away

BOAT

A fast passenger ferry connects Montezuma to Jacó in only one hour. At ₡20,000 or so, it's not cheap, but it'll save you a day's worth of travel. Boats depart at 9:30am daily and the price includes van transfer from the beach to Jacó bus terminal. Book in advance from any tour operator. Dress appropriately; you will get wet.

BUS

Buses depart Montezuma from the sandy lot on the beach, across from the soccer field. Buy tickets directly from the bus driver. To get to Mal País and Santa Teresa, go to Cóbano and change buses.

Cabo Blanco via Cabuya ₡600; 45 minutes; departs 8:15am, 10:15am, 2:15pm and 6:15pm.

Cóbano ₡400; 30 minutes; departs every two hours from 8am to 8pm.

Paquera ₡1300; 1½ hours; departs 5:30am, 8am, 10am, noon, 2:15pm and 4pm.

San José ₡5800; six hours; departs 6:15am and 2:30pm.

CAR & TAXI

During the rainy season, the stretch of road between Cóbano and Montezuma is likely to require a 4WD. In the village itself, parking can be a problem, though it's easy enough to walk everywhere.

A 4WD taxi can take you to Mal País (₡15,000) or Cóbano (₡4000).

Montezuma Expeditions (www.montezumaexpeditions.com) operates private shuttles to San José (US$40), La Fortuna (US$45), Tamarindo (US$40) and Sámara (US$40).

CABUYA

This tiny village is scattered along a dirt road about 9km south of Montezuma. Although it's rather uninteresting, it's worth visiting the town **cemetery**, which is on Isla Cabuya and can only be reached when a natural land bridge magically appears at low tide. Here you'll find a few modest graves marked by crosses, though make sure you keep an eye on the tides!

Aside from visiting the cemetery, most travelers either pass through Cabuya on their way to Cabo Blanco or use the town as a base for exploring Cabo Blanco.

Coming from Montezuma, the first hotel you'll come to is the Belgian-owned **Hotel Celaje** (2642-0374; www.celaje.com; s/d incl breakfast US$78/90; P), which has a collection of beautiful A-frame, thatched bungalows that sleep four. Neatly standing beside a nice pool and Jacuzzi, each lovely bungalow has its living quarters above, and an open ground floor with its own hammock. Real Belgian beer is readily available.

Turning down the signed side road, you'll find the **Howler Monkey Hotel** (2642-0303; www.howlermonkeyhotel.com; bungalows US$60; P). These are cute A-frame bungalows with kitchenettes. They are perfectly clean and comfortable, and the place is right on a slice of very quiet, rocky beach. This decent midrange

ALONG THE WEST COAST BY 4WD

If you are truly adventurous, have a lot of time on your hands and some experience driving in places where there is nary a road in sight, you might be ready to take on the southern Pacific coast of Península de Nicoya. Make sure you have a 4WD with high clearance though, as well as a comprehensive insurance policy. Do *not* attempt this drive during the rainy season.

Mal País, Montezuma and Cabo Blanco are most frequently reached by the road that follows the eastern part of the peninsular coast and connects with the ferry from Puntarenas in Playa Naranjo. However, if you're looking for some adventure in your life, it's possible to take a 4WD from Playa Carrillo along the southeast coast to Islita, Playa Coyote, south to Mal País and points beyond. Again, don't even think of trying to do any of this in a regular car.

As the crow flies, it's about 70km of 'road' from Playa Carrillo to Mal País, though you should allow at least five hours for the trip (provided you encounter no delays). Several rivers have to be forded, including the Río Ora about 5km east of Carrillo, which is impassable at high tide during the dry season, even for 4WDs; check tide schedules.

From Playa Coyote, drivers will cross a few more rivers, including the Ríos Bongo and Arío, and pass by Playas Caletas, Arío and Manzanillo (you can camp on any of these beaches if you're self-sufficient). There are some pretty hairy river crossings throughout this stretch, so it certainly helps to talk to locals before setting out. In some cases the road doesn't cross directly through the river, and you'll have to drive up the river a bit to find the egress. In these cases, it is best to walk the river first, double-check the egress and then drive in so that you don't plunge your rental car into thigh-deep mud or onto a pile of rocks. Many a rental vehicle has been lost to this stretch of road, so it definitely pays to be cautious (see boxed text, p548).

From Playa Manzanillo head inland to Cóbano, which is well connected to Montezuma, Mal País and Cabo Blanco by reasonable dirt roads.

For the majority of the trip there are a couple of villages, no facilities, and few people that can help you if you get stuck. Also, the roads are unsigned, so getting lost will be part of the deal, though you can always navigate with a compass and the sun. Take a jerry can of gas, your favorite snack foods and plenty of water – if you break down, plan on spending some quality time on your own or with your traveling companion.

For very good reason, Costa Rica's tourist office recommends against undertaking this journey.

hotel is run by friendly US expats and was undergoing renovation during our visit.

For everything else, make a pit stop at **Café Coyote** (mains ₡2800-3400; 💻). The owners serve pizza, seafood and veggie meals, and offer internet access. **Panadería Cabuya** (☎ 2642-1184; 🕑 6am-9pm; 📶) is a local landmark serving fresh bread and strong coffee.

RESERVA NATURAL ABSOLUTA CABO BLANCO

Just 11km south of Montezuma is Costa Rica's oldest protected wilderness area. **Cabo Blanco** is comprised of 12 sq km of land and 17 sq km of surrounding ocean, and includes the entire southern tip of the Península de Nicoya. The moist microclimate present on the tip of the peninsula fosters the growth of evergreen forests, which are unique when compared with the dry tropical forests typical of the Nicoya. The park also encompasses a number of pristine white-sand beaches and offshore islands that are favored nesting areas for various bird species.

The park was originally established by a Danish-Swedish couple, the late Karen Mogensen and Nicholas Olof Wessburg, who settled in Montezuma in the 1950s and were among the first conservationists in Costa Rica. In 1960 the couple was distraught when they discovered that sections of Cabo Blanco had been clear-cut. At the time, the Costa Rican government was primarily focused on the agricultural development of the country (see boxed text, p238), and had not yet formulated its modern-day conservation policy. However, Karen and Olof were instrumental in convincing the government to establish a national park system, which eventually led to the creation of the Cabo Blanco reserve in 1963. The couple continued to fight for increased conservation of ecologically rich areas, but tragically Olof was murdered in 1975 during a campaign in the Península de

Osa. Karen continued their work until her death in 1994, and today they are buried in the Reserva Absoluta Nicolás Wessburg, which was the site of their original homestead.

Cabo Blanco is called an 'absolute' nature reserve because prior to the late 1980s visitors were not permitted. Even though the name hasn't changed, a limited number of trails have been opened to visitors, but the reserve remains closed on Monday and Tuesday to minimize environmental impact.

Information

The **ranger station** (☎ 2642-0093; admission US$10; 8am-4pm Wed-Sun) is 2km south of Cabuya at the entrance to the park, and trail maps are available. It is not possible to overnight in the park, though there are plenty of options in nearby Cabuya or Montezuma. Bring drinks and snacks as there is no food or water available.

The average annual temperature is about 27°C (80°F) and annual rainfall is some 2300mm at the tip of the park. Not surprisingly, the trails can get muddy, so it's best to visit in the dry season, from December to April.

Activities

WILDLIFE-WATCHING

Monkey, squirrel, sloth, deer, agouti and raccoon are usually present, and armadillo, coati, peccary and anteater are occasionally sighted.

The coastal area is known as an important nesting site for the brown booby, mostly found 1.6km south of the mainland on **Isla Cabo Blanco** (White Cape Island). The name 'Cabo Blanco' was coined by Spanish conquistadors when they noticed that the entire island consisted of guano-encrusted rocks. Other seabirds in the area include the brown pelican and the magnificent frigate bird.

HIKING

From the ranger station, the **Swedish Trail** and **Danish Trail** lead 4.5km down to a wilderness beach at the tip of the peninsula. Note that both trails intersect at various points, and it's possible to follow one down and return via the other. Be advised that the trails can get very muddy (especially in the rainy season), and are fairly steep in certain parts – plan for about two hours in each direction. From the beach at the end of the trails it's possible to follow another trail to a second beach, though check first with park rangers as this trail is impassable at high tide.

Getting There & Away

Buses (₡600, 45 minutes) depart from the park entrance for Montezuma at 7am, 9am, 1pm and 4pm. A taxi from Montezuma to the park costs about ₡7000.

During dry season, you can drive (4WD required) for 7km from Cabuya to Mal País via the stunningly scenic Star Mountain Road, so called because it passes by the Star Mountain Eco Resort (p308).

MAL PAÍS & SANTA TERESA

Mal País (Bad Country) refers to the southwestern corner of Península de Nicoya that's famous among surfers for its consistent waves. The area lies more or less north to south along the coastline, with Santa Teresa being the largest village in the area. Further south is the smaller village of Playa El Carmen, and more southerly still is Mal País, the village. *¿Comprende*? Don't worry if it doesn't make sense at first; the villages have pretty much merged into one surf community lining the coast, and are collectively known as Mal País.

The legendary waves at Mal País have been attracting surfers since the 1970s, so it's not surprising that many of them grew up and decided to stay. In the last several years, this once isolated corner of the peninsula has become something of the backpackers' version of Nosara – surf session in the morning, yoga in the afternoon and cruising at night. This laid-back surfers' paradise has even become a hideaway for A-list celebrities; supermodel Giselle Bündchen and US football star Tom Brady were married here in 2009.

Widespread development is rapidly carving up the beachfront but the town still retains its old fishing-village roots. The coastal dust road remains unpaved and there are few transportation links to the outside world.

If you're an experienced surfer looking for a 'scene,' throw away your itinerary because you're going to get stuck here. And even if you're not a surfer, no worries, because there's plenty to see and do in Mal País, one of the most beautiful beaches in the world.

Orientation & Information

The road from Cóbano meets the beach road next to Frank's Place (see p306), on the western side of the peninsula. To the left (south) lies Mal País and to the right (north) is Santa Teresa.

Next door to Frank's Place, **Banco de Costa Rica** (9am-4pm Mon-Fri) has a 24-hour ATM. Directly across the street at the new Centro Comercial Playa El Carmen, you'll find a branch of **Banco Nacional** (2640-0598; 1-7pm) that can change US dollars and has an ATM.

You can find internet access all over Mal País, but for a start, try Frank's Place on the main intersection and **Beach Break Surf Hotel** (2640-0612; www.beachbreakcr.net; 7am-10pm) in Santa Teresa.

There are several grocery stores along the coast. The largest is **Super La Hacienda** (7am-8pm), located 100m north of Cuesta Arriba hostel.

A useful website for local info is www.malpais.net.

Activities

Surfing is usually the be-all and end-all for most visitors to Mal País, but the beautiful beach stretches north and south for kilometers on end – many accommodations can arrange horseback-riding tours and fishing trips.

SURFING

The following beaches are listed from north to south. If you choose a lodge that has 'surf camp' in its name, chances are it's right in front of a good break. At the very least, it can point you to the best nearby spots.

About 8km north of the intersection, **Playa Manzanillo** is a combination of sand and rock that's best surfed when the tide is rising and there's an offshore wind.

The most famous break in the Mal País area is at **Playa Santa Teresa**, and is characterized as being fast and powerful. This beach can be surfed virtually any time of day, though be cautious as there are scattered rocks.

Playa El Carmen, which is at the end of the road leading down from the main intersection, is a good beach break that can also be surfed anytime.

The Mal País area is saturated with surf shops, and competition has kept the prices low – this is a good place to pick up an inexpensive board, and you can probably get most of your money back if you sell it elsewhere. Most of the local shops also do rentals and repairs, and may let you in on some good surf spots. This is by no means an exhaustive list:

Alex Surf Shop (2640-0364) Rent or buy a board here, or take a lesson; 250m north of the intersection.

Corduroy to the Horizon (2640-0173; 8am-6pm) Shapers Andy and Aaron create custom epoxy boards and also do ding repairs. Find their shop 50m west of Frank's Place.

Jobbie's Surf Camp (www.surfjobbie.com) Not a shop per se, but kooky local Canuck Josh (aka 'Jobbie') is a brand in and of himself, and he gives surfing lessons.

Shit Hole (8887-9144) Yep, that's really what it's called, 200m north of the main intersection. It rents and sells boards as well as gives lessons – also, it claims to make crepes.

Tuanis (2640-0370) Has internet access, various gifts and sundries, and can help book taxi services around the area. It's 2km north of Frank's Place.

YOGA

Yoga naturally complements surfing – at the very least, if you haven't been in the water for a while, the stretching can be the perfect antidote to sore paddling arms.

Casa Zen (p307) Offers three- to seven-day yoga retreats; the instructor here teaches a variety of styles, from Ashtanga to Vinyasa.

Horizon Yoga Hotel (2640-0524; www.horizon-yogahotel.com) Offers three classes daily, in a serene environment overlooking the ocean.

Milarepa (p307) Offers classes in Hatha yoga, Swasthya yoga and partner yoga for all levels of practice.

Sleeping & Eating

The following places are listed in relation to the main intersection in Playa El Carmen, where Frank's Place occupies the corner. For simplicity's sake, though the nomenclature isn't technically accurate, listings north of the intersection appear in the Santa Teresa section, and those around and south of the intersection are in the Mal País section.

SANTA TERESA

You'll find all of the following places heading north into Santa Teresa – they're ordered according to their distance from Frank's Place.

Frank's Place (2640-0096/155; www.franksplacecr.com; s US$55-75, d US$60-95; P) Coming into town from Cóbano, the first place you'll see is this local landmark and historic surfer outpost, which has taken over the entire corner with lots of rooms and an internet cafe. Frank has grown up, and this is no longer the backpackers' paradise it once was. Spacious, tiled *cabinas* are comfortable. The free-form pool, whirlpool and restaurant are great places to hang out and get the latest surf report.

Las Piedras (☎ 2640-0453; mains ₡1700-4000; ⌚ lunch & dinner) This Argentine-run chicken shack proclaims 'Our chicken is the sh%t.' One bite and you'll agree.

Trópico Latino Lodge (☎ 2640-0062; www.hoteltropicolatino.com; d US$120, bungalows US$160-180; P ✻ ᯤ ◙) Beautifully decorated with dark wood and deep, saturated colors, the roomy bungalows here are peppered around a tropical garden and along the beach, and feature air-con, king-sized beds, hammock-strung patios and hot-water bathroom (one bungalow also has a full kitchen). There's a dreamy pool fringed with palms and heliconia, and a surfside restaurant (dishes ₡2100 to ₡4200) that specializes in Italian food.

Luz de Vida (☎ 2640-0568; www.luzdevida-resort.com; d US$75-85; P ✻ ◙) The Light of Life is an apt name for this bright tropical refuge. All of the rooms and bungalows have air-con and bathroom, and the common areas have a pool and cozy *palapa* (shelter with a thatched, palm-leaf roof and open sides) bar.

Casa Zen (☎ 2640-0523; www.zencostarica.com; dm US$12, d without bathroom US$24-45, apt from US$55; P) This recommended Asian-inspired guesthouse is decked out in Zen art, celestial murals and enough happy Buddha sculptures to satisfy all your belly-rubbing needs. The owner, Kelly, is committed to helping guests 'chill and recreate on their own time.' She also runs an eclectic restaurant (mains ₡2000 to ₡4400) that has everything from veggie sandwiches and burgers to fresh sushi and Thai curries. Casa Zen also offers a variety of yoga retreats; check the website for current offerings.

Don Jon's (☎ 2640-0700; grupodonjons@gmail.com; dm/d/apt from US$12/35/60; P ✻ ᯤ) This friendly spot run by Colombian brothers Jon and Jeison offers several rustic teak bungalows and modern apartments plus dorm accommodations. The two-bedroom apartment has a full kitchen and is roomy enough for four. The onsite restaurant serves burritos, tacos and sandwiches.

Funky Monkey Lodge (☎ 2640-0272; www.funky-monkey-lodge.com; r/bungalows/ste/apt US$50/80/85/120; P ✻ ▣ ◙) Up the hill from Tuanis (p306), this funky lodge is situated at the top of a natural-rock hill, and has sweet, rustic-style bungalows built out of bamboo. Each one has an open-air shower, and the larger ones have a fully equipped kitchen. A popular bar-restaurant (sushi rolls ₡2200 to ₡4500) packs in the crowds with good international food and excellent sunsets.

Hostal Brunela (☎ 2640-0321; hostalbrunela.com; dm with bathroom US$12; P) This big hostel feels very homey, maybe because there are so many long-term surf slaves living here, or because the owner has a kind, paternal air about him – the lounge area feels like a giant living room with, uh, *sleepy* surfers sprawled out watching TV. Comfortable, colorful rooms all have four beds, lockers and bathroom. The kitchen is huge and fully equipped – with free coffee – and the place is right next to a great surf break.

our pick Cuesta Arriba (☎ 2640-0607; www.santateresahostels.com; dm with bathroom US$13, d US$35, all incl breakfast; P ᯤ) Up a hill across from one of Santa Teresa's best surf breaks, this drop-dead gorgeous hostel is a gem – each bright, colorful room sleeps six and has a hot-water bathroom. There's a big, beautiful kitchen area with a breezy wood-floored terrace upstairs with a TV and DVDs. It also has boards for rent, laundry service, free breakfast and secure parking. There are hammocks in the garden, lots of places to lounge, and the vibe is happy and relaxed. Friendly hosts Barbara and Martin are a wealth of local information and will make you feel at home. The bus from San José terminates 100m south of the hostel.

Milarepa (☎ 2640-0023; www.milarepahotel.com; bungalows from US$198; P ᯤ ◙) This is a self-proclaimed 'small hotel of luxurious simplicity,' with Asian-inspired bungalows made of bamboo and Indonesian teak. Each one is furnished with four-poster beds draped in voluminous mosquito nets, and comes complete with a shower open to the sky. The restaurant (mains ₡4400 to ₡6700) serves international cuisine that emphasizes the fresh local seafood. The owners can arrange tours and activities and offer several types of yoga classes.

Florblanca (☎ 2640-0232; www.florblanca.com; villas incl breakfast US$552-989; P ✻ ▣ ◙) The most sumptuous hotel in Santa Teresa is truly in a class of its own – not surprisingly, it belongs to the group of Small Distinctive Hotels of Costa Rica. Ten romantic villas are scattered around three hectares of land next to a pristine white-sand beach. Each villa is lit by warm hues, with indoor-outdoor spaces such as open-air sunken bathtub and living area. Complimentary yoga and Pilates classes are offered, as are free use of bikes, surfboards and snorkeling equipment. Transfers to and from Tambor airport are included in the rates. Its Asian-fusion restaurant, Nectar (mains ₡5500 to ₡12,000), is open to the public and is highly recommended for its innovative dishes and unbelievably fresh sushi. Children under 13 are not allowed.

MAL PAÍS

Frank's Place marks the spot – this is the main intersection, where shuttles will drop you off and pick you up. The following places are listed in order of their distance south of Frank's Place.

Umi Sushi (☎ 2640-0968; sushi ₡1800-5000; ⏰ noon-10pm) In the courtyard of the Centro Comercial Playa El Carmen, this sushi bar has a pleasant dining room and tables outside. If you're lucky, it will have a surf movie projected on the outside wall while you savor your Mal País roll. Beer drinkers, beware: it only serves Japanese beers, at exorbitant prices.

The Place (☎ 2640-0101; www.theplacemalpais.com; d incl breakfast US$68-136, bungalows US$224; P ✻ ≋ ♨) Cheaper rooms in this Swiss-run guesthouse are air-conditioned and have a hot-water bathroom, but it's absolutely worth it to splurge on the more expensive bungalows – each one is creatively decorated according to a different theme (check the website for pictures). Rooms ring a small pool amid the somewhat random landscaping. The owners can arrange surfing lessons and tours, and the small restaurant serves Mediterranean-style seafood by candlelight in the evenings.

Malpaís Surf Camp & Resort (☎ 2640-0061; www.malpaissurfcamp.com; campsite per person US$13, cabinas/villas/casas US$40/107/130; P ✻ ♨) Whether you're looking for a breezy bunkhouse or a poolside villa, this 'surfers' lodge' caters to travelers of all budget levels. However, regardless of how much you're paying each night, you can wander the landscaped tropical grounds, swim in the lavish pool or grab a cold beer in the open-air bar-restaurant.

our pick **Soda Piedra Mar** (☎ 2640-0069; mains ₡1800-8500; ⏰ breakfast, lunch & dinner) This is one of the best local places to eat in Mal País, with generous portions of fresh seafood and, as the name suggests, a rocky location right by one of the most beautiful blue beaches on the entire peninsula. Make sure you bring your camera!

Blue Jay Lodge (☎ 2640-0089; www.bluejaylodgecostarica.com; d/tr/q incl breakfast US$80/100/115, extra person US$20; P ♨) These charming stilt bungalows are built along a forest-covered hillside, each with its own hot-water bathroom and a huge, screened-in veranda with hammocks. The bamboo-and-wood bungalows sleep three, and though they're a bit on the rustic side, the luxury is in their spaciousness and openness to the surroundings. The lodge is 200m from the beach.

our pick **Beija Flor** (☎ 2640-1007; www.beijaflorresort.com; r US$96-135, ste/villas US$153/210; P ≋ ♨) One of the loveliest new properties in Mal País, Beija Flor is a luxurious, Balinese-styled boutique hotel. The clean and spacious rooms are decorated in minimalist stone and wood interiors and have outdoor showers. Onsite amenities include a small pool, spa and a beautiful open-air yoga studio. It's also home to one of the area's best restaurants with a daily changing, French and Asian-influenced menu.

Mary's Restaurant (☎ 2640-0153; mains ₡3000-7000; ⏰ 5:30-10pm Thu-Tue) Hidden in a jungly garden on the south end of town, this charming restaurant is locally known for the scrumptious wood-fired pizzas, plus fish tacos, burritos, quesadillas and other yummies.

Star Mountain Eco Resort (☎ 2640-0101; www.starmountaineco.com; s/d/tr incl breakfast US$50/70/90, casitas US$130; P ✻ 💻 ≋ ♨) This intimate and secluded lodge was built without cutting down a single tree, and today the grounds of the resort abound with wildlife. There are trails leading through the property that offer good bird-watching, and a viewpoint overlooks both sides of the peninsula. There are four hillside rooms, each simply and thoughtfully decorated in muted tropical colors. Only the *casita* (cottage) has air-con and wi-fi access. The resort is off the rough road (4WD only) between Mal País and Cabuya, alongside the Cabo Blanco reserve (follow the signs), 5.5km south of Frank's Place. It's closed in September and October.

Drinking & Entertainment

Artemis Café (☎ 2640-0579; www.artemiscafe.com; mains ₡3600-4800; ⏰ 7am-2am; ≋) Come for the free wi-fi, stay for the coffee. Located in Centro Comercial Playa El Carmen, Artemis has fantastic coffee (best iced mocha ever), smoothies and juices, plus salads, sandwiches and panini. After dark, Artemis transforms into a groovy lounge with DJs spinning cool tracks and occasional live music.

D&N Day & Night Beach Club (☎ 2640-0353; dayandnightbeachclub.com; 9am-2am;) This beachfront, thatched-roof, two-level building is the hottest new place in town. By day, you'll find volleyball, beach beds and *bocas*. At night it's the biggest party on the beach with DJs, live music and occasional fire-dancing and belly-dancing shows. It's on the beach, about 100m north of Frank's Place.

Getting There & Away

All buses begin and end at Ginger Café, 100m south of Cuesta Arriba hostel; you can flag the bus down anywhere along the road up to Frank's Place, at which point buses turn left and head inland.

A new direct bus from Mal País to San José via the Paquera ferry departs at 6am and 2pm (₡6800, six hours). Local buses to Cóbano depart at 7am, 11:30am, 2pm and 6:30pm (₡800, 45 minutes).

A taxi to or from Cóbano costs approximately ₡12,000. **Montezuma Expeditions** (☎ 2642-0919; www.montezumaexpeditions.com; Centro Comercial Playa El Carmen) organizes shuttle-van transfers to San José, Tamarindo or Sámara (US$40), plus La Fortuna and Monteverde (US$45).

Central Pacific Coast

Stretching from the rough and ready port city of Puntarenas to the tiny town of Uvita on the shores of Bahía Drake, the central Pacific coast is home to both wet and dry tropical rainforests, sun-drenched sandy beaches and a healthy dose of rare wildlife. On shore, national parks protect endangered animals such as the squirrel monkey and the scarlet macaw, while offshore waters are home to migrating whales and pods of dolphins.

With so much biodiversity packed into a small geographic area, it's no wonder the coastal area is often thought of as Costa Rica in miniature. Given its close proximity to San José and the Central Valley and highlands, and its well-developed system of paved roads, the region has traditionally served as a weekend getaway for everyone from sun-worshippers and sportfishers to tree-huggers and outdoors enthusiasts.

Centered on the boomtown of Jacó, and to an increasing extent Manuel Antonio and Dominical, urbanization is primed to transform the coastline. Foreign investment and expats alike have flooded in, catapulting the region into the ranks of Costa Rica's wealthiest and most cosmopolitan regions. This socioeconomic shift has resulted in drastically improved infrastructure and job creation, though vocal critics in the local media are concerned about future sustainability.

While threats of unregulated growth and environmental damage are very real, it's also important to see the bigger picture, namely the stunning nature that first put the central Pacific coast on the map. Although at times it can be hard to look beyond the towering construction cranes, spotting a troop of monkeys swinging through the canopy will quickly renew your faith in the natural beauty of Costa Rica.

HIGHLIGHTS

- Watching troops of squirrel monkeys scamper along the beaches at **Parque Nacional Manuel Antonio** (p349)
- Listening to squawking pairs of rare scarlet macaws flying overhead at **Parque Nacional Carara** (p318)
- Surfing the breaks at **Jacó** (p322), **Playa Hermosa** (p332) and **Dominical** (p354)
- Spotting pods of breaching humpback whales at **Parque Nacional Marino Ballena** (p359)
- Clambering up the canopy platforms at **Hacienda Barú National Wildlife Refuge** (p354)

History

Prior to the tourism boom in Costa Rica, the central Pacific coast – particularly the Quepos port area – was historically one of the country's largest banana-producing regions. However, in response to the 1940 banana blight that affected most of Central America, the United Fruit Company (also known as Chiquita Banana) introduced African palms to the area. Native to West Africa, these palms are primarily cultivated for their large, reddish fruits, which are pressed to produce a variety of cooking oils.

Although the banana blight finally ended in the 1960s, the palm plantations were firmly entrenched and starting to turn a profit. Since palm oil is easily transported in tanker trucks, Quepos was able to close its shipping port in the 1970s, which freed up resources and allowed the city to invest more heavily in the palm oil industry. In 1995 the plantations were sold to Palma Tica, which continues to operate the plantations today. With the exception of commercial fishing and tourism, the palm oil plantations serve as the primary source of employment in the Quepos area.

In more recent years, this stretch of the Pacific has grown increasingly popular with the package-holiday crowd, as it's quite easy – particularly for North Americans – to squeeze in a one-week retreat and be back to work on Monday. Unable to resist the draw of paradise, a good number of baby boomers nearing retirement have relocated to warmer climes.

This demographic shift has been facilitated by the Costa Rican government's decades-old policy of offering tax incentives and legal residence to foreigners who buy property or start business and enterprises in the country. Foreign investment has thus far blessed this region with vitally needed economic stimuli, though the rising cost of living has priced a significant percentage of local Ticos out of the market.

During the shelf life of this book, a sparkling new marina at Quepos will bring in a larger volume of tourists visiting Costa Rica on cruise ships, and several exclusive high-end gated communities will attract an even greater number of wealthy immigrants. Things are indeed changing quickly along this stretch of coastline, though it's difficult to imagine that the authenticity of the coastal fishing villages, agricultural plantations and protected areas could ever be lost.

Climate

West of the Cordillera Central, rains fall heavily between April and November. The hillsides are particularly lush and green during this time, while in summer (December to March) little rain falls, leaving the countryside dry and barren-looking.

Parks & Reserves

The central Pacific coast is home to a number of parks and reserves, including the most visited national park in Costa Rica.

Hacienda Barú National Wildlife Refuge (p354) A small reserve that encompasses a range of tropical habitats and is part of a major biological corridor that protects a wide range of species.

Parque Nacional Carara (p318) Home to no less than 400 different species of birds, including the rare scarlet macaw, which is amazingly a commonly sighted species in the park.

Parque Nacional Manuel Antonio (p349) The pristine beaches, rainforest-clad mountains and dense wildlife never fail to disappoint in Costa Rica's most touristed national park.

Parque Nacional Marino Ballena (p359) A vitally important marine park, this is the country's premier destination for both whale- and dolphin-watching.

Getting There & Around

The best option for exploring the coast in depth is to have your own form of private transportation. With the exception of a few odd unpaved stretches of dirt, the central Pacific coast has some of the country's best roads.

Major cities and towns along the coast, such as Puntarenas, Jacó, Quepos, Dominical and Uvita, are serviced by regular buses. Generally speaking, public transportation is frequent and efficient, and is certainly more affordable than renting a car.

Both **NatureAir** (www.natureair.com) and **Sansa** (www.flysansa.com) service Quepos, which is the base town for accessing Manuel Antonio. Prices vary according to season and availability, though you can expect to pay a little less than US$75 for a flight from San José or Liberia.

PUNTARENAS TO QUEPOS

The northern reaches of the central Pacific coast extend from the maritime port of Puntarenas, a historic shipping hub that has fallen on harder times, to the booming town

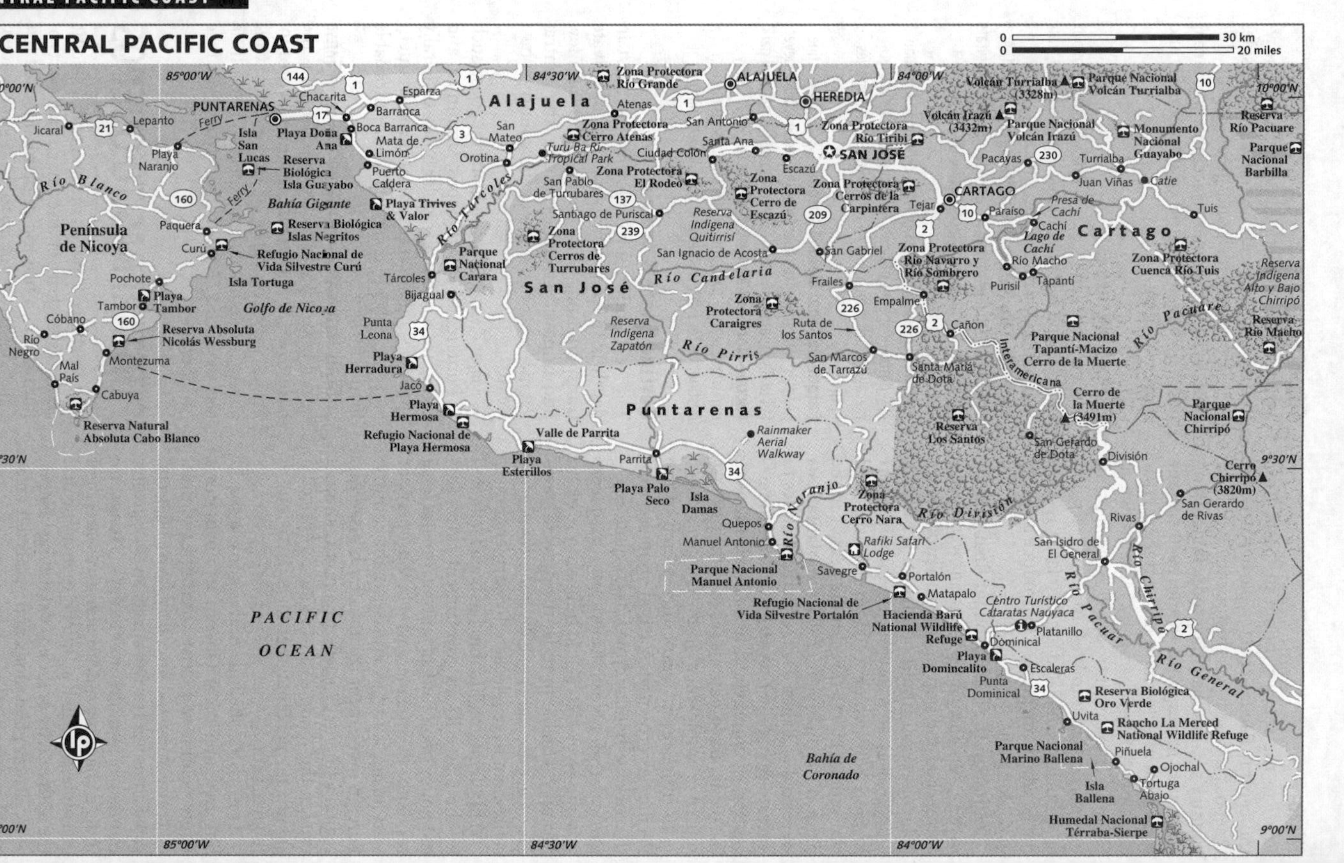
CENTRAL PACIFIC COAST
0 30 km
0 20 miles
10°00'N
9°30'N
9°00'N
85°00'W
84°30'W
84°00'W
PACIFIC
OCEAN
Golfo de Nicoya
Bahía Gigante
Bahía de Coronado
Península de Nicoya
Alajuela
San José
Puntarenas
Cartago
PUNTARENAS
ALAJUELA
HEREDIA
SAN JOSÉ
CARTAGO
Jicaral
Lepanto
Playa Naranjo
Paquera
Curú
Pochote
Tambor
Playa Tambor
Montezuma
Cabuya
Cóbano
Mal País
Río Negro
Reserva Natural Absoluta Cabo Blanco
Reserva Absoluta Nicolás Wessburg
Isla Tortuga
Refugio Nacional de Vida Silvestre Curú
Reserva Biológica Islas Negritos
Reserva Biológica Isla Guayabo
Isla San Lucas
Ferry
Chacarita
Playa Doña Ana
Boca Barranca
Barranca
Esparza
Mata de Limón
Puerto Caldera
Playa Tivives & Valor
Tárcoles
Bijagual
Punta Leona
Playa Herradura
Jacó
Playa Hermosa
Refugio Nacional de Playa Hermosa
Playa Esterillos
Valle de Parrita
Parrita
Playa Palo Seco
Isla Damas
Quepos
Manuel Antonio
Parque Nacional Manuel Antonio
Refugio Nacional de Vida Silvestre Portalón
Savegre
Portalón
Matapalo
Hacienda Barú National Wildlife Refuge
Playa Dominicalito
Dominical
Punta Dominical
Escaleras
Platanillo
Centro Turístico Cataratas Nauyaca
Uvita
Parque Nacional Marino Ballena
Isla Ballena
Piñuela
Ojochal
Tortuga Abajo
Humedal Nacional Térraba-Sierpe
Rancho La Merced National Wildlife Refuge
Reserva Biológica Oro Verde
Rafiki Safari Lodge
Zona Protectora Cerro Nara
Rainmaker Aerial Walkway
Parque Nacional Carara
San Mateo
Orotina
Turu Ba Ri Tropical Park
Atenas
Zona Protectora Cerro Atenas
Zona Protectora Río Grande
Zona Protectora El Rodeo
Ciudad Colón
Santa Ana
San Antonio
Escazú
San Pablo de Turrubares
Santiago de Puriscal
Zona Protectora Cerros de Turrubares
Reserva Indígena Quitirrisí
Zona Protectora Cerro de Escazú
San Ignacio de Acosta
Reserva Indígena Zapatón
Zona Protectora Caraigres
Ruta de los Santos
San Gabriel
Frailes
San Marcos de Tarrazú
Santa María de Dota
Empalme
Cañon
Zona Protectora Cerros de la Carpintera
Zona Protectora Río Tiribí
Zona Protectora Río Navarro y Río Sombrero
Tejar
Paraíso
Cachí
Presa de Cachí
Lago de Cachí
Río Macho
Purisil
Tapantí
Parque Nacional Tapantí-Macizo Cerro de la Muerte
Interamericana
Cerro de la Muerte (3491m)
San Gerardo de Dota
Reserva Los Santos
División
San Isidro de El General
Rivas
San Gerardo de Rivas
Cerro Chirripó (3820m)
Parque Nacional Chirripó
Reserva Indígena Alto y Bajo Chirripó
Reserva Río Macho
Zona Protectora Cuenca Río Tuis
Tuis
Turrialba
Juan Viñas
Catie
Pacayas
Volcán Irazú (3432m)
Parque Nacional Volcán Irazú
Volcán Turrialba (3328m)
Parque Nacional Volcán Turrialba
Monumento Nacional Guayabo
Parque Nacional Barbilla
Reserva Río Pacuare
Río Blanco
Río Tárcoles
Río Candelaria
Río Pirris
Río Naranjo
Río División
Río Pacuar
Río Chirripó
Río General
Río Pacuare
1
2
3
10
17
21
34
137
144
160
209
226
230
239

of Quepos, which is a gateway to Parque Nacional Manuel Antonio. In between are vast swathes of forested hillsides and wilderness beaches, which together protect large concentrations of remarkable wildlife. However, the local spotlight is fixed firmly on the surf city of Jacó, which plays host to a colorful cast of characters.

PUNTARENAS

Port cities the world over have a reputation for polluted waters, seedy environs and slow decay, which is pretty much a good way to sum up Costa Rica's gateway to the Pacific. As the closest coastal town to San José, Puntarenas has long been a popular escape for landlocked Ticos, especially since it takes just a few hours to reach here from San José and surrounding environs. However, although the city council has done a commendable job in cleaning the beaches and renovating the boardwalk, it's hard to escape the feeling that you're sunning yourself in a container yard.

Despite serving as the main cruise-ship port along Costa Rica's Pacific stretch, Puntarenas is struggling to reap the benefits of increased tourism, and has rather tragically failed to capture the interest (or the dollars) of foreign investors. Adding insult to injury, the opening of the Pez Vela Marina in Quepos will pull the vast majority of cruise-ship traffic further south, and is very likely to sound the death knell on Puntarenas' tourism ambitions.

Although the future outlook of Puntarenas is anything but rosy, the city's ferry terminal will continue to serve as a convenient way to access the more pristine beaches further south in southern Nicoya. While few travelers are keen to spend any more of their time here than it takes to get on and off the boat, stopping through here is something of a necessary evil en route to greener pastures and bluer seas.

History

Prior to the mid-20th century, Puntarenas was the largest and most significant openwater port in Costa Rica. Some of the finest coffees to grace European tables and coffee cups were carried to the continent on Puntarenas-registered freighters, and the steady flow of capital back into the city transformed Puntarenas into the 'Pearl of the Pacific.' However, after the construction of the railway leading from the Central Valley to Puerto Limón in 1890, the establishment of a more direct shipping route to Europe initiated the city's decline in importance, though Puntarenas did manage to remain a major port on the Pacific coast.

Orientation

Situated at the end of a sandy peninsula (8km long but only 100m to 600m wide), Puntarenas is Costa Rica's most significant Pacific coastal town, and is just 110km west of San José by paved highway. The city has 60 *calles* (streets) running north to south, but only five *avenidas* (avenues) running west to east at its widest point. As in all of Costa Rica, street names are largely irrelevant, and landmarks are used for orientation (see boxed text, p534, for an explanation).

Information

The major banks along Av 3, to the west of the market, exchange money and are equipped with 24-hour ATMs.

Banco de San José (cnr Av 3 & Calle 3) Connected to the Cirrus network.

Coonatramar (☎ 2661-9011/1069; cnr Calle 31 & Av 3; per hr ₡550; ⏰ 8am-5pm) Internet access.

Hospital Monseñor Sanabria (☎ 2663-0033; 8km east of town)

Puntarenas tourism office (Catup; ⏰ 8am-5pm Mon-Fri) Opposite the pier on the 2nd floor above Bancredito. It closes for lunch.

Sights & Activities

La Casa de la Cultura (☎ 2661-1394; Av Central btwn Calles 3 & 5; ⏰ 10am-4pm Mon-Fri) has an art gallery with occasional exhibits as well as a performance space offering seasonal cultural events.

Behind the Casa is the **Museo Histórico Marino** (☎ 2661-5036, 2256-4139; admission free; ⏰ 8am-1pm & 2-5pm Tue-Sun). The museum describes the history of Puntarenas through audiovisual presentations, old photos and artifacts.

The **Puntarenas Marine Park** (☎ 2661-5272; www.parquemarino.org; adult/child under 12yr US$7/4; ⏰ 9am-5pm Tue-Sun) has an aquarium that showcases manta rays and other creatures from the Pacific. The park sits on the site of the old train station and has a tiny splash pool, snack bar, gift shop and information center.

You can stroll along the beach or the aptly named **Paseo de los Turistas** (Tourists' Stroll), a pedestrian boulevard stretching along the southern edge of town. Cruise ships make

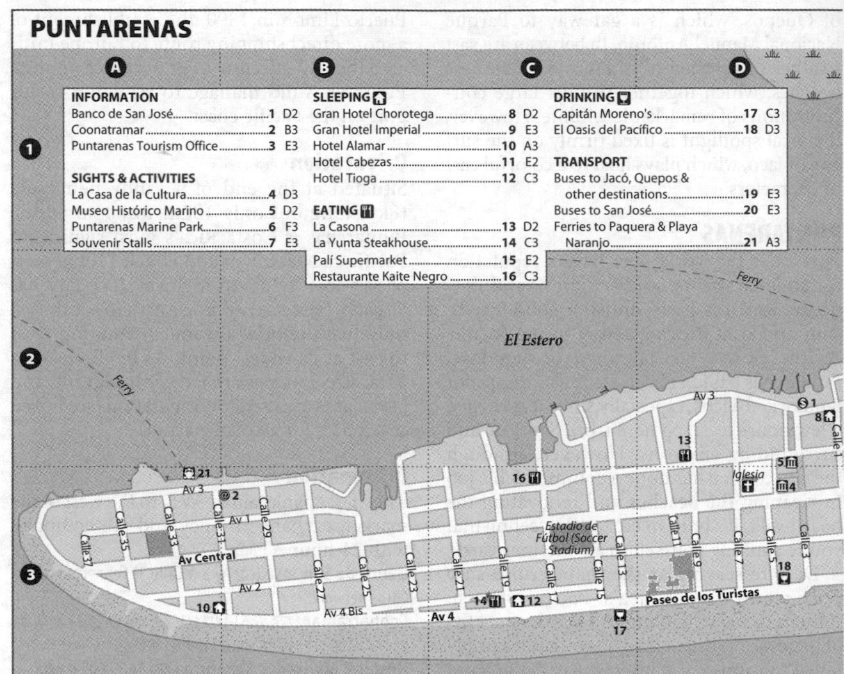

day visits to the eastern end of this road, and a variety of **souvenir stalls** and *sodas* (informal lunch counters) are there to greet passengers.

For information on sights on offer around Puntarenas, see p317.

Tours

Coonatramar (☎ 2661-9011/1069; www.coonatramar.com; cnr Av 3 & Calle 31) can organize tours to the islands in and around Bahía Gigante as well as fishing charters. Prices vary depending on the size of your party and the nature of your trip.

Festivals & Events

Puntarenas is one of the seaside towns that celebrate the **Fiesta de La Virgen del Mar** (Festival of the Virgin of the Sea) on the Saturday closest to July 16. Fishing boats and elegant yachts are beautifully bedecked with lights, flags and all manner of fanciful embellishments as they sail around the harbor, seeking protection from the Virgin as they begin another year at sea. There are also boat races, a carnival, and plenty of food, drinking and dancing.

Sleeping

There's no shortage of accommodations in Puntarenas, though like in most port cities the world over, finding a secure place that doesn't charge by the hour isn't always an easy proposition. However, we have tried to list places that we would be comfortable bringing our own mother to, so you can sleep easy knowing that there won't be any unwanted midnight visitors.

BUDGET

Hotel Cabezas (☎ 2661-1045; Av 1 btwn Calles 2 & 4; s/d from US$20/25; P) This no-nonsense budget option is an excellent choice. Pastel-painted rooms have functional overhead fans and screened windows, which means you'll sleep deeply without needing air-con. Although you certainly shouldn't leave your valuables strewn about, this hotel is safe and secure.

Gran Hotel Chorotega (☎ 2661-0998; cnr Av 3 & Calle 1; r with/without bathroom US$25/20) Fairly basic rooms are clean and well kept with rickety overhead fans and buzzing TVs, though you'd be wise to opt for a room with bathroom as the shared facilities leave a lot to be desired.

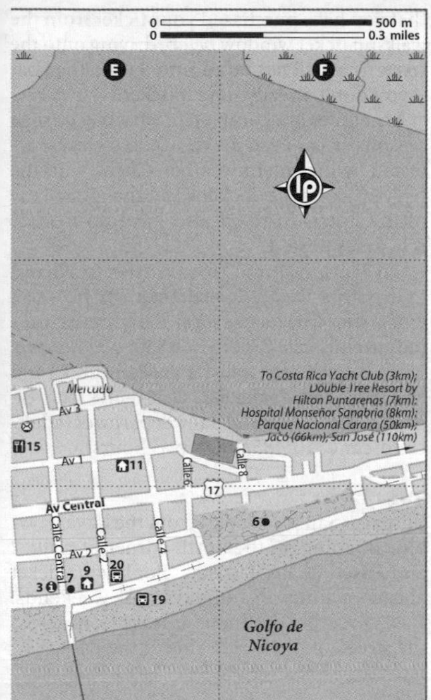

While this budget crash pad is certainly nothing to write home about, it's perfectly adequate if you're just passing through town.

Gran Hotel Imperial (☎ 2661-0579; Paseo de los Turistas btwn Calles Central & 2; s/d from US$25/40; (P)) Well situated near the bus stations, this dilapidated and rickety wooden structure still manages to retain a little old-world charm. Cavernous rooms (some with a spacious balcony) are cool and clean, and have subtle colonial flourishes, such as wooden furniture and dated paintings to help set the atmosphere. A beer cooler of Imperial (Costa Rica's favorite beer) greets you when you enter.

MIDRANGE & TOP END

Costa Rica Yacht Club (☎ 2661-0784; www.costaricayachtclub.com; s/d from US$75/85, villas with air-con US$175; (P)) Some 3km east of downtown, in Cocal at the narrowest portion of the peninsula, this somewhat historic yacht club caters to members of both local and foreign yachters as well as the public. Considering that wealthy yachters are fairly discerning when it comes to accommodations, rooms at the club are surprisingly plain. If you're traveling in a group, the modern villas can easily accommodate a gaggle of five yachties.

Hotel Tioga (☎ 2661-0271; www.hoteltioga.com; Paseo de los Turistas btwn Calles 17 & 19; d deluxe/executive incl breakfast from US$80/90; (P)) Opened in 1959, this is the most established hotel in Puntarenas, and arguably the best place in the city to lie down for the night. Prices vary according to the room, though it's worth spending a few extra dollars for the larger ones, which have sweeping views of the sea. However, you really can't go wrong as all of the rooms feature modern amenities and generally good vibes.

Hotel Alamar (☎ 2661-4343; www.alamarcr.com; cnr Paseo de los Turistas & Calle 31; d/tr/q standard US$80/100/120, d/q apt US$135/160; (P)) If you're looking for a bit more space to stretch your legs, this upmarket hotel (for Puntarenas at least) offers enormous family-style rooms and apartments at surprisingly affordable prices. Rooms are all spotless, with attractive tiled floors and tropical flourishes scattered about, while apartments have a fully equipped kitchen with everything you could want to whip up a feast. As family fun is the theme of the Alamar, there are two pools (one for kiddies) where guests congregate.

Double Tree Resort by Hilton Puntarenas (☎ 2663-0808; http://doubletree.hilton.com; all-inclusive packages from US$290 per person, child under 12yr free; (P)) A family-friendly option that gets top billing for its enormously curvaceous swimming pool, immense offering of water sports and around-the-clock entertainment, this all-inclusive resort is boasting a fresh new look and a new name to boot. While there are certainly nicer beaches down the coastline, there is excellent value to be had here, especially if you book in advance through the internet.

Eating

The cheapest food is available in the small stands and restaurants near the Palí supermarket. This area is also inhabited by sailors, drunks and prostitutes, but it seems raffish rather than dangerous – during the day, at least. Restaurants along the Paseo de los Turistas are, predictably, filled with *turistas* (tourists).

There's a row of fairly cheap *sodas* on the beach by the Paseo de los Turistas, between Calle Central and Calle 3. They are good for people-watching, and serve snacks and nonalcoholic drinks. You'll also find a collection of Chinese restaurants on Av 1 east of the church.

Self-caterers can head to the **Palí supermarket** (Calle 1 btwn Avs 1 & 3) to stock up on just about anything.

La Casona (cnr Av 1 & Calle 9; casados ₡2500-6000) This bright-yellow house is marked with a small, modest sign, but it's an incredibly popular lunch spot, attracting countless locals who jam onto the large deck and into the interior courtyard. Portions are heaped, and soups are served in bathtub-sized bowls – bring your appetite.

Restaurante Kaite Negro (☎ 2661-2093; cnr Av 1 & Calle 17; dishes ₡3000-6500) On the north side of town, this rambling restaurant is popular with locals, and serves good seafood and a good variety of tasty *bocas* (appetisers). If you really want to see the place swinging, the open-air courtyard comes to life on weekends with live music and all-night dancing.

La Yunta Steakhouse (☎ 2661-3216; Paseo de los Turistas btwn Calles 19 & 21; meals ₡3500-7000) Your culinary mecca for every imaginable cut of meat has professional service, great ocean views and enough hunks of dead animal to arouse your doctor's anger.

Drinking & Entertainment

Entertainment in the port tends to revolve around boozing and flirting, though the occasional cultural offering does happen at La Casa de la Cultura (p313). If you're looking for the more traditional liquid entertainment, do as the Ticos do and head for the countless bars that line Paseo de los Turistas.

A time-honored spot for shaking some booty is **Capitán Moreno's** (cnr Paseo de los Turistas & Calle 13), which has a huge dance floor right on the beach.

Another popular spot is **El Oasis del Pacífico** (cnr Paseo de los Turistas & Calle 5), which has a lengthy bar and a warehouse-sized dance floor.

Getting There & Away

BOAT

Car and passenger ferries bound for Paquera and Playa Naranjo depart several times a day from the **northwestern dock** (Av 3 btwn Calles 31 & 33). (Other docks are used for private boats.) If you are driving and will be taking the car ferry, arrive at the dock early to get in line. The vehicle section tends to fill up quickly and you may not make it on. In addition, make sure that you have purchased your ticket from the walk-up ticket window *before* driving onto the ferry. You will not be admitted onto the boat if you don't already have a ticket.

Schedules are completely variable, change seasonally (or even at whim), and can be affected by inclement weather. Check with the ferry office by the dock for any changes. Many of the hotels in town also have up-to-date schedules posted.

To Playa Naranjo (for transfer to Nicoya and points west), **Coonatramar** (☎ 2661-1069; northwestern dock) has several daily departures (adult/child/car ₡860/515/1850, two hours).

To Paquera (for transfer to Montezuma and Mal País), **Ferry Peninsular** (☎ 2641-0118; northwestern dock) also has several daily departures (adult/child/car ₡810/485/1900, two hours).

BUS

Buses for San José depart from the large navy-blue building on the north corner of Calle 2 and Paseo de los Turistas. Book your ticket ahead of time on holidays and weekends. Buses for other destinations leave from across the street, on the beach side of the Paseo.

Jacó ₡800; 1½ hours; departs 5am, 11am, 2:30pm and 4:30pm.

Quepos ₡2100; 3½ hours; departs 5am, 11am, 2:30pm and 4:30pm.

San José ₡1500; 2½ hours; departs every hour from 4am to 9pm.

Santa Elena, Monteverde ₡1500; 2½ hours; departs 1:15pm and 2:15pm.

Getting Around

Buses marked 'Ferry' run up Av Central and go to the ferry terminal, 1.5km from down-

FIVE AGAINST THE SEA

In January 1988 five fishermen from Puntarenas set out on a trip that was meant to last seven days. Just five days into the voyage, their small vessel was facing 9m waves triggered by northerly winds known as El Norte. Adrift for 142 days, they would face sharks, inclement weather, acute hunger and parching thirsts. They were finally rescued – 7200km away – by a Japanese fishing boat. The book *Five Against the Sea* by US reporter Ron Arias recounts in gripping detail the adversities they faced and how they survived.

town. The taxi fare from the San José bus terminal in Puntarenas to the northwestern ferry terminal is about ₡1000.

Buses for the port of Caldera (also going past Playa Doña Ana and Mata de Limón) leave from the market about every hour and head out of town along Av Central.

AROUND PUNTARENAS

The road heading south from Puntarenas skirts along the coastline, and a few kilometers out of town you'll start to see the forested peaks of the Cordillera de Tilaran in the distance. Just as the port city fades into the distance, the water gets cleaner, the air crisper and the vegetation more lush. At this point, you should take a deep breath and heave a sigh of relief – the Pacific coastline gets a whole lot more beautiful as you head further south.

About 8km south of Puntarenas is **Playa San Isidro**, the first 'real' beach on the central Pacific coast. Although it is popular with beachcombers from Puntarenas, surfers prefer to push on 4km south to **Boca Barranca**, which boasts what is reportedly the third-longest left-hand surf break in the world. Conditions here are best at low tide, and it is possible to surf here year-round. However, be advised that there isn't much in the way of services out here, so be sure that you're confident in the water and seek local advice before hitting the break.

Just beyond the river mouth is a pair of beaches known as **Playa Doña Ana** and **El Segundo**, which are relatively undeveloped and have an isolated and unhurried feel to them. Surfers can find some decent breaks here, too, though like Playa San Isidro, they are more popular for Tico beachcombers on day trips from Puntarenas, especially during weekends in high season. There are snack bars, picnic shelters and changing areas, and supervised swimming areas.

The next stop along the coast is **Mata de Limón**, a picturesque little hamlet that is situated on a mangrove lagoon, and locally famous for its bird-watching. If you arrive during low tide, flocks of feathered creatures descend on the lagoon to scrounge for tasty morsels. Mata de Limón is divided by a river, with the lagoon and most facilities on the south side.

A major port on the Pacific coast is **Puerto Caldera**, which you pass soon after leaving Mata de Limón. There aren't any sights here, and the beach is unremarkable unless you're a surfer, in which case there are a few good breaks to be had here (though be careful as the beach is rocky in places).

Buses heading for the Caldera port depart hourly from the market in Puntarenas, and can easily drop you off at any of the spots listed above. If you're driving, the break at Boca Barranca is located near the bridge on the Costanera Sur (South Coastal Hwy), while the entrance to Playa Doña Ana and El Segundo is a little further south (look for a sign that says 'Paradero Turístico Doña Ana'). Also, the turnoff for Mata de Limón is located about 5.5km south of Playa Doña Ana.

TURU BA RI TROPICAL PARK & AROUND

The **Turu Ba Ri Tropical Park** (☎ 2250-0705; www.turubari.com; admission US$15; 🕑 8:30am-5pm Tue-Sun; 🚸) is a collection of botanical gardens reflecting each of the topographic zones native to Costa Rica. As you walk along impeccably manicured trails, you'll pass through palm forests, pasture lands, herbariums, cactus fields, bamboo groves, bromeliad gardens, orchid beds and a loma canopy. The gardens are accessed by an aerial cable car, which is included in the price of admission.

If you're an adrenaline junkie, there is also a canopy tour (adult/child US$55/40) that has you swinging through the trees, as well as opportunities for horseback riding and rock climbing. If you're traveling with the little ones, they'll be content for hours either playing in the two hedge mazes or checking out the exhibits in the reptile house.

Although there are no accommodations in the park, there is a wonderfully intimate B&B in the nearby town of San Pablo de Turrubares, namely **Ama Tierra** (☎ 2419-0110; www.amatierra.com; s/d incl breakfast US$127/149; P ✕ 💻 🏊). Accommodations are in a handful of warm and wooden *casitas* that are scattered along landscaped trails and manicured gardens, though the highlight is its onsite holistic center, yoga studio and organic restaurant. If you're interested in detoxing the body and clearing the mind, Ama Tierra offers a number of multiday packages that are dedicated to improving your well-being. San Pablo de Turrubares is located approximately 10km east of Orotina on the road to Santiago de Puriscal – once in town, follow the signs for the B&B.

The park can be easily accessed by bus from Orotina (₡600, 30 minutes), which departs at 5:30am, noon and 4:30pm. However, most tourists organize private transportation to the park either from Puntarenas or San José. If you're driving, look for a road to the east, just south of Orotina, signed 'Coopebaro, Puriscal.' This road goes over an Indiana Jones–worthy wooden suspension bridge to the park. The park is located about 9km beyond the bridge, and half the road is paved.

PARQUE NACIONAL CARARA

Straddling the transition between the dry forests of Costa Rica's northwest and the sodden rainforests of the southern Pacific lowlands, this **national park** is a biological melting pot of the two. Acacias intermingle with strangler figs, and cacti with deciduous kapok trees, creating heterogeneity of habitats with a blend of wildlife to match. The significance of this national park cannot be understated – surrounded by a sea of cultivation and livestock, it is one of the few areas in the transition zone where wildlife finds sanctuary.

Carara is also the famed home to one of Costa Rica's most charismatic bird species, namely the scarlet macaw (see boxed text, p320). While catching a glimpse of this tropical wonder is a rare proposition in most of the country, macaw sightings are virtually guaranteed at Carara. And, of course, there are more than 400 other avian species flitting around the canopy, as well as Costa Rica's largest crocodiles in the waterways – it's best to leave your swimming trunks at home!

Orientation

Situated at the mouth of the Río Tárcoles, the 52-sq-km park is only 50km southeast of Puntarenas by road or about 90km west of San José via the Orotina highway.

The dry season from December to April is the easiest time to go, though the animals are still there in the wet months. March and April are the driest months. Rainfall is almost 3000mm annually, which is less than in the rainforests further south. It's fairly hot, with average temperatures of 25°C (77°F) to 28°C (82°F), but it's cooler within the rainforest. An umbrella is important in the wet season and occasionally needed in the dry months. Make sure you have insect repellent.

Dangers & Annoyances

Increased tourist traffic along the Pacific coast has unfortunately resulted in an increase in petty theft. Vehicles parked at the trailheads are routinely broken into, and although there may be guards on duty, it is advised that drivers leave their cars in the lot at the Carara ranger station and walk along the Costanera Sur for 2km north or 1km south. Alternatively, park beside Restaurante y Cabinas El Cocodrilo (p320).

Sadly, armed robberies, which in the past were unheard of outside San José, have been reported both along the trails and on the peripheries of the park. Police presence in the area has subsequently increased, but there is no substitute for your own vigilance. Whenever possible, travel in a group, don't carry unnecessary valuables and, if things do take a turn for the worse, never resist or try to fight off a mugger.

Sights

With the help of a hired guide, it's possible to visit the archaeological remains of various indigenous **burial sites** located within the park, though they're tiny and unexciting compared to anything you might see in Mexico or Guatemala. At the time of the Europeans' arrival in Costa Rica, these sites were located in an area inhabited by an indigenous group known as the Huetar (Carara actually means 'crocodile' in the Huetar language). Unfortunately, not much is known about this group, as little cultural evidence was left behind. Today, the few remaining Huetar are confined to several small villages in the Central Valley.

If you're driving from Puntarenas or San José, pull over to the left immediately after crossing the Río Tárcoles bridge, also known as **Crocodile Bridge**. If you scan the sandbanks below the bridge, you'll have a fairly good chance of seeing as many as 30 basking crocodiles. Although they're visible year-round, the best time for viewing is low tide during the dry season. Binoculars will help a great deal.

Crocodiles this large are generally rare in Costa Rica as they've been hunted vigorously for their leather. However, the crocs are tolerated here as they feature prominently in a number of wildlife tours that depart from Tárcoles. And of course, the crocs don't mind as they're hand-fed virtually every day.

Activities

WILDLIFE-WATCHING

The most exciting bird for many visitors to see, especially in June or July, is the brilliantly patterned scarlet macaw, a rare bird that is common to Parque Nacional Carara. Their distinctive call echoes loudly through the canopy, usually moments before a pair of these soaring birds appear against the blue sky. If you're having problems spotting them, it may help to inquire at the ranger's station, which keeps tabs on where nesting pairs are located.

Dominated by open secondary forest punctuated by patches of dense, mature forest and wetlands, Carara offers some superb bird-watching. More than 400 different species of birds inhabit the reserve, though your chances of spotting rarer species will be greatly enhanced with the help of an experienced guide. Some commonly sighted species include orange-billed sparrow, five kinds of trogon, crimson-fronted parakeet, blue-headed parrot, golden-naped woodpecker, rose-throated becard, gray-headed tanager, long-tailed manikin and rufous-tailed jacamar (just to name a few!).

Birds aside, the trails at Carara are home to several mammal species, including red brocket, white-tailed deer, collared peccary, monkey, sloth and agouti. The national park is also home to one of Costa Rica's largest populations of tayra, a weasel-like animal that scurries along the forest floor. And, although most travelers aren't too keen on stumbling upon an American crocodile, some truly monstrous specimens can be viewed from a safe distance at the nearby Crocodile Bridge.

According to the park rangers, the best chance of spotting wildlife is at 7am, when the park opens.

HIKING

Some 600m south of the Crocodile Bridge on the left-hand side is a locked gate leading to the **Sendero Laguna Meándrica** trail. This trail penetrates deep into the reserve and passes through open, secondary forest and patches of dense, mature forest and wetlands. About 4km from the entrance is Laguna Meańdrica, which has large populations of heron, smooth-bill and kingfisher. If you continue past the lagoon, you'll have a good chance of spotting mammals and the occasional crocodile, though you will have to turn back to exit.

Another 2km south of the trailhead is the **Carara ranger station** (admission US$10; 7am-4pm), where you can get information and enter the park. There are bathrooms, picnic tables and a short nature trail. Guides can be hired for US$20 per person (two minimum) for a two-hour hike.

About 1km further south are two loop trails. The first, **Sendero Las Araceas**, is 1.2km long and can be combined with the second, **Sendero Quebrada Bonita** (another 1.5km). Both trails pass through primary forest, which is characteristic of most of the park.

Sleeping & Eating

Camping is not allowed, and there's nowhere to stay in the park. As a result, most people

GARABITO

The area encompassed by Parque Nacional Carara was once home to a legendary indigenous hero, a local *cacique* (chief) named Garabito. Commanding a vast area from the Golfo de Nicoya to the Central Valley, he led a fierce struggle against the Spanish.

A favorite tactic of the Spanish to weaken native resistance was to decapitate the tribal leadership – literally. In 1560 the Guatemalan high command dispatched a military force to arrest Garabito. The wily chieftain used the forest to elude capture, but the Spanish managed to seize his wife, Biriteka, as a hostage. Garabito countered by having one of his followers dress up as the chieftain who allowed himself to be captured. While the camp celebrated catching who they thought was Garabito, the real Garabito escaped with his wife.

Garabito's ploy, however, was the exception. The more common fate of captured *caciques* was to star in an imperial morality play. In Act One, the shackled chief sat through a trial at which his numerous transgressions against God and king were expounded. The chief responded to the charges, then was sentenced to death. In Act Two, a public execution was staged, whereby the guilty chief had his eyes and tongue cut out, was shot with a crossbow, was beheaded with an axe, had his severed head displayed on a pike, and finally had his body burned to ashes. The End.

come on day trips from neighboring towns and cities such as Jacó (p322).

Restaurante y Cabinas El Cocodrilo (☎ 2661-8261; d from US$25; P) Located on the north side of the Río Tárcoles bridge, this is the nearest place to stay and eat. Rooms are unexciting, though it's a cheap and convenient base for getting to the park before the tour buses arrive. Its restaurant has meals for a few thousand colones, and is extremely popular with travelers stopping to check out the crocodiles. It is open from 6am to 8pm. If you're nervous about leaving your car at the trailhead, there is secure parking here in a guarded lot.

Getting There & Away

Any bus traveling between Puntarenas and Jacó can leave you at the park entrance. You can also catch buses headed north or south in front of the Restaurante y Cabinas El Cocodrilo. This may be a bit problematic on weekends, when buses are full, so go midweek if you are relying on a bus ride. If you're driving, the entrance to Carara is right on the Costanera and is clearly marked.

TÁRCOLES & AROUND

The small, unassuming town of Tárcoles is little more than a few rows of houses strung along a series of dirt roads that parallel the ocean. As you'd imagine, this tiny Tico town isn't exactly a huge tourist draw, though the surrounding area is perfect for fans of the superlative, especially if you're interested in seeing the country's tallest waterfall and its largest crocodiles. Here, intrepid hikers can penetrate virgin forest in search of remote swimming holes and ample wildlife, while aspiring crocodile hunters can get an up-close and personal view of these exquisite predators.

Orientation

About 2km south of the Carara ranger station is the Tárcoles turnoff to the right (west) and the Hotel Villa Lapas turnoff to the left. To get to Tárcoles, turn right and drive for 1km, then go right at the 'T' junction to the village.

Sights & Activities

A 5km dirt road past Hotel Villa Lapas leads to the primary entrance to the **Catarata Manantial de Agua Viva** (☎ 8831-2980; admission US$20; 8am-3pm), which is a 200m-high waterfall, claimed to be the highest in the country. From here, it's a steep 3km hike down into the valley, though there are plenty of benches and viewpoints where you can rest. Be sure to keep an eye out for the beautiful (but deadly) poison-dart frog as well as the occasional scarlet macaw. The falls are more dramatic in the rainy season when they're fuller, though the serene rainforest setting is beautiful any time of year. At the bottom of the valley, the river continues through a series of natural swimming holes where you can take a dip and cool off. A camping area and outhouse are located at the bottom. Local buses between Orotina and Bijagual can drop you off at the entrance to the park.

Some 2km further up the road is the 70-hectare **Jardín Pura Vida** (☎ 2637-0346; admission US$20; 8am-5pm) in the town of Bijagual. This private botanical garden offers great vistas of Manantial de Agua Viva cascading down the side of a cliff, and there are some easy but altogether pleasant hiking trails. There is a small

SCARLET MACAWS

The scarlet macaw *(Ara macao)* is one of the most visually arresting birds in the neotropical rainforest. Flamboyantly colored with bright-red body, blue-and-yellow wings, long red tail and white face, these macaws make their presence known with signature squeaks and squawks that echo for kilometers across the forest canopy. With life spans reaching up to 75 years, they have an undeniable air of both beauty and wisdom.

Prior to the 1960s, the scarlet macaw was distributed across much of Costa Rica, though trapping, poaching, habitat destruction and the increased use of pesticides devastated the population. By the 1990s, the distribution was reduced to two isolated pockets: the Península de Osa and Parque Nacional Carara.

Fortunately, these charismatic creatures are thriving in large colonies at both locales, and sightings are virtually guaranteed if you have the time and patience to spare. Furthermore, despite this fragmentation, the World Conservation Union continues to evaluate the species as 'Least Concern,' which bodes well for the future of this truly emblematic rainforest denizen.

restaurant on the grounds, and you can also arrange horseback riding and tours through the area. As with to the Catarata Manantial de Agua Viva, local buses between Orotina and Bijagual can drop you off at the entrance to the park.

Tours

If you want to get the adrenaline pumping, check out a crocodile tour on the mudflats of the Río Tárcoles. Bilingual guides in boats will take you out on the river for croc-spotting and some hair-raising croc tricks. And you know it's going to be good when the guide gets *out* of the boat and *into* the water with these massive beasts.

Although the tours are definitely a spectacle to behold, it's a bit frustrating to watch the crocodiles being hand-fed by the tour guides. Furthermore, several travelers report that these tours may not be worth it if you've already been to Tortuguero (p458). Tours usually cost US$25 per person for two hours.

Both **Crocodile Man** (☎ 2637-0771; www.crocodilemantour.com) and **Jungle Crocodile Safari** (☎ 2637-0338; www.junglecrocodilesafari.com) have offices in Tárcoles. The tours leave from town or you can arrange for them to pick you up at your hotel.

Sleeping & Eating

Hotel Villa Lapas (☎ 2221-5191; www.villalapas.com; all inclusive r from US$130; P) Located on a private reserve comprised both of secondary rainforest and expansive tropical gardens, this all-inclusive resort is a classy retreat for anyone who wants their eco-fun served up in a fruity cocktail with an umbrella on top. With a modest number of rooms housed in an attractive Spanish colonial–style lodge, guests can unwind in relative comfort in between guided hikes, bird-watching trips, canopy tours and the obligatory soak in the infinity pool. If this kind of luxury is your cup of shade-grown coffee, check out the website as discounted packages are available if you book in advance.

Getting There & Away

There are no buses to Tárcoles, but any bus between Puntarenas and Jacó can leave you at the entrance. If you're driving, the entrance to the town is right on the Costanera Sur and is clearly marked. If you're staying at Hotel Villa Lapas, it's possible to arrange a pick-up from either San José or Jacó with an advance reservation.

PLAYA HERRADURA AREA

Until the mid-1990s, Playa Herradura was a rural, palm-sheltered beach of grayish-black sand that was popular mainly with campers and local fishermen. In the late 1990s, however, Herradura was thrown into the spotlight when it was used as the stage for the movie *1492*. Rapid development ensued, resulting in the construction of one of the most high-profile hotels in the country, namely the Los Sueños Marriott Beach and Golf Resort.

While parts of the beach today look like one giant gravel pit, Playa Herradura represents one possible future face of the central Pacific coast. Sprawling complexes of condos and high-rise apartments are slowly encircling the bay and snaking up the mountainside, while the marina boasts rows of luxury yachts and sportfishing vessels. Although opinionated detractors of Playa Herradura are quick to lob insults, there are some truly world-class hotels on the beach and high up in the surrounding mountains that are worth seeking out.

Sleeping

You have to pay to play in Playa Herradura, so consider moving further down the coast to Jacó if you're not prepared to bunk down in the top end price bracket.

our pick **Hotel Villa Caletas** (☎ 2637-0505; www.hotelvillacaletas.com; r US$178-470; P) One of only eight hotels in all of Costa Rica belonging to the Small Distinctive Hotels of Costa Rica group, this complex of ultraexclusive accommodations is located on the tiny headland of Punta Leona. Since it's perched high on a dramatic hillside, you'll first have to navigate a 1km-long serpentine driveway adorned with cacti and Victorian lanterns. The drive will be worth it as upon entering the property, you'll be rewarded with panoramic views of the Pacific coastline. But, what makes the hotel truly unique is its fusion of architectural styles, incorporating elements as varied as tropical Victorian, Hellenistic and French colonial. Villa Caletas consists of 35 units, each sheltered in a tropical garden and dense foliage that gives the appearance of total isolation. The interiors of the rooms are individually decorated with art and antiques, but nothing is nearly as magnificent as the views you'll have from your room. There is also a French-influenced restaurant, a striking infinity pool and a private 1km trail leading down the hillside to the beach.

Los Sueños Marriott Beach and Golf Resort (☎ 2630-9000; www.lossuenosresort.com; r from US$410; P ⛶ 💻 📶 🍽 ♿) This is the US$40 million hotel, marina and condo project that completely transformed this once-secluded bay into one of Costa Rica's most exclusive destinations. The centerpiece of the project is a 250-berth yacht marina that unfolds onto a lush golf course, upscale shopping center, resort hotel and ultraelite residential development. The entire Spanish colonial complex is a five-star class act from check-in to checkout, but its mass-market approach lacks the intimacy and personality found at Villa Caletas.

Zephyr Palace (☎ 2637-0505; www.zephyrpalace.com; r US$550-1500; P ⛶ 💻 📶 🍽) Need more proof that Costa Rica is experiencing some monumental changes? Welcome to the Zephyr Palace, the sister hotel (and pet project) of the Villa Caletas. While the older sibling woos guests with subtle notes of elegance and sophistication, Zephyr whops them over the head with the hedonism mallet. At this veritable marble palace of unchecked luxury, individually decorated theme rooms that wouldn't look out of place in Las Vegas evoke the splendor of ancient Rome, pharaonic Egypt and the Orient.

Getting There & Away

The Herradura turnoff is on the Costanera Sur, 3.5km north of the turnoff to Jacó. From here, a paved road leads 3km west to Playa Herradura. There are frequent local buses (₡1200, 20 minutes) connecting Playa Herradura to Jacó.

JACÓ

Few places in Costa Rica generate as broad a range of opinions and emotions as the beach town of Jacó. In one camp, you have the loyal surfing contingent, resident North American expats and international developers who bill Jacó as the ultimate central Pacific destination and one of the country's most rapidly developing cities. Truth be told, the surfing is excellent, the restaurants and bars are cosmopolitan, and a skyline of future high-rise apartments and luxury hotels is rapidly being constructed.

However, there is another camp of dissatisfied tourists, concerned environmentalists and marginalized Ticos who would urge you to steer clear of Jacó and make an effort to spread the word to others. Again, truth be told, there is a burgeoning drug and prostitution problem, questions of sustainability and the fear that Ticos are being priced out of their homes.

Like all cases concerning the delicate balance between conservation and development, Jacó is steeped in its fair share of controversy. However, it's probably best to ignore the hype and the stereotypes alike, and make your own decisions about the place. Although the US-style cityscape of shopping malls and gated communities may be off-putting to some, it's impossible to deny the beauty of the beach and the surrounding hillsides, and the consistent surf that first put the beach on the map is still as good as it ever was.

History

Jacó has a special place in the hearts of Ticos as it is the quickest oceanside escape for landlocked denizens of the Central Valley. Many Ticos recall fondly the days when weekend shuttle buses would pick up beach-seekers in the city center and whisk them away to the undeveloped Pacific paradise of Jacó. With warm water, year-round consistent surf, world-class fishing and a relaxed, beachside setting, it was hard to believe that a place this magical was only a short bus ride away from San José.

The secret got out in the early 1990s when Canadians on package tours started flooding Jacó, though for the most part tourism remained pretty low-key. Things picked up a bit in the late 1990s when surfers and anglers the world over started visiting Costa Rica en masse, though Jacó remained the dominion of Central Valley Ticos looking for a little fun and sun. However, things changed dramatically as soon as retiring baby boomers in search of cheap property began to colonize this once tiny Costa Rican beach town.

In only a few years' time, Jacó became the most rapidly developing town (some would argue city) in all of Costa Rica. Plots of land were subdivided, beachfronts were cleared, hillsides were leveled and almost overnight Jacó became the exclusive enclave of moneyed expats. Ticos were happy that development brought coveted Western institutions such as paved roads and fast-food restaurants, but as the initial flash of cash and glitz started to fade, some began to wonder if they had inadvertently sold the doormat beneath their feet.

It's anybody's guess as to where the future of Jacó lies. Optimists point out that the town is simply experiencing growing pains, and argue that the drugs and prostitution will subside just as soon as the infrastructure stabilizes and the town residents begin to clamp down on illicit vices. Pessimists are quick to retort that wealth attracts opportunism, especially of the illicit kind, and that the problems in Jacó are just getting started.

Regardless of which camp you fall into, one thing is for certain: all of Costa Rica is casting a watchful eye on Jacó, and will ultimately point to the city as either an example of development gone awry, or a success story of wealth creation.

Orientation

Playa Jacó is about 2km off the Costanera, 3.5km past the turnoff for Herradura. The beach itself is about 3km long, and hotels and restaurants line the road running behind it. The areas on the northern and southern fringes are the most tranquil and attractive, and are the cleanest.

In an effort to make foreign visitors feel more at home, the town has placed signs with street names on most streets. These names are shown on the map, but the locals continue to use the traditional landmark system (see boxed text, p534).

Information

Jacó is relatively expensive and during the high season it's jam-packed with tourists, so reservations are recommended, especially around the winter holidays.

There's no independent tourist information office, though several tour offices will give information. Look for the free monthly *Jaco's Guide*, which includes tide charts and up-to-date maps, or go to www.jacoguide.com. The free monthly magazine *Central Pacific Way* has information on tourist attractions up and down the coastline.

Banco de San José (Map p328; Av Pastor Díaz, north of Calle Cocal; 🕑 8am-5pm Mon-Fri, 8am-noon Sat) Has a Cirrus ATM open during bank hours on the 2nd floor of the Il Galeone shopping center.

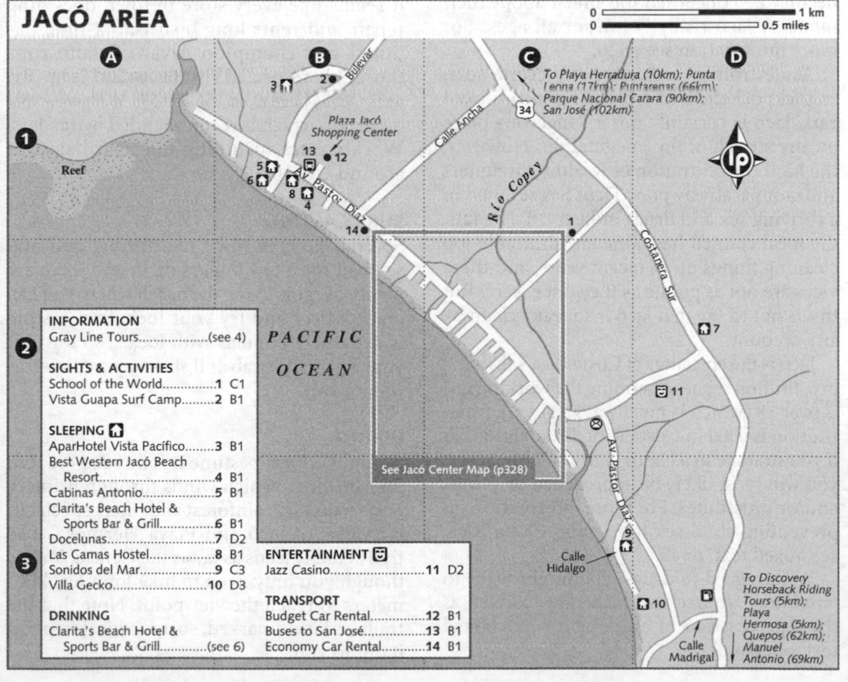

Banco Popular (Map p328; cnr Av Pastor Díaz & Calle La Central) Exchanges US dollars and traveler's checks.
Books & Stuff (Map p328; Av Pastor Díaz btwn Calles Las Olas & Bohío) Has books in several languages as well as US newspapers.
Mexican Joe's (Map p328; Av Pastor Díaz btwn Calles Las Olas & Bohío; per hr ₡500; 9am-9pm Mon-Sat, 10am-8pm Sun) The best place to check email; has multiple computers with high-speed connections and air-con.
Red Cross (Map p328; ☎ 2643-3090; Av Pastor Díaz btwn Calles Hicaco & Las Brisas) Medical clinic.

Dangers & Annoyances

First, let's clear up some common misconceptions: Jacó bills itself as a fun-in-the-sun and family-friendly and holiday destination, and – for the most part – this is anything but false advertising. Tourist infrastructure here is among the best in the country, and all around the greater Jacó area, you can expect some very high-quality goods and services for your hard-earned money.

Furthermore, even though it's often stereotyped as a brash party destination for young surfers and retired cruisers, Jacó is also proud to equally cater to families and young children. If you're traveling with little tykes, you needn't be concerned too much about their safety as Jacó really is fun for all ages. For more information see p326.

Aside from occasional petty crime such as pickpocketing and breaking into locked cars, Jacó is certainly not a dangerous place by any stretch of the imagination. However, the high concentration of wealthy foreigners and comparatively poor Ticos has resulted in a thriving sex and drugs industry. To be fair, the local council has done an admirable job cleaning things up in recent years, and these vices are not as public as they once were. But this is not to say that Jacó is squeaky clean by any account.

Jacó is the epicenter of Costa Rica's thriving prostitution scene. Assuming the working girl is over 18 (which is not always a given), prostitution is legal in Costa Rica. Be advised that if you're alone in a bar or club at night in Jacó, you will most likely be approached by pimps and/or prostitutes. For more information on preventing child-sex tourism in Costa Rica, see boxed text, p540.

With regard to drugs, you might want to familiarize yourself with the law, as well as the repercussions of breaking it – see boxed text, opposite).

Activities

SWIMMING

Jacó is generally safe for swimming, though you should avoid the areas near the estuaries, which are polluted. Be advised that the waves can get crowded with beginner surfers who don't always know how to control their boards, so be smart and stay out of their way. Riptides do occasionally occur, especially when the surf gets big, so inquire about local conditions and keep an eye out for red flags marking the paths of rips.

SURFING

Although the rainy season is considered best for Pacific coast surfing, Jacó is blessed with consistent year-round breaks. Even though more advanced surfers head further south to Playa Hermosa, the waves at Jacó are strong, steady and a lot of fun. Jacó is also a great place to start a surf trip as it's easy to buy and sell boards here. If you're looking to rent a board for the day, shop around as the better places will rent you a board for US$15 to US$20 for 24 hours, while others will try to charge you a few dollars per hour.

There are too many surf shops to list, and it seems like every store in town does ding repair and rents long boards. Six-time national surf champion Álvaro Solano runs the highly respected **Vista Guapa Surf Camp** (Map p323; ☎ 2643-2830, in USA 409-599-1828; www.vistaguapa.com), which is recommended by readers. Weekly rates including full board start at around US$1000.

SURF CASTING

Several shops in town rent fishing gear and sell bait for a few dollars each, and there are plenty of spots along the beach where you can crack a beer and try your luck. Surf casting is extremely popular with locals, so dust off your Spanish vocab and strike up a conversation or two.

HIKING

A popular local pastime is following the trail up Mt Miros, which winds through primary and secondary rainforest and offers spectacular views of Jacó and Playa Hermosa. The trail actually leads as far as the Central Valley, though you only need to hike for a few kilometers to reach the viewpoint. Note that the trailhead is unmarked, so ask a local to point it out to you.

GOT DRUGS, WILL TRAVEL

Drugs are plentiful in Costa Rica, and a good number of tourists would never give a second thought to lighting up a joint on the beach (or, more recently, blowing a line of coke in a discotheque). However, drugs are 100% illegal in Costa Rica, and if you are charged with possession, you can be fined and imprisoned depending on the severity of the offense. There are currently foreigners serving out lengthy prison terms, and occasionally a big drug bust will make the headlines. The bad news is that there is little your embassy can do on your behalf. The good news is that, as far as Latin American penal systems are concerned, there are places a hell of a lot worse than a Costa Rican jail.

Based on reports we've heard on the ground, the reality is that some police officers would rather collect a bribe than incarcerate a bunch of backpackers. Unlike other destinations on the fabled hippie trail, notably Morocco, Thailand and India, Costa Rica has a squeaky clean, ecofriendly image that it needs to uphold. Case in point: the last thing the government tourist board wants is the mugs of a bunch of teenagers plastered on the front pages of the international papers.

However, things are changing rapidly, and as more foreigners start packing their bags and heading to Costa Rica, you can expect that the supply will meet the demand. On beaches with a growing international party scene such as Jacó and Tamarindo, it's possible to buy just about any drug on any street corner in any language. While marijuana once dominated the scene, the drug of choice has quite suddenly become cocaine. While travelers report that the price is cheap and the quality is high, it's much harder for the authorities to turn a blind eye to coke possession.

The moral of the story is that at some point during your travels in Costa Rica, there is a good chance that you will be offered drugs. And there's also a chance that if you're reading this right now, you might say yes. So, remember to use your judgment, consider the consequences and don't kid yourself: other travelers much like yourself have had their lives ruined by drugs or imprisonment, and they most definitely will not be the last.

HORSEBACK RIDING

Readers have reported incidents of horse abuse in Jacó, specifically operators using malnourished and mistreated animals. However, one recommended company is **Discovery Horseback Tours** (off Map p323; ☎ 8838-7550; www.horseridecostarica.com; from $60), which is run by an English couple and offers an extremely high level of service and professionalism.

KAYAKING

If you're interested in organized kayaking and sea canoeing trips that include snorkeling excursions to tropical islands, contact **Kayak Jacó Costa Rica Outriggers** (☎ 2643-1233; www.kayakjaco.com), which offers a wide variety of customized day and multiday trips. This outfit does not have an office in Jacó, so it's best to either phone them, or have your accommodations do so for you.

CANOPY TOURS

In Jacó there are two competing companies offering similar products: **Canopy Adventure Jacó** (☎ 2643-3271; www.adventurecanopy.com; tours adult/child US$60/45) and **Waterfalls Canopy Tour** (☎ 2632-3322; www.waterfallscanopy.com; tours adult/child US$60/45). These outfits do not have formal offices in Jacó, so it's best to either phone them, or have your accommodations do so for you.

HANG GLIDING

HangGlide Costa Rica (☎ 2643-4200; www.hangglidecr.com; from $100) will pick you up in Jacó and shuttle you to an airstrip south of Playa Hermosa where you can tandem-ride in a hang glider or fly in a three-seat ultralight plane. There's no office in town.

SPAS

A branch of the exceedingly professional **Serenity Spa** (Map p328; ☎ 2643-1624; Av Pastor Díaz, east of Calle Bohio) offers the full range of spa services.

Courses

School of the World (Map p323; ☎ 2643-1064; www.schooloftheworld.org; 1-4 week packages US$525-1680; P) is a popular school and cultural studies center offering classes in Spanish, surfing, art and photography. The impressive building and activities center also houses a cafe and art gallery. Rates include kayaking and hiking field trips and onsite lodging. Spanish and surfing are the most popular programs.

Tours

Tours around the area include visits to Parque Nacional Carara (from US$45) as well as longer-distance trips around the country. Another popular destination is **Isla Damas** – you can organize tours here or in Quepos, further south. Isla Damas is not technically an island, but the tip of a pointed mangrove forest that juts out into a small bay just south of Parrita. During high tide, as the surrounding areas fill with water, this point becomes an island – offering an incredible opportunity for bird- and other wildlife-watchers. Boating tours can be arranged from Jacó for around US$65 per person, but more avid adventurers can opt for a sea-kayaking expedition with Amigo Tico Complete Adventure Tours in Quepos (see p338).

Virtually every shop, hotel and restaurant in town books tours, as Jacó operates on a lucrative commission-based system. As you'd imagine, it's hard to actually know who is greasing whose palms and who is actually running tours, though usually it all works out – assuming you use your judgment and book from places that look reliable. Needless to say, you shouldn't book anything from touts on the streets, and if an offer from a vendor seems too good to be true, then most likely it is.

One long-standing agent that receives good reviews from readers is **Gray Line Tours** (Map p323; ☎ 2220-2126; www.graylinecostarica.com; Best Western Jacó Beach Resort, Av Pastor Díaz), which books tours throughout the country as well as private intercity transportation.

Jacó for Children

Jacó has long been on the radar screens of Tico families looking to swap the congestion of San José for the ocean breezes of the central Pacific coast. Therefore, you'll find that your own children are very well cared for in Jacó, and there is enough on offer to keep even those with the shortest attention spans amused for days on end.

Families flock to the beach in Jacó, and compared with more famed surfing destinations up and down the coast, the waves here are modest. As with any water-based activities, the usual amount of parental watch is required, though young children can safely splash about on most days. However, strong surges often accompany ill weather, so it's always best to survey the scene and inquire locally about conditions.

Beyond the beach, you'll find a grocery list of activities on offer in Jacó, and a good number of operators offer discounts for young children. For more information, see the activities listings, p324.

There is a tremendous diversity of accommodations in the Jacó area, and aside from the more backpacker-oriented youth hostels and the upmarket boutique hotels, the vast majority welcome children. Smaller, more intimate B&B types are good for maintaining a comfortable, familial atmosphere, while larger resorts have a range of child-friendly amenities on offer. If possible, book in advance if you need to reserve child beds or have other special requests. Hotels with outdoor pools can save the day, especially when the mercury starts to rise.

Eating out in Jacó with children is a breeze, since nearly all of the places in town offer English menus and/or have English-speaking staff. If your children aren't accustomed to eating typical Costa Rican food (such as rice and beans), you can easily find more US-style fast-food items as well as pizza and pasta. Fruit smoothies are an excellent way to keep your kids properly hydrated, and Jacó is one place in Costa Rica where you definitely don't need to worry too much about the drinking water.

GOING TOPLESS?

Though it's the cultural norm in several corners of the globe, going topless is heavily frowned upon in Costa Rica. This of course shouldn't be surprising, as more than two-thirds of Ticos are practicing Catholics. Sure, if you bare it all the guys on the beach will hoot and holler, but remember that families often frequent Costa Rican beaches. If the temptation to get a little extra sun is too much to bear, be considerate and move to an isolated stretch of sand.

Just for the record, there is one place in the central Pacific where topless sunbathing is tolerated, namely La Playita in Manuel Antonio. However, it's worth mentioning that this beach is predominantly a pick-up scene for gay men on vacation – for more information, see boxed text, p348.

One last thing: it's worth taking the time to read Dangers & Annoyances (p324) as Jacó has something of a dirty underbelly that children should be sheltered from. Generally speaking, most of the ill happenings occur under the cover of dark, at which point you might want to keep the young ones safely inside the confines of your hotel or a nearby restaurant. Once again though, it's worth pointing out that aside from a few rough edges, Jacó is regarded as a safe and family-friendly destination through and through.

Sleeping

The center of town, with its many bars and discos, can mean that noise will be a factor in where you choose to stay. The far northern and southern ends of town have more relaxed and quieter accommodations.

Reservations are highly recommended on weekends in the dry season and become critical during Easter and the week between Christmas and New Year's Eve.

The rates given are high-season rates, but low-season rates could be as much as 30% to 40% lower. If you plan on a lengthy stay (more than five days), ask about long-term rates.

HOSTELS

Las Camas Hostel (Map p323; Av Pastor Díaz; dm/d US$14/30; P) With little more than the word 'Hostel' scribbled onto a whitewashed exterior wall, this young backpacker start-up is an understated but highly personable shoestring offering. Centrally located next to the KFC, Las Camas puts you steps away from the beach and the nightlife, yet guests seem content spending more of their time on the expansive rooftop deck. Rooms are a bit rough around the edges, but shabbiness is easy to forgive at this price range.

Hotel de Haan (Map p328; ☎ 2643-1795; www.hoteldehaan.com; Calle Bohío; dm/d from US$19/48; P) This Dutch-Tico outpost is one of the top budget bets in town, and is perennially popular with backpackers from around the world. Freshly tiled rooms with steamy hot-water showers (dorms have shared bathrooms) are clean and secure, and there's a shared kitchen with fridge, plus a pool and free internet around the clock. The highlight of the property, however, is the upstairs balcony where you can congregate with fellow backpackers, and swap travel stories over a few cans of Imperial until the wee hours of the morning.

BUDGET

Cheap budget hotels are scattered around the Jacó area, though we constantly receive reports from travelers about petty theft. Indeed, sometimes it's worth spending a few extra dollars for the safety and peace of mind that comes with having a secure room. In keeping with this theme, we have tried to list only places that meet our high standards. However, since there is no substitute for your own vigilance, always lock up your valuables (even at top-end places), and never give anyone a reason to wonder what you're keeping inside your room.

Camping El Hicaco (Map p328; ☎ 2643-3004; Calle Hicaco; campsites per person US$3; P) The only proper campground in town: there are picnic tables, bathrooms and a lockup for gear, though its proximity to the bars and clubs means you might not get much shut-eye. Don't leave valuables in your tent as theft is a big problem here.

Cabinas Antonio (Map p323; ☎ 2643-3043; cnr Av Pastor Díaz & Blvr; r per person from US$15; P) Something of an institution among shoestringers and local Tico families, this clutch of cabins at the northern end of Jacó is one of the best deals in town. Basic rooms are uninteresting at best, but they are clean and cozy, and come with private cold shower and cable TV. And of course, when you're just steps from the surf, it's hard to be too fussy about your surroundings.

MIDRANGE

Jacó is chock-a-block with midrange hotels, and our list is by no means comprehensive. However, we have tried to select places that have a certain *je ne sais quoi,* while still offering safety, security and comfortable surroundings to slightly more discerning travelers.

Clarita's Beach Hotel and Sports Bar and Grill (Map p323; ☎ 2643-3327; www.claritashotel.com; western end of Blvr; s/d from US$60/70; P) The three most important rules in the real-estate business are location, location and location. If you subscribe to this mantra, Clarita's beachfront location is difficult to top. Basic rooms with cutesy flourishes are modestly priced, especially if you can sleep easy with just a fan at night, while more expensive rooms come with 'luxuries,' such as hot-water shower, cable TV and air-con. The attached sports bar and grill is a fun and friendly open-air joint that serves up your typical beer and nachos fare.

AparHotel Vista Pacífico (Map p323; ☎ 2643-3261; www.vistapacifico.com; top of the hill off Blvr; d incl breakfast from US$68; P ⊠ 💻 🚘) Located on the crest of a hill just outside Jacó, this Canadian-run hotel is an absolute gem that is worth seeking out. The views of the coastline from here are phenomenal, particularly at sunset when you'll have panoramic vistas of a fiery sky, and the mountaintop location also means that it's a few degrees cooler (and a whole lot quieter) than neighboring Jacó. Homey rooms of varying sizes and shapes cater to all budgets, and are made all the better by the warm and caring hosts. There is even a BBQ pit where you can grill up some killer eats while chatting with other guests.

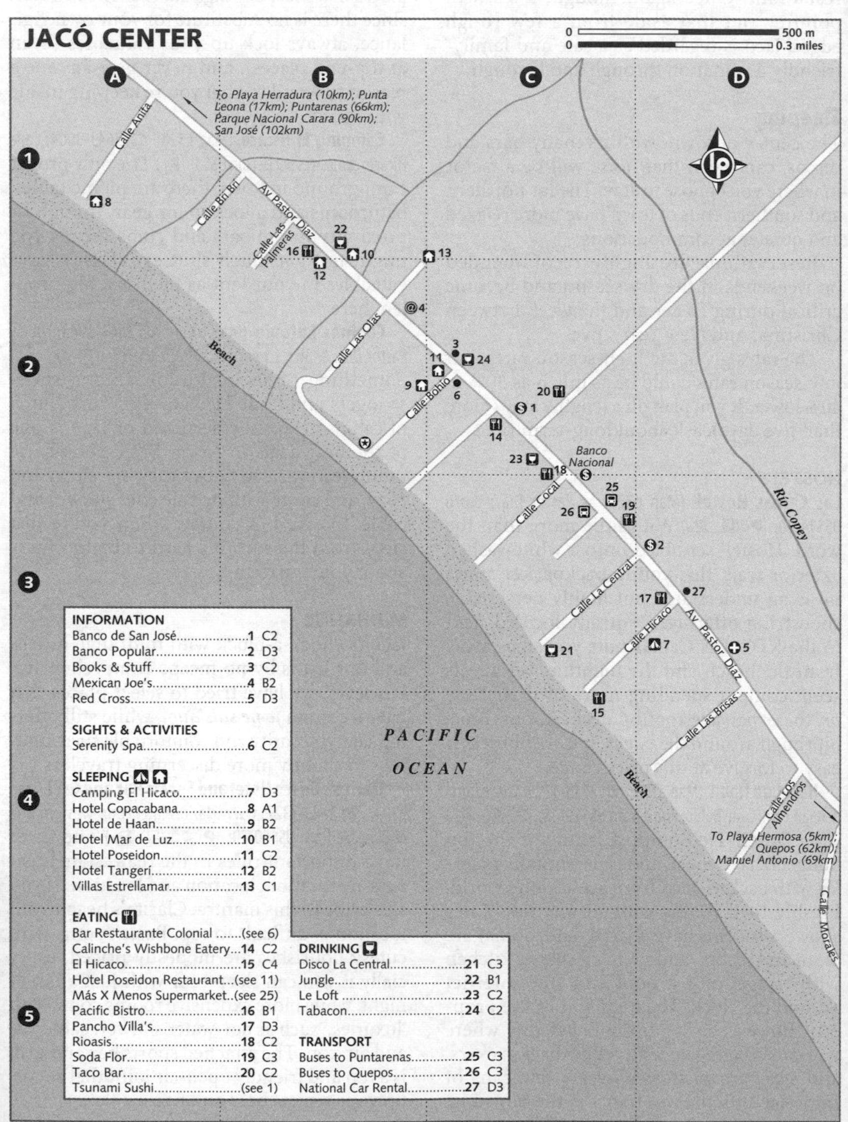

Villas Estrellamar (Map p328; ☎ 2643-3102; www.estrellamar.com; eastern end of Calle Las Olas; s/d US$75/85, 1-/2-bedroom villas US$85/100; P) While the spacious rooms at the Estrellamar are certainly good value considering they boast a massive bathroom and private balcony, it really is worth paying the small bit of extra cash for your own personal villa. Depending on the size of your party, you can choose from one- and two-bedroom villas that have a full kitchen and plenty of space for stretching out after a day at the beach or a night on the town. Regardless of which accommodations option you choose, be sure to take a relaxing swing in the hammock pavilion, and keep an eye out for the huge iguanas that live on the grounds and feed off the mango tree.

Hotel Mar de Luz (Map p328; ☎ 2643-3259; www.mardeluz.com; Av Pastor Díaz btwn Calles Las Palmeras & Las Olas; d/tr/q incl breakfast US$78/98/118; P) This adorable little hotel with Dutch-inspired murals of windmills and tulips has tidy and attractive air-conditioned rooms that are perfect for a little family fun in the sun. Since it can be difficult sometimes to appease the little ones, the friendly Dutch owners (who also speak Spanish, English, German and Italian) offer two swimming pools, several BBQ grills and plenty of useful information on how to best enjoy the area. The owners are also extremely committed to fighting drugs and prostitution in Jacó, and are at the forefront of an admirable campaign to clean up the city.

Villa Gecko (Map p323; ☎ 2643-1314; www.villagecko.net; Calle Hidalgo; 2-3 person studios US$80, 3-5 person ste US$150; P) By far the most charming accommodations on the beach, Villa Gecko is managed by a French artist whose touch can be seen throughout the property. From stenciled drawings on the walls to mosaic murals in the bathrooms, every corner of the property projects European sensibility and imaginative design. Rooms have air-con and hot water, and there's a shared kitchen and a pool.

Hotel Copacabana (Map p328; ☎ 2643-1005; www.copacabanahotel.com; Calle Anita; r/ste from US$95/159; P) This three-story resort hotel gets good marks for offering a variety of rooms and suites to meet the size and needs of your party. If you're traveling either by yourself or with your significant other, fairly modern standard rooms are well priced considering the hotel's convenient beachfront location and rich offerings of amenities, including an attractive pool and hot tub. Of course, the hotel really packs in the value with its larger suites that come equipped with a well-stocked kitchenette and spacious private balcony from where you can get a personal view of the Pacific sunset.

Best Western Jacó Beach Resort (Map p323; ☎ 2643-1000; www.bestwestern.com; Av Pastor Díaz btwn Blvr & Calle Ancha; r from US$97; P) Despite whatever preconceived notions you may have about the Best Western, this particular establishment in the famous US chain is the original full-service beach resort in Jacó. With that said, dark and dingy rooms are certainly showing their age, though you can't beat the impressive grounds, convenient beach access and the laundry list of resort activities on offer. Of course, these days gringos prefer to bed down in some of the newer top-end resorts, though the Best Western does attract a loyal Tico-family following. If you're planning on spending the night here, it pays to check the internet for special discount rates.

TOP END

Jacó is in the midst of going upscale, though it's still going to be a few years before some of the proposed top-end resorts and hotels open up to the tourist masses. In the meantime, however, there are a number of all-inclusive–style resorts and a few boutique hotels and guesthouses where your dollars can buy you a nice slice of luxury.

Hotel Poseidon (Map p328; ☎ 2643-1642; www.hotel-poseidon.com; Calle Bohío; d from US$105; P) It's hard to miss the huge Grecian wood carvings that adorn the exterior of this small European-run hotel. On the inside, sparkling rooms are perfectly accented with stylish furniture and mosaic tiles, though the highlight of the property is the elegant open-air restaurant that specializes in fresh fish – it's one of the best spots in town. There's a pool with a convenient swim-up bar, as well as a small Jacuzzi for getting to know your neighbors.

Hotel Tangerí (Map p328; ☎ 2643-3001; www.hoteltangeri.com; Av Pastor Díaz btwn Calles Las Palmeras & Las Olas; r from US$115, villas from US$190; P) This low-key resort complex is smack-dab in the middle of it all, but surprisingly manages to remain tranquil despite the ensuing craziness surrounding it. The tropical-infused grounds are extremely well manicured, and home to no less than three pools where you can soak up the rays while floating the daylight away. Rooms are fairly standard, though they do boast ocean views and are brightened up a bit by the colorful linens. However, if you have a bit of extra cash to burn, larger villas with full kitchens are certainly worth the splurge and help you make the necessary transition to resort living.

Docelunas (Map p323; ☎ 2643-2277; ww.docelunas.com; Costanera Sur; d/junior ste incl breakfast US$140/160; P ⊠ ✲ 💻 ≋ 🏊) Situated in the foothills across the highway, 'Twelve Moons' is a heavenly mountain retreat consisting of only 20 rooms sheltered in a pristine landscape of tropical rainforest. Each teak-accented room is intimately decorated with original artwork that's available for purchase, and the luxurious bathrooms feature double sinks and bathtubs. Yoga classes are given daily, there's a full spa which uses the hotel's own line of beauty products, and you can dip in a free-form pool that's fed by a waterfall. The open-air restaurant serves everything from marlin *ceviche* (raw but well-marinated seafood) to vegan delicacies. To reach the hotel, make a left off the Costanera between the two entrances for Playa Jacó.

Sonidos del Mar (Map p323; ☎ 2643-3924/12; www.sonidosdelmar.com; Calle Hidalgo; house US$250; P ✲ 💻 ≋ 🏊) Howard and Lauri, a South African–American couple, will welcome you to their guesthouse as if you were family. And when you see their house, you'll wish you were! Set within a mature garden at the bend of a river, 'Sounds of the Ocean' may be one of the most beautiful guesthouses in Costa Rica. Lauri is a skilled artist and a collector who has lovingly filled each room with original paintings, sculptures and indigenous crafts. The house itself is impeccable, incorporating stylistic elements such as vaulted Nicaraguan hardwood ceilings and black, volcanic-rock showers. Guests have free use of kayaks and surfboards, and the beach is only 50m away. Full spa services are also available. The house can accommodate up to six people, and cheaper weekly and monthly rates are available.

Eating

The quality of fare in Jacó is surprisingly good, and aside from the Quepos and Manuel Antonio area, the city proudly boasts the most eclectic offering of international cuisine on the central Pacific coast. While the vast majority of eateries cater primarily to Western palettes, there are still a few local spots that have weathered the storm of change.

It's worth pointing out that hours can fluctuate wildly, especially in the rainy season when many shops close sporadically, so it's best to eat early.

BUDGET

If you're counting your colones, head to **Más X Menos** (Map p328; Av Pastor Díaz), a Western-style supermarket that has an impressive selection of fresh produce, local and international culinary items and a surprisingly good outdoors section. And for the record, the name is pronounced *mas por menos,* which means 'more for less.'

Soda Flor (Map p328; Av Pastor Díaz, north of Calle La Central; casados ₡2000-3000) This Jacó institution is a perennial favorite of locals and budget travelers alike. Remarkably, the menu hasn't changed in years despite the fact that nearly every other place in town is now offering everything from sushi to sirloin. Food is fresh, tasty, cheap and 100% Costa Rican, and the portions here are huge.

Pancho Villa's (Map p328; cnr Av Pastor Díaz & Calle Hicaco; dishes ₡2500-5000) The food here certainly isn't gourmet by any stretch of the imagination, but it caters to every conceivable taste from Tico and Western to Asian and Mexican. Even if you skip dinner, you'll probably end up here at some point since the kitchen is open until the wee hours of the morning.

MIDRANGE

Bar Restaurante Colonial (Map p328; cnr Av Pastor Díaz & Calle Bohío; dishes ₡3000-5000) Centered on a large bar facing the alfresco table settings, this breezy tapas-style bar and restaurant is perfect for some light noshing followed up by a crafted cocktail or two. Fast-food staples arc balanced out by local seafood options, while signature drinks make excellent use of regional liquors and fresh fruit juices.

Taco Bar (Map p328; mains ₡3000-6000) A one-stop shop for Mexican, seafood, salads and smoothies. Get your drink with the gargantuan 1L sizes, or your greens at the salad bar featuring more than 20 different kinds of exotic and leafy combinations. And of course, there's the obligatory fish taco, which may be one of the planet's greatest food combinations.

Tsunami Sushi (Map p328; Av Pastor Díaz, north of Calle Cocal; sushi ₡3500-6500) If you've got a hankering for raw fish, don't miss Tsunami, a modern and lively restaurant that serves up an exquisite assortment of sushi, sashimi and Californian rolls. The Far East may be a long way away, but the nearby Pacific is home to some seriously tasty sport fish, such as dolphinfish, tuna and wahoo.

Rioasis (Map p328; cnr Calle Cocal & Av Pastor Díaz; pizzas ₡4500-8000) There's pizza, and then there's *pizza* – this much loved pizzeria definitely falls into the latter category, especially considering that there are more than 30 different kinds of pies on the menu. Of course, considering that each one emerges from an authentic wood-fired oven, and is topped with gourmet ingredients from both Costa Rica and abroad, you really can't go wrong here.

Calinche's Wishbone Eatery (Map p328; Av Pastor Díaz, south of Calle Bohío; meals ₡4500-9000) Overseen by the charming Calinche, this is the most famous restaurant in town, and has been so for years and years. The eclectic menu includes pizzas, pitas, stuffed potatoes, pan-seared sea bass and tuna-sashimi salads, though its justifiable fame comes from the fact that everything is quite simply fresh, delicious and good value.

El Hicaco (Map p328; ☎ 2643-3226; Calle Hicaco; mains ₡5000-10,000) It's hard not to be impressed by the innovative offerings at this oceanside spot brimming with casual elegance, generally regarded as one of the finer dining experiences in Jacó. Although the menu is entirely dependent on seasonal offerings, both from the land and the sea, the specialty of the house is seafood, prepared with a variety of special sauces highlighted by Costa Rica's tropical produce.

TOP END

Hotel Poseidon Restaurant (Map p328; ☎ 2643-1642; Calle Bohío; meals ₡10,000-14,000) This is one of the most sophisticated restaurants in town, and the specialty here is fresh seafood served up with Asian flare. Sauces are inventive, the staff professional and the atmosphere upscale yet relaxing. A good bet for top-quality food and refined European-style dining that consistently receives good marks from travelers.

our pick **Pacific Bistro** (Map p328; Av Pastor Díaz, south of Calle Las Palmeras; meals ₡10,000-16,000) This deservedly popular place is run by a gourmet chef from California who specializes in Pan-Asian–style fusion dishes. Whether you're partial to Indonesian-style noodles and fiery Thai curries, or more refined Japanese soba and fish fillets topped with exotic Chinese sauces, one thing is for certain: this gem of a restaurant really hits the spot, especially if you've been craving fine Asian cuisine.

Drinking & Entertainment

Jacó may not be the cultural capital of Costa Rica, but it's without a doubt a great place to get hammered and party the night away. There are numerous raging bars and dance clubs that cater to good times–seeking expats and travelers, but be advised that a good portion of the nightlife in Jacó revolves around prostitution (see Dangers & Annoyances, p324). Gentlemen's clubs have sprung up all over town, so be sure to survey both the premises and the clientele before walking into a dodgy scene. Still, if you can find the right group of people (and stay away from the wrong group of people!), a night out in Jacó is – more often than not – a fun time for all!

Le Loft (Map p328; Av Pastor Díaz) A highly touted addition to Jacó's nightlife offering, the Loft aims to balance out the mix of beach clubs and girly bars with some much needed urban sophistication. Live DJs spin essential mixes while glam-aspiring customers do their best to look beautiful and act fabulous.

Tabacon (Map p328; Av Pastor Díaz) Definitely one of the more modest night spots in town, Tabacon is a casually elegant lounge that occasionally hosts live music. The mature crowd passes the night away with carefully measured doses of hard liquor, while younger hotheads can let off a bit of steam at the pool tables and foosball.

Clarita's Beach Hotel and Sports Bar and Grill (Map p323; western end of Blvr) Part hotel and part watering hole, this sports bar sets the table with ample pub grub, and quenches the thirst with copious draft beer. Sports fans will appreciate being able to catch the game on the big screen, not to mention the cheerleader-esque bartenders and wait staff.

Jungle (Map p328; Av Pastor Díaz) The 2nd-story terrace gives you a good vantage point for sizing up your prey, which is a good thing as this place can turn into an unabashed meat market. But, the vast majority of people here are looking for a hookup rather than opting to pay for one, so it definitely earns a small measure of respectability in our book.

Disco La Central (Map p328; Calle La Central) This unintentionally retro disco sets the volume at 11 (whether or not there's anyone on the dance floor), though it's an old-timer on the

Jacó scene that still draws in a strong local following. Very much an after-hours spot, Disco La Central doesn't really get going until the restaurants and bars have emptied out, sending inebriated patrons out in search of flashing lights and heavy bass.

Jazz Casino (Map p323) is located in Hotel Amapola at the southern reaches of town. This full-on casino is in the business of squeezing the last few colones out of your pocket. That is, of course, assuming your luck isn't riding high, so why not add a dash of excitement to your night by trying your hand at slots, blackjack, roulette and craps?

Getting There & Away

AIR

NatureAir (www.natureair.com) and **Alfa Romeo Aero Taxi** (www.alfaromeoair.com) offer charter flights. Prices are dependent on the number of passengers, so it's best to try to organize a larger group if you're considering this option.

BOAT

Travelers are increasingly taking advantage of the jet-boat transfer service that connects Jacó to Montezuma. Several boats per day cross the Golfo de Nicoya, and the journey only takes about an hour. At US$37 it's definitely not cheap, but it'll save you about a day's worth of travel. Reservations can be made at most tour operators in town. It's a beach landing, so wear the right shoes.

BUS

Buses for San José stop at the Plaza Jacó mall, north of the center. The bus stop for other destinations is opposite the Más X Menos supermarket. (Stand in front of the supermarket if you're headed north; stand across the street if you're headed south.) The departure times listed here are approximate since buses originate in Puntarenas or Quepos. Get to the stop early!

Puntarenas ₡800; 1½ hours; departs 6am, 9am, noon and 4:30pm.

Quepos ₡800; 1½ hours; departs 6am, noon, 4:30pm and 6pm.

San José ₡2000; three hours; departs 5am, 7:30am, 11am, 3pm and 5pm.

Getting Around

BICYCLE & SCOOTER

Several places around town rent bicycles, mopeds and scooters. Bikes can usually be rented for about US$3 to US$5 an hour or US$8 to US$15 a day, though prices can change depending on the season. Mopeds and small scooters cost from US$25 to US$50 a day (many places ask for a cash or credit card deposit of about US$200).

CAR

There are several rental agencies in town, so shop around for the best rates.

Budget (Map p323; ☎ 2643-2665; Plaza Jacó Mall; 🕑 8am-6pm Mon-Sat, to 4pm Sun)

Economy (Map p323; ☎ 2643-1719; Av Pastor Díaz, south of Calle Ancha; 🕑 8am-6pm)

National (Map p328; ☎ 2643-1752; cnr Av Pastor Díaz & Calle Hicaco; 🕑 7:30am-6pm)

TAXI

Taxis to Playa Hermosa from Jacó cost upwards of ₡3000. To arrange for a pick-up, call **Taxi 30-30** (☎ 2643-3030), or negotiate with any of the taxis along Av Pastor Díaz.

PLAYA HERMOSA

While newbies struggle to stand up on their boards in Jacó, a few kilometers south in Playa Hermosa seasoned veterans are thrashing their way across the faces of some truly monster waves. Regarded as one of the most consistent and powerful breaks in the whole country, Hermosa serves up serious surf that commands the utmost respect. Of course, you really need to know what you're doing in these parts – huge waves and strong riptides are unforgiving, and countless surfboards here have wound up shattered to pieces and strewn about on the shoreline.

Meaning 'Pretty Beach' in Spanish, Playa Hermosa is a 10-km long strip of grayish sand that has seen significant investment in recent years, primarily in the form of several brand-new upmarket hotels. In comparison with neighboring Jacó and Playa Herradura, the development here is modest by all accounts. Rather than striving to achieve city status, Hermosa is still very much a slow-paced beach town edged by the Costanera Sur and the surf-washed shores of the Pacific. It's also surprisingly well to do, targeting older adults that balance their surfing hobby with real professions elsewhere in the world.

If you're looking for the 'other' Playa Hermosa on the Península de Nicoya, see p253.

Activities

SURFING

Most of the adrenaline-soaked action takes place at the northern reaches, where there are no less than half a dozen clearly defined beach breaks. Conditions are highly variable, but you can expect the maximum height to top out around high tide. Swell size is largely dependent on unseen factors such as current and offshore weather patterns, but when it gets big, you'll know. At times like these, you really shouldn't be paddling out unless you have some serious experience under your belt. Playa Hermosa is not for beginners, and even intermediate surfers on occasion get chewed up and spit out here.

YOGA

High in the hills above Playa Hermosa lies the **Vida Asana Retreat Center** (☎ 2643-7108; www.vidaasana.com), which offers fully customizable packages combining yoga, surfing, rustic jungle accommodations and healthy organic meals. Advanced reservations are highly recommended, and prices are dependent on the size of your party, the season and the extent of requested instruction.

CANOPY TOURS

Playa Hermosa is, surprisingly enough, home to a canopy tour, which blends the usual forested surrounds with panoramic views of the central Pacific coastline. **Chiclets Canopy Tour** (☎ 2643-3271; per person US$60), located 500m north of town on the main highway, is comprised of 13 platforms, 11 zip lines and a suspension bridge.

Festivals & Events

If you don't think you can hack it with the aspiring pros, you might want to give the surf on this beach a miss. However, consider stopping by in August when local and international pro surfers descend on Hermosa for the annual **surf competition**. Dates vary, though the event is heavily advertised around the country, especially in neighboring Jacó.

Sleeping

The highway is the only road, and all of the accommodations listed below are just off it. While there aren't proper addresses to speak of, everything is clustered along an easy-to-identify stretch unofficially known as 'Playa Hermosa Village.'

BUDGET

Cabinas Brisa del Mar (☎ 2643-2076; http://cabinasbrisadelmar.com; s/d/tr US$25/40/45; P) If your wallet is looking a bit thin these days, consider bunking down at this Floridian-run crash pad, which is decidedly more budget-friendly than the vast majority of options in Hermosa. Brisa del Mar has a few rooms of varying sizes with air-con, private hot shower and cable TV, as well as a communal kitchen where you can self-cater. If the surf is looking too small (or too big!), you can pass the time on the basketball court or with a few games of table tennis.

Cabinas Las Arenas (☎ 2643-7013; www.cabinaslasarenas.com; s/d/tr/q US$37/49/55/62; P) Another one of just a handful of hotels in Hermosa that cater exclusively to the backpacking surfer crowd, Las Arenas sticks to the basics in an effort to keep prices on the low side. The property comprises 10 cabins that can each sleep up to four, providing tremendous bang for your buck if you're traveling in a group. The premises are also home to a full restaurant, surf supply shop and a small beach BBQ pit.

MIDRANGE

Cabinas Las Olas Hotel (☎ 2643-7021; www.lasolashotel.com; r US$45-75, ranchos US$100, skybox US$100; P) This distinctive three-story A-frame building is home to the awesome 'skybox room,' a teak-accented, ocean-facing penthouse where you can fall asleep and wake up to the sounds of the surf. If heights aren't your thing, you can also rent one of several beachside *ranchos* (small houses) that come equipped with kitchenette and sleep several people comfortably. Alternatively, price-conscious travelers can snag a cheap but cheerful room in the main house.

Posada Playa Hermosa (☎ 2643-2640; www.fbsurfboards.com/surfcamp; r from US$50; P) This Argentine-run compound is decked out in vibrant oil paintings courtesy of the painter, surfer and owner extraordinaire, Eduardo Fischer. But the focus is very much on the nearby breaks as evidenced by the adjacent Fischer Bros Surf Shop, where you can repair dings, buy or sell boards and get reliable advice on local conditions. The rooms themselves are all unique in design, though we're partial to the ones with the richly hued exposed wooden beams.

Costanera Bed and Breakfast (☎ 2643-1942; www.costaneraplayahermosa.com; r from US$55; P) For a bit of European flair, this well-priced Italian-run B&B has a very sophisticated ambience. Five rooms of various sizes and shapes have vaulted wooden ceilings and beachfront terraces, each offering a fair degree of privacy and intimacy. Of course, the undisputed highlight of these accommodations is the authentic handmade pasta and rich Italian sauces served at the onsite restaurant each evening.

Tortuga del Mar (☎ 2643-7132; www.tortugadelmar.net; r US$75, studios from US$85; P) Top-end accommodations with a recession-proof midrange price tag, this brand-new lodge is sheltered amid shady grounds, and comprised of just a handful of rooms housed in a two-story building. Tropical modern is the style at hand, making excellent use of local hardwoods to construct lofty ceilings that catch every gust of the Pacific breezes. The larger studios are spacious by all accounts, and even feature minikitchenettes that make self-catering a real possibility within this budget bracket.

TOP END

Terraza del Pacífico (☎ 2643-3222; www.terrazadelpacifico.com; r/ste from US$115/175; P) The granddaddy of top-end hotels is this standout property, located on prime beachfront overlooking some seriously killer breaks at the northern end of town. With Spanish colonial accents and luxurious tiled-floor rooms throughout, this Hermosa establishment is strictly for upscale surfers. Assuming you can pry yourself away from the beach, there is also a whole list of impressive amenities on offer ranging from a pool with swim-up bar to a small but energetic casino.

Backyard Hotel (☎ 2643-7011; www.backyardhotel.com; r/ste from US$130/180; P) Despite being a new addition to the Hermosa scene, the Backyard is a premium boutique hotel that has substantially raised the bar on quality. The highlight of the property is the Backyard Bar, a bustling bar and restaurant that is also open to the public, and serves as the nexus for nightlife in formerly sleepy Hermosa. Rooms themselves are well appointed with modern home furnishings that reflect good taste, and face either the beach or the forested hillsides inland.

Eating & Drinking

Jungle Surf Café (meals ₡1500-5000; 7am-9pm) If you're looking for a quick bite between sets, this terminally laid-back cafe is a local institution that offers everything from burritos to kebabs, though locals swear by the seriously gourmet fish tacos. There is also a small bar decorated with the obligatory surf paraphernalia that makes for a refreshing sundowner after a long day of thrashing about in the waves.

Jammin Café (meals ₡2000-5000; 7am-9pm) While you're somewhat far from the shores of the Caribbean, this Rasta-inspired eatery brings a much welcome dose of mellow to the Pacific. It's particularly popular for its generous breakfasts, which combine US-style omelets and pancakes with Costa Rican standards, namely tropical fruits, coconut-scented *gallo pinto* (rice and beans) and shade-grown coffee.

Backyard Bar (☎ 2643-7011; meals ₡2500-7000; noon-late) A proper eatery unlike any that Hermosa has ever known, this is where you should head for an expansive menu that reaches beyond the usual surfer fare. As the town's de facto nightspot, the Backyard Bar occasionally hosts live music, and you can also count on a happy hour here every night of the week.

Getting There & Away

Located only 5km south of Jacó, Playa Hermosa can be accessed by any bus heading south from Jacó. Frequent buses running up and down the Costanera Sur can easily pick you up, though determined surfers can always hail a taxi (with surf racks) or stick out a thumb if there is a rush.

Since Jacó serves as the regional transportation hub, see p332 for detailed information on getting there and away.

PLAYA ESTERILLOS

Just 22km south of Jacó is this beautiful stretch of pale gray sand, which can easily be reached by short side roads from the Costanera Sur. Although the beach is relatively undiscovered and little visited, there are a few great surf spots here, which should be evident once you see the small groups of surfers camping underneath the trees at the northern edge of the beach.

For anyone not keen on exposing themselves to the elements, there's always the long-standing **Pélican Hotel** (☎ 2778-8105; www.pelicanhotelcr.com; r from US$45; P), a homey, beachfront spot that has a handful of rustic rooms, and is only steps away from the surf. And of course, there are plenty of hammocks onsite – perfect for lounging – as well as free surfboards, body boards and bikes for guests.

If it's possible for you to stretch your budget for a night or two, do not miss the chance to stay at the **Xandari by the Pacific** (☎ 2778-7070; ww.xandari.com; villas US$295-440; P), a visually stunning resort that is aiming to put Playa Esterillos on the map. There is no shortage of attractive resorts along this stretch of the Pacific, but what makes Xandari so unique is the incredible architectural scheme that is evident from the moment you step foot on the property. Each individually designed villa encompasses a range of intriguing design elements including wooden-lattice ceilings, sheer walls of glass framing private gardens, concrete-poured furniture done up with custom leatherwork and impossibly intricate mosaic tile work. As if all of this wasn't enough to make you postpone your onward travel plans, there is also an onsite restaurant specializing in gourmet and organic healthy fare, as well as an immaculate palm-fringed infinity pool that faces the crashing surf.

The Playa Esterillos area can be a little confusing to navigate as there are three towns with access to the beach: Esterillos Oeste, Esterillos Centro and Esterillos Este. These towns are all off the Costanera about 22km, 25km and 30km southeast of Jacó, respectively, and can all be reached by any bus heading south from Jacó.

PARRITA

A bustling town on a river of the same name, Parrita is home to a tremendous palm oil processing plant. If the wind is blowing right, the plant can be smelled from several kilometers away, though the odor is somewhat pleasant if you're a fan of fried foods. Although palm oil doesn't have the immediate recognition as olive oil perhaps, the product finds its way into just about everything, from chocolate bars and french fries to baked goods and snack foods.

While you're driving through the area, watch the workers in the fields on the sides of the road as the palm oil industry is a fascinating one. In terms of day-to-day maintenance, workers spend hours keeping the palms clear of insects, which is accomplished by clearing growth on the forest floor and applying poison to the trunks. In addition, fronds must be regularly clipped in order to encourage fruit growth and to provide easy access to the pod. Workers must also collect mature pods and transport them to processing plants where the fruits are separated and pressed. This last step is perhaps most evident in the huge big-rig trucks stacked full of reddish fruit that come flying down this relatively poor stretch of the Costanera Sur – be careful if you're on the road out there!

The primary reason for visiting Parrita is to visit **Playa Palo Seco**, a quiet, unhurried black-sand beach located near mangrove swamps that provide good opportunities for bird-watching. A 6km dirt road connects the eastern edge of town to the beach. Another popular excursion is to visit **Isla Damas**, which is actually the tip of a mangrove peninsula that becomes an island at high tide. Most people arrive here on package tours from Jacó or Quepos, though you can hire a boat to bring you to and from the island for a few thousand colones each way.

If you're looking to stay on Playa Palo Seco, **Beso del Viento B&B** (☎ 2779-9674; www.besodelviento.com; s/d/q US$87/112/136; P) has four modest but comfortable apartments for rent that have a tiled bathroom, fully stocked kitchen and breezy grounds. Kayaks, bikes and horses can be rented if you're interested in exploring this off-the-beaten-path area. The French owners are extremely warm and accommodating, and go out of their way to make guests feel more like visiting family.

Parrita is about 40km south of Jacó, and can be reached by any bus heading south from Jacó. After Parrita, the coastal road dips inland through more palm oil plantations on the way to Quepos. If you're driving, the road is a mix of badly potholed pavement and stretches of dirt, with several rickety one-way bridges.

RAINMAKER AERIAL WALKWAY

Rainmaker was the first **aerial walkway** through the forest canopy in Central America, though it is still regarded as one of the region's best. From its tree-to-tree platforms, there are spectacular panoramic views of the surrounding primary and secondary rainforest, as well as occasional vistas out to the Pacific Ocean. The reserve is also home to the full complement of tropical wildlife, which means that there are myriad opportunities here for great bird-watching as well as the occasional monkey sighting.

Tours with naturalist guides leave hotels in Manuel Antonio and Quepos daily except Sunday; reservations can be made at most hotels or by calling the **Rainmaker office** (Map p337; ☎ in Quepos 2777-3565; www.rainmakercostarica.org). Standard tours cost US$70 and include a light breakfast and lunch, though there are also bird-watching (US$90) and night tours (US$60) available. Binoculars are invaluable for watching wildlife, as are water and sun protection for staying hydrated and sunburn-free.

Rainmaker also offers opportunities for volunteers to participate for two weeks to one month in one of the four departments needed to run and preserve the project. There are also opportunities to work with local schools and various community outreach programs. Contact them for more information regarding fees and placements.

From the parking lot and orientation area, visitors walk up a beautiful rainforest canyon with a pristine stream tumbling down the rocks. A wooden boardwalk and series of bridges across the canyon floor lead to the base of the walkway. From here, visitors climb several hundred steps to a tree platform, from which the first of six suspension bridges spans the treetops to another platform. The longest span is about 90m, and the total walkway is about 250m long. At the highest point, you are some 20 stories above the forest floor.

In addition, there are short interpretive trails that enable the visitor to identify some of the local plants, and some long and strenuous trails into the heart of the 20-sq-km preserve. Keep your eye out for poison-dart frogs, which are very common along the trails!

A large colorful sign marks the turnoff for Rainmaker on the Costanera Sur at the northern end of Pocares (10km east of Parrita or 15km west of Quepos). From the turnoff, it is 7km to the parking area.

QUEPOS & MANUEL ANTONIO

The sleepy, provincial town of Quepos never had ambitions of being anything more than a community of fishers, merchants and plantation workers. However, as the international spotlight began to shine on nearby Parque Nacional Manuel Antonio, Quepos suddenly found itself with an opportunity to cash in on something even more lucrative than fish and palm oil: tourism. With rainforested hills sweeping down to the sea, the Manuel Antonio park is a stunning destination worthy of the tourist hype, while decidedly more relaxed Quepos is admirably maintaining its roots despite ongoing socioeconomic transformation.

Note that this section is divided into Quepos proper, the road from Quepos to Manuel Antonio, the village of Manuel Antonio and the national park itself.

QUEPOS

Located just 7km from the entrance to Manuel Antonio, the small town of Quepos serves as the gateway to the national park, as well as a convenient port of call for travelers in need of goods and services. Although the Manuel Antonio area was rapidly and irreversibly transformed following the ecotourism boom, Quepos has largely remained an authentic Tico town. Exuding a traditional Latin American charm that is absent from so much of the central Pacific, Quepos is a low-key alternative to the tourist-packed gringo trail not far beyond.

While most visitors to the Manuel Antonio area prefer to stay outside Quepos, accommodations are generally cheaper in town, though you will need to organize transportation to both the national park and the beaches. However, Quepos can be an appealing place to stay, especially since it's home to a burgeoning restaurant scene that belies its small size. Quepos is also gridded with easy-to-walk streets, which provides the opportunity to interact with the friendly locals, who have thus far weathered the storm of change with cheerfulness and optimism.

History

The town's name was derived from the indigenous Quepoa, a subgroup of the Brunka (Boruca), who inhabited the area at the time of the Spanish conquest. As with many indigenous populations across the region, the Quepoa were quickly decimated by newly introduced European diseases. By the end of the 19th century, no pure-blooded Quepoa were left, and the area proceeded to be colonized by farmers from the highlands.

Quepos first came to prominence as a banana-exporting port in the early 20th century, though crops declined precipitously in subsequent decades due to disease and labor issues. African oil palms, which currently stretch toward the horizon in dizzying rows around Quepos, soon replaced bananas as the major local crop, though unfortunately they generated a lot less employment for the locals.

The future, on the other hand, is looking bright for locals as foreign visitors are coming to the Manuel Antonio area by the boatload, and more people means more jobs in the area's rapidly expanding tourism industry. The opening of the Pez Vela Marina during the life of this book will have profound effects on this humble town, though questions of sustainability and the need for balanced growth continue to be fiercely debated in the local media.

Orientation

Downtown Quepos is a small checkerboard of dusty streets that are lined with a mix of local- and tourist-oriented shops, businesses, markets, restaurants and cafes. The town loses its well-ordered shape as it expands outward, but the sprawl is kept relatively in check by the mountains to the east and the water to the west.

Southeast of the town center is the brand-new Pez Vela Marina, a shimmering jewel of architectural prowess that – to be frank – seems a bit out of place in drowsy Quepos. In 2010 the marine slips opened up to the public

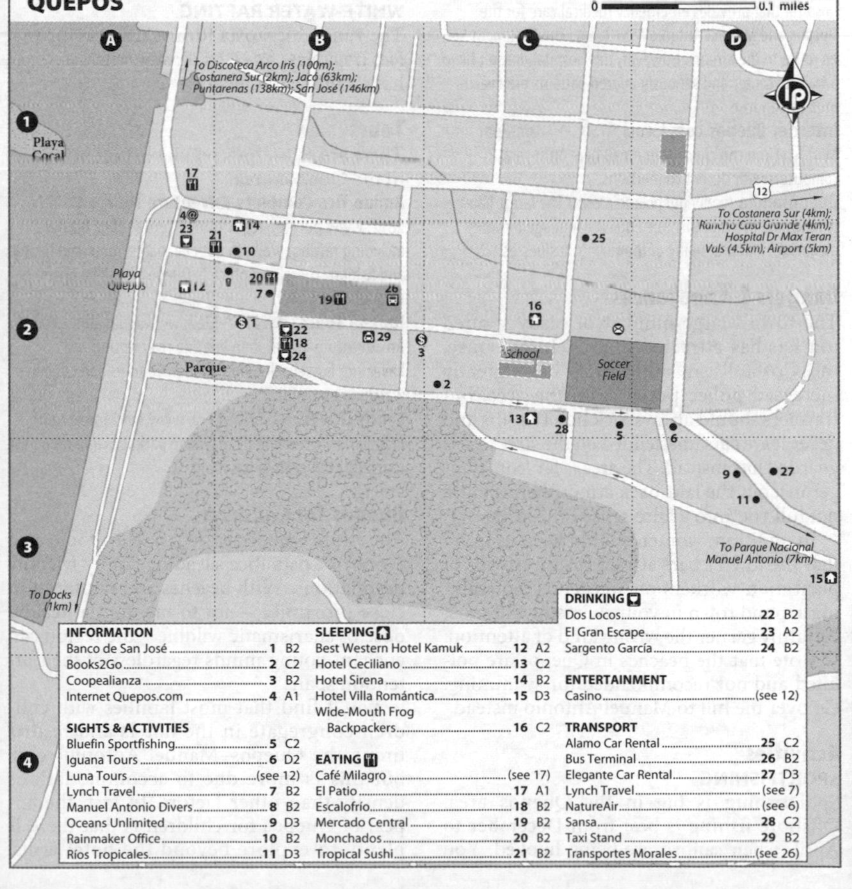

with much fanfare, though it will still be a few years before the construction subsides. The subsequent phase will include large residential communities, shopping complexes and boutique hotels, which may eventually reshift the town's orientation.

Information

Both Banco de San José and Coopealianza have 24-hour ATMs on the Cirrus and Plus systems. Other banks will all change US dollars and traveler's checks.

Books2Go (☎ 2777-1754, 8371-3476; tours2go@racsa.co.cr; 🕒 10am-6pm) Susan runs a quaint little bookstore that also serves as the travelers' meeting place. You can post messages, store your bags, burn photos to CDs, use the internet (₡1000 per hour), or just hang out and read a good book.

Hospital Dr Max Teran Vals (☎ 2777-0200) A hospital that provides emergency medical care for the Quepos and Manuel Antonio area. It's on the Costanera Sur en route to the airport. However, this hospital doesn't have a trauma center and seriously injured patients are evacuated to San José.

Internet Quepos.com (per hr ₡750; 🕒 8am-8pm Mon-Sat) You can check your email here on several computers with decent connections.

Quepolandia (www.quepolandia.com) The latest happenings are listed in this free English-language monthly magazine, found at many of the town's businesses.

Dangers & Annoyances

The town's large number of easily spotted tourists has attracted thieves. In response, the Costa Rican authorities have greatly increased police presence in the area, but travelers should always lock hotel rooms and never leave cars unattended on the street – use guarded lots instead. The area is far from dangerous, but the laid-back atmosphere should not lull you into a false sense of security.

In addition, women should keep in mind that the town's bars attract rowdy crowds of plantation workers on weekends. So walking around town in your swimsuit will most certainly garner the wrong kind of attention.

Note that the beaches in Quepos are polluted and not recommended for swimming. Go over the hill to Manuel Antonio instead.

Activities

SPORTFISHING

Sportfishing is big in the Quepos area. Offshore fishing is best from December to April, when sailfish are being hooked. You can expect to pay upwards of US$1000 to hire a boat for the day.

Bluefin Sportfishing (☎ 2777-2222; www.bluefinsportfishing.com) Across from the soccer field.

Luna Tours (☎ 2777-0725; www.lunatours.net) Located in Best Western Hotel Kamuk.

DIVING

The dive sites are still being developed in the Quepos and Manuel Antonio area, though the following operators have both been recommended by readers. The dive sites are away from the contaminated beaches, so water pollution is not a problem when diving.

Manuel Antonio Divers (☎ 2777-3483; www.manuelantoniodivers.com)

Oceans Unlimited (☎ 2777-3171; www.oceansunlimitedcr.com)

WHITE-WATER RAFTING

The venerable Costa Rican rafting company, **Ríos Tropicales** (☎ 2777-4092; www.riostropicales.com), has an office in Quepos.

Tours

There are numerous reputable tour operators in the Quepos area.

Amigo Tico Complete Adventure Tours (☎ 2777-2812; www.puertoquepos.com) Offers a range of tours, including rafting, walks in national parks, mountain biking and fishing. There's no office in Quepos; book by phone or through your hotel.

Iguana Tours (☎ 2777-1262; www.iguanatours.com) An adventure-travel shop offering river rafting, sea kayaking, horseback riding, mangrove tours and dolphin-watching excursions.

Lynch Travel (☎ 2777-1170; www.lynchtravel.com) From airline reservations to fishing packages and rainforest tours, this travel shop has it all.

Quepos for Children

The entire Quepos and Manuel Antonio area is one of Costa Rica's leading family-friendly destinations. With beaches and rainforest in close proximity – not to mention a healthy dose of charismatic wildlife – the region can enchant young minds regardless of their attention spans.

You'll find that most families with children congregate in the hotels and resorts lining the Quepos–Manuel Antonio road, but this is more due to accommodations density than other factors. In fact, the appeal of Quepos for children is that there is plenty to explore beyond the hotel walls,

X MARKS THE SPOT

Locals have long believed that a treasure worth billions and billions of dollars lies somewhere in the Quepos and Manuel Antonio area, waiting to be discovered. The lore was popularized by the English pirate John Clipperton, who befriended the coastal Quepoa during his years of sailing to and from the South Pacific. Clipperton's belief stemmed from a rumor that in 1670 a number of Spanish ships laden with treasure escaped from Panama City moments before it was burned to the ground by Captain Henry Morgan. Since the ships were probably off-loaded quickly to avoid being raided at sea, a likely destination was the San Bernadino de Quepo Mission, which had a strong loyalty to the Spanish crown.

John Clipperton died in 1722 without ever discovering the legendary treasure, and the mission closed permanently in 1746 as most of the Quepoa had succumbed to European diseases. Although the ruins of the mission were discovered in 1974, they were virtually destroyed and were long since looted. However, if the treasure was indeed as large as it's described in lore, it is possible that a few gold doubloons could still be lying somewhere, waiting to be unearthed.

which can give parents a bit of fresh air and breathing room.

All in all, the town's excellent restaurant scene is kid-friendly, and the local Ticos in town are very welcoming to little ones. And finally, while you're not exactly on the beach or up in the forest, it's just a short and uneventful ride out to Manuel Antonio if your kids are in dire need of a little fun in the sun.

Sleeping

Staying in Quepos offers a cheaper alternative to the sky-high prices at many lodges on the road to Manuel Antonio. It can also be more convenient, as all the banks, supermarkets and bus stops are in Quepos. Reservations are recommended during high-season weekends and are necessary during Easter and the week between Christmas and New Year's Eve.

For more accommodations options, see the Quepos to Manuel Antonio section, p343, as well as the Manuel Antonio Village section, p348.

HOSTELS

our pick Wide-Mouth Frog Backpackers (☎ 2777-2798; www.widemouthfrog.org; dm US$11, r with/without bathroom US$40/30; P) This backpacker outpost is run by a welcoming British–New Zealand couple who are determined to make their little spot one of the best accommodations in Costa Rica – and so far, they've done everything right. Brightly tiled rooms are centered on an inviting pool with plenty of lounge chairs where backpackers can congregate and swap stories. There's also a communal kitchen with a huge dining area, a TV lounge with a free DVD rental library and free internet. But what makes this place so memorable are the generally good vibes that radiate throughout the premises, especially in the evenings when everyone unwinds and lets loose over a few drinks.

BUDGET

Hotel Ceciliano (☎ 2777-0192; r from US$20; P) There is no shortage of budget hotels in Quepos catering primarily to Tico travelers, though this family-friendly spot gets good marks for its comfortable rooms and welcoming owners. Although the Ceciliano isn't the newest hotel on the block, everything here is kept spic-and-span, and the welcoming staff ensure that Costa Rican hospitality reigns true during the entirety of your stay.

MIDRANGE

Hotel Sirena (☎ 2777-0572; www.lasirenahotel.com; s/d/tr US$60/75/85; P) An unexpectedly Zen-inducing hotel, the Sirena has whitewashed walls with soft pastel trims that are subtly lit by blue Tiffany lamps. The Mediterranean ambience is soothing, and a world away from the rough-and-ready Quepos street scene. The hotel is also perfectly accented with potted plants and original artwork, and is highlighted by a quaint tiki bar overlooking a tranquil swimming pool.

Hotel Villa Romántica (☎ 2777-0037; www.villaromantica.com; s/d from US$65/85; P) A short walk southeast from the town center brings you to this peaceful garden oasis, which is overflowing with verdant greens and tropical flowers. If you're looking for a compromise between the convenience of staying in Quepos and the intimate proximity to nature found in Manuel Antonio, this is an excellent choice. The rooms themselves are designed to be light and open, which is a nice departure from the cloistered feel found at many other midrange spots.

Best Western Hotel Kamuk (☎ 2777-0379; www.kamuk.co.cr; r from US$95; P ❄ 💻 🏊 ♿) This upmarket Quepos stalwart bears the somewhat stale Best Western brand name, though in reality the Hotel Kamuk is a surprisingly refreshing historic building that provides excellent value. The Best Western label ensures that service is professional from check-in to checkout, though once you get past reception, the hotel is anything but American in ambience. In fact, the core of the hotel is a winding wooden staircase that fans out to breezy hallways adorned with colonial flourishes. Rooms are a bit on the small side, but you can always head to the attractive pool or Western-style restaurant if you want a bit more breathing space. If you're planning on staying here, check the internet as discount rates are sometimes available.

TOP END

Rancho Casa Grande (☎ 2777-3130; www.ranchocasagrande.com; ste/bungalows/villas from US$118/146/280; P ❄ 💻 🏊 ♿) This resort hotel, located out on the road to the Quepos airport, benefits from an expansive concession that is crisscrossed by hiking and horseback-riding trails. Luxury here is of the low-key variety, and the *rancho* is most definitely not in the same league as some of the more posh places found further out along the Quepos–Manuel Antonio road. But if you're looking for bucolic ambience without having to sacrifice customer service, you'll feel right at home here.

Eating

For a small Tico town (albeit on the edge of a major tourist attraction), Quepos is home to a surprising number of eateries that aspire to meet international standards of quality. In fact, one of the main appeals of staying in the town center is having so many excellent places virtually right on your doorstep.

For more eating options, see the Quepos to Manuel Antonio section, p346, as well as the Manuel Antonio Village section, p348.

If you want to go local, you can't go wrong with the **mercado central** (central market; 🕑 hours vary), a vast complex in the center of town that hosts plenty of budget-friendly *sodas* and cafes in addition to fruit and vegetable vendors.

Café Milagro (dishes ₡1000-3000; 🕑 6am-10pm Mon-Fri) Serving some of the country's best cappuccino and espresso, this is a great place to perk up in the morning – try the *perezoso* (meaning 'lazy' or 'sloth'), which is a double espresso poured into a large cup of drip-filter coffee. Or, if you want to simply relax and read the English-language newspapers that are available, you can indulge in a baked good or a freshly made deli sandwich.

Escalofrío (gelato ₡1000, meals ₡3000-5500; 🕑 Tue-Sun) Here you'll find more than 20 different flavors of gelato, which may just be the perfect way to beat the tropical heat. There is also a spacious alfresco seating area where you can sample other Italian treats including espressos and cappuccinos as well as an assortment of pizzas and pastas.

Monchados (dishes ₡4000-7500; 🕑 5pm-midnight) Something of a Quepos institution, this long-standing Mex-Carib spot is always bustling with dinner-goers who line up to try traditional Limón-style dishes and Mexican standards. Food here is eclectic, innovative and never bland, a theme that is also reflected in the vibrant decorations and fairly regular live music.

Tropical Sushi (meals ₡4500-8000; 🕑 5-10pm) Quepos has gone cosmopolitan – for authentic Japanese (yes, the sushi chef is from Japan!), try this colorfully decorated restaurant, which occasionally has all-you-can-eat specials. If you're a purist, you can stick to the tuna sashimi spreads, though it's worth venturing out a bit and sampling some of the local Costa Rican–style rolls.

El Patio (meals ₡5500-12,000; 🕑 6am-10pm) This Nuevo Latino spot is adored by locals and tourists alike, in part because its menu changes daily yet never fails to entice and surprise. The unspoken rule here is fresh and local, which means that meats, seafood and produce are always of the highest quality, and always prepared in a way that highlights their natural flavors. If you're a fan of tapas, sample a few dishes here, though go slow and enjoy your meal over a few glasses of imported wine.

Drinking & Entertainment

Nightlife in Quepos has a good blend of locals and travelers, and it's cheaper than anything you'll find in the Manuel Antonio area. If you are looking for something a bit more sophisticated, however, it's easy enough to jump in a taxi.

Dos Locos (☎ 2777-1526; 🕑 7am-11pm Mon-Sat, 11am-10pm Sun) This popular Mexican restaurant also serves as a regular drinking spot for the local expat community, and as a venue for the occasional live band.

El Gran Escape (☎ 2777-0395; 🕑 6am-11pm) A fishermen-friendly bar and restaurant that is good for cold beer, warm pub grub and some light-hearted chit-chat about the one that got away.

Sargento García (☎ 2777-2960; 🕑 9am-9pm) This Stars-and-Stripes tribute bar may be a bit heavy on the Americana for some, but look no further if you're craving a Budweiser.

Discoteca Arco Iris (🕑 10pm-late) An industrial-sized discotheque just north of town that brings out the locals with thumping dance beats.

If you feel like putting your cash on the line, there's a small but suitable casino at the Best Western Hotel Kamuk (p340).

Getting There & Away

AIR

Both **NatureAir** (www.natureair.com) and **Sansa** (www.sansa.com) service Quepos, which is the base town for accessing Manuel Antonio. Prices vary according to season and availability, though you can expect to pay a little less than US$75 for a flight from San José or Liberia. Flights are packed in the high season, so book (and pay) for your ticket well ahead of time and reconfirm often.

Lynch Travel (☎ 2777-1170; www.lynchtravel.com) can book charter flights to and from the Quepos area.

The airport is 5km out of town, and taxis make the trip for a few thousand colones, depending on traffic.

BUS

All buses arrive and depart from the main terminal in the center of town. Buy tickets for San José well in advance at the **Transportes Morales ticket office** (☎ 2777-0263; 🕑 7-11am & 1-5pm Mon-Sat, 7am-1pm Sun) at the bus terminal. Buses from Quepos depart for the following destinations:

Jacó ₡800; 1½ hours; departs 4:30am, 7:30am, 10:30am and 3pm.
Puntarenas ₡2100; 3½ hours; departs 8am, 10:30am and 3:30pm.
San Isidro, via Dominical ₡2000; three hours; departs 5am and 1:30pm.
San José (Transportes Morales) ₡3500 to ₡3700; four hours; departs 5am, 8am, 10am, noon, 2pm, 4pm and 7:30pm.
Uvita, via Dominical ₡4000; 4½ hours; departs 10am and 7pm.

Getting Around

BUS

Buses between Quepos and Manuel Antonio (₡200) depart roughly every 30 minutes from the main terminal between 6am and 7:30pm, and less frequently after 7:30pm. The last bus departs Manuel Antonio at 10:25pm. There are more frequent buses in the dry season.

CAR

The following car-rental companies operate in Quepos; reserve ahead and reconfirm to guarantee availability:

Alamo (☎ 2777-3344; 🕑 7:30am-noon & 1:30-5:30pm)
Elegante (☎ 2777-0115; 🕑 7:30am-5pm Mon-Fri)

TAXI

Colectivo taxis between Quepos and Manuel Antonio will usually pick up extra passengers for a few hundred colones. A private taxi will cost a few thousand colones. Call **Quepos Taxi** (☎ 2777-0425/734) or catch one at the taxi stand south of the market.

QUEPOS TO MANUEL ANTONIO

From the port of Quepos, the road swings inland for 7km before reaching the beaches of Manuel Antonio village and the entrance to the national park. This serpentine route passes over a number of hills awash with picturesque views of forested slopes leading down to the palm-fringed coastline. Although this area is anything but cheap, it is home to some of Costa Rica's finest hotels and restaurants. While shoestringers and budget travelers are somewhat catered for, this is one part of the country where those with deep pockets can bed down and dine out in the lap of luxury.

Orientation

Note that the road to Manuel Antonio is steep, winding and very narrow. Worse, local bus drivers love to careen through at high velocities, and there are almost no places to pull over

SAVING THE SQUIRREL MONKEY

With its expressive eyes and luxuriant coat, the *mono tití* (Central American squirrel monkey) is arguably the most beautiful of Costa Rica's four monkey species. It is also in danger of extinction as there are roughly 1500 of these animals left in Manuel Antonio, one of its last remaining native habitats.

Unfortunately, the area is nearing environmental jeopardy due to constant threats of overdevelopment. To remedy this problem, a conservation project known as **Saving Mono Tití** (www.savingmonotiti.com) is taking bold measures to prevent further decline. This coalition of various organizations is helping to create a sustainable wildlife corridor between Parque Nacional Manuel Antonio and the Zona Protectora Cerro Nara in the northeast.

To achieve this aim, they are reforesting the Río Naranjo, a key waterway linking the two locations. More than 10,000 trees have already been planted along 8km of the Naranjo. This not only has the effect of extending the monkeys' habitat, but also provides a protected area for other wildlife to enjoy. Scientists at the Universidad Nacional de Costa Rica have mapped and selected sites for reforestation, and business owners in the area as well as private donations support the project financially.

in the event of an emergency. At all times, you should exercise caution and drive and walk with care, especially at night.

Information

Banco Promerica (☉ 8am-5pm Mon-Fri, 9am-1pm Sat) Has a 24-hour ATM on the Cirrus network and can exchange US dollars.
Cantina Internet Café (per hr ₡750; ☉ 8am-8pm Mon-Sat)
El Chante Internet (per hr ₡750; ☉ 8am-8pm Mon-Sat)
La Buena Nota (☎ 2777-1002; buennota@racsa.co.cr; Manuel Antonio) A good source of tourist information for this area.

Sights & Activities

You can relax after a day's activities at the **Serenity Spa** (☎ 2777-0777, ext 220; Hotel Sí Como No), a good place for couple's massages, sunburn-relief treatments, coconut body scrubs and tasty coffee.

Also belonging to the Hotel Sí Como No and situated just across the street is **Fincas Naturales** (☎ 2777-0850; www.butterflygardens.co.cr; adult/child US$15/8), a private rainforest preserve and butterfly garden. About three dozen species of butterfly are bred here. The garden has a sound-and-light show at night (US$35 per person) and is surrounded by nature trails.

Amigos del Río (☎ 2777-1084; www.adventuremanuelantonio.com) runs white-water rafting trips for all skill levels on the Ríos Savegre and Naranjo. Prices vary depending on the size of the party and the nature of your trip.

Courses

Escuela de Idiomas D'Amore (☎ 2777-1143, in USA 310-435-9897, 262-367-8589; www.escueladamore.com) has Spanish immersion classes at all levels; local homestays can be arranged. Two-week classes with/without homestay start at US$995/845, though significant discounts are available for longer periods of study. This institute comes recommended by a large number of readers for its high level of service and professionalism.

Quepos to Manuel Antonio for Children

The Quepos to Manuel Antonio stretch of road is home to the lion's share of accommodations and restaurants in these parts, and you will see plenty of vacationing families wherever you go. But it's worth pointing out that many of the high-end boutique hotels and upscale eateries are not always very welcoming of babies and young children. Assuming, however, that you avoid anything with obvious over-the-top glitz and glamour, your children will be well catered for at many of the establishments covered in this section.

A word of caution: driver visibility is limited along parts of the narrow, steep and winding road, particularly during low-light and foul-weather conditions. If you find yourself walking along the road (there is no shoulder), keep a close eye on your children at all times, and warn them to be careful of passing cars. Likewise, always drive carefully, and return the favor by keeping an eye out for pedestrians.

Sleeping

The Quepos–Manuel Antonio road is heavily skewed towards ultra top-end hotels, but there are plenty of noteworthy midrange accommodations as well as an excellent budget hostel. High-season rates are provided throughout this section, though it's worth knowing that low-season rates can be as much as 40% lower in some hotels. Reservations are an absolute must for busy weekends and holiday seasons.

For more accommodations options, see Quepos section, p339, and Manuel Antonio Village, p348.

HOSTELS

our pick **Vista Serena Hostel** (☎ 2777-5162; www.vistaserena.com; 3-/4-bed dm US$10/15, bungalows without bathroom US$50; P) In an area that is hopelessly overpriced, it's a relief to find such a great budget hostel. Perched scenically on a quiet hillside, this truly memorable spot allows guests to enjoy spectacular ocean sunsets from a hammock-filled terrace. Unsurprisingly, most travelers find themselves getting stuck here for longer than they planned, especially when you can spend your days hiking down from the hostel through a farm to a remote wilderness beach. Catering to the needs of backpackers, Vista Serena offers spic-and span white-tiled dorms with shared bathrooms, a communal kitchen and a TV lounge, as well as affordable private bungalows for couples that want a bit more privacy. Sonia and her son Conrad, the super-helpful Tico owners, speak fluent English, and are commendable for their efforts in assisting countless travelers.

MIDRANGE

Hotel Mono Azul (☎ 2777-2572; www.monoazul.com; r US$40-65, child under 12yr free; P) This is a great family option, as the entire hotel is decorated with animal murals and rainforest paraphernalia, not to mention the three pools and games room. You'll also sleep well at night knowing that your money is going to a good cause. The Mono Azul is home to 'Kids Saving the Rainforest' (KSTR), started by two local schoolchildren who were concerned about the endangered *mono tití* (Central American squirrel monkey). Many of these adorable critters were run over on the narrow road to the national park, or electrocuted on overhanging electrical cables, so KSTR purchased and erected monkey 'bridges' across the road (you can see them, often in use, as you head to the park). Ten percent of hotel receipts are donated to the organization.

Hotel Plinio (☎ 2777-0055; www.hotelplinio.com; d with/without air-con US$75/65, 2-/3-story ste US$85/110, jungle house US$100; P) This cozy hotel is nestled on the verdant edge of the rainforest, and is the perfect retreat from all of your stresses. Rooms have superhigh ceilings, which create a tranquil, relaxed atmosphere. Larger suites are two and three stories tall, and have great polished-wood decks for lounging, while groups of up to five can live it up in the jungle house. The grounds boast 10km of trails into the forest, where you'll find a 17m-high lookout tower (open to the public).

Mimo's Hotel (☎ 2777-2217; www.mimoshotel.com; d/ste from US$65/95; P) Run by a delightful Italian couple, this whitewashed and wood-trimmed hotel has spacious, clean, terra-cotta–tiled rooms that are positively lit up with bright, colorful murals. Highlights here include the palm-fringed swimming pool, a fiber-optically lit Jacuzzi and restaurant-bar serving Italian-influenced dishes. The owners speak half a dozen languages, and

EXPLORE MORE: FILA CHONTA MOUNTAINS

If you're looking for an off-the-beaten-path experience in the Quepos and Manuel Antonio area, consider a day trip to the inland Fila Chonta mountain range. Excursions can be arranged through the **Hotel Sí Como No** (☎ 2777-0777; www.sicomono.com/tours/santa_juana.php; adult/child US$95/50), and include round-trip transportation by 4WD Land Cruiser, a bilingual guide and a traditional *campesino* (farmer) lunch. The tour stops at the village of Santa Juana, which is working in close collaboration with the owner of Hotel Sí Como No to develop various community-based ecotourism initiatives. You'll get the opportunity to swim in waterfalls, try your hand at tilapia fishing, learn about citrus growing and coffee production, and even participate in a tree-planting initiative. This tour is not only a wonderful example of how tourism can empower local communities, but also a nice day out for you and your friends or family!

can share with you a wealth of knowledge about Costa Rica.

Hotel Las Tres Banderas (2777-1871; www.hoteltresbanderas.com; d/ste/apt US$80/120/250;) This welcoming roadside inn is owned by a Polish-born US citizen who lives in Costa Rica – hence the very appropriate moniker, *tres banderas* (three flags). Fourteen doubles and three suites are spacious affairs with imported tiles and local woods, while a private apartment built up with natural stones is available for groups of up to five. Guests congregate around the central pool, Jacuzzi and bar-restaurant, lending a festive and communal flourish to the property.

BaBaLoo Inn (2777-3461; www.babalooinn.com; d standard/king US$90/185;) This US-run establishment offers standard rooms with private balcony overlooking a lush, tropical garden. However, we're partial to the larger king rooms featuring dramatic ocean views, a comfortable sitting area, oversized beds and shower, a small kitchenette and enough space for a family of four. All rooms come with small extras, like a fully stocked minibar and DVD player, which means that there is plenty to do on a rainy day.

TOP END

our pick **Hotel Costa Verde** (2777-0584; www.costaverde.com; efficiency/studios from US$115/149, Boeing 727 fuselage home US$500;) This collection of rooms, studios and – believe it or not – a fully converted Boeing 727 fuselage occupies a lush, tropical setting that is frequented by regular troops of primate visitors. Efficiency units are attractively tiled, and face the encroaching forest, while slightly more expensive studios have full ocean views. But the real kicker here is the airplane–tree house hybrid, which gives new life to a previously decommissioned Boeing. The fuselage has been completely retrofitted with wooden paneling, and now houses two bedrooms, a fully functional master bathroom, and a chandelier-lit balcony that branches off the wing. It's one of the most surreal accommodations we've ever seen, especially when toucans flit by the cockpit! In case you're wondering where the idea came from, the owners of Hotel Costa Verde were also the masterminds behind El Avión (see p346).

Hotel Casitas Eclipse (2777-0408/1738; www.casitaseclipse.org; standard r/ste/casitas from US$140/190/330;) The soothing curves of this architecturally arresting, pure-white complex hint at the beauty within. The hotel consists of nine attractive, split-level houses spread around three swimming pools. The bottom floor of each house is an enormous junior suite, while the upper floor is a standard room with private terrace. These have a separate entrance but a staircase (with lockable door) combines the two and, voilà, you have a sumptuous *casita* (apartment) sleeping five.

Hotel Sí Como No (2777-0777; www.sicomono.com; r US$210-265, ste US$305-340, child under 6yr free;) This flawlessly designed hotel is an example of how to build a resort while maintaining environmental sensibility. Buildings are insulated for comfort and use energy-efficient air-con units; water is recycled into the landscape, and solar-heating panels are used to heat the water. No surprise here that the Sí Como No is one of only four hotels in the country to have been awarded five out of five leaves by the government-run Certified Sustainable Tourism campaign. Ecofriendliness aside, the hotel is also gorgeous and packed full of family-friendly amenities. The rooms themselves are accented by rich woods and bold splashes of tropical colors, and feature enormous picture windows and sweeping balconies – you'll never feel closed in from the surrounding rainforest and distant ocean. The hotel has two pools (one with a slide for kids, one for adults only, both with swim-up bars), two solar-heated Jacuzzis, a health spa, THX movie theater and two excellent restaurants.

Hotel La Mariposa (2777-0355; www.lamariposa.com; r US$215-450, ste US$450;) This internationally acclaimed hotel was the area's first luxury accommodations option, so unsurprisingly it snatched up the best view of the coastline. Fifty-plus pristine rooms of various sizes are elegantly decorated with hand-carved furniture – big spenders should check out the penthouse suite, which has a Jacuzzi on the terrace facing the sea. This hotel was listed in the book *1000 Places to See Before You Die*, principally for the immaculate gardens and world-class views that hug every corner of the property.

Makanda by the Sea (2777-0442; www.makanda.com; studios/villas incl breakfast from US$265/400;) Comprised of just six villas and five studios, Makanda has an unmatched air of intimacy and complete privacy. Villa 1 (the largest) will take your breath away – the

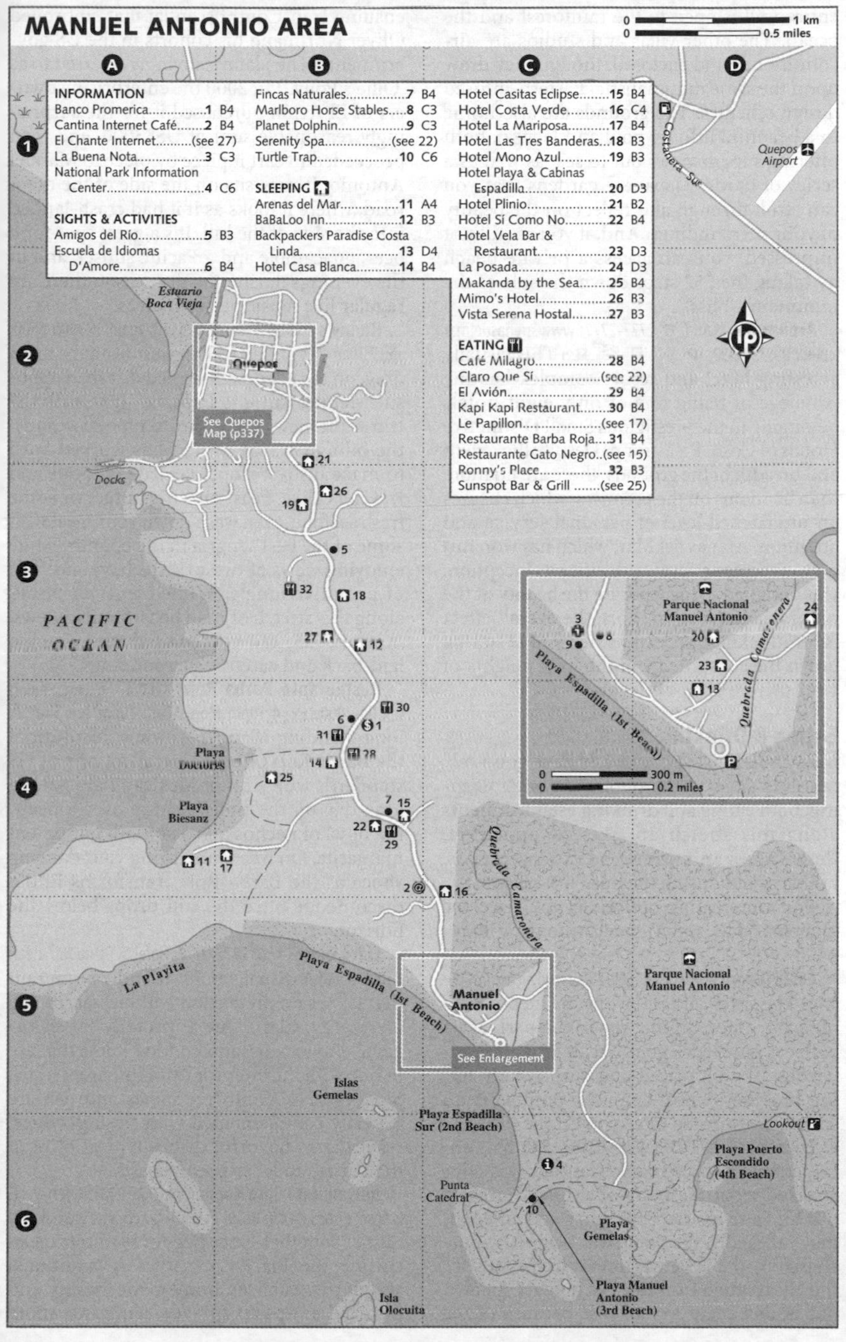
MANUEL ANTONIO AREA
0 1 km
0 0.5 miles
A
B
C
D
1
2
3
4
5
6
INFORMATION
Banco Promerica..........1 B4
Cantina Internet Café........2 B4
El Chante Internet..........(see 27)
La Buena Nota..................3 C3
National Park Information Center..........4 C6
SIGHTS & ACTIVITIES
Amigos del Rio..................5 B3
Escuela de Idiomas D'Amore..........6 B4
Fincas Naturales..................7 B4
Marlboro Horse Stables.....8 C3
Planet Dolphin..................9 C3
Serenity Spa..................(see 22)
Turtle Trap..................10 C6
SLEEPING
Arenas del Mar..................11 A4
BaBaLoo Inn..................12 B3
Backpackers Paradise Costa Linda..................13 D4
Hotel Casa Blanca..................14 B4
Hotel Casitas Eclipse........15 B4
Hotel Costa Verde..........16 C4
Hotel La Mariposa..........17 B4
Hotel Las Tres Banderas...18 B3
Hotel Mono Azul..........19 B3
Hotel Playa & Cabinas Espadilla..........20 D3
Hotel Plinio..........21 B2
Hotel Sí Como No..........22 B4
Hotel Vela Bar & Restaurant..........23 D3
La Posada..........24 D3
Makanda by the Sea..........25 B4
Mimo's Hotel..........26 B3
Vista Serena Hostal..........27 B3
EATING
Café Milagro..........28 B4
Claro Que Sí..........(see 22)
El Avión..........29 B4
Kapi Kapi Restaurant..........30 B4
Le Papillon..........(see 17)
Restaurante Barba Roja....31 B4
Restaurante Gato Negro..(see 15)
Ronny's Place..........32 B3
Sunspot Bar & Grill ....(see 25)
Costanera Sur
Quepos Airport
Estuario Boca Vieja
Quepos
See Quepos Map (p337)
Docks
PACIFIC OCEAN
Playa Dulces
Playa Biesanz
Parque Nacional Manuel Antonio
Playa Espadilla (1st Beach)
Quebrada Camaronera
0 300 m
0 0.2 miles
La Playita
Manuel Antonio
See Enlargement
Islas Gemelas
Playa Espadilla Sur (2nd Beach)
Lookout
Playa Puerto Escondido (4th Beach)
Punta Catedral
Playa Gemelas
Playa Manuel Antonio (3rd Beach)
Isla Olocuita

entire wall is open to the rainforest and the ocean. The other villas and studios are air-conditioned and enclosed, though they draw upon the same minimalistic, Eastern-infused design schemes. The grounds are also home to a beautiful infinity pool and Jacuzzi, both offering superb views out to sea, as well as a series of flawless Japanese gardens that you can stroll through and reflect on the beauty of your surroundings. And, if you're still not impressed, you can access a private beach by taking the 552 steps down the side of the mountain – bliss!

Arenas del Mar (☎ 2777-2777; www.arenasdelmar.com; r US$330-550; P) This visually arresting hotel and resort complex has the privilege of being one of only eight hotels belonging to the prestigious Small Distinctive Hotels of Costa Rica group. Despite the extent and breadth of the grounds, there are no more than 40 rooms on the premises, which ensures an unmatched level of personal service and attention. Arenas del Mar, which has won numerous ecotourism awards since its inception, was designed to incorporate the beauty of the natural landscape. In short, the overall effect is breathtaking, especially when you're staring down the coastline from the lofty heights of your private open-air Jacuzzi.

Eating & Drinking

Many hotels listed previously have good restaurants open to the public. As with sleeping, both eating and drinking establishments along this stretch are skewed upmarket. Reservations are recommended on weekends, holidays and during the busy dry season.

For more eating options in the area, see Quepos, p340, and Manuel Antonio Village, p348.

Café Milagro (breakfast ₡1500-2500, sandwiches ₡2000-3000) The sister cafe of the one in Quepos is an obligatory stop on the way to the park as its coffee is pure black gold. Breakfast and sandwiches are well priced and surprisingly filling, and they'll most definitely put that extra spring in your step once you hit the trails.

El Avión (☎ 2777-3378; dishes ₡3000-6500) This unforgettable airplane bar-restaurant was constructed from the body of a 1954 Fairchild C-123. Here is where the story gets interesting – allegedly, the plane was originally purchased by the US government in the '80s for the Nicaraguan Contras, but it never made it out of its hangar in San José because of the ensuing Iran-Contra scandal that embroiled Oliver North and his cohorts in the US government. (The plane is lovingly referred to as 'Ollie's Folly.') In 2000 the enterprising owners of El Avión purchased it for the surprisingly reasonable sum of US$3000, and then proceeded to cart it piece by piece to Manuel Antonio. It now sits on the side of the main road, where it looks as if it had crash-landed into the side of the hill. It's a great spot for a beer, guacamole and a Pacific sunset, and in the evenings during the dry season there are regular live music performances.

Ronny's Place (☎ 2777-5120; mains ₡3000-6500; 7:30am-10pm) Head 800m west from the main drag, on the good, well-signed dirt road opposite Manuel Antonio Experts – it's worth the trip as the view here won't disappoint. Ronny, the bilingual Tico owner, has worked hard to make his rest stop a favorite of locals and travelers alike. Feast on a big burger or some fresh seafood, then wash down your meal with some of the best sangría in the country while enjoying views of two pristine bays and 360° of primitive jungle. While plenty of places along this stretch of road boast similar views, nowhere else can you enjoy them in such a laid-back and carefree surroundings.

Restaurante Barba Roja (☎ 2777-0331; meals ₡3500-7000; 4-10pm Mon, 10am-10pm Tue-Sun) A long-standing Manuel Antonio institution, the Barba Roja offers an excellent mix of US standards with a bit of Mexican flair. After a long day on the trails, recoup over a heaping bowl of nachos and a smooth but potent margarita. On weekends, bring your dancing shoes as the Barba Roja transforms into a discotheque once the sun drops below the horizon.

Claro Que Sí (☎ 2777-0777; Hotel Sí Como No; meals ₡4000-8000) A casual, family-friendly restaurant that passes on pretension without sacrificing on quality, Claro Que Sí proudly serves organic and locally sourced food items that are in line with the philosophy of its parent hotel, Sí Como No. Guilt-free meats and fish are expertly complemented with fresh produce, resulting in flavorful dishes typical of both the Pacific and Caribbean coasts.

Restaurante Gato Negro (☎ 2777-0408; Hotel Casitas Eclipse; dishes ₡4500-8000) An elegant yet subdued dinner spot that specializes in Mediterranean cuisine, the 'Black Cat' serves up traditional standards, such as homemade pastas and assorted antipasto spreads, alongside more inventive Costa Rican–influenced tapas-style dishes. The bar also bustles during the busy dry season, drawing in lovers of crafted cocktails and chilled wines.

Le Papillon (☎ 2777-0355; Hotel La Mariposa; lunch ₡5000-10,000, dinner ₡10,000-20,000) The featured restaurant at Manuel Antonio's landmark luxury hotel is perfectly perched to take in the daily sunset over the vast expanse of the Pacific Ocean. As you'd imagine, you're paying for the view at this world-class institution, though when the sun dips below the horizon and lights up the sky, you'll stop caring about the price. The food is largely continental cuisine that takes advantage of Costa Rica's rich bounty of fresh seafood and tropical produce – if you're trying to keep to your budget, the lunch menu is a good deal.

Sunspot Bar & Grill (☎ 2777-0442; Makanda by the Sea; dishes ₡6000-15,000) OK, so your budget won't allow you to stay at Makanda by the Sea, but trust us – it's worth checking out the exclusive little poolside restaurant here for its breathtaking rainforest and ocean views. The kitchen whips up delicious seafood, sandwiches and salads, though the real reason you're stopping by is to soak up the atmosphere of one of the most beautiful hotels on the Pacific coast. After all, just because you can't afford to lie down in the lap of luxury doesn't mean you can't sit on it from time to time.

our pick **Kapi Kapi Restaurant** (☎ 2777 5049; dishes ₡7500-20,000) While there is some stiff competition for the title of best restaurant in the Manuel Antonio area, this Californian creation certainly raises the bar on both quality and class. Kapi Kapi, which is a traditional greeting of the indigenous Maleku people, welcomes diners with soft lights, flush earthy tones and soothing natural decor, which perfectly frame the dense forest lying just beyond the perimeter. The menu is no less ambitious, spanning the globe from America to Asia, and making several pivotal stops along the way. Pan-Asian–style seafood is featured prominently on the menu, and brought to life with rich Continental-inspired sauces, while South American wines and Costa Rican coffees complete this globetrotting culinary extravaganza.

Getting There & Away

A good number of visitors who stay in this area arrive by private or rented car. For buses and taxis between Manuel Antonio and Quepos, see p341.

MANUEL ANTONIO VILLAGE

The hordes descend on this tiny oceanside village with good reason – it marks the entrance to Parque Nacional Manuel Antonio, one of the country's most celebrated tourist destinations. Of course, before arriving all bright-eyed and bushy-tailed, it's worth dissecting a few kernels of truth out from all the hype. If you're coming here expecting deserted beaches frequented by hundreds of monkeys, then you're in for a bit of a surprise. Higher primates tend to be the most frequently sighted species, especially during the congested dry season when tour groups arrive en masse.

While it can be difficult at times to have a quiet moment to collect your thoughts, the environs here really do look as glossy and polished as the travel brochures suggest. And, when troops of monkeys climb down from the forest canopy to the tropical sands, you really can get up close and personal with some marvelous wildlife. So in short, the moral is to arrive in Manuel Antonio with some realistic expectations, though, more often than not, you're going to have a memorable visit.

Information

La Buena Nota (☎ 2777-1002), at the northern end of Manuel Antonio village, serves as an informal tourist information center. It sells maps, guidebooks, books in various languages, English-language newspapers, beach supplies and souvenirs; it also rents body boards. You can inquire here about guesthouses available for long-term stays. Look for a free copy of the English-language *Quepolandia,* which details everything to see and do in the area.

Sights & Activities

There's a good beach, **Playa Espadilla**, near the entrance to the park, though you need to be wary of rip currents. There are some lifeguards working at this beach, though not at the other beaches in the area.

At the far western end of Playa Espadilla, beyond a rocky headland (wear sandals) is **La Playita**, a gay beach frequented primarily by young men and offering nude sunbathing (use lashings of sunscreen). This point is inaccessible one hour before and after the high tide, so time your walk well or you'll get cut off. Don't be fooled – you do not need to pay to use the beaches as they're outside the park.

GAY GUIDE TO MANUEL ANTONIO

For jet-setting gays the world over, Manuel Antonio is regarded as something of a dream destination.

Homosexuality has been decriminalized in Costa Rica since the 1970s, which is indeed a rarity in the all too often machismo-fueled conservative Central America. As a result, gays and lesbians have had Costa Rica on their travel wish list for decades, though the blossoming gay scene in Manuel Antonio is unlike any other in the country.

It's not hard to understand why Manuel Antonio first started attracting gays, especially since the area is stunningly beautiful, and has long attracted liberal-minded and tolerant individuals. There is also a burgeoning artist community, a sophisticated restaurant scene and one of the country's few nudist beaches.

So, without further ado, here is your concise gay guide to Manuel Antonio…

Sights & Activities

During the daylight hours, the epicenter of gay Manuel Antonio is the famous **La Playita**, one of the few beaches in Costa Rica where nude sunbathing and skinny dipping are tolerated. Although there are a few women here, who come to sunbathe topless in relative safety and comfort, La Playita is widely regarded as a playful pick-up scene for gay men on the prowl.

Sleeping

A significant number of hotels in the Manuel Antonio area advertise themselves as being gay-friendly. Even at the ones that don't, it is rather unlikely that you'll face any outright discrimination. Of course, if you want to enjoy the freedom and peace of mind that comes with staying at exclusively gay accommodations, then look no further than **Hotel Casa Blanca** (☎ 2777-0523; http://hotel-casablanca.server1.de/en_welcome.shtml; r/apt/ste US$100/140/220; P ✻ 💻 ♿). With more than two decades in this business, Casa Blanca offers an assortment of pools, hot tubs and sundecks to help create a flirtatious yet light-hearted resort ambience. Accommodations are in a variety of rooms, apartments and suites that cater to differing group sizes and budgets.

Eating & Drinking

The Manuel Antonio area has always been proud to host one of the most sophisticated and cosmopolitan restaurant scenes on the central Pacific coast. While there are no exclusively gay restaurants and bars, you'll have no problems enjoying a romantic dinner and drinks at any of the upmarket listings we provide in this section. However, you should use a bit of discretion at any of the local spots since some rural Costa Ricans may not be accustomed to public displays of affection, especially from gays and lesbians.

Snorkeling gear, body boards and kayaks can be rented all along the beach at Playa Espadilla. If you're looking to surf, the gentle ankle-slappers here are perfect for getting your sea legs. **Manuel Antonio Surf School** (☎ 2777-4842; www.masurfschool.com) has a kiosk on the beach.

Steve Wofford at **Planet Dolphin** (☎ 2777-2137; www.planetdolphin.com; Cabinas Piscis) offers dolphin- and whale-watching tours; starlight sailing cruises are also available. Prices vary depending on the size of your group and your itinerary.

The Tico-run **Marlboro Horse Stables** (☎ 2777-1108) rents horses, and can organize trips through the rainforest for variable prices.

White-water rafting and sea kayaking are both popular in this area – see p342 for more information.

Sleeping & Eating

The village of Manuel Antonio is the closest base for exploring the national park, though the selection of eating and sleeping options is not as varied as in Quepos proper (see p339) or the Quepos to Manuel Antonio stretch of road (see p343).

Backpackers Paradise Costa Linda (☎ 2777-0304; www.costalinda-backpackers.com; dm or r without bathroom per person from US$10, meals ₡2500-4500; P ✻ 💻) While it's most definitely not in the same class as competing hostels in Quepos and along the Quepos–Manuel Antonio Road, this shoestringers' crash pad is decent enough for a night or two, especially considering the rock-bottom price tag. The beachside location, however, is excellent, and the small garden cafe serves up some satisfying comfort food, but the rooms lack personality and style, and are in desperate need of an update.

Hotel Vela Bar & Restaurant (☎ 2777-0413; www.velabar.com; s/d US$43/53, meals ₡3000-6500; P ❄ 💻) Hotel Vela is primarily known in these parts for its justifiably famous bar and restaurant, which serves up some of the freshest seafood in the Manuel Antonio area. However, the hotel is also a surprisingly affordable spot to post up for a night or two – rooms here are fairly basic, but it's hard to beat the price considering that you can literally wake up, have your morning coffee and stroll over to the entrance to the national park before your caffeine perk sets in.

Hotel Playa & Cabinas Espadilla (☎ 2777-0903/416; www.espadilla.com; cabins/r from US$65/160; P ❄ 🏊) Two properties in one: the hotel is centered on a large swimming pool and tennis courts, but the rooms are fairly bland considering the hefty price tag. The cabins are very affordable, however, and while they're a bit worn for wear, you have access to all the facilities at Hotel Playa. While there are certainly swisher properties up the road en route to Quepos, you can't beat the convenience factor that comes with staying here.

La Posada (☎ 2777-1446; www.laposadajungle.com; bungalows US$115-225; P ❄) Your private jungle bungalow can accommodate you and several of your friends, though you might have some furry visitors as – quite literally – you're on the edge of the national park. From the comfort of your fully equipped home away from home, which is jam-packed with modern amenities, including a fully stocked kitchen, you can view wildlife as it scurries across your front yard (or across your rooftop in the middle of the night!).

There are a number of stands on the beach that cater to hungry tourists, though everything is expectedly overpriced and of dubious quality. Plus, it leads to the temptation to feed the monkeys, which isn't exactly good for their little digestive systems. Here are a few reasons why:

- Monkeys are susceptible to bacteria transmitted from human hands.
- Irregular feeding will lead to aggressive behavior as well as create a dangerous dependency.
- Bananas are not their preferred food, and can cause serious digestive problems.
- Increased exposure to humans facilitates illegal poaching.

Once again, while it should go without saying, don't feed the monkeys. And, if you do happen to come across someone doing so, take the initiative and ask them politely to stop. *Gracias.*

Getting There & Away

Buses depart Manuel Antonio for San José (₡3500 to ₡3700, four hours) at 6am, 9:30am, noon and 5pm. These will pick you up in front of your hotel if you are on the road to flag them down, or from the Quepos bus terminal, after which there are no stops. Buy tickets well in advance at the Quepos bus terminal. This bus is frequently packed and you will not be able to buy tickets from the driver. Buses for destinations other than San José also leave from the main terminal in Quepos (see p341).

PARQUE NACIONAL MANUEL ANTONIO

Parque Nacional Manuel Antonio was declared a national park in 1972, preserving it (with just minutes to spare) from being bulldozed and razed to make room for a coastal development project. Although Manuel Antonio was enlarged to its present-day size of 16 sq km in 2000, it is still the country's second-smallest national park. Space remains a premium, and as this is one of Central America's top tourist destinations, you're going to have to break free from the camera-clicking tour groups and actively seek out your own idyllic spot of sand.

With that said, Manuel Antonio is absolutely stunning, and on a good day, at the right time, it's easy to convince yourself that you've died and gone to a coconut-filled paradise. The park's clearly marked trail system winds through rainforest-backed tropical beaches and rocky headlands, and the views across the bay to the pristine outer islands are unforgettable. As if this wasn't enough of a hard sell, add to the mix iguanas, howlers, capuchins, sloths and squirrel monkeys, which may be the gosh-darn cutest little fur balls you've ever seen.

Orientation & Information

Visitors must leave their vehicles in the parking lot near the national park entrance; the charge is US$3, but there have been reader reports of break-ins and thefts. Note that the road here is also very narrow and congested, so it's suggested that you leave your car at your hotel, and take an early morning bus to the park entrance instead, then simply walk in.

The **park entrance** (admission US$10; 7am-4pm Tue-Sun) is a few meters south of the rotunda. Count your change carefully as many tourists complain about being ripped off by staff with sticky fingers. Here you can hire naturalist guides to take you into the park; see Tours, following, for more information.

To reach the entrance, you'll have to wade through the Camaronera estuary, which can be anywhere from ankle- to thigh-deep, depending on the tides and the season. However, in an impressive display of opportunism, there are boaters here to transport you 100m for the small fee of about ₡500.

The ranger station and **national park information center** (☎ 2777-0644) is just before Playa Manuel Antonio. Drinking water is available, and there are toilets, beach showers, picnic tables and a refreshment stand. There is no camping and guards will come around in the evening to make sure that no one has remained behind.

The beaches are often numbered – most people call Playa Espadilla (outside the park) '1st beach,' Playa Espadilla Sur '2nd beach,' Playa Manuel Antonio '3rd beach,' Playa Puerto Escondido '4th beach' and Playa Playita '5th beach.' Some people begin counting at Espadilla Sur, which is the first beach in the park, so it can be a bit confusing trying to figure out which beach people may be talking about. Regardless, they're all equally pristine, and provide ample opportunities for snorkeling or restful sunbathing. There is a refreshment stand on Playa Manuel Antonio.

The average daily temperature is 27°C (80°F) and average annual rainfall is 3875mm. The dry season is not entirely dry, merely less wet, so you should be prepared for rain (although it can also be dry for days on end). Make sure you carry plenty of drinking water, sun protection and insect repellent. Pack a picnic lunch if you're spending the day.

Tours

Hiring a guide costs US$20 per person for a two-hour tour. The only guides allowed in the park are members of Aguila (a local association governed by the park service), who have official ID badges, and recognized guides from tour agencies or hotels. This is to prevent visitors from getting ripped off and to ensure a good-quality guide – Aguila guides are well trained and multilingual. (French-, German- or English-speaking guides can be requested.) Visitors report that hiring a guide virtually guarantees wildlife sightings.

Sights & Activities

HIKING

After the park entrance, it's about a 30-minute hike to **Playa Espadilla Sur**, where you'll find the park ranger station and information center; watch out for birds and monkeys as you walk. West of the station, follow an obvious trail through forest to an isthmus separating Playas Espadilla Sur and Manuel Antonio. This isthmus is called a tombolo and was formed by the accumulation of sedimentary material between the mainland and the peninsula beyond, which was once an island. If you walk along Playa Espadilla Sur, you will find a small mangrove area. The isthmus widens into a rocky peninsula, with a forest in the center. A trail leads around the peninsula to **Punta Catedral**, from where there are good views of the Pacific Ocean and various rocky islets that are bird reserves and form part of the national park. Brown boobies and pelicans are among the seabirds that nest on these islands.

TOP PICKS: KIDDY FUN IN MANUEL ANTONIO

Here are some suggestions for enjoying nature with the little ones:

- Buy a wildlife picture book, and make a game out of spotting animals.
- Teach your kids how to read a map and use a compass to navigate.
- If your older children have an adventurous streak, take them rafting.
- Cool off by splashing in the gentle surf at Playa Manuel Antonio.
- When in doubt, even the fussiest of tykes love playing in the sand.

You can continue around the peninsula to **Playa Manuel Antonio**, or you can avoid the peninsula altogether and hike across the isthmus to this beach. At the western end of the beach, during the low tide, you can see a semicircle of rocks that archaeologists believe were arranged by pre-Columbian indigenous people to function as a **turtle trap**. (Turtles would swim in during high tide, but when they tried to swim out after the tide started receding, they'd be trapped by the wall.) The beach itself is an attractive one of white sand and is popular for swimming. It's protected and safer than the Espadilla beaches.

Beyond Playa Manuel Antonio, the trail divides. The lower trail is steep and slippery during the wet months and leads to the quiet Playa Puerto Escondido. This beach can be more or less completely covered by high tides, so be careful not to get cut off. The upper trail climbs to a **lookout** on a bluff overlooking Puerto Escondido and Punta Serrucho beyond – a stunning vista. Rangers reportedly limit the number of hikers on this trail to 45.

The trails in Manuel Antonio are well marked and heavily traversed, though there are some quiet corners near the ends of the trails. Off-trail hiking is not permitted without prior consent from the park service.

Watch out for the manchineel tree *(Hippomane mancinella)* it has poisonous fruits that look like little crab apples, and the sap exuded by the bark and leaves is toxic, causing the skin to itch and burn. Warning signs are prominently displayed beside examples of this tree near the park entrance.

WHITE-WATER RAFTING & KAYAKING

While not as popular as Turrialba (see boxed text, p148), Manuel Antonio is something of an emerging white-water rafting and sea kayaking center. Although you shouldn't expect the same level of world-class runs here as in other parts of the country, there are certainly some adrenaline kicks to be had. For more information, see p342.

WILDLIFE-WATCHING

Increased tourist traffic has taken its toll on the park's wildlife as animals are frequently driven away or – worse still – taught to scavenge for tourist handouts. To its credit, the park service has reacted by closing the park on Monday and limiting the number of visitors to 600 during the week and 800 on weekends and holidays.

Even though visitors are funneled along the main access road, you should have no problem seeing animals here, even as you line up at the gate. White-faced capuchins are very used to people, and normally troops feed and interact within a short distance of visitors – they can be encountered anywhere along the main access road and around Playa Manuel Antonio.

You'll probably also hear mantled howler monkeys soon after sunrise and, like capuchins, they can be seen virtually anywhere inside the park and even along the road to Quepos – watch for them crossing the monkey bridges that were erected by several local conservation groups.

Agoutis and coatis can be seen darting across various paths, and both three-toed and two-toed sloths are also common in the park. Guides are extremely helpful in spotting sloths as they tend not to move around all that much.

However, the movements of the park's star animal and Central America's rarest primate, namely the Central American squirrel monkey, are far less predictable. These adorable monkeys are more retiring than capuchins, and though they are occasionally seen near the park entrance in the early morning, they usually melt into the forest well before opening time. With luck, however, a troop could be encountered during a morning's walk, and they often reappear in beachside trees and on the fringes of Manuel Antonio village in the early evening.

Offshore, keep your eyes peeled for pantropical spotted and bottle-nosed dolphins, as well as humpback whales passing by on their regular migration routes. Other possibilities include orcas (killer whales), false killers and rough-toothed dolphins.

Big lizards are also something of a featured sighting at Manuel Antonio – it's hard to miss the large ctenosaurs and green iguanas that bask along the beach at Playa Manuel Antonio and in the vegetation behind Playa Espadilla Sur. To spot the well-camouflaged basilisk, listen for the rustle of leaves along the edges of the trails, especially near the lagoon.

Manuel Antonio is not usually on the serious bird-watchers' trail of Costa Rica, though the bird list is respectable nevertheless. The usual suspects include the blue-gray and palm tanagers, great-tailed grackles, bananaquits, blue dacnises and at least 15 different species of hummingbirds. Among the regional endemics you should look out for are the fiery-billed aracaris, black-hooded antshrikes, Baird's trogons, black-bellied whistling-ducks, yellow-crowned night-herons, brown pelicans, magnificent frigate birds, brown boobies, spotted sandpipers, green herons and ringed kingfishers.

Getting There & Away

The entrance and exit to Parque Nacional Manuel Antonio lies in Manuel Antonio village – for more information, see p350.

QUEPOS TO UVITA

South of Quepos, the well-trodden central Pacific tourist trail slowly tapers off, though this certainly shouldn't deter you from pushing on to lesser-known locales. In fact, this stretch of coastline is a great place to get a feel for the Costa Rica of yesteryear, and if you're an intrepid traveler, you can have your pick of any number of deserted beaches and great surf spots. The region is also home to a great bulk of Costa Rica's African palm oil industry, which should be immediately obvious after the few dozen kilometers of endless plantations lining the sides of the Costanera.

RAFIKI SAFARI LODGE

Nestled into the rainforest, with a prime spot right next to the Río Savegre, the **Rafiki Safari Lodge** (☎ 2777-2250/5327; www.rafikisafari.com; s/d/ste incl all meals US$203/350/400, child under 5yr free; P) combines all the comforts of a hotel with the splendor of a jungle safari – all with a little bit of African flavor. The owners, who are from South Africa, have constructed nine luxury tents on stilts equipped with bathroom, hot water, private porch and electricity. All units are screened in, which allows you to see and hear the rainforest without actually having creepy-crawlies in your bed. There's a spring-fed pool with a waterslide and ample opportunity for horseback riding, bird-watching (more than 350 species have been identified), hiking and white-water rafting. And of course, South Africans are masters on the *braai* (BBQ), so you know that you'll eat well alongside other guests in the *rancho*-style restaurant.

The entrance to the lodge is located about 15km south of Quepos in the small town of Savegre. From here, a 4WD dirt road parallels the Río Savegre and leads 7km inland, past the towns of Silencio and Santo Domingo, to the lodge. However, if you don't have private transportation, the lodge can arrange all of your transfers with advanced reservations.

MATAPALO

Matapalo is off most travelers' radar screens, though without good reason as this palm-fringed, grey-sand beach has some truly awesome surf. With two river-mouth breaks generating some wicked waves, Matapalo is recommended for intermediate to advanced surfers who are comfortable dealing with rapidly changing conditions. As you might imagine, Matapalo is not the best beach for swimming as the transient rips here are about as notorious as they come.

Just south of Matapalo are the **Terciopelo Waterfalls**, which are famous for their swimming pools. The falls are located a few kilometers south of Rió Hatillo Viejo, though it's best to ask someone to point out the trailhead for you as it's tough to find.

The first hotel you'll see after turning off the Costanera is the German-run **El Coquito del Pacífico** (☎ 2787-5028, 8384-7220; www.elcoquito.com; bungalows from US$65; P), which consists of a small batch of bungalows highlighted by their beaming whitewashed walls and rustic furnishings. The entire complex is attractively landscaped with shady gardens of almond and mango trees, and centered on an open-air bar and restaurant serving up the obligatory traditional German specialties.

The US-owned **Jungle House** (☎ 2787-5005, 2777-2748; www.junglehouse.com; r from US$65; P) provides the epitome of relaxation, with five polished-wood quarters decorated with a good smattering of rustic knick-knacks. If you're traveling with your better half, the bamboo 'honeymoon' cabin in the back is a large open-air unit with incredible views of the distant hills. Charlie, the friendly owner, is active locally and supports local education initiatives and trash pick-up efforts on the beach. Significant discounts are available for weekly and monthly stays.

Dreamy Contentment (☎ 2787-5223; www.dreamycontentment.com; r/bungalows/house US$25/75/200; P) is a beautiful, Spanish-colonial property with impressive woodworking and

ANDRES POVEDA ON COSTA RICAN PRIDE

Andres Poveda, the founder of the Costa Rican Hostel Network, has spent the last several years raising the bar for backpacker haunts throughout the country. Over an ice-cold Imperial lager and a bowl of nachos, Andrés shared his thoughts on being Costa Rican.

How did you end up owning backpacker hostels? That's a good story, especially since the honest truth is that I always dreamed of becoming a lawyer. As a kid I used to get into a lot of trouble, so I thought that I should probably learn how to properly defend myself! Anyway, after finishing law school and landing a high-powered job with the government, I learned that wearing a suit and dealing with papers wasn't the kind of life that I wanted. So, together with my identical twin brother Adrian, we decided to create a place where travelers could experience the real side of Costa Rica. Today, we are proud of the fact that we are one of the few Costa Rican–owned businesses in this country catering exclusively to backpackers from around the world.

What does it mean to be Costa Rican? To understand this, all you need to do is spend some time hanging out with us Costa Ricans, or as we prefer to call ourselves, Ticos. I think one of the most infectious qualities of Ticos is that we don't think too much about the future, and instead prefer to have a great time and simply enjoy the moment for what it is. Ticos are also extremely family-oriented, which means that we are really quick to treat friends as if they were our own kin. You know, almost immediately upon arriving in this country, travelers are greeted with the words *pura vida,* which really is a catch-all phrase for Ticos. Although it directly translates as 'pure life,' *pura vida* really is a philosophy of living that all of us strive to uphold.

What makes Costa Rica so unique? Costa Rica is such a tiny country with only a few million people, so you would think that it would be hard for us to have a strong identity. On the contrary, there are so many unique things about Costa Rica that give us Ticos a strong sense of pride and love for our country. For instance, everyone knows that our country is home to some of the world's most virgin rainforest, and that we haven't had a standing army for decades. To me, however, what makes this country so unique is that we are honest people who work hard for what we have. The reality is that we will never be one of the world's largest economies, though people here are extremely satisfied with their lives, which is why we are so passionate about having fun!

What is the best way for travelers to experience Costa Rica? The great thing about this country is that it has a youthful spirit, so you don't have to be 18 or 21 to have a good time here. In Costa Rica the great social equalizer is beer, so all you have to do is grab a bottle and just interact with the people around you.

What is the best part of being in the hostel business? The answer is definitely meeting backpackers from all around the world, and knowing that, at the end, we are all human beings. When you work in an international environment like a hostel, it's a daily affirmation to learn that we all share the same wants, needs and desires.

What is the most challenging part of the hostel business? Keeping it real, keeping it Costa Rican. This is the way our business has always been, the way it is, and the way that it will always be. Others may be motivated by profit, but for me, it's about sharing my pride in being Tico with every single backpacker that steps foot through the front door.

Costa Rican Hostel Network accommodations: Hostel Pangea (p82), Hostel Toruma (p102), Arenal Backpackers Resort (p165), Monteverde Backpackers (p201) and Tamarindo Backpackers (p267).

towering trees throughout. The bungalows are equipped with functional kitchenettes, though the real star attraction is the main house, which has the kitchen of your dreams, a beachfront veranda and a princely bathroom complete with hot tub. For those on a budget, there are basic but reasonably conformable backpacker rooms that put you in front of the surf without having to dig too deep.

At the end of the road you'll find the **Bahari Beach Bungalows** (☎ 2787-5014; www.baharibeach.com; cabins/tents US$55/105; Ⓟ) with luxury safari-style beachfront tents and a small clutch of cabins. All of the tents are fully furnished and have electricity, tiled bathroom with hot shower, hand-painted sink and ocean views. The cabins, across the road, are also beautifully decorated and come ornamented with fresh flowers. There's a pool overlooking the ocean, a spa and an excellent restaurant featuring continental cuisine.

Buses between Quepos and Dominical can drop you off at the turnoff to the village; from there it's a couple of kilometers to the beach.

HACIENDA BARÚ NATIONAL WILDLIFE REFUGE

Located on the Pacific coast 3km northeast of Dominical on the road to Quepos, this **wildlife refuge** (☎ 2787-0003; www.haciendabaru.com; admission US$6, each extra day US$2) forms a key link in a major biological corridor called 'the Path of the Tapir.' It comprises more than 330 hectares of private and state-owned land that has been protected from hunting since 1976. The range of tropical habitats that may be observed here include pristine beaches, riverbanks, mangrove estuaries, wetlands, selectively logged forests, secondary forests, primary forests, tree plantations and pastures.

This diversity of habitat plus its key position in the Path of the Tapir biological corridor accounts for the multitude of species that have been identified in Hacienda Barú. These include 351 birds, 69 mammals, 94 reptiles and amphibians, 87 butterflies and 158 species of trees, some of which are more than 8.5m in circumference. Ecological tourism provides this wildlife refuge with its only source of funds with which to maintain its protected status, so guests are assured that money spent here will be used to further the conservation of tropical rainforest.

There is an impressive number of guided tours (US$20 to US$60) on offer. You can experience the rainforest canopy in three different ways – a platform 36m above the forest floor, tree climbing and a zip line called 'the Flight of the Toucan.' In addition to the canopy activities, Hacienda Barú offers bird-watching tours, hiking tours, and two overnight camping tours in both tropical rainforest and lowland beach habitats. Hacienda Barú's naturalist guides come from local communities and have lived near the rainforest all of their lives.

For people who prefer to explore the refuge by themselves, there are 7km of well-kept and marked, self-guided trails, a bird-watching tower, 3km of pristine beach, an orchid garden and a butterfly garden.

The **Hacienda Barú Lodge** (d US$60, extra person US$10, child under 10yr free) consists of six clean, two-bedroom cabins located 350m from Barú beach. The red-tile–roofed, open-air restaurant (meals ₡3000 to ₡5000) serves a variety of tasty Costa Rican dishes.

The Quepos–Dominical–San Isidro bus stops outside the hacienda entrance. The San Isidro–Dominical–Uvita bus will drop you off at the Río Barú bridge, 2km from the hacienda office. A taxi from Dominical costs about ₡2500.

If you're driving, the El Ceibo gas station, 50m north of the Hacienda Barú Lodge, is the only one for a good distance in any direction. Groceries, fishing gear, tide tables and other useful sundries are available, and there are clean toilets.

DOMINICAL

With monster waves, chilled-out vibes and a freewheelin' reputation for reefer madness, Dominical is the kind of place where travelers get stuck for longer than they intended – so long as the surf's up and the spliff isn't out. As proud residents are quick to point out, Dominical recalls the mythical 'old Costa Rica,' namely a time when the legions of international jet-setters had yet to jump onto the ecotourism bandwagon. And in part, they've got a valid point, as evidenced by the town's motley crew of surfers, backpackers and do-nothings alike.

But the overall picture is more complex, especially since Dominical is at long last stretching its legs, and seeking to attract more than the college-aged and shoestringer sets. Case in point: the completion of the Costanera Sur is facilitating the spread of development further south along the coast, which has brought along with it an intense wave of foreign investment. Boutique hotels and luxury residences are springing up along the coastline, foretelling a much more grown-up future. In the meantime, however, Dominical remains the sort of place where it's best to just slow down, unwind and take things as they come.

Orientation & Information

The Costanera Sur bypasses Dominical; the entrance to the village is immediately past the Río Barú bridge. There's a main road through the village, where many of the services are found, and a parallel road along the beach. For the most part, development remains low-key. The few roads around the village are still dusty

BATTLING THE BLOOD SUCKERS

Whether you call them skeeters, mozzies or midges, everyone can agree that fending off mosquitoes is one of the most annoying parts of traveling in the tropics. Although the scientific evidence surrounding effective mosquito-bite prevention is circumstantial at best, the following is a list of road-tested combat strategies for battling the blood-suckers.

- Wear socks, long trousers and a long-sleeve shirt, especially at dusk when mosquitoes feed.
- Eat lots of garlic (not recommended if you're traveling with your significant other).
- Fill your room with the smoke of the ever present burnable Costa Rican mosquito coils.
- Invest in a good-quality mosquito net, preferably one that has been chemically treated.
- Never underestimate the power of spraying yourself with vast quantities of DEET.

and potholed, and forests – not fast-food outlets – front the majority of the beach.

There are no banking facilities, but San Clemente Bar & Grill will exchange traveler's checks. It also has a postal service upstairs.

Dominical Internet (per hr ₡1000; 9:30am-7pm Mon-Sat) Check email here, above the San Clemente Bar & Grill.

Police (☎ 2787-0011)

Dangers & Annoyances

Waves, currents and riptides in Dominical are very strong, and there have been drownings in the past. Watch for red flags (which mark riptides), follow the instructions of posted signs and swim at beaches that are patrolled by lifeguards.

Dominical attracts a heavy-duty party crowd, which in turn has led to a burgeoning drug problem. For more information on the potential repercussions of drug use in Costa Rica, see boxed text, p325.

Sights

Just north of the turnoff for Dominical is the junction for San Isidro – if you turn left toward San Isidro and travel for about 10km, you'll see an entrance to the right that leads to **Centro Turístico Cataratas Nauyaca** (☎ 2787-0198, 2771-3187; www.cataratasnauyaca.com). This Costa Rican family-owned and operated tourist center is home to a series of wonderful waterfalls that cascade through a protected reserve of both primary and secondary forest.

There's no vehicle access to this tourist center, but you can hire horses for a guided ride to two waterfalls that plunge into a deep swimming hole. With advance notice, a tour can be arranged, including the guided ride, swimming and country meals with the local family. Tours leave at 8am, take six to seven hours and cost US$50 per person. There's a campground with changing rooms and toilets. Accommodations in Dominical can also arrange tours to the falls.

Another worthwhile diversion is the aptly named **Parque Reptilandia** (☎ 2787-8007; www.crreptiles.com; admission adult/child US$10/1; 9am-4:30pm), also located 10km outside of Dominical in the town of Platanillo. If you're traveling with kids who love slick and slimy reptiles, or you yourself just can't get enough of these prehistoric creatures, don't miss the chance to get face to face with Costa Rica's most famous reptiles. The animal park is home to everything from alligators and crocodiles to turtles and poison dart frogs. Of course, our favorite section is the viper section, home to such infamous critters as the deadly fer-de-lance. For an added bonus, stop by on Friday for feeding time – we promise you won't be disappointed.

Activities

Dominical owes its fame to its seriously sick point and beach breaks, though surf conditions here are variable. In general, however, it pays to have a bit of board experience, as you can really get trashed out here if you don't know what you're doing. If you're just getting started, the nearby beach of Domincalito is tamer.

Of course, one great way to get a bit more experience under your belt is by heading to the reader-recommended **Green Iguana Surf Camp** (☎ 8815-3733; www.greeniguanasurfcamp.com). Located on a side road leading to the beach, this camp is run by experienced surfers Jason and Karla Butler, and offers a variety of surf lessons and tours as well as seven- to 10-day surfing camps.

Courses

Adventure Spanish School (☎ 2787-0023, in USA & Canada 800-237-730; www.adventurespanishschool.com) runs one-week Spanish-language programs starting at US$400, without homestay. Private lessons are available, as are discounts for longer periods of study.

Tours

Dominical has emerged as a jumping-off point for trips to Parque Nacional Corcovado (p421) and Parque Nacional Marino Ballena (p359). Get details at **Southern Expeditions** (☎ 2787-0100; www.southernexpeditionscr.com) at the entrance to the village. The staff can also organize trips to the Guaymí indigenous reserve near Boruca (p378), and all tours can be individually customized to meet your interests.

Sleeping

Dominical proper is home to the majority of the area's budget accommodations, while midrange and top-end places are popping up on the outskirts of town. The rates given here are for high season, but low-season rates could be as much as 30% to 40% lower. Note that there are additional accommodations options in the nearby mountaintop village of Escaleras (p357).

IN TOWN

Antorchas Camping (☎ 2787-0307; campsites per person US$5, dm US$10; P) Just a few meters from the beach, this campground is one of the most secure in town, though you should still be extremely diligent about locking up your valuables in the provided lockers. Campers can take advantage of basic amenities, including cold showers and a shared kitchen, while more finicky shoestringers can bed down in spartan dorms for a few extra dollars a night.

Cabinas San Celemente (☎ 2787-0158; r per person US$10-40; P) Backpackers gravitate to this classic Dominical spot, which is actually comprised of a variety of different accommodations options. The highlight of the property are the private beach houses that are just steps from the surf, though more budget-conscious travelers can choose from either shiny wooden *cabinas* or simple dorm rooms at the adjacent Dominical Backpackers Hostel.

Tortilla Flats (☎ 2787-0033; r US$25-40; P) Another popular option, this budget hotel contains 20-odd rooms of varying shapes and sizes, though all feature a hot-water shower as well as a hammock-strung patio and terrace – a nice option considering the cheap price tag. The downstairs restaurant can get a bit noisy at night, but on the other hand it serves up one of the town's best breakfasts.

Domilocos (☎ 787 0244; www.domilocos.net; r US$50; P) This Italian-owned property is a solid midrange option, with Mediterranean-inspired grounds, an attractive swimming pool lined with potted plants and one of the town's best restaurants. Fairly ordinary rooms with solid beds and bamboo furniture are nothing to write home about, but they're definitely a step up in comfort from the budget hotels.

Hotel DiuWak (☎ 2787-0087; www.diuwak.com; r US$75-120, ste US$140-160; P) This proper resort complex offers low-key luxury as opposed to unchecked hedonism. Still, the grounds surrounding the waterfall-fed pool are palm-fringed, which makes for relaxing days of idle laziness, and there are some great onsite amenities, including bars, restaurants, a fitness center and health spa. Inquire about the size of the room as some are larger than others, and can easily accommodate you and a few of your friends.

AROUND DOMINICAL

Albergue Alma de Hatillo B&B (☎ 8850-9034; www.cabinasalma.com; r US$60; P) One of the most loved B&Bs on the entire Pacific coast, this hidden gem is run by Sabina, a charming Polish woman who has legions of dedicated fans the world over. If you're looking for a quiet base from which to explore the Dominical area, this tranquil spot is home to immaculate cabins spread among several hectares of fruit trees. Guests rave about the organic produce on offer at Sabina's restaurant, as well as the daily yoga classes in her open-air studio. Alma de Hatillo is located about 6km north of town along the Constanera Sur.

Hotel Villas Río Mar (☎ 787 0052; www.villasriomar.com; bungalows US$75-95, ste US$130-140; P) Just beyond the edge of town, a sign points under the bridge to this property about 800m from the village. Here you'll find a few dozen polished-wood bungalows, each with a private hammock-strung terrace, as well as a handful of luxury suites that accommodate small groups. Río Mar also functions as a miniresort, offering a pool, Jacuzzi, tennis court, equipment rental, restaurant and bar.

Hotel y Restaurante Roca Verde (☎ 2787-0036; www.rocaverde.net; r US$85; P) Overlooking the beach about 1km south of town, this chic and stylish US-owned hotel is decorated with hardwoods, tile mosaics, festive murals and rock inlays. The 12 tropical-themed rooms are superbly comfortable places to unwind, though the real action takes place in the festive communal areas, which include an open-air bar and infinity pool. On certain nights, the hotel turns into a theater when local theater groups and dancers perform in the hotel lobby.

Cascadas Farallas (☎ 2787-8378; www.waterfallvillas.com; ste/villas from US$125/225; P) Although it's a bit outside Dominical proper, this spiritual retreat is located beside a series of cascading waterfalls. Balinese-style suites and villas are decked out from floor to ceiling with Zen-inducing Asian art, and regular yoga and meditation sessions help guests seek peace and tranquility. To reach the property, take the San Isidro fork (just north of the Dominical turnoff) for 3km, and look out for the Balinese dragon banners marking the entrance.

Eating & Drinking

Complejo Arena y Sol (dishes ₡1500-4500) A local eatery that serves up a hearty *gallo pinto* (rice and beans) breakfast spread, this is where you can carbo-load before a serious surf session. Stop by in the afternoon or evening for typical *casados* (cheap set meals), or the usual assortment of Western-style fast foods.

San Clemente Bar & Grill (dishes ₡2000-4500, drinks ₡500-1500) This classic Dominical watering hole complete with broken surfboards on the walls serves up big breakfasts and Tex-Mex dishes. It's also one of the more popular places around to get absolutely tanked with like-minded travelers from around the world.

Maracutú (dishes ₡3000-5500, drinks ₡1000-2000; V) The self-proclaimed 'world-music beach bar and Italian kitchen' serves up an eclectic culinary offering that is highlighted by some delicious vegetarian and vegan fare. Each night of the week it features a different genre of music, a good amount of which is live.

Thrusters Bar (sushi ₡4500-8000, drinks ₡500-1500) The local party people congregate here for good times around the pool tables. Next door is a small sushi bar that's definitely worth checking out, as raw fish and tap beer are a blissful combination.

ConFusione (meals ₡5500-12,000) Italian-Latin fusion gets top billing at the Domilocos' main dining room, which has a warm candlelit Mediterranean ambience and a nice selection of Chianti. You can stick to classics from the peninsula such as penne pasta and flatbread pizzas, stay local with freshly caught seafood and aged tenderloin, or strike a healthy balance – authentic gelato with tropical fruits.

Getting There & Away

BUS

Buses pick up and drop off passengers along the main road in Dominical.

Quepos ₡3200; three hours; departs 7:30am, 8am, 10:30am, 1:45pm, 4pm and 5pm.

Uvita ₡800; one hour; departs 4:30am, 10:30am, noon and 6:15pm.

TAXI

Taxis to Uvita cost ₡7500 to ₡10,000, while the ride to San Isidro costs ₡12,500 to ₡15,000, and ₡27,500 to ₡30,000 for Quepos. Cars accommodate up to five people, and can be hailed easily in town from the main road.

ESCALERAS

Escaleras, a small community scattered around a steep and narrow dirt loop-road that branches off the Costanera, is famed for its sweeping views of the coastline and the crashing surf. Of course, if you want to make it up here, you're going to need a 4WD to navigate one of the country's most notoriously difficult roads. Needless to say, the locals weren't kidding when they named the place *escaleras* (staircase). Aside from the scenic views, travelers primarily brave the road to either have a relaxing mountain retreat in any of the places listed in this section, or to catch a 'Movie in the Jungle' (see boxed text, p358).

The first entrance to Escaleras is 4km south of the San Isidro turnoff before Dominical, and the second is 4.5km past the first one. Both are on the left-hand side of the road and poorly signed.

One of the first places you'll come to along the main road is the **Bella Vista Lodge** (☎ 3888-0155, in USA 800-909-4469; www.bellavistalodge.com; r/cabins incl breakfast US$45/75; P), a remote farm owned by longtime resident Woody Dyer. The lodge itself is in a revamped farmhouse (surrounded by a balcony providing superb ocean views) that contains four shiny-wood rooms with private, solar-heated shower. The grounds are also home to a two-storied private cabin with a full kitchen and living room and enough space to comfortably accommodate six. Rates include breakfast or an evening snack of beer and chips, and there are tasty home-cooked meals (and pies!) available. If you don't have a 4WD, Woody will pick you up in Dominical for a small fee.

About 1km further up the Escaleras road, **Villa Escaleras** (☎ 8823-0509, in USA 773-279-0516; www.villa-escaleras.com; villa for 4/6/8 people US$240/280/320; P) is a spacious four-bedroom villa accented by cathedral ceilings, tiled floors, colonial furnishings and a palatial swimming pool. Twice-weekly maid service and a wraparound balcony awash with panoramic views make the setting complete. If you're planning on staying here long-term, inquire about discounted weekly and monthly rates.

Located on a different access road that's 1.2km south of the first entrance is **Pacific Edge** (☎ 2531-8000; www.pacificedge.info; cabins/bungalows from US$60/85; P). The owners are a worldly North American–British couple who delight in showing guests their slice of paradise. Four cabins are perched on a knife-edge ridge about 200m above sea level, while larger family-friendly bungalows accommodate up to six and come with fully stocked kitchen. Of course, if you're not one for cooking, there is a wonderful onsite restaurant specializing in international cuisine.

Escaleras is best accessed by private vehicle, though any of the accommodations listed previously can arrange a pick-up service with advanced notice. If you're coming for Movies in the Jungle, a taxi from Dominical shouldn't cost more than ₡5000.

MOVIES IN THE JUNGLE

Every Friday night, a resident expat named Toby in the town of Escaleras invites locals and travelers to watch his favorite flicks. **Cinema Escaleras** (☎ 2787-8065) is built on a hilltop with panoramic views of jungle-fronted coastline and features state-of-the-art projection equipment and surround sound. Seriously, this guy loves his movies! Films are shown every Friday at 6pm, with a potluck dinner preceding the screening at 5pm. To get to the cinema, follow the first entrance to Escaleras a few hundred meters up the mountain and look for a white house on the left-hand side. Note that a small donation to pay for the projector bulbs is requested.

UVITA

Just 17km south of Dominical, this little hamlet is really nothing more than a loose straggle of farms, houses and tiny shops, though it should give you a good idea of what the central Pacific coast looked like before the tourist boom. Uvita does, however, serve as the base for visits to Parque Nacional Marino Ballena (p359), a pristine marine reserve famous for its migrating pods of humpback whales, in addition to its virtually abandoned wilderness beaches.

Orientation

The area off the main highway is referred to locally as Uvita, while the area next to the beach is called Playa Uvita and Playa Bahía Uvita (the southern end of the beach). The beach area is reached through two parallel dirt roads that are roughly 500m apart. The first entrance is just south of the bridge over the Río Uvita and the second entrance is in the center of town. At low tide you can walk out along Punta Uvita, but ask locally before heading out so that the rising water doesn't cut you off.

Sights & Activities

Uvita is a perfect base for exploring Parque Nacional Marino Ballena, which is home to some truly spectacular beaches that don't see anywhere near the number of tourists that they should attract. Then again, perhaps this is a good thing as you'll have plenty of space to sprawl out and soak up the sun without having to worry about someone stealing your beach chair.

Surfers passing through the area tend to push on to more extreme destinations further south, though there are occasionally some swells at **Playa Hermosa** to the north and **Playa Colonia** to the south. However, if you've just come from Dominical, or you're planning on heading to Pavones (p435), you might be a bit disappointed with the mild conditions here.

A few kilometers before Uvita, you'll see a signed turnoff to the left on a rough dirt road (4WD only) that leads 3.5km up the hill (look over your shoulder for great views of Parque Nacional Marino Ballena) to **Reserva Biológica Oro Verde** (☎ 2743-8072, 8843-8833). This private reserve is on the farm of the Duarte family, who have lived in the area for more than three decades. Two-thirds of the 150-hectare property is rainforest, and there are guided hikes, horseback-riding tours and bird-watching walks. Tour prices are variable.

Opposite the turnoff to Oro Verde is **Rancho La Merced National Wildlife Refuge** (☎ 2771-4582; www.rancholamerced.com; d incl full board per person US$80), a 506-hectare national wildlife refuge (and former cattle ranch) with primary and secondary forests and mangroves lining the Río Morete. Here you can take guided nature hikes, horseback-riding tours to Punta Uvita and bird-watching walks. You can also stay at La Merced in a 1940s farmhouse, which can accommodate up to 10 people in double rooms of various sizes. Tour prices vary.

Sleeping & Eating

The main entrance to Uvita leads inland, east of the highway, where you'll find the following places. For more accommodations options, also check out the sections on Parque Nacional Marino Ballena (p360) and Ojochal (p360).

Tucan Hotel (☎ 2743-8140; www.tucanhotel.com; tents/hammocks/tree house US$5/6/12, dm US$10, d US$25-30; P) Located 100m inland from the main highway, this is the most popular hostel in Uvita – and with good reason. Run by a delightful family that has made some major changes here in the last few years, the Tucan is home to a variety of accommodations to suit all budgets, from simple tents and hammocks to dorms, private rooms and the lofty tree house. Even though the beach is right down the road, most guests never escape the evil clutches of the hammock movie theater, a spectacular creation that needs to be treated with respect unless you want to defer your future travel plans.

Cabinas Los Laureles (☎ 2743-8235; www.cabinasloslaureles.com; campsites US$10, s/d from US$20/25; P) About 200m up the road you'll find this pleasant, locally run spot which has eight clean, polished-wood cabins that are set in a beautiful grove of laurels. If you're looking for a bit of local flavor and authentic Costa Rican hospitality, this is a good choice. The friendly and accommodating family can arrange horseback rides, boat tours and any other activities you might be interested in.

Cascada Verde (☎ 2743-8191; www.cascadaverde.org; dm US$12, shared loft per person US$12, s/d from US$16/25; P) About 2km inland and uphill from Uvita, this organic permaculture farm and holistic retreat attracts legions of dedicated alternative lifestylers, who typically spend weeks here searching for peace of mind and sound body. Accommodations are extremely basic and somewhat exposed to the elements, though there is ample outdoor communal space for yoga and quiet meditation, and you'll sleep deeply at night if you've spent any time here working on the farm. Cascada Verde is also home to a restaurant that serves vegetarian and raw-food specialties, which take advantage of produce grown on the property. A taxi here costs about ₡1500 from the highway area.

Las Terrazas de Ballena (☎ 2743-8034; www.terrazasdeballena.com; ste US$150-170; P) Located about 1.5km up in the hills about Uvita, this secluded Balinese-style boutique hotel quickly transports you to the other end of the Earth. Three luxury suites are given life through exposed stone and thatch, indigenous artwork and minimalist furnishings, and they open up to expansive views of the marine national park below. Chilled-out common areas with plush pillows, soft electronic music and ample Buddha statues complete the ensemble. Even if you're not staying here, stop by for some Pan-Asian fusion that combines freshly caught seafood and flavorful spices from the Orient.

Getting There & Away

Most buses depart from the two sheltered bus stops on the Costanera in the main village.

San Isidro de El General ₡800; 1½ hours; departs 6am and 2pm.

San José ₡2500; seven hours; departs 5am, 6am and 2pm.

PARQUE NACIONAL MARINO BALLENA

This stunner of a **marine park** protects coral and rock reefs surrounding Isla Ballena. Despite its small size, the importance of this area cannot be overstated, especially since it protects migrating humpback whales, pods of dolphins and nesting sea turtles, not to mention colonies of sea birds and several terrestrial reptiles.

Although Ballena is essentially off the radar screens of most coastal travelers, this can be an extremely rewarding destination for beach-lovers and wildlife-watchers alike. The lack of tourist crowds means that you can enjoy a quiet day at the beach – something that is not always possible in Costa Rica. And, with a little luck and a bit of patience, you just might catch a glimpse of a humpback breaching or a few dolphins gliding through the surf.

Orientation & Information

Heading southeast from Punta Uvita, the park includes 13km of sandy and rocky beaches, mangrove swamps, estuaries and rocky headlands. All six kinds of Costa Rican mangrove occur within the park. There are coral reefs near the shore, though they were heavily damaged by sediment run-off from the construction of the coastal highway. Entrance is at the **ranger station** (☎ 2743-8236; admission US$6; ⌚ dawn-dusk) in Playa Bahía Uvita, the seaside extension of Uvita.

Sights & Activities

The beaches at Parque Nacional Marino Ballena are a stunning combination of golden sand and polished rock. All of them are virtually deserted and perfect for peaceful swimming and sunbathing. And the lack of visitors means you'll have a number of quiet opportunities for good bird-watching.

From the station, you can walk out onto Punta Uvita and snorkel (best at low tide). Boats from Playa Bahía Uvita to Isla Ballena can be hired for up to US$30 per person for a two-hour snorkeling trip, though you are not allowed to stay overnight on the island.

If you're looking to get under the water, **Mystic Dive Center** (☎ 2788-8636; www.mysticdivecenter.com; Playa Ventanas) is a PADI operation that offers scuba trips in the national park.

There is also some decent surfing near the river mouth at the southern end of Playa Colonia.

WILDLIFE-WATCHING

Although the park gets few human visitors, the beaches are frequently visited by a number of different animal species, including nesting seabirds, bottle-nosed dolphins and a variety of lizards. And from May to November, with a peak in September and October, both olive ridley and hawksbill turtles bury their eggs in the sand nightly. However, the star attraction are the pods of humpback whales that pass through the national park from August to October and December to April.

Scientists are unsure as to why humpback whales migrate here, though it's possible that Costa Rican waters may be one of only a few places in the world where humpback whales mate. There are actually two different groups of humpbacks that pass through the park – whales seen in the fall migrate from California waters, while those seen in the spring originate from Antarctica.

Sleeping

The park is home to a free campground just 300m from the entrance, which has toilets and showers but no electricity. Keep in mind that the campsite is not secure, so do not leave any valuables lying around inside your tent. As such, the vast majority of travelers prefer to stay in nearby Uvita (p359) or Ojochal (below), and visit the marine park on a day trip.

Getting There & Away

Parque Nacional Marino Ballena is best accessed from Uvita or Ojochal, either by private vehicle or a quick taxi ride – inquire at your accommodations for the latter.

OJOCHAL AREA

Beyond Uvita, the Costanera Sur follows the coast as far as Palmar (p380), approximately 40km away. This route provides a coastal alternative to the Interamericana, as well as convenient access to points in the Península de Osa (p390).

Remote beaches along this stretch are slowly being discovered as more and more travelers head this way, though the pace of life remains calm and unhurried. The Ojochal area also serves as a convenient base for exploring nearby Parque Nacional Marino Ballena, and there are plenty of accommodations here to choose from, in addition to a couple of excellent restaurants that are destinations themselves.

Orientation

About 14km south of Uvita is the wilderness beach of Playa Tortuga, which is largely undiscovered and virtually undeveloped, but it's home to some occasional bouts of decent surf. One kilometer further south is the small village of Ojochal, which offers a couple of accommodations and restaurants, and serves as the main reference point along this part of the coastline.

Sleeping

Note that accommodations in this section are listed from north to south.

La Cusinga (☎ 2770-2549; www.lacusingalodge.com; Finca Tres Hermanas; s/d US$118/149; Ⓟ)

About 5km south of Uvita, this beachside ecolodge is admirably powered by the hydroelectric energy provided by a small stream, and centered on a working organic farm. Accommodations are in natural-style wooden rooms that epitomize simple and uncomplicated living, though guests tend to spend most of their time on boat trips to the national park, hiking and bird-watching on the onsite network of trails, and snorkeling and swimming in the national park. If you work up an appetite, head to the farmhouse and dine on rural Tico-style food that includes locally raised chicken, fresh seafood and organic produce.

Finca Bavaria (☎ 8355-4465; www.finca-bavaria.de; s/d from US$60/70; P) This quaint German-run inn comprises a handful of pleasing rooms with wood accents, bamboo furniture and romantic mosquito net–draped beds. The lush grounds are hemmed by forest, though you can always ascend to the hilltop pool and take in the sweeping views of the open ocean. And of course, there's plenty of great German beer served by the stein. Look for the signed dirt road on the inland side of the road just beyond La Cusinga.

Lookout at Playa Tortuga (☎ 2786-5074; www.hotelcostarica.com; d US$70-80; P) A signed turnoff on the eastern side of the road just after mile marker 175 leads to this beautiful hilltop sanctuary, where you'll find a dozen brightly painted rooms awash in calming pastels. The grounds are traversed by a series of paths overlooking the beaches below, but the highlight is the large wooden deck in a tower above the pool. Here you can pursue some early morning bird-watching, or perhaps better yet, indulge in some late-afternoon slothful lounging.

Hotel Villas Gaia (☎ 8382-8240; www.villasgaia.com; r from US$80; P) Along the beach side of the road is this beautifully kept collection of shiny wooden cabins, set in tranquil forested grounds. There is also an excellent restaurant serving a wide variety of international standards, as well as a hilltop pool where you can swim a few laps while enjoying the panoramic view of Playa Tortuga. The beach itself is a pleasant 20-minute hike along a dirt path that winds down the hillside.

Diquis el Sur (☎ 2786-5012; diquiscostarica.com; r per day/week from US$50/300; P) In Ojochal proper, this French Canadian–run bed and breakfast is a home away from home, by the night or by the week. Accommodations are in a variety of fairly modest rooms that are priced by amenities, though all have kitchenettes conducive to self-catering. An interesting side fact: the property is named after the 'Diquis Spheres,' which are pre-Columbian stone balls that were rumored to have come from Atlantis. They are currently being displayed in the courtyard of the Museo Nacional de Costa Rica in San José (p73).

Eating

The restaurants listed below are located in the town of Ojochal. Advanced reservations are recommended as they both command strong local followings.

our pick **Restaurante Exótica** (☎ 2786-5050; dishes ₡5000-15,000) While rural Ojochal isn't exactly a hot spot of cosmopolitan urbanity, this phenomenal gourmet restaurant certainly sets a benchmark for comparison. Despite the humble thatched roof and wooden tables, the menu features a mind-blowing array of nouveau French dishes, each emphasizing a breadth of ingredients that are brought together in masterful combinations. Some of the highlights include oil-drizzled fish carpaccio, wild-duck breast topped with tropical-fruit tapenades, and homemade desserts that taste as if they were shipped directly from Parisian patisseries. With more than a decade in the business, yet only nine tables for diners to choose from, this is an intimate culinary experience that is certainly worth seeking out.

Citrus (☎ 2786-5175; dishes ₡5000-15,000) While it is the something of the new kid in town, Citrus has the potential to equal (some would argue top) Restaurante Exótica in due time. Offering New World dishes that are heavily influenced by Southeast Asian and North African culinary traditions, and benefiting from its candlelit riverside location, Citrus welcomes patrons with a heaping spoon of flair and bravado.

Getting There & Away

Daily buses between Dominical and Palmar can drop you off near any of the places described here. However, given the infrequency of transportation links along this stretch of highway, it's recommended that you explore the area by private car.

Southern Costa Rica

In southern Costa Rica, the Cordillera de Talamanca descends dramatically into agricultural lowlands carpeted with sprawling plantations of coffee beans, bananas and African palms. Here, *campesinos* (farmers) work their familial lands, maintaining agricultural traditions that have been passed down through the generations. While the rest of Costa Rica embraces globalization, life in the southern zone remains constant, much as it has for decades, and in some places, centuries on end.

In a country where little pre-Columbian influence remains, southern Costa Rica is where you'll find the most pronounced indigenous presence. The region is home to large populations of Bribrí, Cabécar and Brunka, largely confined to private reservations, who are largely succeeding in maintaining their traditions despite outside pressures to modernize.

Costa Rica's well-trodden tourist trail seems to have bypassed the southern zone, though this isn't to say that the region doesn't have any traveler appeal. On the contrary, southern Costa Rica is home to the country's single largest swath of protected land, namely Parque Internacional La Amistad. Largely unexplored, this national park extends across the border into Panama and is one of Central America's last true wilderness areas.

And while Monteverde is the country's most iconic cloud forest, southern Costa Rica offers many equally enticing opportunities to explore this mystical habitat. If you harbor any hope of spotting the elusive resplendent quetzal, you can start by looking in the cloud forest in Parque Nacional Los Quetzales. Or, if you want to stand on top of the Cordillera Central, you can climb the cloud-capped heights of Cerro Chirripó (3820m), Costa Rica's highest peak.

HIGHLIGHTS

- Wondering why you're the only one around in the pristine but untouristed **Parque Internacional La Amistad** (p385)
- Trekking to the top of Costa Rica's highest summit at **Cerro Chirripó** (p374)
- Catching a glimpse of the Maya bird of paradise in **Parque Nacional Los Quetzales** (p367)
- Getting a history lesson at the vibrant Fiesta de los Diablitos at the **Reserva Indígena Boruca** (p378)
- Following the steps of one of Costa Rica's greatest ornithologists at **Los Cusingos Bird Sanctuary** (see boxed text, p372)

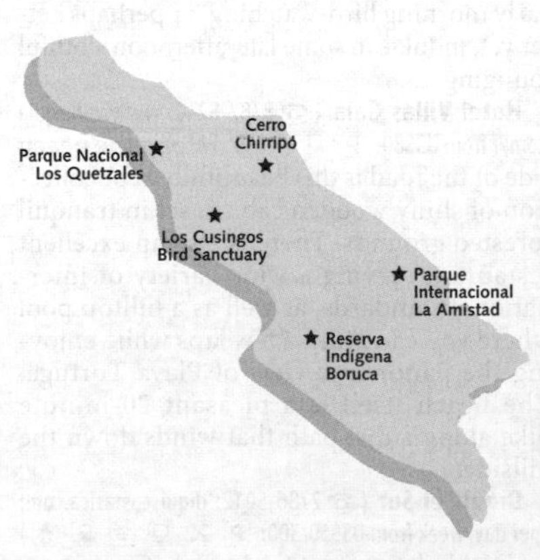

History

Costa Rica's indigenous population was almost entirely wiped out through both the direct and indirect effects of colonization. Spanish conquistadors eventually gave way to Catholic missionaries, though the end result was the same, namely the complete disruption of pre-Columbian life in the New World.

Even as late as the 20th century, indigenous groups were actively excluded from the Spanish-dominated society and pushed to the fringes. In fact, citizenship was not granted to the indigenous population until 1949, and reservations were not organized until 1977. Fortunately, in the last three decades, indigenous groups have finally been allowed to engage in their traditional languages and customs.

However, an increasing number of indigenous youths are finding themselves unable to subsist on their ancestral lands, and many are choosing to shed their native ways in favor of employment in the agricultural sector. Others have turned to the tourism sector for work, though as a population group, economic gains have been modest.

Climate

Given its geographic diversity, the climate varies considerably throughout the southern zone. In the lowlands, it remains hot and humid year-round, with marked rainfall from mid-April through mid-December. In the highlands, however, you can expect much cooler temperatures year-round (getting as low as 4°C or 40°F at times).

Parks & Reserves

The parks and reserves of southern Costa Rica offer great opportunities for wildlife-watching and hiking.

Cloudbridge Nature Preserve (p373) A tiny private reserve on the slopes of Cerro Chirripó that is operated by two New Yorkers, and is the site of an ongoing reforestation project.

Parque Internacional La Amistad (p385) This enormous bi-national park is shared with Panama and protects a biological corridor of incredible ecological significance.

Parque Nacional Chirripó (p374) Home to Costa Rica's highest and most famous peak, which offers views of both the Pacific and the Caribbean on a clear day.

Parque Nacional Los Quetzales (p367) Costa Rica's newest national park is extremely rich in birdlife and offers a good chance of spotting the quetzal in all its resplendent glory.

Reserva Biológica Dúrika (p378) This private reserve within Parque Internacional La Amistad is home to an independent, sustainable community committed to conservation.

Getting There & Around

The best way to explore the region in depth is with your own form of private transportation, though you will have to leave your wheels behind if you plan on trekking through La Amistad or scaling Chirripó. Note that this chapter refers to the numbered posts along the Carretera Interamericana, which count the kilometers from San José.

Major towns in the southern zone are serviced by regular buses, though public transportation can get sporadic once you leave these major hubs.

NatureAir (www.natureair.com) and **Sansa** (www.sansa.com) service Palmar, which is a jumping-off point for the southern zone. Prices vary according to season and availability, but usually you can expect to pay a little less than US$75 for a flight from San José or Liberia.

THE ROAD TO CHIRRIPÓ

Traveling south, the road to Parque Nacional Chirripó passes through stunning countryside of redolent coffee plantations and cool cloud forests. The first major area of interest is the Zona Santa or 'Saint's Zone,' a collection of highland villages that famously bear sainted names: San Pablo de León Cortés, Santa María de Dota, San Marcos de Tarrazú, San Cristóbal Sur and San Gerardo de Dota. Further south in the Valle de El General, family-run *fincas* (farms) dot the fertile valley, though the action tends to center on San Isidro de El General, southern Costa Rica's largest town and major transportation hub.

SANTA MARÍA & VALLE DE DOTA

Centered on a green, grassy soccer field and surrounded by lavish plantations, Santa María de Dota is a charming Tico (Costa Rican) town that merits at least a quick stop. As you'd imagine, coffee production is the economic lifeblood of Santa María, especially since the Coopedota processing facility employs much of the town.

Coopedota (☎ 2541-2828; www.coopedota.com) can give you the complete picture of where your caffeine fix comes from: the Coffee Experience

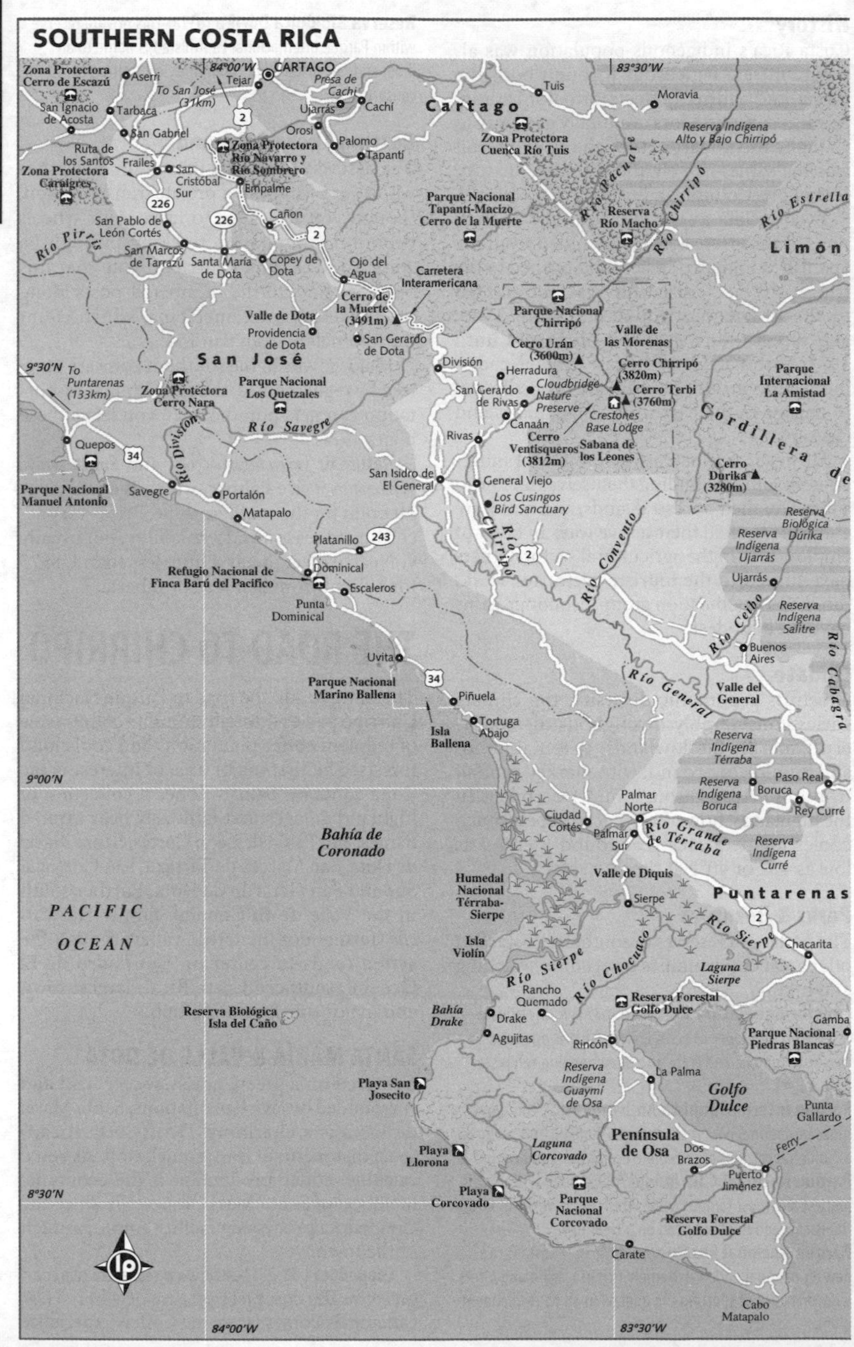
SOUTHERN COSTA RICA
84°00'W
83°30'W
CARTAGO
Cartago
San José
Limón
Puntarenas
PACIFIC OCEAN
Bahía de Coronado
Golfo Dulce
Península de Osa
Zona Protectora Cerro de Escazú
Aserrí
Tejar
To San José (31km)
Presa de Cachí
Ujarrás
Cachí
San Ignacio de Acosta
Tarbaca
San Gabriel
Orosi
Palomo
Tapantí
Ruta de los Santos
Frailes
San Cristóbal Sur
Zona Protectora Río Navarro y Río Sombrero
Empalme
Zona Protectora Caraigres
San Pablo de León Cortés
Cañon
San Marcos de Tarrazú
Santa María de Dota
Copey de Dota
Río Pirrís
Ojo del Agua
Cerro de la Muerte (3491m)
Carretera Interamericana
Valle de Dota
Providencia de Dota
San Gerardo de Dota
Tuis
Moravia
Zona Protectora Cuenca Río Tuis
Reserva Indígena Alto y Bajo Chirripó
Parque Nacional Tapantí-Macizo Cerro de la Muerte
Río Pacuare
Reserva Río Macho
Río Chirripó
Río Estrella
Parque Nacional Chirripó
Valle de las Morenas
Cerro Urán (3600m)
Cerro Chirripó (3820m)
Cerro Terbi (3760m)
Crestones Base Lodge
Cerro Ventisqueros (3812m)
Sabana de los Leones
Herradura
Cloudbridge Nature Preserve
San Gerardo de Rivas
Canaán
División
Rivas
9°30'N
To Puntarenas (133km)
Zona Protectora Cerro Nara
Parque Nacional Los Quetzales
Río Savegre
Río División
Quepos
Parque Nacional Manuel Antonio
Savegre
Portalón
Matapalo
San Isidro de El General
General Viejo
Los Cusingos Bird Sanctuary
Platanillo
Río Chirripó
Río Convento
Parque Internacional La Amistad
Cordillera de
Cerro Durika (3280m)
Reserva Biológica Dúrika
Reserva Indígena Ujarrás
Ujarrás
Reserva Indígena Salitre
Río Ceibo
Buenos Aires
Río Cabagra
Río General
Valle del General
Refugio Nacional de Finca Barú del Pacifico
Dominical
Escaleros
Punta Dominical
Uvita
Parque Nacional Marino Ballena
Piñuela
Tortuga Abajo
Isla Ballena
9°00'N
Reserva Indígena Térraba
Reserva Indígena Boruca
Boruca
Paso Real
Rey Curré
Palmar Norte
Palmar Sur
Ciudad Cortés
Río Grande de Térraba
Reserva Indígena Curré
Valle de Diquis
Humedal Nacional Térraba-Sierpe
Sierpe
Río Sierpe
Isla Violín
Río Chocuaco
Chacarita
Laguna Sierpe
Rancho Quemado
Reserva Forestal Golfo Dulce
Bahía Drake
Drake
Agujitas
Reserva Biológica Isla del Caño
Rincón
Gamba
Parque Nacional Piedras Blancas
Reserva Indígena Guaymí de Osa
La Palma
Playa San Josecito
Punta Gallardo
Playa Llorona
Laguna Corcovado
Dos Brazos
Ferry
Puerto Jiménez
8°30'N
Playa Corcovado
Parque Nacional Corcovado
Reserva Forestal Golfo Dulce
Carate
Cabo Matapalo
lp

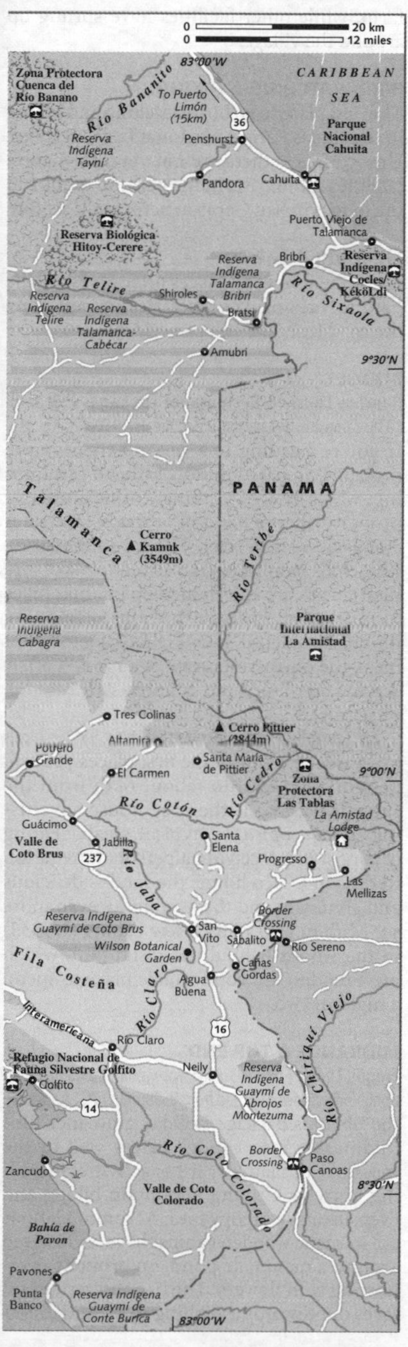

is a half-day tour (US$10) that takes guests to an organic coffee farm, visits the production facility and – most importantly – offers tastings of several different kinds of coffee. The cofounder and manager of the cafe previously won third place in a national barista competition and is locally famous for her signature coffee drinks.

A great place to spend the night is at **El Toucanet Lodge** (☎ 2541-3131; www.eltoucanet.com; Copey de Dota; s/d from US$55/71; **P**) a lovely country lodge that is perched at 1850m and offers seven rustic hardwood cabins with wonderful views of Valle de Dota. The valley and the surrounding cloud forest are excellent for bird-watching and co-owner Gary leads daily tours – fruit birds are commonly sighted, as well as the resplendent quetzal and the namesake toucanet. The Flintstones-style hot tub is an excellent place to recover from the day's activities. To reach the lodge, drive east from Santa María or turn off the Interamericana at Km 58.

If you are traveling south on the Interamericana, **Café de los Santos** (Interamericana Km 52; 🕓 10:30am-5:30pm), is a convenient place to stop and sample the fruits of the region, including fancy espresso drinks for less than a thousand colones. Incidentally, the gas station at this intersection is the last place to fill your tank before San Isidro de El General.

Most drivers from San José take the Interamericana south to Empalme, almost 30km from Cartago. Just south of the station a signed turnoff leads west on a paved road and turns to Santa María de Dota (10km away), San Marcos de Tarrazú (7km beyond) and San Pablo (4km further). Six daily buses (₡1500, 2½ hours) connect these towns to San José.

SAN GERARDO DE DOTA

Bird-watchers from around the world flock to this small mountain town – no pun intended – as the area surrounding San Gerardo de Dota is famed for attracting rare high-altitude species. In fact, the elusive resplendent quetzal is such a celebrity in these parts that in 2005, the national government demarcated a national park in its honor. For anyone serious about catching a glimpse of the fabled Maya bird of paradise, there is no better spot in the country than nearby Parque Nacional Los Quetzales (see p367 for more information).

Since the national park lacks permanent infrastructure, the town of San Gerardo not only provides easy access to the trailheads, but also offers a wide assortment of tourist lodges. Beyond bird-watching, the surrounding countryside is famous for its abundant trout fishing, and locals are quick to point out that their humble little town may be one of the most beautiful spots in the whole country. With fresh mountain air, bountiful fruit orchards, heaps of bucolic charm and plenty of smiles to boot, we're inclined to agree.

History

The banks of the Río Savegre were long protected by the steep flanks of the Talamanca mountains, prohibiting settlement in this area. It was not until 1952 that Efrain Chacón and his brothers – driven by drought – made their way south from Copey de Dota, and established a farm on the western slopes of Cerro de la Muerte – which would eventually become the village of San Gerardo.

In the early days, they planted *cubano* beans, a typical subsistence crop in this region. That's as far as the Chacón family followed the typical trend, however. Eschewing coffee (which would not thrive at these high altitudes) and beef cattle (which would destroy the surrounding cloud forest), the Chacón family instead raised dairy cattle.

Later, they supplemented dairy-farm activity by stocking their streams with trout and planting apple orchards and other fruit trees. The former had the effect of attracting anglers from San José, while the latter (along with the abundant wild avocado trees) attracted the resplendent quetzal, in turn attracting bird-watchers.

As tourism in Costa Rica flourished, so did San Gerardo. Today, this little farming village has become famous for highland bird-watching. Quetzals are spotted frequently every April and May (during breeding season) and are fairly common throughout the rest of the year.

Activities

SPORTFISHING

The trout fishing in the Río Savegre is excellent: May and June is the time for fly-fishing and December to March for lure-fishing (see boxed text, opposite). And the Chacón family, now several generations deep, operates the well-established Savegre Hotel de Montaña (opposite) on the grounds of their productive farm, while other facilities have sprung up around the village.

BIRD-WATCHING & HIKING

The best place to go bird-watching and hiking in the area is Parque Nacional Los Quetzales. Unfortunately there are not yet information facilities for tourists in the park, so inquire at the lodges in San Gerardo before you set out.

Sleeping & Eating

All of the following places offer access to the Parque Nacional Los Quetzales and are along the road from the Interamericana.

BUDGET

Ranchos La Isla & Restaurante Los Lagos (☎ 2740-1038; campsites per person US$4, meals ₡1500-2500; P) If you're heading to Chirripó then you're probably prepared to do a little bit of camping, which is a good thing as this attractive property offers a handful of shady campsites alongside a small river. The accommodating Chinchilla families also go all out to make sure their guests are entertained by guiding hikes to nearby waterfalls in the hope of spotting the elusive quetzal. If you're looking for a hot meal, the onsite restaurant is a modest affair serving up wholesome, country-style *casados*, or set meals.

La Comida Típica Miriam (cabins US$35, meals ₡1500-3500; P) One of the first places you will pass in San Gerardo (about 6km from the Interamericana) is the cozy house advertising *comida típica*, or 'typical meals.' Eating is almost like receiving a personal invitation to dine in a Tico home: the food is delicious and abundant and the hospitality even more so. Miriam also rents a few cabins (US$35) in the woods behind the restaurant, which are a modest but comfortable place to spend a night or two.

MIDRANGE & TOP END

Trogon Lodge (☎ 2293-8181; www.grupomawamba.com/trogonlodge/index.html; s/d from US$86/80; P) Despite the obvious package-holiday ambience, this midmarket resort lodge caters well to the masses with a laundry list of activities including horseback riding, mountain biking and even an onsite canopy tour. Accommodations are in rustic wooden cabins that are clustered around a manmade pond, on grounds overflowing with flowers. The bar and restaurant faces out towards a gushing river, and diners congregate at massive tables constructed from fallen trees.

Savegre Hotel de Montaña (☎ 2740-1028; www.savegre.co.cr; s/d/ste incl 3 meals US$125/179/254; P) Set on a 160-hectare orchard and reserve, this justifiably famous lodge has been owned and operated by the Chacón family since 1957. It's now something of a Costa Rican institution, especially among bird-watchers keen to catch a glimpse of the quetzal. Of course, this isn't a difficult proposition in these parts, especially since the edges of the grounds are lined with avocado trees, the favorite perch of the bird of paradise. The suites are simply gorgeous: wrought-iron chandeliers hang from the high wooden ceilings, while rich wooden furniture surrounds a stone fireplace.

our pick Dantica Lodge and Gallery (☎ 8352-2761; www.dantica.com; r/ste from US$142/180; P) Definitely the slickest place in San Gerardo, if not the whole southern zone, this upscale lodge consists of beautiful natural wood and stone cabins that are bedecked with artwork displayed in glass cases from the owner's native Colombia. The modern twist comes in the form of luxurious black leather sofas, flat-screen plasma TVs, Jacuzzi bathtubs and sophisticated track lighting. The kicker, though, is the wall of picture windows that provides extraordinary vistas over the cloud forest. A romantic breakfast is served each morning on your private terrace, which will most likely be frequented by countless species of tropical birds. You also have a nature reserve complete with private trails at your doorstep, as well as a health spa where you can pamper your feet after hiking.

Getting There & Away

The turnoff to San Gerardo de Dota is near Km 80 on the Interamericana. From here, the dirt road descends 8km to the village. The road is very steep: be careful if you're in an ordinary car. Buses between San José and San Isidro de El General can drop you at the turnoff.

PARQUE NACIONAL LOS QUETZALES

This **national park**, formerly known as the Reserva Los Santos, was made official in 2005 in honor of the very quetzal that first put this region of Costa Rica on the tourist map. Spread along both banks of the Río Savegre, at an altitude of 2000m to 3000m, Los Quetzales covers 50 sq km of rain and cloud forest lying along the slopes of the Cordillera de Talamanca.

TALAMANCA TROUT FISHING

While most sportfishers flock to the coast for the thrill of the big catch, the mountain rivers of the Cordillera de Talamanca offer a different kind of fishing experience. The crystal-clear waters and the cool air of the cloud forest are a delightfully tranquil setting, and the fish – here, rainbow trout – are no less tasty.

Interestingly, the trout that populate these rivers are not endemic. Supposedly, they were first introduced to Central American rivers by the US military in Panama and the healthy fish made their way north into Costa Rican waters. The most popular spot for trout fishing is the Río Savegre, although the nearby Río Blanca and Río Dota also attract local anglers.

In order to maintain healthy populations, fishers are strongly encouraged to limit stream fishing to catch and release. If you want to take home your trout for dinner, fish in one of the local spring-fed ponds, which are well stocked with 30cm to 50cm trout. Success is guaranteed and you just pay for what you take home (about US$4 per kilogram). This is a great option for kids and folk with poor fishing karma.

Finca Madre Selva (☎ 2224-6388; Copey de Dota) A popular local fishing spot that is home to a well-stocked trout pond as well as hiking trails – good for a full day of fun.

Pesca Deportiva Río Blanca (☎ 2541-1818/6; Copey de Dota) Near Santa María de Dota, this is another local spot that is popular among Tico families.

Ranchos La Isla (☎ 2740-1038; San Gerardo de Dota) Borrow equipment to fish in the river and ponds, then bring your catch back and have the staff fry it up for dinner.

Savegre Hotel de Montaña (☎ 2740-1028; San Gerardo de Dota) This lodge provides equipment and guides for fly-fishing in Río Savegre, or you can fish in the picturesque pond and pay for what you catch. See above for more information.

The lifeblood of the park is the Río Savegre, which starts high up on the Cerro de la Muerte and feeds several mountain streams and glacial lakes at a range of altitudes before pouring into the Pacific near the coastal town of Savegre. Although it covers a relatively small area, this region is remarkably biodiverse – the Savegre watershed contains approximately 20% of all the registered bird species in Costa Rica.

As the park's new name implies, this area is extremely rich in birdlife – the resplendent quetzal is only one of the many species that call this park home. Trogon, hummingbird, great tinamou and sooty robin are some bird favorites. Avians aside, the park is home to several other endangered species including jaguars, Baird's tapirs and squirrel monkeys.

While hiking through the higher altitudes, take notice of the fact that the flora is very different from what you will see in the lowland forests. The park, which is classified as montane and premontane forests (the latter being the second-most endangered life zone in Costa Rica), is home to massive oak trees and alpine plants.

The park does not have any facilities for tourists, aside from a small **ranger station** (☎ 2200-5354; admission US$10; 🕑 8am-4pm) where you must pay your park fees. From here, a modest network of bird-watching trails radiates out into the forest beyond.

All of the lodges around San Gerardo de Dota (see p366) organize hiking and bird-watching tours. With advanced reservations, it is sometimes possible to gain entrance to the park at sunrise, which will put you in the center of the action just in time for morning song.

The national park is bordered by the Interamericana, with the entrance lying just past Km 76 en route to Cerro de la Muerte. Any bus along this route can drop you off at the ranger station, though most people arrive with their guide in a private car or coach.

EXPLORE MORE: LOS QUETZALES

The area around San Gerardo is full of unofficial hiking trails that skirt the perimeter of Los Quetzales. As an example, if you follow the road to San Gerardo to its end, an unmarked trail will lead you through lush forest to a spectacular waterfall. With that said, it's worth inquiring locally for more specific directions – or better yet hire a local guide – before you set out into the forest as the going can get difficult in these parts.

CERRO DE LA MUERTE

Along the stretch between Empalme and San Isidro de El General, the highway passes the highest point along the Interamericana, the famed **Cerro de la Muerte** (3491m). The so-called 'Hill of Death' received this moniker before the paved road was built, though the steep, fog-shrouded highway, which climbs high into the clouds, is still considered one of the most dangerous in Costa Rica. When the fog clears, however, this area offers exquisite panoramic views of the Cordillera de Talamanca – but only for a moment, as the fog undoubtedly rolls back in almost immediately.

Cerro de la Muerte marks the northernmost extent of the *páramo,* a highland shrub and tussock grass habitat typical of the southern zone. This Andean-style landscape is extremely rich in wildlife and is home to many of the same species found in nearby Parque Nacional Chirripó (p374). The area is also part of the Parque Nacional Tapantí-Macizo Cerro de la Muerte, which offers even more opportunities for hiking and bird-watching.

Orientation

The road itself is paved and smooth, but it twists and turns around the mountain, which can make overtaking treacherous and potentially life-ending. During the rainy season, landslides may partially or completely block the road. As in most places in rural Costa Rica, it's best to avoid driving at night.

Parque Nacional Tapantí-Macizo Cerro de la Muerte is also accessible from the Central Valley & Highlands region. For more information, see p144.

Sleeping & Eating

Iyök Ami (☎ 8387-2238, 2772-0222; www.ecotourism.co.cr/iyokami/index.htm; Interamericana Km 71; reserve admission US$5, s/d from US$30/40; Ⓟ) Meaning 'Mother Earth' in the Bribri language, Iyök Ami is a private cloud-forest reserve, ecolodge, quaint coffee shop and volunteer opportunity, all in one. Considering that one Tica woman manages everything, this is an extremely impressive operation that is certainly worthy of a measure of your support. Rustic, no-frills cabins are tucked away on the edge of the forest, providing easy access to 6km of hiking trails, while delicious country-style meals await you on your return. If you'd like to extend your stay and help with the operation, a one-month volunteer placement costs US$650, which includes lodging and all of your meals.

Mirador Vista del Valle (☎ 8384-4685, 8836-6193; www.ecotourism.co.cr/vistadelvalle; Interamericana Km 119; s/d US$41/47; Ⓟ) Aptly named, the 'View of the Valley Lookout' boasts a windowed restaurant offering panoramic views that perfectly complement local specialties such as fried trout fillet, and fresh-brewed coffee. Below the restaurant, cabins built entirely from cultivated wood are brightened by colorful indigenous tapestries. Guests can also take advantage of nearly 11km of onsite trails that allow for excellent bird-watching.

Mirador de Quetzales (☎ 2771-8456; www.exploringcostarica.com/mirador/quetzales.html; Interamericana Km 70; cabins per person incl 2 meals US$50; Ⓟ) Commonly known as Eddie Serrano's farm, this excellent-value lodging option is located about 1km west of the Interamericana. Painted wood walls and colorful curtains brighten up the eight cozy cabins that line the farm's ridge (and electric heaters warm them up). Prices also include an early-morning 'quetzal walk' – the bright beauties reside in these forested hills year-round, but sightings are virtually guaranteed between November and April.

Bosque del Tolomuco (☎ 8847-7207; www.bosquedeltolomuco.com; Interamericana Km 118; d from US$65; Ⓟ) Named for the sly tayra (tree otter) spotted on the grounds, this cutesy B&B is run by a lovely, loquacious Canadian couple. There are four spacious, light-filled cabins, the most charming of which is the secluded 'Hummingbird Cabin.' The grounds offer 5km of hiking trails, ample opportunities to indulge in bird-watching and some magnificent views of Los Cruces. A made-to-order gourmet dinner is also available with advance notice.

Getting There & Away

Frequent buses running between San José and San Isidro de El General can drop you off at any of the lodges listed here.

SAN ISIDRO DE EL GENERAL

Considering that most settlements in the southern zone are mere mountain villages, it doesn't take much in these parts to be called a 'big city.' Truth be told, with a population

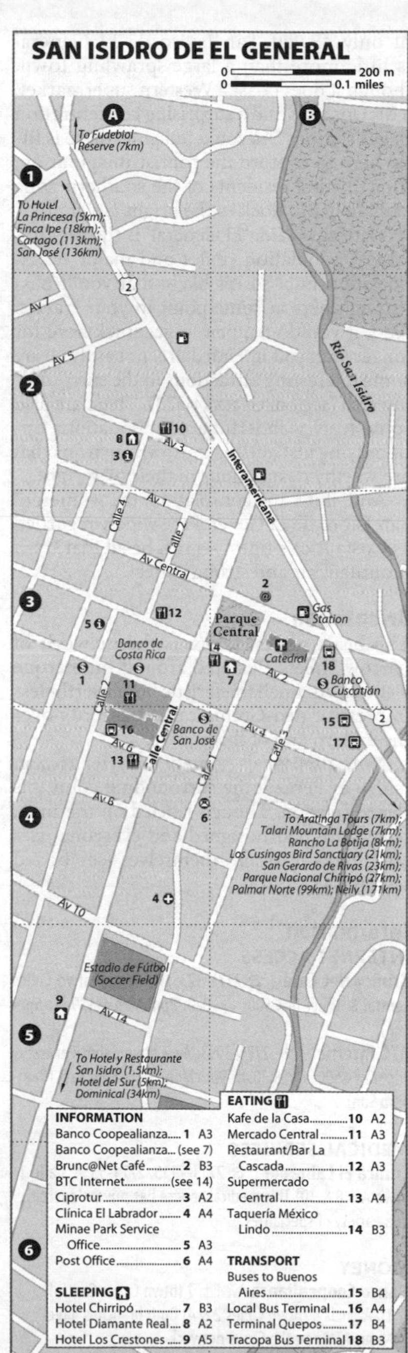

of only 45,000, San Isidro de El General is little more than a large sprawling town, though it does boast a Western supermarket, a McDonald's and a surprising concentration of gas stations. As you'd imagine, there is little here to capture the tourist imagination, though rural residents of the southern zone can't help but flock to the bright city lights.

With that said, 'El General' is the region's largest population center and major transportation hub, so it's likely that you'll pass through here at some point in your travels. And, if you do happen to get stuck here for longer than you intended, fret not as there are some interesting attractions in the surrounding area (see boxed text, p372). There are also some truly wonderful accommodations options lying just outside the town environs that are worthy destinations in their own right.

And, if it's any consolation, the women of San Isidro de El General are widely regarded as Costa Rica's finest – must be all that fresh mountain air and strong coffee!

Orientation

The heart of San Isidro is the network of narrow streets clustered around the Parque Central. An uncharacteristic but nevertheless impressive neo-Gothic cathedral lords over the eastern end of this square.

Note that locals sometimes refer to San Isidro as Pérez – the surrounding county is Pérez Zeledón. Though labeled on the map, streets are poorly signed and everyone uses landmarks to orient themselves (see boxed text, p534).

Information

INTERNET ACCESS

Brunc@Net Café (☎ 2771-3235; Av Central btwn Calles Central & 1; per hr ₡500; 🕑 8am-8pm Mon-Sat, 9am-5pm Sun)

BTC Internet (☎ 2771-3993; Av 2 btwn Calles Central & 1; per hr ₡500; 🕑 8:30am-9pm Mon-Fri, to 8pm Sat, 10am-4pm Sun)

MEDICAL SERVICES

Clínica El Labrador (☎ 2771-7115, 2771-5354; Calle 1 btwn Avs 8 & 10) This medical service has private doctors in a variety of specialties.

MONEY

Banco Coopealianza Avenida 2 (btwn Calles Central & 1); Avenida 4 (btwn Calles 2 & 4) Both branches have 24-hour ATMs on the Cirrus network.

POST

Post office (Calle 1 btwn Avs 6 & 8)

TOURIST INFORMATION

Ciprotur (☎ 2770-9393; www.ecotourism.co.cr; Calle 4 btwn Avs 1 & 3; 🕑 7:30am-5pm Mon-Fri, 8am-noon Sat) Tourist office with information about the southern Pacific region.

Minae park service office (Sinac; ☎ 2771-3155; aclap@sinac.go.cr; Calle 2 btwn Avs 2 & 4; 🕑 8am-noon & 1-4pm Mon-Fri) Dispenses very basic information about Parque Nacional Chirripó. Here is where you can make reservations for the mountaintop hostel at Chirripó – see p377 for details.

Tours

Pieter Westra runs the highly recommended **Aratinga Tours** (☎ 2574-2319; www.aratinga-tours.com) and specializes in bird tours in his native Dutch, but he is fluent in English, Spanish and many dialects of bird. His website provides an excellent introduction to bird-watching in Costa Rica. He is based at Talari Mountain Lodge (p371).

Sleeping

Options in San Isidro proper serve as one-night crash pads of varying levels of style and sophistication, while options outside the town generally have more character and warrant a longer stay.

IN TOWN

Hotel Chirripó (☎ 2771-0529; Av 2 btwn Calles Central & 1; s/d from US$17/22; P) Popular with discerning budget travelers, here you'll find bare, whitewashed rooms that are utterly barren but surprisingly dirt- and grime-free. A few flowering plants and a festive mural in the lobby brighten otherwise stark surroundings.

Hotel y Restaurante San Isidro (☎ 770 3444; Interamericana; s/d from US$24/34; P) This roadside motel does not have much character, but it is clean, comfortable and convenient for those travelers who have to do business in San Isidro. Everything you need – from bank to internet to pizza place – is right here in this complex, 2km south of the center.

Hotel Los Crestones (☎ 2770-1200, 2770-1500; www.hotelloscrestones.com/es/index.php; Calle Central at Av 14; s/d from US$36/48; P) This sharp motor court is decked with blooming flowerboxes and climbing vines outside, which is indeed a welcome sight to the road-weary traveler. Inside, functional rooms feature modern furnishings and fixtures, which are made all the better by the attentive staff that keep this place running efficiently.

Hotel Diamante Real (☎ 2770-6230; www.hoteldiamantereal.com; cnr Av 3 & Calle 4; standard/luxury r US$40/60; P) 'Executive Elegance' is the boast of this upscale business hotel, which is surprisingly swish for fairly understated San Isidro. The classy quarters are painted bright yellow and fitted with shiny black-lacquer furniture to complete the executive package.

Hotel del Sur (☎ 771 3033; http://hoteldelsur.net; standard/superior r US$53/75; P) This business complex has modern rooms with nondescript decor, several conference rooms and an upscale restaurant and bar. Located several kilometers south of the center, right off the highway, it's good for guests who don't want to leave the hotel.

AROUND SAN ISIDRO

Hotel La Princesa (☎ 2772-0324; www.laprincesahotel.com; San Rafael; d/q US$35/45; P) If sitting in the hot tub watching the sun drop behind the Talamanca sounds appealing, La Princesa is for you, especially if you're looking for affordable luxury and quieter surrounds than downtown San Isidro. Eight sparkling rooms are decorated with wood furniture and bright linens, while lovely gardens are filled with blooms and birds. To reach the property, turn off the Interamericana 5km north of San Isidro in the *barrio* (district) of San Rafael.

Talari Mountain Lodge (☎ 2771-0341; www.talari.co.cr; Rivas; s/d US$49/72; P) This secluded mountain lodge exudes an incredible amount of charm, as does the Dutch-Tica couple that runs the place. They are ever-accommodating, also offering arrangements for treks to Chirripó and customized bird-watching tours – Pieter Westra of Aratinga Tours in San Isidro is their son. Accommodations are in simple wooden cabins on the edge of the forest, though the real attraction here is the prolific birdlife on the grounds, as well as the 2km of trails that wind through the forest. To get here, drive 7km south of San Isidro on the road from San Gerardo de Rivas.

Finca Ipe (☎ no phone; www.fincaipe.com/conall.html; 2-bedroom house rental per week/month from US$300/900; P) Located approximately 20km west of San Isidro, this entirely self-sufficient and sustainable organic farm draws its name from the Ipe tree, the bark of which is used by the local indigenous population for medicine. Here a group of devoted staff and volunteers experiment with ways of alternative living in order be happier and healthier. If you want to catch a small glimpse of their long-term project, weekly or monthly house rentals give you a comfortable base right in the middle of the action. However, the best way to live the Ipe dream is to roll up your sleeves, bury your hands into some warm compost and volunteer your time and energy – US$400 a month gets you a dorm bed, clean sheets and all the seasonal produce you can stomach.

Eating & Drinking

Taquería México Lindo (☎ 2771-8222; Av 2 btwn Calles Central & 1; dishes ₡1500-4000; 10am-8.30pm) For a welcome change of pace, stop by this *taquería* (taco shop) for tasty tacos as well as burritos, nachos and fajitas, not to mention homemade guacamole and several kinds of salsa. Photos of Mexico and festive *piñatas* set the ambience.

Restaurant/Bar La Cascada (☎ 2771-6479; cnr Calle 2 & Av 2; dishes ₡2500-4500; 11pm-late) Pleasant restaurant by day, happening bar by night. The well-stocked bar, massive TV screens showing music videos, and an extensive menu of pub grub attract plenty of local youth, who spend quality time getting to know the beer, the burgers and each other.

our pick **Kafe de la Casa** (Av 3 btwn Calles 2 & 4; meals ₡3000-6500; 7am-8pm) Set in an old Tico house, this bohemian cafe features brightly painted rooms decorated with eclectic artwork, an open kitchen and shady garden seating. With a menu featuring excellent breakfasts, light lunches, gourmet dinners and plenty of coffee drinks, this funky place receives a stream of regulars.

Travelers watching their colones should head for inexpensive *casados* in the **Mercado Central** (Central Market; Av 4 btwn Calles Central & 2), while self-caterers can shop at the **Supermercado Central** (Av 6 btwn Calles Central & 2; 7am-9pm Mon-Sat, 8am-2pm Sun), one block south.

Getting There & Away

BUS

In San Isidro the local bus terminal is on Av 6 and serves nearby villages. Long-distance buses leave from various points near the Interamericana and are frequently packed, so buy tickets early.

From Tracopa Terminal

You will find **Tracopa bus terminal** (☎ 2771-0468) on the Interamericana, just southwest of Av Central.

Neily ₡3500; six hours; departs 4:45am, 7:30am, 12:30pm and 3pm.
Palmar Norte ₡2000; three hours; departs 4:45am, 7:30am, 12:30pm and 3pm.
Paso Canoas ₡3000; five hours; departs 8:30am, 10:30am, 2:30pm, 4pm, 7:30pm and 9pm.
San José ₡2100; three hours; departs 7:30am, 8am, 9:30am, 10:30am, 11am, 1:30pm, 4pm, 5:45pm and 7:30pm.
San Vito ₡2100; three hours; departs 5:30am and 2pm.

From Terminal Quepos

Terminal Quepos (☎ 2771-2550) is on the side street south of the Tracopa terminal.

Dominical ₡1800; 2½ hours; departs 7am, 8am, 1:30pm and 4pm.
Palmar Norte ₡2000; three hours; departs 6:30am and 3pm.
Palmar Norte/Puerto Jiménez ₡3000; five hours; departs 6:30am and 3pm.
Quepos ₡2000; three hours; departs 7am and 1:30pm.
Uvita ₡800; 1½ hours; departs 8:30am and 4pm.

From Other Bus Stops

The following buses originate in San Isidro.

Buenos Aires (Gafeso) ₡650; 1 hour; departs hourly 5am to 5pm from north of Terminal Quepos.
San Gerardo de Rivas, for Parque Nacional Chirripó ₡1800; 2½ hours; departs from Parque Central at 5am and from the local terminal on Av 6 at 2pm.

TAXI

A 4WD taxi to San Gerardo de Rivas will cost between ₡10,000 and ₡15,000. To arrange one, it's best to inquire through your accommodations.

SAN GERARDO DE RIVAS

If you have plans to climb to the summit of Chirripó, then you're in the right place – the tiny but tranquil town of San Gerardo de Rivas marks the entrance to the national park. Here, you can make reservations for accommodations within the park, pick up a few last-minutes supplies and – perhaps most important of all – get a good night's rest, a decent meal and a hot shower before embarking on the trek.

DAY TRIPS AROUND SAN ISIDRO DE EL GENERAL

The following day trips are great ways to pass the time in El General:

- **Fudebiol Reserve** (☎ 2771-4131; admission US$2, lodging per person incl 3 meals US$24; 🕒 8am-4pm Tue-Sun) North of El General, Fudebiol is a community reserve along the Río Quebradas. Its 750-hectare grounds include extensive hiking trails, some with rewarding lookout spots, a cooling pond and a butterfly farm (always a treat for kids). Fudebiol offers volunteer opportunities for travelers who want to live with a local family and work at the reserve; this educational facility also has lodging for visiting groups. For more information, contact Ciprotur (p370).
- **Los Cusingos Bird Sanctuary** (☎ 2200-5472; www.cct.or.cr; Quizarrá; adult/child US$10/5; 🕒 7am-4pm Tue-Sun) This sanctuary and museum are on the grounds of the farm that was once home to the great ornithologist Dr Alexander Skutch. Author of the bird-watcher's bible, *A Guide to the Birds of Costa Rica,* Dr Skutch enjoyed a long and fruitful career studying the birds of the tropics. Much of his work took place at this 78-hectare reserve, which is now open to the public. The grounds are wonderful for watching wildlife, wandering the trails and meditating on the mysteries of nature, as Dr Skutch often did. The great scientist's home is due to open as a museum dedicated to his life and work. To get to Los Cusingos, drive 8km north on the road to San Gerardo de Rivas. Turn right at Rivas and continue 5km through General Viejo, then turn east to Quizarrá. Aratinga Tours (p370) leads bird-watching walks here.
- **Rancho La Botija** (☎ 2770-2146, 2770-2147; www.rancholabotija.com; Rivas; admission US$5, r incl meals from US$65; 🕒 8:30am-5pm Tue-Sun; 👶) A great option for families with kids, this is a working coffee and sugar farm. Trails traverse the grounds, and a daily guided hike departs at 9am and leads to the famous 'Indian Rock,' an ancient stone carved with pre-Columbian petroglyphs. There is entertainment for all ages, whether you paddle a kayak around the lake or a raft around the swimming pool. A restaurant and a few cabins are onsite. The *rancho* is 7km from the Interamericana along the road to San Gerardo de Rivas.

Although hikers are understandably keen to press on to the park as quickly as possible, San Gerardo has its own merits. The backdrop to this village scene is the rushing Río Chirripó and the rocky peak of the same name, which is characterized by breathtaking alpine scenery and home to bountiful birdlife. And of course, you don't have to climb the mountain to be able to walk around with your head in the clouds – Cloudbridge Nature Preserve (below) is a perfect alternative for those who don't have the time (or energy) to go all the way to the summit.

Orientation & Information

The road to San Gerardo de Rivas winds its way 22km up the valley of the Río Chirripó. The road is paved for the first 10km or so; after the town of Rivas, however, it is a gravel road that is bumpy, narrow and steep. The 'center' of San Gerardo – as it is – consists merely of the soccer field and the *pulpería* (corner grocery store) opposite. Otherwise, there's not much to this village – just the family-run farms and *cabinas* that are strung along this road.

The **Chirripó ranger station** (Sinac; ☎ 2200-5348; ⏲ 6:30am-noon & 1-4:30pm) is located about 1km below the soccer field on the road from San Isidro. Stop by here (the earlier the better) to check for space and availability at Crestones Base Lodge (p377), and to confirm and pay your fee before setting out.

Sights & Activities

About 2km past the trailhead to Cerro Chirripó you will find the entrance to the mystical, magical **Cloudbridge Nature Preserve** (☎ in USA 212-362-9391; www.cloudbridge.org; admission by donation; ⏲ sunrise-sunset). Covering 182 hectares on the side of Cerro Chirripó, this private reserve is an ongoing reforestation and preservation project, spearheaded by New Yorkers Ian and Genevieve Giddy. A network of trails traverses part of the property, which is easy to explore independently; maps are available. Hike to two waterfalls, including the magnificent Catarata Pacifica close to the entrance. You are bound to see some amazing birdlife, including the vibrant emerald toucanet, the endangered black guan and many other cloud-forest species. Also, be sure to inquire if you are interested in volunteering on the reforestation program at Cloudbridge. You can drive up here if you have a 4WD; otherwise it's a steep but rewarding hike.

If you need to recuperate after hiking, consider a soak in the **thermal hot springs** (☎ 8391-8107; Herradura; admission US$3; ⏲ 7am-6pm) that are about 2km north of San Gerardo. Just above the ranger station the road forks; take the left fork and walk for about 1km on a paved road. Turn right and take the rickety suspension bridge over the river. A switchback trail will lead you another 1km to a house with a *soda* (inexpensive eatery), which is the entrance to the springs.

Sleeping

The listings below are all situated along the narrow road that runs parallel to the river. The majority rent mountaineering equipment (sleeping bags, air mattresses, cooking stoves etc), though supplies are limited and quality varies considerably. Given that most Chirripó-bound travelers are of the shoestring mindset, accommodations in this part of the country are skewed towards the budget end.

HOSTELS

El Urán Hotel y Restaurante (☎ 2742-5003; www.hoteluran.com; dm US$10, s/d US$25/35; Ⓟ) Just 50m below the trailhead, this no-nonsense youth hostel is something of an institution for hikers heading to/from Chirripó. Budget-friendly rooms are perfect for a restful snooze, while the onsite restaurant, grocery store and laundry facility all cater to the shoestring set.

Casa Mariposa (☎ 2742-5037; www.hotelcasamariposa.net; dm US$13, s/d US$17/30; Ⓟ 💻) This warm and welcoming backpacker hostel offers an excellent communal atmosphere that is conducive to picking up a few travel companions for the Chirripó trek. Carved out the side of the mountain, the close but cozy quarters have stone walls and plenty of character.

BUDGET

Cabinas y Restaurante El Descanso (☎ 2742-5061; campsites per person US$5, s/d US$10/30; Ⓟ) This quaint and quiet homestead, run by the ever-accommodating Elizondo family, is an excellent budget option. Skip the cheaper, cell-like single rooms and spring for a brighter, more spacious unit on the 2nd floor, with bathroom and balcony. Transportation to the park entrance for trekkers is included in the rate.

Cabinas Roca Dura (☎ 2262-7218; campsites per person US$5, r US$15-35; Ⓟ) Located in the center of town just opposite the soccer field, this hip hostelry is built right into the side of a giant boulder, lending a Flintstones ambience to the quarters. Wall murals brighten the smallest stone rooms, while pricier rooms have tree-trunk furniture and fixtures and views of forested hillsides.

Cabinas y Restaurante El Bosque (☎ 2742-5021; r per person US$10-15) Set in the midst of overflowing gardens, this family affair offers decent rooms without bathrooms, as well as newer, more spacious units with facilities. Some kitsch art by a local painter adorns the restaurant-bar, where you can enjoy great views of the forest and river from the outdoor deck.

Albergue de Montaña El Pelicano (☎ 8382-3000; r/cabins from US$20/40; Ⓟ) About 300m below the ranger station, this simple but functional budget lodge has a collection of spartan but spotless rooms that overlook the river valley. The highlight of the property is the gallery of the owner, a late-blooming artist who sculpts whimsical wood pieces.

MIDRANGE & TOP END

Talamanca Reserve (☎ 2772-1715; www.talamancareserve.com; r/ste US$70/80; Ⓟ) This sprawling 16-sq-km private reserve is dotted with Talamanca indigenous sculptures that pose ominously among the stone cabins. Spacious interiors are furnished with lacquered wood and highlighted by picture windows, which open up to an impressive network of hiking trails. This full-service lodge also lures in nonguests with its decidedly modern restaurant that is surprisingly gourmet. The entrance is about 1km south of the trailhead for Chirripó.

Río Chirripó Retreat (☎ 2742-5109; www.riochirripo.com; Canaán; r per person incl 3 meals from US$80; Ⓟ) About 1.5km below the ranger station, in Canaán, this upscale lodge is centered on both a beautiful yoga studio overlooking the river, and a vast open-air, Santa Fe–style communal area. You can hear the rush of the river from eight secluded cabins, where woven blankets and stenciled walls evoke the southwest USA. Grounds include hiking trails, a heated swimming pool and a hot tub with sweeping mountain views.

Getting There & Away

Buses to San Isidro depart from the soccer field at 7am and 4pm (₡1800, 2½ hours). Any of the hotels can call a taxi for you.

Driving from San Isidro, head south on the Interamericana and cross the Río San Isidro at the southern end of town. About 500m further cross the unsigned Río Jilguero and take the first, steep turn up to the left, about 300m beyond the Jilguero. Note that this turnoff is not marked.

The ranger station is about 18km up this road from the Interamericana. The road is paved as far as Rivas but beyond that it is steep and graveled. It is passable to ordinary cars in the dry season, but a 4WD is recommended. If you are driving past the village of San Gerardo de Rivas, to Albergue Urán or to Cloudbridge Nature Preserve, you will need a 4WD.

PARQUE NACIONAL CHIRRIPÓ

Costa Rica's mountainous spine runs the length of the country in four distinct *cordilleras* (ranges), of which the Cordillera de Talamanca is the highest, longest and most remote. While most of the Talamanca highlands are difficult to access, Costa Rica's highest peak, Cerro Chirripó, at 3820m above sea level, is the focus of this popular **national park**. Of course, while Chirripó is the highest and most famous summit in Costa Rica, it is not unique: two other peaks inside the park top 3800m, and most of the park's 502 sq km lies above 2000m.

Like a tiny chunk of the South American Andes, Parque Nacional Chirripó is an entirely unexpected respite from the heat and humidity of the rainforest. Above 3400m, the landscape is *páramo,* which is mostly scrubby trees and grasslands, and supports a unique spectrum of highland wildlife. Rocky outposts punctuate the otherwise barren hills, and feed a series of glacial lakes that earned the park its iconic name: Chirripó means 'eternal waters.'

The bare *páramo* contrasts vividly with the lushness of the cloud forest, which dominates the hillsides between 2500m and 3400m. Oak trees (some more than 50m high) tower over the canopy, which also consists of evergreens, laurels and lots of undergrowth. Epiphytes – the scraggy plants that grow up the trunks of larger trees – thrive in this climate. However, the low-altitude cloud forest is being en-

TOP PICKS: ONLY IN CHIRRIPÓ

While Costa Rica's national parks stretch from valley floor to mountain top, only in Chirripó can you do the following:

- Lord over the Costa Rican landscape while standing at the country's highest point.
- Spot highland endemics including the volcano hummingbird and green spiny lizard.
- Catch glimpses of both the Caribbean and the Pacific in a single panoramic gaze.
- Zip up the sleeping bag just as the mercury drops below the freezing point.
- Experience a slice of the Andes without ever leaving Central America.

croached upon by agricultural fields and coffee plantations in the areas near San Gerardo de Rivas.

The only way up to Chirripó is by foot. Although the trekking routes are long and challenging, watching the sunrise over the Caribbean from such lofty heights is an undeniable highlight of Costa Rica. You will have to be prepared for the cold – and at times wet – slog to the top, though your efforts will be rewarded with some of the most sweeping vistas that Costa Rica can offer.

ORIENTATION

The dry season (from late December to April) is the most popular time to visit Chirripó. February and March are the driest months, though it may still rain. On weekends, and especially during holidays, the park is crowded with Tico hiking groups, and the mountaintop hostel is often full. The park is closed in May, but the early months of the rainy season are still good for climbing as it usually doesn't rain in the morning. In any season, temperatures can drop below freezing at night, so warm clothes (including hat and gloves), rainwear and a three-season sleeping bag are necessary. In exposed areas, high winds make it seem even colder. The ranger station in San Gerardo de Rivas is a good place to check on the weather conditions.

The maps available at the ranger station are fine for the main trails. However, more detailed topographical maps are available from the Instituto Geográfico Nacional in San José (p534). Frustratingly, Chirripó lies at the corner of four separate 1:50,000-scale maps, so you need maps 3444 II *San Isidro* and 3544 III *Dúrika* to cover the area from the ranger station to the summit of Chirripó, and maps 3544 IV *Fila Norte* and 3444 I *Cuerici* to cover other peaks in the massif.

INFORMATION

It is essential that you stop at the **Chirripó ranger station** (Sinac; ☎ 2200-5348; 🕑 6:30am-noon & 1-4:30pm) at least one day before you intend to climb Chirripó so that you can check availability at the mountaintop hostel and pay your park entry fee (US$15 for two days, plus US$10 for each additional day). Space at the hostel is limited, so it's best to arrive early – first thing in the morning – to inquire about space on the following day. Even if you have a reservation, you must stop here the day before to confirm (bring your reservation and payment confirmation). You can also make arrangements here to hire a porter (about US$30 to US$50 for up to 15kg of luggage) or to store your luggage while you hike.

WILDLIFE-WATCHING

The varying altitude means an amazing diversity of fauna in Parque Nacional Chirripó. Particularly famous for its extensive birdlife, the national park is home to several endangered species, including the harpy eagle and the resplendent quetzal (especially visible between March and May). Even besides these highlights, you might see highland birds including the three-wattled bellbird, black guan and tinamou. The Andean-like *páramo* guarantees volcano junco, sooty robin, slaty finch, large-footed finch and the endemic volcano hummingbird, which is found only in Costa Rica's highlands.

In addition to the prolific birdlife, the park is also home to some unusual high-altitude reptiles, such as the green spiny lizard and the highland alligator lizard. Mammals include puma, Baird's tapir, spider monkey, capuchin and – at higher elevations – Dice's rabbit and the coyotes that feed on them.

Although spotting rarer animals is never a guaranteed proposition, here are few tips to

CHIRRIPÓ CHECKLIST

Costa Rica might be in the tropics, but Chirripó lies at some chilly altitudes. Don't get caught without the necessities when hiking Costa Rica's highest mountain. Check the Chirripó checklist before you head off:

- water bottle (there is one water stop between the trailhead and the base camp)
- food (including snacks for the hike)
- warm jacket, gloves and hat (temperatures can dip below freezing)
- good sleeping bag (also available to rent at the lodge)
- rain gear (even when it's not raining, the summit is misty)
- plastic bags (to protect your clothing and personal items from the rain)
- sunblock (it may be chilly but the sun is powerful, and much of the route is not shaded)
- flashlight (there's no electricity for much of the evening at the mountaintop hostel)
- compass and map (especially if you are planning to hike one of the lesser-used trails)
- camera (photographic evidence that you reached the top!)

maximize your chances: pumas stick to the savannah areas and use the trails at dawn and dusk to move about; Baird's tapirs gravitate to various highland lagoons, mainly in the rainy season, so stake out the muddy edges at dawn or dusk if you see recent tracks; at nighttime, coyotes can be seen feeding at the rubbish bins near Crestones Base Lodge.

HIKING

Climbing Chirripó

The park entrance is at San Gerardo de Rivas, which lies 1350m above sea level; from here the summit is 2.5km straight up! An easy-to-follow 16km trail leads all the way to the top and no technical climbing is required.

Allow seven to 14 hours to cover the 10km from the trailhead to the hostel, depending on how fit you are: the recommended departure time is 5am or 6am. The trailhead lies 50m beyond Albergue Urán in San Gerardo de Rivas (about 4km from the ranger station). The main gate is open from 4am to 10am to allow climbers to enter; no one is allowed to begin the ascent after 10am. Inside the park the trail is clearly signed at every kilometer.

The open-sided hut at **Llano Bonito**, halfway up, is a good place for a lunch break. There is shelter and water, but it is intended for emergency use, not overnight stays.

About 6km from the trailhead, the **Monte Sin Fe** (which translates as 'Mountain Without Faith'; this climb is not for the faint of heart) is a preliminary crest that reaches 3200m. You then enjoy 2km with gravity in your favor, before making the 2km ascent to the Crestones Base Lodge at 3400m.

Reaching the hostel is the hardest part. From there the hike to the summit is about 6km on relatively flatter terrain (although the last 100m is very steep): allow at least two hours if you are fit, but carry a warm jacket, rain gear, water, snacks and a flashlight just in case. From the summit on a clear day, the vista stretches to both the Caribbean Sea and the Pacific Ocean. The deep-blue lakes and the plush-green hills carpet the Valle de las Morenas in the foreground. Readers recommend leaving the base camp at 3am to arrive in time to watch the sunrise from the summit.

A minimum of two days is needed to climb from the ranger station in San Gerardo to the summit and back, leaving no time for recuperation or exploration. It is definitely worthwhile to spend at least one extra day exploring the trails around the summit and/or the base lodge.

Other Trails

Most trekkers follow the main trail to Chirripó and return the same way, but there are several other attractive destinations that are accessible by trails from the base camp. An alternative, longer route between the base lodge and the summit goes via **Cerro Terbi** (3760m), as well as **Los Crestones**, the moonlike rock formations that adorn many postcards. If you are hanging around for a few days, the glorious, grassy **Sabana de los Leones** is a popular destination that offers a stark contrast to the otherwise alpine scenery. Peak-baggers will want to visit **Cerro Ventisqueros** (3812m), which is also within a day's walk of Crestones. These trails are fairly well maintained, but it's worth inquiring about conditions before setting out.

For hardcore adventurers, an alternative route is to take a guided three- or four-day loop trek that begins in Herradura and spends a day or two traversing cloud forest and *páramo* on the slopes of Fila Urán. Hikers ascend **Cerro Urán** (3600m) before the final ascent of Chirripó and then descend through San Gerardo. This trip requires bush camping and a local guide must accompany you at all times. **Costa Rica Trekking Adventures** (☎ 2771-4582; www.chirripo.com) can make arrangements for this tour.

TOURS

Most travelers prefer to access the park either independently or by hiring a local guide, though **Costa Rica Trekking Adventures** (☎ 2771-4582; www.chirripo.com) is highly recommended if you prefer organized adventure. This well-established company offers several different guided excursions around Chirripó, ranging from a one-day trek to Llano Bonito to a four-day trek around the Urán loop. Note that prices are variable, and ultimately dependant on the size of the party and the time of year.

CHIRRIPÓ FOR CHILDREN

Children come in all different shapes and sizes, and patient parents know that it can take a lot of energy to keep up with your kid's stamina. But, if we're permitted to make a sweeping generalization, it's that Chirripó – and indeed much of the southern zone – is not one of Costa Rica's more kid-friendly corners. Rough trails and foul weather aside, nature here is wild and difficult to access, which means that it's probably best to bring the kids elsewhere in the country – or least wait until they grow up a little bit.

SLEEPING & EATING

The only accommodations in Parque Nacional Chirripó are at **Crestones Base Lodge** (Centro Ambientalista el Parámo; dm US$10), housing up to 60 people in dorm-style bunks. The basic stone building has a solar panel that provides electric light from 6pm to 8pm and sporadic heat for showers. The lodge rents a variety of gear including sleeping bags, blankets, cooking equipment and gas canisters for a few dollars per day.

Reservations are absolutely necessary at Crestones Base Lodge. Your tour company will likely make reservations for you; but for those traveling independently, it is virtually impossible to make reservations before your arrival in Costa Rica. Once in Costa Rica, however, it is necessary to contact the **Minae office** (☎ 2771-3155; fax 2771-3297; aclap@sinac.go.cr) in San Isidro. If space is available, you will be required to pay by credit card in order to confirm the reservation. You must present your reservation and payment confirmation at the ranger station in San Gerardo de Rivas on the day before you set out.

Fortunately, the lodge reserves 10 spaces per night for travelers who show up in San Gerardo and are ready to hike on the following day. This is the more practical option for most travelers, although there is no guarantee that there will be space available on the days you wish to hike. Space is at a premium during holiday periods and on weekends during the dry season. The ranger station opens at 6:30am – the earlier you arrive, the more likely you will be able to hike the following day.

Crestones Base Lodge provides drinking water, but no food. Hikers must bring all of their own provisions.

Camping is allowed only at a special designated area near Cerro Urán – not at Crestones or anywhere else in the park.

GETTING THERE & AROUND

See details under San Gerardo de Rivas (p373) for directions on how to get here. From opposite the ranger station, in front of Cabinas El Bosque, there is free transportation to the trailhead at 5am. Also, several hotels offer early morning trailhead transportation for their guests.

THE ROAD TO LA AMISTAD

From San Isidro de El General, the Interamericana winds its way southeast through some glorious geography of rolling hills and coffee plantations backed by striking mountain facades, towering as much as 3350m above. Along this stretch, a series of narrow, steep, dirt roads lead to some of the country's most remote areas – some nearly inaccessible due to the prohibitive presence of the Cordillera de Talamanca. But it's worth enduring the thrilling road for the chance to visit Parque International La Amistad, a true wilderness of epic scale.

BUENOS AIRES

All it takes is a quick glance at the town's Del Monte processing plant to realize that pineapples are big business in Buenos Aires. Unless you're interested in getting a good price on a truckload of sweetened pineapple rings, there is little reason to give the town more than a passing glance.

However, if you are planning to visit the Reserva Biológica Dúrika (below), you should either contact – or, alternatively, stop by – the office of **Fundación Dúrika** (☎ 2730-0657; www.durika.org), which is in charge of administering the biological reserve.

Buses that travel between Palmar Norte, San Vito, San Isidro and San José pass by without stopping in Buenos Aires, though you can flag them down on the Interamericana. However, there is no marked bus shelter, so be sure that you are visible otherwise the bus driver won't stop for you.

If you have your own transportation, Buenos Aires can be reached by turning off the Interamericana just south of the Del Monte plant – a paved road leads 3km north to Buenos Aires. This main road into town forks about 1km south of town: the left fork passes the Fundación Dúrika office and heads into the center of town, near the Parque Central.

RESERVA BIOLÓGICA DÚRIKA

A perfect example of sustainable tourism in action, this 75-sq-km **biological reserve** is home to a small but thriving community of Ticos and resident foreigners who are committed to local conservation, natural medicine and the preservation of indigenous culture. Since 1992 Dúrika has opened its arms to any travelers interested in partaking in their inspiring social experiment.

Tours of the working farm demonstrate the principles and processes of organic agriculture that Dúrika employs, such as fertilizer made from chili peppers. Guests can also arrange short hikes into the reserve, day-long forays to the Cabécar indigenous village of **Ujarrás**, and/or multiday treks. Travelers with a strong interest in indigenous cultures or medicinal plants should inquire about the **Shaman Tour**, a week-long journey that visits several communities and focuses on traditional healing methods.

Visitors are also welcome to stay closer to home, participating in the life of the farm, checking out local waterfalls (which fuel the community's hydroelectric power) and otherwise exploring the grounds. Accommodations are also available in **cabins** (per person from US$45) of various sizes sleeping two to eight people. As an added bonus, rates include organic vegetarian meals made from locally grown foods. Note that discounted rates are available for large groups and students, and volunteer opportunities are available.

Reservations and information are available from the **Fundación Dúrika office** (☎ 2730-0657; www.durika.org) in Buenos Aires. If possible, it is advised that you make reservations as early as possible since accommodations fill up quickly in the high season.

Although it is possible to drive to Dúrika in a 4WD, the office in Buenos Aires can easily arrange transportation to the reserve and watch over your car while you're staying at the reserve. This is a highly recommended option as the road out to the reserve is extremely challenging and potentially dangerous, especially if there has been heavy rainfall.

RESERVA INDÍGENA BORUCA

The picturesque valley of the Río Grande de Térraba is the setting for the various towns that comprise the **indigenous reserve** of Brunka (Boruca) peoples. At first glance it is difficult to differentiate these towns from a typical Tico village, aside from a few artisans selling their handiwork. In fact, these towns hardly cater to the tourist trade, which is one of the main reasons why traditional Brunka life is continuing on without much distraction.

In any case, be particularly sensitive when visiting indigenous communities – always dress modestly, avoid taking photographs of people without asking permission, and take time to appreciate the fact that these living communities are struggling to maintain their traditional culture amid a changing world.

History

Historians believe that the present-day Brunka have evolved out of several different indigenous groups, including the Coto,

THE BORUCA DAM THAT ALMOST WAS

Over the past few decades, electricity consumption in Costa Rica (and throughout much of Latin America) has spiked significantly, putting pressure on both the public and private sectors to meet increasing energy needs. One proposal that made international headlines after prompting major environmental and social justice concerns was the Boruca Dam. At 220m tall, this enormous hydroelectric project – if completed – would have spanned the Río Grande de Térraba at Rey Curré, and been dubbed the largest dam in Central America.

Controversy arose when engineers announced that the dam would flood 25 sq km of land and displace thousands of local residents, the majority of which are members of the Brunka (Boruca) indigenous group. The Brunka have strong ties to their land, not only due to their subsistence from agriculture and dependence on plants for medicinal use, but also due to the presence of ancestral burial grounds. Furthermore, the Brunka recognized that relocation would inevitably result in the physical division of their community, something they have already experienced – to a smaller degree – with the construction of the Interamericana highway.

According to Costa Rican law, the hydroelectric project could not go forward without the consent of the residents, but many of the Brunka felt helpless and hopeless in the face of the ICE: a government-owned electricity company that has an incredible amount of weight and capital behind them. However, despite the odds stacked against them, community-based organizations sprung to action, and actively campaigned against the ICE's initiative with great success. After several years of tense negotiations, the ICE abandoned the project entirely, and agreed to build a smaller dam in a different region.

Quepos, Turrucaca, Burucac and Abubaes, whose territories stretched all the way to the Península de Osa in pre-Columbian times. Today, however, the entire Brunka population is largely confined to the small villages of Rey Curré, which is bisected by the Carretera Interamericana, and Boruca, 8km north.

Orientation & Information

Rey Curré (usually just 'Curré' on maps) is about 30km south of Buenos Aires, right on the Interamericana. Drivers can stop to visit a small **cooperative** (9am-5pm Mon-Fri, 2-5pm Sat) that sells handicrafts. In Boruca, local artisans post signs outside their homes advertising their handmade balsa masks and woven bags. Exhibits are sometimes on display in the informal **museum** (hours vary), a thatch-roof *rancho* 100m west of the *pulpería*.

Galería Namu (☎ 2256-3412; www.galerianamu.com; Av 7 btwn Calles 5 & 7, San José; per person per day US$45) This San José gallery – which specializes in indigenous art – can arrange tours to Boruca, which include homestay, hiking to waterfalls, handicraft demonstrations and storytelling. Transportation to Boruca is not included. For more information, see p95.

Festivals & Events

The **Fiesta de los Diablitos** is a three-day Brunka event that symbolizes the struggle between the Spanish and the indigenous population. Sometimes called the Danza de los Diablitos, or 'dance of the little devils,' the culmination of the festival is a choreographed battle between the opposing sides. Villagers wearing wooden devil masks and burlap costumes play the role of the natives in their fight against the Spanish conquerors. The Spaniards, represented by a man in a bull costume, lose the battle. This festival is held in Boruca from December 31 to January 2 and in Curré from February 5 to 8.

Many outsiders descend on Boruca and Curré during these events. While the Brunka welcome visitors, they request that guests respect their traditions. Tourists are generally required to pay a fee for the right to take photographs or video. No flash photography or artificial lighting is allowed, and tourists are not allowed to interfere with the program.

The lesser-known **Fiesta de los Negritos**, held during the second week of December, celebrates the Virgin of the Immaculate Conception. Traditional indigenous music (mainly drumming and bamboo flutes) accompanies dancing and costumes.

Sleeping & Eating

The only regular place to stay in the area is at the Tico-owned **Bar Restaurante Boruca** (☎ 2730-2454; d from US$10) in Boruca, which consists of five basic rooms with cold-water bathroom.

However, for a more in-depth understanding of the Brunka culture and lifestyle, it's recommended that you arrange a homestay through **Pedro Rojas Morales** (☎ 506-362-2545; saribu@yahoo.com). A soft-spoken Brunka artist who is certainly a local expert, Señor Morales can help you arrange a wide range of activities on the reservation. Prices are negotiable.

Shopping

The Brunka are celebrated craftspeople and their traditional art plays a leading role in the survival of their culture. While most people make their living from agriculture, some indigenous people have begun producing fine handicrafts for tourists. The tribe is most famous for its ornate masks, carved from balsa or cedar, and sometimes colored with natural dyes and acrylics. Brunka women also use pre-Columbian backstrap looms to weave colorful, natural cotton bags, placemats and other textiles.

Getting There & Away

Buses (₡1650, one hour) leave the central market in Buenos Aires at noon and 3:30pm daily, traveling to Boruca via a very poor dirt road. The bus returns the following morning, which makes Boruca difficult for a day trip relying on public transportation. A taxi from Buenos Aires to Boruca is about ₡10,000.

Drivers will find a better road that leaves the Interamericana about 3km south of Curré – look for the sign. In total, it's about 8km to Boruca from Curré, though the going is slow, and a 4WD is recommended.

PALMAR

At the intersection of the country's two major highways, the unremarkable village of Palmar is a transportation hub that serves as a gateway to the Osa peninsula and Golfo Dulce (for more information, see p390). Although the town also serves as an important banana-growing center, for the average traveler there is little reason to spend any more time here than it takes to get off the plane or change buses. Quite simply, it's a hot, dusty and altogether uneventful place.

Orientation & Information

Palmar is actually split in two – to get from Palmar Norte to Palmar Sur, take the Interamericana southbound over the Río Grande de Térraba bridge, then take the first right beyond the bridge. Most facilities are in Palmar Norte, clustered around the intersection of the Carretera Interamericana and the Costanera Sur (Pacific Coast Hwy), while Palmar Sur is the locale of the airstrip.

In Palmar Norte you can grab some cash at the **Banco Coopelianza** (🕒 8am-5pm Mon-Fri, 8am-noon Sat) or **Banco Popular** (☎ 2786-7033), both on the Interamericana.

Sights

Lack of charm aside, Palmar is one of the best sites in the country to see the **granite spheres**, or *esferas de piedra*, a legacy of pre-Columbian cultures – some of which exceed 2m in diameter. They are scattered all over town, including at the airstrip – some of the largest and most impressive are in front of the peach-colored *el colegio* (school) on the Interamericana.

Sleeping & Eating

You'll not want to linger in Palmar, but if you miss a connection you may find yourself spending the night.

Hotel Vista al Cerro (☎ 2786-6663; www.vistaalcerro.com; s/d from US$30/35, apt negotiable; P ❄ 💻 📶) On the western edge of town, the Vista al Cerro is a modest family-run hotel with all the required amenities and a decent restaurant to boot. Long-term apartment rentals are available if you find yourself needing a cheap base in the region.

Brunka Lodge (☎ 2786-7489; www.brunkalodge.com; s/f from US$35/45; ❄ 💻 📶 🏊) The Brunka Lodge is undoubtedly the most inviting option in Palmar Norte. Sun-filled, clean-swept bungalows are clustered around a swimming pool and a popular, pleasant open-air restaurant, and all rooms have hot-water bathrooms, cable TV and high-speed internet connections.

Self-caterers will want to visit the **Supermercado Térraba** (Transportes Térraba bus stop) before heading to the Osa, as shopping opportunities are limited in Bahía Drake. The **Panadería Palenquito** (Tracopa bus stop) is a useful breakfast spot if you are catching an early-morning bus.

Getting There & Away

AIR

Departing from San José, **NatureAir** (www.natureair.com) and **Sansa** (www.sansa.com) have daily

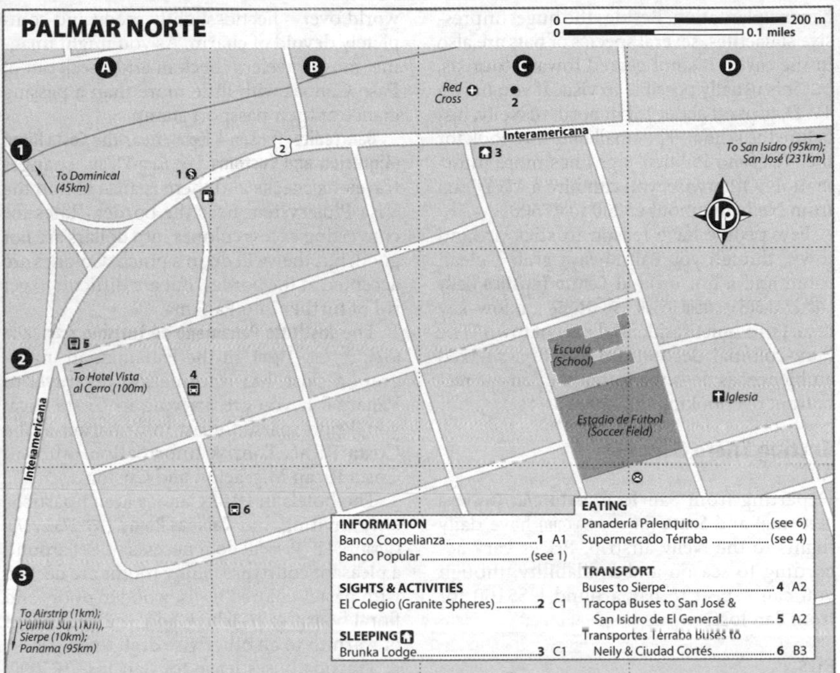

flights to the Palmar airstrip. Prices vary according to season and availability, though you can expect to pay around US$100 to/from San José.

Taxis meet incoming flights and charge up to ₡2500 to Palmar Norte and ₡7500 to ₡12,500 to Sierpe. Otherwise, the infrequent Palmar Norte–Sierpe bus goes through Palmar Sur – you can board it if there's space available.

BUS

Buses to San José and San Isidro stop on the east side of the Interamericana. Other buses leave from in front of Panadería Palenquito or Supermercado Térraba a block apart on the town's main street. The bus ticket office is inside the Palenquito.

Neily (Transportes Térraba) ₡800; 1½ hours; departs 5am, 6am, 7am, 9:30am, noon, 1pm, 2:20pm & 4:50pm.

San Isidro (Tracopa) ₡2000; three hours; departs 8:30am, 11:30am, 2:30pm and 4:30pm.

San José (Tracopa) ₡2800; five hours; departs 5:25am, 6:15am, 7:45am, 10am, 1pm, 3pm and 4:45pm.

Sierpe ₡650; one hour; departs 4:30am, 7am, 9:30am, 11:30am, 2:30pm and 5:30pm.

NEILY

Although it is southern Costa Rica's second-largest 'city,' Neily has retained the friendly atmosphere of a rural town, much like neighboring Palmar. At just 50m above sea level, steamy Neily also serves as a regional transportation hub and agricultural center, though it is decidedly lacking in tourist appeal.

Neily is located on the west bank of the Río Corredor, on the north side of the Interamericana. From here the Interamericana continues 17km to Panama, while Rte 16 makes a beeline north to the attractive mountain village of San Vito.

To the south, the lowlands are carpeted in the banana and palm plantations of the Valle de Coto Colorado, and in the north, the Fila Costeña is the source of spectacular mountain scenery.

There is a **Banco Coopealianza** (🕑 8am-3pm Mon-Fri), just southwest of the *mercado* (market), that has a 24-hour ATM on the Cirrus network.

About 15km north of Neily on the road to San Vito, **Las Cavernas de Corredores** are a network of little-explored caverns on a private banana plantation. Besides the huge, impressive stalactites, several species of bats are also in the caves. It's not geared toward tourists, but it is usually possible to visit. If you have a 4WD, turn off about 15km north of Neily, just before the school. The small *pulpería* (look for the 'Teléfono Público' sign) has more information. Otherwise, you can hire a 4WD taxi from Neily for about ₡5000 to ₡7500.

Few people have reason to stick around town, though you can always grab a clean room and a hot meal at **Centro Turístico Neily** (☎ 2783-3031; r from US$30; P), a low-key resort in a quiet residential part of town. The faux-colonial decorations create a relaxed ambience, as does the tranquil open-air restaurant overlooking the grounds.

Getting There & Away

AIR

Departing from San José, **NatureAir** (www.natureair.com) and **Sansa** (www.sansa.com) have daily flights to the Neily airstrip. Prices vary according to season and availability, though you can expect to pay around US$100 to/from San José.

BUS

The following buses leave from the main terminal on the east side of town:

Airport ₡250; 30 minutes; departs 7:30am, 9:15am, 11:30am, 1:15pm, 3:15pm, 5:30pm and 6pm.
Golfito ₡800; 1½ hours; departs hourly 6am to 7:30pm.
Palmar ₡800; 1½ hours; departs 4:45am, 9:15am, noon, 12:30pm, 2:30pm, 4:30pm and 5:45pm.
Paso Canoas ₡250; 30 minutes; departs every half-hour 6am to 6pm.
Puerto Jiménez ₡2000; three hours; departs 7am and 2pm.
San Isidro (Tracopa) ₡3500; six hours; departs 7am, 10am, 1pm and 3pm.
San José (Tracopa) ₡5000; eight hours; departs 4:30am, 5am, 8:30am, 11:30am and 3:30pm.
San Vito ₡250; 30 minutes; departs 6am, 7:30am, 9am, noon, 1pm, 4pm and 5:30pm.
Zancudo ₡2000; three hours; departs 9:30am and 2:15pm.

TAXI

Taxis with 4WD wait at the taxi stand southeast of the park. The fare from Neily to Paso Canoas is about ₡3000.

PASO CANOAS

The main port of entry between Costa Rica and Panama is like most border outposts the world over – hectic, slightly seedy and completely devoid of charm. As you might imagine, most travelers check in and check out of Paso Canoas with little more than a passing glance at their passport stamp.

Báncredito (🕒 8am-4:30pm), near the **Costa Rican Migración and Customs** (🕒 6am-11pm), changes traveler's checks and there is an ATM on the Visa Plus system near the border. Rates for converting excess colones into dollars are not good, but they will do in a pinch. Colones are accepted at the border, but are difficult to get rid of further into Panama.

The **Instituto Panameño de Turismo** (☎ 2727-6524; 🕒 6am-11pm), in the Panamanian immigration post, has information on travel to Panama. If you are arriving in Costa Rica, you'll find sparse tourist information at the Costa Rican Tourist Information office in Costa Rican Migración and Customs.

The hotels in Paso Canoas aren't particularly inviting, but **Cabinas Romy** (☎ 2732-2873; r from US$12; P) will do if necessary. Set around a pleasant courtyard, shiny rooms are decked with pastel-colored walls, wooden doors and floral bedspreads, which add a surprising bit of warmth to an otherwise drab town.

Tracopa buses leave for San José (₡5000, six hours) at 4am, 7:30am, 9am and 3pm. The **Tracopa bus terminal** (☎ 2732-2201), or window really, is north of the border post, on the east side of the main road. Sunday-afternoon buses are full of weekend shoppers, so buy tickets as early as possible. Buses for Neily (₡800, 30 minutes) leave from in front of the post office at least once an hour from 6am to 6pm. Taxis to Neily cost about ₡3000 and to the airport about ₡4000.

For more information on border-crossing specifics, see boxed text, opposite.

WILSON BOTANICAL GARDEN

Wilson Botanical Garden (☎ 2773-4004; www.esintro.co.cr; Las Cruces Biological Station; admission US$8, guided tours half-/full-day US$18/24; 🕒 8am-4pm) lies about 6km south of San Vito. Covering 12 hectares and surrounded by 254 hectares of natural forest, this world-class garden was established by Robert and Catherine Wilson in 1963 and thereafter became internationally known for its collection.

In 1973 the area came under the auspices of the Organization for Tropical Studies (OTS) and today the well-maintained garden – part of Las Cruces Biological Station – holds more

GETTING TO PANAMA

To David

On the Carretera Interamericana, Paso Canoas is the major border crossing with Panama. Although it is conveniently open 24 hours, it is crowded and confusing, especially during holiday periods, when hordes of Ticos arrive for shopping sprees. Note that it's very easy to walk across the border without realizing it. No harm done, but don't go too far without getting the proper stamps in your passport.

Costa Rican *migración* (immigration) is on the eastern side of the highway, north of the Tracopa bus terminal. After securing an exit visa, walk 300m east to the Panamanian immigration post, in the huge new yellow cement block. Here you can purchase the necessary tourist card (price varies by nationality) to enter Panama. You might be asked for an onward ticket and evidence of financial solvency (presenting a credit card usually does the trick). From here, dozens of minivans make the 90-minute trip to the city of David for a couple of dollars.

If you are in a private vehicle, you must have your car fumigated. Keep a copy of the fumigation ticket as roadside checkpoints often request it. Note that you cannot cross the border in a rental vehicle without having made prior arrangements.

To Río Sereno

East of San Vito (see below), a little-transited road leads to the border crossing at Río Sereno, from where you can continue on to the village of Volcán near Parque Nacional Volcán Barú in Panama. Río Sereno is a tranquil, pleasant place – atypical of most border towns. The crossing here is largely hassle-free as there aren't the usual touts hanging around.

Migración (🕑 8am-6pm) is beside the police station. Once again, Panamanian immigration officials may require an onward ticket, and some foreigners will need to purchase a tourist card, which is sold at the bank, about 100m past the *migración* office.

There are no facilities on the Costa Rican side, but Río Serena in Panama has a decent hotel, a good pizza place and internet access. Once across the border, regular minibuses make the hour-long trip from Río Sereno to Volcán for a couple of dollars.

than 1000 genera of plants from about 200 families. As part of the OTS, the garden plays a scientific role as a research center. Species threatened with extinction are preserved here for possible reforestation in the future.

The gardens are well laid out, many of the plants are labeled and a trail map is available for self-guided walks, featuring exotic species such as orchids, bromeliads, palms and medicinal plants. The many ornamental varieties are beautiful, but the tours explain that they are useful too (eg the delicate cycad, used by Cabécar and Bribrí people as a treatment for snakebites). The gardens are very popular among bird-watchers, who may see scarlet-thighed dacni, silver-throated tanager, violaceous trogon, blue-headed parrot, violet sabre-wing hummingbird and turquoise cotinga.

If you want to stay overnight at the botanical gardens, make your reservations well in advance: facilities are often filled with researchers and students. Accommodations are in comfortable **cabins** (s/d incl meals US$88/164) in the midst of the gorgeous grounds. The rooms are simple, but they each have a balcony with an amazing view of the surrounding flora. Rates include entry to the gardens.

Buses between San Vito and Neily pass the entrance to the gardens. Take the bus that goes through Agua Buena, as buses that go through Cañas Gordas do not stop here. A taxi from San Vito to the gardens costs up to ₡2500.

SAN VITO

Founded by Italian immigrants in the 1950s, San Vito is home to their descendants, who have retained their language and culture (not to mention their cuisine!). Of course, this is no small feat considering that this remote mountain town is located on the edge of Parque Internacional La Amistad, one of Central America's last great frontier areas. As such, the town serves as a base for travelers in need of a hot meal and a good night's sleep before descending into the deep wilderness.

In addition to the descendants of the original Italian founders, San Vito is also home to a large population of Guaymí people. The proximity of the town to the Reserva Indígena Guaymí de Coto Brus means that indigenous peoples pass through this region (Guaymí enclaves move back and forth undisturbed across the border with Panama). You might spot women in traditional clothing – long, solid-colored *pollera* dresses trimmed in contrasting hues – riding the bus or strolling the streets.

Orientation

Tucked in between the Cordillera de Talamanca and the Fila Costeña, the Valle de Coto Brus offers some glorious geography, featuring the green, rolling hills of the coffee plantations backed by striking mountain facades, towering as much as 3350m above. The principal road leaves the Interamericana at Paso Real (near Curré) and follows the Río Jaba to San Vito, then continues south to rejoin the Interamericana at Neily. This winding mountain road (paved, but poorly maintained) offers spectacular scenery and a thrilling ride.

Information

If you're planning on heading to Parque Internacional La Amistad, San Vito is home to the **Minae parks office** (☎ 2773-3955; ⌚ 9am-4pm), which can help you get your bearings before heading to the national park.

Sights

About 3km south of town, **Finca Cántaros** (☎ 2773-3760; admission US$1, campsites per person US$6; ⌚ 9:30am-5pm Tue-Sun; 👶) is a recreation center, campground and reforestation project. The 10 hectares of grounds – which used to be coffee plantations and pasture land – are now a lovely park with garden trails, picnic areas and a dramatic lookout over the city. The reception is housed in a pretty, well-maintained cabin that contains a small but carefully chosen selection of local and national crafts.

Sleeping & Eating

In addition to the following accommodations options, camping is also available at Finca Cántaros (see above).

RAINFOREST MEDICINE

Indigenous groups use tropical flowers, herbs and plants to treat all kinds of illnesses, from diabetes to a slipped disk. Here are a few of our favorites, courtesy of Paradise Tropical Garden (see below):

- Most doctors treat stomach ulcers with antibiotics, but natural-medicine connoisseurs recommend the seeds from the spiny red annatto pod. Remove the seeds from the pod and wash away the red paste. You can eat the seeds straight from the pod, or dry them and grind them into your food.
- The leaves of the avocado tree are said to cure high blood pressure. Just boil them for three minutes and let them steep for another three. Strain the murky drink and store it in the fridge. Apparently you should drink three cups a day, but beware: this brew is a diuretic.
- If you suffer from a slipped disk, you might try this natural remedy, made from the bracts of the beautiful red plume ginger *(Alpinia purpurata)*, which is bountiful in the rainforest. The bracts are the small leaves at the base of the bloom. Pull them off the stem of the ginger and stuff as many as you can fit into a small bottle, then fill the bottle with rubbing alcohol. Let it sit for three days, before rubbing this tincture onto your sore back. This remedy should ease your pain within a few days.

If you would like to learn more, pay a visit to the **Paradise Tropical Garden** (☎ 2789-8746; www.paradise-garden.travelland.biz; Río Claro; admission by donation; ⌚ 6am-5pm), where Robert and Ella Beatham have created a wonderfully sensual introduction to tropical fruits and rainforest remedies that they call the 'Tropical Fruit See, Smell, Taste & Touch Experience.' Besides this interactive display, visitors also learn about the production of African palm oil and how it came to be the dominant crop of this region following the collapse of the banana industry. Robert and Ella are wonderful hosts, but you should call a day in advance if you want their full attention. The gardens are located just west of the town of Río Claro – follow the Interamericana for 1km, cross the Río Lagarto and turn right at the end of the bridge. From here, the garden is just 200m beyond.

Cabinas Rino (☎ 2773-3071; s/d from US$12/20; P) This 2nd-floor hotel is located above a block of shops on the main road, though it's fairly well insulated from the street noise below. Basic rooms with whitewashed walls are reasonably clean and comfortable, and staff are polite and courteous.

Hotel El Ceibo (☎ 2773-3025; s/d from US$35/45; P) The best option in town – though fairly subdued by any account – is El Ceibo, conveniently located about 100m west of the main intersection. Here, you can sleep easy in simple but functional rooms (some with forest views) and dig into some truly authentic Italian pastas and wines.

Pizzería Restaurante Lilliana (pizzas ₡2000-4500; 10:30am-10pm) This great spot for Italian fare is proud to offer more than a dozen different kinds of pizza, all of which are made from scratch. The lovely mountain views and old-world environs make this a pleasant place to spend an afternoon.

Getting There & Away

AIR

Alfa Romeo Aero Taxi (www.alfaromeoair.com) offers charter flights to San Vito from Puerto Jiménez and Golfito – prices vary according to the number of people and season. The airstrip is 1km east of town. Otherwise, the nearest airports with scheduled services are at Neily and Golfito.

BUS

The main **Tracopa bus terminal** (☎ 2773-3410) is at the northern end of the main street.

San Isidro ₡2100; three hours; departs 6:45am and 1:30pm.

San José ₡4200; seven hours; departs 5am, 7:30am, 10am and 3pm.

A local bus terminal at the northwest end of town runs buses to Neily and other destinations.

Neily ₡250; 30 minutes; departs 5:30am, 7am, 7:30am, 9am, 11am, noon, 2pm and 5pm.

Río Sereno ₡800; 1½ hours; departs 7am, 10am, 1pm and 4pm.

CAR

The drive north from Neily is a scenic one, with superb views of the lowlands dropping away as the road winds up the hillside. The paved road is steep, narrow and full of hairpin turns. You can also get to San Vito from San Isidro via the Valle de Coto Brus – an incredibly scenic and less-used route with fantastic views of the Cordillera de Talamanca to the north and the lower Fila Costeña to the south.

PARQUE INTERNACIONAL LA AMISTAD

This 4070-sq-km **international park** was established jointly in 1988 by Panama and Costa Rica – hence its Spanish name, La Amistad (Friendship). It is by far the largest protected area in Costa Rica, and stands as a testament to the possibilities of international cooperation in the name of environmental conservation. In 1990 La Amistad was declared a Unesco World Heritage Site, and later became part of the greater Mesoamerican Biological Corridor, which protects a great variety of endangered habitats.

Although most of the park's area is high up in the Talamanca, and remains virtually inaccessible, there is no shortage of hiking and camping opportunities available for intrepid travelers at lower altitudes. However, tourist infrastructure within the park is virtually nonexistent, which means that trekkers are limited to specific areas, and strongly encouraged (in some places required) to make use of local guides.

While tourists flock to Costa Rica's better-known parks in the hopes of having an eco-adventure, La Amistad is truly as rugged as it comes. Tackling this pristine yet potentially treacherous environment is no easy task, but La Amistad is brimming with possibilities for wilderness exploration – if you're afraid of growing old in an urban jungle, spend some time in this verdant one.

ORIENTATION

The backbone of this park is the Cordillera de Talamanca, which not only includes the peaks of the Chirripó massif, but also numerous other mountains higher than 3000m. At this altitude, the landscape is characterized by the shrubby, stunted vegetation of the *páramo*, while slightly lower altitudes yield impressive oaks and the thick vegetation of the cloud forest. The lowlands of the Talamanca valley are fertile rainforest – a canopy of cedar, cypress and oak trees, with a thick undergrowth of palms, ferns and epiphytes. This diversity of altitude and habitat creates unprecedented biological diversity, thus attracting the attention of ecologists and conservationists worldwide.

INFORMATION

Limited information is available at local **Minae offices** (San Isidro ☎ 2771-3155/4836/5116; San Vito ☎ 2773-3955; Calle 2 btwn Avs 4 & 6), but generally speaking, they're minimally helpful.

To make reservations to camp or to stay in a refuge, it's better to call directly to park headquarters at **Altamira** (☎ 2200-5355; park fee per person per day US$7). This is the best-developed area of the park, with a camping area, showers and drinking water, electric light and a lookout tower. A group of parataxonomists studying insects in this area has created a small display of butterflies and moths.

The thickly forested northern Caribbean slopes and southern Pacific slopes of the Talamanca are protected in the park, but it is only on the Pacific side that ranger stations are found. Besides the headquarters at Altamira, there are additional, little-used ranger stations at Potrero Grande, north of Paso Real; and Santa María de Pittier on the slopes of Cerro Pittier (2844m).

ACTIVITIES

Hiking

Behind Altamira station, **Los Gigantes del Bosque** is a short 3km circuit that is named for the 40m trees along the way. Signposts in Spanish

RESPONSIBLE TREKKING GUIDELINES

Consider the following tips to help preserve the ecology and beauty of La Amistad.

Rubbish

- Carry out all your rubbish. Don't overlook easily forgotten items, such as silver paper, orange peel, cigarette butts and plastic wrappers. Empty packaging should be stored in a dedicated rubbish bag. Make an effort to carry out rubbish left by others.
- Never bury your rubbish – digging disturbs soil and ground cover and encourages erosion. Buried rubbish will likely be dug up by animals, which may be injured or poisoned by it. It may also take years to decompose.
- Minimize waste by taking minimal packaging and no more food than you will need. Take reusable containers or stuff sacks.
- Sanitary napkins, tampons, condoms and toilet paper should be carried out despite the inconvenience. They burn and decompose poorly.

Human Waste Disposal

- Contamination of water sources by human feces can lead to the transmission of all sorts of nasties. Where there is a toilet, please use it. Where there is none, bury your waste. Dig a small hole 15cm deep and at least 100m from any watercourse. Cover the waste with soil and a rock. In snow, dig down to the soil.

Washing

- Don't use detergents or toothpaste in or near watercourses, even if they are biodegradable.
- For personal washing, use biodegradable soap and a water container (or even a lightweight, portable basin) at least 50m away from the watercourse. Disperse the waste water widely to allow the soil to filter it fully.
- Wash cooking utensils 50m from watercourses using a scourer or sand (not detergent).

Fires & Low-Impact Cooking

- Don't depend on open fires for cooking. The cutting of wood for fires in popular trekking areas can cause rapid deforestation. Cook on a lightweight kerosene, alcohol or Shellite provide simple explanations of some of the flora, and the trail is an easy means of seeing some ancient rainforest. It passes two lookout points, one on the edge of the primary forest, and the other overlooking the rural landscape outside the park. Note that this trail is marked, but it is not well maintained. Be prepared to climb over fallen branches and wade through high grass. More importantly, make sure you bring plenty of water and snacks and pay close attention to the markers. Normally the loop takes two hours, but it can be much longer if you lose the trail.

The longest trail (approximately 20km) – known as the **Valle del Silencio** – departs from the Estación Altamira, and winds its way through pristine and hilly primary forest before ending up at a camping area and refuge at the base of **Cerro Kamuk** (3549m). The walk takes anywhere from eight to 12 hours, provided you are in very good physical condition. It is spectacular, and traverses one of the most isolated areas in all of Costa Rica, but a local guide is required to make the journey.

Contact the association of guides, **Asoprola** (☎ 2743-1184) in Altamira to inquire about these arrangements. Rates vary depending on the size of your party and your intended course. Asoprola can also arrange food and lodging in the village of Altamira, just below the park headquarters – see p388, for more information.

Hardy adventurers can also hike to the summit of Cerro Kamuk from the village of

(white gas) stove and avoid those powered by disposable butane gas canisters. If you are trekking with a guide and porters, supply stoves for the whole team. In alpine areas, ensure that all members are outfitted with enough clothing so that fires are not a necessity for warmth.

- If you patronize local accommodations, select those places that do not use wood fires to heat water or cook food.
- Fires may be acceptable below the tree line in areas that get very few visitors. If you light a fire, make sure you use an existing fireplace. Don't surround fires with rocks. Use only dead, fallen wood. Remember the saying 'the bigger the fool, the bigger the fire.' Use minimal wood – just what you need to use for cooking. In huts, leave wood for the person that comes after you.
- Ensure that you fully extinguish a fire after use. Spread the embers and flood them with water.

Wildlife Conservation

- Do not feed the wildlife as this can lead to animals becoming dependent on handouts, to unbalanced populations and to diseases.
- Discourage the presence of wildlife by not leaving food scraps behind you. Place gear out of reach and tie packs to rafters or trees.
- Do not engage in or encourage hunting. It is illegal in all parks and reserves.
- Don't buy items made from endangered species.
- Don't attempt to exterminate animals in huts. In wild places, they are likely to be protected native animals.

Erosion

- Hillsides and mountain slopes, especially at high altitudes, are prone to erosion. Stick to existing trails and avoid short cuts.
- If a well-used trail passes through a mud patch, walk through the mud so as not to increase the size of the patch.
- Avoid damaging or removing the plant life that keeps topsoil in place.

Potrero Grande or Tres Colinas. This journey requires three days to ascend and two days to descend and – again – the services of a guide. Lodging is in tents and hikers must transport all of their own supplies and provisions.

Visiting Indigenous Groups

Besides the countless animal species, La Amistad is also home to five different indigenous reservations for the Cabécar and Bribrí groups. These tribes originally inhabited lands on the Caribbean coast (and many still do), but over the past century they have migrated west into the mountains and as far as the Pacific coast. It is possible to visit the Cabécar via the Reserva Biológica Dúrika (p378) and the Bribrí via ATEC (p482) in Puerto Viejo de Talamanca.

The reserves see few foreign visitors, and as a result the Cabécar and Bribrí tend to view tourists with equal parts respect and awe – at times you will be amazed at the hospitality of your hosts. Although they are tough peoples that have made a life for themselves in an unforgiving habitat, the Cabécar and Bribrí have smiles that could melt gold.

Of course, you should still make an effort to respect the sensibilities of your hosts. Although some men and women still walk around topless in the village, these are still fairly conservative societies, and it's recommended that you cover up as a sign of respect.

With regard to photography, most villagers will be happy to pose for a photo, but you should always ask before sticking your camera where it doesn't belong. Generally speaking, you will not be asked to pay for a photo, though it's best to ask your guide what is expected from you.

Tourism has a long way to develop in the region, which is one reason why a visit to a Cabécar or Bribrí village is so refreshing.

Wildlife-Watching

Although most of Parque Internacional La Amistad is inaccessible terrain high up in the Talamanca, the park is home to a recorded 90 mammal species and more than 400 bird species. The park has the nation's largest population of Baird's tapirs (see boxed text, p428), as well as giant anteaters, all six species of neotropical cats – jaguar, puma (mountain lion), margay, ocelot, oncilla (tiger cat) and jaguarundi – and many more-common mammals.

Bird species (49 unique) that have been sighted – more than half of the total in Costa Rica – include the majestic but extremely rare harpy eagle (see boxed text, opposite). In addition, the park protects 115 species of fish, 215 different reptiles and amphibians, as well as innumerable insect species.

SLEEPING & EATING

Besides the options listed here, see also the Reserva Biológica Dúrika (p378), which is contained within the borders of the park.

All of the ranger stations, including Altamira, have **camping facilities** (per person US$5). There are **basic hostels** (per person US$6) at Santa María de Pittier and at the base of Cerro Kamuk. These camps and hostels offer drinking water and toilets, and – in the case of Altamira – electricity. All food and supplies must be packed in and out.

Asoprola (☎ 2743-1184) can make arrangements for lodging in local homes in the village of Altamira for a negotiable fee. For an intimate look at the lives of people living on the fringes of the rainforest, there is no better way than to arrange a homestay.

West of Santa María de Pittier, in the village of El Carmen, **Soda y Cabinas La Amistad** (☎ 2743-1080; r per person US$8) has simple cabins with cold-water showers. The cabins are useful if you want one last night's rest before heading in or out of the park.

our pick **La Amistad Lodge** (☎ 2200-5037, in San José 2289-7667; www.laamistad.com; s/d US$100/175; P) is about 3km by poor dirt road from the village of Las Mellizas, and sits on 100 sq km of wilderness and organic farmland that constitutes Costa Rica's third-largest reserve. Since 1940, the congenial Montero family has operated this organic coffee farm, and has long worked to balance the needs of development with protecting the environment. The main lodge has tropical hardwood cabins with hot water and electricity provided by a low-impact hydroelectric plant. Four additional jungle camps have been built at different altitudes and habitats, allowing visitors to do a multiday trek around the area without leaving the comforts of a solid bed and good cooking. The staff will transport your belongings from one site to another and provide meals at each camp, which have full-sized walk-in tents, toilets and running water. The extensive network of trails (40km) is excellent for bird-watching and horseback riding. Guests are also invited

THE MOTHER OF ALL EAGLES

The harpy eagle, Central America's most striking raptor, is considered by many to be the most powerful bird of prey in the world. Unfortunately, opportunities to see the bird in the wild are limited as they are rare throughout most of their range and are hard to spot in the canopy even when they are present. Fortunately you're in La Amistad, which is home to a healthy nesting population. Although the chances of spotting one are still low, your chances are better here than anywhere else in Costa Rica.

Harpy eagles are enormous birds with a wingspan of 2m and a height of 1.5m – they are immediately recognizable. Adults tend to have white breasts with a broad black chest band and faint leg barring as well as gray upperparts. They also have piercing yellow eyes that can be seen from the forest floor, as well as powerful yellow talons and a hooked bill.

Anyone who has had the privilege to watch a harpy eagle hunt will tell you that it is simply awesome. For instance, a harpy seen with a large male howler writhing in her grip will shift her talons with a resounding 'pop' in order to crush the monkey's skull and carry it back to the nest unhindered. With massive claws as big as a grizzly bear's and legs as big as man's wrist, the harpy is an undeniable killing machine.

A female harpy can weigh up to 9kg, and such a large predator obviously has high energy requirements. As a result, harpies hunt all but the largest forest mammals, as well as other large birds and a whole slew of snakes and lizards. As an apex predator (like the jaguar), the harpy eagle probably never occurred in high densities, though deforestation has removed much of its prey base and its habitat. Furthermore, its habit of perching for long spells, even when people approach, makes it vulnerable to poachers.

Harpies rarely soar above the treetops and usually hunt by rapidly attacking prey through the canopy. Monkeys are plucked from the foliage, unwary birds are taken from tree limbs and snakes are swept off the forest floor. However, the majority of the harpy's diet consists of sloths, which are extremely vulnerable in the morning when they are basking in the sun. A harpy will sit nearby – sometimes for days – until it is hungry, and then snatch the sloth at its leisure.

to participate in the harvesting and processing (and drinking) of the homegrown coffee. Rates include three meals a day (and lots of fresh-brewed coffee), as well as the entry fee into the park. Buses to Las Mellizas can get you close to the lodge, but the owners will come get you if you call ahead.

GETTING THERE & AWAY

To reach Altamira, you can take any bus that runs between San Isidro and San Vito and get off in the town of Guácimo (often called Las Tablas). From Guácimo buses depart at noon and 5pm daily and travel the 16km to the town of El Carmen; if the road conditions permit, they continue 4km to the village of Altamira. From the village of Altamira, follow the Minae sign (near the church) leading to the steep 2km hike to the ranger station. To return to Guácimo, buses depart from Altamira at 5am and 2:30pm daily.

Vehicles with 4WD go all the way to Altamira station. In theory, it is possible to hire a 4WD taxi to bring you here, either from San Vito or from Buenos Aires. Keep in mind, however, that the roads are grueling, and bad conditions can make it pretty tough for anyone to get there. If you are driving here, inquire about road conditions prior to your departure.

Península de Osa & Golfo Dulce

Locals and tourists alike regard this remote enclave in the extreme southwestern corner of the country as the most picturesque, the most pristine and the most perfect spot in Costa Rica. Centered on Parque Nacional Corcovado, which contains one of the continent's last remaining patches of Pacific rainforest, and shaped by the serene waters of the wildlife-rich Golfo Dulce, the entire peninsula operates as a vast biological corridor. Not surprisingly, *National Geographic* famously labeled Corcovado as 'the most biologically intense place on earth.'

Although much of the rainforest in Costa Rica is protected by the national park system, no other region of the country can offer the breadth and extent of wildlife found in Osa. In Corcovado, it's sometimes possible to see all four native species of monkey swinging in the canopy overhead, while rare animals such as Baird's tapir can be spotted regularly. Indeed, the Osa peninsula is Costa Rica at its finest, and striking evidence that there is an intrinsic value and beauty of the rainforest that is worth saving.

Beyond Corcovado, the Osa peninsula captivates travelers with its abandoned wilderness beaches, world-class surf and endless opportunities for rugged exploration. In a country where adventure is all too often downgraded and packaged for tourist consumption, Osa is the real deal. Simply put, it's a place for travelers with youthful hearts, intrepid spirits and a yearning for something truly wild. If you've been growing old in a concrete jungle, spend some time in this verdant one – just be sure to bring a good pair of boots, a sturdy tent and some serious quantities of bug spray!

HIGHLIGHTS

- Testing your survival skills by trekking across **Parque Nacional Corcovado** (p421), the country's premier wilderness experience
- Exploring the dense jungles that fringe the crystalline waters of **Bahía Drake** (p395)
- Catching a ride on the world's longest left break at the undiscovered surfing paradise that is **Pavones** (p435)
- Watching the sun rise over the Golfo Dulce and set over the Pacific from the deserted beaches on **Cabo Matapalo** (p418)
- Diving off the coastlines of the far-flung **Isla del Cocos** (p438), the on-screen location of *Jurassic Park*

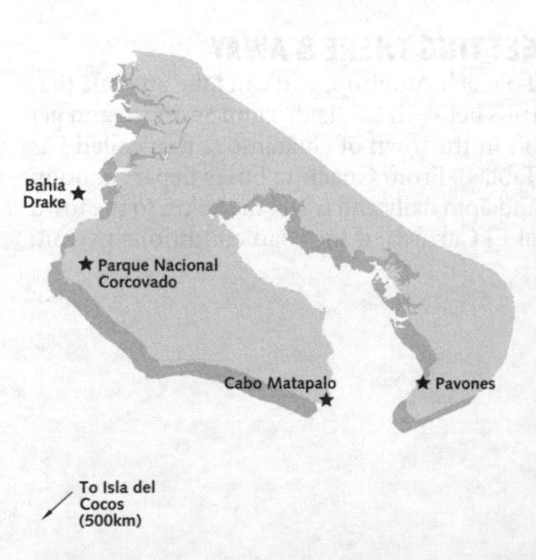

History

While the Guaymí were the earliest inhabitants of the Osa (for more information see boxed text, p413), the vast majority of the peninsula was never populated or developed by Ticos (Costa Ricans). In fact, because of the remoteness of the region, commercial logging was never a threat until the early 1960s.

Although this tumultuous decade saw the destruction of much of Costa Rica's remaining primary forests, Osa was largely spared. By 1975, however, international companies were greedily eyeing the peninsula's natural resources, namely its vast timber and gold reserves. Fortunately, these self-interested ambitions were halted when researchers petitioned President Daniel Oduber to establish a national park. Following the creation of Parque Nacional Corcovado, Oduber received the Albert Schweitzer Award from the Animal Welfare Institute for his much-applauded actions.

In recent years, the peninsula has attracted the attention of wealthy foreigners who want to trade in their workaday world for a piece of paradise. Prime real estate is being snatched up, and it's inevitable that things are set to change in Osa as they have in the rest of Costa Rica. However, there is hope that development will be more sustainable in this part of the country, particularly since there is a vested interest in keeping the peninsula green. For a local perspective on the changes in the region, see boxed text, p436.

Climate

The Osa peninsula has two drastically different seasons: the rainy season and the dry season. During the rainy season (mid-April to mid-December) the amount of precipitation is astounding, with most months boasting more than 500mm. Even in the dry season, better described as the 'less rainy season,' you can expect a good downfall every now and again, especially while trekking through Corcovado.

Parks & Reserves

As the country's premier ecotourism destination, the Península de Osa is home to a plethora of parks, reserves and wildlife refuges.

Humedal Nacional Térraba-Sierpe (p393) Approximately 330 sq km of protected mangrove wetlands that harbor numerous species of aquatic birds.

Parque Nacional Corcovado (p421) This national park, which occupies a great bulk of the peninsula, is Osa's shining crown jewel, and one of Costa Rica's last true wilderness areas.

Parque Nacional Isla del Cocos (p438) Visually stunning, utterly pristine and – by far – the country's most remote and difficult spot to access.

Parque Nacional Piedras Blancas (p432) Formerly known as Parque Nacional Esquinas, this contains one of the last remaining stretches of lowland rainforest in the country.

Refugio Nacional de Fauna Silvestre Golfito (p429) This tiny 28-sq-km reserve surrounding the town of Golfito is home to rare cycads or living plant fossils.

Reserva Biológica Isla del Caño (p402) A tiny marine and terrestrial park in Bahía Drake that is a popular destination for snorkelers, divers and biologists.

Reserva Forestal Golfo Dulce (p403) On the northern shore of Golfo Dulce, this is an important biological corridor for migrating wildlife.

Reserva Indígena Guaymí (see boxed text, p413) Home to the vast majority of the peninsula's indigenous communities, though most of the reserve is not open to tourism.

Dangers & Annoyances

The greatest hazard in Osa is the difficult environment, particularly in Parque Nacional Corcovado. Trails are generally well marked but it can be difficult going at times, especially if you're not accustomed to wilderness navigation. Also, the many large rivers that run through the park create their own hazards, especially if they're running swift in the rainy season. Any help at all, much less medical help, is very far away – if you get lost out here, you have a serious problem on your hands.

To minimize these risks, it's recommended that you explore Corcovado either as part of an organized tour or with the help of a local guide. Hiring a knowledgeable guide will also provide up-to-date information on potential hazards, and it provides safety through numbers.

Areas of Corcovado are also prime territory for the deadly fer-de-lance snake. The chance of getting bitten is remote, but you should be careful – always wear boots while walking in the forest.

Although they don't carry Lyme disease, ticks are also everywhere in Corcovado. In reality, they're nothing more than a nuisance, though you'd be wise to bring a good pair of tweezers and a few books of matches. If you're not traveling with a buddy, a pocket mirror will also help as these little buggers have a habit of turning up in some rather uncomfortable places.

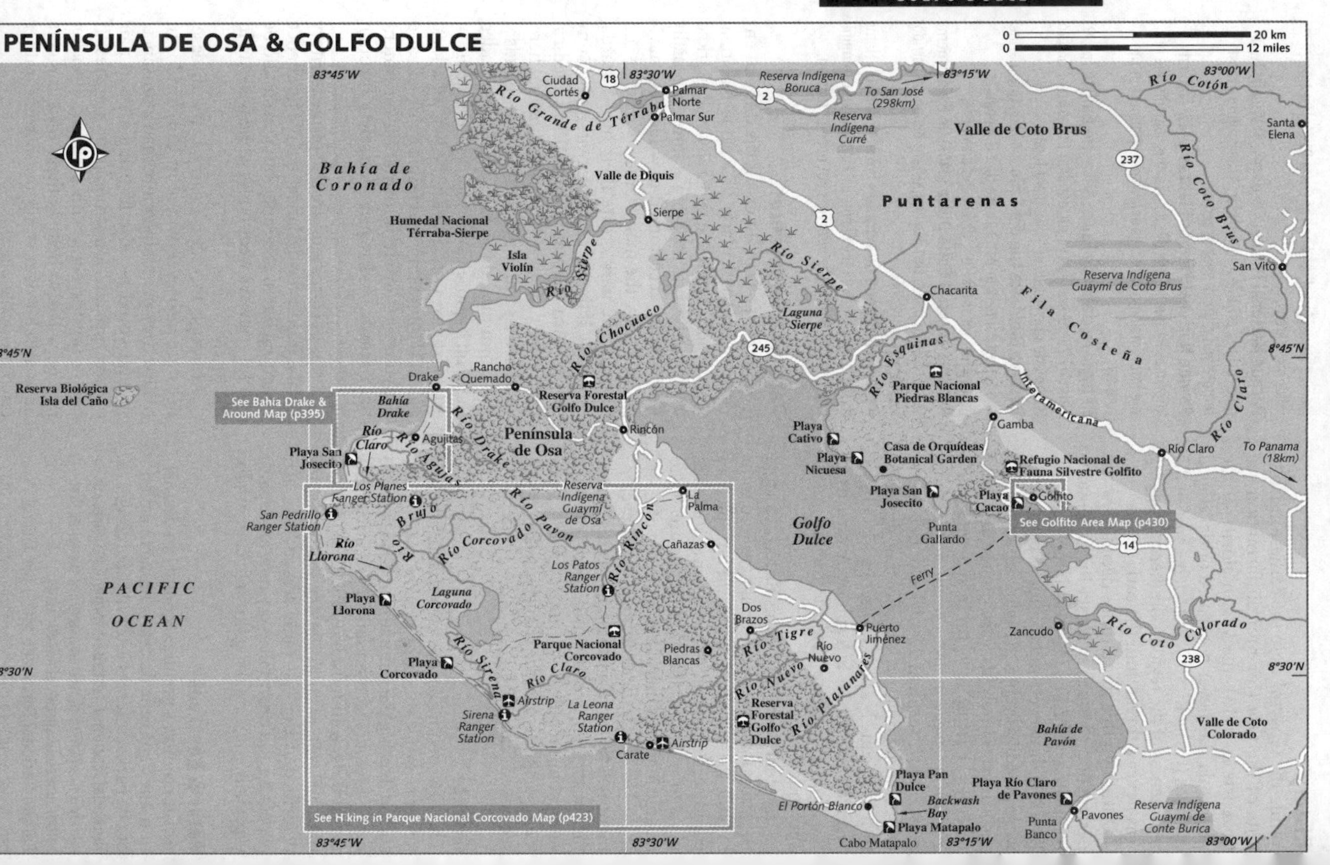
PENÍNSULA DE OSA & GOLFO DULCE
0 20 km
0 12 miles
83°45'W
83°30'W
83°15'W
83°00'W
8°45'N
8°30'N
Ciudad Cortés
Palmar Norte
Palmar Sur
Reserva Indígena Boruca
To San José (298km)
Reserva Indígena Curré
Valle de Coto Brus
Río Cotón
Santa Elena
Río Coto Brus
San Vito
Río Grande de Térraba
Bahía de Coronado
Valle de Diquis
Puntarenas
Humedal Nacional Térraba-Sierpe
Sierpe
Isla Violín
Río Sierpe
Chacarita
Reserva Indígena Guaymí de Coto Brus
Fila Costeña
Laguna Sierpe
Río Chocuaco
Río Esquinas
Reserva Biológica Isla del Caño
Drake
Rancho Quemado
Reserva Forestal Golfo Dulce
Parque Nacional Piedras Blancas
Interamericana
Río Claro
See Bahía Drake & Around Map (p395)
Bahía Drake
Río Claro
Agujitas
Río Drake
Península de Osa
Rincón
Gamba
Playa Cativo
Playa Nicuesa
Casa de Orquídeas Botanical Garden
Refugio Nacional de Fauna Silvestre Golfito
To Panama (18km)
Playa San Josecito
Río Agujas
Los Planes Ranger Station
Reserva Indígena Guaymí de Osa
La Palma
Playa San Josecito
Playa Cacao
Golfito
San Pedrillo Ranger Station
Río Brujo
Río Pavon
Río Rincón
Golfo Dulce
Punta Gallardo
See Golfito Area Map (p430)
Río Llorona
Río Corcovado
Cañazas
Los Patos Ranger Station
Ferry
PACIFIC OCEAN
Playa Llorona
Laguna Corcovado
Dos Brazos
Puerto Jiménez
Zancudo
Río Coto Colorado
Río Sirena
Parque Nacional Corcovado
Piedras Blancas
Río Tigre
Río Nuevo
Playa Corcovado
Río Claro
Río Platanares
Airstrip
La Leona Ranger Station
Reserva Forestal Golfo Dulce
Valle de Coto Colorado
Sirena Ranger Station
Carate
Bahía de Pavón
Playa Pan Dulce
Playa Río Claro de Pavones
Backwash Bay
El Portón Blanco
Pavones
Reserva Indígena Guaymí de Conte Burica
Playa Matapalo
Punta Banco
Cabo Matapalo
See Hiking in Parque Nacional Corcovado Map (p423)
18
2
237
245
14
238

Getting There & Around

The best option for exploring the peninsula in depth is to have your own private transportation. However, you will need to bring a spare tire (and plenty of patience): roads in Osa are extremely poor, as most of the peninsula is still off the grid.

Major towns in Osa such as Golfito and Puerto Jiménez are serviced by regular buses, though public transportation can get sporadic once you leave these major hubs. Unpaved roads can also make for a long and jarring bus ride, so it's probably best to bring a rolled-up fleece for your bottom and an mp3 player for your sanity.

If you're planning on hiking through Corcovado or visiting one of the lodges in Bahía Drake, another excellent option is to fly. Both **NatureAir** (www.natureair.com) and **Sansa** (www.sansa.com) service the Osa peninsula, namely Bahía Drake, Puerto Jiménez and Golfito. Prices vary according to season and availability, though you can expect to pay around US$100 to/from San José.

Alfa Romeo Aero Taxi (☎ 2735-5353; www.alfaromeoair.com) offers charter flights connecting Puerto Jiménez, Drake and Golfito to Carate and Sirena. Flights are best booked at the airport in person, and one-way fares are typically less than US$100.

TO CORCOVADO VIA BAHÍA DRAKE

The first of two principal overland routes to Parque Nacional Corcovado, the Bahía Drake route starts in the Valle de Diquis at the northern base of the Península de Osa, which is named for the indigenous group of this area. From here, the valley stretches west to the basin of the Río Grande de Térraba and south to Sierpe, from where the Río Sierpe flows out to Bahía Drake. The route also takes in the Humedal Nacional Térraba-Sierpe, a vast reserve that protects an amazing array of jungle swampland and overgrown mangroves.

SIERPE

This sleepy village on the Río Sierpe is the gateway to Bahía Drake, and if you've made a reservation with any of the jungle lodges further down the coast, you will be picked up here by boat. Beyond its function as a transit point, there is little reason to spend any more time here than it takes for your captain to arrive, though fortunately you won't have to if you time the connection right.

The **Centro Turístico Las Vegas** (🕑 6am-10pm), next to the boat dock, is a catch-all place for tourist information, distributing a wide selection of maps and brochures. It also offers internet access and serves a broad range of food to waiting passengers.

If you get stuck for the night, the only real accommodations option in town is **Hotel Oleaje Sereno** (☎ 2786-7580; www.hoteloleajesereno.com; s/d from US$45/70; P ❄). This surprisingly stylish little motel has a prime dockside location overlooking the Río Sierpe, and is home to pleasant rooms with wood floors, sturdy furniture and crisp, mismatched linens. The open-air restaurant is one of Sierpe's most welcoming, with linen tablecloths and lovely river views. If you make prior arrangements with the manager, you can safely and conveniently leave your car here when you continue on to Drake.

Getting There & Away

AIR

Scheduled flights and charters fly into Palmar Sur (see p380), 14km north of Sierpe.

BOAT

If you are heading to Bahía Drake, your lodge will make arrangements for the boat transfer. If for some reason things go awry, there is no shortage of water taxis milling about, though you will have to negotiate to get a fair price.

BUS & TAXI

Buses to Palmar Norte (₡300, 30 minutes) depart from in front of Pulpería Fenix at 5:30am, 8:30am, 10:30am, 12:30pm, 3:30pm and 6pm. A taxi to Palmar costs about ₡10,000.

HUMEDAL NACIONAL TÉRRABA-SIERPE

The Ríos Térraba and Sierpe begin on the southern slopes of the Talamanca mountains and flow toward the Pacific Ocean. Once near the sea, however, they form a network of channels and waterways that weave around the country's largest mangrove swamp. This river delta comprises the Humedal Nacional Térraba-Sierpe, which protects approximately 330 sq km of wetland and is home to red, black and tea mangrove species. The

FLOATING FOREST

As many as seven different species of mangrove, or *manglar,* thrive in Costa Rica. Comprising the vast majority of tropical coastline, mangroves play a crucial role in protecting it from erosion. Mangroves also serve as a refuge for countless species of animals, especially fish, crab, shrimp and mollusks, and as a sanctuary for roosting birds seeking protection from terrestrial predators.

Mangroves are unique among plants in that they have distinct methods for aeration (getting oxygen into the system) and desalination (getting rid of the salt that is absorbed with the water). Red mangroves, which are the most common species in Costa Rica, use their web of aboveground prop roots for aerating the plant's sap system. Other species, such as the black mangrove, have vertical roots that stick out above the mud, while buttonwood mangroves have elaborate buttresses.

The most amazing feature of the mangrove is its tolerance for salt, which enables the plant to thrive in brackish and saltwater habitats. Some species, such as the Pacific coast black mangrove, absorb the salinated water, then excrete the salt through their leaves and roots, leaving behind visible crystals. Other species filter the water as it is absorbed – the mangrove root system is so effective as a filter that the water from a cut root is drinkable!

Despite their ecological importance, mangrove habitats the world over are being increasingly threatened by expanding human habitats. Furthermore, mangrove wood is an easily exploitable source of fuel and tannin (used in processing leather), which has also hastened their destruction. Fortunately in the Humedal Nacional Térraba-Sierpe, this fragile yet vitally important ecosystem is receiving the respect and protection that it deserves.

reserve also protects a plethora of birdlife, especially waterbirds such as herons, egrets and cormorants.

Information

The Térraba-Sierpe reserve has no facilities for visitors, though the lodges listed in the following section can organize tours to help you explore the wetlands.

Sleeping

Veragua River House (☎ 2788-1460; www.hotelveragua.com/en; 3km north of Sierpe; r from US$55; Ⓟ) This wonderfully memorable bed and breakfast is centered on a Victorian-style river house that is hidden behind blooming hibiscus and shady fruit trees. Inside are inviting common areas decked out with antique furnishing and original artwork, and there is even a mock period library, a pool table and a discrete plunge pool. Guests stay in the four garden bungalows, which feature hand-painted tiles that are the work of the talented owner.

Estero Azul Lodge (☎ 2786-7422; esteroazul@hotmail.com; 2km north of Sierpe; r per person incl meals from US$90; Ⓟ) Named for the peaceful flowing river, the Estero Azul Lodge is set on several hectares of primary forest along the road to Palmar. Safari-style rooms have hardwood floors, screened porches and tile bathrooms, while delectable gourmet meals highlight fresh river fish and local seafood.

Sábalo Lodge (☎ 2770-1457; www.sabalolodge.com; r from US$95, 4-day package incl meals & tours US$545) Accepting less than 10 guests at a time in order to maximize the chance of getting up close and personal with wildlife, this highly personalized lodge receives much love from our readers. Guests are treated to a variety of activities, including guided hikes, horseback riding and ocean kayaking, and a portion of your accommodation fee helps to fund a local school. The lodge is only accessible by boat, and transportation from Sierpe is included in the package price.

Río Sierpe Lodge (☎ 2253-5203, 8384-5595; www.riosierpelodge.com; 3-/4-day package incl meals & tours per person from US$245/325) The Río Sierpe's namesake lodge is nestled in this remote spot near where the river meets the sea. Breezy rooms with hardwood floors overlook the waterways that wind through the Sierpe delta, while hiking trails radiate from the lodge into the surrounding primary forest. Transportation from Sierpe is included in the price as the lodge is only accessible by boat.

Getting There & Away

Estero Azul Lodge and Veragua River House are 2km and 3km, respectively, north of Sierpe along the road to Palmar, and can easily be reached by car. If you don't have private transportation, ring the lodges and arrange for a pick-up.

Río Sierpe Lodge and Sábalo Lodge are only accessible by boat; make prior arrangements to be picked up in Sierpe.

BAHÍA DRAKE

Parque Nacional Corcovado aside, the jungle-fringed crystalline waters of Bahía Drake are arguably Península de Osa at its best. As one of the peninsula's (and the country's) most isolated destinations, Bahía Drake is a veritable Lost World filled with tropical landscapes and abundant wildlife. In the rainforest canopy, howlers greet the rising sun with their haunting bellows, while pairs of macaws soar between the treetops, filling the air with their cacophonous squawking. Offshore in the bay itself, schools and pods of migrating dolphins flit through turquoise waters.

Of course, one of the reasons why Bahía Drake is brimming with wildlife is that it remains largely cut off from the rest of the country. With little infrastructure beyond dirt roads and the occasional airstrip, most of the area remains off the grid. However, Bahía Drake is home to a number of stunning wilderness lodges, which all serve as ideal bases for exploring this veritable ecological gem. And of course, if you're planning on visiting Sirena ranger station in Corcovado (p422), you can trek south along the coastline and enter the park at San Pedrillo ranger station.

History

The bay is named for Sir Francis Drake himself, who visited this area in March 1579, during his circumnavigation in the *Golden Hind*. History has it that he stopped on the nearby Isla del Caño, but locals speculate that he probably landed on the continent as well. A monument at Punta Agujitas, located on the grounds of the Drake Bay Wilderness Resort (see p399), states as much.

Orientation

The shores of Bahía Drake are home to two settlements: Agujitas, a tiny town of 300 residents spread out along the southern shore of the bay, and Drake, a few kilometers to the north, which is little more than a few houses alongside the airstrip.

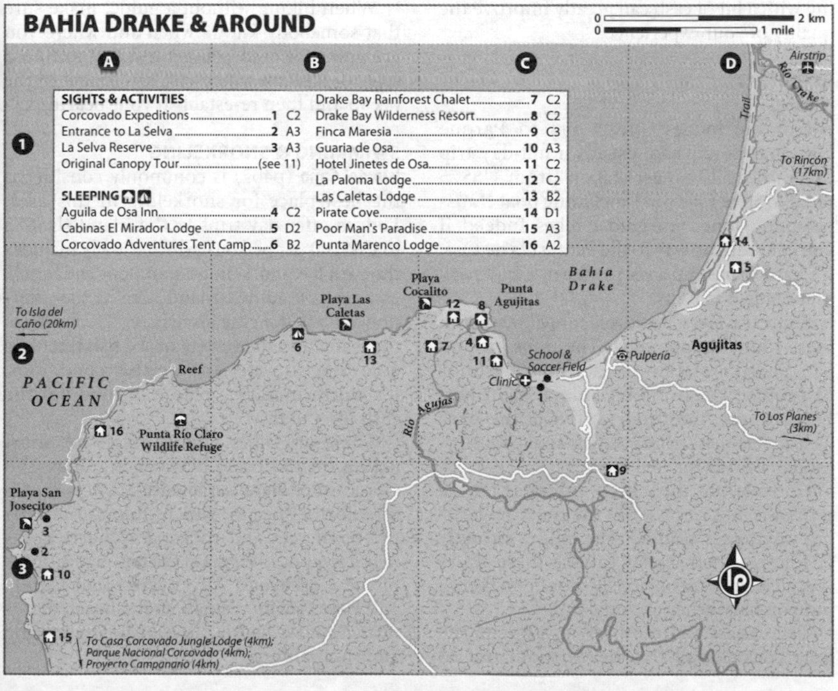

Agujitas is a one-road town (and not a very good road at that). It comes south from Rincón and past the airstrip in Drake. At the T, the right branch dead-ends at the water, where the *pulpería* (grocery store), clinic and school constitute the heart of Agujitas; the left branch heads out of town southeast to Los Planes. From the eastern end of Agujitas, a path follows the shoreline out of town. A swinging, swaying pedestrian bridge crosses the Río Agujitas to Punta Agujitas. From here, the trail picks up and continues south along the coast, all the way to Parque Nacional Corcovado.

The only way to get around the area is by boat or by foot. Fortunately, both forms of transportation are also recreation, as sightings of macaws, monkeys and other wildlife are practically guaranteed

Information

It's not easy to visit Bahía Drake if you're a backpacker since only a few shoestring options exist in Agujitas. Also, supplies, food and just about everything else are shipped in, which is reflected in local prices. However, Bahía Drake is one destination where parting with a bit of cash can greatly improve the quality of your experience.

Activities

HIKING

All of the lodges offer tours to Parque Nacional Corcovado, usually a full-day trip to San Pedrillo ranger station (from US$75 to US$150 per person), including boat transportation, lunch and guided hikes. Indeed, if you came all the way to the Península de Osa, it's hard to pass up a visit to the national park that made it famous.

Some travelers, however, come away from these tours disappointed. The trails around San Pedrillo station attract many groups of people, which inhibit animal sightings. Furthermore, most tours arrive at the park well after sunrise, when activity in the rainforest has already quieted down.

Considering their hefty price tag, these tours are not necessarily the most rewarding way to see wildlife. The lodges strongly encourage their guests to take these tours (because they are obviously money-makers), but you have other options.

The easiest and most obvious one is the long coastal trail that heads south out of Agujitas and continues about 10km to the border of the national park. Indeed, a determined hiker could make it all the way to San Pedrillo ranger station on foot in three to four hours (make sure you reserve a spot at the ranger station if you intend to spend the night). From here, you can follow the coastal route south to wildlife-rich Sirena ranger station, which is undoubtedly the highlight of Corcovado.

Of course, if you don't have the time (or the inclination) for this challenging trek, you can take comfort in the fact that most of the same species that inhabit the park are frequently spotted in the surrounding buffer zone. In fact, macaws, monkeys and other exotic species travel this trail as often as humans!

In addition to Corcovado, other popular day trips include nearby **Playa San Josecito** (p433), a stunningly remote beach where you can slow down and soak up the beauty of the bay. If you want to head inland, you can also explore the **Punta Río Claro Wildlife Refuge** (also called the Marenco Rainforest Reserve; p401), which can be accessed from the Río Claro trail or from Playa San Josecito.

When hiking without a guide, make sure that somebody knows when and where you are going. Should you get lost, try to find a river or stream, which you can follow to the ocean and then re-establish your bearings.

SWIMMING & SNORKELING

Isla del Caño (p402) is commonly considered the best place for snorkeling in this area. Lodges offer day trips to the island (US$75 to US$100 per person), which usually includes the park fee, snorkeling equipment and lunch, as well as a guided island hike in the afternoon. As is the case anywhere, the clarity of the water and the variety of the fish fluctuate according to water and weather conditions: it's worth inquiring before dishing out the cash for a tour.

There are other opportunities for snorkeling on the coast between Agujitas and Corcovado. **Playa San Josecito** attracts scores of colorful species, which hide out among the coral reef and rocks. Another recommended spot is **Playa Las Caletas**, just in front of the Corcovado Adventures Tent Camp, and **Playa Cocalito**, a small, pretty beach that is near Agujitas and is pleasant for swimming and sunbathing.

SCUBA DIVING

About 20km west of Agujitas, **Isla del Caño** is one of Costa Rica's top spots for diving, with attractions including intricate rock and coral formations and an amazing array of underwater life, teeming with colorful reef fish and incredible coral formations. Divers report that the schools of fish swimming overhead are often so dense that they block the sunlight from filtering down.

While the bay is rich with dive sites, a local highlight is undoubtedly the **Bajo del Diablo** (Devil's Rock), an astonishing formation of submerged mountains that attracts an incredible variety of fish species, including jack, snapper, barracuda, puffer, parrotfish, moray eel and shark.

A two-tank dive runs from US$100 to US$150 depending on the spot, or you can do an open-water course for US$325 to US$400. Most of the upscale lodges in the area either have onsite dive centers or can arrange trips and courses through a neighboring lodge.

KAYAKING & CANOEING

A fantastic way to explore the region's biodiversity is to paddle through it. The idyllic **Río Agujitas** attracts a huge variety of birdlife and lots of scaly reptiles. The river conveniently empties out into the bay, which is surrounded by hidden coves and sandy beaches ideal for exploring in a sea kayak. Paddling at high tide is recommended because it allows you to explore more territory. Most accommodations in the area have kayaks and canoes for rent for a small fee.

HORSEBACK RIDING

The **coastal trail** running between Agujitas and Corcovado is perfect for horseback riding, especially if you relish the idea of galloping wildly across deserted beaches while the waves crash below you. **Los Planes** is another popular destination for horseback riders, with ample opportunities for wildlife-watching along the way. Again, most of the upscale lodges in the area offer guided rides (from US$75), or can arrange trips through a neighboring lodge.

SPORTFISHING

Bahía Drake claims more than 40 fishing records, including sailfish, marlin, yellowfin tuna, wahoo, cubera snapper, mackerel and roosterfish. Fishing is excellent year-round, although the catch may vary according to the season. The peak season for tuna and marlin is from August to December. Sailfish are caught year-round, but experience a slow-down in May and June. Dorado and wahoo peak between May and August. Other species are abundant year-round, so you are virtually assured to reel in something. Many lodges can arrange fishing excursions, but you need to be prepared to pay heavily – half-/full-day excursions cost around US$600/1000.

DOLPHIN- & WHALE-WATCHING

As of 2006, swimming with dolphins and whales is illegal in Costa Rica. These measures are a result of an increase in tourist activity, often led by inexperienced guides who did not respect the best interests of these amazing creatures. However, dolphin- and whale-watching tours still provide opportunities to get up close and personal with these sea creatures – but only from the comfort and safety of the boat.

Bahía Drake is rife with marine life, including more than 25 species of dolphin and whale that pass through on their migrations throughout the year. This area is uniquely suited for whale watching: humpback whales come from both the northern and the southern hemispheres to calve, resulting in the longest humpback whale season in the world. Humpbacks can be spotted in Bahía Drake year-round (except May), but the best months to see whales are late July through early November.

Several of the lodges are involved with programs that protect and preserve marine life in Bahía Drake, as well as programs that offer tourists a chance for a close encounter. Tours generally cost about US$100 per person.

The program at Drake Bay Wilderness Resort (see p399) is highly recommended. Marine biologist Shawn Larkin has an infectious enthusiasm about marine mammals. He spends his time researching and filming dolphins and whales for his educational organization, the **Costa Cetacea Research Institute** (www.costacetacea.com).

CANOPY TOURS

Original Canopy Tour (☎ 8371-1598; admission US$60; ⏰ 8am-4pm) at Hotel Jinetes de Osa has nine platforms, six cables and one 20m-observation deck from where you can get a new perspective on the rainforest.

JUNGLE NIGHTS

As night falls in the jungle, an amazing transformation takes place. That is, all the birds that were squawking all day long are suddenly quiet. And a whole new host of noises fills the air. The sounds of crickets, cicadas and other tropical bugs, awakening at dusk, are utterly overwhelming: the buzz emanates from all sides, vibrating throughout the forest. This is also when the aptly named vesper bats come out, seemingly flying in circles around your head.

As the darkness engulfs you, your other senses are heightened. That is the only way to explain the amazing otherworldly quality of the exotic night sounds, like the mournful coo of the pauraque calling his mate, or the scream of fighting coatis in the distance.

Most of the night tours in Bahía Drake focus on finding nocturnal critters such as river shrimps, frogs, spiders and insects. But many mammals are nocturnal: night tours around Sirena station in Corcovado (p422) are the best way to spot Baird's tapir, kinkajou and skunk, as well as American crocodile. It doesn't happen often, but if you're going to see a feline it will likely be at night.

Tours

Corcovado Expeditions (☎ 8818-9962; www.corcovadoexpeditions.net) Offers competitively priced tours to Corcovado and Isla del Caño, as well as a wide variety of specialty hikes including unique excursions to look for rare tropical birds and poison-dart frogs.

our pick Night Tour (☎ 8382-1619; www.thenighttour.com; tours US$35; 7:45-10pm) Tracie the 'Bug Lady' has created quite a name for herself with this fascinating nighttime walk in the jungle. Tracie is a walking encyclopedia on bug facts, and not just the boring scientific detail – one of her fields of research is the military use of insects! Participants use night-vision scopes as an added bonus. Make reservations well in advance.

Bahía Drake for Children

The remote location and difficult access are two major hurdles in planning a family visit to Bahía Drake, particularly if your children are very young. However, assuming they're a bit older, and they have a healthy sense of adventure, this is one corner of Costa Rica where their imagination can really run wild. With so much virgin nature at their disposal, kids can be kids as they swim, snorkel, hike, ride and boat their way through the great outdoors. Accommodations are also varied, allowing you to either spoil your family with eco-luxury, or win them over with rustic charm.

Sleeping & Eating

This area is off the grid, so many places do not have electricity (pack a flashlight) or hot water. Reservations are recommended in the dry season (mid-November to the end of April).

While budget and midrange options are available, accommodations in Bahía Drake are heavily skewed toward the top end. But, you can expect tremendous quality and service for your dollars, especially as you ascend the price ladder.

High-season rates are quoted; prices are per person, including three meals, unless otherwise stated. Note that three daily meals are also included in the price at all midrange and top-end lodges because stand-alone eating options are virtually nonexistent in this part of the peninsula.

At budget places, affordably priced food is available onsite at the restaurant/cantina. Most hotels and lodges also have small shops that sell snacks and drinks. If you're planning on hiking, be sure to stock up on lots of fresh water as well as your favorite form of trail mix – once you're out on the trail, options are decidedly limited.

All of the midrange and top-end accommodations listed in this section provide transportation (sometimes free, sometimes not) from either Agujitas or the airstrip in Drake with prior arrangements.

For other accommodations, check out the stretch of coastline from Bahía Drake to Corcovado (p401).

BUDGET & MIDRANGE

our pick Finca Maresia (☎ 8832-6730; www.fincamaresia.com; dm US$18, s/d US$25/36, standard/superior bungalow US$55/75) After traveling the world for more than 20 years, the owners of this absolute gem of a hotel decided to settle down in their own veritable slice of paradise. Here amid a large *finca* (farm) that stretches across a series of hills, Finca Maresia beckons to shoestringers and budget travelers alike by offering a combination of low prices, high value and good design sense. All seven rooms overlook lush environs, and play a near-continuous audio track of jungle sounds. Beyond the show-stopping natural setting, the internationalism of the owners is evident as you walk from room to room and view the transition from modernist glass walls to Japanese-style sliding rice-paper doors.

Cabinas El Mirador Lodge (☎ 8836-9415; www.miradordrakebay.com; r US$45; P) High on a hill at the northern end of Agujitas, El Mirador (Lookout Point) lives up to its name, offering spectacular views of the bay from its eight cozy cabins – catch the sunset from the balcony, or climb to the lookout that perches above. The hospitable Vargas family ensures all guests receive a warm welcome, as well as three square meals a day of hearty, home-cooked Costa Rican fare.

Hotel Jinetes de Osa (☎ 8371-1598, 2236-5637, in USA 800-317-0333; www.costaricadiving.com; s/d from US$66/110;) The reasonably priced Jinetes de Osa boasts a choice bayside location that is literally a few steps from the ocean – you can sip your morning coffee from your hotel room while staring out across the bay. Jinetes also has a canopy tour, as well as one of the peninsula's top PADI dive facilities, which means that guests have plenty of adrenaline-soaked activities on the roster. In fact, true diving aficionados would balk at staying elsewhere, especially since discount dive packages with full equipment rental are always available.

TOP END

Pirate Cove (☎ 2234-6154; www.piratecovecostarica.com; r per person from US$90;) Breezy, tent-like bungalows and spacious hardwood cabins both offer an element of laid-back luxury at the appropriately named Pirate Cove (Sir Francis Drake wasn't exactly the most honorable of captains!). With private terraces that are strung up with hammocks, most guests seem content to just swing the day away, though there are 2km of deserted coastline in front of the property to explore. There is also a very reputable dive center on the premises should you feel the need to move beyond the beach.

Aguila de Osa Inn (☎ 2296-2190; www.aguiladeosa.com; s/d 2-night package US$623/1048) On the east side of the Río Agujitas, this swanky lodge consists of roomy quarters with shining wood floors, cathedral ceilings and private decks overlooking the ocean. The vast centerpiece of the lodge, however, is the comfortable yet elegant open-air *rancho* (small house-like building), which serves up signature cocktails and innovative *bocas* (savory bar snacks) throughout the day and into the evening. Diving and sportfishing charters are available to guests, as are significant discounts if you extend your stay beyond two nights.

Drake Bay Wilderness Resort (☎ 2770-8012; www.drakebay.com; 4-day package per person from US$770;) Sitting pretty on Punta Agujitas, this relaxed resort occupies the optimal piece of real estate in all of Bahía Drake. Naturalists will be won over by the lovely landscaping, from flowering trees to the ocean-fed pool, while history buffs will appreciate the memorial to Drake's landing. Accommodations are in comfortable cabins, which have mural-painted walls and private patios with ocean views, while family-style meals feature ingredients from your congenial host's organic farm.

La Paloma Lodge (☎ 2239-7502; www.lapalomalodge.com; 3-/4-/5-day package from US$1100/1245/1390;) Perched on a lush hillside, this exquisite lodge provides guests with an incredible panorama of ocean and forest, all from the comfort of the sumptuous, stylish quarters. Rooms have shiny hardwood floors and queen-sized orthopedic beds, draped in mosquito netting, while shoulder-high walls in all the bathrooms offer rainforest views while you bathe. Each room has a large balcony (with hammock, of course) that catches the cool breeze off the ocean.

our pick **Drake Bay Rainforest Chalet** (☎ 8382-1619; www.drakebayholiday.com; 3-/4-/5-/6-/7-day package from US$1150/1275/1400/1525/1650) Set on 18 hectares of pristine rainforest, this jungle getaway is a remote, romantic adventure. Huge French windows provide a panoramic view of the surrounding jungle, enjoyed from almost every room in the house. Sleeping quarters have a king-sized bed with giant mosquito net, flanked by a luxurious tile bathroom with a sunken shower and a decadent two-person hot tub. In an innovative twist on luxury, the Moroccan-themed kitchen is fully stocked for self-catering, though chef service is available for the culinary impaired.

Getting There & Away

AIR

Departing from San José, **NatureAir** (www.natureair.com) and **Sansa** (www.sansa.com) have daily flights to the Drake airstrip, which is 2km north of Agujitas. Prices vary according to season and availability, though you can expect to pay around US$100 to/from San José.

Alfa Romeo Aero Taxi (☎ 2735-5353; www.alfaromeoair.com) offers charter flights connecting Drake to Puerto Jiménez, Golfito, Carate and Sirena. Flights are best booked at the airport in person, and one-way fares are typically less than US$100.

Most lodges provide transportation to/from the airport, which involves a jeep or a boat or both, but advanced reservation is necessary.

BOAT

All of the hotels offer boat transfers between Sierpe and Bahía Drake with prior arrangements. The trip to Drake is scenic and at times exhilarating. Boats travel along the river through the rainforest and the mangrove estuary. Captains then pilot boats through tidal currents and surf the river mouth into the ocean. Most hotels in Drake have beach landings, so wear the appropriate footwear.

If you have not made advance arrangements with your lodge for a pick-up, you can always grab a private water taxi in Sierpe for a negotiable price.

BUS & CAR

A rough dirt road links Agujitas to Rincón, from where you can head south to Puerto Jiménez or north to the Interamericana. A 4WD is recommended for this route, especially from June to November, as there are several river crossings. The most hazardous crossing is the Río Drake, and locals fish many a water-logged tourist vehicle out of the river – see boxed text, p548 for some tips on not destroying your rental.

Once in Agujitas, you will likely have to abandon your car as most places are accessible only by boat or by foot. As theft or vandalism is always a very real possibility in Costa Rica, you should park your car in a secure place, and pay someone to watch it for a few days. There are several small *pulperías* where the management would be happy to watch over your 4WD for a nice tip.

If you are hiking through Parque Nacional Corcovado, but you want to avoid the arduous San Pedrillo trail, you can hire a 4WD vehicle to La Palma (US$50 to US$75) and start the hike there. In theory, a bus also goes to La Palma, departing Drake at 4am during the dry season only, but it's best to inquire locally as it's not reliable.

HIKING

From Bahía Drake, it's a four- to six-hour hike along the beachside trail to San Pedrillo ranger station at the north end of Corcovado. If you are heading into the park, make sure you have reservations to camp at the ranger stations – for more information, see our full coverage of Parque Nacional Corcovado, p421.

BAHÍA DRAKE TO CORCOVADO

This craggy stretch of coastline is home to sandy inlets that disappear at high tide, leaving only the rocky outposts and luxuriant rainforest. Virtually uninhabited and undeveloped beyond a few tourist lodges, the setting here is magnificent and wild. If you're looking to spend a bit more time along the shores of Bahía Drake before penetrating the depths of

POISON DARTS & HARMLESS ROCKETS

Traversed by many streams and rivers, Corcovado is a hot spot for exquisitely beautiful poison-dart frogs. Two species here, the granular poison-dart frog and the Golfo Dulce poison-dart frog, are Costa Rican endemics – indeed, the latter only occurs in and around Corcovado. A search of the leaf litter near Sirena ranger station readily turns up both species, as well as the more widespread green and black poison-dart frog.

You might also find some other members of the family that have one important difference: they're not poisonous! Called rocket frogs because of their habit of launching themselves into streams when disturbed, they are essentially poison-dart frogs without the poisonous punch.

Why the difference? It probably arises from their diets. Poison-dart frogs have a diet dominated by ants, which are very rich in alkaloids, and are thought to give rise to their very formidable defenses. Rocket frogs also eat ants, but in far lower quantities, and rely instead on their astounding leaps to escape predation. They also lack the dazzling warning colors of their toxic cousins, but it's safer (and kinder to the frog) to observe, rather than handle, any species you might encounter.

Parque Nacional Corcovado, consider a night or two in some of the country's most remote accommodations.

Orientation & Information

A public trail follows the coastline for the entire spectacular stretch, and it's conducive to spotting wonderful wildlife. Among the multitude of bird species, you're likely to spot (and hear) squawking scarlet macaw, often traveling in pairs, and the hooting chestnut-mandible toucan. White-faced capuchin and howler monkeys inhabit the treetops, while eagle-eyed hikers might also spot a sloth or a kinkajou.

The only way to get around the area is by boat or by foot, which means that travelers are more or less dependent on their lodges.

Sights & Activities

Scenic little inlets punctuate this entire route, each with a wild, windswept beach. Just west of Punta Agujitas, a short detour off the main trail leads to the picturesque **Playa Cocalito**, a secluded cove perfect for sunning, swimming and body surfing. With no lodges in the immediate vicinity, it's often deserted. **Playa Las Caletas**, in front of the Corcovado Adventures Tent Camp, is excellent for snorkeling.

Further south, the Río Claro empties out into the ocean. Water can be waist deep or higher, and the current swift, so take care when wading across. This is also the start of the Río Claro trail, which leads inland into the 400-hectare **Punta Río Claro Wildlife Refuge** (formerly known as the Marenco Rainforest Reserve) and passes a picturesque waterfall along the way. Be aware that there are two rivers known as the Río Claro: one is located near Bahía Drake, while the other is inside Corcovado near Sirena station.

South of Río Claro, the **Playa San Josecito** is the longest stretch of white-sand beach on this side of the Península de Osa. It is popular with swimmers, snorkelers and sunbathers, though you'll rarely find it crowded.

From here you can access another private reserve, **La Selva**. A short, steep climb leads from the beach to a lookout point, offering a spectacular view over the treetops and out to the ocean. A network of trails continues inland, and eventually connects La Selva to the Río Claro reserve. Be advised that La Selva does not have any facilities: the trails are not labeled; there is no water or maps; you'll likely meet nobody along the way. If you choose to continue past the lookout point, make sure you have food, water and a compass.

The border of Parque Nacional Corcovado is about 5km south of here (it takes three to four hours to hike the entire distance from Agujitas to Corcovado). The trail is more overgrown as it gets closer to the park, but it's a well-traveled route.

Sleeping & Eating

Reservations are recommended in the dry season (mid-November to the end of April). High-season rates are quoted; prices are per person, including three meals, unless otherwise stated. Many places in this area don't have electricity (pack a flashlight) or hot water. Stand-alone eating options are virtually nonexistent in this part of the peninsula.

With prior arrangements, all of the accommodations listed in this section provide transportation (free or for a charge) from either Agujitas or the airstrip in Drake.

Las Caletas Lodge (☎ 8381-4052, 8326-1460; www.caletas.co.cr; r per person from US$70; 💻 📶 🚸) This adorable little hotel is set on the picturesque beach of the same name and consists of five cozy wooden cabins that are awash with sweeping views. The Swiss-Tico owners are warm hosts who are passionate about environmental sustainability, which means you can rest easy knowing that solar and hydroelectric power provides electricity around the clock.

Corcovado Adventures Tent Camp (☎ 8384-1679; www.corcovado.com; r per person from US$80, 3-/4-day package per person US$400/535; 🚸) Less than an hour's walk from Drake brings you to this fun, family-run spot. It's like camping, but comfy: spacious, walk-in tents are set up on covered platforms and fully equipped with sturdy wood furniture. Twenty hectares of rainforest offer plenty of opportunity for exploration, and the beachfront setting is excellent for water sports.

Poor Man's Paradise (☎ 2771-4582; www.mypoormansparadise.com; 3-day package per person from US$315) Sportfishing can be an expensive prospect, but local fisherman Pincho Amaya aims to make it more accessible. Here at the aptly named Poor Man's Paradise, guests can take advantage of Bahía Drake's most reasonably priced fishing excursions. Accommodations are in large canvas tents, which are elevated on sturdy wooden platforms to protect you from the cold, wet ground. You can also choose rooms in the rustic ranch houses and cabins, which have private en suite facilities.

Punta Marenco Lodge (☎ 2234-1308, 2234-1227; www.puntamarenco.com; 3-day package per person US$339;) This intimate family-run lodge shares access to the Punta Río Claro Wildlife Refuge, providing excellent opportunities for independent hiking and wildlife-watching. Accommodations are in thatch-roof *cabañas* (cabins) in the style of the Brunka indigenous peoples and have private terraces, ocean views and 360 degrees of screened windows, which affords a wonderful cross-breeze.

Guaria de Osa (☎ 2235-4313, in USA 510-235-4313; www.guariadeosa.com; 3-day package per person US$395) Cultivating a new-age ambience, this Asian-style retreat center offers yoga, tai chi and all kinds of massage, along with the more typical rainforest activities. The lovely grounds include an ethnobotanical garden, which features exotic local species used for medicinal and other purposes. The architecture of this place is unique: the centerpiece is the Lapa Lapa Lounge, a spacious multistory pagoda, built entirely from reclaimed hardwood.

Proyecto Campanario (☎ 2258-5778; www.campanario.org; 4-day package per person US$436) Run by a former Peace Corps volunteer, this biological reserve is more of an education center than a tourist facility, as evidenced by the dormitory, library and field station. Behind the main facility, five spacious platform tents with 'garden' bathrooms offer a bit more privacy and comfort. Ecology courses and conservation camps are scheduled throughout the year, but individuals are also invited to take advantage of the facilities. The whole place is set on 150 hectares of tropical rainforest, which provides countless opportunities for exploration and wildlife observation.

our pick Casa Corcovado Jungle Lodge (☎ 2256-3181, in USA 888-896-6097; www.casacorcovado.com, 3-day package per person from US$955;) A spine-tingling boat ride takes you to this luxurious lodge on 175 hectares of rainforest bordering the national park. Each bungalow is tucked away in its own private tropical garden, and artistic details including antique Mexican tiles and handmade stained-glass windows make the Casa Corcovado one of this area's classiest accommodation options. Guests can also stretch their legs at any time on the lodge's extensive network of hiking rails, which winds through the forest and passes by a number of refreshing watering holes. On site, the Margarita Sunset Bar lives up to its name, serving up 25 different 'ritas and great sunset views over the Pacific. Discounts are available for longer stays.

Getting There & Away

BOAT

All of the hotels offer boat transfers between Sierpe and Bahía Drake with prior arrangements. If you haven't made advance arrangements with your lodge for a pick-up, grab a private water taxi in Sierpe for a negotiable price.

HIKING

From Bahía Drake, it's a four- to six-hour hike along the beachside trail to San Pedrillo ranger station at the north end of Corcovado. If you're heading into the park, make sure you have reservations to camp at the ranger stations – for more information, see p421.

RESERVA BIOLÓGICA ISLA DEL CAÑO

The centerpiece of this biological reserve is a 326-hectare island that is the tip of numerous underwater rock formations. Along the rocky coastline, towering peaks soar as high as 70m, which provide a dramatic setting for anyone who loves secluded nature.

The submarine rock formations are among the island's main attractions, drawing divers to explore the underwater architecture. Snorkelers can investigate the coral and rock formations along the beach right in front of the ranger station. The water is much clearer here than along the mainland coast, though rough seas can cloud visibility. Fifteen different species of coral have been recorded, as well as threatened animal species that include the Panulirus lobster and the giant conch. The sheer numbers of fish attract dolphins and whales, which are frequently spotted swimming in outer waters. Hammerhead sharks, manta rays and sea turtles also inhabit these waters.

A steep but well-maintained trail leads inland from the ranger station. Once the trail plateaus, it is relatively flat, winding through evergreen forest to a lookout point at about 110m above sea level. These trees are primarily milk trees (also called 'cow trees' after the drinkable white latex they exude), believed to be the remains of an orchard planted by pre-Columbian indigenous

A BEGINNER'S GUIDE TO PARQUE NACIONAL CORCOVADO

If you're confused about the best way to access Parque Nacional Corcovado, don't be. With a little prior planning, and a good idea as to the kind of trip you're interested in, you'll find yourself trekking through the rainforest, fording rivers and (hopefully!) spotting tapirs in no time at all!

For starters, it helps to know that there are two major centers where tourists tend to organize their expeditions: Bahía Drake (p398) and Puerto Jiménez (p415). Both of these areas are home to hotels, lodges and tour operators where you can arrange your onward plans, hire guides and purchase supplies.

Each area has its own unique flair and tourist draws, though for the most part travelers choose Puerto Jiménez since it's closer to the famed Sirena ranger station, where most of the wildlife action happens. However, staying in a remote jungle lodge along the coastline of Bahía Drake is truly one of the highlights of Osa.

If you start the trek from Bahía Drake, your entry into the park will most likely be at San Pedrillo ranger station, from where you easily trek to either Sirena or the more remote Los Planes ranger station. If you start the trek from Puerto Jiménez, your entry into the park will most likely be at either La Leona or Los Patos ranger station, both of which are good bases for accessing Sirena.

A third option for accessing the park is to fly direct to the airstrips in either Carate or Sirena. See p428 for details on how to fly from Puerto Jiménez or Drake to Carate or Sirena. This option is certainly more expensive, but it can be a huge time-saver if you're dealing with a time-crunched itinerary.

Be advised that if you're planning on sleeping in Corcovado, you must register in advance with the park headquarters in Puerto Jiménez. This can be done either in person, by phone or often through your tour operator.

For information on the Bahía Drake route, see p396. For information on the Puerto Jiménez route, go to p413. For information on the park itself, check out p421.

inhabitants. Near the top of the ridge, there are several pre-Columbian granite spheres. Archaeologists speculate that the island may have been a ceremonial or burial site for the same indigenous tribes.

Camping is prohibited, and there are no facilities except a ranger station by the landing beach. Most visitors arrive on tours arranged by the nearby lodges – admission is US$10 per person, plus a US$4 additional charge for divers, although this fee is usually included in your tour price.

TO CORCOVADO VIA PUERTO JIMÉNEZ

The second of two principal overland routes to Parque Nacional Corcovado, the Puerto Jiménez route on the eastern side of the peninsula is much more 'developed.' Of course, as this is Osa, developed means a single road and a sprinkling of villages along the coast of Golfo Dulce. The landscape is cattle pastures and rice fields, while the Reserva Forestal Golfo Dulce protects much of the inland area. The largest settlement in the area is the town of Puerto Jiménez, which has transitioned from a boomtown for gold miners to an emerging ecotourism hot spot.

RESERVA FORESTAL GOLFO DULCE

The northern shore of the Golfo Dulce is home to this vast **forest reserve**, which links Parque Nacional Corcovado to the Parque Nacional Piedras Blancas. This connecting corridor plays an important role in preserving the biodiversity of the peninsula, and allowing the wildlife to migrate to the mainland. Although much of the reserve is not easily accessible, there are several area lodges that are doing their part to preserve this natural resource by protecting their own little pieces of this wildlife wonderland.

Sights & Activities

About 9km southeast of Rincón, the town of **La Palma** is the origin of the rough road that turns into the trail to the Los Patos ranger station. If you're hiking across Corcovado, this will likely be the starting point or ending point of your trek. Before heading out, however, don't miss the chance to get some sun at the beautiful sand and coral beach, known as **Playa Blanca**, at the east end of town.

The **Reserva Indígena Guaymí** (see boxed text, p413) is southwest of La Palma, on the border of Parque Nacional Corcovado.

About 8km south of La Palma, the Tico-run **Finca Köbö** (☎ 8351-8576; www.fincakobo.com/finca.html; 3hr tour US$28) is a chocolate-lover's dream come true (in fact *köbö* means 'dream' in Guaymí). The 50-hectare *finca* is dedicated to organic cultivation of fruits and vegetables and – the product of choice – cacao. Tours in English give a comprehensive overview of the life cycle of cacao plants and the production of chocolate (with degustation!). But, this *finca* (farm) isn't just a *finca* – more than half of the territory is dedicated to protecting natural ecosystems, and experimenting with different methods of reforestation. To really experience the beauty and vision of this *finca*, you can stay in simple, comfortable teak **cabins** (s/d US$33/60, meals ₡4000-6500), and indulge in the opportunity to view the merits of the forest and the land through a farmer's eyes.

Just before entering Puerto Jiménez, a turnoff in the road leads 16km to the hamlet of **Río Nuevo**, also in the forest reserve. A good trail network leads to spectacular mountain viewpoints, some with views of the gulf. Birdwatching is excellent in this area: you can expect to see the many species that you would find in Corcovado. Most of the following lodges offer day-long excursions in this area.

Fully customizable and utterly unique **artists retreats** can be arranged through Sombre de la Lapa (see right).

Sleeping

Accommodations are also available at Finca Köbö.

Danta Corcovado Lodge (☎ 8378-9188, 8819-1860; www.dantacorcovado.net; cabins per person US$35) Conveniently located midway between Los Patos and La Palma, this low-key lodge is set on the *finca* of the congenial Sanchez family. Rustic wood cabins are painted in warm hues and furnished with handcrafted pieces. The highlight of the lodge, however, is the family's traditional wood stove, which fires up some delicious, home-cooked meals.

Suital Lodge (☎ 8826-0342; www.suital.com; 15km east of Rincón; s/d/tr US$45/62/70; Ⓟ) Lots of love has gone into the construction of this tiny clutch of *cabinas* on the northern shores of Golfo Dulce. It's situated on 30 hectares of hilly, forested property (not a single tree has been felled), and guests can take advantage of a network of trails that winds through the property and down to the beach.

Bosque del Río Tigre (☎ in Puerto Jiménez 2735-5062, 8824-1372, in USA 888-875-9453; www.osaadventures.com; Dos Brazos; s/d US$135/155, 4-day package per person from US$528; Ⓟ) On the edge of the Reserva Forestal Golfo Dulce, in the midst of a 13-hectare private reserve, this off-the-beaten-track ecolodge is a bird-watcher's paradise. Four well-appointed guest rooms and one private, open-air *cabaña* have huge windows for viewing the feathered friends that come to visit. In case you want to brush up on your taxonomy, the lodge contains a library well stocked with wildlife reference books.

Villa Corcovado (☎ 8817-6969; www.villacorcovado.com; Rincón; s/d incl meals US$325/446; Ⓟ) Rincón seems an unlikely setting for a top-of-the-line resort, but you'll understand when you glimpse the 30 hectares of exquisite, unspoiled rainforest and the magnificent unobstructed vista of the Golfo Dulce. Eight light-filled, luxurious villas have private porches, wood-beamed ceilings and hardwood floors, not to mention classy, contemporary decor. Gourmet meals (included) feature organic produce straight from the garden; you can request yours packed in a picnic to enjoy on a nearby deserted beach.

our pick **Sombre de la Lapa** (☎ 8378-3013, in USA 508-714-0622; www.costaricaartretreat.com; 1-week house rental low/high season US$1200/1600, 9-day artist retreat per person from US$1995; Ⓟ) Further south along the coast toward Puerto Jiménez is this hidden gem in the jungle, a phenomenal fantasy-inspired artistic retreat that has to be seen to be believed. The pet project of two expat artists, Sombre de la Lapa is a vast private reserve complete with expansive hiking trails, natural springs, pre-Columbian burial grounds and abandoned gold mines. While it's certainly an expensive proposition – albeit a bit cheaper if you can get six to eight friends together and fill all three bedrooms – the Sombre de la Lapa rental house was built entirely from naturally felled lumber, and is covered from floor to ceiling in artisanal masonry, hand-carved furnishing and original artwork. Not to be outdone by the main house, there is also a six-level, three-bedroom, two-bathroom tree house that wraps around

(Continued on page 413)

Costa Rica Outdoors

Lazy strolls along the beach or more active pursuits – in Costa Rica, the choice is yours.

MARK NEWMAN

Exploring the *páramo* (scrubby trees and grasslands) of Parque Nacional Chirripó (p374).

LUKE

Costa Rica's lofty tally of national parks and reserves provides an incredible stage for lovers of the outdoors. Natural spaces are so entwined with Costa Rica's ecofriendly image that it's difficult to envisage the country without them. Since the designation of the Reserva Natural Absoluta Cabo Blanco in 1963, Costa Rica has lured countless travelers in search of the pristine.

Despite all of the high-octane activities on offer, casual hiking and more intense trekking remain two of the country's most enduring outdoor activities. For the vast majority of travelers, Costa Rica equates with rainforest, and you're certain to encounter charismatic wildlife including primates, birdlife and butterflies galore. As first-time visitors quickly discover, no two rainforests are created equal, providing a constantly shifting palette of nature.

Of course, if you want to experience all that this country has to offer, you're going to have to get wet. Costa Rica proudly boasts some of the world's finest surfing, white-water rafting and kayaking. If thrills and spills aren't exactly your thing, fret not as you can always don a mask, fins and snorkel, or alternatively pass the time with rod and reel in hand.

What truly distinguishes Costa Rica from other competing destinations is the diversity and accessibility of the outdoors. While hard-core enthusiasts can seek out complete solitude in absolute wilderness, families and novices alike are equally well catered for. From jungle treks and beachcombing to rafting snaking rivers and surfing crashing waves – whatever you're looking for, Costa Rica has most definitely got it.

This chapter provides a brief overview of Costa Rica's share of the great outdoors. However, if you're looking for more specific information, including detailed lists of recommended operators, check out the Activities section of the Directory on p524.

HIKING & TREKKING

Whether you're interested in taking a walk in the park, or embarking on a rugged mountaineering circuit, there is no shortage of hiking opportunities around Costa Rica. At tourist-packed destinations such as Monteverde and Santa Elena, trails are clearly marked, and even lined with cement blocks in parts. This is very appealing if you're traveling with the little ones, or if you're lacking navigational prowess. Sun-drenched coastlines also invite ambling walks through the crashing waves.

Opportunities for moderate hiking are available in most parks and reserves, particularly once you leave the well-beaten tourist path. As this is Costa Rica, you can – for the most part – still rely on signs and maps for orientation, though it helps to have a bit of experience under your belt. Good hiking shoes, plenty of water and a confidence in your abilities will enable you to combine several shorter day hikes into a lengthier expedition. Tourist information centers at park entrances are great resources for planning out your intended route.

If you're properly equipped with the various camping essentials (tent, sleeping bag, air mattress etc), the country's longer and more arduous multiday treks are at your disposal. Costa Rica's top challenges are scaling Cerro Chirripó, traversing Corcovado and penetrating deep into the heart of La Amistad. While all three endeavors can be undertaken either solo or with trusted companions, local guides provide an extra measure of safety, and can help in identifying flora and fauna.

top five

SPOTS TO HIKE & TREK

Reserva Santa Elena (p214) and **Reserva Biológica Bosque Nuboso Monteverde** (p211) Costa Rica's most famous cloud-forest reserves.

Parque Nacional Corcovado (p421) The last remaining strand of coastal Pacific rainforest.

Cerro Chirripó (p374) Home to the highest mountain in Costa Rica at 3820m.

Parque Internacional La Amistad (p385) A heavily forested yet rarely traversed park.

WILDLIFE- & BIRD-WATCHING

Costa Rica's biodiversity is legendary, so it should come as no surprise that the country offers unparalleled opportunities for wildlife- and bird-watching. As a bonus, people of all ages are already familiar with Costa Rica's most famous yet commonly spotted animals.

A proud basilisk shows off its prehistoric figure.

MARK NEWMAN

top five

SPOTS TO WATCH WILDLIFE

Parque Nacional Corcovado (p421) At the heart of the Península de Osa, this is the country's richest wildlife area.

Parque Nacional Santa Rosa (p234) The tropical dry forest along the Pacific coast harbors a unique ecosystem.

Parque Nacional Tortuguero (p458) Canals and waterways provide for excellent bird-watching.

Caño Negro (p516) Expansive wetlands provide refuge for reptiles and avians alike.

Monteverde and Santa Elena (p191) The reserves provide unique insight into the cloud-forest ecosystem.

You'll instantly recognize monkeys bounding through the treetops, sloths clinging to branches and toucans gliding beneath the canopy. Young children, even if they've been to the zoo dozens of times, typically enjoy the thrill of spotting creatures in the wild.

For the slightly older, keeping checklists is a fun way to add an education element to your travels. Want to move beyond the novice level? Check out your local bookstore prior to landing in Costa Rica, and be sure to pick up wildlife and bird guides – look for ones with color plates that make positive identification a cinch. For a quick but informative overview of native wildlife (including birds), check out the Costa Rica Wildlife Guide on p181.

A quality pair of binoculars is highly recommended, and can really make the difference between far-off movement and a veritable face-to-face encounter. For expert bird-watchers, a spotting scope is essential, and multipark itineraries will allow you to quickly add dozens of new species to your all-time list. Finally, it's worth pointing out that Costa Rica is brimming with wildlife at every turn, so always keep your eyes open and your ears peeled – you never know what's waiting for you just ahead!

SURFING

Point and beach breaks, lefts and rights, reefs and river mouths, warm water and year-round waves make Costa Rica a favorite surfing destination. For the most part, the Pacific coast has bigger swells and better waves during the latter part of the rainy season, but the Caribbean cooks from November to May. Basically, there is a wave somewhere waiting to be surfed at any time of the year. See the surfer's map opposite for an idea of what's around.

For the uninitiated, lessons are available at almost all of the major surfing destinations – especially popular towns include Jacó (p322) and Tamarindo (p263) on the Pacific coast. Surfing definitely has a steep learning curve, and can be potentially dangerous

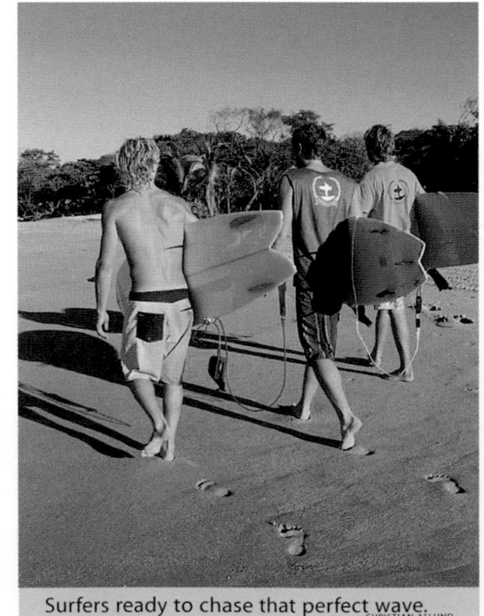

Surfers ready to chase that perfect wave. CHRISTIAN ASLUND

SURFER'S MAP

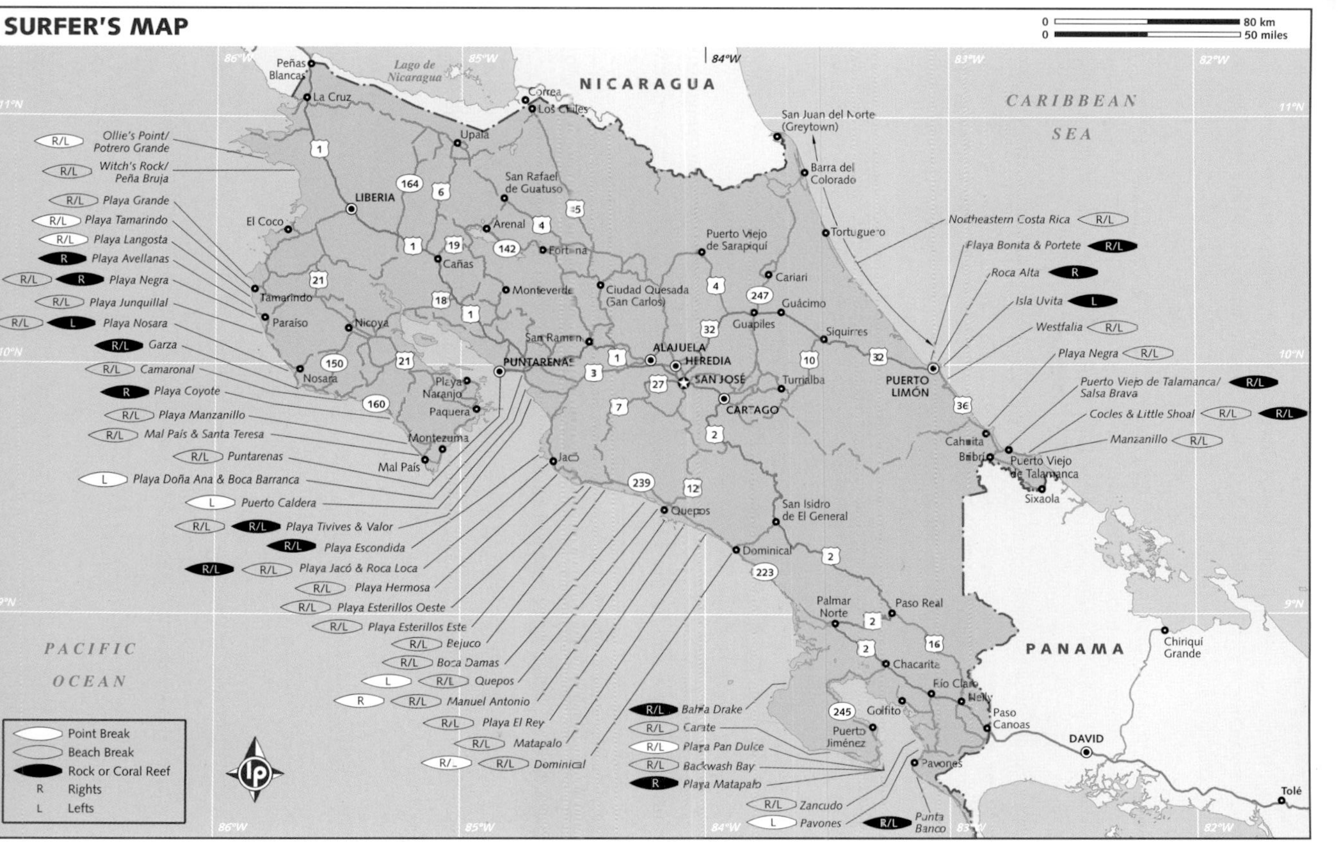
0 80 km
0 50 miles
NICARAGUA
CARIBBEAN SEA
PACIFIC OCEAN
PANAMA
Lago de Nicaragua
86°W
85°W
84°W
83°W
82°W
11°N
10°N
9°N
Ollie's Point/ Potrero Grande
Witch's Rock/ Peña Bruja
Playa Grande
Playa Tamarindo
Playa Langosta
Playa Avellanas
Playa Negra
Playa Junquillal
Playa Nosara
Garza
Camaronal
Playa Coyote
Playa Manzanillo
Mal País & Santa Teresa
Puntarenas
Playa Doña Ana & Boca Barranca
Puerto Caldera
Playa Tivives & Valor
Playa Escondida
Playa Jacó & Roca Loca
Playa Hermosa
Playa Esterillos Oeste
Playa Esterillos Este
Bejuco
Boca Damas
Quepos
Manuel Antonio
Playa El Rey
Matapalo
Dominical
Bahía Drake
Carate
Playa Pan Dulce
Backwash Bay
Playa Matapalo
Zancudo
Pavones
Punta Banco
Northeastern Costa Rica
Playa Bonita & Portete
Roca Alta
Isla Uvita
Westfalia
Playa Negra
Puerto Viejo de Talamanca/ Salsa Brava
Cocles & Little Shoal
Manzanillo
Peñas Blancas
La Cruz
Correa
Los Chiles
Upala
LIBERIA
El Coco
Tamarindo
Paraíso
Nicoya
Nosara
San Rafael de Guatuso
Arenal
Cañas
Monteverde
Ciudad Quesada (San Carlos)
Puerto Viejo de Sarapiquí
San Juan del Norte (Greytown)
Barra del Colorado
Cariari
Guácimo
Guapiles
Siquirres
Turrialba
PUNTARENAS
ALAJUELA
HEREDIA
SAN JOSÉ
CARTAGO
PUERTO LIMÓN
Playa Naranjo
Paquera
Montezuma
Mal País
Quepos
San Isidro de El General
Dominical
Palmar Norte
Paso Real
Chacarita
Golfito
Puerto Jiménez
Pavones
Paso Canoas
Puerto Viejo de Talamanca
Sixaola
Chiriquí Grande
DAVID
Tolé
Point Break
Beach Break
Rock or Coral Reef
R Rights
L Lefts

if the currents are strong. With that said, the sport is accessible to children and novices, though it's always best to inquire locally about conditions before you paddle out. Having trouble standing up? Here is a tip: long boards readily maintain their stability, even in heavy crashing surf.

Throughout Costa Rica, waves are big (though not Hawaii-big), and many offer hollow and fast rides that are perfect for intermediates. As a bonus, Costa Rica is one of the few places on the planet where you can surf two different oceans in the same day. Advanced surfers with plenty of experience under their belts can tackle some of the sport's most famous waves. The top ones include: world-famous Ollie's Point and Witch's Rock, off the coast of Parque Nacional Santa Rosa (p234); Mal País and Santa Teresa (p305), with a groovy scene to match the powerful waves; Playa Hermosa (p332), whose bigger, faster curls attract a more determined (and experienced) crew of wave-chasers; Pavones (p435), a legendary long left across the sweet waters of the Golfo Dulce; and the infamous Salsa Brava (p481) in Puerto Viejo de Talamanca (p479), which is for experts only.

WHITE-WATER RAFTING & KAYAKING

Since the birth of the ecotourism-based economy in the mid-1980s, white-water rafting has emerged as one of Costa Rica's top-billed outdoor pursuits. Ranging from family-friendly Class II swells to borderline unnavigable Class V rapids, Costa Rica's rivers offer highly varied white-water experiences.

First-time runners are catered for year-round, while seasoned enthusiasts arrive en masse during the wildest months from June through to October. There is also much regional variation, with gentler rivers located near Manuel Antonio along the central Pacific coast, and truly world-class runs along the Ríos Pacuare and Reventazón in the Central Valley. Since all white-water rafting in Costa Rica requires the presence of a certified guide, you will need to book all trips through a reputable tour agency (see p527 for listings).

SPOTS TO RAFT & KAYAK

Turrialba (p146) Home to the country's most popular rafting rivers, the Pacuare and Reventazón.

La Virgen (p499) The base town for rafting and kayaking on the Río Sarapiquí.

Manuel Antonio (p341) A tourist mecca that offers family-friendly rafting year-round.

Parque Nacional Tortuguero (p458) Boasts 310 sq km of wildlife-rich and kayak-friendly lagoons and canals.

Bahía Drake (p395) Extensive mangrove patches are optimally explored by kayak.

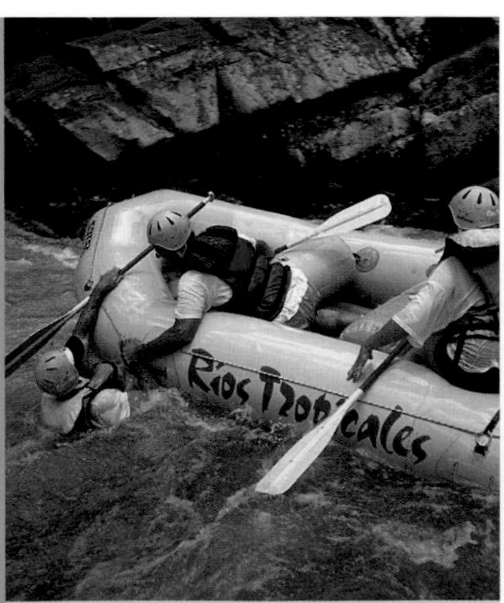

Plunging down the challenging Río Pacuare.
MARK NEWMAN

River kayaking is not as popular as rafting, though it has its fair share of loyal fans. The tiny village of La Virgen in the northern lowlands is the unofficial kayaking capital of Costa Rica, and the best spot to hook up with other like-minded lovers of the sport. The Río Sarapiquí has an impressive variety of runs that cater to all ages and skill levels.

With 1228km of coastline, two gulfs and plentiful mangrove estuaries, Costa Rica is also an ideal destination for sea kayaking. This is a great way for paddlers to access remote areas and catch rare glimpses of birds and wildlife. Difficulty of access varies considerably, and is largely dependent on tides and currents.

top five

SPOTS TO DIVE & SNORKEL

Playa del Coco (p247) Home to manta rays, sharks and dozens of species of fish, all in large numbers.

Isla del Caño (p402) A top dive spot famous for giant schools of fish.

Puerto Viejo de Talamanca (p479) An emerging dive center that is good for snorkelers and novice divers.

Isla del Cocos (p438) A truly world-class destination inhabited by an astonishing amount of marine life.

Cahuita (p469) and **Manzanillo** (p492) Popular Caribbean reefs that are good for snorkelers.

Dive deeper than the fish near Isla del Caño.
JOHNNY HAGLUND

DIVING & SNORKELING

There's good news and there's bad news. The good news is that Costa Rica offers body-temperature water with few humans and abundant marine life. The bad news is that the visibility is low because of silt and plankton, and soft corals and sponges are dominant. If you are looking for turquoise waters and plenty of hard coral, head for Belize and Honduras.

However, if you're looking for fine opportunities to see massive schools of fish, as well as larger marine animals such as turtles, sharks, dolphins and whales, then you have arrived in exactly the right place. It's also worth pointing out that there are few places in the world where you can dive in the Caribbean and the Pacific on the same day, albeit with a good amount of effort and some advanced planning.

The Caribbean Sea is better for novice divers and snorkelers, with the beach towns of Manzanillo and Cahuita particularly well suited to youngsters. Puerto Viejo lays claim to a few decent sites that can be explored on a discovery dive. Along the Pacific, Playa del Coco and Isla del Caño up the ante slightly, offering a variety of beginner- and intermediate-level sites.

Isla del Cocos is the exception to the rule – this remote island floating in the deep Pacific is regarded by veteran divers as one of the best dive spots in the world. In order to

top five

SPOTS TO FISH

Tamarindo (p263) Pacific sailfish swim in these waters between December and April.

Puerto Jiménez (p413) Costa Rica's top spot for fishing, especially for dorado, marlin, sailfish and tuna.

Zancudo (p434) Excellent for snook, which inhabit the surrounding mangrove swamps.

Bahía Drake (p395) Claims more than 40 fishing records, including sailfish, three kinds of marlin, yellowfin tuna and wahoo.

Caño Negro (p516) Another good inland spot that harbors snook.

catch a glimpse of the underwater world of Cocos, you'll need to visit on a liveaboard, and have some serious experience in your logbook.

FISHING

Sportfishing enthusiasts flock to both of Costa Rica's coasts for the thrill of reeling in mammoth marlins and supersized sailfish. Add dorado, wahoo and dolphin to the list, and you can easily understand why the country has produced so many record-breaking catches. Of course, Costa Rica has an eco-image to maintain, which is why the vast majority of sportfishing companies encourage 'catch and release' practices in an effort to maintain existing fish populations.

The ocean is always open for fishing. As a general rule, the Pacific coast is best in June and July, though you'll get better fishing on the south coast during that period, while the Caribbean is best from September to November. Unless you have your own boat and tackle, you will need to book a trip through an operator (see p525 for listings).

Sportfishing is a very expensive proposition, with baseline trips starting at several hundred dollars per outing. Assuming you have a serious pile of cash to burn, anyone can enjoy the thrill of getting a bite, though it definitely takes a bit of practice (and muscle) to reel in the big one. And, even if you're traveling with nonanglers, few people can resist the pleasure of an open-water cruise on a stylish fishing vessel.

For those on a more modest budget, there are several inland spots where you can hook freshwater fish. Finally, if you want to do as the locals do, try your hand at surfcasting, which simply involves standing on a beach and casting a hook and line into the crashing waves.

Enjoy the thrill of going for the record 'catch and release' in Costa Rican waters. RICHARD CUMMINS

(Continued from page 404)

an ancient guanacaste tree – the glass-bottom shower is not for the faint of heart! You'll find Sombre de la Lapa at Agujas, off the main La Palma–Puerto Jiménez road before the Dos Brazos turnoff.

Getting There & Away

The easiest way to travel the eastern coast of the peninsula is by car. Otherwise, frequent buses ply the sole road between La Palma and Puerto Jiménez (₡250, 30 minutes).

PUERTO JIMÉNEZ

Puerto Jiménez is something of a natural wonder in itself. Sliced in half by the swampy, overgrown Quebrada Cacao, and flanked on one side by the emerald waters of the Golfo Dulce, this untamed environment is shared equally by local residents and wildlife. While walking through the dusty streets of Port Jim (as the gringos call it), it's not unusual to spot scarlet macaws roosting on the soccer field, or white-faced capuchins swinging in the treetops adjacent to the main street.

Then again, it's not too hard to understand why Puerto Jiménez is brimming with wildlife, mainly because the town lies on the edge of Parque Nacional Corcovado (p421). As the preferred jumping-off point for travelers heading to the famed Sirena ranger station, the town is a great place to organize an expedition, stock up on supplies, eat a hot meal and get a good night's rest before hitting the trails.

Indeed, Puerto Jiménez is known as the 'big city' in these parts, and here you'll find the region's largest and most diverse offering of hotels, restaurants and other tourist services. But don't be mistaken. Port Jim is very much a close-knit community at its core, and its small-town charm and languid pace are surprisingly infectious. While it is understandably difficult to resist the pull of the deep jungle just beyond, consider putting the brakes on and lingering here for a few days – it will surely do you good.

History

Although it appears on maps dating to 1914, Puerto Jiménez was little more than a cluster of houses built on a mangrove swamp. With the advent of logging in the 1960s and

GUAYMÍ

The earliest inhabitants of Costa Rica's far southern corner were the Guaymí, or Ngöbe, who migrated over generations from neighboring Panama. The Guaymí inhabit indigenous reserves in the Valle de Coto Brus, the Osa peninsula and southern Golfo Dulce, though they retain some semi-nomadic ways and are allowed to pass freely over the border into Panama. This occurs frequently during the coffee harvesting season, when many Guaymí travel to work on plantations.

The Guaymí have been able to preserve – to some degree – their customs and culture, and it is not unusual to see women wearing traditional dress. These vibrant, solid-color *pollera* dresses hang to the ankles, often trimmed in contrasting colors and patterns. Unlike other indigenous groups, the Guaymí still speak their native language and teach it in local schools.

The Guaymí traditionally live in wooden huts with palm roofs and dirt floors, although most families have now upgraded to wooden houses on stilts. However, they still live off the land, cultivating corn, rice and tubers, while fruit and palmitos grow in the wild.

The Guaymí reserves are largely inaccessible, which may be one reason why the culture persists. However, as tourism filters into the furthest corners of the country, there is a growing interest in indigenous traditions and handicrafts, and this demand may actually encourage their preservation. But, the reserves are also at a precipitous point – without proper management and community participation, an influx of tourists (and tourist dollars) can also lead to cultural dilution.

The best way to visit the reserve is through **Tamandu Lodge** (☎ 8821-4525; www.tamandu-lodge.com; r per person US$55), which is run by the Carreras, a Guaymí family. This unique lodge provides a rare chance to interact directly with an indigenous family and experience firsthand the Guaymí lifestyle. This is hands-on stuff: gather crabs and fish with palm rods; hunt for palmito or harvest yucca; learn how to prepare these specialties over an open fire. Accommodations are in rustic, wooden houses, built on stilts with thatch roofs. Home-cooked meals are included in the price. A member of the Carrera family will meet you in La Palma, from where it is a two-hour journey on horseback to the lodge – getting there is half the fun!

the subsequent discovery of gold in the local streams, Jiménez became a small boomtown. The logging industry still operates in parts of the peninsula, but the gold rush has quieted down in favor of the tourist rush.

Even so, the town has a frontier feel. Now, instead of gold miners descending on its bars on weekends, it's outdoors and fishing types who come to have a shot of *guaro* (local firewater) and brag about the snakes, sharks and alligators they've allegedly tousled with.

Orientation

The compact, gridded and easily walkable 'downtown' is located to the west of the Río Platanares, which feeds a modest estuary and mangrove forest before reaching the Golfo Dulce. On the east side are the headquarters for Parque Nacional Corcovado and a small airstrip. There is also a tiny access road leading to Playa Platanares, which is lined with a few upmarket properties (see p417).

Information

INTERNET RESOURCES

Cafenet El Sol (☎ 2735-5719; per hr ₡1000; ⌚ 7am-10pm)

MEDICAL SERVICES

Red Cross (☎ 2735-5109) For medical emergencies.

MONEY

Banco Nacional de Costa Rica (⌚ 8:30am-3:45pm Mon-Fri)

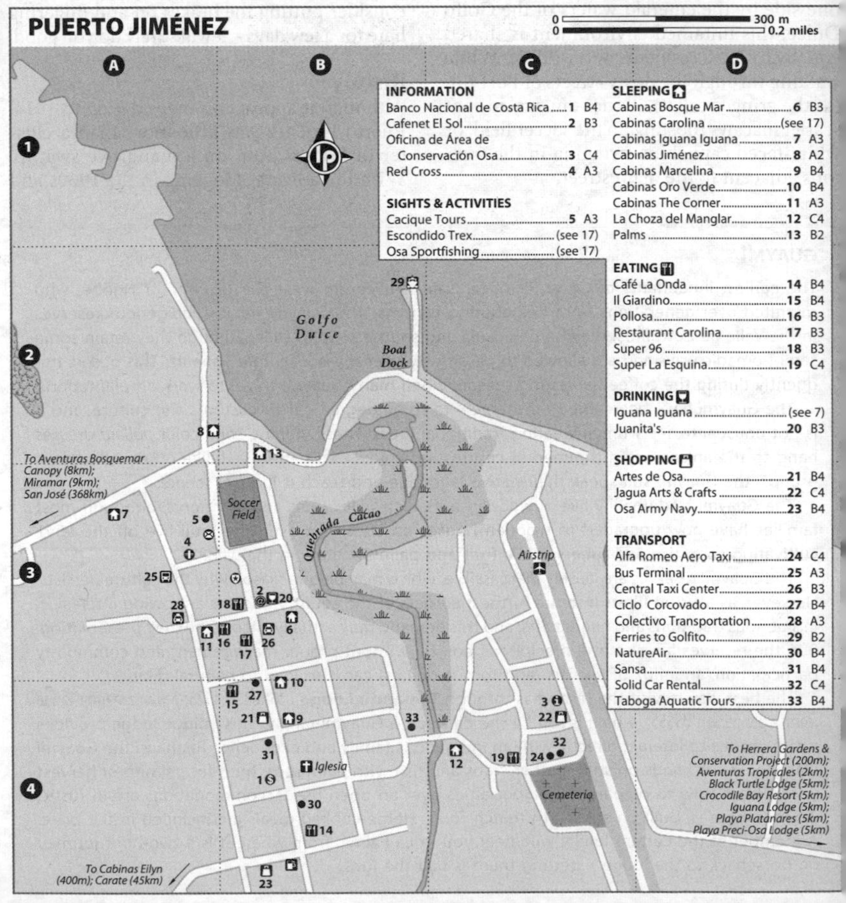

TOURIST INFORMATION

Oficina de Área de Conservación Osa (Osa Conservation Area Headquarters; ☎ 2735-5580; 🕑 8am-noon & 1-4pm Mon-Fri) Information about Corcovado, Isla del Caño, Parque Nacional Marino Ballena and Golfito parks and reserves. Make reservations here to camp in Corcovado.

Sights & Activities

About 5km east of town, the secluded – and often deserted – **Playa Platanares** is excellent for swimming, sunning and recovering from too much adventure. The nearby mangroves of Río Platanares are a paradise for kayaking and bird-watching.

On the east side of the airstrip, **Herrera Gardens & Conservation Project** (☎ 2735-5267; admission US$5, 2hr guided tour US$15; 🕑 6am-5pm) is a 100-hectare reserve with beautiful botanical gardens. This innovative, long-term reforestation project offers an ecologically and economically sustainable alternative to cattle-grazing. Visitors can explore the 5km of garden trails or 15km of well-marked forest trails. Guided tours focus on bird-watching, botany or even tree climbing! Stop by Jagua Arts & Crafts (p418) to buy a map or arrange your tour.

If you prefer to tour the rainforest at high speed, the thrilling **Aventuras Bosquemar Canopy** (☎ 2735-5102; www.goodcostarica.com/canopy.html; Miramar; admission US$75) is the only zip-line canopy tour on this side of the peninsula. Five lines stretch between five platforms, winding 500m through primary forest. It's about 8km from Jiménez near the village of Miramar – prices include transportation from Puerto Jiménez.

Boat tours around the Golfo Dulce are becoming increasingly popular. The all-day outing often includes a mangrove tour, snorkeling excursion and dolphin-watching. Remember that it is illegal to swim with the dolphins, despite your tour guide's best intentions. These outings are typically booked either through your accommodations, or by simply stopping by the waterfront and chartering your own boat and captain. As such, rates are variable depending on the nature of your trip.

Tours

Aventuras Tropicales (☎ 2735-5195; www.aventurastropicales.com) A Tico-run operation that offers all sorts of tropical adventures.

Cacique Tours (☎ 8815-8919; www.lasosas.com/index_tours.htm) The affable Oscar Cortés offers a variety of wildlife tours, his specialty being an early-morning bird-watching walk.

Escondido Trex (☎ 2735-5210; www.escondidotrex.com; Restaurant Carolina) Specializes in kayak tours, including mangrove paddles, night paddles, sunset tours and kayak-snorkel combos.

Osa Sportfishing (☎ 2735-5675; www.costa-rica-sportfishing.com; Restaurant Carolina) Transplanted Florida fishers who organize sportfishing vacations and dolphin- and whale-watching on the 15m double-decker *Delfín Blanco*.

Puerto Jiménez for Children

Compared to Bahía Drake (p395), the alternative access point for Parque Nacional Corcovado, Puerto Jiménez is much more family-friendly in the sense that you can rely on a wider range of goods and services. The simple fact that you're 'on-the-grid' can be very comforting to parents. Of course, Port Jim doesn't attract as many families as some of the more mainstream tourist destinations along the Central Pacific Coast and in the Nicoya peninsula, though your children will nevertheless be well catered for here.

The wide range of sleeping listings gives you choice when it comes to comfort, quality and the all-important price. As a disclaimer, the majority of the budget options in town have some rough edges, so you might want to dig a bit deeper into your pockets. Regardless of where you stay, however, there are plenty of activities on the roster, which can help keep your kids busy and – hopefully – out of trouble!

Sleeping

Puerto Jiménez is fairly quiet most times of the year, though reservations are always a good idea on weekends and during busy holidays. Unlike other destinations in the Osa peninsula, backpackers and shoestringers are well catered for, and you'll find the greatest diversity of accommodations at the budget and midrange levels. Top-end options also abound, but they tend to be located on the outskirts of town.

BUDGET

Cabinas The Corner (☎ 2735-5328; www.jimenezhotels.com/cabinasthecorner; dm US$5, d US$12) While this ultra-budget crash pad provides little more than a bed in a fan-cooled room for the night, the Corner is kept admirably clean and secure, and resultantly has a growing legion

DAY TRIPPER

You've got a free day in Port Jim and you don't want to hang around town? Here's what you can do:

- Catch a wave and you're sittin' on top of the world. Check out the point break at Playa Pan Dulce in **Cabo Matapalo** (p418).
- Indulge your sweet tooth. See (and taste) where chocolate comes from at **Finca Köbö** (p404).
- Slow down and get some sun. Have a picnic on the deserted wilderness beach of **Playa Blanca** (p404).
- Get a bird's eye view from the top of a 60m ficus tree. Tree-climbing tours are offered by **Everyday Adventures** (p418).
- Experience tropical paradise among the orchids, bromeliads and heliconia at the **Casa de Orquídeas** (p433).

of devoted fans. It'll do just fine if all you need is a bit of shut-eye before heading out to Corcovado, and this is as good a place as any to link up with other potential trekkers, form an expedition party and stock up on invaluable local advice.

Cabinas Oro Verde (☎ 2735-5241; r per person US$15) Simple and central: this is what you're looking for in a budget hotel. Rooms are clean, if a little musty, and the bars on the windows are not pretty, but at least you know the place is safe. All in all, this is a good place to stumble back to late at night, but don't be surprised if you're woken up in the morning by early-bird shoppers.

Cabinas Iguana Iguana (☎ 2735-5158; r per person US$20; P) Wood cabins are set on quiet and shady grounds here on the northern edge of town. The rooms are slightly dank, and the swimming pool bears a striking resemblance to a frog swamp, but the overall atmosphere is pleasant. The onsite bar is among the town's hottest spots on weekend nights so light sleepers should probably stay elsewhere.

Cabinas Carolina (☎ 2735-5696; d with/without air-con US$40/35) The lack of windows makes this low-priced stalwart feel something like a concrete prison, but at least it's got air-con and a central location. The attached *soda,* Restaurant Carolina, is a Jiménez institution, so even if you're looking for something in a higher price bracket, don't miss the stellar *casados* (set meals) on offer here.

Cabinas Bosque Mar (☎ 2735-5681; d with/without air-con US$40/35; P) This hot-pink motel-style building is one of the best bargains in Jiménez, especially considering that all the rooms are large and airy. Although the atmosphere is nothing to write home about, there is a decent onsite restaurant for those feeling too lazy to head into town, as well as a helpful onsite tour agency.

Cabinas Eilyn (☎ 2735-5465; d with/without air-con US$40/35; P) Hospitality is a family affair at these quiet quarters on the edge of town. High ceilings, tile floors and a comfy porch enhance the decor of the four cozy *cabinas* that are attached to the Tico owners' home. Prices include a home-cooked breakfast of hearty *gallo pinto* (rice and beans) and fresh fruit.

MIDRANGE

Cabinas Jiménez (☎ 2735-5090; www.cabinasjimenez.com; s/d from US$35/50; P) The efforts of the recent change in ownership are evident at this long-standing clutch of cabins. All of the rooms have jungle scenes painted on the walls and underwater murals in the hot-water bathrooms. Refrigerators and safes are practical, while details such as carved wooden furniture, woven textiles and batik curtains add an elegant flair. The pricier rooms have fantastic views of the lagoon.

La Choza del Manglar (☎ 2735-5002; www.manglares.com; r US$40-99; P) Set on the edge of the mangrove swamp, this tropical inn is – as it claims – 'a *very* natural place.' Wildlife sightings are de rigueur on these beautifully landscaped grounds – from crocodiles to kinkajous, monkeys to macaws. Bright and airy rooms have hand-carved furniture and mural-painted walls, as well as large windows overlooking the lush surroundings.

Cabinas Marcelina (☎ 2755-5286; d with/without air-con US$50/45; P) Marcelina's place is a long-standing favorite among budget travelers looking for a peaceful night of sleep. The concrete building is painted salmon pink and surrounded by blooming trees, lending it a homey atmosphere that invites good dreams. Rooms have modern furniture, fluffy towels and tile bathrooms, which are certainly a welcome sight at this price range.

Palms (☎ 2735-5012; www.thepalmscostarica.com; r US$45-85; P) A modest attempt at approximating boutique *cabinas*, the Palms offers rooms of varying sizes and shapes with artsy touches – from the hand-painted sinks and murals to the soft lighting and fine linens. The biggest draw, however, is Mother Nature, who regularly provides cooling breezes that sweep through the well-situated waterside property.

Playa Preci-Osa Lodge (☎ 8818-2959; www.playa-preciosa-lodge.de; Playa Platanares; s/d from US$45/70; P) All of the options at this romantic beach lodge on nearby Playa Platanares offer excellent value: four spacious thatch-roof bungalows have a sleeping loft and plenty of living space (great for families), while eight screened platform tents are set in the secluded garden. The grounds are filled with fruit trees and flowering plants that attract loads of birdlife, monkeys and iguanas, while the ocean is literally a few feet from your doorstep.

TOP END

Black Turtle Lodge (☎ 2735-5005; www.blackturtlelodge.com; Playa Platanares; s/d from US$85/140; P) A peaceful yoga retreat along Playa Platanares, this ecolodge offers the choice of two-story *cabinas*, which have magnificent views over the treetops to the Golfo Dulce, and the less-spacious *cabinettas* (small cabins) nestled into the tropical garden below. All have bamboo furniture and hardwood floors, but the *cabinettas* share hot-water bathrooms.

Iguana Lodge (☎ 2735-5205; www.iguanalodge.com; Playa Platanares; casitas per person US$155, villas US$450; P) This luxurious lodge fronting Playa Platanares has the most architecturally alluring cabins in the area: four two-story bungalows have huge breezy decks, bamboo furniture, orthopedic beds draped in mosquito netting and lovely stone bathrooms with garden showers. Rates include three delectable meals a day: the creative cuisine is a highlight. If you're traveling in a large group, consider renting the three-room Villa Villa Kula, a charming tropical colonial house with a fully stocked kitchen.

Crocodile Bay Resort (☎ 2735-5631; www.crocodilebay.com; Playa Platanares; 3-day all-inclusive fishing package per person from US$2195; P) Sportfishing is never a cheap proposition, but this all-inclusive anglers' resort offers competitive packages to help cushion the blow to your wallet. Accommodations are in fairly standard *cabinas* that are scattered around an attractive pool and well-cared-for gardens. But, you're here to fish, which is an easy prospect given the 40-plus fishing-boat fleet, highly trained crews and veritable arsenal of professional-grade gear at your disposal.

Eating

The restaurant scene in Puerto Jiménez is surprisingly subdued considering all the tourist traffic passing through. While there is no shortage of cheap *sodas* serving up typical Tico staples, for slightly fancier fare your options are much more limited.

Stock up on food items, bug repellent and other necessities at the Super La Esquina or the smaller Super 96.

Café La Onda (light meals ₡1000-3500) A funky and eclectic travelers' cafe that's equally suited for chilling out or chatting up, la Onda sets the stage with homemade pastries accompanied by excellent coffees and fruit smoothies. While you're a long way from Manhattan, bagels and deli items add a dash of cosmopolitanism to sleepy Port Jim.

Restaurant Carolina (dishes ₡1500-4000) This is *the* hub in Puerto Jiménez. Expats, nature guides, tourists and locals all gather here for food, drinks and plenty of carousing. The food is famous locally and the fresh-fruit drinks and cold beers go down pretty easily on a hot day.

Pollosa (☎ 2735-5667; meals ₡2000-4500; noon-9pm Sun-Fri) Pollosa is renowned among locals for juicy, delectable rotisserie chicken, but it also has a good selection of salads, sandwiches and spaghetti. Take-away is available, making this is an excellent option for picnicking.

Il Giardino (☎ 2735-5129; meals ₡3500-6000; 10am-2pm & 5-10pm) The specialties of the house at Il Giardino are homemade pasta and fresh seafood. Considering that you're on the edge of the wilderness in a far-flung corner of Costa Rica, there is a fair measure of Italian authenticity here.

Drinking

You can get decent Mexican food at **Juanita's** (5pm-2am), but it's more popular for the margaritas. **Iguana Iguana** (4pm-midnight), at the cabins of the same name, is another popular watering hole, especially on weekends when the locals join in the action.

Shopping

Artes de Osa (☎ 2735-5429; 🕑 8am-5pm) This cutesy souvenir shop has the usual knick-knacks in addition to some attractive handcrafted furniture and hand-painted pottery.

Jagua Arts & Crafts (☎ 2735-5267; 🕑 8am-5pm) A great collection of art and jewelry by local and expat craftspeople, including some amazing painted masks.

Osa Army Navy (🕑 8am-7pm Mon-Sat, 9am-4pm Sun) Your one-stop shop for sportswear, boogie boards, fishing gear, bug nets, knives, backpacks and other outdoor gear.

Getting There & Around

AIR

NatureAir (www.natureair.com) and **Sansa** (www.sansa.com) have daily flights to/from San José; one-way flights are approximately US$100.

Alfa Romeo Aero Taxi (☎ 2775-5353; www.alfaromeoair.com) has light aircraft (three and five passengers) for charter flights to Golfito, Carate, Drake, Sirena, Palmar Sur, Quepos and Limón. Prices are dependent on the number of passengers, so it's best to try to organize a larger group if you're considering this option.

BICYCLE

Rent a bike at **Ciclo Corcovado** (☎ 2735-5429; per hr ₡500; 🕑 8am-5pm).

BOAT

Two passenger ferries travel to Golfito (₡3000, 1½ hours), departing at 6am and 10am daily. Note that these times are subject to change; in this part of the country, schedules often fall prey to the whims of the captain.

A better option than chugging away on the ferries is to hire a private water taxi to shuttle you across the bay. You will have to negotiate, but prices are generally reasonable, especially considering that you'll be free of having to rely on the ferry. Fortunately, waters in the Golfo Dulce are sheltered and generally calm, though it's still good to have a reasonable degree of faith in the seaworthiness of both your captain and his ship before you set out.

Taboga Aquatic Tours (☎ 2735-5265) runs water taxis to Zancudo for ₡25,000.

BUS

Most buses arrive at the peach-color terminal on the west side of town. All of these pass La Palma (23km away) for the eastern entry into Corcovado. Buy tickets to San José in advance.

Neily ₡2000; three hours; departs 5:30am and 2pm.
San Isidro ₡3000; five hours; departs 1pm.
San José, via San Isidro (Autotransportes Blanco Lobo) ₡5900; eight hours; departs 5am and 11am.

CAR & TAXI

Colectivo Transportation (☎ 8837-3120, 8832-8680; Soda Deya) runs a collective jeep-taxi service to Cabo Matapalo (₡2000) and Carate (₡3500) on the southern tip of the national park. Departures are from Soda Deya at 6am and 1:30pm, returning at 8:30am and 4pm.

Otherwise, you can call and hire a 4WD taxi from **Taxi 348** (☎ 8849-5228; taxicorcovado@racsa.co.cr) or from the **Central Taxi Center** (☎ 2735-5481). Taxis usually charge up to ₡37,500 for the ride to Carate, up to ₡15,000 for the ride to Matapalo, and more than ₡50,000 for the overland trek to Drake.

You can also rent a vehicle from **Solid Car Rental** (☎ 2735-5777).

CABO MATAPALO

The tip of the Osa peninsula and the entrance to Golfo Dulce lies just 17km south of Puerto Jiménez, but this heavily forested and beach-fringed cape is a vastly different world. A network of trails traverses the foothills, which are uninhabited except for migrating wildlife from the Reserva Forestal Golfo Dulce. Along the coastline, miles upon miles of beaches in pristine wilderness are virtually abandoned, except for handfuls of surfers in the know.

Although facilities in this remote corner are extremely limited, Cabo Matapalo is home to a number of luxurious lodges that cater to travelers searching for peace and seclusion. Of course, it's hard to feel lonely out here given the breadth of animals about: scarlet macaw, brown pelican and all breeds of heron are frequently sighted on the beaches, while four species of monkey, sloth, coati, agouti and anteater roam the woods.

Tours

Naturalist Andy Pruter runs **Everyday Adventures** (☎ 8353-8619; www.psychotours.com), which offers all kinds of not-so-everyday adventures in Cabo Matapalo. His signature tour

EXPLORE MORE: CABO MATAPALO

Cabo Matapalo is an attractive destination for adventurers who wish to go it alone. All of the lodges have easy access to miles of **trails**, which you can explore without a guide. Indeed, you are likely to spot a good selection of wildlife just walking along the Cabo's tree-lined dirt road.

A fantastic and easy hiking destination is **King Louis**, a magnificent, 28m-tall waterfall that can be accessed by a trail from **Playa Matapalo**. For ocean adventures, most of the lodges also offer **kayaks**, and the wild, beautiful beach – surrounding on three sides – is never more than a short walk away.

These pristine beaches around Cabo Matapalo offer three breaks that are putting this little peninsula on the surfing map. **Playa Pan Dulce** is a double point break. The inside break is a small wave that is ideal for beginners; experts can find the point on the outside break and ride it all the way into shore. **Backwash Bay** offers a nice beach break at low tide. The steep beach makes it excellent for long-boarding. **Playa Matapalo** also has an A-plus right break, with the biggest and best waves in the area. Conditions are usually good with a west swell; surfing season coincides with the rainy season, which is April to October.

So put your guidebook down for a day or – even better – a week. Follow your own path, catch your own wave and paddle up your own stream. It is bound to be an adventure more memorable than any one you'll find along the well-trodden tourist trail.

is tree climbing (US$55 per person): scaling a 60m ficus tree, aptly named 'Cathedral.' Also popular – and definitely adrenaline inducing – is waterfall rappelling (US$85) down cascades ranging from 15m to 30m. For the tamer of heart, excellent three to four hour guided nature walks (US$45) tap into Andy and his staff members' extensive knowledge base.

Sleeping

This area is off the grid, so many places do not have electricity around the clock or hot water. Reservations are recommended in the dry season (mid-November to the end of April). In the following listings high-season rates are quoted; prices include three meals, unless otherwise stated.

Ojo del Mar (☎ 2735-5531; www.ojodelmar.com; s/d from US$65/110; P) Tucked in amid the windswept beach and the lush jungle, this is a little plot of paradise. The four beautifully handcrafted bamboo bungalows are entirely open-air, allowing for all the natural sounds and scents to seep in (thatch roofs and mosquito nets provide protection from the elements). Solar power provides electricity in the *casa grande* (main house). Hammocks swing from the palms, while howler monkeys swing above. Rates include breakfast, but Niko – co-owner and cook – also serves an excellent, all-organic dinner. Look for this gem on the road to Carate, just before the Buena Esperanza Bar.

Ranchos Almendros (Kapu's Place; ☎ 2735-5531; http://home.earthlink.net/~kapu/; Cabo Matapalo; r per person from US$75; P) This is the end of the line on Cabo Matapalo, where the road stops pretending and turns into a sandy beach path. The property includes three cozy *cabañas* that are equipped with solar power, large screened windows, full kitchens and garden showers. As per the name, 'Almond Tree Ranch' is part of an ongoing project dedicated to the reforestation of Indian almond trees to create habitat for the endangered scarlet macaw.

El Remanso Lodge (☎ 2735-5569; www.elremanso.com; road to Carate, 18km; s/d from US$180/300; P) Set on 56 hectares of rainforest, El Remanso is yet another tropical paradise. Constructed entirely from fallen tropical hardwoods, the secluded, spacious and sumptuous cabins have shiny wood floors and beautifully finished fixtures. Several units have folding French doors that open to unimpeded vistas of the foliage and the ocean in the distance.

Casa Bambú (www.casabambu.addr.com; Cabo Matapalo; 2-/3-/4-person cottages without meals US$195/205/215; P) This property on the pristine Playa Pan Dulce has three secluded *casas*. All have solar power, bamboo-and-hardwood construction and screen-free half-walls, allowing nothing to come between you and the ocean breezes (except maybe a mosquito net). Fully equipped kitchens and twice-weekly maid service make this an excellent option for longer-term guests who want to get back to nature (weekly rates available). Meals are not included; kayaks, boogie boards and other beach toys are.

Bosque del Cabo (☎ 8381-4847, in Puerto Jiménez 2735-5206; www.bosquedelcabo.com; road to Carate, 18km; s/d from US$195/300; P) Nine quaint cabins are perched on a bluff here overlooking the ocean. Modern bathrooms, garden showers and personal hammocks in lush surroundings are the norm; deluxe cabins have added perks like king-sized beds, dressing rooms and wraparound porches. Explore the surrounding 200 hectares of rainforest at canopy level (by zip line or by suspension bridge) or at ground level (on miles of marked trails).

ourpick **Lapa Ríos** (☎ 2735-5130; www.laparios.com; road to Carate, 17km; s/d US$495/610; P) A few hundred meters beyond El Portón Blanco along the road to Carate, this top-notch all-inclusive wilderness resort combines the right amount of luxury with a rustic, tropical ambience. Scattered over the site are 16 spacious, thatch bungalows, all decked out with queen-sized beds, bamboo furniture, garden showers and private decks with panoramic views. An extensive trail system allows exploration of the 400-hectare reserve, while swimming, snorkeling and surfing are at your doorstep. As one of the select few hotels in Costa Rica to earn five leaves in the government-run Certified Sustainable Tourism program, Lapa Ríos also serves as a living classroom. If you need substantial proof that ecotourism can be a profitable and successful vehicle for ensuring wilderness preservation and empowering local communities with increased economic opportunities, look no further.

Eating & Drinking

About 1km before El Portón Blanco, you'll find the trendy, tropical **Buena Esperanza Bar** (☎ 2735-5531; road to Carate, Carbonera; meals ₡2500-5500; 9am-midnight; V), a festive, open-air tropical bar on the east side of the road. The limited menu includes lots of sandwiches and vegetarian items, plus a full bar. It's Cabo Matapalo's only place to eat or drink, and so often attracts a decent crowd of locals, resident expats and tourists.

Most hotels and lodges also have small shops that sell snacks and drinks. If you're planning on hiking, be sure to stock up on lots of fresh water as well as your favorite form of trail mix – once you're out in the woods or on the beach, options are decidedly limited.

Getting There & Away

From the Puerto Jiménez–Carate road, the turnoff for Cabo Matapalo is on the left-hand side, through a white cement gate (called 'El Portón Blanco'). If you are driving, a 4WD is highly recommended – even in the dry season – as roads frequently get washed out. Otherwise, the transport *colectivo* will drop you here; it passes by at about 6:30am and 2pm heading to Carate, and 10am and 5:30pm heading back to Jiménez. A taxi will come here from Port Jim for about ₡15,000.

CARATE

About 45km south of Puerto Jiménez, the dirt road that rounds the peninsula comes to an abrupt dead end in the village of Carate, which is literally nothing more than an airstrip and a *pulpería*. Carate may not rate high on the list of Osa's top tourist destinations, but it does serve as the southwestern gateway for anyone hiking into Sirena ranger station (p422) in Parque Nacional Corcovado.

With that said, there are a handful of recommended wilderness lodges in the area, any of which can provide a good night's rest for travelers heading to/from Corcovado. The ride from Puerto Jiménez to Carate is also an adventure in itself as the narrow, bumpy dirt road winds its way around dense rainforest, through gushing rivers and across windswept beaches. Birdlife and other wildlife are prolific along this stretch: keep your eyes peeled and hang on tight.

Sleeping & Eating

Many places in Carate don't have 24-hour electricity or hot water. Reservations are recommended in the dry season – communication is often through Puerto Jiménez, so messages may not be retrieved every day. High-season rates are quoted; prices are per person, including three meals, unless otherwise stated.

West of Carate is the national park, so if you're planning on hiking into Corcovado, you must be self-sufficient from here on out. The *pulpería* is the last chance you have to stock up on food and water.

La Leona Eco-Lodge (☎ 2735-5704; www.laleonaecolodge.com; s/d from US$95/160; P) On the edge of Parque Nacional Corcovado 2km west of the *pulpería*, this friendly lodge offers all of the thrills of camping, without the hassles. Sixteen comfy forest-green tents are nestled between the palm trees, with decks facing the beach. All are fully screened and comfortably furnished; solar power provides electricity in the restaurant. Behind the accommodations, 30 hectares of virgin rainforest property offer opportunities for waterfall hiking, horseback riding and wildlife-watching.

Lookout Inn (☎ 2735-5431; www.lookout-inn.com; r per person from US$115; Ⓟ 💻 🏊) A deep wilderness retreat, Lookout Inn has comfortable quarters with mural-painted walls, hardwood floors, beautifully carved doors and unbeatable views. Accommodations are in 'tiki huts,' which are open-air, A-frame huts accessible only by a wooden walkway winding through the giant joba trees (prime bird-watching territory). Behind the inn, 360 steps – known as the 'Stairway to Heaven' – lead straight up the side of the mountain to four observation platforms and a waterfall trail. And here's an interesting twist: if you don't spot a scarlet macaw during your stay, your lodging is free!

Luna Lodge (☎ 8380-5036, in USA 888-409-8448; www.lunalodge.com; s/d US$120/210; Ⓟ) A steep road goes through the Río Carate and up the valley to this enchanting mountain retreat, located about 2km north of the *pulpería*. Taking full advantage of the vista, the high-roofed, open-air restaurant is a marvelous place to indulge in the delights of the gardens and orchards on the grounds. Seven spacious, thatch-roof bungalows each have a huge garden shower and private patio. The open-air meditation studio is nothing less than inspirational.

Getting There & Away

NatureAir (www.natureair.com) and **Alfa Romeo Aero Taxi** (www.alfaromeoair.com) offer charter flights. Prices are dependent on the number of passengers, so it's best to try to organize a larger group if you're considering this option.

Transportation Colectivo (₡3000, 2½ hours) departs Puerto Jiménez for Carate at 6am and 1:30pm, returning at 8:30am and 4pm. Note that the *colectivo* often fills up on its return trip to Puerto Jiménez, especially during the dry season. Arrive at least 30 minutes ahead of time or you might find yourself stranded.

Alternatively, catch a taxi from Puerto Jiménez (₡30,000). If you are driving, you'll need a 4WD – even in the dry season as there are a couple of river crossings. Assuming you don't have valuables in sight, you can leave your car at the *pulpería* (per night ₡2500) and hike to La Leona station (1½ hours), or at any of the tented camps listed above (with prior arrangements).

PARQUE NACIONAL CORCOVADO

Famously labeled by *National Geographic* as 'the most biologically intense place on earth,' this **national park** is the last great original tract of tropical rainforest in Pacific Central America. The bastion of biological diversity is home to Costa Rica's largest population of scarlet macaws, as well as countless other endangered species, including Baird's tapir, the giant anteater and the world's largest bird of prey, the harpy eagle. Corcovado's amazing biodiversity has long attracted a devoted stream of visitors who descend from Bahía Drake and Puerto Jiménez to explore the remote location and spy on a wide array of wildlife.

HISTORY

Because of its remoteness, Corcovado remained undisturbed until loggers invaded in the 1960s. The destruction was halted in 1975 when the area was established as government-administered parklands. The early years were a challenge, as park authorities, with limited personnel and resources, sought to deal with illegal clear-cutting, poaching and gold mining, the latter of which was causing severe erosion in the park's rivers and streams. By 1986,

TOP PICKS: ONLY IN CORCOVADO

While Costa Rica's national parks can stretch from coast to coast, only in Corcovado can you do the following:

- Spot all four of the country's primate species in a single outing.
- Be virtually guaranteed an up-close-and-personal encounter with a tapir.
- Add more than a dozen endemic subspecies to your bird-watching list.
- Explore the country's largest remaining tract of Pacific tropical rainforest.
- Pass through no less than 25 unique and varied terrestrial and marine ecosystems.

the number of gold miners had exceeded 1000, which promptly caused the government to evict them (and their families) entirely from the park environs.

Unfortunately, poaching remains a severe problem in Corcovado to this day. The highest-profile victims are the highly endangered Central American jaguar and its main food source, the white-lipped peccary. Heavily armed hunters regularly gun down peccaries en masse and sell their meat, which has resulted in a drastic decline in population size over the last decade. Jaguars, suffering from a diminishing food supply, prey on domestic animals in the area, making them a target of local residents (not to mention the fact that jaguar pelts and bones fetch hefty sums, as well). The Ministry of Environment and Energy (Minae; Ministerio del Ambiente y Energía) has stepped up its police patrols, but has been unable to completely stop the poaching.

On the bright side, illegal logging has all but subsided, primarily since increased tourism has lead to an increased human presence in the park. Furthermore, in an effort to control hunting, agencies such as Conservation International, the Nature Conservancy and the World Wildlife Fund, as well as various other NGOs and charities, have banded together to help organize and fund the park's anti-poaching units.

Since 2003, Corcovado has – much to the chagrin of Minae – remained stagnant on the 'tentative list' of Unesco World Heritage Sites. While no official disclosure has been released as to the reason behind the park's perennial failure to achieve recognition, local media speculates that mismanagement, poor funding and the inability to control illegal poaching may serve as contributing factors.

ORIENTATION & INFORMATION

The 425-sq-km park is nestled in the southwestern corner of the Península de Osa, and protects habitat ranging from mangrove swamps to primary and secondary rainforest to low-altitude cloud forest. The most accessible and visible habitat is the 46km of sandy coastline.

Information and maps are available at the **Oficina de Área de Conservación Osa** (Osa Conservation Area Headquarters; ☎ 2735-5580; park fee per person per day US$10; 🕐 8am-noon & 1-4pm) in Puerto Jiménez. Contact this office to make reservations for lodging and meals at all of the ranger stations and to pay your park fee. Be sure to make these arrangements a few days in advance as facilities are limited, and they do fill up on occasion in the dry season.

Park headquarters are at **Sirena ranger station** on the coast in the middle of the park. Other ranger stations are located on the park boundaries: **San Pedrillo station** in the northwest corner on the coast; the new **Los Planes station** on the northern boundary (near the village of the same name); **La Leona station** in the southeast corner on the coast (near the village of Carate); and **Los Patos ranger station** in the northeast corner (near the village of La Palma).

Always check with rangers before setting out about trail conditions and possible closures (especially during the wettest months, from June to November).

ACTIVITIES

Wildlife-Watching

The best wildlife-watching in Corcovado is at Sirena, but the coastal trails have two advantages: they are more open, and the constant crashing of waves covers the sound of noisy walkers. White-faced capuchin, red-tailed squirrel, collared peccary, white-nosed coati and northern tamandua are regularly seen on both of the following trails.

On the less-traveled San Pedrillo–Sirena trail, Playa Llorona is a popular nesting spot for marine turtles, including leatherback, olive ridley and green turtles. Nesting turtles attract ocelot, jaguar and other predators, though they are hard to spot.

Both coastal trails produce an endless pageant of birds. Pairs of scarlet macaws are guaranteed, as the tropical almond trees lining the coast are a favorite food. The sections along the beach shelter mangrove black hawk by the dozens and numerous waterbird species. The little rock island opposite Punta Salsipuedes serves as a roost for hundreds of birds, including the magnificent frigate bird and brown booby.

The Los Patos–Sirena trail attracts lowland rainforest birds such as great curassow, chestnut-mandibled toucan, fiery-billed aracari, turquoise cotinga and rufous piha; trogon, hummingbird and wood creeper are plentiful. Encounters with mixed flocks are common. Mammals are similar to those sighted on the coastal trails, but Los Patos is better for primates and white-lipped peccary.

For wildlife-watchers frustrated at the difficulty of seeing rainforest mammals, a stay at Sirena ranger station is a must. Topping the list, Baird's tapirs are practically assured – that is a statement that can be made at few other places in the world. This endangered and distant relative of the rhinoceros is frequently spotted grazing along the airstrip after dusk. Sirena is excellent for other herbivores, particularly red brocket (especially on the Los Platos–Sirena trail) and both species of peccary. Agouti and tayra are also common.

The profusion of meat on the hoof means there are predators aplenty, but they are not nearly as confiding. Jaguars are occasionally sighted near the airstrip in the very early morning (midnight to 4am). While spotlighting at night you are more likely to see kinkajou and crab-eating skunk (especially at the mouth of the Río Sirena). Ocelot represents your best chance for observing a cat, but again, it's difficult.

Corcovado is the only national park in Costa Rica with all four of the country's primate species. Spider monkey, mantled howler and white-faced capuchin can be encountered anywhere, while the Los Platos–Sirena trail is best for the fourth and most endangered species, the Central American squirrel monkey. Sirena also has fair chances for the extremely hard-to-find silky anteater, a nocturnal animal that frequents the beachside forests between the Río Claro and the station.

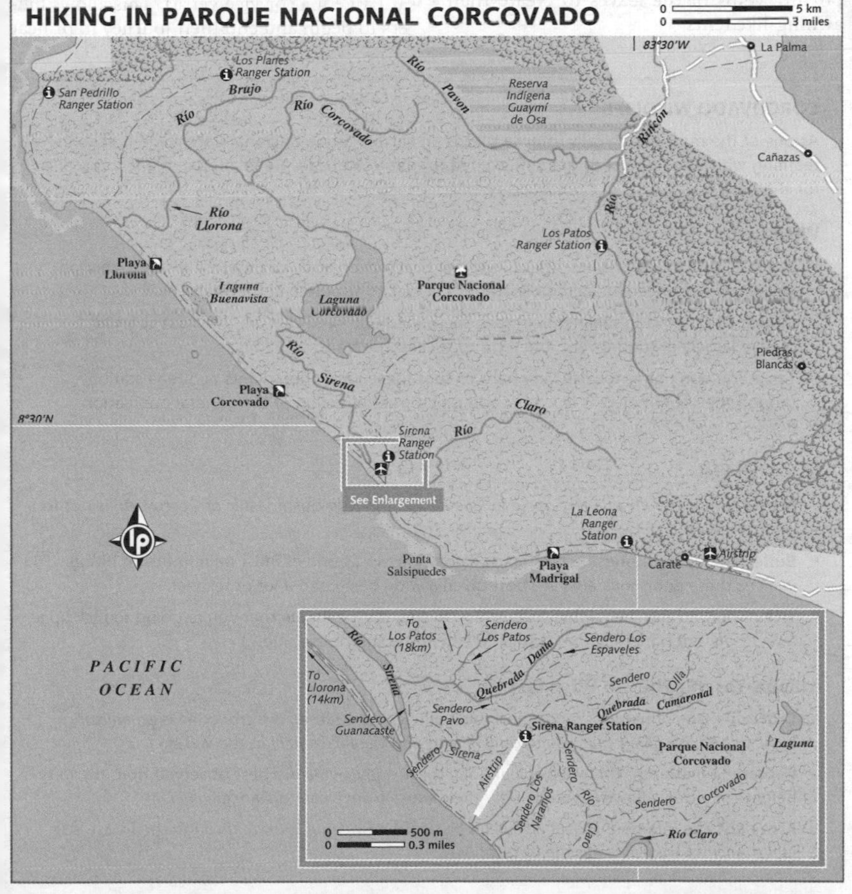

The Río Sirena is a popular spot for all kinds of heron, as well as waders such as ruddy turnstone and western sandpiper. However, you may be more excited to spot the other riverside regulars, which include the American crocodile, three-toed sloth and bull shark.

Here's a good tip: the abundant banana trees along the coastal trails are not indigenous to Costa Rica (bananas are Asian in origin), but they serve as huge magnets for wildlife. In addition to the more obvious visitors, namely monkeys, there are a few other interesting species to be on the lookout for. For instance, hermit crabs dine on the fallen fruit, while rufous-tailed hummingbirds build their nest under banana leaves. Thomas' fruit-eating bats also snip the supporting veins of the leaves to create their awning-like tents.

Hiking

Paths are primitive and the hiking is hot, humid and insect-ridden, but the challenge of the trek and the interaction with wildlife at Corcovado are thrilling. Hiring a local guide is highly recommended. Obviously, your guide will know the trails well, thus avoiding the unmitigated disaster of getting lost; furthermore, he or she will have a keen eye for spotting and identifying wildlife.

Otherwise, travel in a small group. Bring a compass, as it is impossible to navigate using the sun or stars underneath the rainforest canopy. Carry plenty of food, water and insect repellent. And always verify your route with the rangers before you depart.

The most popular route traverses the park from Los Patos to Sirena, then exits the park at La Leona (or vice versa). This allows hikers to begin and end their journey in or near

CORCOVADO WILDLIFE

As one of the most biologically intense places on earth, Parque Nacional Corcovado is absolutely teeming with wildlife. Just to get you excited for the trek ahead, we've prepared a few top picks for the best (and worst) of Corcovado wildlife.

Wish List

- **Jaguar** These elusive felines sit at the top of nearly everybody's rainforest wish list, though you're going to need an incredible amount of luck to spot one in the wild.
- **Ocelot** Of Corcovado's feline predators, these medium-sized cats are the most spotted – they're largely ground-lovers, and tend to stick to the trails.
- **Tapir** You don't have to wish very hard to spot these lumbering giants at Sirena station, though their commonness in Corcovado isn't a true reflection of the general population figure.

No-Wish List

- **Fer-de-lance** Known as a *terciopelo* in Costa Rica, the true bushmaster of Corcovado is not to be toyed with.
- **Bullet ant** Sitting alongside the tarantula hawk wasp as one of most pain-inducing biting insects, these enormous ants are best given a wide berth and a lot of respect.
- **Ticks** Approaching megalithic sizes in Corcovado; it's inevitable that you're going to pick up a few dozen, but hopefully they'll stick to where the sun does shine.

Maybe-Yes, Maybe-No Wish List

- **Crocodile** One of nature's oldest and most efficient predators, the crocodile is an amazing sight to behold, given that you're on the land and they're mostly in the water.
- **Peccary** Something akin to a tropical boar, these surly swine are best observed from the lofty heights of a tree, allowing you to view their antics from a safe distance.
- **Army ant** The infamous insect army can be heard crunching its way through the forest, so you'd be wise to give them the right of way.

Puerto Jiménez, offering easy access to La Leona and Los Patos. The trek between Sirena and San Pedrillo is more difficult, both physically and logistically. The travel times listed are conservative: fit hikers with light packs can move faster, unless you spend a lot of time bird-watching or taking photos.

Hiking is best in the dry season (from December to April), when there is still regular rain but all of the trails are open. It's still muddy, but you won't sink quite as deep.

SIRENA TO SAN PEDRILLO/LOS PLANES

The route between Sirena and San Pedrillo/Los Planes is the longest trail in Corcovado. The vast majority of this hike is along the beach, which means loose sand and little shade – grueling, especially with a heavy pack. One local guide recommends starting this hike at night in order to avoid the hot sun.

Another tricky factor is the three river crossings, which become very difficult or impossible at high tide. As a result, the time of departure from Sirena station depends on the tides; the recommended departure time is about two hours before low tide.

The first river crossing – Río Sirena – is about 1km north of Sirena. The largest river on the hike, it is the neighborhood hangout for sharks and crocodiles, and it can sometimes spawn swift currents, so cross with extreme caution. The final river, the cascading Río Llorona, marks the end of the beach trail, and lies just before the trail splits and diverges.

Hikers generally prefer to turn left and follow the coast to San Pedrillo, a route that covers 23km in 10 to 15 hours, and is awash with stunning beachside scenery. Following the coastline is also easier to navigate and ultimately safer than heading inland, though the Los Planes route is most definitely less trafficked and more wild. Detouring inland, however, will add a couple of kilometers (and hours) to your hike.

This trail is only open from December through April, since heavy rains can make the Río Sirena impassable. Due to the complexity of this route, taking a guide is strongly recommended, particularly if you're heading to Los Planes.

SIRENA TO LA LEONA

The 16km hike from Sirena to La Leona is another sizzler, following the shoreline through coastal forest and along deserted beaches. It involves one major river crossing at Río Claro, just south of Sirena station.

The journey between Sirena and La Leona takes six or seven hours. You can camp at La Leona; otherwise, it takes another hour to hike the additional 3.5km to Carate, where you can stay in a local lodge or catch the collective taxi to Puerto Jiménez.

SIRENA TO LOS PATOS

The route to Los Patos goes 18km through the heart of Corcovado, affording the opportunity to pass through plenty of primary and secondary forest. The trail is relatively flat for the first 12km. You will hike through secondary forest and wade through two river tributaries before reaching the Laguna Corcovado. From this point, the route undulates steeply (mostly uphill!) for the remaining 6km. One guide recommends doing this hike in the opposite direction – from Los Patos to Sirena – to avoid this exhausting, uphill ending. Near Los Patos, a lovely waterfall provides a much-needed shower at the end of a long trek.

The largest herds of peccary are reportedly on this trail. Local guides advise that peccary sense fear, but they will back off if you act aggressively. Alternatively, if you climb up a tree – about 2m off the ground – you'll avoid being bitten or trampled in the event of running into a surly bunch. Hint: peccary herds emit a strong smell of onions, so you usually have a bit of a heads-up before they come crashing through the bush.

You can camp at Los Patos, or continue an additional 14km to the village of La Palma. This four-hour journey is a shady and muddy descent down the valley of the Río Rincón. If you are traveling from La Palma to Los Patos, be prepared for a steep climb.

If you don't plan on traversing the park, a 6km day hike from Los Patos to the Laguna Corcovado is feasible, though this requires spending two nights at Los Patos.

It is highly recommended that you take a guide with you on this route as getting lost – or much worse – is a very real possibility.

TOURS

The main routes across Parque Nacional Corcovado are well marked and well traveled, making the journey easy enough to complete independently. However, hiring a guide can greatly enhance this experience, not only because you will not have to worry about taking a

IT'S A JUNGLE OUT THERE

The birds are brilliant, the animals are enchanting and the forest is fantastic. But Parque Nacional Corcovado is the real deal, 100% wilderness, and the dangers should not be underestimated. Every season, travelers to Corcovado become injured, sick or even dead; take some precautions to make sure this is not you:

- The number one danger for hikers is heat exhaustion and dehydration. This is the rainforest: it is hot and humid and you are going to sweat more than you realize. Make sure you carry enough water: a 1L or 1.5L bottle (which you can refill at each ranger station) is the bare minimum per person.
- Do not drink untreated water from any stream – this is a surefire way to get a nasty case of giardia. However, prior to setting out for Costa Rica, you should consider investing in a water treatment device, such as a filter and pump system, a UV wand or even a bottle of old-fashioned iodine tablets.
- Wear a hat, sunblock and insect repellent. The number two danger for hikers is sunburn and subsequently sunstroke, especially while traveling on the exposed coastal trails. Although malaria and dengue are relatively minor risks in Costa Rica, mosquitoes are a huge nuisance in Corcovado so take precautions and cover up.
- Travel light, as the pleasure of the hike is inversely proportionate to the weight of your pack. Although it's tempting to carry gear for every conceivable type of situation, overloading your pack is a surefire way to succumb to all of the risks we've previously mentioned.
- Always check with the rangers about trail conditions and tide charts before setting out. This is extremely valuable, so that not only are you up-to-date on this information, but also the rangers know the route you are planning to follow and your time of departure. Pay attention to their recommendations as river crossings can be very dangerous.
- If you're hiking without a guide, bring a compass and know how to use it! Also recommended is a topography map or a modern GPS navigation system. If you have limited wilderness experience, hire a guide – you will get your money back many times over in peace of mind.

wrong turn. Besides their intimate knowledge of the trail, local guides are amazingly knowledgeable about flora and fauna, including the best places to spot various species. Many guides also carry telescopes, allowing for up-close inspection of the various creatures.

Guides are most often hired through the park office in Puerto Jiménez, at any of the ranger stations heading into the park, or near the airstrip in either Carate or Sirena. You can also inquire with tour operators and hotels in Puerto Jiménez and Bahía Drake. As you'd imagine, prices vary considerably depending on the season, availability, the size of your party and the type of expedition you want to arrange. In all cases, you will need to negotiate a price that is inclusive of park fees, meals and transportation to the park.

Generally speaking, it is difficult to recommend a particular agency or guide as things change quickly in this part of the country. On top of that, we constantly receive mixed reports from travelers detailing life-changing and life-threatening experiences in Corcovado, which means that this is one destination where it pays to put the book down and do things yourself.

Although there is no hard and fast rule for sizing up the quality of a guide, the three things you want to measure are their communicative ability, professionalism and park knowledge. Perhaps most important of all is their English ability, especially if you don't have a strong command of Spanish. Trekking through the rainforest can be a dangerous activity, though it doesn't have to be if both you and your guide stay in constant communication.

Professionalism is best assessed by using your common sense – simply put, ask yourself whether or not this is the kind of person you would trust your life with. Professional guides are also usually outfitted with modern and well-maintained gear, and are quick to reassure travelers of the length and breadth of their experience.

On that note, the final factor in choosing a guide is park knowledge. No matter how many guidebooks you've read or maps you've studied, Corcovado can be a tricky place to access. Before choosing your guide, talk to them about your intended route, and be sure that they are knowledgeable about the trek ahead.

Finally, don't stress – Corcovado is truly a world-class trekking destination, and so long as you're comfortable with your guide, you're guaranteed to have an amazing experience here.

CORCOVADO FOR CHILDREN

While so many natural spaces in Costa Rica are undeniably kid-friendly, Corcovado is raw wilderness that commands a healthy amount of respect. As such, the decision to bring your children along for the adventure is not to be taken lightly, and you should carefully weigh the potential risks before doing so.

At the bare minimum, your children should be old enough to fend for themselves. Carrying a toddler on your back through the jungle is a taxing, not to mention potentially dangerous, feat of endurance. You should also make the call as to whether or not your children will be able to endure the rough conditions in the park. Tropical sun, creepy crawlies, strenuous exercise and the lack of bathroom facilities can quickly overwhelm inexperienced city slickers.

However, if your kids are the outdoors type, then feel free to choose a trail that is appropriate to their skill level. Day hikes around Sirena or San Pedrillo offer curious young minds a glimpse of the unknown, while longer inter-station treks provide older children and teenagers an unforgettable experience. Whichever trail you opt for, strongly consider taking along a guide – it's always wise to have an extra pair of eyes watching over your loved ones!

SLEEPING & EATING

Camping costs US$4 per person per day at any station; facilities include potable water and latrines. Sirena station has a covered platform, but other stations have no such luxuries. Remember to bring a flashlight or a kerosene lamp, as the campsites are pitch black at night. Camping is not permitted in areas other than the ranger stations.

Simple dormitory lodging (US$12) and meals are available at Sirena station only. Food and cooking fuel have to be packed in, so reserve at least 15 to 30 days in advance through the **Oficina de Área de Conservación Osa** (Osa Conservation Area Headquarters; ☎ 2735-55800) in Puerto Jiménez. Scientists and researchers working at the Sirena biological station get preference over travelers for accommodations and meals, but if you secure a reservation, you will be taken care of.

Otherwise, campers must bring all their own food. Note that ranger stations face a challenge with trash disposal, so all visitors are required to pack out all of their trash.

GETTING THERE & AWAY

From Bahía Drake

From Bahía Drake, you can walk the coastal trail that leads to San Pedrillo station (about four hours from Agujitas), or any lodge can drop you here as a part of their regular tours to Corcovado. Alternatively, you can

PENÍNSULA DE OSA & GOLFO DULCE

GREEN GRASSROOTS

The **Fundación Corcovado** (☎ 2297-3013; www.corcovadofoundation.org) is a network of local businesspeople – mostly hoteliers – who have teamed up to raise both money and awareness to support their most valuable resource: the biodiversity of the national park. Through their own fund-raising efforts, they have hired additional rangers to crack down on poaching, implemented various community education programs and worked toward establishing a sustainable-tourism code for local businesses. Fundación Corcovado has also been spearheading an increasingly high-profile campaign to designate Parque Nacional Corcovado as a Unesco World Heritage Site.

The Fundación Corcovado invites volunteers to work in the community and in the park. Tasks might include teaching about waste management and conservation at local schools, maintaining trails and bridges in the park, patrolling beaches and collecting data during turtle season, and providing assistance and expertise to visiting tourists. The daily fee of US$24 for volunteers includes transportation from San José as well as room and board with a local family. Note that there is a two-week minimum commitment for all service projects.

BAIRD'S TAPIR PROJECT

The **Baird's Tapir Project** (http://savetapirs.org) has been studying the populations of Baird's tapir around Sirena station since 1994 in the hope of enhancing conservation efforts. Scientists use radio telemetry (that's radio collars to us) to collect data about where the tapirs live, how far they wander, whom they associate with and how often they reproduce. So far, several dozen tapirs around Sirena are wearing collars, which allows scientists to collect the data without disrupting the animals.

Sirena station is an ideal place to do such research, because there is no pressure from deforestation or hunting, which gives researchers the chance to observe a healthy, thriving population. The animals' longevity and slow rate of reproduction mean that many years of observation are required before drawing conclusions.

So, what have we learned about these river rhinos so far? The nocturnal animals spend their nights foraging – oddly, they prefer to forage in 'disturbed habitats' (like along the airstrip), not in the dense rainforest. They spend their days in the cool waters of the swamp, out of the hot sun. Tapirs are not very social, but a male-female pair often shares the same 'home range,' living together for years at a time. Scientists speculate that tapirs may in fact be monogamous – who knew these ungainly creatures would be so romantic!

consider heading inland to the Los Planes station, though this is a longer, more heavily forested route.

You can also charter a boat to San Pedrillo (US$80 to US$125) or Sirena (US$125 to US$165). If you have a car, most hotels and lodges along Bahía Drake can watch over it for you for a few dollars a day.

From La Palma

From the north, the closest point of access is the town of La Palma, from where you can catch a bus or taxi south to Puerto Jiménez or north to San José.

Heading to Los Patos, you might be able to find a taxi to take you partway; however, the road is only passable to 4WD vehicles (and not always), so be prepared to hike the 14km to the ranger station. The road crosses the river about 20 times in the last 6km. It's easy to miss the right turn shortly before the ranger station, so keep your eyes peeled.

If you have a car, it's best to leave it with a hotel or lodge in La Palma instead of traversing the route to Los Patos, though it certainly is an adventure. Furthermore, once in Los Patos, there is no reliable place to park your car while trekking in the park.

From Carate

In the southeast, the closest point of access is Carate, from where La Leona station is a one-hour, 3.5km hike west along the beach.

Carate is accessible from Puerto Jiménez via a poorly maintained, 45km dirt road. This journey is an adventure in itself, and often allows for some good wildlife-spotting along the way. A collective 4WD taxi travels this route twice daily for ₡3500. Otherwise you can hire a 4WD taxi; prices depend on the size of your party, the season (prices increase in the rainy months) and your bargaining skills.

If you have your own car, the *pulpería* in Carate is a safe place to park for a few days, though you'll have some extra piece of mind if you tip the manager before setting out.

By Air

Alfa Romeo Aero Taxi (☎ 2735-5353; www.alfaromeoair.com) offers charter flights connecting Puerto Jiménez, Drake and Golfito to Carate and Sirena. Flights are best booked at the airport in person, and one-way fares are typically less than US$100. Note that long-term parking is not available at any of these locations, so it's best to make prior arrangements if you need to leave your car somewhere.

GOLFO DULCE

While Golfo Dulce is certainly less celebrated than the Península de Osa, an increasing number of travelers are making the arduous journey in search of the world's longest left-hand break at Pavones. The region is also home to Parque Nacional Piedras Blancas, a stunning tract of rainforest that used to be part of Corcovado, and still protects the same amazing biodiversity. This far corner of Costa Rica is also home to significantly large indigenous populations, which live in the Reserva Indígena Guaymí de Conte Burica near Pavones.

GOLFITO

A historic banana port that is slowly fading into obscurity, Golfito is a rough-and-ready town struggling to find a purpose beyond yellow gold. Although Golfito has temporarily postponed its demise by implementing duty-free shopping for domestic tourists, the jungle behind it is slowly creeping in, and local residents hardly seem concerned about it.

As the largest town in Golfo Dulce, Golfito is a major transportation hub for hikers heading to Corcovado, surfers heading to Pavones and sportfishers docking for the night. Although it's unlikely that you'll want to stick around for any longer than you have to, there is a certain charm to Golfito that isn't lost on everyone. Case in point – the verdant slopes of the Refugio Nacional de Fauna Silvestre Golfito surround the town, and provide a picturesque backdrop to the crumbling buildings.

History

From 1938 to 1985, bustling Golfito was the headquarters of United Fruit's operations in the southern part of Costa Rica. In the 1980s, declining markets, rising taxes, worker unrest and banana diseases forced the company's departure. Although some of the plantations now produce oil from the African oil palm, the collapse of the banana industry has not alleviated the economic hardship caused by United Fruit's departure.

In an attempt to boost the region's economy, the federal government built a duty-free facility *(depósito libre)* in the northern part of Golfito. This surreal shopping center attracts Ticos from around the country, who descend on the otherwise dying town for 24-hour shopping sprees.

Not so fast: the duty-free shopping is for Costa Rica residents only, so you can put away your credit card. Worse yet, the primary impact on foreign tourists is that tax-free shoppers are required to spend the night in Golfito, so hotel rooms can be in short supply on weekends and during holiday periods.

Orientation

Golfito is named after a tiny gulf that forms an inlet into the eastern shore of the much larger Golfo Dulce. The town is strung out along a dusty coastal road with a backdrop of steep, thickly forested hills. The southern part of town is where you find most of the bars and businesses, including a seedy red-light district. Nearby is the so-called Muellecito (Small Dock), from where the daily ferry to Puerto Jiménez departs.

The northern part of town was the old United Fruit Company headquarters, and it retains a languid, tropical air, with its large, veranda-decked homes. Now, the so-called Zona Americana is home to the airport and the duty-free zone.

Information

Banco Coopealianza (⌚ 8am-5pm Mon-Fri, 8am-noon Sat) Has a 24-hour ATM on the Cirrus network and a Western Union office.

Golfito On-line (☎ 2775-2424; per hr ₡600; ⌚ 8am-9pm Mon-Sat, noon-6pm Sun) Speedy internet connections and delicious air-con.

Hospital de Golfito (☎ 2775-0011) Emergency medical attention.

Immigration office (Migración; ☎ 2775-0423; ⌚ 8am-4pm) Situated away from the dock, in a 2nd-floor office above Soda Pavas.

Port captain (☎ 2775-0487; ⌚ 7:30-11am & 12:30-4pm Mon-Fri) Opposite the large Muelle de Golfito.

Sights

REFUGIO NACIONAL DE FAUNA SILVESTRE GOLFITO

The small, 28-sq-km **reserve** encompasses most of the steep hills surrounding Golfito. It was originally created to protect the town's watershed, though it has also had the wonderful side effect of conserving a number of rare and interesting plant species. For example, the reserve is home to several cycads, which are 'living fossils,' and are regarded as the most primitive of plants. The reserve also attracts a variety of tropical birds, four species of monkey and several small mammals.

There are no facilities for visitors, save a gravel access road and a few poorly maintained trails. About 2km south of the center of Golfito, a gravel road heads inland, past a soccer field, and winds 7km up to some radio towers (Las Torres) 486m above sea level. This access road is an excellent option for hiking, as it has very little traffic. In any case, you'll

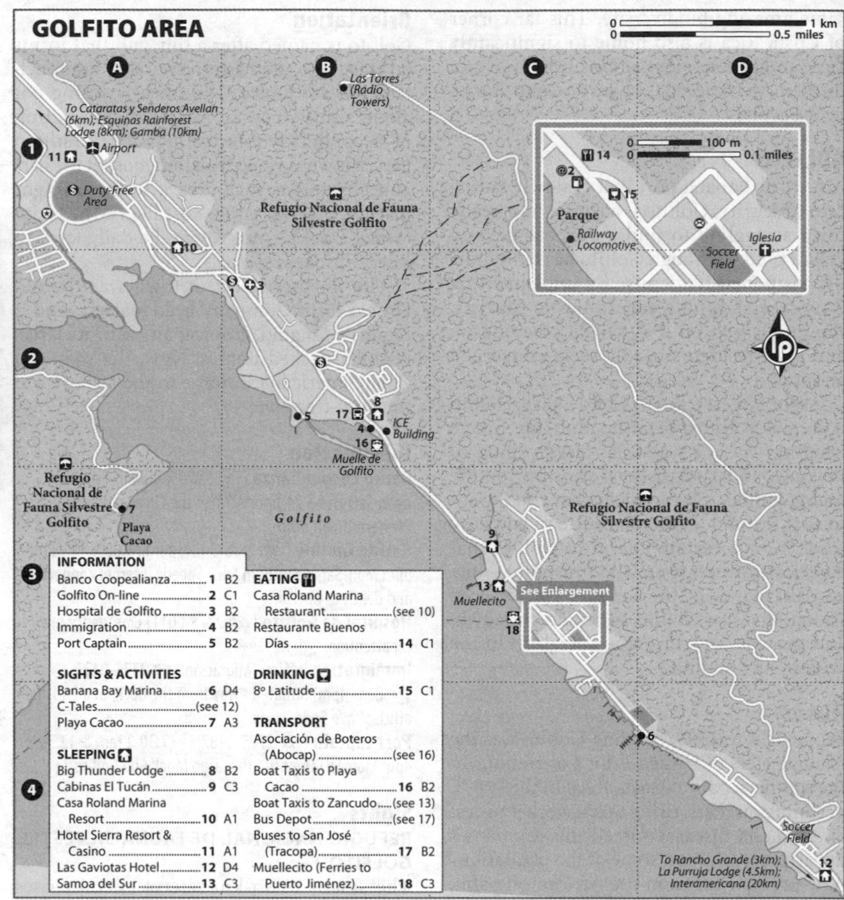

probably see more from the cleared road than from the overgrown trails.

A very steep hiking trail leaves from Golfito, almost opposite the Samoa del Sur hotel. A somewhat strenuous hike (allow about two hours) will bring you out on the road to the radio towers. The trail is easier to find in Golfito than at the top.

Another option is to walk along the poor dirt road heading toward Gamba. This road begins a couple of kilometers northwest of the duty-free area and crosses through part of the refuge. The local bus stops at the beginning of this dirt road, from where it is about 10km to Gamba.

Finally, there are several trails off the road to Playa Cacao. Hikers on these routes will be rewarded by waterfalls and views of the gulf. However, the trails are often obscured, so it's worth asking locally about maps and trail conditions before setting off.

As always, be sure that somebody knows when and where you are going before you set off on an independent hike.

PLAYA CACAO

Just a hop, skip and a jump across the bay, this small beach offers a prime view of Golfito stretched out along the coast, with the rainforest as a backdrop. If you're stuck in Golfito for the day, Playa Cacao is perhaps the most appealing spot from which to enjoy the old port. To reach the beach, catch a water taxi from Golfito for around ₡1000 per person.

You can also get to Playa Cacao by walking or driving about 6km along a dirt road west and then south from the airport – a 4WD is recommended.

Activities

CATARATAS Y SENDEROS AVELLÁN

This Tico family-run **reserve and adventure camp** (☎ 8378-7895; admission US$5; ⌚ 10am-4pm) is an excellent option for adventurers who like a little guidance. Guided hikes and horseback-riding tours (prices vary) explore the extensive, rainforest-covered grounds, including three impressive waterfalls. Camping (US$10 per site) and basic cabins (US$10 per person) and meals are also available.

SPORTFISHING & YACHTING

Golfito is home to several full-service marinas that attract coastal-cruising yachters. If you didn't bring your own boat, you can hire local sailors for tours of the gulf at any of the docks. You can fish year-round, but the best season for the sought-after Pacific sailfish is from November to May.

Banana Bay Marina (☎ 2775-0838; www.bananabaymarina.com) Charters can be arranged, and a full day of all-inclusive fishing starts at around US$750.

C-Tales (☎ in USA 772-335-9425; www.c-tales.com) Operating out of Las Gaviotas Hotel, this company offers a two-day package per person from US$2000.

Sleeping

Note that the area around the soccer field in town (not far east of the Muellecito) is Golfito's red-light district, so you'd be wise to spend a few more dollars and stay elsewhere.

BUDGET

Cabinas El Tucán (☎ 2775-0553; r per person with/without air-con US$15/10; P ❄) This friendly, family-run hotel is a wonderfully welcoming place to stay, and you don't have to worry about there being any funny business going on around you. Clean spacious rooms of varying sizes and shapes are clustered around the shady tiled courtyard.

La Purruja Lodge (☎ 2775-1054; www.purruja.com; 4.5km south of Golfito; s/d/tr incl breakfast US$30/40/50; P) A delightful Swiss-Tica couple runs this secluded lodge, which is home to five simple but sparkling cabins that have all the necessary comforts. The tranquil and tree-filled grounds are renowned for bird sightings, and the personable owners can organize tours throughout the area.

Samoa del Sur (☎ 2775-0233, 2775-0264; www.samoadelsur.com; r from US$40; P ❄) This French-run facility offers handsome lodgings that are outfitted with tiled floors and stylish wood furniture. The bar is a popular spot in the evenings, when guests congregate to play pool or darts. The kiddies, meanwhile, seem content to pass the time in the swimming pool, play area and (on rainy days) the onsite shell museum.

MIDRANGE

Las Gaviotas Hotel (☎ 2775-0062; s/d/tr US$65/75/85; P ❄) This decidedly low-key resort hotel comprises a clutch of stucco cabins set amid a lovely tropical garden. Here, you can pass the time in Golfito proper by sipping rum on your private porch or doing a few laps in the inviting pool.

Hotel Sierra Resort & Casino (☎ 2775-0666, 2775-0336; www.hotelsierra.com; s/d/tr US$68/80/92; P ❄) Appropriate to its location in the Zona Americana, this place feels like an US-style motor lodge, though its sterility shouldn't deter you from staying here. Far removed from the grit and grime of Golfito, the Hotel Sierra is a mini-island where you can pass the night in relative ease, especially since there is a good restaurant and a small casino onsite.

Big Thunder Lodge (☎ 2775-9191; www.bigthunder-lodge.com; opposite Muelle de Golfito; d from US$85; P ❄) Colorful depictions of marlin and sailfish adorn the walls of this upmarket lodge, which is a pleasant alternative to the more anonymous resorts in town. Backed by the forested hills of the reserve, the property was formerly the home of a banana manager, but now houses just a handful of individually decorated rooms.

TOP END

Casa Roland Marina Resort (☎ 2775-0180; www.casarolandgolfito.com; d from US$125; P ❄) A brand-new construction in the Zona Americana, the Casa Roland is now Golfito's most expensive hotel, and primarily caters to duty-free shoppers looking for an amenity-laden base. You can expect to find all the usual top-end standards including a swimming pool, restaurants and bars, tennis courts and a health spa, as well as a few extras such as a movie theatre and a casino. Rooms themselves lack the character typically found at this price range, but they're by far the most comfortable in town.

Eating & Drinking

Restaurante Buenos Días (meals ₡2500-5000; 6am-10pm) Rare is the visitor who passes through Golfito without stopping at this cheerful spot opposite the Muellecito. Brightly colored booths, bilingual menus and a super convenient location ensure a constant stream of guests – whether for an early breakfast, a typical Tico *casado* or a good old-fashioned burger.

Rancho Grande (dishes ₡2500-5000) About 3km south of Golfito, this rustic, thatch-roof place serves country-style Tico food cooked over a wood stove. Margarita, the Tica owner, is famous for her *patacones* (fried plantain chips). Her hours are erratic, so stop in during the day to let her know you're coming for dinner.

8° Latitude (dishes ₡3000-6000; 11am-late) Northwest of the soccer field, this popular expat bar is frequented by North Americans seriously into their sportfishing. Its laid-back and friendly atmosphere makes it the perfect place to tipple a few and listen to fish tales.

Casa Roland Marina Restaurant (dishes ₡4000-8500; 11am-10pm) The main restaurant at the Casa Roland Marina Resort isn't particularly inventive, but it does justice to the classics. Steaks and seafood are an excellent bet, as are pizzas, pastas and lighter salads.

Getting There & Away

AIR

The airport is 4km north of the town center near the duty-free zone. **NatureAir** (www.natureair.com) and **Sansa** (www.sansa.com) have daily flights to/from San José. One-way tickets are approximately US$100.

BOAT

There are two main boat docks for passenger service: the Muellecito is the main dock in the southern part of town. There is a smaller dock north of the Muelle Bananero (opposite the ICE building) where you'll find the **Asociación de Boteros** (Abocap; ☎ 2775-0357), an association of water taxis that can provide service anywhere in the Golfo Dulce area.

Two passenger ferries travel to Puerto Jiménez from the Muellecito (₡3000, 1½ hours), departing at 6am and 10am daily. Note that these times are subject to change; in this part of the country, schedules often fall prey to the whims of the captain.

A better option than chugging away on the ferries to Puerto Jiménez is to hire a private water taxi to shuttle you across the bay. You'll have to negotiate, but prices are generally reasonable given that you won't have to rely on the ferry. Waters in the Golfo Dulce are sheltered and generally calm, but it's still best if you feel comfortable with both your captain and ship.

The boat taxi for Zancudo (₡2500, 45 minutes) departs from the dock at Samoa del Sur hotel at noon, Monday through Saturday. The return trip is at 7:30am the next day (except Sunday).

If you're staying at any of the coastal lodges north of Golfito and you've made prior arrangements for transportation, the lodge will send a boat to pick you up at the docks. In the event that your boat doesn't arrive, simply give the name of the lodge to any of the boat captains, and they should be able to get you where you're going.

BUS

Most buses stop at the depot near the Muelle de Golfito.

Neily ₡800; 1½ hours; departs hourly from 6am to 7pm.

Pavones ₡2500; three hours; departs 10am and 3pm. This service may be affected by road and weather conditions, especially in the rainy season.

San José, via San Isidro (Tracopa) ₡4700; seven hours; departs from the terminal near Muelle Bananero at 5am and 1:30pm.

Zancudo ₡2500; three hours; departs1:30pm.

Getting Around

City buses and collective taxis travel up and down the main road of Golfito. Although the payment system seems incomprehensible to anyone else but the locals, it shouldn't cost you more than a few coins.

PARQUE NACIONAL PIEDRAS BLANCAS

Formerly known as Parque Nacional Esquinas, this **national park** was established in 1992 as an extension of Corcovado. Currently, Piedras Blancas or 'White Rocks' covers an area of 120 sq km of undisturbed tropical primary rainforest, as well as 20 sq km of secondary forests, pasture land and coastal cliffs and beaches.

As one of the last remaining stretches of lowland rainforest on the Pacific, Piedras

Blancas is also home to a vast array of flora and fauna. According to a study conducted at the biological station at Gamba, the biodiversity of trees in Piedras Blancas is the densest in all of Costa Rica, even surpassing Corcovado.

Orientation & Information

Parque Nacional Piedras Blancas borders the Refugio Nacional Fauna Silvestre Golfito at its east. At its west, the Reserva Forestal Golfo Dulce connects Piedras Blancas with Corcovado, forming an important biological corridor for resident wildlife, especially large mammals and predators that cover vast areas. Unfortunately, the forests around Rincón are threatened by illegal logging, jeopardizing this route.

Parque Nacional Piedras Blancas does not yet have facilities for visitors. However, it is possible to access the park from the Esquinas Rainforest Lodge in Gamba, as well as any of the coastal lodges lining the beaches north of Golfito.

Wildlife-Watching

Because Piedras Blancas is so remote and so little-visited, it is the site for several ongoing animal projects, including the reintroduction of scarlet macaws with the hopes of establishing a self-sustaining population, as well as the re-integration of wild cats like ocelot and margay, which were confiscated from private homes. Look for all of the wildlife that you might see in Corcovado: all five big cats and all four species of monkey, herds of collared and white-lipped peccary, crocodiles, various species of poison-dart frogs (including the endemic Golfo Dulce poison-dart frog) and more than 330 species of bird.

Sleeping

our pick **Esquinas Rainforest Lodge** (☎ 2741-8001; www.esquinaslodge.com; Gamba; s/d/tr incl meals US$149/226/279; P) This lodge was founded by the nonprofit Rainforest for the Austrians, which was also vital in the establishment of Piedras Blancas as a national park. Now, surrounded by the primary and secondary rainforest of the park, Esquinas is integrally connected with the community of Gamba, employing local workers and reinvesting profits in community projects. Accommodations at Esquinas Lodge are in spacious, high-ceilinged cabins with ceiling fans and private porches. The lodge's extensive grounds comprise a network of well-marked trails and a welcoming stream-fed pool. Gamba is 8km north of Golfito and 6km south of the Interamericana.

Getting There & Away

Piedras Blancas is best accessed from the Esquinas Rainforest Lodge, which has an extensive trail network onsite and can easily arrange guided hikes deeper into the park. If you don't have your own transportation, any bus heading north from Golfito can drop you off at the lodge.

If you're staying at any of the coastal lodges north of Golfito (see p434), you can inquire about transportation to/from the park as well as guided hikes into the interior.

PLAYAS SAN JOSECITO, NICUESA & CATIVO

Idyllic deserted beaches, backed by the pristine rainforest of Parque Nacional Piedras Blancas, define the northeastern shore of the Golfo Dulce. The appeal of this area is only enhanced by its inaccessibility: part of the charm is that very few people make it to this untouched corner of Costa Rica. If you're looking for a romantic retreat or a secluded getaway, all of the lodges along this stretch of coastline are completely isolated and serve as perfect spots for quiet reflection.

Sights

CASA DE ORQUÍDEAS

This private **botanical garden** (Playa San Josecito; admission & tour US$8; tours 8:30am Sat-Thu), surrounded on three sides by primary rainforest, is a real-life Eden. The garden's plants have been lovingly collected and tended by Ron and Trudy MacAllister, who have lived in this remote region since the 1970s. Self-taught botanists, they've amassed a wonderful collection of tropical fruit trees, bromeliads, cycads, palms, heliconias, ornamental plants and more than 100 varieties of orchid, after which their garden is named. The two-hour guided tours stimulate all of the senses: chew on a 'magic' seed that makes lemons taste sweet; smell vanilla beans; see insects trapped in bromeliad pools; or touch ginger in its flower.

Casa de Orquídeas is at the west end of Playa San Josecito and can be reached from the lodges on that beach by foot. Otherwise, it's accessible only by boat; inquire at your accommodations to make these arrangements.

Activities

The beaches along this stretch are excellent for swimming, snorkeling and sunning. Lodges also provide kayaks for maritime exploration. Hiking and wildlife-watching opportunities are virtually unlimited, as the lodges provide direct access to the wilds of Piedras Blancas. Miles of trails lead to secluded beaches, cascading waterfalls and other undiscovered attractions.

Sleeping

If you're planning on staying at any of the lodges listed here, advanced reservations via the internet are strongly recommended, especially since it can be difficult to contact them by phone.

All of these lodges are extremely isolated and are accessible only by boat – you can expect a beach landing, so make sure you're wearing the right kind of shoes! Prices include three meals per day and transportation to/from either Golfito or Puerto Jiménez.

Dolphin Quest (☎ 2775-8630, 2775-0373; www.dolphinquestcostarica.com; Playa San Josecito; s/d campsites US$30/55, cabins US$60/100, houses US$70/120) This jungle lodge offers as much privacy as a mile of beach and 280 hectares of mountainous rainforest can offer. Three round, thatch-roof cabins and one large house are spread out around two hectares of landscaped grounds. Meals – featuring many organic ingredients from the garden – are served communally in an open-air pavilion near the shore. Access to many miles of trails is free after an introductory tour outlining the beauties (and dangers) of the forest.

Playa Nicuesa Rainforest Lodge (☎ 2735-5237, in USA 866-348-7610; www.nicuesalodge.com; Playa Nicuesa; s/d from US$225/380) Nestled into a 65-hectare private rainforest reserve north of Casa de Orquídeas, this lodge is barely visible from the water (though its dock gives it away). The rustic, natural accommodations are beautifully decorated with canopied beds and indigenous textile spreads; private hot-water bathrooms have garden showers. Meals are served in a thatched *rancho* featuring a sparkling, polished wood bar. Electricity is provided by solar power, but the lodge usually uses candlelight to conserve energy and enhance the romantic atmosphere.

Golfo Dulce Lodge (☎ 8821-5398; www.golfodulcelodge.com; Playa San Josecito; standard/deluxe 4-day package per person from US$345/570; 🅿) Set back from the rocky beach, this Swiss-owned place is on the edge of a 275-hectare property, much of which is primary rainforest. The owners are clued in about local flora and fauna, dedicating their efforts to a nearby wildcat rehabilitation project. The five deluxe units are individual wooden cabins, each with a large veranda containing a rocking chair and hammock; three standard adjoining rooms with smaller verandas surround the spring-fed pool.

Getting There & Away

All of the lodges offer boat transportation from Puerto Jiménez and/or Golfito with prior arrangements, though you can always grab a water taxi if plans go awry.

ZANCUDO

Occupying a slender finger of land that juts into the Golfo Dulce, the tiny village of Zancudo is about as laid-back a beach destination as you'll find in Costa Rica. On the west side of town, gentle, warm Pacific waters lap onto black sands, and seeing more than a handful of people on the beach means it's crowded. On the east side, a tangle of mangrove swamps attracts birds, crocodiles and plenty of fish, which in turn attract fishers hoping to reel them in. Unlike nearby Pavones, an emerging surf destination, Zancudo is content to remain a far-flung village in a far-flung corner of Costa Rica.

Orientation & Information

Zancudo consists of one dirt road, which leads from the boat dock in the north, past the lodges that are strung along the shore, and out of town south toward Pavones. There is no bank in town and very few places accept credit cards, so bring your cash from Golfito.

Activities

The main activities at Zancudo are undoubtedly swinging on hammocks, strolling on the **beach** and swimming in the aqua-blue waters of the Golfo Dulce. Here, the surf is gentle, and at night the water sometimes sparkles with bioluminescence – tiny phosphorescent marine plants and plankton that light up if you sweep a hand through the water. The effect is like underwater fireflies.

The **mangrove swamps** offer plenty of opportunities for exploration: birdlife is prolific, while other animals such as crocodile, caiman, monkey and sloth are also frequently spotted. The boat ride from Golfito gives a glimpse of these waters, but you can also paddle them yourself: rent kayaks from any of the accommodations listings following.

Zancudo is a base for inshore and offshore **fishing**, river fishing (mangrove snapper, snook and corbina) and fly-fishing. The best sportfishing is from December to May for sailfish and May to September for snook, though many species bite year-round. Trips are best organized through the Zancudo Lodge (see right).

Sleeping & Eating

Cabinas Sol y Mar (☎ 2776-0014; www.zancudo.com; campsites per person US$3, cabins US$25-50; P 🖳) This popular place offers various budget lodging options: smallish economy dwellings that are further from the water, larger standard units with a shared terrace overlooking the beach, and private, deluxe units with fancy tile showers and unobstructed ocean views. Even if you're not staying here, the open-air restaurant and thatched bar is a Zancudo favorite.

Cabinas Los Cocos (☎ 2776-0012; www.loscocos.com; cabins US$60; P) This unique beachfront lodge is home to two historic cabins that used to be banana-company homes in Palmar but were transported to Zancudo, reassembled and completely refurbished. The other two more spacious cabins are also charming, with loft sleeping areas under palm-frond roofs.

Oceano (☎ 2776-0921; http://bestcostaricavacations.com; r US$79; P) With its back to the beach, this friendly little Canadian-run inn has just two rooms, both spacious and airy with wood-beamed ceilings, tile bathrooms and quaint details such as throw pillows and folk art. The open-air restaurant is also inviting for dinner or drinks, especially if the sea has been kind to the local fishermen.

Playa Zancudo Bed and Breakfast (☎ 2776-0006; www.playazancudobedandbreakfast.com; r from US$80; P ❄ 🖳) This US-run B&B also has just two rooms in a vaulted plantation-style house adorned with rich hardwoods and accentuated by sweeping verandas. Another highly personable option; guests receive intimate and attentive service throughout their stay.

Zancudo Lodge (☎ 2776-0008; www.thezancudolodge.com; 4-day all-inclusive s/d US$4195/6390; P ❄ 🖳 ♿) This newly refurbished lodge is completely dedicated to sportfishing, and offers multiday packages that include everything from boat charters and equipment rental to all-you-can-eat meals and a 24/7 open bar. While nonanglers might feel a bit out of place here, the Zancudo Lodge is regarded as one of the definitive fishing spots in Golfo Dulce, and your surest bet for hooking the big one.

Getting There & Away

BOAT

The boat dock is near the north end of the beach on the inland, estuary side. A water taxi to Golfito (₡2500, 45 minutes) departs from this dock at 7am, returning at noon, Monday through Saturday. Inquire locally, however, as times are subject to change, though you can always find a local boat captain willing to take you for a negotiable price.

BUS

A bus to Neily leaves from the *pulpería* near the dock at 5:30am (₡2500, three hours). The bus for Golfito (₡2500) leaves at 5am for the three-hour trip, with a ferry transfer at the Río Coto Colorado. Service is erratic in the wet season, so inquire before setting out.

CAR

It's possible to drive to Zancudo by taking the road south of Río Claro for about 10km. Turn left at the Rodeo Bar and go another 10km to the Río Coto Colorado ferry, which carries three vehicles (₡1000 per car) and runs all day except during the lowest tides. From there, 30km of dirt road gets you to Zancudo. To get to Pavones, take a right at the first major intersection, instead of a left. A 4WD is necessary in the rainy season.

PAVONES

Home to what is reportedly the longest left-hand surf break on the planet, Pavones is a legendary destination for surfers the world over. As this is Costa Rica's southernmost point, you'll need to work hard to get down here. However, the journey is an adventure in its own right, especially since the best months for surfing coincide with the rainy season (think river crossings!).

Although the village remains relatively off the beaten path, both foreigners and Ticos

MARSHALL & ANGELA MCCARTHY ON THE FUTURE OF GOLFO DULCE

Marshall and Angela McCarthy, the owners and managers of Cabinas La Ponderosa in Pavones (see p438), have spent 19 and 11 years, respectively, living in Golfo Dulce. Over a hearty breakfast of eggs and potatoes, Marshall and Angela shared their thoughts on the past, present and future of their adopted home.

What was it you found about this remote corner of the country that made you both want to settle down in Golfo Dulce? Marshall: Having grown up in the cities throughout North and South America, I immediately fell in love with the nature here. There is so much open space here, and instead of clutter and congestion you have empty beaches and thick jungles. When I first arrived, Costa Rica was off the tourist map, and I could have easily chosen any part of the country to settle in. However, I chose Golfo Dulce because it was, and still is, the most virgin corner of the country.

Angela: I've traveled throughout all of Central America, but I chose Costa Rica specifically because everything here is so accessible. Even in a place as remote as Golfo Dulce, you literally have the beach, the mountains and the rainforest on your doorstep. Also, I just love the way this place smells! After the rains have fallen, the air here is heavy with the scent of the jungle. It's difficult to describe, but once you spend time here, it's impossible to forget.

Why do you think it is that Golfo Dulce has been spared from hasty development? Angela: People have always been attracted to Golfo Dulce because of its nature, and fortunately the local government is well attuned to this reality. In fact, tourism officials are actually marketing the pristine beauty of the region, which is attracting the right types of foreign investment. Here in Golfo Dulce, the product is the environment, so the impetus is for developers is to keep everything green.

Marshall: Because the local government has a strict regulatory and development plan, this municipality is growing a lot slower than others. As a direct result, wealthy foreigners who want to come down here and build an enormous condo project or a sprawling resort hotel face intense scrutiny, and eventually decide to invest elsewhere.

Do you think that Golfo Dulce attracts a certain type of person? Marshall: Simply put, Golfo Dulce is old Costa Rica. The beauty of this area is that it's overgrown and sparsely populated, which tends to attract more educated people who are aware of the broader environmental picture. For the most part, tourists and concerned locals such as ourselves are extremely conscientious about saving the forest, and are passionate about preserving the natural beauty of the gulf.

Angela: People are attracted to the region by big wildlife and even bigger trees. Although much of Costa Rica is packaged for tourist consumption, the rainforest in Golfo Dulce is as real as it gets. The kind of people who come down here are the kind of people who want to be in the jungle. Almost everyone down here is extremely sensitive to development, and the last thing we want is for the peninsula to develop along the same lines as Cancún.

Are you optimistic about the future of Golfo Dulce? Angela: Development may be inevitable, but I am optimistic because the market is demanding sustainability. People are coming to the region because they want to see green, and in the end, I believe that developers here must always keep this market force in mind.

Marshall: This region is home to one of the last rainforests on the planet, and it is just something that we need to protect. It is a special place, and its value is too much to destroy, though fortunately people are finally starting to catch on to this fact.

are transforming Pavones from a relative backwater into a hip and happening hot spot. Fortunately, development is progressing slowly and sustainably, which means that the palm-lined streets are still not paved, the pace of life is slow and the overall atmosphere remains tranquil.

Orientation & Information

The name Pavones is used to refer to both Playa Río Claro de Pavones and Punta Banco, which is 6km south.

The road into Pavones comes south and dead-ends at the Río Claro, which is where you'll find a small soccer field. About 200m to the east, a parallel road crosses the Río Claro and continues the 6km to Punta Banco.

Pavones has no bank or gas station, so make sure you have plenty of money and gas prior to arrival.

Sights

Set on a verdant hillside between Pavones and Punta Banco, the **Tiskita Jungle Lodge** (☎ in San José 2296-8125; www.tiskita-lodge.co.cr; guided hike US$15) consists of 100 hectares of virgin forest and a huge orchard, which produces more than 100 varieties of tropical fruit with origins from all over the world. Fourteen trails wind through surrounding rainforest, which contains waterfalls and freshwater pools suitable for swimming. The combination of rainforest, fruit farm and coastline attracts a long list of birds. About 300 species have been recorded here. The fruit farm is particularly attractive to fruit-eating birds such as parrot and toucan. The forest is home to more reticent species such as yellow-billed cotinga, fiery-billed aracari, green honeycreeper and lattice-tailed trogon. The owners – personable conservationists and conversationalists Peter and Elizabeth Aspinall – or their son usually guide hikes. Reservations are recommended.

Activities

SURFING

Pavones is one of Costa Rica's most famous **surf breaks** – when the surf's up, this tiny beach town attracts hordes of international wave riders and Tico surfer dudes. Conditions are best with a southern swell, usually between April and October. However, because Pavones is inside Golfo Dulce, it is protected from many swells so surfers can go for weeks without seeing any waves.

Pavones has become legendary among surfers for its wicked long left. Some claim it is among the world's longest, offering a two- or three-minute ride on a good day. Legend has it that the wave passes so close to the Esquina del Mar Cantina that you can toss beers to surfers as they zip by. Be warned: when the wave is big, it can deposit surfers on the sharp rocks at the far end of the bay.

Locals know that when Pavones has nothing (or when it's too crowded), they can head south to **Punta Banco**, a reef break with decent rights and lefts. The best conditions are at mid or high tide, especially with swells from the south or west.

YOGA

Yoga Farm (www.yogafarmcostarica.org; dm/r per night US$35/40, per week US$175/240) This yoga retreat center and working farm is a unique and welcome addition to Pavones. The price includes accommodations in simple and clean rooms with wood bunk beds; three vegetarian meals, prepared primarily with ingredients from the organic garden; and daily yoga classes, which take place in a fabulous open-air studio overlooking the ocean. This place is a 15-minute walk from Rancho Burica in Punta Banco: take the road going up the hill to the left, go through the first gate on the left and keep walking up the hill. Inquire about volunteer opportunities.

Sleeping

PLAYA RÍO CLARO DE PAVONES

Cabinas Casa Olas (☎ 8826-3693; r per person from US$15; P) About 100m east of the soccer field, five cabins of varying sizes have wide-plank wood floors, brightly painted walls and an attractive unfinished feel that is appealing if you're one of the laid-back surfer set. All the rooms share access to outdoor kitchen facilities and a covered hammock lounge.

Cabinas Mira Olas (☎ 8393-7742; www.miraolas.com; r US$30-45; P) This 4.5-hectare farm is full of wildlife and fruit trees, and cabins to suit all tastes. The 'rustic' cabin, incidentally, boasted the first flush toilet in Pavones, though it's quite different from the 'jungle deluxe,' a beautiful, open-air lodging with a huge balcony and elegant cathedral ceiling. To find Mira Olas, turn off at the fishing boats and follow the signs up the steep hill: it's worth the climb!

Riviera Riverside Villas (☎ 8823-5874; www.pavonesriviera.com; s/d US$85/90; P) This clutch of exclusive villas in Pavones proper offers fully equipped kitchens, cool tile floors and attractive hardwood ceilings. Big shady porches overlook the landscaped gardens, which offer a degree of intimacy and privacy found at few other places in town.

Casa Siempre Domingo (☎ 8820-4709; www.casa-domingo.com; d/tr US$100/150; P) The most unbelievable views of Golfo Dulce are from this luxurious bed and breakfast, perched high in the hills above Pavones. Lodgings at the 'Always Sunday House' are elegant and glorious, with soaring cathedral ceilings and an overwhelming sense of openness. Flowerbeds that border on expansive stretches of verdant jungle frame the grounds. You'll need a car to get here: take the left fork at the Río Claro crossing.

PUNTA BANCO

Rancho Burica (www.ranchoburica.com; r per person US$8-22; P) Backpackers can't stop raving about this friendly and youthful Dutch-run outpost, which is literally the end of the road in Punta Banco. All rooms have bathrooms and fans, while the pricier ones have mosquito-netted beds and attractive wood furniture. Hammocks interspersed around the property offer ample opportunity for chilling out. Reservations are not accepted: 'Just show up…like everyone else does.'

Sotavento (☎ 8391-3468; www.sotaventoplantanal.com; houses US$60-80; P) These two tropical hardwood, furnished houses are set on a picturesque pepper and cacao plantation perched above Punta Banco. Casa Poinsetta and the larger Casa Vista Grande both have rustic, open-air architecture that takes advantage of the breeze and the views. The houses sleep six to eight people, so they are a great deal if you can get a pack of friends together to split costs. The personable US surfer Harry, who custom-designs his own boards, manages the property.

Cabinas La Ponderosa (☎ 8824-4145, in USA 954-771-9166; www.cabinaslaponderosa.com; r US$60-200; P) Housed on six lovely landscaped hectares, these cozy cabins are tenderly cared for by Marshall and Angela McCarthy, who have spent years living in their adopted home of Pavones (see boxed text, p436). The common lounge offers all kinds of entertainment, including a ping-pong table and a massive video library, but the real appeal of staying here is the warm hospitality of the McCarthys.

our pick Tiskita Jungle Lodge (☎ in San José 2296-8125; www.tiskita-lodge.co.cr; s/d from US$155/275; P) Set amid extensive gardens and orchards, this lodge is arguably the most beautiful and intimate in all of Golfo Dulce. Accommodations are in a clutch of stunning wooden cabins accented by stone garden showers that allow you to freshen up while you go bird-watching. Daily rates include fresh home-cooked meals and guided walks. Reservations must be made in advance as the lodge fills up quickly. Even if you're not spending the night here, stop by for a guided tour of the property – for more information, see p437.

Eating & Drinking

Esquina del Mar Cantina (dishes ₡1500-2500) A Pavones institution that has great views of the left break, this is where you should grab a drink after your last ride.

Café de la Suerte (dishes ₡2000-4500; V) Animal-lovers and the health-conscious will appreciate this open-air vegetarian joint, which serves tropical-fruit smoothies and heart-healthy fare.

La Manta (dishes ₡2500-6000) This airy *rancho*, which catches the breezes off the bay, offers an impressive variety of Mediterranean food.

Restaurante La Piña (dishes ₡4500-8000) Located in Punta Banco, this Italian-run spot has authentic pastas and pizzas from the peninsula (Italy, not Osa).

Getting There & Away

NatureAir (www.natureair.com) and **Alfa Romeo Aero Taxi** (www.alfaromeoair.com) offer charter flights. Prices are dependent on the number of passengers, so it's best to try to organize a larger group if you're considering this option.

Two daily buses go to Golfito (₡2500, three hours). The first leaves at 5:30am and departs from the end of the road at Rancho Burica (but you can pick it up at the bus stop opposite the Riviera); the second leaves at 12:30pm from the Esquina del Mar Cantina. Buses from Golfito depart at 10am (to Pavones) and 3pm (to Punta Banco via Pavones) from the stop at the Muellecito.

A 4WD taxi will charge about US$50 from Golfito, though you can also take a water taxi for about the same price. If you're driving, follow the directions to Zancudo and look for the signs to Pavones.

PARQUE NACIONAL ISLA DEL COCOS

In the opening minutes of the classic film *Jurassic Park*, a small helicopter swoops over and around Isla Nublar, a lushly forested island with dramatic tropical peaks descending straight into clear blue waters. The inspiration for this silver-screen island was none other than Isla del Cocos, and that single scene turned Costa Rica's most remote **national park** into much more than a figment of our collective imagination.

Isla del Cocos is around 500km southwest of the mainland in the middle of the eastern Pacific, and is often referred to as the 'Costa Rican Galápagos' due to both its total isolation and unique ecosystem. As it's the most far-

NEW 7 WONDERS OF NATURE SHORT-LIST CANDIDATE

Although you may or may not have agreed with their choices, the **New 7 Wonders** (www.new7wonders.com) campaign made international headlines in 2007. From the statue of Christ the Redeemer in Rio de Janeiro to the Taj Mahal in Agra, the New 7 Wonders campaign sought to modernize the list of departed ancient wonders – with the sole exception of the Great Pyramids at Giza, of course.

Following the surprising success of its original campaign, the Swiss foundation proceeded to nominate 300 natural wonders of the world, which will eventually be honed down to seven by popular vote in 2011. While Isla del Cocos didn't make it to the finalist round, it did receive international recognition as a short-list candidate, much to the pleasure of Costa Rican tourism officials. Despite the fact that the island has been a Unesco World Heritage Site since 1967, few people know anything about Isla del Cocos beyond its association with resurrected dinosaurs.

According to a published interview with Danny Gonzalez, the spokesperson for **MarViva** (www.marviva.net/#/en/home), a conservation organization that helps protect Cocos: 'The island houses great nature and cultural riches. It's home to many endemic species and is, along with the islands of Coiba, Malpelo and the Galápagos, part of the East Pacific Tropical Marine Corridor, which allows the movement of many migratory marine species from North and South America. This nomination [helped] people learn about serious problems that affect Isla del Cocos' marine ecosystems, such as illegal fishing, shark finning and other human activities that put pressure on natural resources. Protecting these resources is a big challenge, and that's why…we will do our best to tell people about the importance of knowing about and contributing to the safeguarding of this heritage site.'

flung corner of Costa Rica, you will certainly have to work hard to get here, though few other destinations in the country are as wildly exotic and visually arresting.

As beautiful as the island may be, its terrestrial environs are believed by many to pale in comparison to what lies beneath. Named by PADI (Professional Association of Diving Instructors) as one of the world's top 10 dive spots, the surrounding waters of Isla del Cocos harbor abundant pelagics including one of the largest known schools of hammerhead sharks in the world.

Since the island remains largely uninhabited, and is completely closed to overnight visitors, you will have to visit either in a private yacht, or, more realistically, on a liveaboard dive vessel. While nondivers are certainly welcome to make the trip out, it definitely pays to have some significant underwater experience in your logbook – dive sites around Isla del Cocos are as challenging as they are breathtaking.

History

In 1526 Spanish explorer Joan Cabezas was the first European to discover Isla del Cocos, though it wasn't noted on maps until its second discovery by French cartographer Nicolas Desliens in 1541. In the centuries that followed, heavy rainfall attracted the attention of sailors, pirates and whalers, who frequently stopped by for fresh water, coconuts and fresh seafood.

Between the late 17th and early 19th century, Isla del Cocos became something of a way station for a band of pirates who supposedly hid countless treasures here. The most famous was the storied Treasure of Lima, which consisted of gold and silver ingots, gold laminae scavenged from church domes and a solid-gold, life-sized sculpture of the Virgin Mary. Isla del Cocos is so renowned for its hidden treasures that authors have speculated it was the inspiration for Robert Louis Stevenson's *Treasure Island*. Nonetheless, more than 500 treasure-hunting expeditions have found only failure.

In fact, in 1869 the government of Costa Rica organized its own official treasure hunt. No gold or jewels were discovered, but this expedition did result in Costa Rica unfurling its flag and taking possession of the island, a treasure in itself.

Settlers arrived on the island in the late 19th and early 20th centuries, though their stay on Isla del Cocos was short-lived. However, they did leave behind domestic animals that have since converted into feral populations of pigs, goats, cats and rats.

Today it's the pigs that are the greatest threat to the unique species native to the island: they uproot vegetation, cause soil erosion and contribute to sedimentation around the island's coasts, which damages coral reefs.

Unregulated fishing also poses further, more ominous, threats, especially to populations of shark, tuna and billfish that get caught in longline nets. The Servicio de Parques Nacionales (Sinac) is aware of the problem, but sadly a lack of funding has made regulation of these illegal activities difficult, if not impossible.

Orientation

Just shy of 24 sq km in area, Isla del Cocos is a rectangular-shaped oceanic island of volcanic origin. Despite its rocky and mountainous topography, large tracts of moist cloud forest cover the island, which are fed by frequent and abundant rainfall. The island is also crisscrossed by two large river systems that feed more than 200 waterfalls, and drain into four prominent bays.

Information

In order to protect the conservation status of the island, all visitors must apply for a permit at the **Área de Conservación de la Isla del Cocos** (Acmic; ☎ 2258-7350; www.acmic.sinac.go.cr) in San José. However, unless you're sailing to the island in a private boat, tour operators will make all of the necessary arrangements for you – for more information, see opposite.

Park fees are US$35 per person per day. On the island, there is a ranger station, with staff surveillance stations at Wafer Bay and Chatham Bay. Drinking water is available, but there is no camping – visitors must spend the night on their boats.

Sights

While hard-core divers tend to eschew landlubbers, trust us on this one – making landfall and exploring Isla del Cocos is most definitely worth your time and effort. Need a second opinion? The famous oceanographer and diving guru Jacques Cousteau famously dubbed Cocos 'the most beautiful island in the world.'

Rugged, heavily forested and punctuating by cascading waterfalls, Cocos is ringed and transected by an elaborate network of trails. The highest point is at **Cerro Iglesias** (634m), where you can soak up spectacular views of the lush, verdant island and the deep blue Pacific.

Note that visitors to the island must first register with the park rangers, though your tour company will most likely make all the necessary arrangements well in advance. Also, given that the island is completely undeveloped, it's highly recommended that you explore the trails with a guide – you're a long way from civilization if problems occur.

Activities

DIVING

As we've mentioned already, the diving here is excellent, and is regarded by most as the main attraction of the island. But strong oceanic currents can lead to treacherous underwater conditions, and Isla del Cocos can only be recommended to intermediate and advanced divers with sufficient experience.

The island has two large bays with safe anchorages and sandy beaches: **Chatham Bay** is located on the northeast side and **Wafer Bay** is on the northwest. Just off Cocos are a series of smaller basaltic rocks and islets, which constitute some of the best dive sites.

Isla Manuelita is a prime spot, home to a wide array of fish, ray and eel. Shark also inhabit these waters, including huge schools of scalloped hammerhead as well as white-tips, which are best spotted at night. **Dirty Rock** is another main attraction – a spectacular rock formation that harbors all kinds of sea creatures.

WILDLIFE-WATCHING

Isla del Cocos is arguably the most pristine national park in the country, and truly one of Costa Rica's great wildlife destinations. Since the island was never linked to the Americas during its comparatively short geological history, Cocos is home to a very large number of rare endemic species.

Heading inland from the coastal forests up to the high-altitude cloud forests, it is possible to find around 235 unique species of flowering plants, 30% of which are only found on the island. This incredible diversity of flora supports more than 400 known species of insects. Sixty-five endemics, as well as a striking range of butterflies and moths, are included in this count. Scientists believe that more remain to be discovered.

Bird-watchers also aspire to visit Cocos, and are primarily interested in spotting the myriad colonies of migratory seabirds that

RESPONSIBLE DIVING & SAFETY GUIDELINES

Help preserve the ecology and beauty of Isla del Cocos by following these guidelines:

- Avoid touching or standing on living marine organisms or dragging equipment across the reef. Polyps can be damaged by even the gentlest contact. If you must hold on to the reef, only touch exposed rock or dead coral.
- Be conscious of your fins. Even without contact, the surge from fin strokes near the reef can damage delicate organisms. Take care not to kick up clouds of sand, which can smother organisms.
- Practice and maintain proper buoyancy control. Descending too fast and colliding with the reef can do major damage.
- Take great care in underwater caves. Spend as little time within them as possible as your air bubbles may be caught within the roof, creating air pockets that will leave organisms high and dry. Take turns to inspect the interior of a small cave.
- Resist the temptation to collect corals or shells from underwater sites.
- Ensure that you take home all your rubbish and any litter you may find as well. Plastics in particular are a serious threat to marine life.
- Minimize your disturbance of marine animals, and please don't feed the fish.

nest here. Of the 87 recorded species on the island and neighboring rocks, the most pronounced are the aquatic birds: brown and red-footed booby, great frigatebird, white tern and brown noddy. There are also three terrestrial endemics, namely the Cocos cuckoo, Cocos flycatcher and Cocos finch.

No amphibians have been reported on the island, though both species of lizards are endemic. Pigs, deer, cats and rats inhabit the island, though humans introduced these mammals long ago, and they are currently the focus of a pest-control campaign aimed at preserving the original ecosystem.

The island's marine life is equally varied, with 18 species of coral, 57 types of crustacean and tropical fish in abundance, not to mention visiting pelagics such as sea turtles, manta rays, dolphins and sharks. The scalloped hammerhead shark receives top billing, especially since it often schools in the hundreds.

Tours

Even if you're normally a fiercely independent traveler, Cocos is one destination where you will have to join up with an organized tour. If it is within your financial means, you may be tempted to visit here on a private sailing vessel, though you'll have an easier time getting the government to grant you access to the island's interior if you join a tour.

Two liveabord dive operators, both of which dock their vessels in Puntarenas, offer guided excursions to the island. Diving and food are included in the tour prices listed below, but daily park fees are not.

Okeanos Aggressor (☎ in USA 866-653-2667; www.aggressor.com/subpage10.php) Offers eight-/10-day land and sea expeditions with room for 22 from US$3335/3735 per person.

Undersea Hunter (☎ 2228-6613, in USA 800-203-2120; www.underseahunter.com) Offers 10-/12-day land and sea expeditions with room for 14 to 18 people from US$4750/5150 per person.

Sleeping

While visitors are permitted to make landfall on Cocos during the day, you must return to the boat at night to sleep.

Getting There & Away

With advanced reservations, both of the tour companies listed above will arrange transfers from either San José or Liberia to Puntarenas, which is the embarkation/disembarkation point for the tour.

Caribbean Coast

When the Spaniards arrived in this neck of the woods in the 16th century, the country's jungle-fringed Caribbean coast was deemed too wild, too impassible and too malarial for settlement. For centuries, it developed at its own pace, with its own unique culture – a mix of indigenous and West Indian. In the 19th century, the arrival of thousands of Jamaican railroad workers infused the area with the traditions of the islands.

But even as the culture evolved, the landscape remained wild. This isn't the postcard-perfect Caribbean stereotype of salt-white beaches and gentle turquoise waters. Here, you'll find brooding, tempestuous seas and one of Costa Rica's most notorious surfing waves. Not to mention black volcanic shores and dense swamps stocked with enough nesting sea-turtles and brilliant birds to keep the *National Geographic* set occupied for a lifetime.

In recent years, North American surfers and Italian hoteliers have emigrated here in droves, adding new flavors to what was always an intriguing cultural stew. Celebrated local cooks now produce spicy Caribbean dishes for a coterie of world travelers. Old cacao farms have been reborn as quaint B&Bs. And once-inaccessible jungle canals are plied by travelers in search of dozing caimans. It is as rugged as it is delicious – a territory you'll never forget.

HIGHLIGHTS

- Taking snaps of brilliantly plumed birds on the canals of **Parque Nacional Tortuguero** (p458)
- Enjoying the wild surf, crazy parties and excellent cuisine scene in **Puerto Viejo de Talamanca** (p479)
- Rolling up your sleeves to help guard the important turtle nesting site of **Parismina** (p457)
- Taking lounging tips from the overhanging sloths and gently rocking the day away in a hammock in **Cahuita** (p469)
- Snorkeling the colorful reef at the **Refugio Nacional de Vida Silvestre Gandoca-Manzanillo** (p494)

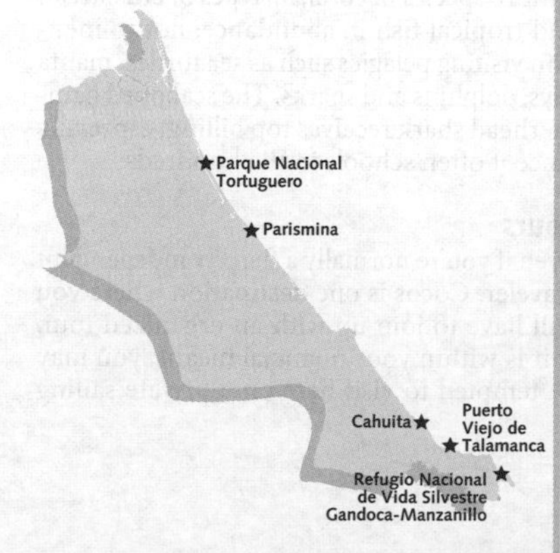

History

In 1502 Christopher Columbus spent a total of 17 days anchored off the coast of Puerto Limón on what would be his fourth and final voyage to the New World. He dropped anchor at an isle he baptized La Huerta (today known as Isla Uvita), loaded up on fresh water, and then continued on his way to Panama and, ultimately back to Spain. It wasn't a good trip: Columbus was imprisoned by a rival in Santo Domingo and shipwrecked in Jamaica. In 1504, unable to discover heaps of gold or a passage to the Far East, he returned to Europe a failure. Within two years he was dead.

For Costa Rica's Caribbean coast, however, this small encounter would foreshadow the colonization that was to come. But it would be centuries before the Europeans would fully dominate the area. Because of the difficult nature of the terrain (all those croc-filled swamps and steep mountain slopes) and the malaria delivered by relentless fleets of mosquitoes, the Spanish steadfastly avoided it. For hundreds of years, in fact, the area remained the province of indigenous ethnicities – the Miskito in the north and the Cabécar, Bribrí and KéköLdi in the south – along with a mix of itinerant Afro-Caribbean turtle hunters from Panama and Colombia.

It was the building of the railroad, beginning in 1871, that would solidify the area's West Indian accent, with the arrival of thousands of former Jamaican slaves in search of employment. The plan was to build a port at the site of a grand old lemon tree (hence the name, Puerto Limón) on the Caribbean Sea, so that coffee barons in the Central Valley could more easily export their crops to Europe. The railway was intended to unify the country, but it was a source of segregation as well. Blacks were not allowed to vote or travel freely around Costa Rica until 1949. Out of isolation, however, sprung an independent culture, with its own musical and gastronomic traditions, and even its own unique language, a creole called Mekatelyu – which is still spoken today.

Climate

The fact that there is no traditional dry season is a mixed blessing. It rains throughout the year, though rains tend to be slighter in February and March, as well as September and October – this latter period happens to conveniently occur when the rest of the country is getting soaked. There's a steady year-round temperature of about 27°C (80°F) to 8°C (46°F). Surfers, note: the biggest swells hit the southern Caribbean from December to March.

Parks & Reserves

Many refuges and parks line the Caribbean coast. Some of the most popular include:

Parque Nacional Cahuita (p477) A patch of coastal jungle is home to armadillos, monkeys and sloths, while the protected reef is one of the most important on the coast.

Parque Nacional Tortuguero (p458) Jungle canals obscure snoozing caimans, while howler, spider and capuchin monkeys traipse overhead. The star attraction, however, are the sea turtles, which nest here from March to October.

Refugio Nacional de Vida Silvestre Barra del Colorado (p467) A remote park that draws fishing enthusiasts who come to hook species such as snook, tarpon and gar.

Refugio Nacional de Vida Silvestre Gandoca-Manzanillo (p494) A rich rainforest and wetland tucked away along the country's southeastern border, with rivers full of manatee, caiman and croc.

Dangers & Annoyances

The Caribbean coast region has had a bad reputation over the years for being more dangerous than other parts of Costa Rica. In reality, crime levels against tourists are no higher here than in any other part of the country. Still, as anywhere else, exercise common sense.

A bigger problem is the sea: rip tides get ferocious (even in shallow water) and, in the north, sharks are a regular presence. Swim in safe areas – and if you're unsure, ask a local.

Getting There & Around

When traveling to Puerto Limón and the southern Caribbean, it's easy enough to hop on any of the regular buses from San José. Buses also connect most towns along the coast, from Sixaola, on the Panamanian border, to Puerto Limón. The roads are in good condition, so driving is also an option.

The north is a little trickier. Much of the area is only linked up by waterways, making boats the sole means of transport. Puerto Limón, Tortuguero and Barra del Colorado all have landing strips, but only Tortuguero has daily commercial flights.

THE ATLANTIC SLOPE

The idea was simple: build a port on the Caribbean coast and connect it to the Central Valley by railroad, thus opening up important shipping routes for the country's soaring coffee production. Construction began in 1871, through 150km of dense jungles and muddy mountainsides along the Atlantic slope. Things didn't exactly go according to plan – it took almost two decades to build the railroad and the first 30km reportedly cost 4000 men their lives. But when the last piece of track was laid down in 1890, the transformation it would unleash would permanently change Costa Rica (and the rest of Central America, for that matter). It was the dawn of the banana boom, an industry that would dominate life, politics and the environment in the region for almost a century.

Today, the railroad is no longer. An asphalt highway (Hwy 32) – through Parque Nacional Braulio Carrillo – links San José to the Caribbean coast, winding down the foothills of the Cordillera Central, through agricultural plantations to the swampy lowlands around Limón. Likewise, banana production is not as mighty as it once was, supplanted in many areas by pineapples and African oil palms.

PARQUE NACIONAL BRAULIO CARRILLO

Enter this underexplored **national park** and you will have an idea of what Costa Rica looked like prior to the 1950s, when 75% of the country's surface area was still covered in forest: steep hills cloaked in impossibly tall trees are interrupted only by cascading rivers and canyons. It has an extraordinary biodiversity due to the range of altitudes, from steamy 2906m cloud forest alongside Volcán Barva to lush, humid lowlands on the Caribbean slope. It's most incredible feature, however, is that this massive park (the size of Rhode Island) is only 30 minutes north of San José.

Founded in the 1970s, Braulio Carrillo's creation was the result of a unique compromise between conservationists and developers. At the time, the government had announced a plan to build a new highway that would connect the capital to Puerto Limón. Back then, San José's only link to its most important port was via a crumbling railway or a slow rural road through Cartago and Turrialba. The only feasible route for the new thoroughfare was along a low pass between the Barva and Irazú volcanoes – an area covered in primary forest. Conservationists were deeply worried about putting a road (and any attendant development) in an area that served as San José's watershed. So a plan was hatched: the road would be built, but the 400 sq km of land to either side of it would be set aside as a national park. Thus, in 1978, Parque Nacional Braulio Carrillo was born.

Orientation & Information

The most popular hiking areas can be accessed from the San José–Guápiles highway. At the southern end of the park, 19km northeast of San José, is the **Zurquí ranger station** (☎ 2257-0992; admission US$8; ⌚ 8am-4pm), while the **Quebrada González station** (☎ 2268-1038/1039; admission US$8; ⌚ 7am-4pm) is at the northeast corner, 22km past the Zurquí tunnel. At both, you'll find guarded parking lots, toilets and well-marked trails. At the latter, look for the dozens of bright webs spun by golden orb-weavers in front of the station's offices.

People who want to climb Volcán Barva on a day trip or camp overnight can stop by the **Barva Sector ranger station** (☎ 2261-2619; ⌚ 8am-3pm), in the southwest of the park, 3km north of Sacramento in Paso Llano. There are also two remote outposts, El Ceibo and Magasay, in the extreme northwest corner.

Temperatures can fluctuate drastically, and annual rainfall can be as high as 8000mm. The best time to go is the 'dry' season (January to April), but it is liable to rain then, too. Bring warm clothing, wet-weather gear and good hiking boots.

Dangers & Annoyances

There have been reports of thefts from cars parked at entrances to the trails, as well as an armed robbery inside the park. Don't leave your car parked anywhere along the main highway. And as a general rule, you should always register at a station before setting out on a hike, and when possible, arrange for a guide.

Activities

WILDLIFE-WATCHING

Bird-watching in the park is excellent, and commonly sighted species include parrots, toucans and hummingbirds; quetzals can be seen at higher elevations, primarily in the Barva sector. Other rare but sighted birds include eagles and umbrella birds.

Mammals are difficult to spot due to the lush vegetation, though deer, monkeys and *tepezcuintle* (agouti, the park's mascot) are frequently seen. Jaguars and ocelots are present but rare.

HIKING

From Zurquí, there is a short, steep 1km trail that leads to a viewpoint. You can also follow the **Sendero Histórico**, which follows the crystal-clear Río Hondura to its meeting point with the Río Sucio (Dirty River), whose yellow waters carry volcanic minerals.

From Quebrada González, you can follow the 2.8km **Sendero La Botella** (about 90 minutes) past a series of waterfalls into Patria Canyon. There are several other unmarked trails that lead through this area, including a few places where you are permitted to camp, though there are no facilities.

Keep an eye out for the distinctive Gunnera plants, which quickly colonize newly exposed parts of montane rainforest. The huge leaves can protect a person from a sudden downpour – hence the plant's nickname *sombrilla de pobre* (poor man's umbrella).

CLIMBING VOLCÁN BARVA

Climbing Volcán Barva is a strenuous five-hour round-trip adventure along a reasonably well-maintained trail. Because of its relative inaccessibility, there is a good chance you will be alone. Begin on the western side of the park, north of Heredia, at Paso Llano. From there a signed track climbs to the summit. Trails are often muddy, and you should be prepared for rain any time of the year.

The trail leads to three lagoons – Lagos Danta, Barva and Copey – at the volcano's summit, and several spur trails lead to waterfalls and other scenic spots along the way. From Barva, it is possible to follow overgrown, poorly marked 'trails' all the way to Estación Biológica La Selva (p508) and La Virgen (p499) – an activity which takes around four days. Hire a guide for this one – as hikers have gotten seriously lost and there are no facilities en route.

If you're visiting on a day trip, get to the entrance as early as possible as afternoons tend to be cloudy. Nighttime temperatures can drop below freezing. Camping is allowed at basic **campsites** (per person US$3) near the chilly but impossibly scenic summit, though you will need to bring your own drinking water.

VOLUNTEERING

Near Monte de la Cruz, in the Barva sector, the **Cerro Dantas Wildlife Refuge** (www.cerrodantas.co.cr) is an education facility that is always seeking volunteers to help out with a variety of administrative, maintenance and research duties. Contact the organization through their website for details.

Getting There & Away

Both the Zurquí and Quebrada González stations are on Hwy 32 between San José and Guápiles. Frequent buses between the two cities can drop you off at these, but pick-up on the road is dangerous and difficult (though not impossible).

The Barva station can be reached by following the decent paved road north from Heredia through Barva and on to San José de la Montaña, Sacramento and, ultimately, Paso Llano, where a signed, 3km-long, 4WD-only trail leads north to the entrance. If you don't have a car, you can take a public bus from Heredia (Calle 1, between Avs 4 and 6; ₡400). These depart at 5:25am, 6:25am, noon and 4pm on weekdays; 6:40am, 11am and 4pm on weekends. For a day-trip, it's best to take the earliest buses. Note: make sure you're catching a bus that goes all the way to Paso Llano – or you'll be left more than 15km from the park's entrance.

El Ceibo and Magasay can be accessed via rough roads from La Virgen (p499).

RAINFOREST AERIAL TRAM

The brainchild of biologist Don Perry, a pioneer of rainforest canopy research, the **Rainforest Aerial Tram** (☎ 2257-5961; www.rainforestrams.com; adult/student & child US$55/28, full-day tour with lunch & guided hike US$89; ♿) is a worthwhile splurge if you want to visit the heights of the forest canopy in a gondola. The 2.6km ride takes 40 minutes each way, affording unusual plant-spotting and bird-watching opportunities. The fee includes a knowledgeable guide, which is helpful since the density of the vegetation can make observing animals difficult. A variety of other tours are also available.

If you are staying in San José, you can easily arrange a shuttle to the tram. The company has a booking office in San José (Map p74), but it's just as easy to make reservations over the phone. If you are driving, look for the well-signed turnoff (it has lots of flags) just north of the Zurquí park entrance, on the east side of the road. From the parking lot, a truck will take you 3km to the tram-loading point, where there is an exhibit area, restaurant and gift shop. Here you can see an orientation video, and there are short maintained hiking trails for independent exploration. Be prepared for rain.

CARIBBEAN COAST

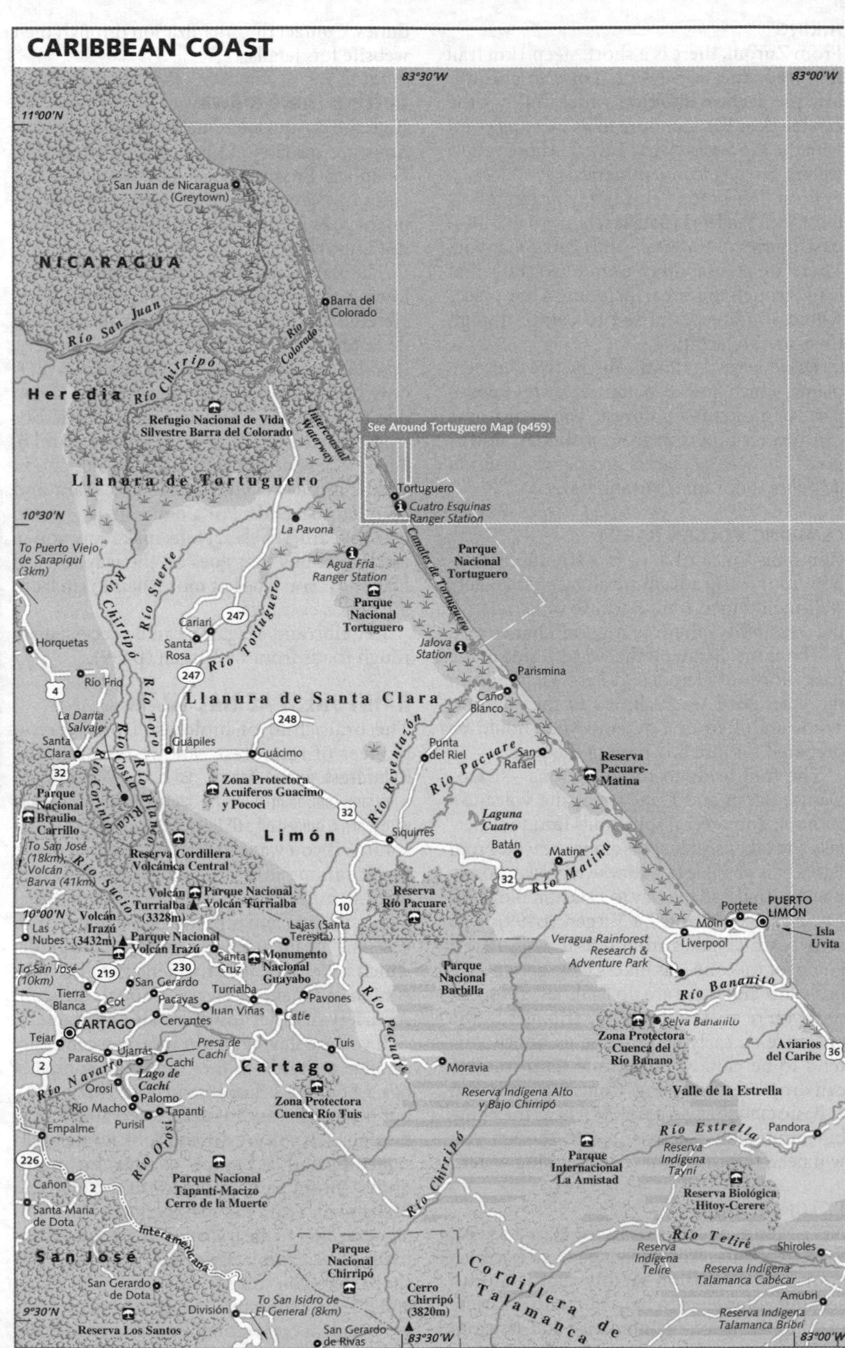

GUÁPILES & AROUND

pop 15,700

A pleasant (if not terribly scenic) lowland agricultural town located at the base of the northern foothills of the Cordillera Central serves as a transport center for the Río Frío banana-growing region. It's a good spot to hang out if you want to avoid the tourism industrial complex. Bustling streets are filled with shoppers, and families gather in a broad, rectangular plaza lined by rows of painted palm trees. A lively agricultural market takes place on Saturdays.

Guápiles serves as a convenient base from which to explore Parque Nacional Braulio Carrillo (p444), which lies just a 20 minute drive away, or to organize excursions to Tortuguero (p461).

The center of town is about 1km north of Hwy 32. The two major streets are one-way, running parallel to each other. Most of the services are on the loop that these streets make through the busy downtown.

Sights & Activities

About 2km east of downtown lies the **Jardín Botánico Las Cusingas**(☎ 2710-2652; guided tour US$5; ⏰ by appointment), a sprawling 20-hectare botanical garden with more than 80 medicinal species, 80 orchid species and 30 bromeliad species – plus, more than 100 bird species have been recorded on the flower-filled property. There are several easy trails for walking, as well as courses, research projects and a library on offer. From the main highway, turn north at the Servicentro Santa Clara, then go 4km by rough paved road to the signed entrance.

North of Guápiles, 3km northeast of the village of Santa Rosa, is the ecological farm **Ecofinca Andar** (☎ 2272-1024; www.andarcr.org; 1-day admission US$14, per person homestay incl meals US$17; P), an impressive educational facility that shows how plants are cultivated for medicinal purposes and used as sources of renewable energy. If you stick around for more than a day you can get your hands dirty by planting in the gardens and maintaining trails. See the website for details.

Sleeping

GUÁPILES

Hotel y Cabinas Wilson (☎ 2710-2217; d with/without air-con US$18/15, tr with air-con US$30; P ❄) A slightly musty, reasonably clean spot has 24 rooms with cool-water showers (not that you'll need hot water in the blistering lowland heat). Get a room in the back to avoid the street noise. To get here: from the main highway, turn north at the Burger King. The hotel will be about 300m in, on your right, on a broad commercial street.

Hotel Country Club Suerre (☎ 2710-7551, 2713-3000; www.suerre.com; s/d US$70/90, each additional person US$20; P ☒ ❄ ☎ ⛄ ♿) Just 1km north of the Servicentro Santa Clara lies this swish spot, popular with fruit company executives. The place has a rather bland Holiday Inn vibe, but the 98 rooms are spacious and tidy, and the grounds are meticulously maintained. There's a restaurant, casino, an Olympic-sized swimming pool, a gym, shaded tennis courts and a children's play area.

AROUND GUÁPILES

West of Guápiles, a 45-minute 4WD trip and three-hour hike will take you 800m above sea level to **La Danta Salvaje** (☎ 2750-0012; www.ladantasalvaje.com; 4-night package per person US$225), a 410-hectare rainforest reserve in a critical buffer zone adjacent to Parque Nacional Braulio Carrillo. The rustic lodge hosts

THE TROUBLED LEGACY OF BANANAS

The banana. Nothing embodies the tumultuous history of Latin America – and its complicated relationship to the United States – quite like this common yellow fruit. They are the crop that has determined the path of current affairs in more than one Central American nation. They are the sobriquet used to describe corrupt, dictatorial regimes – 'the banana republic.' They are a symbol of frivolity, the raw material for Carmen Miranda hats and Busby Berkeley dance numbers. (Want to blow your mind? Look up 'The Lady with the Tutti Frutti Hat' from the 1942 musical flick, *The Gang's All Here* – it's a hallucinogenic panorama of dancing bananas.)

It was in Costa Rica, interestingly, where the idea of bananas as an industry was born. Imported from the Canary Islands by sailors during the colony, the fruit had long been a basic foodstuff in the Caribbean islands. But it was 19th-century railroad baron Minor Keith who turned it into a booming international business (see p37). After building the railroad between San José and Limón, Keith proceeded to carpet vast swaths of Central America in bananas. Over the course of the 20th century, the company he founded – United Fruit – would become an integral part of the region's economies and a behind-the-scenes puppet master in its political systems. (For a highly readable history on this topic, pick up *Bananas: How the United Fruit Company Shaped the World,* by journalist Peter Chapman.)

Part of the reason bananas became a continent-wide crop boils down to profit and biology. Bananas – a fruit afflicted with a high rate of spoilage – require a vast economy of scale (and cheap labor) to be profitable. It's also an inordinately delicate fruit to cultivate, partly because bananas are clones. The fruit doesn't grow from seeds; it spawns by taking a cutting from an existing plant and putting it into the ground. This makes them incredibly vulnerable to illness – what kills one banana, kills all bananas. A fungus can devastate entire networks of plantations, such as the diseases that swept through Costa Rica's southern Caribbean coast in the 1910s and '20s.

Over the years, this weakness has led growers to turn to a veritable arsenal of chemicals to protect their crops. This, in turn, has taken a toll on the workers who spray them, some of whom have been rendered sterile by powerful fungicides such as DBCP (now banned). Groups of workers in various countries have filed numerous lawsuits against fruit companies and chemical manufacturers – and won – but these victories are generally short-lived. Even when Central American courts rule in workers' favor, it is practically impossible for plaintiffs to secure payouts. One suit has made it to the US legal system, but has been derailed by questions about evidence gathering.

There have been some attempts at growing bananas organically, but those efforts are not enough – and according to some experts, will never be enough – to replace the intense agribusiness that currently supplies the world with its fourth major foodstuff, after rice, wheat and milk. Costa Rica likes to think of itself as a country of coffee producers, a nation built on the work of humble, independent farmers. But the fact is that bananas remain the country's number one agricultural export – as they have been for decades. They are an inextricable part of the country's DNA. And, unless everyone suddenly starts putting sliced apples into their cereal, that likely won't change any time soon.

small groups (no more than eight people) for four days of hiking in the jungle, splashing around in swimming holes and spotting spider monkeys, tapirs and silky anteaters. Prices include three meals a day and guided hikes. Reservations must be made in advance.

Hotel Cabinas Lomas del Toro (☎ 2710-2934; d US$13-18; P ❄) Located about 3km east of Guápiles, on a hill above the northern side of the highway, an efficient roadside hotel has clean guestrooms, a restaurant serving local food and a recreation room with pool tables.

our pick **Casa Río Blanco B&B** (☎ 2710-4124; www.casarioblanco.com; d/tr/q incl breakfast US$65/80/90; P) A rustic inn, run by the personable Annette and Herbie, has four little wood *cabinas* on a two-hectare hillside that rises above the Río Blanco. It is devoid of niceties such as cable TV and wi-fi – making this a throwback to a time when travel to Costa Rica was all about unplugging. Late-night entertainment consists of listening to frogs croak and watching the lightning bugs put on a spectacle. The best part: the inn has a private trail that leads down to the river, where a spectacular swimming hole awaits. The helpful owners can organize off-the-beaten path area hikes as well as excursions to Tortuguero. Call ahead for reservations; additional meals (including vegetarian options) can be arranged. It is located 7km west of Guápiles. From Hwy 32, turn south onto the dirt road immediately west of the Río Blanco bridge. Follow the rocky road for 1km.

Eating

Deleites (100m west of Hotel y Cabinas Wilson) An attractive, well-stocked bakery sells, cookies, cakes, bread and even cappuccino.

Soda Buenos Aires (☎ 2710-1768; Hwy 32; ⏲ Mon-Sat) Situated 1km west of Guápiles, on the south side of the main highway, is this popular *soda* (cheap, informal lunch counter) that comes highly recommended for its well-prepared fish dishes.

El Rubio (☎ 2710-2323; 100m north of Hwy 32; mains ₡1800-4800) The clutter of pick-up trucks out front is a clue that you have stumbled onto this popular family eatery. It offers a wide selection of grilled fish and roasted meats (the *churrasco* – flank steak – is truly excellent). And there is a good selection of *bocas* (savory bar snacks), including our favorite: *chifrijo*, a pile of rice and pinto beans studded with fried pork and capped with fresh tomato salsa and corn chips. From the Burger King, go 100m north, then 100m east on the dirt road.

Restaurante El Campesino (Hwy 32; mains ₡2700-5000; ⏲ 7am-8pm Tue-Sun;) You'll find good ol' country cooking at this wholesome family spot (no alcohol sold) across the highway from the Burger King. Dip into tasty *chorreadas* (savory fresh-corn pancakes), *arroz con pollo* (chicken and rice) and *torta de queso* (a pile of cubed beef or chicken doused in melted cheese and served with corn tortillas).

There's a huge **Más X Menos** (⏲ 7am-9pm Mon-Sat, until 8pm Sun) supermarket, 200m north of the bus terminal.

Getting There & Away

The bus terminal is about 200m north of the main highway from the Burger King turn-off.

Cariari (Guapileños; ☎ 2766-6141) ₡400; 20 minutes; departs every 15 minutes from 6am to 10pm.

Puerto Limón via Guácimo & Siquirres (Tracasa) ₡1600; two hours; departs hourly from 6am to 7pm.

Puerto Viejo de Sarapiquí (Guapileños; ☎ 2766-6141) ₡800; 45 minutes; departs at 5:30am, 8am, 9am, 10:30am, noon, 1.15pm, 2:30pm, 4pm, 5pm and 6:30pm.

San José (Guapileños; ☎ 2766-6141) ₡1100; 1¼ hours; departs every 30 minutes from 6:30am to 7pm.

CARIARI

pop 12,100

Due north of Guápiles, Cariari is a blue-collar, rough-around-the-edges banana town, cluttered with tin-roof shops, hardware stores, bakeries and vegetable stands. Most travelers make their way quickly through town, en route to Tortuguero. If you are headed there, this will be your last opportunity to get cash.

There's a gas station and a branch of **Banco de Costa Rica** (opposite the San José bus terminal; ⏲ 9am-4pm Mon-Fri), with a 24-hour ATM on the Cirrus system.

If you get stuck, spend the night at **Hotel El Trópico** (☎ 2767-7186; 300m north of Terminal Caribeño; d with/without air-con US$20/17; P ❄), on the main road, which has 15 tidy rooms in a motor court-style layout with bathroom, hot showers and fans. A **restaurant** (⏲ 7am-10pm) serves local dishes.

Getting There & Away

If you are driving, the turnoff for the paved road to Cariari is about 1km east of Guápiles, at the Servicentro Santa Clara. If you are heading to Tortuguero, you can leave your car at the guarded parking by the boat dock on the Río La Suerte in La Pavona (about 30km north of Cariari).

To get to La Pavona, take the main road north out of Cariari, through Campo Dos and Cuatro Esquinas. At Abastecidor Palacio, make a left. It is generally well-signed. Casa Marbella in Tortuguero has posted a very helpful map of the exact route on its website at http://casamarbella.tripod.com/id6.html.

Buses from San José and Guápiles have a regular service to Cariari. Note that Cariari has two terminals: the one serving San José (known as the *estación nueva* – new station) is at the southern end of town, while the one serving Guápiles and Caribbean destinations is about five blocks to the north, just west of the main road. This latter station is known as the *estación vieja* (old bus station) or Terminal Caribeño.

For transfer to Puerto Limón, take a bus to Guápiles and then transfer to one of the regular hourly buses to Limón.

To reach Tortuguero, you will have to take a bus to the dock at La Pavona from the *estación vieja*. From here, you can transfer to one of several boat services that make multiple daily trips to Tortuguero. There are two public companies (Clic Clic and Coopetraca), which are the cheapest, and one private one (Viajes Bananero). In recent years, there has been a great deal of confusion as to how these services operate. For precise details on making the Cariari–Tortuguero transfer, see boxed text, p466.

Guápiles (Estación vieja) ₡400; 20 minutes; departs every 20 minutes from 5:30am to 7pm.

La Pavona for boat transfer to Tortuguero (Estación vieja) ₡1000; one hour; departs at 6am, 11:30am and 3pm.

Puerto Lindo (for Barra del Colorado) (Estación vieja) Bus-boat combo ₡2400; departs 4am and 2pm.

San José (Estación nueva) ₡1300; three hours; departs at 5:30am, 6:30am, 7:30am, 8:30am, 11:30am, 1pm, 3pm and 5:30pm

GUÁCIMO

pop 6100

Twelve kilometers east of Guápiles, off Hwy 32, lies this diminutive agricultural town. A popular destination of the Limón cruise-ship crowd is **Costa Flores** (☎ 2717-6457; 90-min guided tour US$18; by reservation; ♿), a huge tropical-flower and palm farm, with incredible heliconia gardens that are a riot of tropical colors. Its 48 hectares include landscaped gardens and fountain-fed ponds (much of it wheelchair-accessible). The farm exports 120 varieties of blossoms to the USA and Europe. To get there follow the main road into Guácimo for 2.5km.

Several kilometers east of the main Guácimo turn-off, is the main entrance to **EARTH** (Escuela de Agricultura de la Región Tropical Húmeda; ☎ 2713-0000; www.earth.ac.cr; guided tours per person US$25). This innovative not-for-profit university attracts students from all over the world to research sustainable agriculture in the tropics. The curriculum focuses on agriculture and integrates various academic disciplines into plenty of hands-on activities at onsite greenhouses and biological labs. Travelers can visit the facilities on guided tours; these must be arranged at least one week in advance. Rates are discounted for groups of seven or more.

Hotel Restaurant Río Palmas (☎ 2760-0330; d with/without air-con on weekdays US$46/36, d with/without air-con on weekends US$75/65; P ⊠ ❄ 🍴) is a hacienda-style roadside inn situated some 500m east of EARTH that comes with lush gardens and hiking trails. It has 25 decent rooms with cable TV and hot showers, and the restaurant is popular with tour buses making their way along Hwy 32.

SIQUIRRES

pop 15,200

The steamy lowland town of Siquirres has long served as an important transportation hub. It sits at the intersection of Hwy 32 (the main road that crosses the Atlantic slope to Puerto Limón) and Hwy 10, the old road that connects San José with Puerto Limón via Turrialba.

Even before the roads were built, it was a significant location – for it was in Siquirres in the early 20th century that the lines of segregation were drawn. At the time, blacks were barred from traveling west of here without special permission. So any train making its way from Limón to San José was required to stop here and change its crew: black conductors and engineers would change places with their Spanish counterparts and the train would continue on its route to the capital. This ended in 1949, when a new constitution outlawed racial discrimination.

Today, Siquirres still marks the place where Costa Rica takes a dip into the Caribbean – and it's not just the geography. It's reflected in the demographics and the culture as well. This is where Costa Rican *casados* (set meals) give way to West Indian *rondón* (a spicy seafood gumbo cooked in coconut milk), where Spanish guitar is replaced with the strains of calypso, and where Costa Rica's inherently *mestizo* race gives way to black features.

There is little reason to stop in Siquirres, unless you are heading north to Parismina – in which case this is a good spot to find banking, internet and telephone services. (Tip: buy phone cards here; they don't sell them at all in Parismina.) For purposes of orientation: the Siquirres church – a highly recognizable round building – is located to the west side of the soccer field.

Banco de Costa Rica (100m north of the park; 9am-4pm) has a 24-hour ATM on the Cirrus network. **Internet Siquirres** (7am-7pm Mon-Sat; per hr ₡350), on a 2nd story across from the Importadora Monge, north of the park, has a dozen terminals with decent connections.

If you need somewhere to crash for the night, head 1km northeast of the park to **Centro Turístico Las Tilapias** (2768-9293; www.tarzantico.com; d with/without air-con US$45/35; P), also known as 'Chito's Place.' It's hard to find, so ask around – or better yet, take a taxi. This sprawling, swampy property – a manmade lagoon in the center is home to a massive, snoozing crocodile – seems to channel the Florida Everglades. There are animal shows every Sunday at 4pm, when local celebrities Chito and Pocho put the moves on said croc. Surrounding the lagoon you'll find 17 clean-but-basic rooms as well as a bar and restaurant.

Sodas and bakeries are plentiful.

Getting There & Away

There are two principal bus terminals in town. At the corner terminal on the east side of the park, you'll find the following buses:

Guápiles ₡700; 45 minutes; departs every 45 minutes 6:30am to 7:30pm.
Limón ₡900; 1½ hours; departs almost hourly 6:30am to 10pm.
San José ₡1600; 1½ hours; departs almost hourly 5am to 6pm.

On the north side of the park, an L-shaped station has buses to Turrialba (₡700; almost hourly 5:30am to 6:30pm).

TO PARISMINA

At the L-shaped station on the park, you'll find buses to Caño Blanco, for transfer by boat to Parismina. **Caño-Aguilar** (2768-8172) operates the route to Caño Blanco (₡900; weekday departures at 4am, noon and 3:15pm, weekend departure at 7:30am). It's a two-hour ride to Caño Blanco, after which you transfer to a water taxi (₡1000) that makes the 10-minute trip to Parismina. (Take small change to pay the boatman.) There is a small restaurant with bathrooms by the dock.

Note: the Caño Blanco bus gets crowded. Get to the station early to buy your ticket and get in the queue. People start lining up to board about 15 minutes before the scheduled departure time.

VERAGUA RAINFOREST RESEARCH & ADVENTURE PARK

In Las Brisas de Veragua, you'll find this bells-and-whistles **rainforest adventure park** (2296-5056; www.veraguarainforest.com; Las Brisas de Veragua; admission adult with/without zip line tour US$89/55, child with/without zip line tour US$65/45), nestled into the foothills of the Talamanca Mountains. A sprawling complex, it has guided tours of the forest along elevated walkways and maintained trails, as well as attractions such as an aerial tram, a reptile vivarium, an insectarium and hummingbird and butterfly gardens. There is also a zip-line canopy tour, available at an extra charge. Installations include a cafeteria and gift shop and many of the attractions are wheelchair-accessible – and a good way of exploring nature if traveling with an elderly person or small children. To get here, take the signed turned-off south from Hwy 32 at Liverpool, 12km west of Puerto Limón.

PUERTO LIMÓN

pop 27,000

The biggest city on Costa Rica's Caribbean coast, the birthplace of United Fruit and capital of Limón Province – this hard-working port city sits removed from the rest of the country. Cruise ships deposit dazed-looking passengers between October and May. We can only hope that they weren't expecting to spot a quetzal – since Limón was never intended as a tourist attraction, but as a strategic shipping center, where containers of tropical fruits could be relayed to New York, London and beyond. Around here, business is measured by truckloads of fruit, not busloads of tourists, so don't expect much pampering.

A general lack of political and financial support from the federal government in San José means that Limón is not a city that has aged gracefully. It is a grid of dilapidated buildings, overgrown parks and sidewalks choked with street vendors. Crime is a problem: the city, distressingly, has as many homicides annually as San José – even though San José has five times the population. It's worth noting, however, that a good deal of this violence is related to organized crime and therefore does not affect travelers. Despite its shortcomings, Limón can nonetheless be a compelling destination for adventurous urban explorers.

History

Until the 1850s, the most frequent visitors to Limón were pirates, who used the area's natural deep-water bays as a regular hideout. At the time, the country's main port was in Puntarenas, on the Pacific, but when the railroad came to town in the late 19th century, Limón would blossom into a full-blown trade hub. From the city's teeming docks, tons of coffee would make their way to Europe, and the city would ultimately serve as the key export point for the country's newest agribusiness: bananas.

Beginning in 1913, a series of blights shut down many Caribbean *fincas* and a large portion of area banana-production moved to the southern Pacific coast (and eventually to Ecuador). Afro-Caribbean workers, however, couldn't follow the jobs as they were forbidden to leave the province. Stranded in the least-developed part of Costa Rica, many turned to subsistence farming, fishing or managing small-scale cocoa plantations. Others organized and staged bloody strikes against United Fruit. Fed up with the status quo, Limón provided key support to José Figueres during the 1948 civil war (see p38). This act was rewarded the following year when the new president enacted a constitution that granted blacks full citizenship and the right to work and travel freely throughout Costa Rica.

Even though segregation was officially dismantled, Limón continues to live with its legacy. The area was the last to get paved roads, the last to get electricity (areas to the south of the city weren't on the grid until the late 1970s) and the region has chronically higher crime and unemployment rates than the rest of the country. However, there have been some improvements in recent years. A police crackdown in 2009 has led to a slight reduction in crime and, that same year, the government launched an US$80 million investment project to help revitalize the city.

Orientation

Limón's streets are poorly marked and most locals use the landmark system to navigate their way around the city (see boxed text, p534). The old Radio Casino (don't expect to see a sign) and Parque Vargas both serve as prominent landmarks.

Information

If traveling onward to Parismina or Tortuguero, Limón will be your last opportunity to get cash. If continuing on to Parismina, also pick up telephone cards as these are not sold in the village.

Banco de Costa Rica (☎ 2758-3166; cnr Av 2 & Calle 1) Exchanges US dollars cash and has an ATM.

Hospital Tony Facio (☎ 2758-2222) On the coast at the northern end of town; serves the entire province.

Multiservices Pascal (☎ 2758-4090; 2nd fl, Av 2, north side of Parque Vargas; per hr ₡1700; 🕓 8am-10pm) A pricey internet and international phone joint with a dozen capable computers.

Post office (Calle 4 btwn Avs 1 & 2; 🕓 9am-4pm)

Scotiabank (☎ 2798-0009; cnr Av 3 & Calle 2; 🕓 9am-5pm Mon-Fri, 9am-1pm Sat) Exchanges cash and traveler's checks and has a 24-hour ATM on the Plus and Cirrus systems that dispenses US dollars.

Dangers & Annoyances

Theft is a problem: take precautions against pickpockets during the day, particularly in the market and along the sea wall. In addition, people do get mugged here, so stick to well-lit main streets at night, avoiding the sea wall and Parque Vargas. If driving, park in a guarded lot and remove everything from the car.

Sights & Activities

The city's main attraction is the waterfront **Parque Vargas**, an incongruous expanse of bench-lined sidewalks beneath a lost little jungle of tall palms and tropical flowers, centered on an appealingly decrepit bandstand.

From here, you can head inland along Av 2, the **pedestrian mall** that caters to the cruise-ship traffic. Keep an eye out for vendors selling home-burned CDs by local bands – Limón is getting a reputation for its growing hip-hop and reggaetón scene. (A band you can definitely expect to see being hawked: Los Trinitarios, a Limón band that has been fusing calypso and salsa since the '70s.)

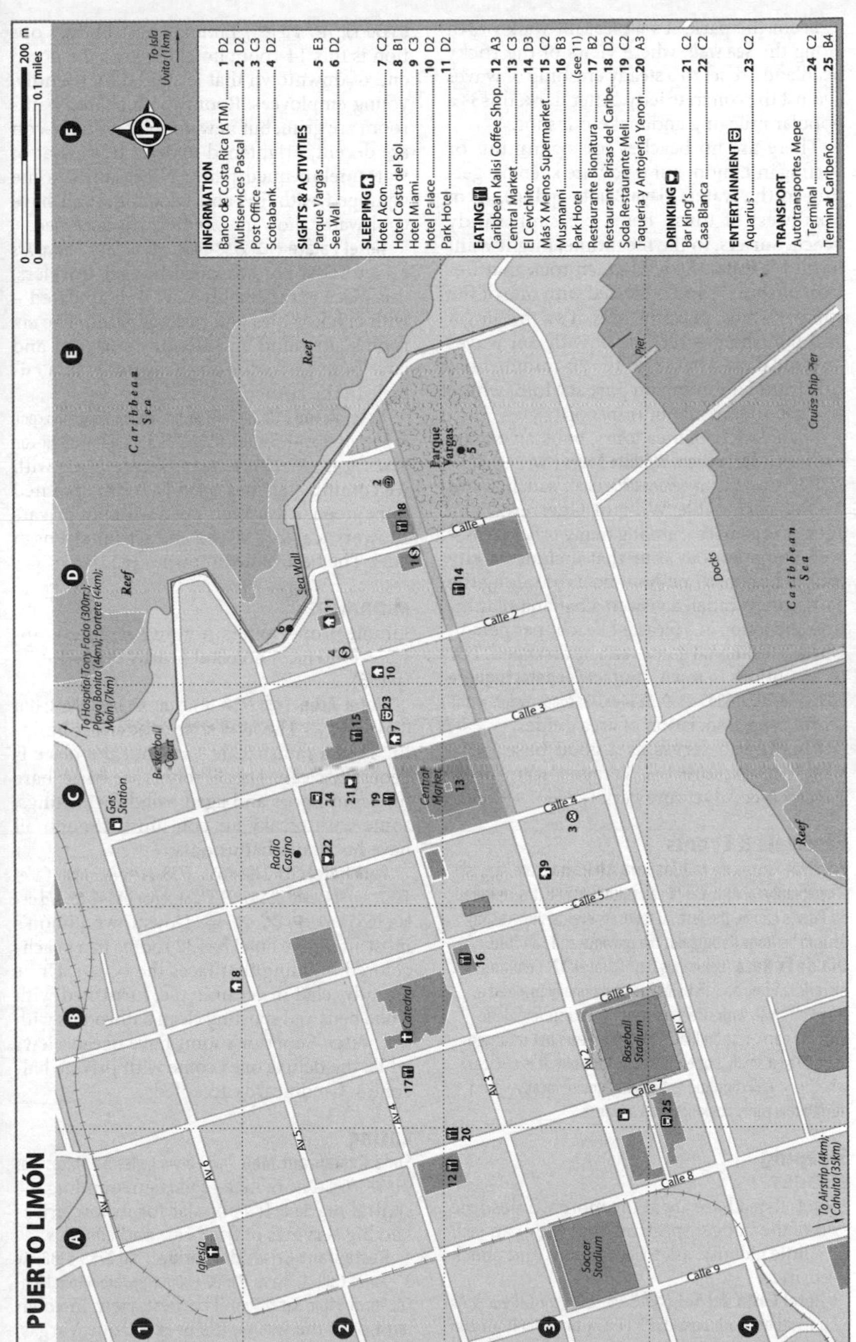
PUERTO LIMÓN
0 200 m
0 0.1 miles
INFORMATION
Banco de Costa Rica (ATM) 1 D2
Multiservices Pascal 2 D2
Post Office 3 C3
Scotiabank 4 D2
SIGHTS & ACTIVITIES
Parque Vargas 5 E3
Sea Wall 6 D2
SLEEPING
Hotel Acon 7 C3
Hotel Costa del Sol 8 B1
Hotel Miami 9 C3
Hotel Palace 10 D2
Park Hotel 11 D2
EATING
Caribbean Kalisi Coffee Shop 12 A3
Central Market 13 C3
El Cevichito 14 D3
Más X Menos Supermarket 15 C2
Musmanni 16 B3
Park Hotel (see 11)
Restaurante Bionatura 17 B2
Restaurante Brisas del Caribe 18 D2
Soda Restaurante Meli 19 C2
Taquería y Antojería Yenori 20 A3
DRINKING
Bar King's 21 C2
Casa Blanca 22 C2
ENTERTAINMENT
Aquarius 23 C2
TRANSPORT
Autotransportes Mepe Terminal 24 C2
Terminal Caribeño 25 B4
To Isla Uvita (1km)
Caribbean Sea
Reef
Sea Wall
Parque Vargas
Pier
Cruise Ship Pier
Docks
Central Market
Radio Casino
Gas Station
Basketball Court
To Hospital Tony Facio (300m); Playa Bonita (4km); Portete (4km); Moín (7km)
Catedral
Baseball Stadium
Soccer Stadium
Iglesia
To Airstrip (4km); Cahuita (35km)
Calle 1
Calle 2
Calle 3
Calle 4
Calle 5
Calle 6
Calle 7
Calle 8
Calle 9
Av 1
Av 2
Av 3
Av 4
Av 5
Av 6
Av 7

CARIBBEAN COAST

From the park, it's a pleasant walk north along the **sea wall**, where views of the rocky headland are set to a steady crashing of waves against the concrete jetty. After dark, this is a popular mugging and make-out spot.

There are no beaches for swimming or surfing in Limón, but if you are keen on getting in the water, **Playa Bonita** (p456), 4km northwest of town, has a pleasant, sandy beach. Surfers, in the meantime, might want to hit **Isla Uvita**, the wild green rock that lies 1km offshore – and is blessed with one of the country's most powerful lefts. It's a thrilling – and punishing – reef break with 3m waves on good days. The island is a 20-minute boat ride from Limón's main port at Moín, where you can inquire about transport.

For a variety of area tours, book an excursion with **Tortuguero Wildlife Tours** (☎ 2798-7027, 2758-2534; www.tortuguero-wildlife.com), which is run by the personable William Guerrero. The agency organizes – among many other trips – a combination day tour that includes a city tour of Limón, a one-hour boat ride along the Tortuguero canal, a visit to a banana plantation and a stop at a pleasant beach (per person US$45). Bilingual guides can be arranged. For other options in town, contact **Coopetortuguero** (☎ 2798-7029, 8865-2190, 8834-0072; coopetortuguero@gmail.com) an association of area guides.

Limón also serves as a good base from which to explore the Veragua Rainforest Research & Adventure Park (p451).

Festivals & Events

Festival Flores de la Diáspora Africana (Late August) A celebration of Afro-Caribbean culture. While it is centered on Puerto Limón, the festival sponsors events showcasing African heritage throughout the province and San José.

Día de la Raza (Columbus Day; October 12) Columbus' historic landing on Isla Uvita has traditionally inspired a small carnival, with street parades, live music and dancing. The party was on hiatus for a few years but returned in 2009 to a small, but enthusiastic turn-out. It is unclear whether it will continue to be held. Inquire locally – and during this time, book hotels in advance.

Sleeping

BUDGET

Hotels listed here are at the more wholesome end of the budget spectrum, but they can still be a little gloomy; ask to see a room and check security.

Hotel Costa del Sol (☎ 2798-0909; cnr Calle 5 & Av 5; s/d without bathroom US$9/11 d with/without air-con US$30/15; P ❄ 📶) Limón's best budget option is this 14-room hotel towards the north end of downtown that is staffed by friendly, young employees. Rooms with shared bathroom are grim, but new doubles with air-con are decent, brightened up by a fresh coat of watermelon-hued paint. Nicer units come equipped with TV and telephones; all have cool-water showers. Credit cards accepted.

Hotel Palace (☎ 2758-1068; 2nd fl, Calle 2 btwn Avs 2 & 3; d US$19) For seasoned budget travelers, this place is reasonably safe, if dilapidated – with cracked tiles and peeling paint. The six rooms surround an interior courtyard and have built-in cold-water bathrooms in a cubicle in the corner.

Hotel Miami (☎ 2758-0490; hmiamilimon@yahoo.com; Av 2 btwn Calles 4 & 5; s/d/tr US$22/28/31, s/d/tr with air-con US$29/39/43; P ❄) A clean, secure place with welcoming staff has 34 tidy rooms painted mint green. All are equipped with hot private showers, cable TV and industrial-strength fans. The best value in town.

MIDRANGE

Limón proper offers nothing remotely upscale. Find nicer hotels at nearby Playa Bonita (p456).

Hotel Acon (☎ 2758-1010; cnr Av 3 & Calle 3; d/tr US$45/56; ❄) The '60s-style Modernist building is in a ramshackle state, but the place is generally clean. The 39 rooms are basic: bare linoleum floors and aged wood furnishings, some with creaky air-con units, though all have hot-water bathrooms.

Park Hotel (☎ 2798-0555, 2758-3476; Av 3 btwn Calles 1 & 2; s/d standard US$45/59, s/d superior US$49/69, s/d deluxe US$53/69; P ⊠ ❄ 💻) Downtown Limón's most attractive hotel has 32 rooms in a peach-colored building that faces the ocean. Units are tidy, clad in ceramic tile, furnished with wood beds and sporting clean bathrooms with hot water. Superior rooms have ocean views while the deluxe ones come with private balconies. Credit cards accepted.

Eating

Soda Restaurant Meli (Av 3 btwn Calles 3 & 4; casados ₡1400-3800) One of many *sodas* surrounding the central market. It's popular for its low prices and big servings of fried rice and *casados*.

Restaurant Brisas del Caribe (☎ 2758-0138; Av 2, east of Calle 1; mains ₡1500-6000; 🕑 7am-11pm Mon-Fri, 10am-11pm Sat & Sun) The best view in town isn't over the waves, it's over Parque Vargas, where outdoor tables and a breezy balcony make for good people-watching and decent Caribbean fare.

Taquería y Antojería Yenori (☎ 2758-8294; Calle 7 btwn Avs 3 & 4; mains ₡2000-5000; 🕑 9am-9pm Mon-Sun) A cute little Mexican spot serves tacos (₡600) and *casados* (₡2000). You have to ring the bell to get buzzed in, where you'll find clean tables, chilled soda and a blaring air-con unit.

Caribbean Kalisi Coffee Shop (☎ 2758-3249; Calle 7 btwn Avs 3 & 4; mains from ₡2200; 🕑 7am-7pm Mon-Sat) A tidy, unremarkable-looking family spot serving a wide variety of local specialties, including Caribbean-style chicken with rice and red beans.

El Cevichito (Av 2 btwn Calles 1 & 2; mains ₡2800) The outdoor patio along the pedestrian mall is one of the city's more pleasant spots. You'll find locals gathering here to guzzle beer, talk soccer and devour tasty garlic fish.

Restaurante Bionatura (☎ 2798-2020; Calle 6 btwn Avs 3 & 4; mains ₡2900-3800; 🕑 8am-8pm Mon-Sat; Ⓥ) In a town where everything seems to be deep-fried, this restaurant stands out for its focus on healthy vegetarian cuisine, including fresh fruit salads, veggie burgers and *bistek de soya* (soy steak) *casados*. There's a health-food store next door.

Park Hotel (☎ 2798-0555; Av 3 btwn Calles 1 & 2; mains ₡3100-14,000; 🕑 6:30am-midnight) Sporting a 1970s Miami vibe, this semi-swanky (for Limón) eatery inside the town's top hotel has bright pink and green linens and ocean views. There is a long menu, but the specialty here is seafood, including fish brochettes, shrimp-studded rice and sea bass served countless ways.

For the cheapest budget eats, hit the **central market** (🕑 6am-8pm Mon-Sat), which has several *sodas* and plenty of groceries. The big supermarket **Más X Menos** (cnr Av 3 & Calle 3; 🕑 8am-9pm), across the avenue, is useful for self-caterers.

For breakfast, you can't go wrong with the baked goods at **Musmanni** (Av 3 btwn Calles 5 & 6; pastries from ₡600; 🕑 6am-6pm), near the cathedral.

Drinking & Entertainment

No one in Limón need ever go thirsty, considering the wide selection of bars. Those by Parque Vargas and a few blocks west are popular hang outs for a variety of coastal characters: banana workers, sailors, ladies of the night, entrepreneurs, boozers, losers and the casually curious. The standard warnings for solo women travelers go double here. (If you feel like having a beer, we recommend hitting a restaurant instead.) This is a lousy town for getting drunk – keep your wits about you.

Bar King's (Calle 3 btwn Avs 3 & 4) More Latin in flavor, it also attracts a few local women.

Casa Blanca (cnr Calle 4 & Av 4) A dark, smoky and air-conditioned dive that is packed from about 5pm onward with a mainly male clientele sipping drinks and watching grainy porn on the telly. It's easy to find: follow the ear-splitting Latin music emanating from the jukebox.

Aquarius (☎ 2758-1010; Av 3 btwn Calles 2 & 3; 🕑 8pm-2am) Inside Hotel Acon, this long-running disco spins salsa, reggaetón and pop on different nights.

Getting There & Away

Puerto Limón is the transportation hub of the Caribbean coast.

AIR

The airstrip is about 4km south of town. There are no regularly scheduled flights, but you can charter a flight to San José through one of the charter companies there (see p97) or to Puerto Jiménez or Golfito through Alfa Romeo Aero Taxi (see p393).

BOAT

Cruise ships occasionally dock in Limón, but most boats providing transportation use the major port at Moín, about 7km west of Limón. For information on boats to Tortuguero, see p456.

BUS

Buses to and from San José, Moín, Guápiles and Siquirres arrive at **Terminal Caribeño** (Av 2 btwn Calles 7 & 8) on the west side of the city by the baseball stadium, where local ladies line up to sell *pan bon*, a type of West Indian fruit cake.

Guápiles via Siquirres & Guácimo (Tracasa; Terminal Caribeño) To Siquerres/Guápiles ₡900/1600; two hours; departs almost hourly 5am to 6pm.

Moín, for boats to Tortuguero (Tracasa; Terminal Caribeño) ₡300; 20 minutes; departs hourly 5:30am to 6:30pm.

San José (Autotransportes Caribeños; Terminal Caribeño) ₡2500; three hours; departs almost hourly 5am to 7pm.

Buses to points south all depart from **Autotransportes Mepe Terminal** (☎ 2758-1572; Mepe; Av 4 btwn Calles 3 & 4), 100m north of the Central Market.

Bribrí & Sixaola ₡2600; three hours; departs hourly between 5am and 6pm.

Cahuita ₡1000; 1½ hours; departs at 5am, 6am, 8am, 10am, 1pm, 2:30pm, 4pm and 6pm.
Manzanillo ₡2000; 2½ hours; departs at 5:30am, 6am 10:30am, 3pm and 6pm.
Puerto Viejo de Talamanca ₡1900; 2½ hours; departs at 5:30am, 6am, 10:30am, 3pm and 6pm.

AROUND PUERTO LIMÓN

Playa Bonita

While not the finest beach in the Caribbean, **Playa Bonita** offers sandy stretches of seashore and good swimming convenient to Limón – and accommodations that are considerably more attractive than anything you'll find in the city. Surfers make their way to Bonita for its point/reef break, which makes for a powerful (and sometimes dangerous) left. Just north, **Portete** is a small bay with a wicked right working off the southerly point. Any Limón–Moín bus will drop you off at these places.

SLEEPING & EATING

The road between Limón and Moín is home to some good accommodations. The following are listed in order from Limón (east to west).

Oasis del Caribe (☎ 2795-0024; d US$35; P) About 3km northwest of Limón, on the inland side of the road, these cozy pink bungalows are decorated with lace curtains, bamboo furniture and worn (but clean) sheets. They are clustered around a small pool, which is critical, as this place does not have beach access.

Hotel Maribú Caribe (☎ 2795-2543/2553; maribu@racsa.co.cr; d/tr US$51/69, d with ocean view US$85; P) A few hundred paces west of Oasis, on the ocean side, is this 52-room hilltop hotel with spacious white-stucco bungalows with thatched roofs dotting a well-maintained garden. Rooms come equipped with simple wood beds, cable TV, minifridge and private hot showers. A popular onsite restaurant (mains ₡3200 to ₡5400) – with incredible water views – dishes out a mix of Costa Rican and Mediterranean specialties.

Hotel Cocori (☎ 2795-1670; s/d/tr incl breakfast & dinner US$38/55/76; P) A freshly renovated seaside hotel with simple, white-washed rooms and private hot showers also has a breezy, ocean-view restaurant that serves everything from burgers (₡2250) to jumbo shrimp (₡12,000). It's about 2.5km from the entrance to the docks at Moín.

About 50m down the road, right on the beach, **Reina's** (☎ 2798-0879; mains ₡3200-6000; 8am-last guest) has loud music, good vibes and plenty of *mariscos* (seafood) and *cerveza* (beer) on the menu.

Moín

This is Puerto Limón's main transportation dock. The reason you're here, no doubt, is to catch a boat through the canals to Parismina or Tortuguero.

GETTING THERE & AWAY

The journey by boat to Tortuguero can take anywhere from three to five hours, depending on how often the boat stops to observe wildlife (many tours also stop for lunch). Indeed, it is worth taking your time. As you wind your way through these jungle canals, you are likely to spot howler monkeys, crocodiles, two- and three-toed sloth and an amazing array of wading birds, including roseate spoonbills.

The route is most often used by tourist boats, which means that if the canal becomes blocked by water hyacinths or logjams, the route might be closed altogether. Schedules exist in theory only and they change frequently depending on demand. If you are feeling lucky, you can just show up in Moín in the morning and try to get on one of the outgoing tour boats. But you are better off reserving in advance.

Asociación de Boteros de los Canales de Tortuguero (Abacat; ☎ 8360-7325) Abacat operates regular service to Tortuguero (per person one-way US$30). Call for departure times.
Caribbean Tropical Tours (☎ 8371-2323, 2798-7027; wguerrerotuca@hotmail.com) A small, well-recommended company run by master sloth-spotter William Guerrero and his wife, it's ideal if you want to book a leisurely ride to Tortuguero with plenty of pit-stops to see wildlife (per person one-way US$35).
Moín–Parismina–Tortuguero water taxi (☎ 2709-8005) Departs Moín at 3pm. Reservations are essential, especially if you are requesting a stop in Parismina. One-way to Tortuguero US$30.
Tropical Wind (☎ 2798-6059, 8313-7164, 8327-0317) Operates almost-daily shuttles between Tortuguero and Moín (per person one-way US$30).
Viajes Bananero (☎ 8833-1066, in San José 2222-8973) Though based in Tortuguero, with an office in San José, this company makes regular (though not daily) trips between Tortuguero and Moín (per person one-way US$35). Call ahead to reserve.

Tracasa buses to Moín from Puerto Limón (₡300, 20 minutes) depart from Terminal Caribeño hourly from 5:30am to 6:30pm. Get off the bus before it goes over the bridge. If you are driving, leave your car in a guarded lot in Limón.

NORTHERN CARIBBEAN

Running north–south along the country's water-logged eastern shore, the Tortuguero Canal serves as the liquid highway that connects Puerto Limón to the lush lowland settlements to the north: Parismina, Tortuguero and Barra del Colorado. This is the wettest region in Costa Rica, a network of rivers and canals that are home to diminutive fishing villages and slick sportfishing camps, raw rainforest and all-inclusive resorts – not to mention plenty of wading birds and sleepy sloths.

Most significantly, the area's long, wild beaches serve as the protected nesting grounds for three kinds of sea turtles. In fact, more green turtles are born here than anywhere else. Much of the region lies only a 15-minute flight from San José – but it nonetheless can feel like the end of the earth.

PARISMINA

If you want to get a sense of what Costa Rica's Caribbean coast was like prior to the arrival of mass tourism, this tiny coastal fishing village, wedged between the Tortuguero Canal and the Caribbean Sea, is an excellent spot to spend a little time. Bereft of zip lines, 4WD adventure tours and wi-fi everything, it's the sort of spot where old men play dominoes on front porches and kids splash in muddy puddles in the street. It's not fancy – but it's real.

Sportfishing is the traditional tourist draw. (The top tarpon season is from January to mid-May, while snook are caught from September to November.) But a smattering of travelers also arrive to see (and protect) endangered sea turtles. Leatherbacks nest on the beach between late February and early October, with the peak season in April and May. Green turtles begin nesting in June, with a peak in August and September. Hawksbills are not as common, but they are sometimes seen between February and September.

In addition, every year around July 16, fishers and local boat captains have a small waterborne procession in honor of the Virgen del Carmen, the patron virgin of sailors.

Information

There are no banks or post offices in Parismina. Credit cards and traveler's checks are not accepted, so make sure you bring plenty of cash. In addition, while the village has a couple of pay phones, no one in town sells phone cards – be sure to bring your own. Internet access is almost nonexistent.

ASTOP (Asociación Salvemos Las Tortugas de Parismina Information Center; Save the Turtles of Parismina; ☎ 2798-2220; www.parisminaturtles.org; 🕑 1-5pm Feb-Oct) A turtle-protection organization run by a former Peace Corps volunteer, ASTOP organizes homestays (per night with three meals US$25), offers internet access (per hour ₡1700) and posts information about local activities, events and tour guides. Staff can arrange horseback-riding trips, bike rentals, as well as turtle-watching tours (per person US$20 in season) and wildlife-viewing excursions by boat (per person US$20 to US$25 for two- to four-hour tours).

Sights & Activities

ASTOP (☎ 2798-2220; www.parisminaturtles.org; 🕑 1-5pm Feb-Oct) has built a guarded **turtle hatchery** to deter poachers and thieves. Travelers can volunteer as turtle guards to patrol the beaches alongside local 'turtle guides.' To volunteer, you'll have to pay a US$30 registration fee, in addition to a daily US$15 lodging fee that includes training, accommodations with a local family and three meals daily. A three night minimum is required. (Note that the US$15 per night rate is for volunteers only. Independent travelers and others who arrange homestays through ASTOP will have to pay the full fee of US$25 per night.)

Villagers have traditionally depended on farming and fishing, but the turtle project has become an important part of the local economy, as many families depend on the income they receive from homestays and other activities. ASTOP can also help organize Spanish lessons, Latin dance lessons, fishing trips and boat tours into Parque Nacional Tortuguero. ASTOP also organizes day trips to Caño Blanco (per person US$25, not including boat transport), where you can visit a traditional Tico farm, milk cows and make cheese.

For a worthwhile day trip, cross the river to Caño Blanco and pay a visit to Don Victor and his wife Isaura, who run **Jardín Tropical** (☎ 2200-5567; admission US$2; 🕑 8am-5pm), an amazing heliconia farm.

You can rent kayaks at Carefree Ranch (per day US$9).

Sleeping & Eating

Cabinas Cariblanco (☎ 2798-1031; r per person US$8) A bare-bones spot on the beach with 11 worn rooms and private cold-water showers. A popular bar is attached – in other words, this place gets LOUD.

Iguana Verde (☎ 2798-0828; s/d US$10/15, d with air-con US$25; ❄) Set around a small courtyard, three tidy rooms have bathrooms and air-con. It will be on your left-hand side as you walk east from the dock.

Parismina Gamefish Lodge (☎ 2758-5456; r per person with/without air-con US$14/10; ❄) Across from Iguana Verde is this new spot, with six simple, tiled rooms surrounding a garden lined with hammocks. The beds are firm and the electric showers may or may not work.

Carefree Ranch (☎ 2710-3149; r per person US$10) Opposite the Catholic church, this basic clapboard house – bright yellow with green trim – has nine tidy rooms with concrete bathrooms and a broad front porch that is ideal for relaxing. In Parismina, it's about as quaint as things get. Family-style meals are available for an additional charge.

Green Gold Ecolodge (☎ 2798-0845; dm per person US$10) A little more than 3km south of the dock, on the beach, is this solar-powered bunk-house set on 36 hectares of forest. Administered by the bilingual Jason, it's raw: expect a dorm bed, a shared outdoor kitchen and basic shared bathrooms. But if you're looking to retreat to an authentic rainforest hideaway, then this is it. Jason leads turtle tours and can organize fishing and wildlife-spotting excursions – but whatever you do, make sure he introduces you to the wonders of coconut sponge. Transport from the dock to the lodge can be arranged (from ₡3000 per person).

ASTOP (☎ 2798-2220; www.parisminaturtles.org; r per person incl 3 meals US$25) Volunteers get first choice of accommodations, but if the village isn't full ASTOP can arrange homestays, including meals, with a local family. All lodging is in private rooms with locking doors, mosquito nets and shared bathroom facilities. Vegetarians can be accommodated with advance notice, though it might be worthwhile to bring produce from Cariari; fruits and veggies are scarce in Parismina.

Don Alex at the hardware store, about 300m north of the dock, has camping (high season only) – with sheltered tent sites and access to showers and bathrooms.

For package sportfishing expeditions to the area organized from the USA, check out the following two companies:

Caribbean Tarpon Lodge (☎ 2798-0964, in USA 888-341-5525; www.caribbeantarponlodge.com) A midrange canal-side hotel with five simple rooms and a private dock. The cost of 4-day/5-night packages including transfers, meals and guided fishing is from US$1700.

Río Parismina Lodge (☎ 2229-7597, in USA 800-338-5688, 210-824-4442; www.riop.com; ⊠ 🅿) A top-of-the line spot across the river from Parismina has swimming pool, Jacuzzi and English-speaking guides. The cost of 4-day/5-night packages including meals and guided fishing is from US$1950.

For meals, hit **Soda Las Palmas** (casados ₡2800; 🕒 6am-7pm Mon-Sat) right next to the dock. Here, no-nonsense doña Amelia serves up fresh and tasty *casados*. She also keeps the small plaster statue of the Virgin that is paraded during the annual boat procession in July.

Getting There & Away

Parismina is only accessible by boat, and the only regular service is to Caño Blanco (for transfer to Siquirres). For directions on how to get here from Siquirres, see p451.

To get to Caño Blanco, take one of the water taxis (₡1000) that leave from the Parismina dock at 5:30am, 1:30pm and 4:30pm Monday through Friday, and at 9am and 1:30pm on Saturday and Sunday. Buses will be waiting at the dock to continue the journey to Siquirres (₡900), where you can find onward transport.

If you want to travel to Puerto Limón or Tortuguero, it is simple enough to secure a seat on one of the tourist boats that travel between the two destinations – provided you reserve in advance. Doña Amelia at Soda Las Palmas (above) can book a seat for you. Likewise, you can call one of the boat companies in Moín (p456) directly to see if any are making the trip. Depending on the company, expect the rate to Tortuguero to be between US$20 to US$25 per person. Note that it may take 24 to 48 hours to secure transport.

PARQUE NACIONAL TORTUGUERO

'Humid' is the driest word that could truthfully be used to describe Tortuguero, a 311-sq-km coastal park that serves as the most important breeding ground of the green sea turtle. With an annual rainfall of up to

6000mm in the northern part of the park, it is one of the wettest areas in the country. In addition, the protected area extends into the Caribbean Sea, covering about 5200 sq km of marine habitat. In other words, plan on spending quality time in a boat.

The famed **Canales de Tortuguero** are the introduction to this important park. A north–south waterway created to connect a series of lazy lagoons and meandering rivers in 1974, this engineering marvel allowed inland navigation between Limón and coastal villages in something sturdier than a dugout canoe. There are regular flights to the village of Tortuguero – but if you fly, you'll be missing half the fun. The leisurely taxi-boat ride, through banana plantations and wild jungle, is equal parts recreation and transportation.

Most visitors, naturally, come to watch sea turtles lay eggs on the area's wild, black-sand beaches. The area attracts four of the world's eight species of sea turtle – making it a crucial habitat for these massive reptiles. It will come as little surprise, then, that these hatching grounds gave birth to the sea turtle–conservation movement. The Caribbean Conservation Corporation (p462), the first program of its kind in the world, has continuously monitored turtle populations here since 1955. Today, green sea turtles are increasing in numbers along this coast, but the leatherback and hawksbill are in decline (see boxed text, p58).

The area, however, is more than just turtles: you'll find sloths and howler monkeys in the treetops, tiny frogs and green iguanas scurrying among buttress roots, and mighty tarpon and endangered manatee swimming in the waters. Tortuguero is thick with wildlife.

Orientation & Information

The park is accessible from the village of Tortuguero (the most common entry point) and Parismina. Park headquarters is at **Cuatro Esquinas** (☎ 2709-8086; admission US$10; 🕑 5:30am-6pm with breaks for breakfast & lunch), just south of Tortuguero village. This is an unusually helpful ranger station, with maps, information and access to a 2km-loop nature trail. Wear boots: it's muddy, even in the dry season.

Jalova Station (🕑 6am-6pm) is on the canal at the south entrance to the national park, accessible from Parismina by boat. Tour boats from Moín often stop here for a picnic; you will find a short nature trail, bathroom, drinking water and rudimentary camping facilities that may or may not be open to campers (and may or may not be flooded).

There is no dry season, although it does rain less in February, March and October.

Activities

HIKING

Behind Cuatro Esquinas station, **El Gavilán Land Trail** is the only public trail through the park that is on solid ground. Visitors can hike the muddy, 2km loop that traverses the tropical humid forest and follows a stretch of beach. Green parrots and several species of monkeys are commonly sighted here. The short trail is well marked and does not require a guide.

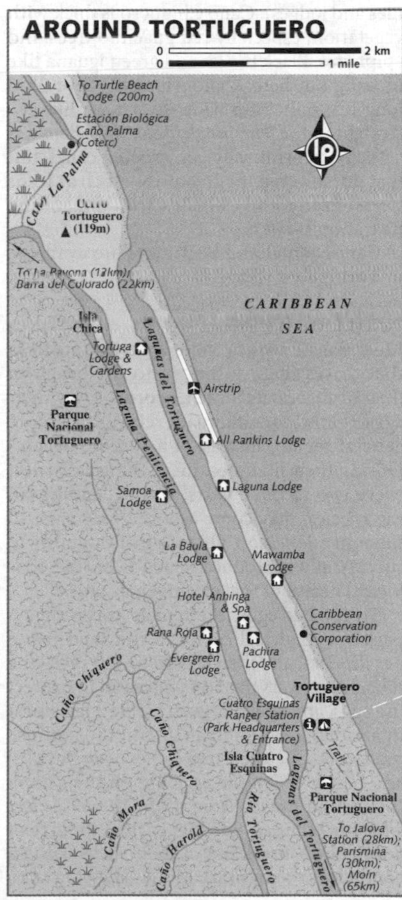

CARIBBEAN COAST

BOATING

Four aquatic trails wind their way through Parque Nacional Tortuguero, inviting waterborne exploration. **Río Tortuguero** acts as the entrance way to the network of trails. This wide, beautiful river is often covered with water lilies and frequented by aquatic birds such as heron (especially the great blue heron and the night heron), kingfisher and anhinga – the latter of which is known as the snakebird for the way its slim, winding neck pokes out of the water when it swims.

Caño Chiquero and **Canõ Mora** are two narrower waterways with good wildlife-spotting opportunities. According to park regulation, only kayaks, canoes and silent electric boats are allowed in these areas (a rule that is constantly violated by many area tour companies and lodges). Caño Chiquero is thick with vegetation, especially red guácimo trees and epiphytes. Black turtles and green iguana like to hang out here. Caño Mora is about 3km long but only 10m wide, so it feels like it's straight out of *The Jungle Book*. **Caño Harold** is actually an artificially constructed canal, but that doesn't stop the creatures – such as Jesus Christ lizards and caiman – from inhabiting its tranquil waters.

Canoe rental and boat tours are available in Tortuguero village.

TURTLE-WATCHING

Most female turtles share a nesting instinct that drives them to return to the beach of their birth, or natal beach, in order to lay their eggs. (Only the leatherback returns to a more general region, instead of a specific beach.) During their lifetimes, they will usually nest every two to three years, and depending on the species, may come ashore to lay eggs 10 times in one season. Often, a turtle's ability to successfully reproduce depends on the ecological health of this original habitat.

To lay her eggs, the female turtle digs a perfect cylindrical cavity in the sand using her flippers, and then lays 80 to 120 eggs. She diligently covers the nest with sand to protect the eggs, and she may even create a false nest in another location in an attempt to confuse predators. She then makes her way back to sea – after which the eggs are on their own. Incubation ranges from 45 to 70 days, after which hatchlings – no bigger than the size of your palm – break out of their shells using a caruncle, or temporary tooth. They crawl to the ocean in small groups, moving as quickly as possible to avoid dehydration and predators. Once they reach the surf, they must swim for at least 24 hours to get to deeper water, away from land-based predators.

Because of the sensitive nature of the habitat and the critically endangered status of some species, tours of this activity are highly regulated. So as to not alarm turtles as they come to shore (a frightened turtle will return to the ocean and dump her eggs), tour groups gather in shelter sites close to the beach and a spotter relays a turtle's location via radio once she has safely crossed the high-tide mark and built her nest. At this time, visitors can then go to the beach and watch the turtle lay her eggs, cover her nest and return to the ocean. Seeing a turtle is not guaranteed. By law, tours can only take place between 8am and midnight. Some guides will offer tours after midnight; these are illegal.

Visitors should wear closed-toe shoes and rain gear. Tours cost US$20 (a flat rate established by the village), which includes the purchase of a US$4 sticker that pays for the patrols that help protect the nesting sites from scavengers and looters. Nesting season runs from March to October, with July and August being prime time. The next best time is April, when leatherback turtles nest in small numbers. Flashlights and cameras (of all kinds) are not allowed on the beach. (See boxed text, p263, for more about this.)

For information about volunteering, see boxed text, p461.

OTHER WILDLIFE-WATCHING

More than 300 bird species, both resident and migratory, have been recorded in Tortuguero – making the park a bird-watchers paradise. Due to the wet habitat, the park is especially rich in waders – including egrets, jacanas, 14 different types of heron, as well as species such as kingfishers, toucans and the great curassow (a type of jungle peacock known locally as the *pavón*). The great green macaw is a highlight – and is most common from December to April, when the almond trees are fruiting. In September and October, look for flocks of migratory species such as eastern kingbird, barn swallows and purple martins. The Caribbean Conservation Corporation (p462) conducts a biannual monitoring program, in which volunteers can help scientists take inventory of local and migratory species.

DOING TIME FOR THE TURTLES

There are many opportunities to volunteer your time to help protect sea turtles – and the many other creatures that inhabit the Caribbean coast. In most cases, organizations require a minimum commitment of a week. A few options:

Asociación Salvemos Las Tortugas de Parismina (☎ 2798-2220; www.costaricaturtles.org) A small, locally run organization coordinates important conservation activities in Parismina (p457).

Asociación Widecast (☎ in San José 8818-2543; www.latinamericanseaturtles.org, www.widecast.org) A grassroots NGO has volunteer opportunities in Cahuita (p478) and Gandoca (p495), on the southern coast.

Canadian Organization for Tropical Education and Rainforest Conservation (☎ 2709-8052, in Canada 905-831 8809; www.coterc.org) A reputable Canadian not-for-profit has various volunteer opportunities at its research station in Tortuguero (p462).

Caribbean Conservation Corporation (☎ 2709-8091, in USA 800-678-7853; www.cccturtle.org) A renowned long-time organization that has myriad volunteer options at its research station in Tortuguero (p462).

Certain species of mammals are particularly evident in Tortuguero, especially mantled howler monkeys, the Central American spider monkey (the most graceful of the local monkey species) and white-faced capuchin. If you've got a good pair of binoculars (and a good guide), you can usually see both two- and three-toed sloth. In addition, normally shy neo-tropical river otters are reasonably habituated to boats. Harder to spot are timid West Indian manatees. The park is also home to big cats such as jaguars and ocelots – but these are savvy, nocturnal animals that can be difficult to see under the best circumstances.

Most wildlife-watching tours are done by boat. To get the best from Tortuguero, be on the water early or go out following a heavy rain – when all the wildlife comes out to sunbathe. It is also highly recommended to take tours by canoe or kayak – since these smaller, silent craft will allow you to get into the park's less trafficked nooks and crannies.

Sleeping

The Cuatro Esquinas ranger station has been closed to camping for the foreseeable future. It may be possible to pitch a tent at Jalova Station at the southern end of the park, but services are limited and the area is often submerged after heavy rains.

Getting There & Away

For information on traveling to and from the area, see p465, and boxed text, p466.

TORTUGUERO VILLAGE

Located within the confines of Parque Nacional Tortuguero, accessible only by air or water, this bustling little village with strong Afro-Caribbean roots is best known for attracting hordes of sea turtles (the name Tortuguero means 'turtle place') – and the hordes of tourists who want to see them. While the peak turtle season is in July and August – the park and village have begun to attract travelers year-round. Even in October, when the turtles have pretty much returned to the sea, caravans of families and adventure travelers arrive to go on jungle hikes and to canoe the area's lush canals.

Information

A solid source of information is the town's website, **Tortuguero Village** (www.tortuguerovillage.com), which lists local businesses and provides comprehensive directions on how to get into the area. It also has a helpful map.

There are no banks or ATMs in town and only a few businesses accept credit cards, so bring all the cash you'll need. Internet connections can be iffy, especially during heavy rains.

Beyetty Internet (☎ 2709-8058; per hr ₡2000; 🕑 8:30am-9pm) You'll find a few vintage machines and a friendly proprietor at this tiny spot on the canal side towards the north end of town.

Paraíso Tropical Store (☎ 2710-0323) A sprawling shop on the north side capped by a giant toucan statue on a pole sells pricey souvenirs and NatureAir tickets; it also cashes traveler's checks.

Tortuguero Info Center (☎ 2709-8055; tortuguero_info@racsa.co.cr; per hr ₡2000; 🕑 8am-7pm) An independent information center that sells Sansa airline tickets and provides internet access. It is across from the Catholic church.

Dangers & Annoyances

Competition for business is fierce in Tortuguero and relentless touts often sell tourists less-than-stellar services. Many so-called 'guides' are unlicensed, others downright unprofessional. Go with recommended guides and, if you're unsure about where you've decided to stay, ask to see a room before putting any money down.

Sights

About 200m north of Tortuguero village, the **Caribbean Conservation Corporation** (CCC; ☎ 2709-8091, in USA 800-678-7853; www.cccturtle.org; admission US$1; ⏲ 10am-noon & 2-5pm Mon-Sat, 2-5pm Sun) operates a research station that has a small visitor center and museum. Exhibits focus on all things turtle-related, including a video about the history of local turtle conservation.

CCC also runs a highly reputable environmental volunteer program, recommended by none other than *National Geographic*. During nesting season, interested folks can assist with turtle tagging and egg counts, and during bird-migration seasons, help with mist-netting and point-counts. Volunteer fees start at US$1450 per week and include bunk-house accommodations, all meals, first and last nights' hotel room in San José and transport to and from the capital.

The **Canadian Organization for Tropical Education and Rainforest Conservation** (Coterc; ☎ 2709-8052, in Canada 905-831 8809; www.coterc.org; admission free) is a not-for-profit organization that operates the Estación Biológica Caño Palma, 7km north of Tortuguero village. This small biological research station houses a diminutive museum that contains, among other things, an impressive collection of skulls. From here, a network of trails wind through the surrounding rainforest. Coterc is surrounded on three sides by water, so you'll have to hire a boat to get here.

The group also runs a volunteer program, in which visitors can assist with upkeep of the station and ongoing research projects, including sea-turtle and bird monitoring and plant-diversity inventories. Volunteer fees start at US$250 and include accommodations in dormitory buildings and three meals per day.

For other volunteer opportunities on the Caribbean coast, see boxed text, p461.

Activities

Besides the usual nature-focused activities, the town is cluttered with more souvenir shops than you can shake a coconut at. Shop around – prices and quality vary.

In addition, Hotel Aningha, across the river, has a spa where you can sign up for massages and exfoliating treatments.

BOATING & CANOEING

Signs all over Tortuguero advertise boat tours and boats for hire. This is obviously the best way to explore the surrounding waterways (see p460). For a list of recommended companies and guides, see below. Our advice: for optimum wildlife-spotting, forego the motors (the noise scares off wildlife) and opt for a guided tour by canoe. (You don't have to row if you don't want to.)

Numerous area businesses rent kayaks and canoes; inquire locally.

HIKING

A number of trails extend from the village into the national park (see p459) and around Coterc (following). Inquire at the agencies listed below for guided tours. Note: night hiking in the national park is not allowed.

Tours

Guides have posted signs all over town advertising their services for canal tours and turtle walks. The **Tortuguero Info Center** (☎ 2709-8055; tortuguero_info@racsa.co.cr) can provide information. Going rates are about US$20 per person for a two-hour turtle tour, and US$15 for a two-hour hiking or boat excursion.

Recommended local guides:

Barbara Hartung (☎ 2709-8004; www.tinamontours.de) Offers hiking, canoe and turtle tours in German, English, French or Spanish. Also offers a unique tour about Tortuguero history, culture and medicinal plants.

Castor Hunter Thomas (☎ 8870-8634; castorhunter.blogspot.com;) A local who has worked as a guide for more than 20 years leads turtle tours (in season), guided hikes and wonderful canoe tours. Ask at Soda Doña María.

Chico (☎ 2709-8033) Chico's hiking and canoe tours receive rave reviews from readers. Ask at Cabinas Miss Miriam.

Daryl Loth (☎ 8833-0827, 2709-8011; safari@racsa.co.cr) A personable Canadian-born naturalist (formerly of Coterc) offers excellent boat trips in a supersilent electric motorboat, as well as turtle tours (in season) and guided hikes.

Sleeping

TORTUGUERO VILLAGE

There is a wide range of budget and midrange options here. The following places are listed in order from south (near the park entrance) to north. Lodgings on the northern half of town are quieter.

Tropical Lodge (☎ 2709-8110/8108, 8826-6246; d US$25; 💻) Behind the Tienda Bambú food shop, this colorful Caribbean setup has 10 somewhat dark, concrete rooms with private electric showers, four of which come with cable TV. The onsite bar is convenient, but inhibits beauty rest.

Cabinas Tortuguero (☎ 2709-8114; cabinas_tortuguero@yahoo.com; s/d without bathroom US$10/16, s/d/tr US$20/25/30) Inland from Tienda Bambú, you'll find 11 brightly painted bungalows surrounding a tidy garden at this popular Tico-run budget spot. Rooms are clean and there are hammocks for lounging.

Cabinas Princesa Resort (☎ 2709-8131; princesaresort08@yahoo.com; r per person with/without breakfast US$20/15; 🏊) There are three Princesa hotels scattered about town; this one, on the ocean, south of the cemetery, is best. A clapboard structure with 23 basic wood-and-concrete rooms faces an open garden with two pools (one for children). An onsite restaurant (open 7am to 9pm) serves Caribbean-Tico cuisine.

La Casona (☎ 2709-8092/8047; d/tr US$25/35, d with kitchenette US$35; 📶) Ten painted cement rooms with rustic touches surround a garden at this family-run spot on the north side of the soccer field. Three units have kitchenettes with hot plates. In addition, Jenny and her sons offer canoe rental, as well as canoe tours to a local farm in Caño Harold. It has a pleasant restaurant that serves Italian meals. Credit cards accepted.

Cabinas Miss Miriam (☎ 2709-8002, 8821-2037; s/d/tr US$20/25/30) Spread out over two buildings (one on the north end of the soccer field, the other south of it), this solid budget option has 16 clean tiled rooms, firm foam mattresses and electric showers. Upstairs rooms in the northern building have great ocean views, while units at the southern annex are bigger. The onsite restaurant, Miss Miriam's, is Tortuguero's top spot for Caribbean fare (see p465).

our pick **Casa Marbella** (☎ 8833-0827, 2709-8011; www.casamarbella.tripod.com; d incl breakfast US$40-60; 💻) Owned by naturalist Daryl Loth, this charming B&B opposite the Catholic church manages to be wonderfully serene while also being in the middle of it all. Ten simple whitewashed rooms have good lighting and ceiling fans, as well as super clean bathrooms with electric showers. Hearty breakfasts (think fresh pancakes with tropical fruit) are served on an outdoor deck with views of the canal. Loth also organizes excellent area tours.

Cabinas Beyetty (☎ 2709-8207, 8332-3304; beyetty@hotmail.com; 💻) Eight basic-but-neat cement-box rooms make up the offerings at this small family-run spot. There is an internet cafe on the ground floor (available at an extra charge). It is located 75m south of the school across the street from the canal.

Hotel Miss Junie (☎ 2709-8029, in San José 2231-6803; www.iguanaverdetours.com; d US$40-60) At the northern end of the village, Miss Junie's place is set on wide grounds, shaded by palm trees and strewn with hammocks. Seventeen spotless rooms in a nicely kept tropical plantation-style building come in various configurations (downstairs units are cheaper), but all are tastefully decorated with wood accents and bright bedspreads. Prices include a full breakfast by one of Tortuguero's most celebrated cooks. Credit cards accepted.

NORTH OF THE VILLAGE

Most of the lodges outside of town cater primarily to high-end travelers on package deals, though most of these will accept walk-ins if they aren't full. The following are listed from south to north; rates include all meals, unless otherwise stated. See Map, p459, for exact locations.

Pachira Lodge (☎ 2709-8172/8222, in San José 2256-7080, in USA 800-644-7438; www.pachiralodge.com; 2-night package per adult/child US$289/100; 📶 🏊 🚸) A sprawling compound set on five hectares of land, this 88-room hotel is a popular family spot, with pristine, brightly painted clapboard bungalows and rooms that sleep up to four. (There are even cribs and children's beds.) All have private terraces, mini-fridge and safe – and there's a downright Disneyesque turtle-shaped pool, in addition to the region's only zip line (US$30). Credit cards are accepted

Hotel Anhinga & Spa (☎ 2709-8190; 2-night package per adult/child US$289/100; 📶 🏊 🚸) Immediately to the north of Pachira Lodge, and run by the same company, the 32-room Anhinga has a pleasant open-air spa (open to the public) with massage services and plunge pools. Accepts credit cards.

Evergreen Lodge (☎ 2709-8213; 2-night package per adult/child US$289/100; 📶 🏊 🚸), Also run by the same company, the 55-room Evergreen Lodge is across the river. Credit cards are accepted.

our pick **Rana Roja** (☎ 2709-8260; www.ranarojatortuguero.com; r per person per night US$55;) This new Tico-run midrange spot offers one of the best valued options in the area. Seventeen small, earth-colored cabins – all with private terraces and rockers – are connected by elevated walkways. The units are immaculate, with tile floors, hot showers and awesome jungle views. Free kayaks are available onsite and guests can make use of the turtle-shaped swimming pool at the neighboring Evergreen Lodge, just a couple of meters away. Credit cards accepted.

Mawamba Lodge (☎ 2709-8181; in San José 2293-8181; www.grupomawamba.com; 2-night package per adult/child US$330/144;) With 58 rooms, pool tables, foosball, a free-form mosaic swimming pool, two butterfly gardens, as well as iguana and frog vivariums, this is one of the most tricked-out lodges in the area. Rooms are simple, wood-paneled affairs with firm beds, good fans and roomy bathrooms with hot water. All are fronted by a wide veranda equipped with hammocks and rocking chairs. Credit cards accepted.

La Baula Lodge (☎ 2231-1404; www.labaulalodge.com; 2-night package per person US$330;) Under new ownership, this pleasant 45-room inn with beautiful gardens has recently received a needed makeover. Freshly painted cottages have simple, wood-floor rooms accented by bright linens and equipped with spacious, tidy bathrooms. An open-air canal-side *rancho* houses a bar and restaurant.

Laguna Lodge (☎ 2709-8082, in San José 2272-4943; www.lagunatortuguero.com; 2-night package per person from US$265;) About 2km north of the village, this expansive lodge, popular with honeymooners, has 110 graceful rooms with high ceilings. It also has a restaurant, two bars (one on the river, one by the pool), a botanical garden with labeled plants, a massage room and – best of all – a reception area that looks like it's straight out of the Dagobah System from the *Empire Strike Back* (let us know if you see Yoda). All guests are greeted with a 'Coco Loco,' the hotel's tasty signature cocktail. Credit cards accepted.

Samoa Lodge (☎ in San José 2258-6244/5790; www.samoalodge.com; 2-night package US$289;) Set on 21 hectares on the far side of the Laguna Penitencia, this lovely Swiss-run spot has red clapboard buildings with 20 airy rooms that come with polished wood floors, brightly painted walls, bamboo beds, folk-art touches, coffee makers and minibars. The grounds are tidy, much of the vegetation is labeled and there is a swimming pool and hammock lounge. The owners can organize night tours on the lodge grounds. Canoes are available for paddlers.

All Rankins Lodge (☎ 2758-4160, 8815-5175; allrankinstours@hotmail.com; per person per night without meals US$25, per person per night incl meals, transport & tours US$140) Run by Tortuguero native Willis Rankin (who has a terrifically dry sense of humor), this simple spot by the airport is quite popular with students. It has 14 basic, wood *cabinas* with bathrooms and electric showers. An onsite restaurant dishes up fresh Caribbean cooking and there are lovely views of the river. Rankin can arrange all manner of excursions.

Tortuga Lodge & Gardens (☎ 2709-8034, in San José 2257-0766, 2222-0333; www.costaricaexpeditions.com; 2-night package per person from US$360;) Tortuguero's most elegant lodge, operated by Costa Rica Expeditions, is set amid 20 hectares of private gardens. Here you'll find a serene environment, as well as 27 demure rooms that channel a 19th-century safari vibe. Units are accented with creamy linens, handmade textiles, vintage photos and broad terraces that invite lounging. The grounds come equipped with private trails, a free-form infinity-edge pool and a riverside bar-restaurant that is a wonderful spot for drinks. An all-around excellent choice. Credit cards accepted.

Turtle Beach Lodge (☎ 2248-0707, after hr 8837-6969; www.turtlebeachlodge.com; 2-night package per adult/child US$288/110;) The northernmost lodge is flanked on either side by beach and river. It is surrounded by 70 hectares of tropical gardens and rainforest. Spacious, wood cabins have terra-cotta tile floors, hardwood furniture and huge screened windows to let in the breeze. You can explore the grounds on the network of jungle trails, or lounge around the turtle-shaped pool or the thatch-roofed hammock hut.

Eating

One of Tortuguero's unsung pleasures is the cuisine: the homey restaurants lure you in from the rain with steaming platters of Caribbean-style food. Listings are from south to north.

Soda Doña María (☎ 2709-8050; dishes ₡1500-3000; 7am-8pm) Recover from a hike in the park at this riverside *soda*, serving fresh *jugos* (juices),

CARIBBEAN COAST

burgers and tasty fish *casados*. It's about 200m north of the park entrance.

La Casona (casados ₡3200, mains ₡3000-5600; 7:30-11am & 1:30-8:30pm; V) On the northern edge of the soccer field, it serves a variety of Italian specialties, including a well-rendered lasagna made with hearts of palm.

our pick **Miss Miriam's** (2709-8002; mains ₡4400-11,000) Right next door to La Casona is this little place, bursting with flavor and character. Run by Miss Miriam's friendly and fabulous daughter, it's so good you'll want to eat all of your meals here. Don't miss the well-spiced Caribbean chicken (the best we tasted on the entire coast), served with heaping sides of sautéed fresh veggies and Caribbean-style rice and beans.

Restaurante Tortuguero (dishes ₡2660-9600; 5am-noon & 5-10pm) A big log cabin offers what the owners claim is 'the Best Breakfast in Costa Rica,' which will set you back ₡1700 to ₡4280. Credit cards accepted.

Buddha Cafe (2709-8084; pizzas ₡3200-4000, dishes ₡3500-9000; noon-8:30pm; V) A riverside spot keeps a hipster vibe with ambient-club music on the sound system and Buddhist 'om' symbols stenciled onto just about everything. It's a lovely spot, with excellent pizzas, rich coffee and scrumptious crepes (both savory and sweet). Grab a table outside or plant yourself in a deck chair for a prime view of the yellow-bellied flycatchers zipping over the canal. Credit cards accepted.

Dorling Bakery (8876-2263; pastries from ₡900; 5am-10pm) Outstanding homemade banana bread, lemon cake and other pastries get you even more wired when combined with a shot of espresso. In the evenings, it sells BBQ meats – of the sort that will keep your mouth watering – along with the mouths of all the local stray dogs. Good times.

Miss Junie's (2709-8029; mains from ₡8500; 7-9am breakfast, 11:30am-2:30pm & 6-9pm) This is Tortuguero's best-known restaurant – serving a bevy of local specialties: chicken, fish, lobster and many other dishes, all served in flavorful Caribbean sauces, with traditional rice and beans.

You can grab groceries at a number of little markets; our favorite is the **Grupo Morpho Pulpería** (2709-8110; 6:30am-9pm Mon-Sat, 8am-8pm Sun) – which is the best stocked and most reasonable. Look for super tasty 'Mmmio' ice-cream bars in the freezer. It's across from the public dock.

Drinking

La Taberna (11am-11pm) Adjacent to Tropical Lodge, overlooking the canal, this popular tavern is mellow in the afternoons, but draws the party people after dark, with cold beer and blaring reggaetón. The highlight, however, is the decor: namely, a life-sized statue of Jar Jar Binks.

La Culebra (8pm-close) The town's only nightclub is a barren concrete space where thumping music makes for a good dance floor, or hang out at the waterside bar area for beer and *bocas*. This place rocks during turtle season. It's next to the public boat dock in the center of town.

Getting There & Away

It's not hard to get here on your own (see boxed text, p466). However, if you don't care to go it alone, these package tours can take care of everything from the moment your plane lands in San José. Costs vary widely depending on accommodations and transportation.

Exploradores Outdoors (2222-6262; www.exploradoresoutdoors.com) Primarily a rafting outfit, this company organizes overnight excursions from San José, Arenal and Puerto Viejo de Talamanca (per person US$169).

Jungle Tom Safaris (2280-0243; www.jungletomsafaris.com) Offers recommended one-day (US$90), overnight (from US$115) and two-night packages (from US$147) or just round-trip transportation (US$45) – useful for independent travelers who want to be free upon arrival.

Riverboat Francesca Nature Tours (2226-0986; www.tortuguerocanals.com) A highly recommended company run by Modesto and Fran Watson, it also offers sportfishing (two-day packages from US$165).

AIR

The small airstrip is 4km north of Tortuguero village. Both **NatureAir** (2220-3054) and **Sansa** (2709-8055) have daily flights to and from San José (the one-way flight is less than 20 minutes). Charter flights land regularly here as well.

BOAT

Tortuguero is accessible by boat from Cariari or Moín. If you are traveling to Parismina, you should be able to get one of the boats to Moín to drop you off on the way. Regular taxi boats ply the waters around Tortuguero – so it's easy enough to get around, even if you aren't staying in town.

To/From Cariari

The most common and least expensive route to Tortuguero is a bus-boat combination trip through Cariari. (See boxed text, below for detailed directions.) There are three main companies that provide transportation along this route – all of whom also offer regular boat-bus service from Tortuguero to Cariari:

Clic Clic (☎ 8844-0463, 2709-8155) ₡2600; departs 6am, 11:30am and 3pm from the main public dock in town.

Coopetraca (☎ 2767-7137/7590) ₡2600; departs 6am, 11:30am and 3pm.

Viajes Bananeros (☎ 2709-8005) ₡5500; departs 6am, 11am and 2:30pm from the private dock on the far south end of town.

GETTING TO TORTUGUERO INDEPENDENTLY

If you want to get to Tortuguero independently, it can be easily done. There are a number of companies that offer bus-boat transport service from Cariari to Tortuguero several times a day. But with competition among rival transport agencies at an all-time high, some companies will say anything to get your fare – including telling you that they are the only transport option in town. Don't believe everything you hear. Here's what to do:

From San José

Take the 6:30am, 9am or 10:30am bus to Cariari (three hours) from San José's Gran Terminal del Caribe. In Cariari, you will arrive at a bus station at the south end of town (known as the *estación nueva*). From here, you can walk or take a taxi 500m north to the *estación vieja* (old station), otherwise referred to as the Terminal Caribeño.

Public Transportation from Cariari

The cheapest option is by public transport on **Clic Clic** (☎ 2709-8155, 8844-0463) or **Coopetraca** (☎ 2767-7590), both of which charge ₡2600 per person for bus-boat service from the *estación vieja* all the way to Tortuguero. For these two options, the bus service will be the same, but the boat service will be different. Buses depart Cariari at 6am, 11:30am and 3pm.

For both of these services, buy only the bus ticket to La Pavona (₡1000). After a ride through banana plantations, you will arrive at the Río La Suerte, where a number of boat companies will be waiting at the dock. (Get ready to be solicited.) We recommend Clic Clic, which is generally prompt and well-run, with experienced boat captains – but you may want to choose based on availability or on the condition of the boats. From this point, you will pay the remainder of your fare (₡1600) to the boatman. Be sure to take small change.

Ticket vendors at the *estación vieja* in Cariari may try to sell you on a combined bus-boat ticket. Note that these are only for Coopetraca, since Clic Clic does not have a sales agent in town. We recommend paying your boat fare at the dock – since it allows you to see what you're getting into – literally.

These companies will ferry you to the public boat dock in Tortuguero.

Private Transportation from Cariari

For a more expensive private service, there is **Viajes Bananero** (☎ 2709-8005), which has an office inside the San José bus terminal in Cariari. Buy your boat ticket here (per person US$10). From this same point, you will then take a bus (per person ₡600) to their proprietary boat dock. Bus departure times are at 11:30am and 2pm. Pay the driver directly; take small change. If you are traveling in a group, Bananero can arrange custom pick-ups. For private service, you will need to reserve ahead.

The trip ends at the company's private dock on the southern edge of the village.

Warning

There have been thefts from the buses that ply the route between Cariari and La Pavona – and a reported armed mugging. Keep important belongings with you and stash your cash in several places. Likewise, be wary of 'guides' that solicit you for tours on the bus – since many of these folks aren't always who they claim to be.

During the peak of the turtle nesting season, we recommend purchasing your tickets at least one day in advance. Many of the information centers sell these. If you are traveling to San José, you are better off taking a 6am boat because bus connections are better earlier in the day.

Transportation schedules and fares for Tortuguero change regularly. Inquire locally before setting out.

To/From Moín

Moín–Tortuguero is primarily a tourist route – and while boats ply these canals frequently, there isn't a scheduled service. The following two Tortuguero-based agencies make the run regularly; both of these can stop in Parismina (one-way US$25):

Tropical Wind (☎ 8313-7164, 2798-6059, 8327-0317; per person one-way US$30)

Viajes Bananeros (☎ 2709-8005; per person one-way US$35)

Likewise, you can always call the companies operating out of Puerto Limón (p455), since they frequently have boats in the area.

Note: it may take at least 24 hours to secure transport – especially in the low season.

BARRA DEL COLORADO

At 904 sq km, including the frontier zone with Nicaragua, Refugio Nacional de Vida Silvestre Barra del Colorado, or 'Barra' for short, is the biggest national wildlife refuge in Costa Rica. It is also one of the most remote – and it just got more so since both of the country's commercial airlines suspended service to the area in 2009. This means that the only way to get to Barra is to take the local bus-boat transport from Cariari or arrange a charter flight from San José.

The area has long been a favorite of sportfishers who arrive to hook gar, tarpon and snook, and hole up in one of the area fishing lodges. But those who aren't into fishing will be rewarded with incredible landscape. The Ríos San Juan, Colorado and Chirripó all wind through the refuge and out to the Caribbean Sea – through a soggy wetland habitat made up of marshes, mangroves and lagoons. Here, you'll find West Indian manatees, caiman, monkeys, tapirs and three-toed sloths, plus a riotous bird population that includes everything from keel-billed toucans to white hawks. There are countless species of waterbird.

The northern border of the refuge is the Río San Juan, the border with Nicaragua (many local residents are Nicaraguan nationals). This area was politically sensitive during the 1980s, due to the Nicaraguan conflict. Today, however, it is possible to journey north along the Río Sarapiquí and east along the Río San Juan, technically entering Nicaragua (see boxed text, p468).

Note: while Costa Ricans have right of use, the San Juan is Nicaraguan territory. Carry your passport when you are out fishing.

Orientation & Information

The village of Barra del Colorado lies near the mouth of the Río Colorado and is divided by the river into Barra del Norte and Barra del Sur. The airstrip is on the south side of the river, but more people live along the north side. The area outside the village is swampy and there are no roads; travel is almost exclusively by boat.

A couple of *pulperías* (corner grocery stores) and a souvenir shop alongside the landing strip sell basic food supplies and dry goods. There is a public phone and patchy internet access. The Servicio de Parques Nacionales (SPN) maintains a small **ranger station** (🕓 6am-6pm; refuge admission US$10, 60-day freshwater fishing license US$30) west of the village, in Barra del Sur. However, there are no facilities here. Bring exact change to pay for your entry fee as the rangers rarely have change.

Activities

Fishing is the bread and butter of area lodges and anglers go for tarpon from January to June and snook from September to December. Fishing is good year-round, however, and other catches include barracuda, mackerel and jack crevalle, all inshore; or bluegill, *guapote* (rainbow bass) and machaca in the rivers. There is also deep-sea fishing for marlin, sailfish and tuna, though this sort of activity is probably better on the Pacific. Dozens of fish can be hooked on a good day, so 'catch and release' is an important conservation policy of all the lodges.

All of the lodges can also organize custom wildlife-watching excursions along mangroves, lagoons and canals (from US$40).

Sleeping & Eating

From the airport, only Tarponland Cabinas and Río Colorado Lodge is accessible on foot.

GETTING TO SAN JUAN DE NICARAGUA

Day trips along the Río San Juan and some offshore fishing trips technically enter Nicaraguan territory. Carry your passport and US$10, in the unlikely event that you are stopped and checked.

If you are planning to head further into Nicaragua, you can make arrangements with your lodge for a water taxi (per person US$60) to take you to the border town of San Juan del Norte – now called San Juan de Nicaragua (formerly Greytown). It's a tranquil village, with few services, but an interesting history. (At various times over the centuries, it has been under the control of Miskito people, Spanish colonists, British troops and even US Marines. Much of it was destroyed during the Contra-Sandinista conflict of the 1980s.)

This is a little-used border crossing, however, so don't make the trip without first checking in with Costa Rican immigration officials in **San José** (☎ 2299-8100) or **Puerto Limón** (☎ 2758-2097). Barra del Colorado does not have an immigration office of its own, so you might have to secure an exit stamp prior to arriving there.

In San Juan, **Río Indio Lodge** (☎ 2231-4299, 2220-3594/3596; www.therioindiolodge.com; d per person incl meals US$168; 💻 🅿) has 34 spacious polished-wood rooms, a restaurant and bar. Fishing is the forte, but you can also go hiking or kayaking.

San Juan is linked to the rest of Nicaragua by irregular passenger boats sailing up the Río San Juan to San Carlos, on the Lago de Nicaragua.

Other lodges will have a boat waiting when you arrive with prior reservation.

Tarponland Cabinas (☎ 8818-9921; r US$30, r with sportfishing, food & lodging US$300; 🅿) This is as far as budget lodgings go in Barra. Situated right next to the airstrip, just a few dozen meters from the dock, a brightly painted building has worn wood rooms with private hot showers. An adjacent restaurant and bar is a local gathering spot and a good place for fish *casados* (mains from ₡2500).

Río Colorado Lodge (☎ 2232-4063, in USA 800-243-9777; www.riocoloradolodge.com; d per person with/without fishing US$475/120; ❄ ♿) Built in 1971, this 18-room lodge is housed in a rambling tropical-style building connected by covered walkways. Rooms are breezy and there is a pool table, an outdoor deck with satellite TV and afternoon happy hours. Situated within walking distance of the landing strip, near the mouth of the Río Colorado, it attracts a local crowd at the bar, which has earned it a reputation as a 'party lodge.' Rates include meals.

Silver King Lodge (☎ 2711-0708, in USA 877-335-0755; www.silverkinglodge.net; 3-day package per person from US$2050; ❄ 💻 🅿) This excellent sportfishing lodge caters to couples and families. Huge hardwood rooms have cane ceilings, colorful tapestries and lots of amenities. Outside, covered walkways lead to a large swimming pool (complete with waterfall). Bounteous meals are served buffet-style and an open-air bar whips up tropical drinks. The lodge closes in July and December; rates include fishing and meals.

Casa Mar Lodge (☎ in USA 800-543-0282; www.casamarlodge.com; r per person US$585, 5-night package per person from US$2500) A pleasant 2.8-hectare garden is dotted with deluxe, bright turquoise wood cabins that come equipped with tiled hot showers. Rates include fishing, meals, open bar, all gear and daily laundry service. There is an onsite tackle shop.

Getting There & Away

There is a regular bus-boat service from Cariari via Puerto Lindo (see p449 for details). Likewise, it is possible to arrange a charter boat service from Tortuguero (prices start somewhere in the vicinity of US$50 to US$100 depending on the season and the number of people). Otherwise, most folks get here on air charters arranged by the individual lodges.

SOUTHERN CARIBBEAN

The southern coast is the heart and soul of Costa Rica's Afro-Caribbean community. Jamaican workers arrived in the middle of the 19th century to build the railroad and then stayed on to serve as labor for United Fruit. After the banana industry began its decline in the 1920s, government-mandated segregation kept the black community here (blacks were not allowed to travel freely around the rest of the country). For more than eight decades, they existed independently of the rest of Costa Rica – managing subsistence farms, speaking English and Mekatelyu, eating spicy Caribbean gumbos and swaying to the beat of calypso. Although the racial borders fell in 1949, the local culture still retains its unique traditions.

Also in this area, to the interior, are some of the country's most prominent indigenous groups – cultures that have managed to remain intact despite several centuries' worth of incursions, first from the Spanish, later from the fruit industry and currently from the globalizing effects of tourism. They principally inhabit the Cocles/KéköLdi, Talamanca Cabécar and Bribrí indigenous territories.

Naturally, this fascinating cultural bubble wouldn't remain isolated forever. Since the 1980s, the southern coast has seen the arrival of surfers, backpackers and adventurous families on holiday – many of whom have stayed, adding Italian, German and North American inflections to the cultural stew. For the traveler, it is a rich and rewarding experience – with lovely beaches to boot.

RESERVA BIOLÓGICA HITOY-CERERE

One of the most rugged and rarely visited reserves in the country, **Hitoy-Cerere** (☎ 2795-1446; admission US$10; 🕓 8am-4pm) is only about 60km south of Puerto Limón. The 99-sq-km reserve sits on the edge of the Cordillera de Talamanca, characterized by varying altitudes, evergreen forests and rushing rivers. This may be one of the wettest reserves in the parks system, inundated with 4000mm to 6000mm of rain annually.

Naturally, wildlife is abundant. The most commonly sighted mammals include gray four-eyed opossums, tayras (a type of weasel), and howler and capuchin monkeys. There are plenty of ornithological delights as well (the area is home to more than 230 avian species), including keel-billed toucans, spectacled owls and the green kingfisher. And, you can hardly miss the Montezuma oropendola, whose massive nests dangle from the trees like twiggy pendulums. The moisture, in the meantime, keeps the place hopping with all manner of poison-dart frog.

The reserve is surrounded by some of the country's most remote indigenous reserves, which you can visit with a local guide.

Although there is a ranger station at the reserve entrance with bathrooms, there are no other facilities nearby. A 9km trail leads south to a waterfall, but it is steep, slippery and poorly maintained. Jungle boots are recommended.

Getting There & Away

By car (4WD recommended), head west on the signed road to Valle de la Estrella and Penshurst (just south of the Río Estrella bridge). Another sign at the bus stop sends you down a good dirt road about 15km to the reserve.

By public transportation, catch a bus from Puerto Limón to Valle de la Estrella. From the end of the bus line (Fortuna/Finca 6) you can hire a taxi to take you the rest of the way and pick you up at a prearranged time (from ₡17,000).

AVIARIOS DEL CARIBE SLOTH SANCTUARY

About 10km northwest of Cahuita, this **wildlife sanctuary** (☎ 2750-0775; www.slothrescue.org; 🕓 6am-5pm; Ⓟ ✖ 📶) sits on an 88-hectare property bordering the Río Estrella. Here, proprietors Luis Arroyo and Judy Avery help injured and orphaned sloths – providing travelers with an opportunity to see these unique animals up close. (Irrefutable fact: there is nothing cuter than a baby sloth.) Though many of the rehabilitated sloths remain on the grounds (animals orphaned at a very young age don't have the skills to return to the wild), Luis and Judy have been successful at releasing more than 80 of them back into area forests. In addition to sloth tours (US$25), they also offer early morning bird-watching tours by canoe (US$30 including breakfast), which include a short presentation on sloths. The couple also maintains a small, seven-room **B&B** (d US$75-85; Ⓟ ✖), with tiled, modern rooms.

Volunteer opportunities are available (US$30 per day, including three meals).

CAHUITA

pop 600

Even as tourism has mushroomed on Costa Rica's southern coast, Cahuita has managed to hold onto its laidback Caribbean vibe. The roads are made of dirt, many of the older houses rest on stilts and chatty neighbors still converse in Mekatelyu. It's not as polished as Puerto Viejo de Talamanca to the south, which sports an air-conditioned strip mall and slick international eateries. But a graceful black-sand beach and a chilled-out demeanor hint at a not-so-distant past, when the area

A STAY IN THE FOREST: SELVA BANANITO

At the foot of Cerro Muchilla, on the edge of Parque Internacional La Amistad, this rustic family-run **farm and lodge** (☎ 2253-8118; www.selvabananito.com; per person from US$130, per person 2-night package from US$432, all incl 3 meals daily; P) is composed of 12 hilly sq km ideal for tree climbing, waterfall rappelling, hiking and horseback riding. (If you are traveling with children, guides can tailor some of these activities to your tyke's abilities.) Above all, this is an environmentally conscious spot: the Stein family employs solar energy and uses biodegradable soaps and cleaning products. Cabins are all crafted from recycled hardwoods and constructed, Caribbean-style on stilts, for optimum ventilation.

Rates are based on double occupancy. Packages include transfers from San José, as well as a waterfall tour, horseback riding and a tree-climbing lesson. If you are driving yourself, take the turnoff south of the Río Vizcaya (about 19km south of Limón). The lodge is located about 8km inland. The route requires river crossings; it's for 4WD only. Detailed driving directions are posted online.

was little more than just a string of cocoa farms.

This is a proud town, too. Cahuita claims the area's first permanent Afro-Caribbean settler – a turtle fisherman named William Smith, who moved his family to Punta Cahuita in 1828. Now his descendants, along with the descendants of so many other West Indian immigrants, run the tasty backyard eateries and brightly painted bungalows that hug this idyllic stretch of coast.

Situated on a pleasant point, the town itself has a waterfront, but no beach. For that, most folks make the jaunt to Playa Negra or into neighboring Parque Nacional Cahuita (p477).

Information

The town's helpful new website, www.cahuita.cr, has all manner of lodging and restaurant information, with pictures of many of the spots listed here. (Interestingly, it also has a 'Cahuita Cam' – which has live shots of the beach at Playa Blanca.)

In addition to the places listed below, the bus station has two internet cafes.

Banco de Costa Rica (9am-4pm Mon-Fri) Located at the bus terminal, it has an ATM that works on Cirrus, Plus and Visa systems.

Centro Turístico Brigitte (☎ 2755-0053; www.brigittecahuita.com; Playa Negra; per hr ₡1000; 7am-6pm) Internet access.

Internet Palmer (per hr ₡1000; 9am-8pm)

Mercado Safari (6am-4pm) Changes US and Canadian dollars, euros and traveler's checks but has a steep commission.

Willie's Tours (☎ 2755-0267; per hr ₡1000; 8am-8pm Mon-Sat, 4-8pm Sun) Internet access.

Sights & Activities

On the highway, at the entrance to town, you'll find **Mariposario de Cahuita** (☎ 2755-0361; admission US$10; 8:30am-3:30pm), a wonderful garden aflutter with lovely butterflies (great for kids). Stroll around the fountain-filled grounds and admire the local residents, including many friendly caterpillars. Descriptions are posted in several languages; guided tours are available.

A new greenhouse space filled with a lush garden, **Ranario** (8:30am-3:30pm; admission US$8) has 14 species of native frog hopping around on the loose. (No cages here.) Admission includes a guided tour – a necessity, since guides know where the frogs like to hide.

At the northwest end of Cahuita, **Playa Negra** is a long, black-sand beach flying the *bandera azul ecológica,* a flag that indicates the beach is kept to the highest ecological standards. This is undoubtedly Cahuita's top spot for swimming. Most importantly, it is generally never crowded. When the swells are big, this spot also has an excellent beach break. It is not one of the regular stops on the Costa Rica surfer circuit, which means more waves for you. Centro Turístico Brigitte in Playa Negra rents boards (half-day US$10) and offers lessons (two hours US$25).

Playa Blanca at the entrance to the national park (see p478) is another good option for swimming.

Tours

Snorkeling, horseback riding, chocolate tours and visits to nearby indigenous territories are standard offerings:

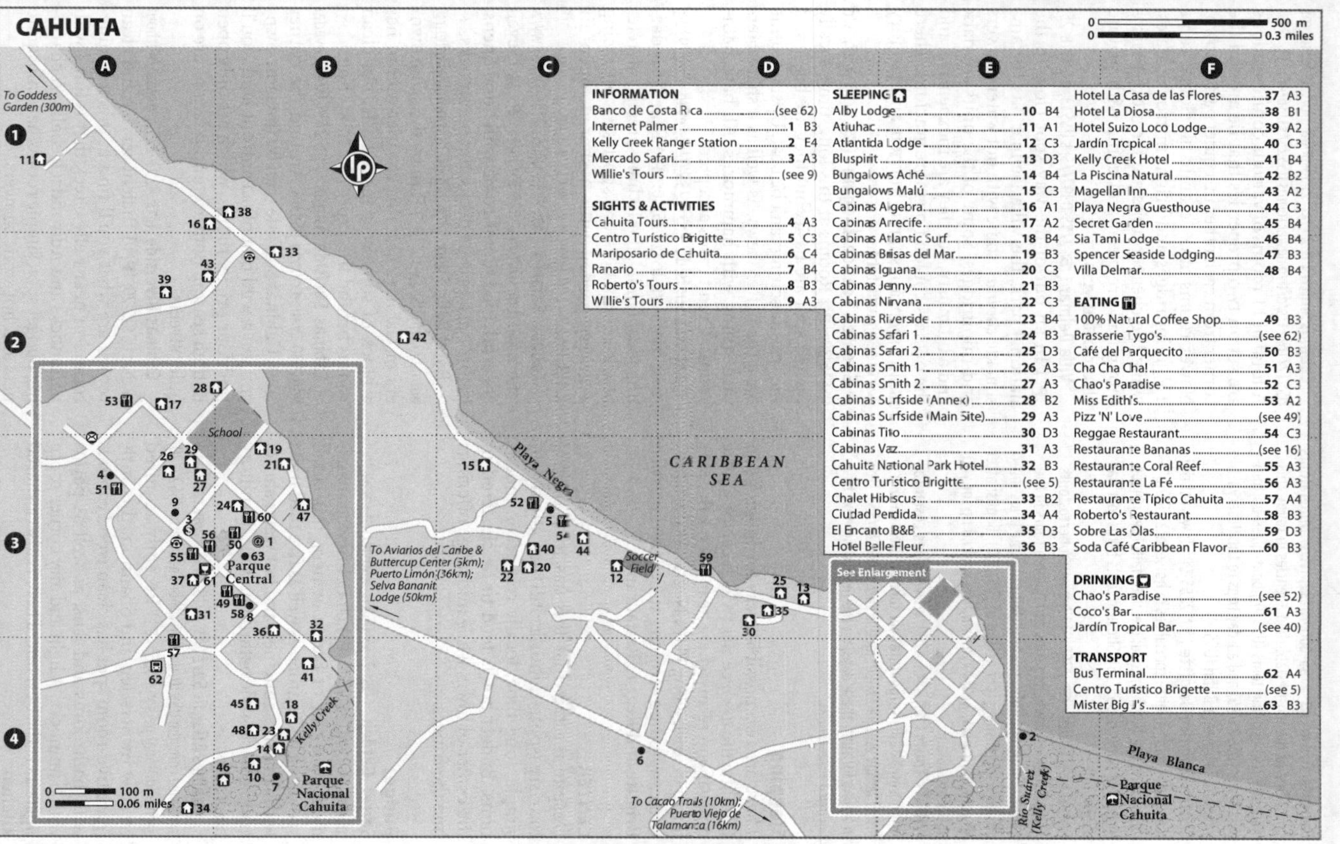
CAHUITA
INFORMATION
Banco de Costa Rica (see 62)
Internet Palmer 1 B3
Kelly Creek Ranger Station 2 E4
Mercado Safari 3 A3
Willie's Tours (see 9)
SIGHTS & ACTIVITIES
Cahuita Tours 4 A3
Centro Turístico Brigitte 5 C3
Mariposario de Cahuita 6 C4
Ranario 7 B4
Roberto's Tours 8 B3
Willie's Tours 9 A3
SLEEPING
Alby Lodge 10 B4
Atiuhac 11 A1
Atlantida Lodge 12 C3
Bluspirit 13 D3
Bungalows Aché 14 B4
Bungalows Malú 15 C3
Cabinas Algebra 16 A1
Cabinas Arrecife 17 A2
Cabinas Atlantic Surf 18 B4
Cabinas Brisas del Mar 19 B3
Cabinas Iguana 20 C3
Cabinas Jenny 21 B3
Cabinas Nirvana 22 C3
Cabinas Riverside 23 B4
Cabinas Safari 1 24 B3
Cabinas Safari 2 25 D3
Cabinas Smith 1 26 A3
Cabinas Smith 2 27 A3
Cabinas Surfside (Annex) 28 B2
Cabinas Surfside (Main Site) 29 A3
Cabinas Tito 30 D3
Cabinas Vaz 31 A3
Cahuita National Park Hotel 32 B3
Centro Turístico Brigitte (see 5)
Chalet Hibiscus 33 B2
Ciudad Perdida 34 A4
El Encanto B&B 35 D3
Hotel Belle Fleur 36 B3
Hotel La Casa de las Flores 37 A3
Hotel La Diosa 38 B1
Hotel Suizo Loco Lodge 39 A2
Jardín Tropical 40 C3
Kelly Creek Hotel 41 B4
La Piscina Natural 42 B2
Magellan Inn 43 A2
Playa Negra Guesthouse 44 C3
Secret Garden 45 B4
Sia Tami Lodge 46 B4
Spencer Seaside Lodging 47 B3
Villa Delmar 48 B4
EATING
100% Natural Coffee Shop 49 B3
Brasserie Tygo's (see 62)
Café del Parquecito 50 B3
Cha Cha Cha! 51 A3
Chao's Paradise 52 C3
Miss Edith's 53 A2
Pizz 'N' Love (see 49)
Reggae Restaurant 54 C3
Restaurante Bananas (see 16)
Restaurante Coral Reef 55 A3
Restaurante La Fé 56 A3
Restaurante Típico Cahuita 57 A4
Roberto's Restaurant 58 B3
Sobre Las Olas 59 D3
Soda Café Caribbean Flavor 60 B3
DRINKING
Chao's Paradise (see 52)
Coco's Bar 61 A3
Jardín Tropical Bar (see 40)
TRANSPORT
Bus Terminal 62 A4
Centro Turistico Brigette (see 5)
Mister Big J's 63 B3
To Goddess Garden (300m)
CARIBBEAN SEA
Playa Negra
Soccer Field
School
Parque Central
Kelly Creek
Parque Nacional Cahuita
See Enlargement
Playa Blanca
Río Suárez (Kelly Creek)
To Aviarios del Caribe & Buttercup Center (3km); Puerto Limón (36km); Selva Bananito Lodge (50km)
To Cacao Trails (10km); Puerto Viejo de Talamanca (16km)
500 m
0.3 miles
100 m
0.06 miles

CARIBBEAN COAST

Cahuita Tours (☎ 2755-0000/0232; www.cahuitatours.com) One of the most established agencies in town, this place offers snorkeling tours (US$30), boat/glass-bottom-boat tours (US$25/35) and all-day trips to the Reserva Indígena Talamanca Bribrí (US$60).

Centro Turístico Brigitte (☎ 2755-0053; www.brigittecahuita.com) Brigitte specializes in horseback-riding tours along the beach or to jungle waterfalls (per person three/five hours US$55/75). She also rents bikes (per day US$8).

Roberto's Tours (☎ 2755-0117; www.robertostours.com) Arranges snorkeling trips and dolphin tours in the national park, but Roberto's real claim to fame is inshore/offshore sportfishing (per person US$75/200). Bonus: after all your hard work, he'll have your haul cooked up for you at his restaurant.

Willie's Tours (☎ 8843-4700; www.willies-costarica-tours.com) Willie's signature tour takes visitors to visit a Bribrí family and a KéköLdi iguana farm (US$25/55). He's in a new location these days, on the main drag next to Cocorico Pizzeria Bar.

CARIBBEAN COAST

Sleeping

There are two possible areas for lodgings in Cahuita: the town center (which can be a little noisy if you're anywhere near Coco's Bar), or north of town along Playa Negra. At the latter, you can finding camping at Centro Turístico Brigitte and Reggae Restaurant.

CENTER

Despite the fact that this has long been a touristy spot, Cahuita still has plenty of simple, long-time, locally run accommodations. Budget hotels tend to be clustered in the center of town, while midrange offerings line the fringes.

Budget

Secret Garden (☎ 2755-0581; koosiecostarica@live.nl; dm US$9, s/d US$15/25; Ⓟ) Under new management by a pair of Dutch owners, this small spot has a lush garden as well as five tiled units with fans, mosquito nets and hot water showers in cubicle-style bathrooms. One dormitory has five beds.

Cabinas Atlantic Surf (☎ 8919-9313; www.cabinasatlanticsurf.com; dm US$10, d with/without hot water US$25/20, each additional person US$5; Ⓟ) Recently acquired by new owners Jen and Shannon, this intimate five-room spot has clean wood *cabinas* with bathrooms and fans, as well as patios with hammocks. A light and airy corner room upstairs is the best one. There is also a shared kitchen.

Cabinas Smith 1 & 2 (☎ 2755-0068; s/d/tr older rooms US$12/16/21, s/d/tr/q newer rooms US$25/31/36/46; Ⓟ) A total of 11 rooms of various configurations are set on two properties that lie around the corner from each other in a quiet part of town. Newer rooms have ceramic tile floors, cable TV, minifridges and bright mirror mosaics, while the cheaper units are far more basic – though all are clean and come with private electric showers.

Villa Delmar (☎ 2755-0392/75; s US$13, d US$18-25; Ⓟ) In an out-of-the-way spot close to the national park, the Villa Delmar has 10 ramshackle *cabinas*, some with hot water showers and minifridges. Some of the units are dark and a bit musty, but they are inexpensive, and the owners couldn't be more gracious. There is an open-air shared kitchen and laundry service is available.

Spencer Seaside Lodging (☎ 2755-0027; s/d US$16/30; Ⓟ) Rooms at this long-time, locally owned spot are basic, but they are big – and the seaside setting can't be beat. Upstairs units have the better views, as well as a shared terrace strung with hammocks. All have bathrooms. Credit cards accepted.

Cabinas Surfside (☎ 2755-0246; evadarling1930@yahoo.com; s/d/tr US$20/25/30; Ⓟ) Run by a darling local family, the 13 lime-green concrete-block rooms here are spotless – all facing a grassy garden with a shared, open-air kitchen.

Cabinas Safari 1 (☎ 2755-0405, 2755-0393; www.cabinasafari.com; s/d/tr/q US$20/25/35/45; Ⓟ) Seven cheerful, tiled rooms come with floral linens, bathrooms, private decks and hammocks.

Hotel Belle Fleur (☎ 2755-0283; hotelbellefleur@hotmail.com; US$25-35; Ⓟ) Run by the same owners of Cabinas Vaz, this cheaper option has a block of somewhat more basic, but clean rooms behind the Super Vaz food shop.

Cabinas Surfside Annex (☎ 2755-0246; evadarling1930@yahoo.com; d US$30) Around the corner from Cabinas Surfside (run by the same owners), on a wild plot of oceanfront land, you'll find four pricier rooms, which are only open in high season. Both accommodations are on quiet streets.

Cabinas Riverside (☎ 8893-2252; d with/without kitchen US$25/20; Ⓟ) Efficient service and clean rooms are what you'll find at this tidy nine-room inn near Kelly Creek that is lined with hammocks and Adirondack chairs. A charming budget spot, simple rooms have mosquito nets and hot stone showers.

Cabinas Safari 2 (☎ 2755-0405, 2755-0393; www.cabinasafari.com; s/d/tr US$30/40/50) Located on the road to Playa Negra, with an annex location, Safari 2 has another five rooms with ocean views and kitchenettes. Credit cards are accepted.

Cabinas Arrecife (☎ 2755-0081; www.cabinasarrecife.com; d/tr/q US$30/35/40; P) Tiled rooms are basic, with polished wood ceilings and fans, but they are comfortable. An onsite *soda* offers Tico breakfasts (₡2200) and ocean breezes, plus there is a small pool.

Cabinas Brisas del Mar (☎ 2755-0011; d/apt US$30/60; P) A tranquil spot run by a charmingly crotchety owner has small cement rooms that are basic, but clean and come equipped with bathrooms, cable TV and hammocks – all within sight of the water. A bigger apartment with two large beds also comes with a full kitchen and TV.

Cabinas Vaz (☎ 2755-0218; hotelvaz@gmail.com; d with/without air-con US$40/35; P) A motor court–style structure that's built in a tropical style surrounds a gravel courtyard and a pool. Twenty-one rooms come with wood furnishings, bright ceramic tiles, cable TV and plenty of daylight.

Midrange

Cabinas Jenny (☎ 2755-0256; www.cabinasjenny.com; d US$40-45, d bungalow US$85; P) A stone's throw from the advancing waves, this place might appear ramshackle on the outside, but its rooms are tidy. Upstairs is best, with units that have wood detailing and ocean views, as well as mosquito nets, coffee makers and toaster ovens. Call in advance to make sure that somebody is here when you arrive.

our pick **Bungalows Aché** (☎ 2755-0119; www.bungalowsache.com; bungalows US$40-60; P) In Nigeria, *Aché* means 'Amen,' and you'll likely say the same thing when you see these spotless octagonal bungalows on a peaceful property bordering the national park. The three charming, polished wood cabins have bright red-and-white linens and come stocked with a lockbox, minifridge, kettle and private decks with hammocks. Configurations vary, but some units can sleep up to four.

Cahuita National Park Hotel (☎ 2755-0244; d/tr/q US$45/55/65, apt US$130; P) A three-story building overlooks the ocean at the entrance to the national park and is equipped with 20 pleasant whitewashed rooms with wood furnishings, cool tile floors and roomy

WHAT HAPPEN: PAULA PALMER REMEMBERS CAHUITA IN THE 1970S

In early 1974, after an epic overland journey through Mexico and Central America, US-born Paula Palmer arrived in Cahuita with no firm plans other than to travel as cheaply as possible. She ended up staying 20 years, in the process recording two absolutely essential cultural histories on the area: *What Happen: A Folk History of the Talamanca Coast,* which tracks the traditions of the Afro-Caribbean community, and *Taking Care of Sibö's Gifts,* which documents indigenous people's beliefs.

What was Cahuita like when you first arrived? It didn't have restaurants, hotels, electricity or telephones. Mail delivery was about once a month. There was also no regular bus service. From Puerto Limón, we'd take the banana train. Then we'd get off at Penshurst, cross the river and get onto a bus. It didn't have windows or headlights. The guy who collected our money stood up front and would shine a flashlight out onto the road. We all had to push it to start. In those days, the area really had a barter economy. Cacao was the only cash crop, and people lived mostly by exchanging goods and services. I helped establish an English school; in exchange, the parents brought me provisions: eggs, fish, bread or whatever they had. I really admired the people's self-reliance and cooperation.

What aspects of the culture might travelers still be able to experience? You can really find it on Sundays, when everyone goes to the Protestant and Catholic churches. And there's the traditional calypso and reggae bands – like Mr Walter Ferguson, who is 89 and doesn't perform anymore, but who has made CDs. Food is obviously the biggest carry-over: rice and beans in the Caribbean style with coconut and *rondón* (seafood gumbo). You'll find it at Miss Edith's in Cahuita (p476) or Soda Miss Sam in Puerto Viejo (p486). The first meal I had in Cahuita in February of 1974 was lobster. I arrived late at night and there was a heavy rain. A woman in her home fed me lobster, rice and beans, cabbage salad and lemonade – for US$1. I was very happy!

bathrooms. They all come equipped with lockbox, minifridge and cable TV. A two-bedroom apartment has a full kitchen and living area, as well as excellent ocean views. There is an onsite restaurant as well.

Alby Lodge (☎ 2755-0031; www.albylodge.com; d/tr/q US$50/55/60; P) This fine German-run lodge on the edge of the park has spacious landscaped grounds, littered with trees that attract howler monkeys. Four thatch-room bungalows are spread out across the grounds, allowing for plenty of privacy. High ceilings, mosquito nets and driftwood details make for a pleasant jungle decor. A common *rancho* (thached gazebo) has excellent communal kitchen facilities.

Kelly Creek Hotel (☎ 2755-0007; www.hotelkellycreek.com; d US$55, extra person US$10; P) This snazzy hotel on a busy stretch of beach is conveniently situated right next to the park entrance. Four graceful, tropical *cabinas* have high ceilings and are accented with cream-colored linens and mosquito nets. Public areas are decorated with paintings by local artists. The onsite Spanish restaurant (dishes ₡2300 to ₡14,000; open from 6:30pm Monday to Saturday) serves up paella for two (₡7000).

Sia Tami Lodge (☎ 2755-0374; www.siatami.com; d/q US$75/85; P) A gravel road leads from town, past the other lodges, to this tranquil spot on the edge of the park. This place is ideal for families, as the 10 casas are fully equipped with two bedrooms, living space and kitchen. From each, a terrace overlooks a large private garden. With rainforest all around, this the next best thing to staying in the park itself.

Hotel La Casa de las Flores (☎ 2755-0326; www.lacasadelasfloreshotel.com; d incl breakfast US$80, additional person US$15; P) Right in the middle of town, this three-year-old Italian-owned spot has 10 large, sleek contemporary rooms (one of which is wheelchair-accessible) equipped with spacious bathrooms, cable TV and efficient air-con. The close proximity to Coco's, however, puts you within thumping distance of the bar's well-endowed speakers. Credit cards accepted.

Ciudad Perdida (☎ 2755-0303; www.ciudadperdidaecolodge.com; s/d/tr incl breakfast US$84/102/168; P) Bordering the national park, you'll find this place, with cute one- and two-room, cotton-candy–colored wood bungalows in a nicely landscaped garden. There are plenty of hammocks, ceiling fans, refrigerators, kitchens and safe boxes. One house has a Jacuzzi, all have cable TV. Credit cards accepted.

PLAYA NEGRA

Northwest of town, along Playa Negra, you'll find the mellowest options. All of these have bathrooms with hot water.

Budget

Cabinas Algebra (☎ 2755-0057; www.cabinasalgebra.com; d US$18, d/tr with kitchen US$25/39; P V) A long-time German-run place has three cabins that channel a rustic *Swiss Family Robinson* vibe. Each of the cozy units is crafted from wood and strung with hammocks. An onsite restaurant serves Tico specialties (mains ₡1100 to ₡6600), including veggie options on request. It's a 2km trek out of town, but the owners will come pick you up in town (for free!) if you call in advance. A solid, family-friendly budget choice.

Cabinas Tito (☎ 2755-0286; www.cahuita-cabinas-tito.com; d US$25, additional person US$8; P) Surrounded by extensive tropical gardens and banana plants, this charming spot offers seven clean, brightly painted cabins. Rooms are furnished in wicker, with mosquito nets and jungle accents. If you absolutely love it, there is a furnished two-bedroom house available for long-term rental.

Centro Turístico Brigitte (☎ 2755-0053; www.brigittecahuita.com; d with/without kitchen US$35/25; P) A couple of basic wood *cabinas* are painted in bright colors. You can also camp on the grounds provided you have your own gear (per person per night US$3).

Cabinas Iguana (☎ 2755-0005; www.cabinas-iguana.com; d US$25, d bungalow US$40; P) Set back from the beach, several bungalows – some older, some newer – are nestled into the lushly forested grounds. Simple wood cabins of various sizes (one of which sleeps six) have ceramic tile floors and beds with mosquito nets. One fully furnished apartment with a kitchen sleeps six (US$80). There is a swimming pool.

Jardín Tropical (☎ 8811-2754; www.jardintropical.ch; d US$30, 2-bedroom house US$45; P) Deep in the middle of an overgrown garden, two basic wood cabins have high ceilings and porch hammocks. A two-bedroom house sleeps four and comes with a full kitchen. It doesn't get more tranquil than this – unless, of course, there's a rowdy crowd at the very popular onsite bar.

our pick **La Piscina Natural** (☎ 2755-0146; d US$35; P) This little gem of a spot – run by inimitable Cahuita native Walter – is the top budget spot in Playa Negra. Painted cement rooms are comfortable and come equipped with bathrooms. But what makes this chilled-out little place so special are the lush grounds and the natural pool (great for a dip) amid the rocks. There is a huge shared kitchen, an outdoor lounge studded with intriguing driftwood sculptures and plenty of chilled beer on hand for guests.

Cabinas Nirvana (☎ 2755-0110; d US$35-60, tr US$55-70; P) Seven *cabinas* come in a variety of arrangements at this lush garden spot surrounding a pool. A couple of units (all of which are built out of wood) have kitchens, one has air-con and one has a broad veranda. Credit cards accepted.

Midrange

Bluspirit (☎ 2755-0122; www.bungalowsbluspirit.com; s/d/tr US$40/50/60; P) Three small but delightful blue A-frame cabins are lined up on a pleasant stretch of rocky, waterfront property. They each have a thatch-roofed porch – hung with a hammock, of course – for maximum breeze-catching.

Bungalows Malú (☎ 2755-0114; d US$55-110, tr US$65-115; P) At this lodge along Playa Negra, seven stone bungalows with varying configurations and amenities surround an open-air *rancho* and a sunken free-form pool with waterfall. Cabin floors are lined with an earthy terra-cotta tile and immaculate showers are crafted from stone. All units feature local art. A perfect spot for families. Credit cards accepted.

Hotel La Diosa (☎ 2755-0055; www.hotelladiosa.net; s/d US$58/63, with air-con US$76/87, with air-con & Jacuzzi US$88/99, all incl breakfast; P) Set amid a tropical garden, La Diosa has 10 spacious, tiled cabins with names such as Aphrodite and Isis, and featuring king-sized beds and Jacuzzi tubs with views. There's a hardwood yoga studio, meditation space and a swimming pool.

Goddess Garden (☎ 2755-0055/0444; www.thegoddessgarden.com; per person incl breakfast/3 meals US$60/100; P) Operated by the same owners as Hotel La Diosa, this place is situated at the end of the Playa Negra road, and is geared more at groups and retreats of up to 100 people. It has a spa, yoga studio and events space. Credit cards accepted.

our pick **Playa Negra Guesthouse** (☎ 2755-0127; www.playanegra.cr; d US$60-80, 2-bedroom cottage US$120; P) This beautiful Caribbean-style plantation house, with several freestanding storybook cottages (equipped with full kitchens), is meticulously decorated and maintained. Guest rooms are painted sherbety colors and feature charming tropical accents – such as colorful mosaics in the bathrooms and cozy wicker lounge chairs on the private decks. Every unit has a minifridge and coffee maker; there is a barbecue and honor bar, plus a lovely free-form pool is set into a well-manicured garden dotted with fan palms. A winner all around. Credit cards accepted.

Chalet Hibiscus (☎ 2755-0021; www.hotels.co.cr/hibiscus.html; d US$60, chalets US$120-140; P) Four free-standing beach cottages that sleep between six and 10 people are stocked with full kitchens and balconies strung with hammocks. The accommodations are simple: spacious units have cool white tile floors and wooden walls. One smaller unit sleeps two.

Atlantida Lodge (☎ 2755-0115; d standard/deluxe US$63/93; P) The 30 standard-issue wood *cabinas* at this long-time lodge are much brighter on the outside than on the inside. The grounds, however, are spacious and pretty, with a small outdoor gym and swimming pool. Credit cards accepted.

Magellan Inn (☎ 2755-0035; www.magellaninn.com; d with fan/air-con US$69/89, all incl breakfast; P) Toward the northern end of Playa Negra, this comfortable six-room inn has six spacious carpeted rooms with rustic wood furnishings, firm mattresses and cable TV. It also has an open-air bar that overlooks a beautiful garden and a free form pool.

El Encanto B&B (☎ 2755-0113; www.elencantocahuita.com; d US$70, d apt US$90, 3-bedroom house US$205, all incl breakfast; P) This charming French-owned B&B is set into lovingly landscaped grounds that are dotted with easy chairs and hammocks. Demure bungalows have high ceilings and firm beds draped in colorful textiles. The apartment and the beach house both have fully equipped kitchens. Credit cards accepted.

Hotel Suizo Loco Lodge (☎ 2755-0349; www.suizolocolodge.com; d incl US$89-110; P) Ten immaculate, whitewashed cabins of various sizes have king-sized beds and folk-art accents at this family-friendly spot. All units come equipped with safe, minifridge, solar-heated showers and small, private terraces – and the hotel's charming owners can supply parents of infants with a crib upon request. Two affectionate pooches patrol the perfectly landscaped grounds, which contain an impressive mosaic-tile pool with a swim-up bar.

Top End

Atiuhac (☎ 8911-1347; www.atiuhac.com; d incl breakfast US$100; P) Four raw wood bungalows surround a large *rancho* with open-air bar stocked with comfy hammock chairs. The cabins are designed to appeal to outdoorsy types: surrounded by foliage, they are rustic, spread out over the property and equipped with roomy private decks, a living area and a shower set into the hollowed trunk of a tree. There's a creaky 5m-tall look-out tower that is a great spot to hang out and catch a breeze. Check the website for last-minute deals.

Eating

CENTER

Brasserie Tygo's (dishes ₡1000-3200; 7am-6pm Wed-Sun; wi-fi) A surprising airy and attractive cafe with wicker furnishings overlooks the bus station. It serves pastries, cappuccino, light sandwiches and *casados* – and it even has wi-fi. It's a perfect spot to wait for the bus.

100% Natural Coffee Shop (☎ 2755-0010; dishes ₡1700-5500; 6:30am-2pm Mon-Fri) There is no better place in Cahuita to greet the morning with a cup o' joe or unwind in the afternoon with a refreshing *jugo*. A lunch menu has tapas and there is a pleasant bar. Try the waffles and ice cream – yum!

Café del Parquecito (☎ 2775-0279; breakfast ₡2000-2900; 6am-3pm & 6pm-close) Early risers come for the coffee at this spot on Parque Central. Most of the menu is so-so, but you won't be disappointed if you stick to the crepes stuffed full of fresh tropical fruit.

Cha Cha Cha! (☎ 8394-4153; mains ₡2200-8000; noon-10pm Tue-Sun; V) In a corner veranda of an old house, this attractive expat favorite offers recommended *cuisine del mundo* (cuisine of the world). Dishes range from Jamaican jerk chicken to Cuban specialties to plenty of vegetarian options, including a 'zen salad' crafted from mandarin oranges, basil, cashews and macadamia nuts.

Restaurante Coral Reef (☎ 2755-0133; mains ₡2200-9000; 11:30am-10pm) This place attracts fish-lovers, who arrive for steaming portions of seafood stew served in a pleasant 2nd-story balcony overlooking the main drag. The place gets packed, especially in high season (make a reservation). It is located right next to Coco's Bar, putting post-dinner drinks within easy reach.

Miss Edith's (☎ 2755-0248; mains ₡2300-12,000; 11am-10pm; V) This long-time local restaurant serves a laundry-list of Caribbean specialties, including jerk chicken, rice and beans, and potatoes stewed in garlic – in addition to a number of vegetarian options. It's a famed spot that sometimes rests on its laurels, with cooking that is off-and-on and somewhat indifferent service.

Roberto's Restaurant (☎ 2755-0117; dishes ₡2500-9000; 7am-10pm) Owned by one of the top fishing guides in the region, you know the seafood is going to be fresh at this charming candlelit spot. The restaurant uses organic ingredients whenever possible.

our pick **Restaurant La Fé** (dishes ₡2500-10,000; 7am-11pm) A basic, cement eatery on the main drag is draped in swinging oropendola nests and illuminated by candlelight in the evenings. Chef and owner Walter, a Cahuita native, speaks English, Spanish and Mekatelyu, and serves up tall tales and tasty meals at this reasonably priced spot. There's a laundry-list of Tico and Caribbean items, but the main reason to come here is to eat anything doused in the restaurant's spicy-delicious coconut sauce. (We still have fantasies about his delicious fish.)

Also good for lunch:

Soda Café Caribbean Flavor (mains ₡1900-5800; 6am-9pm) Caribbean-style standards, fresh juices and *gallo pinto* (meal of blended rice and beans).

Restaurant Típico Cahuita (☎ 2755-0017; mains ₡2000-5800; 8am-close) A spacious spot beneath a palm-thatched *palapa* has a wide-ranging menu, from *casados* to pricey lobster (₡25,000).

Pizz 'N' Love (breakfast ₡1800-2300, casados ₡2500-3000) It may serve pizza, but the *gallo pinto* at breakfast is tops.

PLAYA NEGRA

Near Playa Negra, you can also head to Restaurant Bananas at Cabinas Algebra or Centro Turístico Brigitte for good breakfasts, including tasty banana pancakes.

Reggae Restaurant (☎ 2755-0269; mains ₡2000-5000; 7-11am & noon-9pm) Exuding a friendly, laidback vibe, this *soda* serves Caribbean-style standards, from basic *casados* to the house specialty, shrimp in coconut milk. This place also has facilities for camping (per person

US$3), plus some comfortable cabins (US$20 to US$30).

Chao's Paradise (☎ 2755-0480; seafood mains ₡3700-7000; ⌚ 11am-11pm) Follow the wafting smell of garlic and simmering sauces to this highly recommended Playa Negra outpost that serves fresh catches cooked up in spicy 'Chao' sauce. The open-air restaurant-bar has a pool table and live music some nights.

Sobre Las Olas (☎ 2755-0109; pastas ₡5500-6500, mains ₡5500-12,500; ⌚ noon-10pm Wed-Mon; V) Cahuita's top option for waterfront dining (an ideal spot for a date) lies only a 100m walk out of town. It is owned by a lively Tico-Italian couple who serve a variety of Mediterranean-influenced specialties, such as Marco's *spaghetti pescatore*, fresh pasta studded with fish and shrimp. There is a decent wine list and tiramisu (₡2400) for dessert.

Drinking

This low-key town is home to one insanely loud drinking hole: **Coco's Bar** (⌚ noon-last man standing). You can't miss it at the main intersection, painted in Rasta red, yellow and green and cranking the reggaetón up to volume 11. On some nights (usually on weekends) there is also live music. If you're not looking to burst your ear drums, try one of the mellower drinking establishments situated right across the street.

Along Playa Negra, Chao's Paradise and Jardín Tropical are both good spots for a beer.

Getting There & Away

All public buses arrive and depart at the bus terminal about 200m southwest of Parque Central.

Bribrí/Sixaola ₡1600; two hours; departs hourly from 6am to 7pm.

Puerto Limón (Autotransportes Mepe) ₡1000; 1½ hours; departs 6am, 9:30pm, 10:45pm, 1:45pm and 6:15pm. (These times are approximate because these buses originate in Manzanillo. Get there early just in case.)

Puerto Viejo de Talamanca/Manzanillo ₡1000; 30 minutes to one hour; departs 6:15am, 6:45am, 11:15am, 3:45pm and 6:45pm.

San José (Autotransportes Mepe) ₡3700; four hours; departs 7am, 8am, 9:30am, 11:30am and 4:30pm.

Getting Around

The best way to get around Cahuita – especially if you're staying out along Playa Negra – is by bicycle. In town, rent bikes at **Mister Big J's** (☎ 8887-4695; per day US$7; ⌚ 7am-6pm); he also rents boogie boards for US$6 per day. On Playa Negra, bikes are available at Centro Turístico Brigitte (see p472) for similar prices.

PARQUE NACIONAL CAHUITA

This small **park** – just 10 sq km – is one of the more frequently visited national parks in Costa Rica. The reasons are simple: the nearby town of Cahuita provides attractive accommodations and easy access; more importantly, the white-sand beaches, coral reef and coastal rainforest are bursting with wildlife.

Declared a national park in 1978, Cahuita is typical of the entire coast (very humid), which results in dense tropical foliage, as well as coconut palms and sea grapes. The area includes the swampy **Punta Cahuita**, which juts into the sea between two stretches of sandy beach. Often flooded, the point is covered with cativo and mango trees and is a popular hang-out spots for birds such as green ibis, yellow-crowned night heron, boat-billed heron and the rare green-and-rufous kingfisher.

The dark Río Perezoso, or 'Sloth River,' bisects Punta Cahuita and sometimes prevents hiking between the ranger stations since it serves as the discharge for the swamp that covers the point. (Check in with the rangers about this before you set out.)

Red land and fiddler crab live along the beaches, attracting mammals such as crab-eating raccoon and white-nosed coati. White-faced capuchin, southern opossum and three-toed sloth also live in these parts. The mammal you are most likely to see (and hear) is the mantled howler monkey, which makes its bellowing presence known. The coral reef represents another rich ecosystem that abounds with life.

Information

The **Kelly Creek ranger station** (☎ 2755-0461; admission by donation; ⌚ 6am-5pm) is convenient to the town of Cahuita, while 1km down Hwy 32 takes you to the well-signed **Puerto Vargas ranger station** (☎ 2755-0302; admission US$10; ⌚ 8am-4pm Mon-Fri, 7am-5pm Sat & Sun).

You do not have to pay the full admission fee if you enter at Kelly Creek. (This is the result of a local stir-up in the 1990s, when locals feared high park fees would deter the tourists.) But note that these fees provide important income for the park service, which is habitually underfunded. Tourist dollars support education, conservation and maintenance programs. Please consider supporting the park to the best of your ability.

Activities

HIKING

An easily navigable 8km **coastal trail** leads through the jungle from Kelly Creek to Puerto Vargas. At times the trail follows the beach; at other times hikers are 100m or so away from the sand. At the end of the first beach, Playa Blanca, hikers must ford the Río Perezoso. Inquire about river conditions before you set out: under normal conditions, this river can be thigh-deep at high tide. During periods of heavy rain, it is often too dangerous to cross.

The trail continues around Punta Cahuita to the long stretch of Playa Vargas. The trail ends at the southern tip of the reef, where it meets up with a road leading to the Puerto Vargas ranger station. From the ranger station, it is another 1.5km along a gravel road to the park entrance. From here, you can hike back to Cahuita along the coastal highway, or you can catch a ride going in either direction.

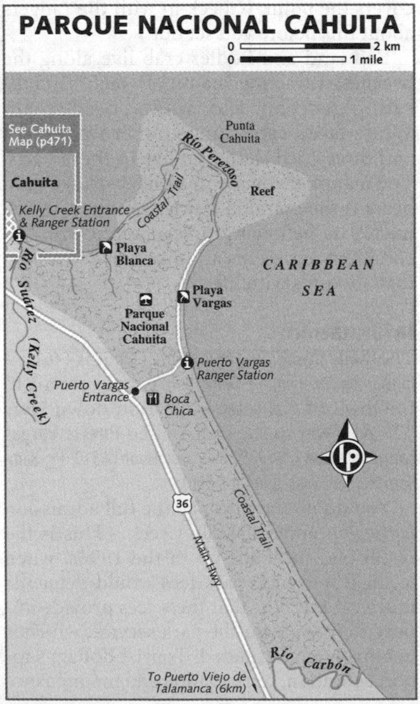

PARQUE NACIONAL CAHUITA

SWIMMING

Almost immediately upon entering the park, you'll see the 2km-long **Playa Blanca** stretching along a gently curving bay to the east. The first 500m of beach may be unsafe for swimming, but beyond that, waves are generally gentle. (Look for green flags marking safe swimming spots.) The rocky Punta Cahuita headland separates this beach from the next one, **Playa Vargas**. It is unwise to leave clothing or other belongings unattended when you swim.

SNORKELING

Parque Nacional Cahuita contains one of the last living coral reefs in Costa Rica. The reef is accessible from the beach, but the best way to see the creatures under the sea is to hire a guide with a boat in Cahuita. If you prefer to walk, hike along the beach trail. After about 6km, you will come to a sandy stretch that is cut off from the coastline by a rocky headland of Punta Cahuita.

While the reef represents some of the area's best snorkeling, it has incurred damage over the years from earthquakes and tourism-related activities. In an attempt to protect the reef from further damage, snorkeling is only permitted with a licensed guide. (The tour companies listed on p472 all offer excursions.) The going rate for one person is about US$30.

You'll find that snorkeling conditions vary greatly, depending on the weather and other factors. In general, the drier months in the highlands (from February to April) are best for snorkeling on the coast, as less runoff occurs in the rivers and there is less silting in the sea. Conditions are often cloudy at other times. Indeed, conditions are often cloudy, period.

VOLUNTEERING

Though not renowned as a sea turtle destination, Cahuita's beaches are nonetheless an important habitat for several breeds. **Asociación Widecast** (☎ in San José 8818-2543; www.latinamericanseaturtles.org, www.widecast.org; volunteer fee per day US$50) has volunteering opportunities for those interested in assisting on in-water research projects and various conservation-related activities. The daily fee includes homestay accommodations and three meals. It runs a similar program in Gandoca, to the south (p495). Reserve in advance.

Eating

After the long, hot hike through the jungle, you may think you are hallucinating when you see **Boca Chica** (☎ 2755-0415; meals ₡3300-10,000; 9am-6pm;), a small, whitewashed family recreation center, at the end of the road. It's not a mirage, just a well-placed bar and eatery, run by a charming Italian owner, and offering cold *jugos*, homemade pasta and Tico and Caribbean specialties. There is a swimming pool.

CACAO TRAILS

Halfway between Cahuita and Puerto Viejo de Talamanca in Hone Creek, this **botanical garden and chocolate museum** (☎ 2756-8186; Hone Creek; guided tour US$25; 7am-4pm;) has a couple of small museums devoted to indigenous and Afro-Caribbean culture, a lush garden bursting with bromeliads and heliconias, as well as an onsite chocolate factory where cacao is processed in traditional ways. Two-hour tours include a visit to all of these spots, plus a hike to a nearby organic farm. Additional expeditions allow for further exploration by kayak on the adjacent Río Carbón. Any bus between Cahuita and Puerto Viejo can drop you at the entrance. This is a great outing for kids.

PUERTO VIEJO DE TALAMANCA

There was a time when the only travelers to the little seaside settlement once known as Old Harbor were intrepid surfers who shacked up in cheap *cabinas* and then lazily flip-flopped around the quiet, dusty streets, board under arm, on their way to ride the Salsa Brava. That, certainly, is no longer the case. This burgeoning Caribbean party town is bustling with tourist activity: street vendors ply Rasta trinkets and Bob Marley T-shirts, stylish eateries serve global fusion everything and intentionally rustic bamboo bars pump dancehall and reggaetón. The scene, in fact, can get downright hedonistic, attracting dedicated revelers who arrive to marinate in ganja and *guaro* (the local cane alcohol).

Despite the reputation for revelry, Puerto Viejo nonetheless manages to hold on to an easy charm. Stray a couple of blocks off the main commercial strip and you might find yourself on a sleepy dirt road, savoring a spicy Caribbean stew in the company of local families. Nearby, you'll find rainforest fruit farms set to a soundtrack of cackling birds and croaking frogs, and wide-open beaches where the daily itinerary revolves around surfing and snoozing. So, chill a little. Party a little. Eat a little. You've come to just the right place.

Dangers & Annoyances

Unfortunately, a cottage industry of drug dealers has become a permanent part of the landscape in Puerto Viejo. In fact, in some spots, it can get quite aggressive. Be firm if you're not interested. And be aware that though the use of marijuana is common in Puerto Viejo, it is nonetheless illegal.

As in other popular tourist centers, theft can be an issue. Stay aware, use your hotel safe, and if you are staying outside of town, it is best not to walk alone late at night. Likewise, the town has a number of independent touts offering all manner of travel services. Choose your accommodations carefully and take tours from recommended agencies and guides.

Information

The websites **Green Coast** (www.greencoast.com) and **Puerto Viejo** (www.puertoviejocr.com) have information on lodging, eating and activities in the area.

ATEC (Asociación Talamanqueña de Ecoturismo y Conservación; ☎ 2750-0191, 2750-0398; www.ateccr.org; 8am-9pm) A reliable source of information on tours and activities in the area also offers a number of vintage desktops with internet access (₡1200 per hour).

Banco de Costa Rica (9am-4pm Mon-Fri) The ATM here works on the Plus and Visa systems. It sometimes runs out of cash on weekends.

David's Library (☎ 2750-0232) This book exchange operates in the lobby of the Lotus Garden hotel.

Jungle Internet (☎ 2750-2086; www.junglec.com; per hr ₡1700; 8am-11pm) Decent laptops and wireless access.

Sights

To the west of town, **Finca La Isla Botanical Garden** (☎ 2750-0046; www.costaricacaribbean.com; self-guided/guided tour US$5/10; 10am-4pm Fri-Mon) is a working tropical farm where the owners have been growing organic pepper, cacao, tropical fruits and ornamental plants for more than a decade. Part of the farm is set aside as a botanical garden, which is also good for bird-watching and for wildlife observation (look for sloths, poison-dart frogs and toucans). The informative guided tour (in English) includes admission, fruit tasting and a glass of fresh juice to finish, or you can buy a booklet (US$1) and take yourself on a self-guided tour.

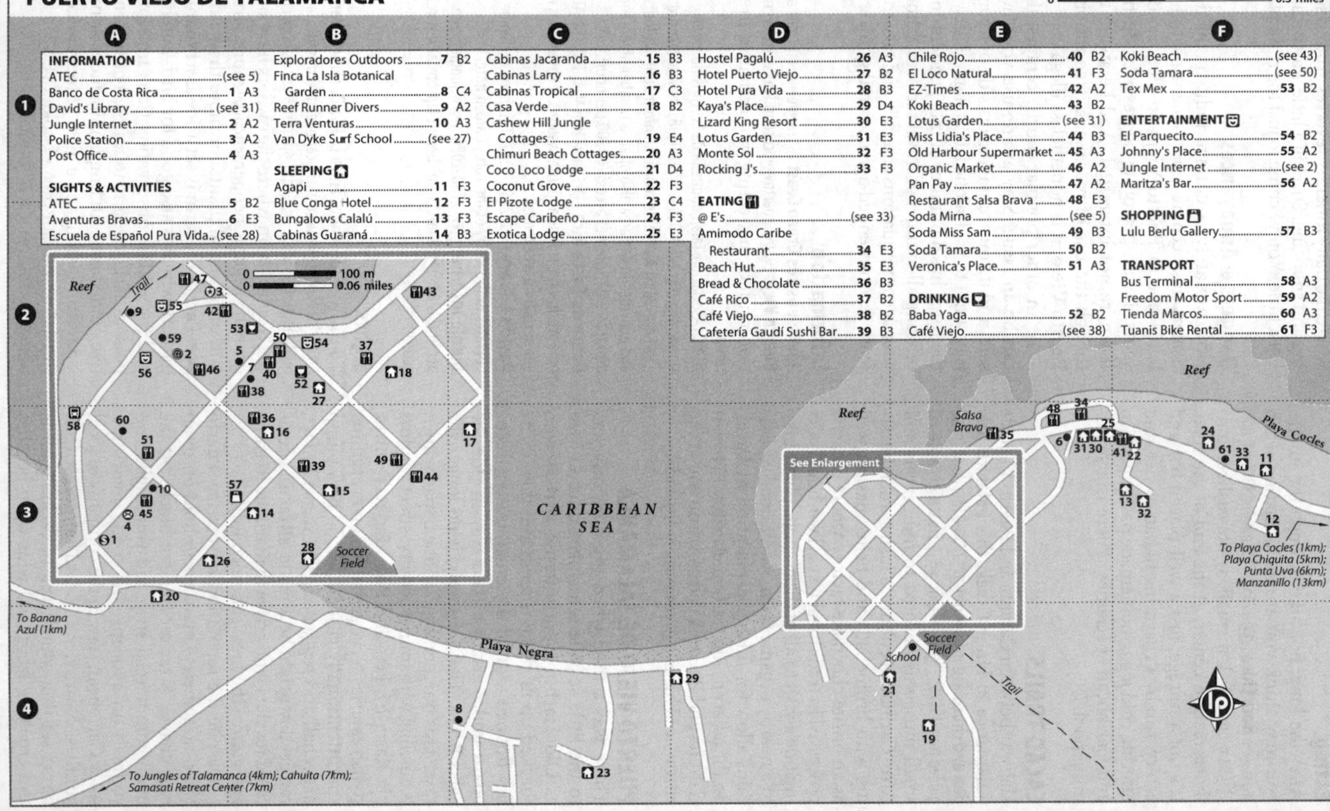
PUERTO VIEJO DE TALAMANCA
500 m
0.3 miles
INFORMATION
ATEC (see 5)
Banco de Costa Rica 1 A3
David's Library (see 31)
Jungle Internet 2 A2
Police Station 3 A2
Post Office 4 A3
SIGHTS & ACTIVITIES
ATEC 5 B2
Aventuras Bravas 6 E3
Escuela de Español Pura Vida (see 28)
Exploradores Outdoors 7 B2
Finca La Isla Botanical Garden 8 C4
Reef Runner Divers 9 A2
Terra Venturas 10 A3
Van Dyke Surf School (see 27)
SLEEPING
Agapi 11 F3
Blue Conga Hotel 12 F3
Bungalows Calalú 13 F3
Cabinas Guaraná 14 B3
Cabinas Jacaranda 15 B3
Cabinas Larry 16 B3
Cabinas Tropical 17 C3
Casa Verde 18 B2
Cashew Hill Jungle Cottages 19 E4
Chimuri Beach Cottages 20 A3
Coco Loco Lodge 21 D4
Coconut Grove 22 F3
El Pizote Lodge 23 C4
Escape Caribeño 24 F3
Exotica Lodge 25 E3
Hostel Pagalú 26 A3
Hotel Puerto Viejo 27 B2
Hotel Pura Vida 28 B3
Kaya's Place 29 D4
Lizard King Resort 30 E3
Lotus Garden 31 E3
Monte Sol 32 F3
Rocking J's 33 F3
EATING
@ E's (see 33)
Amimodo Caribe Restaurant 34 E3
Beach Hut 35 E3
Bread & Chocolate 36 B3
Café Rico 37 B2
Café Viejo 38 B2
Cafetería Gaudí Sushi Bar 39 B3
Chile Rojo 40 B2
El Loco Natural 41 F3
EZ-Times 42 A2
Koki Beach 43 B2
Lotus Garden (see 31)
Miss Lidia's Place 44 B3
Old Harbour Supermarket 45 A3
Organic Market 46 A2
Pan Pay 47 A2
Restaurant Salsa Brava 48 E3
Soda Mirna (see 5)
Soda Miss Sam 49 B3
Soda Tamara 50 B2
Veronica's Place 51 A3
DRINKING
Baba Yaga 52 B2
Café Viejo (see 38)
Koki Beach (see 43)
Soda Tamara (see 50)
Tex Mex 53 B2
ENTERTAINMENT
El Parquecito 54 B2
Johnny's Place 55 A2
Jungle Internet (see 2)
Maritza's Bar 56 A2
SHOPPING
Lulu Berlu Gallery 57 B3
TRANSPORT
Bus Terminal 58 A3
Freedom Motor Sport 59 A2
Tienda Marcos 60 A3
Tuanis Bike Rental 61 F3
Reef
Trail
100 m
0.06 miles
Soccer Field
CARIBBEAN SEA
Playa Negra
Salsa Brava
See Enlargement
School
Playa Cocles
To Banana Azul (1km)
To Jungles of Talamanca (4km); Cahuita (7km); Samasati Retreat Center (7km)
To Playa Cocles (1km); Playa Chiquita (5km); Punta Uva (6km); Manzanillo (13km)

SALSA BRAVA

One of the biggest breaks in Costa Rica, the Salsa Brava is named for the heaping helping of 'spicy sauce' it serves up on the sharp, shallow reef, continually collecting its debt of fun in broken skin, boards and bones. The wave makes its regular, dramatic appearance when the swells pull in from the east, pushing a wall of water against the reef, in the process, generating a thick and powerful curl. There's no gradual build up here: the water is transformed from swell to wave in a matter of seconds. Ride it out and you're golden. Wipe-out and you'll rocket head-first into the reef. In his memoir, *In Search of Captain Zero,* surfer and screenwriter Allen Weisbecker describes it as 'vicious.' Some mordant locals have baptized it 'the cheese-grater.'

Interestingly, this storied wave helped turn Puerto Viejo into a destination. More than 30 years ago, the town was barely accessible. But that did not dissuade dogged surfers from the bumpy bus rides and rickety canoes that hauled them and their boards on the week-long trip from San José. They camped on the beach and shacked up with locals, carbo-loading at cheap *sodas*. Other intrepid explorers – biologists, Peace Corps volunteers, disaffected US veterans looking to escape the fallout of the Vietnam War – also materialized during this time, helping spread the word about the area's luminous sunsets, lush rainforests and monster curls. Today, Puerto Viejo has a fine paved road, global eateries and wi-fi. The fierceness of the Salsa Brava, however, remains unchanged.

West of Puerto Viejo, the **Jungles of Talamanca** is actually a small tropical nursery and cacao *finca*. This Bribrí family welcomes visitors to its home, where you can see cacao toasted over an open fire then hand-ground into delicious chocolate or rich cocoa butter. Nutmeg, black pepper or cinnamon, all grown onsite, may be added. The resulting product is truly decadent – it's amazing that something so luscious comes from such humble origins. This place is 4km out of town, on the road to Bribrí; look for the sign just past the clinic.

Activities

SURFING

Breaking on the reef that hugs the village, you will find the famed **Salsa Brava**, a shallow break that is also one of the country's most infamous waves (see boxed text above). It's a tricky ride – if you lose it, the waves will plow you straight into the reef – but it's a rush (and most definitely not for beginners). Salsa Brava offers both rights and lefts, although the right is usually faster. Conditions are best with an easterly swell.

For a softer landing, try the beach break at **Playa Cocles** – where the waves are almost as impressive and the landing, far less-damaging. Cocles is about 2km east of town. Conditions are usually best early in the day, before the wind picks up.

Waves in the area generally peak from December to March, and there is a surfing mini-season from June to July. From late March to May, and in September and October, the sea is at its calmest.

There are several surf schools around town, charging about US$40 for two hours of lessons. Stands around town rent boards from about US$20 per day. Surf schools around town include:

Caribe Surf (☎ 8357-7703; www.caribesurf.com) Run by super-smiley surf instructor, Hershel, who is widely considered the best teacher in the town. Call Hershel to organize a lesson (the school has no office).

Van Dyke Surf School (☎ 2750-0620; hotelpuertoviejocr.com) Long-time surfer Kurt Van Dyke – who has lived in Puerto Viejo for decades (and who, coincidentally, is the nephew of legendary big wave surfer Fred Van Dyke) – runs this new outfit, which offers lessons for beginners and workshops for experienced riders who want to sharpen their skills. Look for the office adjacent to Hotel Puerto Viejo (Van Dyke is the proprietor there as well).

SWIMMING

The entire southern Caribbean coast – from Cahuita all the way south to Punta Mona – is lined with unbelievably beautiful beaches. Just northwest of town, **Playa Negra** offers the area's safest swimming.

Southeast of town you will find some gems – stretches of smooth white sand (quite slender at high tide), fringed by jungle and ideal for surfing, body surfing and, when the swell is low, swimming. **Playa Cocles** (2km east of town), **Playa Chiquita** (4km east), **Punta Uva** (6km east) and **Manzanillo** (see p495) all offer postcard-perfect beach paradises (think: swaying palm trees and exotic birds). Swimming conditions vary greatly, however, and the surf can get dangerous. Riptides and powerful undertows can be deadly. Inquire at your hotel or with local tour operators about conditions before setting out.

SNORKELING

The waters from Cahuita to Manzanillo are protected by Costa Rica's only two living reef systems, which form a naturally protected sanctuary, home to some 35 species of coral and 400 species of fish, not to mention dolphins, sharks and, occasionally, whales. Generally, underwater visibility is best when the sea is calm – in other words, when surfing is bad.

Just south of **Punta Uva**, in front of the Arrecife restaurant, is a decent spot for snorkeling, when conditions are calm. The reef is very close to the shore and features include stunning examples of reindeer coral, sheet coral and lettuce coral. The reef at **Manzanillo** is also easily accessible. Rent equipment at Aquamor Talamanca Adventures (p495). Most of the dive companies offer snorkeling trips of varying lengths for about US$35 to US$45 per person.

DIVING

Divers in the southern Caribbean will discover upward of 20 dive sites, from the coral gardens in shallow waters to deeper sites with amazing underwater vertical walls. Literally hundreds of species of fish swim around here, including angelfish, parrotfish, triggerfish, shark and different species of jack and snapper.

In Puerto Viejo the principal operator is **Reef Runner Divers** (☎ 2750-0480; www.reefrunnerdivers.net; 1-/2-tank dive US$65/90; 🕑 8am-6pm). If you are not certified, you can use a temporary license for US$65 or spring for the full PADI certification for US$325. In Punta Uva, check in with Punta Uva Dive Center (p488), and in Manzanillo book trips with the highly reputable Aquamor Talamanca Adventures (p495).

HIKING

The immediate vicinity of Puerto Viejo is not prime hiking territory: the proximity of the Parque Nacional Cahuita and the Refugio Nacional de Vida Silvestre Gandoca-Manzanillo means that most trekkers will head to these protected areas to look for toucan and sloth. Getting to the indigenous reserves often requires a pretty serious trek, usually with a guide (see Tours, below).

If you are up for some independent exploring, pack a picnic and follow the town's most southerly road, which goes past the soccer field and the Cashew Hill Jungle Cottages. Once out of the village, the road dwindles to a path and leads straight up into the hills.

WHITE-WATER RAFTING

Plenty of rafters head straight for Turrialba (see boxed text, p148) but it's possible to do rafting from the southern Caribbean. **Exploradores Outdoors** (☎ 2750-2020; www.exploradoresoutdoors.com; one-day trip incl 2 meals & transport from US$99) offers one- and two-day trips on the Ríos Pacuare, Reventazón and Sarapiquí. Staff can pick you up and drop you off in either Cahuita, Puerto Viejo San José or Arenal, and you're free to mix and match your pick-up and drop-off points. They also organize overnight excursions to Tortuguero.

Courses

Escuela de Español Pura Vida (☎ 2750-0002; www.idiomas.hotel-puravida.com), located at the Hotel Pura Vida, offers everything from private hourly tutoring (from US$18) to intensive five-hour-a-day sessions (from US$350 per week).

Tours

Tour operators generally require a minimum of two people on any excursion. Rates are per person, but they may be discounted for larger groups.

ATEC (☎ 2750-0191, 2750-0398; www.ateccr.org; 🕑 8am-9pm) This highly reputable not-for-profit promotes environmentally sensitive tourism by working with local guides and supporting local communities. Hiking, horseback riding and canoe trips involve bird-watching and visiting indigenous territories and local farms. Depending on the activity, half-day excursions start at about US$20 and go up to US$80 for overnight trips.

Aventuras Bravas (☎ 2750-2000, 8849-7600; www.braveadventure.net) With offices in town and at Rocking J's hostel, this company works largely as a booking agent arranging almost every tour imaginable. Popular activities include kayak trips (US$25), rafting excursions (US$75) and canopy tours (US$55).

Terra Venturas (☎ 2750-0750/489; www.terraventuras.com; 🕑 8am-7pm) Offers overnights in Tortuguero (US$179-239), hiking (US$45) and snorkeling (US$49) in

CARIBBEAN COAST

Cahuita, tours of chocolate *fincas* (US$60), white-water rafting (US$100), plus it has its very own 23-platform, 2.1km-long canopy tour (US$55) – complete with Tarzan swing.

Sleeping

Puerto Viejo has a little bit of everything. In the village, accommodations off the main drag are quietest.

HOSTELS

Rocking J's (☎ 2750-0657; www.rockingjs.com; camping per person US$4, hammock US$5, dm US$7, d US$20-30, 3-person king ste US$60, apt US$350; P) Puerto Viejo's grooviest hostel and 'hammock hotel' is owned by the charismatic, mischievous 'J,' who organizes full-moon toga parties and round-the-table drinking games. If you're looking for good times, you'll find them here – along with plenty of new friends. The accommodations are basic. Tight rows of tents, hammocks, snug dorms and private doubles share rickety showers in a concrete structure that is brightened by a veritable explosion of psychedelic mosaics. Save up your pennies and rent out J's Palace, a pimpin' three-story apartment that sleeps six and is equipped with private kitchen and retractable roof. Surfboards, snorkels and bikes are available for rent and there is a popular restaurant, @E's.

Hostel Pagalú (☎ 2750-1930; www.pagalu.com; dm US$10, d with/without bathroom US$28/22; P) A brand new hostel on a quiet street, this place offers a break from Puerto Viejo's party scene. Super clean, airy dorms and half a dozen private doubles are painted white and come with polished-wood accents. Niceties include large lockers, charging stations for MP3 players and reading lamps installed above each bunk. Private doubles are spacious (one is wheelchair-accessible) and there is a shared, open-air kitchen and a quiet lounge with tables and hammocks. In addition, the owners supply spring water on an honor system – so that you can refill your reusable plastic bottles, rather than constantly be buying new ones.

BUDGET

All budget spots have private hot-water bathrooms unless otherwise stated.

Hotel Puerto Viejo (☎ 2750-0620; hotelpuertoviejocr.com; dm US$8, r per person with shared bathroom US$10, d US$30; P) No shoes, no shirt, no problem. This dedicated surfer crash pad administered by hardcore wave rider Kurt Van Dyke has a warren of 68 wooden rooms, some of which sleep up to eight. Units are basic, but very clean and come equipped with strong fans and bathrooms that run on recycled rainwater. Onsite, you'll find an extravagantly large shared kitchen, a chilled-out bar where the talk is all about waves and a surf school (p481). Credit cards accepted.

Kaya's Place (☎ 2750-0690/0060; www.kayasplace.com; s/d with shared bathroom US$19/27, d with/without ocean views US$40/35, s/d with garden views US$40/50, 2-/5-person apt US$70/85; P) A small US-run inn just west of town has 17 snug, basic rooms and apartments (some of which share cool-water showers). A few units are rather dim, though the ones facing the garden are airy. A 2nd-floor lounge is filled with hammocks and offers prime views of the ocean. Beach cruisers are available for rent; credit cards are accepted.

Monte Sol (☎ 2750-0098; www.montesol.net; d US$20-30, d/q bungalows with kitchen US$45/65, 4-person house US$70; P) Set back from the main road, this laidback German-run place east of town has six cabins painted a pleasing mustard yellow. Units are rustic, with tile floors, cubicle bathrooms and mosquito nets – but are clean and have hammocks. A full house with kitchen sleeps up to eight and available for long-term rentals.

Cabinas Larry (☎ 2750-0964; d US$24; P) Cheap, tidy, bright and clean. This locally run spot behind a dental office has eight functional, concrete rooms that surround a gravel courtyard. The public deck is stocked with hammocks.

Coconut Grove (☎ 2750-0093; d without bathroom US$25, d/tr US$45/55; P) Four efficient wood-beam rooms and one small apartment (sleeping five) make up this basic spot on the east side of town. For an extra US$5 per day, owner Heidi will throw in a breakfast of eggs or German pancakes.

our pick **Hotel Pura Vida** (☎ 2750-0002; www.hotel-puravida.com; s/d/tr without bathroom US$25/30/40, s/d/tr US$32/38/50; P) Though this place has budget prices, the atmosphere and amenities are solidly midrange. Ten breezy, immaculate rooms, clad in polished wood, bright linens and ceramic tile floors make up this homey Chilean-German run inn on a quiet street. (Unit 6 is best – offering incredible views of town right from the solar-heated shower.) Alongside a lovingly tended garden, you'll find a serene lounge studded with easy chairs and hammocks. Simple breakfasts, light snacks and chilled beers are available at an additional charge. A great spot for couples; credit cards accepted.

Bungalows Calalú (☎ 2750-0042; www.bungalowscalalu.com; s/d/tr US$26/36/44, with kitchen US$45/55/65; P ❄ 🏊) Set in a blooming garden, this family-friendly inn has five bungalows that surround a tranquil courtyard with a roomy stone-lined pool fed by a gushing waterfall. The bungalows themselves are simple, with tiled floors and wood-beam ceilings, but all have private porches.

Cabinas Jacaranda (☎ 2750-0069; www.cabinasjacaranda.net; d/tr/q from US$30/36/50; P 📶) In a blooming garden intersected by mosaic walkways, this tidy local spot – run by a terrifically friendly staff – has 15 simple wood *cabinas* with lockboxes, spotless ceramic tile floors and murals of flowers. There is yoga and massage available onsite, as well as a shared kitchen and a garden patio for lounging. Credit cards accepted.

Lizard King Resort (☎ 2750-0614; lizardkingresort@net.com; s/d/tr/q US$35/45/60/75, d with air-con US$75; P ❄ 📶 🏊) A two-storey wooden building on the eastern edge of town houses 15 spacious hardwood cabins that overlook a roomy pool. Upstairs units are nicer – and more private. Rates include a hearty Tico or US-style breakfast. The onsite restaurant serves three meals a day. Credit cards accepted.

Cabinas Guaraná (☎ 2750-0244; www.hotelguarana.com; s/d/tr/q US$33/41/51/58; P 💻 📶) Set amid a riotous tropical garden, you'll find 10 brightly painted concrete cabins at this charming Italian-run inn. Units are decorated with wooden furniture and colorful folk tapestries, and each one comes with a small private terrace with hammock. There is a spacious shared kitchen, free internet, laundry service and a vertigo-inducing tree house that offers spectacular views of the Caribbean Sea. This place is excellent value; credit cards are accepted.

Cabinas Tropical (☎ 2750-0283; www.cabinastropical.com; s/d/tr US$35/40/48, d with air-con US$48; P ⊠ ❄ 📶) Ten spacious rooms – decorated with varnished wood and shiny tiles – surround a primly landscaped garden on the edge of town. The comfortable quarters are just part of the appeal: biologist owner Rolfe Blancke leads excellent bird-watching hikes at dawn (per person US$50, minimum three people, breakfast provided).

Casa Verde (☎ 2750-0015; www.cabinascasaverde.com; s/d without bathroom from US$38/40; s/d/tr/q US$56/70/86/102; P 📶 🏊) Tiled walkways wind through gardens with 17 tidy rooms, each with high ceilings, stained wood furniture, folk-art touches and private terraces with hammocks. Cheaper rooms are more basic, but the shared bathrooms shine. A pool and hot tub – encrusted with rock formations – are straight out of *Fantasy Island*. Credit cards accepted.

Chimuri Beach Cottages (☎ 2750-0119; www.chimuribeach.com; d/q US$39/55; P 📶) On the road to Playa Negra, the charming Colocha and Mauricio keep three sherbet-colored beach cottages in various sizes that are clean and simple, each with its own private deck and hammock – as well as a bed draped in a mosquito net. They can organize walks through their *finca* in the mountains, which abuts the KéköLdi indigenous territory. This is a wonderfully serene spot.

MIDRANGE

Exotica Lodge (☎ 2750-0542; www.exoticalodge.com; s/d US$40/50, additional person US$10; P ❄) A row of clean, simple whitewashed rooms with wicker furnishings, bright linens, decorative textiles, minifridge and cable TV. Some are equipped with air-con as well.

Lotus Garden (☎ 2750-0232; thelotusgarden.net; d US$40, 2-person ste US$70-90; P ❄ 📶 🏊) Channeling the Far East (by way of Puerto Viejo), the nine large, stone-lined suites at this inn come with king-sized four-poster beds, cable TV, air-con, lockbox, Jacuzzi tubs, gobs of Asian textiles and Japanese names such as 'Shogun.' (Cue the zither music.) Several smaller doubles have simple decor and ceiling fans. To complete the mood, there's the recommended Lotus Garden Restaurant.

Coco Loco Lodge (☎ 2750-0281; www.cocolocolodge.com; 2-person r/bungalow/apt US$45/50/60; P 📶) You'll find various accommodations at this quiet, Austrian-run hotel southwest of the soccer field. The most charming of these are the palm-thatched bungalows, equipped with shining wood floors, minifridge and coffee makers. All of these have private terraces with hammocks, offering views of the expansive garden. Credit cards accepted.

El Pizote Lodge (☎ 2750-0227; d/q US$50/70, bungalows US$70/90; P ❄ 🏊) On a quiet back road about 500m west of town, this mellow hotel popular with Tico families is about a

PUERTO VIEJO: ¡NO A LA MARINA!

Drive around the Puerto Viejo area and you are bound to see signs that read, *¡No a la marina!* These refer to a proposed US$40 million, 398-slip marina proposed by a consortium of US and Costa Rican investors. The plan – which would lay waste to the famous Salsa Brava surf break (see boxed text, p481) – would include two breakwaters, a shopping center and a yacht maintenance center.

There is staunch local opposition to the project (hence the signs) – including Bribrí leaders, who have publicly decried the idea because of its possible cultural and environmental impact. In addition, some local activists are concerned that a marina would consume vast amounts of freshwater for the purpose of boat maintenance – at a time when the area (and the country) is struggling with freshwater shortages.

For now, with the global economy sputtering along – and tourism down on all fronts – the project appears to be on hold. There's no telling, however, when the idea could be resurrected. Watch this space…

10-minute walk from the village. Standard rooms are basic wooden *cabinas* with bathrooms and a shared deck, while more private concrete bungalows come with terraces, minifridge, coffee maker and toaster. There is both an adult and children's pool as well as a restaurant. Credit cards accepted.

Agapi (☎ 2750-0446; www.agapisite.com; d standard/apt US$60/80, additional person US$10; P) In a prime seaside location east of town, this sweet 18-room spot with a lovingly tended garden is run by a friendly Greek-Tica couple. Simple units vary in size and configuration, from wood-paneled cabins to spacious apartments with ocean views. Grown-ups will love the free-form mosaic pool and outdoor Jacuzzi, while the tykes will go crazy in the brand new kiddie splash pool. Breakfast and bicycle rental are available for an additional charge. Credit cards accepted.

our pick **Banana Azul** (☎ 2750-2035; www.bananaazul.com; d incl breakfast US$69-94, 2-person apt US$129; P) Lost in the jungle at the far end of Playa Negra this wonderfully wild hotel run by Roberto Vreña and Colin Brownlee sits at the edge of a blissfully tranquil black-sand beach. The 13 rooms are all done up in the finest jungle chic: shining wooden floors, white linens, mosquito nets and private decks with views – as well as graceful touches such as bromeliads in the showers. There is a two-bedroom apartment that comes stocked with private decks and a small fish pond. An onsite restaurant-bar serves light meals and snacks, as well as sensational fruity cocktails, ideal for sipping by the free-form pool. No children under 15; credit cards accepted.

Escape Caribeño (☎ 2750-0103; www.escapecaribeno.com; d with/without ocean view US$80/70, additional person US$15; P) Charming Italian owners keep 14 spic-and-span bungalows with spotless bathrooms, some of which lie close to the beach and others of which are set back into a tidy garden. More expensive units are in lovely Caribbean-style structures, but all of them have stocked minifridges, cable TV, fans and, most importantly, hammocks. Breakfast is available with advance reservation. Credit cards accepted.

Blue Conga Hotel (☎ 2750-0681; www.bluecongacr.com; d/tr incl breakfast US$80/90; P) A graceful new B&B east of town has 10 sparkling rooms in a tropical-style building, all of which are named after local flora. Airy units have high ceilings, clerestory windows, canopy beds with mosquito nets, handcrafted lamps, private terraces, as well as plenty of tables to sit at and hammocks to lounge in. Breakfast is served in a large open-air *rancho* facing a beautifully tended garden. Credit cards accepted. Recommended.

Samasati Retreat Center (☎ 2750-0315, in USA 800-563-9643; www.samasati.com; per person guesthouse/bungalow incl 3 meals from US$85/135; P V) Set on a hillside 8km west of Puerto Viejo, this attractive yoga retreat center has sweeping views of the coast as well as nine wooden bungalows with wraparound screened windows and a guesthouse stocked with single beds (for solo travelers on a budget). Meals are vegetarian, with an organic focus (including organic chocolate cake) and are served buffet-style on a terrace with views. Hiking trails lead from the lodge into the hills and guided trips can be arranged. Rates are all based on double occupancy.

Cashew Hill Jungle Cottages (☎ 2750-0001; www.cashewhilllodge.co.cr; 1-/2-/3-bedroom cottages

US$90/110/150; (P) (wi-fi) (pool) (child-friendly)) Set on a lush hillside studded with pre-Columbian style statuary, the seven cottages at this lovely, family-friendly jungle spot are bright, colorful and comfortable. The wood houses are painted in vivid shades and come with full kitchens, loft-style sleeping areas and charming rustic touches such as shell-encrusted sinks. All of the units have private decks or patios stocked with comfy chairs and hammocks, while one two-bedroom cabin offers exquisite ocean views. It's a bit of a trek from town, but it's worth it. Credit cards accepted.

Eating

With what is perhaps the most impressive restaurant scene on the coast, Puerto Viejo has the cure for *casado* overkill.

BUDGET

Café Rico (coffee from ₡800; 8am-4pm) Dark, rich coffee – iced, even – is served alongside light breakfasts and lunches. Bonus: you earn yourself a free mug by doing your laundry (₡3500 for 4kg) onsite. Also on offer: beach cruisers, snorkel gear and 'conspiracy consultations.' (Just ask.)

Veronica's Place (2750-0132; dishes ₡1200-3200; 7am-9pm Sun-Thu, until 4:30pm Fri; (V)) A delightful vegetarian cafe offers fresh, healthy interpretations of Caribbean food, using fresh fruits and vegetables, as well as soy products. Veronica rents cabins and has a macrobiotic health food store onsite.

Pan Pay (2750-0081; dishes ₡1500-2800; 7am-7pm) This popular beachside spot is excellent for strong coffee, fresh baked goods and hearty wedges of fluffy Spanish omelet served with crisp tomato-bread. There are sandwiches and other light meals, but it's thoughts of their flaky chocolate croissants that make us want to jump out of bed in the morning.

Soda Tamara (2750-0148; breakfast ₡1500-2800, seafood mains ₡4200-4800; 7am-10pm) With its signature red, green and yellow paint job, this is a popular spot to grab breakfast and watch the village wake up. During the day seafood is the specialty, but don't miss out on the moist coconut bread. Yum!

Bread & Chocolate (8830-3223; breakfast ₡1500-3800; 6:30am-6:30pm Wed-Sat, 6:30am-2:30pm Sun; (V)) This cafe invites early risers to sit on the spacious, covered porch, sip fresh-brewed coffee and chill. Favorites include old-school oatmeal, fluffy omelets and crunchy granola and yogurt.

Cafetería Gaudí Sushi Bar (dishes ₡2000-4000; 7-11am & 5-11pm) A pleasant blue-and-white painted spot on a quiet side road has a menu stocked with Japanese-influenced specialties, including sushi, rice noodles and tuna tataki. Breakfast is served as well.

our pick **Soda Mirna** (mains ₡2200-3500; noon-10pm) This humble little *soda* on the main drag offers excellent people-watching and highly tasty (and inexpensive) Caribbean-style dishes. Try the smoked pork chops with marinated onions or the zesty stewed chicken served with rice and beans – and whatever you do, don't forget to sample the fiery homemade hot sauce.

EZ-Times (mains ₡2800-5600; 10am-2:30am) The reggae music and groovy vibe lure in hungry beach bums for pizza, pasta and salads. The outdoor terrace is a good place to sit back and enjoy the munchies, not to mention the live music on Friday nights.

@E's (2750-0657; mains ₡3000-4200; 7:30am-11pm) The restaurant and bar at Rocking J's is much more than just a travelers hang-out. Run by a Cordon Bleu–trained chef, Eric, the menu is a pan-everything fusion of Thai, Mexican and US cuisine – covering the gamut from burgers to stir-fries as well as fancier dishes, like seared marlin.

Other excellent places for Caribbean cooking are **Soda Miss Sam** (2750-0108; dishes ₡1000-8000) and **Miss Lidia's Place** (2750-0598; dishes ₡1000-10,000; 9am-9pm), local favorites that dish up plenty of spicy coconut sauce. Red snapper dishes cost ₡8000 and lobster in garlic will set you back ₡20,000. Both ladies have been around for years, pleasing the palates and satisfying the stomachs of locals and tourists alike.

The best spot for groceries is **Old Harbour Supermarket** (6:30am-8:30pm). Don't miss the weekly **Organic Market** (6am-6pm Sat), when area vendors and growers sell snacks typical of the region.

MIDRANGE

Chile Rojo (2750-0025; chilerojopuertoviejo.com; mains ₡2800-7500; noon-10pm; (V)) If you are craving a little Asian fusion, head to this trendy, 2nd-storey spot that offers excellent views of the main drag (ideal at sunset). Here you'll find everything from sushi to Thai curries to Indian samosas stuffed full

CARIBBEAN COAST

of veggies. Arrive early in the evening for wallet-friendly two-for-one beer specials.

Lotus Garden Restaurant (mains ₡3000-7800; 7am-11pm) Serving a mix of sushi, noodles and stir-fries, this pleasant garden restaurant is a good spot if you are in the mood for something Asian.

ourpick **El Loco Natural** (2750-0530; meals ₡3200-9000; 5-10pm Wed-Mon; V) A pleasant candle-lit patio cafe located 200m east of town serves up creative fusion cuisine, combining elements of Caribbean, Indian, Mexican and Thai cooking. Steamed spicy mussels in red-curry sauce and tandoori chicken in coconut are just a couple of standouts. But if you really want to give your tastebuds a joy ride, try the exquisite fish tacos – excellent with an icy *guaro* sour (₡2800) from the bar. Owner and chef Stash Golas is a rock star in the kitchen and an artist to boot. There is an encyclopedic list of vegetarian items (with Friday nights featuring additional vegan specialties). Do not miss.

Beach Hut (2750-0895; mains from ₡4000; noon-midnight) A lovely yellow-and-blue garden restaurant on the east end of the village with stellar views of the Salsa Brava and highly recommended fusion cuisine (think: tuna with wasabi, ratatouille and poached pears in chocolate sauce). It is very popular with locals and travelers alike – promising its customers 'love at first bite.'

Restaurant Salsa Brava (2750-0241; mains ₡4400-10,000; noon-10pm) A recommended hot spot specializes in fresh seafood and open-grill cooking. The ever-popular 'juice joint' is an oasis for thirsty beachcombers and the sangria is refreshingly good, too.

Amimodo Caribe Restaurant (2750-0257; meals ₡4700-14,500; 4-10pm Mon-Thu, noon-10pm Fri-Sun; V) Listen to the waves crash at this local Italian favorite, where you can chow down on pizzas and homemade pasta dishes – such as lobster spaghetti (₡14,500). A cheaper 'surfing menu' (₡3800) features carb-heavy specialties such as fish and chips and chicken-fried steak with rice.

TOP END

Koki Beach (2275-0902; www.kokibeach.com; meals ₡5500-13,000; 2pm-midnight Wed-Sun) Doing its best to channel Miami Beach, this sleek spot cranking reggae-lite classics has fruit-colored paper lanterns and Adirondack chairs that face the ocean from an elevated wooden platform. There's a decent selection of Peruvian-inflected *ceviches,* meat and seafood dishes as well as some watery cocktails. If you're going to snack, the yucca chips and guacamole are quite good.

Café Viejo (2750-0817; mains ₡5000-16,000; noon-close) A pricey, sceney Mediterranean lounge and restaurant that gets good marks for fresh pastas, tasty pizzas and fancy cocktails. The upscale, romantic ambience makes it a safe bet for important dates – and its location right on the main drag makes for excellent people-watching.

Drinking

Restaurants often metamorphose into rollicking bar scenes after the tables are cleared. For excellent people-watching over beer, try Soda Tamara. If you want to see and be seen, hit Koki Beach or Café Viejo.

Tex-Mex (6am-2am) A rowdy open-air bar on the main drag has live music, pool tables and movies on big screens playing most nights. Minty mojitos and Bloody Marys made with fresh tomato juice make this a popular place.

Baba Yaga (8388-4359) Go on Tuesday for ladies' night, Sunday for reggae night.

Entertainment

There is plenty to do after the sun goes down – including drink, dance and drink some more.

CINEMA

Jungle Internet (p479) plays outdoor movies on the street on most nights after sunset. Pop in during the day to find out what's playing.

LIVE MUSIC & DANCING

Maritza's Bar (2750-0003) This nonfancy local spot has regular live bands and DJs that play reggae, rock and salsa, and all the funky beats in between. If you're lucky, you might just hear a reggae version of the Cuban classic *Guantanamera.*

Johnny's Place (1pm-3am) A Puerto Viejo institution, where DJs spin reggaetón, hip hop and salsa to a mix of locals and travelers who take up the dance floor and surround the late-night beach bonfires outside.

El Parquecito (7pm-midnight) On the other side of town, this pleasant outdoor lounge features jamming weekend bands that play reggae and calypso classics – among many other things.

Shopping

Makeshift stalls clutter the main road, selling all manner of knick-knacks and Rasta-colored accoutrement. For finer crafts, try **Lulu Berlu Gallery** (☎ 2750-0394; 9am-9pm), which carries folk art, one-of-a-kind clothing and mosaic mirrors, among many other items.

Getting There & Away

All public buses arrive and depart from the bus stop half a block southwest of Maritza's Bar. **Grayline** (☎ 2262-3681; www.graylinecostarica.com) runs a private daily bus service departing Puerto Viejo at roughly 2:15pm bound for San José (US$35). Reserve ahead.

Bribrí/Sixaola ₡1100; 30 minutes/1½ hours; departs roughly every hour from 6:30am to 7:30pm.

Cahuita/Puerto Limón ₡400; 30 minutes/1½ hours; departs roughly every hour from 5:30am to 7:30pm.

Manzanillo ₡400; 30 minutes; departs 7:30am, noon, 4:30pm and 7:30pm.

San José ₡4100; five hours; departs 7:30am, 9am, 11am and 4pm.

Getting Around

A bicycle is a fine way to get around town, and pedaling out to other beaches east of Puerto Viejo is one of the highlights of this corner of Costa Rica. You'll find rentals all over town (in addition to many hotels):

Freedom Motorsport (☎ 2750-0728; per half-day US$55; 8am-5pm) Motorized four-wheelers for rent seven days a week.

Tienda Marcos (☎ 2750-0303; bicycles per day US$5; 8:30am-5pm)

Tuanis Bike Rental (bicycles per half-/full-day US$4/5; 7am-6pm)

PUERTO VIEJO TO PUNTA UVA

A 13km road winds east from Puerto Viejo, through rows of coconut palms, alongside coastal lodges and through lush lowland rainforest before coming to a dead end at the sleepy town of Manzanillo. The road was paved for the first time in 2003 – dramatically shortening the amount of time it took to drive or cycle the route. The weather and buses, however, have since done a number on the tarmac and it is now an extravaganza of crater-sized potholes. (Take your time driving, unless you want to lose an axle.)

If you want to stay close to Puerto Viejo while having access to a nice beach, Playa Cocles has a good mix of isolation and amenities, offering a wide variety of places to stay and eat. After that, the pickings get thin until you get closer to Punta Uva, where you'll find a cluster of lodges and restaurants – as well as one of the prettiest beaches in the region.

Buses heading from Puerto Viejo to Manzanillo will drop you at any of these places along the way.

Sights

Admittedly, **Echo Books** (11am-6pm Fri-Tue;) is a strange place for a bookstore – buried in the jungle off the main road – but this tiny store (really the 1st floor of a private home) has a decent selection of used paperbacks, including literature and nonfiction. It also has air-con, sweets and excellent coffee.

The **Mariposario Punta Uva** (☎ 2750-0086; adult/child under 6 US$5/free; 8am-4pm) in Punta Uva is more of a butterfly-breeding center than a tourist attraction (though it does have wonderful ocean views). Some 70 species of butterfly are bred annually, including four species that the staff says exist in captivity nowhere else in the world. What you'll see depends on the time of year. Bilingual guided tours are available.

Nearby, the **Crazy Monkey Canopy Tour** (☎ 2759-9057/56, in USA 800-317-4108; www.crazymonkeycanopytour.com; per person US$40; 8am-2pm), affiliated with Punta Uva's Almonds and Corals Lodge, will zip you through the tree-tops from rainforest to beach. Staff can arrange transport to and from Puerto Viejo for an extra US$10.

Activities

The region's biggest draws involve surf, sand, wildlife-watching and attempts to get a decent tan between downpours. **Playa Cocles** is known for its great surfing and organized lifeguard system, which helps offset the dangers of the frequent riptides, while **Punta Uva** features the best and safest beaches for swimming.

In Playa Chiquita, find the **Jaguar Centro de Rescate** (☎ 2750-0710; www.jaguarrescue.com; admission US$10; 9:30-11:30am), a grassroots animal-rescue center founded by a Spanish zoologist.

For all manner of underwater excursions, check in with the **Punta Uva Dive Center** (☎ 2759-9191; www.puntauvadivecenter.com; 1-tank dives from US$60), which can set you up with snorkels and scuba equipment. It is located at the first turn-off into Punta Uva.

INDIGENOUS COMMUNITIES IN THE SOUTHERN CARIBBEAN

The area is home to a number of thriving indigenous communities, many of which can be visited by travelers. Brush up on a little local knowledge first:

Bribrí & Cabécar

At least two indigenous groups occupied the territory on the Caribbean side of the country from pre-Columbian times. The Bribrí tended to inhabit lowland areas, while the Cabécar made their home high in the Talamanca Mountains. Over the last century, members of both ethnic groups have migrated to the Pacific side. But many have stayed on the coast, inter-marrying with Jamaican immigrants and even working in the banana industry. Today the Bribrí tend to be more acculturated, while the Cabécar are more isolated.

The groups have distinct languages (which are preserved to some degree), though they share similar architecture, weapons and canoe style. They also share the spiritual belief that the planet – and the flora and fauna contained within it – are gifts from Sibö, or God. *Taking Care of Sibö's Gifts*, by Juanita Sánchez, Gloria Mayorga and Paula Palmer, is a remarkable record of Bribrí oral history.

Visiting Indigenous Communities

There are several reserves on the Caribbean slopes of the Cordillera de Talamanca, including the Talamanca Cabécar territory (which is more difficult to visit) and the Bribrí territory, where locals are more equipped to handle visitors.

The most interesting destination is **Yorkín**, in the Reserva Indígena Yorkín (it's a long trip, so it's best to spend the night). While you are there, you can meet with a local women's artisan group, **Mujeres Artesanas Stibrawpa** (☎ 2248-9470, in USA 866-393-5899; artesanasdeyorkin.org; day trips from US$74), who offer demonstrations in roof thatching, cooking and basket-weaving (the latter of which provides plenty of fine examples for purchase). The group organizes all manner of day trips and can arrange for pick-up in San José, though it may be easier to make arrangements at **ATEC** (☎ 2750-0191/398; www.greencoast.com/atec.htm; 🕒 8am-9pm), right in Puerto Viejo. It's a rewarding trip, but it's not easy to get there (part of the trip is by canoe).

Alternately, you can visit the larger, modern village of **Shiroles**, about 20km west of Bribrí, where you can observe and participate in local chocolate production. ATEC organizes half-day tours to the area (from US$35). The agency also organizes visits to an iguana farm (from US$25) on the KéköLdi territory (this is a tiny ethnicity related to the Bribrí). Other more vigorous excursions – with hiking and bird-watching – are also available.

Note: it is not recommended to visit these territories independently. Not only are some spots difficult to reach, in most cases, villages do not have the infrastructure to accommodate streams of tourists. Overnight stays should to be arranged in advance. Please be respectful – these are people's private homes and workspaces, not tourist attractions.

Sleeping & Eating

All of the places below are listed from west (Puerto Viejo) to east (Punta Uva). Accommodations have hot water, unless otherwise noted. Note that some restaurants may have reduced hours or close down entirely during the low season.

PLAYA COCLES

A broad stretch of white-sand beach lies just 1.5km east of Puerto Viejo – offering proximity to the village and its many restaurants – but plenty of peace and quiet, too.

Cabinas El Tesoro (☎ 2750-0128; www.puertoviejo.net/cabinaselteroro.htm; dm US$7, d standard US$48-80, d executive US$64-100, bungalows from US$48; P ✈ 💻 📶) The rooms are rather dim, but they are clean and the location is excellent – especially for the surfer set. Located right on the beach break at Playa Cocles, the 12 simple units have tile floors, queen beds with floral spreads and cable TV. Private bungalows can accommodate up to 11 people. Next door, you'll find bikes and surfboards for rent. The small open-air bar hosts grooving live music jams on Wednesdays. Credit cards accepted.

La Isla Inn (☎ 2750-0109; www.laislainn.com; d with/without air-con US$96/68; P ✈ 📶 🏊) Opposite the lifeguard tower at the main hub of the beach lies this functional wooden lodge with

CARIBBEAN COAST

12 expansive rooms, all of which are equipped with safes, cable TV and handmade wood furnishings crafted from the slightly curved outer boards that are discarded during lumber processing. The service is efficient and there is a pool that faces the ocean. Credit cards accepted.

our pick **Totem** (☎ 2750-0758; www.totemhotelresort.com; d with/without air-con US$90/80, junior ste/2-room ste US$90/110, additional person US$18, all incl breakfast; P) Just beyond La Isla – and just steps from the beach – you'll find this smartly decorated 20-room inn set back into a lush, tropical garden. Rooms are painted in soothing colors, decked out with bamboo furnishings, folk-art touches, and spotless bathrooms clad in earth-tone ceramic tile. Nicer suites (one of which is wheelchair-accessible) are even roomier – with a couple that open straight out on the pool. There is a surf shop, board rentals and the beachfront Osteria (mains ₡3500 to ₡6000), an Italian restaurant serving tasty pasta dishes. Credit cards accepted; no charge for children under 12.

Cariblue (☎ 2750-0035/0518; www.cariblue.com; d standard/deluxe/superior US$95/110/120, additional person US$30, all incl breakfast; P) Set in lovely gardens (with labeled plants for the botanically curious), this popular family spot has a mix of 22 individual rooms and bungalows (some with air-con), all of which are crisply painted, with hardwood accents, bright linens and private decks equipped with hammocks and easy chairs. There is a pool table, an open-air lounge and a lovely mosaic pool, complete with swim-up bar. Credit cards accepted.

Cabinas Garibaldi (☎ 2750-0101; d/tr US$30/40, d with kitchenette US$40; P) A basic surfer crash pad – and the cheapest stay in the area – offers a row of reasonably clean *cabinas* that share a porch with sea views. The waves are right across the street.

Azania Bungalows (☎ 2750-0540; www.azania-costarica.com; d incl breakfast US$85, additional person US$20; P) Ten spacious but dark thatch-roofed bungalows are brightened up by colorful linens at this charming inn set on landscaped jungle grounds. Nice details including woven bedspreads, well-designed bathrooms and wide-plank hardwood floors. Plus, some units sleep up to four. You'll find a free-form pool and a hot tub nestled into the greenery, as well as an Argentine restaurant and bar. Credit cards accepted.

La Costa de Papito (☎ 2750-0704; www.lacostadepapito.com; d incl breakfast US$89, additional person US$13; P) Relax in rustic comfort in the sculpture-studded grounds at this popular Cocles outpost, which has wood and bamboo bungalows decked out with hand-carved furniture, stone bathrooms straight out of *The Flintstones* and roomy porches draped with hammocks. The Que Rico Papito Restaurant (mains US$9 to US$15) serves Italian-influenced specialties – and for an extra US$8 per day can arrange to have breakfast delivered to your room. At the entrance, find the rustic, palm-thatched Pure Jungle Spa (☎ 2750-0536; www.purejunglespa.com; one-hour massage US$70), which offers massages, exfoliating treatments and facials using hand-mixed local products.

El Tucán Jungle Lodge (☎ 2750-0026; www.eltucanjunglelodge.com; s/d/tr incl breakfast US$45/60/70; P) You may wonder if you missed the turn, as you follow the signs in search of this little lodge on the banks of the Caño Negro; it's only 1km off the road, but it feels miles from anywhere – making it ideal for bird-watchers. Four super-clean wooden *cabinas* buried in the forest have bright linens and share a broad patio with hammocks. The welcoming German owner organizes walks in the area.

Hotel Yaré (☎ 2750-0106; www.hotelyare.com; s/d US$41/58, d bungalow US$70; P) Facing the soccer field, a network of elevated walkways lead through a marshy jungle filled with croaking frogs to one of 22 private rooms and bungalows at this locally run spot. The units are somewhat worn, but clean; more expensive rooms with kitchens are best. Credit cards accepted.

our pick **La Pecora Nera** (☎ 2750-0490; mains ₡5600-15,000; 5pm-close Tue-Sun; V) If you splurge for a single fancy meal during your trip, do it here. A lovely, candle-lit patio off the main road is home to this romantic eatery run by Tuscan-born Ilario Giannoni and serving deftly prepared Italian seafood and pasta dishes, such as tender handmade ravioli filled with pumpkin and shrimp. A must-have: the delicate *carpaccio di carambola,* transparent slices of starfruit topped with shrimp, tomatoes and balsamic vinaigrette. And, for dessert, don't miss the profiteroles, layered with homemade vanilla ice-cream and doused in a rich chocolate sauce. There is an extensive wine list (from ₡8000 a bottle), but you can't go wrong with the well-chosen and relatively inexpensive house wines.

Gatta Ci Cova (sandwiches ₡3000-5500, mains ₡4000-5500; noon-10pm Tue-Sun; V) Right next door, and also run by Giannoni, is this informal 2nd-story trattoria cooking up basic Italian dishes. The pizzas are forgettable, but the *paninis* (pressed sandwiches) are excellent, served on fresh Tuscan bread and brimming with ingredients such as mozzarella and salami. A new ground-floor bar and lounge (open from 4pm to midnight) has drinks and light snacks.

Le Cameleon (2750-0501; www.lecameleonhotel.com; d from US$200; P) In a super-sleek structure that seems to have been airlifted straight from West Hollywood, this trendy new boutique inn has 23 all-white rooms accented by colorful throw pillows. Units all have air-con and are stocked with all the requisite high-end goodies and services. There is a pool and an uber-contemporary restaurant-lounge that serves so-so cocktails and fusion cuisine. It's not on the beach, but a private beach club keeps patrons plied with lounge chairs and cold drinks. Credit cards accepted.

PLAYA CHIQUITA

It isn't exactly clear where Playa Cocles ends and Playa Chiquita begins, but conventional wisdom applies the name to a series of beaches 4km to 6km east of Puerto Viejo.

Villas del Caribe (2750-0202, in San José 2233-2200; www.villasdelcaribe.com; d standard/junior villa/villa US$89/99/119; P) Lovely, brightly painted rooms have comfortable beds, sitting areas, roomy bathrooms with Spanish tile and air-con. More expensive junior villas also come with toasters, microwave ovens and coffee makers, while the two-storey villas have ocean views, king-sized beds, kitchens and BBQ. All have private decks with hammocks. Credit cards accepted.

Aguas Claras (2750-0131; www.aguasclaras-cr.com; 1-/2-/3-room cottages from US$70/130/220; P) Five tropical Victorian cottages painted in bright, candy colors have fully equipped kitchens and easy access to the beach. The delightful gazebo out front is Miss Holly's Kitchen (breakfast ₡3800; open from 8am to 4pm), which serves breakfast (think French toast and tropical fruit), sandwiches and baked goods.

Cabinas Slothclub (2750-0358; d US$50; P) The best and only budget option along Playa Chiquita: five simple, clean wooden cabins have great views, beach access and a snorkeling reef out the front. These little places often attract long-term renters, so call in advance.

Kashá (2750-0205, in USA 800-521-5200; www.costarica-hotelkasha.com; d/tr/q US$90/120/140, s/d bungalows with air-con US$90/110, all incl breakfast; P) Simple wood bungalows with whitewashed interiors are somewhat basic given the prices. All-inclusive packages are available. The on-site restaurant, Magic Ginger (mains ₡3900 to ₡7200; open from noon to 2pm and from 6pm to 10pm Monday to Saturday), is well recommended for global fusion specialties, including seared tuna and spicy Jamaican-style pork.

Miraflores Lodge (2750-0038; www.mirafloreslodge.com; d incl breakfast US$30-60) You'll find a mix of 10 rooms with various configurations spread out over a couple of structures at this simple, homey spot run by long-time resident Pamela Carpenter, an expert on botany and medicinal plants. (Check out the garden labyrinth.) Upstairs rooms are best, with garden views, and a small open-air lounge has a library. Breakfast includes seasonal fruits grown on the grounds.

Jungle Love Garden Café (2750-0162; meals ₡4300-6500; 5-9.30pm Tue-Sun; V) American bohemian meets the Caribbean at this popular porch-front cafe that serves fusion dishes such as mango chicken with cilantro, creamy shrimp pasta with brandy and an eponymous Jungle Love Milkshake, a very grown-up blend of Bailey's, *guaro* and local ice cream. The menu has veggie options and vegan items can be prepared on request. There are only eight tables; reserve ahead.

C&J Marketplace (2750-0904; www.candjcostarica.com; s/d/tr/q US$25/50/75/100; P) A small supermarket and juice joint (perfect for fresh-made juice) also has a handful of clean, wood *cabinas* on offer at wallet-friendly rates.

Playa Chiquita Lodge (2750-0408; www.playachiquitalodge.com; d incl breakfast US$60; P) A row of eight brightly painted wooden cabins are slightly worn, but come with bathrooms (with questionable water pressure) and a broad deck equipped with hammocks. Though not on the beach, this hotel has direct access – a short 200m walk through the forest to get there. Credit cards accepted.

Shawandha Lodge (2750-0018; www.shawandhalodge.com; d incl breakfast US$105; P) Run by the wonderfully serene and stylish Mako, this upscale lodge has 13 private, spacious, demure bungalows painted in soothing earth tones and equipped with expansive mosaic-tiled bathrooms, each of which boasts a different natural theme. A meticulously maintained thatched *rancho* serves as an open-air lounge (perfect for cocktails) and the French-Caribbean restaurant (mains ₡6900 to ₡8600; open from 7am to 9:30pm) serves fusion dishes such as ginger sea bass cooked in banana leaves. Credit cards accepted.

PUNTA UVA

Punta Uva is known for the region's most swimmable beaches, each lovelier than the next. Don't miss the turnoff to the point, about 7km east of Puerto Viejo.

our pick **Costa Rica Tree House Lodge** (☎ 2750-0706; www.costaricatreehouse.com; d from US$200-390, extra person US$50; P) For adventurers that like their lodgings rustic and whimsical, this wonderful spot run by energetic former economist Edsart Besier is the place for you. Five units of various sizes dot four jungle-filled hectares, including a literal 'tree house' – a two-storey cabin built around the base of a living sangrillo tree. All are open-air and come equipped with mosquito nets, kitchens, BBQs and spacious decks with easy chairs and hammocks. Each unit has a private path that leads to a small, white-sand beach. Proceeds support an iguana breeding program; credit cards accepted.

Itaitá Villas (☎ 2750-0414; www.costaricaitaitavillas.com; d incl breakfast US$85-145; P) Eight bright green-and-yellow wood *cabinas* with no-nonsense rooms are nestled into the forest along the beach. Units each come with a small outdoor kitchen and deck, as well as a safe. A few rooms accommodate four people. Credit cards accepted.

Selvin's Restaurant (mains ₡2800-8000; 8am-8pm Wed-Sun) Selvin is a member of the extensive Brown family, noted for their charm, and his place is considered one of the region's best, specializing in shrimp, lobster and a succulent chicken *caribeño* (chicken stewed in a spicy Caribbean sauce).

Casa Viva (☎ 2750-0089; www.puntauva.net; d per night/week from US$100/600; P) Enormous well-constructed, fully furnished hardwood houses, each with tiled shower, kitchen and wraparound veranda, are set on a property that fronts the beach – an ideal spot in which to chill out in a hammock and observe the local wildlife.

Arrecife Restaurant (☎ 2759-9200; www.arrecifepuntauva.net; mains ₡3500-8000; 8am-10pm) Located on the second turn-off into Punta Uva, this popular beachside restaurant attracts expats and locals for a mix of Tico and international specialties, including tasty looking sandwiches. It also rents a few tiled *cabinas* (doubles US$60) with tiled floors and bathrooms.

Cabinas Angela (☎ 2759-9092; r per person US$10) The lap of luxury, it isn't. But if you're counting colones and *have* to be near the beach, these bare-bones, super basic, adequately clean *cabinas* with cool-water showers will probably do just fine. It's about 100m to the east of Arrecife Restaurant.

Korrigan Lodge (☎ 2759-9103; www.korriganlodge.com; d incl breakfast US$70; P) Four beautiful wood and concrete bungalows are topped with thatched roofs and nestled into a patch of lush jungle. All units have minibar, safe, modern bathrooms and private terraces with hammocks, plus all guests have access to free bikes. Breakfast is served in an open-air *rancho* surrounded by gardens. Credit cards accepted.

El Colibrí Lodge (☎ 2759-9036; www.elcolibrilodge.com; d/tr incl breakfast US$65/85, 2-bedroom house US$150; P) Perfect for couples and small families, you'll find four gracious, well-tended rooms with private terraces at this lovely, locally run spot nestled into the rainforest – ideal for wildlife-watching. Breakfast is served on the terrace or in the privacy of your room. A 300m trail winds through the rainforest to the beach. Recommended.

Almonds & Corals Lodge (☎ 2759-9057/56, in San José 2272-2024; www.almondsandcorals.com; s/d US$235/300, s/d master ste US$315/400, additional child/adult from US$40/93, all incl breakfast & dinner; P) Buried deep in the woods, this long-time luxury spot popular with honeymooners has 24 sparkling wood suites of various sizes with four-poster beds, Jacuzzi tubs and private patios with hammocks. Rooms are screened-in, making them comfortable, but you'll still be able to enjoy the nightly serenade of insects and frogs. Meals are served family-style in an open-air dining room. Credit cards accepted.

MANZANILLO

The idyllic little village of Manzanillo has long been an off-the-beaten-track destination. Despite the fact that the paved roads arrived in 2003, this little town remains a vibrant outpost of Afro-Caribbean culture. It has also remained pristine – thanks to the

1985 establishment of the Refugio Nacional de Vida Silvestre Gandoca-Manzanillo, which includes the village and imposes strict regulations on development of the region.

Activities are of a simple nature: there are fine opportunities to hike, snorkel and kayak – depending on the swells. (As with other parts, ask about riptides before heading out.) Other than that, the rowdiest scene you might come across is the sight of children playing ball in the street. Not that there aren't occasional parties – courtesy of the locally renowned Maxi's bar and restaurant, which lies in view of the water at the end of the road. This is where all buses to Manzanillo arrive.

Information

Aquamor Talamanca Adventures(☎ 2759-9012, 8835-6041; www.greencoast.com/aquamor.htm, www.costacetacea.com; 1-hr beach dive US$25, 2-tank boat dive from US$59) In addition to organizing scuba excursions, this reputable long-time outfit run by marine biologist Shawn Larkin and his wife Vanessa Schot is an excellent source of information on the refuge, the environment and the community. (Don't let the gringo looks fool you: Larkin is half-Tico.) He also organizes dolphin-watching trips (US$40), kayak fishing excursions (US$30) and rents snorkel gear (per hour US$3). Highly recommended.

Casa de Guías (☎ 2759-9064) Opposite the Minae (Ministry of Environment and Energy) office, on the way into town, this small operation provides information on local guides, as well as internet access (per hour ₡1500). Ask about camping onsite.

Sleeping & Eating

The following hotels have hot water, unless otherwise noted, and are listed from east to west.

Maxi's Cabinas (☎ 2759-9042/9061/9073; r with/without air-con US$50/35; P) This family-owned standard-bearer close to the entrance of the park has half a dozen functional *cabinas* with clean, ceramic tile floors, minifridge, bathrooms and hot-water showers. Expect some noise from the bar on party nights.

Cabinas Something Different (☎ 2759-9014/97; d from US$35; P) About 200m south of Aquamor, you'll find 18 simple *cabinas* named after local fauna. Rooms are equipped with minifridge and the welcoming owners can help organize tours.

Cabinas Las Veraneras (☎ 2759-9050; d from US$30; P) About 100m off the main drag, these 13 clean, simple *cabinas* smell of disinfectant. They are all equipped with TVs and hot water. The pleasant *soda* (breakfast ₡1800, mains ₡2200 to ₡5000) serves Caribbean and Tico standards.

our pick **Cabinas Manzanillo** (☎ 2759-9033, 8839-8386; d/tr US$20/30; P) Run by the ever-helpful Sandra Castillo and Pablo Bustamante, these eight *cabinas* on the western end of town are so spic and span, you could eat off the shining tile floors. Rooms have big beds and are painted bright pastel colors, with industrial-strength ceiling fans and spacious bathrooms. Ask about discounts for extended stays. From Maxi's, travel 300m along the main road in the direction of Punta Uva, then make a left onto the dirt road that leads to the southern part of town. Do not confuse with the dilapidated Hotel Manzanillo on the beach.

Cabinas Bucus (☎ 2759-9143; www.costa-rica-manzanillo.com; s US$20, d US$25-30; P) Four tidy, brightly painted tiled rooms in a two-storey mustard-yellow structure have mosquito nets and private bathrooms – and share a small kitchen with coffee maker and hot plate. Find them just beyond Cabinas Manzanillo. Omar, one of the co-owners, is one of Manzanillo's top guides.

Congo Bongo (☎ 2759-9016; www.congo-bongo.com; d/tr/q US$125/150/175, per week US$750/900/1050; P) Just outside of town, on the road to Punta Uva, you'll find six charming wooden cottages set in a reclaimed cacao plantation (now dense forest). They offer fully equipped kitchens and plenty of living space, including open-air terraces and strategically placed hammocks that are perfect for spying on the wildlife. A network of trails leads through the six hectares of grounds to the beautiful beach.

Maxi's Restaurant (mains ₡2500-21,000, lobster from ₡9000; 6am-close; V) The most famous restaurant in Manzanillo attracts travelers from all over for large platters of tender, grilled seafood, whole red snappers *(pargo rojo)*, steaks and Caribbean-style lobsters (the latter are expensive and not necessarily worth it). It also serves veggie grills and *casados*. Despite the scampering tourist hordes (especially at lunch), this is still a wonderful spot for a meal and a seaside beer – and the bar can get hopping on weekends, with live music and DJs cranking out everything from R&B to reggaetón.

Two good family-operated *sodas* for cheap, tasty *casados* are **Mi Rinconcito Alegre** (casados ₡2200), right across from Aquamor, and **Soda Miskito** (casados ₡2200; 7am-9pm), which is decorated with lamps and lots of greenery.

Need a break from *casados*? Try **Oh La La** (☎ 2759-9055; ⏰ breakfast & lunch), a French cafe facing the beach that serves recommended crepes.

Getting There & Away

Buses to Manzanillo depart from Puerto Viejo (₡400, 30 minutes) at 7:30am, noon, 4:30pm and 7:30pm. They return to Puerto Viejo at 5am, 8:15am, 12:45pm and 5:15pm. These buses all continue to Puerto Limón (₡2000, 2½ hours) for onward transfers.

REFUGIO NACIONAL DE VIDA SILVESTRE GANDOCA-MANZANILLO

This little-explored **refuge** – called Regama for short – protects nearly 70% of the southern Caribbean coast, extending from Manzanillo all the way to the Panamanian border. It encompasses 50 sq km of land plus 44 sq km of marine environment. The peaceful, pristine stretch of sandy white beach is one of the area's main attractions. It's the center of village life in Manzanillo, and stretches for miles in either direction – from Punta Uva to Punta Mona in the east. Offshore, a 5-sq-km coral reef is a teeming habitat for lobster, sea fan and long-spined urchin.

Other than the village itself, and the surrounding farmland areas (these were grandfathered in when the park was created in 1985), the wildlife refuge is composed largely of rainforest. Cativo trees form the canopy, while there are many heliconia in the undergrowth. A huge, 400-hectare swamp – known as **Pantano Punta Mona** – provides a haven for waterfowl, as well as the country's most extensive collection of holillo palms and sajo trees. Beyond Punta Mona, protecting a natural oyster bank, is the only red mangrove swamp in Caribbean Costa Rica. In the nearby Río Gandoca estuary there is a spawning ground for Atlantic tarpon, and caiman and manatee have been sighted.

The variety of vegetation and the remote location of the refuge attract many tropical birds; sightings of the rare harpy eagle have been recorded here. Other birds to look out for include the red-lored parrot, the red-capped manikin and the chestnut-mandibled toucan, among hundreds of others. The area is also known for incredible raptor migrations, with more than a million birds flying overhead during autumn.

Despite the idyllic nature of the environment, there has been some political squabbling between the Minae (the government agency that administers the national parks in Costa Rica) and some local businesses over the management of the refuge. Some local operators are trying to get the village excluded from the confines of the refuge – which would open the door to increased development in the area. (In fact, unapproved constructions have already materialized – some within 50m of the high tide line, a zone in which construction is prohibited by national law.) Others oppose it. It will likely take years – and armies of lawyers – to sort the mess out.

Information

An excellent photo book on the area, with commentary in Spanish and English, is *Refugio Nacional de Vida Silvestre Gandoca-Manzanillo* by Juan José Puccí, available locally.

Minae (☎ 2759-9100; ⏰ 8am-noon & 1-4pm) is located in the green wooden house as you enter town, and generally has trail maps of the refuge.

Aquamor Talamanca Adventures and Casa de Guías (see opposite) are also good sources of information on what to do in the park.

Activities

HIKING

A coastal trail heads 5.5km east out of Manzanillo to **Punta Mona**. The first part of this path leads from Manzanillo to Tom Bay (about a 40-minute walk) is well-trammeled and clearly marked and doesn't require a guide. Once you pass Tom Bay, however, the path gets murky and it's easy to get lost – so ask about conditions before you set out or, if you're unsure, hire a guide. It's a rewarding walk – with amazing scenery, as well as excellent (and safe) swimming and snorkeling at the end.

Another more difficult 9km trail leaves from just west of Manzanillo and skirts the southern edges of the Pantano Punta Mona, continuing to the small community of **Gandoca**. This trail is not commonly walked, as most people access Punta Mona and Gandoca from the park entrance at the northern edge of the refuge, which is located on the road to Sixaola. If you want to try and hike this, be sure to hire a guide.

SNORKELING & DIVING

The undersea portion of the park cradles one of two living coral reefs in the country. Comprising five different types of coral, the reefs begin in about 1m of water and extend 5km offshore to a barrier reef that local fishers have long relied on and researchers have only recently discovered. This colorful undersea world is home to some 400 species of fish and crustaceans. **Punta Mona** is a popular destination for snorkeling, though it's a trek so you may wish to hire a boat (see below). Otherwise, you can snorkel offshore at **Manzanillo** at the eastern end of the beach (the riptide can be dangerous here; inquire about conditions before setting out).

As at Punta Uva and in Cahuita, conditions vary widely, and clarity can be adversely affected by weather changes. Visit the excellent **coral reef information center** (☎ 2759-9012, 8835-6041; www.greencoast.com/aquamor.htm, www.costacetacea.com; Aquamor Talamanca Adventures; 1-hr beach dive US$25, 2-tank boat dive from US$59, PADI certification US$350), housed at Aquamor Talamanca Adventures, where you can rent snorkeling equipment (per hour US$3) and organize dive excursions.

KAYAKING

You can explore some of the area's waterways by kayak, available from Aquamor Talamanca Adventures (per hour US$5). Paddle out to the reef, or head up the **Quebrada Home Wark**, in the west of the village, or the tiny **Simeon Creek**, at the east end of the village. These are short paddles – ideal if you've got kids.

DOLPHIN-WATCHING

In 1997 a group of local guides in Manzanillo identified tucuxi dolphins, a little-known species previously not found in Costa Rica, and began to observe their interactions with the bottlenose dolphins. A third species – the Atlantic spotted dolphin – is also common in this area. This unprecedented activity has attracted the attention of marine biologists and conservationists, who are following these animals with great interest. Learn more about this work through the **Talamanca Dolphin Foundation** (☎ 2759-0715/612; www.dolphinlink.org), a not-for-profit dedicated to the study and preservation of local dolphin populations.

Aquamor Talamanca Adventures (see Tours, following) organizes dolphin-watching excursions for US$40 per person.

TURTLE-WATCHING

Marine turtles – especially leatherback but also green, hawksbill and loggerhead – all nest on the beaches between Punta Mona and the Río Sixaola. Leatherbacks nest from March to July, with a peak in April and May. Local conservation efforts are underway to protect these nesting grounds since the growth of the area's human population has led to increased theft of turtle eggs.

During turtle season, no flashlights, beach fires or camping are allowed on the beach. All tourists must be accompanied by a local guide to minimize the disturbance to the nesting turtles.

Asociación Widecast (☎ in San José 8818-2543; www.latinamericanseaturtles.org, www.widecast.org; volunteer fee per day about US$40) is a grassroots NGO with opportunities for volunteers on turtle-protection projects. Volunteers can assist in patrols, hatchery maintenance as well as research and beach clean-up efforts. Rates include training, homestay accommodations and three meals per day.

Tours

Sure, you can explore the refuge on your own, but without a guide you'll probably be missing out on the refuge's incredible diversity of medicinal plants, exotic birds and earthbound animals. Most guides charge US$35 per person for a four- to five-hour trek, depending on the size of the group. Ask around at Maxi's (p493) or at the Casa de Guías (below).

Recommended local guides include **Florentino Grenald** (☎ 2759-9043, 8841-2732), who used to serve as the reserve's administrator; **Omar** (☎ 2759-9143), at Cabinas Bucus, who leads recommended rainforest hikes and turtle-watching tours; and **Abel Bustamante** (☎ 2759-9043).

Aquamor Talamanca Adventures (☎ 2759-9012; www.greencoast.com/aquamor.htm) Shawn Larkin's highly recommended outfit is devoted as much to conservation as recreation. As well as diving packages, staff also lead kayak and snorkeling tours (per person US$40) and rent equipment for independent use.

ATEC (Map p480; ☎ 2750-0191/398; www.ateccr.org; half-day/full-day hikes US$35/50) This community organization, based in Puerto Viejo, offers a variety of tours into the refuge. Check the website for the latest offerings.

Casa de Guías (☎ 2759-9064) A much-needed, though poorly organized initiative to hook up travelers with local guides. Offers guided hikes (four hours US$35) and turtle-watching. Also, enquire about boat tours and sportfishing.

Sleeping & Eating

There are many options for sleeping and eating in the village of Manzanillo (p492). Five kilometers southeast of the village, you'll find **Punta Mona** (☎ 8321-8788; www.puntamona.org; dm incl 3 meals US$45, transportation US$10; V), an organic farm and retreat center that is an experiment in permaculture design and sustainable living. Covering some 40 hectares, it grows more than 200 varieties of edible fruits and veggies, which comprise about 85% of the huge vegetarian meals that are included in the daily rate. Check the website for myriad volunteer opportunities here. To arrange accommodations and transport, email ahead or visit the farm's office in Puerto Viejo, which is located behind ATEC (Map p480).

BRIBRÍ

This bustling, no-stoplight town in the foothills of the Talamanca mountains lies at a bend in the paved road that connects Cahuita to Sixaola and the Panama border. There is little in the way of traveler trappings here – the village is primarily an agricultural center and a spot for nearby indigenous communities to take care of errands. Though it has little in the way of sights, it makes for a pleasant place to break away from the tourism industrial complex that dominates the coast.

From Bribrí, a 34km road – mostly paved – takes the traveler to the border.

Information

Banco Nacional (100m north of the bus stop; 8:30am-3:45pm) Changes US dollars; plan on standing in a long line.

Internet Veloz (per hr ₡500; 8am-6pm) Up a flight of rickety stairs from the bus stop.

Sights & Activities

Nestled into the Talamanca Mountains, 2km outside the village (just beyond the Volio waterfall), is **Aiko-logi** (☎ 2750-2084, 8997-6869; www.aiko-logi-tours.com; day tour incl transport & lunch US$60, overnight stay per person incl meals US$99; P), a private 135-hectare reserve centered around the site of what was once a small *finca,* on a piece of land fringed with dense primary rainforest. It's an ideal spot for bird-watching, hiking and splashing around in crisp, clean swimming holes. Day tours from Puerto Viejo and Cahuita can be arranged, as can overnight stays at Aiko-logi's tent platform. This is a small outfit; reserve ahead.

On the road between Bribrí and Cahuita, just north of the Sixaola turn-off, find the **studio of Fran Vásquez** (☎ 2751-0205), a self-taught folk painter whose colorful acrylic landscapes are well known in Puerto Viejo and San José. Look for a brightly painted sign outside a small, one-story house with chickens in the yard.

You can inquire about tours to indigenous villages at Restaurant Bribrí.

Sleeping & Eating

There are a few basic lodging options, a supermarket and the requisite Musmanni bakery. Accommodations tend to fill up on market days (Monday and Tuesday).

Cabinas El Piculino (☎ 2751-0130; d with/without air-con US$41/28; P) has 22 clean, simple brightly painted rooms with private hot showers; all have TV and most have air-con. Credit cards are accepted. A recommended **soda** (casados ₡2500; 6:15am-8:30pm Mon-Sat), run by the same family, serves a fine *sopa consomé de pollo* (chicken soup) as well as good rice dishes.

Complejo Turístico Mango (☎ 2751-0115; tr with/without air-con US$28/15; P) has various configurations of basic rooms with cool-water showers and an attached **restaurant** (casados ₡1700-2500; 7am-11pm). It is located right on the main road, on the way into town.

Run by the helpful Carlos and Miriam, the busy **Restaurante Bribrí** (☎ 2751-0044; casados ₡2000, mains ₡2500; 5am-5pm Mon-Sat) serves *casados,* chicken with rice, fried plantains and *gallos* (an open-faced taco). But it's also an excellent place to ask about tours to indigenous villages, where local guides lead hikes and boat rides through the area's jungle and rivers.

our pick **Restaurante Kaya Chökök Mlas Mlas** (casados ₡1750-3500; mains ₡1750-4450; 7:30am-4pm Mon-Sat) is a pleasant 2nd-story terrace restaurant located near the Banco Nacional. It serves up superdelicious cooking, including lightly crisp fish in garlic sauce as well as the delectably carnivorous 'Arroz Kaya' (₡2500) – a steaming pile of fried rice studded with bacon, ham, chicken and steak, and served with salad and fried plantains. Don't miss the searing pickled chili vegetables, which is an ideal meal in case you need to clear your sinuses.

GETTING TO GUABITO & BOCAS DEL TORO, PANAMA

Welcome to Costa Rica's most entertaining border crossing! An old railroad bridge that spans the churning waters of the Río Sixaola connects Costa Rica with Panama amid a sea of agricultural plantations. The best part: oversized buses and trucks also ply this route – which means that, if you're lucky, you'll get to watch one of these vehicles clatter along the wood planks as hapless pedestrians scatter to the edges to let them pass.

From here, most travelers make for Bocas del Toro, in Panama, a picturesque archipelago of jungle islands that is home to lovely beaches, endangered red frogs and a dilapidated set from the TV show *Survivor*. There is a wide range of accommodations in the area – all of it easily accessible by regular water taxis from the docks at Almirante.

The border is open 7am to 5pm (8am to 6pm in Guabito, Panama, which is an hour ahead of Costa Rica) – though one or both sides may close for lunch at around 1pm. At the entrance to the bridge, on the right-hand side, get your exit stamp at **Costa Rica migración** (☎ 2754-2044). Once over the bridge, stop at Panama *migración* on the left-hand side to get your passport stamped. US citizens will have to purchase a tourist card for US$5. Personal cars can cross here (not rentals). If you are driving, be prepared for a *loooong* wait.

Guabito has no hotels or banks, but in a pinch you can exchange colones at the market across the street. From the border, half-hourly buses (US$1, one hour) ply the route to the Terminal Piquera in Changuinola, where you can transfer to one of the frequent buses to Almirante (US$1, 45 minutes) for the water taxi. Alternately, from Guabito, you can take a collective taxi (per person US$5, one hour) straight to Almirante. From this point, hourly water taxis (per person US$5, 20 minutes) make the trip to Bocas del Toro between 6:30am and 10pm.

Getting There & Away

Buses arrive and depart hourly from in front of Restaurante Bribrí.

Puerto Limón, via Cahuita ₡1800; three hours; departs hourly from 6am to 7pm.

San José ₡4800; 5½ hours; departs 6:30am, 8:30am, 10:30am and 3:30pm.

Sixaola ₡800; 30 minutes; departs from 6am to 8pm.

SIXAOLA

pop 1500

This is the end of the road – literally. A bumpy tarmac leads to an old railroad bridge over the Río Sixaola that serves as the border crossing into Panama. Like most border towns, Sixaola is hardly scenic: set into the midst of sprawling banana plantations, it's an extravaganza of dingy bars and roadside stalls selling rubber boots. You're also likely to find plenty of expats without residency visas here, needing to take their required 72-hour visa vacations in nearby Bocas del Toro.

Sixaola is centered on the optimistically named Mercado Internacional de Sixaola, a gravelly square where you can find taxis and a handful of *sodas*. The market is about two blocks from the border crossing.

For details on crossing into Panama, see boxed text above.

Sleeping & Eating

Accommodations and restaurants are basic, but acceptable for any seasoned budget traveler. Don't expect hot water (even if it's advertised).

Cabinas Viajero (2nd fl, Soda Mi Sabor) Located on the north side of the highway, about 100m west of the bus station, you'll find four new (if bare bones) tiled *cabinas* over a *soda* of the same name.

Cabinas Imperio (☎ 2754-2289; d US$20) About 1km from the border, across from the police checkpoint, this quiet motor-court style hotel has eight clean rooms with cool water showers.

Soda Nabbi (mains ₡1500-2500; 🕑 6am-9pm) Facing the Mercado Internacional, north of the highway, this ramshackle spot serves up plenty of *gallo pinto* (beans and rice) and fried fish.

Getting There & Away

The bus station is one block north of the border crossing, on the east side of the main drag. Buses to either San José or Puerto Limón all stop at Bribrí and Cahuita.

Puerto Limón ₡2600; three hours; departs hourly from 5am to 6pm.

San José ₡5300; six hours; departs 6am, 8am, 10am and 3pm.

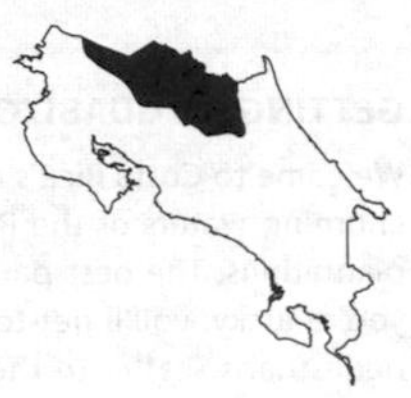

Northern Lowlands

It's getting harder and harder to get away from it all in Costa Rica – it's only natural for a country this richly blessed with varied gifts to be such a desirable destination. So the saturation point of popular *playas* (beaches) means spillover to the next not-so-secret sliver of coast, and zip lines continue to proliferate over the canopies from Monteverde to Manzanillo. But travelers who stray to the wild rivers and tropical jungle of the northern lowlands find that in these places, the getting away is still good.

Tourism has certainly touched the lowlands, creating added revenue for a local economy whose living has historically been made from agriculture. Plantations of bananas, sugarcane and pineapples roll across the humid plains from the Cordillera Central to the Nicaraguan border; these plantations are fringed by the tropical forest which was slashed to create the plantations. But green is the color of budding tourism around these parts. Conservationists team with landowners and local governments to make ecotourism work for all parties involved – whether it's the family farmer, the naturalist or the endangered great green macaw.

Bird-watchers, hoping to spot this macaw in the wild, flock to remote lodges in the verdant rainforests of the San Juan–La Selva Biological Corridor, while paddlers who are in the know show up to run the fun rapids of the Río Sarapiquí. Wildlife-watchers and fisherfolk alike head to the lagoons of Caño Negro, and travelers of all stripes are hopping launches up the Río Frío for the languid, fauna-rich river crossing to Nicaragua. This is real-life Costa Rica, where the balance of agricultural commerce and ecological conservation converge to create a contemporary work in green progress.

HIGHLIGHTS

- Exploring the lagoons of **Refugio Nacional de Vida Silvestre Caño Negro** (p516) to take a gander at spoonbills or a stab at tarpon
- Rafting the wildlife-rife **Río Sarapiquí** (p501) near La Virgen
- Keeping your eyes peeled for crocs and sloths as you float to the **Río San Juan** (see boxed text, p515) at the Nicaraguan border
- Slip-sliding through swampy jungle to spot poison-dart frogs and rare green macaws at **Laguna del Lagarto Lodge** (p512)
- Exploring the ruins of **Centro Neotrópico Sarapiquís** (p503) and traipsing the suspension bridges of nearby **Tirimbina Rainforest Center** (p503)

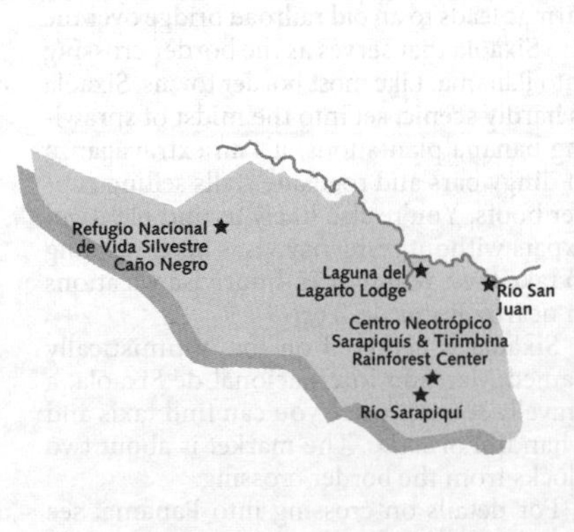

History

Life in the northern lowlands has always followed the rhythms of seasonal rains – when riverbanks swelled and flooded across the plains the landscape was transformed into a vast swamp that enabled people to subsist on fish, fowl and small game. However, as populations flourished and resources were strained, the earth was altered with the swing of a hoe, and the lowlands were slowly reshaped by farming interests.

In the early 1900s the United Fruit Company planted bananas across Costa Rica and built a railroad from the Caribbean coast to transport them. Many locales in the northern lowlands were originally established by, or branched off from, the banana trade and these settlements continue to make agriculture their business.

Climate

As in most of Costa Rica, the climate varies within this region. From the hot, dry Llanura de Guatusos along the Nicaraguan border, the northern plains roll southward to swampy lowlands and tropical hardwood forests. In the northern lowlands the dry season runs from April to November. However, the lush jungles surrounding the rivers in the region, such as the Río Frío and the Río Sarapiquí, receive rainfall at almost any time of year.

Parks & Reserves

Several notable refuges and parks are found in the northern lowlands, offering opportunities for low-key, crowd free boat tours and wildlife-watching.

Parque Nacional Braulio Carrillo (p508) Ecolodges in the Sarapiquí area can arrange rainforest tours and have accommodations at the northern end of Braulio Carrillo.

Refugio Nacional de Vida Silvestre Caño Negro (p516) The lagoons of Caño Negro attract a wide variety of birds year-round, though prime time for bird-watchers is between January and July.

Refugio Nacional de Vida Silvestre Mixto Maquenque (see boxed text, p510) Though there isn't much in the way of infrastructure at this recently formed refuge, local lodges can take you into this remote rainforest.

Getting There & Around

Transportation hubs in the lowlands include Puerto Viejo de Sarapiquí and San Miguel to the southeast, and Upala and Los Chiles to the northwest, all of which are served by daily buses from San José. If you're not in a hurry, you can get around with little hassle via public bus, but having your own vehicle will allow you greater ease in getting to the appealingly far-flung reaches of this relatively tourist-free region. In the far north, the border outpost of Los Chiles serves as a launching point for lovely river trips across the border to San Carlos, Nicaragua (see boxed text, p515).

THE SARAPIQUÍ VALLEY

This flat, steaming stretch of *finca*-dotted lowlands was once part of the United Fruit Company's cash-cow of banana holdings. Harvests were carried from the plantations to Puerto Viejo de Sarapiquí where they were packaged and shipped down the river on boats destined for the lucrative North American market. However, with the advent of the railway in 1880 that connected much of the country to the new shipping port in Puerto Limón, Puerto Viejo de Sarapiquí became a sleepy backwater.

Banana harvesting continued in the area through most of the 20th century, though in recent years farmers have switched to a more lucrative cash crop – sugarcane. Although Puerto Viejo de Sarapiquí has never managed to recover its faded glory, the area around the town is still one of the premier destinations in Costa Rica for kayakers and rafters. There are also a number of stellar ecolodges in the region that are open to nonguests, and feature everything from rainforest hiking and suspension bridges to pre Columbian ruins and chocolate tours.

From San José, the road north of San Miguel drops for 12km to the village of La Virgen and then flattens out as it bisects agricultural country for an additional 13km to Bajos de Chilamate. The old port town of Puerto Viejo de Sarapiquí lies 6km further along this road. Buses linking either San José or Ciudad Quesada with Puerto Viejo de Sarapiquí are the primary means of public transportation along this route.

LA VIRGEN

Tucked into the densely jungled shores of the wild and scenic Río Sarapiquí, La Virgen was one of a number of small towns that grew and prospered during the heyday of the banana trade. Although United Fruit has long since packed up and shipped out, the town is still

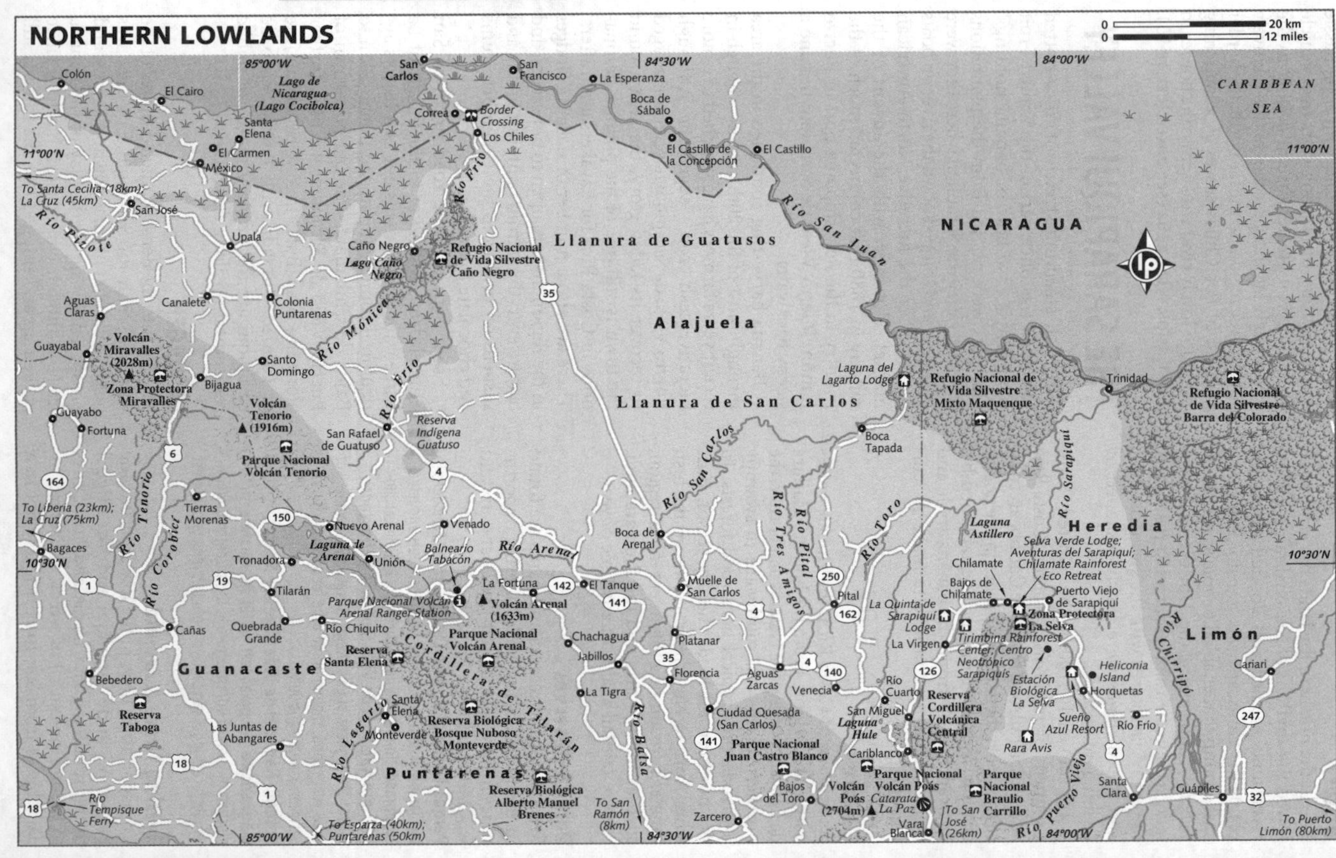
NORTHERN LOWLANDS
0 20 km
0 12 miles
CARIBBEAN SEA
NICARAGUA
Lago de Nicaragua (Lago Cocibolca)
Río San Juan
Río Sarapiquí
Río Chirripó
Río Toro
Río Pital
Río Tres Amigos
Río San Carlos
Río Frío
Río Mónica
Río Arenal
Río Balsa
Río Lagarto
Río Corobicí
Río Tenorio
Río Pizote
Río Puerto Viejo
Llanura de Guatusos
Llanura de San Carlos
Alajuela
Heredia
Limón
Guanacaste
Puntarenas
Cordillera de Tilarán
Refugio Nacional de Vida Silvestre Barra del Colorado
Refugio Nacional de Vida Silvestre Mixto Maquenque
Refugio Nacional de Vida Silvestre Caño Negro
Laguna del Lagarto Lodge
Laguna Astillero
Lago Caño Negro
Laguna de Arenal
Reserva Indígena Guatuso
Volcán Tenorio (1916m)
Parque Nacional Volcán Tenorio
Volcán Miravalles (2028m)
Zona Protectora Miravalles
Volcán Arenal (1633m)
Parque Nacional Volcán Arenal
Parque Nacional Volcán Arenal Ranger Station
Balneario Tabacón
Reserva Santa Elena
Reserva Biológica Bosque Nuboso Monteverde
Reserva Biológica Alberto Manuel Brenes
Reserva Taboga
Parque Nacional Juan Castro Blanco
Reserva Cordillera Volcánica Central
Parque Nacional Volcán Poás
Volcán Poás (2704m)
Catarata La Paz
Laguna Hule
Parque Nacional Braulio Carrillo
Rara Avis
Sueño Azul Resort
Estación Biológica La Selva
Tirimbina Rainforest Center; Centro Neotrópico Sarapiquís
Heliconia Island
La Quinta de Sarapiquí Lodge
Selva Verde Lodge; Aventuras del Sarapiquí; Chilamate Rainforest Eco Retreat
Zona Protectora La Selva
Puerto Viejo de Sarapiquí
Chilamate
Bajos de Chilamate
La Virgen
Border Crossing
Colón
El Cairo
El Carmen
Santa Elena
México
San José
Aguas Claras
Guayabal
Guayabo
Fortuna
Bagaces
Canalete
Upala
Bijagua
Colonia Puntarenas
Santo Domingo
Caño Negro
San Carlos
Correa
Los Chiles
San Francisco
La Esperanza
Boca de Sábalo
El Castillo de la Concepción
El Castillo
Trinidad
Boca Tapada
Boca de Arenal
Muelle de San Carlos
Platanar
Florencia
Ciudad Quesada (San Carlos)
Aguas Zarcas
Venecia
Pital
San Miguel
Río Cuarto
Cariblanco
Vara Blanca
Bajos del Toro
Zarcero
La Tigra
Jabillos
Chachagua
El Tanque
La Fortuna
Venado
San Rafael de Guatuso
Nuevo Arenal
Unión
Río Chiquito
Tronadora
Tilarán
Quebrada Grande
Tierras Morenas
Cañas
Las Juntas de Abangares
Bebedero
Monteverde
Santa Elena
Horquetas
Río Frío
Santa Clara
Guápiles
Cariari
To Santa Cecilia (18km); La Cruz (45km)
To Liberia (23km); La Cruz (75km)
To Esparza (40km); Puntarenas (50km)
To San Ramón (8km)
To San José (26km)
To Puerto Limón (80km)
Río Tempisque Ferry
85°00'W
84°30'W
84°00'W
11°00'N
10°30'N

dependent on the river, though most people today earn a living by either mongering fish or guiding gringos through the rapids.

Welcome to one of the premier kayaking and rafting destinations in Costa Rica. Surprisingly, most travelers have never even heard about La Virgen, and those who have would be hard-pressed to find it on a map. But, to the dedicated groups of hard-core rafters and kayakers that spend days running the Río Sarapiquí, La Virgen is a relatively off-the-beaten-path paradise. As an added bonus, the three luxurious lodges east of town feature a number of interesting attractions including museums, private trails and a Malcku archaeological site – so there's plenty to do in the area even on a rest day.

Information

Most of La Virgen's businesses are strung out along the highway, including a gas station, a **Banco Nacional** (☎ 2212-2000) with 24-hour ATM, a couple of small supermarkets, several internet cafes and many bars. The blue **Almacenes El Colono** (🕒 7am-noon & 1-6pm Mon-Fri, to 4:30pm Sat) building contains a Western Union, money exchange and another 24-hour ATM. Across the street, **Internet La Virgen** (per hr ₡400; 🕒 8am-8pm) has fast connections.

Sights & Activities

WHITE-WATER RAFTING

The Río Sarapiquí isn't as wild as the white water on the Río Pacuare near Turrialba, though it will still get your heart racing, and the dense jungle that hugs the riverbank is lush and primitive. You can run the Sarapiquí year-round, but July through December are considered peak months. Although it's possible to get a rafting trip on short notice, it's far better to make reservations at least two days in advance. Several tour operators in La Fortuna and San José organize trips. You can also call directly to the companies listed in this section.

There are three basic runs offered by several companies, and all have a minimum age of nine or 10; prices and times vary a bit, but the following are average. The Class I-II Chilamate put-in (US$60 per person, three hours) is a gentle float more suited to younger kids and wildlife-watching. The Class III-IV Lower Sarapiquí (US$75, three hours) puts in close to La Virgen and is a scenic and challenging trip that's a good choice for healthy people without white-water experience. The Class IV-V Upper Sarapiquí (US$85, five hours) is 11km of serious white water – perfect for thrill-seekers.

In addition to offering rafting trips from La Virgen, San José and La Fortuna, **Aguas Bravas** (☎ 2292-2072; www.aguas-bravas.co.cr) is a safety-oriented, Tico-run outfit that can also arrange horseback rides and bike tours.

Aventuras del Sarapiquí (☎ 2766-6768; www.sarapiqui.com) near Chilamate, and **Hacienda Pozo Azul Adventures** (☎ 2438-2616, in USA & Canada 877-810-6903; www.haciendapozoazul.com) are also reputable local professionals who organize rafting trips.

KAYAKING

If you're a kayaker, several accommodations in town are directly on the river, which means that you can roll out of bed, brush your teeth and have a quick paddle before breakfast. **Rancho Leona** (☎ 2761-1019; www.rancholeona.com) is something of a meeting spot for kayakers, which isn't surprising as its prime riverside location allows for easy launches and free kayak storage (see p502 for more information). Staff can provide information regarding launches in the area before you set out on the river.

HIKING

For truly rugged do-it-yourself adventurers, it's possible to hike from La Virgen to the southernmost ranger stations in Parque Nacional Braulio Carrillo. For more information on hiking in Parque Nacional Braulio Carrillo, see p445.

OTHER ACTIVITIES

Hacienda Pozo Azul Adventures (☎ 2438-2616, in USA & Canada 877-810-6903; www.haciendapozoazul.com) specializes in adventure activities, including horseback-riding tours starting from two-hour jaunts (US$40) to multiday treks. It also runs a canopy tour (US$50) over the lush jungle and river, can take you rappelling (US$31), and leads mountain-bike tours (half-day US$50, full day US$70) and guided hikes (US$18).

SERPENTARIO

A great, locally run attraction is La Virgen's famous **snake garden** (☎ 2761-1059; adult/student & child US$7/6; 🕒 9am-5pm), where you can get face-to-face with more than 60 different species of reptiles and amphibians, including poison-dart frog, anaconda and the star attraction, an 80kg Burmese python. The owner of the *serpentario*, Lydia, gives impromptu tours and takes certain snakes out of their cages for big hugs and memorable photo ops. The mural outside is most definitely tattoo-worthy.

CENTRO BIOLÓGICO SANTUARIO DE MARIPOSAS AGUAS SILVESTRES

You'll need your own wheels, or you can make arrangements through Rancho Leona (below), to visit this **butterfly sanctuary** (☎ 2761-1095) in the mountains, run by the energetic Edgar Corrales. Guided hikes (in Spanish; US$12) take you through the rainforest along a waterfall trail and include a tour of the butterfly garden. You can also stay overnight in the rustic **bunkhouse** (per person US$40); the rate includes dinner, breakfast, a half-day tour of the local rainforest with a swim in the lagoon, and lunch on your return. However long your stay, be sure to bring bug repellent, as butterflies are not the only insects living up there.

To get here on your own, turn onto the Pozo Azul road and follow the brown wood signs to the sanctuary, which is about 10km up the mountain, near the village of San Ramón.

Sleeping & Eating

Sarapiquí Outdoor Center (☎ 2761-1123; www.costaricaraft.com; campsites US$5, r US$25; Ⓟ) Riverside campsites here have access to showers and bathrooms. Private rooms are simple and have river views, though they're a bit overpriced for what they are. There's also a communal kitchen and a covered terrace in case of rain. Contrary to the signs out front, this location no longer offers rafting excursions, but staff can help get you in touch with the tour office.

our pick **Bar & Cabinas El Río** (☎ 2761-0138; r with fan/air-con US$10/15; Ⓟ) About 1km from Pozo Azul at the southern edge of town, these seven A-frame bungalows have tiled floors, clean hot-water bathroom and TV – they're cute as heck and bordered with hedges and flowers. About 100m further down the steep hill is the lovely open-air Bar El Río, on rough-hewn stilts high above the river. This is the best nightlife spot in town, especially on Fridays when it's karaoke night. The family-run bar also has a great dinner menu such as grilled local tilapia and sides for just ₡3000.

Rancho Leona (☎ 2761-1019; www.rancholeona.com; r without bathroom per person US$12; Ⓟ) This shady, riverside spot is a gem – kayakers congregate here to swap tales of white-water adventure, bird-watchers linger over huge breakfasts (₡3500) as the local color of avian life flits by, and artistically minded travelers admire the lodge's incredible stained glass, which was handmade by the owners. The handful of simple, spotless rooms in the wood-plank lodge share hot-water bathrooms, and there's a small bathing pool for taking a cool dip; spa services are also available. The superfriendly staff sometimes prepare family-style dinners in the evenings, and they can take you out on inflatable 'ducky' or kayak trips, as well as arrange rafting tours for you.

Hacienda Pozo Azul Adventures (☎ 2438-2616, in USA & Canada 877-810-6903; www.haciendapozoazul.com; s/d/tr luxury tents US$80/92/115; Ⓟ) If you've ever dreamed of camping in the rainforest, this is your chance to do it in style. Located near the south end of La Virgen, Pozo Azul features luxurious, recently remodelled 'tent suites' scattered on the edge of the treeline, all on raised, polished-wood platforms and outfitted with luxurious bedding, bathroom and mosquito nets. At night, the frogs and wildlife sing you to sleep as raindrops patter on the tent top. For large groups there's also the 10-room Magsasay Jungle Lodge (single/double/triple US$60/96/132) deep in the jungle, perched at the edge of Parque Nacional Braulio Carrillo. All showers at both locations have hot water. The onsite adventure activities include canopy tours, horseback riding, white-water rafting, hiking and rappelling. Pozo Azul also boasts the best restaurant-bar (mains ₡3000 to ₡7000) in town for lunch and dinner, with an outdoor veranda alongside the river, but skip the bland breakfast.

Restaurante y Cabinas Tía Rosita (☎ 2761-1032/125; www.restaurantetiarosita.com; meals ₡900-3000; breakfast, lunch & dinner; Ⓟ) Tía Rosita is the most highly recommended *soda* (lunch counter) in La Virgen, with excellent *casados* (set meals), Costa Rican–style *chiles rellenos* (stuffed fried peppers) and *horchata* (sweet rice shake), and service with a smile. The family also rents several *cabinas* (single/double/triple US$11/17/23) with private hot shower, TV, fan and plenty of breathing space. There's an onsite internet cafe (₡300 per hour).

Restaurante Mar y Tierra (☎ 2761-1603; mains ₡2200-5250; 8am-10pm) La Virgen's favorite fine-dining (but still very relaxed) option is this comfortable seafood and steak restaurant that's popular with both locals and travelers. The specialty here is shrimp, and it's damn good.

Getting There & Away

La Virgen lies on Hwy 126, about 8km from San Miguel, to the south, and 17km from Puerto Viejo de Sarapiquí, to the northeast. Buses originating in either San José, San Miguel or Puerto Viejo de Sarapiquí make regular stops in La Virgen. If you're driving, the curvy road is paved between San José and Puerto Viejo de Sarapiquí, though irregular maintenance can make for a bumpy ride.

LA VIRGEN TO PUERTO VIEJO DE SARAPIQUÍ

This scenic stretch of Hwy 126 is home to a few lovely ecolodges that are extremely popular among well-heeled tourists. However, if you're the kind of traveler that scraps together a few hundred colones every morning to buy a loaf of bread from Palí supermarket, fear not, as these places do allow nonguests to see their unusual attractions and private trails for a small fee. Any bus between La Virgen and Puerto Viejo de Sarapiquí can drop you off at the entrances, while a taxi from La Virgen (or Puerto Viejo for Selva Verde) will cost from ₡2300 to ₡3500.

Centro Neotropico Sarapiquís

About 2km north of La Virgen is **Centro Neotrópico Sarapiquís** (☎ 2761-1004; www.sarapiquis.org; d/tr US$105/130; P ⊠ ⁂ ☐), a unique ecolodge that aims to foster sustainable tourism by educating its guests about environmental conservation and pre-Columbian history and culture. The entire complex consists of *palenque*-style, thatched-roof buildings modeled after a 15th-century pre-Columbian village, and contains a clutch of luxuriously appointed hardwood rooms with huge, solar-heated bathroom and private terrace. However, the main reason guests rave about this ecolodge is the variety of exhibits and attractions located on the grounds.

Even if you're not staying at the lodge, it's worth stopping by just to visit its real claims to fame, namely the **Alma Ata Archaeological Park**, **Rainforest Museum of Indigenous Cultures** and **Sarapiquís Gardens** (adult/child under 8yr US$15/free; ⌚ 9am-5pm). The admission price includes entry to all three places, though alternatively, you can purchase tickets for the individual attractions. The archaeological site is estimated to be around 600 years old, and is attributed to the Maleku (see boxed text, p521). Currently, about 70 small stone sculptures marking a burial field are being excavated by Costa Rican archaeologists who have revealed a number of petroglyphs and pieces of pottery. Although the site is modest, and definitely not comparable in size or scope to other Central American archaeological sites, it's one of the few places in Costa Rica where you can get a sense of its pre-Columbian history.

The museum chronicles the history of the rainforest (and of human interactions with it) through a mixture of displays and videos, and also displays hundreds of Costa Rican indigenous artifacts including some superbly crafted musical instruments. Finally, the gardens boast the largest scientific collection of medicinal plants in Costa Rica.

An onsite **restaurant** (mains ₡4000-12,000; ⌚ breakfast, lunch & dinner) serves meals incorporating fruits, vegetables, spices and edible flowers used in indigenous cuisine, many of which are grown on the premises.

Tirimbina Rainforest Center

A working environmental research and education center, **Tirimbina Rainforest Center** (☎ 2761-0055/333; www.tirimbina.org; r incl breakfast US$60) also provides tours and accommodations for visitors. The 350-hectare private reserve of Tirimbina and the nearby Centro Neotrópico Sarapiquís are connected by two suspension bridges, 267m and 117m long, that span the Río Sarapiquí. Halfway across, a spiral staircase drops down to a large island in the river. Tirimbina reserve has more than 9km of trails with suspension bridges; some of the trails are paved or wood-blocked. There are also several different guided tours on offer (US$17 to US$27) including bird-watching, frog and bat tours, night walks and a recommended guided chocolate tour, which lets you explore a working cacao plantation and learn about the harvesting, fermenting and drying processes. Child and student discounts are available. Tirimbina is about 2km north of La Virgen, next door to Centro Neotrópico Sarapiquís.

La Quinta de Sarapiquí Lodge

About 5km north of La Virgen, this pleasant family-run **lodge** (☎ 2761-1052; www.laquintasarapiqui.com; s/d/tr/ste US$110/110/125/140; P ⁂ ☐ ♿) is on the banks of the Río Sardinal, which branches off from the Sarapiquí in the north and runs to the west of it. The lodge has covered paths through the landscaped garden connecting thatched-roof, hammock-strung rooms. All rooms have a terrace, ceiling fan and private hot shower. You can also get meals in the open-air restaurant (mains ₡4640 to ₡7540).

Owner Beatriz Gámez is active in local environmental issues and helps administer the Cámara de Turismo de Sarapiquí (Cantusa), which works to balance conservation and tourism in the area. Activities at the lodge include swimming in the pretty pool or river (there's a good swimming hole nearby), fishing, boat trips and bird-watching, and you can spend time in the large **butterfly garden** or hike the 'frog land' trail where poison-dart frogs are commonly seen.

On the hotel grounds, **La Galería** (admission US$6, lodge guests free) features an eclectic collection of regional ephemera, including an extensive collection of insect specimens such as the *machaca* (also known as the lantern bug), a bizarre-looking insect about 7.5cm long. Even more interesting are the unusual exhibits on Costa Rican history. Indigenous artifacts, including some worthwhile copies of the area's more important archaeological finds, are a treat. The collection of Spanish-colonial relics is even more impressive, featuring not only antiques collected by the owners, but interesting family heirlooms as well – Gámez' great-grandmother was pen pals with famed Nicaraguan poet Rubén Darío. The fee also includes access to the lodge's private trails and gardens.

Collin Street Bakery Pineapple Plantation

You won't find any bread at Collin Street Bakery (its name reflects the ownership). Instead, you'll discover the sweetest, most delicious pineapples, grown right here at the world's largest organic pineapple plantation. Collin Street offers **tours** (☎ 2551-5804; www.collinstreet.com/pages/finca_corsicana; tours adult/child US$31/27; ⌚ 8am, 10am & 2pm Mon-Fri) through its 12 sq km of pineapple fields plus the processing and packing plant that ships 38 million pineapples a year. The interesting but pricey tour ends with a tasting of fresh pineapple, washed down with a piña colada. Yum! The plantation is located 2km north of La Quinta and is well signed from the highway.

Selva Verde Lodge

In Chilamate, about 7km west of Puerto Viejo, this former *finca* (plantation) is now an elegant **lodge** (☎ 2766-6800, in USA & Canada 800-451-7111; www.selvaverde.com; s/d incl breakfast US$107/125, incl all meals US$137/184; P) that protects over 200 hectares of rainforest. Guests can choose to stay at the river lodge, which is elevated above the rainforest floor on wooden platforms, or in a private bungalow, quietly tucked away in the nearby rainforest. Wood-floored rooms have private hot shower, screened windows, in-room safe and, of course, your very own hammock.

The lodge works closely with a tour company for over-55-year-olds called Exploritas and offers educational opportunities, guided tours and other interesting diversions, many of which nonguests can enjoy for a fee.

There are several kilometers of walking trails through the grounds and into the premontane tropical wet forest; you can either get a trail map or hire a bilingual guide from the lodge (US$17 per person, three hours). There's also a garden of medicinal plants, as well as a **butterfly garden** (admission US$6, lodge guests free). Various boat tours on the Río Sarapiquí are also available, from rafting trips to guided canoe tours; locally guided horseback rides (US$29 for two to three hours) can also be arranged.

The Holbrook family, who own the lodge, fund the nonprofit **Sarapiquí Conservation Learning Center** (www.learningcentercostarica.org), through which guests can participate in cultural-exchange activities such as a *charla* (chat) over coffee, homestays or salsa-dancing lessons with locals. The center also partners with student groups to serve as a base for conservation and environmental education.

Chilamate Rainforest Eco Retreat

Founded in 2009 by Sarapiquí native Davis Azofeifa and his Irish-Canadian wife Meghan Casey, **Chilamate** (☎ 2766-6949, 8842-1171; www.chilamaterainforest.com; dm US$17, s/d incl breakfast US$35/65; P) is the most exciting new ecolodge project in the area. The young couple have spent three years building their little piece of paradise on 20 hectares of prime virgin rainforest. See also boxed text, p506.

The four large cabins built by Davis and friends are basic but full of character, with comfy hand-crafted furniture, private bathroom, fan and traditional architectural style that provides natural air-cooling. Out back, the bunkhouse has 12 dorm beds with shared bathroom and kitchen, perfect for groups or those on a tight budget. Other resort amenities include a small bar, restaurant and laundry facilities. Davis and Meghan have two young children, so the resort is naturally quite kid-friendly. Covered, flat walkways allow you to move between buildings in the complex without ever getting wet (after all, this is the rainforest!).

Throughout the resort, sustainability is the key feature. Everything has been built with wood and other sustainable materials. The buildings are all designed to take advantage of natural lighting, cooling and insulation. Solar power provides much of the resort's electrical needs, waste is recycled or composted and rainwater is recycled for cleaning and washing purposes.

Behind the cabins, 6km of paths wind through the jungle, where you might spot sloths, monkeys, toucans, frogs, snakes and more. The resort provides rubber boots for sloshing through the rainforest. Davis is a wealth of local information and can help arrange excursions in the area. For those who want a true ecolodge experience without the high ecotourism prices, we highly recommend Chilamate.

PUERTO VIEJO DE SARAPIQUI & AROUND

At the scenic confluence of Ríos Puerto Viejo and Sarapiquí, Puerto Viejo de Sarapiquí was once the most important port in Costa Rica. Boats laden with bananas, coffee and other commercial exports plied the Sarapiquí as far as the Nicaraguan border, then turned east on the Río San Juan to the sea. Today, Puerto Viejo (the full name distinguishes it from Puerto Viejo de Talamanca on the Caribbean coast) is simply a jungle border town – slightly seedy in a film-noir sort of way. There are, however, numerous opportunities in the surrounding area for bird-watching, rafting, boating and jungle exploration.

Migración (immigration) is near the small wooden dock, sometimes avoided by visiting Nicaraguans who share the river with local fishers and visiting bird-watchers. Adventure-seekers can still travel down the Sarapiquí in motorized dugout canoes.

There is no dry season, but from late January to early May is the 'less wet' season. On the upside, when it rains here there are fewer mosquitoes.

Banco Popular (☎ 2766-6815) has an ATM and changes money. **Banco de Costa Rica** at the entrance of town also has an ATM. **Cruz Roja** (☎ 2766-6212) provides medical care. Of the many internet cafes in town, **Gecko.Net** (☎ 2766-7007; per hr ₡400; 8:30am-7pm Mon-Fri, 9am-6pm Sun), across from Cruz Roja, is the newest and fastest game in town.

Activities

Grassroots environmental activity is strong in this area. Local guide Alex Martínez (owner of the Posada Andrea Cristina B&B), who speaks excellent English, maintains an **ecotourism center** (☎ 2766-6265; 8am-3pm), which focuses on conservation activities and wilderness tours – **bird-watching** trips in particular. You can also arrange transportation and make other reservations here, as well as learn about worthwhile volunteer opportunities in the region. Alex arrived here 40 years ago as a tough young hunter exploring what was virgin forest, and saw the jungle's rapid destruction at the hands of humankind. He changed his philosophy and is now a volunteer game warden – who will abandon a Saturday-night soccer match to chase down poachers on the river. He helped found Asociación para el Bienestar Ambiental de Sarapiquí (Abas), a local environmental-protection and education agency, and can tell you as much as you want to know about environmental issues in the area. One of his latest projects involves identifying nesting sites of breeding green macaw, and purchasing living almendro trees from property owners, who are then honor-bound to protect the trees.

If you're looking to organize a rafting or kayaking trip, a branch of **Aguas Bravas** (☎ 2292-2072; www.aguas-bravas.co.cr) is across the road from the bank. You can also try **Costa Rica Fun Adventures** (☎ 2290-6015; www.crfunadventures.com), which is 2km north of town and offers a good variety of guided hiking and horseback-riding trips.

Taking the launch trip from Puerto Viejo to the Trinidad Lodge (p506), at the confluence of the Ríos Sarapiquí and San Juan, provides a rich opportunity to see crocodiles, sloths, birds, monkeys and iguanas sunning themselves on the muddy riverbanks or gathering in the trees. This river system is a historically important gateway from the Caribbean into the heart of

A FAMILY AFFAIR ON THE RÍO SARAPIQUÍ

Sarapiquí native Davis Azofeifa and his Irish-Canadian wife Meghan Casey are the founders of Chilamate Rainforest Eco Retreat and actively involved in the local community.

How and why did you create Chilamate Rainforest Eco Retreat? Davis: We were interested in doing something that would allow us to live simple and well, while also assisting the community, generating quality jobs and helping reduce the devastation of development. We were originally looking for a farm when, by chance, we stumbled on Chilamate jungle with its beautiful forest, river and, most importantly, a great community. It was love at first sight. With much passion and love of nature, we began Chilamate Rainforest Retreat, which has become a sustainable, forward-looking project and a living example of the future.

Meghan: Davis and I are both passionate nature-lovers. Now that we have children, we are especially worried about problems of deforestation and loss of biodiversity and habitat. Our dream was to start a family business that would allow us to work together, make enough money to get by and allow us to contribute positively to the environment and our community and receive visits from our friends from all over the world.

Why should people visit the Sarapiquí region? Meghan: There are many beautiful places in Costa Rica, but to me, the Sarapiquí Valley is the most special area of all. In Sarapiquí, the tourists traditionally come to enjoy the biodiversity, birds, adventure, or to study and share with the community. The harmony and good vibes between the locals and foreigners here in Sarapiquí is very distinct and special, the climate here is beautiful, the people are warm and friendly, the air is fresh and clean, the water crystalline and wildlife abounds. Sarapiquí is a haven for anyone looking for an authentic tourism experience.

Davis: The people, security, location, national parks, rivers and mountains are some of the many reasons to visit Sarapiquí instead of, say, the Pacific resorts. Locals practice sustainable development and simple living with nature. Visiting the area will help the people of Sarapiquí to continue their conservation efforts. Sarapiquí is the best rainforest experience in Costa Rica.

Is Costa Rica a good travel destination for children? Davis: One of the most important values of Costa Rica is the family, the essential basis for living in harmony. People are very friendly and love children. It's completely normal to see men and women lovingly doting on children. Most places offer special attention, service and discounts for children. The food and weather are ideal for families of all ages to have a wonderful time anywhere in Costa Rica.

What's it like raising two young children in the rainforest? Meghan: It's been a blessing. It is much easier to get away from the pressures of consumerism and the material here in the rainforest. The colours, tastes, smells and sounds of our natural surroundings provide an endless natural wonderland…and reinforce our children's innate love for nature and help them learn creative solutions for a sustainable future. Throuought this experience, they have taught us that we really do need less 'stuff,' and the time we spend together and immersed in nature is priceless.

Central America, and it's still off the beaten tourist track, giving a glimpse of rainforest and ranches, wildlife and old war zones, deforested pastureland and protected areas.

Sleeping

This stretch of jungle boasts quite a range of accommodations, from budget bunks in town, designed for local long-term plantation workers, to several extraordinary lodges on the outskirts, the most exclusive of which are on the road to La Virgen. Lodges in the area north of Puerto Viejo are also listed, including one in the river town of Trinidad, on the Nicaraguan border.

BUDGET

Trinidad Lodge (☎ 2213-0661, 8381-0621; r per person US$10) Situated on the Río San Juan in the community of Trinidad, this budget lodge is right across from the Nicaraguan border crossing and is pretty much the only gig in town. Though on the rustic side, the bamboo-walled bungalows are charming and very clean, with cold-water bathroom. Candle power provides light when the generator shuts off at the end of the night, and meals (₡2300 to ₡4600) are available at the *rancho*, with a pool table besides. The lodge is accessible only by boat (₡5800), which departs once daily at 2pm from the main dock of Puerto

Viejo de Sarapiquí (35km away). The motorized launches leave Trinidad daily at (yawn) 5am. Due to the launch schedules, consider staying two nights to fully appreciate a hike, horseback-riding tour or boat trip through this lush, remote sector of jungle.

Mi Lindo Sarapiquí (☎ 2766-6281; s/d US$18/30; P ✕ 💻) On the south side of the soccer field, this is the best budget option in the town center. Rooms here are simple but spacious and clean, and have a private hot shower and fan. The onsite restaurant (mains ₡1700 to ₡5800; open 10am to 10pm) is slightly pricey, though it offers some of the freshest seafood in town.

our pick Posada Andrea Cristina B&B (☎ 2766-6265; www.andreacristina.com; s/d incl breakfast US$28/48, tree-house d US$55, extra guests per person US$15; P) About 1km west of the center, this recommended B&B has eight quiet, immaculate cabins in its garden, each with fan, private hot-water bathroom, hammock and outdoor table and chairs. It's also situated on the edge of the rainforest, so there are plenty of opportunities for bird-watching while you sit outside and eat breakfast. The newest accommodations option is a funky living tree house with bathroom and canopy-level balcony from which you can spy on the sloth family living in the nearby trees. The owner, Alex Martínez, is an excellent, amiable guide as well as a passionate frontline conservationist who runs an onsite ecotourism center (for details, see p505).

MIDRANGE

El Gavilán (☎ 2766-6743; www.gavilanlodge.com; d standard/superior US$60/75; P) Sitting on a 100-hectare reserve about 4km northeast of Puerto Viejo, this former cattle hacienda is cozy, quaint and a bird-watching haven. Each of the spacious rooms has a big hot-water shower and fan; all rooms have porches, some with river views. The grounds feature 5km of private trails and a good restaurant, plus a nice outdoor Jacuzzi to relax in after a long hike. Although the accommodations don't quite live up to the price, bird-watching and boat trips are the draw here. Trips range from short jaunts down the Río Sarapiquí to overnights in Tortuguero. Multiday package deals are available that include meals, tours and transportation from San José.

Hotel Ara Ambigua (☎ 2766-7101; www.hotelaraambigua.com; s/d/tr incl breakfast from US$65/75/82; P ✕ 💻 🏊) About 1km west of Puerto Viejo near La Guaíra, this countryside retreat offers cozy rooms that are well equipped with private hot-water shower and cable TV. The superior rooms feature log-style furniture and flagstone floors. There are also a few standard rooms that cost US$17 less. The real draw are the varied opportunities for wildlife-watching – you can see poison-dart frogs in the *ranario* (frog pond), caimans in the small lake, and the birds that come to feed near the onsite Restaurante La Casona, which is open for breakfast, lunch and dinner.

Hotel El Bambú (☎ 2766-6005; www.elbambu.com; r standard/deluxe incl breakfast US$67/79; P ✕ 📶 🏊) You really can't miss the sign for downtown Puerto Viejo's finest lodging, which caters mostly to package tourists looking for a clean and comfortable base when they're not out on 'adventure tours.' Rooms are all equipped with air-con and hot water, and there's a big, inviting pool and a popular restaurant open to the main road. Spring for one of the quieter deluxe rooms out back, whose raised platform paths take you through the trees.

Eating

Most of the lodgings in and around Puerto Viejo have onsite restaurants or provide meals.

There are several *sodas* in Puerto Viejo de Sarapiquí, including the excellent **Soda Judith** (mains ₡1160-2320; 🕑 6am-7pm), one block off the main road, where early risers grab brewed coffee and big breakfasts or an *empanada* (turnover stuffed with meat or cheese) to start their day. Or you can grab a coffee and fresh bread at **Panadería Cafetería Musmanni** (snacks ₡100-600; 🕑 4:30am-8:30pm), across from the bus terminal. **Restaurante La Casona** (meals ₡2320-5800; 🕑 breakfast, lunch & dinner) at the Hotel Ara Ambigua is particularly recommended for its oven-baked pizza and typical, homemade cuisine served in an open-air *rancho*.

There's also a **Palí supermarket** (🕑 8am-9pm) at the west end of town, and the local Super Sarapiquí on the way to the port.

Getting There & Away

Puerto Viejo de Sarapiquí has been a transportation center longer than Costa Rica has been a country, and is easily accessed by paved major roads from San José, the Caribbean coast and other population centers. There is a taxi stop across from the bus terminal, and taxis will take you to the nearby lodges and Estación Biológica La Selva for ₡2320 to ₡4060.

BOAT

The small port has a regular service to the Trinidad Lodge in Trinidad, and you can arrange transportation anywhere along the river (seasonal conditions permitting) through independent boat captains. Short trips cost about ₡5800 per hour per person for a group of four, or ₡11,600 per hour for a single person. Serious voyages to Tortuguero or Barra del Colorado and back cost about ₡203,000 for a boat holding five.

BUS

Right across from the park, the **bus terminal** (☎ 2233-4242; 🕑 5am-7pm) sells tickets and stores backpacks (₡870 per day). Local buses run frequently between La Virgen and Puerto Viejo de Sarapiquí. The 30-minute trip costs ₡350.

Ciudad Quesada/San Carlos via La Virgen (Empresarios Guapileños) ₡1230; three hours; departs 5:30am, 8:30am, 10:30am, 12:15pm, 2:30pm, 4pm, 6pm and 7:10pm.

Guápiles (Empresarios Guapileños) ₡780; one hour; departs 5:30am, 6:45am, 7:10am, 9:40am, 10:30am, 12:10pm, 2:30pm, 3:45pm, 4:45pm and 7pm.

San José (Autotransportes Sarapiquí) ₡1650; two hours; departs 6:30am, 7:30am, 10am, 11:30am, 1:30pm, 2:30pm, 3:30pm, 4:30pm and 6pm.

SOUTH OF PUERTO VIEJO DE SARAPIQUÍ

South of Puerto Viejo de Sarapiquí, banana and other plantations line Hwy 4 and sprawl all the way to the marshes and mangroves of the Caribbean coast. To the west, the rugged hills of the Cordillera Central mark the northeastern boundary of Parque Nacional Braulio Carrillo. Most travelers on this scenic stretch of highway are either heading to the Caribbean coast or to the Central Valley. However, some are pulling off the road to visit the working research center Estación Biológica La Selva, the world-class botanical garden called Heliconia Island, or Rara Avis, one of the most isolated lodges in Costa Rica.

About 12 smoothly paved kilometers from Puerto Viejo de Sarapiquí is the village of Horquetas, around which you'll find the turnoffs for Heliconia Island and Rara Avis. From Horquetas it's another 15km to Hwy 32, which connects San José to the Caribbean coast and bisects Parque Nacional Braulio Carrillo on the way to San José.

ESTACIÓN BIOLÓGICA LA SELVA

Not to be confused with Selva Verde Lodge in Chilamate, **Estación Biológica La Selva** (☎ 2524-0697, 2766-6565; s/d incl meals US$88/166; Ⓟ) is a working biological research station that is well equipped with laboratories, experimental plots, a herbarium and an extensive library. On any given day, the station is usually teeming with scientists and students, who use the station as a headquarters for researching the nearby private reserve. Although most guests are affiliated with an institution of higher learning, La Selva does welcome drop-ins, though it's best to phone ahead and reserve your accommodations. Rooms are simple but comfortable, and rates include all meals and guided hikes.

La Selva is operated by the **Organization for Tropical Studies** (OTS; ☎ 2524-0607; www.ots.ac.cr), a consortium founded in 1963 to provide leadership in the education, research and wise use of tropical natural resources. In fact, many well-known tropical ecologists have trained at La Selva. Twice a year OTS offers a grueling eight-week course open mainly to graduate students of ecology, along with various other courses and field trips that you can apply for.

The area protected by La Selva is 16 sq km of premontane wet-tropical rainforest, much of which is undisturbed. It's bordered to the south by the 476-sq-km **Parque Nacional Braulio Carrillo** (p444), creating a protected area large enough to support a great diversity of life. More than 445 bird species have been recorded at La Selva, as well as 120 mammal species, 1850 species of vascular plants (especially from the orchid, philodendron, coffee and legume families) and thousands of insect species.

Hiking

Reservations are required for guided **hikes** (adult/child full day US$43/32, half-day US$34/25; 🕑 8am & 1:30pm daily; ♿) with a bilingual naturalist guide. You'll head across the hanging bridge and into 57km of well-developed jungle trails, some of which are wheelchair-accessible. Unguided hiking is forbidden, although you'll be allowed to wander a bit after your guided tour. Make reservations for the popular guided bird-watching hikes, led at 5:45am and 7pm, depending on demand. Profits from these walks help to fund the research station.

No matter when you visit La Selva, it will probably be raining. Bring rain gear and footwear that's suitable for muddy trails. Insect repellent and a water bottle are also essential.

For the truly rugged do-it-yourself adventurers, it's possible to hike from La Selva to the southernmost ranger stations in Parque Nacional Braulio Carrillo. For more information on hiking in Braulio Carrillo, see p445.

Getting There & Away

Public buses between Puerto Viejo and Río Frío/Horquetas can drop you off 1km from the entrance to La Selva. It's about 4km from Puerto Viejo, where you can catch a taxi for around ₡2320 to ₡3480.

OTS runs buses (₡5800) from San José on Monday. Make reservations when you arrange your visit, and note that researchers and students have priority.

SUEÑO AZUL RESORT

Yoga-retreat groups make up the majority of guests at **Sueño Azul** (☎ 2764-1000; www.suenoazulresort.com; s/d/ste US$100/122/174; P ✻ ≋), a top-end resort upon a hill. Independent travelers interested in honing their yoga practice will appreciate the appeal of this peaceful place, especially at the secluded bamboo yoga platform if no groups have scheduled a stay. Spacious, airy rooms have a hot-water shower and bamboo furnishings, and are nestled on the grounds of this private jungle reserve. Hiking trails offer jungle walks to waterfalls, and the reserve can also be explored on horseback.

HELICONIA ISLAND

This self-proclaimed 'oasis of serenity' is arguably the most beautiful garden in all of Costa Rica. **Heliconia Island** (☎ 2764-5220; www.heliconiaisland.com; s/d incl breakfast US$55/72, d with air-con US$85; P ✻) is a masterpiece of landscape architecture that was started in 1992 by New York City native Tim Ryan, a former professor of art and design. Today, this 2.3-hectare island is owned by Dutch couple Henk and Carolien, and is home to more than 80 varieties of heliconias, tropical flowers, plants and trees. The grounds are a refuge for 228 species of birds (hummingbirds are the sole pollinators of heliconias). There are also resident howler monkeys, river otters and a few friendly dogs that will greet you upon arrival.

Henk and Carolien will guide you through the property, showing off a number of memorable plants including the Madagascar traveling palm, rare hybrids of heliconia found only on the island, and the *Phenakospermum guyannense* (Phenomenal sperm), a unique flowering plant native to Guyana. The admission fee (self-guided/guided tours US$11/17) is waived for overnight guests. You can stay in this oasis in immaculate raised cabins, which have stone floors, hot-water showers and breezy balconies.

Heliconia Island is about 5km north of Horquetas, and there are signs along the highway pointing to the entrance. When you arrive at the entrance, park your car, walk across the metal bridge and turn left on the island to reach the gardens.

RARA AVIS

When they say remote, they mean remote: this **private reserve** (☎ 2764-3131; www.rara-avis.com; P), which is comprised of 13 sq km of high-altitude tropical rainforest, is accessible only to overnight guests willing to make the three-hour tractor ride (seriously!) up a steep, muddy hill to get there.

Rara Avis was founded by Amos Bien, an American who came to Costa Rica as a biology student in 1977. Amos is dedicated to environmental conservation, and has been involved in a number of ongoing sustainability projects since his arrival. The private reserve borders the eastern edge of Parque Nacional Braulio Carrillo and has no real dry season. **Bird-watching** here is excellent, with more than 350 species sighted so far, while mammals including monkeys, coatis, anteaters and pacas are often seen. Visitors can use the trail system alone, or on guided hikes included in the cost of lodging. A popular jaunt is the short trail leading from the lodge to **La Catarata**, a 55m-high waterfall that cuts an impressive swath through the forest.

The accommodations, although lovely, are rustic – most don't have electricity, though the kerosene lamps and starry skies are unforgettable. Room prices, which include all meals, transportation and a guided hike, seem high, but it's because of the remote location – you, the groceries and the guides all have to be hauled up that mountain from Horquetas.

A GREEN-GREEN SITUATION

The gorgeous green plumage, electric-blue wing tips and red forehead of the great green macaw *(Ara ambiguus)* have long attracted collectors of exotic birds. The illegal sale of just one green macaw can fetch several thousand dollars, despite the fact that the species' nervous personality causes them to fare poorly in captivity. International trade has depleted the population, though fortunately, the great green macaw is protected by the Convention on International Trade in Endangered Species (Cites).

In addition to illegal poaching, deforestation also threatens the great green macaw. The northern lowlands have suffered from heavy deforestation in recent years due to the demand for increased agricultural and pasture land. Furthermore, the almendro tree *(Dipteryx panamensis)*, whose nut provides 90% of the macaw's diet and whose high hollows are far and away the preferred nesting tree for breeding pairs, is highly sought after as a luxury hardwood. Extensive logging of the almendro has severely cut back potential nesting sites, and as a result, the great green macaw has made it onto the endangered species list. It's estimated that Costa Rica's population of great green macaws is as low as 200 individuals, with as few as 30 breeding pairs left.

But all is not lost! A coterie of nonprofit organizations and government agencies formed a committee to establish the **San Juan–La Selva Biological Corridor** (www.lapaverde.or.cr), which aims to protect existing green macaw populations as well as other species in the area. The proposed corridor would bridge the gap between the Reserva Cordillera Volcánica Central, Refugio Nacional de Vida Silvestre Barra del Colorado, Parque Nacional Tortuguero and the Indio-Maíz, Punta Gorda and Cerro Silva reserves in Nicaragua. Eventually, the hope is that all of these protected areas will form a part of a Mesoamerican biological corridor that will stretch from Mexico through Central America.

In 2005 the **Refugio Nacional de Vida Silvestre Mixto Maquenque** was officially declared by then-President Abel Pacheco. Owing to this victory, Maquenque now protects an estimated 6000 species of vascular plants, 139 mammals, 515 birds, 135 reptiles and 80 amphibians. And as a 'mixed-use' wildlife refuge, the first of its kind in Costa Rica, it allows human residents to continue living and working within the boundaries of the refuge. However, most of the refuge's approximately 500 sq km, which are privately owned, are now bound to certain regulations, such as the drastic reduction of activities such as logging. So where does this leave the residents, who depend on forestry and agriculture for subsistence?

Enter the **Costa Rican Bird Route** (www.costaricanbirdroute.com), a project initiated by the nonprofit Rainforest Biodiversity Group in partnership with several other nonprofit organizations. The Costa Rican Bird Route has been working with and educating communities within these protected areas to help create viable and sustainable ecotourism opportunities, as economic alternatives to habitat-destructive agriculture and logging. While promoting existing locally owned lodges throughout the region, the Costa Rican Bird Route is also helping to establish new, community-based ecolodges from Río San Juan to Parque Nacional Braulio Carrillo. The hope is that green tourism – a field in which Costa Rica shines – will not only be more financially beneficial to these poor communities, but will also be salvation for the great green macaw.

The great news for travelers is that this blossoming bird-watching route offers a rare chance for a wilder bird-watching experience in one of the least developed regions of Costa Rica. Not only do you get to interact in a real way with the local people and contribute directly to their communities, but traveling way out here may lead you right into the path of a beautiful great green macaw.

We've listed some lodges participating in the Costa Rican Bird Route, in the Boca Tapada area (p512) and around Puerto Viejo de Sarapiquí (p506). Check the website for specific lodges, as well as for current volunteer opportunities.

Very basic **cabins** (per person US$50) in the woods sleep four and have shared cold-water bathrooms, while nicer rooms in the **Waterfall Lodge** (s/d/tr US$80/150/195) have a private hot-water shower and a balcony overlooking the rainforest. Even when it's pouring outside you can watch the birds from your private balcony. The **River-Edge Cabin** (s/d US$80/160) is the nicest spot, with solar-powered electricity, hot water and separate rooms. It's a dark (or romantic, depending on the company) 10-minute hike from the rest of the lodge.

Because getting here is time-consuming and difficult, a two-night stay is recommended. The bus to Puerto Viejo de Sarapiquí leaves San José (₡1160, 1½ hours) from the Guápiles-Limón terminal at 6:30am, and you'll need to get off at Horquetas. Here, you'll embark on the famed tractor ride. You can also arrange to be taken by jeep or on horseback, both of which require hiking the last 3km yourself.

HWY 126 TO SAN MIGUEL

Curving up the slopes of the Cordillera Central, Hwy 126 leaves behind the urban bustle of Heredia and Alajuela and leads to the foot of Volcán Poás before descending again into the bougainvillea-laced greenery of *fincas* and pastureland. This is *campesino* (farmer) country, where the plodding hoofbeat of cattle is about the speed of life, as the hard-to-spot rural speedbumps will remind you if you take those curves too quickly.

The highway passes through a number of small towns and villages before reaching San Miguel, which is the main transportation hub in the southeast corner of the region. From San Miguel, you can head northwest toward Los Chiles or northeast toward Puerto Viejo de Sarapiquí. Buses from San José to Puerto Viejo de Sarapiquí follow this route.

Hwy 126 climbs to just more than 2000m before reaching the tiny village of Vara Blanca, and, if you are lucky, on a clear day you can see Volcán Poás to the west and Volcán Barva to the east. At the gas station in town, continue straight if you're heading to Poás or make a right turn for San Miguel. A few kilometers past the turnoff, the road starts to descend at a dizzying speed. If you're on a tour or driving your own car, there are numerous viewpoints to stop for a photograph as well as ample opportunities for high- and middle-elevation bird-watching.

About 8km north of Vara Blanca, Río La Paz is crossed by a bridge on a hairpin bend; to your left you will find an excellent view of the absolutely spectacular Catarata La Paz. Several other waterfalls may also be seen, particularly on the right-hand side (if you are heading north) in the La Paz Valley, which soon joins up with the Sarapiquí Valley.

In January 2009 a massive earthquake (see boxed text, p126) struck the Vara Blanca area, destroying the road from Vara Blanca to San Miguel. At the time of writing, a new road was under construction and scheduled for completion in late 2010. Check with locals for updates. Until the new road opens, the best way to drive from San José to Sarapiquí is to go counterclockwise, taking Hwy 32 to Santa Clara, then Hwy 4 north to Sarapiquí.

SAN MIGUEL TO LOS CHILES

The route from San Miguel to Muelle de San Carlos is trimmed by papaya plantations and jungles and winds through the mountains in a series of hairpin turns. But just as the patchwork of *fincas* and wildflowers gives way entirely to sugarcane, the road opens to a long, straight and usually steaming-hot stretch across the lowlands to Caño Negro and hot, dusty Los Chiles. This is the principal route to the border crossing with Nicaragua, which is a straightforward trip by riverboat from Los Chiles.

If, instead of heading northwest, you travel north through the small town of Pital, you'll find yourself bumping along the back roads of one of the least-touristed parts of Costa Rica. This northern zone makes up part of the San Juan–La Selva Biological Corridor, an ongoing collaborative project involving nonprofit conservation organizations and local communities to create a wildlife refuge, with the Refugio Nacional de Vida Silvestre Mixto Maquenque (see boxed text, p510) at its heart.

VENECIA & AROUND

The westbound road traces the northern limits of the Cordillera Central as flowering vines scramble down the mountains and threaten to overtake the road. In the distance, the northern lowlands appear as a patchwork quilt of cane fields and rice paddies. The road momentarily straightens out as it enters the rural town of Venecia, 14km west of San Miguel, though the town passes by in a heartbeat as the road continues its dizzying wind toward Muelle de San Carlos.

If you're looking to break up the driving, what better place to spend the night than Venecia's famous 'medieval castle' of **Torre Fuerte Cabinas** (☎ 2472-2424; s/d US$30/60; P), behind the big church. Though it looks like it would feel more at home on the Las Vegas Strip, rooms are clean and have a bathroom with hot water. Plus, if you stay there you can tell all your friends and family that you spent the night in a Costa Rican castle.

A great place to relax and rejuvenate your body after a long drive is **Recreo Verde** (☎ 2472-1020; www.recreoverde.com; campsites US$15, s/d incl breakfast US$35/55; P), which has a number of rustic *cabinas* near a river bend, all with private bathroom. Guests have access to four mineral baths featuring a variety of different-colored mud, as well as three cold-water pools fed by mountain spring water. There's also a soccer pitch for a quick pick-up game, and a number of rainforest trails that you can hike and explore. You can also go spelunking in the Cueva de la Muerte (Cave of Death), though the only real danger is the risk of catching a cold.

Halfway between San Miguel and Venecia is the hamlet of Río Cuarto, from where an unpaved road heads southeast past the beautiful **waterfall** near Bajos del Toro, through Parque Nacional Juan Castro Blanco, and on to Zarcero.

BOCA TAPADA AREA

Don't bother venturing out here if Tico time ticks you off; the rocky roads and lack of signage (even less than usual!) could mean a few unintended detours. On the roads that pass pineapple fields and packing plants, your fellow travelers will be commuting *caballeros* (cowboys) and *campesinos* (farmers) going about their day-to-day business. And at the end of the road, you'll be rewarded with a luxuriant bit of rainforest replete with frog songs, rare avian residents and an inkling of the symbiosis that can happen when humans make the effort. Local ecolodges offer rainforest tours into the Refugio Nacional de Vida Silvestre Mixto Maquenque; for more information, see boxed text, p510.

Sleeping & Eating

Laguna del Lagarto Lodge (☎ 2289-8163; www.lagarto-lodge-costa-rica.com; s/d/tr US$45/59/68; P) This environmentally sensitive, German-run lodge is surrounded by 13 sq km of virgin rainforest and is something of a legend among birdwatchers. Simple but pleasant screened rooms have private bathroom and fan and share large, hammock-strung verandas. Package tours include transportation from San José, all meals and guided tours. Otherwise, breakfast is ₡3480, lunch ₡4060 and dinner ₡8120. Room rates include an afternoon guided hike through the jungle and a nighttime caiman-feeding walk.

Most of the 500-hectare 'grounds' of the lodge is rainforest, some of which is swamp – as a result the area's 10km of trails can get quite mucky. Canoes are available to explore the surrounding lagoons, where caimans dwell and Jesus Christ lizards make tracks across the water's surface. Horseback-riding trips and boat tours along the Nicaraguan border can be arranged.

The lodge is about 9km from Boca Tapada, and the staff can also arrange round-trip transportation from San José for ₡70,000 per person (two-person minimum).

Tico-run lodges near Boca Tapada include **Mi Pedacito de Cielo** (☎ 8308-9595; www.pedacitodecielo.net; s/d/tr US$65/75/85; P), whose name charmingly means 'my little piece of heaven.' The lodge has several rustic wooden bungalows built into the semiwild forest. Opened in 2009, **Maquenque Eco-Lodge** (☎ 2479-8200; www.maquenqueecolodge.com; r US$85/105; P) is located on 60 hectares with easy access to the new Refugio Nacional de Vida Silvestre Mixto Maquenque. The 14 bungalows feature bathroom with hot water and private deck. The tropical garden has a lovely swimming pool, and there's also an onsite bar and restaurant. Both lodges offer bird-watching, boating and horseback-riding tours in the Maquenque refuge.

Getting There & Away

If you're driving, getting to Boca Tapada is an adventure in itself. The nearest town of note is Pital, north of Aguas Zarcas. After passing through Pital, turn right after the church on the right and soccer field on the left and continue through the village of Veracruz. At the Del Huerto pineapple packing plant, hang a left and continue along the paved road. About 10km later, where the pavement ends, turn right at the intersection. When you come to the gas station, turn right at the intersection and follow the signs for Mi Pedacito del Cielo to Boca Tapada.

Buses from San José (₡2600, six hours) depart from the Atlántico Norte terminal at 5:30am and 12:30pm daily, with a connection to Boca Tapada, where most lodges can pick you up by prior request.

MUELLE DE SAN CARLOS

This small crossroads village is locally called Muelle, which means 'dock,' seemingly because 'Cañas' was already taken – this is sugarcane country. Breaks in the sweet scenery include huge sugarcane-processing facilities, always interesting to ponder over a soda, and very slow sugarcane-hauling trucks, so drive carefully. This was, actually, an important dock (hence the shipping infrastructure still here) as it's the most inland spot from which the Río San Carlos is navigable.

The main tourist activity in Muelle is pulling over to have a look at the map. A 24-hour gas station lies at the intersection of Hwy 4 (which connects Ciudad Quesada and Upala) and Hwy 35 (running from San José to Los Chiles). From Hwy 4 you can easily catch Hwy 32, the main artery serving the Caribbean coast. Can't decide? A range of accommodations will let you sleep on it, and they're convenient to just about everything.

Sleeping & Eating

Cabinas Beitzy (☎ 2469-9100; campsites US$4, d without bathroom US$10; P) The cheapest accommodations option in town is on the road to Los Chiles. It's perfectly acceptable if you need a place to crash, and the pool is surprisingly well maintained. Rooms are (not surprisingly) bare and share cold showers. If you're counting every dollar, you can also pitch a tent here and save yourself a few bucks.

La Quinta Lodge (☎ 2475-5260, fax 2475-5921; s/d US$35/40, cabinas per person US$10; P) About 5km south of Muelle in the tiny community of Platanar, this friendly Tico-run inn has a pool with a small water slide and sauna. Birds have adopted the grounds, and there's a small river behind the inn where fish and caimans can be seen. This is a popular option with Tico families as the atmosphere is warm and inviting.

SUGAR IN THE RAW

The origins of the sugar industry lie in the European colonization of the Americas, particularly on the Caribbean islands. Although it was possible for Europeans to import sugar from the colonies in Asia, the advent of slavery in the New World meant that sugarcane could be grown for a fraction of the cost. This in turn led to lower prices for the European consumer, which took precedent over the lives of the slaves forced to work in the fields.

During the 18th century, European diets started to change dramatically as sugar increased in popularity. Coffee, tea and cocoa were consumed in greater frequency, and processed foods such as candies and jams became commonplace items. The demand for increased production fueled the slave trade, though the actual process of refining sugar became increasingly mechanized.

Today, sugar is one of the most heavily subsidized agricultural products in industrial countries. Sugar prices in the USA, the EU and Japan are on average three times the international market cost as governments maintain elevated price floors by subsidizing domestic production and imposing high tariffs on imports. As a result, sugar-exporting countries are excluded from these markets, and thus receive lower prices than they would under a system of free trade. Brazil, which exports more than a quarter of the world's supply of refined sugar and heads a coalition of sugar-exporting nations, has repeatedly lobbied the World Trade Organization to reform the market.

For countries such as Costa Rica, sugar production is mainly a domestic industry because it's not profitable to export sugar to countries that levy a high tariff on imports – true even with the ratification of Cafta (US–Central American Free Trade Agreement), or TLC (Tratado de Libre Comercio), as the USA is loathe to open its sugar market to lower-priced imports.

Harvesting sugarcane manually is exhausting work as the stalks can grow to a height of 4m and they are thick, fibrous and difficult to cut down. It's becoming increasingly common in Costa Rica for sugarcane to be harvested using self-propelled harvesting machines, which has made it difficult for rural Ticos to find employment.

The next time you're driving through cane country, support the local industry and look for signs advertising *jugo de caña* – there's nothing quite like a cool glass of fresh sugarcane juice.

Hotel La Garza (☎ 2475-5222; www.hotellagarza.com; d/tr incl breakfast US$85/100, extra person US$15; P ⊠) Also near Platanar, this attractive, upscale lodge sits on a 700-hectare working dairy ranch and citrus plantation with views of the Río Platanar and far-off Volcán Arenal. Visitors enter the landscaped reception and restaurant area via a graceful suspension footbridge, and the 12 polished wooden bungalows with big porch, ceiling fan, telephone and good-sized private bathroom have a touch of class. Tennis, basketball and volleyball courts are available, as are 4km of private trails, a swimming pool and Jacuzzi. Tours are available, including horseback rides through primary and secondary tropical forest land (US$28/45 for two/four hours).

our pick **Tilajari Resort Hotel** (☎ 2469-9091; www.tilajari.com; s/d incl breakfast from US$99, extra person US$20; P ⊠) This former country club turned luxury resort has well-landscaped grounds overlooking the Río San Carlos, and it offers an impressive number of tours and activities. Comfortable, well-appointed rooms are accented with wood details and have private hot shower, cable TV, refrigerator and private terrace. A few of the rooms and private trails are wheelchair-accessible. Other amenities include a lovely pool area, racquetball and tennis courts, a restaurant, sauna, spa and butterfly garden (admission US$3.50), plus access to the neighboring 400-hectare private rainforest reserve with several trails. The resort is 800m west of the intersection at Muelle, on the road to Ciudad Quesada.

There are a number of *sodas* and a small supermarket on the road toward Los Chiles that will do just fine if you're looking for your *casado* fix. However, one recommended spot is **Restaurant-Bar La Subasta** (☎ 2467-8087; mains ₡1740-4000; 11am-11pm), which overlooks a bullpen and is bustling with hungry *campesinos*. It has an expansive menu of local dishes, and it's a great spot for a cold beer. If you speak Spanish, strike up a conversation here as you're bound to meet some interesting characters.

LOS CHILES

Seventy kilometers north of Muelle on a smooth, paved road through the sugarcane, and just three dusty, red and heavily rutted kilometers south of the Nicaraguan border, lies the sweltering farming and fishing town of Los Chiles. The humid lowland village, arranged with dilapidated grace around a grassy soccer field and along the unmanicured banks of the leisurely Río Frío, is pleasant enough – almost charming by border-town standards. It was originally settled by merchants and fisherfolk who worked on the nearby Río San Juan, much of which forms the Nicaragua–Costa Rica border. In recent history, Los Chiles served as an important supply route for the Contras in Nicaragua, and was home to a strong US military presence throughout the 1980s.

Gringo traffic is on the rise in Los Chiles as it's a great base for enjoying the scenic water route to Caño Negro, and an early morning excursion by small motorized boat is an adventure in itself. The second big draw is the scenic route to Nicaragua, a one-hour boat ride across the border that is becoming increasingly popular among foreign tourists. Crossing the border via the river is a relaxing, hassle-free way to go.

Although the road continues past Los Chiles to Nicaragua, this border post is closed to pretty much everyone. The police patrolling this line in the sand are heavily armed and extremely bored, so don't waste your time and energy trying your luck there.

Information & Orientation

The last stretch of paved road along Hwy 35 is home to a few restaurants, the post office and a gas station. If you continue north past Los Chiles on the rutted dirt road, you'll find yourself in the dusty no-man's-land en route to a border crossing you won't be allowed to use.

Drivers will want to hang a left (west) off the highway when you see the sign for Pali grocery store to reach the town center and docks of the Río Frío. Most services are located along this road. The **bus terminal** is tucked behind Soda Pamela. One block west is the **post office** (8am-noon & 1-5:30pm Mon-Fri). **Banco Nacional** (☎ 2212-2000), close to the central park and soccer field, changes cash and traveler's cheques and has a 24-hour ATM. Just down the road, around the side of the pink boutique, is **Multiservicios J&Q Internet Cafe** (☎ 2471-1636; per hr ₡600; 8:30am-noon & 2-8pm Mon-Sat). There's a **Cruz Roja** (Red Cross; ☎ 2471-1037/2025) on the west side of the plaza if you need some basic medical assistance or supplies.

NORTHERN LOWLANDS

The **docks** are located about 1km west of the bus terminal. If you're going by foot from the bus terminal, turn right onto the main street, walk one block past Cruz Roja, turn left, then make an immediate right downhill to the waterfront.

Before hopping on the boat to Nicaragua, you need to stop at the **migración** (immigration; ☎ 2471-1233; 🕑 8am-noon & 1:30-4pm), across the street from Hotel Tulipán. See boxed text, p515, for details on crossing into Nicaragua.

Tours

Los Chiles is a convenient base to organize your tours to Caño Negro. You'll be able to get on the river early, which means you'll probably see more wildlife than folks being shuttled in from La Fortuna and San José. The port is also a good jumping-off point for exploring the islands of Lago de Nicaragua (Lake Nicaragua), and if you miss the early boat, the local tour companies can sometimes arrange private transportation to San Carlos, Nicaragua.

You can arrange tours with Oscar Rojas at **Heliconia Tours & Restaurant** (☎ 2471-2096, 8307-8585), on the road between the *migración* and the dock, or at **Rancho Tulipán** (☎ 2471-1414; www.ranchotulipan.com). **Viajes y Excursiones Cabo Rey** (☎ 2471-1251, 8839-7458) provides a boat service to the refuge (from US$51) as well as to El Castillo and the islas Solentiname in Nicaragua. Cabo himself can usually be found by the dock.

GETTING TO SAN CARLOS, NICARAGUA

Although there's a 14km dirt road between Los Chiles and San Carlos, Nicaragua, using this crossing requires special permission generally reserved for federal employees. Most regular folk go across by boat on the Río Frío, which is easily arranged in Los Chiles. You must first get an exit stamp in your passport at the **migración** (immigration; ☎ 2471-1223; 🕑 8am-noon & 1:30-4pm), about 100m east of the dock and directly across the street from Hotel Tulipán. If you are coming from Nicaragua, you must make *migración* your first stop.

Regular boats (₡5800, 90 minutes) leave Los Chiles at 12:30pm and 3:30pm daily, with extra boats at 11am and 2:30pm if demand is high. Boats leave San Carlos for Los Chiles at 10:30am and 1pm, with extra boats scheduled as needed. Of course, the Nicaragua–Costa Rica border is not known for its reliability, so confirm these times before setting out. Nicaragua charges a US$7 entry fee and US$2 exit fee. Los Chiles municipality charges a ₡500 exit and entry fee; after getting your passport stamped at *migración*, walk down to the docks and pay the exit fee at the yellow Recaudador Municipal office. Reverse this procedure if you are arriving here from Nicaragua.

Your boat will make a stop at the actual border post about halfway through the trip; note the psychedelic 'camouflage' paint job on the building where your friendly, gun-wielding Nicaraguan border personnel are based.

When you hit the confluence of the Río San Juan, consider keeping your fingers and toes in the boat as there are river sharks (seriously!). Sharks are one of several euryhaline species that are able to survive in both fresh- and saltwater conditions. Every year, sharks that have been tagged by scientists in the Caribbean Sea are later found swimming in Lake Nicaragua. Although the rapids of the Río San Juan are a deterrent for most species of marine fish, sharks are apparently able to negotiate the river without problems, and presumably head for fresh water in search of food.

From San Carlos, which has a similar range of services to Los Chiles, you can arrange bus, boat or plane transportation to Managua, Granada and other destinations in Nicaragua. If you're looking to experience the Nica side of life, here's a quick list of the country's nearby highlights:

- Float down to **El Castillo**, one of Nicaragua's historical fortresses, accessible only by boat and one of the most chilled-out spots.
- Explore the twin volcanoes of **Isla Ometepe**, a strong contender for the world's most beautiful island.
- Pay a visit to the local artists on the **Islas Solentiname**, where art is truly the heartbeat of the community.

See boxed text, p242, for more information on southwestern Nicaragua.

At the boat dock you can also hire boat captains to take you up the Río Frío during the dry season and all the way into Lago Caño Negro during the rainy season, as well as to San Carlos, Nicaragua (see boxed text, p515). Three- to four-hour trips cost about US$50 to US$90 for a small group, depending on the size and type of boat.

Festivals & Events

This sleepy little town bursts to life during the October 4 **Feast of San Francisco**. Occasionally, festivities are held in Los Chiles during the irregularly scheduled **Binational Green Macaw Festival**, so look out for information.

Sleeping & Eating

Accommodations in town are surprisingly limited, though most people aren't too keen on sticking around anyhow.

Cabinas Jabirú (☎ 2471-1496, 8898-6357; r US$17; P ❄) Named for the rare, large jabiru stork *(Jabiru mycteria)* that can sometimes be seen at Caño Negro, this worn but clean spot near the bus terminal has bare rooms with hot-water bathrooms.

No Frills Hotel, Bar & Restaurant (☎ 2471-1200/410; r US$20; P ❄) This hotel, about 1km south of Los Chiles just past the gas station, is not, in fact, completely frill-free. Though basic, rooms here are clean and quiet (except for the honking of resident geese), with air-con and TV; some even have a full-sized fridge. The restaurant-bar is open for lunch and dinner, and the proprietors can also arrange fishing and boat tours.

our pick **Hotel Tulipán** (☎ 2471-1414; www.ranchotulipan.com; s/d/tr US$20/25/35; P ⊠ ❄ 🖳 ≋) Remodeled in 2009, Hotel Tulipán is the most respectable accommodations in town, though it's also home to a very popular (read: noisy!) bar that becomes a discotheque on Wednesdays and Fridays. All the rooms have air-con, hot-water bathroom and cable TV, and it's conveniently located right across from the immigration office. The onsite restaurant (mains ₡2700 to ₡4000; open 6am to late) has great local seafood and other specialties. Don't miss the teriyaki chicken fajitas.

Soda Juanita (☎ 2471-1607; mains ₡1100-3000; 🕑 6am-6pm) Right next to the dock, this cheery, bright-green *soda* serves up tasty *casados*, the usual deep-fried fast foods, *batidos* (fruit shakes) and coffee. Seating at the counter or at one of the thatch-shaded tables makes a sweet spot to watch the world go by and await your boat to Nicaragua.

Restaurante El Parque (☎ 2471-1373/090; mains ₡1800-4000; 🕑 6am-9pm) This popular spot facing the plaza has some of the best eats in town, and it's open early if you're looking to get your coffee fix before setting out on the river.

There's a Palí two blocks north of the bus stop, and the local Almacén de Los Chiles on the west side of the soccer field to meet all of your grocery and bakery needs.

Getting There & Away

Drivers usually get here via Hwy 35 from Muelle, about 70 paved, straight kilometers where you're likely to get passed by big-rig drivers with lead feet. Skid marks and roadkill iguanas do break up the monotony of endless sugarcane plantations. More scenic, if a little harder on your chassis, is the decent dirt road running for 50km from Upala, through Caño Negro, passable for normal cars throughout the dry season.

Regular boat transportation is limited to quick shuttles across the Nicaraguan border (₡5800) and various day trips throughout the region.

All buses arrive and leave from the terminal behind Soda Pamela, near the intersection of Hwy 35. Timetables are flexible, so play it safe and inquire locally.

Ciudad Quesada ₡1700; two hours; departs 12 times daily from 5am to 7pm.
San José ₡3000; five hours; departs 5am and 3pm.
Upala via Caño Negro ₡1400; 2½ hours; departs 5am & 4pm.

REFUGIO NACIONAL DE VIDA SILVESTRE CAÑO NEGRO

Because of the region's relative remoteness (although this has changed in recent years with the improvement of roads), this 102-sq-km **refuge** has long been frequented primarily by two sorts of specialists. Anglers come in search of that elusive 18kg snook, though they abandon ship April through July, when the park is closed to fishing (a good time to get a bargain price on accommodations). Bird-watchers alight on the refuge each year from January through March to spot an unequalled assortment of waterfowl. During the dry season water levels drop, with the effect of concentrating the birds (and fish) in photogenically (or tasty) close quarters. From January to March, when migratory birds land in large numbers, avian density is most definitely world-class.

The Río Frío defines the landscape – a table-flat, swampy expanse of marsh that is similar in appearance to other famous wetlands such as the Florida Everglades or the Mekong Delta. During the wet season, the river breaks its banks to form an 800-hectare lake, and then contracts during the dry months from January through April, when water levels drop to the point where the river is barely navigable. By April it has almost completely disappeared – until the May rains begin. This cycle has proceeded without fail for millennia, and the small fishing communities that live around the edges of the reserve have adapted to each seasonal nuance of their environment.

Thanks to improved roads, dozens of tour operators are now able to offer relatively inexpensive trips to Caño Negro from all over the country. However, it's advisable to book your trip through a reputable tour company as it's fairly common practice for operators to save on park fees by taking tourists on a boat ride through swampy private property that is by all accounts lovely, though not Caño Negro. If you're more independently minded, you'll save yourself a little money (and have a much better experience) by heading directly to the park without a tour operator, and hiring a local guide in town. This practice is recommended as it puts money directly in the hands of locals, and encourages communities in the area to protect the wildlife.

Orientation & Information

Caño Negro refuge is part of the Area de Conservación Arenal–Huetar Norte and is accessible primarily by boat. Close to the park entrance (that'd be the dock) is the tiny community of Caño Negro, which has no banks or gas stations. All visitors to the park must go to the **Minae office and ranger station** (☎ 2471-1309; adult/child under 12yr US$10/1; ⌚ 8am-4pm) to pay the entrance fees; it's located about 150m behind (north) of the green and pink *pulpería* (corner grocery store).

The ranger station can provide information and arrange guided tours. In addition to administering the refuge, rangers are contact points for local guides and a few community projects, including a butterfly garden put together by a local women's association (Asomucan). You can **camp** (per person US$2) by the river, or stay in the rangers' house for US$6 with advance reservations. There are cold showers, and meals can be arranged. At the time of writing, all park offices, research labs and accommodations were scheduled to move in late 2010 to the new **Estación Biológica Caño Negro**, located 6km north of the church at the end of the gravel road past the radio tower.

Local guides for fishing and ecological tours can also be arranged at most hotels and restaurants in town. You can usually find a guide (US$10 to US$20 per hour) on short notice, but they can get booked up during peak fishing and bird-watching seasons.

Wildlife-Watching

Caño Negro is regarded among bird-watchers as one of the premier destinations in Central America. During the dry season, the sheer density of birds in the park is astounding, and you'll be impressed with the number and variety of different species that inhabit the park. In the winter months, migratory duck congregations can be enormous, and very well represented groups include kingfisher, heron, egret, ibis, rail, anhinga, roseate spoonbill and stork. The refuge is also the only reliable site in Costa Rica for olivaceous cormorant, Nicaraguan grackle and lesser yellow-headed vulture.

Reptiles are easily seen in the park, especially spectacled caiman, green iguana and striped basilisk. Commonly sighted mammals in Caño Negro include howler monkey, white-faced capuchin and two-toed sloth. Despite increasing incursions from poachers, puma, jaguar and tapir have also been recorded here in surprising numbers.

Caño Negro also possesses an abundant number of river turtles, which were historically an important part of the Maleku diet (see boxed text, p521). Prior to a hunt, the Maleku would appease the turtle god Javara by fasting and abstaining from sex. If the hunt was successful, the Maleku would later celebrate by feasting on smoked turtle meat and consuming large quantities of *chicha,* or alcohol derived from maize.

Mosquitoes in Caño Negro are huge, abundant and most definitely classifiable as wildlife. Bring bug spray, or suffer the consequences.

Tours

If you don't have your own car or you're not a fan of public transportation, it's easiest to

THE WEEPING FOREST

Extensive deforestation of the Caño Negro area began in the 1970s in response to an increase in population density and the subsequent need for more farmland. Although logging was allowed to proceed in the area for almost 20 years, the government took action in 1991 with the creation of the Refugio Nacional de Vida Silvestre Caño Negro. Since its creation, Caño Negro has served as a safe habitat for the region's aquatic and terrestrial birds, and has acted as a refuge for numerous migratory birds.

However, illegal logging and poaching have continued around the perimeter of the park, and the wildlife has accordingly suffered. In the last two decades, one-time residents of the park including ocelot, manatee, shark and macaw have vanished. Tarpon and caiman populations are decreasing, and fewer migratory birds are returning to the park each year. Additionally, anglers are reporting record lows in both the size and number of their catches.

Satellite images show that the lake is shrinking each year, and that water levels in the Río Frío are dropping rapidly. It's difficult to say with certainty what is causing these changes, though the farms surrounding Caño Negro require extensive irrigation, and sugarcane is nearly 10 times as water-intensive as wheat.

Locals are extremely worried about the stability of the park as entire communities are dependent on fishing and tourism for their survival. In response to the growing need to regulate development in the region, area residents have formed a number of organizations aimed at controlling development in the northern lowlands. If you want to support the Caño Negro community, avoid booking your tour in another town and spend your tourist dollar locally.

organize a day trip to Caño Negro from La Fortuna, San José or any hotel within a 150km radius. Tours are geared toward wildlife-watching, although travelers report that a boatload of noisy tourists tends to scare away most animals. If you're looking to do a little sportfishing, it's best to organize your trips through one of the lodges in the park. Fishing licenses, valid for two months, can be arranged through the lodges or at the ranger station for US$34; you will need a photocopy of your passport and a small photo.

Caño Negro is not as difficult to access as it once was, and you'll have a much better experience if you avoid the tour operators and head directly to the park. Hiring a local guide is quick, easy and full of advantages – you'll be supporting the local economy, you'll have more privacy when you're out on the water and, of course, there's the satisfaction of doing things independently. You can usually find indie guides hanging around in the park or at the docks during the day. A recommended company is **Pantanal Tours** (8816-3382, 8825-0193), which offers boat trips through the park, plus fishing, kayaking and horseback-riding tours.

Either way, the key to Caño Negro is to get there as early in the morning as possible when wildlife is still active, and it's worth paying extra for an overnight adventure that puts you in the water by 7am. Folks staying in town basically have the refuge to themselves at daybreak, with boat-trippers from Puerto Viejo de Sarapiquí and Los Chiles arriving by 9am.

Sleeping & Eating

There are a few budget lodging options in town, plus a handful of nicer accommodations down the road, most of which are geared toward fishing.

Albergue Caño Negro (☎ 2471-2029; r without bathroom per person US$12; P) The cheapest accommodations in the area is this family-run venture of small *cabinas* overlooking the lagoon. Rooms are simple and share cold-water bathrooms, but the proprietors, Manuel and Isabel, are relaxed and friendly. Look for the little blue 'cabinas' sign and the stilt *cabinas* past the bend in the road after the Caño Negro Natural Lodge.

Kingfisher Lodge (☎ 2471-1116/369; s/d from US$25/50; P) These rustic *cabinas* are about 100m from the town center, and there is a variety of rooms to accommodate travelers of all budgets. They're owned and operated by the Sequera brothers, who are recommended refuge guides and boat captains. Two-hour fishing or naturalist trips for up to five people cost US$55, and you can also arrange horseback riding here. Stop by the pink house with the sign advertising the *cabinas* to have a look.

Hotel de Campo Caño Negro (☎ 2471-1012; www.hoteldecampo.com; s/d incl breakfast US$75/95; P ✖ 🏊) Set in an orchard of mango and citrus trees next to one of Caño Negro's lagoons, this Italian-run hotel is a fisherman's paradise. You can rent any combination of boats, guides (who speak English, Spanish, French and Italian), kayaks and fishing equipment here at the well-stocked tackle shop. And after angling for gargantuan tarpon all day, relax in comfortable, high-ceilinged rooms with air-con and private hot shower, or soak in the grotto-like Jacuzzi. There's also a restaurant (mains ₡4000 to ₡7000; open 7:30am to 9:30pm) specializing in, yep, fish.

Caño Negro Natural Lodge (☎ 2471-1000/426; www.canonegrolodge.com; s/d incl breakfast US$90/100; P ✖ 🏊) Perched on land that becomes a virtual island in the Río Frío during the rainy season, this lodge is surprisingly upscale considering its remote location. Well-appointed rooms have hot shower, air-con and satellite TV. The friendly staff can arrange all your trips while you relax in the pleasant pool, Jacuzzi or game room. The onsite restaurant, Jabirú, is open to the public and a great place for breakfast if you're weary of *gallo pinto* (rice and beans).

Soda La Palmera (☎ 2471-1045; mains ₡1700-5800; 🕒 6am-9pm) Right at the entrance to the refuge, this pleasant *soda* serves Tico standards and fresh fish, including your personal catch of the day. The staff can also arrange local guides for fishing and naturalist trips (US$45, two hours, up to three people). Advance reservations are recommended in the high season.

El Caiman Bar & Restaurante (☎ 8399-4164; mains ₡2320-5800; 🕒 10am-10pm Tue-Sun) At the bridge over the Río Frío just outside the village is this pleasant riverside eatery run by Canoa Aventura, a tour operator based in La Fortuna. Sit among the bamboo groves and feast on fresh sea bass or tilapia while you watch the caimans drift idly by, or rent a canoe and paddle into their territory.

Getting There & Away

The village of Caño Negro and the entrance to the park lie on the rough road connecting Upala and Los Chiles, which is passable to all cars during the dry season. However, this road is frequently washed out during the rainy season, when a 4WD is usually required.

There are three buses per day to Los Chiles (₡1000) and Upala (₡1200). Both buses pass through town and circle the village square at approximately 7am, 12:30pm and 6pm; ask around as this schedule changes frequently.

During the rainy season and much of the dry season, you can also catch a boat (₡8500) here from Los Chiles. This is becoming increasingly popular, especially as more travelers are crossing into and out of Nicaragua on the Río Frío (see boxed text, p515).

UPALA

Just 9km south of the Nicaraguan border in the northwestern corner of the northern lowlands, Upala is a small but thriving town that serves a widespread community of some 15,000 people. A center for the area's cattle and rice industries, Upala enjoys some apparent affluence. Most visitors are Costa

TOP WATERWAYS FOR WILDLIFE-WATCHERS

Head to some of the following waterways for an up-close glimpse of the local wildlife.

- Whether you're resting between rapids or traveling up to Trinidad, keep your eyes peeled for somnolent sloths or mud-covered caimans as you float up the **Río Sarapiquí** (p501).
- Wake up early to savor a quiet view of breakfasting birds on the lagoons of **Caño Negro** (p516).
- Not only is the **Río Frío** the kinder, gentler border crossing into Nicaragua (see boxed text, p515), but you'll see trees filled with howler monkeys, and caimans on the riverbanks along the way.
- Lodges in the Boca Tapada area (see p512) can get you on the **Río San Carlos**, where the slow flow near the Río San Juan affords good opportunities for bird-watching.
- Float on the **Río Medio Queso**, an off-the-beaten-track tributary that runs parallel to Río Frío (see p515), with much better opportunities for viewing birds and other wildlife.

Rican businesspeople, who arrive in town to negotiate for a few dozen calves or a truck-load of grain, but travelers who need to stop for the night between Caño Negro and the northwestern coast will find it nice enough.

Sleeping

Hotel Buena Vista (☎ 2470-0186; r with/without air-con US$19/14; P ❄) This cute yellow compound is a steal, with clean but unremarkable rooms that come with hot-water bathroom and TV. There's a shaded courtyard and secure parking at this family-run spot. Find it 150m south of the metal bridge.

Hotel Upala (☎ 2470-0169; s/d US$14/20; P ❄) The most established hotel in town is always a good choice as all rooms are spotless and bright, and you can watch the soccer games from your private porch. Rooms have a cold-water shower and cable TV.

Cabinas Maleku (☎ 2470-0142; s/d with air-con US$22/26, with fan US$16/22; P ❄) Though it's a few dollars more, this is the best option in town. Big, high-ceilinged rooms with colorful cartoon murals have folksy furniture, including cheery Sarchí-style wooden chairs in front of the rooms. All rooms have a bathroom and a large TV with cable.

Eating

The busy market, just behind the bus terminal, opens early with several nice *sodas* dishing up good *gallos* (tortilla sandwiches), *empanadas* (corn turnovers filled with meat, cheese or fruit) and just about everything else. There are also a few Chinese restaurants and produce vendors.

Restaurant Buena Vista (☎ 2470-0063; mains ₡1700-4300; 🕑 11am-9pm) This breezy spot serves a good mix of typical Chinese food. It's also aptly named (Good View) as the river views are wonderful, although customer service leaves much to be desired.

Soda Norma (☎ 8819-7048; mains ₡2320-3500; 🕑 6:30am-9pm) With outdoor tables overlooking the park, this is a seriously top-notch *soda*, serving some of the most beautiful *casados* (with all the trimmings) you've ever seen.

Rancho Don Horacio (☎ 2470-0905; mains ₡3500-5220; 🕑 11am-10pm) Right off the plaza, and far more atmospheric, is this romantic restaurant with red tablecloths, mood lighting and a nice bar. The specialty is steak, and chances are it was born, raised and slaughtered right here in Upala.

Getting There & Away

Upala is connected to the Interamericana north of Cañas by Hwy 6, an excellent paved road, and also to La Fortuna and Laguna de Arenal by the somewhat more potholed Hwy 4. A rough, unpaved road, usually passable to all cars, skirts the Refugio Nacional de Vida Silvestre Caño Negro on the way to Los Chiles, the official border crossing with Nicaragua.

Other dirt roads cross the Nicaraguan border, 9km away, but these are not official entry points into either Costa Rica or Nicaragua.

The bus terminal is right off the park; a **ticket booth** (🕑 4:30-5:15am, 7:30am-1pm & 6:45-8pm Mon-Sat) has information and can store bags for ₡580. Taxis congregate just outside the bus terminal. The following buses depart from Upala:

Los Chiles, via Caño Negro ₡2200; two hours; departs 5am, 11am and 4pm.

San José, via Cañas ₡3500; five hours; 4:30am, departs 5:15am and 9:30am.

San José, via Ciudad Quesada/San Carlos ₡3500; five hours; departs 9am.

SAN RAFAEL DE GUATUSO AREA

The small town of Guatuso (shown on some maps as San Rafael) is 19km northeast of Nuevo Arenal and 40km east of Fortuna (not to be confused with the town of La Fortuna), and is the main population center of this predominantly agricultural area. Although the town itself is rather unremarkable, it's a good base for exploring the fantastic Venado Caves and Parque Nacional Volcán Tenorio (p219). The area is also home to the few remaining Maleku (see boxed text, p521), one of Costa Rica's indigenous groups, and Guatuso makes a good base for visiting the nearby *palenques* (indigenous settlements).

Venado Caves

Four kilometers south of Venado (Spanish for 'deer') along a good dirt road, the **caves** (☎ 2478-8008; admission US$17; 🕑 7am-4pm, last admission 2:30pm) are a popular rainy-day attraction that can be organized as a day trip from La Fortuna, San José and many other cities for US$45 to US$70 per person (including transportation and lunch). It's cheaper and easier to visit with your own car, as bus service is inconvenient.

The caves were discovered by chance in 1945 when a farmer fell through a hole in the ground and found himself in an underground

A BRIEF HISTORY OF THE MALEKU

The Maleku (colloquially referred to as the Guatuso) are one of the few remaining indigenous groups in Costa Rica. Unlike other pre-Columbian populations, the Maleku are closer in stature to Europeans, and their skin tone is comparatively lighter than that of other groups in Central America. Historically, the Maleku were organized into 12 communities that were scattered around the Tilarán-Guanacaste range and the Llanura de San Carlos.

Although their numbers dwindled following the arrival of Spanish colonists, the population survived relatively intact until the early 20th century. With the invention of the automobile, the US rubber industry started searching for new reserves to meet the increasing demand for tires. With the aid of Nicaraguan mercenaries, industry representatives scoured Central America for stable reserves, which were found on Maleku-inhabited land. The resulting rubber war virtually wiped out the population, and confined the survivors to a handful of communities. Today, the Maleku number around 400, and live in the three *palenques* (settlements) of Sol, Margarita and Tonjibe.

As is the situation with most indigenous groups in Costa Rica, the Maleku are among the poorest communities in the country, and they survive by adhering to a subsistence lifestyle. Their diet revolves around corn and the *tipuisqui* root, a traditional food source that grows wild in the region. Fortunately, since the Maleku have a rich artisan tradition, they are able to earn a small income by selling traditional crafts to tourists. Although their modern crafts primarily consist of pottery, jewelry, musical instruments and other small trinkets that are desirable to tourists, historically they were renowned for their impressive jade work and arrow craftsmanship.

The Maleku are also famous for their unique style of clothing known as *tana*. Although it's rare to see modern Maleku wearing anything other than Western-style clothing, *tana* articles are often offered to tourists for purchase. *Tana* is actually tree bark that has been stripped of its outer layer, soaked in water and then pounded thin on wooden blocks. After it has been dried and bleached in the sun, it can be stitched together like leather, and has a soft texture similar to suede.

Despite being small in number, the Maleku have held on to their cultural heritage, perhaps more than any other indigenous group in Costa Rica. This is especially evident in their language, which is one of the oldest in the Americas and linguistically distinct from the Amazonian and Maya dialects. Today, the Maleku still speak their language among themselves, and a local radio station, Radio Sistema Cultural Maleku, airs daily programs in the Maleku language. The Maleku have also maintained their ceremonial traditions, such as the trimonthly custom of crying out to Mother Nature for forgiveness through ritualistic song and dance.

As with all indigenous reservations in Costa Rica, the Maleku welcome tourists as craft sales are vital to their survival. You can access the *palenques* via Rte 143, though it's best to inquire locally for directions as the roads are poorly maintained and unsigned. While you're at the *palenque*, please be sensitive to their situation and buy a few small crafts. If you can, you might also consider bringing some small, useful gifts such as pencils, pens and paper, for the schools. And of course, avoid giving handouts such as money and candies, as this will only create a culture of begging.

chamber surrounded by stalactites (hanging *tight* to the ceiling) and stalagmites (that *might* reach the ceiling…get it?). The exploration that followed uncovered an eight-chamber limestone labyrinth which extends for almost 3km. The cavern system, composed of soft, malleable limestone, was carved over the millennia by a series of underground rivers.

The caves get rave reviews from folks fond of giant spiders, swarms of bats and eyeless fish. A guide takes you through the caves, including a few tight squeezes, pointing out various rock formations and philosophizing about what they sort of look like.

Drop-ins are welcome, but it's best to make reservations so you don't need to wait around for a group. You're provided with a guide (some speak English), lights, helmets and showers afterward. You'll definitely want to bring a change of clothes. There's a small onsite *soda*, and a few restaurants in Venado, but no lodging.

We don't recommend coming by bus; the 'early' bus from Ciudad Quesada drops you off at a steep 4km slog to the cave entrance at about 2pm, too late to make the last admission into the caves. A taxi from San Rafael de Guatuso will cost about ₡11,000.

If you're driving, the caves are well signed from Hwy 4.

Sleeping & Eating

There are several clean, basic *cabinas* in San Rafael de Guatuso, sometimes used on a long-term basis by farm workers, as well as a good selection of *sodas* and stores.

Cabinas Milagro (☎ 2464-0037; s/d US$6/10; P) This quiet, family-run place on the edge of town is a tranquil budget option. From the center, go past the church toward the Río Frío bridge and turn right just past the soccer field. Rooms have cold showers and fan.

Cabinas Tío Henry (☎ 2464-0344; r per person US$9; P ❄) Big, clean, air-conditioned rooms here are relatively plush, with cable TV and private hot shower. The *cabinas* are centrally located in town, though the reception is at the vet and feed store next door.

Soda La Macha (☎ 2464-0393; mains ₡1740; 🕑 breakfast, lunch & dinner) You don't exactly get a menu at this fine *soda*, on the main road across from the bus stop. Everything here is cooked using a wood-fired oven. Just request your *casado* (set meal) or *gallo* (tortilla sandwich) preferences and they'll be made on the spot.

Getting There & Away

Guatuso lies on Hwy 4, about 40km from both Upala, to the northwest, and Muelle de San Carlos, to the southeast. Buses leave about every two hours for either Tilarán or Ciudad Quesada, some of which continue to San José. Ciudad Quesada is the most frequent destination.

Directory

CONTENTS

ACCOMMODATIONS

The hotel situation in Costa Rica ranges from luxurious ecolodges and sparkling all-inclusive resorts to backpacker palaces and I-can't-believe-I'm-paying-for-this barnyard-style quarters. Given this astounding variety of accommodations, it's rare to arrive in a town and find nowhere to sleep.

High- or dry-season (December to April) prices are provided throughout this book, though many lodges lower their prices during the low or rainy season (May to November). Keep in mind that prices change quickly in Costa Rica, so it's best to see the prices in this book as approximations rather than facts.

Throughout this book, sleeping options are listed in order of budget, unless otherwise specified. Prices are inclusive of tax and given in US dollars, which is the preferred currency for listing rates in Costa Rica. However, colones are accepted everywhere, and are usually exchanged at current rates without an additional fee.

B&Bs

Almost unknown in the country prior to the ecotourism boom, the B&B phenomenon has swept through Costa Rica in the past two decades, primarily fueled by the increasing number of resident European and North American expats. Generally speaking, B&Bs in Costa Rica tend to be midrange to top-end affairs. While some B&Bs are reviewed in this guide, you can also find this type of accommodations on several websites (although they are far from exhaustive):

BedandBreakfast.com (www.bedandbreakfast.com/costa-rica.html)
Costa Rica Innkeepers Association (www.costaricainnkeepers.com)
Pamela Lanier's Worldwide Bed and Breakfasts Directory (www.lanierbb.com)

Camping

Camping is the way that many Ticos (Costa Ricans) can enjoy the more expensive seaside towns, especially since these days most accommodations cater specifically to foreigners. As a result, most major tourist destinations have at least one campsite, and if not, most budget hotels outside San José accommodate campers on their grounds. Although these sites usually include toilets, cold showers and basic self-catering facilities

BOOK YOUR STAY ONLINE

For more accommodations reviews and recommendations by Lonely Planet authors, check out the online booking service at www.lonelyplanet.com/hotels. You'll find the true, insider low-down on the best places to stay. Reviews are thorough and independent. Best of all, you can book online.

(a sink and a BBQ pit), they can be crowded, noisy affairs.

In most national parks, however, campsites are generally of excellent quality and are rigorously cleaned and maintained by dedicated staff. As a general rule, you will need to carry in all of your food and supplies, and carry out all of your trash.

Hostels

Although there are still a handful of Hostelling International (HI) hostels left in Costa Rica, the backpacker scene has gone increasingly top market in recent years. Compared to other destinations in Central America, hostels in Costa Rica tend to be fairly expensive affairs, though the quality of service and accommodations is unequalled.

Hotels

It is always advisable to ask to see a room – and a bathroom – before committing to a stay, especially in budget lodgings.

BUDGET

For the most part, this guide's budget category covers lodging in which a typical double costs up to US$40. The cheapest places generally have shared bathrooms, but it's still possible to get a double with a bathroom for US$25 in some towns off the tourist trail. (Note that 'private bathroom' in some low-end establishments consists of a stall in the corner of your hotel room.) On the top end of the budget scale, rooms will frequently include a fan and bathroom that may or may not have hot water. At the cheapest hotels, rooms will frequently be a stall, with walls that don't go to the ceiling.

Hot water in showers is often supplied by electric showerheads (affectionately termed the 'Costa Rican suicide shower'). Contrary to traveler folklore, they are perfectly safe – provided you don't fiddle with the showerhead while it's on. The electric showerhead will actually dispense hot water if you keep the pressure low.

> **HOSTEL & HOTEL SECURITY**
>
> Although hotels give you room keys, it is recommended that you carry a padlock for your backpack or suitcase for extra security. Furthermore, don't invite trouble by leaving valuables, cash or important documents lying around your room or in an unlocked bag. Upmarket hotels will have safes where you can keep your money and passport, so it's advised that you take advantage of them. If you're staying in a basic place, it's probably wise to take your valuables with you at all times. Theft is perhaps the number-one complaint of travelers in Costa Rica, so it can't hurt to take a few extra precautions.

MIDRANGE & TOP END

Midrange generally covers hotels that charge between US$40 and US$100. These rooms will be more comfortable than budget options, and will generally include a bathroom with gas-heated hot water, a choice between fans and air-con, and cable or satellite TV. Some places will also offer tour services, and many will have an onsite restaurant or bar and a swimming pool or Jacuzzi. In this price range, many hotels offer kitchenettes or even full kitchens, and using them is a great way to save money if you're traveling in a large group or as a family.

Anything more than US$100 is considered top end, and includes ecolodges, all-inclusive resorts, business and chain hotels, in addition to a strong network of more intimate boutique hotels, remote jungle camps and upmarket B&Bs. Many such lodging options will include amenities such as hot-water bath tubs, private decks, satellite TV and air-con as well as concierge, tour and spa services.

Most midrange and top-end places charge 13% in taxes. This book has attempted to include taxes in the prices listed throughout. Note that many hotels charge per person, rather than per room – read rates carefully. For information on reserving hotels by credit card, see boxed text, p525.

ACTIVITIES

For a full-color teaser of some of Costa Rica's top-billed activities, see the Costa Rica Outdoors feature on p405.

Bungee Jumping

No vacation appears to be complete without a head-first, screaming plunge off a bridge. **Tropical Bungee** (☎ 2248-2212, 8398-8134; www.bungee.co.cr) in San José has been organizing jumps off the Río Colorado bridge since 1992.

RESERVING BY CREDIT CARD

Some of the pricier hotels will require that you confirm your reservation with a credit card. Before doing so, note that some top-end hotels require a 50% to 100% payment upfront when you reserve. Unfortunately, many of them don't communicate this rule clearly.

Sometimes visitors end up 'reserving' a room only to find out that they have actually paid for it in advance. Technically, reservations can be canceled and refunded with enough advance notice. (Again, ask the hotel about its cancellation policy.) However, in Costa Rica it's a lot easier to make the reservation than to unmake it. In addition, many hotels charge a hefty service fee for credit card use.

Have the hotel fax or email you a confirmation. Hotels often get overbooked, and if you don't have confirmation, you could be out of a room.

Canopy Tours

Life in the rainforest takes place at canopy level. But with trees extending 30m to 60m in height, the average human has a hard time getting a look at what's going on up there. Indeed, it was only a matter of time before someone in Costa Rica invented the so-called 'canopy tour.'

Some companies have built elevated walkways through the trees that allow hikers to stroll through. **SkyTrek** (p200) near Monteverde and **Rainmaker** (p335) near Quepos are two of the most established operations in the country. A somewhat newer but equally popular operation is Actividades Arboreales near Santa María de Dota.

You can also take a ski lift-style ride through the tree tops, such as the **Rainforest Aerial Tram** near Braulio Carrillo (p445) or the smaller **Monteverde Trainforest** (p200) in Monteverde.

Diving & Snorkeling

Costa Rica doesn't pretend to rank alongside regional diving and snorkeling heavyweights such as Belize, the Cayman Islands and Bonaire. However, Costa Rica's underwater world does offer sheer number and variety of underwater life.

As a general rule, water visibility is not good during the rainy months, when rivers swell and their outflow clouds the ocean. At this time, boats to locations offshore offer better viewing opportunities.

The water is warm – around 24°C (75°F) to 29°C (84°F) at the surface, with a thermocline at around 20m below the surface where it drops to 23°C (73°F). If you're keeping it shallow, you can skin-dive (ie no wetsuit).

If you want to maximize your diving time, it's advisable to get diving accreditation beforehand. For more information, check out the **Professional Association of Diving Instructors** (PADI; ☎ in USA 949-858-7234, 800-729-7234, in Canada 604-552-5969, 800-565-8130, in Switzerland 52-304-1414; www.padi.com). **Divers Alert Network** (☎ in USA 800-446-2671, 919-684-2948; www.diversalertnetwork.org) is a nonprofit organization that provides diving insurance and emergency medical evacuation.

If you are interested in diving but are not accredited, you can usually do a one-day introductory course that will allow you to do one or two accompanied dives. If you love it, which most people do, consider getting certified, which takes three to four days and costs around US$350 to US$500.

The following dive companies offer liveaboard tours in Costa Rica:

JD's Watersports (☎ in USA 970-356-1028, 800-477-8971; www.jdwatersports.com)

Okeanos Aggressor (☎ in USA 985-385-2628, in USA & Canada 800-348-2628; www.aggressor.com)

Undersea Hunter (☎ 2228-6613, in USA 800-203-2120; www.underseahunter.com)

Fishing

Sportfishing is tremendously popular in Costa Rica, though the 'catch-and-release' mantra is strongly encouraged.

A good fishing resource is **Costa Rica Outdoors** (☎ 2282-6743, in USA 800-308-3394; www.costaricaoutdoors.com), a magazine available online or in hard copy that carries information on adventure travel, with a focus on fishing.

The following companies offer fishing tours in Costa Rica:

Discover Costa Rica (☎ 2257-5780, in USA 888-484-8227; www.discover-costa-rica.com) Offers six-day fishing packages and is based in Quepos.

JD's Watersports (☎ in USA 970-356-1028, 800-477-8971; www.jdwatersports.com)

Rod & Reel Adventures (☎ in USA 800-356-6982; www.rodreeladventures.com)

Hiking & Trekking

With mountains, valleys, jungles, cloud forests and two coastlines, Costa Rica is one of Central America's most varied hiking and trekking destinations. The country also boasts an extensive number of national parks that have well-developed hiking and trekking networks in even the most remote areas.

For long-distance hiking and trekking, it's best to travel in the dry season (December to April). Outside this narrow window, rivers become impassable and trails are prone to flooding. In the highlands, journeys become more taxing in the rain, and the bare landscape offers little protection. And then there are the mosquitoes which, needless to say, are enough to put a damper on your fun.

Costa Rica is hot and humid: hiking in these tropical conditions can really take it out of you. Overheating and dehydration are the main sources of misery on the trails, so be sure to bring plenty of water and don't be afraid to stop and rest. Make sure you have sturdy, comfortable footwear and a lightweight rain jacket.

Unfortunately, some readers have told us horror stories of getting robbed while on some of the more remote hiking trails. Although this is certainly not a common occurrence, it is always advisable to hike in a group for added safety. Hiring a local guide is another excellent way to enhance your experience, avoid getting lost and learn an enormous amount about the flora and fauna in your midst.

Some of the local park offices have maps, but this is the exception rather than the rule. If you are planning to do independent hiking on long-distance trails, be sure to purchase your maps in San José in advance (see p67).

The following companies offer trekking tours in Costa Rica:

Costa Rica Trekking Adventures (☎ 2771-4582; www.chirripo.com; San Isidro de El General) Offers multi-day treks in Chirripó, Corcovado and Tapanti.

Ocarina Expeditions (☎ 2229-4278; www.ocarinaexpeditions.com) Naturalist-led treks in Corcovado and Chirripó, as well as volcano and cloud-forest hiking.

Osa Aventura (☎ 2735-5670; www.osaaventura.com) Specializes in treks through Corcovado.

Horseback Riding

Wherever you go in Costa Rica, you will inevitably find someone giving horseback-riding trips. Rates vary from US$25 for an hour or two to more than US$100 for a full day. Overnight trips with pack horses can also be arranged, and are a popular way of accessing remote destinations in the national parks. Riders weighing more than 100kg cannot expect small local horses to carry them very far.

THESE BOOTS WERE MADE FOR WALKING

With its ample supply of mud, streams and army ants, hiking through Costa Rica's parks can be quite an adventure – particularly for your shoes. Footwear is a personal issue, but here are some options for keeping your feet happy in the jungle.

- Do as the locals do and invest in galoshes (rubber boots), especially for the rainy season. Rubber boots are indestructible, protect you from snakes and ticks, provide excellent traction and can be easily hosed off at the end of the day. The downside of rubber boots is that they are not very comfortable. Plus, river crossings guarantee that the boots will fill up with water at some point, and then your feet are wet for the rest of the day. If you are larger than a size 44 – men's 10 in the US – consider buying them abroad. Price: approximately US$6.
- High-end sport sandals (like Chacos or Tevas) are used by climbers to scramble up boulders to the starting points for climbing routes. These are great for crossing rivers, as the water runs right off them (and your feet). However, be aware that there are lots of creepy crawlies living in the rainforest, some of which might like to make lunch out of your toes, and sandals offer little protection. Price: US$50 to US$150.
- There is something to be said for good, solid, waterproof hiking boots. You don't have to pay an arm and a leg for sturdy boots that offer strong support and keep your feet marginally dry. If you can't stand the idea of walking around with wet feet, consider tossing a pair of sandals into your pack too, and change your shoes for the river crossings. Price: US$100 to US$250.

Travelers should continue to recommend good outfitters (and give the heads up on bad ones) by writing to Lonely Planet.

The following companies organize horseback riding in Costa Rica:

Sarapiquí Aguas Bravas (☎ 2292-2072; www.aguas-bravas.co.cr) Offers rafting, biking and horseback-riding day trips around Puerto Viejo de Sarapiquí and La Virgen.

Serendipity Adventures (☎ 2558-1000, in USA 734-995-0111, 800-635-2325; www.serendipityadventures.com) Creates quality horseback-riding itineraries, including journeys to a Cabécar indigenous reserve.

Mountain Biking & Motorcycling

Some cyclists claim that the steep, narrow, winding and potholed roads and aggressive Costa Rican drivers add up to a poor cycling experience. This may be true of the main roads, but there are numerous less-trafficked roads that offer plenty of adventure – from winding and scenic mountain paths with sweeping views to rugged trails that take riders through streams and by volcanoes.

Outfitters in Costa Rica and the USA can organize multiday mountain-biking trips around Costa Rica that cover stretches of highland and beach. Gear is provided on trips organized by local companies, but US outfitters require that you bring your own.

Most international airlines will fly your bike as a piece of checked baggage if you box it (remember to pad it well, because the box is liable to be roughly handled). Some airlines might charge you an extra handling fee.

You can rent mountain bikes in almost any tourist town, but the condition of the equipment varies. Another option is to buy a decent bike and sell it back at a reduced rate at the end of your trip. It is advisable to bring your own helmet and water bottle as the selection of such personalized items may be wider in your home country. For a monthly fee, **Trail Source** (www.trailsource.com) can provide you with information on trails all over Costa Rica and the world.

The following companies organize bike tours in Costa Rica:

Backroads (☎ in USA 510-527-1555, 800-462-2848; www.backroads.com) Offers a variety of excursion including a six-day cycling trip around Arenal and the Pacific coast.

Coast to Coast Adventures (☎ 2280-8054; www.ctocadventures.com) Everything from short cycling excursions to 14-day coast-to-coast multisport trips.

Costa Rica Expeditions (☎ 2257-0766, 2222-0333; www.costaricaexpeditions.com) Multisport itineraries including cycling, hiking, rafting and other adventures.

Lava Tours (☎ 2281-2458; www.lava-tours.com) Reader-recommended tours include a bike ride (mostly downhill) from the Cerro de la Muerte to Manuel Antonio. Offers day trips, multiday packages and riding clinics.

MotoDiscovery (☎ in USA 800-233-6564, 830-438-7744; www.motodiscovery.com) Organizes motorcycle tours through Central America, including an annual one from the Río Grande (known locally as Río Bravo del Norte) in Mexico to the Panama Canal.

Serendipity Adventures (☎ 2558-1000, in USA 734-995-0111, 800-635-2325; www.serendipityadventures.com) Creates custom cycling itineraries to fit your schedule and your group.

Western Spirit Cycling (☎ in USA 800-845-2453; www.westernspirit.com) Offers a few different eight-day cycling itineraries.

Wild Rider (☎ 2258-4604; www.wild-rider.com) Motorcycle tours; see p100.

River Rafting & Kayaking

The months between June and October are considered to be the wildest time for river rafting and kayaking, though some rivers offer good trips all year. Rafters and kayakers should bring sunblock, a spare change of clothes, a waterproof bag for a camera, and river sandals for foot protection. The government regulation of outfitters is poor, so make sure that your guide is well versed in safety and has had emergency medical training.

River kayaking can be organized in conjunction with white-water rafting trips if you are experienced; sea kayaking is a popular activity year-round.

The Costa Rica Outdoors chapter (p410) has more detailed information on destinations to raft and kayak.

Many companies specialize in kayaking and rafting trips:

Aventuras Naturales (☎ 2225-3939, 2224-0505, in USA 800-514-0411; www.toenjoynature.com)

BattenKill Canoe Ltd (☎ in USA 802-362-2800, 800-421-5268; www.battenkill.com) Trips include a six-day canoe journey around Monteverde and an 11-day paddle through Talamanca.

Coast to Coast Adventures (☎ 2280-8054; www.ctocadventures.com) Trips incorporate rafting, biking and trekking.

Costa Rica Expeditions (☎ 2257-0766, 2222-0333; www.costaricaexpeditions.com) Multisport itineraries including rafting and other adventures.

Costa Rica Sun Tours (☎ 2296-7757; www.crsuntours.com)

Exploradores Outdoors (☎ 2222-6262; www.exploradoresoutdoors.com) With offices in San José and Puerto Viejo de Talamanca, offers one- and two-day rafting trips.
Gulf Islands Kayaking (☎ in Canada 250-539-2442; www.seakayak.ca) Tours on offer include five days of sea kayaking in Corcovado.
H2O Adventures (☎ 2777-4092; www.aventurash2o.com) Two- and five-day adventures on the Río Savegre. Also offers day-long river-rafting and sea-kayaking excursions.
Mountain Travel Sobek (☎ in USA 510-594-6000, 888-687-6235; www.mtsobek.com) Offers a 10-day adventure that incorporates sea kayaking and river rafting.
Ocarina Expeditions (☎ 2229-4278; www.ocarinaexpeditions.com)
Ríos Tropicales (☎ 2233-6455; www.riostropicales.com) Offers many day-long river-rafting trips, as well as some two- and three-day adventures on the Río Pacuare and two days of kayaking in Tortuguero.
Safaris Corobicí (☎ 2669-6191; www.nicoya.com) These slow-moving rafting trips are less for adventurers and more for bird-watchers.
Sarapiquí Aguas Bravas (☎ 2292-2072; www.aguas-bravas.co.cr) Offers rafting, biking and horseback-riding day trips around Sarapiquí and La Virgen.

Surfing

Most international airlines accept surfboards (they must be properly packed in a padded board bag) as one of the two pieces of checked luggage, though this is getting more difficult (and expensive) in the age of higher fuel tariffs. Domestic airlines offer more of a challenge. They will accept surfboards (for an extra charge), but the board must be under 2.1m in length. If the plane is full, there's a chance your board won't make it on because of weight restrictions.

In recent years, it's becoming more popular to buy a board (new or used) in Costa Rica, and then sell it before you leave. Great places to start your search include **Jacó** (p324), **Mal País** and **Santa Teresa** (p306), and **Tamarindo** (p266). It's usually possible to buy a cheap long board for about US$250 to US$300, and a cheap short board for about US$150 to US$200. Most surf shops will buy back your board for about 50% of the price you paid.

Outfitters in many of the popular surf towns rent short and long boards, fix dings, give classes and organize excursions. **Jacó** (p324), **Tamarindo** (p266), **Pavones** (p437) and **Puerto Viejo de Talamanca** (p481) are good for these types of activities.

For detailed surfing information, including a comprehensive surfer's map, see p408. The following companies organize tours and/or courses:

Costa Rica Rainforest Outward Bound (☎ 2278-6058, in USA 800-676-2018; www.crrobs.org) Multiweek courses cover surf spots in Nicaragua, Panama and Costa Rica.
Discover Costa Rica (☎ 2257-5780, in USA 888-484-8227; www.discover-costa-rica.com) Budget surf packages center on Tamarindo, Jacó and the Caribbean coast.
Pura Vida Adventures (☎ in USA 415-465-2162; www.puravidaadventures.com; Mal País) Multiday packages catered exclusively for women.
Tico Travel (☎ in USA 800-493-8426; www.ticotravel.com) Offers a great variety of surfing packages and camps.
Venus Surf Adventures (☎ 8840-2365, in USA 800-793-0512; www.venussurfadventures.com; Pavones) Offers a six-day surf camp for women only, including lessons, yoga and other activities.

Wildlife- & Bird-Watching

Any of Costa Rica's national parks are good places for observing wildlife, as are the various private reserves scattered around the country. The following Costa Rican–based companies come highly recommended by our readers. These companies can book everything, from gentle hikes to expeditions in remote wilderness.

Aratinga Tours (☎ 2770-6324; www.aratinga-tours.com) Pieter Westra specializes in bird tours in his native Dutch, but he is fluent in English, Spanish and many dialects of bird. His website provides an excellent introduction to bird-watching in Costa Rica.
Costa Rica Expeditions (☎ 2257-0766, 2222-0333; www.costaricaexpeditions.com) Offers custom itineraries and a network of ecolodges.
Expediciones Tropicales (☎ 2257-4171; www.costaricainfo.com) Offers a variety of one- and two-week itineraries.
Horizontes (☎ 2222-2022; www.horizontes.com) An 11-day itinerary (US$1706) visits Tortuguero, Arenal, Monteverde and Manuel Antonio.

Windsurfing & Kitesurfing

Laguna de Arenal is the nation's undisputed windsurfing (and kitesurfing) center. From December to April, winds are strong and steady, averaging 20 knots in the dry season, with maximum winds of often 30 knots, and windless days are a rarity. The lake has a year-round water temperature of 18°C (64°F) to 21°C (70°F) with 1m-high swells. For more information see boxed text, p179.

For warmer water (but more inconsistent winds), try Puerto Soley in the Bahía Salinas (p241).

BUSINESS HOURS

Restaurants are usually open from 7am and serve dinner until 9pm, though upscale places may open only for dinner. In remote areas, even the small *sodas* (inexpensive eateries) might open only at specific meal times. See other business hours on the inside front cover of this book. Unless otherwise stated, count on sights, activities and restaurants to be open daily.

CHILDREN

Costa Rica is a kid-friendly country, especially since Ticos themselves are extremely family-orientated, and will go out of their way to lavish attention on children. Although you will have to take certain precautions to ensure the health and safety of your little ones, Costa Rica is arguably the most popular family destination in Latin America. As such, we have tried to highlight the best of 'Costa Rica for children' throughout this book – see various destinations for more information, as well as p21.

For starters, children under the age of 12 receive a 25% discount on domestic-airline flights, while children under two fly free (provided they sit on a parent's lap). Children pay full fare on buses (except for those under the age of three). Car seats for infants are not always available at car-rental agencies, so bring your own.

Most midrange and top-end hotels have reduced rates for children under 12, provided the child shares a room with parents. Top-end hotels will provide cribs and usually have activities for children.

If you're traveling with an infant, bring disposable diapers (nappies), baby creams or toiletries, baby aspirin and a thermometer from home, or stock up in San José. In rural areas, supplies may be difficult to find, though cloth diapers are more widespread (and friendlier to the environment).

For a near-infinite number of other travel suggestions, check out Lonely Planet's *Travel with Children*.

CLIMATE CHARTS

For a small country, Costa Rica's got an awful lot of weather going on. The highlands are cold, the cloud forest is misty and cool, San José and the Central Valley get an 'eternal spring' and both the Pacific and Caribbean coasts are pretty much sweltering year-round. Get ready for some bad-hair days!

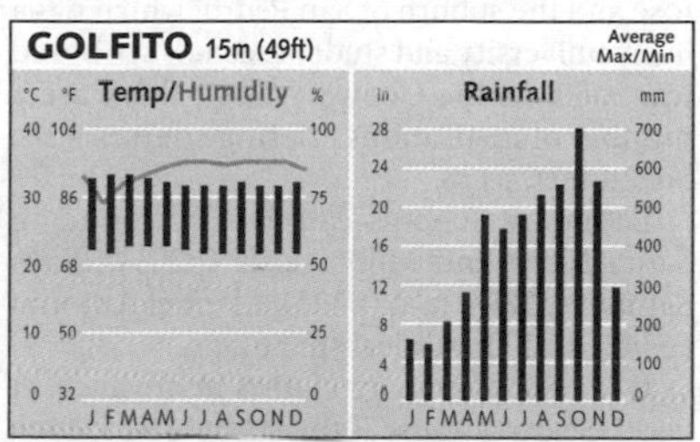

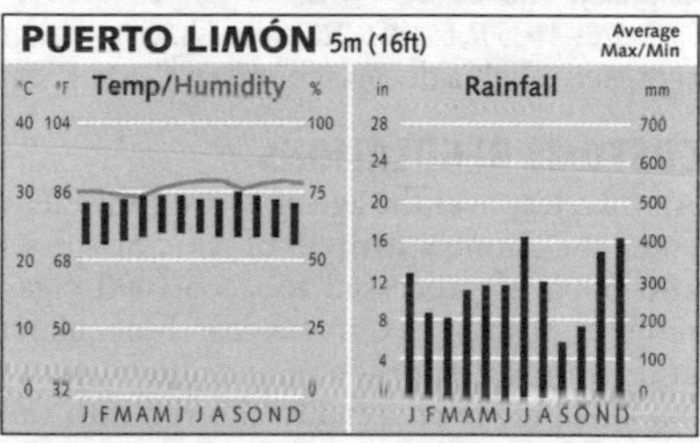

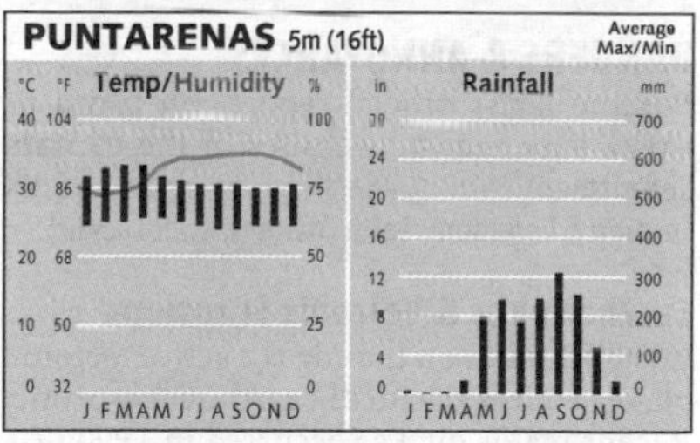

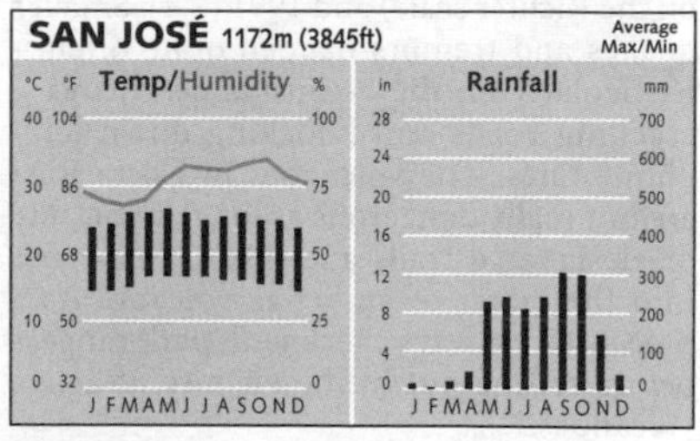

COURSES

Language

Spanish-language schools operate all over Costa Rica, and they charge by the hour for instruction. Lessons are usually intensive, with class sizes varying from two to five pupils and classes meeting for several hours every weekday.

Courses are offered mainly in central San José and the suburb of San Pedro, which has a lively university and student scene – see boxed text, p80. In the Central Valley, there are a number of institutions offering courses – see boxed text, p128.

Language schools can also be found in Santa Elena and Monteverde (p201), Playa Sámara (p287), Jacó (p325), Manuel Antonio (p342) and Dominical (p356).

It is best to arrange classes in advance. A good clearing house is the **Institute for Spanish Language Studies** (ISLS; ☎ 2258-5111, in USA 800-765-0025, 626-441-3507, 858-456-9268; www.isls.com), which represents half a dozen schools in Costa Rica.

CUSTOMS REGULATIONS

All travelers over the age of 18 are allowed to enter the country with 5L of wine or spirits and 500g of processed tobacco (400 cigarettes or 50 cigars). Camera gear, binoculars, and camping, snorkeling and other sporting equipment are readily allowed into the country.

DANGERS & ANNOYANCES

For the latest official reports on travel to Costa Rica see the websites of the **US State Department** (www.travel.state.gov/travel) or the **UK Foreign & Commonwealth Office** (www.fco.gov.uk).

Earthquakes & Volcanic Eruptions

Costa Rica lies on the edge of active tectonic plates, so it is decidedly earthquake-prone. Recent major quakes occurred in 1990 (7.1 on the Richter scale) and 1991 (7.4). Smaller quakes and tremors happen quite often – particularly on the Península de Nicoya – cracking roads and knocking down telephone lines. The volcanoes in Costa Rica are not really dangerous as long as you stay on designated trails and don't try to peer into the crater of an active volcano. As a precaution, always check with park rangers before setting out in the vicinity of active volcanoes.

Hiking Hazards

Hikers setting out into the wilderness should be adequately prepared for their trips. Most importantly, don't bite off more than you can chew. If your daily exercise routine consists of walking from the fridge to the TV, don't start your trip with a 20km trek. There are plenty of 3km and 5km trails that are ideally suited to the less active.

In addition, carry plenty of water, even on very short trips. The hiking is hot and dehydration sets in quickly. In Corcovado, hikers have died from exhaustion on the scorching trail between San Pedrillo and Sirena. Hikers have also been known to get lost in rainforests, so carry maps, extra food and a compass. Let someone know where you are going, so they can narrow the search area in the event of an emergency.

There is also wildlife to contend with. Central America's most poisonous snakes, the fer-de-lance (the 'Costa Rican landmine') and the bushmaster, are quite assertive, and crocodiles are a reality at many estuaries. As if these creatures weren't enough to make you worried, it's also worth mentioning that bull sharks love to lounge at the mouth of Río Sirena in Corcovado.

See also boxed text, p386.

Ocean Hazards

Approximately 200 drownings a year occur in Costa Rican waters, 90% of which are caused by riptides, which are strong currents that pull the swimmer out to sea. Many deaths in riptides are caused by panicked swimmers struggling to the point of exhaustion. If you are caught in a riptide, do not struggle. Simply float and let the tide carry you out beyond the breakers, after which the riptide will dissipate, then swim parallel to the beach and allow the surf to carry you back in. For more information on riptides see boxed text, p272.

River-Rafting Hazards

River-rafting expeditions may be particularly risky during periods of heavy rain – flash floods have been known to capsize rafts. Reputable tour operators will ensure conditions are safe before setting out; see p527 for a list of operators.

Thefts & Muggings

The biggest danger that most travelers face is theft, primarily from pickpockets. There is a lot of petty crime in Costa Rica so keep your wits about you at all times and don't let your guard down.

DISCOUNT CARDS

Students with an International Student Identity Card (ISIC) or a valid ID from a university are generally entitled to discounts on museum or guided-tour fees. Cards supplied by language schools are not accepted.

EMBASSIES & CONSULATES

Mornings are the best time to go to embassies and consulates. Australia and New Zealand do not have consular representation in Costa Rica; their closest embassies are in Mexico City. For visa information see p537. All of the following are located in San José.

Canada (☎ 2242-4400; Oficentro Ejecutivo La Sabana, 3rd fl, Edificio 3, Sabana Sur) Behind La Contraloría.
El Salvador (☎ 2257-7855) Head 500m north and 25m west of the Toyota dealership on Paseo Colón.
France (off Map p102; ☎ 2234-4167) On the road to Curridabat, 200m south and 50m west of the Indoor Club.
Germany (Map p79; ☎ 2232-5533; 8th fl, Torre La Sabana, Sabana Norte) About 300m west of the ICE building.
Guatemala (off Map p102; ☎ 2283-2555; Curridabat) Casa Izquierda, 500m south and 30m west of Pops.
Honduras (☎ 2291-5147; Urbanización Trejos Montealegre) About 100m west of Banca Promérica, Escazú.
Israel (Map p79; ☎ 2221-6444; 11th fl, Edificio Centro Colón, Paseo Colón btwn Calles 38 & 40)
Italy (Map p102; ☎ 2234-2326; cnr Av Central & Calle 41, Los Yoses)
Mexico (☎ 2257-0633) About 250m south of the Subaru dealership, Los Yoses.
Netherlands (☎ 2296-1490; Oficentro Ejecutivo La Sabana, 3rd fl, Edificio 3, Sabana Sur) Behind La Contraloría.
Nicaragua (☎ 2283-8222; Av Central 2540 btwn Calles 25 & 27, Barrio La California)
Panama (☎ 2281-2442) Head 200m south and 25m east from the *antiguo higuerón* (old fig tree), San Pedro.
Spain (Map p79; ☎ 2222-1933; Calle 32 btwn Paseo Colón & Av 2)
Switzerland (Map p79; ☎ 2221-3229; 10th fl, Edificio Centro Colón, Paseo Colón btwn Calles 38 & 40)
UK (Map p79; ☎ 2258-2025; 11th fl, Edificio Centro Colón, Paseo Colón btwn Calles 38 & 40)
USA (☎ 2220-3939; Carretera a Pavas) Opposite Centro Commercial del Oeste.

FESTIVALS & EVENTS

The following events are of national significance in Costa Rica:

JANUARY/FEBRUARY

Fiesta de Santa Cruz (mid-January) Held in Santa Cruz, there is a religious procession, rodeo, bullfight, music, dances and a beauty pageant.
Las Fiestas de Palmares (mid-January) Ten days of beer drinking, horse shows and other carnival events in the tiny town of Palmares.
Fiesta de los Diablitos (December 31 to January 2 in Boruca; February 5 to 8 in Curré) Men wear carved wooden devil masks and burlap masks to re-enact the fight between the indigenous people and the Spanish. In this one, the Spanish lose.

MARCH

Día del Boyero (second Sunday of the month) A parade is held in Escazú in honor of oxcart drivers.
Día de San José (St Joseph's Day; March 19) This day honors the patron saint of the capital.
Feria de la Mascarada (dates vary) Residents of Barvia don massive colorful masks (many of which weigh up to 20kg), and gather to dance around the town square.

JUNE

Día de San Pedro & San Pablo (Sts Peter & Paul's Day; June 29) Celebrations with religious processions held in villages of the same name.

JULY

Fiesta de La Virgen del Mar (Festival of the Virgin of the Sea; mid-July) Held in Puntarenas and Playa del Coco, it involves colorful regattas and boat parades.
Día de Guanacaste (July 25) Celebrates the annexation of Guanacaste from Nicaragua. There's a rodeo in Santa Cruz on this day.

AUGUST

La Virgen de los Ángeles (August 2) The patron saint is celebrated with an important religious procession from San José to Cartago.

OCTOBER

Día de la Raza (Columbus' Day; October 12) Puerto Limón celebrates with gusto the explorer's landing at nearby Isla Uvita. The four-or five-day carnival is full of colorful street parades and dancing, music, singing and drinking.

NOVEMBER

Día de los Muertos (All Souls' Day; November 2) Families visit graveyards and have religious parades in honor of the deceased.

DECEMBER

La Inmaculada Concepción (Immaculate Conception; December 8) An important religious holiday.
Las Fiestas de Zapote (December 25 to January 1) A week-long celebration of all things Costa Rican (namely rodeos, cowboys, carnival rides, fried food and a whole lot of drinking) in Zapote, southeast of San José.

PRACTICALITIES

- **Electricity** Electrical current is 110V AC at 60Hz; plugs are two flat prongs (same as in the US).
- **Emergency** The local tourism board, Instituto Costarricense de Turismo (ICT; www.visitcostarica.com), is located in San José and distributes a helpful brochure with up-to-date emergency numbers for every region.
- **Magazines** The Spanish-language *Esta Semana* is the best local weekly news magazine.
- **Newspapers** The most widely distributed newspaper is *La Nación* (www.nacion.co.cr), followed by *Al Día* (a tabloid), *La República* (www.larepublica.net) and *La Prensa Libre* (www.prensalibre.co.cr). *Tico Times* (www.ticotimes.net), the English-language newspaper, hits the streets every Friday afternoon.
- **Radio** The English-language radio station on 107.5FM plays current hits and provides a regular BBC news feed.
- **TV** Cable and satellite TV are widely available for a fix of CNN, French movies or Japanese news, and local TV stations have a mix of news, variety shows and *telenovelas* (Spanish-language soap operas).
- **Video Systems** Videos on sale use the NTSC image registration system (same as in the US). DVDs in Costa Rica are region 4.
- **Weights & Measures** Costa Ricans use the metric system for weights, distances and measures.

FOOD

Throughout this book, eating listings are given in order of budget, according to the average price of a meal. The budget category covers meals costing up to ₡5000, midrange is between ₡5000 and ₡12,500, while top-end category includes prices over ₡12,500.

GAY & LESBIAN TRAVELERS

Let's start with the good news. In Costa Rica, the situation facing gay and lesbian travelers is better than in most Central American countries. Homosexual acts between two consenting adults (aged 18 and over) are legal, though note that travelers may be subject to the laws of their own country in regard to sexual relations. Most Costa Ricans are tolerant of homosexuality only at a 'don't ask, don't tell' level. This is undoubtedly a side effect of the strong role of Catholicism and the persistence of traditionalism in society.

Here's the bad news. In the past decade, there has been an increasing number of outward acts of prejudice. In 1998 a gay-and-lesbian festival planned in San José was canceled following heavy opposition from Catholic clergy. The church also forced the cancellation of a gay-and-lesbian tour to Manuel Antonio, and encouraged the boycott of a coastal hotel hosting a gay group. Things took an embarrassing turn in 1999 when the tourism minister said that Costa Rica should not be a destination for sex tourism or gays. The gay community made it clear that it was against sex tourism, and that linking gay tourism with sex tourism was untrue and defamatory. The official position in Costa Rica was then modified, stating that gay tourism was neither encouraged nor prohibited.

Although homosexual acts between consenting adults are legal in Costa Rica, gays and lesbians continue to suffer from discrimination in society. Fortunately, discrimination usually takes the role of subtle nonacceptance, as opposed to violence or outright persecution. Homophobia has declined in recent years, especially in heavily touristy areas – one positive result of the influx of foreigners.

Thankfully, Costa Rica's gays and lesbians have made some strides. In the 1990s the Supreme Court ruled against police harassment in gay nightspots and guaranteed medical treatment to people living with HIV/AIDS. And in June 2003 the first ever gay-pride festival in San José drew more than 2000 attendants. Gays and lesbians traveling in Costa Rica are unlikely to be confronted with poor treatment; nonetheless, outside of gay spots, public displays of affection are not recommended.

The undisputed gay and lesbian capital of Costa Rica is Manuel Antonio – for more information, see boxed text, p348.

The monthly newspaper *Gayness* and the magazine *Gente 10* (in Spanish) are both available at gay bars in San José (see p93). There are a number of other resources for gay travelers:

Agua Buena Human Rights Association (☎ 2280-3548; www.aguabuena.org, in Spanish) This noteworthy nonprofit organization has campaigned steadily for fairness in medical treatment for people living with HIV/AIDS in Costa Rica.

Cipac (☎ 2280-7821; www.cipacdh.org, in Spanish) The leading gay activist organization in Costa Rica.

International Gay & Lesbian Travel Association (IGLTA; ☎ in USA 800-448-8550, 954-776-2626; www.iglta.org) Maintains a list of hundreds of travel agents and tour operators all over the world.

Tiquicia Travel (☎ 2256-9682; www.tiquiciatravel.com) Makes arrangements at gay-friendly hotels.

Toto Tours (☎ in USA 800-565-1241, 773-274-8686; www.tototours.com) Gay-travel specialists who organize regular trips to Costa Rica, among other destinations.

HOLIDAYS

Días feriados (national holidays) are taken seriously in Costa Rica. Banks, public offices and many stores close. During these times, public transport is tight and hotels are heavily booked. Many festivals (see p531) coincide with public holidays.

New Year's Day January 1

Semana Santa (Holy Week; March or April) The Thursday and Friday before Easter Sunday is the official holiday, though most businesses shut down for the whole week. From Thursday to Sunday bars are closed and alcohol sales are prohibited; on Thursday and Friday buses stop running.

Día de Juan Santamaría (April 11) Honors the national hero who died fighting William Walker in 1856; major events are held in Alajuela, his hometown.

Labor Day May 1

Día de la Madre (Mother's Day; August 15) Coincides with the annual Catholic feast of the Assumption.

Independence Day September 15

Día de la Raza Columbus' Day; October 12

Christmas Day (December 25) Christmas Eve is also an unofficial holiday.

Last week in December The week between Christmas and New Year is an unofficial holiday; businesses close and beach hotels are crowded.

INSURANCE

No matter where you travel to in the world, getting a comprehensive travel-insurance policy is a good idea. For travel to Costa Rica, a basic theft/loss and medical policy is recommended. Read the fine print carefully as some companies exclude dangerous activities from their coverage, which can include scuba diving, motorcycling and even trekking. You may prefer a policy that pays doctors or hospitals directly rather than you having to pay on the spot and make a claim later. See also p548 for details on car insurance, and p552 for more on health insurance.

INTERNET ACCESS

Internet cafes abound in Costa Rica, and you don't have to look very far to find cheap and speedy internet access. The normal access rate in San José and tourist towns is US$1 to US$2 per hour, though you can expect to pay upwards of US$5 per hour in the hard-to-reach places.

Wi-fi access is on the rise in Costa Rica. If you keep your eyes open (and computer on), you'll find wireless hot spots in San José, Alajuela, Jacó, Monteverde and Santa Elena, La Fortuna, Tamarindo, Puerto Jiménez and Puerto Viejo de Talamanca. Furthermore, the majority of top-end hotels and backpacker hostels offer secure wireless networks to their customers.

LEGAL MATTERS

If you get into legal trouble and are jailed in Costa Rica, your embassy can offer limited assistance. This may include an occasional visit from an embassy staff member to make sure your human rights have not been violated, letting your family know where you are and putting you in contact with a Costa Rican lawyer, who you must pay yourself. Embassy officials will not bail you out and you are subject to Costa Rican laws, not the laws of your own country.

In Costa Rica the legal age for driving, voting and having heterosexual sex is 18 years, and you can get married when you are 15 years old. There is no specific legal age for homosexual sex but sex with anyone under 18 is not advisable. Keep in mind that travelers may be subject to the laws of their own country in regard to sexual relations.

Drivers & Driving Accidents

Drivers should carry their passport and driver's license at all times. If you have an accident, call the police immediately to make a report (required for insurance purposes) or attend to any injured parties. Leave the vehicles in place until the report has been made and do not make any statements except to members of law-enforcement agencies. The injured should only be moved by medical professionals.

Keep your eye on your vehicle until the police arrive and then call the car-rental company to find out where you should take the vehicle for repairs (do not have it fixed yourself). If the accident results in injury or death, you could be jailed or prevented from leaving the country until legalities are handled.

Emergency numbers are listed on the inside front cover of this book.

MAPS

Detailed maps are unfortunately hard to come by in Costa Rica. An excellent option is the 1:330,000 *Costa Rica* sheet produced by **International Travel Map** (ITMB; www.itmb.com; 530 W Broadway, Vancouver, BC, V5Z 1E, Canada), which is waterproof and includes a San José inset.

The **Fundación Neotrópica** (www.neotropica.org) publishes a 1:500,000 map showing national parks and other protected areas. These are available in San José bookstores and over the internet.

The Instituto Costarricense de Turismo (ICT; see p72) publishes a 1:700,000 *Costa Rica* map with a 1:12,500 *Central San José* map on the reverse. These are free at ICT offices in San José.

Online, **Maptak** (www.maptak.com) has maps of Costa Rica's seven provinces and their capitals.

Don't count on any of the national park offices or ranger stations having maps for hikers. Topographical maps are available for purchase from **Instituto Geográfico Nacional** (IGN; ☎ 2257-7798; Calle 9 btwn Avs 20 & 22, San José; 🕑 7:30am-noon & 1-3pm Mon-Fri). In the USA, contact **Omni Resources** (☎ in USA 336-227-8300; www.omnimap.com).

The *Mapa-Guía de la Naturaleza Costa Rica* is an atlas published by Incafo that includes 1:200,000 topographical sheets, as well as English and Spanish descriptions of Costa Rica's natural areas. It is available at Lehmann's (p67) bookstore in San José.

MONEY

ATMs

It's increasingly easy to find *cajeros automáticos* (ATMs) in Costa Rica, even in the smallest towns. The Visa Plus network is the standard, but machines on the Cirrus network, which accepts most foreign ATM cards, can be found in larger cities and tourist towns. In these areas, ATMs also dispense US dollars, which is convenient for payments at hotels and tour agencies. Note that some machines will only accept cards held by their own customers.

Cash & Currency

The Costa Rican currency is the colón (plural colones, ₡), named after Cristóbal Colón (Christopher Columbus). Bills come in 500, 1000, 5000 and 10,000 notes, while coins come in denominations of 5, 10, 20, 25, 50 and 100. Note that older coins are larger and silver, while newer ones are smaller and gold-colored – this is often a source of confusion for travelers fresh off the plane.

Paying for things in US dollars should be free of hassle, and at times is encouraged since the currency is viewed as being more stable than colones (see boxed text, p535). Newer US dollars (ie big heads) are preferred throughout Costa Rica.

WHAT'S THAT ADDRESS?

Though some larger cities have streets that have been dutifully named, signage is rare in Costa Rica and finding a Tico who knows what street they are standing on is even rarer. Everybody uses landmarks when providing directions; an address may be given as 200m south and 150m east of a church. A city block is *cien metros* – literally 100m – so *250 metros al sur* means '2½ blocks south,' regardless of the distance. Churches, parks, office buildings, fast-food joints and car dealerships are the most common landmarks used – but these are often meaningless to the foreign traveler who will have no idea where the Subaru dealership is to begin with. Better yet, Ticos frequently refer to landmarks that no longer exist. In San Pedro, outside San José, locals still use the sight of an old fig tree *(el antiguo higuerón)* to provide directions.

Confused? Get used to it…

At the time of writing, Costa Rica was about to roll out new banknotes in 2010, including two new denominations: 20,000 and 50,000 colones. Old banknotes will subsequently be collected and destroyed, and no longer deemed legal tender. Fortunately, it should be easy enough for foreign tourists to tell the two sets apart, since the new bills will each have different colors, shapes and images than their predecessors.

Credit Cards

You can expect a transaction fee on all international credit-card purchases. Holders of credit and debit cards can buy colones and sometimes US dollars in some banks, though you can expect to pay a high transaction fee. Cards are widely accepted at some midrange and most top-end hotels, as well as top-end restaurants and some travel agencies. All car-rental agencies accept credit cards.

Exchanging Money

All banks will exchange US dollars, and some will exchange euros and British pounds; other currencies are more difficult. Most banks have excruciatingly long lines, especially at the state-run institutions (Banco Nacional, Banco de Costa Rica, Banco Popular), though they don't charge commission on cash exchanges. Private banks (Banex, Banco Interfin, Scotiabank) tend to be faster. Make sure the bills you want to exchange are in good condition or they may be refused.

Taxes

Travelers will notice a 13.39% sales tax at midrange and top-end hotels and restaurants, while hotels also charge an additional 3% tourist surcharge. Everybody must pay a US$26 airport tax upon leaving the country. It is payable in US dollars or in colones, and credit cards are accepted at the Juan Santamaría airport in San José.

Tipping

It is customary to tip the bellhop/porter (US$1 to US$5 per service) and the housekeeper (US$1 to US$2 per day) in top-end hotels, less in budget places. On guided tours, tip the guide US$5 to US$15 per person per day. Tip the tour driver about half of what you tip the guide. Naturally, tips depend upon quality of service. Taxi drivers are not normally tipped, unless some special service is provided. Top-end restaurants may add a 10% service charge onto the bill. If not, you might leave a small tip to show your appreciation, but it is not required.

DOLLARS VS COLONES

While colones are the official currency of Costa Rica, US dollars are virtually legal tender. Case in point: most ATMs in large towns and cities will dispense both currencies. However, it pays to know where and when you should be paying with each currency.

In Costa Rica you can use US dollars to pay for hotel rooms, midrange to top-end meals, admission fees for sights, tours, domestic flights, international buses, car hire, private shuttle buses and large-ticket purchase items. Local meals and drinks, domestic bus fares, taxis and small-ticket purchase items should be paid for in colones.

Throughout this book, all of our listings for hotels, sights and activities contain prices in US dollars. For information, eating, drinking and entertainment listings, prices are given in colones. With regard to transportation, our use of either dollars or colones reflects the preferred currency for a given mode.

Traveler's Checks

Most banks and exchange offices will cash traveler's checks at a commission of 1% to 3%. Some hotels will accept them as payment, but check policies carefully as many hotels do not. US dollar traveler's checks are preferred. It may be difficult or impossible to change traveler's checks of other currencies.

PHOTOGRAPHY

Costa Ricans make wonderful subjects for photos. However, most people resent having cameras thrust in their faces, and some attach price tags to their mugs. As a rule, you should ask for permission if you have an inkling your subject would not approve.

Since most people use digital cameras these days, it can be quite difficult to purchase high-quality film in Costa Rica. However, most internet cafes in the country can burn your digital pictures on CD, and cheap media is available for purchase in most large towns and cities.

POST

Airmail letters cost about US$0.35 for the first 20g. Parcels can be shipped at the rate of US$7 per kilogram. You can receive mail at the main post office of major towns. Mail to San José's central post office should be addressed: (Name), c/o Lista de Correos, Correo Central, San José, Costa Rica.

Letters usually arrive within a week from North America, longer from more distant places. The post office will hold mail for 30 days from the date it's received. Photo identification is required to retrieve mail and you will only be given correspondence with your name on it.

Note that in addresses, *apartado* (abbreviated 'Apdo') means 'PO Box'; it is not a street or apartment address.

SHOPPING

Avoid purchasing animal products, including turtle shells, animal skulls and anything made with feathers, coral or shells. Wood products are also highly suspicious: make sure you know where the wood came from.

Coffee & Alcohol

Coffee is the most popular souvenir, and deservedly so. It is available at gift shops, the Mercado Central (p96) in San José and at any supermarket throughout the country.

The most popular alcohol purchases are Ron Centenario, Café Rica (the coffee liqueur) and *guaro* (the local firewater). All are available at duty-free shops inside the airport, or in supermarkets and liquor stores in every town and city.

> **BARGAINING**
>
> A high standard of living along with a steady stream of international tourist traffic means that the Latin American tradition of haggling is fast dying out in Costa Rica. In tourist towns especially, fixed prices on hotels cannot be negotiated, and you can expect business owners to be offended if you try. Some smaller hotels in the interior regions still accept the practice.
>
> Negotiating prices at outdoor markets is acceptable, and bargaining is accepted when hiring long-distance taxis. Overall, Ticos respond well to good manners and gentle inquiries. If you demand a service, chances are you won't get it.

Handicrafts & Ceramics

Tropical-hardwood items include salad bowls, plates, carving boards, jewelry boxes and a variety of carvings and ornaments. The most exquisite woodwork is available at Biesanz Woodworks (p112) in Escazú. All of the wood here is grown on farms expressly for this purpose, so you needn't worry about forests being chopped down for your salad bowl.

Uniquely Costa Rican souvenirs are the colorfully painted replicas of *carretas* (traditional oxcarts) produced in Sarchí (p130).

SOLO TRAVELERS

Costa Rica is a fine country for solo travelers, especially if you get in with the backpacking community. Inexpensive hostels with communal kitchens encourage social exchange, while a large number of language schools, tours and volunteer organizations will provide every traveler with an opportunity to meet others. However, it isn't recommended to undertake long treks in the wilderness by yourself.

Most female travelers experience little more than a *'mi amor'* ('my love') or an appreciative hiss from the local men in Costa Rica. But in general, Costa Rican men consider foreign women to have looser morals and to be easier conquests than Ticas (female Costa Ricans). Men will often make flirtatious comments to single women, particularly blondes. Women traveling together are not exempt from this. The best way to deal with this is to do what the Ticas do – ignore it completely. Women who firmly resist unwanted verbal advances from men are normally treated with respect.

In small highland towns, dress is usually conservative. Women rarely wear shorts, but belly-baring tops are all the rage. On the beach, skimpy bathing suits are OK, but topless and nude bathing are not.

As in any part of the world, the possibilities of rape and assault do exist. Use your normal caution: avoid walking alone in isolated places or through city streets late at night, and skip the hitchhiking. Do not take unlicensed 'pirate' taxis (licensed taxis are red and have medallions) as there have been reports of assaults against women by unlicensed drivers.

Birth-control pills are available at most pharmacies (without a prescription) and tampons can be difficult to find in rural areas – bring some from home or stock up in San José.

TELEPHONE

Public phones are found all over Costa Rica and Chip or Colibrí phone cards are available in 1000, 2000 and 3000 colón denominations. Chip cards are inserted into the phone and scanned. Colibrí cards (more common) require you to dial a toll-free number (☎ 199) and enter an access code. Instructions are provided in English or Spanish. Colibrí is the preferred card of travelers since it can be used from any phone. Cards can be found just about everywhere, including supermarkets, pharmacies, newsstands, *pulperías* (corner grocery stores) and gift shops.

The cheapest international calls from Costa Rica are direct-dialed using a phone card. To make international calls, dial '00' followed by the country code and number. Pay phones cannot receive international calls.

Make sure that no one is peeking over your shoulder when you dial your code. Some travelers have had their access numbers pilfered by thieves.

To call Costa Rica from abroad, use the country code (☎ 506) before the eight-digit number. Find other important phone numbers on the inside front cover of this book.

Due to the increasing popularity of voice-over IP services such as Skype, it's sometimes possible to skip the middle man and just bring a headset along with you to an internet cafe. Ethernet connections and wireless signals are becoming more common in accommodations, so if you're traveling with a laptop you can just connect and call for pennies.

TIME

Costa Rica is six hours behind GMT, so Costa Rican time is equivalent to Central Time in North America. There is no daylight-saving time.

TOILETS

Public restrooms are rare, but most restaurants and cafes will let you use their facilities, sometimes for a small charge – never more than ₡500. Bus terminals and other major public buildings usually have toilets, also at a charge.

If you're particularly fond of toilet paper, carry it with you at all times as it is not always available. Just don't flush it down! Costa Rican plumbing is often poor and has very low pressure in all but the best hotels and buildings. Dispose of toilet paper in the rubbish bin inside the bathroom.

TOURIST INFORMATION

The government-run tourism board, the ICT, has two offices in the capital (see p72). However, don't expect to be wowed with any particularly insightful travel advice as it's the staff's job to tell you that it's all good in Costa Rica. That said, the ICT can provide you with free maps, a master bus schedule and information on road conditions in the hinterlands. English is spoken.

Consult the ICT's flashy English-language website (www.visitcostarica.com) for information, or in the USA call the ICT's toll-free number (☎ in USA 800-343-6332) for brochures and information.

TRAVELERS WITH DISABILITIES

Independent travel is difficult for anyone with mobility problems. Although Costa Rica has an equal-opportunity law for disabled people, the law applies only to new or newly remodeled businesses and is loosely enforced. Therefore, very few hotels and restaurants have features specifically suited to wheelchair use. Many don't have ramps, while room or bathroom doors are rarely wide enough to accommodate a wheelchair.

Outside the buildings, streets and sidewalks are potholed and poorly paved, making wheelchair use frustrating at best. Public buses don't have provisions to carry wheelchairs and most national parks and outdoor tourist attractions don't have trails suited to wheelchair use. Notable exceptions include Volcán Poás (p124), INBio (p135) and the Rainforest Aerial Tram (p445). Lodges with wheelchair accessibility are indicated in the reviews with this symbol: ♿.

The following organizations offer specially designed trips for travelers with disabilities:

Accessible Journeys (☎ in USA 800-846-4537; www.disabilitytravel.com) Organizes independent travel to Costa Rica for people with disabilities.

Vaya con Silla de Ruedas (☎ 2454-2810; www.gowithwheelchairs.com) Offers specialty trips for the wheelchair-bound traveler. The company has specially designed vans and its equipment meets international accessibility standards.

VISAS

Passport-carrying nationals of the following countries are allowed 90 days' stay with no visa: Argentina, Canada, Israel, Japan, Panama, the USA, and most Western European countries. Citizens of Australia, Iceland, Ireland, Mexico, New Zealand, Russia, South Africa and Venezuela are allowed to stay for 30 days with no visa. Others require a visa from a Costa Rican embassy or consulate.

For the latest info on visas, check the websites of the **ICT** (www.visitcostarica.com) or the **Costa Rican embassy** (www.costarica-embassy.org) in Washington, DC.

If you are in Costa Rica and need to visit your embassy or consulate, see p531 for contact information.

Extensions

Extending your stay beyond the authorized 30 or 90 days is a time-consuming hassle. It is far easier to leave the country for 72 hours and then re-enter. Otherwise, go to the office of **Migración** (Immigration; ☎ 2220-0355; ⌚ 8am-4pm) in San José, opposite Channel 6, about 4km north of Parque La Sabana. Requirements for extensions change, so allow several working days.

Onward Tickets

Travelers officially need onward tickets before they are allowed to enter Costa Rica. This requirement is not often checked at the airport, but travelers arriving by land should anticipate a need to show an onward ticket.

If you're heading to Panama, Nicaragua or another Central or South American country from Costa Rica, you may need an onward or round-trip ticket before you will be allowed entry into that country or even allowed to board the plane if you're flying. A quick check with the appropriate embassy – easy to do via the internet – will tell you whether the country you're heading to has an onward-ticket requirement.

VOLUNTEERING

The sheer number of volunteer opportunities in Costa Rica is mind-blowing. 'Voluntourism' is a great way to travel sustainably and make a positive contribution to the local community. Volunteer work is also an amazing forum for self-exploration, especially if you touch a few lives and make a few new friends along the way. Generally speaking, you will get as much out of volunteering as you put in, and the majority of volunteers in Costa Rica walk away from their experiences content.

The following volunteer opportunities provide a general overview of what is currently available in Costa Rica.

English Teaching

Although many travelers in Costa Rica are extremely keen to learn and/or perfect their Spanish, you can give a lot back by teaching English to kids and adults of all ages. With that said, once class ends and you're outside the school, your students will be happy to swap roles and teach you a bit of Spanish along the way.

Amerispan Study Abroad (www.amerispan.com) Offers a variety of educational travel programs in specialized areas.

Cloud Forest School (www.cloudforestschool.org) A bilingual school (kindergarten to 11th grade) in Monteverde offering creative and experiential education.

Sustainable Horizon (www.sustainablehorizon.com) Arranges volunteering trips such as guest-teaching spots and orphanage placements.

Forestry Management

Despite its relatively small size, Costa Rica is home to an impressive number of national parks, a good number of which protect some of the most pristine rainforest on the planet. If you're interesting in helping to save this threatened ecosystem, and perhaps gaining a valuable skill set in the process, consider a placement in a forest-management program.

Bosque Eterno de los Niños (Children's Eternal Forest; www.acmcr.org) Volunteers are needed to help manage this remarkable achievement – a rainforest purchased by children who raised money to buy and protect it.

Cloudbridge Nature Preserve (www.cloudbridge.org) A private reserve where an ongoing reforestation project is being spearheaded by two New Yorkers.

Fundación Corcovado (www.corcovadofoundation.org) An impressive network of people and organizations committed to preserving Parque Nacional Corcovado.

Monteverde Institute (www.mvinstitute.org) A nonprofit educational institute offering training in tropical biology, conservation and sustainable development.

Organic Farming

The entire world is going organic, and Costa Rica is certainly at the forefront of this highly admirable and sustainable movement. Home to virtual living laboratories of self-sufficient farms and plantations, Costa Rica is perfectly

HOW TO KNOW IF A BUSINESS IS REALLY ECOFRIENDLY

Ecotourism means big business in Costa Rica, and sometimes it can seem like every hotel, restaurant, souvenir stall, bus company, surf shop and ATV tour operator is claiming to be a friend and protector of Mother Earth. It's certainly easy to dupe your average package tourist with business cards printed on recycled paper and a bunch of tree-frog stickers plastered on an office wall, but sometimes in Costa Rica it's difficult even for the discerning traveler to know whether a business is truly 'eco.' Sure, you didn't cut down a single tree when you built your canopy tour, but can you explain why your gray water trickles down the hillside into the stream below?

The guiding principle behind ecotourism is striking a balance between the positive and negative impacts of tourism, specifically traveling in a manner that is sensitive to the conditions of your destination while simultaneously minimizing negative impacts on the environment. Unfortunately, the problem is that it is becoming increasingly popular for destinations to label themselves as 'ecodestination,' yet there are no universal guidelines dictating exactly what it means to be 'eco.' However, there are various environmental, economic and sociocultural aspects of running an ecofriendly business that every traveler should be aware of.

Since most ecotourism destinations are in areas where the natural environment is relatively untouched, it is important for a business to adhere to strict conservation guidelines. At the bare minimum, an ecofriendly business should participate in recycling programs, effectively manage their wastewater and pollutants, implement alternative energy systems, use natural illumination whenever possible and maintain pesticide-free grounds using only native plants. When it is possible, a business should also participate in environmental conservation programs as well as be an active member of regional or local organizations that work on solving environmental problems.

The economics of an ecotourist destination is a major issue concerning tourists, local communities and developers as the maldistribution of economic benefits generated by a business can have harmful consequences on the sustainability of an area. This is especially important as tourists are increasingly interested in visiting the most undeveloped areas possible, which is a problem as the individuals living in these locales are relatively removed from the greater economy. An ecofriendly business can address these realities by hiring a majority of its employees from the local population, associating with locally owned businesses, providing places where native handicrafts can be displayed for sale, serving foods that support local markets and using local materials and products in order to maintain the health of the local economy.

The sociocultural aspect of ecotourism refers to the ability of a community to continue functioning without social disharmony as a result of its adaptation to an increased volume of tourists. Although tourism contributes to the loss of cultural integrity, it can also alleviate poverty and help maintain natural resources that might otherwise be exploited. An ecofriendly business can achieve these goals by fostering indigenous customs; protecting sites of historical, archaeological and/or spiritual importance; educating visitors about local customs and practices; regulating the tourist flow to indigenous areas; and, when possible, donating a portion of profits to the local community.

For a complete listings of businesses that meet our 'eco' stamp of approval, check out the GreenDex on p586.

suited for volunteers interested in greening their thumbs.

Finca La Flor de Paraíso (www.la-flor.org) Offers programs in a variety of disciplines from animal husbandry to medicinal-herb cultivation.

Punta Mona (www.puntamona.org) An organic farm and retreat center that is based on organic permaculture and sustainable living.

Rancho Margot (www.ranchomargot.org) This self-proclaimed life-skills university offers a natural education emphasizing organic farming and animal husbandry.

Reserva Biológica Dúrika (www.durika.org) A sustainable community that is centered upon a 75-sq-km biological reserve.

Wildlife Conservation

If you're interested in sea turtles or rehabilitating rescued animals, Costa Rica is one of the best places in the world to get hands-on experience with wild animals. Whether you're an aspiring veterinarian or just concerned with the plight of endangered species, there

PREVENTING CHILD-SEX TOURISM IN COSTA RICA *ECPAT/Beyond Borders*

Tragically, the exploitation of local children by tourists is becoming more prevalent throughout Latin America, including Costa Rica. Various socioeconomic factors make children susceptible to sexual exploitation, and some tourists choose to take advantage of their vulnerable position.

Sexual exploitation has serious, lifelong effects on children. Sexual exploitation of children is a crime and a violation of human rights, and Costa Rica has laws against it. Many countries have enacted extraterritorial legislation that allows travelers to be charged as though the exploitation happened in their home country.

Travelers can help stop child-sex tourism by reporting it – it is important not to ignore suspicious behavior. **Cybertipline** (www.cybertipline.com) is a website where the sexual exploitation of children can be reported, you can also report it to local authorities, and if you know the nationality of the perpetrator, you can report it to their embassy.

Travelers interested in learning more about how to fight against the sexual exploitation of children can go to **Ecpat International** (End Child Prostitution and Trafficking; www.ecpat.org) or **Beyond Borders** (www.beyondborders.org), the Canadian affiliate of Ecpat. Ecpat aims to advance the rights of children and help them to be free from abuse and exploitation without regard to race, religion, gender or sexual orientation. **Ecpat USA** (☎ in USA 718-935-9192; www.ecpatusa.org) is part of a global network working on these issues with more than 70 affiliate organizations around the world. The US headquarters is located in New York.

are some programs that can help you get a little closer to some of Mother Nature's charismatic creatures.

CCC (www.cccturtle.org) Assist scientists with turtle-tagging and research on green and leatherback turtles.

Profelis (www.grafischer.com/profelis) A feline conservation program that takes care of confiscated wild cats, both big and small.

WORK

It's difficult for foreigners to find work in Costa Rica. The government doesn't like anyone taking jobs away from Costa Ricans and the labor laws reflect this sentiment. Basically, the only foreigners legally employed in Costa Rica are those who work for their own businesses, possess skills not found in the country, or work for companies that have special agreements with the government.

Getting a bona fide job necessitates obtaining a work permit – a time-consuming and difficult process. The most likely source of paid employment is as an English teacher at one of the language institutes, or working in the hospitality industry in a hotel or resort. Naturalists or river guides may also be able to find work with either private lodges or adventure-travel operators, though you shouldn't expect to make more than survival wages from these jobs.

Transportation

CONTENTS

GETTING THERE & AWAY

ENTERING THE COUNTRY

A few people arrive in Costa Rica by sea, either on fishing or scuba charters or as part of a brief stop on a cruise. Others travel in by bus from neighboring countries. But the vast majority of travelers land at the airport in San José, with a growing number arriving in Liberia.

Entering Costa Rica is usually hassle-free (with the exception of some long queues). For more information on crossing the border, see p543. Some foreign nationals will require a visa. Be aware that those who need visas can't get them at the border. For information on visas, see p537.

Passport

Citizens of all nations are required to have a passport that is valid for at least six months beyond the dates of your trip. When you arrive, your passport will be stamped. The law requires that you carry your passport at all times during your stay in Costa Rica.

Onward Ticket

Travelers officially need a ticket out of Costa Rica before they are allowed to enter, but the rules are enforced erratically. Those arriving by land can generally meet this requirement by purchasing an outward ticket from the TICA bus company, which has offices in Managua (Nicaragua) and Panama City.

AIR

Airports & Airlines

International flights arrive at Aeropuerto Internacional Juan Santamaría (p96), 17km northwest of San José, in the town of Alajuela. As a result, an increasing number of travelers are bypassing the capital altogether, and choosing instead to strike out into the country from Alajuela.

Aeropuerto Internacional Daniel Oduber Quirós (p229) in Liberia also receives international flights from the USA and Canada. At the time of research, Liberia was being served by Air Canada, American Airlines, Continental, Delta, Northwest, United Airlines and US Airways. Private charter flights were also starting to arrive with increasing frequency from London Gatwick.

There has been a lot of talk about expanding Daniel Oduber Quirós, primarily since the airport is convenient for travelers visiting the Península de Nicoya. However, thus far progress has been extremely slow, and it will still be several years before major ground is broken. In the meantime, however, a few European charters have announced their intention to fly direct to Liberia, which would mean that travelers from the continent will no longer need to lay over in the USA or Canada.

Costa Rica is well connected by air to other Central and South American countries, as well as the USA. The national airline, Lacsa (part

> **THINGS CHANGE...**
>
> The information in this chapter is particularly vulnerable to change. Check directly with the airline or a travel agent to make sure you understand how a fare (and ticket you may buy) works and be aware of the security requirements for international travel. Shop carefully. The details given in this chapter should be regarded as pointers and are not a substitute for your own careful, up-to-date research.

of the Central American Airline consortium Grupo TACA), flies to the USA and Latin America, including Cuba. The US Federal Aviation Administration has assessed Costa Rica's aviation authorities to be in compliance with international safety standards.

Airlines flying to and from Costa Rica include the following companies; see p96 for details of those with offices in San José.

Air Canada (airline code AC; ☎ in Canada 514-393-3333; www.aircanada.ca) No office in Costa Rica.
Air France (airline code AF; ☎ 2220-4111; www.airfrance.com)
America West (airline code HP; ☎ in USA 480-693-6718; www.americawest.com) No office in Costa Rica.
American Airlines (airline code AA; ☎ 2248-9010; www.americanairlines.co.cr)
Avianca (airline code AV; ☎ 2441-2827/2776; www.avianca.com)
Continental (airline code CO; ☎ 2296-4911; www.continental.com)
COPA (airline code CM; ☎ 2222-6640; www.copaair.com)
Cubana de Aviación (airline code CU; ☎ 2221-7625/6918; www.cubana.cu)
Delta (airline code DL; ☎ 2256-7909; www.delta.com)
Grupo TACA (airline code TA; ☎ 2299-8222; www.taca.com)
Iberia (airline code IB; ☎ 2431-5633; www.iberia.com)
JetBlue Airways (airline code JB; ☎ in USA 800-538-2583; www.jetblue.com) No office in Costa Rica.
Lacsa (see Grupo TACA)
Mexicana (airline code MX; ☎ 2295-6969; www.mexicana.com)
Northwest (airline code NW; ☎ in USA 800-225-2525; www.nwa.com) No office in Costa Rica.
United Airlines (airline code UA; ☎ 2220-4844; www.united.com)
US Airways (airline code US; ☎ toll-free reservations in Costa Rica 800-011-0793, 800-011-4114; www.usairways.com) No office in Costa Rica.

DEPARTURE/ARRIVAL TAX

There is a US$26 departure tax on all international outbound flights, payable in cash (US dollars or colones, or a mix of the two). At the Juan Santamaría airport you can pay with credit cards, and Banco de Costa Rica has an ATM (on the Plus system) by the departure-tax station. Note that you will not be allowed through airport security without paying.

At the time of research, the government had recently declared a US$15 tax on international inbound flights, though this is included in the price of your ticket. The fee was designed to replace the 3% hotel tax, which didn't capture the increasing amount of condominium and other private rentals.

Tickets

Airline fares are usually more expensive during the Costa Rican high season (from December through April), with December and January the most expensive months to travel.

Central & Latin America

American Airlines, Continental, Delta, Northwest, United and US Airways have connections to Costa Rica from many Central and Latin American countries. Grupo TACA usually offers the most flights on these routes.

In the last few years the domestic Costa Rican airlines have begun offering a few international flights. **Nature Air** (www.natureair.com) now flies from Liberia to Granada, Nicaragua, four times a week, and to Bocas del Toro, Panama, two times a week. Note that rates vary considerably on season and availability.

Grupo TACA offers daily direct flights to Caracas, Guatemala City and San Salvador. TACA and Mexicana have daily flights to Mexico City, while both TACA and COPA have several flights a day to Panama City. Again, rates vary considerably on season and availability.

Other Countries

More than one-third of all travelers to Costa Rica come from the USA, so finding a nonstop flight from Houston, Miami or New York is quite simple. Schedules and prices are competitive – a little bit of shopping around can get you a good fare.

From Canada, most travelers to Costa Rica connect through US gateway cities, though Air Canada has direct flights from Toronto.

Most flights from the UK and Europe connect either in the USA or in Mexico City, although this may change once the new airport in Liberia starts attracting more flights. High-season fares may still apply during the northern summer, even though this is the beginning of the Costa Rican rainy season.

From Australia and New Zealand, travel routes usually go through the USA or Mexico. Again, fares tend to go up in June and July

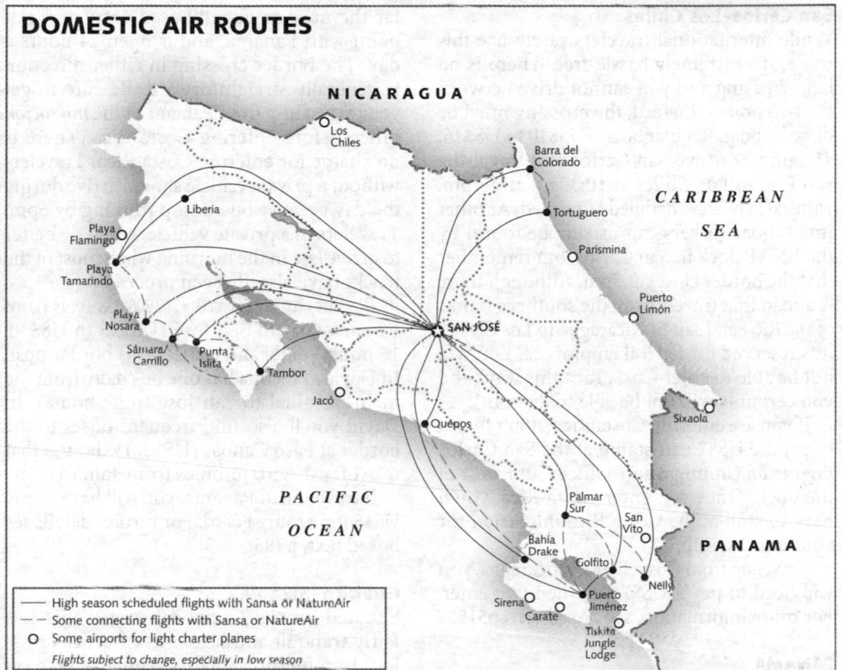

even though this is the beginning of the rainy season in Costa Rica.

LAND

Border Crossings

Costa Rica shares land borders with Nicaragua and Panama. There is no fee for travelers to enter Costa Rica. However, some local Tico towns have recently added their own entry/exit fees, usually US$1. For more information on visa requirements for entering Costa Rica, see p537.

NICARAGUA

Sapoá–Peñas Blancas

Situated on the Interamericana, this is the most heavily trafficked border station between Nicaragua and Costa Rica. Virtually all international overland travelers from Nicaragua enter Costa Rica through here. The border station is open from 6am to 8pm daily on both the Costa Rican and Nicaraguan sides – though local bus traffic stops in the afternoon. This is the only official border between Nicaragua and Costa Rica that you can drive across.

The **Tica Bus** (☎ in Managua 222-6094), **Nica Bus** (☎ in Managua 228-1374) and **TransNica** (☎ in Managua 278-2090) all have daily buses to Costa Rica. The fare is around US$15, and the trip takes approximately nine to 10 hours. From Rivas (37km north of the border) twice-hourly buses depart for Sapoá from 5am to 4:30pm. Regular buses depart Peñas Blancas, on the Costa Rican side, for La Cruz, Liberia and San José.

The Costa Rican and Nicaraguan immigration offices are almost 1km apart; most people travel through by bus or private car. Travelers without a through bus will find golf carts (a small tip is requested) running between the borders, but walking is not a problem. While Costa Rica does not charge visitors to cross the border, Nicaragua does: people leaving Nicaragua pay US$2, while folks entering Nicaragua will be charged US$7 until noon, after which the fee becomes US$9. All fees must be paid in US dollars.

Note that Peñas Blancas is only a border post, not a town, so there is nowhere to stay. For more information see boxed text, p242.

San Carlos–Los Chiles

While international travelers rarely use this route, it's extremely hassle-free. There is no land crossing and you cannot drive between the two points. Instead, the crossing must be done by boat. Regular boats (US$10 to US$15, 45 minutes) leave San Carlos and travel the Río Frío to Los Chiles at 10:30am and 4pm, with extra boats scheduled as needed. At other times, boatworkers can usually be found by the ENAP dock in San Carlos, but remember that the border closes at 5pm. Although there is a road that travels from the southern banks of the Río San Juan in Nicaragua to Los Chiles, it is reserved for federal employees. You will not be able to enter Costa Rica this way (and you certainly will not be able to drive in).

If you are entering Costa Rica, don't forget to get the US$2 exit stamp at the San Carlos *migración* (immigration) office, 50m west of the dock. Once you enter Costa Rica, you'll have to stop at the Costa Rica *migración* for your entry stamp.

Traveling from Costa Rica to Nicaragua, you will need to pay a US$7 fee when you enter. For more information, see boxed text, p515.

PANAMA

Paso Canoas

This border crossing on the Carretera Interamericana (Pan-American Hwy) is by far the most frequently used entry and exit point with Panama, and is open 24 hours a day. The border crossing in either direction is generally straightforward. Be sure to get your exit stamp from Panama at the *migración* office before entering Costa Rica. There is no charge for entering Costa Rica. Travelers without a private vehicle should arrive during the day because buses stop running by 6pm. Travelers in a private vehicle would do better to arrive late in the morning when most of the trucks have already been processed.

Tica Bus (☎ in Panama City 262 2084) travels from Panama City to San José (US$25 to US$30, 15 hours) daily and crosses this border post. In David, Tracopa has one bus daily from the main terminal to San José (nine hours). In David you'll also find frequent buses to the border at Paso Canoas (US$2, 1½ hours) that take off every 10 minutes from 4am to 8pm.

If traveling to Panama, you will have to pay US$5 for a tourist card. For further details see boxed text, p383.

Guabito–Sixaola

Situated on the Caribbean coast, this is a fairly tranquil and hassle-free border crossing. Immigration guards regularly take off for lunch and you may have to wait a while to be processed. The border town on the Panamanian side is Guabito.

CLIMATE CHANGE & TRAVEL

Climate change is a serious threat to the ecosystems that humans rely upon, and air travel is the fastest-growing contributor to the problem. Lonely Planet regards travel, overall, as a global benefit, but believes we all have a responsibility to limit our personal impact on global warming.

Flying & Climate Change

Pretty much every form of motor travel generates CO_2 (the main cause of human-induced climate change) but planes are far and away the worst offenders, not just because of the sheer distances they allow us to travel, but because they release greenhouse gases high into the atmosphere. The statistics are frightening: two people taking a return flight between Europe and the US will contribute as much to climate change as an average household's gas and electricity consumption over a whole year.

Carbon Offset Schemes

Climatecare.org and other websites use 'carbon calculators' that allow jetsetters to offset the greenhouse gases they are responsible for with contributions to energy-saving projects and other climate-friendly initiatives in the developing world – including projects in India, Honduras, Kazakhstan and Uganda.

Lonely Planet, together with Rough Guides and other concerned partners in the travel industry, supports the carbon offset scheme run by climatecare.org. Lonely Planet offsets all of its staff and author travel.

For more information check out our website: lonelyplanet.com.

The border is open from 8am to 6pm in Panama and from 7am to 5pm in Costa Rica. (Panama is one hour ahead.) Both sides close for an hour-long lunch at around 1pm, which means that there are potentially two hours each day when you'll be unable to make it across the border quickly. Get to Sixaola as early as possible; while there are a couple of sleeping options, it won't be the highlight of your trip if you have to spend the night. Before crossing the bridge, stop at the Costa Rica **migración** (☎ 2754-2044) to process your paperwork. Walking across the bridge is kind of fun, in a vertigo-inducing sort of way.

If you are coming from Bocas del Toro, it's faster and cheaper to take the ferry to Changuinola (US$5 to US$7, 45 minutes), from where you can take a quick taxi to the border or to the bus station (US$5). One daily bus travels between Changuinola and San José at 10am (US$15, eight hours). Otherwise, you can walk over the border and catch one of the hourly buses that go up the coast from Sixaola. For details, see boxed text, p497.

Río Sereno–San Vito

This is a rarely used crossing in the Cordillera de Talamanca. The border is open from 8am to 6pm in Panama and from 7am to 5pm in Costa Rica. The small village of Río Sereno on the Panamanian side has a hotel and a place to eat; there are no facilities on the Costa Rican side.

Regular buses depart Concepción and David in Panama for Río Sereno. Local buses (four daily) and taxis go from the border to San Vito. See also boxed text, p383.

Bus

A lot of travelers, particularly shoestringers, enter the country by bus. Furthermore, an extensive bus system links the Central American capitals and it's vastly cheaper than flying.

If crossing the border by bus, note that international buses may cost slightly more than taking a local bus to the border, then another onwards from the border, but they're worth it. These companies are familiar with border procedures and will tell you what's needed to cross efficiently.

There will be no problems crossing, provided your papers are in order. If you are on an international bus, you'll have to exit the bus and proceed through both border stations. Bus drivers will wait for everyone to be processed before heading on.

If you choose to take local buses, it's advisable to get to border stations early in the day to allow time for waiting in line and processing. Note that onward buses tend to wind down by the afternoon.

International buses go from San José to Changuinola (Bocas del Toro), David and Panama City in Panama; Guatemala City in Guatemala; Managua in Nicaragua; San Salvador in El Salvador; and Tegucigalpa in Honduras. For approximate schedules and fares, see p97.

Car & Motorcycle

The cost of insurance, fuel and border permits makes a car journey significantly more expensive than buying an airline ticket. Also, the mountain of paperwork required to drive into Costa Rica from other countries deters many travelers, who prefer to arrive here and then buy or rent a vehicle. To enter Costa Rica by car, you'll need the following items:

- valid registration and proof of ownership
- valid driver's license or International Driving Permit
- valid license plates
- recent inspection certificate (not essential, but a good idea)
- passport
- multiple photocopies of all these documents in case the originals get lost

Sometimes border guards can be overzealous when examining a vehicle, so make sure that it doesn't violate any potential or existing safety regulations or you may have to pay a hefty fee to get it processed. Before departing, check that the following elements are present and in working order:

- blinkers, head- and taillights
- spare tire
- jerry can for extra gas (petrol)
- well-stocked toolbox including parts, such as belts, that are harder to find in Central America
- emergency flares, roadside triangles and a fire extinguisher

Insurance from foreign countries isn't recognized in Costa Rica, so you'll have to buy a policy locally. At the border it will cost about US$15 a month. In addition, you'll probably have to pay a US$22 road tax to drive in.

DRIVING TO COSTA RICA FROM NORTH AMERICA

Every year, readers send us letters detailing their long-haul road trip across the continent. If you think you're game for a little overland adventure, here is a selection of reader-tested tips for making the most of the big drive:

- **Think it through** Driving yourself through Central America is *not* a cheap option. Having your own car will afford you greater comfort and flexibility, though you will spend more than you expect on gas, insurance and import fees. Unless you are planning to spend a lot of time off the beaten track or detest the idea of slumming it on local buses, public transportation will probably be a cheaper and easier way to go.
- **Buy a Japanese car** Toyotas, Hondas and Nissans are extremely popular in Central America, which makes them substantially easier to service if problems arise.
- **Learn to service your car** A degree of mechanical know-how will allow you to make minor repairs yourself, and help you avoid being ripped off by unscrupulous mechanics. If you do need to repair your vehicle, be advised that mechanics charge much more in Costa Rica than in other Central American countries.
- **Be prepared** It's a good idea to plan for the worst, so make sure that you bring along a good tool kit, an emergency jerry can of gas, plenty of emergency food and water, and a roll of industrial-strength duct tape for reattaching bits of your battered car. A spare tire or two is also a good idea, especially if you're planning to go off-road or traveling over rough terrain.
- **Know the law** Costa Rican law requires that all vehicles be fitted with a catalytic converter. Bear this in mind if you remove your catalytic converter elsewhere in Central America due to the poorer grades of fuel that can cause the converter to get clogged.
- **And most importantly – drive defensively** As one reader put it, 'Understand that many drivers are clinically insane.' Driving in Costa Rica and the rest of Central America is not for the faint of heart – be smart, be safe and arrive alive.

You are not allowed to sell the car in Costa Rica. If you need to leave the country without the car, you must leave it in a customs warehouse in San José.

For tips on driving to Costa Rica from North America, importing your car and selling it afterwards, see the boxed text above.

SEA

Cruise ships stop in Costa Rican ports and enable passengers to make a quick foray into the country. Typically, ships dock at either the Pacific port of Caldera (near Puntarenas, p317) or the Caribbean port of Puerto Limón (p455).

It is also possible to arrive in Costa Rica by private yacht.

GETTING AROUND

AIR

Scheduled Flights

Costa Rica's domestic airlines are **NatureAir** (☎ 2220-3054; www.natureair.com) and **Sansa** (☎ 2290-4100; www.flysansa.com); the latter is linked with Grupo TACA.

Both airlines fly small passenger planes, and you're allocated a baggage allowance of no more than 12kg. Space is limited and demand is high in the dry season, so reserve and pay for tickets in advance.

In Costa Rica schedules change constantly and delays are frequent because of inclement weather. Be patient: Costa Rica has small planes and big storms – you don't want to be in them at the same time. You should not arrange a domestic flight that makes a tight connection with an international flight back home.

All domestic flights originate and terminate at San José. Destinations reached from San José include Bahía Drake, Barra del Colorado, Golfito, Liberia, Neily, Palmar Sur, Playa Nosara, Playa Sámara/Carrillo, Playa Tamarindo, Puerto Jiménez, Quepos, Tambor and Tortuguero.

Charters

If you've got some serious cash to burn – or you're traveling as part of a large party – chartering a private plane is by far the quickest way to travel around the country. Destinations include Carrillo, Bahía Drake, Golfito, Jacó, La Fortuna, Liberia, Limon, Nosara, Palmar Sur, Parismina, Pavones, Puerto Jiménez, Punta Islita, Quepos, Sixaola, Tamarindo, Tambor and Tortuguero. It takes on average 45 to 90 minutes to fly to most destinations, though weather conditions can significantly speed up or delay travel time.

While there are a good number of charter companies serving Costa Rica, the most reputable in terms of safety is the domestic carrier, **NatureAir** (☎ 2220-3054; www.natureair.com). **Alfa Romeo Aero Taxi** (www.alfaromeoair.com) also gets good marks. You can book either directly through the company, through a tour agency or even your accommodations, especially if it's a high-end property.

For a King Air plane capable of seating one to seven passengers, you can expect to pay anywhere from US$850 to US$2250. For a Twin Otter holding one to 19 passengers, the price range is US$1750 to US$4000.

You should be aware that luggage space is extremely limited, so pack light if you're planning on chartering private planes.

BICYCLE

Mountain bikes and beach cruisers can be rented in towns with a significant tourist presence at US$10 to US$15 per day. A few companies organize bike tours around Costa Rica (see p527).

BOAT

Ferries cross the Golfo de Nicoya connecting the central Pacific coast with the southern tip of Península de Nicoya. The **Countermark ferry** (☎ 2661-1069) links the port of Puntarenas with Playa Naranjo four times daily. The **Ferry Peninsular** (☎ 2641-0118) travels between Puntarenas and Paquera every two hours, for a bus connection to Montezuma (see p316).

On the Golfo Dulce, a daily passenger ferry links Golfito with Puerto Jiménez on the Península de Osa, and a weekday water taxi travels to and from Playa Zancudo (see p432). On the other side of the Península de Osa, water taxis connect Bahía Drake with Sierpe (see p393).

On the Caribbean coast, there is a bus and boat service that runs several times a day, linking Cariari and Tortuguero (p466), while another links Parismina and Siquirres (p458).

Boats also ply the canals that run along the coast from Moín to Tortuguero, although no regular service exists. A daily water taxi connects Puerto Viejo de Sarapiquí with Trinidad on the Río San Juan (p508). The San Juan is Nicaraguan territory, so take your passport. You can try to arrange boat transportation in any of these towns for Barra del Colorado.

BUS

Local Buses

Local buses are the best (if rather slow) way of getting around Costa Rica. You can take one just about everywhere, and they're frequent and cheap, with the longest domestic journey out of San José costing less than US$15.

San José is the transportation center for the country (see p97), though there is no central terminal. Bus offices are scattered around the city: some large bus companies have big terminals that sell tickets in advance, while others have little more than a stop – sometimes unmarked.

Normally there's room for everyone on a bus, and if there isn't, someone will squeeze you on anyhow. The exceptions are days before and after a major holiday, especially Easter, when buses are ridiculously full. Note that there are no buses from Thursday to Saturday before Easter Sunday.

There are two types of bus: *directo* and *colectivo*. The *directo* buses should go from one destination to the next with few stops, though it goes against the instincts of most Costa Rican bus drivers to not pick up every single roadside passenger. As for the *colectivo,* you know you're on one when the kids outside are outrunning your bus.

Trips longer than four hours usually include a rest stop as buses do not have toilets. Space is limited on board, so if you have to check luggage make sure that it gets loaded and that it isn't 'accidentally' given to someone else at intermediate stops. Keep your day pack with important documents on you at all times. Theft from overhead racks is rampant.

Bus schedules fluctuate wildly, so always confirm the time when you buy your ticket. If you are catching a bus that picks you up somewhere along a road, get to the roadside early. Departure times are estimated and if the bus comes early, it will leave early.

For information on departures from San José, pay a visit to the Instituto Costarricense de Turismo (ICT) office (p72) to pick up the

DRIVING THROUGH RIVERS

You know all those great ads where 4WD monster trucks splash through rivers full speed ahead? Forget you ever saw them.

Driving in Costa Rica will likely necessitate a river crossing at some point. Unfortunately, too many travelers have picked up their off-road skills from watching TV, and every season Ticos (Costa Ricans) get a good chuckle out of the number of dead vehicles they help wayward travelers fish out of waterways.

If you're driving through water, follow the rules below:

- **Only do this in a 4WD** Don't drive through a river in a car. (It may seem ridiculous to have to say this, but it's done all the time.) Getting out of a steep, gravel riverbed requires a 4WD. Besides, car engines flood very easily – *adiós* rental car.
- **Check the depth of the water before driving through** To accommodate an average rental 4WD, the water should be no deeper than above the knee. In a sturdier vehicle (Toyota 4-Runner or equivalent), water can be waist-deep. If you're not sure, ask a local.
- **The water should be calm** If the river is gushing so that there are white crests on the water, do not try to cross. Not only will the force of the water flood the engine, it could sweep your car away.
- **Drive slooooowly** Taxi drivers all over Costa Rica make lots of money towing tourists who think that slamming through a river at full speed is the best way to get across. This is a huge mistake. The pressure of driving through a river too quickly will send the water right into the engine and you'll be cooking that electrical system in no time. Keep steady pressure on the accelerator so that the tail pipe doesn't fill with water, but take it slow.
- **Err on the side of caution** Car-rental agencies in Costa Rica do not insure for water damage, so if you drown your vehicle, you're paying – in more ways than one.

(sort of) up-to-date copy of the master schedule, which is also available online at www.visitcostarica.com.

Shuttle Buses

The tourist-van shuttle services (aka the gringo buses) are an alternative to the standard intercity buses. Shuttles are provided by **Grayline's Fantasy Bus** (☎ 2220-2126; www.graylinecostarica.com) and **Interbus** (☎ 2283-5573; www.interbusonline.com). Both companies run overland transportation from San José to the most popular destinations, as well as directly between other destinations (see their websites for the comprehensive list). These services will pick you up at your hotel and reservations can be made online, or through local travel agencies and hotel owners.

CAR & MOTORCYCLE

If you plan to drive in Costa Rica, your driver's license from home is normally accepted for up to 90 days. Many places will also accept an International Driving Permit (IDP), issued by the automobile association in your country of origin. After 90 days, however, you will need to get a Costa Rican driver's license.

Gasoline (petrol) and diesel are widely available, and 24-hour service stations dot the entire stretch of the Interamericana. The price of gas is about US$0.75 per liter, although it can fluctuate to more than US$1 per liter. In more remote areas, fuel will likely be more expensive and might be sold from a drum at the neighborhood *pulpería* (corner grocery store); look for signs that say *'Se vende gasolina'* ('We sell gas'). Spare parts may be hard to find, especially for vehicles with sophisticated electronics and emissions-control systems.

Hire & Insurance

Most car-rental agencies can be found in San José and in popular tourist destinations on the Pacific coast. Car rental is not cheap, but if you are going to be doing even a small amount of driving, invest in a 4WD. Many agencies will insist on 4WD for extended travel, especially in the rainy season, when driving through rivers is a matter of course. In fact, ordinary cars are pointless as soon as you leave the Interamericana.

To rent a car you need a valid driver's license, a major credit card and a passport. The minimum age for car rental is 21. Carefully inspect rented cars for minor damage and make sure that any damage is noted on the rental agreement. If your car breaks down, call the rental company. Don't attempt to get the car fixed yourself – most companies won't reimburse expenses without prior authorization.

Prices vary considerably, but on average you can expect to pay about US$350 to US$650 per week for an SUV, including *kilometraje libre* (unlimited mileage), and as little as US$200 per week for a standard car. Basic insurance will cost an additional US$15 to US$25 per day, and rental companies won't rent you a car without it. The roads in Costa Rica are rough and rugged, meaning that minor accidents or car damage are common. On top of this, you can pay an extra fee (about US$10 to US$15 per day) for a Collision Damage Waiver, or CDW, which covers the driver and a third party with a US$750 to US$1500 deductible.

Above and beyond this, you can purchase full insurance (about US$30 to US$50 per day), which is expensive, but well worth it. Note that if you pay basic insurance with a gold or platinum credit card, the company will usually take responsibility for damages to the car, in which case you can forego the cost of the full insurance. Make sure you verify this with your credit card company ahead of time.

Finally, note that most insurance policies do not cover damages caused by flooding or driving through a river (even though this is sometimes necessary in Costa Rica!), so be aware of the extent of your policy.

Rental rates fluctuate wildly, so make sure you shop around before you commit to anything. Some agencies offer discounts if you reserve online or if you rent for long periods of time. Note that rental offices at the airport charge a 12% fee in addition to regular rates.

Thieves can easily recognize rental cars, and many thefts have occurred from them. *Never* leave anything in sight in a parked car – nothing! – and remove all luggage from the trunk overnight. Park the car in a guarded parking lot rather than on the street. We cannot stress enough how many readers send letters to us each year detailing thefts from their cars.

Motorcycles (including Harleys) can be rented in San José (p100) and Escazú (p112).

All of the major international car-rental agencies have outlets in Costa Rica, but you can usually get a better deal from one of the local companies:

Adobe (☎ 2259-4242, in USA 800-769-8422; www.adobecar.com) Reader-recommended with offices in Liberia, Tamarindo and Quepos.

Dollar (☎ 2443-2950, in USA 866-767-8651; www.dollarcostarica.com) One of the cheapest companies in Costa Rica with offices in both airports.

Poas (☎ 2442-6178, in USA 888-607-POAS; www.carentals.com) Service centers in Liberia, Tamarindo, La Fortuna and Guápiles.

Solid (☎ 2442-6000; www.solidcarrental.com) The only agency with offices in Puerto Jiménez and Golfito.

TRANSPORTATION

ROAD DISTANCES (KM)

	Golfito	Liberia	Monteverde	Puerto Limón	Quepos	San Isidro de El General	San José
Liberia	447						
Monteverde	396	112					
Puerto Limón	449	379	318				
Quepos	194	255	118	334			
San Isidro de El General	180	329	294	294	77		
San José	339	220	160	168	174	134	
Turrialba	364	287	227	136	241	159	67

Road Conditions & Hazards

Overall, driving in Costa Rica is for people with nerves of steel. The roads vary from quite good (the Interamericana) to barely passable (just about everywhere else). Even the good ones can suffer from landslides, sudden flooding and fog. Most roads are single-lane and winding, lacking hard shoulders; others are dirt-and-mud affairs that climb mountains and traverse rivers.

Drive defensively. Always expect to come across cyclists, a broken-down vehicle, a herd of cattle, slow-moving trucks or an oxcart around the next bend. Unsigned speed bumps are placed on some stretches of road without warning. (The locals lovingly refer to them as *muertos*, 'the dead.')

Most roads (except around the major tourist towns) are inadequately signed and will require at least one stop to ask for directions. Always ask about road conditions before setting out, especially in the rainy season; a number of roads become impassable in the rainy season.

Road Rules

There are speed limits of 100km/h or less on all primary roads and 60km/h or less on secondary roads. Traffic police use radar, and speed limits are enforced with speeding tickets. You can get a traffic ticket for not wearing a seat belt. It's illegal to stop in an intersection or make a right turn on a red. At unmarked intersections, yield to the car on your right. Driving in Costa Rica is on the right and passing is allowed only on the left.

If you are issued with a ticket, you have to pay the fine at a bank; instructions are given on the ticket. If you are driving a rental car, the rental company may be able to arrange your payment for you – the amount of the fine should be on the ticket. A portion of the money from these fines goes to a children's charity.

Police have no right to ask for money, and shouldn't confiscate a car, unless: the driver cannot produce a license and ownership papers; the car lacks license plates; the driver is drunk; or the driver has been involved in an accident causing serious injury. (For more on what to do in an accident, see p533.)

If you are driving and see oncoming cars with headlights flashing, it often means that there is a road problem or a radar speed trap ahead. Slow down immediately.

HITCHHIKING

Hitchhiking is never entirely safe in any country and Lonely Planet doesn't recommend it. Travelers who hitchhike should understand that they are taking a small but potentially serious risk. People who do hitchhike will be safer if they travel in pairs and let someone know where they are planning to go. Single women should use even greater discretion.

Hitchhiking in Costa Rica is not common on main roads that have frequent buses. On minor rural roads, hitchhiking is easier. To get picked up, most locals wave to cars in a friendly manner. If you get a ride, offer to pay when you arrive by saying *¿Cuánto le debo?* (How much do I owe you?). Your offer may

THE CASE OF THE FLAT TIRE & THE DISAPPEARING LUGGAGE

A serious scam is under way on the streets around Aeropuerto Internacional Juan Santamaría. Many readers have reported similar incidents, so take precautions to ensure this doesn't happen to you. Here's how it goes…

After picking up a rental car and driving out of the city, you notice that it has a flat tire. You pull over to try to fix it. Some friendly locals, noticing that a visitor to their fair land is in distress, pull over to help out. There is inevitably some confusion with the changing of the tire, and everybody is involved in figuring it out, but eventually the car repair is successfully accomplished and the friendly Ticos (Costa Ricans) give you a wave and drive off. That's when you get back in your car and discover that your wallet – or your luggage, or everything – is gone.

This incident has happened enough times to suggest that somebody may be tampering with rental cars to 'facilitate' these flat tires. It certainly suggests that travelers should be very wary – and aware – if somebody pulls over to help. Keep your wallet and your passport on your person whenever you get out of a car. If possible, let one person in your party stay inside the car to keep a watchful eye. In any case, lock your doors – even if you think you are going to be right outside. There's nothing like losing all your luggage to put a damper on a vacation.

USING TAXIS IN REMOTE AREAS

Taxis are considered a form of public transportation in remote areas that lack good public-transportation networks. They can be hired by the hour, the half-day or full day, or you can arrange a flat fee for a trip. Meters are not used on long trips, so arrange the fare ahead of time. Fares can fluctuate due to worse-than-expected road conditions and bad weather in tough-to-reach places.

The condition of taxis varies from basic sedans held together by rust, to fully equipped 4WDs with air-con. In some cases, taxis are pick-up trucks with seats built into the back. Most towns will have at least one licensed taxi, but in some remote villages you may have to get rides from whoever is offering – ask at *pulperías* (corner grocery stores).

be waved aside, or you may be asked to help with money for gas.

LOCAL TRANSPORTATION

Bus

Local buses operate chiefly in San José, Puntarenas, San Isidro, Golfito and Puerto Limón, connecting urban and suburban areas. Most local buses pick up passengers on the street and on main roads. The vehicles in service are usually converted school buses imported from the USA, and they are often packed.

Taxi

In San José taxis have meters, called *marías*, but many drivers try to get out of using them, particularly if you don't speak Spanish. With that said, it is illegal not to use the meter, so don't be afraid to point this out if you feel as if you're about to be scammed. Outside of San José, however, most taxis don't have meters and fares tend to be agreed upon in advance – some bargaining is quite acceptable.

In some towns, there are *colectivos* (taxis that several passengers are able to share). Although *colectivos* are becoming increasingly difficult to find, the basic principle is that the driver charges a flat fee (usually about US$0.50) to take passengers from one end of town to the other.

In rural areas, 4WD jeeps are often used as taxis and are a popular means for surfers (and their boards) to travel from their accommodations to the break. Prices vary wildly depending on how touristy the area is, though generally speaking a 10-minute ride should cost between US$5 and US$15.

Taxi drivers are not normally tipped unless they assist with your luggage or have provided an above-average service. However, owing to the increasing number of North American travelers, don't be surprised if drivers in tourist towns are quick to hold out their palm.

Health

Dr David Goldberg

CONTENTS

Travelers to Central America need to be vigilant about food-borne and mosquito-borne infections. Most of these illnesses are not life-threatening, but they can certainly ruin your trip. Besides getting the proper vaccinations, it's important to use a good insect repellent and exercise care in what you eat and drink.

BEFORE YOU GO

Since most vaccines don't produce immunity until at least two weeks after they're given, visit a physician four to eight weeks before departure. Ask your doctor for an International Certificate of Vaccination (otherwise known as the 'yellow booklet'), which will list all the vaccinations you've received. This is mandatory for countries that require proof of yellow-fever vaccination upon entry, but it's a good idea to carry it wherever you travel.

Bring medications in their original containers, clearly labeled. A signed, dated letter from your physician describing all medical conditions and medications, including generic names, is also a good idea. If carrying syringes or needles, be sure to have a physician's letter documenting their medical necessity.

INSURANCE

Most doctors and hospitals expect payment in cash, regardless of whether you have travel health insurance or not. If you develop a life-threatening medical problem, you'll probably want to be evacuated to a country with state-of-the-art medical care. As this may cost tens of thousands of dollars, make sure you have insurance to cover this before you leave home. A list of medical evacuation and travel insurance companies is on the website of the **US State Department** (www.travel.state.gov/medical.html).

If your health insurance does not cover you for medical expenses while you are abroad, you should consider supplemental insurance. Check the Travel Services section of the Lonely Planet website at www.lonelyplanet.com for more information. It might pay to find out in advance if your insurance plan will make payments directly to providers or if they reimburse you later for any overseas health expenditures.

MEDICAL CHECKLIST

- acetaminophen (Tylenol) or aspirin
- adhesive or paper tape
- antibacterial ointment (eg Bactroban) for cuts and abrasions
- antibiotics
- antidiarrheal drugs (eg loperamide)
- antihistamines for hay fever and allergic reactions
- anti-inflammatory drugs (eg ibuprofen)
- bandages, gauze, gauze rolls
- insect repellent (containing DEET) for the skin
- insect spray (containing permethrin) for clothing, tents and bed nets
- iodine tablets for water purification
- oral rehydration salts
- pocket knife
- scissors, safety pins, tweezers
- steroid cream or cortisone for poison ivy and other allergic rashes
- sunblock
- syringes and sterile needles
- thermometers

INTERNET RESOURCES

There is a wealth of travel health advice on the internet. For further information, the website of **Lonely Planet** (www.lonelyplanet.com) is a good place to start. A superb book called

International Travel and Health, which is revised annually and available online at no cost, is published by the **World Health Organization** (www.who.int/ith). Another website of general interest is **MD Travel Health** (www.mdtravelhealth.com), which provides complete travel health recommendations for every country, updated daily, also at no cost.

It's usually a good idea to consult your government's travel health website before departure, if one is available:

Australia (www.dfat.gov.au/travel)
Canada (www.phac-aspc.gc.ca/tmp-pmv/pub_e.html)
UK (http://www.dh.gov.uk/en/Publichealth/Communicablediseases/Communicablediseasesgeneralinformation/index.htm)
USA (www.cdc.gov/travel)

FURTHER READING

For further information, see *Healthy Travel Central & South America* from Lonely Planet. If you're traveling with children, Lonely Planet's *Travel with Children* will be useful. The *ABC of Healthy Travel,* by E Walker et al, is another valuable resource.

IN TRANSIT

DEEP VEIN THROMBOSIS (DVT)

Blood clots (deep vein thrombosis) may form in the legs during plane flights, chiefly because of prolonged immobility. The longer the flight, the greater the risk. Though most blood clots are reabsorbed uneventfully, some may break off and travel through the blood vessels to the lungs, where they could cause life-threatening complications.

The chief symptom of DVT is swelling or pain of the foot, ankle or calf, usually but not always on just the one side. When a blood clot travels all the way to the lungs, it may cause chest pain and difficulty in breathing. Travelers with any of these symptoms should immediately seek out medical attention.

To prevent the development of DVT on long flights, you should walk about the cabin, perform isometric compressions of the leg muscles (ie contract the leg muscles while sitting), drink plenty of fluids and avoid alcohol and tobacco.

JET LAG & MOTION SICKNESS

Jet lag is common when crossing more than five time zones, resulting in insomnia, fatigue, malaise or nausea. To avoid jet lag, try drinking plenty of fluids (nonalcoholic) and eating light meals. Upon arrival, get exposure to natural sunlight and readjust your schedule (for meals, sleep etc) as soon as possible.

Antihistamines such as dimenhydrinate (Dramamine) and meclizine (Antivert, Bonine) are usually the first choice for treating motion sickness. Their main side effect is drowsiness. Ginger is a herbal alternative that apparently works like a charm for some people.

IN COSTA RICA

AVAILABILITY & COST OF HEALTH CARE

Good medical care is available in most major cities, but may be limited in rural areas. In a medical emergency, you should call one of the following numbers:

CIMA San José (☎ 2208-1000; Autopista Próspero Fernández, San José) It's 500m west of the tollbooths on the highway to Santa Ana.
Clínica Bíblica (☎ 2522-1000/1030; www.clinicabiblica.com; Av 14 btwn Calles Central & 1, San José)
Hospital Nacional de Niños (☎ 2222-0122; Calle 14 & Av Central, San José) Only for children under 12 years.
Poison Center (☎ 2223-1028)
Red Cross Ambulance (☎ 128, in San José 2221-5818)
San Juan de Dios Hospital (☎ 2257-6282; cnr Paseo Colón & Calle 14, San José)

For an extensive list of physicians, dentists and hospitals go to the US embassy website (http://usembassy.or.cr). If you're pregnant, be sure to check this site before departure to find the name of one or two obstetricians, just in case.

Most pharmacies are well supplied and the pharmacists are licensed to prescribe medication. If you're taking any medication on a regular basis, make sure you know its generic (scientific) name, since many pharmaceuticals go under different names in Costa Rica. The following pharmacies are open 24 hours:

Farmacia Clínica Bíblica (☎ 2522-1000; cnr Calle 1 & Av 14, San José)
Farmacia Clínica Católica (☎ 2283-6616; Guadalupe, San José)
Farmacia El Hospital (☎ 2222-0985)

INFECTIOUS DISEASES

Chagas' Disease

Chagas' disease is a parasitic infection that is transmitted by triatomine insects (reduviid bugs), which inhabit crevices in the walls and roofs of substandard housing in South and Central America. In Costa Rica most cases occur in Alajuela, Liberia and Puntarenas. The triatomine insect lays its feces on human skin as it bites, usually at night. A person becomes infected when they unknowingly rub the feces into the bite wound or any other open sore. Symptoms of the disease include fever and swelling of the spleen, liver and lymph nodes. Chagas' disease is extremely rare in travelers. However, if you sleep in a poorly constructed house, especially one made of mud, adobe or thatch, you should make sure you protect yourself with a bed net and a good insecticide.

Dengue Fever (Breakbone Fever)

Dengue fever is a viral infection found throughout Central America. In Costa Rica outbreaks involving thousands of people occur every year. Dengue is transmitted by aedes mosquitoes, which prefer to bite during the daytime and are usually found close to human habitations, often indoors. They breed primarily in artificial water containers such as jars, barrels, cans, cisterns, metal drums, plastic containers and discarded tires. As a result, dengue is especially common in densely populated, urban environments.

Dengue usually causes flulike symptoms including fever, muscle aches, joint pains, headaches, nausea and vomiting, often followed by a rash. The body aches may be quite uncomfortable, but most cases resolve uneventfully in a few days. Severe cases usually occur in children under the age of 15 who are experiencing their second dengue infection.

There is no real treatment for dengue fever except taking analgesics such as acetaminophen/paracetamol (Tylenol) and drinking plenty of fluids. Severe cases may require hospitalization for intravenous fluids and supportive care. There is no vaccine. The key to prevention is taking insect protection measures (see p556).

Hepatitis A

Hepatitis A is the second most common travel-related infection (after traveler's diarrhea). It's a viral infection of the liver that is usually acquired by ingestion of contaminated water, food or ice, though it may also be acquired by direct contact with infected persons. The illness occurs throughout the world, but the incidence is higher in developing nations. Symptoms may include fever, malaise, jaundice, nausea, vomiting and abdominal pain. Most cases resolve without complications, though hepatitis A occasionally causes severe liver damage. There is no treatment.

The vaccine for hepatitis A is extremely safe and highly effective. If you get a booster six to 12 months later, it lasts for at least 10 years. You should get vaccinated before you go to Costa Rica or any other developing nation. Because the safety of hepatitis A vaccine has not been established for pregnant women or children under the age of two, they should instead be given a gammaglobulin injection.

Hepatitis B

Like hepatitis A, hepatitis B is a liver infection that occurs worldwide but is more common in developing nations. Unlike hepatitis A, the disease is usually acquired by sexual contact or by exposure to infected blood, generally through blood transfusions or contaminated needles. The vaccine is recommended only for long-term travelers (on the road for more than six months) who expect to live in rural areas or have close physical contact with the local population. Additionally, the vaccine is recommended for anyone who anticipates sexual contact with the local inhabitants or a possible need for medical, dental or other treatments while abroad, especially if a need for transfusions or injections is expected.

Hepatitis B vaccine is safe and highly effective. However, a total of three injections are necessary to establish full immunity. Several countries added hepatitis B vaccine to the list of routine childhood immunizations in the 1980s, so many young adults are already protected.

HIV/AIDS

The HIV/AIDS virus occurs in all Central American countries. Be sure to use condoms for all sexual encounters.

Leishmaniasis

Leishmaniasis occurs in the mountains and jungles of all Central American countries. The infection is transmitted by sand flies, which are about one-third the size of mosquitoes. Most cases occur in newly cleared forest or areas of secondary growth. The highest incidence is in Talamanca. In Costa Rica it is generally limited to the skin, causing slow-growing ulcers over exposed parts of the body, but more severe infections may occur in those with HIV. There is no vaccine for leishmaniasis. To protect yourself from sand flies, follow the same precautions as for mosquitoes (p556), except that netting must be finer mesh (at least 18 holes to the linear inch).

Leptospirosis

Leptospirosis is acquired by exposure to water contaminated by the urine of infected animals. White-water rafters are at particularly high risk. In Costa Rica most cases occur in Puerto Limón, Turrialba, San Carlos and Golfito. Cases have been reported among residents of Puerto Limón who have bathed in local streams. Outbreaks can occur at times of flooding, when sewage overflow may contaminate water sources. The initial symptoms, which resemble a mild flu, usually subside uneventfully in a few days, with or without treatment, but a minority of cases are complicated by jaundice or meningitis. There is no vaccine. You can minimize your risk by staying out of bodies of fresh water that may be contaminated by animal urine. If you're engaging in high-risk activities, such as river rafting, in an area where an outbreak is in progress, you can take 200mg of doxycycline once weekly as a preventative measure. If you actually develop leptospirosis, the treatment is 100mg of doxycycline twice daily.

Malaria

Malaria occurs in every country in Central America. It's transmitted by mosquito bites, usually between dusk and dawn. The main symptom is high spiking fevers, which may be accompanied by chills, sweats, headache, body aches, weakness, vomiting or diarrhea. Severe cases may involve the central nervous system and lead to seizures, confusion, coma and death.

Taking malaria pills is recommended for the provinces of Alajuela, Limón (except for Puerto Limón), Guanacaste and Heredia. The risk is greatest in the cantons of Los Chiles (Alajuela province), and Matina and Talamanca (Limón province).

For Costa Rica the first-choice malaria pill is chloroquine, taken once weekly in a dosage of 500mg, starting one to two weeks before arrival and continuing through the trip and for four weeks after departure. Chloroquine is safe, inexpensive and highly effective. Side effects are typically mild and may include nausea, abdominal discomfort, headache, dizziness, blurred vision or itching. Severe reactions are uncommon.

Protecting yourself against mosquito bites (see p556) is just as important as taking malaria pills, since no pills are 100% effective.

If you may not have access to medical care while traveling, you should bring along additional pills for emergency self-treatment, which you should take if you can't reach a doctor and you develop symptoms that suggest malaria, such as high spiking fevers. One option is to take four tablets of Malarone once daily for three days. If you start self-medication, you should try to see a doctor at the earliest possible opportunity.

If you develop a fever after returning home, see a physician as malaria symptoms may not occur for months.

Rabies

Rabies is a viral infection of the brain and spinal cord that is almost always fatal. The rabies virus is carried in the saliva of infected animals and is typically transmitted through an animal bite, though contamination of any break in the skin with infected saliva may result in rabies.

Rabies occurs in all Central American countries. However, in Costa Rica only two cases have been reported over the last 30 years. Rabies vaccine is therefore recommended only for those at particularly high risk, such as spelunkers (cave explorers) and animal handlers.

All animal bites and scratches must be promptly and thoroughly cleansed with large amounts of soap and water. Local health authorities should be contacted to determine whether or not further treatment is necessary (see p556).

Typhoid

Typhoid fever is caused by ingestion of food or water contaminated by a species of salmonella known as *Salmonella typhi*. Fever occurs in virtually all cases. Other symptoms may include headache, malaise, muscle aches, dizziness, loss of appetite, nausea and abdominal pain. Either diarrhea or constipation may occur. Possible complications include intestinal perforation, intestinal bleeding, confusion, delirium or (rarely) coma.

Unless you expect to take all your meals in major hotels and restaurants, a typhoid vaccine is a good idea. It's usually given orally, but is also available as an injection. Neither vaccine is approved for use in children under the age of two.

The drug of choice for typhoid fever is usually a quinolone antibiotic such as ciprofloxacin (Cipro) or levofloxacin (Levaquin), which many travelers carry for treatment of traveler's diarrhea. However, if you self-treat for typhoid fever, you may also need to self-treat for malaria, since the symptoms of the two diseases may be indistinguishable.

TRAVELER'S DIARRHEA

To prevent diarrhea, you should only eat fresh fruit or vegetables if cooked or peeled; be wary of dairy products that might contain unpasteurized milk; and be highly selective when eating food from street vendors. Tap water is generally OK, but when you're off the beaten path it's best to drink bottled and avoid tap water unless it has been boiled, filtered or chemically disinfected (iodine tablets).

If you develop diarrhea, be sure to drink plenty of fluids, preferably with an oral rehydration solution containing lots of salt and sugar. A few loose stools don't require treatment, but if you start having more than four or five stools a day, you should begin taking an antibiotic (usually a quinolone drug) and an antidiarrheal agent (such as loperamide). If diarrhea is bloody or persists for more than 72 hours, or is accompanied by fever, shaking chills or severe abdominal pain, you should seek medical attention.

ENVIRONMENTAL HAZARDS

Animal Bites

Do not attempt to pet, handle or feed any animal, with the exception of domestic animals known to be free of any infectious disease. Most animal injuries are directly related to a person's attempt to touch or feed the animal.

Any bite or scratch by a mammal, including bats, should be promptly and thoroughly cleansed with large amounts of soap and water, followed by application of an antiseptic such as iodine or alcohol. The local health authorities should be contacted immediately for possible postexposure rabies treatment, whether or not you've been immunized against rabies. It may also be advisable to start an antibiotic, since wounds caused by animal bites and scratches frequently become infected. One of the newer quinolones, such as levofloxacin (Levaquin), which many travelers carry in case of diarrhea, would be an appropriate choice.

Insect Bites

No matter how much you safeguard, getting bitten by mosquitoes is part of every traveler's experience in the country. While there are occasional outbreaks of dengue fever (see p554) in Costa Rica, for the most part the greatest worry you will have with bites is the general discomfort that comes with them, namely itching.

The best prevention is to stay covered up – wearing long pants, long sleeves, a hat and shoes (rather than sandals). Unfortunately, Costa Rica's sweltering temperatures might make this a bit difficult. Therefore, the best measure you can take is to invest in a good insect repellent, preferably one containing DEET. (These repellents can also be found in Costa Rica.) This should be applied to exposed skin and clothing (but not to eyes, mouth, cuts, wounds or irritated skin).

In general, adults and children over the age of 12 can use preparations containing 25% to 35% DEET, which usually lasts about six hours. Children between two and 12 years of age should use preparations containing no more than 10% DEET, applied sparingly, which will usually last about three hours. Neurologic toxicity has been reported from DEET, especially in children, but appears to be extremely uncommon and generally related to overuse. Compounds containing DEET should not be used on children under age the age of two.

Insect repellents containing certain botanical products, including eucalyptus and soybean oil, are effective but last only 1½ to two hours.

A particularly good item for every traveler to take is a bug net to hang over beds (along with a few thumbtacks or nails with which to hang it). Many hotels in Costa Rica don't have windows (or screens), and a cheap little net will save you plenty of nighttime aggravation. The mesh size should be less than 1.5mm.

Dusk is the worst time for mosquitoes, so it's best to take extra precautions once the sun starts to set.

Snake Bites

Costa Rica is home to all manner of venomous snakes and any foray into forested areas will put you at (a very slight) risk of snake bite.

The best prevention is to wear closed, heavy shoes or boots and to keep a watchful eye on the trail. Snakes like to come out to cleared paths for a nap, so watch where you step. (For more on Costa Rica's fer-de-lance and bushmaster, see p185).

In the event of a bite from a venomous snake, place the victim at rest, keep the bitten area immobilized and move the victim immediately to the nearest medical facility. Avoid tourniquets, which are no longer recommended.

Sun

To protect yourself from excessive sun exposure, you should stay out of the midday sun, wear sunglasses and a wide-brimmed hat, and apply sunblock with SPF 15 or higher, with both UVA and UVB protection. Sunblock should be generously applied to all exposed parts of the body approximately 30 minutes before sun exposure and should be reapplied after swimming or vigorous activity. Travelers should also drink plenty of fluids and avoid strenuous exercise when the temperature is high.

Water

It's generally safe to drink tap water in Costa Rica, except in the most rural and undeveloped parts of the country. However, if you prefer to be cautious, buying bottled water is your best bet. If you have the means, vigorous boiling for one minute is the most effective means of water purification. At altitudes greater than 2000m, boil for three minutes. Another option is to disinfect water with iodine pills: add 2% tincture of iodine to 1L of water (five drops to clear water, 10 drops to cloudy water) and let stand for 30 minutes. If the water is cold, longer times may be required.

TRAVELING WITH CHILDREN

In general, it's safe for children and pregnant women to go to Costa Rica. However, because some of the vaccines listed previously are not approved for use by children or during pregnancy, these travelers should be particularly careful not to drink tap water or consume any questionable food or beverage. Also, when traveling with children, make sure they're up to date on all routine immunizations. It's sometimes appropriate to give children some of their vaccines a little early before visiting a developing nation. You should discuss this with your pediatrician.

Lastly, if pregnant, bear in mind that should a complication such as premature labor develop while abroad, the quality of medical care may not be comparable to that in your home country.

See p529 for some general information on traveling with children.

Language

CONTENTS

Spanish is the official language of Costa Rica and the main language the traveler will need. Indigenous languages are spoken in isolated areas, but unless you're getting off the beaten track you'll rarely encounter them. The indigenous languages Bribrí and Cabécar are understood by an estimated 18,000 people living on both sides of the Cordillera de Talamanca.

English is often spoken in the upmarket hotels, airline offices and tourist agencies, and some other European languages are spoken in hotels run by Europeans. On the Caribbean coast, many of the locals speak some English (with a local creole dialect).

Every visitor to Costa Rica should make the effort to learn at least a few basic phrases in Spanish. Spanish language courses are available in all parts of the country (see p529). Don't hesitate to practice your new skills – in general, Latin Americans meet attempts to communicate in the vernacular with enthusiasm and appreciation.

Lonely Planet's *Costa Rican Spanish* phrasebook will be very helpful during your trip. If you're traveling outside Costa Rica, Lonely Planet's *Latin American Spanish* phrasebook is also a handy language guide.

SPANISH IN COSTA RICA

These colloquialisms and slang *(tiquismos)* are frequently heard, and are for the most part used only in Costa Rica.

¡Adiós! – Hi! (used when passing a friend in the street, or anyone in remote rural areas; also means 'Farewell!' but only when leaving for a long time)
bomba – gas station
buena nota – OK/excellent (literally 'good note')
chapulines – a gang, usually of young thieves
chunche – thing (can refer to almost anything)
cien metros – one city block
¿Hay campo? – Is there space? (on a bus)
machita – blonde woman (slang)
mae – buddy (pronounced 'ma' as in 'mat' followed with a quick 'eh'; it's mainly used by boys and young men)
mi amor – my love (used as a familiar form of address by both men and women)
pulpería – corner grocery store
¡Pura vida! – Super! (literally 'pure life,' also an expression of approval or even a greeting)
sabanero – cowboy, especially one who hails from Guanacaste Province
salado – too bad; tough luck
soda – cafe or lunch counter
¡Tuanis! – Cool!
¡Upe! – Is anybody home? (used mainly in rural areas at people's homes, instead of knocking)
vos – you (singular and informal, same as *tú*)

Another useful resource is the *University of Chicago Spanish-English, English-Spanish Dictionary*. For a comprehensive food and drink glossary, see p53.

LATIN AMERICAN SPANISH

The Spanish of the Americas comes in many regional varieties. Slang and regional vocabulary, much of it derived from indigenous languages, adds to the linguistic richness. The boxed text above gives you a few insights into the local lingo of Costa Rica.

Throughout Latin America, the Spanish language is referred to as *castellano* more often than *español*. Unlike in Spain, the plural of the familiar *tú* (you) form is *ustedes* rather than *vosotros;* the latter term will sound quaint and archaic in the Americas. Another notable difference is that the letters **c** and **z** are never pronounced as lisped in Latin America.

PRONUNCIATION

Spanish spelling is phonetically consistent, meaning that there's a clear and consistent relationship between what you see in writing and how it's pronounced. Also, most Spanish sounds have English equivalents, so English speakers shouldn't have trouble being understood. The phrases in this language guide are all accompanied by guides to pronunciation, so the task of getting your message across is made even simpler. Even if you read our pronunciation guides as if they were English, you will be understood.

Vowels

a	as the 'a' in 'father'
ai	as in 'aisle'
ay	as in 'say'
e	as the 'e' in 'met'
ee	as the 'ee' in 'meet'
o	as the 'o' in 'more' (without the 'r')
oo	as the 'oo' in 'zoo'
ow	as in 'how'
oy	as in 'boy'

Consonants

Pronunciation of Spanish consonants is similar to their English counterparts. The exceptions are given in the following list.

kh	as the throaty 'ch' in the Scottish *loch*
ll	in Costa Rica, as the 'y' in 'yes'
ny	as the 'ny' in 'canyon'
r	as in 'run' but stronger and rolled, especially at the beginning of a word and in all words with *rr*
s	not lisped (unlike in Spain)

The letter 'h' is invariably silent (ie never pronounced) in Spanish.

Note also that the Spanish **b** and **v** sounds are very similar – they are both pronounced as a very soft 'v' in English (somewhere between 'b' and 'v').

There are some variations in spoken Spanish as part of the regional accents across Latin America in general. The most notable of these variations is the pronunciation of the letter *ll*. In some parts of Latin America it's pronounced as the 'll' in 'million,' but in Costa Rica it's pronounced as 'y' (eg as in 'yes'), and this is how it's represented in our pronunciation guides.

WORD STRESS

In general, words ending in vowels or the letters **n** or **s** have stress on the next-to-last syllable, while those with other endings have stress on the last syllable. Thus *vaca* (cow) and *caballos* (horses) both carry stress on the next-to-last syllable, while *ciudad* (city) and *infeliz* (unhappy) are both stressed on the last syllable.

Written accents will almost always appear in words that don't follow the rules above, eg *sótano* (basement), *América* and *porción* (portion). When counting syllables, be sure to remember that diphthongs (vowel combinations, such as the **ue** in *puede*) constitute only one. When a word with a written accent appears in capital letters, the accent is often not written, but is still pronounced.

GENDER & PLURALS

Spanish nouns are either masculine or feminine, and there are rules to help determine gender (with the obligatory exceptions). Feminine nouns generally end with **-a** or with the groups **ción**, **-sión** or **-dad**. Other endings typically signify a masculine noun. Endings for adjectives also change to agree with the gender of the noun they modify (masculine/feminine **-o**/**-a**). Where both masculine and feminine forms are included in this chapter, they are separated by a slash, with the masculine form given first, eg *perdido/a*.

If a noun or adjective ends in a vowel, the plural is formed by adding **-s** to the end. If it ends in a consonant, the plural is formed by adding **-es** to the end.

ACCOMMODATIONS

Where's a ...?	*¿Adónde hay ...?*	a·*don*·de ai ...
cabin	*una cabina*	*oo*·na ka·*bee*·na
camping ground	*una área para acampar*	*oo*·na *a*·re·a *pa*·ra a·kam·*par*
ecolodge	*un ecolodge*	oon e·ko·loj
guesthouse	*una casa de huéspedes*	*oo*·na *ka*·sa de *wes*·pe·des
hostel	*un hospedaje*	oon os·pe·*da*·khe
hotel	*un hotel*	oon o·*tel*
youth hostel	*un albergue juvenil*	oon al·*ber*·ge khoo·ve·*neel*

MAKING A RESERVATION

(for phone or written requests)

To …	*A …*
From …	*De …*
Date	*Fecha*
I'd like to book …	*Quisiera reservar …*
in the name of …	*en nombre de …*
for the nights of …	*para las noches del …*
credit card	*tarjeta de crédito*
number	*número*
expiry date	*fecha de vencimiento*
Please confirm …	*¿Puede confirmar …?*
availability	*la disponibilidad*
price	*el precio*

Do you have a room available?
¿Tiene una habitación? tye·ne *oo*·na a·bee·ta·*syon*

Does it include breakfast?
¿Incluye el desayuno? een·*kloo*·ye el de·sa·*yoo*·no

May I see the room?
¿Puedo ver la habitación? *pwe*·do ver la a·bee·ta·*syon*

I'd like a … room.	*Quisiera una habitación …*	kee·*sye*·ra *oo*·na a·bee·ta·*syon* …
double	*doble*	*do*·ble
single	*sencilla*	sen·*see*·ya
twin	*con dos camas*	kon dos *ka*·mas
How much is it per …?	*¿Cuánto cuesta por …?*	*kwan*·to *kwes*·ta por …
night	*noche*	*no*·che
person	*persona*	per·*so*·na
week	*semana*	se·*ma*·na
cheaper	*más barato*	mas ba·*ra*·to
discount	*descuento*	des·*kwen*·to
full board	*pensión completa*	pen·*syon* kom·*ple*·ta
private/shared bathroom	*baño privado/ compartido*	*ba*·nyo pree·*va*·do/ kom·par·*tee*·do
too expensive	*demasiado caro*	de·ma·*sya*·do *ka*·ro
I don't like it.	*No me gusta.*	no me *goos*·ta
It's fine.	*Está bien.*	es·*ta* byen
I'll take it.	*La tomo.*	la *to*·mo
I'm leaving now.	*Me voy ahora.*	me voy a·*o*·ra

CONVERSATION & ESSENTIALS

Latin Americans are very conscious of civilities. Never approach a stranger for information without extending a greeting, such as *buenos días* or *buenas tardes*, and use only the polite form of address, especially with the police and public officials.

Central America is generally more formal than many of the South American countries. The polite form *usted* (you), rather than the informal *tú*, is used in all cases in this chapter; where options are given, the form is indicated by the abbreviations 'pol' and 'inf.'

The three most common greetings are often abbreviated to simply *buenos* (for *buenos días*) and *buenas* (for *buenas tardes* and *buenas noches*).

Hi.	*Hola.*	o·la
Good morning.	*Buenos días.*	*bwe*·nos *dee*·as
Good afternoon.	*Buenas tardes.*	*bwe*·nas *tar*·des
Good evening/ night.	*Buenas noches.*	*bwe*·nas *no*·ches
Goodbye.	*Adiós.*	a·*dyos*
Bye.	*Chao.*	chow
Yes.	*Sí.*	see
No.	*No.*	no
Please.	*Por favor.*	por fa·*vor*
Thank you.	*Gracias.*	*gra*·syas
Many thanks.	*Muchas gracias.*	*moo*·chas *gra*·syas
You're welcome.	*Con mucho gusto.*	kon *moo*·cho *goo*·sto
Excuse me. (to get past/to get attention)	*Con permiso.*	kon per·*mee*·so
Excuse me. (apology)	*Discúlpeme.*	dees·*kool*·pe·me
I'm sorry.	*Lo siento.*	lo *syen*·to

How are you?
¿Cómo va/vas? *ko*·mo va/vas (pol/inf)

Fine, and you?
¿Bien, y usted/vos? byen ee oos·*ted*/vos (pol/inf)

What's your name?
¿Cómo se llama? *ko*·mo se *ya*·ma (pol)
¿Cómo te llamas? *ko*·mo te *ya*·mas (inf)

My name is …
Me llamo … me *ya*·mo …

It's a pleasure to meet you.
Mucho gusto. *moo*·cho *goos*·to

Where are you from?
¿De dónde es/sos? de *don*·de es/sos (pol/inf)

I'm from …
Soy de … soy de …

Do you live here?
¿Vive/Vivís por aqui? *vee*·ve/vee·*vees* por a·*kee* (pol/inf)

Can I take a photo?
¿Puedo tomar una foto? *pwe*·do to·*mar* *oo*·na *fo*·to

LANGUAGE

DIRECTIONS

How do I get to ...?
¿Cómo llego a ...? ko·mo *ye*·go a ...
What's the address?
¿Cuál es la dirección? kwal es la dee·rek·*syon*
Can you show me (on the map)?
¿Me puede enseñar (en el mapa)? me *pwe*·de en·se·*nyar* (en el *ma*·pa)
How far is it?
¿Qué tan largo está? ke tan *lar*·go es·*ta*
It's straight ahead.
Está aquí directo. es·*ta* a·*kee* dee·*rek*·to
Turn left.
Doble a la izquierda. *dob*·le a la ees·*kyer*·da
Turn right.
Doble a la derecha. *dob*·le a la de·*re*·cha

north	*norte*	*nor*·te
south	*sur*	soor
east	*este*	*es*·te
west	*oeste*	o·*es*·te

avenue	*avenida*	a·ve·*nee*·da
block	*cuadra*	*kwa*·dra
here	*aquí*	a·*kee*
street	*calle*	*ka*·ye
there	*ahí*	a·*ee*

EATING OUT

Can you recommend a bar/restaurant?
¿Podría recomendar un bar/restaurante? po·*dree*·a re·ko·men·*dar* oon bar/res·tow·*ran*·te
Do you have an English menu?
¿Hay un menú en inglés? ai oon me·*noo* en een·*gles*
What would you recommend?
¿Qué me recomienda? ke me re·ko·*myen*·da
What's the local specialty?
¿Cuál es la especialidad local? kwal es la es·pe·sya·lee·*dad* lo·*kal*
I'll have (that).
Yo quiero (eso). yo *kye*·ro (*e*·so)
I'd like it with/without ...
Lo quiero con/sin ... lo *kye*·ro kon/seen ...
I'm a vegetarian.
Soy vegetariano/a. soy ve·khe·ta·*rya*·no/a
That was delicious.
Estuvo delicioso. es·*too*·vo de·lee·*syo*·so
I'll buy you a drink.
Te invito a un trago. te een·*vee*·to a oon *tra*·go
Please bring the drink list.
Tráigame la lista de tragos, por favor. *trai*·ga·me la *lees*·ta de *tra*·gos por fa·*vor*
Cheers!
¡Salud! sa·*lood*
The bill, please.
La cuenta, por favor. la *kwen*·ta por fa·*vor*

EMERGENCIES

Help!	*¡Socorro!*	so·*ko*·ro
Stop!	*¡Pare!*	*pa*·re
Fire!	*¡Incendio!*	een·*sen*·dyo
Thief!	*¡Ladrón!*	lad·*ron*
Go away!	*¡Váyase!*	*va*·ya·se
Watch out!	*¡Cuidado!*	*kwee*·da·do

Call ...	*Llame a ...*	*ya*·me a ...
a doctor	*un doctor*	oon dok·*tor*
an ambulance	*una ambulancia*	*oo*·na am·boo·*lan*·sya
the police	*la policía*	la po·lee·*see*·a

It's an emergency.
Es una emergencia. es *oo*·na e·mer·*khen*·sya
Could you help me, please?
¿Me podría ayudar, por favor? me po·*dree*·a a·yoo·*dar* por fa·*vor*
I'm lost.
Estoy perdido/a. es·*toy* per·*dee*·do/a
Where are the toilets?
¿Dónde está el baño? *don*·de es·*ta* el *ba*·nyo

HEALTH

I'm sick.
Estoy enfermo/a. es·*toy* en·*fer*·mo/a
I need a doctor.
Necesito un doctor. ne·se·*see*·to oon dok·*tor*
Where's the hospital?
¿Adónde está el hospital? a·*don*·de es·*ta* el os·pee·*tal*
I'm pregnant.
Estoy embarazada. es·*toy* em·ba·ra·*sa*·da
I've been vaccinated.
Estoy vacunado/a. es·*toy* va·koo·*na*·do/a

I'm allergic to ...	*Soy alérgico/a a ...*	soy a·*ler*·khee·ko/a a ...
antibiotics	*los antibióticos*	los an·tee·*byo*·tee·kos
bees	*las abejas*	las a·*be*·khas
nuts	*las nueces*	las *nwe*·ses
penicillin	*la penicilina*	la pe·nee·see·*lee*·na

I'm ...	*Soy ...*	soy ...
asthmatic	*asmático/a*	as·*ma*·tee·ko/a
diabetic	*diabético/a*	dya·*be*·tee·ko/a
epileptic	*epiléptico/a*	e·pee·*lep*·tee·ko/a

I have (a) ...	*Tengo ...*	*ten*·go ...
diarrhea	*diarrea*	dya·*re*·a
headache	*dolor de cabeza*	do·*lor* de ka·*be*·sa
nausea	*náuseas*	*now*·se·as
sore throat	*dolor de garganta*	do·*lor* de gar·*gan*·ta

LANGUAGE DIFFICULTIES

Do you speak English?
¿Habla/Hablas inglés? a·bla/a·blas een·*gles* (pol/inf)
Does anyone here speak English?
¿Alguien habla inglés? al·gyen *a*·bla een·*gles*
I (don't) understand.
(No) Entiendo. (no) en·*tyen*·do
How do you say ...?
¿Cómo se dice ...? ko·mo se *dee*·se ...
What does ...mean?
¿Qué significa ...? ke seeg·nee·*fee*·ka ...

Could you please ...?	*¿Puede ..., por favor?*	*pwe*·de ... por *fa*·vor
repeat that	*repetir eso*	re·pe·*teer e*·so
speak more slowly	*hablar más despacio*	a·*blar* mas des·*pa*·syo
write it down	*escribirlo*	es·kree·*beer*·lo

NUMBERS

0	*cero*	*se*·ro
1	*uno*	*oo*·no
2	*dos*	dos
3	*tres*	tres
4	*cuatro*	*kwa*·tro
5	*cinco*	*seen*·ko
6	*seis*	says
7	*siete*	*sye*·te
8	*ocho*	*o*·cho
9	*nueve*	*nwe*·ve
10	*diez*	dyes
11	*once*	*on*·se
12	*doce*	*do*·se
13	*trece*	*tre*·se
14	*catorce*	ka·*tor*·se
15	*quince*	*keen*·se
16	*dieciséis*	dye·see·*says*
17	*diecisiete*	dye·see·*sye*·te
18	*dieciocho*	dye·see·*o*·cho
19	*diecinueve*	dye·see·*nwe*·ve
20	*veinte*	*vayn*·te
21	*veintiuno*	vayn·tee·*oo*·no
30	*treinta*	*trayn*·ta
31	*treinta y uno*	*trayn*·ta ee *oo*·no
40	*cuarenta*	kwa·*ren*·ta
50	*cincuenta*	seen·*kwen*·ta
60	*sesenta*	se·*sen*·ta
70	*setenta*	se·*ten*·ta
80	*ochenta*	o·*chen*·ta
90	*noventa*	no·*ven*·ta
100	*cien*	syen
101	*ciento uno*	*syen*·to *oo*·no
200	*doscientos*	do·*syen*·tos
1000	*mil*	meel
5000	*cinco mil*	*seen*·ko meel

SIGNS

Abierto	Open
Cerrado	Closed
Entrada	Entrance
Estación Policial	Police Station
Información	Information
Prohibido	Prohibited
Salida	Exit
Servicios/Baños	Toilets
Hombres/Varones	Men
Mujeres/Damas	Women

PAPERWORK

birth certificate	*certificado de nacimiento*	ser·tee·fee·*ka*·do de na·see·*myen*·to
car-owner's title	*título de propiedad*	*tee*·too·lo de pro·pye·*dad*
car registration	*registro del carro*	re·*khees*·tro del *ka*·ro
customs	*aduana*	a·*dwa*·na
departure tax	*impuesto de salida*	eem·*pwe*·sto de sa·*lee*·da
driver's license	*licencia de conductor*	lee·*sen*·sya de kon·dook·*tor*
immigration	*migración*	mee·gra·*syon*
insurance	*seguro*	se·*goo*·ro
passport	*pasaporte*	pa·sa·*por*·te
temporary vehicle import permit	*permiso de importación temporal de vehículo*	per·*mee*·so de eem·por·ta·*syon* tem·po·*ral* de ve·*ee*·koo·lo
tourist card	*tarjeta de turista*	tar·*khe*·ta de too·*rees*·ta
visa	*visa*	*vee*·sa

SHOPPING & SERVICES

I'd like to buy ...
Quiero comprar ... *kye*·ro kom·*prar* ...
I'm just looking.
Sólo estoy viendo. *so*·lo es·*toy vyen*·do
Can I look at it?
¿Puedo verlo? *pwe*·do *ver*·lo
How much is it?
¿Cuánto cuesta? *kwan*·to *kwes*·ta
That's too expensive for me.
Es demasiado caro para mí. es de·ma·*sya*·do *ka*·ro *pa*·ra mee
Could you lower the price?
¿Podría bajarle el precio? po·*dree*·a ba·*khar*·le el *pre*·syo
I don't like it.
No me gusta. no me *goos*·ta
I'll take it.
Lo llevo. lo *ye*·vo

Do you accept ...?	*¿Acepta ...?*	a·*sep*·ta ...
American dollars	*dólares americanos*	*do*·la·res a·me·ree·*ka*·nos
credit cards	*tarjetas de crédito*	tar·*khe*·tas de *kre*·dee·to
traveler's checks	*cheques de viajero*	*che*·kes de vya·*khe*·ro

more	*más*	mas
less	*menos*	*me*·nos
large	*grande*	*gran*·de
small	*pequeño/a*	pe·*ke*·nyo/a

Where's a/an/the ...?	*¿Adónde esta ...?*	a·*don*·de es·*ta* ...
ATM	*un cajero automático*	oon ka·*khe*·ro ow·to·*ma*·tee·ko
bank	*un banco*	oon *ban*·ko
bookstore	*la librería*	la lee·bre·*ree*·a
chemist	*la farmacia*	la far·*ma*·sya
exchange office	*una casa de cambio*	*oo*·na *ka*·sa de *kam*·byo
general store	*una tienda*	*oo*·na *tyen*·da
laundry	*la lavandería*	la la·van·de·*ree*·a
market	*el mercado*	el mer·*ka*·do
post office	*el correo*	el ko·*re*·o
supermarket	*el supermercado*	el soo·per·mer·*ka*·do
tourist office	*la oficina de turismo*	la o·fee·*see*·na de too·*rees*·mo

What time does it open/close?
¿A qué hora abre/cierra? a ke *o*·ra *a*·bre/*sye*·ra

I want to change some money.
Quiero cambiar dinero. *kye*·ro kam·*byar* dee·*ne*·ro

What is the exchange rate?
¿A cómo está el tipo de cambio? a *ko*·mo es·*ta* el *tee*·po de *kam*·byo

I want to call ...
Quiero llamar a ... *kye*·ro ya·*mar* a ...

airmail	*correo aéreo*	ko·*re*·o a·e·re·o
cell phone	*teléfono celular*	te·*le*·fo·no se·loo·*lar*
letter	*carta*	*kar*·ta
registered mail	*correo certificado*	ko·*re*·o ser·tee·fee·*ka*·do
stamps	*estampillas*	es·tam·*pee*·yas

TIME & DATES

What time is it?	*¿Qué hora es?*	ke *o*·ra es
It's one o'clock.	*Es la una.*	es la *oo*·na
It's (10) o'clock.	*Son las (diez).*	son las (dyes)
Half past (two).	*(Dos) y media.*	(dos) ee *me*·dya
noon	*mediodía*	me·dyo·*dee*·a
now	*ahora*	a·*o*·ra
tonight	*hoy en la noche*	oy en la *no*·che
midnight	*medianoche*	me·dya·*no*·che

yesterday	*ayer*	a·*yer*
today	*hoy*	oy
tomorrow	*mañana*	ma·*nya*·na

Monday	*lunes*	*loo*·nes
Tuesday	*martes*	*mar*·tes
Wednesday	*miércoles*	*myer*·ko·les
Thursday	*jueves*	*khwe*·ves
Friday	*viernes*	*vyer*·nes
Saturday	*sábado*	*sa*·ba·do
Sunday	*domingo*	do·*meen*·go

January	*enero*	e·*ne*·ro
February	*febrero*	fe·*bre*·ro
March	*marzo*	*mar*·so
April	*abril*	a·*breel*
May	*mayo*	*ma*·yo
June	*junio*	*khoo*·nyo
July	*julio*	*khoo*·lyo
August	*agosto*	a·*gos*·to
September	*septiembre*	se·*tyem*·bre
October	*octubre*	ok·*too*·bre
November	*noviembre*	no·*vyem*·bre
December	*diciembre*	dee·*syem*·bre

TRANSPORTATION

Public Transportation

What time does the ... leave/arrive?	*¿A qué hora sale/llega ...?*	a ke *o*·ra *sa*·le/*ye*·ga ...
boat	*el barco*	el *bar*·ko
bus	*el bus*	el boos
minibus	*el colectivo/ la buseta/ el microbús*	el ko·lek·*tee*·vo/ la boo·*se*·ta/ el mee·kro·*boos*
plane	*el avión*	el a·*vyon*
train	*el tren*	el tren

airport	*aeropuerto*	a·e·ro·*pwer*·to
bus station	*estación de buses*	es·ta·*syon* de *boo*·ses
bus stop	*parada de bus*	pa·*ra*·da de boos
left-luggage office	*consigna para equipaje*	kon·*seeg*·na *pa*·ra e·kee·*pa*·khe
ticket office	*ventanilla*	ven·ta·*nee*·ya
timetable	*itinerario*	ee·tee·ne·*ra*·ryo
train station	*estación de tren*	es·ta·*syon* de tren
transfer	*cambio*	*kam*·byo
travel agent	*agente de viajes*	a·*khen*·te de *vya*·khes

A ticket to ..., please.
Un tiquete para ..., por favor. oon tee·*ke*·te *pa*·ra ... por fa·*vor*
What's the fare to ...?
¿Cuánto cuesta para ...? *kwan*·to *kwe*·sta *pa*·ra ...

1st class	*primera clase*	pree·*me*·ra *kla*·se
2nd class	*segunda clase*	se·*goon*·da *kla*·se
one way	*solo de ida*	*so*·lo de *ee*·da
round trip	*de ida y vuelta*	de *ee*·da ee *vwel*·ta
student's	*de estudiante*	de es·too·*dyan*·te
taxi	*taxi*	*tak*·see

Private Transportation

I'd like to hire a ... *Quiero alquilar ...* *kye*·ro al·kee·*lar* ...

4WD	*un cuatro por cuatro*	oon *kwa*·tro por *kwa*·tro
bicycle	*una bicicleta*	*oo*·na bee·see·*kle*·ta
car	*un carro*	oon *ka*·ro
motorcycle	*una motocicleta*	*oo*·na *mo*·to·see·*kle*·ta

hitchhike	*pedir un aventón*	pe·*deer* oon a·ven·*ton*
truck	*camión*	ka·*myon*

Where's a gas station?
¿Adónde hay una bomba? a·*don*·de ai *oo*·na *bom*·ba
How much is a liter of gas?
¿Cuánto cuesta un litro de gasolina? *kwan*·to *kwes*·ta oon *lee*·tro de ga·so·*lee*·na
Please fill it up.
Lleno, por favor. *ye*·no por fa·*vor*
I'd like (2000 colones) worth.
Quiero (dos mil colones) en gasolina. *kye*·ro (dos meel ko·*lo*·nes) en ga·so·*lee*·na

diesel	*diesel*	*dee*·sel
gas	*gasolina*	ga·so·*lee*·na
leaded (regular)	*con plomo*	kon *plo*·mo
unleaded	*sin plomo*	seen *plo*·mo

oil	*aceite*	a·*say*·te
puncture	*agujero*	a·goo·*khe*·ro
tire	*llanta*	*yan*·ta

Is this the road to ...?
¿Por aquí se va a ...? por a·*kee* se va a ...
(How long) Can I park here?
¿(Cuánto tiempo) Puedo parquear aquí? (*kwan*·to *tyem*·po) *pwe*·do par·ke·*ar* a·*kee*

ROAD SIGNS

Though Costa Rica mostly uses the familiar international road signs, be prepared to encounter these other signs as well:

Acceso	Entrance
Acceso Permanente	24-Hour Access
Acceso Prohibido	No Entry
Alto	Stop
Ceda el Paso	Give Way
Construcción de Carreteras	Roadworks
Curva Peligrosa	Dangerous Curve
Derrumbes	Landslides
Despacio	Slow
Desviación	Detour
Desvío	Detour
Mantenga Su Derecha	Keep to the Right
No Adelantar	No Passing
No Hay Paso	No Entry
No Pase	No Overtaking
Pare	Stop
Peaje	Toll
Peligro	Danger
Prohibido el Paso	No Entry
Prohibido Estacionar	No Parking
Puente Angosto	Narrow Bridge
Salida de Autopista	Exit Freeway
Una Vía	One Way

Where do I pay?
¿Dónde pago? *don*·de *pa*·go
I need a mechanic.
Necesito un mecánico. ne·se·*see*·to oon me·*ka*·nee·ko
The car has broken down at ...
El carro se varó en ... el *ka*·ro se va·*ro* en ...
The motorbike won't start.
La moto no arranca. la *mo*·to no a·*ran*·ka
I have a flat tire.
Se me estalló una llanta. se me es·ta·*yo* *oo*·na *yan*·ta
I've run out of gas.
Me quedé sin gasolina. me ke·*de* seen ga·so·*lee*·na
I've had an accident.
Tuve un accidente. *too*·ve oon ak·see·*den*·te
Can you fix it (today)?
¿Lo puede arreglar (hoy)? lo *pwe*·de a·reg·*lar* (oy)
How long will it take?
¿Cuánto va a durar? *kwan*·to va a doo·*rar*

TRAVEL WITH CHILDREN

Do you mind if I breast-feed here?
¿Le molestaría si doy de mamar aquí? le mo·le·sta·*ree*·a see doy de ma·*mar* a·*kee*
Are children allowed?
¿Se permiten niños? se per·*mee*·ten *nee*·nyos

Is there a/an ...?	*¿Tienen ...?*	tye·nen ...
(English-speaking) babysitter	*una niñera (que hable inglés)*	oo·na nee·*nye*·ra (ke *a*·ble een·*gles*)
child-minding service	*una guardería*	*oo*·na gwar·de·*ree*·a
children's menu	*un menú para niños*	oon me·*noo* *pa*·ra nee·nyos
discount for children	*un descuento para niños*	oon des·*kwen*·to *pa*·ra nee·nyos

I need (a) ...	*Necesito ...*	ne·se·*see*·to ...
baby seat	*una silla para bebé*	*oo*·na *see*·ya *pa*·ra be·*be*
(disposable) diapers/nappies	*pañales (desechables)*	pa·*nya*·les (de·se·*cha*·bles)
milk formula	*leche en polvo*	*le*·che en *pol*·vo
potty	*una vacenilla*	*oo*·na va·see·*nee*·ya
stroller	*un coche sombrilla*	oon *ko*·che som·*bree*·ya

LANGUAGE

Glossary

See p53 for a glossary of food and drink terms, and the Language chapter (p558) for other useful words and phrases.

adiós – means 'goodbye' universally, but used as a greeting in rural Costa Rica
almuerzo ejecutivo – literally 'executive lunch'; a more expensive version of a set meal or *casado*
alquiler de automóviles – car rental
apartado – post-office box (abbreviated 'Apdo')
artesanía – handicrafts
ATH – *a toda hora* (open all hours); used to denote ATMs
automóvil – car
avenida – avenue
avión – airplane

bahía – bay
barrio – district or neighborhood
batido – fresh fruit drink, similar to smoothie
biblioteca – library
bocas – small savory dishes served in bars
bomba – short, funny verse; also means 'gas station' and 'bomb'
bosque – forest
bosque nuboso – cloud forest
buena nota – excellent, OK; literally 'good note'

caballo – horse
cabaña – cabin; see also *cabina*
cabina – cabin; see also *cabaña*
cajero automático – ATM
calle – street
cama, cama matrimonial – bed, double bed
campesino – peasant, farmer or person who works in agriculture
carreta – colorfully painted wooden oxcart, now a form of folk art
carretera – road
casado – inexpensive set meal; also means 'married'
casita – cottage or apartment
catedral – cathedral
caverna – cave; see also *cueva*
cerro – mountain or hill
cerveza – beer
ceviche – local dish of raw, marinated seafood
Chepe – affectionate nickname for José; also used when referring to San José
cine – cinema
ciudad – city
cocina – kitchen or cooking
colectivo – bus, minivan or car operating as shared taxi
colibrí – hummingbird
colina – hill
colón – Costa Rican unit of currency; plural *colones*
comida típica – typical local food
cordillera – mountain range
correo – mail service
Costarricense – Costa Rican; see also *Tico/a*
cruce – crossing
cruda – often used to describe a hangover; literally 'raw'
cueva – cave; see also *caverna*
culebra – snake; see also *serpiente*

Dios – God
directo – direct; refers to long-distance bus with few stops

edificio – building
estación – station, eg ranger station or bus station; also means 'season'

farmacia – pharmacy
fauna silvestre – wildlife
fiesta – party or festival
finca – farm or plantation
floresta – forest
frontera – border
fútbol – soccer (football)

gallo pinto – stir-fry of rice and beans
garza – cattle egret
gasolina – gas (petrol)
gracias – thanks
gringo/a (m/f) – US or European visitor; can be affectionate or insulting, depending on the tone used
guaro – local firewater made from sugarcane

hacienda – rural estate
hielo – ice

ICT – Instituto Costarricense de Turismo; Costa Rica Tourism Board, which provides tourist information
iglesia – church
indígena – indigenous
Interamericana – Pan-American Hwy; the nearly continuous highway running from Alaska to Chile (it breaks at the Darién Gap between Panama and Colombia)
invierno – winter; the rainy season in Costa Rica
isla – island

jardín – garden
josefino/a (m/f) – resident of San José

lago – lake
lavandería – laundry facility, usually offering dry-cleaning services
librería – bookstore
llanura – tropical plain

machismo – an exaggerated sense of masculine pride
macho – literally 'male'; figuratively also 'masculine,' 'tough.' In Costa Rica *macho/a* (m/f) also means 'blonde.'
macrobiótica – health-food store
maría – local name for taxi meter
mercado – market
mercado central – central town market
Meseta Central – Central Valley or central plateau
mestizo/a (m/f) – person of mixed descent, usually Spanish and indigenous
metate – flat stone platform, used by Costa Rica's pre-Columbian populations to grind corn
migración – immigration
Minae – Ministerio de Ambiente y Energía; Ministry of Environment and Energy, in charge of the national park system
mirador – lookout point
mole – rich chocolate sauce
mono – monkey
mono tití – squirrel monkey
motocicleta – motorcycle
muelle – dock
museo – museum

niño – child
normal – refers to long-distance bus with many stops

obeah – sorcery rituals of African origin
ola(s) – wave(s)
OTS – Organization for Tropical Studies

pájaro – bird
palapa – shelter with a thatched, palm-leaf roof and open sides
palenque – indigenous settlement
panadería – bakery
páramo – habitat characterized by highland shrub and tussock grass
parque – park
parque central – central town square or plaza
parque nacional – national park
pastelería – pastry shop
perezoso – sloth
perico – mealy parrot
playa – beach
posada – country-style inn or guesthouse
puente – bridge
puerto – port
pulpería – corner grocery store
punta – point
pura vida – super; literally 'pure life'

quebrada – stream
queso – cheese

rana – frog or toad
rancho – small house or house-like building
refugio nacional de vida silvestre – national wildlife refuge
río – river

sabanero – cowboy from Guanacaste
selva – jungle
Semana Santa – the Christian Holy Week that precedes Easter
sendero – trail or path
serpiente – snake; see also *culebra*
Sinac – Sistema Nacional de Areas de Conservación; National System of Conservation Areas
soda – informal lunch counter or inexpensive eatery
supermercado – supermarket

telenovela – Spanish-language soap opera
Tico/a (m/f) – Costa Rican; see also *Costarricense*
tienda – store
tiquismos – typical Costa Rican expressions or slang
tortuga – turtle

valle – valley
verano – summer; the dry season in Costa Rica
vino – wine
volcán – volcano

zoológico – zoo

The Authors

MATTHEW D FIRESTONE

Coordinating Author, Central Pacific Coast, Southern Costa Rica, Península de Osa & Golfo Dulce

Matthew is a trained anthropologist and epidemiologist, though he postponed his academic career to spend his youth living out of a backpack. To date he has authored more than 20 guidebooks for Lonely Planet, and covered far-flung destinations from the Darién Gap to the Dead Sea. When he's not in graduate school, out in the field or on assignment, he likes to spend his time exploring the American West with his parents, or catching up with the in-laws in the foothills of Mt Fuji.

CAROLINA A MIRANDA

San José, Central Valley & Highlands, Caribbean Coast

Carolina has traveled Costa Rica top to bottom and east to west on numerous occasions over more than a half-dozen years. During these sojourns, she has eaten ungodly amounts of *chifrijo* (rice and beans with fried pork and salsa) and seen some of the most spectacular scenery on earth. When she isn't getting lost along jungle trails in Costa Rica, she works as a freelance writer in New York City, where she contributes stories to *Time, Budget Travel, Travel + Leisure, Florida Travel + Life* and the public radio station WNYC. She is the author of the uncouth and saucy cultural blog C-Monster.net. Find her on Twitter at @cmonstah.

CÉSAR G SORIANO

Northwestern Costa Rica, Península de Nicoya, Northern Lowlands

Bitten by the wanderlust bug at birth, César has based all his life decisions on the travel opportunities they would afford. Desperate to flee his Virginia hometown after college, he joined the US Army – and was promptly deployed to war-torn Bosnia and Hercegovina. As a career journalist, César landed his first dream job at *USA Today*, where he covered everything from celebrity gossip to the Iraq and Afghanistan wars. In 2006 César changed gear and became a London-based freelance writer. This is his eighth and final guidebook for Lonely Planet; in 2010 César switched careers again and is now a US Foreign Service Officer.

LONELY PLANET AUTHORS

Why is our travel information the best in the world? It's simple: our authors are passionate, dedicated travelers. They don't take freebies in exchange for positive coverage so you can be sure the advice you're given is impartial. They travel widely to all the popular spots, and off the beaten track. They don't research using just the internet or phone. They discover new places not included in any other guidebook. They personally visit thousands of hotels, restaurants, palaces, trails, galleries, temples and more. They speak with dozens of locals every day to make sure you get the kind of insider knowledge only a local could tell you. They take pride in getting all the details right, and in telling it how it is. Think you can do it? Find out how at **lonelyplanet.com**.

CONTRIBUTING AUTHORS

Dr David Goldberg wrote the Health chapter. He completed his training in internal medicine and infectious diseases at Columbia-Presbyterian Medical Center in New York City, where he has also served as voluntary faculty. At present he is an infectious-diseases specialist in Scarsdale, New York, and the editor in chief of the website MDtravelhealth.com.

David Lukas wrote the Environment chapter. He is an avid student of natural history who has traveled widely to study tropical ecosystems in locations such as Borneo and the Amazon. He has also spent several years leading natural-history tours to all corners of Costa Rica, Belize and Guatemala.

Behind the Scenes

THIS BOOK

This 9th edition of Costa Rica was written by Matthew D Firestone (coordinating author), Carolina A Miranda and César G Soriano. David Lukas penned the Environment chapter and Dr David Goldberg wrote the Health chapter. Some of the content in the Wildlife Guide was based on David Lukas' text from the previous edition. Matthew D Firestone, Guyan Mitra and Wendy Yanagihara wrote the 8th edition, and Mara Vorhees and Matthew D Firestone wrote the 7th edition. The 6th edition was written by Paige R Penland and Carolina A Miranda, while the first five editions were written by Rob Rachowiecki. This guidebook was commissioned in Lonely Planet's Oakland office, and produced by the following:

Commissioning Editor Catherine Craddock
Coordinating Editors Martine Power, Branislava Vladisavljevic
Coordinating Cartographers Mark Griffiths, Valentina Kremenchutskaya
Coordinating Layout Designer Jim Hsu
Managing Editor Annelies Mertens
Managing Cartographers Alison Lyall, Herman So
Managing Layout Designers Indra Kilfoyle, Celia Wood
Assisting Editors Carolyn Bain, Laura Crawford, Evan Jones, Trent Holden
Cover Research Sabrina Dalbesio, lonelyplanetimages.com
Internal Image Research Aude Vauconsant, lonelyplanetimages.com
Project Manager Rachel Imeson

Thanks to Lucy Birchley, Daniel Corbett, Bruce Evans, Mark Germanchis, Michelle Glynn, Craig Kilburn, Yvonne Kirk, Lisa Knights, Rebecca Lalor, John Mazzocchi, Daniel Moore, Kirsten Rawlings, Averil Robertson, Fiona Siseman, John Taufa, Nick Thorpe, Juan Winata

THANKS

MATTHEW D FIRESTONE

My family has gotten bigger since the publication of this book, so first off, I'd like to extend a warm welcome to my wonderful wife, Aki. We've traveled the world from east to west, but there is still so much more for us to discover together. And of course, I can't overlook the overwhelming support that my parents and sister have shown me over the years, which has guided me over more hurdles and around more obstacles than I care to mention. At Lonely Planet, a tip of the hat to commissioning editor extraordinaire Catherine Craddock for getting behind the steering wheel of yet another edition of Costa Rica. And finally, a sincere *muchísimas gracias* to Carolina and César, who are two of the most diligent and

THE LONELY PLANET STORY

Fresh from an epic journey across Europe, Asia and Australia in 1972, Tony and Maureen Wheeler sat at their kitchen table stapling together notes. The first Lonely Planet guidebook, *Across Asia on the Cheap,* was born.

Travelers snapped up the guides. Inspired by their success, the Wheelers began publishing books to Southeast Asia, India and beyond. Demand was prodigious, and the Wheelers expanded the business rapidly to keep up. Over the years, Lonely Planet extended its coverage to every country and into the virtual world via lonelyplanet.com and the Thorn Tree message board.

As Lonely Planet became a globally loved brand, Tony and Maureen received several offers for the company. But it wasn't until 2007 that they found a partner whom they trusted to remain true to the company's principles of traveling widely, treading lightly and giving sustainably. In October of that year, BBC Worldwide acquired a 75% share in the company, pledging to uphold Lonely Planet's commitment to independent travel, trustworthy advice and editorial independence.

Today, Lonely Planet has offices in Melbourne, London and Oakland, with over 500 staff members and 300 authors. Tony and Maureen are still actively involved with Lonely Planet. They're traveling more often than ever, and they're devoting their spare time to charitable projects. And the company is still driven by the philosophy of *Across Asia on the Cheap*: 'All you've got to do is decide to go and the hardest part is over. So go!'

SEND US YOUR FEEDBACK

We love to hear from travelers – your comments keep us on our toes and help make our books better. Our well-traveled team reads every word on what you loved or loathed about this book. Although we cannot reply individually to postal submissions, we always guarantee that your feedback goes straight to the appropriate authors, in time for the next edition. Each person who sends us information is thanked in the next edition and the most useful submissions are rewarded with a free book.

To send us your updates – and find out about Lonely Planet events, newsletters and travel news – visit our award-winning website: **lonelyplanet.com/contact**.

Note: we may edit, reproduce and incorporate your comments in Lonely Planet products such as guidebooks, websites and digital products, so let us know if you don't want your comments reproduced or your name acknowledged. For a copy of our privacy policy visit lonelyplanet.com/privacy.

high-spirited authors I've ever had the privilege to work with.

CÉSAR G SORIANO

Thank you to the Poveda twins, Andrés and Adrian, at Costa Rica Hostel Network, for your invaluable guidance and assistance during my journey. In Fortuna, thanks to Diego, Joanna, Alonso and the rest of the staff at Arenal Backpackers for your help and friendship – *¡Viva El Rey!* In Tamarindo, thanks to Roberto and his awesome dog Diego, and Arnoldo at iOne Mac repair for saving my MacBook from certain death. At Lonely Planet, huge thanks to my cowriters Matthew and Carolina, and commissioning editor Catherine Craddock. It's been an honor. And last but not least, eternal gratitude to my wife and favorite travel partner, Marsha, for her love and support. The world is our oyster.

CAROLINA A MIRANDA

To the readers who sent tips on hidden gems and the awesome Lonely Planet team (Catherine, Matt and César) – you guys rock. For sharing their time and knowledge: Matthew Cook, Daryl Loth, Annette and Herbie, the Walters in Cahuita, María Barquero, J, Shawn Larkin, everyone at Wild Rider in San José, not to mention Toñito, my 10-year-old boat captain – thank you. *A mis ma'es que laboran en la granja de los chompipes, un requete fuerte abrazo.* Above all, I'd like to express a deep gratitude to my husband Ed Tahaney, without whom I'd be a mess of papers and a pile of bad ideas. This one's for you.

OUR READERS

Many thanks to the travelers who used the last edition and wrote to us with helpful hints, useful advice and interesting anecdotes:

Carolien Amperse, Michael Anderson, Alexander Anyfandakis, Ana Carina Araujo, Marina Asenjo, Martine Baars, Manon Baas, Jason Bachman, Isabelle Banner, Ed Benjamin, Hilary Benson, Fosco Bernasconi, Ashvy Bhardwaj, Stephen Blau, Paul Boehlen, Esmeralda Borgo, Philipp Braune, Florence Broder, Derek Byrne, Adriana Calambas, Kathryn Callan, Lindsay Campbell, Charles Carriere, Emma Cases Moller, Brian Cassidy, Roy Clagg, Sean Clare, Edwin Colebunders, Dirk Cordes, Kristen Corrigan, Emma Cox, Simon Crosbie, Todd Cumming, Ami Dehne, Stéphane Desrochers, Ingrid Døskeland Thaule, Karin Drach, Monica Drake, Sam Dratch, Eckerle, Miriam Eglinton, Kikki Eilertsen, Koos En Willeke, Hunter Essex, Maryjka Faecett, Hakan Fahleryd, Chris Frings, Audrey Furnell, Matt Gaither, Guillermo García, Sascha Giest, Amy Gode, Mollie Goldstein, Maarten Golterman, Veronica Halderson, Barbara Hartung, Kurt Headrick, Jennifer Helsper, Sandra Herms, Therese Hoerstroem, Andreas Hoferichter, Diane Jacobs, Jack James, Adrienne Janssen, Manon Jetten, Laura Johnson, Mary Jones, Maurice Kappelhof, Sebastian Katz, Natalie Keen, Tom and Teri Kinnier, Rebecca Kirkwood, Ruediger Klanck, Lisa Knappich, Nicole Kollermann, Arnold Koning, Anna Korbut, Joey La Penna, Aaron Langolf, Ali Lemer, Noel Levin, Conrad Lichota, Ann Lipkin, Kimberley Little, Donna Magdalina, Pamela Malo, Nicole Maniglia, Emily Mao, Mareike, Corina Marty, Joe McDonald, Tom McDorman, Laurie McLaughlin, Leo Meyer, Matt Milbrandt, Kate Nakfoor, Brian Nett, Joann Newton, Alex Owen, Micah Paysinger, Melissa Picoli, Malcolm Pittman, Rae and Sylvain Plante, Sabine Puckert, Chris Raleigh, Leah Rathbun, Maud Renaud, Juan Carlos Rodríguez, Jaime Rodríguez, Brenna Rose, Liam Rosen, Dennis Rucker, Konrad Rusch, Eva Ruttkay, Tal S, Alvaro Salazar, Adam Saltzman, Brian Scales, Petra Schreiber, Edwin Schuller, Rachel Seidelman, Lisa Severin, Eric Shamas, Joe Shurgold, Lisel Sjögren, Ivanka Smitsmans, Judith Steenbrugge, Christoffer Steffen, Judith Stenroos,

Amy Stensberg, Brian Stepanek, Julie Stevenson, Martin Sumening, Jaap Teunissen, Sam Tomlinson, JF Tremblay, Nathalie Van Doorn, Robert Van Iren, Hannah Van Winkle, David Vander Pluym, Peter Vansumere, Manuel Vering, Jörgen Verstralen, Moritz Von Schweinitz, Sebastein Wains, Jonathan Walczak, David Walker, Elizabeth Walters, Meghan Ward, Tony Wheeler, Bronwynn Whiteley, Cindy Williams, Kim Williams, Maartje Winkler, Claudia Wolff, Claudia Wolff, Lise Zersch

ACKNOWLEDGMENTS

Many thanks to the following for the use of their content:

Globe on title page ©Mountain High Maps 1993 Digital Wisdom, Inc.

BEHIND THE SCENES

Index

INDEX

000 Map pages
000 Photograph pages

INDEX

INDEX

000 Map pages
000 Photograph pages

GreenDex

GOING GREEN

It seems like everyone's going 'green' these days, but how can you know which businesses are actually ecofriendly and which are simply jumping on the sustainable bandwagon?

Lonely Planet authors have selected all of the following listings because they demonstrate an active sustainable-tourism policy. Some are involved in conservation or environmental education, and many are owned and run by local and indigenous operators, thereby maintaining and preserving regional identity and culture. Some of the listings below have also been certified by the Instituto Costarricense de Turismo (ICT; Costa Rica Tourism Board; www.visitcostarica.com), which means they meet high standards of environmental sustainability, business ethics and cultural sensitivity.

We want to keep developing our sustainable-tourism content. If you think we've omitted someone who should be listed here, or if you disagree with our choices, email us at talk2us@lonelyplanet.com.au. For more information about sustainable tourism and Lonely Planet, see www.lonelyplanet.com/responsibletravel.

PENÍNSULA DE NICOYA

PENÍNSULA DE OSA & GOLFO DULCE

SAN JOSÉ

SOUTHERN COSTA RICA

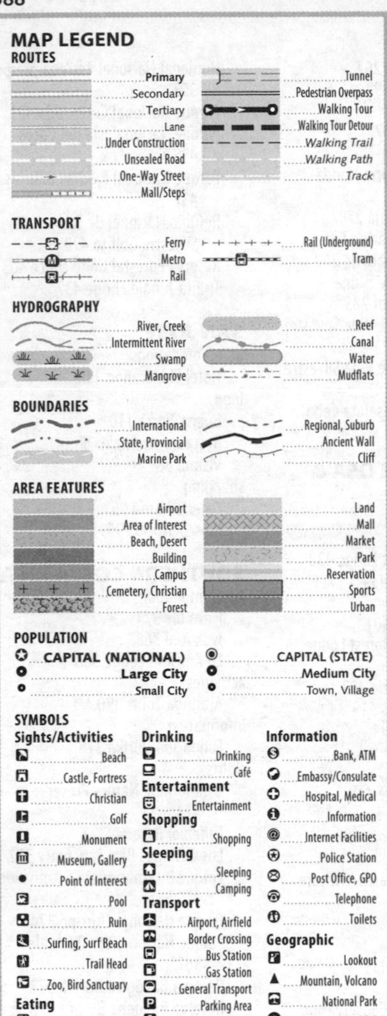

LONELY PLANET OFFICES

Australia (Head Office)
Locked Bag 1, Footscray, Victoria 3011
☎ 03 8379 8000, fax 03 8379 8111
talk2us@lonelyplanet.com.au

USA
150 Linden St, Oakland, CA 94607
☎ 510 250 6400, toll free 800 275 8555
fax 510 893 8572
info@lonelyplanet.com

UK
2nd fl, 186 City Rd,
London EC1V 2NT
☎ 020 7106 2100, fax 020 7106 2101
go@lonelyplanet.co.uk

Published by Lonely Planet
ABN 36 005 607 983

Cover photograph: Pair of Scarlet Macaw (Ara macao) preening, Ralph Hopkins/Lonely Planet Images. Many of the images in this guide are available for licensing from Lonely Planet Images: lonelyplanetimages.com.

Printed by Hang Tai Printing Company, Hong Kong
Printed in China